Frequently Used Symbols in Managerial Finance

a	periodic level payment or annuity
b	proportion of net income (NI) retained by the firm
B	the market value of the firm's debt
β (beta)	beta of a security, a measure of its riskiness
c	coupon payment for a bond
Cov_{jM}	covariance of security j returns with market returns
CV	coefficient of variation
$CVIF$	compound value interest factor
$CVIF_a$	compound value interest factor for an annuity
d	dividend payment per share of common equity
D	total dividend payments of the firm for common equity
Dep	depreciation
EPS	earnings per share; also e
F	net after-tax cash flows for capital budgeting analysis of projects
g	growth rate or growth factor
i	interest rate
I	amount of investment
k	in general, the discount factor; more specifically, the weighted average cost of capital

k_b	cost of debt
k_c	cost of a convertible issue
k_j	returns to firm j or on security j
k_s	cost of common equity for the levered firm
k_{ps}	cost of senior equity, e.g., preferred stock
k_u	cost of capital for the unlevered firm
k_M	return on the market portfolio

λ (lambda)	slope of the security market line $= (\bar{k}_M - R_F)/\sigma_M^2$
n	number of shares outstanding
N	life of a project; also terminal year of decision or planning horizon
p	price of a security
P	sales price per unit of product sold
P_s	probability for state of the world s
$PVIF$	present value interest factor
$PVIF_a$	present value interest factor for an annuity
Q	quantity produced or sold
r	rate of return on new investments; also internal rate of return (IRR)
R_F	risk-free rate of interest
ρ_{jk} (rho)	correlation coefficient
s	subscript referring to alternative states of the world
S	market value of a firm's common equity
σ (sigma)	standard deviation
σ^2	variance
t	time period
T	the marginal corporate income tax rate
TR	total revenues $\equiv$ sales $\equiv$ PQ
V	market value of a firm
w	weights in capital structure or portfolio proportions
X	net operating income of the firm; also equals EBIT $\equiv$ NOI

Managerial Finance

Sixth Edition

Managerial Finance

J. Fred Weston
Professor of Managerial Economics and Finance
University of California, Los Angeles

Eugene F. Brigham
Professor of Finance
University of Florida

The Dryden Press
Hinsdale, Illinois

Text and cover design by Jim Buddenbaum

Preface

Financial management has undergone many changes in recent years. Strong inflationary pressures have pushed interest rates to unprecedented heights, and the resulting high cost of capital has led to profound changes in corporate financial policies and practices. Academic researchers have made significant advances, especially in the areas of capital budgeting and the cost of capital. At the same time, business practitioners are making increasing use of financial theory, and feedback from the "real world" has led to revisions in financial theory. To a large extent, these trends dictated the revisions made in this Sixth Edition of *Managerial Finance*.

The changes in the Sixth Edition of *Managerial Finance* continue the basic philosophy of previous editions. This is to provide users with coverage of all important areas of managerial finance and financial management, while providing flexibility in the use of the materials. At present, the major theoretical chapters on the cost of capital and valuation are near the end of the book in order to work up to the most difficult material as an increasing challenge to the reader. However, some users tell us they start with these chapters so they can use the concepts in their treatment of the materials in the earlier chapters. Different sequencing patterns have been reported by other professors. Still others use different combinations of the materials in the first, second or subsequent courses in a finance sequence. Since faculty, students and curriculum needs and personalities vary among different schools, we believe this flexibility is an important strength of *Managerial Finance*—and it is no accident; we have planned for it.

This flexibility objective has guided the placement of some new materials in the Sixth Edition. Three important recent developments in finance are the Capital Asset Pricing Model (CAPM), the Options Pricing Model (OPM) and the State-Preference Model (SPM). The Capital Asset Pricing Model is discussed in Appendix D to Chapter 10 and in Appendix C to Chapter 19. The Option Pricing Model has been set forth in Appendix A to Chapter 16. We utilize the State-Preference Model to provide a wrap-up of the discussion of financial leverage in Appendix D to Chapter 19. These and other materials continue the up-to-date coverage of *Managerial Finance* while providing flexibility in the sequence and in the courses in which the topics are treated.

In addition to containing new materials, the revision reflects our experience, and that of others, in teaching business finance. Organizational changes have been made to provide for smoother flow and greater continuity; points that proved troublesome to students have been clarified; a few outright errors have been corrected; and, of course, descriptive materials have been updated. Moreover, the end-of-chapter questions, problems, and references have been clarified and strengthened.

Much of the specific content of the book is the result of our experience in executive development programs over a number of years. This experience, in addition to our consulting with business firms on financial problems and policies, has helped us to identify the most significant responsibilities of financial managers, the most fundamental problems facing firms, and the most feasible approaches to practical decision-making. Some topics are conceptually difficult, but so are the issues faced by financial managers. Business managers must be prepared to handle complex problems, and finding solutions to these problems necessarily involves the use of advanced tools and techniques.

We have not sought to avoid the many unresolved areas of business financial theory and practice. Although we could have simplified the text in many places by avoiding the difficult issues, we preferred to provide a basic framework based on the "received doctrine," then to go on (often in appendixes) to present materials on a number of important but controversial issues. It is hoped that our presentation, along with the additional references provided at the end of each chapter, will stimulate the reader to further inquiry.

We acknowledge that the level and difficulty of the material is uneven. Certain sections are simply descriptions of the institutional features of the financial environment and, as such, are not difficult to understand. Other parts—notably the material on capital budgeting, uncertainty, and the cost of capital—are by nature rather abstract, and, as such, are difficult for those not used to thinking in abstract terms. In some of the more complex sections, we have simply outlined procedures in the main body of the text, then justified the procedures in the chapter appendixes.

The appendixes permit great flexibility in the use of *Managerial Finance*. The book can be used in a basic course by omitting selected appendix topics. If instructors wish to cover selected topics from the appendixes, they may do so, and the more interested or mature student may also choose to select appendix topics for independent study. Alternatively, the book may be used in a two-semester course, supplemented, as the instructor sees fit, with outside readings or cases, or both. At both UCLA and Florida we use the basic chapters plus a very few appendixes in the introductory course, then cover selected appendixes plus cases and some articles in the advanced course. In fact, some of the appendixes were written specifically to help bridge the gap between basic texts and journal literature.

Changes in the Sixth Edition

The Sixth Edition of *Managerial Finance* differs from the Fifth in several key respects.

1. We have updated all materials that have a time aspect.
2. A listing of "Frequently Used Symbols" in *Managerial Finance* has been developed which relates and makes consistent all symbols used in the capital budgeting, cost of capital, uncertainty, valuation and other basic conceptual themes that run through the book. The symbols used seek to reflect the widest usage found in the journal literature. This has a number of advantages. The reader has the assurance that on the central conceptual materials one set of symbols is consistently used. Furthermore, this will help the reader increase his familiarity with the symbols used in the general literature. It will thereby facilitate the access of the reader to the journal literature. Another benefit of the list of "Frequently Used Symbols" is that it provides a perspective which allows some simplification and reduction in the number of symbols employed in *Managerial Finance*.
3. Chapter 1 has been rewritten to focus more directly and fully on the nature of the finance function and to discuss the goals of the firm in a broader perspective.
4. We have added an appendix to Chapter 2 to discuss accounting under inflation and its implications for financial ratio analysis.
5. We have added a section to Chapter 10 for comparing mutually exclusive projects with unequal lives.
6. An appendix has been developed for Chapter 10, utilizing the Capital Asset Pricing Model for measuring the required risk adjusted return for new investment projects.
7. Another appendix to Chapter 10 describes the adjustments required for capital budgeting under inflation.
8. The section on leasing has been reworked to reflect the important development in the recent new articles on the subject.
9. An appendix to Chapter 17 uses the market price of risk relationships to show how the risk premium in the returns to investments and to securities can be measured.
10. The new and complex formulas for option pricing are shown to use a combination of materials already covered in *Managerial Fi-*

nance; simple, clear applications of the Black and Scholes formulas are made to pricing options as well as to other corporate securities. This is placed as an appendix to Chapter 16.

11. Some recent work on state-preference theory is applied in discussing the determination of optimal financial leverage. Again the material is presented in clear, easy-to-follow examples, and its use in a managerial finance decision-framework is demonstrated in an appendix to Chapter 19.

12. Capital investment decisions are explicitly integrated with the valuation of the firm.

13. The materials on capital budgeting are further developed and clarified.

14. A correct conceptualization of multi-period stock valuation models is presented in Chapter 17.

15. New institutional materials are added to continue up-to-date coverage related to real world developments.

16. We have added new problems to round out the coverage of concepts as well as to provide appropriate emphasis to areas of central importance.

Several reviewers suggested that it might be desirable to reduce the total length of the book. The idea was appealing, but we did not follow their suggestion for several reasons. We want the book to cover the entire field of business finance and to deal with all the functions of the financial manager. Eliminating institutional material and concentrating on theory and technique would give the student an unrealistic, sterile view of finance. Some of the more advanced theory and techniques could have been eliminated on the ground that they probably would not be covered in basic courses, but it is useful to show where this material fits into the scheme of things and to provide the student with a bridge to the journal literature. Finally, our verbosity results, to a large extent, from a deliberate addition of statements, examples, and other materials to clarify points that our students have found difficult; eliminating these would have reduced the clarity of the book. These factors, *together with the fact that the book is structured so that instructors do not have to assign all the material,* caused us to forego a marked reduction in the book's length.

Ancillary Materials

Several items are available to supplement *Managerial Finance.* First, there are two casebooks, *Cases in Managerial Finance,* 3rd Edition, and *Decisions in Financial Management: Cases,* by Eugene F. Brigham et al. Second, there are a number of readings books which can be used to supplement the text. One book in particular, *Issues in Managerial Fi-*

nance, edited by E. F. Brigham and R. E. Johnson, is a useful supplement to *Managerial Finance.* Finally, many students will find the *Study Guide* useful. The *Study Guide* highlights the key points in the text and presents a comprehensive set of problems similar to those at the end of each chapter. Each problem is solved in detail, so a student who has difficulty working the end-of-chapter problems can be aided by reviewing the *Study Guide.*

Acknowledgments In its several revisions, the book has been worked on and critically reviewed by numerous individuals, and we have received many detailed comments and suggestions from instructors (and students) using the book in our own schools and elsewhere. All this help has improved the quality of the book, and we are deeply indebted to the following individuals, and others, for their help: M. Adler, E. Altman, J. Andrews, R. Aubey, P. Bacon, W. Beranek, V. Brewer, W. Brueggeman, R. Carleson, S. Choudhury, P. Cooley, C. Cox, D. Fischer, R. Gray, J. Griggs, R. Haugen, S. Hawk, R. Hehre, J. Henry, A. Herrmann, G. Hettenhouse, R. Himes, C. Johnson, R. Jones, D. Kaplan, M. Kaufman, D. Knight, H. Krogh, R. LeClair, W. Lee, D. Longmore, J. Longstreet, H. Magee, P. Malone, R. Moore, T. Morton, T. Nantell, R. Nelson, R. Norgaard, J. Pappas, R. Pettit, R. Pettway, J. Pinkerton, G. Pogue, W. Regan, F. Reilly, R. Rentz, R. Richards, C. Rini, R. Roenfeldt, W. Sharpe, K. Smith, P. Smith, R. Smith, D. Sorenson, M. Tysseland, P. Vanderheiden, D. Woods, J. Yeakel, and D. Ziegenbein for their careful reviews of this and previous editions.

We owe special thanks to V. Apilado, J. Dran, M. Ertell, G. Laber, G. Hettenhouse, J. Longstreet, R. Melicher, and G. Pinches for providing us with detailed reviews of the manuscript of this edition. Particularly helpful in the present revision was the assistance of L. Dann, H. DeAngelo, J. Kiholm, M. McElroy, P. Scharf, and I. Woodward. We would like to thank C. Barngrover S. Manshinghka, W. Eckardt, H. Rollins, H. Alwan, D. Wort, and J. Zumwalt for their assistance in helping us to develop the acetate program; we would also like to express our appreciation to Bob LeClair and to The American College for their help in preparing the transparencies, available from The Dryden Press. (Note to instructors: a set of additional problems with solutions developed with the assistance of Professors Roger Bey, Keith Johnson and Ramon Johnson will be made available to adoptors by The Dryden Press.)

The Universities of California and Florida, and our colleagues on these campuses, provided us with intellectual support in bringing the book to completion. Finally, we are indebted to the Dryden Press staff— principally Garret White, Paul R. Jones, Jo-Anne Naples, and Ray Ashton—for their special efforts in getting the manuscript into production and for following through to the bound book.

The field of finance will continue to experience significant changes. It is stimulating to participate in these exciting developments, and we sincerely hope that *Managerial Finance* will contribute to a better understanding of the theory and practice of finance.

Los Angeles, California   J. Fred Weston
Gainesville, Florida   Eugene F. Brigham

December 1977

Contents

Sixth Edition **Managerial Finance**

Part I

Overview of Finance:
Analysis, Planning
and Control

Part I consists of five chapters. The first describes the scope and nature of managerial finance and serves as an introduction to the book. In Chapter 2 we examine the construction and use of the basic ratios of financial analysis; through ratio analysis, the firm's strengths and weaknesses can be pinpointed. Chapter 3 explains two key tools used in financial planning: break-even analysis and the sources and uses of funds statement. In Chapter 4 we take up financial forecasting: given a projected increase in sales, how much money must the financial manager raise to support this level of sales? Finally, in Chapter 5, we consider the budget system through which management controls and coordinates the firm.

Finance deals, in the main, with very specific questions: Should we lease or buy the new machine? Should we expand capacity at the Hartford plant? Should we raise capital this year by long-term or short-term debt or by selling stock? Should we go along with the marketing department, which wants to expand inventories, or with the production department, which wants to reduce them? Specific questions such as these, which are typical of the types of decisions facing the financial manager, are considered in the remainder of the book. But here in Part I we take an *overview* of the firm. Because all specific decisions are made within the context of the firm's overall position, this overview is critical to an understanding of any specific proposal.

1 Scope and Nature of Managerial Finance

What is managerial finance? What is the finance function in the firm? What specific tasks are assigned to the financial manager? What tools and techniques are available to him, and how does one go about measuring his performance? On a broader scale, what is the role of finance in the American economy, and how can managerial finance be used to further national goals? Providing at least tentative answers to these questions is the principal purpose of this book.

The Finance Function

Financial management is defined by the functions and areas of responsibilities of financial managers. While the specifics vary among individual organizations, some finance tasks are basic. Funds are raised from external financial sources. Funds are allocated among different uses. The flows of funds involved in the operations of the enterprise are managed. Benefits are returned to sources of financing in the form of returns, repayments or products and services. These key financial functions must be performed in any kind of organization whether it be a business firm, a governmental unit or governmental agency, an aid group such as the Red Cross or Salvation Army, or other nonprofit organizations such as an art museum or theater group.

In Figure 1–1, the functions of financial managers are shown to link the financing of an organization to its financing sources *via* the financial markets. The major parts of Figure 1–1 will be explained in the remaining sections of this discussion of the finance function. Funds for conducting the operations of organizations are obtained from a wide range of financial institutions. The funds are obtained in the form of loans, bonds, common stocks, etc. The financial manager has primary responsibilities for acquiring funds and participates in the allocation of the funds among alternative projects and to specific forms such as inventories, plant, and equipment. The cash flow cycle must be managed. Payments are made for labor, materials, and capital goods purchased from the external markets. Products and services are created which generate fund inflows. In managing cash inflows and cash outflows, some cash is recycled and some returned to financing sources.

Figure 1–1
Financial Markets, the
Financial Manager,
and the Firm

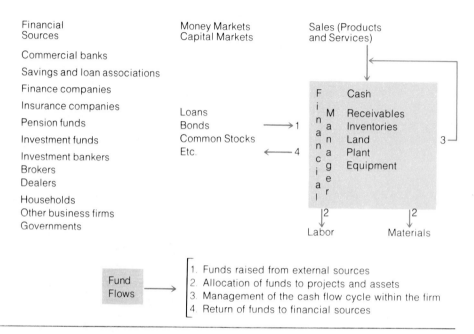

Financial Markets

Financial Sources	Money Markets Capital Markets	Sales (Products and Services)
Commercial banks		
Savings and loan associations		
Finance companies		Cash
Insurance companies	Loans	Receivables
Pension funds	Bonds	Inventories
Investment funds	Common Stocks	Land
Investment bankers	Etc.	Plant
Brokers		Equipment
Dealers		
Households Other business firms Governments		Labor Materials

Fund Flows

1. Funds raised from external sources
2. Allocation of funds to projects and assets
3. Management of the cash flow cycle within the firm
4. Return of funds to financial sources

Financial Markets

The financial manager functions in a complex financial network because the savings and investment functions in a modern economy are performed by different economic agents. For savings surplus units, savings exceed their investment in real assets and they own financial assets. For savings deficit units, current savings are less than investment in real assets so they issue financial liabilities. The savings deficit units issue a wide variety of financial claims such as promissory notes, bonds, and common stocks.

The transfer of funds from a savings surplus unit or the acquisition of funds by a savings deficit unit involves the creation of a financial asset *and* a financial liability. For example, when a person places funds in a savings account in a bank or savings and loan association, his deposit represents a financial asset in his personal balance sheet along with real assets such as an automobile or household goods. The savings deposit is a liability account of the financial institution and represents a financial liability. When the funds are loaned to aid another person in the purchase of a home, for example, the loan by the financial institution represents a financial asset on its balance sheet. The borrower has incurred a financial liability represented by the loan owed to the financial institution. Consider another example. When a person buys goods on credit from a department store, this adds to "accounts receivable" on the books of the department store. The amounts payable by the person who has purchased goods on credit represents a financial liability that he has incurred.

A financial transaction results in the creation simultaneously of a financial asset and a financial liability. The creation and transfer of financial assets and financial liabilities constitute *financial markets.* The nature of financial markets can be further explained by analogy to the market for actual goods such as the automobile. "The automobile market" is defined by all transactions in automobiles. Some transactions take place at the auto dealer's location; there are also places at which wholesale auctions of used cars take place; in addition trades between individuals may occur. These constitute "the automobile market" because all the transactions make up a part of the total demand and supply curves for autos.

Similarly, financial markets are comprised of all trades that result in the creation of financial assets and financial liabilities. Some trades may be made through organized institutions such as the New York Stock Exchange or various regional stock exchanges. A large volume of transactions also takes place through the thousands of brokers and dealers throughout the country who buy and sell securities, making up what is called the "over-the-counter market." Our own individual transactions with department stores, savings banks, or other financial institutions also create financial assets and financial liabilities as we have illustrated above. Thus financial markets are not just specific physical structures, nor are they remote—all of us are involved in them in one way or another in various degrees.

Continuing the auto analogy, just as a distinction is made between a new car market and a used car market because somewhat different demand and supply influences are operating in each segment, different segments of the financial markets have been placed into categories and given names. When the financial claims and financial obligations bought and sold have a maturity of less than one year, such transactions constitute *money markets.* When the maturities of the instruments traded are more than one year, the markets are referred to as *capital markets.* The latter term is somewhat confusing because real capital in an economy is represented by such things as plant, machinery, and equipment. But long-term financial instruments are regarded as ultimately representing claims on the real resources in an economy and for that reason the markets in which long-term financial instruments are traded are referred to as capital markets.

**Financing
Sources and
Financial
Intermediation**

The financial markets, composed of money markets and capital markets, provide a mechanism through which the financial manager obtains funds from a wide range of financing sources. The nature of each of these financing sources is now briefly described.

Commercial banks are defined by their ability to accept demand deposits subject to transfer by check by the depositor. Such checks represent a widely accepted medium of exchange, accounting for over 90 percent of transactions that take place. Savings and loan associations receive funds from passbook savings, using such funds to invest primarily in real estate mortgages representing long-term borrowings mostly by individuals. Finance companies are business firms whose main activity is making loans to other business firms and to households. Life insurance companies sell protection against the loss of income from premature death or disability. The insurance policies they sell typically have a savings element in them. Pension funds collect contributions from employees and/or employers to make periodic payments upon the employee's retirement. Investment funds or mutual funds sell shares to investors and use the proceeds to purchase already existing equity securities.

Investment bankers are financial firms who buy new issues of securities from business firms at a guaranteed agreed upon price and who seek immediately to resell the securities to other investors. Related financial firms, which function simply as agents linking buyers and sellers, are called investment brokers. Investment dealers are those who purchase for their own account from sellers and ultimately make resales to other buyers. Investment banking (discussed in Chapter 14) functions in the new issue market. Brokers and dealers are engaged in transactions in already issued securities.

Finally, on the left hand side of Figure 1–1, other sources of funds are households, other business firms, and governments. At any point in time some of these will be borrowers and others will be lenders.

Financial intermediation is accomplished through the transactions in the financial markets, which bring the savings surplus units together with the savings deficit units so that savings can be redistributed into their most productive uses. The specialized business firms whose activities include the creation of financial assets and financial liabilities are called financial intermediaries. Without financial intermediaries and the processes of financial intermediation described above, the allocation of savings into real investment would be limited by whatever the distribution of savings happened to be. With financial intermediation, savings are transferred to economic units that have opportunities for profitable investment of the savings. In the process real resources are allocated more effectively and real output for the economy as a whole is increased.

Financial managers have important responsibilities in the financial intermediation process described. They are part of the process by which funds are allocated to their most productive uses.

We can, therefore, now re-state the functions of financial managers in the perspective of this broader social framework. In the aggregate, business firms are savings deficit units that obtain funds to make investments to increase the supply of goods and services. Financial managers utilize financial markets to obtain external funds. How shall the funds be acquired efficiently? What is the most economical mix of financing to be obtained? From what alternative sources and in what specific forms should the funds be raised? What should be the timing and forms of returns and repayments to financing sources?

Since funds are acquired as a part of the process by which resources are allocated to their most productive uses, financial managers have responsibilities for the effective use of funds. To what projects and products should the funds be allocated? What assets and resources should the organization acquire in order to produce its products and services? What standards and controls should be utilized to monitor the effective utilization of funds allocated among the segments of operating activities? How should the planning and control of funds be managed so that the organization will produce and sell its products and services most efficiently?

In summary, the main functions of financial managers are to plan for, acquire, and utilize funds to make the maximum contribution to the efficient operation of an organization. This requires knowledge of the financial markets from which funds are drawn. It requires a knowledge of how to make sound investment decisions and to stimulate efficient operations in the organization. A large number of alternative sources and uses of funds will have to be considered. There are always alternative choices involved in financial decisions. The choices include the use of internal versus external funds, long-term projects versus short-term projects, long-term fund sources versus short-term fund sources, a higher rate of growth versus a lower rate of growth, etc.

Up to this point, much of our discussion of the finance function applies to all types of organizations. What is unique about business organizations is that they are directly and measurably subject to the discipline of the financial markets. The financial markets are continuously making determinations of the valuations of the securities of business firms, which provide measures of the performance of business firms.[1] As a consequence of the continuous reassessment of the managerial

1. The financial markets provide continuous valuations of firms whose shares are traded. The relationships established between returns and risk provide the basis for the valuation as well of smaller companies whose ownership shares are not actively traded.

performance of business firms by the capital markets, the relative valuation levels of business firms will change. Changes in valuations signal changes in performance. Valuations, therefore, provide a stimulus to the efficiency of business firms and provide incentives to business managers to improve their performance. It is difficult to formulate tests of the efficiency and performance of organizations other than business firms because of the lack of financial markets for continuously placing valuations on these other organizations and thereby providing a continuous assessment of their performance. This leads to a consideration of financial goals.

Goals of the Firm

It is in the context of the valuation processes of the financial markets in evaluating business firms that the objectives of financial management have been formulated. The goal of financial management is to maximize shareholder wealth. By formulating the firm's objectives in terms of the shareholder's interest, the discipline of the financial markets is implemented. This means that firms with better performance will have higher stock prices. Additional funds can be raised under more favorable terms. If funds go to firms with favorable stock price trends, the economy's resources are being directed to their efficient allocation and use. Hence, throughout this book we operate on the assumption that management's primary goal is to maximize the wealth of its shareholders.

Just how good is this assumption—does management really try to maximize stockholder wealth, or is it equally interested in profits, in sales, in survival, in the personal satisfaction of the managers themselves, in employees' welfare, or in the good of the community and society at large? Further, does management really try to *maximize?* Or does it "satisfice"; that is, does it seek satisfactory rather than optimal results?

Profit versus Wealth Maximization

Let us consider the question of profits versus wealth. Suppose management is interested primarily in stockholders, making its decisions so as to maximize their welfare. Will profit maximization be best for stockholders?

Total Profits. In answering this question, we must consider first the matter of total corporate profits versus earnings per share. Suppose a firm raises capital by selling stock and then invests the proceeds in government bonds. Total profits will rise, but more shares will be outstanding. Earnings per share would probably decline, pulling down the value of each share of stock and, hence, the existing stockholders' wealth. Thus, to the extent that profits are important, management should concentrate on earnings per share rather than on total corporate profits.

Earnings per Share. Will maximization of earnings per share maximize stockholder welfare, or should other factors be considered? Consider the timing of the earnings. Suppose one project will cause earnings per share to rise by $.20 per year for five years, or $1.00 in total, while another project has no effect on earnings for four years but increases earnings by $1.25 in the fifth year. Which project is better? The answer depends upon which project adds the most to the value of the stock, and this in turn depends upon the time value of money to investors. In any event, timing is an important reason to concentrate upon wealth as measured by the price of the stock rather than upon earnings alone.

Risk. Still another issue relates to risk. Suppose one project is expected to increase earnings per share by $1.00, while another is expected to raise earnings by $1.20 per share. The first project is not very risky; if it is undertaken, earnings will almost certainly rise by about $1.00 per share. The other project is quite risky, so while our best guess is that earnings will rise by $1.20 per share, we must recognize the possibility that there may be no increase whatever. Depending upon how averse stockholders are to risk, the first project may be preferable to the second.

Recognizing all those factors, managers interested in maximizing stockholder welfare seek to maximize the value of the firm's common stock. The price of the stock reflects the market's evaluation of the firm's prospective earnings stream over time, the riskiness of this stream, and a host of other factors. The higher the price of the stock, the better is management's performance from the standpoint of the stockholders; thus, market price provides a performance index by which management can be judged.[2]

Maximizing Stockholder Wealth versus Other Goals

In theory, stockholders own the firm and elect the management team; management, in turn, is supposed to operate in the best interests of the stockholders.

Might not managements pursue goals other than maximizing stockholder wealth? Some alternative goals are examined in this section.

---

2. A firm's stock price might, of course, decline because of factors beyond management's control. Accordingly, it is useful to look at comparative statistics; even though a firm's stock declines by ten percent, management will have performed well if other firms in the industry decline by 20 percent.

Maximizing versus "Satisficing." First, consider the question of *maximizing*, which involves seeking the best possible outcome, versus "satisficing," which involves a willingness to settle for something less.[3] A firm that is on the brink of bankruptcy may be forced to operate as efficiently as possible. But some argue that the management of a large, well-entrenched corporation could work to keep stockholder returns at a fair or "reasonable" level and then devote part of its efforts and resources to public service activities, to employee benefits, to higher management salaries, or to golf.

Similarly, an entrenched management could avoid risky ventures, even when the possible gains to stockholders are high enough to warrant taking the gamble. The theory behind that argument is that stockholders are generally well-diversified, holding portfolios of many different stocks, so if one company takes a chance and loses, the stockholders lose only a small part of their wealth. Managers, on the other hand, are not diversified, so setbacks affect them more seriously. Accordingly, some argue that the managers of widely held firms tend to play it safe rather than aggressively seek to maximize the prices of their firms' stocks.

It is extremely difficult to determine whether a particular management team is trying to maximize shareholder wealth or is merely attempting to satisfice on this factor while pursuing other goals. For example, how can we tell whether or not voluntary employee or community benefit programs are in the long-run best interests of the stockholders? Are relatively high management salaries really necessary to attract and retain excellent managers who, in turn, will keep the firm ahead of its competition? When a risky venture is turned down, does this reflect management conservatism or a correct judgment that the risks of the venture outweigh the potential rewards?

It is impossible to give definitive answers to these questions — several studies have suggested that managers are not completely stockholder-oriented, but the evidence is cloudy.[4] It is true that more and more firms are tying management's compensation to the company's performance, and research suggests that this motivates management to operate in a

---

3. J. Fred Weston, *The Scope and Methodology of Finance* (Englewood Cliffs, N.J.: Prentice-Hall, 1966), chap. 2; Herbert A. Simon, "Theories of Decision Making in Economics and Behavioral Science," *American Economic Review*, June 1959, pp. 253–83.

4. W. J. Baumol, *Business Behavior, Value, and Growth* (New York: Macmillan, 1959), argues that firms may seek to maximize sales subject to a minimum profit constraint. J. W. Elliott, "Control, Size, Growth, and Financial Performance in the Firm," *Journal of Financial and Quantitative Analysis*, January 1972, concludes that firms managed by the owners hold fewer liquid assets; this suggests a greater propensity to take risks. On the other hand, W. G. Lewellen in "Management and Ownership in the Large Firm," *Journal of Finance*, May 1969, concluded that top managers of large firms have most of their wealth tied to their firms' fortunes, hence they behave more like owners than earlier literature would suggest.

manner consistent with stock price maximization.[5] Additionally, in recent years tender offers and proxy fights have removed a number of supposedly entrenched managements; the recognition that such actions can take place has doubtless stimulated many other firms to attempt to maximize share prices.[6] Finally, a firm operating in a competitive market, or almost any firm during an economic downturn, will be forced to undertake actions that are reasonably consistent with shareholder wealth maximization. Thus, while managers may not seek only to maximize stockholder wealth, there are reasons to view this as a dominant goal for most firms. And even though a management group may pursue other goals, stockholder wealth is bound to be of considerable importance. Often the same types of actions that could maximize wealth are also necessary to keep it at a satisfactory level; it may therefore be difficult, in practice, to determine which goal is dominant.

Maximizing Wealth versus Utility. In many formulations, the objective is stated in terms of utility—the satisfactions enjoyed by individuals that result in a set of preferences. But the utility patterns or utility functions of individuals vary greatly. For example, some individuals receive positive gratification from the excitement of exposure to risks; for other individuals even moderate risks may cause nervousness and even illness. Who is to determine or to interpret the risk attitudes of individual investors? What would the financial manager do if shareholders have widely divergent utility preferences?

Again the capital markets come to the rescue. Whatever the individual attitudes that may be held toward risk, the market returns in relation to various measures of risk establish that investors on the average exhibit risk aversion—the bearing of risk is considered a "bad" rather than a "good." Furthermore, capital market relationships make it possible to quantify the relationships between required returns and measures of risk. From the returns-to-risks relationships methods of valuation are provided.

Thus the maximization of shareholder wealth as an objective can be made a usable or operational guide to financial decisions. But since it is utility maximization that is ultimately involved, the formal statement of the firm's objective may be expressed in the form of a utility function to be maximized. From such formal statements of the firm's objective,

---

5. See R. T. Masson, "Executive Motivations, Earnings, and Consequent Equity Performance," *Journal of Political Economy*, November 1971.

6. A tender offer is a bid by one company to buy the stock of another, while a proxy fight involves an attempt to gain control by getting stockholders to vote a new management group into office. Both actions are facilitated by low stock prices, so self-preservation can lead management to try to keep the stock value as high as possible.

analytical solutions may be reached and theorems or propositions set forth. Such results may lead to development of theories that may in turn be useful for decisions by financial managers. While such theoretical formulations provide the basis for some of the concepts utilized in this book, our emphasis is on practical financial decision making. We find that the decision criteria and decision rules for financial management are more operational and usable when the analysis is formulated in terms of the objective of shareholder wealth maximization rather than utility maximization.

Social Responsibility. Another viewpoint that deserves consideration is *responsibility:* Should businesses operate strictly in stockholders' best interests, or are they also partly responsible for the welfare of society at large? This is a complex issue with no easy answers. As economic agents whose actions have considerable impact, business firms should take into account the effects of their policies and actions on society as a whole. No one and especially large firms can ignore their obligations for responsible citizenship. Furthermore, it may even be good for wealth maximization in the long run to develop goodwill by being viewed as a "good corporate citizen" that has made substantial contributions to social welfare. Even more fundamentally, some amount of social responsibility by business firms may be required for the survival of a private enterprise system in which business firms can operate.

But many different views of what is best for society are held by different people. By what authority do businessmen have the right to allocate funds in terms of their own views of the social good? In addition, if some firms attempt to be socially responsible and their costs thereby increase substantially, they will be at a disadvantage if their competitors do not incur the same additions to costs. Because of these considerations, an argument can be made that social programs should be formulated through the processes of representative government in our democracy. This implies that most cost-increasing programs would be enacted by the government and put on a mandatory rather than voluntary basis, at least initially, to insure that the burden of such action falls uniformly across all businesses. Thus, fair hiring practices, minority training programs, product safety, pollution abatement, antitrust actions, and the like are more likely to be effective if realistic rules are established initially and enforced by governmental agencies.[7]

---

7. What is first imposed by government may be too much and too fast and after some experience the requirements may be modified. An example is the initial requirement of interlocked seat belts so that a car could not be started until the seat belts were fastened. This requirement was later modified. What is required by government may later become general and customary patterns of behavior by business firms.

It is critical that industry and government cooperate in establishing the rules of corporate behavior and that firms follow the spirit as well as the letter of the law in their actions. Thus, the rules of the game become constraints, and firms should strive to maximize shareholder wealth subject to these constraints. Throughout the book, we shall assume that managements operate in this manner.

Changing Role of Financial Management

As with many things in the contemporary world, financial management has undergone significant changes over the years. When finance first emerged as a separate field of study in the early 1900s, the emphasis was on legalistic matters such as mergers, consolidations, the formation of new firms, and the various types of securities issued by corporations. Industrialization was sweeping the country, and the critical problem firms faced was obtaining capital for expansion. The capital markets were relatively primitive, and transfers of funds from individual savers to businesses were quite difficult. Accounting statements of earnings and asset values were unreliable, and stock trading by insiders and manipulators caused prices to fluctuate wildly; consequently, investors were reluctant to purchase stocks and bonds. In this environment, it is easy to see why finance concentrated so heavily on legal issues relating to the issuance of securities.

The emphasis remained on securities through the 1920s; however, radical changes occurred during the depression of the 1930s. Business failures during that period caused finance to focus on bankruptcy and reorganization, on corporate liquidity, and on governmental regulation of securities markets. Finance was still a descriptive, legalistic subject, but the emphasis shifted to survival rather than expansion.

During the 1940s and early 1950s, finance continued to be taught as a descriptive, institutional subject, viewed from the outside rather than from within the firm's management. However, some time was devoted to budgeting and other internal control procedures, and, stimulated by the work of Joel Dean, capital budgeting was beginning to receive attention.[8]

The evolutionary pace quickened during the late 1950s. Whereas the right-hand side of the balance sheet (liabilities and capital) had received more attention in the earlier era, increasing emphasis was being placed on asset analysis during the last half of that decade. Mathematical models were developed and applied to inventories, cash, accounts receivable, and fixed assets. Increasingly, the focus of finance shifted from the

---

8. Joel Dean, *Capital Budgeting* (New York: Columbia University Press, 1951).

outsider's to the insider's point of view, as financial decisions within the firm were recognized to be the critical issues in corporate finance. Descriptive, institutional materials on capital markets and financing instruments were still studied, but these topics were considered within the context of corporate financial decisions.

The emphasis on decision making has continued in recent years, with the increasing belief that sound capital budgeting procedures require accurate measurements of the cost of capital. Accordingly, ways of quantifying the cost of capital now play a key role in finance. Second, capital has been in short supply, rekindling the old interest in ways of raising funds. Third, there has been continued merger activity, which has led to renewed interest in take-overs. Fourth, accelerated progress in transportation and communications has brought the countries of the world closer together; this, in turn, has stimulated interest in international finance. Fifth, inflation is now recognized as a critical problem, as so much of the financial manager's time is presently devoted to coping with high wages, prices, and interest rates at a time when stock prices are relatively low. Finally, there is an increasing awareness of such social ills as air and water pollution, urban blight, and unemployment among minorities. Finding his firm's realistic role in efforts to solve these problems demands much of the financial manager's attention.

The Impact of Inflation on Financial Management

During the 1950s and 1960s, prices rose at an average rate of about 1½ to 2 percent per year, but in the 1970s the rate of inflation in some years has been more than 10 percent. This "double digit inflation" has had a tremendous impact on business firms, especially on their financial operations. As a result, many established financial policies and practices are undergoing dramatic changes, some of which are outlined below.

1. *Interest rates.* The rate of interest on U.S. government securities (called the default-free rate) consists of a "real rate of interest" of 1 to 3 percent plus an "inflation premium" that reflects the expected long-run rate of inflation. Accordingly, an increase in the rate of inflation is quickly translated into higher default-free interest rates.

   The cost of money to firms is the default-free rate plus a risk premium, so inflation-induced increases in the default-free rate are also reflected in business borrowing rates.

2. *Planning difficulties.* Businesses operate on the basis of long-run plans. For example, a firm builds a plant only after making a thorough analysis of expected costs and revenues over the life of the plant. Reaching such estimates is not easy under the best of conditions, but during rapid inflation, when labor and materials costs are

changing dramatically, accurate forecasts are especially important yet exceedingly hard to make. Efforts are, of course, being made to improve forecasting techniques, and financial planning must include more flexibility to reflect the increased level of uncertainty in the economy. Incidentally, the increased uncertainty in many industries tends to raise the risk premiums for firms in those industries, driving their costs of capital still higher.

3. *Demand for capital.* Inflation increases the amount of capital required to conduct a given volume of business. When inventories are sold, they must be replaced with more expensive goods. The costs of expanding or replacing plants are also greater, while workers demand higher wages. All of these things put pressure on financial managers to raise additional capital. At the same time, in an effort to hold down the rate of inflation, the Federal Reserve System tends to restrict the supply of loanable funds. The ensuing scramble for limited funds drives interest rates still higher.

4. *Bond price declines.* Long-term bond prices fall as interest rates rise, so, in an effort to protect themselves against such capital losses, lenders are beginning (a) to put more funds into short-term than into long-term debt, and (b) to insist upon bonds whose interest rates vary with "the general level of interest rates" as measured by an index of interest rates. Brazil and other inflation-plagued South American countries have used such index bonds for years. Unless inflation in the United States is controlled, their use is likely to increase in this country.

5. *Investment planning.* High interest rates, as well as a general shortage of capital, are causing firms to be especially wary in planning long-term investment outlays. Indeed, headlines such as "ITT Cuts '74 Spending Plan $106 Million Because of Difficulties in Raising Funds," or "Detroit Edison to Fight Cash Shortage by Sale-Lease-back of Coal Equipment,"[9] have become commonplace.

6. *Accounting problems.* With high rates of inflation, reported profits are distorted. The sale of low-cost inventories results in higher reported profits, but cash flows are held down as firms restock with higher-cost inventories. Similarly, depreciation charges are inadequate, as they do not reflect the new costs of replacing plant and equipment. If a firm is unaware of the "shakiness" of profits that reflect inventory valuation and inadequate depreciation charges, and if it plans dividends and capital expenditures on the basis of such figures, then it could develop serious financial problems.

9. *Wall Street Journal*, 18, July 1974.

Double digit inflation is a disturbing and challenging new experience for United States financial managers. Although no one knows what the full impact of continued inflation will be, one thing is clear — if double digit inflation does continue, many financial policies and practices will have to be modified to meet this new situation.

Increased Importance of Financial Management

Those evolutionary changes have greatly increased the importance of financial management. In earlier times, the marketing manager would project sales; the engineering and production staffs would determine the assets necessary to meet these demands; and the financial manager would simply raise the money necessary to purchase the plant, equipment, and inventories. This mode of operation is no longer prevalent — today decisions are made in a much more coordinated manner, with the financial manager directly responsible for the control process. The direction in which business is moving, as well as the increasing importance of finance, is well illustrated by the following quotation.[10]

General Motors Corporation [on December 6, 1971] named Richard C. Gerstenberg, a tough-minded financial man, as its chairman and chief executive officer. The main reason Mr. Gerstenberg got the job, it's believed, is his strong financial background, making him the man of the hour when GM is increasingly worried about its profit margins and its ability to finance its growth internally.

The biggest surprise in the executive reorganization was the naming of T. A. Murphy [another finance man] to the powerful post of vice chairman. Observers expressed some surprise that none of the top assignments given out was to an executive whose career had been in sales or manufacturing.

Similar events are occurring throughout the business world; as the emphasis continues to shift toward closer internal controls, financial managers will play larger and larger roles in business firms.

Organization of a Firm's Finance Department

In the typical firm, the chief financial officer, who has the title of vice-president-finance, reports to the chief executive officer and has accountable to him two key officers, the treasurer and the controller. The treasurer and his staff are responsible for raising capital and dealing with suppliers of capital, as well as for the firm's credit policy. The controller and his staff are responsible for the accounting and budgeting

---

10. *Wall Street Journal*, 7 December 1971.

systems, including capital budgeting. In a sense, the treasurer handles the outside finance functions and the controller, the inside functions, while the vice-president-finance has the overall responsibility for both.

Financial Decisions: Risk-return Tradeoff

Financial decisions affect the value of a firm's stock by influencing both the size of the earnings stream, or profitability, and the riskiness of the firm. These relationships are diagrammed in Figure 1–2. Policy decisions, which are made subject to government constraints, affect both profitability and risk; these two factors jointly determine the value of the firm.

Figure 1–2
Valuation as the Central Focus of the Finance Function

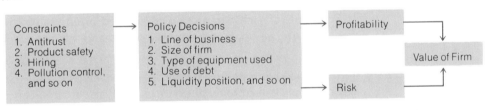

The primary policy decision is that of choosing the industry in which to operate—the product-market mix of the firm. When this choice has been made, both profitability and risk are determined by decisions relating to the size of the firm, the types of equipment used, the extent to which debt is employed, the firm's liquidity position, and so on. Such decisions generally affect both risk and profitability. An increase in the cash position, for instance, reduces risk; however, since cash is not an earning asset, converting other assets to cash also reduces profitability. Similarly, the use of additional debt raises the rate of return, or the profitability, on the stockholders' net worth; at the same time, more debt means more risk. The financial manager seeks to strike the particular balance between risk and profitability that will maximize the wealth of the firm's stockholders. That is called a *risk-return trade-off*, and most financial decisions involve such trade-offs between risk and return.

Organization And Structure Of this Book

The optimal structure for a finance text, if one exists, is most elusive. On the one hand, it is desirable to set out a theoretical structure first, then use the theory in later sections to explain behavior and to attack real-world decision problems. On the other hand, it is easier to understand the theoretical concepts of finance if one has a working knowledge of certain institutional details. Given this conflict, what should come first, theory or institutional background? We have wrestled with this problem, experimenting with both approaches in our own classes, and the following outline of the six parts of the book reflects our own experience and that of others who shared their ideas and preferences with us.

I. Overview of finance: financial analysis, planning, and control
II. Working capital management
III. Decisions involving long-term assets
IV. Sources and forms of long-term financing
V. Financial structure, the cost of capital, and dividend policy
VI. Integrated topics in financial management

The contents of each part are next discussed briefly to provide an overview of both the book and the field of managerial finance.

Part I: Overview of Finance: Financial Analysis, Planning, and Control

Part I, which consists of Chapters 1–5, develops certain key concepts and commonly used tools of financial analysis. Included are such topics as ratio analysis, operating leverage, sources and uses of funds analysis, financial forecasting, and financial control techniques. The material provides a useful overview of finance, and the ideas and terminology developed facilitate an understanding of all the other parts of the book.

Part II: Working Capital Management

Financial management involves the acquisition and use of assets, and to a large extent these actions are reflected in the firm's balance sheet. Accordingly, to a degree, the book is organized in a balance sheet sequence, with Part II focusing on the top part of the balance sheet, or the "working capital" section. Working capital refers to the firm's short-term, or current, assets and liabilities, and the emphasis is placed on determining optimal levels for these items. Chapter 6 is on the theory of working capital, Chapter 7 concerns current assets, and Chapter 8 discusses current liabilities. The theory chapter sets forth a rational framework within which to consider decisions affecting the specific balance sheet items that make up working capital. Firms make two kinds of working capital decisions: (1) *strategic* decisions relating to target working capital levels, and (2) *tactical* decisions that relate to day-to-day operations. The strategic decisions are fundamentally related to the trade-off between risk and return we discussed earlier, to alternative sources of capital, to management's view of the term structure of interest rates, to the effectiveness of internal control procedures (that is, inventory control), to credit policy decisions, and so forth. The tactical operating decisions involve short-run adjustments in current assets and current liabilities to meet temporary conditions. The most obvious short-run adjustment relates to changing sales levels—fixed assets and long-term liabilities are inflexible in the short run, so changes in market demand must be met by working capital adjustments. Working capital is also adjusted from the target levels to reflect changes in long- and short-run interest rates and other changes in the availability of, and the need for, funds.

In Chapter 7 we discuss some factors bearing on (1) target levels of each kind of current asset and (2) methods for economizing on the investment in each kind of current asset. For example, the target inventory level is determined jointly by costs of stock-outs, costs of carrying and ordering inventories, order lead times and usage rates, and the probability distributions of each of those factors. With this in mind, we base our discussion of inventories on the standard EOQ-plus-safety-stock inventory model. Then, in Chapter 8, we examine the sources and forms of short-term credit.

**Part III:
Decisions
Involving Long-
Term Assets**

In Part III we move into the lower part of the left-hand side of the balance sheet, examining the decisions involved in fixed-asset acquisitions. After a discussion of compound interest in Chapter 9, we take up capital budgeting techniques, explaining in some detail the mechanics of capital budgeting in Chapter 10. Next, in Chapter 11, we expand the discussion to include uncertainty, covering the basic concepts of probability distributions, the trade-off between risk and rate of return, decision trees, and simulation.

**Part IV:
Sources and
Forms of
Long-Term
Financing**

In Part IV we move to the lower right-hand side of the balance sheet, examining the various kinds of long-term capital available to finance long-term investments. Chapter 12 presents an overview of the capital markets, explaining briefly certain institutional material without which no basic finance course is complete. Chapter 13 analyzes the financial characteristics of common stock, Chapter 14 examines bonds and preferred stock, Chapter 15 analyzes term loans and leases, and Chapter 16 discusses the nature and use of warrants and convertibles.

Part V:
Financial
Structure, the
Cost of Capital,
and Dividend
Policy

In Part V we pull together the threads developed in earlier chapters. We show how (1) financial structure affects both risk and expected returns; (2) risk and return interact to determine the optimal capital structure; (3) the cost of capital, which is required when making fixed-asset decisions, is calculated; and (4) investment opportunities and cost of capital considerations interact to determine the way the firm should distribute its profits between dividends and retained earnings.

Part VI:
Integrated
Topics in
Financial
Management

In the final five chapters we take up important but somewhat specialized topics that draw upon the concepts developed in the earlier sections. In Chapter 21 we introduce dynamics into the decision process, showing how financial managers react to changing conditions in the capital markets. We next discuss the external growth of firms through mergers and holding companies, as well as the factors affecting this development, in Chapter 22. Throughout most of the text we deal with growing and successful firms; however, many firms face financial difficulties, so the causes and possible remedies to these difficulties are discussed in Chapter 23. Chapter 24 deals with an increasingly important aspect of financial management—the finance function in a multinational corporation. Finally, in Chapter 25, we discuss the financial situation facing the small business firm and show how the tools of financial analysis may be applied to such a company.

Questions

1-1. What activities of financial managers are depicted by Figure 1-1?

1-2. What are financial intermediaries and what economic functions do they perform?

1-3. What are the main functions of financial managers?

1-4. Why is wealth maximization a better operating goal than profit maximization?

1-5. What role does utility maximization perform in finance theory?

1-6. What role does social responsibility have in formulating business and financial goals?

1-7. What have been the major developmental periods in the field of finance and what circumstances led to the evolution of the emphasis in each period?

1-8. What is the nature of the risk-return trade-off faced in financial decision making?

Selected References

Anthony, Robert N. "The Trouble with Profit Maximization." *Harvard Business Review* 38 (Nov.–Dec. 1960):126–34.

Branch, Ben. "Corporate Objectives and Market Performance." *Financial Management* 2 (Summer 1973):24–29.

Brigham, Eugene F., and Pappas, James L. *Managerial Economics*. Hinsdale, Ill.: Dryden Press, 1972, chap. 1.

Davis, Keith. "Social Responsibility Is Inevitable." *California Management Review* 19 (Fall 1976):14–20.

De Alessi, Louis. "Private Property and Dispersion of Ownership in Large Corporations." *Journal of Finance* 28 (Sept. 1973):839–51.

Donaldson, Gordon. "Financial Goals: Management versus Stockholders." *Harvard Business Review* 41 (May–June 1963):116–29.

———. "Financial Management in an Affluent Society." *Financial Executive* 35 (Apr. 1967):52–56, 58–60.

Elliott, J. W. "Control, Size, Growth, and Financial Performance in the Firm." *Journal of Financial and Quantitative Analysis* 7 (Jan. 1972):1309–20.

Findlay, Chapman M., and Whitmore, G. A. "Beyond Shareholder Wealth Maximization." *Financial Management* 3 (Winter 1974):25–35.

Gaskill, William J. "What's Ahead for Corporations in Social Responsibility?" *Financial Executive* 39 (July 1971):10–18.

Gerstner, Louis V., and Anderson, M. Helen. "The Chief Financial Officer as Activist." *Harvard Business Review* 54 (Sept.–Oct. 1976):100–06.

Gordon, Myron J. "A Portfolio Theory of the Social Discount Rate and the Public Debt." *The Journal of Finance* 31 (May 1976):199–214.

Grabowski, Henry G., and Mueller, Dennis C. "Managerial and Stockholder Welfare Models of Firm Expenditures." *Review of Economics and Statistics* 54 (Feb. 1972):9–24.

Haley, Charles W., and Schall, Lawrence D. *The Theory of Financial Decisions*. New York: McGraw-Hill, 1973, chap. 5.

Harkins, Edwin P. *Organizing and Managing the Corporate Financial Function*. Studies in Business Policy, no 129. New York: National Industrial Conference Board, Inc., 1969.

Hettenhouse, George W. "A Rationale for Restructuring Stock Plans." *Financial Management* 1 (Summer 1972):30–35.

Hill, Lawrence W. "The Growth of the Corporate Finance Function." *Financial Executive* 44 (July 1976):38–43.

Lewellen, Wilbur G. "Management and Ownership in the Large Firm." *Journal of Finance* 24 (May 1969):299–322.

Masson, Robert Tempest. "Executive Motivations, Earnings, and Consequent Equity Performance." *Journal of Political Economy* 79 (Nov.–Dec. 1971): 1278–92.

Merton, Robert C. "Distinguished Speaker Series." *The Journal of Financial and Quantitative Analysis* 10 (Nov. 1975):659–74.

Moag, Joseph S.; Carleton, Willard T.; and Lerner, Eugene M. "Defining the Finance Function: A Model-Systems Approach." *Journal of Finance* 22 (Dec. 1967):543–56.

Mobraaten, William L. "Social Responsibility of the Treasurer," in *The Treasurer's Handbook*. Edited by J. Fred Weston and Maurice B. Goudzwaard. Homewood, Illinois: Dow Jones-Irwin, 1976, pp. 1144–63.

Rosenberg, Ernest S. "Standards and Industry Self-Regulation." *California Management Review* 19 (Fall 1976):79–90.

Scanlon, John J. "Bell System Financial Policies." *Financial Management* 1 (Summer 1972):16–26.

Simkowitz, Michael A., and Jones, Charles P. "A Note on the Simultaneous Nature of Finance Methodology." *Journal of Finance* 27 (Mar. 1972):103–8.

Solomon, Ezra. *The Theory of Financial Management*. New York: Columbia University Press, 1963.

Trivoli, George W. "Evaluation of Pollution Control Expenditures by Leading Corporations." *Financial Management* 2 (Winter 1973):19–24.

Weston, J. Fred. "New Themes in Finance." *Journal of Finance* 24 (Mar. 1974): 237–43.

———. *The Scope and Methodology of Finance*. Englewood Cliffs, N.J.: Prentice-Hall, 1966.

———. "Toward Theories of Financial Policy." *Journal of Finance* 10 (May 1955): 130–43.

2   Ratio Analysis

Planning is the key to the financial manager's success. Financial plans may take many forms, but any good plan must be related to the firm's existing strengths and weaknesses. The strengths must be understood if they are to be used to proper advantage, and the weaknesses must be recognized if corrective action is to be taken. For example, are inventories adequate to support the projected level of sales? Does the firm have too heavy an investment in accounts receivable, and does this condition reflect a lax collection policy? The financial manager can plan his future financial requirements in accordance with the forecasting and budgeting procedures we will present in succeeding chapters, but his plan must begin with the type of financial analysis developed in this chapter.

Basic Financial Statements

Because ratio analysis employs financial data taken from the firm's balance sheet and income statement, it is useful to begin this chapter with a review of these accounting reports. For illustrative purposes, we shall use data taken from the Walker-Wilson Manufacturing Company, a producer of specialized machinery used in the automobile repair business. Formed in 1961, when Charles Walker and Ben Wilson set up a small plant to produce certain tools they had developed while in the army, Walker-Wilson grew steadily and earned the reputation of being one of the best small firms in its line of business. In December 1976, both Walker and Wilson were killed in a crash of their private plane, and for the next two years the firm was managed by Walker-Wilson's accountant.

In 1978 the widows, who are the principal stockholders in Walker-Wilson, acting on the advice of the firm's bankers and attorneys, engaged David Thompson as president and general manager. Although Thompson is experienced in the machinery business, especially in production and sales, he does not have a detailed knowledge of his new company, so he has decided to conduct a careful appraisal of the firm's position and, on the basis of this position, to draw up a plan for future operations.

Balance Sheet

Walker-Wilson's balance sheet, given in Table 2–1, shows the value of the firm's assets, and of the claims on these assets, at two particular points in time, December 31, 1977, and December 31, 1978. The assets are arranged from top to bottom in order of decreasing liquidity; that is, assets toward the top of the column will be converted to cash sooner than those toward the bottom of the column. The top group of assets— cash, marketable securities, accounts receivable, and inventories, which are expected to be converted into cash within one year—is defined as *current assets*. Assets in the lower part of the statement—plant and equipment—are not expected to be converted to cash within one year; these are defined as *fixed assets*.

The right side of the balance sheet is arranged similarly. Those items toward the top of the Claims column mature and must be paid off relatively soon; those further down the column are due in the more distant future. Current liabilities must be paid within one year; because the firm never has to "pay off" common stockholders, common stock and retained earnings represent "permanent" capital.

Income Statement

Walker-Wilson's income statement is shown in Table 2–2. Sales are shown at the top of the statement; various costs, including income taxes, are deducted to arrive at the net income available to common stockholders. The figure on the last line represents earnings per share (EPS), calculated as net income divided by number of shares outstanding.

Statement of Retained Earnings

Earnings may be paid out to stockholders as dividends or retained and reinvested in the business. Stockholders like to receive dividends, of course, but if earnings are plowed back into the business, the value of the stockholders' position in the company increases. Later in the book we shall consider the pros and cons of retaining earnings versus paying them out in dividends, but for now we are simply interested in the effects of dividends and retained earnings on the balance sheet. For this purpose, accountants use the statement of retained earnings, illustrated for Walker-Wilson in Table 2–3. Walker-Wilson earned $120,000 during the year, paid $100,000 in dividends to stockholders, and plowed $20,000 back into the business. Thus the retained earnings at the end of 1978, as shown both on the balance sheet and on the statement of retained earnings, is $400,000, which is $20,000 larger than the year-end 1977 figure.

Table 2-1
Walker-Wilson Company
Illustrative Balance Sheet (Thousands of Dollars)

Assets

	Dec. 31, 1977	Dec. 31, 1978
Cash	$ 52	$ 50
Marketable securities	175	150
Receivables	250	200
Inventories	355	300
Total current assets	$ 832	$ 700
Gross plant and equipment	$1,610	$1,800
Less depreciation	400	500
Net plant and equipment	1,210	1,300
Total assets	$2,042	$2,000

Claims on Assets

	Dec. 31, 1977	Dec. 31, 1978
Accounts payable	$ 87	$ 60
Notes payable, 10%	110	100
Accruals	10	10
Provision for federal income taxes	135	130
Total current liabilities	$ 342	$ 300
First mortgage bonds, 8%*	520	500
Debentures, 10%	200	200
Common stock (600,000 shares)	$600	$600
Retained earnings	380	400
Total net worth	980	1,000
Total claims on assets	$2,042	$2,000

*The sinking fund requirement for the mortgage bonds is $20,000 a year.

Table 2–2
Walker-Wilson
Company
Illustrative Income
Statement
for Year Ended
December 31, 1978

Net sales		$3,000,000
Cost of goods sold		2,555,000
Gross profit		$ 445,000
Less: Operating expenses		
Selling	$22,000	
General and administrative	40,000	
Lease payment on office building	28,000	90,000
Gross operating income		$ 355,000
Depreciation		100,000
Net operating income		$ 255,000
Add: Other income		
Royalities		15,000
Gross income		$ 270,000
Less: Other expenses		
Interest on notes payable	$10,000	
Interest on first mortgage	40,000	
Interest on debentures	20,000	70,000
Net income before income tax		$ 200,000
Federal income tax (at 40%)		80,000
Net income, after income tax, available to common stockholders		$ 120,000
Earnings per share *(EPS)*		$ .20

Table 2–3
Walker-Wilson
Company
Statement of Retained
Earnings for Year
Ended December 31,
1978 (Thousands of
Dollars)

Balance of retained earnings, December 31, 1977	$380
Add: Net income, 1978	120
	$500
Less: Dividends to stockholders	100
Balance of retained earnings, December 31, 1978	$400

**Relationship
among the
Three
Statements**

It is important to recognize that the balance sheet is a statement of the firm's financial position *at a point in time*, whereas the income statement shows the results of operations *during an interval of time*. Thus, the balance sheet represents a snapshot of the firm's position on a given date, while the income statement is based on a flow concept, showing what occurred between two points in time.

The statement of retained earnings indicates how the retained earnings account on the balance sheet is adjusted between balance sheet dates. Since its inception, Walker-Wilson had retained a total of $380,000 by December 31, 1977. In 1978 it earned $120,000, and $20,000 of this amount was retained. Thus, the retained earnings shown on the balance sheet for December 31, 1978, is $400,000.

When a firm retains earnings, it generally does so to expand the business—that is, to finance the purchase of assets such as plant, equipment, and inventories. As a result of operations in 1978, Walker-Wilson has $20,000 available for that purpose. Sometimes retained earnings will be used to build up the cash account, but retained earnings as shown on the balance sheet are *not* cash. Through the years they have been invested in bricks and mortar and other assets, so retained earnings as shown on the balance sheet are not "available" for anything. The earnings *for the current year* may be available for investment, but the *past retained earnings* have already been employed.

Stated another way, the balance sheet item "retained earnings" simply shows how much of their earnings the stockholders, through the years, have elected to retain in the business. Thus, the retained earnings account shows the additional investment the stockholders as a group have made in the business, over and above their initial investment at the inception of the company and through any subsequent issues of stock.

Basic Types of Financial Ratios

Each type of analysis has a purpose or use that determines the different relationships emphasized in the analysis. The analyst may, for example, be a banker considering whether or not to grant a short-term loan to a firm. He is primarily interested in the firm's near-term, or liquidity, position, so he stresses ratios that measure liquidity. In contrast, long-term creditors place far more emphasis on earning power and on operating efficiency. They know that unprofitable operations will erode asset values and that a strong current position is no guarantee that funds will be available to repay a 20-year bond issue. Equity investors are similarly interested in long-term profitability and efficiency. Management is, of course, concerned with all those aspects of financial analysis—it must be able to repay its debts to long- and short-term creditors as well as earn profits for stockholders.

It is useful to classify ratios into four fundamental types:

1. *Liquidity ratios*, which measure the firm's ability to meet its maturing short-term obligations.
2. *Leverage ratios*, which measure the extent to which the firm has been financed by debt.
3. *Activity ratios*, which measure how effectively the firm is using its resources.
4. *Profitability ratios*, which measure management's overall effectiveness as shown by the returns generated on sales and investment.

Specific examples of each ratio are given in the following sections, where the Walker-Wilson case history is used to illustrate their calculation and use.

Liquidity Ratios

Generally, the first concern of the financial analyst is liquidity: Is the firm able to meet its maturing obligations? Walker-Wilson has debts totaling $300,000 that must be paid within the coming year. Can these obligations be satisfied? Although a full liquidity analysis requires the use of cash budgets (described in Chapter 5), ratio analysis, by relating the amount of cash and other current assets to the current obligations, provides a quick and easy-to-use measure of liquidity. Two commonly used liquidity ratios are presented below.

Current Ratio. The current ratio is computed by dividing current assets by current liabilities. Current assets normally include cash, marketable securities, accounts receivable, and inventories; current liabilities consist of accounts payable, short-term notes payable, current maturities of long-term debt, accrued income taxes, and other accrued expenses (principally wages). The current ratio is the most commonly used measure of short-term solvency, since it indicates the extent to which the claims of short-term creditors are covered by assets that are expected to be converted to cash in a period roughly corresponding to the maturity of the claims.

The calculation of the current ratio for Walker-Wilson at year-end 1978 is shown below.

$$\text{Current ratio} = \frac{\text{current assets}}{\text{current liabilities}} = \frac{\$700,000}{\$300,000} = 2.3 \text{ times.}$$

$$\text{Industry average} = 2.5 \text{ times.}$$

The current ratio is slightly below the average for the industry, 2.5, but not low enough to cause concern. It appears that Walker-Wilson is about in line with most other firms in this particular line of business. Since current assets are near maturing, it is highly probable that they could be liquidated at close to book value. With a current ratio of 2.3, Walker-Wilson could liquidate current assets at only 43 percent of book value and still pay off current creditors in full.[1]

Although industry average figures are discussed later in the chapter, it should be stated at this point that the industry average is not a magic number that all firms should strive to maintain. In fact, some very well

---

1. $(1/2.3) = .43$, or 43 percent. Note that $(.43)(\$700,000) \approx \$300,000$, the amount of current liabilities.

managed firms will be above it, and other good firms will be below it. However, if a firm's ratios are very far removed from the average for its industry, the analyst must be concerned about why this variance occurs; that is, a deviation from the industry average should signal the analyst to check further.

Quick Ratio or Acid Test. The quick ratio is calculated by deducting inventories from current assets and dividing the remainder by current liabilities. Inventories are typically the least liquid of a firm's current assets and the assets on which losses are most likely to occur in the event of liquidation. Therefore, this measure of the firm's ability to pay off short-term obligations without relying on the sale of inventories is important.

$$\text{Quick, or acid test, ratio} = \frac{\text{current assets} - \text{inventory}}{\text{current liabilities}} = \frac{\$400,000}{\$300,000}$$

$$= 1.3 \text{ times.}$$

$$\text{Industry average} = 1.0 \text{ times.}$$

The industry average quick ratio is 1, so Walker-Wilson's 1.3 ratio compares favorably with other firms in the industry. Thompson knows that if the marketable securities can be sold at par and if he can collect the accounts receivable, he can pay off his current liabilities without selling any inventory.

Leverage Ratios

Leverage ratios, which measure the funds supplied by owners as compared with the financing provided by the firm's creditors, have a number of implications. First, creditors look to the equity, or owner-supplied funds, to provide a margin of safety. If owners have provided only a small proportion of total financing, the risks of the enterprise are borne mainly by the creditors. Second, by raising funds through debt, the owners gain the benefits of maintaining control of the firm with a limited investment. Third, if the firm earns more on the borrowed funds than it pays in interest, the return to the owners is magnified. For example, if assets earn 10 percent and debt costs only 8 percent, there is a 2 percent differential accruing to the stockholders. Leverage cuts both ways, however; if the return on assets falls to 3 percent, the differential between that figure and the cost of debt must be made up from equity's share of total profits. In the first instance, where assets earn more than the cost of debt, leverage is favorable; in the second, it is unfavorable.

Firms with low leverage ratios have less risk of loss when the economy is in a downturn, but they also have lower expected returns when the economy booms. Conversely, firms with high leverage ratios run the risk of large losses but also have a chance of gaining high profits. The prospects of high returns are desirable, but investors are averse to risk. Decisions about the use of leverage, then, must balance higher expected returns against increased risk.[2]

In practice, leverage is approached in two ways. One approach examines balance sheet ratios and determines the extent to which borrowed funds have been used to finance the firm. The other approach measures the risks of debt by income statement ratios designed to determine the number of times fixed charges are covered by operating profits. These sets of ratios are complementary, and most analysts examine both leverage ratios.

Total Debt to Total Assets. The ratio of total debt to total assets, generally called the *debt ratio*, measures the percentage of total funds provided by creditors. Debt includes current liabilities and all bonds. Creditors prefer moderate debt ratios, since the lower the ratio, the greater the cushion against creditors' losses in the event of liquidation. In contrast to the creditors' perference for a low debt ratio, the owners may seek high leverage either (1) to magnify earnings or (2) because raising new equity means giving up some degree of control. If the debt ratio is too high, there is a danger of encouraging irresponsibility on the part of the owners. The stake of the owners can become so small that speculative activity, if it is successful, will yield a substantial percentage return to the owners. If the venture is unsuccessful, however, only a moderate loss is incurred by the owners because their investment is small.

$$\text{Debt ratio} = \frac{\text{total debt}}{\text{total assets}} = \frac{\$1,000,000}{\$2,000,000} = 50\%.$$

$$\text{Industry average} = 33\%.$$

Walker-Wilson's debt ratio is 50 percent; this means that creditors have supplied half the firm's total financing. Since the average debt ratio for this industry — and for manufacturing generally — is about 33 percent, Walker-Wilson would find it difficult to borrow additional funds without first raising more equity capital. Creditors would be reluctant to lend the firm more money, and Thompson would probably be sub-

---

2. The problem of determining optimum leverage for a firm with given risk characteristics is examined extensively in Chapters 17, 18, and 19.

jecting the stockholders to undue dangers if he sought to increase the debt ratio still more by borrowing.[3]

Times Interest Earned. The times-interest-earned ratio is determined by dividing earnings before interest and taxes (gross income in Table 2–2) by the interest charges. The times-interest-earned ratio measures the extent to which earnings can decline without resultant financial embarrassment to the firm because of inability to meet annual interest costs. Failure to meet this obligation can bring legal action by the creditors, possibly resulting in bankruptcy. Note that the before-tax profit figure is used in the numerator. Because income taxes are computed after interest expense is deducted, the ability to pay current interest is not affected by income taxes.

$$\text{Times interest earned} = \frac{\text{gross income}}{\text{interest charges}}$$

$$= \frac{\text{profit before taxes} + \text{interest charges}}{\text{interest charges}}$$

$$= \frac{\$270,000}{\$70,000} = 3.9 \text{ times.}$$

Industry average = 8.0 times.

Walker-Wilson's interest charges consist of three payments totaling $70,000 (see Table 2–2). The firm's gross income available for servicing these charges is $270,000, so the interest is covered 3.9 times. Since the industry average is 8 times, the company is covering its interest charges by a minimum margin of safety and deserves only a poor rating. This ratio reinforces the conclusion based on the debt ratio that the company is likely to face some difficulties if it attempts to borrow additional funds.

Fixed Charge Coverage. This ratio is similar to the times-interest-earned ratio, but it is somewhat more inclusive in that it recognizes

---

3. The ratio of debt to equity is also used in financial analysis. The debt to assets (B/A) and debt to equity (B/S) ratios are simply transformations of one another:

$$B/S = \frac{B/A}{1 - B/A} \quad \text{and} \quad B/A = \frac{B/S}{1 + B/S}$$

Both ratios increase as a firm of a given size (total assets) uses a greater proportion of debt, but B/A rises linearly and approaches a limit of 100 percent while B/S rises exponentially and approaches infinity.

that many firms lease assets and incur long-term obligations under lease contracts.[4] As we show in Chapter 15, leasing has become quite widespread in recent years, making this ratio preferable to the times-interest-earned ratio for most financial analyses. "Fixed charges" are defined as interest plus annual long-term lease obligations, and the fixed charge coverage ratio is defined as

$$\text{Fixed charge coverage} = \frac{\begin{matrix}\text{profit} & \text{interest} & \text{lease} \\ \text{before taxes} + \text{charges} + \text{obligations}\end{matrix}}{\text{interest charges} + \text{lease obligations}}$$

$$= \frac{\$200,000 + \$70,000 + \$28,000}{\$70,000 + \$28,000} = \frac{298,000}{98,000}$$

$$= 3.04 \text{ times.}$$

Industry average $= 5.5$ times.

Walker-Wilson's fixed charges are covered 3.04 times, as opposed to an industry average of 5.5 times. Again, this indicates that the firm is somewhat weaker than creditors would prefer it to be, and it further points up the difficulties Thompson would likely encounter if he should attempt additional borrowing.[5]

Activity Ratios

Activity ratios measure how effectively the firm employs the resources at its command. These ratios all involve comparisons between the level of sales and the investment in various asset accounts. The activity ratios presume that a "proper" balance should exist between sales and the various asset accounts—inventories, accounts receivable, fixed assets, and others. As we shall see in the following chapters, this is generally a good assumption.

Inventory Turnover. The inventory turnover is defined as sales divided by inventories.

---

4. Generally, a long-term lease is defined as one extending at least three years into the future. Thus, rent incurred under a one-year lease would not be included in the fixed charge coverage ratio, but rental payments under a three-year or longer lease would be defined as fixed charges.

5. A still more complete coverage ratio is the *debt service coverage ratio*, defined similarly to the fixed charge coverage except that mandatory annual payments to retire long-term debt (amortization payments, discussed in Chapter 15) are also included in the denominator. This ratio is not widely used, primarily because sinking fund obligations are not generally known to outside analysts. Moreover, it is difficult to develop industry averages for this ratio because of the absence of data. The information on lease obligations, in contrast, is almost always available in footnotes to financial statements.

$$\text{Inventory turnover} = \frac{\text{sales}}{\text{inventory}} = \frac{\$3,000,000}{\$300,000} = 10 \text{ times.}$$
$$\text{Industry average} = 9 \text{ times.}$$

Walker-Wilson's turnover of 10 compares favorably with an industry average of 9 times. This suggests that the company does not hold excessive stocks of inventory; excess stocks are, of course, unproductive and represent an investment with a low or zero rate of return. This high inventory turnover also reinforces Thompson's faith in the current ratio. If the turnover was low—say 3 or 4 times—Thompson would wonder whether the firm was holding damaged or obsolete materials not actually worth their stated value.

Two problems arise in calculating and analyzing the inventory turnover ratio. First, sales are at market prices; if inventories are carried at cost, as they generally are, it would be more appropriate to use cost of goods sold in place of sales in the numerator of the formula. Established compilers of financial ratio statistics such as Dun & Bradstreet, however, use the ratio of sales to inventories carried at cost. To develop a figure that can be compared with those developed by Dun & Bradstreet, it is therefore necessary to measure inventory turnover with sales in the numerator, as we do here.

The second problem lies in the fact that sales occur over the entire year, whereas the inventory figure is for one point in time. This makes it better to use an average inventory, computed by adding beginning and ending inventories and dividing by 2. If it is determined that the firm's business is highly seasonal, or if there has been a strong upward or downward sales trend during the year, it becomes essential to make some such adjustment. Neither of these conditions holds for Walker-Wilson; to maintain comparability with industry averages, Thompson did not use the average inventory figure.

Average Collection Period. The average collection period, which is a measure of the accounts receivable turnover, is computed in two steps: (1) annual sales are divided by 360 to get the average daily sales[6]; (2) daily sales are divided into accounts receivable to find the number of days' sales tied up in receivables. This is defined as the average collection period, because it represents the average length of time that the firm must wait after making a sale before receiving cash. The cal-

---

6. Because information on credit sales is generally unavailable, total sales must be used. Since all firms do not have the same percentage of credit sales, there is a good chance that the average collection period will be somewhat in error. Also, note for convenience, the financial community generally uses 360 rather than 365 as the number of days in the year for purposes such as these.

culations for Walker-Wilson show an average collection period of 24 days, slightly above the 20-day industry average.

$$\text{Sales per day} = \frac{\$3,000,000}{360} = \$8,333. \tag{1}$$

$$\text{Average collection period} = \frac{\text{receivables}}{\text{sales per day}} = \frac{\$200,000}{\$8,333} = 24 \text{ days}. \tag{2}$$

$$\text{Industry average} = 20 \text{ days}.$$

This ratio can also be evaluated by comparison with the terms on which the firm sells its goods. For example, Walker-Wilson's sales terms call for payment within 20 days, so the 24-day collection period indicates that customers, on the average, are not paying their bills on time. If the trend in the collection period over the past few years had been rising while the credit policy had not changed, this would be even stronger evidence that steps should be taken to expedite the collection of accounts receivable.

One nonratio financial tool should be mentioned in connection with accounts receivable analysis—the *aging schedule*, which breaks down accounts receivable according to how long they have been outstanding. The aging schedule for Walker-Wilson is given below.

Age of Account (Days)	Percent of Total Value of Accounts Receivable
0–20	50
21–30	20
31–45	15
46–60	3
over 60	12
Total	100

The 24-day collection period looked bad by comparison with the 20-day terms, and the aging schedule shows that the firm is having especially serious collection problems with some of its accounts. Fifty percent are overdue, many for over a month. Others pay quite promptly, bringing the average down to only 24 days, but the aging schedule shows this average to be somewhat misleading.

Fixed Asset Turnover. The ratio of sales to fixed assets measures the turnover of plant and equipment.

$$\text{Fixed assets turnover} = \frac{\text{sales}}{\text{net fixed assets}} = \frac{\$3,000,000}{\$1,300,000} = 2.3 \text{ times.}$$

$$\text{Industry average} = 5.0 \text{ times.}$$

Walker-Wilson's turnover of 2.3 times compares poorly with the industry average of 5 times, indicating that the firm is not using its fixed assets to as high a percentage of capacity as are the other firms in the industry. Thompson should bear this fact in mind when his production people request funds for new capital investments.

Total Assets Turnover. The final activity ratio measures the turnover of all the firm's assets—it is calculated by dividing sales by total assets.

$$\text{Total assets turnover} = \frac{\text{sales}}{\text{total assets}} = \frac{\$3,000,000}{\$2,000,000} = 1.5 \text{ times.}$$

$$\text{Industry average} = 2.0 \text{ times.}$$

Walker-Wilson's turnover of total assets is well below the industry average. The company is simply not generating a sufficient volume of business for the size of its asset investment. Sales should be increased, or some assets should be disposed of, or both steps should be taken.

Profitability Ratios

Profitability is the net result of a large number of policies and decisions. The ratios examined thus far reveal some interesting things about the way the firm is operating, but the profitability ratios give final answers about how effectively the firm is being managed.

Profit Margin on Sales. The profit margin on sales, computed by dividing net income after taxes by sales, gives the profit per dollar of sales.

$$\text{Profit margin} = \frac{\text{net profit after taxes}}{\text{sales}} = \frac{\$120,000}{\$3,000,000} = 4\%.$$

$$\text{Industry average} = 5\%.$$

Walker-Wilson's profit margin is somewhat below the industry average of 5 percent, indicating that the firm's sales prices are relatively low or that its costs are relatively high or both.

Return on Total Assets. The ratio of net profit to total assets measures the return on total investment in the firm, or the ROI, as it is frequently called.[7]

$$\text{Return on total assets} = \frac{\text{net profit after taxes}}{\text{total assets}} = \frac{\$120,000}{\$2,000,000} = 6\%.$$

$$\text{Industry average} = 10\%.$$

Walker-Wilson's 6 percent return is well below the 10 percent average for the industry. This low rate results from the low profit margin on sales and from the low turnover of total assets.

Return on Net Worth. The ratio of net profit after taxes to net worth measures the rate of return on the stockholders' investment.

$$\text{Return on net worth} = \frac{\text{net profit after taxes}}{\text{net worth}} = \frac{\$120,000}{\$1,000,000} = 12\%.$$

$$\text{Industry average} = 15\%.$$

Walker-Wilson's 12 percent return is below the 15 percent industry average but not as far below as the return on total assets. In a later section of this chapter, where the du Pont method of analysis is applied to the Walker-Wilson case, we will see why this is so.

Summary of the Ratios

The individual ratios, which are summarized in Table 2–4, give Thompson a reasonably good idea of Walker-Wilson's main strengths and weaknesses. First, the company's liquidity position is reasonably good — its current and quick ratios appear to be satisfactory by comparison with the industry averages. Second, the leverage ratios suggest that the company is rather heavily indebted. With a debt ratio substantially higher than the industry average, and with coverage ratios well below the industry averages, it is doubtful that Walker-Wilson could do much additional debt financing except on relatively unfavorable terms. Even if Thompson could borrow more, to do so would be subjecting the com-

---

7. In calculating the return on total assets, it is sometimes desirable to add interest to net profits after taxes to form the numerator of the ratio. The theory here is that since assets are financed by both stockholders and creditors, the ratio should measure the productivity of assets in providing returns to both classes of investors. We have not done so at this point because the published averages we use for comparative purposes exclude interest. Later in this book, however, when we deal with leverage decisions, we do add back interest. For example, this addition has a material bearing on the value of the ratio for utilities (which have large amounts of fixed assets financed by debt), and the revised ratio is the one normally used for them.

Table 2–4
Summary
of Financial
Ratio Analysis

Ratio	Formula for Calculation	Calculation	Industry Average	Evaluation
Liquidity				
Current	$\dfrac{\text{current assets}}{\text{current liabilities}}$	$\dfrac{\$\,700{,}000}{\$\,300{,}000} = 2.3$ times	2.5 times	Satisfactory
Quick, or acid, test	$\dfrac{\text{current assets} - \text{inventory}}{\text{current liabilities}}$	$\dfrac{\$\,400{,}000}{\$\,300{,}000} = 1.3$ times	1.0 times	Good
Leverage				
Debt to total assets	$\dfrac{\text{total debt}}{\text{total assets}}$	$\dfrac{\$1{,}000{,}000}{\$2{,}000{,}000} = 50$ percent	33 percent	Poor
Times interest earned	$\dfrac{\text{profit before taxes plus interest charges}}{\text{interest charges}}$	$\dfrac{\$\,270{,}000}{\$\,70{,}000} = 3.9$ times	8.0 times	Poor
Fixed charge coverage	$\dfrac{\text{income available for meeting fixed charges}}{\text{fixed charges}}$	$\dfrac{\$\,298{,}000}{\$\,98{,}000} = 3.04$ times	5.5 times	Poor
Activity				
Inventory turnover	$\dfrac{\text{sales}}{\text{inventory}}$	$\dfrac{\$3{,}000{,}000}{\$\,300{,}000} = 10$ times	9 times	Satisfactory
Average collection period	$\dfrac{\text{receivables}}{\text{sales per day}}$	$\dfrac{\$\,200{,}000}{\$\,8{,}333} = 24$ days	20 days	Satisfactory
Fixed assets turnover	$\dfrac{\text{sales}}{\text{fixed assets}}$	$\dfrac{\$3{,}000{,}000}{\$1{,}300{,}000} = 2.3$ times	5.0 times	Poor
Total assets turnover	$\dfrac{\text{sales}}{\text{total assets}}$	$\dfrac{\$3{,}000{,}000}{\$2{,}000{,}000} = 1.5$ times	2 times	Poor
Profitability				
Profit margin on sales	$\dfrac{\text{net profit after taxes}}{\text{sales}}$	$\dfrac{\$\,120{,}000}{\$3{,}000{,}000} = 4$ percent	5 percent	Fair
Return on total assets	$\dfrac{\text{net profit after taxes}}{\text{total assets}}$	$\dfrac{\$\,120{,}000}{\$2{,}000{,}000} = 6.0$ percent	10 percent	Poor
Return on net worth	$\dfrac{\text{net profit after taxes}}{\text{net worth}}$	$\dfrac{\$\,120{,}000}{\$1{,}000{,}000} = 12.0$ percent	15 percent	Fair

pany to the danger of default and bankruptcy in the event of a business downturn.

Turning to the activity ratios, the inventory turnover and average collection period both indicate that the company's current assets are pretty well in balance, but the low fixed asset turnover suggests that there has been too heavy an investment in fixed assets. This low fixed asset turnover means, in effect, that the company probably could have operated with a smaller investment in fixed assets. Had the excessive fixed asset investment not been made, the company could have avoided some of its debt financing and would now have lower interest payments. This, in turn, would have led to improved leverage and coverage ratios.

The profit margin on sales is low, indicating that costs are too high or that prices are too low or both. In this particular case, the sales prices are in line with other firms; high costs are, in fact, the cause of the low margin. Further, the high costs can be traced to (1) high depreciation charges and (2) high interest expenses. Both these costs are, in turn, attributable to the excessive investment in fixed assets.

Returns on both total investment and net worth are also below the industry averages. These relatively poor results are directly attributable to the low profit margin on sales, which lowers the numerators of the ratios, and to the excessive investment, which raises the denominators.

Trend Analysis

While the preceding ratio analysis gives a reasonably good picture of Walker-Wilson's operation, it is incomplete in one important respect — it ignores the time dimension. The ratios are snapshots of the picture at one point in time, but there may be trends in motion that are in the process of rapidly eroding a relatively good present position. Conversely, an analysis of the ratios over the past few years may suggest that a relatively weak position is being improved at a rapid rate.

The method of trend analysis is illustrated in Figure 2–1, which shows graphs of Walker-Wilson's sales, current ratio, debt ratio, fixed assets turnover, and return on net worth. The figures are compared with industry averages; industry sales have been rising steadily over the entire period, and the industry average ratios have been relatively stable throughout. Thus, any trends in the company's ratios are due to its own internal conditions, not to environmental influences affecting all firms. In addition, Walker-Wilson's deterioration since the death of the two principal officers is quite apparent. Prior to 1973, Walker-Wilson was growing more rapidly than the average firm in the industry; during the following two years, however, sales actually declined.

Walker-Wilson's liquidity position as measured by its current ratio has also gone downhill in the past two years. Although the ratio is only

Figure 2–1
Illustration of Trend
Analysis

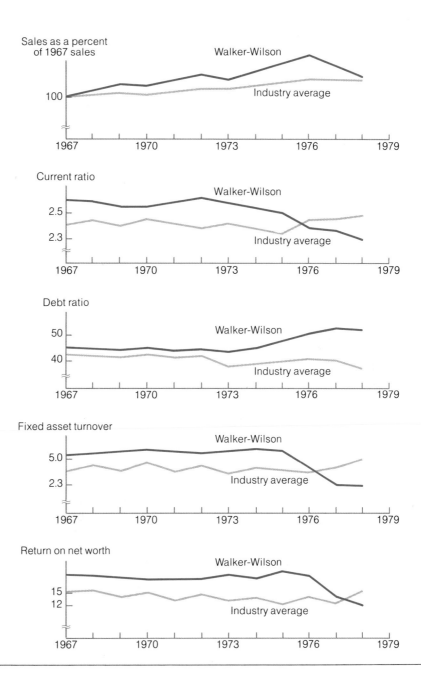

slightly below the industry average at the present time, the trend suggests that a real liquidity crisis may develop during the next year or two unless corrective action is taken immediately.

The debt ratio trend line shows that Walker-Wilson followed industry practices closely until 1976, when the ratio jumped to a full 10 percentage points above the industry average. Similarly, the fixed assets turnover declined during 1976, even though sales were still rising. The records reveal that the company borrowed heavily during 1976 to finance a major expansion of plant and equipment. Walker and Wilson had intended to use this additional capacity to generate a still higher volume of sales and to retire the debt out of expected high profits. Their untimely death, however, led to a decrease in sales rather than an increase, and the expected high profits that were to be used to retire the debt did not materialize. The analysis suggests that the bankers were correct when they advised Mrs. Walker and Mrs. Wilson of the need for a change in management.

du Pont System of Financial Analysis

The du Pont system of financial analysis has achieved wide recognition in American industry, and properly so. It brings together the activity ratios and profit margin on sales and shows how these ratios interact to determine the profitability of assets. The nature of the system, modified somewhat, is set forth in Figure 2–2.

The right side of the figure develops the turnover ratio. That section shows how current assets (cash, marketable securities, accounts receivable, and inventories), when added to fixed assets, gives total investment. Total investment divided into sales gives the turnover of investment.

The left side of the figure develops the profit margin on sales. The individual expense items plus income taxes are subtracted from sales to produce net profits after taxes. Net profits divided by sales gives the profit margin on sales. When the asset turnover ratio on the right side of Figure 2–2 is multiplied by the profit margin on sales developed on the left side of the figure, the product is the return on total investment (ROI) in the firm. This can be seen from the following formula:

$$\frac{profit}{sales} \times \frac{sales}{investment} = ROI.$$

Walker-Wilson's turnover was seen to be 1.5 times, as compared to an industry average of 2 times; its margin on sales was 4 percent, as compared to 5 percent for the industry. Multiplied together, turnover and profit margin produced a return on assets equal to 6 percent, a rate well

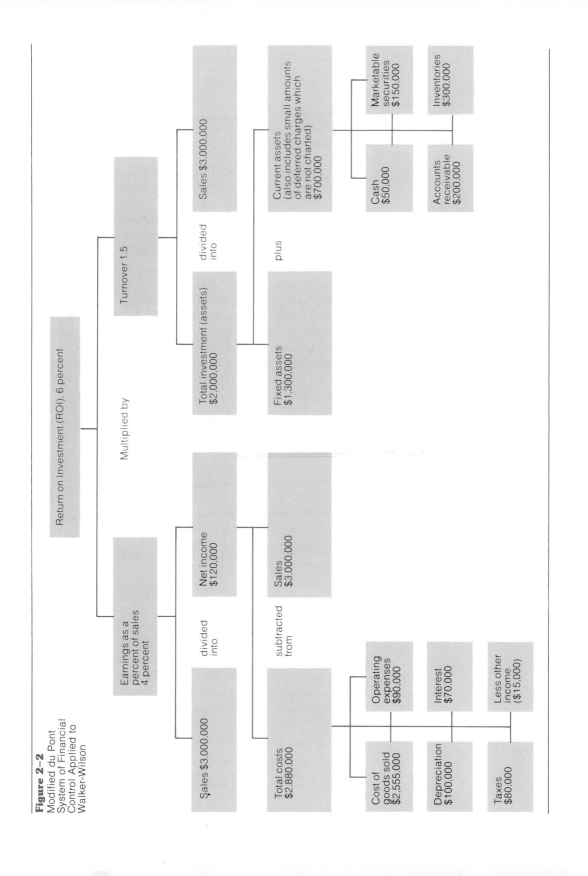

Figure 2-2
Modified du Pont System of Financial Control Applied to Walker-Wilson

Return on Investment (ROI), 6 percent

Earnings as a percent of sales 4 percent

Multiplied by

Turnover 1.5

Net income $120,000

divided into

Sales $3,000,000

Sales $3,000,000

subtracted from

Total costs $2,880,000

Cost of goods sold $2,555,000

Operating expenses $90,000

Depreciation $100,000

Interest $70,000

Taxes $80,000

Less other income ($15,000)

Total investment (assets) $2,000,000

divided into

Sales $3,000,000

Fixed assets $1,300,000

plus

Current assets (also includes small amounts of deferred charges which are not charted) $700,000

Cash $50,000

Marketable securities $150,000

Accounts receivable $200,000

Inventories $300,000

below the 10 percent industry average. If Thompson is to bring Walker-Wilson back to the level of the rest of the industry, he should strive to boost both his profit margin and his total asset turnover. Tracing back through the du Pont system should help him in this task.

Extending the du Pont System to Include Leverage

Although Walker-Wilson's return on total assets is well below the 10 percent industry average, the firm's 12 percent return on net worth is only slightly below the 15 percent industry average. How can the return on net worth end up so close to the industry average when the return on total assets is so far below the average? The answer is that Walker-Wilson uses more debt than the average firm in the industry.

Only half of Walker-Wilson's assets is financed with net worth; the other half is financed with debt. This means that the entire 6 percent return on assets (which is computed after interest charges on debt) goes to the common stockholders, so their return is boosted substantially. The precise formula for measuring the effect of financial leverage on stockholder returns is shown below.

$$\text{Rate of return on net worth} = \frac{\text{return on assets (ROI)}}{\text{percent of assets financed by net worth}}$$

$$= \frac{\text{return on assets (ROI)}}{1.0 - \text{debt ratio}}.$$

Calculation for Walker-Wilson:

$$\text{Return on net worth} = \frac{6\%}{1.0 - 0.50} = \frac{6\%}{0.5} = 12\%.$$

Calculation for the industry average:

$$\text{Return on net worth} = \frac{10\%}{1.0 - 0.33} = \frac{10\%}{0.67} = 15\%.$$

This formula is useful for showing how financial leverage can be used to increase the rate of return on net worth.[8] But increasing returns on net worth by using more and more leverage causes the leverage ratios to rise higher and higher above the industry norms. Creditors resist this tendency, so there are limitations to the practice. Moreover, greater leverage increases the risk of bankruptcy and thus endangers the firm's stockholders. Since widows Walker and Wilson are entirely dependent

8. There are limitations on this statement—specifically, the return on net worth increases with leverage only if the return on assets exceeds the rate of interest on debt, after considering the tax deductibility of interest payments. This whole concept is explored in detail in Chapter 18, which is devoted entirely to financial leverage.

on income from the firm for their support, they would be in a particularly bad position if the firm goes into default. Consequently, Thompson would be ill-advised to attempt to use leverage to boost the return on net worth much further.

Rates of Return in Different Industries

Would it be better to have a 5 percent margin on sales and a total asset turnover of 2 times, or a 2 percent sales margin and a turnover of 5 times? It makes no difference—in either case the firm has a 10 percent return on investment. Actually, most firms are not free to make the kind of choice posed in the above question. Depending on the nature of its industry, the firm *must* operate with more or fewer assets, and it will experience a turnover that depends on the characteristics of its particular line of business. In the case of a dealer in fresh fruits and vegetables, fish, or other perishable items, the turnover should be high—every day or two would be most desirable. In contrast, some lines of business require very heavy fixed investment or long production periods. A hydroelectric utility company, with its heavy investment in dams and transmission lines, requires heavy fixed investment; a shipbuilder or an aircraft producer needs a long production period. Such companies necessarily have a low asset turnover rate but a correspondingly higher profit margin on sales.

If a grocery chain has a high turnover, and a chemical producer, with its heavy investment in fixed assets, a low turnover, would you expect to find differences in their profit margins on sales? In general, you would—the chemical producer should have a considerably higher profit margin to offset its lower turnover. Otherwise, the grocery business would be much more profitable than the chemical, investment would flow into the grocery industry, and profits in this industry would be eroded to the point where the rate of return was about equal to that in the chemical industry.

We know, however, that leverage must be taken into account when considering the rate of return on net worth. If the firms in one industry have a somewhat lower return on total assets but use slightly more financial leverage than do those in another industry, both sets of firms may end up with approximately the same rate of return on net worth.[9]

These points, which are all necessary for a complete understanding of ratio analysis, are illustrated in Table 2–5. There we see how turnover and profit margins interact with each other to produce varying returns on assets, and also how financial leverage affects the returns on net worth. Crown-Zellerbach, Kroger, and the average of all manufacturing

---

9. The factors that make it possible for firms to use more leverage are taken up in Chapters 14 and 18. It may be stated now, however, that the primary factor favoring leverage is sales and profit stability.

Table 2–5 **Turnover,** **Profit Margins** **and Returns on** **Net Worth**		Sales to Total Assets (Times)	× Profit to Sales (Percent)	= Profit to Total Assets (Percent)	Debt to Total Assets (Percent)	Profit to Net Worth[a] (Percent)
	All manufacturing firms	1.42	5.3	7.5	46	13.9
	Crown-Zellerbach (forest products)	1.30	4.59	5.97	48.8	11.7
	Kroger (food retailer)	8.43	0.65	5.48	32.8	8.1

[a]The figures in this column may be found as

$$\text{Profit to net worth} = \frac{\text{profit to total assets}}{1 - \text{debt to total assets}}$$

Sources: FTC Quarterly Financial Reports and Company Annual Reports for 1976.

firms are compared. Crown-Zellerbach, with its very heavy fixed asset investment, is seen to have a relatively low turnover; Kroger, a typical chain food store, has a very high sales-to-assets ratio. Crown-Zellerbach, however, ends up with about the same rate of return on assets because its high profit margin on sales compensates for its low turnover. Both Kroger and Crown-Zellerbach use financial leverage to increase their return on net worth.

Sources of Comparative Ratios

In our analysis of the Walker-Wilson Company, industry average ratios were frequently used. Where may such averages be obtained? Some important sources are listed below.

Dun & Bradstreet

Probably the most widely known and used of the industry average ratios are those compiled by Dun & Bradstreet, Inc. D&B provides fourteen ratios calculated for a large number of industries. Sample ratios and explanations are shown in Table 2–6. The complete data give the fourteen ratios, with the interquartile ranges,[10] for 125 lines of business activity based on their financial statements. The 125 types of business activity consist of 71 manufacturing and construction categories, 30 categories of wholesalers, and 24 categories of retailers.

10. The median and the quartile ratios can be illustrated by an example. The median ratio of current assets to current debt of manufacturers of airplane parts and accessories, as shown in Table 2–6, is 1.81. To obtain this figure, the ratios of current assets to current debt for each of the 59 concerns were arranged in a graduated series, with the largest ratio at the top and the smallest at the bottom. The median ratio of 1.81 is the ratio halfway between the top and the bottom. The ratio of 2.40, representing the upper quartile, is one quarter of the way down the series from the top (or halfway between the top and the median). The ratio 1.42, representing the lower quartile, is one quarter of the way up from the bottom (or halfway between the median and the bottom).

Robert Morris Associates

Another group of useful ratios can be found in the annual *Statement Studies* compiled and published by the Robert Morris Associates, which is the national association of bank loan officers. These are representative averages based on financial statements received by banks in connection with loans made. Eleven ratios are computed for 156 lines of business.

Quarterly Financial Report for Manufacturing Corporations

The Federal Trade Commission (FTC) publishes quarterly financial data on manufacturing companies. Both balance sheet and income statement data are developed from a systematic sample of corporations. The reports are published perhaps six months after the financial data have been made available by the companies. They include an analysis by industry groups and by asset size and financial statements in ratio form (or common-size analysis) as well. The FTC reports are a rich source of information and are frequently used for comparative purposes.

Individual Firms

Credit departments of individual firms compile financial ratios and averages on their (1) customers in order to judge their ability to meet obligations and (2) suppliers in order to evaluate their financial ability to fulfill contracts. The First National Bank of Chicago, for instance, compiles semiannual reports on the financial data for finance companies. The NCR, Inc. gathers data for a large number of business lines.

Trade Associations and Public Accountants

Financial ratios for many industries are compiled by trade associations and constitute an important source to be checked by a financial manager seeking comparative data. These averages are usually the best obtainable. In addition to balance sheet data, they provide detailed information on operating expenses, which makes possible an informed analysis of the efficiency of the firms.

Use of Financial Ratios in Credit Analysis

In this chapter we have discussed a rather long list of ratios and have learned what each ratio is designed to measure. Sometimes it will be unnecessary to go beyond a few calculations to determine that a firm is in very good or very bad condition, but often the analysis is equivalent to a detective-story investigation—what one ratio will not indicate, another may. Also, a relation vaguely suggested by one ratio may be corroborated by another. For these reasons, it is often useful to calculate a number of different ratios.

In numerous situations, however, a few ratios will tell the story. For

Table 2–6
Dun & Bradstreet Ratios for Selected Industries

Line of Business (and Number of Concerns Reporting)	Current Assets to Current Debt (Times)	Net Profits on Net Sales (Percent)	Net Profits on Tangible Net Worth (Percent)	Net Profits on Net Working Capital (Percent)	Net Sales to Tangible Net Worth (Times)	Net Sales to Net Working Capital (Times)	Collection Period (Days)
3522* Agricultural Implements and Machinery (74)	3.78 2.27 1.52	7.15 4.12 3.23	21.44 14.59 8.30	36.82 20.68 14.95	5.27 3.21 2.34	8.13 4.60 2.98	25 39 52
3722–23–29 Airplane Parts & Accessories (59)	2.40 1.81 1.42	8.12 5.25 3.10	27.78 18.11 11.90	44.96 32.21 17.76	4.46 3.43 2.72	8.27 5.29 4.20	34 46 61
3714 Automobile Parts and Accessories (84)	3.77 2.58 2.03	6.75 4.59 3.22	18.89 14.60 8.65	32.11 20.32 14.09	3.89 2.99 2.19	6.54 4.63 3.23	35 42 51
2515 Bedsprings and Mattresses (49)	3.60 2.33 1.87	2.69 2.06 0.80	11.53 6.46 2.71	15.03 10.95 5.11	5.85 3.48 2.61	8.52 5.79 4.34	30 42 55
2082 Breweries (27)	3.34 2.59 1.88	6.48 4.75 1.28	15.15 10.38 2.55	63.72 34.27 8.23	3.23 2.49 1.72	11.34 8.51 5.13	8 16 24
287 Chemicals, Agricultural (33)	2.98 1.73 1.33	3.87 2.02 0.95	11.78 7.58 1.56	44.91 17.73 2.80	5.11 3.46 1.98	13.41 6.72 4.15	32 55 87
281 Chemicals, Industrial (60)	2.77 2.28 1.51	8.15 5.53 3.93	16.07 12.45 9.03	50.01 30.32 17.95	3.09 1.95 1.52	7.05 5.03 3.39	39 50 59
1511 Contractors, Building Construction (188)	2.06 1.49 1.27	3.14 1.38 0.74	19.04 12.39 6.20	33.04 16.38 9.14	12.51 8.09 4.32	20.41 11.52 5.79	† † †

*Standard Industrial Classification (SIC) categories.
†Building trades contractors have no inventories in the credit sense of the term. As a general rule, they have no customary selling terms, such contracts being a special job for which individual terms are arranged.
Source: *Key Business Ratios in 125 Lines* (New York: Dun & Bradstreet, Inc.). Reprinted by permission of Dun & Bradstreet.

example, a credit manager who has a great many invoices flowing across his desk each day may limit himself to three ratios as evidence of whether the prospective buyer of his goods will pay promptly: (1) He may use either the current or the quick ratio to determine how burdened the prospective buyer is with current liabilities; (2) he may use the debt to total assets ratio to determine how much of the prospective buyer's own funds are invested in the business; (3) he may use any one of the profitability ratios to determine whether or not the firm has favorable prospects. If the profit margin is high enough, it may justify the

Table 2–6 Continued
Dun & Bradstreet Ratios for Selected Industries

Line of Business (and Number of Concerns Reporting)	Net Sales to Inventory (Times)	Fixed Assets to Tangible Net Worth (Percent)	Current Debt to Tangible Net Worth (Percent)	Total Debt to Tangible Net Worth (Percent)	Inventory to Net Working Capital (Percent)	Current Debt to Inventory (Percent)	Funded Debts to Net Working Capital (Percent)
3522*	6.1	21.5	22.5	47.5	71.3	44.6	17.8
Agricultural Implements	3.9	33.5	49.3	80.0	104.9	72.0	37.0
and Machinery (74)	3.1	63.6	115.3	149.6	161.4	98.4	50.9
3722–23–29	8.6	27.9	43.2	58.0	73.8	87.9	14.1
Airplane Parts &	5.9	48.4	61.5	103.5	103.4	100.0	47.5
Accessories (59)	3.9	75.5	112.5	179.1	154.7	141.9	65.8
3714	8.0	25.7	23.5	47.3	60.5	56.5	14.6
Automobile Parts and	5.3	39.6	38.0	77.8	86.2	79.7	41.6
Accessories (84)	4.2	55.5	63.4	116.9	100.5	113.7	59.9
2515	11.7	15.6	22.9	48.7	54.8	55.6	3.6
Bedsprings and	8.2	28.1	45.9	72.8	76.8	93.6	26.6
Mattresses (49)	5.5	49.3	76.3	133.9	114.5	154.8	52.1
2082	21.6	53.7	13.1	20.4	33.3	108.2	9.6
Breweries (27)	16.4	59.4	21.3	38.6	46.5	137.8	118.6
	11.4	81.9	34.1	97.5	87.7	194.9	176.2
287	10.4	29.5	33.6	58.4	62.1	89.5	24.1
Chemicals, Agricultural	6.6	53.6	73.1	111.0	106.6	122.9	47.9
(33)	5.0	71.2	123.0	165.9	160.5	237.3	75.2
281	10.1	42.6	20.1	31.8	65.2	76.1	44.0
Chemicals, Industrial	6.9	68.8	30.0	58.9	84.7	98.5	94.2
(60)	5.5	88.9	50.0	106.0	100.1	128.7	152.4
1511	†	9.5	61.7	119.4	†	†	11.9
Contractors, Building	†	22.2	138.0	188.4	†	†	27.4
Construction (188)	†	42.1	239.8	318.0	†	†	83.4

risk of dealing with a slow-paying customer—profitable companies are likely to grow and thus to become better customers in the future. However, if the profit margin is low in relation to other firms in the industry, if the current ratio is low, and if the debt ratio is high, a credit manager probably will not approve a sale involving an extension of credit.[11]

11. Statistical techniques have been developed to improve the use of ratios in credit analysis. One such development is the discriminant analysis model reported by Edward I. Altman in "Financial Ratios, Discriminant Analysis, and the Prediction of Corporate Bankruptcy," *Journal of Finance* 23 (September 1968). In his model, Altman combines a number of liquidity, leverage, activity, and profitability ratios to form an index of a firm's probability of going bankrupt. His model has predicted bankruptcy quite well one or two years in the future. See also Altman, Haldeman, and Narayanan, "ZETA Analysis: A New Model to Identify Bankruptcy Risk of Corporations," *Journal of Banking and Finance* 1 (June 1977):29–54.

Of necessity, the credit manager is more than a calculator and a reader of financial ratios. Qualitative factors may override quantitative analysis. For instance, oil companies, in selling to truckers, often find that the financial ratios are adverse and that if they based their decisions solely on financial ratios, they would not make sales. Or, to take another example, profits may have been low for a period, but if the customer understands why profits have been low and can remove the cause of the difficulty, a credit man may be willing to approve a sale to him. The credit man's decision is also influenced by his own firm's profit margin. If the selling firm is making a large profit on sales, it is in a better position to take credit risks than if its own margin is low. Ultimately, the credit manager must judge a customer with regard to his character and management ability, and intelligent credit decisions must be based on careful consideration of conditions in the selling firm as well as in the buying firm.

Use of Financial Ratios in Security Analysis

We have emphasized the use of financial analysis by the financial manager and by outside credit analysts. However, this type of analysis is also useful in security analysis, that is, in the analysis of the investment merits of stocks and bonds. When the emphasis is on security analysis, the principal focus is on judging the long-run profit potential of the firm. Profitability is dependent in large part on the efficiency with which the firm is run; because financial analysis provides insights into this factor, it is useful to the security analyst.

Some Limitations of Ratio Analysis

Although ratios are exceptionally useful tools, they do have limitations and must be used with caution. Ratios are constructed from accounting data, and accounting data are subject to different interpretations and even to manipulation. For example, two firms may use different depreciation methods or inventory valuation methods; depending on the procedures followed, reported profits can be raised or lowered. Similar differences can be encountered in the treatment of research and development expenditures, pension plan costs, mergers, product warranties, and bad-debt reserves. Further, if firms use different fiscal years, and if seasonal factors are important, this can influence the comparative ratios. Thus, if the ratios of two firms are to be compared, it is important to analyze the basic accounting data upon which the ratios were based and to reconcile any major differences.

A financial manager must also be cautious when judging whether a particular ratio is "good" or "bad" and in forming a composite judgment about a firm on the basis of a set of ratios. For example, a high inventory turnover ratio could indicate efficient inventory management, but it could also indicate a serious shortage of inventories and suggest the likelihood of stock-outs. Further, there is nothing sacred about the industry average figures — after all, any management worth its salt will try to be better than average.

Ratios, then, are extremely useful tools. But as with other analytical methods, they must be used with judgment and caution, not in an unthinking, mechanical manner.

Summary

Ratio analysis, which relates balance sheet and income statement items to one another, permits the charting of a firm's history and the evaluation of its present position. Such analysis also allows the financial manager to anticipate reactions of investors and creditors and thus gives him a good insight into how his attempts to acquire funds are likely to be received.

Basic Types of Ratios. Ratios are classified into four basic types: (1) liquidity, (2) leverage, (3) activity, and (4) profitability. Data from the Walker-Wilson Manufacturing Company were used to compute each type of ratio and to show how a financial analysis is made in practice. An almost unlimited number of ratios may be calculated, but in practice a limited number of each type is sufficient. We have discussed in this chapter what are probably the 12 most common ratios.

Use of Ratios. A ratio is not a meaningful number in and of itself — it must be compared with something before it becomes useful. The two basic kinds of comparative analysis are (1) trend analysis, which involves computing the ratio of a particular firm for several years and comparing the ratios over time to see if the firm is improving or deteriorating, and (2) comparisons with other firms in the same industry. These two comparisons are often combined in the graphic analysis illustrated in Figure 2-1.

du Pont System. The du Pont system shows how the return on investment is dependent upon asset turnover and the profit margin. The system is generally expressed in the form of the following equation:

$$\frac{\text{profit}}{\text{sales}} \times \frac{\text{sales}}{\text{investment}} = \text{ROI}.$$

The first term, the profit margin, times investment turnover equals the rate of return on investment. The kinds of actions we discussed in this chapter can be used to effect needed changes in turnover and the profit margin and thus improve the return on investment.

The du Pont system can be extended to encompass financial leverage and to examine the manner in which turnover, sales margins, and leverage all combine to determine the rate of return on net worth. The following equation is used to show this relationship:

$$\text{Rate of return on net worth} = \frac{\text{return on assets (ROI)}}{1.0 - \text{debt ratio}}.$$

Rates of Return in Different Industries. The extended du Pont system shows why firms in different industries—even though they have widely different turnovers, profit margins, and debt ratios—may end up with very similar rates of return on net worth. In general, firms dealing with relatively perishable commodities are expected to have high turnovers but low profit margins; firms whose production processes require heavy investments in fixed assets are expected to have low turnover ratios but high profit margins.

Questions

2-1. "A uniform system of accounts, including identical forms for balance sheets and income statements, would be a most reasonable requirement for the SEC to impose on all publicly owned firms." Discuss.

2-2. We have divided financial ratios into four groups: liquidity, leverage, activity, and profitability. We could also consider financial analysis as being conducted by four groups of analysts: management, equity investors, long-term creditors, and short-term creditors.
a. Explain the nature of each type of ratio.
b. Explain the emphasis of each type of analyst.

2-3. Why can norms with relatively well-defined limits be stated in advance for some financial ratios but not for others?

2-4. How does trend analysis supplement the basic financial ratio calculations and their interpretation?

2–5. Why would you expect the inventory turnover figure to be more important to a grocery store than to a shoe repair store?

2–6. How can a firm have a high current ratio and still be unable to pay its bills?

2–7. "The higher the rate of return on investment (ROI), the better the firm's management." Is this statement true for all firms? Explain. If you disagree with the statement, give examples of instances in which it might not be true.

2–8. What factors would you, as a financial manager, want to examine if a firm's rate of return (a) on assets or (b) on net worth is too low?

2–9. Profit margins and turnover rates vary from industry to industry. What industry characteristics account for these variations? Give some contrasting examples to illustrate your answer.

2–10. Which relation would you, as a financial manager, prefer: (a) a profit margin of 10 percent and a capital turnover of 2, or (b) a profit margin of 20 percent and a capital turnover of 1? Can you think of any firm with a relation similar to b?

Problems

2–1. The following data were taken from the financial statements of the Michigan Furniture Company for the calendar year 1975. The norms given below are based on industry averages for the Dun & Bradstreet category "Wood household furniture and upholstered" taken from *Dun's Review*, December 1976.
   a. Fill in the ratios for the Michigan Furniture Company.
   b. Indicate by comparison with industry norms the possible errors in management policies reflected in these financial statements.

Michigan Furniture Company
Balance Sheet
December 31, 1975

Cash	11,000	Accounts payable	45,000
Receivables	104,000	Notes payable (8%)	21,000
Inventory	250,000	Other current liabilities	39,000
Total current assets	365,000	Total current liabilities	105,000
Net fixed assets	110,000	Long term debt (9%)	115,000
		Net worth	255,000
Total assets	475,000	Total claims on assets	475,000

Michigan Furniture Company
Income Statement
for Year Ended December 31, 1975

Sales		760,000
Cost of goods sold		
Material	240,000	
Labor	210,000	
Heat, light and power	25,600	
Indirect labor	30,000	
Depreciation	22,000	527,600
Gross profit		232,400
Selling expense	80,000	
General and administrative expense	110,000	190,000
Operating profit (EBIT)		42,400
Less: Interest expense		12,000
Net profit before tax		30,400
Less: Federal income tax (50%)		15,200
Net profit		15,200

Ratio	Michigan Furniture Company Ratio	Industry Norm
$\dfrac{\text{current assets}}{\text{current liabilities}}$	_____	3.1 times
$\dfrac{\text{debt}}{\text{total assets}}$	_____	45%
times interest earned	_____	4.8 times
$\dfrac{\text{sales}}{\text{inventory}}$	_____	5.2 times
average collection period	_____	46 days
$\dfrac{\text{sales}}{\text{total assets}}$	_____	2.0 times
$\dfrac{\text{net profit}}{\text{sales}}$	_____	2.8%
$\dfrac{\text{net profit}}{\text{total assets}}$	_____	5.6%
$\dfrac{\text{net profit}}{\text{net worth}}$	_____	10.2%

2–2. The following data were taken from the financial statement of Midland
Drug and Proprietary Company, a wholesaler of drugs, drug proprietaries,

and sundries, for the calendar year 1975. The norms given below are the industry averages for wholesale drugs, drug proprietary, and sundries.

a. Fill in the ratios for Midland Drug and Proprietary Company.

b. Indicate by comparison with the industry norms the possible errors in management policies reflected in these financial statements.

Midland Drug and Proprietary Company
Balance Sheet
December 31, 1975
(Figures in Thousands)

Cash	$ 193	Accounts payable	$ 316
Receivables	820	Notes payable (6%)	206
Inventory	592	Other current liabilities	283
Total current assets	1,605	Total current liabilities	805
Net fixed assets	715	Long-term debt (5%)	633
		Net worth	882
Total Assets	$2,320	Total claims on assets	$2,320

Midland Drug and Proprietary Company
Income Statement
for Year Ended December 31, 1975
(Figures in Thousands)

Sales	$3,936	
Cost of goods sold	3,411	
Gross profit		$525
Operating expenses	282	
Depreciation expense	79	
Interest expense	44	
Total expenses		405
Net income before tax		120
Taxes (50%)		60
Net income		$ 60

Ratio	Midland Ratio	Norm
current assets / current liabilities	———	1.97 times
debt / total assets	———	60%
times interest earned	———	3.79 times
sales / inventory	———	6.7 times

Midland

Ratio	Ratio	Norm
average collection period	_____	36 days
$\dfrac{\text{sales}}{\text{total assets}}$	_____	2.94 times
$\dfrac{\text{net profit}}{\text{sales}}$	_____	1.14%
$\dfrac{\text{net profit}}{\text{total assets}}$	_____	3.35%
$\dfrac{\text{net profit}}{\text{net worth}}$	_____	8.29%

2–3. The following data were taken from the financial statement of Springfield Car and Truck Company, a retail motor vehicle dealer, for the calendar year 1975. The norms given below are the industry averages for motor vehicle dealers.

a. Fill in the ratios for Springfield Car and Truck.

b. Indicate by comparison with the industry norms the possible errors in management policies reflected in these financial statements.

Springfield Car and Truck Company
Balance Sheet
December 31, 1975

Cash	$ 5,030	Accounts payable	$105,015
Receivables	88,740	Notes payable (10%)	4,025
Inventory	105,700	Other current liabilities	33,290
Total current assets	199,470	Total current liabilities	142,330
Net fixed assets	35,000	Long-term debt (10%)	30,370
		Net worth	61,770
Total assets	$234,470	Total claims on assets	$234,470

Springfield Car and Truck Company
Income Statement
For year ended December 31, 1975

Sales	$497,000	
Cost of goods sold	$424,680	
		72,320
Operating expenses	51,412	
Depreciation expense	4,820	
Interest expense	7,440	
Total expenses		63,672
Net income before tax		8,648
Taxes (50%)		4,324
Net income		$4,324

Ratio	Springfield Ratio	Norm
$\dfrac{\text{current assets}}{\text{current liabilities}}$	_____	1.43 times
$\dfrac{\text{debt}}{\text{total assets}}$	_____	66%
times interest earned	_____	3.5 times
$\dfrac{\text{sales}}{\text{inventory}}$	_____	6.6 times
average collection period	_____	63 days
$\dfrac{\text{sales}}{\text{total assets}}$	_____	2.95 times
$\dfrac{\text{net profit}}{\text{sales}}$	_____	1.02%
$\dfrac{\text{net profit}}{\text{total assets}}$	_____	3.01%
$\dfrac{\text{net profit}}{\text{net worth}}$	_____	9.09%

2–4. Silicon Valley Electronic Supply Company, a closely held family manufacturer of electronic components, has upon the death of its founder/president Marilyn Hickley two years ago been managed by her nephew Ron, formerly a company salesman. Ed Smith, the firm's account manager at their bank has received numerous complaints about Ron's actions from the family and has asked you to evaluate his performance. The most recent financial statements are reproduced below.
   a. Calculate the relevant financial ratios for this analysis.
   b. Apply a du Pont chart for analysis to Silicon Valley similar to the one in Figure 2–2.
   c. Evaluate Ron's performance and specific areas to be improved.

	Industry Average Ratios
Current ratio	2.2
Quick ratio	1.0
Debt to total assets	50%
Times interest earned	5.2 times
Inventory turnover	5.1 times
Average collection period	52 days
Fixed assets turnover	9.25 times
Total assets turnover	1.85 times
Net profit on sales	3.19%
Return on total assets	5.90%
Return on net worth	10.8%

Common-size balance sheets:

Assets	Norm %	Liabilities	Norm %
Cash	6.8	Due to banks—short term	7.6
Marketable securities	3.5	Due to trade	11.3
Receivables net	24.9	Income taxes	2.3
Inventory net	33.8	Current maturities LT debt	2.3
All other current	2.5	All other current	8.6
Total current	71.5	Total current debt	32.1
Fixed assets net	25.0	Noncurrent debt, unsubordinated	13.9
All other noncurrent	3.5	Total unsubordinated debt	46.0
		Subordinated debt	1.7
		Tangible net worth	52.3
Total assets	100.0	Total claim on assets	100.0

Common-size income statements:

Net sales	100%	
Cost of sales	77.9	
Gross profit		22.1%
Selling and delivery expenses	4.2	
Officers' salaries	2.5	
Other general administrative expenses	8.5	
All other expenses net	1.1	
Operating expenses		16.3
Net income before tax		5.8%
Taxes 45% (assumed)		2.61
Net income		3.19%

Source: *Annual Statement Studies*—1976 edition; Robert Morris
Associates. Balance Sheet, p. 71; 101 firms of asset size greater
than $1,000,000 and less than $10,000,000. Income statement, p.
216; 13 firms of asset size greater than $1,000,000 and less than
$10,000,000.

Silicon Valley Electronic Supply Company
Balance Sheet
December 31, 1975
(thousands of dollars)

Cash	$ 90	Accounts payable	$450
Marketable securities	40	Notes payable (11%)	380
Receivables	1,550	Other current liabilities	280
Inventory	1,190	Total current liabilities	$1,110
Total current assets	2,870	Long-term debt (9%)	880
Net fixed assets	1,130	Total liabilities	1,990
		Net worth	2,010
Total assets	$4,000	Total claims on assets	$4,000

Silicon Valley Electronic Supply Company
Income Statement
For year ended December 31, 1975
(thousands of dollars)

Sales		$6,200
Cost of goods sold		
Materials	$2,440	
Labor	1,540	
Heat, light, and power	230	
Indirect labor	370	
Depreciation	140	4,720
Gross profit		1,480
Selling expenses	490	
General and administrative expenses	530	1,020
Operating profit		460
Less: interest expense		121
Net profit before taxes		339
Less: federal income taxes		
(assumed 45% rate)		152
Net profit		$ 187

2–5. Indicate the effects of the transactions listed below on each of the following: total current assets, working capital, current ratio, and net profit. Use + to indicate an increase, − to indicate a decrease, and 0 to indicate no effect. State necessary assumptions and assume an initial current ratio of more than 1 to 1.

	Total Current Assets	Net Working Capital*	Current Ratio	Net Profit
1. Cash is acquired through issuance of additional common stock.	_____	_____	_____	_____
2. Merchandise is sold for cash.	_____	_____	_____	_____
3. Federal income tax due for the previous year is paid.	_____	_____	_____	_____
4. A fixed asset is sold for less than book value.	_____	_____	_____	_____
5. A fixed asset is sold for more than book value.	_____	_____	_____	_____
6. Merchandise is sold on credit.	_____	_____	_____	_____
7. Payment is made to trade creditors for previous purchases.	_____	_____	_____	_____
8. A cash dividend is declared and paid.	_____	_____	_____	_____
9. Cash is obtained through short-term bank loans.	_____	_____	_____	_____
10. Short-term notes receivable are sold at a discount.	_____	_____	_____	_____
11. Previously issued stock rights are				

	Total Current Assets	Net Working Capital*	Current Ratio	Net Profit
exercised by company stockholders.	___	___	___	___
12. A profitable firm increases its fixed assets depreciation allowance account.	___	___	___	___
13. Marketable securities are sold below cost.	___	___	___	___
14. Uncollectible accounts are written off against the allowance account.	___	___	___	___
15. Advances are made to employees.	___	___	___	___
16. Current operating expenses are paid.	___	___	___	___
17. Short-term promissory notes are issued to trade creditors for prior purchases.	___	___	___	___
18. Ten-year notes are issued to pay off accounts payable.	___	___	___	___
19. A wholly depreciated asset is retired.	___	___	___	___
20. A cash sinking fund for the retirement of bonds is created; a reserve for bond sinking fund is also created.	___	___	___	___
21. Bonds are retired by use of the cash sinking fund.	___	___	___	___
22. Accounts receivable are collected.	___	___	___	___
23. A stock dividend is declared and paid.	___	___	___	___
24. Equipment is purchased with short-term notes.	___	___	___	___
25. The allowance for doubtful accounts is increased.	___	___	___	___
26. Merchandise is purchased on credit.	___	___	___	___
27. Controlling interest in another firm is acquired by the issuance of additional common stock.	___	___	___	___
28. Earnings are added to the reserve for bond sinking fund.	___	___	___	___
29. An unconsolidated subsidiary pays the firm a cash dividend from current earnings.	___	___	___	___
30. The estimated taxes payable are increased.	___	___	___	___

*Net working capital is defined as current assets minus current liabilities.

2–6.[1] Jeff Jones, vice-president and loan officer of the First National Bank of Kansas City, was recently alerted to the deteriorating financial position of one of his clients, Midwest Cannery, by his bank's newly instituted computer loan analysis program. The bank requires quarterly financial statements—balance sheets and income statements—from each of its

1. This problem was adopted from Brigham et al., *Cases in Managerial Finance*, second edition.

Table P2–1 **Midwest Cannery** **Balance sheets**	Year Ended December 31	1967	1973	1974	1975
	Cash	$ 51,000	$ 76,500	$ 35,700	$ 25,500
	Accounts receivable	204,000	306,000	346,800	484,500
	Inventory	255,000	382,500	637,500	1,032,800
	Total current assets	$510,000	$ 765,000	$1,020,000	$1,542,800
	Land and building	76,500	61,200	163,200	153,000
	Machinery	102,000	188,700	147,900	127,500
	Other fixed assets	61,200	35,700	10,200	7,600
	Total assets	$749,700	$1,050,600	$1,341,300	$1,830,900
	Notes payable, bank	—	—	$ 127,500	$ 357,000
	Accounts and notes payable	112,200	$ 122,400	193,800	382,500
	Accruals	51,000	61,200	71,400	96,900
	Total current liabilities	$163,200	$ 183,600	$ 392,700	$ 836,400
	Mortgage	76,500	56,100	51,000	45,900
	Common stock	459,000	459,000	459,000	459,000
	Retained earnings	51,000	351,900	438,600	489,600
	Total liabilities and equity	$749,700	$1,050,600	$1,341,300	$1,830,900

major loan customers. This information is punched on cards and fed into the computer, which then calculates the key ratios for each customer, charts trends in these ratios, and compares the statistics on each company with the average ratios and trends of other firms in the same industry. If any ratio of any company is significantly poorer than the industry average, the computer output makes note of this fact. Moreover, if the terms of a loan require that certain ratios be maintained at specified minimum levels, and if these minimums are not being met by a company, the computer output notes the deficiency.

When an analysis was run on Midwest three months earlier, Jones saw that certain of Midwest's ratios were showing downward trends and were dipping below the averages for the canning industry. Jones sent John Herndon, president of Midwest, a copy of the computer output, together with a note voicing his concern. Although Herndon acknowledged receipt of the material, he took no action to correct the situation.

While problems appeared to be developing in the financial analysis three months ago, no ratio was below the level specified in the loan agreement between the bank and Midwest. However, the latest analysis, which was based on the data given in Tables P2.1, P2.2, and P2.3, showed that the current ratio was below the 2.0 times specified in the loan agreement. Legally, according to the loan agreement, the Kansas City Bank could call upon Midwest for immediate payment of the entire bank loan, and, if payment was not forthcoming within ten days, the bank could force the company into bankruptcy. Jones had no intention of enforcing the contract to the full extent that he legally could, but he did intend to use

Table P2–2
Midwest Cannery
Income statements

Year Ended December 31	1973	1974	1975
Net sales	$3,315,000	$3,442,500	$3,570,000
Cost of goods sold	2,652,000	2,754,000	2,856,000
Gross operating profit	$ 663,000	$ 688,500	$ 714,000
General administration and selling	255,000	280,500	306,000
Depreciation	102,000	127,500	153,000
Miscellaneous	51,000	107,100	153,000
Net income before taxes	$ 255,000	$ 173,400	$ 102,000
Taxes (50%)	127,500	86,700	51,000
Net income	$ 127,500	$ 86,700	$ 51,000

the loan agreement provision to prompt Midwest to take some decisive action to improve its financial picture.

Midwest is a medium-sized cannery whose products—canned fruits, vegetables, and juices—are sold to distributors throughout the midwestern states. Seasonal working capital needs have been financed primarily by loans from the Kansas City Bank, and the current line of credit permits the cannery to borrow up to $360,000. In accordance with standard banking practices, however, the loan agreement requires that the bank loan be repaid in full at some time during the year, in this case by February 1976. Interest expense for 1975 was $48,000.

A limitation on prices of canned goods, coupled with higher costs, caused a decline in Midwest's profit margin and net income during the last half of 1974 as well as during most of 1975. Sales increased during both these years, however, because of the cannery's aggressive marketing program.

When Herndon received a copy of Jones' latest computer analysis and his blunt statement that the bank would insist on immediate repayment of the entire loan unless Midwest presented a program showing how its poor current financial picture could be improved, Herndon tried to determine what could be done. He rapidly concluded that the present level

Table P2–3

Canning Industry Ratios (1975)*

Quick ratio	1.0
Current ratio	2.7
Inventory turnover†	7 times
Average collection period	32 days
Fixed asset turnover†	13.0 times
Total asset turnover†	2.6 times
Return on total assets	9%
Return on net worth	18%
Debt ratio	50%
Profit margin on sales	3.5%

*Industry average ratios have been constant for the past three years.
†Based on year-end balance sheet figures.

of sales could not be continued without an *increase* in the bank loan from $360,000 to $510,000 since payments of $150,000 for construction of a plant addition would have to be made in January 1976. Although the cannery had been a good customer of the Kansas City Bank for over 50 years, Herndon was concerned whether the bank would continue to supply the present line of credit, let alone increase the outstanding loan. Herndon was especially troubled in view of the fact that the Federal Reserve had recently tightened bank credit considerably, forcing the Kansas City Bank to ration credit even to its best customers.

1. Calculate the key financial ratios for Midwest and plot trends in the firm's ratios against the industry averages.
2. What strengths and weaknesses are revealed by the ratio analysis?

Questions to be answered at the option of the instructor:
3. What sources of *internal* funds would be available for the retirement of the loan? If the bank grants additional credit and extends the increased loan from a due date of February 1, 1976, to June 30, 1976, would the company be able to retire the loan on June 30, 1976? *Hint:* To answer this question, consider profits and depreciation, as well as the amount of inventories and receivables that would be carried if Midwest's inventory turnover and average collection period were at industry average levels; that is, how much funds would be released if Midwest's current assets were at industry average levels?
4. In 1975, Midwest's return on equity was 5.38 percent versus 18 percent for the industry. Use the du Pont equation to pinpoint the factors causing Midwest to fall so far below the industry average.
5. On the basis of your financial analysis, do you believe that the bank should grant the additional loan and extend the entire line of credit to June 30, 1976?
6. If the credit extension is not made, what alternatives are open to Midwest?
7. Under what circumstances is the validity of comparative ratio analysis questionable?

Selected References

Altman, Edward I. "Financial Ratios, Discriminant Analysis and the Prediction of Corporate Bankruptcy." *Journal of Finance* 23 (Sept. 1968):589–609.
———. "Railroad Bankruptcy Propensity." *Journal of Finance* 26 (May 1971): 333–45.
Altman, Edward I.; Haldeman, R. G.; and Narayanan, P., "ZETA Analysis: A New Model to Identify Bankruptcy Risk of Corporations," *Journal of Banking and Finance* 1 (June 1977):29–54.
Beaver, William H. "Financial Ratios as Predictors of Failure." *Empirical Research in Accounting: Selected Studies* in *Journal of Accounting Research* (1966): 71–111.

Benishay, Haskel. "Economic Information on Financial Ratio Analysis." *Accounting and Business Research* 2 (Spring 1971):174–79.

Bierman, Harold, Jr., "Measuring Financial Liquidity." *Accounting Review* 35 (Oct. 1960):628–32.

Brinkman, Donald R., and Prentiss, Paul H. "Replacement Cost and Current-Value Measurement: How to Do it." *Financial Executive* 43 (Oct. 1975):20–26.

Davidson, S., and Weil, R. L. "Predicting Inflation-Adjusted Results." *Financial Analysts Journal* 31 (Jan.–Feb. 1975):27–31.

———. "Inflation Accounting and 1974 Earnings." *Financial Analysts Journal* 31 (Sept.–Oct. 1975):42–54.

———. "Replacement Cost Disclosure." *Financial Analysts Journal* 32 (Mar.–Apr. 1976):57–66.

Donaldson, Gordon. "New Framework for Corporate Debt Capacity." *Harvard Business Review* 40 (Mar.–Apr. 1962).

Edmister, Robert O. "An Empirical Test of Financial Ratio Analysis for Small Business Failure Predictions." *Journal of Financial and Quantitative Analysis* 7 (Mar. 1972):1477–93.

Helfert, Erich A. *Techniques of Financial Analysis.* 3rd ed. Homewood, Ill.: Irwin, 1972.

Horrigan, James C. "A Short History of Financial Ratio Analysis." *Accounting Review* 43 (Apr. 1968):284–94.

———. "The Determination of Long-Term Credit Standing with Financial Ratios." *Empirical Research in Accounting: Selected Studies* in *Journal of Accounting Research* (1966):44–62.

Johnson, Craig C. "Ratio Analysis and the Prediction of Firm Failure." *Journal of Finance* 25 (Dec. 1970):1116–68. See also Edward I. Altman. "Reply." *ibid.*: 1169–72.

Terborgh, George. "Inflation and Profits." *Financial Analysts Journal* 30 (May-June 1974):19–23.

Theil, Henri. "On the Use of Information Theory Concepts in the Analysis of Financial Statements." *Management Science* 15 (May 1969):459–80.

Weston, Frank T. "Adjust your Accounting for Inflation." *Harvard Business Review* 53 (Jan–Feb. 1975):22–29.

Weston, J. Fred, and Goudzwaard, Maurice B. "Financial Policies in an Inflationary Environment." In *The Treasurer's Handbook*, J. Fred Weston and Maurice B. Goudzwaard, eds. (Homewood, Illinois: Dow Jones-Irwin, 1976), pp. 20–42.

Appendix A to Chapter 2
Implications of Changes
in Price Levels

Immediately after World War II with the removal of price controls that had held prices to arbitrary levels, there was a burst of inflation. Annual price increases thereafter stayed mostly within 3 to 5 percent per annum until the escalation of hostilities in Southeast Asia in 1966 when inflation again erupted in the United States. In 1971, the U.S. departed from the convertibility of the dollar into gold, and the major nations adopted floating exchange rates in place of nominally fixed exchange rates.

Double digit inflation as measured by the wholesale price index or consumer price index has been an actuality or a threat in the United States for more than a decade. As a consequence proposals have been made to modify accounting procedures to recognize that the traditional postulate of a stable measuring unit is no longer valid. In December 1974, the Financial Accounting Standards Board issued an exposure draft of a proposed statement entitled "Financial Reporting in Units of General Purchasing Power." On March 23, 1976, the Securities and Exchange Commission issued Accounting Series Release No. 190. SEC Release 190 requires disclosure of replacement costs for inventory items and depreciable plant from registrants with $100 million or more (at historical cost) of gross plant assets and inventories constituting 10 percent or more of its total assets. For 1977 and thereafter, the SEC will require additional details on the replacement costs of plant assets and inventories.

In its Status Report No. 37, issued June 4, 1976, the Financial Accounting Standards Board announced that action was being deferred on the issuance of a Statement on Financial Reporting in Units of General Purchasing power. The Board stated that the action did not have any implications for the merits of the proposal. Rather, the Board stated, ". . . general purchasing power information is not now sufficiently well understood by preparers and users and the need for it is not now sufficiently well demonstrated to justify imposing the cost of implementation upon all preparers of financial statements at this time."

Thus while the requirement for disclosure of current replacement costs is now effective, the proposal for general purchasing power accounting is still under development. Nevertheless, both approaches have implications for financial statement analysis so will be reviewed.

It has been pointed out that in a period of inflation distortions will result from the use of the historical cost postulate. Assets are recorded at cost, but revenue and other expense flows are in dollars of different purchasing power. The amortization of fixed costs does not reflect the current cost of these assets.[1] Furthermore, net income during periods when assets are held do not reflect the effects of management's decision to hold the assets rather than sell them. Assets are not stated on the balance sheet at their current values, so that the firm's financial position cannot be accurately evaluated. And when assets are sold, gains or losses are reported during that period even though these results reflect decisions in prior periods to hold the assets.[2]

Procedures in Replacement Cost Accounting

In replacement cost accounting, two major categories of problems must be solved. One is to decide upon a measure of the current value of assets. A second is to measure income after the first problem is solved. Each is considered in turn.

Three methods of measuring the current value of assets have been identified:

1. Current replacement costs.
2. Net realizable value.
3. Present value of future cash flows.

Current replacement costs have been referred to as an entry value. Current replacement cost may be defined as the current cost of an identical asset or of an asset equivalent in capacity and service. The SEC requirement is not of current values in general, but one specific measure of current values — replacement costs. Other measures of current value may be disclosed in addition to, but not as a substitute for, replacement costs.

However, if a company were to be liquidated by selling off its assets, the relevant measure of value is the net realizable values of the individual assets. But in applying this approach, the only assets for which current market values are quoted are those continuously traded such as marketable securities. Consequently, exit values are hardly relevant for a going concern for which liquidation is not contemplated.

The present values of future cash flows or the discounted cash flows are considered by many to represent economic values. Their practical implementation requires dependable forecasts and the selection of the applicable discount rates. For most companies new investments continue to be made, seeking to add to the earning power of existing assets.

1. Thompson and Koons, "Accounting for Changes in General Price Levels and Current Values," *Modern Accountant's Handbook*, ed. Edwards and Black (Homewood, Ill.: Dow Jones-Irwin, 1976), pp. 560–61.

2. Davidson et al., *Financial Accounting* (Hinsdale, Ill.: Dryden Press, 1975), p. 441.

Hence it becomes difficult to segregate the future cash flows of the firm between the firm's existing assets and its new investments. Thus the discounted cash flow method, while widely and effectively used in evaluating individual investment projects, is more difficult to apply in placing values upon the physical assets of the firm as a whole.

It has been stated that in judging the ability of a business to do the same kinds of things in the future as in the past and to pay dividends or to finance expansion without requiring new external financing, "replacement costs are perhaps the most useful measure of current value."[3] It might also be argued that the discounted cash flow method, soundly applied, yields results consistent with current replacement values.

Postulating that a measure of replacement costs has been achieved, the second task, that of measuring income and financial position, is considered. A number of concepts of income are involved. The simplified illustration presented by Falkenstein and Weil is utilized here. Their illustration and three concepts of income are reproduced in Table 2A – 1.

Pretax distributable income is defined as revenues less expenses based on replacement costs. It is a measure of income that can be distributed as taxes and returns to owners without impairing the firm's physical capacity to remain in business at current levels.

Realized income is distributable income plus holding gains that have been realized during the period. The realized holding gain is the replacement value of goods sold less their historical costs. The sum of the distributable income and the realized holding gain is the realized income. This is the same as the conventional measure of income which is based on the realization principle. Replacement cost data make it possible to separate distributable income and realized holding gains.

The sum of realized income plus unrealized holding gains has been called economic income. This view holds that an increase in the value of assets is economic income whether or not the asset has been sold. The economic measure of income has been defined as the income that can be consumed during the period leaving the person as well off at the end of the period as at the beginning. This leads to an emphasis on the physical capacity of the firm. Thus a company may be said to be as well off at the end of the period as at the beginning only if it has sufficient physical assets to carry on the same level of business activity. Under this view, holding gains, whether or not realized, are tied up in the net assets required to conduct the operations of the firm at the current physical levels of activity. Thus it might be more appropriate to label

3. A. Falkenstein and R. L. Weil, "Replacement Cost Accounting," *Financial Analysts Journal* 33 (January – February 1977), pp. 47 – 48.

Table 2A–1 **Replacement Cost** **Income Statement** **Simple Illustration**	Assumed Data	(Historical) Acquisition Cost	Replacement Cost
	Inventory, 1/1/76	$ 900	$1,100
	Inventory, 12/31/76	1,200	1,550
	Cost of Goods Sold for 1976	4,000	4,500
	Sales for 1976	$5,200	
	Income Statement for 1976		
	Sales		$5,200
	Cost of Goods Sold, replacement cost basis		4,500
	1. Distributable Income		$ 700
	Realized Holding Gains		500[a]
	2. Realized Income		$1,200
	Unrealized Holding Gains		150[b]
	3. Economic Income		$1,350

[a]Realized holding gain during a period is replacement cost of goods sold less historical cost of goods sold; for 1976 the realized holding gain is $500 = $4,500 − $4,000.

[b]The total unrealized holding gain at any time is replacement cost of inventory on hand at that time less historical cost of that inventory. The unrealized holding gain during a period is the unrealized holding gain at the end of the period less the unrealized holding gain at the beginning of the period. The unrealized holding gain prior to 1976 is $200 = $1,100 − $900. The unrealized holding gain during 1976 = (1,550 − $1,200) − (1,100 − $900) = $350 − $200 = $150.

Source: A. Falkenstein and R. L. Weil, "Replacement Cost Accounting." *Financial Analysts Journal* 33 (January–February, 1977), p. 49.

the third measure of income, "realized plus unrealized income unadjusted for general purchasing power changes."

Taking distributable income as the most relevant measure of income, Falkenstein and Weil make comparisons with the use of income as conventionally reported for the Dow Jones industrials for 1975. Income as conventionally reported, approximated $14.5 billions. Using replacement costs, the cost of goods sold increases by $2.2 billions and depreciation by $6.5 billions. Distributable income drops to somewhat under $6 billion, representing 40 percent of the conventionally measured income.

While dividends were about 50 percent of conventional income, they were 127 percent of distributable income. Income taxes currently payable were 63 percent of pre-tax conventional income, but almost 81 percent of distributable income. A wide variation was found among the individual companies reflecting variations in the economic characteristics of their industries, the extent of use of LIFO accounting methods and other individual circumstances. Thus the impact of inflation was different on individual companies.

Therefore the use of current replacement costs in calculating a distributable income measure can result in substantial changes in income as well as in financial position. When economic changes are so large that current values of assets differ greatly from their historical values, it is argued that major distortions will result if these changes are not taken into account in accounting procedures and practices.

General Purchasing Power Reporting

Because both the realized holding gains and unrealized holding gains in the use of replacement accounting may simply reflect a declining value of the unit of account, it has been proposed that more general adjustments are needed. These adjustments would recognize that the assumption of a stable unit of account is no longer valid in most parts of the world. This has resulted in the proposals for General Purchasing Power Reporting (GPPR) along the lines of the FASB draft proposal of December 1974.

The GPPR would seek to adjust the current value of nonmonetary items by a general price index. The historical cost basis of accounting is retained but adjusted by a price index. GPPR adjusts original cost data to compensate for changes in the purchasing power of the dollar and capital consumption expenses and the value of goods sold from inventory are adjusted accordingly. A new entry would be introduced to financial reports: net holding gains on monetary items. Operationally, monetary and nonmonetary items must be separated in financial statements and a price index must be selected. Cash, claims to cash, and claims on cash fixed in terms of dollars are designated as monetary items.

While the adjustments can be quite detailed, some simplifications can be made. When income and expenses are spread relatively uniformly throughout the year, a roughly accurate measure of monetary gain or loss can be calculated on the basis of the average balance of monetary items rather than on the transactions that created them. Consider the following balance sheets, for which the general price level rose 10 percent between the two balance sheet dates.

GPPR Company
Balance Sheets for
19X1 and 19X2

	19X1	19X2
Monetary Assets		
Cash	$ 8,000	$ 10,000
Receivables	12,000	20,000
Nonmonetary assets		
Inventories	30,000	40,000
Net fixed assets	50,000	60,000
Total Assets	$100,000	$130,000

Monetary liabilities

Current liabilities	$ 10,000	$ 15,000
Deferred income taxes	2,000	3,000
Long-term debt	28,000	36,000
Net holding gains on monetary items		2,000

Nonmonetary liabilities

Net worth	60,000	74,000
Total claims	$100,000	$130,000

The net balance of monetary items was ($20,000) in 19X1 and ($24,000) in 19X2. The average net monetary liability was $22,000. The rate of inflation during the year was 10 percent. Hence the value of the net monetary liability at the end of the year price index was $22,000 divided by 1.10 or $20,000. Thus the constant dollar value of the net monetary liabilities decreased by $2,000. Hence the net holding gains on monetary items was $2,000.[4]

The broad significance of the two major forms of adjustments can be indicated by some aggregate measures that have been made. We have

**Table 2A–2
Selected Financial
Ratios For U.S.
Nonfinancial
Corporations**

	Conventional Reporting				**Current-Value Reporting**			
	Debt/ Equity	Operating Income/ Interest Liability	Operating Income/ Equity	Taxes/ Operating Income	Debt/ Equity	Operating Income/ Interest Liability	Operating Income/ Equity	Taxes/ Operating Income
	(1)	(2)	(3)	(4)	(5)	(6)	(7)	(8)
1965	.97	5.3	.15	.42	.91	5.4	.15	.41
1966	1.02	4.8	.15	.42	.92	4.4	.14	.42
1967	1.08	3.9	.13	.43	1.02	3.4	.13	.43
1968	1.14	3.7	.14	.47	.96	3.0	.12	.49
1969	1.21	2.7	.12	.50	.94	2.1	.09	.53
1970	1.28	1.8	.09	.49	1.01	1.4	.07	.57
1971	1.30	2.0	.10	.47	1.06	1.6	.08	.54
1972	1.29	2.2	.11	.44	1.07	1.9	.09	.48
1973	1.32	2.1	.13	.43	1.00	1.7	.08	.52
1974	1.36	1.8	.13	.42	.95	0.9	.05	.77
1975	1.34	1.7	.12	.42	.92	1.1	.06	.60

Source: R. W. Kepcke, "Current Accounting Practices and Proposals for Reform," *New England Economic Review,* *Federal Reserve Bank of Boston (September/October, 1976) p. 23.*

---

4. See the similar illustration in Thompson and Koons, "Accounting for Changes," pp. 580–81.

already seen the major impact of current replacement accounting on financial measures for the Dow Jones Industrial Averages. We will illustrate further from some other aggregate measures.

Table 2A–2 shows the effects on selected financial ratios for U.S. Nonfinancial Corporations over the last 11 years from utilizing current-value reporting as contrasted to conventional reporting. Note that debt to equity ratios of over 130 percent under conventional reporting, fell below 100 percent under current-value reporting.

However, the operating income coverage of interest liability dropped from somewhat less than two to approximately one. This is because the operating income to equity ratio dropped from about 12 percent to 6 percent in recent years. The ratio of taxes to operating income which had been in the region of 42 percent under conventional reporting rose to 60 percent or more under current value.

This illustrates how the use of current value reporting can have a substantial impact on ratios involving the operating performance and financial position of business firms. Given the substantial changes that have taken place in the American economy during the past decade and that the inflation rate has been in the two-digit range, supplemental accounting information is necessary. Without taking into account changes in the purchasing power of the monetary unit and changes in the relative values of assets held by different business firms in the same industry and the differential impact of change on different industries, conventional accounting reporting based on historical cost postulates can be seriously misleading. A reworking of financial ratio analysis based on current values therefore becomes a highly desirable check on financial ratio analysis utilizing conventional accounting reports.

Limitations of Financial Statement Analysis

For a number of reasons, therefore, we cannot place absolute reliance upon the results of financial ratio analysis. In general, "window dressing" practices that will improve profitability in the short run may be utilized. Such practices include the postponement of the maintenance of fixed assets, which will decrease costs and increase profitability in the short run, but which will impact the firm severely when machine breakdowns occur and production processes are interrupted. A policy of delaying the purchase of more modern equipment will decrease capital outlays and reduce depreciation expenditures in the short run. However, failure to keep pace with competitors who are installing the most modern and efficient, low cost machinery will result in a cost disadvantage at some point in time.

In addition, we have seen how changing price levels and changes in the current values of assets can produce distortions in accounting measures of performance and financial position. It is desirable, therefore, to have made available the kinds of additional information that will be forthcoming under the SEC's Accounting Release No. 190 requiring information on current replacement values. Further information would be provided by the FASB's program for general purchasing power reporting.

Nevertheless, even with the additional supplementary information, we do not take the position that financial ratio analysis is the complete answer to evaluating the performance of a firm. When financial ratio analysis indicates that the patterns of a firm depart from industry norms, this is not an absolutely certain indication that something is wrong with the firm. Departures from industry norms provide a basis for raising questions and further investigation and analysis. Additional information and discussions may establish sound explanations for the differences between the pattern for the individual firm and industry composite ratios. Or the differences may reveal forms of mismanagement calling for correction.

Conversely, conformance to industry composite ratios does not establish with certainty that the firm is performing normally and is managed well. In the short run many tricks can be used to make the firm "look good" in relation to industry standards. The analyst must develop first-hand knowledge of the operations of the firm and of its management to provide a check on the financial ratios. In addition, the analyst must develop a sense, a touch, a smell, and a feel of what is going on in the firm. Sometimes it is this sixth sense kind of business judgment that uncovers weaknesses in the firm. The analyst should not be anesthetized by financial ratios that appear to conform with normality.

Thus financial ratios are a useful part of an investigative and analytic process. They are not the complete answer to questions about the performance of firms.

3   **Profit Planning**

The preceding chapter described how ratios are used in financial analysis and showed how the basic ratios are related to one another. A major area of financial management involves a continuous review of these ratios to insure that no aspects of the firm's existing operations are getting out of control—this key element of the system of financial controls designed to maximize operating efficiency is discussed in Chapter 4. Still other tools are available to aid the financial manager in the planning and control process. Two of these—(1) break-even analysis, which is especially useful when considering plant expansion and new product decisions, and (2) the sources and uses of funds statement, which is an important aid in seeing how the firm has obtained funds and how these funds have been used—are discussed in this chapter.

Break-even Analysis

Break-even analysis is an analytical technique for studying the relations among fixed costs, variable costs, and profits. If a firm's costs were all variable, the problem of break-even volume would seldom arise; by having some variable and some fixed costs, the firm must suffer losses until a given volume has been reached.

Break-even analysis is a formal profit-planning approach based on established relations between costs and revenues. It is a device for determining the point at which sales will just cover total costs. If the firm is to avoid losses, its sales must cover all costs—those that vary directly with production and those that do not change as production levels change. Costs that fall into each of those categories are outlined in Table 3–1.

The nature of break-even analysis is depicted in Figure 3–1, the basic break-even chart. The chart is on a unit basis, with volume produced shown on the horizontal axis and costs and income measured on the vertical axis. Fixed costs of $40,000 are represented by a horizontal line; they are the same (fixed) regardless of the number of units produced. Variable costs are assumed to be $1.20 a unit. Total costs rise by $1.20, the amount of the variable costs, for each additional unit produced. Production is assumed to be sold at $2 a unit, so the total income is pictured as a straight line, which must also increase with production. The slope (or the rate of ascent) of the total-income line is steeper than that

Table 3–1 **Fixed and Variable** **Costs**	Fixed Costs*	Direct or Variable Costs
	Depreciation on plant and equipment	Factory labor
	Rentals	Materials
	Interest charges on debt	Sales commissions
	Salaries of research staff	
	Salaries of executive staff	
	General office expenses	

*Some of these costs—for example, salaries and office expenses—could be varied to some degree; however, firms are reluctant to reduce these expenditures in response to temporary fluctuations in sales. Such costs are often called *semivariable* costs.

of the total-cost line. This must be true, because the firm is gaining $2.00 of revenue for every $1.20 paid out for labor and materials, the variable costs.

Up to the break-even point, found at the intersection of the total-in-

Figure 3–1
Break-even Chart

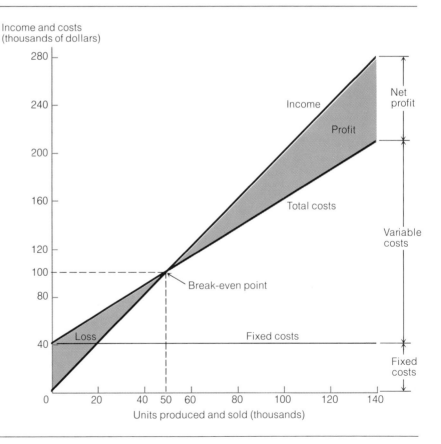

come and total-cost lines, the firm suffers losses. After that point, the firm begins to make profits. Figure 3–1 indicates a break-even point at a sales and cost level of $100,000 and a production level of 50,000 units.

More exact calculations of the break-even point can be carried out algebraically or by trial and error. In section A of Table 3–2, profit and loss relations are shown for various levels of sales; in section B the algebraic calculations are carried out.

Nonlinear Break-even Analysis

In break-even analysis, linear (straight-line) relationships are generally assumed. Although introducing nonlinear relationships complicates matters slightly, it is easy enough to extend the analysis in this manner. For example, it is reasonable to think that increased sales can be obtained only if sales prices are reduced. Similarly, empirical studies suggest that the average variable cost per unit falls over some range of output and then begins to rise. These assumptions are illustrated in Figure 3–2. There we see a loss region when sales are low, then a profit region

Table 3–2
Relations among Units Sold, Total Variable Costs, Fixed Costs, Total Costs, and Total Income

A. Trial-and-error Calculations

Units sold	Total variable costs	Fixed costs	Total costs	Sales	Net profit (loss)
20,000	$ 24,000	$40,000	$ 64,000	$ 40,000	$(24,000)
40,000	48,000	40,000	88,000	80,000	(8,000)
50,000	60,000	40,000	100,000	100,000	—
60,000	72,000	40,000	112,000	120,000	8,000
80,000	96,000	40,000	136,000	160,000	24,000
100,000	120,000	40,000	160,000	200,000	40,000
120,000	144,000	40,000	184,000	240,000	56,000
140,000	168,000	40,000	208,000	280,000	72,000

B. Algebraic Solution to Break-even Point

1. The break-even quantity is defined as that volume of output at which revenue is just equal to total costs (fixed costs plus variable costs).

2. Let: P = sales price per unit
   Q = quantity produced and sold
   FC = fixed costs
   vc = variable costs per unit.

3. Then: $P \cdot Q = FC + vc \cdot Q$
   $P \cdot Q - vc \cdot Q = FC$
   $Q(P - vc) = FC$
   $Q = \dfrac{FC}{P - vc}$ at break-even Q.

4. Illustration: $Q = \dfrac{\$40,000}{\$2.00 - \$1.20}$
   $= 50,000$ units.

(and a maximum profit), and finally another loss region at very high output levels.

Although nonlinear break-even analysis is intellectually appealing, linear analysis is probably more appropriate for the uses to which it is put. Break-even charts allow focus to be placed on the key elements: sales, fixed costs, and variable costs. Even though linear break-even

Figure 3–2
Nonlinear Break-even
Chart

Note: The angle of a line from the origin to a point on the total income line measures price (that is, total income/units sold = price), and a line from the origin to the total costs curve measures cost per unit. It can be seen that the angle of the line to the income curve declines as we move toward higher sales, which means that price reductions are necessary to obtain higher unit sales volume. Unit costs (total costs/units produced) declines to point *X*, the tangency point of a line from the origin to the total costs curve, then begins to rise.

The slopes of the total costs and total income lines measure marginal cost (MC) and marginal revenue (MR), respectively. At the point where the slopes of the two total curves are equal, MR = MC, and profits are at a maximum.

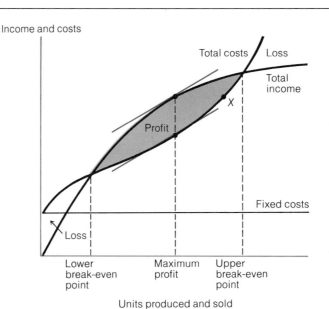

charts are drawn extending from *zero* output to very high output levels, no one who uses them would ordinarily be interested in or even consider the high and low extremes. In other words, users of break-even charts are really interested only in a "relevant range"; within this range linear functions are for the most part reasonably accurate.

**An Example of
Break-even
Analysis: New
Product
Decision**

Break-even analysis can be used in three separate but related ways:

1. To analyze a program to modernize and automate, where the firm would be operating in a more mechanized, automated manner and substituting fixed costs for variable costs. This topic is covered later in this chapter under the section on operating leverage.
2. To study the effects of a general expansion in the level of operations. This topic is covered in the section entitled "Break-even Point Based on Dollar Sales."

3. In new product decisions: How large must the sales volume on a new product be if the firm is to break even on the proposed project? This topic is illustrated in this section.

The textbook publishing business provides a good example of the effective use of break-even analysis for new product decisions. To illustrate, consider the hypothetical example of the analysis of the production costs of a college textbook as described in Table 3–3. The costs and revenues are graphed in Figure 3–3.

The fixed costs can be estimated quite accurately; the variable costs, most of which are set by contracts, can also be estimated precisely (and they are linear). The sales price is variable, but competition keeps prices within a sufficiently narrow range to make a linear total revenue curve

Table 3–3 Hypothetical Cost and Revenue Figures for a Textbook	Fixed costs	
	Copy editing	$ 6,000
	Art work	2,000
	Type setting	72,000
	Total fixed costs	$80,000
	Variable costs per copy	
	Printing and binding	$ 2.20
	Bookstore discounts	4.00
	Salesmen's commissions	.50
	Author's royalties	2.00
	General and administrative costs	1.00
	Total variable costs per copy	$ 9.70
	Sales price per copy	$20.00

Figure 3–3
Break-even Chart for a Hypothetical Textbook

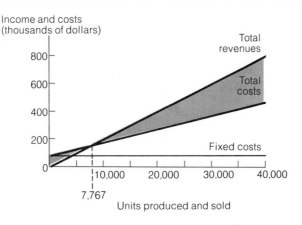

reasonable. Applying the formula, we find the break-even sales volume to be 7,767 copies.

Publishers know the size of the total market for a given book, the competition, and so forth. With these data as a base, they can estimate the possibility that sales of a given book will reach or exceed the break-even point. If the estimate is that they will not, the publisher may consider cutting production costs by spending less on art work and editing, using a lower grade of paper, negotiating with the author on royalty rates, and so on. In this particular business—and for new product decisions in many others—linear break-even analysis has proved itself to be a useful tool.

Break-even Point Based on Dollar Sales

Calculating break-even points on the basis of dollar sales instead of on units of output is frequently useful. The main advantage of this method, which is illustrated in Table 3–4, is that it enables one to determine a general break-even point for a firm that sells many products at varying prices. Furthermore, the procedure requires a minimum of data. Only three values are needed: sales, fixed costs, and variable costs. Sales and total-cost data are readily available from annual reports of corporations and from investment manuals. Total costs must then be segregated into fixed and variable components. The major fixed charges (rent, interest, depreciation, and general and administrative expenses) may be taken from the income statement. Finally, variable costs are calculated by deducting fixed costs from total costs.

Operating Leverage

To a physicist, leverage implies the use of a lever to raise a heavy object with a small force. In business terminology, a high degree of leverage implies that a relatively small change in sales results in a large change in profits. We can divide leverage into two categories: (1) *financial leverage*, discussed briefly in Chapter 2 (and much more extensively in Chapter 18), and (2) *operating leverage*, the subject of this section.

The significance of the degree of operating leverage is clearly illustrated by Figure 3–4. Three firms, A, B, and C, with differing degrees of leverage, are contrasted. Firm A has a relatively small amount of fixed charges—it does not have much automated equipment, so its depreciation cost is low. Note, however, that A's variable cost line has a relatively steep slope, denoting that its variable costs per unit are higher than those of the other firms. Firm B is considered to have a normal amount of fixed costs in its operations. It uses automated equipment (with which one operator can turn out a few or many units at the same labor cost) to about the same extent as the average firm in the industry. Firm B breaks even at a higher level of operations than does firm A. At a production level of 40,000 units, B is losing $8,000 but A breaks even.

Table 3–4 **Calculation of** **Break-even Point** **Based on Dollar** **Sales**	Break-even point (sales volume) $= \dfrac{\text{total fixed costs}}{1 - \dfrac{\text{total variable costs}}{\text{total sales volume}}} = \dfrac{FC}{1 - \dfrac{VC}{P \cdot Q}}$

Procedure

Take any sales level and use the related data to determine the break-even point. For example, assume that 20,000 units were actually produced and sold, and use the data related to that output in Table 3–2:

$$\text{Break-even point} = \frac{\$40,000}{1 - \dfrac{\$24,000}{\$40,000}} = \frac{\$40,000}{0.4} = \$100,000.$$

Rationale

1. At the break-even point, sales ($P \cdot Q^*$) are equal to fixed cost (FC) plus total variable cost (VC):

$$P \cdot Q^* = FC + VC. \tag{3–1}$$

2. Because both the sales price and the variable cost per unit are assumed to be constant in break-even analysis, the ratio $VC/P \cdot Q$ for *any* level of sales is also constant and may be found from the annual income statement.

3. Since variable cost is a constant percentage of sales, equation 3–1 can be rewritten as:

$$P \cdot Q^* = FC + \frac{VC}{P \cdot Q} (P \cdot Q^*)$$

$$P \cdot Q^* \left(1 - \frac{VC}{P \cdot Q}\right) = FC$$

$$P \cdot Q^* = \frac{FC}{1 - \dfrac{VC}{P \cdot Q}}$$

On the other hand, firm C has the highest fixed costs. It is highly automated, using expensive, high-speed machines that require very little labor per unit produced. With such an operation, its variable costs rise slowly. Because of the high overhead resulting from charges associated with the expensive machinery, firm C's break-even point is higher than that for either firm A or firm B. Once firm C reaches its break-even point, however, its profits rise faster than do those of the other firms.

Degree of Operating Leverage

Operating leverage can be defined more precisely in terms of the way a given change in volume affects profits. For this purpose we use the following definition: *The degree of operating leverage is defined as the percentage change in operating income that results from a percentage change in units sold.* Algebraically:

Figure 3–4
Operating Leverage

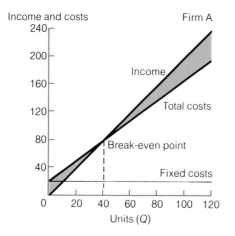

Income and costs   Firm A

Selling price = $2.00
Fixed costs   = $20,000
Variable costs = $1.50 Q

Units sold (Q)	Sales	Costs	Profit
20,000	$ 40,000	$ 50,000	−$10,000
40,000	80,000	80,000	0
60,000	120,000	110,000	10,000
80,000	160,000	140,000	20,000
100,000	200,000	170,000	30,000
120,000	240,000	200,000	40,000

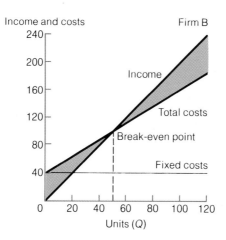

Income and costs   Firm B

Selling price = $2.00
Fixed costs   = $40,000
Variable costs = $1.20 Q

Units sold (Q)	Sales	Costs	Profit
20,000	$ 40,000	$ 64,000	−$24,000
40,000	80,000	88,000	− 8,000
60,000	120,000	112,000	8,000
80,000	160,000	136,000	24,000
100,000	200,000	160,000	40,000
120,000	240,000	184,000	56,000

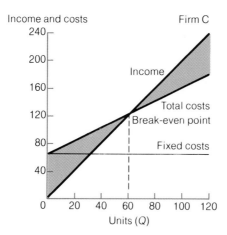

Income and costs   Firm C

Selling price = $2.00
Fixed costs   = $60,000
Variable costs = $1.00 Q

Units sold (Q)	Sales	Costs	Profit
20,000	$ 40,000	$ 80,000	−$40,000
40,000	80,000	100,000	− 20,000
60,000	120,000	120,000	0
80,000	160,000	140,000	20,000
100,000	200,000	160,000	40,000
120,000	240,000	180,000	60,000

$$\text{Degree of operating leverage} = \frac{\text{percentage change in operating income}}{\text{percentage change in units sold}}$$

For firm B in Figure 3–4, the degree of operating leverage (OL_B) at 100,000 units of output is:

$$OL_B = \frac{\dfrac{\Delta \text{ income}}{\text{income}}}{\dfrac{\Delta Q}{Q}}$$

$$= \frac{\dfrac{\$56,000 - \$40,000}{\$40,000}}{\dfrac{120,000 - 100,000}{100,000}} = \frac{\dfrac{\$16,000}{\$40,000}}{\dfrac{20,000}{100,000}}$$

$$= \frac{40\%}{20\%} = \boxed{2.0}.$$

Here Δ income is the increase in income, Q is the quantity of output in units, and ΔQ is the increase in output. For this calculation we assume an increase in volume from 100,000 to 120,000 units, but the calculated OL would have been the same for any other increase from 100,000 units.

For linear break-even, a formula has been developed to aid in calculating the degree of operating leverage at any level of output, Q:

$$\text{Degree of operating leverage at point } Q = \frac{Q(P - vc)}{(P - vc)Q - FC} \qquad (3\text{–}2)[1]$$

$$= \frac{P \cdot Q - VC}{P \cdot Q - VC - FC} \qquad (3\text{–}2a)$$

Here P is the price per unit, vc is the variable cost per unit, FC is fixed costs, $P \cdot Q$ is total sales, and VC is total variable costs. Equation 3–2

---

1. Equation 3–2 is developed as follows:
The change in output is defined as ΔQ. Fixed costs are constant, so the change in profits is $\Delta Q(P - vc)$, where P = price per unit and vc = variable cost per unit. The initial profit is $Q(P - vc) - FC$, so the percentage change in profit is:

$$\frac{\Delta Q(P - vc)}{Q(P - vc) - FC}$$

The percentage change in output is $\Delta Q/Q$, so the ratio of the change in profits to the change in output is:

$$\frac{\dfrac{\Delta Q(P - vc)}{Q(P - vc) - FC}}{\dfrac{\Delta Q}{Q}} = \frac{\Delta Q(P - vc)}{Q(P - vc) - FC} \cdot \frac{Q}{\Delta Q} = \frac{P \cdot Q - VC}{P \cdot Q - VC - FC}$$

expresses the relationship in terms of units, while equation 3–2a expresses it in terms of total dollar figures. Using the equations, we find firm B's degree of operating leverage at 100,000 units of output to be:

$$OL_B \text{ at } 100,000 \text{ units} = \frac{100,000(\$2.00 - \$1.20)}{100,000(\$2.00 - \$1.20) - \$40,000}$$

$$= \frac{\$200,000 - \$120,000}{\$200,000 - \$120,000 - \$40,000}$$

$$= \frac{\$80,000}{\$40,000} = \boxed{2.0}.$$

The two methods must, of course, give consistent answers.

Equation 3-2 can also be applied to firms A and C. When this is done, we find A's degree of operating leverage at 100,000 units to be 1.67 and that of C to be 2.5. Thus, for a 100 percent increase in volume, firm C, the company with the most operating leverage, will experience a profit increase of 250 percent; for the same 100 percent volume gain, firm A, the one with the least leverage, will have only a 167 percent profit gain.

In summary, the calculation of the degree of operating leverage shows algebraically the same pattern that Figure 3–4 shows graphically — that the profits of firm C, the company with the most operating leverage, are most sensitive to changes in sales volume, while those of firm A, which has only a small amount of operating leverage, are relatively insensitive to volume changes. Firm B, with an intermediate degree of leverage, lies between the two extremes.[2]

Cash Break-even Analysis

Some of the firm's fixed costs are noncash outlays, and for a period some of its revenues may be in receivables. The cash break-even chart for firm B, constructed on the assumption that $30,000 of the fixed costs from the previous illustration are depreciation charges and, therefore, a noncash outlay, is shown in Figure 3–5.[3] Because fixed cash outlays are only $10,000, the cash break-even point is at 12,500 units rather than 50,000 units, which is the profit break-even point.

---

2. The degree of operating leverage is a form of *elasticity concept* and, thus, is akin to the familiar price elasticity developed in economics. Since operating leverage is an elasticity, it varies depending upon the particular part of the break-even graph that is being considered. For example, in terms of our illustrative firms the degree of operating leverage is greatest close to the break-even point, where a very small change in volume can produce a very large percentage increase in profits simply because the base profits are close to zero near the break-even point.

3. The nature of depreciation as a noncash charge is explained later in this chapter.

Figure 3–5
Cash Break-even
Analysis

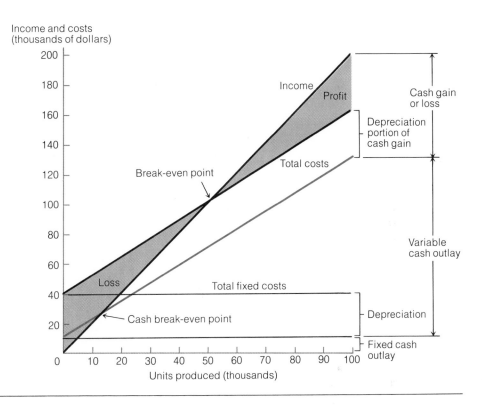

Cash break-even analysis does not fully represent cash flows — for this a cash budget is required. But cash break-even analysis is useful because it provides a picture of the flow of funds from operations. A firm could incur a level of fixed costs that would result in losses during periods of poor business but large profits during upswings. If cash outlays are small, even during periods of losses the firm might still be operating above the cash break-even point. Thus, the risks of insolvency, in the sense of inability to meet cash obligations, would be small. This allows a firm to reach out for higher profits through automation and operating leverage.

**Limitations of
Break-even
Analysis**

Break-even analysis is useful in studying the relations among volume, prices, and costs; it is thus helpful in pricing, cost control, and decisions about alternative expansion programs. It has limitations, however, as a guide to managerial actions.

Linear break-even analysis is especially weak in what it implies about the sales possibilities for the firm. Any linear break-even chart is based on a constant sales price. Therefore, in order to study profit possibilities under different prices, a whole series of charts is necessary, one chart for each price. Alternatively, nonlinear break-even analysis can be used.

With regard to costs, break-even analysis is also deficient — the relations indicated by the chart do not hold at all outputs. As sales increase, existing plant and equipment are worked to capacity; both this situation and the use of additional workers and overtime pay cause variable costs to rise sharply. Additional equipment and plant are required, thus increasing fixed costs. Finally, over a period the products sold by the firm change in quality and quantity. Such changes in product mix influence the level and slope of the cost function. Linear break-even analysis is useful as a first step in developing the basic data required for pricing and for financial decisions. But more detailed analysis, perhaps including nonlinear analysis is required before final judgments can be made.

Sources and Uses of Funds Statement

When a firm requests a loan, the bank's loan officer will doubtless pose these three questions: What has the firm done with the money it had? What will it do with the new funds? How will it repay the loan? The sources and uses statement helps provide answers to these questions, as well as to questions that other interested parties may have about the firm. This information may indicate that the firm is making progress or that problems are arising.

Depreciation as a Source of Funds

Before going on to construct a sources and uses of funds statement, it is useful to pause and consider why, in financial analysis, we consider depreciation to be a source of funds. First, what is depreciation? In effect, it is an annual charge against income that reflects the cost of the capital equipment used in the production process. For example, suppose a machine with an expected useful life of 10 years and a 0 expected salvage value was purchased in 1970 for $100,000. This $100,000 cost must be charged against production during those 10 years; otherwise, profits will be overstated. If the machine is depreciated by the straight-line method, the annual charge is $10,000. This amount is deducted from sales revenues, along with such other costs as labor and raw materials, to determine income. *However, depreciation is not a cash outlay — funds were expended back in 1970, so the depreciation charged against income in 1974 is not a cash outlay, as are labor or charges for raw materials.*

To illustrate the significance of depreciation in cash flow analysis, let us consider the Dallas Fertilizer and Chemical Company, which has the following income statement for 1978:

Sales	$300,000,000
Costs excluding depreciation	$270,000,000
Depreciation	10,000,000
Profit before tax	$ 20,000,000
Taxes	8,000,000
Profit after tax	$ 12,000,000

Assuming that sales are for cash and that all costs except depreciation are paid during 1978, how much cash was available from operations to pay dividends, retire debt, or make investments in fixed or current assets or both? The answer is $22 million, the sum of profit after tax plus depreciation. The sales are all for cash, so the firm took in $300 million in cash money. Its costs other than depreciation were $270 million, and these were paid in cash, leaving $30 million. Depreciation *is not* a cash charge—the firm does not pay out the $10 million of depreciation expenses—so $30 million of cash money is still left after depreciation. Taxes, on the other hand, are paid in cash, so $8 million for taxes must be deducted from the $30 million gross operating cash flow, leaving a net cash flow from operations of $22 million. This $22 million is, of course, exactly equal to profit after tax plus depreciation: $12 million plus $10 million equals $22 million.

This example shows the rationale behind the statement that depreciation is a source of funds. However, we should note that without sales revenues, depreciation would *not* be a source of funds. If a strike idles the plant, the $300 million of sales revenues would vanish; cash flows from depreciation would evaporate.[4] Nevertheless, most firms do not suffer shutdowns for long periods, so normally a firm's depreciation does indeed constitute a source of funds as we use the term.

Sources and Uses Analysis

Several steps are involved in constructing a sources and uses statement. First, the changes in balance sheet items from one year to the next must be tabulated and then classified as either a source or a use of funds, according to the following pattern:

4. This potential problem was brought to the authors' attention in connection with a project involving a financial plan for Communications Satellite Corporation. Comsat has very healthy projected cash flows that would seem able to support a substantial amount of debt. However, Comsat's revenues are derived almost entirely from three satellites (over the North Atlantic, Pacific, and Indian Oceans), and if these satellites failed it would take months to replace them. Thus, when we recognized the degree of uncertainty about these cash flows, we adjusted downward our estimates of how much debt Comsat could safely carry.

Source of funds: (1) decrease in asset item or (2) increase in liability item
Use of funds: (1) increase in asset item or (2) decrease in liability item.

Table 3−5 gives Dallas Chemical's comparative balance sheets for 1977
and 1978 and also net changes in each item classified as to source or use.

Table 3−5
Dallas Fertilizer and
Chemical Company
Comparative balance
sheets and sources
and uses of funds
(millions of dollars)

	Dec. 31, 1977	Dec. 31, 1978	Sources	Uses
Cash	$ 10	$ 5	$ 5	
Marketable securities	25	15	10	
Net receivables	15	20		$ 5
Inventories	25	30		5
Gross fixed assets	150	180		30
Less: Accumulated depreciation*	(40)	(50)	10	
Net fixed assets	110	130		
Total assets	$185	$200		
Accounts payable	$ 10	$ 6		$ 4
Notes payable	15	10		5
Other current liabilities	10	14	4	
Long-term debt	60	70	10	
Preferred stock	10	10	—	—
Common stock	50	50	—	—
Retained earnings	30	40	10	
Total claims on assets	$185	$200		

*The accumulated depreciation is actually a "liability" account (a contra-asset) that appears on the
left side of the balance sheet. Note that it is deducted, not added, when totaling the column.

The next step in constructing a sources and uses statement involves
(1) making adjustments to reflect net income and dividends and (2) iso-
lating changes in working capital (current assets and current liabilities).
These changes are reflected in the sources and uses statement shown in
Table 3−6. Net income in 1978 amounted to $12 million, and dividends
of $2 million were paid. The $12 million is treated as a source, the $2
million as a use. The $10 million retained earnings shown in Table 3−5
is deleted from Table 3−6 to avoid double counting. Notice that Dallas
Chemical had no net change in working capital − the increases were
exactly equal to the decreases. This was merely a coincidence; ordinarily
there will be some change in net working capital.

What does this statement of sources and uses of funds tell the financial manager? It tells him that plant size was expanded and that fixed
assets amounting to $30 million were acquired. Inventories and net re-
ceivables also increased as sales increased. The firm needed funds to
meet working capital and fixed assets demands.

Table 3–6	Amount		Percent	
Dallas Fertilizer and Chemical Company Statement of sources and uses of funds, 1978 (millions of dollars)				
Sources				
Net Income		$12	23.5	
Depreciation		10	19.6	
Decreases in working capital				43.1
Reduction in cash	$ 5		9.8	
Sale of marketable securities	10		19.6	
Increase in other liabilities	4		7.9	
Total decrease in working capital		19		37.3
Increase in long-term debt		10		19.6
Total sources of funds		$51		100.0
Uses				
Increases in working capital:				
Inventory investment	$ 5		9.8	
Increase in receivables	5		9.8	
Reduction in notes payable	5		9.8	
Reduction in accounts payable	4		7.9	
Total increases in working capital		$19		37.3
Gross fixed assets expansion		30	58.8	
Dividends to stockholders		2	3.9	62.7
Total uses of funds		$51		100.0

Previously, Dallas has been financing its growth through bank credit (notes payable). In the present period of growth, management decided to obtain some financing from permanent sources (long-term debt). It obtained enough long-term debt not only to finance some of the asset growth but also to pay back some of its bank credit and to reduce accounts payable. In addition to the long-term debt, funds were obtained from earnings and from depreciation charges. Moreover, the firm had been accumulating marketable securities in anticipation of this expansion program, and some were sold to pay for new buildings and equipment. Finally, cash had been accumulated in excess of the firm's needs and was also worked down. In summary, this example illustrates how the sources and uses of funds statement can provide both a fairly complete picture of recent operations and a good perspective on the flow of funds within the company.

Pro Forma Sources and Uses of Funds

A *pro forma*, or projected, sources and uses of funds statement can also be constructed to show how a firm plans to acquire and employ funds during some future period. In the next chapter we will discuss financial forecasting, which involves the determination of future sales, the level of assets necessary to generate these sales (the left side of the projected balance sheet), and the manner in which these assets will be financed (the right side of the projected balance sheet). Given the projected balance sheet and supplementary projected data on earnings, dividends, and depreciation, the financial manager can construct a pro forma sources and uses of funds statement to summarize his firm's projected operations over the planning horizon. Such a statement is obviously of much interest to lenders as well as to the firm's own management.

Summary

This chapter analyzes two important financial tools, *break-even analysis* and the *sources and uses of funds statement*, and the key concept of *operating leverage*.

Break-even Analysis. Break-even analysis is a method of relating fixed costs, variable costs, and total revenues to show the level of sales that must be attained if the firm is to operate at a profit. The analysis can be based on the number of units produced or on total dollar sales. It can also be used for the entire company or for a particular product or division. Further, with minor modifications, break-even analysis can be put on a cash basis instead of a profit basis. Ordinarily, break-even analysis is conducted on a linear, or straight-line, basis. However, this is not necessary—nonlinear break-even analysis is feasible and at times desirable.

Operating Leverage. Operating leverage is defined as the extent to which fixed costs are used in operations. The *degree of operating leverage*, defined as the percentage change in operating income that results from a specific percentage change in units sold, provides a precise measure of how much operating leverage a particular firm is employing. Break-even analysis provides a graphic view of the effects of changes in sales on profits; the degree of operating leverage presents the same picture in algebraic terms.

Sources and Uses of Funds Statement. The sources and uses of funds statement indicates where cash came from and how it was used. When a firm wishes to borrow funds, one of the first questions posed by the bank's loan officer is "What has the firm done with the money it had?" This question is answered by the sources and uses of funds statement. The information it provides may indicate that the firm is making progress or that problems are arising. Sources and uses data may also be analyzed on a *pro forma*, or projected, basis to show how a firm plans to acquire and employ funds during some future period.

Questions

3-1. What benefits can be derived from break-even analysis?

3-2. What is operating leverage? Explain how profits or losses can be magnified in a firm with high operating leverage as opposed to a firm without this characteristic.

3-3. What data are necessary to construct a break-even chart?

3-4. What is the general effect of each of the following changes on a firm's break-even point?
   a. An increase in selling price with no change in units sold.
   b. A change from the leasing of a machine for $5,000 a year to the purchase of the machine for $100,000. The useful life of this machine will be 20 years, with no salvage value. Assume straight-line depreciation.
   c. A reduction in variable labor costs.

3-5. In what sense can depreciation be considered a source of funds?

Problems

3-1. Mayer Corporation produces toasters, which it sells for $18. Fixed costs are $110,000 for up to 24,000 units of output. Variable cost is $10 per unit.
   a. What is the firm's gain or loss at sales of 12,000 units? of 18,000 units?
   b. What is the break-even point? Illustrate by means of a chart.
   c. What is Mayer's degree of operating leverage at sales of 12,000 and 18,000 units?
   d. What happens to the break-even point if selling price falls to $16? What is the significance of the change to financial management? Illustrate by means of a chart.
   e. How does the break-even point change when the selling price falls to $16 but variable cost falls to $8 a unit? Illustrate by means of a chart.

3-2. For Martin Industries the following relations exist: each unit of output is sold for $75; for output up to 25,000 units the fixed costs are $240,000; variable costs are $35 a unit.
   a. What is the firm's gain or loss at sales of 5,000 units? of 8,000 units?
   b. What is the break-even point? Illustrate by means of a chart.
   c. What is Martin's degree of operating leverage at sales of 5,000 and 8,000 units?
   d. What happens to the break-even point if the selling price rises to $85? What is the significance of the change to financial management? Illustrate by means of a chart.
   e. What occurs to the break-even point if the selling price rises to $85 but variable costs rise to $45 a unit? Illustrate by means of a chart.

3-3. The Ohio Tire Company is currently considering two possible mutually exclusive plant modernizations. Under the first, newer and more efficient machinery would be added; this would tend to reduce labor costs and, because of much less waste, raw material usage. The other alternative would involve a more extensive changeover in the plant to an entirely new process for forming and curing rubber. The second procedure would involve a more extensive investment in both plant and equipment, but it would result in larger savings in labor and materials costs.

The current sales level is about 76,500 units a year at a price of $40 each, but volume has fluctuated from year to year with changes in general economic conditions. The firm's management is primarily concerned with the extent to which profitability will be affected by each alternative project in relation to risk. (For current purposes, riskiness may be considered to be a function of the probability of not reaching the break-even point.) A breakdown of costs for the current sales volume is given below, together with estimates of what each item would be after each of the modernization proposals.

Estimated costs	Currently	Modernization I	Modernization II
Depreciation on plant and equipment	$513,000	$630,000	$787,500
Depreciation on building	288,000	360,000	468,000
Property taxes	36,000	45,000	63,000
Salary expense	639,000	693,000	778,500
Other fixed expenses	54,000	72,000	99,000
Factory labor	625,500	468,000	270,000
Raw materials	450,000	378,000	270,000
Variable selling expenses	72,000	72,000	72,000

a. Determine the break-even point in units for the firm, assuming (1) no modernization is undertaken, (2) the first program is undertaken, and (3) the second program is undertaken.
b. Compute the degree of operating leverage at the current volume (76,500 units) for each of the three possibilities.
c. Compute profits for each alternative, assuming future sales of 76,500 units. Profits for each alternative at other sales levels have been calculated (to save you work) and are given below:

Unit Sales	Profits
No modernization	
65,000	$ 95,000
90,000	720,000
100,000	970,000
Modernization I	
65,000	$ 20,000
90,000	720,000
100,000	1,000,000
Modernization II	
65,000	$ (116,000)
90,000	684,000
100,000	1,004,000

d. Rank the alternatives in terms of potential riskiness.
e. How would the decision if and how to modernize be affected by the expectation of large fluctuations in future sales?
f. (To be worked at the option of the instructor.) Suppose we have estimated the following probability distribution for sales:

Probability	Sales (in Units)
.1	65,000
.3	76,500
.3	90,000
.3	100,000

Use this information to determine the expected values of the three alternative courses of action.
g. Which project is best? What factors would influence your decision?

3–4. The consolidated balance sheets for the Norton Corporation at the beginning and end of 1978 are shown below.

Norton Corporation
Balance sheet
Beginning and end 1978
(millions of dollars)

	Jan. 1	Dec. 31	Source	Use
Cash	$ 45	$ 21	_____	_____
Marketable securities	33	0	_____	_____
Net receivables	66	90	_____	_____
Inventories	159	225	_____	_____
Total current assets	$303	$336	_____	_____
Gross fixed assets	225	450	_____	_____
Less: reserve for depreciation	(78)	(123)	_____	_____
Net fixed assets	147	327	_____	_____
Total assets	$450	$663		

	Jan. 1	Dec. 31	Source	Use
Accounts payable	$ 45	$ 54	_____	_____
Notes payable	45	9	_____	_____
Other current liabilities	21	45	_____	_____
Long-term debt	24	78	_____	_____
Common stock	114	192	_____	_____
Retained earnings	201	285	_____	_____
Total claims on assets	$450	$663	_____	_____

The company bought $225 million worth of fixed assets. The charge for current depreciation was $45 million. Earnings after taxes were $114 million, and the company paid out $30 million in dividends.
a. Fill in the amount of source or use in the appropriate column.

b. Prepare a percentage statement of sources and uses of funds.

c. Briefly summarize your findings.

3–5. Transistor Electronics is considering developing a new miniature calculator. The quantity (Q) sold is a function of the price (P) where

$$Q = 2,000 - 10P$$

Fixed costs are $24,000 and variable cost per unit is $60.

a. Graphically determine the break-even points for the calculator in units and dollars.

b. What is the company's price at an output of 700 units?

c. What is its profit at that output?

d. What happens to the price and profits if the company sells 1,000 units?

Selected References

Helfert, Erich A. *Techniques of Financial Analysis.* 3rd ed. Homewood, Ill.: Irwin, 1972, chap. 2.

Jaedicke, Robert K., and Robichek, Alexander A. "Cost-Volume-Profit Analysis under Conditions of Uncertainty." *Accounting Review* 39 (Oct. 1964):917–26.

Jaedicke, Robert K., and Sprouse, Robert T. *Accounting Flows: Income, Funds, and Cash.* Englewood Cliffs, N.J.: Prentice-Hall, 1965.

Kelvie, William E., and Sinclair, John M. "New Techniques for Breakeven Charts." *Financial Executive* 36 (June 1968):31–43.

Morrison, Thomas A., and Kaczka, Eugene. "A New Application of Calculus and Risk Analysis to Cost-Volume-Profit Changes." *Accounting Review* 44 (Apr. 1969):330–43.

Raun, D. L. "The Limitations of Profit Graphs, Break-even Analysis, and Budgets." *Accounting Review* 39 (Oct. 1964):927–45.

Reinhardt, U. E. "Break-Even Analysis for Lockheed's Tri Star: An Application of Financial Theory." *Journal of Finance* 28 (Sept. 1973):821–38.

Searby, Frederick W. "Return to Return on Investment." *Harvard Business Review* 53 (Mar.–Apr. 1975):113–19.

Soldofsky, R. M. "Accountant's versus Economist's Concepts of Break-even Analysis." *N.A.A. Bulletin* 41 (Dec. 1959):5–18.

4   Financial Forecasting

The planning process is an integral part of the financial manager's job. As we will see in subsequent chapters, long-term debt and equity funds are raised infrequently and in large amounts, primarily because the cost per dollar raised by selling such securities decreases as the size of the issue increases. Because of these considerations, it is important that the firm have a working estimate of its total needs for funds for the next few years. It is therefore useful to examine methods of forecasting the firm's overall needs for funds, and this is the subject of the present chapter.

Cash Flow Cycle

We must recognize that firms need assets to make sales; if sales are to be increased, assets must also be expanded. Growing firms require new investments—immediate investment in current assets and, as full capacity is reached, investment in fixed assets as well. New investments must be financed, and new financing carries with it commitments and obligations to service the capital obtained.[1] A growing, profitable firm is likely to require additional cash for investments in receivables, inventories, and fixed assets. Such a firm can, therefore, have a cash flow problem. The nature of this problem, as well as the cause and effect relationship between assets and sales, is illustrated in the following discussion, in which we trace the consequences of a series of transactions.

Effects on the Balance Sheet

1. Two partners invest a total of $50,000 to create the Glamour Galore Dress Company. The firm rents a plant; equipment and other fixed as-

Balance Sheet 1

Assets		Liabilities	
Current Assets		Capital stock	$50,000
Cash	$20,000		
Fixed Assets			
Plant and equipment	30,000		
Total assets	$50,000	Total liabilities and net worth	$50,000

---

1. "Servicing" capital refers to the payment of interest and principal on debt and to dividends on common stocks.

sets cost $30,000. The resulting financial situation is shown by Balance Sheet 1.

2. Glamour Galore receives an order to manufacture 10,000 dresses. The receipt of an order in itself has no effect on the balance sheet, but in preparation for the manufacturing activity, the firm buys $20,000 worth of cotton cloth on terms of net 30 days. Without additional investment by the owners, total assets increase by $20,000, financed by the trade accounts payable to the supplier of the cotton cloth.

After the purchase, the firm spends $20,000 on labor for cutting the cloth to the required pattern. Of the $20,000 total labor cost, $10,000 is paid in cash and $10,000 is owed in the form of accrued wages. These two transactions are reflected in Balance Sheet 2, which shows that total

Balance Sheet 2

Assets			Liabilities	
Current Assets			Accounts payable	$20,000
Cash		$10,000	Accrued wages payable	$10,000
Inventories			Total current liabilities	$30,000
Work in process				
Materials		20,000	Capital stock	50,000
Labor		20,000		
Total current assets		$50,000		
Fixed Assets				
Plant and equipment		30,000		
Total assets		$80,000	Total liabilities and net worth	$80,000

assets increase to $80,000. Current assets are increased; net working capital—total current assets minus total current liabilities—remains constant. The current ratio declines to 1.67, and the debt ratio rises to 38 percent. The financial position of the firm is weakening. If it should seek to borrow at this point, Glamour Galore could not use the work in

Balance Sheet 3

Assets			Liabilities	
Current Assets			Accounts payable	$20,000
Cash		$ 5,000	Notes payable	15,000
Inventory			Accrued wages payable	10,000
Finished goods		60,000	Total current liabilities	$45,000
Total current assets		$65,000		
			Capital stock	50,000
Fixed Assets				
Plant and equipment		30,000		
Total assets		$95,000	Total liabilities and net worth	$95,000

process inventories as collateral, because a lender could find little use for partially manufactured dresses.

3. In order to complete the dresses, the firm incurs additional labor costs of $20,000 and pays in cash. It is assumed that the firm desires to maintain a minimum cash balance of $5,000. Since the initial cash balance is $10,000, Glamour Galore must borrow an additional $15,000 from its bank to meet the wage bill. The borrowing is reflected in notes payable in Balance Sheet 3. Total assets rise to $95,000, with a finished goods inventory of $60,000. The current ratio drops to 1.4, and the debt ratio rises to 47 percent. These ratios show a further weakening of the financial position.

4. Glamour Galore ships the dresses on the basis of the original order, invoicing the purchaser for $100,000 within 30 days. Accrued wages and accounts payable have to be paid now, so Glamour Galore must borrow an additional $30,000 in order to maintain the $5,000 minimum cash balance. These transactions are shown in Balance Sheet 4.

Balance Sheet 4

Assets			Liabilities	
Current Assets			Notes payable	$ 45,000
Cash		$ 5,000	Total current liabilities	$ 45,000
Accounts receivable		100,000	Capital stock	$ 50,000
Total current assets		$105,000	Retained earnings	40,000
			Total net worth	$ 90,000
Fixed Assets				
Plant and equipment		30,000		
Total assets		$135,000	Total liabilities and net worth	$135,000

Note that in Balance Sheet 4, finished goods inventory is replaced by receivables, with the markup reflected as retained earnings. This causes the debt ratio to drop to 33 percent. Since the receivables are carried at the sales price, current assets increase to $105,000 and the current ratio rises to 2.3. Compared with the conditions reflected in Balance Sheet 3, most of the financial ratios show improvement. However, the absolute amount of debt is large.

Whether the firm's financial position is really improved depends upon the credit worthiness of the purchaser of the dresses. If the purchaser is a good credit risk, Glamour Galore may be able to borrow further on the basis of the accounts receivable.

5. The firm receives payment for the accounts receivable, pays off the bank loan, and is in the highly liquid position shown by Balance Sheet 5. If a new order for 10,000 dresses is received, it will have no effect on the balance sheet, but a cycle similar to the one we have been describing will begin.

Balance Sheet 5

Assets		Liabilities	
Current Assets		Capital stock	$50,000
Cash	$60,000	Retained earnings	40,000
Fixed Assets			
Plant and equipment	$30,000		
Total assets	$90,000	Total liabilities and net worth	$90,000

6. The idea of the cash flow cycle can now be generalized. An order that requires the purchase of raw materials is placed with the firm. The purchase in turn generates an account payable. As labor is applied, work-in-process inventories build up. To the extent that wages are not fully paid at the time labor is used, accrued wages will appear on the liability side of the balance sheet. As goods are completed, they move into finished goods inventories. The cash needed to pay for the labor to complete the goods may make it necessary for the firm to borrow.

Finished goods inventories are sold, usually on credit, which gives rise to accounts receivable. As the firm has not received cash, this point in the cycle represents the peak in financing requirements. If the firm did not borrow at the time finished goods inventories were at their maximum, it may do so as inventories are converted into receivables by credit sales. Income taxes, which were not considered in the example, can add to the problem. As accounts receivable become cash, short-term obligations can be paid off.

Financing Patterns

The influence of sales on current asset levels has just been illustrated. Over the course of several cycles, the fluctuations in sales will be accompanied in most industries by a rising long-term trend. Figure 4–1 shows the consequences of such a pattern. Total permanent assets increase steadily in the form of current and fixed assets. Increases of this nature should be financed by long-term debt, by equity, or by "spontaneous" increases in liabilities, such as accrued taxes and wages and accounts payable, which naturally accompany increasing sales. However, temporary increases in assets can be covered by short-term liabilities. The distinction between temporary and permanent asset levels may be difficult to make in practice, but it is neither illusory nor unimportant. Short-term financing for the financing of long-term needs is dangerous. A profitable firm may become unable to meet its cash obligations if funds borrowed on a short-term basis have become tied up in permanent asset needs.

Figure 4–1
Fluctuating versus
Permanent Assets

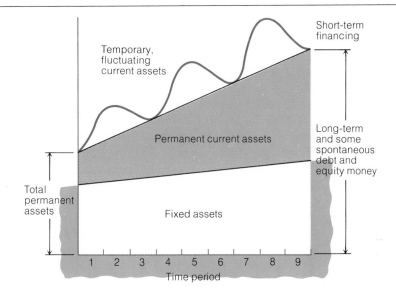

Percent-of-Sales Method

It is apparent from the preceding discussion that *the most important variable that influences a firm's financing requirements is its projected dollar volume of sales. A good sales forecast is an essential foundation for forecasting financial requirements.* In spite of its importance, we shall not go into sales forecasting here; rather, we simply assume that a sales forecast has been made, then estimate financial requirements on the basis of this forecast.[2] The principal methods of forecasting financial requirements are described in this and the following sections.

The simplest approach to forecasting financial requirements express-

Table 4–1	**Assets**		**Liabilities**	
The Moore Company	Cash	$ 10,000	Accounts payable	$ 50,000
Balance sheet	Receivables	85,000	Accrued taxes and wages	25,000
December 31, 1978	Inventories	100,000	Mortgage bonds	70,000
	Fixed assets (net)	150,000	Common stocks	100,000
			Retained earnings	100,000
	Total assets	$345,000	Total liabilities and net worth	$345,000

2. For a discussion of demand forecasting, see E. F. Brigham and J. L. Pappas, *Managerial Economics* (Hinsdale, Ill.: Dryden Press, 1972).

es the firm's needs in terms of the percentage of annual sales invested in each individual balance sheet item. As an example, consider the Moore Company, whose balance sheet as of December 31, 1978, is shown in Table 4–1. The company's sales are running at about $500,000 a year, which is its capacity limit; the profit margin after tax on sales is 4 percent. During 1978, the company earned $20,000 after taxes and paid out $10,000 in dividends, and it plans to continue paying out half of net profits as dividends. How much additional financing will be needed if sales expand to $800,000 during 1979? The calculating procedure, using the percent-of-sales method, is explained below.[3]

First, isolate those balance sheet items that can be expected to vary directly with sales. In the case of the Moore Company, this step applies to each category of assets—a higher level of sales necessitates more cash for transactions, more receivables, higher inventory levels, and additional fixed plant capacity. On the liability side, accounts payable as well as accruals may be expected to increase with increases in sales. Retained earnings will go up as long as the company is profitable and does not pay out 100 percent of earnings, but the percentage increase is not constant. However, neither common stock nor mortgage bonds would increase spontaneously with an increase in sales.

The items that can be expected to vary directly with sales are tabulated as a percentage of sales in Table 4–2. For every $1.00 increase in

Table 4–2
The Moore Company
Balance sheet items expressed as a percent of sales
December 31, 1978
(percent)

Assets		Liabilities	
Cash	2.0	Accounts payable	10.0
Receivables	17.0	Accrued taxes and wages	5.0
Inventories	20.0	Mortgage bonds	na*
Fixed assets (net)	30.0	Common stock	na*
		Retained earnings	na*
Total assets	69.0	Total liabilities and net worth	15.0

Assets as percent of sales	69.0
Less: Spontaneous increase in liabilities	15.0
Percent of each additional dollar of sales that must be financed	54.0

*Not applicable.

3. We recognize, of course, that as a practical matter, business firms plan their needs in terms of specific items of equipment, square feet of floor space, and other factors, and not as a percentage of sales. However, the outside analyst does not have access to this information; the manager, even though he has the information on specific items, needs to check his forecasts in aggregate terms. The percent-of-sales method serves both these needs surprisingly well.

sales, assets must increase by $.69; this $.69 must be financed in some manner. Accounts payable will increase spontaneously with sales, as will accruals; these two items will supply $.15 of new funds for each $1.00 increase in sales. Subtracting the 15 percent for spontaneously generated funds from the 69 percent funds requirement leaves 54 percent. Thus, for each $1.00 increase in sales, the Moore Company must obtain $.54 of financing either from internally generated funds or from external sources.

In the case at hand, sales are scheduled to increase from $500,000 to $800,000, or by $300,000. Applying the 54 percent developed in the table to the expected increase in sales leads to the conclusion that $162,000 will be needed.

Some of that need will be met by retained earnings. Total revenues during 1979 will be $800,000; if the company earns 4 percent after taxes on this volume, profits will amount to $32,000. Assuming that the 50 percent dividend payout ratio is maintained, dividends will be $16,000 and $16,000 will be retained. Subtracting the retained earnings from the $162,000 that was needed leaves a figure of $146,000—this is the amount of funds that must be obtained through borrowing or by selling new common stock.

This process may be expressed in equation form:

$$\text{External funds needed} = \frac{A}{TR}(\Delta TR) - \frac{B}{TR}(\Delta TR) - bm(TR_2) \qquad (4\text{--}1)$$

Here

$\dfrac{A}{TR}$ = assets that increase spontaneously with total revenues or sales as a percent of total revenues or sales

$\dfrac{B}{TR}$ = those liabilities that increase spontaneously with total revenues or sales as a percent of total revenues or sales

ΔTR = change in total revenues or sales

m = profit margin on sales

TR_2 = total revenues projected for the year

b = earnings retention ratio

For the Moore Company, then,

$$\begin{aligned}
\text{External funds needed} &= .69\,(300{,}000) - .15\,(300{,}000) - .04\,(800{,}000)\,(.5) \\
&= .54\,(300{,}000) - .02\,(800{,}000) \\
&= \$146{,}000.
\end{aligned}$$

The $146,000 found by the formula method must, of course, equal the amount derived previously.

Notice what would have occurred if the Moore Company's sales forecast for 1979 had been only $515,000, or a 3 percent increase. Applying the formula, we find the external funds requirements as follows:

External funds needed $= .54\ (15{,}000) - .02\ (515{,}000)$
$$= \$8{,}100 - \$10{,}300$$
$$= (\$2{,}200).$$

In this case, no external funds are required. In fact, the company will have $2,200 in excess of its requirements; it should therefore plan to increase dividends, retire debt, or seek additional investment opportunities. The example shows not only that higher levels of sales bring about a need for funds but also that while small percentage increases can be financed through internally generated funds, larger increases cause the firm to go into the market for outside capital. In other words, a certain level of growth can be financed from internal sources, but higher levels of growth require external financing.[4]

Note that the increase in sales equals $(1 + g)TR_1$ where g equals the growth rate in sales. The increase in sales can therefore be written:

$$\Delta TR = (1 + g)TR_1 - TR_1 = TR_1(1 + g - 1) = gTR_1$$

Let us next take the expression for external funds needed, equation 4–1, and use it to derive the percentage of the increase in sales that will have to be financed externally (PEFR) as a function of the critical variables involved. In equation 4–1 let $\left(\dfrac{A}{TR} - \dfrac{B}{TR}\right) = I$, substitute for ΔTR and TR_2, and divide both sides by $\Delta TR = gTR_1$

$$PEFR = I - \frac{m}{g}\ (1 + g)b \qquad\qquad (4-2)$$

Using equation 4–2, we can now investigate the influence of factors such as an increased rate of inflation on the percentage of sales growth required to be financed externally. Based on the relationships for all manufacturing industries, some representative values of the terms on the right hand side of the equation are: $I = .5$, $m = .05$, and $b = .60$.

During the period before the onset of inflation in the United States after 1966, the economy was growing at about 6 to 7 percent per annum. If a firm was in an industry that grew at the same rate as the economy as a whole and if a firm maintained its market share position in its industry, the firm would be growing at 6 to 7 percent per annum as well. Let us see what the implications for external financing requirements would

---

4. At this point, one might ask two questions: "Shouldn't depreciation be considered as a source of funds, and won't this reduce the amount of external funds needed?" The answer to both questions is no. In the percent-of-sales method, we are implicitly assuming that funds generated through depreciation (in the sources and uses of funds sense) must be used to replace the assets to which the depreciation is applicable. Accordingly, depreciation does not enter the calculations in this forecasting technique; it is netted out.

be. With a growth rate of 6 or 7 percent the percentage of an increase in sales that would have to be financed externally would be as follows:

$$\text{PEFR} = .5 - \frac{.05}{.06}(1.06)(.6)$$
$$= .50 - .53 = -.03 = -3\%$$
$$\text{PEFR} = .5 - \frac{.05}{.07}(1.07)(.6)$$
$$\text{PEFR} = .50 - .46 = .04 = 4\%$$

Thus at a growth rate of 6 percent the percentage of external financing to sales growth would be a negative 3 percent. In other words, the firm would have excess funds with which it could increase dividends or increase its investment in marketable securities. With a growth rate of 7 percent the firm would have a moderate 4 percent requirement of external financing as a percentage of sales increase.

Following 1966 the inflation rate in some particular years was in the two digit range; that is, 10 percent or more. Suppose we add sufficient percentage points per annum of an inflation rate to the previous 6 to 7 percent growth rate to obtain a growth rate of 15 or 20 percent for a firm. Then the external financing requirements will be as follows:

$$\text{PEFR} = .5 - \frac{.05}{.15}(1.15)(.6)$$
$$= .50 - .23 = .27 = 27\%$$
$$\text{PEFR} = .5 - \frac{.05}{.20}(1.20)(.6)$$
$$= .50 - .18 = .32 = 32\%$$

With a growth rate in sales of 15 percent, external financing rises to 27 percent of the firm's sales growth. If inflation caused the growth rate of the firm to rise to 20 percent, then the external financing percentage rises to 32 percent. The substantial increase in the growth rate of sales of firms measured in inflated dollars in recent years points up why external financing has become more important for firms. It underscores also why the finance function in firms has taken on increased importance in recent years. There is just a much bigger job to be done, particularly in requirements for using external financing sources to maintain the sales growth of a firm. Even though the firm were not growing in real terms, an inflation rate of 10 percent, for example, would make it necessary for the firm to raise external financing of 17 percent of its growth in sales of inflated dollars even though the real growth of the firm were zero. This, again, underscores why financing has come to the fore as an important function in the firm.

The percent-of-sales method of forecasting financial requirements is neither simple nor mechanical, although an explanation of the ideas requires simple illustrations. Experience in applying the technique in practice suggests the importance of understanding (1) the basic technology of the firm and (2) the logic of the relation between sales and assets for the particular firm in question. A great deal of experience and judgment is required to apply the technique in actual practice.

The percent-of-sales method is most appropriately used for forecasting relatively short-term changes in financing needs. It is less useful for longer term forecasting for reasons that are best described in connection with the analysis of the regression method of financial forecasting discussed in the next sections.

Scatter Diagram, or Simple Regression, Method

An alternative method used for forecasting financial requirements is the *scatter diagram*, or *simple regression*, method. A scatter diagram is a graphic portrayal of joint relations. Proper use of the scatter diagram method requires practical but not necessarily statistical sophistication.

Table 4–3 and Figure 4–2 illustrate the use of the scatter diagram method and also demonstrate its superiority over the percent-of-sales method for long-range forecasting. As in all financial forecasting, the sales forecast is the starting point. The financial manager is given the sales forecast, or he may participate in formulating it. Suppose he has data through 1979 and is making a forecast of inventories for 1984, as indicated in Table 4–3. If he is using the simple regression method, he draws a line through the points for 1974 through 1979, as shown in Figure 4–2. The line that fits the scatter of points in this example is a straight line. It is called the *line of best fit*, or the *regression line*. Of

Table 4–3
Relationship between Inventory and Sales

Year	Sales	Inventory	Inventory as a Percent of Sales
1974	$ 50,000	$22,000	44
1975	100,000	24,000	24
1976	150,000	26,000	17
1977	200,000	28,000	14
1978	250,000	30,000	12
1979	300,000	32,000	11
.	.	.	.
.	.	.	.
.	.	.	.
1984 (estimated)	500,000	40,000	8

Figure 4–2
Illustrative Relation
between Sales and
Inventory

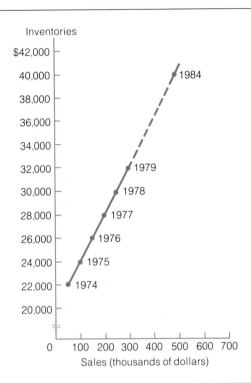

course, all points seldom fall exactly on the regression line, and the line itself may be curved as well as linear.[5]

If the percent-of-sales method had been used, some difficulties would have arisen immediately. Table 4–3 gives percent of sales for 1974 through 1979. What relation should be used? The 44 percent for 1974? The 11 percent for 1979? Or some average of the relations? If the relation for 1979 had been used, a forecast of $55,000 for inventories in 1984 would have been made, compared with $42,000 by the scatter diagram method. That forecast represents a large error.

The regression method is thus seen to be superior for forecasting fi-

5. In these illustrations, inventories are used as the item to be forecast. Much theory suggests that inventories increase as a square root of sales. This characteristic would tend to turn the regression line between inventories and sales slightly downward. Also improvements in inventory control techniques would curve the line downward. However, the increased diversity of types, models, and styles tends to increase inventories. Applications by the authors' students of the regression method to hundreds of companies indicate that the linear straight-line relations frequently represent the line of best fit or, at worst, involve only a small error. If the line were in fact curved over, a curved line could be fitted to the data and used for forecasting purposes.

nancial requirements, particularly for longer term forecasts. When a firm is likely to have a base stock of inventory or fixed assets, the ratio of the item to sales declines as sales increase. In such cases, the percent-of-sales method results in large errors.[6]

Multiple Regression Method

A more sophisticated approach to forecasting a firm's assets calls for the use of *multiple regression analysis.* In simple regression, sales are assumed to be a function of only one variable; in multiple regression, sales are recognized to depend upon a number of variables. For example, in simple regression we might state that sales are strictly a function of GNP. With multiple regression, we might say that sales are dependent upon both GNP and a set of additional variables. For example, sales of ski equipment depend upon (1) the general level of prosperity as measured by GNP, personal disposable income, or other indicators of aggregate economic activity; (2) population increases; (3) number of lifts operating; (4) weather conditions; (5) advertising, and so forth.

We shall not go into detail on the use of multiple regression analysis at this time. However, most computer installations have "canned" regression programs incorporated into their systems, making it extremely easy to use multiple regression techniques; multiple regression is widely used by at least the larger corporations.

Comparison of Forecasting Methods

Thus far we have considered four methods used in financial forecasting: (1) percent of sales, (2) scatter diagram, or simple linear regression, (3) curvilinear simple regression, and (4) multiple regression. In this section we will summarize and compare those methods.

Percent of Sales

The percent-of-sales method of financial forecasting assumes that certain balance sheet items vary directly with sales; that is, that the ratio of a given balance sheet item to sales remains constant. The postulated relationship is shown in Figure 4–3. *Notice that the percent-of-sales method implicitly assumes a linear relationship that passes through the origin.* The slope of the line representing the relationship may vary, but the line always passes through the origin. Implicitly, the relationship is established by finding one point, or ratio, such as that designated as X in

---

6. The widespread use of the percentage method makes for lax control. It would be easy to reduce inventories below the $55,000 percent-of-sales forecast level and still be inefficient because the correct target amount is closer to $40,000.

Figure 4–3
Percent-of-sales

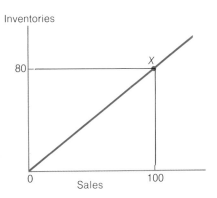

Figure 4–3, and then connecting this point with the origin. Then, for any projected level of sales, the forecasted level of the particular balance sheet item can be determined.

Scatter Diagram, or Simple Linear Regression

The scatter diagram method differs from the percent-of-sales method principally in that it does not assume that the line of relationship passes through the origin. In its simplest form, the scatter diagram method calls for calculating the ratio between sales and the relevant balance sheet item at two points in time, extending a line through these two points, and using the line to describe the relationship between sales

Figure 4–4
Scatter Diagram, or
Simple Linear
Regression

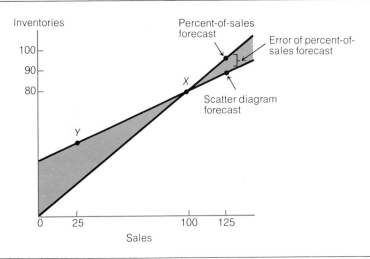

and the balance sheet item. The accuracy of the regression is improved if more points are plotted, and the regression line can be fitted mathematically (by a technique known as the method of least squares) as well as drawn in by eye.

The scatter diagram method is illustrated in Figure 4–4, where the percent-of-sales relationship is also shown for comparison. The error induced by the use of the percent-of-sales method is represented by the gap between the two lines. At a sales level of 125, the percent-of-sales method would call for an inventory of 100 versus an inventory of only 90 using a scatter diagram forecast. *Notice that the error is very small if sales continue to run at approximately the current level, but the gap widens and the error increases as sales deviate in either direction from current levels, as they probably would if a long-run forecast was being made.*

**Curvilinear
Simple
Regression**

Linear scatter diagrams, or linear regressions, assume that the slope of the regression line is constant. Although this condition does frequently exist, it is not a universal rule. Figure 4–5 illustrates the application of curvilinear simple regression to forecasting financial relationships. We have drawn this hypothetical illustration to show a flattening curve, which implies a decreasing relationship between sales and inventory

Figure 4–5
Curvilinear Simple
Regression

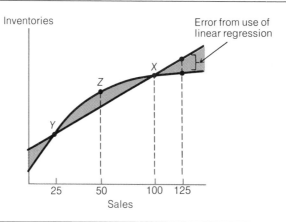

beyond point X, the current level of operations. In this case, the forecast of inventory requirements at a sales level of 125 would be too high if the linear regression method was used (but too low if sales declined from 100 to 50).

Multiple Regression

In our illustrations to this point, we have been assuming that the observations fell exactly on the relationship line. This implies perfect correlation, something that, in fact, seldom occurs. In practice, the actual observations would be scattered about the regression line as shown in Figure 4–6. What causes the deviations from the regression line? One answer, if linear regression is used, is that the actual line of relationship

Figure 4–6
Multiple Regression: Deviations in the Forecast

might be curvilinear. But if curvilinear regression is used and deviations still occur, we must seek other explanations for the scatter around the regression line. The most obvious answer is that inventories are determined by other factors in addition to sales. Inventory levels are certainly influenced by work stoppages at the plants of suppliers. If a steel fabricator anticipates a strike in the steel industry, he will stock up on steel products. Such hedge buying would cause actual inventories to be above the level forecast on the basis of sales projections. Then, assuming a strike does occur and continues for many months, inventories will be drawn down and may end up well below the predicted level. Multiple regression techniques, which introduce additional variables (such as work stoppages) into the analysis, are employed to further improve financial forecasting.

The need to employ more complicated forecasting techniques varies from situation to situation. For example, the percent-of-sales method may be perfectly adequate for making short-run forecasts where conditions are relatively stable, while curvilinear multiple regression may be deemed essential for longer run forecasts in more dynamic industries. As in all other applications of financial analysis, the cost of using more refined techniques must be balanced against the benefits of increased accuracy.

Summary

Firms need assets to make sales; if sales are to be increased, assets must also be expanded. The first section of this chapter illustrates the relationship between sales and assets and shows how even a growing, profitable firm can have a cash flow problem.

The most important causal variable in determining financial requirements is a firm's projected dollar volume of sales; a good sales forecast is an essential foundation for forecasting financial requirements. The two principal methods used for making financial forecasts are (1) the percent-of-sales method and (2) the regression method. The first has the virtue of simplicity—the forecaster computes past relationships between asset and liability items and sales, assumes these same relationships will continue, and then applies the new sales forecast to get an estimate of the financial requirements.

However, since the percent-of-sales method assumes that the balance-sheet-to-sales relationships will remain constant, it is only useful for relatively short-run forecasting. When longer range forecasts are being made, the regression method is preferable because it allows for changing balance-sheet-to-sales relationships. Further, linear regression can be expanded to curvilinear regression, and simple regression to multiple regression. These more complex methods are useful in certain circumstances, but their increased accuracy must be balanced against the increased costs of using them.

The tools and techniques we have discussed in this chapter are generally used in the following manner: As a first step, one of the long-range forecasting techniques is used to make a long-run forecast of the firm's financial requirements over a 3- to 5-year period. This forecast is then used to make the strategic financing plans during the planning period. Long lead times are necessary when companies sell bonds or stocks; otherwise financial managers might be forced to go into the market for funds during unfavorable periods.

In addition to the long-run strategic forecasting, the financial manager must also make accurate short-run forecasts to be sure that bank funds will be available to meet seasonal and other short-run requirements. We consider this topic in the following chapter.

Questions

4–1. What should be the approximate point of intersection between the sales-to-asset regression line and the vertical axis (Y-axis intercept) for the following: inventory, accounts receivable, fixed assets? State your answer in terms of positive, zero, or negative intercept. Can you think of any accounts that might have a negative intercept?

4–2. How does forecasting financial requirements in advance of needs assist the financial manager to perform his responsiblities more effectively?

4–3. Explain how a downturn in the business cycle could either cause a cash shortage for a firm or have the opposite effect and generate excess cash.

4–4. Explain this statement: "Current assets to a considerable extent represent permanent assets."

4–5. What advantages might multiple regression techniques have over simple regression in forecasting sales? What might be some drawbacks in the actual use of this technique?

Problems

4–1. The Universal Supply Company is a wholesale steel distributor. It purchases steel in carload lots from more than 20 producing mills and sells to several thousand steel users. The items carried include sheets, plates, wire products, bolts, windows, pipe, and tubing.

The company owns two warehouses, each housing 15,000 square feet, and contemplates the erection of another warehouse of 20,000 square feet. The nature of the steel supply business requires that the company maintain large inventories to take care of customer requirements in the event of mill strikes or other delays.

In examining patterns from 1972 through 1977, the company found a rather consistent relation between the following accounts as a percent of sales.

Current assets	60%
Net fixed assets	30%
Accounts payable	5%
Other current liabilities, including accruals and provision for income taxes but not bank loans	5%
Net profit after taxes	3%

The company's sales for 1978 were $3 million, and its balance sheet on December 31, 1978, was as follows:

Universal Supply Company
Balance sheet
December 31, 1978

Current assets	$ 1,800,000	Accounts payable	$	150,000
Fixed assets	900,000	Notes payable		400,000
		Other current liabilities		150,000
		Total current liabilities	$	700,000
		Mortgage loan		300,000
		Common stock		550,000
		Retained earnings		1,150,000
Total assets	$2,700,000	Total liabilities and net worth		$2,700,000

The company expects its sales to increase by $400,000 each year. If this is achieved, what will its financial requirements be at the end of the 5-year period? Assume that accounts not tied directly to sales (for example, notes payable) remain constant. Assume also that the company pays no dividends.

a. Construct a pro forma balance sheet for the end of 1983, using "additional financing needed" as the balancing item.

b. What are the crucial assumptions made in your projection method?

4-2. One useful test, or guide, for evaluating a firm's financial structure in relation to its industry is by comparison with financial ratio composites for the industry. A new firm, or one contemplating entering a new industry, may use such composites as a guide to what its financial position is likely to approximate after the initial settling-down period.

The following data represent ratios for the publishing and printing industry for 1975.

Sales to net worth	2.3 times
Current debt to net worth	42%
Total debt to net worth	75%
Current ratio	2.9 times
Net sales to inventory	4.7 times
Average collection period	64 days
Fixed assets to net worth	53.2%

a. Complete the pro forma balance sheet (round to nearest thousand) for Creative Printers if its 1975 sales are $3,200,000.

b. What does the use of the financial ratio composites accomplish?

c. What other factors will influence the financial structure of the firm?

Creative Printers, Inc.
Pro forma balance sheet
December 31, 1975

Cash	_____	Current debt	_____
Accounts receivable	_____	Long term debt	_____
Inventory	_____	Total debt	_____
Current assets	_____		
Fixed assets	_____	Net worth	_____
Total assets	_____	Total liabilities and net worth	_____

4-3. The 1978 sales of Electrosonics, Inc., amounted to $12 million. Common stock and notes payable are constant. The dividend payout ratio is 50 percent. Retained earnings as shown on the December 31, 1977, balance sheet were $60,000. The percent of sales in each balance sheet item that varies directly with sales are expected to be as follows:

Cash	4%
Receivables	10
Inventories	20
Net fixed assets	35
Accounts payable	12
Accruals	6
Profit rate (after taxes) on sales	3

a. Complete the balance sheet given.

Electrosonics, Inc.
Balance sheet
December 31, 1978

Cash	_____	Accounts payable	_____
Receivables	_____	Notes payable	630,000
Inventory	_____	Accruals	_____
Total current assets	_____	Total current liabilities	_____
Fixed assets	_____	Common stock	5,250,000
		Retained earnings	_____
Total assets	_____	Total liabilities and net worth	_____

b. Now suppose that in 1979 sales increased by 10 percent over 1978 sales. How much additional (external) capital will be required?

c. Construct the year-end 1979 balance sheet. Set up an account for "financing needed" or "funds available."

d. What would happen to capital requirements under each of the following conditions?

1. The profit margin went (i) from 3 percent to 6 percent? (ii) from 3 percent to 1 percent? Set up an equation to illustrate your answer.

2. The dividend payout rate (i) was raised from 50 percent to 80 percent? (ii) was lowered from 50 percent to 30 percent? Set up an equation to illustrate your answer.

3. Slower collections caused receivables to rise to 45 days of sales.

4–4. Jones Klein, Inc., a large drug manufacturer had the following balance sheet and income statement for 1975. Also shown is the industry norm for each item based on RMA Statement Studies of the drug industry.

Jones Klein, Inc.
Balance Sheet
December 31, 1975

	Firm	Norm
Cash and securities	$186,700	12.5%
Receivables	125,100	22.8
Inventories	105,700	28.0
Other current assets	9,900	1.2
Total current assets	427,400	64.5

Balance Sheet Continued	Firm	Norm
Net fixed assets	143,300	31.5
Other tangible assets	16,200	4.0
Total assets	$586,900	100.0%
Accounts payable	$ 33,400	10.0%
Notes payable	77,700	8.0
Other current liabilities	52,600	8.3
Total current liabilities	163,700	26.3
Long term debt	111,000	22.6
Net worth	312,200	51.1
Total claims on assets	$586,900	100.0%

Jones Klein, Inc.
Income Statement
for Year Ended December 31, 1975

	Firm	Norm
Sales	$606,300	100.0
Cost of goods sold	228,000	60.2
Gross profit	378,300	39.8
Selling and administrative expense	269,800	21.6
Operating Income	108,500	18.2
Less: Interest expense	14,200	1.4
Net income before tax	94,300	16.8
Less: Federal income tax	30,600	8.4
Net income	$ 63,700	8.4

This industry norm for sales to assets is 1.5 times.

a. Given only the total sales figure of $606,300, project a balance sheet and income statement using the above format. Show liabilities below assets as above. (Round to hundreds).

b. For each item compute the percent difference between actual and pro forma in the form (actual/pro forma)-1.

c. Comment on the difference between the actual and the pro forma account based on the·industry norms.

4–5. A firm has the following relationships. The ratio of assets to sales is 60 percent. Liabilities that increase spontaneously with sales are 15 percent. The profit margin on sales after taxes is 5%. The firm's dividend payout ratio is 40 percent.

a. If the firm's growth rate on sales is 10 percent per annum, what percentage of the sales increase in any year must be financed externally?

b. If the firm's growth rate on sales increases to 20 percent per annum, what percentage of the sales increase in any year must be financed externally?

c. How will your answer to part a change if the profit margin increased to 6 percent?

d. How will your answer to part b change if the firm's dividend payout is reduced to 10 percent.

e. If the profit margin increased from 5 percent to 6 percent and the dividend payout ratio is 20 percent, at what growth rate in sales would the external financing requirement percentage be exactly zero?

Selected References

Ansoff, H. Igor. "Planning as a Practical Management Tool." *Financial Executive* 32 (June 1964):34–37.

Chambers, John C.; Mullick, Satinder K.; and Smith, Donald D. "How to Choose the Right Forecasting Technique." *Harvard Business Review* 49 (July–Aug. 1971):45–74.

Gentry, James A., and Pyhrr, Stephen A. "Stimulating an EPS Growth Model." *Financial Management* 2 (Summer 1973):68–75.

Gershefski, George W. "Building a Corporate Financial Model." *Harvard Business Review* (July–Aug. 1969):61–72.

Gordon, Myron J., and Shillinglaw, Gordon. *Accounting: A Management Approach.* 4th ed. Homewood, Ill.: Irwin, 1969, chap. 16.

Myers, Stewart C., and Pogue, Gerald A. "A Programming Approach to Corporate Financial Management." *The Journal of Finance* 29 (May 1974):579–99.

Pappas, James L., and Huber, George P. "Probabilistic Short-Term Financial Planning." *Financial Management* 2 (Autumn 1973):36–44.

Parker, George G. C., and Segura, Edilberto L. "How to Get a Better Forecast." *Harvard Business Review* 49 (Mar.–Apr. 1971):99–109.

Smith, Gary, and Brainard, William. "The Value of a Priori Information in Estimating a Financial Model." *The Journal of Finance* 31 (Dec. 1976):1299–1322.

Wagle, B. "The Use of Models for Environmental Forecasting and Corporate Planning." *Operational Research Quarterly* 22, no. 3:327–36.

Warren, James M., and Shelton, John P. "A Simultaneous Equation Approach to Financial Planning." *Journal of Finance* 26 (Dec. 1971):1123–42.

Weston, J. Fred. "Forecasting Financial Requirements." *Accounting Review* 33 (July 1958):427–40.

5 Financial Planning and Control-Budgeting

In the preceding chapter we first examined the relationship between assets and sales, then we considered several procedures the financial manager can use to forecast his requirements. In addition to his long-range forecasts, the financial manager is also concerned with short-term needs for funds. It is embarrassing for a corporate treasurer to "run out of money." Even though he may be able to negotiate a bank loan on short notice, his plight may cause the banker to question the soundness of the firm's management and, accordingly, to reduce the company's line of credit or raise the interest rate. Therefore, attention must be given to short-term budgeting, with special emphasis on cash forecasting, or *cash budgeting*, as it is commonly called.

The cash budget is, however, only one part of the firm's overall budget system. The nature of the budget system, and especially the way it can be used for both planning and control purposes, is also discussed in this chapter.

Budgeting

A budget is simply a financial plan. A household budget itemizes the family's sources of income and describes how this income will be spent: so much for food, housing, transportation, entertainment, education, savings, and so on. Similarly, the federal budget indicates the government's income sources and allocates funds to defense, welfare, agriculture, education, and the like. By the same token, a firm's budget is a plan detailing how funds will be spent on labor, raw materials, capital goods, and so on, and also how the funds for these expenditures will be obtained. Just as the federal budget can be used as a device to insure that the Department of Defense, Department of Agriculture, and others limit their expenditures to specific amounts, the corporate budget can also be used as a device for formulating the firm's plans and for exercising control over the various departments.

Budgeting is, thus, a management tool used for both *planning* and *control*. Depending on the nature of the business, detailed plans may be formulated for the next few months, the next year, the next five years, or even longer. A company engaged in, say, heavy construction is constantly extending bids that may or may not be accepted; it cannot, and indeed need not, plan as far ahead as an electric utility company. The electric utility can base its projections on population growth, which is predictable for 5- to 10-year periods, and it *must* plan asset acquisitions years ahead because of the long lead times involved in constructing dams, nuclear power plants, and the like.

Nature of the Budgeting Process

Fundamentally, the budgeting process is a method to improve operations; it is a continuous effort to specify what should be done to get the job completed in the best possible way. Corporate budgeting should not be thought of as a device for limiting expenditures: the budgeting process is a tool for obtaining the most productive and profitable use of the company's resources. The budget requires a set of performance standards, or targets, that can be compared to actual results; this process is called "controlling to plan." It is a continuous monitoring procedure, reviewing and evaluating performance with reference to the previously established standards.

Establishing standards requires a realistic understanding of the activities carried on by the firm. Arbitrary standards, set without a basic understanding of the minimum costs as determined by the nature of the firm's operations, can do more harm than good. Budgets imposed in an arbitrary fashion may represent impossible targets at the one extreme or standards that are too lax at the other. If standards are unrealistically high, frustrations and resentment will develop. If standards are unduly low, costs will be out of control, profits will suffer, and morale will deteriorate. However, a set of budgets based on a clear understanding and careful analysis of operations can play an important, positive role for the firm.[1]

Budgets can provide valuable guides to both high-level executives and middle-management personnel. Well-formulated and effectively developed budgets make subordinates aware that top management has a realistic understanding of the nature of the operations in the business firm, and such a budget can be an important communication link between top management and the divisional personnel whom they guide.

---

1. The authors are familiar with one case where an unrealistic budget ruined a major national corporation. Top management set impossible performance and growth goals for the various divisions. The divisions, in an effort to meet the sales and profit projections, expanded into high-risk product lines (especially real estate development ventures), employed questionable accounting practices that tended to overstate profits, and the like. Debt financing was emphasized in order to leverage earnings. Things looked good for several years, but eventually the true situation became apparent. Top management brought in a team of consultants in an attempt to correct the problems, but it was too late—the firm was beyond help. The interesting point, to us, is that the consultants traced the firm's difficulties *directly* back to the unrealistic targets that were established by top management without adequate consultation with the division managers.

Budgets also represent planning and control devices that enable management to anticipate change and adapt to it. Business operations in today's economic environment are complex and are subject to heavy competitive pressures. In such an environment many kinds of changes take place. The rate of growth of the economy as a whole fluctuates, and these fluctuations affect different industries in a number of different ways. If a firm plans ahead, the budget and control process can provide management with a better basis for understanding the firm's operations in relation to the general environment. This increased understanding leads to faster reactions to developing events, thus increasing the firm's ability to perform effectively.

The budgeting process, in summary, improves internal coordination. Decisions for each product at every stage — at the research, engineering, production, marketing, personnel, and financial levels — all have an impact on the firm's profits. Planning and control are the essence of profit planning, and the budget system provides an integrated picture of the firm's operations as a whole. Therefore, the budget system enables the manager of each division to see the relation of his part of the enterprise to the totality of the firm. For example, a production decision to alter the level of work-in-process inventories, or a marketing decision to change the terms under which a particular product is sold, can be traced through the entire budget system to show its effects on the firm's overall profitability. The budgeting system is thus a most important financial tool.

Budget System

The overall nature of the budget process is outlined in Figure 5 – 1. Budgeting is a part of the total planning activity in the firm, so we must begin with a statement of corporate goals or objectives. The statement of goals (shown in the box at the top of the figure) determines the second section of the figure, the corporate long-range plan. Moving down the figure, we see that a segment of the corporate long-range plan includes a long-range sales forecast. This forecast requires a determination of the number and types of products that will be manufactured both at present and in the future years encompassed by the long-range plan: this is the product mix strategy.

Short-term forecasts and budgets are formulated within the framework of the long-range plan. For example, one might begin with a sales forecast covering six months or one year. The short-term sales forecast provides a basis for (and is dependent on) the broad range of policies indicated in the lower portion of Figure 5 – 1. *First*, there are manufacturing policies covering the choice of types of equipment, plant layout, and production-line arrangements. In addition, the kind of durability built into the products and their associated costs will be considered.

Figure 5–1
Overall View of the
Total Budgeting
Process and Relations

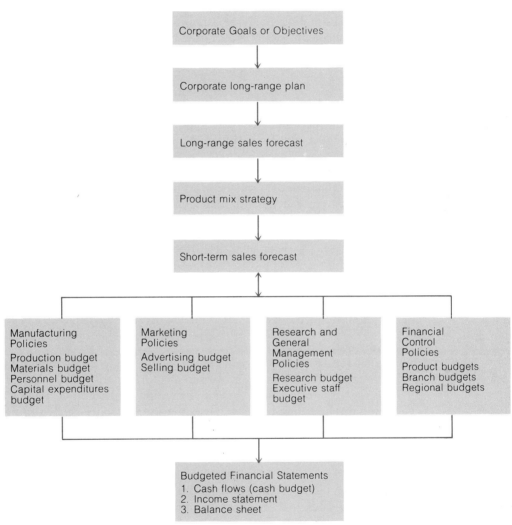

Second, a broad set of marketing policies must be formulated. These relate to such items as the development of the firm's own sales organization versus the use of outside sales organizations; the number of salesmen, and the method by which they will be compensated; the forms of, types of, and amounts spent on advertising; and other factors. *Third* are the research and general management policies. Research policies relate to relative emphasis on basic versus applied research and the product areas emphasized by both types of research. *Fourth* are financial policies, the subject of this chapter. The four major policy sets must be established simultaneously, as each affects the other. We shall concentrate on financial control policies, but it is important to realize the interdependencies between financial and other policies.

Financial Control Policies

Financial control policies include the organization and content of various kinds of financial control budgets. These include a budget for individual products and for every significant activity of the firm. In addition, budgets will be formulated to control operations at individual branch offices. Those budgets, in turn, are grouped and modified to control regional operations.

In a similar manner, policies established at the manufacturing, marketing, research, and general management levels give rise to a series of budgets. For example, the production budget will reflect the use of materials, parts, labor, and facilities; each of the major elements in a production budget is likely to have its own individual budget program. There will be a materials budget, a labor or personnel requirements budget, and a facilities or long-run capital expenditures budget. After the product is produced, the next step in the process will call for a marketing budget. Related to the overall process are the general office and executive requirements, which will be reflected in the general and administrative budget system.

The results of projecting all those elements of cost are reflected in the budgeted (also called "pro forma" or "projected") income statement. The anticipated sales give rise to the various types of investments needed to produce the products; these investments, plus the beginning balance sheet, provide the necessary data for developing the assets side of the balance sheet.

Those assets must be financed, and a cash flow analysis—the cash budget—is required. The cash budget indicates the combined effects of the budgeted operations on the firm's cash flows. A positive net cash flow indicates that the firm has ample financing. However, if an increase in the volume of operations leads to a negative cash flow, additional financing will be required. And that will lead directly to choices of financing, which is the subject of a considerable portion of the remainder of the book.

Since the structures of the income statement and the balance sheet have already been covered in Chapter 2, the rest of this section will deal with the two remaining aspects of the budgeting process—the cash budget and the concept of variable, or flexible, budgets.

Cash Budgeting

The cash budget indicates not only the total amount of financing that is required but its timing as well. This statement shows the amount of funds needed month by month, week by week, or even on a daily basis; it is one of the financial manager's most important tools. Because a clear understanding of the nature of cash budgeting is important, the process is described by means of an example that makes the elements of the cash budget explicit.

Marvel Toy is a medium-sized toy manufacturer. Sales are highly seasonal, with the peak occurring in September when retailers stock up for the Christmas season. All sales are made on terms that allow a cash discount on payments made within 30 days; if the discount is not taken, the full amount must be paid in 60 days. However, Marvel, like most other companies, finds that some of its customers delay payment up to 90 days. Experience shows that on 20 percent of the sales, payment is made within 30 days; on 70 percent of the sales, payment is made during the second month after the sale; while on 10 percent of the sales, payment is made during the third month.

Marvel's production is geared to future sales. Purchased materials and parts, which amount to 70 percent of sales, are bought the month before the company expects to sell the finished product. Its own purchase terms permit Marvel to delay payment on its purchases for one month. In other words, if August sales are forecast at $30,000, then purchases during July will amount to $21,000, and this amount will actually be paid in August.

Wages and salaries, rent, and other cash expenses are given in Table 5–1. The company also has a tax payment of $8,000 coming due in August. Its capital budgeting plans call for the purchase in July of a new machine tool costing $10,000, payment to be made in September. Assuming the company needs to keep a $5,000 cash balance at all times and has $6,000 on July 1, what are Marvel's financial requirements for the period July through December?

The cash requirements are worked out in the cash budget shown in Table 5–1. The top half of the table provides a worksheet for calculating collections on sales and payments on purchases. The first line in the worksheet gives the sales forecast for the period May through January—May and June sales are necessary to determine collections for July and August. Next, cash collections are given. The first line of this section shows that 20 percent of the sales during any given month are collected that month. The second shows the collections on the prior month's sales—70 percent of sales in the preceding month. The third line gives collections from sales two months earlier—10 percent of sales in that month. The collections are summed to find the total cash receipts from sales during each month under consideration.

Table 5–1
Marvel Toy Company *Cash Budget*

Worksheet

	May	June	July	Aug.	Sept.	Oct.	Nov.	Dec.	Jan.
Sales (net of cash discounts)	$10,000	$10,000	$20,000	$30,000	$40,000	$20,000	$20,000	$10,000	$10,000
Collections									
First month (20%)	$ 2,000	$ 2,000	$ 4,000	$ 6,000	$ 8,000	$ 4,000	$ 4,000	$ 2,000	$ 2,000
Second month (70%)		7,000	7,000	14,000	21,000	28,000	14,000	14,000	7,000
Third month (10%)			1,000	1,000	2,000	3,000	4,000	2,000	2,000
Total	$ 2,000	$ 9,000	$12,000	$21,000	$31,000	$35,000	$22,000	$18,000	$11,000
Purchases (70% of next month's sales)	$ 7,000	$14,000	$21,000	$28,000	$14,000	$14,000	$ 7,000	$ 7,000	
Payments (one month lag)		7,000	14,000	21,000	28,000	14,000	14,000	7,000	7,000

Cash budget

	July	Aug.	Sept.	Oct.	Nov.	Dec.	Jan.
Receipts							
Collections	$12,000	$21,000	$31,000	$35,000	$22,000	$18,000	$11,000
Payments							
Purchased	14,000	21,000	28,000	14,000	14,000	7,000	
Wages and salaries	1,500	2,000	2,500	1,500	1,500	1,000	
Rent	500	500	500	500	500	500	
Other expenses	200	300	400	200	200	100	
Taxes	—	8,000	10,000	—	—	—	
Payment on machine	—	—	—	—	—	—	
Total payments	$16,200	$31,800	$41,400	$16,200	$16,200	$ 8,600	
Net cash gain (loss) during month	$(4,200)	$(10,800)	$(10,400)	$18,800	$ 5,800	$ 9,400	
Cash at start of month if no borrowing is done	6,000	1,800	(9,000)	(19,400)	(600)	5,200	
Cumulative cash (= cash at start plus gains or minus losses)	$ 1,800	$(9,000)	$(19,400)	$ (600)	$ 5,200	$14,600	
Less: Desired level of cash	(5,000)	(5,000)	(5,000)	(5,000)	(5,000)	(5,000)	
Total loans outstanding to maintain $5,000 cash balance	$ 3,200	$14,000	$24,400	$ 5,600	—	—	
Surplus cash	—	—	—	—	$ 200	$ 9,600	

With the worksheet completed, the cash budget itself can be considered. Receipts from collections are given on the top line. Next, payments during each month are summarized. The difference between cash receipts and cash payments is the net cash gain or loss during the month; for July, there is a net cash loss of $4,200. The initial cash on hand at the beginning of the month is added to the net cash gain or loss during the month to yield the cumulative cash that will be on hand if no financing is done; at the end of July, Marvel Toy will have cumulative cash equal to $1,800. The desired cash balance, $5,000, is subtracted from the cumulative cash balance to determine the amount of financing that the firm needs if it is to maintain the desired level of cash. At the end of July we see that Marvel will need $3,200; thus, loans outstanding will total $3,200 at the end of July.

This same procedure is used in the following months. Sales will expand seasonally in August; with the increased sales will come increased payments for purchases, wages, and other items. Moreover, the $8,000 tax bill is due in August. Receipts from sales will go up too, but the firm will still be left with a $10,800 cash deficit during the month. The total financial requirements at the end of August will be $14,000 — the $3,200 needed at the end of July plus the $10,800 cash deficit for August. Thus, loans outstanding will total $14,000 at the end of August.

Sales peak in September, and the cash deficit during this month will amount to another $10,400. The total need for funds through September will increase to $24,400. Sales, purchases, and payments for past purchases will fall markedly in October; collections will be the highest of any month because they reflect the high September sales. As a result, Marvel Toy will enjoy a healthy $18,800 cash surplus during October. This surplus can be used to pay off borrowings, so the need for financing will decline by $18,800 to $5,600.

Marvel will have another cash surplus in November, and this extra cash will permit the company to eliminate completely the need for financing. In fact, the company is expected to have $200 in surplus cash by the month's end, while another cash surplus in December will swell the extra cash to $9,600. With such a large amount of unneeded funds, Marvel's treasurer will doubtless want to make investments in some interest-bearing securities or put the funds to use in some other way.[2]

Variable, or Flexible, Budgets

Budgets are planned allocations of a firm's resources, based on forecasts for the future. Two important elements influence actual performance. One is the impact of external influences over which the firm has little or

---

2. Types of investments for excess funds are discussed in Chapter 7.

Table 5–2
Hubler Department Store
Relationship between Sales and Employees

Month	Sales (in Millions of Dollars)	Number of Employees
January	4	42
February	5	51
March	6	60
April	7	75
May	10	102
June	8	83
July	5	55
August	9	92

no control—developments in the economy as a whole and competitive developments in the firm's own industry. The second element, which is controllable by the firm, is its level of efficiency at a given volume of sales. It is useful to separate the impact of these two elements, as this separation is necessary for evaluating individual performances.

The essence of the variable budget system is to introduce flexibility into budgets by recognizing that certain types of expenditures will vary at different levels of output. Thus, a firm might have an alternative level of outlay budgeted for different volumes of operation—high, low, medium. One of management's responsibilities is to determine which of the alternative budgets should be in effect for the planning period under consideration.

The regression method, which we described in the preceding chapter in connection with financial forecasting, may also be used to establish

Figure 5–2
Scatter Diagram and
Regression Line:
Hubler Department
Store

Table 5–3
Hubler Department Store
Budget Allowance

Sales (Millions of Dollars)	Number of Employees	Weekly Payroll Estimate (Average Wage, $100)
$ 6	62	$ 6,200
7	72	7,200
8	82	8,200
9	92	9,200
10	102	10,200
11	112	11,200

the basis for flexible budgeting. The use of the concept can be illustrated by a specific example. Suppose that a retail store, the Hubler Department Store, has had the experience indicated by the historical data set forth in Table 5–2. It is apparent from the data that the number of employees the firm needs is dependent upon the dollar volume of sales that occurs during a month. This is seen more easily from a scatter diagram such as that in Figure 5–2. The freehand regression line is sloped positively because the number of employees increases as the volume of sales increases. The independent variable, dollar volume of sales, is called the *control variable*. Variations in the control variable cause changes in total expenses. The volume of sales can be forecast, and the number of employees can be read from the regression chart. The relations are expressed in tabular form in Table 5–3. Given the forecast of sales, standards are provided for the expected number of employees and the weekly payroll.[3]

Problems of Budgeting

Four major problems are encountered when using budget systems. First, budgetary programs can grow to be so complete and so detailed that they become cumbersome, meaningless, and unduly expensive. Overbudgeting is dangerous.

Second, budgetary goals may come to supersede enterprise goals. A

---

3. Note that regression analysis provides even more flexibility in budgeting than do the high, medium, and low levels mentioned earlier. Also, it is possible to include *confidence levels* when using the regression method. For example, Table 5–3 shows that when volume is at $8 million, we expect to have 82 employees and a weekly payroll of $8,200. Although this relationship would probably not hold *exactly*, we might find that actual observations lie within 78 and 86 employees at this sales volume 95 percent of the time. Thus, 95 percent confidence levels would encompass the range 78–86. Similar ranges could be determined for other volumes; management might, as a matter of control policy, investigate whenever actual performances were outside this expected range.

budget is a tool, not an end in itself. Enterprise goals by definition supersede subsidiary plans of which budgets are a part. Moreover, budgets are based on future expectations that may not be realized. There is no acceptable reason for neglecting to alter budgets as circumstances change. This reasoning is the core of the argument in favor of more flexible budgets.

Third, budgets can tend to hide inefficiencies by continuing initial expenditures in succeeding periods without proper evaluation. Budgets growing from precedent usually contain undesirable expenditures. They should not be used as umbrellas under which slovenly, inefficient management can hide. Consequently, the budgetary process must contain provision for reexamination of standards and other bases of planning by which policies are translated into numerical terms.

Finally, case study evidence suggests that the use of budgets as a pressure device defeats their basic objectives. Budgets, if used as instruments of tyranny, cause resentment and frustrations, which in turn lead to inefficiency. In order to counteract this effect, it has been recommended that top management increase the participation of subordinates during the preparatory stages of the budgets.

Use of Financial Plans and Budgets

Forecasts, or long-range plans, are necessary in all the firm's operations. The personnel department must have a good idea of the scale of future operations if it is to plan its hiring and training activities properly. The production department must be sure that the productive capacity is available to meet the projected product demand, and the finance department must be sure that funds are on hand to meet the firm's financial requirements.

The tools and techniques discussed in this and the preceding chapters are actually used in several separate, but related, ways. First, the percent-of-sales method or, preferably, the regression method is used to make a long-range forecast of financial requirements over a projected 3- to 5-year period. This forecast is then used to draw up the strategic financing plans during the planning period. The company might, for example, plan to meet its financial requirements with retained earnings and short-term bank debt during, say, 1978 and 1979, float a bond issue in 1980, use retained earnings in 1981, and finally sell an issue of common stock in 1982. Fairly long lead times are necessary when companies sell bonds or stocks; otherwise, they might be forced to go into the market during unfavorable periods.

In addition to the long-run strategic planning, the financial manager must also make accurate short-run forecasts to be sure that funds will be available to meet seasonal and other short-run requirements. He might, for example, have a meeting with his bank's loan officer to discuss his company's need for funds during the coming year. Prior to the meeting, he would have his accountants prepare a detailed cash budget showing the need for money during each of the coming 12 months. The cash budget would show the maximum amount that would be needed during the year, how much would be needed during each month, and how cash surpluses would be generated at some point to enable the firm to repay the bank loan.

The financial manager would also have his firm's most recent, and its pro forma, balance sheets and income statements. He would have calculated the key financial ratios to show both his actual and his projected financial positions to the banker. If the firm's financial position is sound and if its cash budget appears reasonable, the bank will commit itself to make the required funds available. Even if the bank decides that the company's request is unreasonable and denies the loan request, the financial manager will have time to seek other sources of funds. While it might not be pleasant to have to look elsewhere for money, it is much better to know ahead of time that the loan request will be refused.

Divisional Control in a Decentralized Firm

In our discussion of the du Pont system of financial control in Chapter 2, we considered its use for the firm as a whole rather than for different divisions of a single firm. The du Pont system can, however, also be used to control the various parts of a multidivisional firm.

For organizational reasons, large firms are generally set up on a decentralized basis. For example, a firm such as General Electric establishes separate divisions for heavy appliances, light appliances, power transformers, fossil fuel generating equipment, nuclear generating equipment, and so on. Each division is defined as a *profit center*. Each profit center has its own investments—its fixed and current assets, together with a share of such general corporate assets as research labs and headquarters buildings—and each is expected to earn an appropriate return on its investment.

The corporate headquarters, or central staff, typically controls the various divisions by a form of the du Pont system. When it is used for divisional control, the procedure is frequently referred to as ROI (return on investment) control. If a particular division's ROI falls below a target figure, then the centralized corporate staff helps the division's own financial staff trace back through the du Pont system to determine the cause of the substandard ROI. Each division manager is judged by his division's ROI, and he is rewarded or penalized accordingly. Therefore, division managers are motivated to keep their ROI up to the target level. These individual actions, in turn, should maintain the total firm's ROI at an appropriate level.

In addition to its use in managerial control, ROI can be used to allocate funds to the various divisions. The firm as a whole has financial resources—retained earnings, cash flow from depreciation, and the ability to obtain additional debt and equity funds from capital markets. Those funds can be allocated to different divisions on the basis of divisional ROI's, with divisions having high ROI's receiving more funds than those with low ROI's.[4]

A number of problems may arise if ROI control is used without proper safeguards. Since the divisional managers are rewarded on the basis of their ROI performance, if their morale is to be maintained it is absolutely essential that the divisional managers feel that their divisional ROI does indeed provide an accurate measure of relative performance. But ROI is dependent on a number of factors in addition to managerial competence. Some of them are listed below.

1. *Depreciation:* ROI is very sensitive to depreciation policy. If one division is writing off assets at a relatively rapid rate, its annual profits and, hence, its ROI will be reduced.

2. *Book value of assets:* If an older division is using assets that have been largely written off, both its current depreciation charges and its investment base will be low. This will make its ROI high in relation to newer divisions.

3. *Transfer pricing:* In most corporations some divisions sell to other divisions. In General Motors, for example, the Fisher Body Division sells to the Chevrolet Division; in such cases the price at which goods are transferred between divisions has a fundamental effect on divisional profits. If the transfer price of auto bodies is set relatively high, then Fisher Body will have a relatively high ROI and Chevrolet a relatively low ROI.

4. *Time periods:* Many projects have long gestation periods—expenditures must be made for research and development, plant construction, market development, and the like; such expenditures will add to the investment base without a commensurate increase in profits for several years. During this period, a division's ROI could be seriously reduced; without proper constraints, its division manager could be improperly penalized. Especially when we recognize the frequency of personnel transfers in larger corporations, we can see that the timing problem

---

4. The point of this procedure is to increase the total firm's ROI. To maximize the overall ROI, marginal ROI between divisions should be equalized.

could possibly cause managers to refrain from making long-term investments that are in the best interests of the firm.

5. *Industry conditions:* If one division is operating in an industry where conditions are favorable and rates of return are high, whereas another is in an industry suffering from excessive competition, such environmental differences may cause the favored division to look good and the unfavored division to look bad, quite apart from any differences in their respective managers. Signal Companies' aerospace division, for example, could hardly be expected to show up as well as their truck division in a year like 1973, when the entire aerospace industry was suffering severe problems and truck sales were booming. External conditions must be taken into account when appraising ROI performance.

Because of those problems, divisions' ROI's must be supplemented with other criteria when evaluating performance. For example, a division's growth rate in sales, profits, and market share, as well as its ROI in comparison with other firms in its own industry, have all been used as a part of the overall control and evaluation procedure.

Although ROI control has been used with great success in American industry, the system cannot be used in a mechanical sense by inexperienced personnel. As with most other tools, it is a good one if used properly, but it is a destructive one if misused.

External Uses of Financial Forecasts and Budgets

We have stressed the use of planning and budgeting for internal purposes, that is, to increase the efficiency of a firm's operations. With relatively minor modifications, those same tools and techniques can be used in both credit analysis and security analysis. For example, outside security analysts can make a forecast of a given firm's sales and, through the income statement and balance sheet relationships, can prepare pro forma (projected) balance sheets and income statements. Credit analysts can make similar projections to aid in estimating the likely need for funds by their customers and the likelihood that borrowers can make prompt repayment.

This kind of analysis has actually been conducted on a large scale in recent years. Very complete financial data going back some 20 years on several thousand large, publicly owned corporations are now available on magnetic tapes (Standard and Poor's Compustat tapes). These tapes are being used by security analysts in highly sophisticated ways. From what we have seen, analyses conducted in such a manner offer large potential benefits. The same tapes, frequently supplemented with additional data, are being used by the major lending institutions — banks and insurance companies — to forecast their customers' needs for funds and, thus, to plan their own financial requirements.

Summary

A budget is a plan stated in terms of specific expenditures for specific purposes. It is used for both planning and control, its overall purpose being to improve internal operations, thereby reducing costs and raising profitability. A budgeting system starts with a set of performance standards, or targets. The targets constitute, in effect, the firm's financial plan. The budgeted figures are compared with actual results — this is the control phase of the budget system, and it is a critical step in well-operated companies.

Although the entire budget system is of vital importance to corporate management, one aspect of the system is especially important to the financial manager — the cash budget. The cash budget is, in fact, the principal tool for making short-run financial forecasts. Cash budgets, if used properly, are highly accurate and can pinpoint the funds that will be needed, when they will be needed, and when cash flows will be sufficient to retire any loans that might be necessary.

A good budget system will recognize that some factors lie outside the firm's control. Especially important here is the state of the economy and its effects on sales, and *flexible budgets* will be set up as targets for the different departments assuming different levels of sales. Also, a good system will insure that those responsible for carrying out a plan are involved in its preparation; this procedure will help guard against the establishment of unrealistic targets and unattainable goals.

As a firm becomes larger, it is necessary for it to decentralize operations to some extent, and decentralized operations require some centralized control over the various divisions. The principal tool used for such control is the return on investment (ROI) method. There are problems with ROI control. But if care is taken in its use, the method can be quite valuable to a decentralized firm.

Questions

5-1. What use might a confidence interval scheme have in variable budgeting?

5-2. Why is a cash budget important even when there is plenty of cash in the bank?

5-3. What is the difference between the long-range financial forecasting concept (for example, the percent-of-sales method) and the budgeting concept? How might they be used together?

5-4. Assume that a firm is making up its long-run financial budget. What period should this budget cover—one month, six months, one year, three years, five years, or some other period? Justify your answer.

5-5. Is a detailed budget more important to a large, multidivisional firm than to a small, single-product firm?

5-6. Assume that your uncle is a major stockholder in a multidivisional firm that uses a naive ROI criterion for evaluating divisional managers and bases managers' salaries in large part on this evaluation. You can have the job of division manager in any division you choose. If you are a salary maximizer, what divisional characteristics would you seek? If, because of your "good performance," you became president of the firm, what changes would you make?

Problems

5-1.[1] The Simmons Company is planning to request a line of credit from its bank. The following sales forecast have been made for 1979 and 1980:

May 1979	$150,000
June	150,000
July	300,000
August	450,000
September	600,000
October	300,000
November	300,000
December	75,000
January 1980	150,000

Collection estimates were obtained from the credit and collection department as follows: collected within the month of sale, 5 percent; collected the month following the sale, 80 percent; collected the second month following the sale, 15 percent. Payments for labor and raw materials costs are typically made during the month following the month in which these costs are incurred. Total labor and raw materials costs are estimated for each month as follows (payments are made the following month):

May 1979	$ 75,000
June	75,000
July	105,000
August	735,000
September	255,000
October	195,000
November	135,000
December	75,000

1. This problem is adapted from *Cases in Managerial Finance*, second edition, Case 5.

General and administrative salaries will amount to approximately $22,500 a month; lease payments under long-term lease contracts will be $7,500 a month; depreciation charges are $30,000 a month; miscellaneous expenses will be $2,250 a month; income tax payments of $52,500 will be due in both September and December; and a progress payment of $150,000 on a new research laboratory must be paid in October. Cash on hand on July 1 will amount to $110,000, and a minimum cash balance of $75,000 should be maintained throughout the cash budget period.

a. Prepare a monthly cash budget for the last six months of 1979.

b. Prepare an estimate of required financing (or excess funds) for each month during the period, that is, the amount of money that the Simmons Company will need to borrow (or will have available to invest) each month.

c. Suppose receipts from sales come in uniformly during the month; that is, cash payments come in 1/30th each day, but all outflows are paid on the fifth of the month. Would this have an effect on the cash budget; that is, would the cash budget you have prepared be valid under these assumptions? If not, what could be done to make a valid estimation of financing requirements?

5-2.[2] Gulf and Eastern, Inc., is a diversified multinational corporation that produces a wide variety of goods and services, including chemicals, soaps, tobacco products, toys, plastics, pollution control equipment, canned food, sugar, motion pictures, and computer software. The corporation's major divisions were brought together in the early 1960s under a decentralized form of management; each division was evaluated in terms of its profitability, efficiency, and return on investments. This decentralized organization persisted through most of the decade, during which Gulf and Eastern experienced a high average growth rate in total assets, earnings, and stock prices.

Toward the end of 1975, however, those trends were reversed. The organization was faced with declining earnings, unstable stock prices, and a generally uncertain future. This situation persisted into 1976, but during that year a new president, Lynn Thompson, was appointed by the board of directors. Thompson, who had served for a time on the financial staff of I.E. du Pont, used the du Pont system to evaluate the various divisions. All showed definite weaknesses.

Thompson reported to the board that a principal reason for the poor overall performance was a lack of control by central management over each division's activities. She was particularly disturbed by the consistently poor results of the corporation's budgeting procedures. Under that system, each division manager drew up a projected budget for the next quarter, along with estimated sales, revenue, and profit; funds were then allocated to the divisions, basically in proportion to their

---

2. This problem is taken from *Cases in Managerial Finance*, second edition.

budget requests. However, actual budgets seldom matched the projections; wide discrepancies occurred, and this, of course, resulted in a highly inefficient use of capital.

In an attempt to correct the situation, Thompson asked the firm's chief financial officer to draw up a plan to improve the budgeting, planning, and control processes. When the plan was submitted, its basic provisions included the following:

1. To improve the quality of the divisional budgets, the division managers should be informed that the continuance of wide variances between their projected and actual budgets would result in dismissal.

2. A system should be instituted under which funds would be allocated to divisions on the basis of their average return on investment (ROI) during the last four quarters. Since funds were short, divisions with high ROI's would get most of the available money.

3. Only about one-half of each division manager's present compensation should be received as salary; the rest should be in the form of a bonus related to the division's average ROI for the quarter.

4. Each division should submit to the central office for approval all capital expenditure requests, production schedules, and price changes. Thus, the company would be *re*centralized.

   a. (1) Is it reasonable to expect the new procedures to improve the accuracy of budget forecasts?
      (2) Should all divisions be expected to maintain the same degree of accuracy?
      (3) In what other ways might the budgets be made?
   b. (1) What problems would be associated with the use of the ROI criterion in allocating funds among the divisions?
      (2) What effect would the period used in computing ROI (that is, four quarters, one quarter, two years, and so on) have on the effectiveness of this method?
      (3) What problems might occur in evaluating the ROI in the crude rubber and auto tires divisions? between the sugar products and pollution control equipment divisions?
   c. What problems would be associated with rewarding each manager on the basis of his division's ROI?
   d. How well would Thompson's policy of recentralization work in a highly diversified corporation such as this, particularly in light of her financial officer's three other proposals?

Selected References

Bacon, Jeremy. *Managing the Budget Function.* Studies in Business Policy, Report No. 131. New York: National Industrial Conference Board, Inc., 1970.

Dearden, John. "The Case Against ROI Control." *Harvard Business Review* 47 (May – June 1969):124 – 35.

Hamermesh, Richard G. "Responding to Divisional Profit Crises." *Harvard Business Review* 55 (Mar. – Apr. 1977):124 – 30.

Henning, Dale A. *Non-Financial Controls in Smaller Enterprises.* Seattle, Wash.: University of Washington, College of Business Administration, 1964.

Hunt, Pearson. "Funds Position: Keystone in Financial Planning." *Harvard Business Review* 53 (May–June 1975):106–15.

Judelson, David N. "Financial Controls That Work." *Financial Executive* 45 (Jan. 1977): 22–27.

Knight, W. D., and Weinwurn, E. H. *Managerial Budgeting.* New York: Macmillan, 1964.

Rappaport, Alfred. "A Capital Budgeting Approach to Divisional Planning and Control." *Financial Executive,* Oct. 1968, pp. 47–63.

Appendix A to Chapter 5
Illustrative Budget System

A complete budget system includes (1) a production budget; (2) a materials purchases budget; (3) a budgeted, or pro forma, income statement; (4) a budgeted, or pro forma, balance sheet; and (5) a capital expenditure budget. Since capital expenditures are related directly to problems of the firm's growth, they have been considered separately in Chapter 10.[1]

Tables A5–1 through A5–7 carry out a hypothetical budget system. In Tables A5–2 through A5–7 the lines are numbered consecutively from 1 to 54. This procedure has the advantage of making it easy to see the relations among the various budgets.

Table A5–1 outlines the highly summarized cost accounting system. It is based on the standard costs of goods sold per unit. Standard costs include direct material, direct labor, and variable and fixed manufacturing expense. Standard costs are the costs of goods produced when the firm is operating at a high level of efficiency and when operations are near a level that may be regarded as "normal."[2]

Table A5–1
Standard Costs Based on Volume of 1,000 Units per Month

	Per Unit
Direct material: 2 pieces—$1 per piece	$2
Direct labor: 1 hour—$2 per hour	2
Variable manufacturing expense: $1 per unit	1
Fixed manufacturing expense: $1,000 per month*	1
Cost of goods produced per unit	$6

*Includes $200 depreciation charges.

Production Budget

The illustrative production budget (Table A5–2) is based directly on the sales forecast and the estimated unit cost of production. It is assumed

---

1. Outlays for capital equipment do, of course, affect the cash budget, the income statement, and the balance sheet.

2. The terminology in this chapter follows accounting usage, but anyone familiar with economics can readily translate it into economic terms. For instance, "$6 per unit at standard output" is "average total (production) cost," "marginal production cost" is $5 per unit; and so on.

Table A5–2
Production Budget

		Estimated 1978, First Quarter			
Item	Monthly Average 1977	First Month	Second Month	Third Month	Source of Data
1. Sales at $10 per unit	$10,000	$10,000	$12,000	$12,000	Assumed
2. Unit sales	1,000	1,000	1,200	1,200	Line 1 divided by $10
3. Beginning inventory (units)	500	500	600	600	One-half of current month's sales
4. Difference (units)	500	500	600	600	Line 2 minus line 3
5. Ending inventory (units)	500	600	600	600	One-half of next month's sales
6. Production in units	1,000	1,100	1,200	1,200	Line 4 plus line 5
7. Estimated cost of goods produced	$ 6,000	$ 6,600	$ 7,200	$ 7,200	Line 6 times $6
8. Burden absorption, under or (over)	0	(100)	(200)	(200)	Line 6 times $1 less $1,000 fixed manufacturing expense
9. Adjusted cost of goods produced	$ 6,000	$ 6,500	$ 7,000	$ 7,000	Line 7 less line 8
9a. Adjusted cost per unit	$ 6	$ 5.91	$ 5.83	$ 5.83	Line 9 divided by line 6
10. Value of ending inventory (finished goods)	$ 3,000	$ 3,545	$ 3,500	$ 3,500	Line 5 multiplied by line 9a (rounded)

that the firm maintains its finished goods inventory at 50 percent of the following month's sales. In any month, the firm must produce the unit sales plus ending inventory less the beginning inventory level.

This example illustrates the financial consequences of a rise in sales from a $10,000-per-month level to a new plateau of $12,000. As production rises in response to increased sales, the (standard) cost of goods produced also rises. But the standard cost of goods produced increases faster than actual costs increase because the unit cost of $6 includes fixed charges of $1 per unit. An increase of one unit of production actually raises total costs by only $5. The estimated total cost, however, increases by $6. Estimates of the cost of goods produced are made and then adjusted by the amount of under- or overabsorbed burden. Of course, the same result for calculating the adjusted cost of goods produced (Table A5–2, line 9) is obtained by multiplying $5 by the number of units produced to get total variable costs, and adding $1,000 in fixed costs to reach total adjusted cost of goods produced.

The per unit adjusted costs of goods produced ($5.91 for the first month) is required to calculate the ending inventory. The first-in, first-out method of inventory costing is employed. The calculation of the ending inventory value is required for the worksheet (Table A5–6) used in developing the budgeted balance sheet (Table A5–7).

Materials Purchases Budget

The level of operations indicated by the production budget in Table A5–2 is based on sales forecast and inventory requirements. The materials purchases budget (Table A5–3) contains estimates of materials

Table A5–3
Materials Purchases Budget

| Item | Monthly Average 1977 | Estimated 1978, First Quarter | | | Source of Data |
		First Month	Second Month	Third Month	
11. Production in units	1,000	1,100	1,200	1,200	Line 6
12. Materials used (units)	2,000	2,200	2,400	2,400	Line 11 times 2
13. Raw materials, ending inventory	2,200	2,400	2,400	2,400	Raw materials requirements next month
14. Total	4,200	4,600	4,800	4,800	Line 12 plus line 13
15. Raw materials, beginning inventory	2,000	2,200	2,400	2,400	Raw material requirements this month
16. Raw materials purchases	$2,200	$2,400	$2,400	$2,400	(Line 14 less line 15) times $1

purchases that will be needed to carry out the production plans. Raw materials purchases depend in turn upon materials actually used in production, material costs (Table A5–1), size of beginning inventories, and requirements for ending inventory.

The example in Table A5–3 does not take into account economical ordering quantities (EOQ's) as discussed in Chapter 7. EOQ's are not integrated, primarily because they assume a uniform usage rate for raw materials, an assumption that is not met in the example. Also, the EOQ analysis assumes a constant minimum inventory, but the desired minimum inventory (Table A5–3, line 13) shifts with production levels. In a practical situation, these assumptions might be approximated. EOQ's can then be used to determine optimum purchase quantities, or more sophisticated operations research techniques may be used.

Cash Budget

The cash budget shown in Table A5–4 is generated from information developed in the production and materials purchases budgets. In addition, estimates for other expense categories are required.[3] In Table

3. These are assumed to be paid in the months the expenses are incurred, in order to reduce the volume of explanatory information.

Table A5–4
Cash Budget

| Item | Monthly Average 1977 | Estimated 1978 | | | Source of Data |
		First Month	Second Month	Third Month	
Receipts					
17. Accounts receivable collected	$10,000	$10,000	$10,000	$12,000	Sales of previous month
Disbursements					
18. Accounts payable paid	$ 2,000	$ 2,200	$ 2,400	$ 2,400	Raw materials purchases of previous month
19. Direct labor	2,000	2,200	2,400	2,400	Line 6 times $2
20. Indirect labor	700	700	700	700	Assumed
21. Variable manufacturing expenses	1,000	1,100	1,200	1,200	Line 6 times $1
22. Insurance and taxes	100	100	100	100	Assumed
23. General and administrative expenses	2,500	2,500	2,500	2,500	Assumed
24. Selling expense	500	500	600	600	5% of line 1
25. Total disbursements	$ 8,800	$ 9,300	$ 9,900	$ 9,900	Sum of lines 18–24
26. Cash from operations	$ 1,200	$ 700	$ 100	$ 2,100	Line 17 less line 25
26a. Initial cash	5,000	6,200	6,900	7,000	Preceding month, line 26b
26b. Cumulative cash	6,200	6,900	7,000	9,100	Line 26 plus line 26a
27. Desired level of cash	5,000	5,000	6,000	6,000	50% of current month's sales; approximately 4.2% of annual sales
27a. Cash available (needed) cumulative	$ 1,200	$ 1,900	$ 1,000	$ 3,100	Line 26b less line 27

A5–4, only cash receipts from operations are considered in order to emphasize the logic of the budget system. No account is taken of receipts or expenditures for capital items. This is because of the emphasis in this illustration on budgeting consequences of short-term fluctuations in the sales volume of the firm, although in practical situations it is a simple matter to incorporate capital expenditures into the cash budget. However, the fact that capital expenditures are ignored does not diminish their impact on cash flows. Capital expenditures occur sporadically and in amounts that sometimes overwhelm operating transactions.

Period

The 3-month period used in the cash budget, Table A5–4, is not necessarily the length of time for which a firm will predict cash flows. Although this period does coincide with the length of traditional 90-day bank loans, the firm is more likely to utilize a six-month or one-year

period. Normally, a six-month forecast is prepared on a monthly basis.
Briefly, the cash budget period will vary with the line of business, credit
needs, the ability to forecast the firm's cash flows for the distant future,
and requirements of suppliers of funds.

**Illustrative
Cash Budget**

The cash flow for a given period is the difference between receipts and
expenditures for that period. In Table A5–4, for the 1977 monthly averages, cash from operations ($1,200) is the difference between accounts
receivable collected ($10,000) and total disbursements ($8,800). Note
that collections from accounts receivable and accounts payable paid
depend upon sales and purchases from the preceding months rather
than on current sales.

The significant figure for the manager is cash available (or needed).
Cash from operations in the first month of 1978, plus the initial cash
balance at the beginning of the month, totals $6,900. The financial man-
ager has previously determined that only $5,000 is needed to handle
this level of sales. Consequently, the firm will have surplus cash of
$1,900 by the end of the month, and $3,100 by the end of the third
month. In the pro forma balance sheet (Table A5–7), it is assumed that
these cash surpluses are used to pay off notes payable.

Use

As mentioned earlier in the chapter, the financial manager uses the cash
budget to anticipate fluctuations in the level of cash. Normally, a growing firm will be faced with continuous cash drains. The cash budget
tells the manager the magnitude of the outflow. If necessary, he can plan
to arrange for additional funds. The cash budget is the primary document presented to a lender to indicate the need for funds and the feasibility of repayment.

In Table A5–4 the opposite situation is illustrated. The firm will have
excess cash of at least $1,000 during each of the three months under con-
sideration. The excess can be invested, or it can be used to reduce outstanding liabilities. In this example, the firm retires notes payable (Table A5–7, line 49). Such a small amount as $1,000 might be held as cash
or as a demand deposit, but the alert financial manager will not allow
substantial amounts of cash to remain idle.

**Budgeted
Income
Statement**

After a cash budget has been developed, two additional financial statements can be formulated—the budgeted income statement (Table
A5–5) and the budgeted balance sheet (Table A5–7). They are prepared

Table A5–5
Budgeted Income Statement

| Item | Monthly Average 1977 | Estimated 1978, First Quarter | | | Source of Data |
		First Month	Second Month	Third Month	
28. Sales	$10,000	$10,000	$12,000	$12,000	Line 1
29. Adjusted cost of sales	6,000	5,955	7,045	7,000	Line 54
30. Gross income	$ 4,000	$ 4,045	$ 4,955	$ 5,000	Line 28 less line 29
31a. General and administrative expenses	2,500	2,500	2,500	2,500	Line 23
31b. Selling	500	500	600	600	5% of line 1
32. Total expenses	$ 3,000	$ 3,000	$ 3,100	$ 3,100	Line 31a plus 31b
33. Net income before taxes	1,000	1,045	1,855	1,900	Line 30 less line 32
34. Federal taxes	500	522	927	950	50% of line 33
35. Net income after taxes	$ 500	$ 522	$ 927	$ 950	Line 33 less line 34

on an accrual rather than a cash basis. For example, the income statement accounts for depreciation charges. Expenses recognized on an accrual basis are included in total expenses (Table A5–5, line 32); thus, calculated net income is lowered. The only accrual item assumed in this exhibit is depreciation, and this is assumed to be $200 monthly. The before-tax profit figure in the third month in the budgeted income statement (line 33) differs from line 26 in the cash budget only by the

Table A5–6
Worksheet

| Item | Monthly Average 1977 | Adjusted Cost of Sales Estimated 1978, First Quarter | | | Source of Data |
		First Month	Second Month	Third Month	
36. Adjusted cost of goods produced	$6,000	$6,500	$ 7,000	$ 7,000	Line 9
37. *Add:* Beginning inventory	3,000	3,000	3,545	3,500	Line 10 lagged one month
38. Sum	$9,000	$9,500	$10,545	$10,500	
39. *Less:* Ending inventory	3,000	3,545	3,500	3,500	Line 10
40. Adjusted cost of goods sold*	$6,000	$5,955	$ 7,045	$ 7,000	Line 52 less line 53

*Note difference from line 9, adjusted cost of goods produced.

amount of depreciation.[4] This illustration makes clear the effect of non-cash expenses on the income statement.

The preparation of the budgeted income statement follows standard accounting procedures. The major calculation involved is adjusted cost of sales, explained in Table A5–6.

The budgeted income statement shows the impact of future events on the firm's net income. Comparison of future income with that of past periods indicates the difficulties that will be encountered in maintaining or exceeding past performance. A forecast indicating low net income should cause management to increase sales efforts as well as to make efforts to reduce costs. Anticipation and prevention of difficulties can be achieved by a sound budgeting system.

Budgeted Balance Sheet

Lenders are interested in the projected balance sheet to see what the future financial position of the firm will be. Balance sheet projections discussed in the body of Chapter 5 were focused on year-to-year forecasts, and they assumed stable underlying relations. The budget technique deals with shorter term projections but is based on the same fundamental kinds of stable relations between the volume of sales and the associated asset requirements. Either method can be used, and each can operate as a check on the other. The budgeted balance sheet presented in Table A5–7, however, is the result of a more detailed and analytical forecast of future operations. It is the logical culmination of the budget system and provides a complete reconciliation between the initial balance sheet, the cash budget, and the income statement.

The required information is readily available from past balance sheets or is contained in other elements of the budget system. For example, the initial balance of notes payable is $3,200. An increase in cash available (Table A5–4, line 27a) is used to repay notes payable; a decrease is met by additional borrowing from a commercial bank. Other new items, such as long-term debt and common stock (Table A5–7, lines 51 and 52), are taken from previous balance sheets.

The foregoing exhibits present a simplified yet complete budget system. It contains all the elements found in a voluminous and complex actual budget system of a firm. If a person understands the logic and flow of this relatively simple budget system, he can approach an actual budget with perspective, looking for the fundamental relations in-

---

4. This close correspondence holds only in a "steady state," that is, when inventories and receivables are not being raised or lowered. Prior to the third month this condition does not hold.

Table A5–7
Budgeted Balance Sheet

		Estimated 1978, First Quarter			
Item	Monthly Average 1977	First Month	Second Month	Third Month	Source of Data
Assets					
41. Cash	$ 5,000	$ 5,000	$ 6,000	$ 6,000	Line 27
42. Government securities					
43. Net receivables	10,000	10,000	12,000	12,000	Sales of current month
44. Inventories					
Raw materials	2,200	2,400	2,400	2,400	Line 13
Finished goods	3,000	3,545	3,500	3,500	Line 10
45. Current assets	$ 20,200	$ 20,945	$ 23,900	$ 23,900	Total lines 36 through 39
46. Net fixed assets	80,000	79,800	79,600	79,400	$80,000 less $200 per month depreciation
47. Total assets	$100,200	$100,745	$103,500	$103,300	Total lines 40 and 41
Liabilities					
48. Accounts payable	$ 2,200	$ 2,400	$ 2,400	$ 2,400	Raw material purchases this month
49. Notes payable $3,200	2,000	1,300	2,200	100	$3,200 less line 27a
50. Provisions for federal income tax	500	1,022	1,950	2,900	
51. Long-term debt	25,000	25,000	25,000	25,000	Cumulation of line 34 Assumed
52. Common stock, $50,000	50,000	50,000	50,000	50,000	Assumed
53. Retained earnings $20,000	$ 20,500	$ 21,023	$ 21,950	$ 22,900	Cumulation line 35 plus $20,000
54. Total claims	$100,200	100,745	103,500	103,300	Sum of lines 43 through 48

volved. He can then apply the patterns to actual budget systems of any
degree of complexity.

Problems

A5–1. Examine carefully the budget system set forth in the appendix, then
answer the following questions:
    a. What advantages can you see to having a budget system such as the
one described? Would such a system be more valuable (assuming a
whole series of budgets where necessary) for a firm with ten employees or for one with 10,000 employees?
    b. What would happen to the system if the sales forecast was far off the
mark? How could variable sales be incorporated into the system?
    c. Would a budget system such as this one be more useful for a firm

whose sales were highly predictable or one whose sales were not very predictable?

d. How might a firm's budget system be computerized? Would such computerization be more useful for a firm with predictable or unpredictable sales?

e. Would such a budget system be more valuable for planning or for control purposes?

Part II

Working Capital Management

In Part I, we analyzed the firm's operations in an overall, aggregate manner. Now we must examine the various aspects of the firm's financial picture in more detail. In Part II, we focus on the top half of the balance sheet, studying current assets, current liabilities, and the interrelationship between these two sets of accounts. This type of analysis is commonly called *working capital management.*

In Chapter 6, we examine some general principles of overall working capital management. Then, in Chapter 7, we consider the determinants of current assets: cash, marketable securities, accounts receivable, and inventories. Finally, in Chapter 8, we discuss current liabilities, considering in some detail the principal sources and forms of short-term funds.

6 **Working Capital Policy**

Working capital refers to a firm's investment in short-term assets—cash, short-term securities, accounts receivable, and inventories. *Net working capital* is defined as current assets minus current liabilities. *Working capital management* refers to all aspects of the administration of both current assets and current liabilities.

No new theories or basic principles are involved in working capital management—rather, this phase of financial management simply requires the application of valuation concepts developed throughout the text. Current asset holdings should be expanded to the point where marginal returns on increases in such assets are just equal to the cost of capital required to finance these increases, while current liabilities should be used in place of long-term debt whenever their use lowers the average cost of capital.

Importance of Working Capital Management

Working capital management includes a number of aspects that make it an important topic for study, and we will now consider some of them.

Time Devoted to Working Capital Management

Surveys indicate that the largest portion of a financial manager's time is devoted to the day-by-day internal operations of the firm; this may be appropriately subsumed under the heading "working capital management." Since so much time is spent on working capital decisions, it is appropriate that the subject be covered carefully in managerial finance courses.

Investment in Current Assets

Characteristically, current assets represent more than half the total assets of a business firm. Because they represent a large investment and because this investment tends to be relatively volatile, current assets are worthy of the financial manager's careful attention.

Importance for Small Firms

Working capital management is particularly important for small firms. A small firm may minimize its investments in fixed assets by renting or leasing plant and equipment, but there is no way it can avoid an investment in cash, receivables, and inventories. Therefore, current assets are particularly significant for the financial manager of a small firm. Further, because a small firm has relatively limited access to the long-term capital markets, it must necessarily rely heavily on trade credit and short-term bank loans, both of which affect net working capital by increasing current liabilities.

Relationship between Sales Growth and Current Assets

The relationship between sales growth and the need to finance current assets is close and direct. For example, if the firm's average collection period is 40 days and if its credit sales are $1,000 a day, it will have an investment of $40,000 in accounts receivable. If sales rise to $2,000 a day, the investment in accounts receivable will rise to $80,000. Sales increases produce similar immediate needs for additional inventories and, perhaps, for cash balances. All such needs must be financed, and since they arise so quickly, it is imperative that the financial manager keep himself aware of developments in the working capital segment of the firm. Of course, continued sales increases will require additional long-term assets, which must also be financed. However, fixed asset investments, while critically important to the firm in a strategic, long-run sense, do not generally have the same urgency as do current asset investments.

Original Concept of Working Capital

The term "working capital" originated at a time when most industries were closely related to agriculture. Processors would buy crops in the fall, process them, sell the finished product, and end up just before the next harvest with relatively low inventories. Bank loans with maximum maturities of one year were used to finance both the purchase and the processing costs, and these loans were retired with the proceeds from the sale of the finished products.

The situation is depicted in Figure 6–1. There fixed assets are shown to be growing steadily over time, while current assets jump at harvest season, then decline during the year, ending at zero just before the next crop is harvested. Short-term credit is used to finance current assets, and fixed assets are financed with long-term funds. Thus, the top segment of the graph deals with working capital.

The figure represents, of course, an idealized situation—current assets build up gradually as crops are purchased and processed; inventories are drawn down less regularly; and ending inventory balances do not decline to zero. Nevertheless, the example does illustrate the general nature of the production and financing process, and working capital management consists of decisions relating to the top section of the

Figure 6–1
Fixed and Current
Assets and Their
Financing

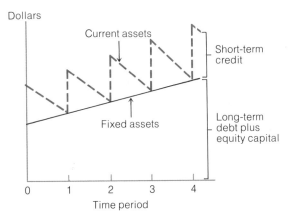

graph—managing current assets and arranging the short-term credit used to finance them.

Extending the Working Capital Concept

As the economy became less oriented toward agriculture, the production and financing cycles of "typical" business changed. Although seasonal patterns still existed, and business cycles also caused asset requirements to fluctuate, it became apparent that current assets rarely, if ever, dropped to zero. This realization led to the development of the idea of "permanent current assets," diagrammed in Figure 6–2. As the figure is drawn, it maintains the traditional notion that permanent assets should be financed with long-term capital, while temporary assets should be financed with short-term credit.

The pattern shown in Figures 6–1 and 6–2 was considered to be desirable because it minimizes the risk that the firm may be unable to pay off its maturing obligations. To illustrate, suppose a firm borrows on a one-year basis and uses the funds obtained to build and equip a plant. Cash flows from the plant (profits plus depreciation) are not sufficient to pay off the loan at the end of the year, so the loan has to be renewed. If for some reason the lender refuses to renew the loan, then the firm has problems. Had the plant been financed with long-term debt, however, cash flows would have been sufficient to retire the loan, and the problem of renewal would not have arisen. Thus, if a firm finances long-term assets with permanent capital and short-term assets with temporary capital, its financial risk is lower than it would be if long-term assets were financed with short-term debt.

Figure 6–2
Fluctuating versus
Permanent Assets

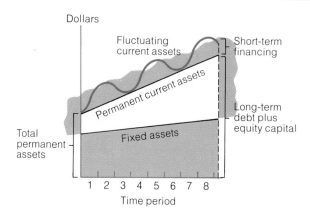

At the limit, a firm can attempt to match the maturity structure of its assets and liabilities exactly. A machine expected to last for five years could be financed by a five-year loan; a 20-year building could be financed by a 20-year mortgage bond; inventory expected to be sold in 20 days could be financed by a 20-day bank loan; and so forth. Actually, of course, uncertainty about the lives of assets prevents this exact maturity matching. We will examine this point in the following sections.

Figure 6–2 shows the situation for a firm that attempts to match asset and liability maturities exactly. Such a policy could be followed, but firms may follow other maturity-matching policies if they desire. Figure 6–3, for example, illustrates the situation for a firm that finances all its

Figure 6–3
Fluctuating versus
Permanent Assets

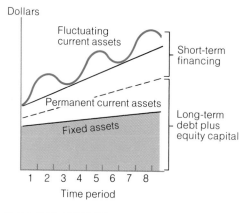

fixed assets with long-term capital but part of its permanent current assets with short-term credit.[1]

The dashed line could have even been drawn *below* the line designating fixed assets, indicating that all the current assets and part of the fixed assets are financed with short-term credit; this would be a highly aggressive, nonconservative position, and the firm would be very much subject to potential loan renewal problems.

Alternatively, as in Figure 6–4, the dashed line could be drawn *above*

Figure 6–4
Fluctuating versus
Permanent Assets
and Liabilities

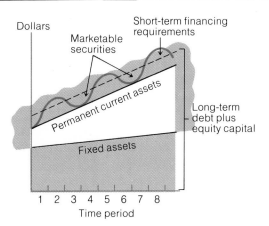

the line designating permanent current assets, indicating that permanent capital is being used to meet seasonal demands. In this case, the firm uses a small amount of short-term credit to meet its peak seasonal requirements, but it also meets a part of its seasonal needs by "storing liquidity" in the form of marketable securities during the off-season. The humps above the dashed line represent short-term financing; the troughs below the dashed line represent short-term security holdings.

**Long-term
versus
Short-term
Debt**

The larger the percentage of funds obtained from long-term sources, the more conservative the firm's working capital policy. The reason for this, of course, is that during times of stress the firm may not be able to renew its short-term debt. This being so, why would firms ever use short-

---

1. Firms generally have some short-term credit in the form of "spontaneous" funds—accounts payable and accruals (see Chapter 4). Used within limits, these constitute "free" capital, so virtually all firms employ at least some short-term credit at all times. We could modify the graphs to take this into account, but nothing is lost by simply abstracting from spontaneous funds, as we do.

term credit (other than spontaneous credit)? Why not just use long-term funds? There are three primary answers to this question: flexibility, cost, and risk.

Flexibility

If the need for funds is seasonal or cyclical, the firm may not want to commit itself to long-term debt. Such debt can be refunded, provided the loan agreement includes a call or prepayment provision, but, even so, prepayment penalties can be expensive. Accordingly, if a firm expects its needs for funds to diminish in the near future, or if it thinks there is a good chance that such a reduction will occur, it may choose short-term debt for the flexibility it provides.

A cash budget is used to analyze the flexibility aspect of the maturity structure of debt. To illustrate, suppose Communications Satellite Corporation (Comsat) is planning to launch a series of satellites in 1977 with an estimated life of seven years. This generation of satellites will provide cash flows—depreciation plus profit—over its seven-year life. If Comsat uses debt to finance the series, it will schedule the debt's retirement to the expected cash flows from the project. A long-term bond issue would not be appropriate.

Cost of Long-Term versus Short-Term Debt

The cost aspect of the maturity decision involves *the term structure of interest rates*, or the relationship between the maturity of debt and the interest rate on the debt. This topic is covered in more detail in the appendix to this chapter, but we may note now that interest rates are frequently lower on short-term debt than on long-term debt. In March 1977, for example, discussions with investment bankers indicated that Comsat could borrow on the following terms:

Loan Maturity	Interest Rate (Percent)
90 days	$6\frac{1}{2}$
6 months	7
1 year	$7\frac{1}{2}$
3 years	8
5 years	$8\frac{1}{4}$
10 years	$8\frac{1}{2}$
20 years	9

These points are graphed in Figure 6–5, a chart commonly called a yield curve, or the term to maturity curve.

While the yield curve presented in Figure 6–5 is a fairly typical one, with short-term rates considerably lower than long-term rates, there are

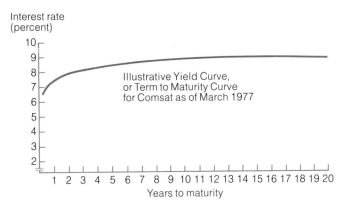

Figure 6–5
Illustrative Term
Structure of Interest
Rates for Comsat,
March 1977

times when the yield curve is downward sloping.[2] At such times, which almost always occur when both long-term and short-term rates are relatively high, short-term money costs more than long-term debt. Nevertheless, since short-term rates have *generally* been lower than long-term rates, a firm's capital will probably be less costly if it borrows short term rather than long term.

Risk of Long-Term versus Short-Term Debt

Even though short-term debt is generally less expensive than long-term debt, use of short-term debt subjects the firm to more risk than does long-term debt. This risk effect occurs for two reasons: (1) If a firm borrows on a long-term basis, its interest costs will be relatively stable over time, but if it borrows on a short-term basis, its interest expenses will fluctuate widely, at times going quite high. For example, from January to June 1974, the short-term rate for large corporations almost doubled, going from 6½ percent to 12 percent. (2) If a firm borrows heavily on a short-term basis, it may find itself unable to repay this debt or it may be in such a shaky financial position that the lender will not extend the loan; thus, the firm could be forced into bankruptcy. We elaborate on these risk factors in the following sections.

Interest Rate Fluctuations. Figure 6–6 shows the pattern of long-term and short-term interest rates during the 1960s and 1970s. The long-

2. In the appendix to this chapter, and in Chapter 21, we spell out these relationships in detail, giving data on the term structure of debt at various points in time and describing the theories that have been advanced to explain the term structure of rates.

Figure 6–6
Long and Short-term
Interest Rates

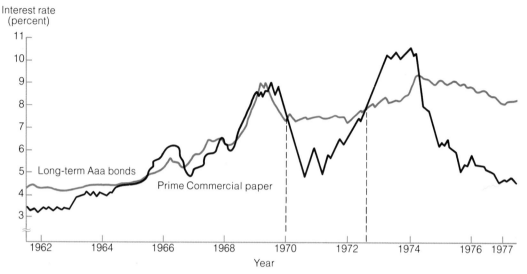

Source: *Federal Reserve Bulletin*, various issues.

term rate is represented by the Aaa bond rate, which is the rate on high-grade, long-term (twenty-five years or more) corporate bonds; the short-term rate is represented by the rate on prime commercial paper, which is the four-to-six month debt of top-quality firms.

Several points should be noted about the graph. *First*, both long-term and short-term rates generally rose over the period. *Second*, short-term rates are more volatile than long-term rates. *Third*, only during 1966 and parts of 1969, 1970, and 1973 were long-term rates below short-term rates. It is worth noting that, except for a period of a few months in the mid-1950s, the long-term rate was consistently above the short-term rate in all years from 1929 to 1966. This confirms the point we made earlier about the yield curve generally sloping upward: whenever the long-term rate in Figure 6–6 is above the short-term rate, the yield curve in Figure 6–5 must be upward sloping.

Impact of a Rise in Rates on Interest Expenses. During a period up to 1970 the yield curve was flat, indicating that long-term and short-term rates were about the same. This can be seen in Figure 6–6, which shows that the long-term and short-term rates were both about 7 percent. Now suppose that in 1970 we were considering two firms, each with $100 million of debt. Firm S has only short-term debt; firm L only long-term debt. Both are stable, mature companies: the total assets of each remain relatively constant from year to year, and the debt of each stays at the $100 million level.

Firm S must "turn over" its debt every year, borrowing at the prevailing short-term interest rate. For simplicity, we assume that firm L's debt will not mature for twenty years, so that its interest rate is fixed at 7 percent for the next 20 years regardless of what happens to either long-term or short-term rates in the intervening years.

Now consider the interest expense of the two firms one year later, in 1971. Firm L still has $100 million of 7 percent debt, so its interest expense is $7 million annually. Firm S, on the other hand, has $100 million of debt that now costs 5 percent, so its interest expense has fallen to $5 million. If other costs and revenues have remained constant between 1970 and 1971, firm L's profits after interest will have remained constant, but those of firm S will have risen sharply. Of course, if we had used as a starting point that date in 1972 when long-term and short-term rates were equal, then things would have worked out better (at least through 1974) for firm L. S would have benefited from the decline in interest rates from 1974 to the end of 1976. The significant point is that while firm L *knows* what its future interest expenses will be, firm S does not, and this very absence of precise knowledge makes firm S the more risky one.

Danger of Being Unable to Refund. In addition to the risk of fluctuating interest charges, firm S faces another risk vis-à-vis firm L: S may run into temporary difficulties that prevent it from being able to refund its debt. Remember that when S's debt matures each year, the firm must negotiate new loans with its creditors. S must, of course, pay the going short-term rate, but suppose the loan comes up for renewal at a time when the firm is facing labor problems, a recession in demand for its products, extreme competitive pressures, or some other set of difficulties that has reduced its earnings.

The creditors will look at firm S's ratios, especially the times-interest-earned and current ratios, to judge its credit worthiness. S's current ratio is, of course, always lower than that of L, but in good times this will be overlooked—if earnings are high, the interest will be well covered and lenders will tolerate a low current ratio. If, however, earnings decline, pulling down the interest coverage ratio, creditors will certainly reevaluate the credit worthiness of firm S. At the very least, because of the perceived increased riskiness of the company, creditors will raise the interest rate charged; at the extreme, they will refuse to renew the loan. In the latter event, the firm will be forced to raise the funds needed to pay off the loan by selling assets at bargain basement prices, borrowing from other sources at exorbitant interest rates, or, in the extreme, going bankrupt.

**Example of the
Risk-Return
Tradeoff**

Thus far we have seen that short-term debt is typically less costly than long-term debt, but that using short-term debt entails greater risk than does using long-term debt. Thus, we are faced with a tradeoff between risk and rate of return. Although we are not prepared to resolve the conflict between risk and rate of return at this point in the book, a further example will help to clarify the issues involved.

Table 6–1 illustrates the nature of the tradeoff. Here, we assume that the firm has $100 million of assets, one-half held as fixed assets and the other half as current assets, and that it will earn 15 percent before interest and taxes on these assets. The debt ratio has been set at 50 percent, but the policy issue of whether to use short-term debt, costing 6 percent, or long-term debt, costing 8 percent, has not been determined. Working through the relationships, we see that a conservative policy of using no short-term credit results in a rate of return on equity of 11 percent, while the more aggressive policy of using only short-term credit boosts the rate of return to 12 percent.

What occurs when uncertainty is introduced into this example? We noted earlier that a firm that makes extensive use of short-term credit may find its earnings fluctuating widely. Suppose, for example, that interest rates rise significantly—a rise from 6 percent to 10 percent is not at all unrealistic. This rise would not affect the firm using the conservative policy, but it would increase the interest expense under the average policy to $4.5 million and under the aggressive policy to $5 million. The rates of return on equity for the three policies would consequently be 11.0 percent, 10.5 percent, and 10.0 percent, respectively—a reversal in

Table 6–1 **Effect of Maturity** **Structure of Debt** **on Return on Equity** **(Millions of Dollars)**	Conservative	Average	Aggressive
Current assets	$ 50.00	$ 50.00	$ 50.00
Fixed assets	50.00	50.00	50.00
Total assets	$100.00	$100.00	$100.00
Short-term credit (6%)	—	25.00	50.00
Long-term debt (8%)	50.00	25.00	—
Current ratio	∞	2:1	1:1
Earnings before interest and taxes (EBIT)	15.00	15.00	15.00
Less interest	4.00	3.50	3.00
Taxable income	$ 11.00	$ 11.50	$ 12.00
Less taxes at 50%	5.50	5.75	6.00
Earnings on common stock	$ 5.50	$ 5.75	$ 6.00
Rate of return on common (%)	11.0	11.5	12.0

relative ranking by rate of return. Of course, a decline in interest rates would have the opposite effect on the rates of return, but it should be clear that the variability of the return under an aggressive policy is more than that under a conservative policy.

Fluctuations in earnings before interest and taxes (EBIT) can pose even more severe problems—if EBIT declines, lenders may simply refuse to renew short-term debt or agree to renew it only at very high rates of interest. To illustrate this, suppose the EBIT of $15 million in Table 6–1 declines to only $5 million. Since the firm's ability to repay has diminished, creditors would certainly be reluctant to lend to it. This would cause creditors to require a higher return on their investment and, thus, raise the interest expense, which would, of course, jeopardize the firm's future even more and, at the same time, compound the effects of the declining EBIT on stockholder returns.

It is possible for the general level of interest rates to rise at the same time a firm's EBIT is falling, and the compound effects could cause the situation to deteriorate so much that the aggressive firm could not renew its credit at any interest rate. The result is bankruptcy.

Notice that if the firm follows a conservative policy of using all long-term debt, it need not worry about short-term, *temporary* changes either in the term structure of interest rates or in its own EBIT. Its only concern is with its long-run performance, and its conservative financial structure may permit it to survive in the short run to enjoy better times in the long run.

Extending the Example

These concepts can be incorporated into our example.[3] A firm has assets of $100 million and is considering the three financial structures, or policies, shown in Table 6–1. Management makes estimates of the future level of riskless interest rates (the Treasury bill rate) and the level of EBIT for the coming year. Management knows that the firm's earnings for next year will be the prime determinant of the risk premium that will be added to the riskless rate.[4]

Probability distributions for riskless rates and EBIT are given in Table 6–2. Assuming that the two probability distributions are independent of each other, we can determine the expected interest rate for the next

---

3. This illustration uses the concept of a probability distribution, a topic discussed at some length in Chapter 11. A probability is the chance of an event occurring, or the odds on the occurrence of the event. The sum of the probabilities must equal 1.0, or 100 percent. The statistical aspects of this section may be omitted without loss of continuity if the statistical concepts are totally new.

4. As we see in detail later in the book, the higher the risk associated with a given loan, the higher the interest rate lenders require on the loan. The difference between the United States government bond rate and the rate the firm must pay is defined as the *risk premium*. Obviously, the risk premium for AT&T or General Motors is lower than that for a smaller, less seasoned borrower.

Table 6–2 **Probability** **Distributions for** **Riskless Rates** **and EBIT**	Treasury Bill Rate One Year Hence		
	(i)	Probability	
	3%	.2	
	5	.3	
	7	.3	
	9	.2	

EBIT for Next Year and Associated Risk
Premiums Expected on Next Year's
Renewal of Short-Term Credit

EBIT	Risk Premium	Probability
(5.00) million	25.0%	.15
5.00	5.0	.20
15.00	2.0	.30
25.00	1.2	.20
35.00	1.0	.15

year by the technique shown in Table 6–3. Column 1 gives the possible riskless rates of return. Column 2 gives the possible risk premiums. Column 3 combines the riskless rates of interest with the risk premiums to give the possible rates of interest the firm may face. Column 4 gives the joint probabilities—the probability of the simultaneous occurrence of each possible riskless rate and risk premium. Column 5 gives the products of each joint probability multiplied by its associated interest rate; the sum of column 5 is the expected interest rate, or 10.8 percent.

Since the expected value of the firm's short-term rate exceeds the long-term rate, 8 percent, the firm should probably use long-term rather than short-term financing. More important, however, is the fact that there is a 15 percent probability that the interest rate will be 28 percent or higher. Because total debt is $50 million, a 28 percent rate of interest would require an EBIT of $14 million to break even. But, at the time when this high rate is applied, EBIT would be *minus* $5 million, so the firm would run a loss before taxes of $19 million. This loss would reduce equity and increase the debt ratio, making the situation even more tense the next time the loan comes up for renewal. Good times might be just around the corner, but the aggressive firm, if its EBIT is subject to wide swings, may not survive until then.

Our example is unrealistic in that few firms will be able to actually generate the data needed to construct a table like Table 6–3. However, the events described are certainly *not* unrealistic, and the example does illustrate that the maturity structure of a firm's debt affects its overall risk. The example also shows that the risk tolerance of the firm with respect to the maturity composition of its liabilities depends to a large extent on the amount of risk already present in the firm owing to indus-

Table 6–3	i	Risk Premium	Interest Rate to Firm	Joint Probability*	Product
Firm's Expected Interest Rate One Year Hence	(1)	(2)	(3) = (1) + (2)	(4)	(5) = (3) × (4)
		1.0%	4.0%	.030	.120%
		1.2	4.2	.040	.168
	3%	2.0	5.0	.060	.300
		5.0	8.0	.040	.320
		25.0	28.0	.030	.840
		1.0	6.0	.045	.270
		1.2	6.2	.060	.372
	5%	2.0	7.0	.090	.630
		5.0	10.0	.060	.600
		25.0	30.0	.045	1.350
		1.0	8.0	.045	.360
		1.2	8.2	.060	.492
	7%	2.0	9.0	.090	.810
		5.0	12.0	.060	.720
		25.0	32.0	.045	1.440
		1.0	10.0	.030	.300
		1.2	10.2	.040	.408
	9%	2.0	11.0	.060	.660
		5.0	14.0	.040	.560
		25.0	34.0	.030	.102
				1.000	

Expected interest rate = 10.822%

*Joint probabilities are developed by multiplying the probabilities contained in Table 6–2 by each other. For example, the joint probability at the top of column 4 is the product .2 × .15 = .03; the second is the product .2 × .20 = .04; and so on. The expected value, or most likely interest rate, is found by multiplying the possible interest rates shown in column 3 by the joint probabilities given in column 4, then adding these products.

try business risk, operating leverage, and overall financial leverage. It is important to keep the overall risk level of the firm within reasonable limits. Thus, a firm with high business risk should probably not use a very aggressive policy in its financial structure and especially not in its maturity structure, but a firm in a stable industry might use such a policy to advantage. Of course, the firm's asset maturity structure has a bearing on its ability to employ short-term debt, and we cover this topic in the next section.

Relationship of Current Assets to Fixed Assets

In the chapters that deal with capital budgeting, we will see that capital budgeting decisions involve estimating the stream of benefits expected from a given project and then discounting these expected cash flows back to the present to find the present value of the project. Although current asset investment analysis is similar to fixed asset analysis in the sense that it also requires estimates of the effects of such investments on profits, it is different in two key respects. *First,* increasing the firm's current assets — especially cash and marketable securities — while holding constant expected production and sales reduces the riskiness of the firm, but it also reduces the overall return on assets. *Second,* although both fixed and current asset holdings are functions of *expected* sales, only current assets can be adjusted to *actual* sales in the short-run; hence, adjustments to short-run fluctuations in demand lie in the domain of working capital management.

Some of these ideas are illustrated in Figure 6–7, which shows the short-run relationship between the firm's current assets and output. The firm's fixed assets are assumed to be $50 million, and they cannot be altered in response to short-run fluctuations in output. Three possible current asset policies are depicted. CA_1 represents a conservative policy: relatively large balances of cash and marketable securities are maintained, large "safety stocks" of inventories[5] are kept on hand, and the firm maximizes sales by adopting a credit policy that causes a high level of accounts receivable. Policy CA_2 is somewhat less conservative than CA_1, while CA_3 represents a risky, aggressive policy.

Current asset holdings are highest at any output level under policy CA_1, lowest under CA_3. For example, at an output of 100,000 units, CA_1 calls for $33 million of current assets versus only $23 million for CA_3. If

Figure 6–7
Relationship between
Current Assets and
Output

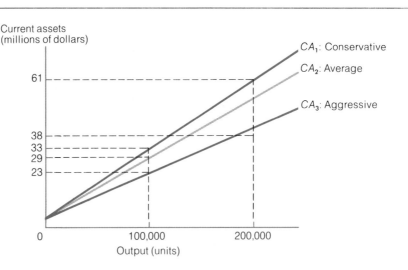

5. The concept of inventory safety stocks is discussed in Appendix A to Chapter 7.

demand strengthens and short-run plans call for production to increase from 100,000 to 200,000 units, current asset holdings will likewise increase. Under policy CA_1, current assets rise to $61 million; under CA_3, the increase is to only $38 million. As we shall see in the following section, the more aggressive policy will lead to a higher expected rate of return; it also entails greater risk.

Risk-Return Tradeoff for Current Asset Holdings

If it could forecast perfectly, a firm would hold *exactly* enough cash to make disbursements as required, *exactly* enough inventories to meet production and sales requirements, *exactly* the accounts receivable called for by an optimal credit policy, and no marketable securities unless the interest returns on such assets exceeded the cost of capital, which is an unlikely occurrence. The current asset holdings under the perfect foresight case would be the theoretical minimum for a profit-maximizing firm. Any larger holdings would, in the sense of the du Pont chart we described in Chapter 2, increase the firm's assets without a proportionate increase in its returns, thus lowering its rate of return on investment. Any smaller holdings would mean the inability to pay bills on time, lost sales and production stoppages because of inventory shortages, and lost sales because of an overly restrictive credit policy.

When uncertainty is introduced into the picture, current asset management involves (1) determination of the minimum required balances of each type of asset and (2) addition of a safety stock to account for the fact that forecasters are imperfect. If a firm follows policy CA_1 in Figure 6–7, it is adding relatively large safety stocks; if it follows CA_3, its safety stocks are minimal. Policy CA_3, in general, produces the highest expected returns on investment, but it also involves the greatest risk—that is, following this policy may actually result in the *lowest* rate of return.

The effect of the three alternative policies on expected profitability is illustrated in Table 6–4. Under the conservative policy, CA_1, the rate of

Table 6–4 **Effects of Alternative Current Asset Policies on Rates of Return and Asset Turnover**		Conservative *(CA₁)*	Average *(CA₂)*	Risky *(CA₃)*
	Sales			
	Units	200,000	200,000	200,000
	Dollars	$100,000,000	$100,000,000	$100,000,000
	EBIT	$ 15,000,000	$ 15,000,000	$ 15,000,000
	Current assets	$ 61,000,000	$ 50,000,000	$ 38,000,000
	Fixed assets	50,000,000	50,000,000	50,000,000
	Total assets	$111,000,000	$100,000,000	$ 88,000,000
	Rate of return on assets (EBIT/assets)	13.5%	15.0%	17.0%

return on assets before interest and taxes is 13.5 percent; the return rises to 15 percent for an average policy and to 17 percent for the risky, aggressive policy, CA_3. However, we know that CA_3 is the most risky policy, since lost sales, lost customer goodwill, and bad credit ratings caused by poor liquidity ratios could combine to bring the actual realized rate of return well below the anticipated 17 percent.

In the real world, things are considerably more complex than this simple example suggests. For one thing, different types of current assets affect both risk and returns differently. Increased holdings of cash do more to improve the firm's risk posture than a similar dollar increase in receivables or inventories; idle cash penalizes earnings more severely than does the same investment in marketable securities. Generalizations are difficult when we consider accounts receivable and inventories, because it is difficult to measure either the earnings penalty or the risk reduction that results from increasing the balances of these items beyond their theoretical minimums. In subsequent chapters, we consider determining the optimal balances of each type of current asset, where *optimal* is defined to include the theoretical minimum plus an optimal safety stock. First, however, we must complete our generalized discussion of working capital policy by combining current asset and current liability management.

Working Capital Policy: Combining Current Asset and Current Liability Management

Table 6–5 illustrates the effect of working capital policy on expected returns and on risk as measured by the current ratio. A conservative policy calling for no short-term debt and large holdings of current assets results in a 9.6 percent expected after-tax return on equity and a very high current ratio. The actual return would probably be quite close to 9.6 percent. An aggressive policy, with minimal holdings of current assets and short-term rather than long-term debt, raises the expected return to 14 percent. But the current ratio under this policy is only .86, a dangerously low level for most industries. Simultaneously, the increasing risks associated with the aggressive policy might adversely affect stock market opinion about the company; therefore, even if working capital policy pushes rates of return up, the net effect still might be to lower stock prices.

Can we resolve this risk-return tradeoff to determine *precisely* the firm's optimal working capital policy, that is, the working capital policy that will maximize the value of existing common stock? In theory, the answer is yes, but in practice, it is no. Determining the optimal policy would require detailed information on a complex set of variables, information that is unobtainable today. Progress is being made in the de-

**Table 6–5
Effects of Working
Capital Policy on
the Rate of Return
on Common Equity**

		Conservative	Average	Aggressive
		Long-Term Debt Large Investment in Current Assets	Average Use of Short-Term Debt; Average Investment in Current Assets	All Short-Term Debt; Minimal Investment in Current Assets
		(CA'_1)	(CA_2)	(CA_3)
Current assets		$ 61,000,000	$ 50,000,000	$ 38,000,000
Fixed assets		50,000,000	50,000,000	50,000,000
Total assets		$111,000,000	$100,000,000	$ 88,000,000
Current liabilities (6%)		—	$ 25,000,000	$ 44,000,000
Long-term debt (8%)		$ 55,500,000	$ 25,000,000	—
Total debt (debt/assets = 50%)		$ 55,500,000	$ 50,000,000	$ 44,000,000
Equity		55,500,000	50,000,000	44,000,000
Total liabilities and net worth		$111,000,000	$100,000,000	$ 88,000,000
Sales in dollars		$100,000,000	$100,000,000	$100,000,000
EBIT		$ 15,000,000	$ 15,000,000	$ 15,000,000
Less: interest		4,400,000	3,500,000	2,640,000
Taxable income		$ 10,600,000	$ 11,500,000	$ 12,360,000
Taxes (50%)		5,300,000	5,750,000	6,180,000
Earnings on equity		$ 5,300,000	$ 5,750,000	$ 6,180,000
Rate of return on equity		9.6%	11.5%	14.0%
Current ratio		*	2:1	.86

*Under policy CA$_1$, the current ratio is shown to be infinitely high. Actually, the firm would doubtless have some spontaneous credit, but the current ratio would still be quite high.

velopment of computer simulation models designed to help determine the effects of alternative financial policy choices, including working capital decisions, but no one using such models would suggest that they can actually reach *optimal* solutions. We can, however, establish guidelines, or ranges of values, for each type of current asset, and we do have ways of examining the various types of short-term financing and their effects on the cost of capital. Because such information, used with good judgment, can be most helpful to the financial manager, we will consider these topics in the remaining chapters of Part II.

Summary

Working capital refers to a firm's investment in short-term assets—cash, short-term securities, accounts receivable, and inventories. *Gross working capital* is defined as the firm's total current assets; *net working capital* is current assets minus current liabilities. *Working capital management* involves all aspects of the administration of both current assets and current liabilities.

Working capital policy is concerned with two sets of relationships among balance sheet items. First is the policy question of the level of total current assets to be held. Current assets vary with sales, but the ratio of current assets to sales is a policy matter. If the firm elects to operate aggressively, it will hold relatively small stocks of current assets. This will reduce the required level of investment and increase the expected rate of return on investment. However, an aggressive policy also increases the likelihood of running out of cash or inventories or of losing sales because of an excessively tough credit policy.

The second policy question concerns the relationship between types of assets and the way these assets are financed. One policy calls for matching asset and liability maturities, financing short-term assets with short-term debt, and long-term assets with long-term debt or equity. This is unsound because current assets are permanent investments as sales grow. If this policy is followed, the maturity structure of the debt is determined by the level of fixed versus current assets. Since short-term debt is frequently less expensive than long-term debt, the expected rate of return may be higher if short-term debt is used. However, large amounts of short-term credit increase the risks (1) of having to renew this debt at higher interest rates and (2) of not being able to renew the debt at all if the firm experiences difficulties.

Both aspects of working capital policy involve risk/return tradeoffs. In the following chapter, we examine methods used to determine the optimal levels of each type of current asset. Then, in Chapter 8, we examine alternative sources and forms of short-term credit.

Questions

6-1. How does the seasonal nature of a firm's sales influence the decision about the amount of short-term credit in the financial structure?

6-2. "Merely increasing the level of current asset holdings does not necessarily reduce the riskiness of the firm. Rather, the composition of the current assets, whether highly liquid or highly illiquid, is the important factor to consider." What is your reaction to this statement?

6-3. What is the advantage of matching the maturities of assets and liabilities?

6-4. There have been times when the term structure of interest rates has been such that short-term rates were higher than long-term rates. Does this necessarily imply that the best financial policy for a firm would be to use all long-term debt and no short-term debt? Explain your answer.

6-5. Assuming a firm's volume of business remained constant, would you expect it to have higher cash balances (demand deposits) during a tight-money period or an easy-money period? Does this situation have any ramifications for federal monetary policy?

Problems   6-1. The Morgan Tile Corporation is attempting to determine an optimal level of current assets for the coming year. Management expects sales to increase to approximately $1.2 million as a result of asset expansion presently being undertaken. Fixed assets total $500,000, and the firm wishes to maintain a 60 percent debt ratio. Morgan's interest cost is currently 8 percent on both short-term debt and the longer term debt, which the firm uses in its permanent structure. Three alternatives regarding the projected current asset level are available to the firm: (1) an aggressive policy requiring current assets of only 45 percent of projected sales; (2) an average policy of 50 percent of sales as current assets; and (3) a conservative policy under which the current asset level would be 60 percent of sales. The firm expects to generate earnings before interest and taxes at a rate of 12 percent on total sales.

a. What is the expected return on equity under each alternative current asset level? (Assume a 50 percent tax rate.)

b. In this problem, we have assumed that (1) level of expected sales is independent of current asset policy and (2) interest rates are independent of this policy. Are these valid assumptions?

c. How would the overall riskiness of the firm vary under each policy? Discuss specifically such questions as the effect of current asset management on demand, expenses, fixed charge coverage, risk of insolvency, and so on.

6-2. The Wilson Cane Company is attempting to project its financial requirements for the next 10-year period. The firm is a relative newcomer to the industry, having been in business only three years. Initially, the firm was totally unknown and found financing, particularly of a permanent nature, quite difficult to obtain. As a result, Wilson was literally "forced" to structure the right-hand side of its balance sheet as follows:

Trade credit payable	$200,000
Short-term bank borrowing	240,000
Common equity	440,000
Total claims	$880,000

In the three years the firm has been very successful, increasing its total capitalization by $120,000 of retained earnings. It is now in a position where it could obtain a long-term loan for ten years from an insurance company at a rate of 10 percent in place of all or any of its present short-term borrowings. Alternatively, it could renew its existing $240,000 loan, or any part thereof, on a one-year loan from the bank at a rate of 8 percent.

George Groves, the financial vice-president, is considering three possible financing plans: (1) to renew the one-year loan with the bank; (2) to borrow $240,000 from the insurance company; and (3) to borrow $120,000 from each. Groves has estimated short-term riskless rates, the premiums that Cane might have to pay over the riskless rate for three possible "states of the economy," and the probability of each possibility. The *average* rates that the firm would likely pay over the next ten years on its short-term borrowings are shown below.

State of Economy	Cane EBIT*	Riskless Rate	Cane Risk Premium	Joint Probability
Good	$300,000	3%	2%	.125
Good	300,000	5%	2	.125
Average	160,000	5%	4	.250
Average	160,000	7%	4	.250
Bad	20,000	7%	10	.125
Bad	20,000	9%	10	.125

*Earnings before interest and taxes.

a. Assuming a 50 percent tax rate, compute expected profits under each of Groves' three alternative financing plans. (Ignore possible growth effects. The expected EBIT is $160,000 under each plan.)

b. On the basis of Groves's estimates, what is the worst profit that could result under each alternative? the best? (Assume no loss carry-back provision in the tax law.) Interpret your results and recommend a financing plan for Cane.

c. Is there anything to prevent Cane from refinancing its short-term debt with the insurance company, thus converting it to long-term debt, at some future date if and when the short-term rate to the firm becomes unreasonably high?

d. In both this problem and the example in the chapter, some very high interest rates were averaged into the computation of an expected short-term interest rate. If such rates would "ruin" a firm, can you see any problem with using them in this computation?

6-3. Three companies (Aggressive, Between, and Conservative) have different working capital management policies as implied by their names. For example, Aggressive employs only minimal current assets and finances almost entirely with current liabilities and equity. This tight ship approach has a dual effect. It keeps total assets lower, which would tend to increase return on assets. But for reasons such as stock-outs total sales are reduced, and since inventory is ordered more frequently and in smaller quantities variable cost is increased. Condensed balance sheets for the three companies are presented below.

Balance Sheets

	Aggressive	Between	Conservative
Current assets	150,000	200,000	300,000
Fixed assets	200,000	200,000	200,000
Total assets	350,000	400,000	500,000
Current liabilities (8%)	200,000	100,000	50,000
Long-term debt (10%)	0	100,000	200,000
Total debt	200,000	200,000	250,000
Equity	150,000	200,000	250,000
Total claims on assets	350,000	400,000	500,000
Current ratio	0.75:1	2:1	6:1

The cost of goods sold functions for the three firms are as follows:

$$\text{Cost of goods sold} = \text{Fixed costs} + \text{Variable costs}$$

Aggressive   Cost of goods sold = \$200,000 + 0.7(sales)
Between   Cost of goods sold = \$250,000 + 0.6(sales)
Conservative   Cost of goods sold = \$300,000 + 0.6(sales)

A company with normal net working capital, such as Between, will sell \$1,000,000 in a year when economic growth is average. If the economy is weak, sales for Between would be reduced by \$100,000; if strong, sales for Between would increase \$100,000. In any given economic condition, Aggressive will sell \$100,000 less than Between, and Conservative will sell \$100,000 more. This is because of the working capital differences.

a. Complete the income statements that follow for strong, average and weak economies.

b. Compare the rates of return (EBIT/Assets and return on equity). Which company is best in a strong economy? an average economy? a weak economy?

c. What are the considerations for management of working capital that are indicated by this problem?

Selected References

Bean, Virginia L., and Griffith, Reynolds. "Risk and Return in Working Capital Management." *Mississippi Valley Journal of Business and Economics* 1 (Fall 1966):28–48.

Beranek, William. *Working Capital Management*. Belmont, Calif: Wadsworth, 1968.

Carr, J. L.; Halpern, P. J.; and McCallum, J. S. "Correcting the Yield Curve: A Re-Interpretation of the Duration Problem." *Journal of Finance* 29 no. 4 (Sept. 1974):1287–94.

Chervany, Norman L. "A Simulation Analysis of Causal Relationships within the Cash Flow Process." *Journal of Financial and Quantitative Analysis* 5 (Dec. 1970):445–68.

Cossaboom, Roger A. "Let's Reassess the Profitability-Liquidity Tradeoff." *Financial Executive* 39 (May 1971):46–51.

Glautier, M. W. E. "Towards a Reformulation of the Theory of Working Capital." *Journal of Business Finance* 3 (Spring 1971):37–42.

Knight, W. D. "Working Capital Management: Satisficing versus Optimization." *Financial Management* 1 (Spring 1972):33–40.

Merville, L. J., and Tavis, L. A. "Optimal Working Capital Policies: A Chance-Constrained Programming Approach." *Journal of Financial and Quantitative Analysis* 8 (Jan. 1973):47–60.

Pettway, Richard H., and Walker, Ernest W. "Asset Mix, Capital Structure, and the Cost of Capital." *Southern Journal of Business* (Apr. 1968):34–43.

Smith, Keith V. *Management of Working Capital: A Reader*. New York: West, 1974.

————. "State of the Art of Working Capital Management." *Financial Management* 2 (Autumn 1973):50–55.

Stancill, James McN. *The Management of Working Capital.* Scranton, Pa.: Intext Educational Publishers, 1971.

Tinsley, P. A. "Capital Structure, Precautionary Balances, and Valuation of the Firm: The Problem of Financial Risk." *Journal of Financial and Quantitative Analysis* 5 (Mar. 1970):33–62.

Van Horne, James C. "A Risk-Return Analysis of a Firm's Working-Capital Position." *Engineering Economist* 14 (Winter 1969):71–89.

Walker, Ernest W. "Towards a Theory of Working Capital." *Engineering Economist* 9 (Jan.–Feb. 1964):21–35.

Walter, James E. "Determination of Technical Solvency." *Journal of Business* 30 (Jan. 1959):30–43.

Appendix A to Chapter 6
Term Structure of Interest Rates

The *term structure of interest rates* describes the relationship between interest rates and loan maturity. When measuring the term structure, we generally use yields on United States government securities. The term structure on other instruments, however, varies similarly.

Figure A6–1 shows the term structure of rates in two years, 1974 and 1976. In the lower curve, for 1976, we see a pattern of rising yields—the shorter the maturity, the lower the rate of interest. This rising yield structure has been typical for most years since 1930. The higher curve, for 1974, shows a yield curve that declines as the term to maturity increases.

Figure A6–1
Term Structure of Rates on U.S. Government Securities, May 1974 and November 1976

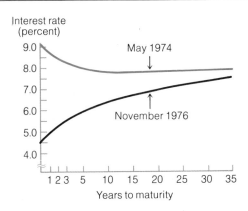

In addition to illustrating the changing term structure of interest rates, Figure A6–1 also reveals a shift in the "level of rates." Between 1974 and 1976, the interest rate on all government securities—long term and short term—decreased. Such movements represent changes in the general level of interest rates.[1] The historical pattern of interest rate

---

1. In addition to the level and term structure of rates on a given class of securities—in this case, government securities—there is also the pattern of relationships among different classes of securities—for example, mortgages, government bonds, corporates, and bank business loans. The relationship among classes of securities is not discussed here. In general, movements in the term structure and level of rates are similar for most classes of securities.

movements depicted in Figure 6–6 in Chapter 6 shows that the general level of interest rates was upward during the 1960s and early 1970s. The tight money period of 1974 represents a peak from which interest rates declined to the end of 1976. A slight rise in the general level of interest rates occurred in the first half of January 1977, but then flattened out through the first half of 1977.

Theoretical Explanation for the Term Structure of Interest Rates

Three theories have been advanced to explain the term structure of interest rates: *the expectations theory, the liquidity preference theory, and the market segmentation theory.* We will consider each in turn.

Expectations Theory

The expectations theory asserts that in equilibrium the long-term rate is a geometric average of today's short-term rate and expected short-term rates in the future. To illustrate, let us consider an investor whose planning horizon is two years. Let r be the short-term interest rate and R be the long-term interest rate. Suppose he has $100 and is considering two alternative investment strategies: (1) purchasing a two-year bond with a yield of 9 percent per year, or (2) purchasing a one-year bond that yields 8 percent, then reinvesting the $108 he will have at the end of the year in another one-year bond. If he choose strategy 1, at the end of two years he will have[2]

Ending value $= \$100 \, (1.09) \, (1.09) = \$118.81$

If he follows strategy 2, his value at the end of two years will depend upon the yield on the one-year bond during the second year, r_2:

Ending value $= \$100 \, (1.08) \, (1 + r_2) = \$108 \, (1 + r_2)$.

Under the expectations theory, the value of r_2 will be 10.01 percent, found as follows:

$\$118.81 = \$108 \, (1 + r_2)$

$1 + r_2 = 1.1001$

$r_2 = .1001 = 10.01\%$

---

2. Compound interest is discussed in more detail in Chapter 9.

Suppose r_2 was greater than 10.01 percent, say 10.5 percent. In that case, our investor (and others) would be better off investing short-term, because he would end up with \$119.34, which is greater than \$118.81. Just the reverse would hold if $r_2 < 10.01$ percent. Thus, according to the expectations theory, capital market competition forces long-term rates to be equal to the (geometric) average of short-term rates over the holding period.

In more formal terminology, let the prefix t represent the year in which a given rate holds, and the postscript t represent the maturity associated with a given rate. Applying this terminology to our previous example, $_tR_{t+1} = {_1R_2} = 9\% =$ the rate today on two-year bonds; $_tr_t = {_1r_1} = 8\% =$ the rate today on one-year bonds; and $_{t+1}r_t = {_2r_1} = 10.01\% =$ the rate expected to prevail next year on one-year bonds. In equilibrium, the expected returns on the two alternatives over the two-year holding period must be equal:

$$(1 + {_tR_2})^2 = (1 + {_tr_1})(1 + {_{t+1}r_1}),$$

or

$$(1 + {_tR_2}) = [(1 + {_tr_1})(1 + {_{t+1}r_1})]^{1/2}.$$

In general,

$$(1 + {_tR_N}) = [(1 + {_tr_1})(1 + {_{t+1}r_1}) \cdots (1 + {_{t+N-1}r_1})]^{1/N}.$$

Thus, if short-term rates are expected to rise in the future, the current

Table A6–1
**Hypothetical Relationship between Short-Term
and Long-Term Interest Rates**

Year	Situation A Expect Rising Rates			Situation B Expect Falling Rates		
	Long-Term[a] (5-Year Note)	Short-Term (1-Year Note)	Intermediate-Term (3-Year Note)[b]	Long-Term[a] (5-Year Note)	Short-Term (1-Year Note)	Intermediate-Term (3-Year Note)[b]
1	8	6	7	8	10	9
2		7			9	
3		8			8	
4		9			7	
5		10			6	

[a]The long-term rate should be a geometric average of short-term rates rather than the arithmetic average that we have used. This refinement is ignored here.
[b]Intermediate terms in this example could be anything between one and five years; for example, two-year notes, three-years notes, or four-year notes. Depending on the definition of intermediate term, different rates would emerge.

long-term rate, $_tR_N$, will be higher than the current short-term rate, and vice versa if rates are expected to decline.

The expectations theory is illustrated in Table A6–1, where "long term" is defined as five years. In situation A, the expected trend in short-term rates is upward — from 6 percent to 10 percent over five years. The long-term rate is thus 8 percent, the mean of that series;[3] a lender could obtain an average yield of 8 percent on his investment either by lending long at 8 percent or by lending short at various increasing rates.

The situation is reversed in section B. There the trend in short-term rates is expected to be downward. Again, however, the mean of the short-term rates is 8 percent, so 8 percent is the effective long-term rate.

The term structure of rates in year 1 under situations A and B is graphed in Figure A6–2. With expectations of rising rates, the yield curve is upward sloping. With expectations of falling rates, the yield curve slopes down.

Figure A6–2
Term Structure of
Rates under Two
Hypothetical Situations

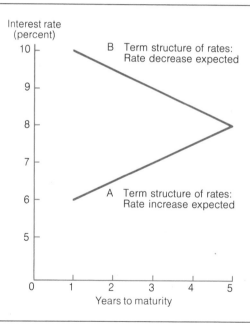

**Liquidity
Preference
Theory**

The future is inherently uncertain, and when uncertainty is considered, the pure expectations theory must be modified. To illustrate, let us consider a situation where short-term rates are expected to remain unchanged in the future. In this case, the pure expectations theory predicts

3. The arithmetic mean is used for ease of exposition.

that short- and long-term bonds sell at equal yields. The liquidity preference theory, on the other hand, holds that long-term bonds must yield more than short-term bonds for two reasons. *First,* in a world of uncertainty, investors will, in general, prefer to hold short-term securities because they are more liquid in the sense that they can be converted to cash without danger of loss of principal. (Short-term bond *prices* are less volatile than long-term bond prices; see Figure 17–1.) Investors will, therefore, accept lower yields on short-term securities. *Second,* borrowers react in exactly the opposite way from investors— business borrowers generally prefer long-term debt because, as we saw in Chapter 6, short-term debt subjects a firm to greater dangers of having to refund debt under adverse conditions. Accordingly, firms are willing to pay a higher rate, other things held constant, for long-term than for short-term funds.

We see, then, that pressures on both the supply and demand sides— caused by liquidity preferences of both lenders and borrowers—will tend to make the yield curve slope upward. Figure A6–3 illustrates this effect.

**Market
Segmentation,
or Hedging-
Pressure,
Theory**

The expectations theory assumes that, in the aggregate, lenders and borrowers are indifferent between long- and short-term investments except for any expected yield differentials between the types of securities.[4] The liquidity preference theory states that an upward bias exists –

Figure A6–3
Term Structure with
Liquidity Preference

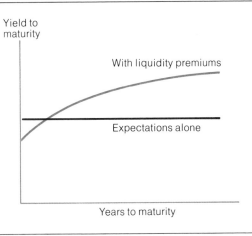

4. In discussing the term structure of interest rates, we are holding constant the risk of default. This is done by using government securities, which presumably have no default risk.

the yield curve slopes upward to a greater extent than is justified by expectations about future rates because investors prefer to lend short while borrowers prefer to borrow long.

The institutional, or hedging-pressure, theory admits the liquidity preference argument as a good description of the behavior of investors with short horizons, such as commercial banks, which regard certainty of principal as more important than certainty of income because of the nature of their deposit liabilities. However, certain other investors with long-term liabilities, such as insurance companies, might prefer to buy long-term bonds because, given the nature of their liabilities, they find certainty of income highly desirable. On the other hand, borrowers typically relate the maturity of their debt to the maturity of their assets— recall the discussion in Chapter 6. Thus, the hedging-pressure theory characterizes market participants as having strong maturity preferences, then argues that interest rates are determined by supply and demand in each segmented market, with each maturity constituting a segment. In the strictest version of this theory, expectations play no role—bonds with different maturities are not substitutes for one another because of different demand preferences or the "preferred habitat" of both lenders and borrowers.

Empirical Evidence

Empirical studies suggest that there is some validity to each of these theories. Specifically, the recent work indicates that if lenders and borrowers have no reason for expecting a change in the general level of interest rates, the yield curve will be upward sloping because of liquidity preferences. (Under the expectations theory, the term structure of interest rates would be flat if there were no expectations of a change in the level of short-term rates.) However, it is a fact that during periods of extremely high interest rates, the yield curve is downward sloping; this proves that the expectations theory also operates. At still other times, when supply and demand conditions in particular maturity sectors change, the term structure seems to be modified, thus confirming the market segmentation theory. In summary, each theory has an element of truth, and each must be employed to help explain the term structure of rates.

References

Cargill, Thomas F. "The Term Structure of Interest Rates: A Test of the Expectations Hypothesis." *The Journal of Finance* 30 (June 1975): 761–71.

Carleton, Willard T., and Cooper, Ian A. "Estimation and Uses of the Term Structure of Interest Rates." *The Journal of Finance* 31 (Sept. 1976): 1067–83.

Dobson, Steven W.; Sutch, Richard C.; and Vanderford, David E. "An Evaluation of Alternative Empirical Models of the Term Structure of Interest Rates." *The Journal of Finance* 31 (Sept. 1976): 1035–65.

Echols, Michael E., and Elliott, Jan Walter. "A Quantitative Yield Curve Model for Estimating the Term Structure of Interest Rates." *The Journal of Financial and Quantitative Analysis* 11 (Mar. 1976): 87–114.

Long, J. B. "Stock Prices, Inflation, and the Term Structure of Interest Rates." *The Journal of Financial Economics* 1 (July 1974): 131–70.

Modigliani, Franco, and Sutch, Richard. "Debt Management and the Term Structure of Interest Rates: An Empirical Analysis," *Journal of Political Economy* 75 (Aug. 1967): 569–89.

Pesando, James E. "Determinants of Term Premiums in the Market for United States Treasury Bills." *The Journal of Finance* 30 (Dec. 1975): 1317–27.

7 Current Asset Management

In the preceding chapter we viewed working capital management in a general, overall sense. Now we focus our attention on the firm's investment in specific current assets, examining cash, marketable securities, accounts receivable, and inventories. According to Federal Trade Commission reports, in 1976 current assets represented approximately 50 percent of manufacturing companies' assets, so current asset management is clearly an important subject.

Cash Management

Controlling the investment in current assets begins with cash management. Cash consists of the firm's holdings of currency and demand deposits, with demand deposits being by far the more important for most firms.

Why Hold Cash?

Businesses or individuals have three primary motives for holding cash: (1) the *transactions motive*, (2) the *precautionary motive*, and (3) the *speculative motive*.

Transactions Motive. The transactions motive for holding cash is to enable the firm to conduct its ordinary business—making purchases and sales. In some lines of business, such as the utilities, where billings can be cycled throughout the month, cash inflows can be scheduled and synchronized closely with the need for the outflow of cash. Hence, we expect the cash-to-revenues ratio and cash-to-total-assets ratio for utility firms to be relatively low. In retail trade, by contrast, sales are more random, and a number of transactions may actually be conducted by physical currency. As a consequence, retail trade requires a higher ratio of cash to sales and of cash to total assets.

The seasonality of a business may give rise to a need for cash for the purchase of inventories. For example, raw materials may be available only during a harvest season and may be perishable, as in the food-canning business. Or sales may be seasonal, as are department store sales around the Christmas and Easter holidays, giving rise to an increase in needs for cash.

Precautionary Motive. The precautionary motive relates primarily to the predictability of cash inflows and outflows. If the predictability is high, less cash must be held against an emergency or any other contingency. Another factor that strongly influences the precautionary motive for holding cash is the ability to borrow additional cash on short notice when circumstances necessitate. Borrowing flexibility is primarily a matter of the strength of the firm's relations with banking institutions and other credit sources.

The precautionary motive for holding cash is actually satisfied in large part by holding near-money assets—short-term government securities and the like.

Speculative Motive. The speculative motive for holding cash is to be ready for profit-making opportunities that may arise. By and large, business accumulations of cash for speculative purposes are not widely found. Holding cash is more common among individual investors. However, the cash and marketable securities account may rise to rather sizable levels on a temporary basis as funds are accumulated to meet specific future needs. For example, at the end of 1975, IBM held $184 million in cash and $4.6 billion in marketable securities. These two items combined represented 31 percent of IBM's year-end total assets of $15.3 billion. Whenever IBM develops and introduces a new computer development, the cash requirements are quite substantial since the total investment and production costs are recovered over several years in monthly rental receipts.

Advantages of Adequate Cash: Specific Points

In addition to these general motives, sound working capital management requires maintenance of an ample amount of cash for several specific reasons. First, it is essential that the firm have sufficient cash to take trade discounts. The payment schedule for purchases is referred to as "the term of the sale." A commonly encountered billing procedure, or term of trade, allows a 2 percent discount if the bill is paid within ten days, with full payment required in thirty days in any event. (This is usually stated as 2/10, net 30.) Since the net amount is due in thirty days, failure to take the discount means paying this extra 2 percent for using the money an additional twenty days. If one were to pay 2 percent for every twenty-day period over the year, there would be eighteen such periods:

$$18 = \frac{360 \text{ days}}{20 \text{ days}}.$$

This represents an annual interest rate of 37 percent.[1] Most firms have a cost of capital that is substantially lower than 37 percent.

Second, since the current and acid test ratios are key items in credit analysis, it is essential that the firm, in order to maintain its credit standing, meet the standards of the line of business in which it is engaged. A strong credit standing enables the firm to purchase goods from trade suppliers on favorable terms and to maintain its line of credit with banks and other sources of credit.

Third, ample cash is useful for taking advantage of favorable business opportunities that may come along from time to time. Finally, the firm should have sufficient liquidity to meet emergencies, such as strikes, fires, or marketing campaigns of competitors.

Using the knowledge about the general nature of cash flows presented in Chapter 4, the financial manager may be able to improve the inflow-outflow pattern of cash. He can do so by better synchronization of flows and by reduction of float, as will be explained in the following sections.

Synchronization of Cash Flows

An example of synchronization demonstrates how cash flows may be improved by more frequent requisitioning of funds by divisional offices from the firm's main or central office. Some Gulf Oil Corporation divisional field offices, for instance, formerly requisitioned funds once a week; now the treasurer's office insists on daily requisitions, thus keeping cash on tap as much as four days longer. On the basis of 20 offices, each requiring $1 million a week, these staggered requisitions

---

1. The following equation may be used for calculating the cost, on an annual basis, of not taking discounts:

$$\text{Cost} = \frac{\text{discount percent}}{(100 - \text{discount percent})} \times \frac{360}{(\text{final due date} - \text{discount period})}.$$

The denominator in the first term (100−discount percent) equals the funds made available by not taking the discount. To illustrate, the cost of not taking a discount when the terms are 2/10, net 30 is computed.

$$\text{Cost} = \frac{2}{98} \times \frac{360}{20} = 0.0204 \times 18 = 36.72\%.$$

Notice that the calculated cost can be reduced by paying late. Thus if the illustrative firm pays in 60 days rather than the specified 30, the credit period becomes 60 − 10 = 50, and the calculated cost becomes

$$\text{Cost} = \frac{2}{98} \times \frac{360}{50} = 0.0204 \times 7.2 = 14.7\%.$$

In periods of excess capacity, some firms may be able to get away with late payments, but such firms may suffer a variety of problems associated with being a "slow-payer" account.

free the equivalent of $40 million for one day each week. At 6 percent interest, this earns better than $336,000 a year.

Moreover, effective forecasting can reduce the investment in cash. The cash flow forecasting at CIT Credit Corporation illustrates this idea. An assistant treasurer forecasts planned purchases of automobiles by the dealers. He estimates daily the number of cars shipped to the 10,000 dealers who finance their purchases through CIT. He then estimates how much money should be deposited in Detroit banks that day to pay automobile manufacturers. On one day he estimated a required deposit of $6.4 million; the actual bill for the day was $6.397 million, a difference of one-half of 1 percent. Although such close forecasting cannot be achieved by every firm, the system enables CIT to economize on the amount of money it must borrow and thereby keeps interest expense to a minimum.

Expediting Collections and Check Clearing

Another important method of economizing on the amount of cash required is to hasten the process of clearing checks. Checks sent from customers in distant cities are subject to delays because of the time required for the check to travel in the mail and the time required for clearing through the banking system.

Even after a check has been received by a firm and deposited in its account, the funds cannot be spent until the check has cleared. The bank in which the check was deposited presents the check to the bank on which it was drawn. Only when this latter bank transfers funds to the bank of deposit are they available for use by the depositor. Checks are generally cleared through the Federal Reserve System or through a clearinghouse set up by the banks in a particular city. Of course, if the check is drawn on the bank of deposit, that bank merely transfers funds by bookkeeping entries from one depositor to another. The length of time required for checks to clear is a function of the distance between the payer's and the payee's banks; in the case of clearinghouses, it can range from one day to three or four days. The maximum time for checks cleared through the Federal Reserve System is two days.

To reduce this delay, a *lock-box plan* can be used. If a firm makes sales in large amounts at far distances, it can establish a lock box in a post office located in the customer's area. It can arrange to have customers send payments to the postal box in their city and then have a bank pick up the checks and deposit them in a special checking account. The bank then has the checks cleared in the local area and remits by wire to the firm's bank of deposit. If the distant customers are scattered, the firm can establish the lock box in its local city and have the checks picked up by its own bank. The bank begins the clearing process, notifying the firm that a check has been received. In this way the clearing process starts before the firm processes the check. By these methods, collection time can be reduced by one to five days. Examples of freeing funds in the amount of $5 million or more by these methods have been cited by firms.

**Slowing
Disbursements**

Just as expediting the collection process conserves cash, slowing down disbursements accomplishes the same thing by keeping cash on hand for longer periods. One obviously could simply delay payments, but this involves equally obvious difficulties. Firms have, in the past, devised rather ingenious methods for "legitimately" lengthening the collection period on their own checks, ranging from maintaining deposits in distant banks to using slow, awkward payment procedures. Since such practices are usually recognized for what they are, there are severe limits to their use.

The most widely publicized of these procedures in recent years is the use of drafts. While a check is payable upon demand, a draft must be transmitted to the issuer, who approves it and deposits funds to cover it, after which it can be collected. AT&T has used drafts: "In handling its payrolls, for instance, AT&T can pay an employee by draft on Friday. The employee cashes the draft at his local bank, which sends it on to AT&T's New York bank. It may be Wednesday or Thursday before the draft arrives. The bank then sends it to the company's accounting department, which has until 3 P.M. that day to inspect and approve it. Not until then does AT&T deposit funds in its bank to pay the draft."[2] Insurance companies also use drafts to pay claims.

Both banks and those who receive drafts dislike them—they represent an awkward, clumsy, costly anachronism in an age when computer transfer mechanisms are reducing the time and expense involved in transfers of funds.

Using Float

Float is defined as the difference between the balance shown in a firm's (or individual's) checkbook balance and the balance on the bank's books. Suppose a firm writes, on the average, checks in the amount of $5,000 each day. It takes about six days for these checks to clear and be deducted from the firm's bank account. Thus, the firm's own checking records show a balance $30,000 less than the bank's records. If the firm

2. "More Firms Substitute Drafts for Checks to Pay, Collect Bills," *The Wall Street Journal* (29 August 1971).

receives checks in the amount of $5,000 daily but loses only four days while these checks are being deposited and cleared, its own books have a balance that is, because of this factor, $20,000 larger than the bank's balance. Thus the firm's float—the difference between the $30,000 and the $20,000—is $10,000.

If a firm's own collection and clearing process is more efficient than that of the recipients of its checks—and this is generally true of larger, more efficient firms—then the firm could show a negative balance on its own records and a positive balance on the books of its bank. Some firms indicate that they *never* have true positive cash balances. One large manufacturer of construction equipment stated that, while its account according to its bank's records shows an average cash balance of about $2 million, its *actual* cash balance is *minus* $2 million; it has $4 million of float. Obviously, the firm must be able to forecast its positive and negative clearings accurately in order to make such heavy use of float.

Cost of Cash Management[3]

We have just described a number of procedures that may be used to hold down cash balance requirements. Implementing these procedures, however, is not a costless operation. How far should a firm go in making its cash operations more efficient? As a general rule, the firm should incur these expenses so long as their marginal returns exceed their marginal expenses.

For example, suppose that by establishing a lock-box system and increasing the accuracy of cash inflow and outflow forecasts, a firm can reduce its investment in cash by $1 million. Further, suppose that the firm borrows at the prime rate, 12 percent. The steps taken have released $1 million, and the cost of capital required to carry this $1 million investment in cash is $120,000.[4] If the costs of the procedures necessary to release the $1 million are less than $120,000, the move is a good one; if the costs exceed $120,000, the greater efficiency is not worth the cost. It is clear that larger firms, with larger cash balances, can better afford to hire the personnel necessary to maintain tight control over their cash positions. Cash management is one element of business operations in which economies of scale are clearly present.

Very clearly, the value of careful cash management depends upon the costs of funds invested in cash, which in turn depend upon the current

---

3. We are abstracting from the security aspects of cash management; that is, the prevention of fraud and embezzlement. These topics are better covered in accounting than in finance courses.

4. The borrowing rate, 12 percent, is used rather than the firm's average cost of capital, because cash is a less risky investment than the firm's average asset. Notice, also, that we are using before-tax figures here; the analysis could employ either before-tax or after-tax figures, so long as consistency is maintained.

rate of interest. In the 1970s, with interest rates at historic highs, firms are devoting more care than ever to cash management.

Determining the Minimum Cash Balance

Thus far we have seen that cash is held primarily for transactions purposes; the other traditional motives for holding cash, the speculative and precautionary motives, are today met largely by reserve borrowing power and by holdings of short-term marketable securities. Some minimum cash balance—which may actually be negative if float is used effectively—is required for transactions, and an additional amount over and above this figure may be held as a safety stock. For many firms the total of transactions balances plus safety stock constitutes the minimum cash balance, the point at which the firm either borrows additional cash or sells part of its portfolio of marketable securities. For many other firms, however, banking relationships require still larger balances.

Compensating Balances

We have seen that banks provide services to firms—they clear checks, operate lock-box plans, supply credit information, and the like. These services cost the bank money, so the bank must be compensated for rendering them.

Banks earn most of their income by lending money at interest, and most of the funds they lend are obtained in the form of deposits. If a firm maintains a deposit account with an average balance of $100,000, and if the bank can lend these funds at a return of $8,000, then the account is, in a sense, worth $8,000 to the bank. Thus, it is to the bank's advantage to provide services worth up to $8,000 to attract and hold the account.

Banks determine first the costs of the services rendered to their larger customers and then the average account balances necessary to provide enough income to compensate for these costs. These balances are defined as *compensating balances* and are often maintained by firms instead of paying cash service charges to the bank.[5]

Compensating balances are also required by some bank loan agreements. During periods when the supply of credit is restricted and interest rates are high, banks frequently insist that borrowers maintain accounts that average some percentage of the loan amount—15 percent is a typical figure—as a condition for granting the loan. If the balance is larger than the firm would otherwise maintain, then the effective cost of

---

5. Banks are compensated for services rendered either by compensating balances or by direct fees.

the loan is increased; the excess balance presumably "compensates" the bank for making a loan at a rate below what it could earn on the funds if they were invested elsewhere.[6]

Compensating balances can be established (1) as *an absolute minimum*, say $100,000, below which the actual balance must never fall, or (2) as *a minimum average balance*, perhaps $100,000 over some period, generally a month. The absolute minimum is a much more restrictive requirement, because the average amount of cash held during the month will be above $100,000 by the amount of transactions balances. The $100,000 in this case is "dead money" from the firm's standpoint. Under the minimum average, however, the balance could fall to zero one day provided it was $200,000 some other day, with the average working out to $100,000. Thus, the $100,000 in this case is available for transactions.

Statistics on compensating balance requirements are not available, but average balances are typical and absolute minimums rare for business accounts. Discussions with bankers, however, indicate that absolute balance requirements are less rare during times of extremely tight money such as prevailed during the late 1960s and early 1970s.

Minimum Cash Balance

The firm's minimum cash balance is set as the larger of (1) its transactions balances plus precautionary balances (that is, safety stocks) or (2) its required compensating balances. Statistics are not available on which factor is generally controlling, but in our experience compensating balance requirements generally dominate, except for firms subject to absolute minimum balances.[7]

Overdraft System

Most countries outside the United States use *overdraft systems.* In such a system a depositor writes checks in excess of his balance, and his bank automatically extends a loan to cover the shortage. The maximum amount of such loans must, of course, be established ahead of time. Statistics are not available on the usage of overdrafts in the United States, but a number of firms have worked out informal, and in some cases

---

6. The interest rate effect of compensating balances is discussed further in Chapter 8.

7. This point is underscored by an incident that occurred at a professional finance meeting. A professor presented a scholarly paper that used operations research techniques to determine "optimal cash balances" for a sample of firms. He then reported that actual cash balances of the firms greatly exceed "optimal" balances, suggesting inefficiency and the need for more refined techniques. The discussant of the paper made her comments short and sweet. She reported that she wrote and asked the sample firms why they had so much cash; they uniformly replied that their cash holdings were set by compensating balance requirements. The model was useful to determine the optimal cash balance in the absence of compensating balance requirements, but it was precisely those requirements that determined actual balances. Since the model did not include compensating balances as a determinant of cash balances, its usefulness is questionable.

formal, overdraft arrangements. Further, the use of overdrafts has been increasing in recent years.

Cash Management Models

Several types of mathematical models designed to help determine optimal cash balances have been developed lately. These models are interesting, and they are beginning to become practical. Examples of cash management models are presented in Appendix B to Chapter 7.

Marketable Securities

Firms sometimes report sizable amounts of such short-term marketable securities as Treasury bills or bank certificates of deposit among their current assets. Why might marketable securities be held? The two primary reasons — as a substitute for cash and as a temporary investment — are considered in this section.

Substitute for Cash

Some firms hold portfolios of marketable securities in lieu of larger cash balances, liquidating part of the portfolio to increase the cash account when cash outflows exceed inflows. Data are not available to indicate the extent of this practice, but our impression is that it is not common. Most firms prefer to let their banks maintain such liquid reserves, with the firms themselves borrowing to meet temporary cash shortages.

Temporary Investment

In addition to using marketable securities as a buffer against cash shortages, firms also hold them on a strictly temporary basis. Firms engaged in seasonal operations, for example, frequently have surplus cash flows during part of the year, deficit cash flows during other months. (See Table 5–1 for an example.) Such firms may purchase marketable securities during their surplus periods, then liquidate them when cash deficits occur. Other firms, particularly in capital goods industries, where fluctuations are violent, attempt to accumulate cash or near-cash securities during a downturn in order to be ready to finance an upturn in business volume.

Firms also accumulate liquid assets to meet predictable financial requirements. For example, if a major modernization program is planned for the near future, or if a bond issue is about to mature, the marketable securities portfolio may be increased to provide the required funds. Furthermore, marketable securities holdings are frequently large immediately preceding quarterly corporate tax payment dates.

Firms may also accumulate resources as a protection against a number of contingencies. When they make uninsurable product warranties, companies must be ready to meet any claims that may arise. Firms in highly competitive industries must have resources to carry them through substantial shifts in the market structure. A firm in an industry in which new markets are emerging—for example, foreign markets— needs to have resources to meet developments; these funds may be on hand for fairly long periods.

Criteria Used in Selecting Security Portfolios

Different types of securities, varying in risk of default, marketability, and length of maturity, are available. We will discuss some of the characteristics of these securities, and the criteria that are applied in choosing among them, here.

Risk of Default. The firm's liquidity portfolio is generally held for a specific, known need; if it should depreciate in value, the firm would be financially embarrassed. Further, most nonfinancial corporations do not have investment departments specializing in appraising securities and determining the probability of their going into default. Accordingly, the marketable securities portfolio is generally confined to securities with a minimal risk of default. However, the lowest risk securities also provide the lowest returns, so safety is bought at the expense of yield.

Marketability. The security portfolio is usually held to provide liquid reserves or to meet known needs at a specific time. In either case, the firm must be able to sell its holdings and realize cash on short notice. Accordingly, the securities held in the portfolio must be readily marketable.

Maturity. We shall see in Chapter 17 that the price of a long-term bond fluctuates much more with changes in interest rates than does the price of a similar short-term security. Further, as we saw in the last chapter, interest rates fluctuate widely over time. These two factors combine to make long-term bonds riskier than short-term securities for a firm's marketable security portfolio. However, partly because of this risk differential, higher yields are more frequently available on long-term than on short-term securities, so again risk-return tradeoffs must be recognized.

Given the motives most firms have for holding marketable security portfolios, it is generally not feasible for them to be exposed to a high degree of risk from interest rate fluctuations. Accordingly, firms generally confine their marketable securities portfolios to the shorter maturities. Only if the securities are expected to be held for a long period, and not be subject to forced liquidation on short notice, will long-term securites be held.

**Investment
Alternatives**

The main investment alternatives open to business firms are given in Table 7–1. Rates vary with the general level of interest rates. Returns are lower on the lower-risk government securities and are generally lower on shorter maturities.

Table 7–1 **Alternative Marketable Securities for Investment**		Approximate Maturities*	Approximate Yields†	
			November 1974	April 1977
	U.S. Treasury bills	91–182 days	7.53%	4.81%
	U.S. Treasury certificates	9–12 months	7.71	5.20
	U.S. Treasury notes	1–5 years	7.85	6.41
	U.S. Treasury bonds	Over 5 years	8.21	7.45
	Negotiable certificates of deposit with U.S. banks	Varies, up to 3 years	8.25	5.35
	Prime commercial paper	Varies, up to 270 days	10.25	4.70
	Eurodollar bank time deposits	Varies, up to 1 year	9.75	5.18
	Bonds of other corporations (AAA)	Varies, up to 30 years	8.85	8.53

*The maturities are those at issue date. For outstanding securities, maturities varying almost by day or week are available.
†Estimated yields for median maturities in the class.

Depending on how long he or she anticipates holding the funds, the financial manager decides upon a suitable maturity pattern for the holdings. The numerous alternatives can be selected and balanced in such a way that the maturities and risks appropriate to the financial situation of the firm are obtained. Commercial bankers, investment bankers, and brokers provide the financial manager with detailed information on each of the forms of investments in the list. Because their characteristics change with shifts in financial market conditions, it would be misleading to attempt to give detailed descriptions of these investment outlets here. The financial manager must keep up to date on these characteristics and should follow the principle of making investment selections that offer maturities, yields, and risks appropriate to the firm.

**Management
of Accounts
Receivable:
Credit Policy**

The level of accounts receivable is determined by (1) the volume of credit sales and (2) the average period between sales and collections. The average collection period is partially dependent upon economic conditions—during a recession or a period of extremely tight money, customers may be forced to delay payment—but it is also dependent upon a set of controllable factors, or *credit policy variables*. The major policy variables include (1) *credit standards*, or the maximum riskiness of acceptable credit accounts; (2) *credit period*, or the length of time for which credit is granted; (3) *discounts* given for early payment; and (4) the firm's *collection policy*. We first discuss each policy variable separately and in qualitative rather than quantitative terms; then we illustrate the interaction of these elements and discuss the actual establishment of a firm's credit policy.

Credit Standards

If a firm makes credit sales to only the strongest of customers, it will never have bad debt losses, and it will not incur much in the way of expenses for a credit department. On the other hand, it will probably be losing sales, and the profit foregone on these lost sales could be far larger than the costs it has avoided. Determining the optimal credit standard involves equating the marginal costs of credit to the marginal profits on the increased sales.

Marginal costs include production and selling costs, but we may abstract from these at this point and consider only those costs associated with the "quality" of the marginal accounts, or *credit quality costs*. These costs include (1) default, or bad debt losses; (2) higher investigation and collection costs; and (3) if less credit-worthy customers delay payment longer than stronger customers, higher costs of capital tied up in receivables.

Since credit costs and credit quality are correlated, it is important to be able to judge the quality of an account. First, how should we define "quality"? Perhaps the best way is in terms of the probability of default. These probability estimates are, for the most part, subjective estimates, but credit rating is a well-established practice, and a good credit manager can make reasonably accurate judgments of the probability of default by different classes of customers.

To evaluate the credit risk, credit managers consider the five Cs of credit: character, capacity, capital, collateral, conditions. *Character* refers to the probability that a customer will *try* to honor his obligations. This factor is of considerable importance, because every credit transaction implies a *promise* to pay. Will the creditor make an honest effort to pay his debts, or is he likely to try to get away with something? Experienced credit men frequently insist that the moral factor is the most important issue in a credit evaluation.

Capacity is a subjective judgment of the ability of the customer. This is gauged by his past record, supplemented by physical observation of the customer's plant or store and business methods. *Capital* is measured by the general financial position of the firm as indicated by a financial ratio analysis, with special emphasis on the tangible net worth of the enterprise. *Collateral* is represented by assets that the customer may offer as a pledge for security of the credit extended to him. Finally, *conditions* refer to the impact of general economic trends on the firm or to special developments in certain areas of the economy that may affect the customer's ability to meet his obligations.

The five Cs of credit represent the factors by which the credit risk is judged. Information on these items is obtained from the firm's previous experience with the customer, supplemented by a well-developed system of information-gathering groups. Two major sources of external information are available. The first is the work of the credit associations. By periodic meetings of local groups and by correspondence, information on experience with creditors is exchanged. More formally, Credit Interchange, a system developed by the National Association of Credit Management for assembling and distributing information of debtors' past performance, is provided. The interchange reports show the paying record of the debtor, the industries from which he is buying, and the trading areas in which his purchases are being made.[8]

The second source of external information is the work of the credit-reporting agencies, the best known of which is Dun & Bradstreet. Agencies that specialize in coverage of a limited number of industries also provide information. Representative of these are the National Credit Office and Lyon Furniture Mercantile Agency. These agencies provide factual data that can be used by the credit manager in his credit analysis; they also provide ratings similar to those available on corporate bonds.

An individual firm can translate its credit information into risk classes, grouped according to the probability of loss associated with sales to a customer. The combination of rating and supplementary information might lead to the following groupings of loss experience:

Risk Class Number	Loss Ratio (in Percentages)
1	None
2	$0-\frac{1}{2}$
3	$\frac{1}{2}-1$
4	$1-2$
5	$2-5$
6	$5-10$
7	$10-20$
8	over 20

If the selling firm has a 20 percent margin over the sum of direct operating costs and all delivery and selling costs, and if it is producing at

8. For additional information, see *Credit Management Handbook, Second Edition*, a publication of the National Association of Credit Management (Homewood, Ill.: Irwin, 1965).

less than full capacity, it may adopt the following credit policies. It may sell on customary credit terms to groups 1 to 5; sell to groups 6 and 7 under more stringent credit terms, such as cash on delivery; and require advance payments from group 8. As long as the bad debt loss ratios are less than 20 percent, the additional sales are contributing something to overhead.

Statistical techniques, especially regression analysis and discriminant analysis,[9] have been used with some success in judging credit worthiness. These methods work best when individual credits are relatively small and a large number of borrowers are involved. Thus, they have worked best in retail credit, consumer loans, mortgage lending, and the like. As the increase in credit cards and similar procedures builds up, as computers are used more frequently, and as credit records on individuals and small firms are developed, statistical techniques promise to become much more important than they are today.[10]

Terms of Credit

The terms of credit specify the period for which credit is extended and the discount, if any, given for early payment. For example, as we saw earlier, if a firm's credit terms to all approved customers are stated as "2/10, net 30," then a 2 percent discount from the stated sales price is granted if payment is made within 10 days, and the entire amount is due 30 days from the invoice date if the discount is not taken. If the terms are stated "net 60," this indicates that no discount is offered and that the bill is due and payable 60 days after the invoice date.

If sales are seasonal, a firm may use seasonal dating. Jensen, Inc., a bathing suit manufacturer, sells on terms of "2/10, net 30, May 1 dating." This means that the effective invoice date is May 1, so the discount may be taken until May 10, or the full amount must be paid on May 30, regardless of when the sale was made. Jensen produces output throughout the year, but retail sales of bathing suits are concentrated in the spring and early summer. Because of its practice of offering seasonal datings, Jensen induces some customers to stock up early, saving Jensen storage costs and also "nailing down sales."

9. Discriminant analysis is similar to multiple regression analysis, except that it partitions a sample into two or more components on the basis of a set of characteristics. The sample, for example, might be loan applicants at a consumer loan company. The components into which they are classified might be those likely to make prompt repayment and those likely to default. The characteristics might be such factors as whether the applicant owns his home, how long he has been with his employer, and so forth.

10. It has been said that the biggest single deterrent to the increased automation of credit processes is George Orwell's classic book, *1984*, in which he described the social dangers of centralized files of information on individuals. Orwell's omnipresent watcher, Big Brother, is mentioned frequently in Congressional sessions discussing mass storage of information relevant to credit analysis.

Credit Period. Lengthening the credit period stimulates sales, but there is a cost to tying up funds in receivables. For example, if a firm changes its terms from net 30 to net 60, the average receivables for the year might rise from $100,000 to $300,000, with the increase caused partly by the longer credit terms and partly by the larger volume of sales. If the cost of capital needed to finance the investment in receivables is 8 percent, then the marginal cost of lengthening the credit period is $16,000 (= $200,000 × 8 percent). If the incremental profit — sales price minus all direct production, selling, and credit costs associated with the additional sales — exceeds $16,000, then the change in credit policy is profitable. Determining the optimal credit period involves locating that period where marginal profits on increased sales are exactly offset by the costs of carrying the higher amount of accounts receivable.

Cash Discounts. The effect of granting cash discounts may be analyzed similarly to the credit period. For example, if a firm changes its terms from ''net 30'' to ''2/10, net 30,'' it may well attract customers who want to take discounts, thereby increasing gross sales. Also, the average collection period will be shortened, as some old customers will pay more promptly to take advantage of the discount. Offsetting these benefits is the cost of the discounts taken. The optimal discount is established at the point where costs and benefits are exactly offsetting.

**Collection
Policy**

Collection policy refers to the procedures the firm follows to obtain payment of past-due accounts. For example, a letter may be sent to such accounts when the account is ten days past due; a more severe letter, followed by a telephone call, may be used if payment is not received within 30 days; and the account may be turned over to a collection agency after 90 days.

The collection process can be expensive in terms of both out-of-pocket expenditures and lost goodwill, but at least some firmness is needed to prevent an undue lengthening in the collection period and to minimize outright losses. Again, a balance must be struck between the costs and benefits of different collection policies.

**Accounts
Receivable
versus
Accounts
Payable**

Whenever goods are sold on credit, two accounts are created — an asset item entitled an *account receivable* appears on the books of the selling firm, and a liability item called an *account payable* appears on the books of the purchaser. At this point, we are analyzing the transaction from the viewpoint of the seller, so we have concentrated on the type of variables under his control. In Chapter 8, we will examine the transaction from the viewpoint of the purchaser. There we will discuss accounts payable as a source of funds and consider the cost of these funds vis-à-vis funds obtained from other sources.

**Establishing a
Credit Policy:
An Illustration[11]**

Rexford Drug and Chemical Company manufactures and distributes drugs and related items to retail drugstores throughout the United States and Canada. At a recent board meeting, several directors voiced concern over the firm's rising bad debt losses and increasing investment in accounts receivable. This group suggested to the financial vice-president that he instruct his credit manager to tighten up the credit policy. Several other directors, including the marketing vice-president, took exception to this suggestion, stating that a tougher credit policy would cause Rexford to lose profitable sales. This group emphasized that the gross profit margin on sales is 50 percent, and stated that, if anything, credit terms should be relaxed. After a heated discussion, the meeting broke up; but before adjournment, the board instructed Jim Nantell, the financial vice-president, to conduct a study of the firm's credit policy. Nantell directed his credit manager, Bob Carleton, to study the firm's policy and to report on the desirability of instituting changes.

Carleton decided to draw up two new credit policies as alternatives to the one currently in use. One could be described as an easy credit policy, the other a tough credit policy. The current policy is an "average" policy in the sense that it closely corresponds to the practices of other drug supply firms.

The new plans require changes in all four credit variables. The "easy" credit policy involves (1) extending credit to a more risky class of customers, (2) extending the allowable payment period, (3) raising the cash discount allowed for prompt payments, and (4) reducing the "pressure" of the collection procedure on overdue accounts. The new terms will be 3/15, net 45, instead of the current 2/10, net 30. Those changes are expected to increase sales, but they will also increase the losses on bad debts and the investment in accounts receivable.

The "tough" credit policy involves tightening credit standards; reducing credit terms to 1/10, net 20; and increasing the collection efforts on overdue accounts. It will result in lower sales but also in lower bad debt losses and a smaller investment in accounts receivable. Working with the sales manager, Carleton developed probability estimates of the

---

11. In part of this example we employ statistical concepts that may be unfamiliar to the reader. However, the "words" are more important than the "numbers," so if the statistics are confusing, just concentrate on the verbal sections.

changes in sales and in costs that could result from the two new policies. This information is represented in Table 7–2, where the expected change in profits under each plan is also computed.

Columns 1, 2, and 3 give alternative sales levels, profit margins, and profits. Column 4 gives the estimated probability of each gross profit outcome; column 5 gives an estimate of the incremental costs, including production, general and administrative, and credit costs, associated with each sales change. Notice that these cost estimates are themselves subject to probability distributions. For example, if sales increase by $100 million, costs may increase by $50, $60, or $70 million; the conditional probability estimate of each cost outcome is given in column 6.

Depending on which sales and cost increases actually occur, net profit will increase or decrease by the amount given in column 7. The joint probabilities, which represent the products of the probabilities in columns 4 and 6, give the probability of each net profit increase, and these joint probabilities are used to derive the expected profits under each proposed credit policy change. Since the easier credit policy produces positive incremental profits, this policy is superior to the present policy and much superior to that of tightening credit.

Two points should be noted. First, this kind of analysis requires that some very difficult judgments be made—estimating the changes in sales and costs associated with changes in credit policies is, to say the least, a highly uncertain business. Second, even if the sales and cost estimates are reasonably accurate, there is no assurance that some other credit policy would not be even better. For instance, an easy credit policy that involved a different mix of the four policy variables might be superior to the one examined in Table 7–2.

For both these reasons, firms usually "iterate" slowly toward optimal credit policies. One or two credit variables are changed slightly, the effect of the changes is observed, and a decision is made to change these variables even more or to retract the changes. Further, different credit policies are appropriate at different times, depending on economic conditions. We see, then, that credit policy is not a static, once-for-all-time decision. Rather, it should be fluid, dynamic, and ever changing in an effort to reach a continually moving optimal target.

Inventory

Manufacturing firms generally have three kinds of inventories: (1) raw materials, (2) work in process, and (3) finished goods. The levels of *raw material inventories* are influenced by anticipated production, seasonality of production, reliability of sources of supply, and efficiency of scheduling purchases and production operations.

Work-in-process inventory is strongly influenced by the length of the

Table 7-2
Incremental Profits from Credit Policy Changes
(Dollars in Millions)

Increase in Sales (1)	Profit Margin (2)	Increase in Gross Profit (3) = (1) × (2)	Probability of Sales Change (4)	Increase (or Decrease) in Cost (5)	Conditional Probability (6)	Increase (or Decrease) in Net Profit (7) = (3) − (5)	Joint Probability (8) = (4) × (6)	Product (9) = (7) × (8)
				Easy credit policy				
$ 100	.50	$ 50	.20	$ 50	.30	—	.06	—
				(60)	.40	$(10)	.08	$(.80)
				70	.30	(20)	.06	(1.20)
200	.50	100	.60	80	.40	20	.18	3.60
				90	.40	10	.24	2.40
				100	.30	—	.18	—
300	.50	150	.20	120	.30	30	.06	1.80
				130	.40	20	.08	1.60
				140	.30	10	.06	.60
			1.00				1.00	
						Expected increase in profit =		$ 8.00
				Tough credit policy				
$(50)	.50	$(25)	.25	$(20)	.20	$(5)	.05	$(.25)
				(30)	.60	5	.15	.75
				(40)	.20	15	.05	.75
(150)	.50	(75)	.50	(50)	.20	(25)	.10	(2.50)
				(60)	.60	(15)	.30	(4.50)
				(70)	.20	(5)	.10	(.50)
(250)	.50	(125)	.25	(90)	.20	(1.75)	.05	(1.75)
				(100)	.60	(3.75)	.15	(3.75)
				(110)	.20	(.75)	.05	(.75)
			1.00				1.00	
						Expected increase in profit =		$(12.5)

production period, which is the time between placing raw material in production and completing the finished product. Inventory turnover can be increased by decreasing the production period. One means of accomplishing this is perfecting engineering techniques to speed up the manufacturing process. Another means of reducing work in process is to buy items rather than make them.

The level of *finished goods inventories* is a matter of coordinating production and sales. The financial manager can stimulate sales by changing credit terms or by allowing credit to marginal risks. Whether the goods remain on the books as inventories or as receivables, the financial manager has to finance them. Many times, firms find it desirable to make the sale and thus take one step nearer to realizing cash. The potential profits can outweigh the additional collection risk.

Our primary focus in this section is control of investment in inventories. *Inventory models* have been developed as an aid in this task and have proved extremely useful in minimizing inventory requirements. As our examination of the du Pont system in Chapter 2 showed, any procedure that can reduce the investment required to generate a given sales volume may have a beneficial effect on the firm's rate of return and hence on the value of the firm.

Determinants of the Size of Inventories

Although wide variations occur, inventory-to-sales ratios are generally concentrated in the 12-to-20 percent range, and inventory-to-total assets ratios are concentrated in the 16-to-30 percent range.

The major determinants of investment in inventory are the following: (1) level of sales, (2) length and technical nature of the production processes, and (3) durability versus perishability, or style factor, in the end product. Inventories in the tobacco industry, for example, are high because of the long curing process. Similarly, in the machinery-manufacturing industries, inventories are large because of the long work-in-process period. However, inventory ratios are low in coal mining and in oil and gas production because no raw materials are used and the goods in process are small in relation to sales. Because of the seasonality of the raw materials, average inventories are large in the canning industry.

With respect to durability and style factors, large inventories are found in the hardware and the precious-metals industries because durability is great and the style factor is small. Inventory ratios are low in baking because of the perishability of the final product. Inventories are low in printing because the items are manufactured to order and require negligible finished inventories.

Within limits set by the economics of a firm's industry, there exists a potential for improvement in inventory control from the use of computers and operations research. Although the techniques are far too diverse and complicated for a complete treatment in this text, the financial manager should be prepared to make use of the contributions of specialists who have developed effective procedures for minimizing the investment in inventory.[12]

Illustrative of the techniques at the practical level is Harris Electronic's inventory system, which works like this: Tabulator cards are inserted in each package of five electronic tubes leaving Harris's warehouse. As the merchandise is sold, the distributor collects the cards and files his replacement order without doing paper work. He simply sends in the cards, which are identified by account number, type of merchandise, and price of the units he orders.

Western Union Telegraph Co. equipment accepts the punched cards and transmits information on them to the warehouse, where it is duplicated on other punched cards. A typical order of 5,000 tubes of varying types can be received in about 17 minutes, assembled in about 90 minutes, and delivered to Boston's Logan Airport in an additional 45 minutes. Orders from 3,000 miles away can be delivered within 24 hours, a saving of 13 days in some cases.

Information on the order also goes into a computer which keeps on file stock-on-hand data for each item. When an order draws the stock down below the *order point*, this triggers action in the production department—additional units of the item are then manufactured for stock. In the next section, we examine both the optimal order point and the number of units that should be manufactured, which is called the *economic ordering quantity* (EOQ).

Generality of Inventory Analysis

Managing assets of all kinds is basically an inventory problem—the same method of analysis applies to cash and fixed assets as applies to inventories themselves. First, a basic stock must be on hand to balance inflows and outflows of the items, with the size of the stock depending upon the patterns of flows, whether regular or irregular. Second, because the unexpected may always occur, it is necessary to have safety stocks on hand. They represent the little extra to avoid the costs of not having enough to meet current needs. Third, additional amounts may be required to meet future growth needs. These are anticipation stocks. Related to anticipation stocks is the recognition that there are optimum purchase sizes, defined as *economic ordering quantities*. In borrowing money, in buying raw materials for production, or in purchasing plants

---

12. The basic inventory model is developed in Appendix A to this chapter.

and equipment, it is cheaper to buy more than just enough to meet immediate needs.

With the foregoing as a basic foundation, we can develop the theoretical basis for determining the optimal investment in inventory, which is illustrated in Figure 7–1. Some costs rise with larger inventories — among these are warehousing costs, interest on funds tied up in inventories, insurance, obsolescence, and so forth. Other costs decline with larger inventories — these include the loss of profits resulting from sales lost because of running out of stock, costs of production interruptions caused by inadequate inventories, possible purchase discounts, and so on.

Figure 7–1
Determination of Optimum Investment in Inventory

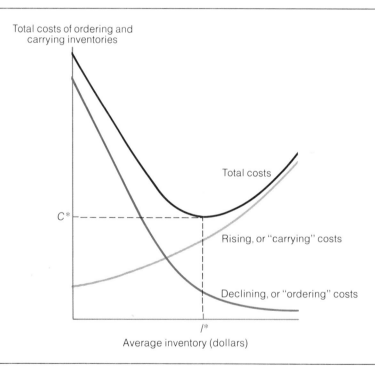

The costs that decline with higher inventories are designated by the declining curve in Figure 7–1; those that rise with larger inventories are designated by the rising curve. The total costs curve is the total of the rising and declining curves, and it represents the total cost of ordering and holding inventories. At the point where the absolute value of the slope of the rising curve is equal to the absolute value of the slope of the declining curve (that is, where *marginal* rising costs are equal to *marginal* declining costs), the total costs curve is at a minimum. This represents the optimum size of investment in inventory.

Inventory Decision Models

The generalized statements in the preceding section can be made much more specific. In fact, it is usually possible to specify the curves shown in Figure 7–1, at least to a reasonable approximation, and actually to find the minimum point on the total cost curve. Since entire courses (in operations research programs) are devoted to inventory control techniques, and since a number of books have been written on the subject, we obviously cannot deal with inventory decision models in a very complete fashion. The model we illustrate, however, is probably more widely used—even by quite sophisticated firms—than any other, and it can be readily expanded to encompass any refinements one cares to make.[13]

The costs of holding inventories—the cost of capital tied up, storage costs, insurance, depreciation, and so on—rise as the size of inventory holdings increases. Conversely, the cost of ordering inventories—the cost of placing orders, shipping and handling, quantity discounts lost, and so on—falls as the average inventory increases. The total cost of inventories is the summation of these rising and declining costs, or the total costs curve in Figure 7–1. It has been shown that, under reasonable assumptions, the minimum point on the total costs curve can be found by an equation called the EOQ formula:

$$EOQ = \sqrt{\frac{2FU}{CP}}.$$

Here

EOQ = the economic ordering quantity, or the optimum quantity to be ordered each time an order is placed.

F = fixed costs of placing and receiving an order.

U = annual usage in units.

C = carrying cost expressed as a percentage of inventory value.

P = purchase price per unit of inventory.

---

13. In the text we simply illustrate the use of the EOQ inventory model; for an explanation of its development see Appendix A to this chapter.

For any level of usage, dividing U by EOQ indicates the number of orders that must be placed each year. The average inventory on hand – the average balance sheet inventory figure – will be

$$\text{Average inventory} = \frac{EOQ}{2}.$$

The derivation of the EOQ model assumes (1) that usage is at a constant rate and (2) that delivery lead times are constant. In fact, usage is likely to vary considerably for most firms – demand may be unexpectedly strong for any number of reasons; if it is, the firm will run out of stock and will suffer sales losses or production stoppages. Similarly, delivery lead times will vary depending on weather, strikes, demand in the suppliers' industries, and so on. Because of these factors, firms add *safety stocks* to their inventory holdings, and the average inventory becomes

$$\text{Average inventory} = \frac{EOQ}{2} + \text{safety stock}.$$

The size of the safety stock will be relatively high if uncertainties about usage rates and delivery times are great, low if these factors do not vary greatly. Similarly, the safety stock will be larger if the costs of running out of stock are great. For example, if customer ill will would cause a permanent loss of business or if an elaborate production process would have to stop if an item were out of stock, then large safety stocks will be carried.[14]

Use of EOQ Model: An Illustration

Let us assume that the following values are determined to be appropriate for a particular firm:

U = usage = 100 units.

C = carrying cost = 20 percent of inventory value.

P = purchase price = $1 per unit.

F = fixed cost of ordering = $10.

Substituting these values into the formula, we obtain

---

14. Formal methods have been developed to assist in striking a balance between the costs of carrying larger safety stocks and the cost of stock-outs (inventory shortages). A discussion of these models, which goes beyond the scope of this book, can be found in most production textbooks.

$$EOQ = \sqrt{\frac{2FU}{CP}}$$

$$= \sqrt{\frac{2 \times 10 \times 100}{0.2 \times 1}} = \sqrt{\frac{2,000}{0.2}} = \sqrt{10,000}$$

$$= 100 \text{ units.}$$

If the desired safety stock is 10 units, then the average inventory *(A)* will be

$$A = \frac{EOQ}{2} + \text{safety stock}$$

$$= \frac{100}{2} + 10$$

$$= 60 \text{ units.}$$

Since the cost of purchasing or manufacturing inventory is $1 a unit, the average inventory in dollars will be $60 for this item.

Cash Management as an Inventory Problem

In our cash budgeting discussion in Chapter 5, we indicated that firms generally have "minimum desired cash balances." Then, in discussing cash management, we considered the various factors that influence cash holdings. We did not, however, attempt to specify optimum cash balances. Optimum cash balances can be found by the use of inventory-type models such as those we discussed just above—examples of such models are given in Appendix B to this chapter. Cash management, together with inventory controls, is perhaps the area of financial management where mathematical tools have proved most useful.

Sophisticated cash management models recognize the uncertainty inherent in forecasting both cash inflows and cash outflows. Inflows are represented, in effect, by the "orders" in our inventory model; they come principally from (1) receipts, (2) borrowing, and (3) sale of securities. The primary "carrying cost" of cash is the opportunity cost of having funds tied up in nonearning assets (or in low-yielding near-cash items); the principal "ordering costs" are brokerage costs associated with borrowing funds or converting marketable securities into cash.

Summary

In this chapter we focused attention on four types of current assets—cash, marketable securities, accounts receivable, and inventories. First, we examined the motives for holding cash and ways of minimizing the investment in cash. With this background, we considered the minimum cash balances a firm is likely to hold. This minimum will be the higher (1) of compensating balance requirements or (2) of transactions balances plus a safety stock.

Marketable securities are held as a substitute for "cash safety stocks" and as temporary investments while the firm is awaiting permanent investment of funds. "Safety stocks" are almost always held in low-risk, short-maturity securities; temporary investments are held in securities whose maturity depends upon the length of time before the funds are permanently employed.

The investment in accounts receivable is dependent (1) upon sales and (2) upon the firm's credit policy. The credit policy, in turn, involves four controllable variables: credit standards, the length of the credit period, cash discounts, and the collection policy. The significant aspect of credit policy is its effect on sales: an easy credit policy will stimulate sales but involves costs of capital tied up in receivables, bad debts, discounts, and higher collection costs. The optimal credit policy is one in which these costs are just offset by the profits on sales generated by the credit policy change.

Inventories—raw materials, work in process, and finished goods—are necessary in most businesses. Rather elaborate systems for controlling the level of inventories have been designed. These systems frequently use computers for keeping records of all the items in stock; an inventory control model that considers anticipated sales, ordering costs, and carrying costs can be used to determine EOQs for each item.

The basic inventory model recognizes that certain costs (carrying costs) rise as average inventory holdings increase but that certain other costs (ordering costs and stock-out costs) fall as average inventory holdings rise. These two sets of costs make up the total cost of ordering and carrying inventories, and the EOQ model is designed to locate an optimal order size that will minimize total inventory costs.

Questions

7-1. How can better methods of communication reduce the necessity for firms to hold large cash balances?

7-2. "The highly developed financial system of the United States, with its myriad of different near-cash assets, has greatly reduced cash balance requirements by reducing the need for transactions balances." Discuss this statement.

7-3. Would you expect a firm with a high growth rate to hold more or less precautionary and speculative cash balances than a firm with a low growth rate? Explain.

7–4. Many firms that find themselves with temporary surplus cash invest these funds in Treasury bills. Since Treasury bills frequently have the lowest yield of any investment security, why are they chosen as investments?

7–5. Assume that a firm sells on terms of net 30 and that its accounts are, on the average, thirty days overdue. What will its investment in receivables be if its annual credit sales are approximately $720,000?

7–6. "It is difficult to judge the performance of many of our employees but not that of the credit manager. If he's performing perfectly, credit losses are zero; and the higher our losses (as a percent of sales), the worse his performance." Evaluate this statement.

7–7. Explain how a firm may reduce its investment in inventory by having its supplier hold raw materials inventories and its customers hold finished goods inventories. What are the limitations of such a policy?

7–8. What factors are likely to reduce the holdings of inventory in relation to sales in the future? What factors will tend to increase the ratio? What, in your judgment, is the net effect?

7–9. What are the probable effects of the following on inventory holdings?
  a. Manufacture of a part formerly purchased from an outside supplier.
  b. Greater use of air freight.
  c. Increase, from 7 to 17, in the number of styles produced.
  d. Your firm receives large price reductions from a manufacturer of bathing suits if they are purchased in December and January.

7–10. Inventory decision models are designed to facilitate the minimization of the cost of obtaining and carrying inventory. Describe the basic nature of the fundamental inventory control model, discussing specifically the nature of increasing costs, decreasing costs, and total costs. Illustrate your discussion with a graph.

Problems

7–1. Gulf Distributors makes all sales on a credit basis. Once each year a routine credit evaluation is made on all its customers. The evaluation procedure allows customers to be ranked in categories from 1 to 5, in order of increasing risk. Results of the ranking are as follows:

Category	Percentage Bad Debts	Average Collection Period	Credit Decision	Annual Sales Lost due to Credit Restrictions
1	None	10 days	Unlimited credit	None
2	1.0	12	Unlimited credit	None
3	3.0	20	Limited credit	400,000
4	9.0	60	Limited credit	200,000
5	16.0	90	No credit	800,000

  a. Using this credit rule, gross profit has averaged 10 percent of sales during the past five years. The opportunity cost of investment in receivables is 12 percent. What would you estimate to be the effect on net profits of extending full credit to each of categories 3, 4 and 5?

b. The implicit assumption in part (a) is that all costs leading to gross profit are variable. Recalculate your answers assuming that variable costs equal 85 percent of sales (excluding bad debts and cost of receivables.)

7-2. A firm issues checks in the amount of $100,000 each day and deducts them from its own records at the close of business on the day they are written. On average, the bank receives and clears (that is, deducts from the firm's bank balance) the checks the evening of the fourth day after they are written; for example, a check written on Monday will be cleared on Friday afternoon. The firm's loan agreement with the bank requires it to maintain a $75,000 minimum average compensating balance; this is $25,000 greater than the cash safety stock the firm would otherwise have on deposit.

a. Assuming that the firm makes deposits in the late afternoon (and the bank includes the deposit in that day's transactions), how much must the firm deposit each day to maintain a sufficient balance?

b. How many days of float does the firm carry?

c. What ending daily balance should the firm try to maintain at the bank and on its own records?

d. Would it make a difference if the compensating balance requirement called for a *minimum* rather than an average of $75,000?

e. What would the firm's average balance on the bank's records and on its own records show if the minimum rather than the average balance is required?

7-3. The Hallaman Distributing Company has mounted an extended sales campaign. In order to move its goods, it has lowered its credit standards somewhat. As a consequence, its average collection period has increased from 20 days to the present level of 50 days under the new credit policies. Credit terms are 2/10, net 30. Gross sales collected over time were as follows, before the sales campaign and during the sales campaign.

Payment By	Percent of Gross Before sale	Sales Collected During sale
Cash Sales	30%	5%
0-10 days (average 5)	20%	10%
11-30 days (average 20)	20%	10%
31-90 days (average 50)	30%	55%
over 90 days (average 100)	0%	20%

As a result of the sales campaign, annual sales increased from $2.0 million to $2.5 million. Profit before credit costs is 8 percent. The cost of capital for receivables is 12 percent. Cash sales are recorded at gross, and the credit discount is given.

a. Calculate the gross profit before and during the sale, and determine the change in gross profit.

b. Compute the change in discount costs.
c. Compute the increased cost of carrying additional receivables outstanding.
d. Compute the change in pretax profits. (Round to the nearest 100.)

7–4. The following relations for inventory purchase and storage costs have been established for the Milton Processing Corporation.
  1. Orders must be placed in multiples of 100 units.
  2. Requirements for the year are 400,000. (Use 50 weeks in a year for calculations.)
  3. The purchase price per unit is $5.
  4. Carrying cost is 20 percent of the purchase price of goods.
  5. Cost per order placed is $25.
  6. Desired safety stock is 10,000 units (on hand initially).
  7. Two weeks are required for delivery.

  a. What is the economic order quantity? (Round to the 100s.)
  b. What is the optimal number of orders to be placed?
  c. At what inventory level should a reorder be made?
  d. If annual unit sales double, what is the percent increase in the EOQ? What is the elasticity of EOQ with respect to sales (% change in EOQ/% change in sales)?
  e. If the cost per order placed doubles, what is the percent increase in EOQ? What is the elasticity of EOQ with respect to cost per order?
  f. If carrying cost declines by 50%, compute the elasticity of EOQ with respect to the change in carrying cost.
  g. If purchase price declines 50%, compute the elasticity of EOQ with respect to the change in purchase price.

Selected References

Andrews, Victor L. "Captive Finance Companies." *Harvard Business Review* 42 (July–Aug. 1964):80–92.

Archer, Stephen H. "A Model for the Determination of Firm Cash Balances." *Journal of Financial and Quantitative Analysis* 1 (Mar. 1966):1–11.

Baumol, William J. "The Transactions Demand for Cash: An Inventory Theoretic Approach." *Quarterly Journal of Economics* 65 (Nov. 1952):545–56.

Baxter, Nevins D. "Marketability, Default Risk, and Yields on Money-Market Instruments." *Journal of Financial and Quantitative Analysis* 3 (Mar. 1968): 75–85.

Benishay, Haskel. "A Stochastic Model of Credit Sales Debt." *Journal of the American Statistical Association* 61 (Dec. 1966):1010–28.

——— "Managerial Controls of Accounts Receivable: A Deterministic Approach." *Journal of Accounting Research* 3 (Spring 1965):114–33.

Beranek, William. *Analysis for Financial Decisions.* Homewood, Ill.: Irwin, 1963, chap. 10.

Brosky, John J. *The Implicit Cost of Trade Credit and Theory of Optimal Terms of Sale.* New York: Credit Research Foundation, 1969.

Brown, Robert G. *Decision Rules for Inventory Management.* New York: Holt, Rinehart and Winston, 1967.

Calman, Robert F. *Linear Programming and Cash Management/CASH ALPHA.* Cambridge, Mass.: M.I.T., 1968.

Chen, Andrew H. Y.; Jen, Frank C.; and Zoints, Stanley. "Portfolio Models with Stochastic Cash Demands." *Management Science* 19 (Nov. 1972):319–32.

Friedland, Seymour. *The Economics of Corporate Finance.* Englewood Cliffs, N.J.: Prentice-Hall, 1966, chapt. 4.

Frost, Peter A. "Banking Services, Minimum Cash Balances and the Firm's Demand for Money." *Journal of Finance* 25 (Dec. 1970):1029–39.

Greer, Carl C. "The Optimal Credit Acceptance Policy." *Journal of Financial and Quantitative Analysis* 2 (Dec. 1967):399–415.

Horn, Frederick E. "Managing Cash." *Journal of Accountancy:* 117. *Instruments of the Money Market.* Richmond, Va.: Federal Reserve Bank of Richmond, 1968.

Jeffers, James R., and Kwon, Jene. "A Portfolio Approach to Corporate Demands for Government Securities." *Journal of Finance* 24 (Dec. 1969):905–20.

King, Alfred M., *Increasing the Productivity of Company Cash.* Englewood Cliffs, N.J.: Prentice-Hall, 1969, chaps. 4 and 5.

Lane, Sylvia. "Submarginal Credit Risk Classification." *Journal of Financial and Quantitative Analysis* 7 (Jan. 1972):1379–85.

Lewellen, Wilbur G. "Finance Subsidiaries and Corporate Borrowing Capacity." *Financial Management* 1 (Spring 1972):21–32.

Long, Michael S. "Credit Screening System Selection." *The Journal of Financial and Quantitative Analysis* 11 (June 1976):313–28.

Mehta, Dileep. "The Formulation of Credit Policy Models." *Management Science* 15 (Oct. 1968):30–50.

———. "Optimal Credit Policy Selection: A Dynamic Approach." *Journal of Financial and Quantitative Analysis* 5 (Dec. 1970).

Miller, Merton H., and Orr, Daniel. "A Model of the Demand for Money by Firms." *Quarterly Journal of Economics* 80 (Aug. 1966):413–35.

———. "The Demand for Money by Firms: Extension of Analytic Results." *Journal of Finance* 23 (Dec. 1968):735–59.

Oh, John S. "Opportunity Cost in the Evaluation of Investment in Accounts Receivable." *Financial Management* 5 (Summer 1976):32–36.

Schwartz, Robert A. "An Economic Model of Trade Credit." *Journal of Financial and Quantitative Analysis* 9 (Sept. 1974):643–57.

Searby, Frederick W. "Cash Management: Helping Meet the Capital Crisis." in *The Treasurer's Handbook,* J. Fred Weston and Maurice B. Goudzwaard, eds. (Homewood, Ill.: Dow Jones-Irwin, 1976):440–56.

Sprenkle, Case M. "The Uselessness of Transactions Demand Models." *The Journal of Finance* 24 (Dec. 1969):835–48.

Wagner, Harvey M. *Principles of Operations Research—with Applications to Managerial Decisions.* Englewood Cliffs, N.J.: Prentice-Hall, 1969, chaps. 9 and 19, and app. 2.

Wrightsman, Dwayne. "Optimal Credit Terms for Accounts Receivable." *Quarterly Review of Economics and Business* 9 (Summer 1969):59–66.

Appendix A to Chapter 7
The Basic Inventory Model

As we noted in Chapter 7, mathematical models have been applied to inventory management with perhaps better results than in any other sphere of business management. In this appendix, we will see how the basic inventory model—the EOQ model—is developed.

The notation used in Chapter 7 and extended in this Appendix is as follows:

A = average inventory
C = carrying cost expressed as a percentage of inventory sales
EOQ = economic order quantity
F = fixed costs of placing and receiving an order
K = total carrying costs
N = number of orders placed per year
P = purchase price per unit of inventory
Q = order quantity
R = total ordering costs
T = total inventory costs
U = annual usage in units
V = variable cost per unit of ordering, shipping, and receiving

This notation is independent of notation used elsewhere in the book.

Nature of the Problem

Recalling Figure 7–1, we find (1) that some costs associated with inventories decline as inventory holdings increase, (2) that other costs rise, and (3) that the total inventory-associated cost curve has a minimum point. The purpose of the basic inventory model is to locate this minimum and the economic order quantity (EOQ) which will lead to minimum costs. We will assume that the Norgaard Company expects to achieve a sales volume of 1,000 widgets during 1978 and that Norgaard is quite confident of hitting this target. Further, these sales are expected to be evenly distributed over the year, so inventories will decline smoothly and gradually. Widgets are purchased for $10 each. No inventory is on hand at the beginning of the year, and none will be held at year's end.

Under these circumstances, the Norgaard Company could place one order for $Q = 1,000$ units at the start of the year. If it did, the average inventory for the year, A, would be equal to

$$A = \frac{Q}{2} = \frac{U}{2} = \frac{1,000}{2} = 500 \text{ units.} \qquad (A7\text{--}1)$$

Since widgets cost $10 each, the average investment in inventories is $5,000.

Alternatively, Norgaard could place two orders for 500 each, in which case average inventories would be

$$A = \frac{500}{2} = 250,$$

or four orders of 250 each for an average inventory of 125, and so on. Inventory investment declines correspondingly.

We can see that average inventories are a function of the number of orders placed per year, N. Specifically, when the number of orders placed is incorporated into the calculation, Equation A7–1 becomes

$$A = \frac{U/2}{N}. \qquad (A7\text{--}1a)$$

By ordering more frequently (increasing N), Norgaard can reduce its average inventory further and further.

How far should inventory reductions be carried? Smaller inventories involve lower *carrying costs* — cost of capital tied up in inventories, storage costs, insurance, and so on — but, since smaller average inventories imply more frequent orders, they involve higher *ordering costs.*

Classification of Costs

The first step in the process of building an inventory model is to specify those costs that rise and those that decline with higher levels of inventory. Table A7–1 gives a listing of some typical costs that are associated with carrying inventories. In the table, we have broken costs down into three categories: those associated with holding inventories, those associated with running short of inventory, and those associated with ordering and receiving inventories.

Although they may well be the most important element, we shall disregard the second category of costs — the costs of running short — at this point. These costs will be considered at a later stage, when we add "safety stocks" to the inventory model. Further, we shall disregard quantity discounts, although it is easy enough to adjust the basic model

Table A7–1 **Costs Associated** **with Inventories**	Carrying Costs 1. Cost of capital tied up 2. Storage costs 3. Insurance 4. Property taxes 5. Depreciation and obsolescence Costs of Running Short 1. Loss of sales 2. Loss of customer goodwill 3. Disruption of production schedules Shipping, Receiving, and Ordering Costs 1. Cost of placing order, including production setup costs 2. Shipping and handling costs 3. Quantity discounts lost

to include discounts.[1] The costs that remain for consideration at this stage, then, are carrying costs and ordering costs.

Carrying Costs

Carrying costs generally rise in direct proportion to the average amount of inventory carried, and this is the case with the Norgaard Company. For example, Norgaard's cost of capital is 10 percent, and depreciation is estimated to amount to 5 percent per year. Lumping together these and Norgaard's other costs of carrying inventory produces a total cost of 25 percent of the investment in inventory. Defining the percentage cost as C, we can, in general, find the total carrying costs as the percentage carrying cost (C) times the price per unit (P) times the average number of units (A):

$$K = \text{total carrying costs}$$
$$= (C)(P)(A).$$

(A7–2)

If Norgaard elects to order only once a year, average inventories will be $1,000/2 = 500$ units; the cost of carrying the inventory will be $.25 \times \$10 \times 500 = \$1,250$. If the company orders twice a year and, hence, has average inventories that are half as large, total carrying costs will decline to 625, and so on.

In an unpublished study, the U.S. Department of Commerce estimated that, on the average, manufacturing firms have an annual cost of carrying inventories that equals 25 percent of original inventory cost. This percentage was broken down as follows:

---

1. See John F. Magee and Harlan C. Meal, "Inventory Management and Standards," *The Treasurer's Handbook,* ed. J. Fred Weston and Maurice B. Goudzwaard (Homewood, Ill.: Dow Jones-Irwin, 1976).

Obsolescence	9.00%
Physical depreciation	5.00
Interest	7.00
Handling	2.50
Property taxes	0.50
Insurance	0.25
Storage	0.75
Total	25.00%

These costs obviously vary from situation to situation, but, with carrying costs of this order of magnitude, inventories deserve careful attention.

**Shipping,
Receiving, and
Ordering Costs**

Although carrying costs are entirely variable and rise in direct proportion to the average size of inventories, ordering costs consist of both a fixed and a variable component. For example, the cost of *placing* an order—interoffice memos, long distance telephone calls, setting up a production run, and so on—are fixed costs per order, so the total cost of placing orders may simply be the cost of placing an order times the number of orders placed. Shipping and receiving costs, on the other hand, generally involve a fixed charge plus a variable charge per unit.[2]

We can lump together all fixed costs of placing and receiving an order and define them as F. Norgaard's total fixed cost *per order*, for example, is $100. The company's per unit variable cost of ordering, shipping, and receiving, which we define as V, depends upon the number of units ordered, and it amounts to $1.00 *per unit ordered*.

Combining the fixed and variable components of ordering costs, we obtain the following equation for R, the total cost of placing and receiving orders:

$$R = (F)(N) + (V)(U), \tag{A7-3}$$

Where F = fixed costs per order; N = number of orders placed; V = variable cost per unit ordered; and U = total number of units ordered during the year, which in this case equals the total sales in units.

Equation A7–1a may be rewritten as $N = U/2A$, then substituted into Equation A7–3 as follows:

---

2. The fixed-versus-variable components in ordering costs can be confusing, so some elaboration on this point might be useful. First, *in toto*, ordering costs are considered to be a variable cost—if the firm does not place any orders, it does not incur any ordering costs. However, some of the costs of each order are fixed and some are variable. It is this fact—that a component of a *variable* cost is *fixed*—that occasionally causes confusion.

$$R = F\left(\frac{U}{2A}\right) + (V)(U). \tag{A7-4}$$

To illustrate, if $F = \$100$, $U = 1{,}000$, $A = 250$, and $V = \$1.00$, then R, the total ordering costs, is

$$R = \$100(2) + \$1(1000) = \$1{,}200.$$

Total Inventory Costs

Inventory carrying costs (K) as defined in Equation A7–2, and ordering costs (R) as defined in Equation A7–4 may be combined to find total inventory costs (T) as follows:

$$T = K + R$$

$$= (C)(P)(A) + F\left(\frac{U}{2A}\right) + (V)(U). \tag{A7-5}$$

Recognizing that $A = Q/2$, or one-half the size of each order quantity, Q, Equation A7–5 may be rewritten as:

$$T = CP\left(\frac{Q}{2}\right) + F\left(\frac{U}{Q}\right) + (V)(U)$$

$$= CP\left(\frac{Q}{2}\right) + \frac{F(U)}{Q} + (V)(U). \tag{A7-6}$$

The next step is to locate an optimal order quantity, or the value of Q that minimizes T. We find this optimal quantity, or the EOQ, by differentiating Equation A7–6 with respect to Q, setting the derivative equal to zero, and obtaining[3] .

$$EOQ = \sqrt{\frac{2FU}{CP}}.$$

In the Norgaard case, we find the EOQ to be

---

3. Proof: differentiate Equation A7–6 with respect to Q and set equal to zero, then solve for Q:

$$\frac{\partial T}{\partial Q} = \frac{CP}{2} - \frac{FU}{Q^2} = 0$$

$$\frac{CP}{2} = \frac{FU}{Q^2}$$

$$Q^2 = \frac{2FU}{CP}$$

$$Q = \sqrt{\frac{2FU}{CP}}$$

$$EOQ = \sqrt{\frac{2(\$100)(1000)}{(.25)(\$10)}}$$

$$= \sqrt{\frac{200,000}{2.5}}$$

$$= \sqrt{80,000}$$

$$\approx 280 \text{ units.} \tag{A7-7}$$

If this quantity is ordered four times a year (1000/280 ≈ 4), or every three months, total costs of ordering and carrying inventories, calculated from Equation A7–6, will be:

$$T = CP\left(\frac{Q}{2}\right) + \frac{FU}{Q} + VU$$

$$= \$2.50(140) + \frac{(\$100)(1,000)}{280} + \$1(1,000)$$

$$= \$350 + \$357 + \$1,000$$

$$= \$1,707.$$

That is the lowest possible cost of ordering and carrying the required amount of inventories.

Equation A7–7 gives us the optimum, or cost minimizing, order quantity for given levels of usage (U), inventory carrying cost (C), and fixed order costs (F). Knowing the EOQ and continuing our assumption of zero beginning and ending inventory balances, we find the optimal average inventory as[4]

$$A = \frac{EOQ}{2} = \frac{280}{2} = 140.$$

Norgaard will thus have an average inventory investment of 140 units at $10 each, or $1,400.

**Relationship
Between
Sales and
Inventories**

Intuitively, we would suppose that the higher the ordering or processing costs, the less frequently orders should be placed. However, the higher the carrying costs of inventory, the more frequently stocks should be ordered. These two features are incorporated in the formula.

4. If we maintain a "safety stock" of inventory to guard against shipping delays, unexpectedly heavy demand, and so on, then average inventories will be higher by this amount, and inventory costs will be higher by CP times this amount. The nature of safety stocks will be considered later in this appendix.

Notice also that if Norgaard's sales had been estimated at 2,000 units, the EOQ would have been 400, while the average inventory would have been 200 units instead of the 140 called for with sales of 1,000 units. Thus, a doubling of sales leads to less than a doubling of inventories. That is, in fact, a general rule: the EOQ increases with the *square root* of sales, so any increase in sales calls for a less-than-proportionate increase in inventories. The financial manager should keep this in mind when he is establishing standards for inventory control.

Extending the EOQ Model to Include "Safety Stocks"

The EOQ model, as we have developed it thus far, assumes that sales can be forecast perfectly and that usage is evenly distributed over the year. Further, the model assumes that orders are placed and received with no delays whatever.

The implications of these assumptions are graphed in Figure A7–1. The Thompson Company, with a demand of 1,000 units per year and an EOQ of 28, places 36 orders each year, or one every 10 days. With a zero beginning and ending inventory balance, the maximum inventory is 28 units and the average is 14 units. The slope of the line in Figure A7–1 measures the daily rate of usage; in this case, 2.8 units of inventory are used each day. The usage line is shown as a step function in the first period, then smoothed in subsequent periods for convenience.

Figure A7–1
Demand Forecast
with Certainty

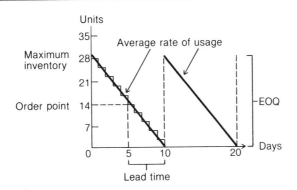

Order Point

We can relax the assumption of instantaneous order and delivery. Let us assume Thompson requires five days to place an order and take delivery. The company, then, must have a five-day stock, or 14 units on hand when it places an order (lead time × daily usage = 5 × 2.8 = 14). The stock that is required to be on hand at time of order is defined as the *order point;* when inventories dip to this point, a new order is placed. If Thompson's inventory control process is automated, the computer will generate an order when the stock on hand falls to 14 units.[5]

Safety Stock

To this point we have assumed that usage (demand) is known with certainty and is uniform throughout time, and that the order lead time never varies. Either or both of these assumptions could be incorrect, so it is necessary to modify the EOQ model to allow for this possibility. This modification generally takes the form of adding a *safety stock* to average inventories.

The safety stock concept is illustrated in Figure A7–2. First, note that the slope of the usage line measures expected daily usage. The company expects a usage of 2.8 units each day, but let us assume a maximum conceivable usage of twice this amount, or 5.6 units each day. It initially orders 42 units, the EOQ of 28 plus a safety stock of 14 units. Subsequently, it reorders the EOQ, 28 units, whenever the inventory level falls to 28 units, the safety stock of 14 units plus the 14 units expected to

Figure A7–2
Demand Forecast
with Safety Stock to
Account for Uncertainty

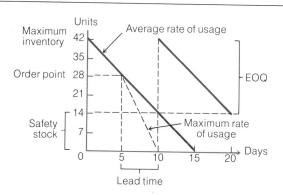

5. We should note that if a new order must be placed before a subsequent order is received—that is, if the normal delivery lead time is longer than the time between orders—then what might be called a "goods-in-transit" inventory builds up. This complicates matters somewhat, but the simplest solution to the problem is to deduct goods in transit when calculating the order point. In other words, the order point would be calculated as

Order point = lead time × daily usage − goods in transit.

This situation arises in the problem at the end of this appendix.

be used while awaiting delivery of the order. Notice that Thompson could, over the five-day delivery period, sell 5.6 units a day ($^{28}/_5$ days = 5.6 units/day), or double its normal expected sales. This maximum rate of usage is shown by the steeper line in Figure A7–2. The event that makes possible this higher maximum rate of usage, of course, is the introduction of a *safety stock* of 14 units.

The safety stock is also useful to guard against delays in receiving orders. The expected delivery time is five days; however, with a 14-unit safety stock, Thompson could maintain sales at the expected rate for an additional five days if shipping delays held up an order.

The actual calculation of optimum safety stocks varies from situation to situation, but it depends upon the following four factors. The optimum safety stock increases with (1) the uncertainty of demand forecasts, (2) the costs in terms of lost sales and lost goodwill that result from inventory shortages, and (3) the probability of delays in receiving shipments; it decreases with (4) the cost of carrying the extra inventory.[6]

Problem

A7–1. Jenjo Sales Company is a retail distributor of living room furniture. As a small firm, with sales under $1,000,000 a year, it has estimated that its cost of capital is a high 16 percent. The firm employs 20 salesmen who average two orders a week. From this information the proprietor, Hank Morris, has estimated his sales volume for the coming year to be 2,000 units. There is some seasonal variation—sales decrease before Christmas, Easter, and Labor Day, as consumers divert their income to purchase of gifts, clothes, and vacations—which Morris ignores in his preliminary inventory planning for the coming year.

In preparing his inventory plans, Morris reviews the following data: Average cost per living room ensemble is $150; depreciation and obsolescence on inventory is estimated at $^1/_2$ of 1 percent a *month*; fire, theft, and all-hazards insurance coverage costs $^1/_2$ of 1 percent a *year*; the current property tax rate is 1 percent a *year*. Each living room set requires 20 square feet of storage space, and warehousing is available at 12 cents a square foot *per month*.

6. For a more detailed discussion of safety stocks, see Magee and Meal, "Inventory Management and Standards." If we knew (1) the probability distribution of usage rates and (2) the probability distribution of order lead times, we could determine joint probabilities of stock-outs with various safety stock levels. With a safety stock of 14 units, for example, the probability of a stock-out for the Thompson Company might be 5 percent. If the safety stock is reduced to 10 units, stock-out probability might rise to 15 percent, while this probability might be reduced to 1 percent with a safety stock of 20 units. If we had additional information on the precise cost of a stock-out, we could compare this with the cost of carrying larger safety stocks. The optimum safety stock is determined at the point where the marginal stock-out cost is equal to the marginal inventory carrying cost.

Morris' cost accountant has provided data revealing that shipping, receiving, and ordering costs are as follows: interoffice memos $4 an order; airmail letter $2 per order (requires four weeks for delivery), or long distance telephone call $7 per order (requires two weeks for delivery). All other shipping, receiving, and handling costs amount to $3 per unit ordered. (Note: this quantity does *not* enter the EOQ calculations.) The desired safety stock is one week's requirements. (Use 50 weeks in a year for your calculations.)

a. Specify values for each element of inventory cost:
   (i) carrying costs per unit
   (ii) fixed ordering costs per unit
b. What is the economic order quantity for each method of ordering?
c. What is the optimal number of orders to be placed for each method of ordering? (Use 50 weeks per year.)
d. Assuming airmail orders, at what inventory level should a reorder be made? (See footnote 5 above before working this part of the problem. Also, note that seven orders, or $3\frac{1}{2}$ weeks of usage, will be in transit at the order point, one order having just been delivered.)
e. What is the total cost of ordering and carrying inventories under each of the two methods? Use the equation $T = CPA + FN + VU$.
f. Why is V omitted from the EOQ solution formula?
g. When should telephone orders be placed with two-week delivery rather than mail orders for four-week delivery? (Use 50 weeks in a year for calculations.)

**Selected
References**

Beranek, William. "Financial Implications of Lot-Size Inventory Models." *Management Science* 13 (Apr. 1967):401–8.

Buchan, Joseph, and Koenigsberg, Ernest. *Scientific Inventory Management.* Englewood Cliffs, N.J.: Prentice-Hall, 1963.

Friedland, Seymour. *The Economics of Corporate Finance.* Englewood Cliffs, N.J.: Prentice-Hall, 1966, chap. 3.

Hadley, G., and Whitin, T. M. *Analysis of Inventory Systems.* Englewood Cliffs, N.J.: Prentice-Hall, 1963.

Magee, John F. "Guides to Inventory Policy, I." *Harvard Business Review* Jan.–Feb. 1956, pp. 34, 49–60.

———. "Guides to Inventory Policy, II." *Harvard Business Review.* Mar.–Apr. 1956, pp. 49–60.

———. "Guides to Inventory Policy, III." *Harvard Business Review.* May–June, 1956, pp. 103–16 and 57–70.

———. and Meal, Harlan C. "Inventory Management and Standards." In *The Treasurer's Handbook,* J. Fred Weston and Maurice B. Goudzwaard, eds. (Homewood, Ill.: Dow Jones-Irwin, 1976) pp. 496–542.

Snyder, Arthur. "Principles of Inventory Management." *Financial Executive* 32 (Apr. 1964).

Starr, Martin K., and Miller, David W. *Inventory Control: Theory and Practice.* Englewood Cliffs, N.J.: Prentice-Hall, 1962.

Vienott, Arthur F., Jr. "The Status of Mathematical Inventory Theory." *Management Science* 12 (July 1966):745–77.

Wagner, Harvey M. *Principles of Operations Research—with Applications to Managerial Decisions.* Englewood Cliffs, N. J.: Prentice-Hall, 1969, chaps. 9 and 19, and app. 2.

Appendix B to Chapter 7
Cash Management Models[1]

Inventory-type models have been constructed to aid the financial manager in determining his firm's optimum cash balances. Four such models—those developed by Baumol, Miller and Orr, Beranek, and White and Norman are presented in this appendix.

Baumol Model

The classic article on cash management by William J. Baumol[2] applies the EOQ model to the cash management problem. Although Baumol's article emphasized the macroeconomic implications for monetary theory, he recognized the implications for business finance and set the stage for further work in this area. In essence, Baumol recognized the fundamental similarities of inventories and cash from a financial viewpoint. In the case of inventories, there are ordering and stock-out costs that make it expensive to keep inventories at a zero level by placing orders for immediate requirements only. But there are also costs involved with *holding* inventories, and an optimal policy balances off the opposing costs of ordering and holding inventory.

With cash and securities the situation is very similar. There are order costs in the form of clerical work and brokerage fees when making transfers between the cash account and an investment portfolio. On the other side of the coin, there are holding costs consisting of interest foregone when large cash balances are held to avoid the costs of making transfers. Further, there are also costs associated with running out of cash, just as there are in the case of inventories. As with inventories, there is an optimal cash balance that minimizes these costs.

In its most operational form, the Baumol model assumes that a firm's cash balances behave, over time, in a sawtooth manner, as shown in Figure B7–1. Receipts come in at periodic intervals, such as time 0, 1, 2, 3, and so forth; expenditures occur continuously throughout the periods. Since the model assumes certainty, the firm can adopt an optimal policy that calls for investing I dollars in a short-term investment port-

1. We would like to acknowledge the assistance of Richard A. Samuelson in the preparation of this appendix.

2. William J. Baumol, "The Transactions Demand for Cash: An Inventory Theoretic Approach," *Quarterly Journal of Economics* 66 (Nov. 1952), pp. 545–56.

Figure B7-1
Baumol's Pattern
of Receipts and
Expenditures

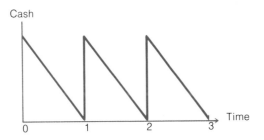

folio at the beginning of each period, then withdrawing C dollars from the portfolio and placing it in the cash account at regular intervals during the period. The model must, of course, take into account both the costs of investment transactions and the costs of holding cash balances.

The decision variables facing the financial manager for a single period can be illustrated in Figure B7-2. At the beginning of the period, he has an amount of cash equal to T. A portion of the initial cash, $R = T - I$, is retained in the form of cash, and the balance, I, is invested in a portfolio of short-term liquid assets that earns a rate of return, i. The retained cash, R, is sufficient to meet expenditures during the period from t_0 to t_1. At time t_1, an additional C dollars will be transferred from the investment portfolio to the cash account to cover expenditures for the period from t_1 to t_2; C dollars will again be withdrawn at time t_2 and t_3. At t_4, receipts of T dollars again flow into the cash account, and the same process is repeated during the following period.

Figure B7-2
Baumol's Transfers
from Securities to
Cash

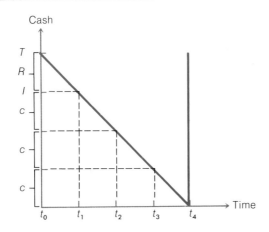

If the disbursements are assumed to be continuous, then $R = T - I$ dollars withheld from the initial cash receipt will serve to meet payments during $(T - I)/T$, a fraction of the period between receipts. Further, since the average cash holding for that time will be $(T - I)/2$, the interest cost (opportunity cost) of withholding that money will be

$$\left(\frac{T - I}{2}\right) i \left(\frac{T - I}{T}\right),$$

where i is the interest rate on invested funds. A brokerage fee is required to invest the I dollars invested, and this fee is equal to $b_a + k_a I$, where b_a and k_a are fixed and variable costs, respectively, of making deposits (investments).

The cost of obtaining cash for the remainder of the period is found, similarly, to be

$$\left(\frac{C}{2}\right) i \left(\frac{I}{T}\right) + (b_w + k_w C) \frac{I}{C}.$$

The first term is the interest (opportunity) cost of holding the average amount $C/2$ of cash over the subperiod, and the second term is the brokerage cost of making withdrawals from the investment account.

Combining these component costs, the total cost function is given by

$$Z = \left(\frac{T - I}{2}\right) i \left(\frac{T - I}{T}\right) + b_a + k_a I + \left(\frac{C}{2}\right) i \left(\frac{I}{T}\right) + (b_w + k_w C) \frac{I}{C}. \tag{B7-1}$$

The optimal value for C is found by differentiating Equation B7–1 with respect to C and setting the derivative equal to zero. This gives

$$C = \sqrt{\frac{2 b_w T}{i}}. \tag{B7-2}$$

R, the optimum cash balance to withhold from the initial receipt, is found by differentiating Equation B7–1 with respect to I, obtaining

$$R = T - I = C + T \left(\frac{k_w + k_a}{i}\right). \tag{B7-3}$$

The financial manager, in order to minimize costs, will then withhold R dollars from the initial receipts to cover expenditures for the beginning of the period and will withdraw C dollars from his investment portfolio I/C times per period.

While the Baumol model captures the essential elements of the problem, its restrictive assumptions about the behavior of cash inflows and outflows are probably more applicable to an individual's situation than to a business firm's. For the firm, inflows are likely to be less lumpy, and outflows are likely to be less smooth. Instead, the behavior of cash balances might resemble the pattern of Figure B7–3. Daily changes in the cash balance may be up or down, following an irregular and somewhat unpredictable pattern. When the balance drifts upward for some length of time, a point is reached at which the financial officer orders a

Figure B7–3
Realistic Pattern
of Receipts and
Expenditures for a
Firm

transfer of cash to the investment portfolio, and the cash balance is returned to some lower level. When disbursements exceed receipts for some period of time, investments are sold and a transfer is made to the cash account to restore the cash balance to a higher level. If this particular behavior is typical, then the certainty assumptions of the Baumol model are too restrictive to make it operational.

Miller-Orr Model

Merton Miller and Daniel Orr[3] expanded the Baumol model by incorporating a stochastic generating process for periodic changes in cash balances so that the cash pattern resembles that shown in Figure B7–3. In contrast to the completely deterministic assumptions of the Baumol model, Miller and Orr assume that net cash flows behave as if they were generated by a "stationary random walk." This means that changes in the cash balance over a given period are random, in both size and direction, and form a normal distribution as the number of periods observed increases. The model allows for a priori knowledge, however, that changes at a certain time have a greater probability of being either positive or negative.

The Miller-Orr model is designed to determine the time and size of transfers between an investment account and the cash account accord-

3. Merton H. Miller and Daniel Orr, "A Model for the Demand for Money by Firms," *Quarterly Journal of Economics* 80 (August 1966), pp. 413–35.

ing to a decision process illustrated in Figure B7–4. Changes in cash balances are allowed to go up until they reach some level h at time t_1; they are then reduced to level z, the "return point," by investing $h - z$ dollars in the investment portfolio. Next, the cash balance wanders aimlessly until it reaches the minimum balance point, r, at t_2, at which time enough earning assets are sold to return the cash balance to its return point, z. The model is based on a cost function similar to Baumol's, and it includes elements for the cost of making transfers to and from cash for the opportunity cost of holding cash. The upper limit, h, which cash balances should not be allowed to surpass, and the return point, z, to which the balance is returned after every transfer either to or from the cash account, are computed so as to minimize the cost function. The lower limit is assumed to be given, and it could be the minimum balance required by the banks in which the cash is deposited.

Figure B7–4
Miller-Orr Cash
Management Model

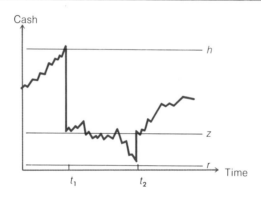

The cost function for the Miller-Orr model can be stated as $E(c) = bE(N)/T + iE(M)$, where $E(N)$ = the expected number of transfers between cash and the investment portfolio during the planning period; b = the cost per transfer; T is the number of days in the planning period; $E(M)$ = the expected average daily balance; and i = the daily rate of interest earned on the investments. The objective is to minimize $E(c)$ by choice of the variables h and z, the upper control limit and the return point, respectively.

The solution as derived by Miller and Orr becomes

$$z^* = \left(\frac{3b\sigma^2}{4i}\right)^{1/3}$$

(B7–4)

$$h^* = 3z^*$$

for the special case where p (the probability that cash balances will increase) equals .5, and q (the probability that cash balances will decrease) equals .5. The variance of the daily changes in the cash balance is represented by σ^2. As would be expected, a higher transfer cost, b, or variance, σ^2, would imply a greater spread between the upper and lower control limits. In the special case where $p = q = \frac{1}{2}$, the upper control limit will always be three times greater than the return point.

Miller and Orr tested their model by applying it to nine months of data on the daily cash balances and purchases and sales of short-term securities of a large industrial company. When the decisions of the model were compared to those actually made by the treasurer of the company, the model was found to produce an average daily cash balance that was about 40 percent *lower* ($160,000 for the model and $275,-000 for the treasurer). Looking at it from another side, the model would have been able to match the $275,000 average daily balance with only 80 transactions as compared to the treasurer's 112 actual transactions.

As with most inventory control models, its performance depends not only on how well the conditional predictions (in this case the expected number of transfers and the expected average cash balance) conform to actuality, but also on how well the parameters are estimated. In this model, b, the transfer cost, is sometimes difficult to estimate. In the study made by Miller and Orr, the order costs included such components as "(a) making two or more long-distance phone calls plus 15 minutes to a half-hour of the assistant treasurer's time, (b) typing up and carefully checking an authorization letter with four copies, (c) carrying the original of the letter to be signed by the treasurer, and (d) carrying the copies to the controller's office where special accounts are opened, the entries are posted and further checks of the arithmetic are made."[4] These clerical procedures were thought to be in the magnitude of $20 to $50 per order. In the application of their model, however, Miller and Orr did not rely on their estimate for order costs; instead they tested the model using a series of "assumed" order costs until the model used the same number of transactions as did the treasurer. They could then determine the order cost implied by the treasurer's own action. The results were then used to evaluate the treasurer's performance in managing the cash balances, and, as such, provided valuable information to the treasurer.

The treasurer found, for example, that his action in purchasing securities was often inconsistent. Too often he made small-lot purchases

4. Merton H. Miller and Daniel Orr, *An Application of Control Limit Models to the Management of Corporate Cash Balances*, Proceedings of the Conference on Financial Research and Its Implications for Management, ed. Alexander A. Robichek (New York: Wiley, 1967).

well below the minimum of $h - z$ computed by the model, while at other times he allowed cash balances to drift to as much as double the upper control limit before making a purchase. If it did no more than give the treasurer some perspective about his buying and selling activities, the model was used successfully.[5]

Beranek Model

William Beranek has devoted a chapter in his text, *Analysis for Financial Decisions*,[6] to the problem of determining the optimal allocation of available funds between the cash balance and marketable securities. His approach differs from Baumol's in that he includes a probability distribution for expected cash flows and a cost function for the loss of cash discounts and deterioration of credit rating when the firm is caught short of cash. The decision variable in Beranek's model is the allocation of funds between cash and investments at the beginning of the period. Withdrawals from investment are assumed possible only at the end of each planning period.

According to Beranek, it is more helpful for the analysis of cash management problems to regard cash *disbursements* as being directly controllable by management and relatively lumpy, and to regard *receipts* as being uncontrollable and continuous. In the certainty case this pattern of cash balance behavior would be the reverse of the sawtooth pattern assumed by Baumol, and it would look similar to the pattern illustrated in Figure B7–5. To rationalize this approach one can argue that institutional customs and arrangements might cause cash outflows to be concentrated at periodic intervals. Wages and salaries are ordinarily paid

Figure B7–5
Beranek's Pattern of Receipts and Expenditures

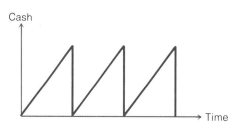

5. For a cash planning approach related to credit decisions by the use of a financial simulation model, see Bernell K. Stone, "Cash Planning and Credit-Line Determination with a Financial Statement Simulator: A Cash Report on Short-Term Financial Planning," *Journal of Financial and Quantitative Analysis* 8 (Nov. 1973), pp. 711–30.
6. William Beranek, *Analysis for Financial Decisions* (Homewood, Ill.: Irwin, 1963), pp. 345–87.

weekly or monthly, credit terms for merchandise purchases may allow
payment on the tenth and final days of the month, and other significant
outflows such as tax and dividend payments will be concentrated at
regular intervals. Insofar as cash outflows are controllable and recur in a
cyclical manner, the financial manager can predict his needs for cash
over a planning period and can invest a portion of the funds that are not
expected to be needed during this period.

In Beranek's model, the financial manager is regarded as having total
resources of k dollars available at the beginning of a planning period.
He expects his net cash drain (receipts less disbursements) at the end of
the period to be y dollars (either positive or negative), with a probability distribution $g(y)$. His objective of maximizing returns by investment
in securities is constrained by transactions costs and the risk of being
short of cash when funds are needed for expenditures. "Short costs" are
regarded by Beranek as consisting of cash discounts forgone and the
deterioration of the firm's credit rating when it is unable to meet payments in time. It might be more realistic, however, to think of "short
costs" as the cost of borrowing on a line of credit, since the company
would undoubtedly prefer short-term borrowing to foregoing cash discounts or allowing its credit rating to deteriorate.

Given the probability distribution of net cash flows, the costs of running short of cash, and the opportunity cost of holding cash balances,
Beranek develops a cost function and differentiates it to find the optimal initial cash balance, or the amount of cash that should be on hand at
the start of the period. His solution calls for setting the cash balance at a
level such that, if this critical level is set, the cumulative probability of
running short of cash is equal to the ratio d/a, where d = net return on
the investment portfolio and a = incremental cost of being short $1 of
cash. Stated in words, this means that the financial manager should
continue shifting resources from the opening cash balance to securities
until the expectation that the ending cash balance will be below the
critical minimum is equal to the ratio of the incremental net return per
dollar of investment to the incremental short cost per dollar.

**White and
Norman
Model**

D. J. White and J. M. Norman[7] developed a model for an English insurance company similar in spirit to the Beranek model. Investment decisions are assumed to be considered periodically, and cash inflows from
premiums and outflows for claims and expenses are assumed to fluc-

---

7. D. J. White and J. M. Norman, "Control of Cash Reserves," *Operational Research Quarterly* 16, no.
3 (September 1965).

tuate randomly according to some known distribution. In addition, another cash outflow for "call-offs" by the stockbrokers is assumed to have an independent distribution function. A penalty rate on overdrafts (borrowings), analogous to Beranek's short-cost function, is also included in the model, while transactions costs are ignored (or implicitly considered in the net rate of return on investments). The opening cash balance that maximizes expected wealth at the end of the period is the relevant decision variable. The optimal solution is a function of Beranek's d, the incremental return per dollar of investment, and the interest rate on overdrafts.

A Comparison of the Models

The models described in this appendix differ primarily in the emphasis given to various costs affecting their solutions. The Baumol and Miller-Orr models give critical emphasis to the costs arising from transfers between the cash account and the investment portfolio. They ignore the alternative of borrowing and concentrate on the liquidation of investments to meet the needs for cash outflows. The Beranek and White-Norman models, on the other hand, give critical emphasis to the costs arising from the shortage of cash (the cost of borrowing, from one viewpoint), while transactions costs are only indirectly considered. The latter models ignore the alternatives of liquidating investments to meet cash needs. A model that directly incorporates both the possibility of borrowing and the possibility of holding a portfolio of liquid assets would be desirable, since it is not clear that liquidation of investments would always be preferable to borrowing or vice versa.

Of all the models, the Miller-Orr version appears to be the easiest to implement, if for no other reason than that its decision rules are so simple. Decision models are more likely to be used when their application is easily understood by management. In addition, the Miller-Orr decision model's planning period covers a longer period of time, so it would not have to be revised as often as the Beranek and White-Norman models. In the Beranek and White-Norman versions, information must be fed into the model and a decision derived each time a transfer between cash and securities is being considered. While this must be counted as a disadvantage of these models, it could result in better decisions by making the models more responsive to conditions existing at the time decisions are made.

The Miller-Orr model has an element of flexibility, however, that should not be overlooked. Expectations that cash balances are more likely to either increase or decrease over a given period can be incorporated into the calculation of the optimal values for the decision variables. Thus, if a business is subject to seasonal trends, the optimal control limits can be adjusted for each season by using different values for p and q, the probabilities that cash will increase and decrease, respectively.

The Miller-Orr model is built on the assumption that cash balances behave as if they were generated by a random walk. To the extent that this assumption is erroneous, the model would be of little use to management. If the timing of cash outflows (and perhaps even cash inflows) can be controlled significantly by management, then a model of the Beranek or White-Norman type may be more suitable. In this case, management should not have too much difficulty in forming the subjective probability distributions that are needed for these models. In reality, it would probably be true that cash flows are partly random and partly controllable, so the applicability of any of the models can be determined only by testing them with actual data.

It should be remembered that decision models of the type discussed in this appendix are not intended to be applied blindly. There are, of course, difficulties in estimating parameters and probabilities, as has been pointed out. But even more important, there is often information available to the financial manager that is not directly incorporated into the model. Thus a model, acting ignorantly and unaware of other relevant information, might provide completely erroneous advice. On the other hand, despite their restrictive assumptions and errors, decision models often perform very well if they capture the essential elements in a decision problem. They should not, however, be used as the final answer to any particular decision; rather, cash management models should be used as a guide to intelligent decision-making, tempered with the manager's own good judgment.

Selected References

Archer, Stephen H. "A Model for the Determination of Firm Cash Balance." *Journal of Financial and Quantitative Analysis* 1 (Mar. 1966):1–11.

Baumol, William J. "The Transactions Demand for Cash: An Inventory Theoretic Approach." *Quarterly Journal of Economics* 65 (Nov. 1952):545–56.

Budin, Morris, and Van Handel, Robert J. "A Rule-of-Thumb Theory of Cash Holdings by Firm." *Journal of Financial and Quantitative Analysis* 10 (Mar. 1975):85–108.

Calman, Robert F. *Linear Programming and Cash Management/CASH ALPHA.* Cambridge, Mass.: M.I.T., 1968.

Constantinides, George M. "Stochastic Cash Management with Fixed and Proportional Transaction Costs." *Management Science* 22 (Aug. 1976):1320–31.

Daellenbach, Hans G. "Are Cash Management Optimization Models Worthwhile?" *Journal of Financial and Quantitative Analysis* 9 (Sept. 1974):607–26.

Eppen, Gary D., and Fama, Eugene F. "Cash Balance and Simple Dynamic Portfolio Problems with Proportional Costs." *International Economic Review* 10 (June 1969):110–33.

Miller, Merton H., and Orr, Daniel. "A Model of the Demand for Money by Firms." *Quarterly Journal of Economics* 80 (Aug. 1966):413–35.

Orgler, Yair E. *Cash Management.* Belmont, Calif.: Wadsworth Publishing Co., 1970.

Sethi, Suresh P., and Thompson, Gerald L. "Application of Mathematical Control Theory to Finance: Modeling Simple Dynamic Cash Balance Problems." *Journal of Financial and Quantitative Analysis* 5 (Dec. 1970):381–94.

8 Major Sources and Forms of Short-term Financing

In Chapter 6 we discussed the maturity structure of the firm's debt and showed how this structure can affect both risk and expected returns. However, a variety of short-term credits are available to the firm, and the financial manager must know the advantages and disadvantages of each. Accordingly, in the present chapter we take up the main forms of short-term credit, considering both the characteristics and the sources of this credit.

Short-term credit is defined as *debt originally scheduled for repayment within one year*. We discuss the three major sources of funds with short maturities in this chapter. Ranked in descending order by volume of credit supplied to business, the main sources of short-term financing are (1) trade credit between firms, (2) loans from commercial banks, and (3) commercial paper.

Trade Credit[1]

In the ordinary course of events, a firm buys its supplies and materials on credit from other firms, recording the debt as an *account payable*. Accounts payable, or *trade credit*, as it is commonly called, is the largest single category of short-term credit, and it represents about 40 percent of the current liabilities of non-financial corporations. This percentage is somewhat larger for small firms; because small companies may not qualify for financing from other sources, they rely rather heavily on trade credit.

Trade credit is a "spontaneous" source of financing in that it arises from ordinary business transactions. For example, suppose a firm makes average purchases of $2,000 a day on terms of net 30. On the average it will owe 30 times $2,000, or $60,000, to its suppliers. If its sales and, consequently, its purchases, double, accounts payable will also double to $120,000. The firm will have spontaneously generated an additional $60,000 of financing. Similarly, if the terms of credit are ex-

---

1. In Chapter 7 we discussed trade credit from the point of view of minimizing investment in current assets. In the present chapter we look at "the other side of the coin," viewing trade credit as a *source* of financing rather than as a *use* of financing. In Chapter 7, the use of trade credit by our customers resulted in an asset investment called *accounts receivable*. In the present chapter, the use of trade credit gives rise to short-term obligations, generally called *accounts payable*.

tended from 30 to 40 days, accounts payable will expand from $60,000 to $80,000; thus, lengthening the credit period, as well as expanding sales and purchases, generates additional financing.

Credit Terms

The terms of sales, or *credit terms*, describe the payment obligation of the buyer. In the following discussion we outline the four main factors that influence the length of credit terms.

Economic Nature of Product. Commodities with high sales turnover are sold on relatively short credit terms; the buyer resells the product rapidly, generating cash that enables him to pay the supplier. Groceries have a high turnover, but perishability also plays a role. The credit extended for fresh fruits and vegetables might run from five to ten days, whereas the credit extended on canned fruits and vegetables would more likely be 15 to 30 days. Terms for items that have a slow retail turnover, such as jewelry, may run six months or longer.

Seller Circumstances. Financially weak sellers must require cash or exceptionally short credit terms. For example, farmers sell livestock to meatpacking companies on a cash basis. In many industries, variations in credit terms can be used as a sales promotion device. Although the use of credit as a selling device could endanger sound credit management, the practice does occur, especially when the seller's industry has excess capacity. Also, a large seller could use his position to impose relatively short credit terms. However, the reverse appears more often in practice; that is, financially strong sellers are suppliers of funds to small firms.

Buyer Circumstances. In general, financially sound retailers who sell on credit may, in turn, receive slightly longer terms. Some classes of retailers regarded as selling in particularly risky areas (such as clothing) receive extended credit terms, but they are offered large discounts to encourage early payment.

Cash Discounts. A cash discount is a reduction in price based on payment within a specified period. The costs of not taking cash discounts often exceed the rate of interest at which the buyer can borrow, so it is important that a firm be cautious in its use of trade credit as a source of financing—it could be quite expensive. If the firm borrows and takes the cash discount, the period during which accounts payable remain on the books is reduced. The effective length of credit is thus influenced by the size of discounts offered.

Illustrative Credit Terms. Credit terms typically express the amount of the cash discount and the date of its expiration, as well as the final due date. Earlier, we noticed that one of the most frequently encountered terms is 2/10, net 30. (If payment is made within ten days of the invoice date, a 2 percent cash discount is allowed. If the cash discount is not taken, payment is due 30 days after the date of invoice.) The cost of not taking cash discounts can be substantial, as shown here.[2]

Credit Terms	Cost of Credit if Cash Discount Not Taken (Percent)
1/10, net 20	36.36
1/10, net 30	18.18
2/10, net 20	73.47
2/10, net 30	36.73

Concept of "Net Credit"

Trade credit has double-edged significance for the firm. It is a source of credit for financing purchases, and it is a use of funds to the extent that the firm finances credit sales to customers. For example, if, on the average, a firm sells $3,000 of goods a day with an average collection period of 40 days, at any balance sheet date it will have accounts receivable of approximately $120,000.

If the same firm buys $2,000 worth of materials a day and the balance is outstanding for 20 days, accounts payable will average $40,000. *The firm is extending net credit of $80,000, the difference between accounts receivable and accounts payable.*

Large firms and well-financed firms of all sizes tend to be net suppliers of trade credit; small firms and undercapitalized firms of all sizes tend to be net users of trade credit. It is impossible to generalize about whether it is better to be a net supplier or a net user of trade credit—the choice depends upon the firm's own circumstances and conditions, and the various costs and benefits of receiving and using trade credit must be analyzed as described here and in Chapter 6.

Advantages of Trade Credit as a Source of Financing

Trade credit, a customary part of doing business in most industries, is convenient and informal. A firm that does not qualify for credit from a financial institution may receive trade credit because previous experience has familiarized the seller with the credit-worthiness of his cus-

---

2. The method of calculating the effective interest rate on accounts payable was described in Chapter 7.

tomer. As the seller knows the merchandising practices of the industry, he is usually in a good position to judge the capacity of his customer and the risk of selling to him on credit. The amount of trade credit fluctuates with the buyer's purchases, subject to any credit limits that may be operative.

Whether trade credit costs more or less than other forms of financing is a moot question. Sometimes trade credit can be surprisingly expensive to the buyer. The user often does not have any alternative forms of financing available, and the costs to the buyer may be commensurate with the risks to the seller. But in some instances trade credit is used simply because the user does not realize how expensive it is. In such circumstances, careful financial analysis may lead to the substitution of alternative forms of financing for trade credit.

At the other extreme, trade credit may represent a virtual subsidy or sales promotion device offered by the seller. The authors know, for example, of cases where manufacturers quite literally supplied *all* the financing for new firms by selling on credit terms substantially longer than those of the new company. In one instance a manufacturer, eager to obtain a dealership in a particular area, made a loan to the new company to cover operating expenses during the initial phases and geared the payment of accounts payable to cash receipts. Even in such instances, however, the buying firm must be careful that it is not really paying a hidden financing cost in the form of higher product prices than could be obtained elsewhere. Extending credit involves a cost to the selling firm, and this firm may well be raising its own prices to offset the "free" credit it extends.

Short-term Financing by Commercial Banks

Commercial bank lending appears on the balance sheet as *notes payable* and is second in importance to trade credit as a source of short-term financing. Banks occupy a pivotal position in the short-term and intermediate-term money markets. Their influence is greater than appears from the dollar amounts they lend because the banks provide nonspontaneous funds. As the financing needs of the firm increase, it requests the banks to provide the additional funds. If the request is denied, often the alternative is to slow down the rate of growth or to cut back operations.

Characteristics of Loans from Commercial Banks

In the following sections, the main characteristics of lending patterns of commercial banks are briefly described.

Forms of Loans. A single loan obtained from a bank by a business firm is not different in principle from a loan obtained by an individual. In fact, it is often difficult to distinguish a bank loan to a small business from a personal loan. A loan is obtained by signing a conventional promissory note. Repayment is made in a lump sum at maturity (when the note is due) or in installments throughout the life of the loan.

A *line of credit* is a formal or an informal understanding between the bank and the borrower concerning the maximum loan balance the bank will allow the borrower. For example, a bank loan officer may indicate to a financial manager that the bank regards his firm as "good" for up to $80,000 for the forthcoming year. Subsequently, the manager signs a promissory note for $15,000 for 90 days — he is said to be "taking down" $15,000 of his total line of credit. This amount is credited to the firm's checking account at the bank. At maturity, the checking account will be charged for the amount of the loan. Interest may be deducted in advance or may be paid at the maturity of the loan. Before repayment of the $15,000, the firm may borrow additional amounts up to a total of $80,000.

A more formal procedure may be followed if the firm is quite large. To illustrate, Chrysler Corporation arranged a line of credit for over $100 million with a group of banks. The banks were formally committed to lend Chrysler the funds if they were needed. Chrysler, in turn, paid a commitment fee of approximately one-quarter of 1 percent of the unused balance of the commitment to compensate the banks for making the funds available.

Size of Customers. Banks make loans to firms of all sizes. The bulk of loans from commercial banks by dollar amount is obtained by firms with total assets of $5 million and more. But, by number of loans, firms with total assets of $50,000 and less account for about 40 percent of bank loans.

Maturity. Commercial banks concentrate on the short-term lending market. Short-term loans make up about two-thirds of bank loans by dollar amount, whereas "term loans" (loans with maturities longer than one year) make up only one-third.

Security. If a potential borrower is a questionable credit risk, or if his financing needs exceed the amount that the loan officer of the bank considers to be prudent on an unsecured basis, some form of security is required. More than one-half the dollar value of bank loans is secured; the forms of security are described later in this chapter. In terms of the number of bank loans, two-thirds are secured or endorsed by a third party who guarantees payment of the loan in the event the borrower defaults.

Compensating Balances. Banks typically require that a regular borrower maintain an average checking account balance equal to 15 or 20 percent of the outstanding loan. These balances, which are commonly called *compensating balances*, are a method of raising the effective interest rate. For example, if a firm needs $80,000 to pay off outstanding obligations, but must maintain a 20 percent compensating balance, it must borrow $100,000 to be able to obtain the required $80,000. If the stated interest rate is 5 percent, the effective cost is actually 6¼ percent —$5,000 divided by $80,000 equals 6.25 percent.[3] These *loan* compensating balances are, of course, added to any *service* compensating balances (discussed in Chapter 6) that the firm's bank may require.

Repayment of Bank Loans. Because most bank deposits are subject to withdrawal on demand, commercial banks seek to prevent firms from using bank credit for permanent financing. A bank may therefore require its borrowers to "clean up" their short-term bank loans for at least one month each year. If a firm is unable to become free of bank debt at least part of each year, it is using bank financing for permanent needs and should develop additional sources of long-term or permanent financing.

Cost of Commercial Bank Loans. Most loans from commercial banks have recently cost from 6 to 12 percent, with the effective rate depending upon the characteristics of the firm and the level of interest rates in the economy. If the firm can qualify as a "prime risk" because of its size and financial strength, the rate of interest will be one-half to three-quarters of 1 percent above the rediscount rate charged by federal reserve banks to commercial banks. On the other hand, a small firm with below-average financial ratios may be required to provide collateral security and to pay an effective rate of interest of more than 12 percent.

"Regular" Interest. Determination of the effective, or true, rate of interest on a loan depends on the stated rate of interest and the method of charging interest by the lender. If the interest is paid at the maturity of the loan, the stated rate of interest is the effective rate of interest. For example, on a $10,000 loan for one year at 7 percent, the interest is $700.

---

3. Note however, that the compensating balance is generally set as a minimum monthly *average:* if the firm would maintain this average anyway, the compensating balance requirement does not entail higher effective rates.

"Regular" loan, interest paid at maturity:

$$\frac{\text{interest}}{\text{borrowed amount}} = \frac{\$700}{\$10,000} = 7\%$$

Discounted Interest. If the bank deducts the interest in advance (*discounts* the loan), the effective rate of interest is increased. On the $10,000 loan for one year at 7 percent, the discount is $700, and the borrower obtains the use of only $9,300. The effective rate of interest is 7.5 percent versus 7 percent on a "regular" loan:

$$\text{Discounted loan:} \frac{\text{interest}}{\text{borrowed amount} - \text{interest}} = \frac{\$700}{\$9,300} = 7.5\%.$$

Installment Loan. If the loan is repaid in 12 monthly installments but the interest is calculated on the original balance, then the effective rate of interest is even higher. The borrower has the full amount of the money only during the first month, and by the last month he has already paid eleven-twelfths of the loan. Thus our hypothetical borrower pays $700 for the use of about half the amount he receives. The amount received is $10,000 or $9,300, depending upon the method of charging interest, but the *average* amount outstanding during the year is only $5,000 or $4,650. If interest is paid at maturity, the approximate effective rate on an installment loan is calculated as follows:

$$\text{Interest rate on original amount of installment loan} = \frac{\$700}{\$5,000} = 14\%.$$

Under the discounting method, the effective cost of the installment loan would be approximately 15 percent:

$$\text{Interest rate on discounted installment loan} = \frac{\$700}{\$4,650} = 15.05\%.$$

The point to note here is that interest is paid on the *original* amount of the loan, not on the amount actually outstanding (the declining balance), and this causes the effective interest rate to be approximately double the stated rate. Interest is calculated by the installment method on most consumer loans (for example, automobile loans), but it is not often used for business loans larger than about $5,000.

Choice of Bank or Banks

Banks have direct relations with their borrowers. There is much personal association over the years, and the business problems of the borrower are frequently discussed. Thus, the bank often provides informal management counseling services. A potential borrower seeking bank relations should recognize the important differences among banks, which are considered in the following discussion.

1. Banks have different basic policies toward risk. Some banks are inclined to follow relatively conservative lending practices; others engage in what are properly termed "creative banking practices." The policies reflect partly the personalities of officers of the bank and partly the characteristics of the bank's deposit liabilities. Thus a bank with fluctuating deposit liabilities in a static community will tend to be a conservative lender. A bank whose deposits are growing with little interruption may follow "liberal" credit policies. A large bank with broad diversification over geographical regions or among industries served can obtain the benefit of combining and averaging risks. Thus, marginal credit risks that might be unacceptable to a small bank or to a specialized unit bank can be pooled by a branch banking system to reduce the overall risks of a group of marginal accounts.

2. Some bank loan officers are active in providing counsel and in stimulating development loans with firms in their early and formative years. Certain banks have specialized departments to make loans to firms expected to become growth firms. The personnel of these departments can provide much counseling to customers.

3. Banks differ in the extent to which they will support the activities of the borrower in bad times. This characteristic is referred to as the degree of *loyalty* of the banks. Some banks may put great pressure on a business to liquidate its loans when the firm's outlook becomes clouded, whereas others will stand by the firm and work diligently to help it attain a more favorable condition.

4. Another characteristic by which banks differ is the degree of deposit stability. Instability arises not only from fluctuations in the level of deposits but also from the composition of deposits. Deposits can take the form of *demand deposits* (checking accounts) or *time deposits* (savings accounts, certificates of deposit, Christmas clubs). Total deposits tend to be more stable when time deposits are substantial. Differences in deposit stability go a long way toward explaining differences in the extent to which the banks are willing or able to help the borrower work himself out of difficulties or even crises.

5. Banks differ greatly in the degree of loan specialization. Larger banks have separate departments specializing in different kinds of loans, such as real estate, installment loans, and commercial loans, among others. Within these broad categories there may be a specialization by line of business, such as steel, machinery, or textiles. The strengths of smaller banks are likely to reflect the nature of the business and the economic environment in which the banks operate. They tend to become specialists in specfic lines, such as oil, construction, and agri-

culture, to name a few. The borrower can obtain more creative cooperation and more active support if he goes to the bank that has the greatest
experience and familiarity with his particular type of business. The financial manager should therefore choose his bank with care. A bank
that is excellent for one firm may be unsatisfactory for another.

6. The size of a bank can be an important characteristic. Since the
maximum loan a bank can make to any one customer is generally limited to 10 percent of capital accounts (capital stock plus retained earnings), it will generally not be appropriate for large firms to develop borrowing relationships with small banks.

7. With the heightened competition between commercial banks and
other financial institutions, the aggressiveness of banks has increased.
Modern commercial banks now offer a wide range of financial and business services. Most large banks have business development departments that provide counseling to firms and serve as intermediaries on a
wide variety of their requirements.

Commercial Paper

Commercial paper consists of promissory notes of *large* firms and is
sold primarily to other business firms, insurance companies, pension
funds, and banks. Although the amounts of commercial paper outstanding are much smaller than bank loans outstanding, this form of
financing has grown rapidly in recent years.

Maturity and Cost

Maturities of commercial paper generally vary from two to six months,
with an average of about five months. The rates on prime commercial
paper vary, but they are generally about one-half of 1 percent below
those on prime business loans. And, since compensating balances are
not required for commercial paper, the *effective* cost differential is still
wider.[4]

Use

The use of the open market for commercial paper is restricted to a com-
paratively small number of concerns that are exceptionally good credit
risks. Dealers prefer to handle the paper of concerns whose net worth is
$10 million or more and whose annual borrowing exceeds $1 million.

---

4. However, this factor is offset to some extent by the fact that firms issuing commercial paper are
sometimes required by commercial paper dealers to have unused bank lines of credit to back up their
outstanding commercial paper, and fees must be paid on these lines.

**Appraisal of
Use**

The commercial paper market has some significant advantages. (1) It permits the broadest and the most advantageous distribution of paper. (2) It provides more funds at lower rates than do other methods. (3) The borrower avoids the inconvenience and expense of financing arrangements with a number of institutions, each of which requires a compensating balance.(4) Publicity and prestige accrue to the borrower as his product and his paper become more widely known. (5) Finally, the commerical paper dealer frequently offers valuable advice to his clients.

A basic limitation of the commercial paper market is that the size of the funds available is limited to the excess liquidity that corporations, the main suppliers of funds, may have at any particular time. Another disadvantage is that a debtor who is in temporary financial difficulty receives little consideration because commercial paper dealings are impersonal. Bank relations, on the other hand, are much more personal; a bank is much more likely to help a good customer weather a temporary storm than is a commercial paper dealer.[5]

**Use of
Security in
Short-term
Financing**

Given a choice, it is ordinarily better to borrow on an unsecured basis, as the bookkeeping costs of secured loans are often high. However, it frequently happens that a potential borrower's credit rating is not sufficiently strong to justify the loan. If the loan can be secured by the borrower's putting up some form of collateral to be claimed by the lender in the event of default, then the lender may extend credit to an otherwise unacceptable firm. Similarly, a firm that could borrow on an unsecured basis may elect to use security if it finds that this will induce lenders to quote a lower interest rate.

Several different kinds of collateral can be employed—marketable stocks or bonds, land or buildings, equipment, inventory, and accounts receivable. Marketable securities make excellent collateral, but few firms hold portfolios of stocks and bonds. Similarly, real property (land and buildings) and equipment are good forms of collateral, but they are

5. This point was emphasized dramatically in the aftermath of the Penn-Central bankruptcy. Penn-Central had a large amount of commercial paper that went into default and embarrassed corporate treasurers who had been holding the paper as part of their liquidity reserves. Immediately after the bankruptcy, the commercial paper market dried up to a large extent, and some companies that had relied heavily on this market found themselves under severe liquidity pressure as their commercial paper matured and could not be refunded. Chrysler, for example, had to seek bank loans of over $500 million because it could not sell commercial paper for a time. Without adequate bank lines, Chrysler might well have been forced into bankruptcy itself, even though it was basically sound, because of the "Penn-Central panic." Incidentally, the Federal Reserve Board recognized that many other firms would be in the same position as Chrysler, so the Fed expanded bank reserves in order to enable the banking system to take up the slack caused by the withdrawal of funds from the commercial paper market.

generally used as security for long-term loans. The bulk of secured short-term business borrowing involves the pledge of short-term assets — accounts receivable or inventories.

In the past, state laws varied greatly with regard to the use of security in financing. In the late 1960s, however, all states passed a *Uniform Commercial Code*, which standardized and simplified the procedure for establishing loan security.

The heart of the Uniform Commercial Code is the *Security Agreement*, a standardized document, or form, on which the specific assets that are pledged are stated. The assets can be items of equipment, accounts receivable, or inventories. Procedures for financing under the Uniform Commercial Code are described in the following sections.

Financing Accounts Receivable

Accounts receivable financing involves either the *assigning of receivables* or the *selling of receivables (factoring)*. The *pledging of accounts receivable* is characterized by the fact that the lender not only has a lien on the receivables but also has recourse to the borrower (seller); if the person or the firm that bought the goods does not pay, the selling firm must take the loss. In other words, the risk of default on the accounts receivable pledged remains with the borrower. Also, the buyer of the goods is not ordinarily notified about the pledging of the receivables. The financial institution that lends on the security of accounts receivable is generally either a commercial bank or one of the large industrial finance companies.

Factoring, or selling accounts receivable, involves the purchase of accounts receivable by the lender without recourse to the borrower (seller). The buyer of the goods is notified of the transfer and makes payment directly to the lender. Since the factoring firm assumes the risk of default on bad accounts, it must do the credit checking. Accordingly, factors provide not only money but also a credit department for the borrower. Incidentally, the same financial institutions that make loans against pledged receivables also serve as factors. Thus, depending on the circumstances and the wishes of the borrower, a financial institution will provide either form of receivables financing.

Procedure for Pledging Accounts Receivable

The financing of accounts receivable is initiated by a legally binding agreement between the seller of the goods and the financing institution. The agreement sets forth in detail the procedures to be followed and the legal obligations of both parties. Once the working relation has been established, the seller periodically takes a batch of invoices to the financing institution. The lender reviews the invoices and makes an appraisal of the buyers. Invoices of companies that do not meet the lender's credit standards are not accepted for pledging. The financial institution seeks to protect itself at every phase of the operation. Selection of sound invoices is the essential first step in safeguarding the financial institution. If the buyer of the goods does not pay the invoice, the lender still has recourse against the seller of the goods. However, if many buyers default, the seller may be unable to meet his obligation to the financial institution.

Additional protection is afforded the lender in that the loan will generally be for less than 100 percent of the pledged receivables; for example, the lender may advance the selling firm 75 percent of the amount of the pledged receivables.

Procedure for Factoring Accounts Receivable

The procedure for factoring is somewhat different from that for pledging. Again, an agreement between the seller and the factor is made to specify legal obligations and procedural arrangements. When the seller receives an order from a buyer, a credit approval slip is written and immediately sent to the factoring company for a credit check. If the factor does not approve the sale, the seller generally refuses to fill the order. This procedure informs the seller, prior to the sale, about the buyer's credit-worthiness and acceptability to the factor. If the sale is approved, shipment is made and the invoice is stamped to notify the buyer to make payment directly to the factoring company.

The factor performs three functions in carrying out the normal procedure as outlined above: (1) credit checking, (2) lending, and (3) risk bearing. The seller can select various combinations of these functions by changing provisions in the factoring agreement. For example, a small or a medium-sized firm can avoid establishing a credit department. The factor's service might well be less costly than a department that may have excess capacity for the firm's credit volume. At the same time, if the firm uses part of the time of a noncredit specialist to perform credit checking, lack of education, training, and experience may result in excessive losses.

The seller may utilize the factor to perform the credit-checking and risk-taking functions but not the lending function. The following procedure is carried out on receipt of a $10,000 order. The factor checks and approves the invoices. The goods are shipped on terms of net 30. Payment is made to the factor, who remits to the seller. But assume that the factor has received only $5,000 by the end of the credit period. He must still remit $10,000 to the seller (less his fee, of course). If the remaining $5,000 is never paid, the factor sustains a $5,000 loss.

Now consider the more typical situation in which the factor performs a lending function by making payment in advance of collection. The goods are shipped and, even though payment is not due for 30 days, the factor immediately makes funds available to the seller. Suppose $10,000 of goods is shipped; the factoring commission for credit checking is 2½ percent of the invoice price, or $250; and the interest expense is computed at a 9 percent annual rate on the invoice balance, or $75.[6] The seller's accounting entry is as follows:

Cash	$9,175	
Interest expense	75	
Factoring commission	250	
Reserve: due from factor on collection of account	500	
Accounts receivable		$10,000

The $500 "due from factor on collection of account" in the entry is a reserve established by the factor to cover disputes between sellers and buyers on damaged goods, goods returned by the buyers to the seller, and failure to make outright sale of goods. The amount is paid to the seller firm when the factor collects on the account.

Factoring is normally a continuous process instead of the single cycle described above. The seller of the goods receives orders; he transmits the purchase orders to the factor for approval; on approval, the goods are shipped; the factor advances the money to the seller; the buyers pay the factor when payment is due; and the factor periodically remits any excess reserve to the seller of the goods. Once a routine is established, a continuous circular flow of goods and funds takes place between the seller, the buyers of the goods, and the factor. Thus, once the factoring agreement is in force, funds from this source are *spontaneous.*

Cost of Receivables Financing

Accounts receivable pledging and factoring services are convenient and advantageous, but they can be costly. The credit-checking commission is 1 to 3 percent of the amount of invoices accepted by the factor. The cost of money is reflected in the interest rate of 8 to 12 percent charged on the unpaid balance of the funds advanced by the factor. Where the

---

6. Since the interest is only for one month, we take one-twelfth of the stated rate, 9 percent, and multiply this by the $10,000 invoice price:

$$1/12 \times 0.09 \times \$10,000 = \$75.$$

Note that the effective rate of interest is really above 9 percent, because a discounting procedure is used and the borrower does not get the full $10,000. In many instances, however, the factoring contract calls for interest to be computed on the invoice price *less* the factoring commission and the reserve account.

risk to the factor is excessive, he purchases the invoices (with or without recourse) at discounts from face value.

Evaluation of Receivables Financing

It cannot be said categorically that accounts receivable financing is always either a good or a poor method of raising funds for an individual business. Among the advantages is, first, the flexibility of this source of financing. As the firm's sales expand and more financing is needed, a larger volume of invoices is generated automatically. Because the dollar amounts of invoices vary directly with sales, the amount of readily available financing increases. Second, receivables or invoices provide security for a loan that a firm might otherwise be unable to obtain. Third, factoring provides the services of a credit department that might otherwise be available to the firm only under much more expensive conditions.

Accounts receivable financing also has disadvantages. First, when invoices are numerous and relatively small in dollar amount, the administrative costs involved may render this method of financing inconvenient and expensive. Second, the firm is using a highly liquid asset as security. For a long time, accounts receivable financing was frowned upon by most trade creditors. In fact, such financing was regarded as confession of a firm's unsound financial position. It is no longer regarded in this light, and many sound firms engage in receivables pledging or factoring. However, the traditional attitude causes some trade creditors to refuse to sell on credit to a firm that is factoring or pledging its receivables, on the grounds that this practice removes one of the most liquid of the firm's assets and, accordingly, weakens the position of other creditors.

Future Use of Receivables Financing

We might make a prediction at this point—in the future, accounts receivable financing will increase in relative importance. Computer technology is rapidly advancing toward the point where credit records of individuals and firms can be kept in computer memory units. Systems have been devised so that a retailer can have a unit on hand that, when an individual's magnetic credit card is inserted into a box, gives a signal that his credit is "good" and that a bank is willing to "buy" the receivable created when the store completes the sale. The cost of handling invoices will be greatly reduced over present-day costs because the new systems will be so highly automated. This will make it possible to use accounts receivable financing for very small sales, and it will reduce the cost of all receivables financing. The net result will be a marked expansion of accounts receivable financing.

Inventory Financing

A rather large volume of credit is secured by business inventories. If a firm is a relatively good credit risk, the mere existence of the inventory may be a sufficient basis for receiving an unsecured loan. If the firm is a relatively poor risk, the lending institution may insist upon security, which often takes the form of a blanket lien against the inventory. Alternatively, *trust receipts* or *field warehouse receipts* can be used to secure the loan. These methods of using inventories as security are discussed below.

Blanket Inventory Lien

The blanket inventory lien gives the lending institution a lien against all inventories of the borrower. However, the borrower is free to sell inventories; thus the value of the collateral can be reduced.

Trust Receipts

Because of the weaknesses of the blanket lien for inventory financing, another kind of security is used — the trust receipt. A trust receipt is an instrument acknowledging that the borrower holds the goods in trust for the lender. When trust receipts are used, the borrowing firm, on receiving funds from the lender, conveys a trust receipt for the goods. The goods can be stored in a public warehouse or held on the premises of the borrower. The trust receipt provides that the goods are held in trust for the lender or are segregated in the borrower's premises on behalf of the lender, and proceeds from the sale of goods held under trust receipts are transmitted to the lender at the end of each day. Automobile dealer financing is the best example of trust receipt financing.

One defect of trust receipt financing is the requirement that a trust receipt must be issued for specific goods. For example, if the security is bags of coffee beans, the trust receipts must indicate the bags by number. In order to validate its trust receipts, the lending institution would have to send a man to the premises of the borrower to see that the bag numbers are correctly listed. Furthermore, complex legal requirements of trust receipts require the attention of a bank officer. Problems are compounded if borrowers are widely separated geographically from the lender. To offset these inconveniences, *warehousing* is coming into wide use as a method of securing loans with inventory.

Warehouse Financing

Like trust receipts, warehouse financing uses inventory as security. A *public warehouse* represents an independent third party engaged in the business of storing goods. Sometimes a public warehouse is not practical because of the bulkiness of goods and the expense of transporting them to and from the borrower's premises. *Field warehouse* financing represents an economical method of inventory financing in which the warehouse is established at the place of the borrower. To provide inventory supervision, the lending institution employs a third party in the arrangement, the field warehousing company. This company acts as the control (or supervisory) agent for the lending institution.

Field warehousing is illustrated by a simple example. Suppose a potential borrower has stacked iron in an open yard on his premises. A field warehouse can be established if a field warehousing concern places a temporary fence around the iron and erects a sign stating: "This is a field warehouse supervised and conducted by the Smith Field Warehousing Corporation." These are minimal conditions, of course.

The example illustrates the two elements in the establishment of a warehouse: (1) public notification of the field warehouse arrangement and (2) supervision of the field warehouse by a custodian of the field warehouse concern. When the field warehousing operation is relatively small, the second condition is sometimes violated by hiring an employee of the borrower to supervise the inventory. This practice is viewed as undesirable by the lending institution, because there is no control over the collateral by a person independent of the borrowing concern.[7]

The field warehouse financing operation is described best by a specific illustration. Assume that a tomato canner is interested in financing his operations by bank borrowing. The canner has sufficient funds to finance 15 to 20 percent of his operations during the canning season. These funds are adequate to purchase and process an initial batch of tomatoes. As the cans are put into boxes and rolled into the storerooms, the canner needs additional funds for both raw materials and labor.

Because of the canner's poor credit rating, the bank decides that a field warehousing operation is necessary to secure its loans. The field warehouse is established, and the custodian notifies the lending institution of the description, by number, of the boxes of canned tomatoes in storage and under his control. Thereupon the lending institution establishes for the canner a deposit on which he can draw. From this point on, the bank finances the operations. The canner needs only enough cash to initiate the cycle. The farmers bring more tomatoes; the

---

7. This absence of independent control was the main cause of the breakdown that resulted in the huge losses connected with the loans to the Allied Crude Vegetable Oil Company headed by Anthony (Tino) DeAngelis. American Express Field Warehousing Company hired men from Allied's staff as custodians. Their dishonesty was not discovered because of another breakdown—the fact that the American Express touring inspector did not actually take a physical inventory of the warehouses. As a consequence, the swindle was not discovered until losses running into the hundreds of millions of dollars had been suffered. See Norman C. Miller, *The Great Salad Oil Swindle* (Baltimore, Md.: Penguin Books, 1965), pp. 72–77.

canner processes them; the cans are boxed, and the boxes are put into the field warehouse; field warehouse receipts are drawn up and sent to the bank; the bank establishes further deposits for the canner on the basis of the receipts; the canner can draw on the deposits to continue the cycle.

Of course, the canner's ultimate objective is to sell the canned tomatoes. As the canner receives purchase orders, he transmits them to the bank, and the bank directs the custodian to release the inventories. It is agreed that, as remittances are received by the canner, they will be turned over to the bank. These remittances by the canner pay off the loans made by the bank.

Typically, a seasonal pattern exists. At the beginning of the tomato harvesting and canning season, the canner's cash needs and loan requirements begin to rise and reach a maximum by the end of the canning season. It is hoped that, just before the new canning season begins, the canner has sold a sufficient volume to have paid off the loan completely. If for some reason the canner has had a bad year, the bank may carry him over another year to enable him to work off his inventory.

Acceptable Products. In addition to canned foods, which account for about 17 percent of all field warehouse loans, many other product inventories provide a basis for field warehouse financing. Some of these are miscellaneous groceries, which represent about 13 percent; lumber products, about 10 percent; and coal and coke, about 6 percent.

These products are relatively nonperishable and are sold in well-developed, organized markets. Nonperishability protects the lender if he should have to take over the security. For this reason a bank would not make a field warehousing loan on perishables such as fresh fish. However, frozen fish, which can be stored for a long time, can be field warehoused. An organized market aids the lender in disposing of an inventory that it takes over. Banks are not interested in going into the canning or the fish business. They want to be able to dispose of an inventory within a matter of hours and with the expenditure of a minimum amount of time.

Cost of Financing. The fixed costs of a field warehousing arrangement are relatively high; such financing is therefore not suitable for a very small firm. If a field warehouse company sets up the field warehouse itself, it will typically set a minimum charge of about $350 to $600 a year, plus about 1 or 2 percent of the amount of credit extended to the borrower. Furthermore, the financing institution will charge from 8 to

12 percent interest. The minimum size of an efficient field warehousing operation requires an inventory of about $100,000.

Appraisal. The use of field warehouse financing as a source of funds for business firms has many advantages. First, the amount of funds available is flexible because the financing is tied to the growth of inventories, which in turn is related directly to financing needs. Second, the field warehousing arrangement increases the acceptability of inventories as loan collateral. Some inventories would not be accepted by a bank as security without a field warehousing arrangement. Third, the necessity for inventory control, safekeeping, and the use of specialists in warehousing has resulted in improved warehouse practices. The services of the field warehouse companies have often saved money for the firm in spite of the costs of financing mentioned above. The field warehouse company may suggest inventory practices which reduce the labor that the firm has to employ, and reduce inventory damage and loss as well.

The major disadvantage of a field warehousing operation is the fixed cost element, which reduces the feasibility of this form of financing for small firms.

Summary

Short-term credit is defined as debt originally scheduled for repayment within one year. This chapter has discussed the three major sources of short-term credit—trade credit between firms, loans from commercial banks, and commercial paper—as well as methods of securing this credit.

Trade Credit. Trade credit, represented by accounts payable, is the largest single category of short-term credit and is especially important for smaller firms. Trade credit is a *spontaneous source of financing* in that it arises from ordinary business transactions; as sales increase, so does the supply of financing from accounts payable.

Bank Credit. Bank credit occupies a pivotal position in the short-term money market. Banks provide the marginal credit that allows firms to expand more rapidly than is possible through retained earnings and trade credit; to be denied bank credit often means that a firm must slow its rate of growth.

Bank interest rates are quoted in three ways—regular compound interest, discount interest, and installment interest. Regular interest needs no adjustment—it is "correct" as stated. Discount interest requires a small upward adjustment to make it comparable to regular compound interest rates. Installment interest rates require a large adjustment, and frequently the true interest rate is double the quoted rate for an installment loan.

Commercial Paper. Bank loans are personal in the sense that the financial manager meets with the banker, discusses the terms of the loan with him, and reaches an agreement that requires direct and personal negotiation. Commercial paper, however, although it is physically quite similar to a bank loan, is sold in a broad, impersonal market. A California firm might, for example, sell commercial paper to a manufacturer in the Midwest.

Only the very strongest firms are able to use the commercial paper markets—the nature of these markets is such that the firm selling the paper must have a reputation so good that buyers of the paper are willing to buy it without any sort of credit check. Interest rates in the commercial paper market are the lowest available to business borrowers.

Use of Security in Short-term Financing. The most common forms of collateral used for short-term credit are inventories and accounts receivable. Accounts receivable financing can be done either by *pledging the receivables* or by selling them outright, frequently called *factoring*. When the receivables are pledged, the borrower retains the risk that the person or firm who owes the receivable will not pay; in factoring, this risk is typically passed on to the lender. Because the factor takes the risk of default, he will investigate the purchaser's credit; therefore, the factor can perform three services—a lending function, a risk-bearing function, and a credit-checking function. When receivables are pledged, the lender typically performs only the first of these three functions.

Loans secured by inventories are not satisfactory under many circumstances. For certain kinds of inventory, however, the technique known as *field warehousing* is used to provide adequate security to the lender. Under a field warehousing arrangement, the inventory is under the physical control of a warehouse company, which releases the inventory only on order from the lending institution. Canned goods, lumber, steel, coal, and other standardized products are goods usually covered in field warehouse arrangements.

Questions

8–1. It is inevitable that firms will obtain a certain amount of their financing in the form of trade credit, which is, to some extent, a free source of funds. What are some other factors that lead firms to use trade credit?

8–2. "Commercial paper interest rates are always lower than bank loan rates to a given borrower. Nevertheless, many firms perfectly capable of selling commercial paper employ higher cost bank credit." Discuss the statement, indicating (a) why commercial paper rates are lower than bank rates and (b) why firms might use bank credit in spite of its higher cost.

8–3. "Trade credit has an explicit interest rate cost if discounts are available but not taken. There are also some intangible costs associated with the failure to take discounts." Discuss.

8–4. A large manufacturing firm that had been selling its products on a 3/10, net 30 basis changed its credit terms to 1/20, net 90. What changes might be anticipated on the balance sheets of the manufacturer and of its customers?

8–5. The availability of bank credit is more important to small firms than to large ones. Why is this so?

8–6. What factors should a firm consider in selecting its primary bank? Would it be feasible for a firm to have a primary deposit bank (the bank where most of its funds are deposited) and a different primary loan bank (the bank where it does most of its borrowing)?

8–7. Indicate whether each of the following changes would raise or lower the cost of a firm's accounts receivable financing, and why this occurs:
   a. The firm eases up on its credit standards in order to increase sales.
   b. The firm institutes a policy of refusing to make credit sales if the amount of the purchase (invoice) is below $100. Previously, about 40 percent of all invoices were below $100.
   c. The firm agrees to give recourse to the finance company for all defaults.
   d. The firm, which already has a recourse arrangement, is merged into a larger, stronger company.
   e. A firm without a recourse arrangement changes its terms of trade from net 30 to net 90.

8–8. Would a firm that manufactures specialized machinery for a few large customers be more likely to use some form of inventory financing or some form of accounts receivable financing? Why?

8–9. "A firm that factors its accounts receivable will look better in a ratio analysis than one that discounts its receivables." Discuss.

8–10. Why would it not be practical for a typical retailer to use field warehousing?

8–11. List an industry, together with your reasons for including it, that might be expected to use each of the following forms of credit:
   a. field warehousing
   b. factoring
   c. accounts receivable discounting
   d. trust receipts
   e. none of these.

Problems

8–1. What is the equivalent annual interest rate that would be lost if a firm failed to take the cash discount under each of the following terms?
a. 1/15, net 30
b. 2/10, net 60
c. 3/10, net 60
d. 2/10, net 40
e. 1/10, net 40

8–2. The balance sheet of the Atlantic Credit Corporation is shown below.

Atlantic Credit Corporation
Balance sheet
(millions of dollars)

Cash	$ 75	Bank loans	$ 250
Net receivables	2,400	Commercial paper	825
Marketable securities	150	Others	375
Repossessions	5	Total due within a year	$1,450
Total current assets	$2,630		
		Long-term debt	1,000
Other assets	170	Total shareholders' equity	350
Total assets	$2,800	Total claims	$2,800

a. Calculate commercial paper (1) as a percentage of short-term financing, (2) as a percentage of total-debt financing, and (3) as a percentage of all financing.
b. Why do finance companies such as Atlantic Credit use commercial paper to such a great extent?
c. Why do they use both bank loans and commerical paper?

8–3. The Shelby Saw Corporation had sales of $4 million last year and earned a 3 percent after tax return on total assets.

Although its terms of purchase are 30 days, accounts payable represent 60 days' purchases. The president of the company is seeking to increase bank borrowings in order to become current in meeting its trade obligations (that is, reduce to 30 days).

The company's balance sheet is shown below:

Shelby Saw Corporation
Balance sheet

Cash	100,000	Accounts payable	600,000
Accounts receivable	300,000	Bank loans	500,000
Inventory	1,400,000	Accruals	400,000
Current assets	1,800,000	Current liabilities	1,500,000
Land and buildings	700,000	Mortgage or real estate	600,000
Equipment	500,000	Net worth	900,000
Total assets	$3,000,000	Claims on assets	$3,000,000

a. How much bank financing is needed to eliminate past-due accounts payable?

b. As a bank loan officer, would you make the loan? Why?

8–4. The Shandow Insulation Company has been growing rapidly, but because of insufficient working capital it has now become slow in paying bills. Of its total accounts payable, $96,000 is overdue. This threatens its relationship with its main supplier of powders used in the manufacture of various kinds of insulation materials for aircraft and missiles. Over 75 percent of its sales are to six large defense contractors. The company's balance sheet, sales, and net profit for the past year are shown below:

Shandow Corporation
Balance sheet

Cash	$ 28,800	Trade credit*	$240,000
Receivables	432,000	Bank loans	192,000
Inventories		Accruals*	48,000
Raw material	38,400		
Work in process	192,000	Total current debt	480,000
Finished goods	57,600	Mortgages on equipment	288,000
		Capital stock	96,000
Total current assets	748,800	Retained earnings	96,000
Equipment	211,200		
Total assets	$ 960,000	Total liabilities and net worth	$960,000
Sales	$1,920,000		
Profit after taxes	96,000		

*Increases spontaneously with sales increases.

a. If the same ratio of sales to total assets continues, and if sales increase to $2,304,000, how much nonspontaneous financing, *including* retained earnings, will be required?

b. Could Shandow Insulation obtain much more funds by use of inventory financing? Explain.

c. Would receivables financing be a possibility for the company? Explain.

d. *Assuming the five facts listed below*, on average what is the total amount of receivables outstanding at any given time when sales are $1,920,000? How much cash does the firm actually receive by factoring the average amount of receivables? What is the average duration of advances, on the basis of 360 days a year? What is the total annual dollar cost of the financing? What is the effective annual financing charge (percentage) paid on the money received?

1. Receivables turn over six times a year. (Sales/receivables = 6.)

2. All sales are made on credit.

3. The factor requires an 8 percent reserve for returns on disputed items.

4. The factor also requires a 2 percent commission on average receiv-

ables outstanding, payable at the time the receivable is purchased, to cover the costs of credit checking.

5. There is a 6 percent annual interest charge based on receivables *less* any reserve requirements and commissions. This payment is made at the beginning of the period and is deducted from the advance.

8–5. The Morton Plastics Company manufactures plastic toys. It buys raw materials, manufactures the toys in the spring and summer, and ships them to department stores and toy stores by late summer or early fall. The company factors its receivables. If it did not, in October 1978, Morton's balance sheet would have appeared as follows:

Morton Company
Pro forma balance sheet
October 31, 1978

Cash	$ 40,000	Accounts payable	$1,200,000
Receivables	1,200,000	Notes payable	800,000
Inventory	800,000	Accruals	80,000
Total current assets	$2,040,000	Total current debt	$2,080,000
		Mortgages	200,000
		Common stock	400,000
Fixed assets	800,000	Retained earnings	160,000
Total assets	$2,840,000	Total claims	$2,840,000

Morton provides advanced dating on its sales; thus its receivables are not due for payment until January 31, 1979. Also, the company would have been overdue on some $800,000 of its accounts payable if the above situation actually existed.

Morton has an agreement with a finance company to factor the receivables for the period October 31 through January 31 of each selling season. The factoring company charges a flat commission of 2 percent, plus 6 percent a year interest on the outstanding balance; it deducts a reserve of 8 percent for returned and damaged materials. Interest and commission are paid in advance. No interest is charged on the reserved funds or on the commission.

a. Show the balance sheet of Morton on October 31, 1978, giving effect to the purchase of all the receivables by the factoring company and the use of the funds to pay accounts payable.

b. If the $1.2 million is the average level of outstanding receivables and if they turn over four times a year (hence the commission is paid four times a year), what are the total dollar costs of financing and the effective annual interest rate?

Selected References

Abraham, Alfred B. "Factoring: The New Frontier for Commercial Banks." *Journal of Commercial Bank Lending* 53 (Apr. 1971): 32–43.

Baxter, Nevins D. *The Commercial Paper Market.* Princeton, N.J.: Princeton University Press, 1964.

Baxter, Nevins D., and Shapiro, Harold T. "Compensating Balance Requirements: The Results of a Survey." *Journal of Finance* 19 (Sept. 1964): 483–96.

Brosky, John J. *The Implicit Cost of Trade Credit and Theory of Optimal Terms of Sale.* New York: Credit Research Foundation, 1969.

Crane, Dwight B., and White, William L. "Who Benefits from a Floating Prime Rate?" *Harvard Business Review* 50 (Jan.–Feb. 1972): 121–29.

Denonn, Lester E. "The Security Agreement." *Journal of Commercial Bank Lending* 50 (Feb. 1968): 32–40.

Hayes, Douglas A. *Bank Lending Policies: Domestic and International.* Ann Arbor, Mich.: University of Michigan Press, 1971.

Nadler, Paul S. "Compensating Balances and the Prime at Twilight." *Harvard Business Review* 50 (Jan.–Feb. 1972): 112–20.

Robinson, Roland I. *The Management of Bank Funds*, Parts III and IV. New York: McGraw-Hill, 1962.

Schadrack, Frederick C., Jr. "Demand and Supply in the Commercial Paper Market." *Journal of Finance* 25 (Sept. 1970): 837–52.

Shay, Robert P., and Greer, Carl C. "Banks Move into High-Risk Commercial Financing." *Harvard Business Review* 46 (Nov.–Dec. 1968): 149–53; 156–61.

Stone, Bernell K. "The Cost of Bank Loans." *Journal of Financial and Quantitative Analysis* 7 (Dec. 1972): 2077–86.

Part III

Decisions Involving Long-term Assets

In Part II, we dealt with the top portion of the firm's balance sheet—the current assets and liabilities, Now, in Part III, we move down to the lower left side of the statement, focusing on the decisions involved in fixed asset acquisitions.

In Chapter 9 we discuss the concepts of compound interest and the time value of money, important subjects in all long-term financial decisions. Capital budgeting—the planning of expenditures whose returns will extend beyond one year—is covered in Chapter 10. Uncertainty about both the costs and the returns associated with a project is introduced in Chapter 11; since projects differ in riskiness, that chapter develops methods of analysis which can be used to incorporate risk into the decision-making process.

9　The Interest Factor in Financial Decisions

Investing in fixed assets should, logically, be taken up at this point. However, the long-term nature of fixed investments makes it necessary to consider first the theory of compound interest—the "math of finance." Compound interest is essential to an understanding of capital budgeting, the topic of the following chapter, and interest rate theory is also an integral part of several other topics taken up later in the text. Financial structure decisions, lease versus purchase decisions, bond refunding operations, security valuation techniques, and the whole question of the cost of capital are some other subjects that cannot be understood without a knowledge of compound interest.

Many people are afraid of the subject of compound interest and simply avoid it. It is certainly true that many successful businessmen—even some bankers—know essentially nothing of the subject. However, as technology advances, as more and more engineers become involved in general management, and as modern business administration programs turn out more and more highly qualified graduates, this "success in spite of yourself" pattern will become more and more difficult to achieve. Furthermore, a fear of compound interest relationships is quite unfounded—the subject matter is simply not that difficult. Almost all problems involving compound interest can be handled satisfactorily with only a few basic formulas.

Compound Value

A person deposits $1,000 in a savings and loan association that pays 4 percent interest compounded annually. How much will he have at the end of one year?

To treat the matter systematically, let us define the following terms:

P_0 = principal, or beginning amount at time 0.

i = interest rate.

$P_0 i$ = total dollar amount of interest earned.

V_t = value at the end of t periods.

When t equals 1, V_t may be calculated as follows:

$$V_1 = P_0 + P_0 i$$
$$= P_0(1 + i).$$

(9–1)

Equation 9–1 shows that the ending amount (V_1) is equal to the beginning amount (P_0) times the factor $(1 + i)$. In the example, where $P_0 = \$1,000$, $i = 4$ percent, and t is one year, V_t is determined as follows:

$$V_1 = \$1,000(1.0 + .04) = \$1,000(1.04) = \$1,040.$$

**Multiple
Periods**

If the person leaves the $1,000 on deposit for five years, to what amount will it have grown at the end of that period? Equation 9–1 can be used to construct Table 9–1, which indicates the answer. Note that V_2, the balance at the end of the second year, is found as follows:

$$V_2 = V_1(1 + i) = P_0(1 + i)(1 + i) = P_0(1 + i)^2.$$

Similarly, V_3, the balance after three years, is found as

$$V_3 = V_2(1 + i) = P_0(1 + i)^3.$$

**Table 9–1
Compound Interest Calculations**

Period	Beginning Amount	× (1 + i) =	Ending Amount (V_t)
1	$1,000	1.04	$1,040
2	1,040	1.04	1,082
3	1,082	1.04	1,125
4	1,125	1.04	1,170
5	1,170	1.04	1,217

In general, V_t, the compound amount at the end of any year t, is found as

$$V_t = P_0(1 + i)^t.$$

(9–2)

Equation 9–2 is the fundamental equation of compound interest. Note that Equation 9–1 is simply a special case of Equation 9–2, where $t = 1$.

While it is necessary to understand the derivation of Equation 9–2 in order to understand much of the material in the remainder of this chapter (as well as material to be covered in subsequent chapters), the concept can be applied quite readily in a mechanical sense. Tables have been constructed for values of $(1 + i)^t$ for wide ranges of i and t. Table

	Period	1%	2%	3%	4%	5%	6%	7%	8%	9%	10%
Table 9–2	1	1.010	1.020	1.030	1.040	1.050	1.060	1.070	1.080	1.090	1.100
Compound Value	2	1.020	1.040	1.061	1.082	1.102	1.124	1.145	1.166	1.188	1.210
of $1 (CVIF)	3	1.030	1.061	1.093	1.125	1.158	1.191	1.225	1.260	1.295	1.331
	4	1.041	1.082	1.126	1.170	1.216	1.262	1.311	1.360	1.412	1.464
	5	1.051	1.104	1.159	1.217	1.276	1.338	1.403	1.469	1.539	1.611
	6	1.062	1.126	1.194	1.265	1.340	1.419	1.501	1.587	1.677	1.772
	7	1.072	1.149	1.230	1.316	1.407	1.504	1.606	1.714	1.828	1.949
	8	1.083	1.172	1.267	1.369	1.477	1.594	1.718	1.851	1.993	2.144
	9	1.094	1.195	1.305	1.423	1.551	1.689	1.838	1.999	2.172	2.358
	10	1.105	1.219	1.344	1.480	1.629	1.791	1.967	2.159	2.367	2.594
	11	1.116	1.243	1.384	1.539	1.710	1.898	2.105	2.332	2.580	2.853
	12	1.127	1.268	1.426	1.601	1.796	2.012	2.252	2.518	2.813	3.138
	13	1.138	1.294	1.469	1.665	1.886	2.133	2.410	2.720	3.066	3.452
	14	1.149	1.319	1.513	1.732	1.980	2.261	2.579	2.937	3.342	3.797
	15	1.161	1.346	1.558	1.801	2.079	2.397	2.759	3.172	3.642	4.177

9–2 is illustrative, while Table D–1, in Appendix D at the end of the book, is a more complete table.

Letting $CVIF$ (= compound value interest factor) = $(1 + i)^t$, Equation 9–2 may be written as $V_t = P_0(CVIF)$. It is necessary only to go to an appropriate interest table to find the proper interest factor. For example, the correct interest factor for the illustration given in Table 9–1 can be found in Table 9–2. Look down the Period column to 5, then across this row to the appropriate number in the 4 percent column to find the interest factor, 1.217. Then, using this interest factor, we find the compound value of the $1,000 after five years as

$$V_5 = P_0(CVIF) = \$1,000(1.217) = \$1,217.$$

Notice that this is precisely the same figure that was obtained by the long method in Table 9–1.

Graphic View of the Compounding Process: Growth

Figure 9–1 shows how the interest factors for compounding increase, or grow, as the compounding period increases. Curves could be drawn for any interest rate, including fractional rates; we have plotted curves for 0 percent, 5 percent, and 10 percent. The curves in the graph were plotted from data taken from Table 9–2.

Figure 9–1 shows how $1 (or any other sum) grows over time at various rates of interest. The higher the rate of interest, the faster the rate of growth. The interest rate is, in fact, the growth rate: if a sum is deposited and earns 5 percent, then the funds on deposit grow at the rate of 5 percent per year.

Figure 9–1
Relationship between
Compound Value
Interest Factors,
Interest Rates, and
Time

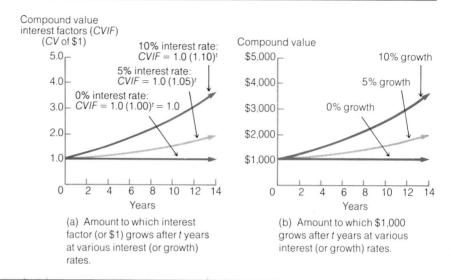

(a) Amount to which interest
factor (or $1) grows after t years
at various interest (or growth)
rates.

(b) Amount to which $1,000
grows after t years at various
interest (or growth) rates.

Present Value

Suppose you are offered the alternative of either $1,217 at the end of five years or X dollars today. There is no question but that the $1,217 will be paid in full (perhaps the payer is the United States government); having no current need for the money, you would deposit it in a savings association paying a 4 percent dividend. (Four percent is defined to be your "opportunity cost.") How small must X be to induce you to accept the promise of $1,217 five years hence?

Table 9–1 shows that the initial amount of $1,000 growing at 4 percent a year yields $1,217 at the end of five years. Thus, you should be indifferent in your choice between $1,000 today and $1,217 at the end of five years. The $1,000 is defined as the *present value* of $1,217 due in five years when the applicable interest rate is 4 percent. It should be noted that the subscript zero in the term P_0 indicates the present. Hence present value quantities may be identified by either P_0 or PV.

Finding present values (or *discounting*, as it is commonly called) is simply the reverse of compounding, and Equation 9–2 can readily be transformed into a present value formula.

$$\text{Present value} = P_0 = \frac{V_t}{(1+i)^t} = V_t\left[\frac{1}{(1+i)^t}\right]. \tag{9–3}$$

Tables have been constructed for the term in brackets for various values of i and t; Table 9–3 is an example. A more complete table, Table D–2, is found in Appendix D at the end of the book. For the illustrative case being considered, look down the 4 percent column in Table 9–3 to the fifth row. The figure shown there, 0.822, is the present value interest factor *(PVIF)* used to determine the present value of $1,217 payable in five years, discounted at 4 percent.

$$P_0 = V_5(PVIF)$$

$$= \$1,217(0.822)$$

$$= \$1,000.$$

Table 9–3
Present Values of $1 (PVIF)

Period	1%	2%	3%	4%	5%	6%	7%	8%	9%	10%	12%	14%	15%
1	.990	.980	.971	.962	.952	.943	.935	.926	.917	.909	.893	.877	.870
2	.980	.961	.943	.925	.907	.890	.873	.857	.842	.826	.797	.769	.756
3	.971	.942	.915	.889	.864	.840	.816	.794	.772	.751	.712	.675	.658
4	.961	.924	.889	.855	.823	.792	.763	.735	.708	.683	.636	.592	.572
5	.951	.906	.863	.822	.784	.747	.713	.681	.650	.621	.567	.519	.497
6	.942	.888	.838	.790	.746	.705	.666	.630	.596	.564	.507	.456	.432
7	.933	.871	.813	.760	.711	.665	.623	.583	.547	.513	.452	.400	.376
8	.923	.853	.789	.731	.677	.627	.582	.540	.502	.467	.404	.351	.327
9	.914	.837	.766	.703	.645	.592	.544	.500	.460	.424	.361	.308	.284
10	.905	.820	.744	.676	.614	.558	.508	.463	.422	.386	.322	.270	.247

Graphic View of the Discounting Process

Figure 9–2 shows how the interest factors for discounting decrease as the discounting period increases. The curves in the figure were plotted from data taken from Table 9–3; they show that the present value of a

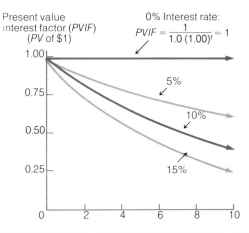

Figure 9–2
Relationship between Present Value Interest Factors, Interest Rates, and Time

sum to be received at some future date decreases (1) as the payment date is extended further into the future and (2) as the discount rate increases. If relatively high discount rates apply, funds due in the future are worth very little today; even at relatively low discount rates, funds due in the distant future are not worth much today. For example, $1,000 due in ten years is worth $247 today if the discount rate is 15 percent, but it is worth $614 today at a 5 percent discount rate. Similarly, $1,000 due in ten years at 10 percent is worth $386 today, but at the same discount rate $1,000 due in five years is worth $621 today.[1]

Compound Value versus Present Value

Because a thorough understanding of compound value concepts is vital in order to follow the remainder of both this chapter and the book, and because compound interest gives many students trouble, it will be useful to examine in more detail the relationship between compounding and discounting.

Notice that Equation 9–2, the basic equation for compounding, was developed from the logical sequence set forth in Table 9–1: the equation merely presents in mathematical form the steps outlined in the table. The present value interest factor $(PVIF_{i,t})$ in Equation 9–3, the basic equation for discounting or finding present values, was found as the *reciprocal* of the compound value interest factor $(CVIF_{i,t})$ for the same i,t combination:

$$PVIF_{i,t} = \frac{1}{CVIF_{i,t}}.$$

For example, the *compound value* interest factor for 4 percent over five years is seen in Table 9–2 to be 1.217. The *present value* interest factor for 4 percent over five years must be the reciprocal of 1.217:

$$PVIF_{4\%,5years} = \frac{1}{1.217} = .822.$$

The *PVIF* found in this manner must, of course, correspond with the *PVIF* shown in Table 9–3.

The reciprocal nature of the relationship between present value and compound value permits us to find present values in two ways—by multiplying or by dividing. Thus, the present value of $1,000 due in five years and discounted at 4 percent may be found as

$$P_0 = PV = V_t\,(PVIF_{i,t}) = V_t\left[\frac{1}{1+i}\right]^t = \$1,000\,(.822) = \$822,$$

---

1. Note that Figure 9–2 is *not* a mirror image of Figure 9–1. The curves in Figure 9–1 approach ∞ as t increases; in Figure 9–2, the curves appraoch zero, not −∞, as t increases.

or

$$P_0 = PV = \frac{V_t}{CVIF_{i,t}} = \frac{V_t}{(1+i)^t} = \frac{\$1{,}000}{1.217} = \$822.$$

In the second form, it is easy to see why the present value of a given future amount (V_t) declines as the discount rate increases.

To conclude this comparison of present and compound values, compare Figures 9–1 and 9–2. Notice that the vertical intercept is at 1.0 in each case, but compound value interest factors rise while present value interest factors decline. The reason for this divergence is, of course, that present value factors are reciprocals of compound factors.

Compound Value of an Annuity

An annuity is defined as a series of payments of a fixed amount for a specified number of years. Each payment occurs at the end of the year.[2] For example, a promise to pay $1,000 a year for three years is a three-year annuity. If you were to receive such an annuity and were to deposit each annual payment in a savings account paying 4 percent interest, how much would you have at the end of three years? The answer is shown graphically in Figure 9–3. The first payment is made at the end of year 1, the second at the end of year 2, and the third at the end of year 3. The last payment is not compounded at all; the next to the last is compounded for one year; the second from the last for two years; and so on back to the first, which is compounded for $t - 1$ years. When the compound values of each of the payments are added, their total is the sum of the annuity. In the example, this total is $3,122.

Expressed algebraically, with S_t defined as the compound sum, a as

Figure 9–3
Graphic Illustration of
an Annuity: Compound
Sum

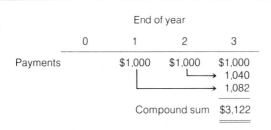

2. Had the payment been made at the beginning of the period, each receipt would simply have been shifted back one year. The annuity would have been called an *annuity due;* the one in the present discussion, where payments are made at the end of each period, is called a *regular annuity* or, sometimes, a *deferred annuity.*

the periodic receipt, t as the length of the annuity, and $CVIF_a$ as the compound value interest factor for an annuity, the formula for S_t is

$$S_t = a(1 + i)^{t-1} + a(1 + i)^{t-2} + \cdots + a(1 + i)^1 + a(1 + i)^0$$

$$= a[(1 + i)^{t-1} + (1 + i)^{t-2} + \cdots + (1 + i)^1 + (1 + i)^0]$$

$$= a[CVIF_a].$$

The expression in brackets, $CVIF_a$, has been given values for various combinations of t and i. An illustrative set of these annuity interest factors is given in Table 9–4; a more complete set may be found in Table

Table 9–4 Period	1%	2%	3%	4%	5%	6%	7%	8%
Sum of an Annuity of $1 for t Years (CVIF$_a$) 1	1.000	1.000	1.000	1.000	1.000	1.000	1.000	1.000
2	2.010	2.020	2.030	2.040	2.050	2.060	2.070	2.080
3	3.030	3.060	3.091	3.122	3.152	3.184	3.215	3.246
4	4.060	4.122	4.184	4.246	4.310	4.375	4.440	4.506
5	5.101	5.204	5.309	5.416	5.526	5.637	5.751	5.867
6	6.152	6.308	6.468	6.633	6.802	6.975	7.153	7.336
7	7.214	7.434	7.662	7.898	8.142	8.394	8.654	8.923
8	8.286	8.583	8.892	9.214	9.549	9.897	10.260	10.637
9	9.369	9.755	10.159	10.583	11.027	11.491	11.978	12.488
10	10.462	10.950	11.464	12.006	12.578	13.181	13.816	14.487

D–3 in Appendix D. To find the answer to the three-year, $1,000 annuity problem, simply refer to Table 9–4, look down the 4 percent column to the row for the third year, and multiply the factor 3.122 by $1,000. The answer is the same as the one derived by the long method illustrated in Figure 9–3:

$$S_t = a \times CVIF_a$$

$$S_3 = \$1,000 \times 3.122 = \$3,122. \tag{9–4}$$

Notice that $CVIF_a$ for the sum of an annuity is always *larger* than the number of years the annuity runs.

Present Value of an Annuity

Suppose you were offered the following alternatives: a three-year annuity of $1,000 a year or a lump-sum payment today. You have no need for the money during the next three years, so if you accept the annuity you would simply deposit the receipts in a savings account paying 4 percent interest. How large must the lump-sum payment be to make it equivalent to the annuity? The graphic illustration shown in Figure 9–4 will help explain the problem.

Figure 9–4
Graphic Illustration of
an Annuity: Present
Value

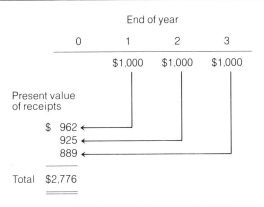

The present value of the first receipt is $a[1/(1 + i)]$; the second is $a[1/(1 + i)]^2$; and so on. Defining the present value of an annuity of t years as PV_{at} and with $PVIF_a$ defined as the present value interest factor for an annuity, we may write the following equation:

$$PV_{at} = a\left[\frac{1}{1+i}\right]^1 + a\left[\frac{1}{1+i}\right]^2 + \cdots + a\left[\frac{1}{1+i}\right]^t$$

$$= a\left[\frac{1}{(1+i)} + \frac{1}{(1+i)^2} + \cdots + \frac{1}{(1+i)^t}\right]$$

$$= a[PVIF_a]. \tag{9–5}$$

Again, tables have been worked out for the $PVIF_a$, the term in the brackets. Table 9–5 is illustrative; a more complete table is found in Table D–4 in Appendix D. From Table 9–5, the $PVIF_a$ for a three-year, 4 percent annuity is found to be 2.775. Multiplying this factor by the $1,000 annual receipt gives $2,775, the present value of the annuity.

Table 9–5 **Present Value of an Annuity of $1**	Period	1%	2%	3%	4%	5%	6%	7%	8%	9%	10%
	1	0.990	0.980	0.971	0.962	0.952	0.943	0.935	0.926	0.917	0.909
	2	1.970	1.942	1.913	1.886	1.859	1.833	1.808	1.783	1.759	1.736
	3	2.941	2.884	2.829	2.775	2.723	2.673	2.624	2.577	2.531	2.487
	4	3.902	3.808	3.717	3.630	3.546	3.465	3.387	3.312	3.240	3.170
	5	4.853	4.713	4.580	4.452	4.329	4.212	4.100	3.993	3.890	3.791
	6	5.795	5.601	5.417	5.242	5.076	4.917	4.766	4.623	4.486	4.355
	7	6.728	6.472	6.230	6.002	5.786	5.582	5.389	5.206	5.033	4.868
	8	7.652	7.325	7.020	6.733	6.463	6.210	6.971	5.747	5.535	5.335
	9	8.566	8.162	7.786	7.435	7.108	6.802	6.515	6.247	5.985	5.759
	10	9.471	8.983	8.530	8.111	7.722	7.360	7.024	6.710	6.418	6.145

This figure departs from the long-method answer shown in Figure 9–4 only by a rounding difference:

$$PV_{at} = a \times PVIF_a$$

$$PV_{a3} = \$1{,}000 \times 2.775$$

$$= \$2{,}775. \tag{9–6}$$

Notice that $PVIF_a$ for the *present value* of an annuity is always *less* than the number of years the annuity runs, whereas $CVIF_a$ for the *sum* of an annuity is *larger* than the number of years.

Annual Payments for Accumulation of a Future Sum

Thus far in the chapter all the equations have been based on Equation 9–2. The present value equation merely involves a transposition of Equation 9–2, and the annuity equations merely take the sum of the basic compound interest equation for different values of t. We now examine some additional modifications of the equations.

Suppose we want to know the amount of money that must be deposited at 5 percent for each of the next five years in order to have $10,000 available to pay off a debt at the end of the fifth year. Dividing both sides of Equation 9–4 by $CVIF_a$, we obtain

$$a = \frac{S_t}{CVIF_a}.$$

Looking up the sum of an annuity interest factor for five years at 5 percent in Table 9–4 and dividing that figure into $10,000 we find

$$a = \frac{\$10{,}000}{5.526} = \$1{,}810.$$

Thus, if $1,810 is deposited each year in an account paying 5 percent interest, at the end of five years the account will have accumulated $10,000. We will employ this procedure in later chapters when we discuss sinking funds set up to provide for bond retirements.

Annual Receipts from an Annuity

Suppose that on September 1, 1978, you receive an inheritance of $7,000. The money is to be used for your education and is to be spent during the academic years beginning September 1979, 1980, and 1981. If you place the money in a bank account paying 5 percent annual interest and make three equal withdrawals at each of the specified dates, how large can each withdrawal be to leave you with exactly a zero balance after the last one has been made?

The solution requires application of the present value of an annuity formula, Equation 9–6. Here, however, we know that the present value of the annuity is $7,000, and the problem is to find the three equal annual payments when the interest rate is 5 percent. This calls for dividing both sides of Equation 9–6 by $PVIF_a$ to make Equation 9–7.

$$PV_{at} = a \times PVIF_a \tag{9–6}$$

$$a = \frac{PV_{at}}{PVIF_a}. \tag{9–7}$$

The interest factor $(PVIF_a)$ is found in Table 9–5 to be 2.723; substituting this value into Equation 9–7, we find the three equal annual withdrawals to be $2,571 a year:

$$a = \frac{\$7,000}{2.723} = \$2,570.69$$

This particular kind of calculation is used frequently in setting up insurance and pension plan benefit schedules; it is also used to find the periodic payments necessary to retire a loan within a specified period. For example, if you want to retire a $7,000 bank loan, bearing interest at 5 percent on the unpaid balance, in three equal annual installments, the amount of each payment is $2,570.69. In this case, you are the borrower, and the bank is "buying" an annuity with a present value of $7,000.

Determining Interest Rates

In many instances the present values and cash flows associated with a payment stream are known, but the interest rate involved is not known. Suppose a bank offers to lend you $1,000 today if you sign a note agreeing to pay the bank $1,469 at the end of five years. What rate of interest would you be paying on the loan? To answer the question we must use Equation 9–2:

$$V_t = P_0(1 + i)^t = P_0(CVIF). \tag{9–2}$$

Simply solve for $CVIF$, then look up this value of $CVIF$ in Table 9–2 (or D–1) under the row for the fifth year:

$$CVIF = \frac{V_5}{P_0} = \frac{\$1,469}{\$1,000} = 1.469.$$

Looking across the row for the fifth year, we find the value 1.469 in the

8 percent column; therefore, the interest rate on the loan is 8 percent.

Precisely the same approach is taken to determine the interest rate implicit in an annuity. For example, suppose a bank will lend you $2,577 if you sign a note in which you agree to pay the bank $1,000 at the end of the next three years. What interest rate is the bank charging you? To answer the question, solve Equation 9–6 for $PVIF_a$, then look up $PVIF_a$ in Table 9–5 (or D–4):

$$PV_{at} = a \times PVIF_a$$

$$PVIF_a = \frac{PV_{a3}}{a} = \frac{\$2,577}{\$1,000} = 2.577. \tag{9–6}$$

Looking across the third-year row, we find the factor 2.577 under the 8 percent column; therefore the bank is lending you money at 8 percent.

Linear Interpolation

The tables give values for even interest rates, e.g., 8 percent, 9 percent, and so on. Suppose you need to find the present value of $1,000 due in 10 years, discounted at $8\frac{1}{4}$ percent. The appropriate $PVIF$ is not in the tables, but a very close approximation to the correct factor can be estimated by the method of *linear interpolation*. The $PVIF$ for 8 percent, 10 years, is .463; that for 9 percent is .422. The difference is .041. Since $8\frac{1}{4}$ is 25 percent of the way between 8 and 9, we can subtract 25 percent of .041 from .463 and obtain .453 as the $PVIF$ for $8\frac{1}{4}$ percent due in 10 years. Thus, if the appropriate discount rate is $8\frac{1}{4}$ percent, $1,000 due in 10 years is worth $453 today.

In general, the formula used for interpolation is as follows:

$$\text{IF for intermediate interest rate} = \left(\frac{i - i_L}{i_H - i_L}\right)(IF_H - IF_L) + IF_L.$$

Here $i =$ the interest rate in question, i_L is the interest rate in the table just lower than i, i_H is the interest rate in the table just higher than i, and IF_H and IF_L are the interest factors for i_H and i_L, respectively. Using the equation with the preceding example, we have

$$PVIF \text{ for } 8\frac{1}{4}\% \text{ due in 10 years} = \left(\frac{8.25 - 8}{9 - 8}\right)(.422 - .463) + .463$$

$$= \left(\frac{.25}{1}\right)(-.041) + .463 = .453,$$

which is the $PVIF$ found above. The equation can be used for each type of factor expression, $PVIF$, $CVIF$, $PVIF_a$, or $CVIF_a$.

Interpolation can also be used to determine interest rates, given interest factors. For example, suppose an investment that costs $163,500 promises to yield $50,000 per year for 4 years, and you want to know the rate of return on the investment. You use Equation 9–6 to find the $PVIF_a$:

$$PVIF_a = \frac{\$163,500}{\$50,000} = 3.27.$$

Looking this value up in Table 9–5, period 4, you see that it lies between 8 and 9 percent. Applying the interpolation formula, but solving for i, we have

$$PVIF_a \text{ for } i\% = 3.27 = \left(\frac{i-8}{9-8}\right)(3.240 - 3.312) + 3.312$$

$$3.27 = (i - 8)(-.072) + 3.312$$

$$-.042 = -.072i + .576$$

$$.072i = .618$$

$$i = 8.58\%.$$

Present Value of an Uneven Series of Receipts

Recall that the definition of an annuity includes the words *fixed amount*—in other words, annuities deal with constant, or level, payments or receipts. Although many financial decisions do involve constant payments, many important decisions are concerned with uneven flows of cash. In particular, the kinds of fixed asset investments dealt with in the following chapter very frequently involve uneven flows. Consequently it is necessary to expand our analysis to deal with varying payment streams. Since most of the applications call for present values, not compound sums or other figures, this section is restricted to the present value *(PV)*.

To illustrate the calculating procedure, suppose someone offers to sell you a series of payments consisting of $300 after one year, $100 after two years, and $200 after three years. How much would you be willing to pay for the series, assuming the appropriate discount rate (interest rate) is 4 percent? To determine the purchase price, simply compute the present value of the series; the calculations are worked out in Table 9–6. The receipts for each year are shown in the second column; the discount factors (from Table 9–3) are given in the third column; and the product of these two columns, the present value of each individual receipt, is given in the last column. When the individual present values in the last

Table 9–6	Period	Receipt	× Interest Factor ($PVIF$) = Present Value (PV or P_o)	
Calculating the	1	$300	.962	$288.60
Present Value of an	2	100	.925	92.50
Uneven Series of	3	200	.889	177.80
Payments				PV of investment $558.90

column are added, the sum is the present value of the investment, $558.90. Under the assumptions of the example, you should be willing to pay this amount for the investment.

Had the series of payments been somewhat different—say $300 at the end of the first year, $200 at the end of the second year, then eight annual payments of $100 each—we would probably want to use a different procedure for finding the investment's present value. We could, of course, set up a calculating table such as Table 9–6, but because most of the payments are part of an annuity we can use a short cut. The calculating procedure is shown in Table 9–7, and the logic of the table is diagrammed in Figure 9–5.

Section 1 of Table 9–7 deals with the $300 and the $200 received at the end of the first and second years respectively; their present values are found to be $288.60 and $185. Section 2 deals with the eight $100 payments. In part (a), the value of a $100, eight-year, 4 percent annuity is

Figure 9–5
Graphic Illustration of
Present Value
Calculations for an
Uneven Series of
Payments That
Includes an Annuity

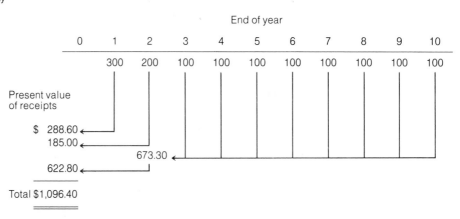

Table 9–7
Calculating Procedure for an Uneven Series of
Payments That Includes an Annuity

1. *PV* of $300 due in 1 year = $300(0.962) =	$ 288.60
PV of $200 due in 2 years = $200(0.925) =	185.00
2. *PV* of eight-year annuity with $100 receipts	
a. *PV* at beginning of year 3: $100(6.733) = $673.30	
b. *PV* of $673.30 = $673.30(0.925) =	622.80
3. *PV* of total series =	$1,096.40

found to be $673.30. However, the first receipt under the annuity comes at the end of the third year, so it is worth less than $673.30 today. Specifically, it is worth the present value of $673.30, discounted back two years at 4 percent, or $622.80; this calculation is shown in part (b) of section 2.[3] When the present values of the first two payments are added to the present value of the annuity component, the sum is the present value of the entire investment, or $1,096.40.

Semiannual and Other Compounding Periods[4]

In all the examples used thus far, it has been assumed that returns were received once a year, or annually. For example, in the first section of the chapter, dealing with compound values, it was assumed that funds were placed on deposit in a savings and loan association and grew by 4 percent a year. However, suppose the advertised rate had been 4 percent compounded *semiannually*. What would this have meant? Consider the following example.

You deposit $1,000 in a bank savings account and receive a return of 4 percent compounded semiannually. How much will you have at the end of one year? Semiannual compounding means that interest is actually paid each six months, a fact taken into account in the tabular calculations in Table 9–8. Here, the annual interest rate is divided by 2, but

Table 9–8
Compound Interest Calculations with Semiannual Compounding

Period	Beginning amount (P_o)	× (1 + i) =	Ending amount (P_t)
1	$1,000.00	(1.02)	$1,020.00
2	1,020.00	(1.02)	1,040.40

3. The present value of the annuity portion, $622.80, could also have been found by subtracting the $PVIF_a$ for a two-year annuity from the $PVIF_a$ for a ten-year annuity, then multiplying the result by $100.
4. This section can be omitted without loss of continuity.

twice as many compounding periods are used, because interest is paid twice a year. Comparing the amount on hand at the end of the second six-month period, $1,040.40, with what would have been on hand under annual compounding, $1,040, shows that semiannual compounding is better from the standpoint of the saver. *This result occurs, of course, because he earns interest on interest more frequently.*

General formulas can be developed for use when compounding periods are more frequent than once a year. To demonstrate this, Equation 9–2 is modified as follows:

$$V_t = P_0(1 + i)^t. \tag{9-2}$$

$$V_t = P_0\left(1 + \frac{i}{q}\right)^{qt}. \tag{9-8}$$

Here, q is the number of times per year compounding occurs. When banks compute daily interest, the value of q is set at 365, and Equation 9–8 is applied.

The interest tables can be used when compounding occurs more than once a year. Simply divide the nominal, or stated, interest rate by the number of times compounding occurs, and multiply the years by the number of compounding periods per year. For example, to find the amount to which $1,000 will grow after five years if semiannual compounding is applied to a stated 4 percent interest rate, divide 4 percent by 2 and multiply the five years by 2. Then look in Table 9–2 (or Table C–1) under the 2 percent column and in the row for the tenth period. You find an interest factor of 1.219. Multiplying this by the initial $1,000 gives a value of $1,219, the amount to which $1,000 will grow in five years at 4 percent compounded semiannually. This compares with $1,217 for annual compounding.

The same procedure is applied in all the cases covered — compounding, discounting, single payments, and annuities. To illustrate semiannual compounding in finding the present value of an annuity, for example, consider the case described in the above section, Present Value of an Annuity: $1,000 a year for three years, discounted at 4 percent. With annual compounding (or discounting) the interest factor is 2.775, and the present value of the annuity is $2,775. For semiannual compounding look under the 2 percent column and in the year-6 row of Table 9–5, to find an interest factor of 5.601. This is now multiplied by half of $1,000, or the $500 received each six months, to get the present value of the annuity, $2,800. The payments come a little more rapidly — the first $500 is paid after only six months (similarly with other payments), so the annuity is a little more valuable if payments are received semiannually rather than annually.

By letting q approach infinity, Equation 9–8 can be modified to the special case of *continuous compounding*. Continuous compounding is extremely useful in theoretical finance, and it also has practical applications. For example, some banks and savings associations pay interest on a continuous basis. Continuous compounding is discussed in the appendix to this chapter.

A Special Case of Semiannual Compounding: Bond Values[5]

Most bonds pay interest semiannually, so semiannual compounding procedures are appropriate for determining bond values. To illustrate, suppose a particular bond pays interest in the amount of $30 each six months, or $60 a year. The bond will mature in ten years, paying $1,000 (the "principal") at that time. Thus, if you buy the bond you will receive an annuity of $30 each six months, or twenty payments in total, plus $1,000 at the end of ten years (or twenty six-month periods). What is the bond worth, assuming that the appropriate market discount (or interest) rate is (A) 6 percent; (B) higher than 6 percent, say 8 percent; and (C) lower than 6 percent, say 4 percent?

PART A.

Step 1. You are buying an annuity plus a lump sum of $1,000. Find the *PV* of the interest payments:
1. Use $i/q = 6\%/2 = 3\%$ as the "interest rate."
2. Look up the $PVIF_a$ in Table D–4 for 20 periods at 3 percent, which is 14.877.
3. Find the *PV* of the stream of interest payments:
   PV of the interest $= \$30 \ (PVIF_a)$
   $$= \$30(14.877) = \$446.$$

Step 2. Find the *PV* of the $1,000 maturity value:
1. Use $i/q = 6\%/2 = 3\%$ as the "interest rate."
2. Look up the *PVIF* in Table D–2 for 20 periods at 3 percent, which is .554.
3. Find the *PV* of that value at maturity:
   PV of the maturity value $= \$1,000(PVIF)$
   $$= \$1,000(.554) = \$554.$$

Step 3. Combine the two component *PV*s to determine the value of the bond:
Bond value $= \$446 + \$554 = \$1,000.$

PART B. Repeating the process, we have
Step 1. $8\%/2 = 4\% =$ the "interest rate."

---

5. This section may be omitted without loss of continuity. The topic is also covered in Chapter 17.

$PVIF_a$ from Table D–4 = 13.59.
$PVIF$ from Table D–2 = .456

Step 2. Bond value = $30(13.59) + $1,000(.456)
= $408 + $456
= $864.

Notice that the bond is worth less when the going rate of interest for investments of similar risk is 8 percent than when it is 6 percent. At a price of $864, this bond provides an annual rate of return of 8 percent; at a price of $1,000, it provides an annual return of 6 percent. If 6 percent is the coupon rate on a bond of a given degree of risk, then whenever interest rates in the economy rise to the point where bonds of this degree of risk have an 8 percent return, the price of our bond will decline to $864, at which price it will yield the competitive rate of return, 8 percent.

PART C. Using the same process produces the following results:
Step 1. 4 percent/2 = 2 percent = the "interest rate."
$PVIF_a$ from Table D–4 = 16.351
$PVIF$ from Table D–2 = .673.

Step 2. Bond value = $30(16.351) + $1,000(.673)
= $491 + $673 = $1,164.

The bond is worth *more* than $1,000 when the going rate of interest is less than 6 percent, because then it offers a yield higher than the going rate. Its price rises to $1,164, where it provides a 4 percent annual rate of return. This calculation illustrates the fact that when interest rates in the economy decline, the prices of outstanding bonds rise.

Appropriate Compounding or Discounting Rates

Throughout the chapter, assumed compounding or discounting rates have been used in the examples. Although we will cover the subject in depth later in the book, it is useful at this point to give some idea of what the appropriate interest rate for a particular investment might be.[6]

The starting point is, of course, the general level of interest rates in the economy as a whole. This level is set by the interaction of supply-and-demand forces, with demand for funds coming largely from businesses, individual borrowers, and the federal government when it is

---

6. For convenience, in this chapter we speak of "interest rates," which implies that only debt is involved. In later chapters this concept is broadened considerably, and the term "rate of return" is used in lieu of "interest rate."

running a deficit. Funds are supplied by individual and corporate savers and, under the control of the Federal Reserve System, by the creation of money by banks. Depending on the relative levels of supply and demand, the basic pattern of interest rates is determined.

There is no one rate of interest in the economy—rather, there is, at any given time, an array of different rates. The lowest rates are found on the safest investments, the highest rates on the most risky ones. Usually, there is less risk on investments that mature in the near future than on longer term investments, so higher rates are usually associated with long-term investments. There are other factors that affect interest rate differentials (also called "yield" differentials), but a discussion of these factors is best deferred until later in the book.

A person faced with the kinds of decisions considered in this chapter must accept the existing set of interest rates found in the economy. If he has money to invest, he can invest in short-term United States government securities and incur no risk whatever. However, he will generally have to accept a relatively low yield on his investment. If he is willing to assume a little more risk, he can invest in high-grade corporate bonds and get a higher fixed rate of return. If he is willing to accept still more risk, he can move into common stocks to obtain variable (and hopefully higher) returns (dividends plus capital gains) on his investment. Other alternatives include bank and savings and loan deposits, long-term governments, mortgages, apartment houses, land held for speculation, and so on.

Risk Premiums

With only a limited amount of money to invest, one must pick and choose among investments; the final selection involves a tradeoff between risk and returns. Suppose, for example, that you are indifferent between a five-year government bond yielding 7 percent a year, a five-year corporate bond yielding 9 percent, and a share of stock on which you can expect a 12 percent return. Given this situation, you can take the government bond as a riskless security, and you attach a 2 percent risk premium to the corporate bond and a 5 percent risk premium to the share of stock. Risk premiums, then, are the added returns that risky investments must command over less risky ones if there is to be a demand for risky assets. The concept of the risk premium is discussed in more detail in Chapter 11 and also in the chapters dealing with the cost of capital.

Opportunity Costs

Although there are many potential investments available in the economy at any given time, a particular individual actively considers only a limited number of them. After making adjustments for risk differentials, he ranks the various alternatives from the most attractive to the least. Then, presumably, our investor puts his available funds in the most attractive investment. If he is offered a new investment, he must compare it with the best of the existing alternatives. If he takes the new investment, he must give up the opportunity of investing in the best of his old alternatives. *The yield on the best of the alternatives is defined as the opportunity cost of investing in the new alternative.* For example, suppose you have funds invested in a bank time deposit that pays 6 percent. Now suppose that someone offers you another investment of equal risk. To make the new investment, you must withdraw funds from the bank deposit; therefore *6 percent is defined as the opportunity cost of the new investment.* You could determine the interest rate on the new investment (using Equation 9–2 or procedures described in the next chapter); if the new investment yields more than 6 percent, make the switch. The interest rates used in the examples throughout this chapter were all determined as opportunity costs available to the person in the example. This concept is also used in the following chapter, where we consider business decisions on investments in fixed assets, or the *capital budgeting decision.*

Summary

A knowledge of compound interest and present value techniques is essential to an understanding of many important aspects of finance: capital budgeting, financial structure, security valuation, and many other topics. The basic principles of compound interest, together with the most important formulas used in practice, were described in this chapter.

Compound Value. Compound value (V_t), or compound amount, is defined as the sum to which a beginning amount of principal (P_0) will grow over t years when interest is earned at the rate of i percent a year. The equation for finding compound values is

$$V_t = P_0(1 + i)^t.$$

Tables giving the compound value of $1 for a large number of different years and interest rates have been prepared. The compound value of $1 is called the compound value interest factor *(CVIF)*; illustrative values are given in Table 9–2, and a more complete set of interest factors is given in Appendix Table D–1.

Present Value (PV). The present value of a future payment *(PV)* is the amount that, if we had it now and invested it at the specified interest rate *(i)*, would equal the future payment *(V_t)* on the date the future payment is due. For example, if you were to receive $1,217 after five years and decide that 4 percent is the appropriate interest rate (it is called *discount rate* when computing present values), then you could find the present value of the $1,217 to be $1,000 by applying the following equation:

$$PV = V_t\left[\frac{1}{(1 + i)^t}\right] = \$1,217[0.822] = \$1,000.$$

The term in brackets is called the present value interest factor *(PVIF)*, and values for it have been worked out in Table 9–3 and Appendix Table D–2.

Compound Value of an Annuity. An annuity is defined as a series of payments of a fixed amount *(a)* for a specified number of years. The compound value of an annuity is the total amount one would have at the end of the annuity period if each payment is invested at a certain interest rate and is held to the end of the annuity period. For example, suppose we have a three-year, $1,000 annuity invested at 4 percent. There are formulas for annuities, but tables are available for the relevant interest factors. The $CVIF_a$ for the compound value of a three-year annuity at 4 percent is 3.122, and it can be used to find the present value of the illustrative annuity:

Compound value $= CVIF_a \times$ annual receipt $= 3.122 \times \$1,000 = \$3,122.$

Thus, $3,122 is the compound value of the annuity.

Present Value of an Annuity. The present value of an annuity is the lump sum one would need to have on hand today in order to be able to withdraw equal amounts *(a)* each year and end up with a balance exactly equal to zero at the end of the annuity period. For example, if you wish to withdraw $1,000 a year for three years, you could deposit $2,775 today in a bank account paying 4 percent interest, withdraw the $1,000 in each of the next three years, and end up with a zero balance. Thus, $2,775 is the present value of an annuity of $1,000 a year for three years when the appropriate discount rate is 4 percent. Again, tables are available for finding the present value of annuities. To use them, one simply looks up the interest factor *(PVIF_a)* for the appropriate number of years and interest rate, then multiplies the $PVIF_a$ by the annual receipt.

PV of annuity $= PVIF_a \times$ annual receipt $= 2.775 \times \$1,000 = \$2,775.$

Relation of Interest Factors to One Another. All interest factors given in the tables are for $1; for example, 2.775 is the $PVIF_a$ for finding the present value of a three-year annuity. It must be multiplied by the annual receipt, $1,000 in the example, to find the actual value of the annuity. Students—and even financial managers—sometimes make careless mistakes when looking up interest factors, using the wrong table for the purpose. This can be avoided if one recognizes the following sets of relations.

1. *Compound value, single payment.* The CVIF for the compound value of a single payment, with the normal interest rates and holding periods generally found, is *always* greater than 1.0 but seldom larger than about 3.0.

2. *Present value, single payment.* The PVIF for the present value of a single payment is *always* less than 1.0; for example, 0.822 is the PVIF for 4 percent held for five years. CVIF is larger than 1.0; the PVIF is less than 1.0.

3. *Compound value of an annuity.* The $CVIF_a$ for the compound value of an annuity is *always* greater than the number of years the annuity has to run. For example, the $CVIF_a$ for a three-year annuity will be greater than 3.0, while the $CVIF_a$ for a ten-year annuity will be greater than 10.0. Just how much greater depends on the interest rate—at low rates the interest factor is slightly greater than N; at high rates it is very much greater.

4. *Present value of an annuity.* The $PVIF_a$ for the present value of an annuity is always less than the number of years it has to run. For example, the $PVIF_a$ for the present value of a three-year annuity is less than 3.0; at high rates it is very much less than 3.0.

Other Uses of the Basic Equations. The four basic interest formulas can be used in combination to find such things as the present value of an uneven series of receipts. The formulas can also be transformed to find (1) the annual payments necessary to accumulate a future sum, (2) the annual receipts from a specified annuity, (3) the periodic payments necessary to amortize a loan, and (4) the interest rate implicit in a loan contract.

Appropriate Interest Rate. The appropriate interest rate to be used is critical when working with compound interest problems. The true nature of the interest rates to be used when working with business problems can be understood only after the chapters dealing with the cost of capital have been examined; this chapter concluded with a brief discussion of some of the factors that determine the appropriate rate of interest for a particular problem—the risk of the investment and the investor's opportunity cost of money.

Questions

9–1. What kinds of financial decisions require explicit consideration of the interest factor?

9–2. Compound interest relations are important for decisions other than financial ones. Why are they important to marketing managers?

9–3. Would you rather have an account in a savings and loan association that pays 5 percent interest compounded semiannually or 5 percent interest compounded daily? Why?

9–4. For a given interest rate and a given number of years, is the interest factor for the sum of an annuity greater or less than the interest factor for the present value of the annuity?

9–5. Suppose you are examining two investments, A and B. Both have the same maturity, but A pays a 6 percent return and B yields 5 percent. Which investment is probably riskier? How do you know it is riskier?

Problems

9–1. Which amount is worth more at 9 percent: $1,000 today or $2,000 after 8 years?

9–2. At a growth rate of 7 percent, how long does it take a sum to double?

9–3. a. What amount would be paid for a $1,000, ten-year bond that pays $40 interest semiannually ($80 a year) and is sold to yield 10 percent, compounded semiannually?
   b. What would be paid if the bond is sold to yield 8 percent?
   c. What would be paid if semiannual interest payments are $50 and the bond is sold to yield 6 percent?

9–4. On December 31, Diane Baker buys a building for $80,000, paying 20 percent down and the balance in 15 equal annual installments that are to include principal plus 8 percent compound interest on the declining balance. What are the equal installments?

9–5. The Family Company is establishing a sinking fund to retire a $900,000 mortgage that matures on December 31, 1988. The company plans to put a fixed amount into the fund each year for ten years. The first payment will be made on December 31, 1979, the last on December 31, 1988. The company anticipates that the fund will earn 9 percent a year. What annual contributions must be made to accumulate the $900,000 as of December 31, 1988?

9–6. You have just purchased a newly issued $1,000, five-year Plug Company bond for $1,000. This bond pays $60 in interest payments semiannually ($120 a year); call this bond A. You are also negotiating the purchase of a $1,000, six-year Plug Company bond which returns $30 in semiannual interest payments and has six years remaining before it matures; call this bond B.
   a. What is the "going rate of return" on bonds of the risk and maturity of Plug Company's bonds?

b. What should you be willing to pay for bond B?

c. How would your answer for the value of bond B change if bond A had paid $40 in semiannual interest instead of $60, but still sold for $1,000? The second bond still pays $30 semiannually and $1,000 at the end of six years.

9-7. You need $129,200 at the end of 17 years. You know that the best you can do is to make equal payments into a bank account on which you can earn 5 percent interest compounded annually.

a. What amount must you plan to pay annually to achieve your objective? The first payment is to be made at the end of the first year.

b. Instead of making annual payments, you decide to make one lump-sum payment today. To achieve your objective of $129,200 at the end of the 17-year period, what should this sum be? You can still earn 5 percent interest compounded annually on your account.

9-8. You can buy a note at a price of $13,420. If you buy the note, you will receive ten annual payments of $2,000, the first payment to be made one year from today. What rate of return, or yield, does the note offer?

9-9. You can buy a bond for $1,000 that will pay no interest during its 8-year life but will have a value of $1,851 when it matures. What rate of interest will you earn if you buy the bond and hold it to maturity?

9-10. A bank agrees to lend you $1,000 today in return for your promise to pay the bank $1,838 nine years from today. What rate of interest is the bank charging you?

9-11. If earnings in 1979 are $2.66 a share, while seven years earlier, in 1972, they were $1, what has been the rate of growth in earnings?

9-12. The Randolf Company's sales last year were $1 million.

a. Assuming that sales grow 18 percent a year, calculate sales for each of the next six years.

b. Plot the sales projections.

c. If your graph is correct, your projected sales curve is nonlinear. If it had been linear, would this have indicated a constant, increasing, or decreasing percentage growth rate?

9-13. You are considering two investment opportunities, A and B. A is expected to pay $400 a year for the first ten years, $600 a year for the next 15 years, and nothing thereafter. B is expected to pay $1,000 a year for ten years, and nothing thereafter. You find that alternative investments of similar risk yield 8 percent and 14 percent for A and B respectively.

a. Find the present value of each investment. Show calculations.

b. Which is the more risky investment? Why?

c. Assume that your rich uncle will give you your choice of investments without cost to you, and that (1) you must hold the investment for its entire life (cannot sell it) or (2) you are free to sell it at its going market price. Which investment would you prefer under each of the two conditions?

9-14. The Bronson Company's common stock paid a dividend of $1 last year.

Dividends are expected to grow at a rate of 18 percent for each of the next six years.

a. Calculate the expected dividend for each of the next six years.

b. Assuming that the first of these six dividends will be paid one year from now, what is the present value of the six dividends? Given the riskiness of the dividend stream, 18 percent is the appropriate discount rate.

c. Assume that the price of the stock will be $27 six years from now. What is the present value of this "terminal value"? Use an 18 percent discount rate.

d. Assume that you will buy the stock, receive the six dividends, then sell the share; how much should you be willing to pay for it?

e. Do not do any calculations for this question, but explain in words what would happen to the price of this stock (1) if the discount rate declined because the riskiness of the stock declined or (2) if the growth rate of the dividend stream increased.

9-15. The Programmatics Consulting Company is considering the purchase of a new computer that will provide the following net cash flow (or profit) stream:

Year

1	$10,000
2	20,000
3	30,000
4	40,000
5	50,000

a. What is the present value of the profit stream, using a 12 percent discount rate?

b. If the computer costs $100,000, should Programmatics purchase it?

9-16. The Martan Company pays $480,000 for a machine that provides savings of $50,000 per year for 20 years. What is the return on the investment in the machine?

9-17. The Gorton Company invests $60,000 in a new item of equipment. The savings from the equipment during the five years of its economic life are:

Year 1	$10,000
Year 2	$10,000
Year 3	$10,000
Year 4	$24,150
Year 5	$24,150

(a) At what discount rate is it profitable for the company to make the purchase?

(b) What changes would simplify the analysis?

9-18. The Brinkner Company has a cost of capital of 12 percent. It invests in a machine which provides savings of $18,000 per year for six years. What is the maximum that can be paid for the machine if it is to earn the required 12 percent cost of capital?

9–19. You are considering the economic value of an MBA. Assuming that you can and do enroll immediately, expenses are $4,000 per year and foregone income $6,000 per year for the required two years; your expected yearly income for the following 18 years is increased by $3,713.

(a) What is the return on investment earned? (Hint: It is worth more than 10 percent.)

(b) What are some of the major complicating factors ignored?

Appendix A to Chapter 9
Continuous Compounding
and Discounting

Continuous Compounding

In Chapter 9 we implicitly assumed that growth occurs at discrete intervals—annually, semiannually, and so forth. For some purposes it is better to assume instantaneous, or *continuous*, growth. The relationship between discrete and continuous compounding is illustrated in Figure A9–1. Figure A9–1(a) shows the annual compounding case, where interest is added once a year; in Figure A9–1(b) compounding occurs twice a year; in Figure A9–1(c) interest is earned continuously.

Figure A9–1
Annual, Semiannual, and Continuous Compounding

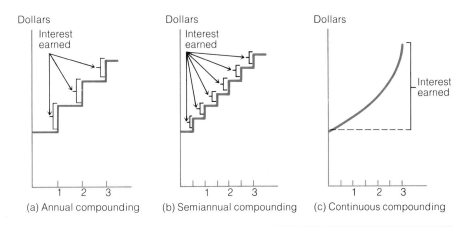

(a) Annual compounding   (b) Semiannual compounding   (c) Continuous compounding

In Chapter 9, Equation 9–8 was developed to allow for any number of compounding periods per year:

$$V_t = P_0\left(1 + \frac{i}{q}\right)^{qt} \tag{9–8}$$

Equation 9–8, in turn, can be modified to allow for continuous compounding. The steps in this modification are developed below. In the literature of finance, where continuous compounding is employed, t is used for years (time). Recognize further that i is an interest rate, discount rate, or growth rate and is also denoted by k, which is used in the following material.

Step 1

First, assume that k, the interest or growth rate, is 100 percent ($k = 100$ percent $= 1.0$); that is, assume that with annual compounding the initial principal (P_0) will double each year:

$$V_t = P_0(1 + k)^t$$
$$= P_0(1 + 1)^t$$
$$= P_0(2)^t.$$

Step 2

Now suppose that $P_0 = 1$ and that k remains at 100 percent, but compounding occurs q times per year. The value after one year will be

$$V_1 = \left(1 + \frac{1}{q}\right)^q \tag{A9-1}$$

If $q = 1$, $V = 2$; if $q = 2$, $V = 2.25$; if $q = 3$, $V = 2.37$. Thus, V increases as q is increased.

Step 3

Returning to Equation 9-8, the general case of compound growth (but using the new notation), we can develop an equation for the special case of continuous compounding. Starting with

$$V_t = P_0\left(1 + \frac{k}{q}\right)^{qt} \tag{9-8}$$

and noting that, since we can multiply qt by k/k, we can set $qt = (q/k)(kt)$ and rewrite Equation 9-8 as

$$V_t = P_0\left[\left(1 + \frac{k}{q}\right)^{(q/k)}\right]^{(kt)} \tag{A9-2}$$

Step 4

Defining $k = q/k$ and noting that $k/q = 1/(q/k) = 1/km$, we can rewrite Equation A9-2 as

$$V_t = P_0\left[\left(1 + \frac{1}{m}\right)^m\right]^{kt} \tag{A9-3}$$

Step 5

As the number of compounding periods, q, increases, k also increases; this causes the term in brackets in Equation A9-3 to increase. At the limit, when q and m approach infinity (and compounding is instantaneous, or continuous), the term in brackets approaches the value $2.718 \cdots$. The value e is defined as this limiting case:

$$e = \operatorname*{Lim}_{m \to \infty} \left(1 + \frac{1}{m}\right)^m = 2.718 \cdots . \tag{A9--4}$$

Thus, we may substitute e for the bracketed term, rewriting Equation A9–3 as

$$V_t = P_0 e^{kt} \tag{A9--5}$$

for the case of continuous compounding (or continuous growth).

Step 6

Interest factors (IF) can be developed for continuous compounding; developing the factors requires the use of natural, or Naperian, logarithms.[1] First, letting $P_0 = 1$, we can rewrite Equation A9–5 as

$$V_t = e^{kt}. \tag{A9--6}$$

Setting Equation A9–6 in log form and noting that ln denotes the log to the base e, we obtain

$$ln \; V_t = kt \; ln \; e. \tag{A9--7}$$

Since e is defined as the base of the system of natural logarithms, $ln \; e$ must equal 1.0 (that is, $e^1 = e$, so $ln \; e = 1.0$). Therefore,

$$ln \; V_t = kt. \tag{A9--8}$$

One simply looks up the product kt in a table of natural logarithms and obtains the value V_t as the antilog. For example, if $t =$ five years and $k =$ 10 percent, the product is .50. Looking up this value in Table A9–1, a table of natural logs, we find .5 to lie between .49470 and .50078, whose antilogs are 1.64 and 1.65 respectively. Interpolating, we find the antilog of .5 to be 1.648. Thus, 1.648 is the interest factor for a 10-percent growth rate compounded continuously for five years; $1 growing continuously at this compound rate would equal $1.648 after five years.

Since continuous compounding is not commonly applied in practice, we have not provided a table of continuous interest factors.[2] It should be noted, however, that the $1.648 obtained for five years of *continuous*

1. Recall that the logarithm of a number is the power, or exponent, to which a specified base must be raised to equal the number; that is, the log (base 10) of 100 is 2 because $(10)^2 = 100$. In the system of natural logs the base is $e \approx 2.718$.
2. Continuous compounding is used extensively in theoretical work. In practice, the major use is by banks and savings and loan associations as a competitive tactic to raise the effective rate on deposits permitted by regulators.

**Decisions Involving
Long-term Assets**

Table A9–1
Natural Logarithms of Numbers between 1.0 and 4.99

N	0	1	2	3	4	5	6	7	8	9
1.0	0.00000	.00995	.01980	.02956	.03922	.04879	.05827	.06766	.07696	.08618
.1	.09531	.10436	.11333	.12222	.13103	.13976	.14842	.15700	.16551	.17395
.2	.18232	.19062	.19885	.20701	.21511	.22314	.23111	.23902	.24686	.25464
.3	.26236	.27003	.27763	.28518	.29267	.30010	.30748	.31481	.32208	.32930
.4	.33647	.34359	.35066	.35767	.36464	.37156	.37844	.38526	.39204	.39878
.5	.40547	.41211	.41871	.42527	.43178	.43825	.44469	.45108	.45742	.46373
.6	.47000	.47623	.48243	.48858	.49470	.50078	.50682	.51282	.51879	.52473
.7	.53063	.53649	.54232	.54812	.55389	.55962	.56531	.57098	.57661	.58222
.8	.58779	.59333	.59884	.60432	.60977	.61519	.62058	.62594	.63127	.63658
.9	.64185	.64710	.65233	.65752	.66269	.66783	.67294	.67803	.68310	.68813
2.0	0.69315	.69813	.70310	.70804	.71295	.71784	.72271	.72755	.73237	.73716
.1	.74194	.74669	.75142	.75612	.76081	.76547	.77011	.77473	.77932	.78390
.2	.78846	.79299	.79751	.80200	.80648	.81093	.81536	.81978	.82418	.82855
.3	.83291	.83725	.84157	.84587	.85015	.85442	.85866	.86289	.86710	.87129
.4	.87547	.87963	.88377	.88789	.89200	.89609	.90016	.90422	.90826	.91228
.5	.91629	.92028	.92426	.92822	.93216	.93609	.94001	.94391	.94779	.95166
.6	.95551	.95935	.96317	.96698	.97078	.97456	.97833	.98208	.98582	.98954
.7	.99325	.99695	.00063*	.00430*	.00796*	.01160*	.01523*	.01885*	.02245*	.02604*
.8	1.02962	.03318	.03674	.04028	.04380	.04732	.05082	.05431	.05779	.06126
.9	.06471	.06815	.07158	.07500	.07841	.08181	.08519	.08856	.09192	.09527
3.0	1.09861	.10194	.10526	.10856	.11186	.11514	.11841	.12168	.12493	.12817
.1	.13140	.13462	.13783	.14103	.14422	.14740	.15057	.15373	.15688	.16002
.2	.16315	.16627	.16938	.17248	.17557	.17865	.18173	.18479	.18784	.19089
.3	.19392	.19695	.19996	.20297	.20597	.20896	.21194	.21491	.21788	.22083
.4	.22378	.22671	.22964	.23256	.23547	.23837	.24127	.24415	.24703	.24990
.5	.25276	.25562	.25846	.26130	.26413	.26695	.26976	.27257	.27536	.27815
.6	.28093	.28371	.28647	.28923	.29198	.29473	.29746	.30019	.30291	.30563
.7	.30833	.31103	.31372	.31641	.31909	.32176	.32442	.32708	.32972	.33237
.8	.33500	.33763	.34025	.34286	.34547	.34807	.35067	.35325	.35584	.35841
.9	.36098	.36354	.36609	.36864	.37118	.37372	.37624	.37877	.38128	.38379
4.0	1.38629	.38879	.39128	.39377	.39624	.39872	.40118	.40364	.40610	.40854
.1	.41099	.41342	.41585	.41828	.42070	.42311	.42552	.42792	.43031	.43270
.2	.43508	.43746	.43984	.44220	.44456	.44692	.44927	.45161	.45395	.45629
.3	.45862	.46094	.46326	.46557	.46787	.47018	.47247	.47476	.47705	.47933
.4	.48160	.48387	.48614	.48840	.49065	.49290	.49515	.49739	.49962	.50185
.5	.50408	.50630	.50851	.51072	.51293	.51513	.51732	.51951	.52170	.52388
.6	.52606	.52823	.53039	.53256	.53471	.53687	.53902	.54116	.54330	.54543
.7	.54756	.54969	.55181	.55393	.55604	.55814	.56025	.56235	.56444	.56653
.8	.56862	.57070	.57277	.57485	.57691	.57898	.58104	.58309	.58515	.58719
.9	.58924	.59127	.59331	.59534	.59737	.59939	.60141	.60342	.60543	.60744

*Add 1.0 to indicated figure.

compounding compares closely with $1.629, the figure for semiannual compounding, and with the $1.611 obtained with annual compounding. Thus, continuous compounding does not produce values materially different from semiannual or annual compounding. As was pointed out earlier, the importance of continuous compounding is its convenience in theoretical work where calculus must be employed.

Continuous Discounting

Equation A9–5 can be transformed into Equation A9–9 and used to determine present values under continuous compounding. Using k as the discount rate (again, this is the standard notation: k is used as the discount rate, and g as the growth rate for compounding), we obtain

$$PV = \frac{V_t}{e^{kt}} = V_t e^{-kt}. \tag{A9-9}$$

Thus, if $1,648 is due in five years and if the appropriate *continuous* discount rate k is 10 percent, the present value of this future payment is

$$PV = \frac{\$1,648}{1.648} = \$1,000.$$

Continuous Compounding and Discounting for Annuities

The treatment of continuous compounding for single values is more complex than that for discrete compounding, but it still involves nothing more than algebra. For continuously compounding and discounting *streams* of payments ("annuities"), however, elementary integral calculus must be employed. The procedures involved are outlined below.

Step 1

First, observe Figure A9–2(a). An amount a is received at the end of each year. The amount received grows at the rate g; thus the accumulated sum of the receipts at the end of any year N is

$$S_t = a(1 + g)^0 + a(1 + g)^1 + a(1 + g)^2 + \cdots a(1 + g)^{t-1}$$

$$= a + a(1 + g)^1 + a(1 + g)^2 + \cdots a(1 + g)^{t-1}$$

$$= \sum_{t=1}^{N} a(1 + g)^{t-1}.$$

The accumulated sum of the receipts, S_t, is equal to the sum of the rectangles in Figure A9–2(a); this is the area under the discontinuous curve formed by the tops of the rectangles.

Figure A9–2
Sum of an "Annuity"
under Discrete and
Continuous
Compounding

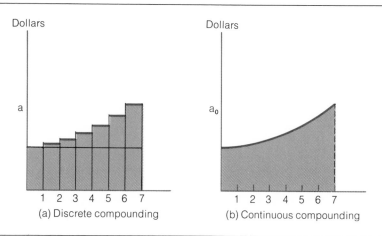

(a) Discrete compounding   (b) Continuous compounding

Step 2

Exactly the same principle is involved in finding the accumulated sum of the continuous equivalent of an annuity, or a stream of receipts received continuously. The accumulated sum is again represented by the area under a curve, but now the curve is continuous as in Figure A9–2(b). In the discrete case, the area under the curve was obtained by adding the rectangles; in the continuous case, the area must be found by the process of integration.

Note that the stream of receipts, or the value of a_t, is found by taking the initial receipt, a_0 *(not a_1)*, and letting it grow at the continuous rate g.

$$a_t = a_0 e^{gt}. \tag{A9–10}$$

Equation A9–10 defines the curve, and the area under the curve (S_t) is represented by the integral

$$S_t = \int_{t=0}^{N} a_0 e^{gt} \, dt = a_0 \int_{t=0}^{N} e^{gt} \, dt. \tag{A9–11}$$

Step 3

Given a discrete series of receipts such as those shown in Figure A9–2(a) and a discount rate, k, we find their *PV* as

$$PV = \sum_{t=1}^{N} a_t (1 + k)^{-t}.$$

If the receipts accrue continuously, as do those in Figure A9–2(b), we must find the present value of the stream of payments by calculus. First, note that by Equation A9–9 we find the *PV* of the instantaneous receipt for period t as

$$PV = a_t e^{-kt}. \tag{A9-9}$$

The present value of the entire stream of receipts is given as the integral

$$PV = \int_{t=0}^{N} a_t e^{-kt} \, dt. \tag{A9-12}$$

Step 4

Although the primary equations (A9-11 and A9-12) developed thus far in this section are seldom used individually, one of the most important theoretical formulations in the field of finance—the Gordon model—is developed by combining them. The Gordon model is discussed at some length in Chapter 17, but we can facilitate that discussion by showing at this point how these equations can be combined.

First, note that $a_t = a_0 e^{gt}$ from Equation A9-10. Next, substitute this value into Equation A9-12, obtaining

$$PV = \int_{t=0}^{N} a_0 e^{gt} e^{-kt} \, dt. \tag{A9-13}$$

Now remove the constant term, a_0, from within the integral and combine the exponents of the e term, obtaining

$$PV = a_0 \int_{t=0}^{N} e^{gt-kt} \, dt$$

$$= a_0 \int_{t=0}^{N} e^{-(k-g)t} \, dt. \tag{A9-14}$$

Therefore, the integration of Equation A9-14 yields an indefinite integral of the form:

$$PV = \frac{a_0 e^{-(k-g)t}}{k-g}$$

that, when evaluated at $t = \infty$, is equal to 0 and when evaluated at $t = 0$, is equal to

$$-\frac{a_0}{k-g}.$$

Subtracting the lower bound from the upper (which is 0) yields:

$$PV = 0 - \left[-\frac{a_0}{k-g} \right]$$

$$= \frac{a_0}{k-g}. \tag{A9-15}$$

Equation A9–15 is, thus, the present value of a continuous stream of receipts growing at a rate g and discounted at a rate k. The basic Gordon model, which is essentially Equation A9–15, is widely used in finance, but its further development is deferred to Chapter 17.

10   Capital Budgeting Techniques

Capital budgeting involves the entire process of planning expenditures whose returns are expected to extend beyond one year. The choice of one year is arbitrary, of course, but it is a convenient cutoff point for distinguishing between kinds of expenditures. Obvious examples of capital outlays are expenditures for land, buildings, and equipment, and for permanent additions to working capital associated with plant expansion. An advertising or promotion campaign, or a program of research and development, is also likely to have an impact beyond one year, so they too can be classified as capital budgeting expenditures.

Capital budgeting is important for the future well-being of the firm; it is also a complex, conceptually difficult topic. As we shall see later in this chapter, the optimum capital budget—the level of investment that maximizes the present value of the firm—is simultaneously determined by the interaction of supply and demand forces under conditions of uncertainty. Supply forces refer to the supply of capital to the firm, or its *cost of capital schedule.* Demand forces relate to the investment opportunities open to the firm, as measured by the *stream of revenues* that will result from an investment decision. *Uncertainty* enters the decision because it is impossible to know exactly either the cost of capital or the stream of revenues that will be derived from a project.

To facilitate an exposition of the investment decision process, we have broken the topic down into its major components. In this chapter, we consider the capital budgeting process and the techniques generally employed by reasonably sophisticated business firms. Here our focus is on the time factor, and the compound interest concepts covered in the preceding chapter are used extensively. Uncertainty is explicitly and formally considered in Chapter 11, and the cost of capital concept is developed and related to capital budgeting in Chapters 17 through 19, after a discussion of the sources and forms of long-term capital in Chapters 12 through 16.

Significance of Capital Budgeting

A number of factors combine to make capital budgeting perhaps the most important decision with which financial management is involved. Further, all departments of a firm—production, marketing, and so on—

are vitally affected by the capital budgeting decisions, so all executives, no matter what their primary responsibility, must be aware of how capital budgeting decisions are made. These points are discussed in this section.

Long-term Effects

First and foremost, the fact that the results continue over an extended period means that the decision maker loses some of his flexibility. He must make a commitment into the future. For example, the purchase of an asset with an economic life of ten years requires a long period of waiting before the final results of the action can be known. The decision maker must commit funds for this period, and, thus, he becomes a hostage of future events.

Asset expansion is fundamentally related to expected future sales. A decision to buy or to construct a fixed asset that is expected to last five years involves an implicit five-year sales forecast. Indeed, the economic life of a purchased asset represents an implicit forecast for the duration of the economic life of the asset. Hence, failure to forecast accurately will result in overinvestment or underinvestment in fixed assets.

An erroneous forecast of asset requirements can result in serious consequences. If the firm has invested too much in assets, it will incur unnecessarily heavy expenses. If it has not spent enough on fixed assets, two serious problems may arise. First, the firm's equipment may not be sufficiently modern to enable it to produce competitively. Second, if it has inadequate capacity, it may lose a portion of its share of the market to rival firms. To regain lost customers typically requires heavy selling expenses, price reduction, product improvements, and so forth.

Timing the Availability of Capital Assets

Another problem is to phase properly the availability of capital assets in order to have them come "on stream" at the correct time. For example, the executive vice-president of a decorative tile company gave the authors an illustration of the importance of capital budgeting. His firm tried to operate near capacity most of the time. For about four years there had been intermittent spurts in the demand for its product; when these spurts occurred, the firm had to turn away orders. After a sharp increase in demand, the firm would add capacity by renting an additional building, then purchasing and installing the appropriate equipment. It would take six to eight months to have the additional capacity ready. At this point the company frequently found that there was no demand for its increased output—other firms had already expanded their operations and had taken an increased share of the market, with the result that demand for this firm had leveled off. If the firm had properly forecast demand and had planned its increase in capacity six months or one year in advance, it would have been able to maintain its market—indeed, to obtain a larger share of the market.

Quality of Capital Assets

Good capital budgeting will also improve the timing of asset acquisitions and the quality of assets purchased. This situation follows from the nature of capital goods and their producers. Capital goods are not ordered by firms until they see that sales are beginning to press on capacity. Such occasions occur simultaneously for many firms. When the heavy orders come in, the producers of capital goods go from a situation of idle capacity to one where they cannot meet all the orders that have been placed. Consequently, large backlogs accumulate. Since the production of capital goods involves a relatively long work-in-process period, a year or more of waiting may be involved before the additional capital goods are available. This factor has obvious implications for purchasing agents and plant managers.

Raising Funds

Another reason for the importance of capital budgeting is that asset expansion typically involves substantial expenditures. Before a firm spends a large amount of money, it must make the proper plans—large amounts of funds are not available automatically. A firm contemplating a major capital expenditure program may need to arrange its financing several years in advance to be sure of having the funds required for the expansion.

Ability to Compete

Finally, it has been said with a great deal of truth that many firms fail, not because they have too much capital equipment but because they have too little. While the conservative approach of having a small amount of capital equipment may be appropriate at times, such an approach may also be fatal if a firm's competitors install modern, automated equipment that permits them to produce a better product and sell it at a lower price. The same thing also holds true for nations: If United States firms fail to modernize but those of other nations do, then the U.S. will not be able to compete in world markets. Thus, an understanding of business investment behavior and of factors that motivate firms to undertake investment programs is vital for congressional leaders and others involved in governmental policy making.

A Simplified View of Capital Budgeting

Capital budgeting is, in essence, an application of a classic proposition from the economic theory of the firm: namely, a firm should operate at the point where its marginal revenue is just equal to its marginal cost. When this rule is applied to the capital budgeting decision, marginal revenue is taken to be the percentage rate of return on investments, while marginal cost is the firm's marginal cost of capital.

A simplified version of the concept is depicted in Figure 10–1(a). Here the horizontal axis measures the dollars of investment during a year, while the vertical axis shows both the percentage cost of capital and the rate of return on projects. The projects are denoted by boxes — project A, for example, calls for an outlay of $3 million and promises a 17 percent rate of return; project B requires $1 million and yields about 16 percent; and so on. The last investment, project G, simply involves buying 4 percent government bonds, which may be purchased in unlimited quantities. In Figure 10–1(b) the concept is generalized to show smoothed investment opportunity schedules (IRR), and three alternative schedules are presented.[1]

Figure 10–1

Illustrative Capital
Budgeting Decision
Process

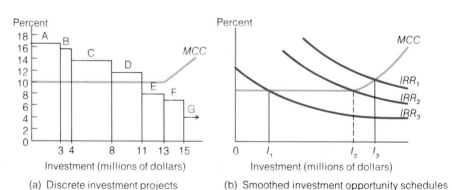

(a) Discrete investment projects

(b) Smoothed investment opportunity schedules

The curve MCC designates the marginal cost of capital, or the cost of each additional dollar acquired for purposes of making capital expenditures. As it is drawn in 10–1(a), the marginal cost of capital is constant

1. The investment opportunity schedules measure the rate of return on each project. The rate of return on a project is generally called the *internal rate of return (IRR)*. This is why we label the investment opportunity schedules *IRR*. The process of calculating the *IRR* is explained later in this chapter.

at 10 percent until the firm has raised $13 million, after which the marginal cost of capital curve turns up.[2] To maximize profits, the firm should accept projects A through D, obtaining and investing $11 million, and reject E, F, and G.

Notice that three alternative investment opportunity schedules are shown in 10–1(b). IRR_1 designates relatively many good investment opportunities, while IRR_3 designates relatively few good projects. The three different curves could be interpreted as applying either to three different firms or to one firm at three different times. As long as the IRR curve cuts the MCC curve to the left of I_2—for example, at I_1—the marginal cost of capital is constant. To the right of I_2—for example, at I_3—the cost of capital is rising. Therefore, if investment opportunities are such that the IRR curve cuts the MCC curve to the right of I_2, the *actual* marginal cost of capital (a single point) varies depending on the IRR curve. In this chapter we generally *assume* that the IRR curve cuts the MCC curve to the left of I_2, thus permitting us to assume that the cost of capital is constant. This assumption is relaxed in Chapter 19, where we show how the MCC varies with the amount of funds raised during a given year.

Application of the Concept

At the applied level, the capital budgeting process is much more complex than the preceding example suggests. Projects do not just appear; a continuing stream of good investment opportunities results from hard thinking, careful planning, and, often, large outlays for research and development. Moreover, some very difficult measurement problems are involved: the sales and costs associated with particular projects must be estimated, frequently for many years into the future, in the face of great uncertainty. Finally, some difficult conceptual and empirical problems arise over the methods of calculating rates of return and the cost of capital.

Businessmen are required to take action, however, even in the face of the kinds of problems described; this requirement has led to the development of procedures that assist in making optimal investment decisions. One of these procedures, forecasting, was discussed in Chapter 4; uncertainty is discussed in formal terms in the next chapter; and the important subject of the cost of capital is deferred to Chapter 19. The essentials of the other elements of capital budgeting are taken up in the remainder of this chapter.

---

2. The reasons for assuming this particular shape for the marginal cost of capital curve are explained in Chapter 19.

**Investment
Proposals**

Aside from the actual generation of ideas, the first step in the capital budgeting process is to assemble a list of the proposed new investments, together with the data necessary to appraise them. Although practices vary from firm to firm, proposals dealing with asset acquisitions are frequently grouped according to the following four categories:

1. Replacements.
2. Expansion: additional capacity in existing product lines.
3. Expansion: new product lines.
4. Other (for example, pollution control equipment).

These groupings are somewhat arbitrary, and it is frequently difficult to decide the appropriate category for a particular investment. In spite of such problems, the scheme is used quite widely and, as we shall see, with good reason.

Ordinarily, replacement decisions are the simplest to make. Assets wear out or become obsolete, and they must be replaced if production efficiency is to be maintained. The firm has a very good idea of the cost savings to be obtained by replacing an old asset, and it knows the consequences of nonreplacement. All in all, the outcomes of most replacement decisions can be predicted with a high degree of confidence.

An example of the second investment classification is a proposal for adding more machines of the type already in use, or the opening of another branch in a city-wide chain of food stores. Expansion investments are frequently incorporated in replacement decisions. To illustrate, an old, inefficient machine may be replaced by a larger and more efficient one.

A degree of uncertainty—sometimes extremely high—is clearly involved in expansion, but the firm at least has the advantage of examining past production and sales experience with similar machines or stores. When it considers an investment of the third kind, expansion into new product lines, little if any experience data are available on which to base decisions. To illustrate, when Union Carbide decided to develop the laser for commercial application, it had very little idea of either the development costs or the specific applications to which lasers could be put. Under such circumstances, any estimates must at best be treated as very crude approximations.

The "other" category is a catchall and includes intangibles; an example is a proposal to boost employee morale and productivity by installing a music system. Mandatory pollution control devices, which must be undertaken even though they produce no revenues, are another example of the "other" category. Major strategic decisions such as plans for overseas expansion, or mergers, might also be included here, but more frequently they are treated separately from the regular capital budget.

Administrative Details

The remaining aspects of capital budgeting involve administrative matters. Approvals are typically required at higher levels within the organization as we move away from replacement decisions and as the sums involved increase. One of the most important functions of the board of directors is to approve the major outlays in a capital budgeting program. Such decisions are crucial for the future well-being of the firm.

The planning horizon for capital budgeting programs varies with the nature of the industry. When sales can be forecast with a high degree of reliability for 10 to 20 years, the planning period is likely to be correspondingly long; electric utilities are an example of such an industry. Also, when the product-technology developments in the industry require an eight-to-ten-year cycle to develop a new major product, as in certain segments of the aerospace industry, a correspondingly long planning period is necessary.

After a capital budget has been adopted, payments must be scheduled. Characteristically, the finance department is responsible for scheduling payments and for acquiring funds to meet payment schedule requirements. The finance department is also primarily responsible for cooperating with the members of operating divisions to compile systematic records on the uses of funds and the uses of equipment purchased in capital budgeting programs. Effective capital budgeting programs require such information as the basis for periodic review and evaluation of capital expenditure decisions—the feedback and control phase of capital budgeting, often called the "post audit."

The foregoing represents a brief overview of the administrative aspects of capital budgeting; the analytical problems involved are considered next.

Capital Budgeting Analysis: Choosing among Alternative Proposals

In most firms there are more proposals for projects than the firm is able or willing to finance. Some proposals are good, others are poor, and methods must be developed for distinguishing between the good and the poor. Essentially, the end product is a ranking of the proposals and a cutoff point for determining how far down the ranked list to go.

In part, proposals are eliminated because they are *mutually exclusive*. Mutually exclusive proposals are alternative methods of doing the same job. If one piece of equipment is chosen to do the job, the others will not be required. Thus, if there is a need to improve the materials handling system in a chemical plant, the job may be done either by conveyer belts or by fork-lift trucks. The selection of one method of doing the job makes it unnecessary to use the others. They are mutually exclusive items.

Independent items are pieces of capital equipment that are being considered for different kinds of projects or tasks that need to be accomplished. For example, in addition to the materials handling system, the chemical firm may need equipment to package the end product. The work would require a packaging machine, and the purchase of equipment for this purpose would be independent of the equipment purchased for materials handling.

To distinguish among the many items that compete for the allocation of the firm's capital funds, a ranking procedure must be developed. This procedure requires, first, calculating the estimated benefits from the use of equipment and, second, translating the estimated benefits into a measure of the advantage of the purchase of the equipment. Thus, an estimate of benefits is required, and a method for converting the benefits into a ranking measure must be developed.

Importance of Good Data

Most discussions of measuring the cash flows associated with capital projects are relatively brief, but it is important to emphasize *that in the entire capital budgeting procedure, probably nothing is of greater importance than a reliable estimate of the cost savings or revenue increases that will be achieved from the prospective outlay of capital funds.* The increased output and sales revenue resulting from expansion programs are obvious benefits. Cost reduction benefits include changes in quality and quantity of direct labor; in amount and cost of scrap and rework time; in fuel costs; and in maintenance expenses, down time, safety, flexibility, and so on. So many variables are involved that it is obviously impossible to make neat generalizations. However, this should not minimize the crucial importance of the required analysis of the benefits derived from capital expenditures. Each capital equipment expenditure must be examined in detail for possible additional costs and savings.

All the subsequent procedures for ranking projects are no better than the data input—the old saying, "garbage in, garbage out," is certainly applicable to capital budgeting analysis. Thus, the data assembly process is not a routine clerical task to be performed on a mechanical basis. It requires continuous monitoring and evaluation of estimates by those competent to make such evaluations—engineers, accountants, economists, cost analysts, and other qualified persons.

After costs and benefits have been estimated, they are utilized for ranking alternative investment proposals. How this ranking is accomplished is our next topic.

Ranking Investment Proposals

The point of capital budgeting — indeed, the point of all financial analysis — is to make decisions that will maximize the value of the firm's common stock. The capital budgeting process is designed to answer two questions: (1) Which of several mutually exclusive investments should be selected? (2) How many projects, in total, should be accepted?

Among the many methods used for ranking investment proposals, three are discussed here:[3]

1. *Payback method (or payback period):* number of years required to return the original investment.
2. *Net present value (NPV) method:* present value of future returns discounted at the appropriate cost of capital, minus the cost of the investment.
3. *Internal rate of return (IRR) method:* interest rate which equates the present value of future returns to the investment outlay.

Future returns are, in all cases, defined as the net income after taxes, plus depreciation, that result from a project. This is also equal to net operating income before deduction of payments to the financing sources but after the deduction of applicable taxes. Thus net operating income after taxes is before deduction of financial payments such as interest on debt and dividends to shareholders. The net operating income after taxes is divided by the value of the firm to obtain the after tax cost of capital of the firm as a whole:

$$\text{Cost of capital} = [\text{Net income plus depreciation}]/\text{Value of the firm}$$
$$= [\text{Net operating cash income } (1 - T) + T \text{ (depreciation)}]/\text{Value of the firm}$$

Note that since interest costs are included in the net operating income, they are reflected in the measurement of the cost of capital for the firm. *In other words, returns are synonymous with net operating cash flows from*

---

3. A number of "average rate of return" methods have been discussed in the literature and used in practice. These methods are generally unsound and, with the widespread use of computers, completely unnecessary. We discussed them in earlier editions, but they are deleted from this edition. We also note that a "benefit/cost" or "profitability index" method is sometimes used; this method is taken up in Appendix A to this chapter.

investments. Next, the nature and characteristics of the three methods are illustrated and explained. To make the explanations more meaningful, the same data are used to illustrate each procedure.

**Payback
Method**

Assume that two projects are being considered by a firm. Each requires an investment of $1,000. The firm's marginal cost of capital is 10 percent.[4] The net cash flows (net operating income after taxes plus depreciation) from investments A and B are shown in Table 10–1.

**Table 10–1
Net Cash Flows**

Year	A	B
1	$500	$100
2	400	200
3	300	300
4	100	400
5		500
6		600

The *payback period* is the number of years it takes a firm to recover its original investment from net cash flows. Since the cost is $1,000, the payback period is two and one-third years for project A and four years for project B. If the firm were employing a three-year payback period, project A would be accepted, but project B would be rejected.

Although the payback period is very easy to calculate, it can lead to the wrong decisions. As the illustration demonstrates, it ignores income beyond the payback period. If the project is one maturing in later years, the use of the payback period can lead to the selection of less desirable investments. Projects with longer payback periods are characteristically those involved in long-range planning—developing a new product or tapping a new market. These are just the strategic decisions which determine a firm's fundamental position, but they also involve investments which do not yield their highest returns for a number of years. This means that the payback method may be biased against the very investments that are most important to a firm's long-run success.

Recognition of the longer period over which an investment is likely to yield savings points up another weakness in the use of the payback

---

4. A discussion of how the cost of capital is calculated is presented in Chapter 19. For now, the cost of capital should be considered as the firm's opportunity cost of making a particular investment; that is, if the firm does not make a particular investment, it "saves" the cost of this investment, and if it can invest these funds in another project that provides a return of 10 percent, then its "opportunity cost" of making the first investment is 10 percent.

method for ranking investment proposals: its failure to take into account the time value of money. To illustrate, consider two assets, X and Y, each costing $300 and each having the following cash flows:

Year	X	Y
1	200	100
2	100	200
3	100	100

Each project has a two-year payback; hence, each would appear equally desirable. However, we know that a dollar today is worth more than a dollar next year, so project X, with its faster cash flow, is certainly more desirable.

The use of the payback period is sometimes defended on the grounds that returns beyond three or four years are fraught with such great uncertainty that it is best to disregard them altogether in a planning decision. However, this is clearly an unsound procedure. Some investments with the highest returns are those which may not come to fruition for eight to ten years. The new product cycle in industries involving advanced technologies may not have a payoff for eight or nine years. Furthermore, even though returns that occur after three, four, or five years may be highly uncertain, it is important to make a judgment about the likelihood of their occurring. To ignore them is to assign a zero probability to these distant receipts. This can hardly produce the best results.

Another defense of the payback method is that a firm that is short of cash must necessarily give great emphasis to a quick return of its funds so that they may be put to use in other places or in meeting other needs. However, this does not relieve the payback method of its many shortcomings, and there are better methods for handling the cash shortage situation.[5]

A third reason for using payback is that, typically, projects with faster paybacks have more favorable short-run effects on earnings per share. Firms that use payback for this reason are sacrificing future growth for current accounting income, and in general such a practice will not maximize the value of the firm. The discounted cash flow techniques discussed in the next section, if used properly, automatically give consideration to the present earnings versus future growth tradeoff and strike the balance that will maximize the firm's value.

Also, the payback method is sometimes used simply because it is so

---

5. We interpret a cash shortage to mean that the firm has a high opportunity cost for its funds and a high cost of capital. We would consider this high cost of capital in the internal rate of return method or the net present value method, thus taking account of the cash shortage.

easy to apply. If a firm is making many small capital expenditure decisions, the costs of using more complex methods may outweigh the benefits of possibly "better" choices among competing projects. Thus, many electric utility companies with very sophisticated capital budgeting procedures use discounted cash flow techniques for larger projects, but they use payback on certain small, routine replacement decisions. When these sophisticated companies do use the payback method, however, they generally do so only after special studies have indicated that the payback method will provide sufficiently accurate answers for the decisions at hand.

Finally, many firms use payback in combination with one of the discounted cash flow procedures described below. The *NPV* or *IRR* method is used to appraise a project's profitability, while the payback is used to show how long the initial investment will be at risk; that is, payback is used as a risk indicator. Recent surveys have shown that when larger firms use payback in connection with major projects, it is almost always used in this manner.

**Net Present
Value Method**

As the flaws in the payback method were recognized, people began to search for methods of evaluating projects that would recognize that a dollar received immediately is preferable to a dollar received at some future date. This recognition led to the development of *discounted cash flow (DCF) techniques* to take account of the time value of money. One such discounted cash flow technique is called the "net present value method," or sometimes simply the "present value method." *To implement this approach, find the present value of the expected net cash flows of an investment, discounted at the cost of capital, and subtract from it the initial cost outlay of the project.*[6] If the net present value is positive, the project should be accepted; if negative, it should be rejected. If the two projects are mutually exclusive, the one with the higher net present value should be chosen.

The equation for the net present value *(NPV)* is[7]

---

6. If costs are spread over several years, this must be taken into account. Suppose, for example, that a firm bought land in 1975, erected a building in 1976, installed equipment in 1977, and started production in 1978. One could treat 1975 as the base year, comparing the present value of the costs as of 1975 to the present value of the benefit stream as of that same date.

7 The second equation is simply a shorthand expression in which sigma (Σ) signifies "sum up" or add the present values of N profit terms. If $t = 1$, then $F_t = F_1$ and $1/(1 + k)^t = 1/(1 + k)^1$; if $t = 2$, then $F_t = F_2$ and $1/(1 + k)^t = 1/(1 + k)^2$; and so on until $t = N$, the last year the project provides any profits. The symbol $\sum\limits_{t=1}^{N}$ simply says "go through the following process: Let $t = 1$ and find the *PV* of F_1; then let $t = 2$ and find the *PV* of F_2. Continue until the *PV* of each individual profit has been found; then add the *PVs* of these individual profits to find the *PV* of the asset."

$$NPV = \left[\frac{F_1}{(1 + k)^1} + \frac{F_2}{(1 + k)^2} + \cdots + \frac{F_N}{(1 + k)^N} \right] - I \qquad (10\text{--}1)$$

$$= \sum_{t=1}^{N} \frac{F_t}{(1 + k)^t} - I.$$

Here F_1, F_2, and so forth, represent the net cash flows; k is the marginal cost of capital; I is the initial cost of the project; and N is the project's expected life.

The net present values of projects A and B are calculated in Table 10–2. Project A has an *NPV* of $92, while B's *NPV* is $400. On this basis, both should be accepted if they are independent, but B should be the one chosen if they are mutually exclusive.

Table 10–2
**Calculating the Net
Present Value (NPV)
of Projects with
$1,000 Cost**

	Project A			Project B		
Year	Net Cash Flow	PVIF (10%)	PV of Cash Flow	Net Cash Flow	PVIF (10%)	PV of Cash Flow
1	$500	.91	$ 455	$100	.91	$ 91
2	400	.83	332	200	.83	166
3	300	.75	225	300	.75	225
4	100	.68	68	400	.68	272
5	10	.62	6	500	.62	310
6	10	.56	6	600	.56	336
		PV of inflows	$1,092			$1,400
		Less: cost	− 1,000			− 1,000
		NPV	$ 92			$ 400

When a firm takes on a project with a positive *NPV*, the value of the firm increases by the amount of the *NPV*. In our example, the value of the firm increases by $400 if it takes on project B, but by only $92, if it takes on project A. Viewing the alternatives in this manner, it is easy to see why B is preferred to A, and it is also easy to see the logic of the *NPV* approach.

**Internal Rate of
Return Method**

The internal rate of return *(IRR)* is defined as the *interest rate that equates the present value of the expected future cash flows, or receipts, to the initial cost outlay*. The equation for calculating the internal rate of return is

$$\frac{F_1}{(1 + r)^1} + \frac{F_2}{(1 + r)^2} + \cdots + \frac{F_N}{(1 + r)^N} - I = 0$$

$$\sum_{t=1}^{N} \frac{F_t}{(1 + r)^t} - I = 0. \qquad (10\text{--}2)$$

Here we know the value of I and also the values of $F_1, F_2, \ldots, F_N$, but we do not know the value of r. Thus, we have an equation with one unknown, and we can solve for the value of r. Some value of r will cause the sum of the discounted receipts to equal the initial cost of the project, making the equation equal to zero, and that value of r is defined as the internal rate of return; that is, the solution value of r is the *IRR*.

Notice that the internal rate of return formula, Equation 10–2, is simply the *NPV* formula, Equation 10–1, solved for that particular value of k that causes the NPV to equal zero. In other words, the same basic equation is used for both methods, but in the *NPV* method the discount rate (k) is specified and the *NPV* is found, while in the *IRR* method the *NPV* is specified to equal zero and the value of r that forces the *NPV* to equal zero is found.

The internal rate of return may be found by trial and error. First, compute the present value of the cash flows from an investment, using an arbitrarily selected interest rate. (Since the cost of capital for most firms is in the range of 10 to 15 percent, projects will hopefully promise a return of at least 10 percent. Therefore, 10 percent is a good starting point for most problems.) Then compare the present value so obtained with the investment's cost. If the present value is higher than the cost figure, try a higher interest rate and go through the procedure again. Conversely, if the present value is lower than the cost, lower the interest rate and repeat the process. Continue until the present value of the flows from the investment is approximately equal to its cost. *The interest rate that brings about this equality is defined as the internal rate of return.*[8]

This calculation process is illustrated in Table 10–3 for projects A and B. First, the 10 percent interest factors are obtained from Table D–2 at the end of the book. These factors are then multiplied by the cash flows for the corresponding years, and the present values of the annual cash flows are placed in the appropriate columns. For example, the *PVIF* of .91 is multiplied by $500, and the product, $455, is placed in the first row of column A.

The present values of the yearly cash flows are then summed to get the investment's total present value. Subtracting the cost of the project from this figure gives the net present value. As the net present values of both investments are positive at the 10 percent rate, increase the rate to 15 percent and try again. *At this point the net present value of investment A is approximately zero, which indicates that its internal rate of return is*

---

8. In order to reduce the number of trials required to find the internal rate of return, it is important to minimize the error at each iteration. One reasonable approach is to make as good a first approximation as possible, then to "straddle" the internal rate of return by making fairly large changes in the interest rate early in the iterative process. In practice, if many projects are to be evaluated or if many years are involved, relatively inexpensive hand calculators can be used to solve for the internal rate of return.

**Table 10–3
Finding the Internal
Rate of Return**

	Cash Flows (F_t Values)	
	Year	F_A	F_B

I = Investment = $1,000

Year	F_A	F_B
$1:F_1 =$	$500	$100
$2:F_2 =$	400	200
$3:F_3 =$	300	300
$4:F_4 =$	100	400
$5:F_5 =$		500
$6:F_6 =$		600

	10 Percent			15 Percent			20 Percent		
		Present Value			Present Value			Present Value	
Year	PVIF	A	B	PVIF	A	B	PVIF	A	B
1	0.91	455	91	0.87	435	87	0.83	415	83
2	0.83	332	166	0.76	304	152	0.69	276	138
3	0.75	225	225	0.66	198	198	0.58	174	174
4	0.68	68	272	0.57	57	228	0.48	48	192
5	0.62	6	310	0.50	5	250	0.40	4	200
6	0.56	6	336	0.43	4	258	0.33	3	198
Present value		1,092	1,400		1,003	1,173		920	985
Net present value = PV − I		92	400		(3)	173		(80)	(15)

approximately 15 percent. Continuing, B is found to have an internal rate of return of approximately 20 percent.[9]

What is so special about the particular discount rate that equates the cost of a project with the present value of its future cash flows? Suppose that the weighted cost of all of the funds obtained by the firm is 10 percent. If the internal rate of return on a particular project is 10 percent, the same as the cost of capital, the firm would be able to use the cash flow generated by the investment to repay the funds obtained, including the costs of the funds. If the internal rate of return exceeds 10 percent, the value of the firm increases. If the internal rate of return is less than 10 percent, taking on the project would cause a decline in the value of the firm. It is this "break-even" characteristic that increases or decreases the value of the firm and makes the internal rate of return of particular significance.

Assuming that the firm uses a cost of capital of 10 percent, the internal rate of return criterion states that, if the two projects are indepen-

---

9. The *IRR* can also be estimated graphically. First, calculate the *NPV* at two or three discount rates as in Table 10–3. Next, plot these *NPVs* against the discount rates — see Figure 10–2 in the next section for an example. The horizontal axis intercept is the *IRR*; with graph paper and a sharp pencil, the *IRR* can be estimated to three decimal places.

dent, both should be accepted—they both do better than "break even."
If they are mutually exclusive, B ranks higher and should be accepted,
while A should be rejected.

A more complete illustration of how the internal rate of return would
be used in practice is given in Table 10–4. Assuming a 10 percent cost
of capital, the firm should accept projects 1 through 7, reject projects 8
through 10, and have a total capital budget of $10 million.

Table 10–4 **The Prospective-** **Projects Schedule** Nature of Proposal	Amount of Funds Required	Cumulative Total	IRR
1. Purchase of leased space	$2,000,000	$ 2,000,000	23%
2. Mechanization of accounting system	1,200,000	3,200,000	19
3. Modernization of office building	1,500,000	4,700,000	17
4. Addition of power facilities	900,000	5,600,000	16
5. Purchase of affiliate	3,600,000	9,200,000	13
6. Purchase of loading docks	300,000	9,500,000	12
7. Purchase of tank trucks	500,000	10,000,000	11
			—10% cutoff
8. Installation of conveyor system	200,000	10,200,000	9
9. Construction of new plant	2,300,000	12,500,000	8
10. Purchase of executive aircraft	200,000	12,700,000	7

IRR for Level Cash Flows

If the cash flows from a project are level, or equal in each year, then the
project's internal rate of return can be found by a relatively simple process. In essence, such a project is an annuity: the firm makes an outlay,
I, and receives a stream of cash flow benefits, F, for a given number of
years. The *IRR* for the project is found by applying Equation 9–6, discussed in Chapter 9.

To illustrate, suppose a project has a cost of $10,000 and is expected to
produce cash flows of $1,627 a year for ten years. The cost of the project,
$10,000, is the present value of an annuity of $1,627 a year for ten years,
so applying Equation 9–6 we obtain

$$\frac{I}{F} = \frac{\$10,000}{\$1,627} = 6.146 = PVIF_a.$$

Looking up $PVIF_a$ in Table D–4, across the ten-year row, we find it (approximately) under the 10 percent column. Accordingly, 10 percent is
the *IRR* on the project. In other words, 10 percent is the value of *r* that
would force Equation 10–2 to zero when F is constant at $1,627 for ten
years and I is $10,000. This procedure works only if the project has con-
stant annual cash flows; if it does not, the *IRR* must be found by trial
and error or by using a calculator.

Basic Differences Between the NPV and IRR Methods[10]

As noted above, the *NPV* method (1) accepts all independent projects whose *NPV* is greater than zero and (2) ranks mutually exclusive projects by their *NPV*s, selecting the project with the higher *NPV* according to Equation 10–3:

$$NPV = \sum_{t=1}^{N} \frac{F_t}{(1 + k)^t} - I. \tag{10-3}$$

The *IRR* method, on the other hand, finds the value of *r* that forces Equation 10–4 to equal zero:

$$NPV = \sum_{t=1}^{N} \frac{F_t}{(1 + r)^t} - I = 0. \tag{10-4}$$

The *IRR* method calls for accepting independent projects where *r*, the internal rate of return, is greater than *k*, the cost of capital, and for selecting among mutually exclusive projects depending on which has the higher *IRR*.

It is apparent that the only structural difference between the *NPV* and *IRR* methods lies in the discount rates used in the two equations—all the values in the equations are identical except for *r* and *k*. Further , we can see that if $r > k$, then $NPV > 0$.[11] *Accordingly, the two methods give the same accept-reject decisions for specific projects—if a project is acceptable under the* NPV *criterion, it is also acceptable if the* IRR *method is used.*

However, under certain conditions the *NPV* and *IRR* methods can *rank* projects differently, and if mutually exclusive projects are involved or if capital is limited, then rankings can be important. The conditions under which different rankings can occur are as follows:

1. The cost of one project is larger than that of the other.
2. The timing of the projects' cash flows differs. For example, the cash flows of one project may increase over time, while those of the other decrease, or the projects may have different expected lives.

The first point can be seen by considering two mutually exclusive projects, L and S, of greatly differing sizes. Project S calls for the invest-

---

10. This section is relatively technical and may be omitted on a first reading without loss of continuity.
11. This can be seen by noting that $NPV = 0$ only when $r = k$:

$$NPV = \sum_{t=1}^{N} \frac{F_t}{(1 + k)^t} - I = \sum_{t=1}^{N} \frac{F_t}{(1 + r)^t} - I = 0,$$

if and only if $r = k$. If $r > k$, then $NPV > 0$, and if $r < k$, then $NPV < 0$. We should also note that, under certain conditions, there may be more than one root to Equation 10–4, hence multiple *IRR*s are found. See appendix A to this chapter for a more detailed discussion of the multiple root problem.

ment of $1.00 and yields $1.50 at the end of one year. Its *IRR* is 50 percent, and at a 10 percent cost of capital its *NPV* is $0.36. Project L costs $1 million and yields $1.25 million at the end of the year. Its *IRR* is only 25 percent, but its *NPV* at 10 percent is $113,625. The two methods rank the projects differently: $IRR_s > IRR_L$, but $NPV_L > NPV_s$. This is, of course, an extreme case, but whenever projects differ in size, the *NPV* and the *IRR* can give different rankings.[12]

The effect of differential cash flows is somewhat more difficult to understand, but it can be illustrated by an example. Consider two projects, A and B, whose cash flows over their three-year lives are given below:

Cash Flow from Project

Year	A	B
1	$1,000	$ 100
2	500	600
3	100	1,100

Project A's cash flows are higher in the early years, but B's cash flows increase over time and exceed those of A in later years. Each project costs $1,200, and their *NPV*s, discounted at the specified rates, are shown below:

NPV

Discount Rate	A	B
0%	$ 400	$ 600
5	300	400
10	200	200
15	100	50
20	50	(85)
25	(25)	(175)
30	(100)	(250)

At a zero discount rate, the *NPV* of each project is simply the sum of its receipts less its cost. Thus, the *NPV* of project A at 0 percent is $1,000 + $500 + $100 − $1,200 = $400; that of project B is $100 + $600 + $1,100 − $1,200 = $600. As the discount rate rises from zero, the *NPV*s of the two projects fall from these values.

The *NPV*s are plotted against the appropriate discount rates in Figure 10–2, a graph defined as a *present value profile*. Notice that the vertical axis intercepts are the *NPV*s when the discount rate is zero, while the horizontal axis intercepts show each project's *IRR*. The internal rate of

---

12. Projects of different size *could* be ranked the same by the *NPV* and *IRR* methods; that is, different sizes do not necessarily mean different rankings.

return is defined as that point where *NPV* is zero; therefore, A's *IRR* is 22 percent, while B's is 17 percent. Because its largest cash flows come late in the project's life, when the discounting effects of time are most significant, B's *NPV* falls rapidly as the discount rate rises. However, since A's cash flows come early, when the impact of higher discount rates is not so severe, its *NPV* falls less rapidly as interest rates increase.

Figure 10-2
Present Value Profile

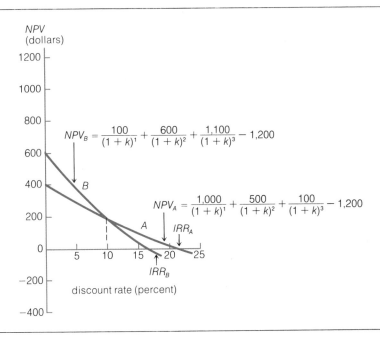

$$NPV_B = \frac{100}{(1 + k)^1} + \frac{600}{(1 + k)^2} + \frac{1,100}{(1 + k)^3} - 1,200$$

$$NPV_A = \frac{1,000}{(1 + k)^1} + \frac{500}{(1 + k)^2} + \frac{100}{(1 + k)^3} - 1,200$$

Notice that if the cost of capital is below 10 percent, B has the higher *NPV* but the lower *IRR*, while at a cost of capital above 10 percent A has both the higher *NPV* and the higher *IRR*. We can generalize these results: *Whenever the* NPV *profiles of two projects cross one another, a conflict will exist if the cost of capital is below the cross-over rate.* For our illustrative projects, no conflict would exist if the firm's cost of capital exceeded 10 percent, but the two methods would rank A and B differently if *k* is less than 10 percent.

How should such conflicts be resolved; for example, when the *NPV* and *IRR* methods yield conflicting rankings, which of two mutually exclusive projects should be selected? Assuming that management is seeking to maximize the value of the firm, the correct decision is to select the project with the higher *NPV*. After all, the *NPV*s measure the projects' contributions to the value of the firm, so the one with the higher *NPV* must be contributing more to the firm's value. *This line of reasoning leads to the conclusion that firms should, in general, use the* NPV *method for evaluating capital investment proposals.*[13] Recognizing this point, sophisticated firms generally rely on the *NPV* method. These firms often calculate (by computer) both the *NPV* and the *IRR*, but they rely on the *NPV* when conflicts arise among mutually exclusive projects.

Capital Budgeting Project Evaluation

Thus far the problem of measuring cash flows — the benefits used in the present value calculations above — has not been dealt with directly. This matter will now be discussed, and a few simple examples given. The procedures developed here can be used both for expansion and for replacement decisions.

Simplified Model for Determining Cash Flows[14]

One way of considering the cash flows attributable to a particular investment is to think of them in terms of comparative income statements. This is illustrated in the following example.

The Widget Division of the Culver Company, a profitable, diversified manufacturing firm, purchased a machine five years ago at a cost of $7,500. The machine had an expected life of 15 years at time of purchase and a zero estimated salvage value at the end of the 15 years. It is being depreciated on a straight-line basis and has a book value of $5,000 at present. The division manager reports that he can buy a new machine for $12,000 (including installation), which, over its ten-year life, will

---

13. The question of *why* the conflict arises is an interesting one. Basically, it has to do with the reinvestment of cash flows — the *NPV* method implicitly assumes reinvestment at the marginal cost of capital *(MCC)*, while the *IRR* method implicitly assumes reinvestment at the internal rate of return. For a value-maximizing firm, reinvestment at the *MCC* is the better assumption. The rationale is as follows: A value-maximizing firm will expand to the point where it accepts all projects yielding more than the *MCC* (these projects will have *NPV* > 0). How these projects are financed is irrelevant — the point is, they will be financed and accepted. Now consider the question of the cash flows from a particular project; if these cash flows are reinvested, at what rate will reinvestment occur? All projects that yield more than the cost of capital have already been accepted; thus, these cash flows can only be invested in physical assets yielding *less than* the *MCC*, or else be used in lieu of other capital with a cost of *MCC*. A rational firm will take the second alternative, so reinvested cash flows will save the firm the cost of capital. This means, in effect, that cash flows are reinvested to yield the cost of capital, which is the assumption implicit in the *NPV* method. For a detailed discussion, see Appendix A to this chapter.

14. The procedure described in this section facilitates an understanding of the capital investment analysis process, but for repeated calculations, the alternative worksheet illustrated in the next section is preferred. Note also that we use straight-line depreciation in the text chapter, but accelerated depreciation in the Appendix B illustration.

expand sales from $10,000 to $11,000 a year. Further, it will reduce labor and raw materials usage sufficiently to cut operating costs from $7,000 to $5,000. The new machine has an estimated salvage value of $2,000 at the end of ten years. The old machine's current market value is $1,000. Taxes are at a 40 percent rate and are paid quarterly, and the firm's cost of capital is 10 percent. Should Culver buy the new machine?

The decision calls for five steps: (1) estimating the actual cash outlay attributable to the new investment, (2) determining the incremental cash flows, (3) finding the present value of the incremental cash flows, (4) adding the present value of the expected salvage value to the present value of the total cash flows, and (5) seeing whether the NPV is positive or whether the IRR exceeds the cost of capital. These steps are explained further in the following sections.

Estimated Cash Outlay. The net initial cash outlay consists of these items: (1) payment to the manufacturer, (2) tax effects, and (3) proceeds from the sale of the old machine. Culver must make a $12,000 payment to the manufacturer of the machine, but its next quarterly tax bill will be reduced because of the loss it will incur when it sells the old machine: tax saving = (loss) (tax rate) = ($4,000) (.4) = $1,600. The tax reduction will occur because the old machine, which is carried at $5,000, will be written down by $4,000 ($5,000 less $1,000 salvage value) immediately if the new one is purchased.

To illustrate, suppose the Culver Company's taxable income in the quarter in which the new machine is to be purchased would have been $100,000 without the purchase of the new machine and the consequent write-off of the old machine. With a 40 percent tax rate, Culver would have had to write a check for $40,000 to pay its tax bill. However, if it buys the new machine and sells the old one, it will take an operating loss of $4,000 — the $5,000 book value on the old machine less the salvage value. (The loss is an operating loss, not a capital loss, because it is in reality simply recognizing that depreciation charges, an operating cost, were too low during the old machine's five-year life.)[15] With this $4,000 additional operating cost, next quarter's taxable income will be reduced from $100,000 to $96,000, and the tax bill from $40,000 to $38,400. This means, of course, that the firm's cash outflow for taxes will be $1,600 less *because* it has purchased the new machine.

In addition, there is to be a cash inflow of $1,000 from the sale of the old machine. The net result is that the purchase of the new machine

---

15. If Culver traded in the old machine as partial payment for the new one, the loss would be added to the depreciable cost of the new machine, and there would be no immediate tax saving.

involves an immediate net cash outlay of $9,400; this is its cost for capital budgeting purposes:

Invoice price of new machine	$12,000
Less: Tax savings	− 1,600
Salvage of old machine	− 1,000
Net cash outflow (cost)	$ 9,400

If additional working capital is required as a result of a capital budgeting decision, as would generally be true for expansion-type investments (as opposed to cost-reducing replacement investments), this factor must be taken into account. The amount of *net* working capital (additional current assets required as a result of the expansion minus any spontaneous funds generated by the expansion) is estimated and added to the initial cash outlay. We assume that Culver will not need any additional working capital; hence this factor is ignored in this example.

Annual Benefits. Column 1 in Table 10–5 shows the Widget Division's estimated income statement as it would be without the new machine; column 2 shows the statement as it will look if the new investment is made. (It is assumed that these figures are applicable for each of the next ten years; if this is not the case, then cash flow estimates must be made for each year.) Column 3 shows the differences between the first two columns.

For capital budgeting analysis the cash flows that are discounted are the net after tax operating cash flows. The data in Table 10–5 represent accounting income and must be adjusted in order (1) to be on a cash rather than accrual basis and (2) to exclude all payments to the sources of financing. In Table 10–5 depreciation is a noncash charge; interest charges and dividends paid are cash flows to the financing sources.

Table 10–5
**Comparative
Accounting Income
Statement
Framework for
Considering
Cash Flows**

	(1) Without new Investment		(2) With new Investment		(3) (2) − (1) Difference
Sales		$10,000		$11,000	$1,000
Operating costs	$7,000		$5,000		($2,000)
Depreciation	500		1,000		500
Interest charges	500		1,000		500
Income before taxes		$ 2,000		$ 4,000	$2,000
Taxes (T = .4)		800		1,600	800
Income after taxes		$ 1,200		$ 2,400	$1,200
Dividends paid		600		1,200	600
Additions to retained earnings		$ 600		$ 1,200	$ 600

While depreciation is a noncash charge, it is deductible for computing income tax, and income tax payments are cash flows. The cash flows must include the depreciation tax benefits.

Table 10–6 shows the operating cash flows without the new investment, with the new investment, and the difference or incremental flows.

**Table 10–6
Net Operating Cash
Flow Statement**

	(1) Without new Investment	(2) With new Investment	(3) (2) − (1) Difference or incremental flows
Sales (P · Q)	$10,000	$11,000	$ 1,000
Operating cash costs (O)*	7,000	5,000	(2,000)
Net operating cash income (NOI)*	$ 3,000	$ 6,000	$ 3,000
Taxes (T = .4)	1,200	2,400	1,200
After tax operating [NOI(1 − T)]	$ 1,800	$ 3,600	$ 1,800
Depreciation tax benefit (T × Dep)	200	400	200
Net cash flows (F)	$ 2,000	$ 4,000	$ 2,000

*Does not include depreciation as a cash cost since this is a cash flow statement and depreciation is not a cash cost.

The incremental cash flows can also be calculated using the following equation. Let ΔSales be the change in sales, ΔO the change in operating costs, ΔNOI the change in operating cash income, ΔDep the change in depreciation, and T the marginal corporate income tax rate. Then

Δ cash flow = change in after-tax operating cash income
+ change in depreciation tax benefit.

$$\Delta F = \Delta NOI\ (1 - T) + T\Delta Dep$$
$$\Delta F = (\Delta Sales - \Delta O)(1 - T) + T\Delta Dep$$
$$\Delta F = [\Delta Sales_2 - Sales_1) - (O_2 - O_1)](1 - T)$$
$$+ T(Dep_2 - Dep_1) \tag{10–5}$$

For the Widget Division analysis:
Δ cash flow = [($11,000 − $10,000) − ($5,000 − $7,000)](1 − .4)
+ (.4)($1,000 − $500)
= [$1,000 − (− $2,000)](.6) + (.4)($500)
$$\Delta F = \$1,800 + \$200 = \$2,000 \tag{10–6}$$

This $2,000 result checks out with the bottom line figure in the last column of Table 10–6. What happens if there is no change in sales? The equation is still valid, but ΔSales = 0. In this case, the problem is a simple replacement decision, with a new machine replacing an old one to reduce costs. The sales levels are the same with and without the investment and do not show up in the incremental column.

Finding the PV of the Benefits. We have explained in detail how to measure the annual benefits. The next step is to determine the present value of the benefit stream. The interest factor for a ten-year, 10 percent annuity is found to be 6.145 from Appendix Table D–4. This factor, when multiplied by the $2,000 incremental cash flow, results in a present value of $12,290.

Salvage Value. The new machine has an estimated salvage value of $2,000; that is, Culver expects to be able to sell the machine for $2,000 when it is retired in ten years. The present value of an inflow of $2,000 due in ten years is $772, found as $2,000 × .386. If additional working capital had been required and included in the initial cash outlay, this amount would be added to the salvage value of the machine because the working capital will be recovered if and when the project is abandoned.

Notice that the salvage value is a return of capital, not taxable income, so it is *not* subject to income taxes. Of course, when the new machine is actually retired ten years hence, it may be sold for more or less than the expected $2,000, so either taxable income or a deductible operating loss may arise, but $2,000 is the best present estimate of the new machine's salvage value.

Determining the Net Present Value. The project's net present value is found as the sum of the present values of the inflows, or benefits, less the outflows, or costs:

Inflows: *PV* of annual benefits	$12,290
PV of salvage value, new machine	772
Less: Net cash outflow, or cost	(9,400)
Net present value *(NPV)*	$ 3,662

Since the *NPV* is positive, the project should be accepted.

Worksheet for Determining Cash Flows

Table 10–7 summarizes the five-step capital budgeting decision process described above. Using the Culver Company investment problem as an example, we first calculate the total outflows for the proposed project by subtracting from the cost of the new machine the sum of the funds received from the sale of the old machine plus the tax savings resulting from that sale. Recall that a $4,000 operating loss will occur if the old machine with a book value of $5,000 is sold for $1,000. Since the old machine is sold at a loss, the $1,000 received from the sale is not taxed. Only the *gain* on the sale of any asset is taxed. Further, the $4,000 loss is a tax deduction for next quarter's tax payment, and it results in a tax saving of $1,600.

Table 10–7 **Worksheet for** **Capital Budgeting** **Project Evaluation**	1. Project Cost, or Initial Outflows Required to Undertake the Project*	
	Investment in new equipment	$12,000
	Receipt from sale of old machine	(1,000)
	Add (or subtract) the taxes (or tax savings) resulting from the gain	
	(or loss) on the old machine: tax rate (T) times gain or loss	(1,600)
	Total project cost	$ 9,400

2. Calculation of Annual Benefits†

Δ Sales	$ 1,000
Less: ΔO	(2,000)‡
Δ Dep	500
Δ Taxable income	$ 2,500
Less: Δ tax at 40%	1,000
Δ After-tax profits	$ 1,500
Plus: Δ Dep	500
Δ Cash flow	$ 2,000

3. Present Value of Benefits

Δ F × Interest factor	
$2,000 × 6.145 =	$12,290

4. Present Value of Expected Salvage

Expected salvage value × interest factor	
$2,000 × .386 =	$ 772

5. Net present Value

PV of inflows: Annual benefits	$12,290
Salvage	772
	$13,062
Less: Project cost	9,400
NPV	$ 3,662

*If project costs are incurred over a number of years, then the present value of project costs must be calculated.

†It should be noted that if the annual cash flows are not level, the annuity format cannot be used. Also, note that if accelerated depreciation is used, the annuity format can almost never be used; in this case, cash flows are unlikely to be uniform from year to year. These restrictions might appear to present serious problems to practical applications in capital budgeting, but they really do not. Most corporations have either computer facilities or time-sharing arrangements with computer service facilities that handle these nonannuity cases without difficulty.

‡Refer to Equation 10–6. We are subtracting the change in cost from the change in sales: ΔC = $5,000 − $7,000 = − $2,000. Therefore, Δ Sales − ΔC = $1,000 − (−$2,000) = $3.000.

Next, we calculate the net annual benefits, then find the present value of this benefit stream, which is $12,290.

We now find the present value of the expected salvage value of the new machine, $772. Since salvage value is a *return of capital*, not taxable income, no taxes are deducted from the salvage value.

Finally, we sum up the PV of the inflows and then deduct the project cost to determine the *NPV*, $3,662 in this example. Since the *NPV* is positive, the project should be accepted.[16]

Alternative Capital Budgeting Worksheet

Table 10–8 presents an alternative worksheet for evaluating capital projects. The top section shows net cash flows at the time of investment; since all these flows occur immediately, no discounting is required and the interest factor is 1.0. The lower section of the table shows future cash flows—benefits from increased sales and/or reduced costs, depreciation, and salvage value. These flows do occur over time, so it is necessary to convert them to present values. The *NPV* as determined in the alternative format, $3,662, agrees with the figure as calculated in Table 10–7.

Capital Rationing

Ordinarily, firms operate as illustrated in Figure 10–1; that is, they take on investments to the point where the marginal returns from investment are just equal to their estimated marginal cost of capital. For firms operating in this way, the decision process is as described above—they make those investments having positive net present values, reject those whose net present values are negative, and choose between mutually exclusive investments on the basis of the higher net present value. However, a firm will occasionally set an absolute limit on the size of its capital budget for any one year that is less than the level of investment it would undertake on the basis of the criteria described above.

The principal reason for such action is that some firms are reluctant to engage in external financing (borrowing or selling stock). One management, recalling the plight of firms with substantial amounts of debt in the 1930s, may simply refuse to use debt. Another management, which

---

16. Alternatively, the internal rate of return on the project could have been computed and found to be 18 percent. Because this is substantially in excess of the 10 percent cost of capital, the internal rate of return method also indicates that the investment should be undertaken. In this case, the *r* is found as follows:

PV of benefit stream + *PV* of salvage − cost = 0.

$$\sum_{t=1}^{10} \frac{\$2,000}{(1+r)^t} + \frac{\$2,000}{(1+r)^{10}} - \$9,400 = 0.$$

$2,000 (*IF* for *PV* of 10-year annuity) + $2,000 (*PV* of $1 in 10 years) − $9,400 = 0.

Try *PVIF*s for 18%:

$2,000 (4.494) + $2,000 (.191) − $9,400 = $8,988 + $382 − $9,400 = $ − 30,

which is very close to zero, indicating that the internal rate of return is approximately equal to 18 percent.

Table 10–8
Alternative Worksheet for Capital Budgeting Project Evaluation

	Amount before Tax	Amount after Tax*	Year Event Occurs	PV Factor at 10%	PV
Outflows at time investment is made					
Investment in new equipment	$12,000	$12,000	0	1.0	$12,000
Salvage value of old	(1,000)	(1,000)	0	1.0	(1,000)
Tax effect of the sale†	(4,000)	(1,600)	0	1.0	(1,600)
Increased working capital (if necessary)	‡	—	0	1.0	—
Total initial outflows (PV of costs)					$ 9,400
Inflows, or annual returns					
Benefits§	$ 3,000	$ 1,800	1–10	6.145	$11,061
Depreciation on new (annual)†	1,000	400	1–10	6.145	2,458
Depreciation on old (annual)†	(500)	(200)	1–10	6.145	(1,229)
Salvage value on new	2,000	2,000	10	.386	772
Return of working capital (if necessary)	‡	—	10	.386	—
Total periodic inflows (PV of benefits)					$13,062

NPV = PV of benefits less PV of cost = $13,062 − $9,400 = $3,662.

*Amount after tax equals amount before tax times T or $(1 - T)$, where T = tax rate.
†Deductions (tax loss and depreciation) are multiplied by T.
‡Not applicable.
§Benefits are multiplied by $(1 - T)$.

has no objection to selling debt, may not want to sell equity capital for fear of losing some measure of voting control. Still others may refuse to use any form of outside financing, considering safety and control to be more important than additional profits. These are all cases of capital rationing, and they result in limiting the rate of expansion to a slower pace than would be dictated by "purely rational profit-maximizing behavior."[17]

17. We should make three points here. First, we *do not* necessarily consider a decision to hold back on expansion irrational. If the owner of a firm has what *he* considers to be plenty of income and wealth, then it might be quite rational for him to "trim his sails," relax, and concentrate on enjoying what he has already earned rather than on earning still more. Such behavior would not, however, be appropriate for a publicly owned firm.

The second point is that it is not correct to interpret as capital rationing a situation where the firm is willing to sell additional securities at the going market price but finds that it cannot because the market will simply not absorb more of its issues. Rather, such a situation indicates that the cost-of-capital curve is rising. If more acceptable investments are indicated than can be financed, then the cost of capital being used is too low and should be raised.

Third, firms sometimes set a limit on capital expenditures, not because of a shortage of funds, but because of limitations on other resources, especially managerial talent. A firm might, for example, feel that its personnel development program is sufficient to handle an expansion of no more than 10 percent a year, then set a limit on the capital budget to insure that expansion is held to that rate. This is not *capital* rationing—rather, it involves a downward reevaluation of project returns if growth exceeds some limit; that is expected rates of return are, after some point, a decreasing function of the level of expenditures.

**Project
Selection under
Capital
Rationing**

How should projects be selected under conditions of capital rationing? First, note that under conditions of true capital rationing, the firm's value is not being maximized—if management was maximizing, then it would move to the point where the marginal project's *NPV* was zero, and capital rationing as defined would not exist. So, if a firm uses capital rationing, it has ruled out value maximization. The firm may, however, want to maximize value *subject to the constraint that the capital ceiling is not exceeded.* Following constrained maximization behavior will, in general, result in a lower value than following unconstrained maximization, but some type of constrained maximization may produce reasonably satisfactory results. Linear programming is one method of constrained maximization that has been applied to capital rationing. To our knowledge, this method has not been widely applied, but much work is going on in the area, and linear programming may, in the future, prove useful in capital budgeting.[18]

If a financial manager does face capital rationing, and if he cannot get the constraint lifted, what should he do? His objective should be to select projects, subject to the capital rationing constraint, such that the

Table 10–9
The Prospective-Projects Schedule

Nature of Proposal	Project's Cost	Cumulative Total of Costs	Internal Rate of Return	PV of Benefits	Project's NPV
1. Purchase of leased space	$2,000,000	$ 2,000,000	23%	$3,200,000	$1,200,000
2. Mechanization of accounting system	1,200,000	3,200,000	19	1,740,000	540,000
3. Modernization of office building	1,500,000	4,700,000	17	2,070,000	570,000
4. Addition of power facilities	900,000	5,600,000	16	1,125,000	225,000
5. Purchase of affiliate	3,600,000	9,200,000	13	4,248,000	648,000
6. Purchase of loading docks	300,000	9,500,000	12	342,000	42,000
7. Purchase of tank trucks	500,000	10,000,000	11	540,000	40,000
⎯⎯⎯⎯⎯⎯⎯⎯⎯cutoff⎯⎯⎯⎯⎯⎯⎯⎯⎯					
8. Installation of conveyor system	200,000	10,200,000	9	186,000	(14,000)
9. Construction of new plant	2,300,000	12,500,000	8	2,093,000	(207,000)
10. Purchase of executive aircraft	200,000	12,700,000	7	128,000	(72,000)

18. For a further discussion of programming approaches to capital budgeting, see Appendix A to this chapter.

sum of the projects' *NPVs* is maximized. Linear programming can be used, but there is really no practical alternative that will approximate the true maximum. Reasonably satisfactory results may be obtained by ranking projects by their internal rates of return and then, starting at the top of this list of projects, by taking investments of successively lower rank until the available funds have been exhausted. However, no investment with a negative *NPV* (or an internal rate of return below the cost of capital) should be undertaken.

A firm might, for example, have the investment opportunities shown in Table 10–9 and only $6 million available for investment. In this situation, the firm would probably accept projects 1 through 4 and project 6, ending with a capital budget of $5.9 million, and a cumulative *NPV* of $2.6 million. Under no circumstances should it accept project 8, 9, or 10, as they all have internal rates of return of less than 10 percent (and also net present values less than zero).

Comparing Mutually Exclusive Projects with Different Lives

To simplify the analysis, the previous capital budgeting examples assumed that alternative investments had equal lives. Suppose, however, that we must choose between two mutually exclusive investments that have different lives. For example, investment 1 has a life of five years while investment 2 has a life of seven years. An illustration would be a wooden bridge that would have a shorter life and lower initial cost than a steel bridge. Both provide about the same quantity of services per year, but the wooden bridge would require more maintenance and more frequent replacement. But since the lives of the two alternative investments are different, the net present value of the cash flows cannot be compared directly. The problem is pictured in Figure 10–3 for a five- and a seven-year alternative.

A computationally easy and theoretically sound method for handling

Figure 10–3

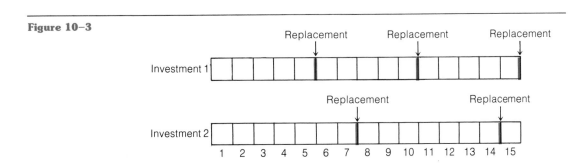

this different length of lives problem is to replace each alternative as it wears out and find the total net present value of each infinitely replaced alternative.[19] Then the net present value of each "infinite" lived alternative can be compared. To find the net present value of each extended alternative (call it NPV_∞):

1. find the net present value NPV_N of the cash flows for each alternative for the original life and for the applicable cost of capital, k,
2. divide NPV_N by the net present value factor for N years at rate k (this gives an equivalent level annuity amount a that will give the same present value NPV_N if invested at rate k for N years),
3. divide the annuity a by the applicable cost of capital k to obtain NPV_∞. (In Chapter 19 it will be shown that the present value of an amount received to infinity is the amount divided by the discount factor.)

(1) and (2) have the effect of normalizing, both by the amount of the investment and by the number of years duration that the cash flows from the investment are received. This makes it possible to compare directly the two streams of normalized annual cash flows.

The third step takes the level annual flows normalized by the amount of investment and discounts them to infinity. When the discount rates are different, we now have a NPV evaluation over infinite lives, so that again direct comparisons can appropriately be made.

The three steps above are summarized and expressed in symbols in Equation 10–7.

$$NPV_\infty = \frac{[NPV_N/PVIF_a(N,k)]}{k} = \frac{a}{k} \tag{10–7}$$

where NPV_∞ is the present value of the "infinite" lived alternative.

a is the equivalent level annuity.

N is the life of the original alternative.

k is the cost of capital.

NPV_N is the net present value of the cash flows for the original life N.

$PVIF_a(N,k)$ is the (net) present value factor for an annuity of $1 at rate k for N years.

The method is illustrated for the mutually exclusive projects 1 and 2 of Table 10–10.

---

19. An alternative method is to equate lives by assuming a reinvestment rate for the shorter-lived project for the additional years required to equate lives.

Table 10-10	Project	Initial Cost (*I*)	Life (*N*)	Cost of Capital (*k*)	Annual Cash Flow (*X*[1 − *T*])
	1	$280	5 years	10%	$100
	2	$350	7 years	12%	$105

For alternative 1, $NPV_N = PVIF_a(N, k)X(1 - T) - I$
$$= PVIF_a(5, .10)\$100 - \$280$$
$$= (3.7908)(\$100) - \$280 = \$99.08,$$
$$a = \frac{NPV_N}{PVIF_a(N, k)} = \frac{\$99.08}{3.7908} = \$26.137,$$

and $$NPV_\infty = \frac{\$26.137}{.10} = \$261.37.$$

Similarly for alternative 2,
$$NPV_N = \$105.00(4.5638) - \$350 = \$129.19,$$
$$a = \frac{\$129.19}{4.5638} = \$28.309,$$

and $$NPV_\infty = \frac{\$28.309}{.12} = \$235.91.$$

Thus alternative 1 is preferable. Note that comparison of the net present value for the original lives would have selected alternative 2 which has an *NPV* of $129.19 compared to the *NPV* of $99.08 for alternative 1.

Some methods for evaluating unequally lived mutually exclusive alternatives compare the annuities *a* in the above analysis. Since NPV_∞ is the quotient of *a* divided by *k*, this method can lead to the wrong choice if the risk classes of the alternatives differ so that the cost of capital, *k*, is different. In the above example a comparison of annuities would have selected alternative 2 of $28.31 versus $26.14 for alternative 1. In most replacement decisions, however, *k* will be the same and the two methods will give the same decision. The above method assumes that the projects can be repeated in perpetual replacement chains. If this assumption is not appropriate, an alternative method is to assume a reinvestment rate for the project of shorter duration to equalize its life with the project of longer duration.

Summary

Capital budgeting, which involves commitments for large outlays whose benefits (or drawbacks) extend well into the future, is of the greatest significance to a firm. Decisions in these areas will, therefore, have a major impact on the future well-being of the firm. This chapter focused on how capital budgeting decisions can be made more effective in contributing to the health and growth of a firm. The discussion stressed the development of systematic procedures and rules for preparing a list of investment proposals, for evaluating them, and for selecting a cutoff point.

The chapter emphasized that one of the most crucial phases in the process of evaluating capital budget proposals is obtaining a dependable estimate of the benefits that will be obtained from undertaking the project. It cannot be overemphasized that the firm must allocate to competent and experienced personnel the making of these judgments.

Determining Cash Flows. The cash inflows from an investment are the incremental change in after-tax net operating cash income plus the incremental depreciation tax benefit; the cash outflow is the cost of the investment less the salvage value received on an old machine plus any tax loss (or less any tax savings) when the machine is sold.

Ranking Investment Proposals. Three commonly used procedures for ranking investment proposals were discussed in the chapter:

Payback is defined as the number of years required to return the original investment. Although the payback method is used frequently, it has serious conceptual weaknesses, because it ignores the facts (1) that some receipts come in beyond the payback period and (2) that a dollar received today is more valuable than a dollar received in the future.

Net present value is defined as the present value of future returns, discounted at the cost of capital, minus the cost of the investment. The *NPV* method overcomes the conceptual flaws noted in the use of the payback method.

Internal rate of return is defined as the interest rate that equates the present value of future returns to the investment outlay. The internal rate of return method, like the *NPV* method, meets the objections to the payback approach.

In most cases, the two discounted cash flow methods give identical answers to these questions: Which of two mutually exclusive projects should be selected? How large should the total capital budget be? However, under certain circumstances conflicts may arise. Such conflicts are caused by the fact that the *NPV* and *IRR* methods make different assumptions about the rate at which cash flows may be reinvested, or the opportunity cost of cash flows. In general, the assumption of the *NPV* method (that the opportunity cost is the cost of capital) is the correct one. Accordingly, our preference is for using the *NPV* method to make capital budgeting decisions.

Questions

10-1. A firm has $100 million available for capital expenditures. Suppose project A involves the purchase of $100 million of grain, shipping it overseas, and selling it within a year at a profit of $20 million. The project has an *IRR* of 20 percent, an *NPV* of $20 million, *and it will cause earnings per share (EPS) to rise within one year.* Project B calls for the use of the $100 million to develop a new process, acquire land, build a plant, and begin processing. Project B, which is not postponable, has an *NPV* of $50 million and an *IRR* of 30 percent, but the fact that some of the plant costs will be written off immediately, combined with the fact that no revenues will be generated for several years, means that accepting project B will *reduce* short-run *EPS.*

    a. Should the short-run effects on *EPS* influence the choice between the two projects?

    b. How might situations such as the one described here influence a firm's decision to use payback as a screening criterion?

10–2. Are there conditions under which a firm might be better off if it chooses a machine with a rapid payback rather than one with the largest rate of return?

10–3. Company X uses the payback method in evaluating investment proposals and is considering new equipment whose additional net after-tax earnings will be $150 a year. The equipment costs $500 and its expected life is ten years (straight-line depreciation). The company uses a three-year payback as its criterion. Should the equipment be purchased under the above assumptions?

10–4. What are the most critical problems that arise in calculating a rate of return for a prospective investment?

10–5. What other factors in addition to rate of return analysis should be considered in determining capital expenditures?

10–6. Would it be beneficial for a firm to review its past capital expenditures and capital budgeting procedures? Why?

10–7. Fiscal and monetary policies are tools used by the government to stimulate the economy. Explain, using the analytical devices developed in this chapter, how each of the following might be expected to stimulate the economy by encouraging investment.

    a. A speed-up of tax-allowable depreciation (for example, the accelerated methods permitted in 1954 or the guideline depreciable life revisions of 1962).

    b. An easing of interest rates.

    c. Passage of a new federal program giving more aid to the poor.

    d. An investment tax credit.

Problems

10–1. Sparkling Beverages is contemplating replacing one of its bottling machines with a newer and more efficient machine. The old machine has a book value of $500,000 and a remaining useful life of five years. The firm does not expect to realize any return from scrapping the old machine in five years, but if it is sold now to another firm in the industry, Sparkling Beverages would receive $300,000 for it.

The new machine has a purchase price of $1.1 million, an estimated useful life of five years, and an estimated salvage value of $100,000. The new machine is expected to economize on electric power usage, labor, and repair costs, and also to reduce defective bottles; in total, an annual saving of $200,000 will be realized if the new machine is installed. (Note: To calculate depreciation, assume that the salvage value *is* deducted from cost to get the depreciable cost.) The company is in the 40 percent tax bracket, has a 10 percent cost of capital, and uses straight-line depreciation.

a. What is the initial cash outlay required for the new machine?

b. What are the cash flows in years 1 to 5?

c. What is the cash flow from the salvage value in year 5?

d. Should Sparkling Beverages purchase the new machine? Support your answer.

e. In general, how would each of the following factors affect the investment decision, and how should each be treated?

(i) The expected life of the existing machine decreases.

(ii) Capital rationing is imposed on the firm.

(iii) The cost of capital is not constant but is rising.

(iv) Improvements in the equipment to be purchased are expected to occur each year, and the result will be to increase the returns or expected savings from new machines over the savings expected with this year's model for every year in the foreseeable future.

10–2. The Feldwyn Company is using a machine whose original cost was $72,000. The machine is two years old and has a current market value of $16,000. The asset is being depreciated over a 12-year original life toward a zero estimated final salvage value. Depreciation is on a straight-line basis, and the tax rate is 50 percent.

Management is contemplating the purchase of a replacement that costs $75,000 and has an estimated salvage value of $10,000. The new machine will have a greater capacity, and annual sales are expected to increase from $1 million to $1.01 million, or by $10,000. Operating efficiencies with the new machine will also produce expected savings of $10,000 a year. Depreciation is on a straight-line basis over a ten-year life, the cost of capital is 8 percent, and a 50 percent tax rate is applicable. The company's total depreciation costs are currently $120,000 and total annual operating costs are $800,000.

a. Should the firm replace the asset? Use the cash flow difference equation shown in Equation 10–5 to solve the problem.

b. How would your decision be affected if a second new machine is available that costs $140,000, has a $20,000 estimated salvage value, and is expected to provide $25,000 in annual savings over its ten-year life? It also increases sales by $10,000 a year. (There are now three alternatives: (1) keep the old machine, (2) replace it with a $75,000 machine, or (3) replace it with a $140,000 machine.) Depreciation is still on a straight-line basis. For purposes of answering this question use both the *NPV*, which you must calculate, and the *IRR*, which you may assume to be 25 percent for the $75,000 project and 17 percent for the $140,000 project.

c. Disregarding the changes in part b—that is, under the original assumption that one $75,000 replacement machine is available—how would your decision be affected if a new generation of equipment is expected to be on the market in about two years that will provide increased annual savings and have the same cost, asset life, and salvage value?

d. What factors in addition to the quantitative factors listed above are likely to require consideration in a practical situation?

e. How would your decision be affected if the asset lives of the various alternatives were not the same?

10-3. The Crassner Company is considering the purchase of a new machine tool to replace an obsolete one. The machine being used for the operation has both a tax book value and a market value of zero; it is in good working order and will last, physically, for at least an additional fifteen years. The proposed machine will perform the operation so much more efficiently that Crassner engineers estimate that labor, material, and other direct costs of the operation will be reduced $4,500 a year if it is installed. The proposed machine costs $24,000 delivered and installed, and its economic life is estimated to be fifteen years with zero salvage value. The company expects to earn 12 percent on its investment after taxes (12 percent is the firm's cost of capital). The tax rate is 50 percent, and the firm uses straight-line depreciation.

a. Should Crassner buy the new machine?

b. Assume that the tax book value of the old machine had been $6,000, that the annual depreciation charge would have been $400, and that it had no sale value. How do these assumptions affect your answer?

c. Change part b to give the old machine a market value of $4,000.

d. Change part b to assume that the annual saving would be $6,000. (The change in part c is not made; the machine is *not* sold for $4,000.)

e. Rework part a assuming that relevant cost of capital is now 6 percent. What is the significance of this? What can be said about parts b, c, and d under this assumption?

f. In general, how would each of the following factors affect the investment decision, and how should each be treated?

  (i) The expected life of the existing machine decreases.

  (ii) Capital rationing is imposed on the firm.

  (iii) The cost of capital is not constant but is rising.

  (iv) Improvements in the equipment to be purchased are expected to occur each year, and the result will be to increase the returns or expected savings from new machines over the saving expected with this year's model for every year in the foreseeable future.

10-4. Each of two mutually exclusive projects involves an investment of $120,000. Cash flows (after-tax profits plus depreciation) for the two projects have a different time pattern although the totals are approximately the same. Project M will yield high returns early with smaller returns in later years (this is a mining type of investment with the expenses of removing the ores lower at the entrance to the mines with easier access). Project O yields smaller returns in the earlier years and larger returns in the later years (this is an orchard type of investment since it takes a number of years for trees to mature and be fully bearing). The cash flow from the two investments are as follows:

	Project O	Project M
Year 1	$10,000	$70,000
Year 2	20,000	40,000
Year 3	30,000	30,000
Year 4	50,000	10,000
Year 5	80,000	10,000

a. Compute the present value of each project if the firm's cost of capital is zero percent, 6 percent, 10 percent, and 20 percent.
b. Compute the internal rate of return for each project.
c. Graph the present values of the two projects, putting net present value (*NPV*) on the Y-axis and the cost of capital on the X-axis.
d. Could you determine the *IRR* of the projects from your graph? Explain.
e. Which project would you select, assuming no capital rationing and a constant cost of capital of (1) 8 percent, (2) 10 percent, (3) 12 percent? Explain.
f. If capital was severely rationed, which project would you select?

10–5. The Waterford Company is considering two mutually exclusive machine purchases. Machine A costs $6,210 and will produce a return of $1,750 per year. Machine B costs $5,130 and will produce a return of $1,375 per year. Both machines have a six-year life and no salvage value.
a. Compute the present value and net present value of each project if the firm's cost of capital is zero percent, 6 percent, 10 percent, and 20 percent.
b. Compute the internal rate of return for each project.
c. Graph the present values of the two projects, putting net present value (*NPV*) on the Y-axis and the cost of capital on the X-axis.
d. Could you determine the *IRR* of the projects from your graph? Explain.
e. Treat the differential cost of Machine A as an investment and its differential cash flows as the return from that investment. Calculate the internal rate of return on the $1,080 investment.

10–6. The Harris Company is analyzing two mutually exclusive machine purchases. One is an electric-powered materials handling unit that costs $10,000 and will produce a return of $3,650 per year for five years. A gas-powered materials handling unit costs $7,000 and produces a return of $2,350 per year also for five years. If the firm's cost of capital is 12 percent, which of the two machines should be purchased?

10-7. A firm is comparing the purchase of two mutually exclusive machine investments. Machine F involves an investment of $40,000, and would produce annual net cash flows after taxes of $12,000 for five years. Machine H would require an investment of $100,000 and would produce annual cash flows after taxes of $30,000 for seven years. Machine H is somewhat more risky and requires a cost of capital of 12 percent, compared to 10 percent for machine F. Which machine would have the greater net present value and should be selected?

**Selected
References**

Baumol, William J., and Quandt, Richard E. "Investment and Discount Rates Under Capital Rationing—A Programming Approach." *The Economic Journal* 75 (June 1965):317–29.

Beenhakker, Henri L. "Sensitivity Analysis of the Present Value of a Project." *The Engineering Economist* 20 (Winter 1975):123–49.

Bernhard, Richard H. "Mathematical Programming Models for Capital Budgeting—A Survey, Generalization, and Critique." *Journal of Financial and Quantitative Analysis* IV (June 1969):111–58.

Bierman, Harold, Jr., and Smidt, Seymour. *The Capital Budgeting Decision.* 3d ed. New York: Macmillan, 1971.

Bower, Richard S., and Jenks, Jeffrey M. "Divisional Screening Rates." *Financial Management* 4 (Autumn 1975):42–49.

Brigham, Eugene F. "Hurdle Rates for Screening Capital Expenditure Proposals." *Financial Management* 4 (Autumn 1975):17–26.

Brigham, Eugene F., and Pettway, Richard H. "Capital Budgeting by Utilities." *Financial Management* 2 (Autumn 1973):11–22.

Dean, Joel. *Capital Budgeting.* New York: Columbia University Press, 1951.

Donaldson, Gordon. "Strategic Hurdle Rates for Capital Investment." *Harvard Business Review* 50 (Mar.–Apr. 1972):50–58.

Elton, Edwin J. "Capital Rationing and External Discount Rates." *Journal of Finance* XXV (June 1970):573–84.

Fogler, H. Russell. "Ranking Techniques and Capital Rationing." *Accounting Review* 47 (Jan. 1972):134–43.

Gordon, Myron J., and Shapiro, Eli. "Capital Equipment Analysis: The Required Rate of Profit." *Management Science* 3 (Oct. 1956):102–10.

Grinyer, J. R. "Relevant Criterion Rates in Capital Budgeting." *The Journal of Business Finance & Accounting* 1 (Autumn 1974):357–74.

Hastie, Larry K. "One Businessman's View of Capital Budgeting." *Financial Management* 3 (Winter 1974):36–44.

Hawkins, Clark A., and Adams, Richard A. "A Goal Programming Model for Capital Budgeting." *Financial Management* 3 (Spring 1974):52–57.

Haynes, W. Warren, and Solomon, Martin B. Jr. "A Misplaced Emphasis in Capital Budgeting." *Quarterly Review of Economics and Business* (Feb. 1962).

Ignizio, James P. "An Approach to the Capital Budgeting Problem with Multiple Objectives." *The Engineering Economist* 21 (Summer 1976):259–72.

Jean, William H. *Capital Budgeting.* Scranton N.J.: International Textbook Company, 1969.

———. "On Multiple Rates of Return." *Journal of Finance* XXIII, no. 1 (Mar. 1968):187–92.

———. "Terminal Value or Present Value in Capital Budgeting Programs." *Journal of Financial and Quantitative Analysis* VI (Jan. 1971):649–52.

Jeynes, Paul H. "The Significance of Reinvestment Rate." *Engineering Economist* XI (Fall 1965):1–9.

Johnson, Robert W. *Capital Budgeting.* Belmont, Calif.: Wadsworth, 1970.

King, Paul. "Is the Emphasis of Capital Budgeting Theory Misplaced?" *Journal of Business Finance & Accounting* 2 (Spring 1975):69–82.

Klammer, Thomas. "Empirical Evidence of the Adoption of Sophisticated Capital Budgeting Techniques." *Journal of Business* 45 (July 1972):387–97.

Lerner, Eugene M., and Rappaport, Alfred. "Limit DCF in Capital Budgeting." *Harvard Business Review* 46 (July–Aug. 1968):133–39.

Lewellen, Wilbur G.; Lanser, Howard P.; and McConnell, John J. "Payback Substitutes for Discounted Cash Flow." *Financial Management* 2 (Summer 1973):17–23.

Lorie, James H., and Savage, Leonard J. "Three Problems in Rationing Capital." *Journal of Business* XXVIII (Oct. 1955).

Lutz, Friederich, and Lutz, Vera. *The Theory of the Investment of the Firm.* Princeton, N.J.: Princeton University Press, 1951.

Mao, James C. T. "The Internal Rate of Return as a Ranking Criterion." *Engineering Economist* XI (Winter 1966):1–13.

———. "Survey of Capital Budgeting: Theory and Practice." *Journal of Finance* 25 (May 1970):349–60.

Martin, John D. and Scott, David F., Jr. "Debt Capacity and the Capital Budgeting Decision." *Financial Management* 5 (Summer 1976):7–14.

Merrett, A. J., and Sykes, Allen. *Capital Budgeting and Company Finance.* London: Longmans, Green & Company, 1966.

Merville, L. J., and Tavis, L. A. "A Generalized Model for Capital Investment." *Journal of Finance* 28 (Mar. 1973):109–18.

Meyers, Stephen L. "Avoiding Depreciation Influences on Investment Decisions." *Financial Management* 1 (Winter 1972):17–24.

Murdick, Robert G., and Deming, Donald D. *The Management of Corporate Expenditures.* New York: McGraw-Hill, 1968.

Nelson, Charles R. "Inflation and Capital Budgeting." *The Journal of Finance* 31 (June 1976):923–31.

Oakford, Robert V. *Capital Budgeting.* New York: Ronald Press, 1970.

Peters, Donald H. "Coupon Rate of Return." *Financial Management* 1 (Winter 1972):25–35.

Petry, Glenn H. "Effective Use of Capital Budgeting Tools." *Business Horizons* 19 (Oct. 1975):57–65.

Petty, J. William; Scott, David F., Jr.; and Bird, Monroe M. "The Capital Expenditure Decision-Making Process of Large Corporations." *The Engineering Economist* 20 (Spring 1975):159–72.

Quirin, G. David. *The Capital Expenditure Decision.* Homewood, Ill.: Irwin, 1967.

Robichek, Alexander A.; Ogilvie, Donald G.; and Roach, John D. C. "Capital Budgeting: A Pragmatic Approach." *Financial Executive* 37 (Apr. 1969):26–38.

Robichek, Alexander A., and Van Horne, James C. "Abandonment Value and Capital Budgeting." *Journal of Finance* XXII (Dec. 1967):577–90.

Sarnat, Marshall, and Levy, Haim. "The Relationship of Rules of Thumb to the Internal Rate of Return: A Restatement and Generalization." *Journal of Finance* XXIV (June 1969):479–89.

Schwab, Bernhard, and Lusztig, Peter. "A Comparative Analysis of the Net Present Value and the Benefit-Cost Ratios as Measures of the Economic Desirability of Investments." *Journal of Finance* XXIV (June 1969):507–16.

———. "A Note on Abandonment Value and Capital Budgeting." *Journal of Financial and Quantitative Analysis* V (Sept. 1970):377–80.

Shore, Barry. "Replacement Decisions Under Capital Budgeting Constraints." *The Engineering Economist* 20 (Summer 1975):243–56.

Solomon, Ezra. *The Management of Corporate Capital.* New York: The Free Press of Glencoe, 1959.

———. *The Theory of Financial Management.* New York: Columbia University Press, 1963.

Stephen, Frank. "On Deriving the Internal Rate of Return from the Accountant's Rate of Return." *The Journal of Business Finance & Accounting* 3 (Summer 1976): 147–50.

Van Horne, James C. "A Note on Biases in Capital Budgeting Introduced by Inflation." *Journal of Financial and Quantitative Analysis* VI (Mar. 1971).

Vickers, Douglas. *The Theory of the Firm: Production, Capital and Finance.* New York: McGraw-Hill, 1968.

Weingartner, H. Martin. "Capital Budgeting of Interrelated Projects: Survey and Synthesis." *Management Science* XII (Mar. 1966), 485–516.

———. "The Generalized Rate of Return." *Journal of Financial and Quantitative Analysis* 1 (Sept. 1966):1–29.

———. *Mathematical Programming and the Analysis of Capital Budgeting Problems.* Englewood Cliffs, N.J.: Prentice-Hall, 1963.

———. "Some New Views on the Payback Period and Capital Budgeting Decisions." *Management Science* 15 (Aug. 1969):594–607.

Williams, John Daniel, and Rakich, Jonathan S. "Investment Evaluation in Hospitals." *Financial Management* 2 (Summer 1973):30–35.

Appendix A to Chapter 10
Further Analysis of Discounted
Cash Flow Selection Criteria

As we indicated in Chapter 10, the *NPV* and *IRR* methods generally give the same "answers" to the important questions in capital budgeting: (1) they usually agree on which of two mutually exclusive projects is "better," and (2) they ordinarily agree on how large the total capital budget should be. We did, however, show that under certain conditions the two methods produce conflicting results and that such conflicts are caused by differences in the assumed reinvestment rate for cash flows implicit in the two methods. In this appendix, we extend the discussion by utilizing the "terminal value" concept to illustrate reinvestment rates. We also define another selection method (the *PI* criterion), consider the problem of multiple internal rates of return, and discuss the use of mathematical programming as a tool to help solve the problem of capital rationing.

More on Capital Rationing: NPV versus IRR

If a firm's management seeks to maximize the value of its stock, then it should use the *NPV* method, choosing among mutually exclusive projects the one that has the highest *NPV*. However, a problem can arise if capital rationing is imposed, that is, if an arbitrary limit is placed on the amount of capital investment during a given year. Consider the situation shown in Figure A10–1. With its cost of capital constant at k_1 and with its investment opportunities given by the *IRR* schedule, this firm should expand its capital budget to I_3, where the marginal cost of capital is equal to the marginal return on investment. Suppose, however, that a management decision limits the capital budget to I_1. Obviously, the firm's value will not be maximized, but how should it select the projects whose total costs will be I_1 dollars?

Notice that no real selection problem exists if all projects have the same time pattern of returns and if all competing projects are about the same size; in this case, the *NPV* and the *IRR* methods will give identical rankings. Neither method will maximize the value of the firm—that would only occur if investment were expanded out to I_3—but the *NPV* and *IRR* methods will lead to identical capital budgeting decisions. However, if different projects have different time patterns or if competing projects differ in size, conflicts can arise. *The resolution of these con-*

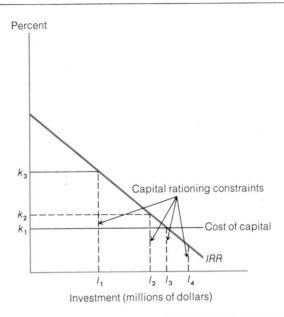

Figure A10–1
Illustration of Capital
Rationing

flicts requires a consideration of the rate of return at which cash flows generated by current investments can be reinvested. This point is explained in
the following section.

**The
Reinvestment
Rate
Assumption**

The *NPV* method assumes that the opportunity exists to reinvest the
cash flows from a project at the cost of capital, while the *IRR* method
assumes reinvestment at the *IRR*. To demonstrate this, consider the following steps.

Step 1

Notice that both the *NPV* and *IRR* methods employ present value interest factors (*PVIFs*) in the solution process; for example, to determine the
NPV, multiply a series of cash flows by appropriate *PVIFs*, subtract the
initial cost, and the result is the *NPV*. Essentially, this method involves
using present value tables.

Step 2

Refer back to Chapter 9, Table 9–1 and Equation 9–2; notice how present value tables are constructed. *The present value of any future sum is*

defined as the beginning amount which, when compounded at a specified and constant interest rate, will grow to equal the future amount over the stated time period. From Table 9–1 we can see that the present value of $1,217 due in five years, when discounted at 4 percent, is $1,000 *because $1,000, when compounded at 4 percent for five years, will grow to $1,217.* Thus, compounding and discounting are reciprocal relationships, and *the very construction of PV tables implies a reinvestment process.*

Step 3

Since both the *NPV* and *IRR* methods involve the use of *IF* tables, and since the very construction of these tables involves an assumed reinvestment process, the concept of reinvestment underlies the two methods.

Step 4

The implicitly assumed reinvestment rate used in the *NPV* method is the cost of capital, k; that used in the *IRR* method is r, which is the *IRR* in the solution process.

Suppose the cash flows from a project are not reinvested but are used for current consumption. No reinvestment is involved, yet an *IRR* for the project could still be calculated—does this show that the reinvestment assumption is not *always* implied in the *IRR* calculation? The answer is no; reinvestment itself is not necessarily assumed, but the *opportunity* of reinvestment *is* assumed. Because that assumption is made in the very construction of the *PV* tables, we simply could not define or interpret the concept of *NPV* without it. Also, the calculation of the *IRR* involves finding the discount rate that makes $NPV = 0$, so the *IRR*, too, depends upon the reinvestment assumption.

**Terminal
Value**

These concepts, and the impact of actual reinvestment rates on the choice of capital budgeting methods, can be made clear through the use of an example involving both *terminal value* (the value of an asset at a future time) and present value. First, note that the value of any asset, or a collection of assets such as a firm, can be estimated at any point in time. We are primarily interested in the value of the asset at the present time, or its present value, because this figure represents stockholders' wealth, which is what management seeks to maximize. However, the terminal value is useful for examining the difference between the *NPV* and the *IRR*.

Assume that a firm is set up with a total capital of $10,000. No additional funds can be brought into the firm, but cash flows from past investments can be reinvested in the business. Thus, the capital rationing constraint is $10,000 in year 1, while in later years it is the available cash flows from prior investments. Assume further that the investors who set up the firm have a 6 percent cost of capital, so this is also the firm's cost of capital. Finally, the investors have mutually agreed to terminate the firm at the end of three years; accordingly, their welfare will be maximized by having the firm attain the highest possible terminal value.

The firm is considering two alternative projects, X and Y, whose salient features are given in Table A10–1. Both projects cost $10,000, but X provides cash flows every year, while Y has no cash flows until year 3. Because of these timing differences, the IRR and NPV methods give conflicting rankings: $IRR_X = 23$ percent $> IRR_Y = 18.2$ percent, but $NPV_Y = \$3,860 > NPV_X = \$3,365$. Which of the two projects should be selected?

The best choice depends upon investment opportunities during years 2 and 3. Project Y has no intermediate cash flows, so its terminal value will be $16,500 regardless of reinvestment rates. However, the terminal values of project X range from $15,920 to $18,750, depending upon the reinvestment rate for cash flows during years 2 and 3. Notice that *the value of the firm today is the present value of the terminal value, discounted at the 6 percent cost of capital.* The value of the firm today is $13,860 if project Y is chosen, but it will range from $13,370 to $15,750, depending upon reinvestment opportunities, if project X is selected.[1] At a reinvestment rate of 10 percent, the two projects are approximately equal. If expected reinvestment rates exceed 10 percent, the management should choose project X. If the expected reinvestment rate is less than 10 percent, Y is preferable. Thus, 10 percent corresponds to the cross-over point in Figure 10–2 of the text.

| **IRR and NPV Redefined** | We can use the terminal value concept to redefine both the NPV and the IRR in the following manner: |

$$NPV^* = \frac{\text{Terminal value}}{(1 + k)^N} - \text{cost,} \qquad\qquad (A10–1)$$

and

$IRR^* =$ solution value of r in the equation

$$\frac{\text{Terminal value}}{(1 + r)^N} - \text{cost} = 0. \qquad\qquad (A10–2)$$

---

1. At first glance, a conflict might seem to exist between Equation 10–3, which states that the value of an asset or collection of assets (a firm) is the *PV* of a series of cash flows, and the statement that the value of the firm is the present value of its terminal value. In fact, no conflict exists because, in the second instance, the only cash flow *to the investors* is the terminal value.

Table A10–1
Analysis of Projects X and Y

Alternative Reinvestment Rates (Percent)	Cost	PV of Cash Flows Discounted at Indicated Rate	NPV	Receipts at End of			Terminal Value at End of Year 3	Present Value of Terminal Value Discounted at 6%
				Year 1	Year 2	Year 3		
Project X	$10,000			$5,000	$5,000	$ 5,000		
6.0		$13,365	$3,365*				$15,920	$13,370†
10.0		12,435	2,435				16,550	13,902
18.2		10,900	900				17,900	15,036
20.0		10,530	530				18,200	15,288
23.0‡		10,000	0				18,750	15,750
Project Y	$10,000			$ 0	$ 0	$16,500		
6.0		$13,860	$3,860*				$16,500	$13,860
10.0		12,391	2,391				16,500	13,860
18.2‡		10,000	0				16,500	13,860
20.0		9,553	(447)				16,500	13,860
23.0		8,415	(1,585)				16,500	13,860

*NPV at the 6 percent cost of capital.
†This value differs from the $13,365 shown in column 3 because of rounding.
‡IRR = discount rate where NPV = 0.

In words, we can define NPV^* as the present value of the terminal value, discounted at the cost of capital, minus the cost, and IRR^* as the value of r that equates the PV of the terminal value to the cost of the project.

To calculate these modified NPVs and IRRs, we need to know the relevant terminal values, and in order to calculate terminal values, we need reinvestment rates. If the pattern of reinvestment rates is known, then we *should* calculate NPV^* and IRR^*—they are clearly more accurate measures of project profitability than the unmodified versions.

For example, for projects X and Y analyzed in Table A10–1, let us assume that the reinvestment rate and the cost of capital, k, are both 6 percent. The present value of the terminal value of X is $13,370, which is less than the present value of the terminal value of Y ($13,860). The value of the IRR^* or the solution value of r in equation A10–2 is 16.76 percent for X, which is less than the 18.17 percent for Y. Note that the NPV^* and the IRR^* give the same rankings. This will always be the case when the reinvestment rate and the cost of capital are equal. For the data in Table A10–1 the IRR^* for project X would be greater than the IRR^* for project Y at reinvestment rates greater than 10 percent. But the NPV^* will also be greater for X than for Y at reinvestment rates greater than 10 percent.[2] The NPV^* and IRR^* may appear to give different rankings only if there is a failure to make the proper adjustment

2. A reliable estimate of the reinvestment rates is therefore of critical importance.

for differences in project scale or size of the initial investment outlay — a critical requirement for the profitability index next discussed.

NPV versus Profitability Index

The profitability index *(PI)*, or the benefit/cost ratio as it is sometimes called, is defined as[3].

$$PI = \frac{PV \text{ benefits}}{\text{cost}}$$

$$= \frac{\displaystyle\sum_{t=1}^{N} \frac{F_t}{(1+k)^t}}{\text{cost}}. \tag{A10-4}$$

The *PI* shows the *relative* profitability of any project, or the *PV* of benefits per dollar of cost.

As was true in the *NPV* versus *IRR* comparison, the *NPV* and *PI* always make the same accept-reject decisions, but *NPV* and *PI* can give different project rankings, which presents problems when mutually exclusive projects are compared. Suppose, for example, that we are comparing project A, which calls for an investment of $1 million in a conveyor-belt system for handling goods in a storage warehouse, with project B, which calls for an expenditure of $300,000 to do the same thing by employing a fleet of fork-trucks. The conveyor-belt system has lower operating costs, so its cash flows are larger; the net present values are found to be $200,000 for A and $100,000 for B. Using the *NPV* criterion on the one hand, we would select project A. However, if we compute the ratio of the present value of the returns on each project to its cost, we find A's ratio to be 1.20 and B's ratio to be 1.33. Thus, on the other hand, using the *PI* for our ranking, we would select project B because it produces higher net returns for each dollar invested.

Given this conflict, which project should be accepted? Alternatively stated: Is it better to use the net present value approach on an absolute basis *(NPV)* or on a relative basis *(PI)? Barring capital rationing, the* NPV *method is preferred.* The differential between the initial outlays of the two projects ($700,000) can be looked upon as an investment itself, project C; that is, project A can be broken down into two components, one identically equal to project B and one a residual project equal to the hypothetical project C. The hypothetical investment has a net present

---

3. If costs are incurred in more than one year, they should be netted against cash inflows in the corresponding years; if costs exceed cash inflows in some years, the denominator must be the *PV* of the costs.

value equal to the differential between the *NPV* of the first two projects, or $100,000. This is shown below:

Project	Cost	NPV
A	$1,000,000	$200,000
B	− 300,000	− 100,000
C	$ 700,000	$100,000

Since the hypothetical project C has a positive net present value, it should be accepted. This amounts to accepting project A.

To put it another way, project A can be split into two components, one costing $300,000 and having a net present value of $100,000, the other costing $700,000 and having a net present value of $100,000. As each of the two components has a positive net present value, both should be accepted; but if project B is accepted, the effect is to reject the second component of project A, the hypothetical project C. As the *PI* method selects project B while the *NPV* method selects project A, we conclude that the *NPV* method is preferable.

Alternatively, we can make an adjustment to make the projects of equal scale or size. We can calculate the *NPV** based on terminal values by assuming an additional investment of $700,000 for project B earning at the firm's cost of capital. If the project cost of capital is 10 percent, for example, the extra investment earns at a 10 percent rate and is discounted at a 10 percent rate. The present value of the inflows must therefore be $700,000. We have added $700,000 to both the gross present value and the investment cost, so the *NPV** of project B is $100,000, the same as its *NPV*. The *PI* method would now take into account the additional $700,000 investment and its present value of $700,000. The original *PV* of benefits was $400,000 (the cost of $300,000 plus the *NPV* of $100,000) to which is added the *PV* of $700,000, for total PV benefits equal to $1,100,000. Next we divide by the cost of $1,000,000 to obtain a *PI* of 1.1, which is less than the 1.2 *PI* calculated for project A. Thus when the *PI* is adjusted for differences in scale or size of investments, it will give the same rankings as the *NPV**.

An extreme example is often cited to argue for the superiority of the *PI* method. Suppose that project L costs $1 million and has a net present value of $100,000, while project S costs $100,000 and has a net present value of $99,000. It may be argued that the benefits from project S are almost as great as for project L, but the amount of funds invested is much smaller. However, if we perform an *NPV** analysis by assuming an investment of an additional $900,000 in project S to make its cost equal with project L's, we find that the *NPV** of project S will be $1,000 less than the *NPV** for project L. It may be argued that project S without the additional investment is less risky because of the smaller investment outlay. However, the operating flows of S are likely to be larger as a substitute for the larger investment outlay for L. For example, a decision to repair a machine will involve a smaller outlay than a replacement. But the repaired machine is likely to involve greater maintenance outlays in the future as compared with the replacement, and the actual size of the maintenance outlays is subject to uncertainty as well. While we have emphasized that, in finance, mechanical rules should not be substituted for judgment, the NPV* generally provides the correct result, which should be set aside only for compelling reasons after all important facets of the evidence have been included in the analysis.

Shifting MCC or IRR Curves

If the *MCC* and *IRR* curves are expected to be reasonably stable over time, then the firm can form a judgment about the reinvestment rate, or opportunity cost of cash flows, and, on the basis of this estimate, it can decide to use either the *NPV* or the *IRR* method. However, if either the *MCC* or the *IRR* curve shifts over time, as in Figure A10–2, then a new problem arises: There is no simple way to prescribe decision rules for a firm faced with such a situation. Probably the most reasonable approach would involve computer simulation, wherein a number of assumptions about future investment opportunities and discount rates are fed into a computer and then present values of the firm are estimated under alternative courses of action. This involves capital budgeting under uncertainty, which is discussed in Chapter 11.

Multiple Solution to the IRR

A totally different problem, unrelated to anything discussed thus far, can arise when the *IRR* is used to rank projects: Under certain circumstances, several different values of *r* can be used to solve Equation A10–3:

$$I = \frac{F_1}{(1 + r)^1} + \frac{F_2}{(1 + r)^2} + \cdots + \frac{F_N}{(1 + r)^N}. \tag{A10–3}$$

Notice that this equation is a polynomial of degree N. Therefore, there are N different roots, or solutions, to the equation. All except one of the roots either are imaginary numbers or are negative when investments are "normal"—a normal investment being one that has one or more outflows (costs) followed by a series of inflows (receipts)—so in the normal case only one positive value of *r* appears. If, however, a project calls for a large outflow either sometime during or at the end of its life,

Figure A10–2
Shifting MCC and IRR
Curves

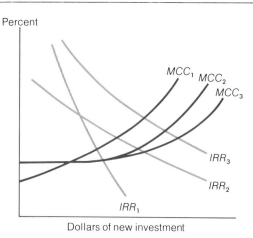

then it is a "nonnormal" project, and the possibility of multiple real roots arises.

To illustrate this problem, suppose the project calls for an expenditure of $1,600 for a pump that will enable the firm to recover $10,000 of oil from a field at the end of one year.[4] If the new pump is not installed, the firm will recover the same $10,000 of oil at the end of two years. Obviously, if the pump is installed and the oil is recovered at the end of year 1, there will be no oil at the end of year 2. Therefore, the project's cash flows are as follows:

Year end	0	1	2
Cash flow	− $1,600	+ $10,000	− $10,000

These values can be substituted into Equation A10–3 to derive the NPV for the investment:

$$NPV = -\$1,600 + \frac{\$10,000}{(1 + r)} - \frac{\$10,000}{(1 + r)^2}.$$

NPV = 0 when r = 25 percent *and* when r = 400 percent, so the IRR of the investment is *both* 25 percent and 400 percent. This relationship is graphically depicted in Figure A10–3. Note that no dilemma would arise if the NPV method were used — we would simply replace r with k in the equation above, find the NPV, and use this for ranking.

A similar situation actually occurred when a major California bank

4. This example is drawn from J. H. Lorie and L. J. Savage, "The Problems in Capital Rationing," *Journal of Business* (October 1955), pp. 236–37.

Figure A10-3
Net Present Value as
a Function of Cost of
Capital

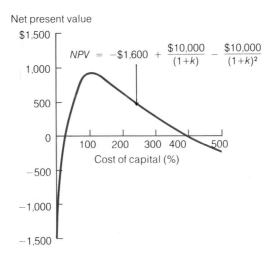

Net present value

$$NPV = -\$1,600 + \frac{\$10,000}{(1+k)} - \frac{\$10,000}{(1+k)^2}$$

borrowed funds from an insurance company, then used these funds (plus an initial investment of its own) to buy a number of jet engines, which it then leased to a major airline. The bank expected to receive positive net cash flows (lease payments minus interest on the insurance company loan) for a number of years, then several large negative cash flows as it repaid the insurance company loan, and, finally, a large inflow from the sale of the engines when the lease expired.

The bank discovered two *IRR*s and wondered which was correct. It could not ignore the *IRR* and use the *NPV* method, as the lease was already on the books; meanwhile, both the bank's senior loan committee and the Federal Reserve Bank examiners wanted to know the return on the lease. The bank's solution called for compounding the cash flows — both positive and negative — at an assumed reinvestment rate of 9 percent, its average return on loans, to arrive at a compounded terminal value for the operation. Then the interest rate that equated this terminal sum to the bank's initial cost was called the *IRR*,* or the rate of return on the lease. This procedure satisfied not only the loan committee but also the bank examiners. Note, however, that the procedure would have been rejected if the bank had borrowed *all* the money to finance the investment. In fact, in most similar situations, the *IRR* becomes larger as the bank's "investment" decreases, with the *IRR* approaching infinity as investment approaches zero.[5]

---

5. For additional insights into the multiple root problem, see James C. T. Mao, *Quantitative Analysis of Financial Decisions* (New York: Macmillan, 1969), chapter 6.

Programming Approaches to Capital Rationing

The problems encountered in capital budgeting that cause conflicts in making decisions are summarized in Table A10–2. If none of the problems listed in the table apply, then the *NPV*, *IRR*, and *PI* methods always provide identical answers to the critical capital budgeting question—What projects should be accepted in the capital budget? However, if any of the project characteristics shown in Part A of Table A10–2 apply, then the three methods can give different rankings to mutually exclusive projects. If none of the firm characteristics in Part B of the table apply, these conflicts really present no problem, as all conflicts should be resolved in favor of the *NPV* method because it selects the set of projects that maximizes the firm's value.

**Table A10–2
Conditions under which NPV, IRR, and PI May Rank Conflicting Projects Differently**

Part A: Project Characteristics
1. The cash flow of one project increases over time, while that of the other decreases.
2. The projects have different expected lives.
3. The cost of one project is larger than that of the other.

Part B: Firm Characteristics
4. Investment opportunities in the future are expected to be different than they are this year, and the direction of change (better or worse) is known.
5. The cost of capital is expected to change in the future, and the direction of change is known.
6. Capital rationing is being imposed upon the firm.

Very serious difficulties can arise when any of the firm characteristics exist, because then future investment opportunities cease to be constant. In that case, *neither the standard* NPV, IRR, *nor* PI *methods will necessarily select a set of projects that maximizes the firm's value.* However, the *NPV* concept can be expanded to take account of both firm and project characteristics through the programming approach outlined below.

The programming approach is, in essence, a methodology that seeks to determine the value of the "modified *NPV*" (*NPV**) discussed above. Initially, consider a procedure that can, at least conceptually, improve our decision. Figure A10–4 gives a matrix of investments in, and cash flows from, alternative projects. The values in the cells of the matrix are the net cash flows attributable to projects A, B, . . . over years 1, 2, . . . , N. The rows of the matrix thus represent the investment opportunities available during the relevant time horizon, while the columns of the matrix represent the net cash flows from all projects during a given year. The cash flows in a particular cell can be either positive or negative; negative cash flow represents an investment, while a positive cash flow represents the benefits resulting from the investment.

Figure A10–4 simply describes the investment opportunities open to

Figure A10–4
Matrix of Future
Investment
Opportunities

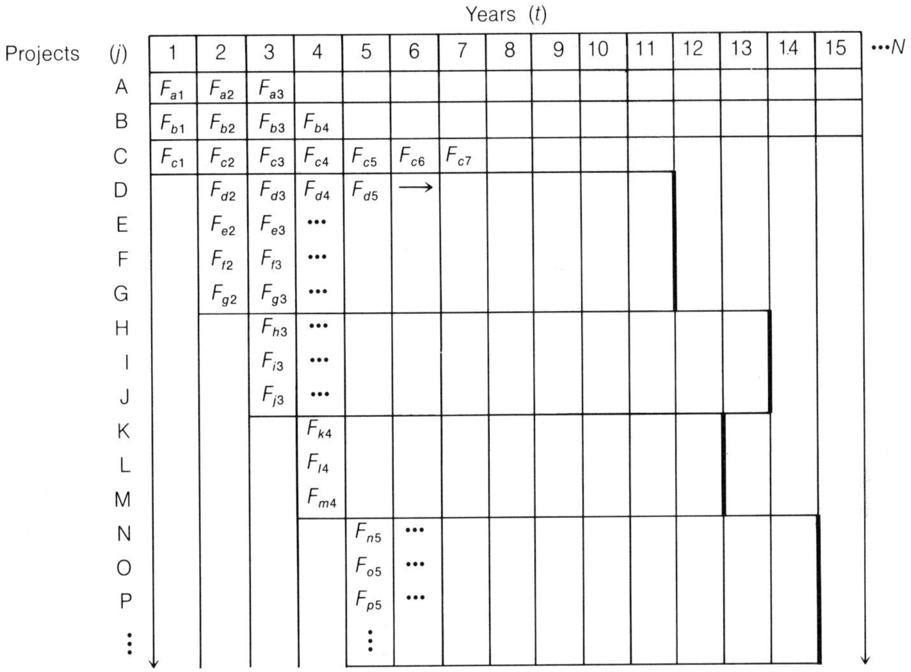

Years (t)

Projects (j)	1	2	3	4	5	6	7	8	9	10	11	12	13	14	15	•••N
A	F_{a1}	F_{a2}	F_{a3}													
B	F_{b1}	F_{b2}	F_{b3}	F_{b4}												
C	F_{c1}	F_{c2}	F_{c3}	F_{c4}	F_{c5}	F_{c6}	F_{c7}									
D		F_{d2}	F_{d3}	F_{d4}	F_{d5}	$\rightarrow$										
E		F_{e2}	F_{e3}	•••												
F		F_{f2}	F_{f3}	•••												
G		F_{g2}	F_{g3}	•••												
H			F_{h3}	•••												
I			F_{i3}	•••												
J			F_{j3}	•••												
K				F_{k4}												
L				F_{l4}												
M				F_{m4}												
N					F_{n5}	•••										
O					F_{o5}	•••										
P					F_{p5}	•••										
$\vdots$					$\vdots$											

the firm — the capital projects it can undertake. If no capital rationing is imposed, the firm will be able to take on all of the projects that have positive *NPVs*. If we make the further assumption that the cost of capital is constant, then the straightforward *NPV* method can be used to determine which of the available projects should be accepted.

Capital Rationing

Suppose, however, that the firm is subject to capital rationing. Specifically, assume that it has an initial amount of money available for investment at the beginning of year 1. It can invest this amount but no more. Further, assume that the funds available for investment in future years must come from cash generated from these same investments. Therefore, the funds available for investment in year 2 will depend upon the profitability of the set of investments chosen in year 1; investment funds available in year 3 will depend upon cash throw-off from investments in years 1 and 2, and so forth.[6]

If the projects available for investment in year 2 are more profitable than those available in year 1—that is, if they have higher internal rates of return—the firm should perhaps select investments in year 1 that will have fast paybacks. This will make funds available for the profitable investment opportunities in year 2. This is, however, only an approximation. Conceptually, the firm should select its investment in each year (subject to the capital rationing constraint) so as to maximize the net present value of future cash flows. These cash flows should, of course, be discounted at the firm's cost of capital. If the investment opportunities were infinitely divisible—for example, if they were securities such as stocks or bonds that could be purchased in larger or smaller quantities—then the firm could use a technique known as *linear programming* to determine the optimal set of investment opportunities. If such opportunities are not infinitely divisible—and in capital budgeting they typically are not—then a more complex procedure known as *integer programming* must be used to find the optimal investment strategy.[7] Regardless of the computational process used to solve the problem, the firm should seek the set of investment opportunities that maximizes the *NPV* of the firm without exceeding the capital rationing constraint.

**Changing Cost
of Capital**

Assuming that the cost of capital is constant, linear or integer programming offers a conceptual solution to the problem of capital budgeting under capital rationing. These methods do not, however, offer a solution to the general case of a changing cost of capital. For example, if the cost of capital is rising at the point where the *IRR* curve cuts the *MCC* curve, the wealth-maximizing set of projects—with regard both to the total budget and to the choices among competing projects—can be determined only by an iterative, or trial-and-error, process. With linear or integer programming, the cost of capital must be given as an input. If, however, the cost of capital *depends* upon the size of the capital budget, then the cost of capital obviously cannot be *assumed* when determining the capital budget. What is required is a dynamic programming model that, through an iterative process, simultaneously determines the capi-

---

6. The concept could also be extended to include any specific amount of external funds during each year. In this case, the capital constraint would be the internally generated funds plus the allowed external funds.

7. H. Martin Weingartner, in *Mathematical Programming and the Analysis of Capital Budgeting Problems* (Englewood Cliffs, N.J.: Prentice-Hall, 1963), has shown how integer programming can be used in capital budgeting decisions.

tal budget and the marginal cost of capital. Such models are quite complex, but they do have practical applications in capital budgeting; these formal aspects may be pursued further in courses in management science or in operations research.

Problems

10A–1. Assume a firm is set up with total capital of $20,000. No additional funds can be brought into the firm, but cash flows can be reinvested in the business. Thus, the *capital rationing* constraint is *$20,000 in year 1*, and in later years it is the *available cash flows* resulting from this and its succeeding investments.

The investors who set up the firm have a *10 percent* cost of capital, and they have mutually agreed to terminate the firm at the end of *three* years. Therefore, the investor's welfare will be maximized by having the firm attain the highest possible *terminal value*. Two projects are available; each costs $20,000 and provides cash flows as follows:

Year	Project A	Project B
1	$10,000	$ 0
2	10,000	0
3	10,000	35,000

a. Calculate IRR^* and NPV^* for each project. Assume cash flows from A are reinvested at 14 percent.
b. Which project should be accepted?
c. Is there a reinvestment rate at which the firm should be indifferent between two projects? If so, what is it?

10A–2. A coal mining firm is considering opening a strip mine, the cost of which is $4.4 million. Cash flows will be $27.7 million, all coming at the end of one year. The land must be returned to its natural state at a cost of $25 million, payable after two years. The *IRR* is found to be either 9.2 percent or 420 percent. Should the project be accepted (a) if $k = 8$ percent, or (b) if $k = 14$ percent? Explain your reasoning.

**Selected
References**

Bernhard, Richard H. "Mathematical Programming Models for Capital Budgeting—A Survey, Generalization, and Critique." *Journal of Financial and Quantitative Analysis* 4 (June 1969):111–58.

Burton, R. M., and Damon, W. W. "On the Existence of a Cost of Capital Under Pure Capital Rationing." *Journal of Finance* XXIX, No. 4 (Sept. 1974): 1165–73.

Findlay, M. Chapman, III, and Williams, Edward E. "Capital Allocation and the Nature of Ownership Equities." *Financial Management* 1 (Summer 1972): 68–76.

Hawkins, Clark A., and Adams, Richard A. "A Goal Programming Model for Capital Budgeting." *Financial Management* 3, No. 1 (Spring 1974):52–57.

Lee, Sang M., and Lerro, A. J. "Capital Budgeting for Multiple Objectives." *Financial Management* 3, No. 1 (Spring 1974):58–66.

Lorie, James H., and Savage, Leonard J. "Three Problems in Rationing Capital." *Journal of Business* 28 (Oct. 1955):227–39.

Myers, Stewart C. "A Note on Linear Programming and Capital Budgeting." *Journal of Finance* 27 (Mar. 1972):89–92.

Sarnat, Marshall, and Levy, Haim. "The Relationship of Rules of Thumb to the Internal Rate of Return: A Restatement and Generalization." *Journal of Finance* 24 (June 1969):479–89.

Sartoris, William L., and Spruill, M. Lynn. "Goal Programming and Working Capital Management." *Financial Management* 3, No. 1 (Spring 1974):67–74.

Schwab, Bernhard, and Lusztig, Peter. "A Comparative Analysis of the Net Present Value and the Benefit Cost Ratios as Measures of the Economic Desirability of Investments." *Journal of Finance* 24 (June 1969):507–16.

Weingartner, H. Martin. *Mathematical Programming and the Analysis of Capital Budgeting Problems.* Englewood Cliffs, N.J.: Prentice-Hall, 1963.

———. "Some New Views on the Payback Period and Capital Budgeting Decisions." *Management Science* 15 (Aug. 1969):594–607.

———. "The Excess Present Value Index—A Theoretical Basis and Critique." *Journal of Accounting Research* 1 (Autumn 1963):213–24.

Appendix B to Chapter 10
Accelerated Depreciation

In the illustrations of capital budgeting given in Chapter 10, it was assumed that straight-line depreciation was used, thus enabling us to derive uniform cash flows over the life of the investment. Realistically, however, firms usually employ *accelerated depreciation* methods; when such is the case, it is necessary to modify the procedures outlined thus far.[1] In terms of the framework given in Table 10–5, accelerated depreciation makes it necessary to recompute the differential cash flow for each year during the life of the investment.

Table 10B–1 contains "present value factors" for accelerated depreciation. The table is constructed as follows:

1. Depreciation is a deductible item for tax purposes, and the taxes saved are equal to TDep. At a 40 percent tax rate, $1 of depreciation saves $0.40; that is, tax saving = .4 ($1) = $0.40.
2. Depreciation is taken over the life of the asset; accordingly, the tax savings occur over this life. For capital budgeting purposes, we want to know the *present value* of the tax savings. To illustrate the calculation of this PV, assume that an asset with a $2 cost, a five-year depreciable life, and zero salvage value is to be depreciated by the sum-of-years-digits method (see Appendix B to this book for an explanation of the method). The firm is taxed at a 40 percent rate, and its cost of capital is 10 percent. Thus, the firm will save taxes of TDep = .4 ($2) = $0.80, but these savings will occur over a five-year period.
3. We first find a new "interest factor," the PV of $1 received in accor-

Year	Depreciation Fraction Applied to Asset Cost	Amount of Depreciation	10% Discount Factor	Product
1	5/15	$0.33333	0.909	$0.303
2	4/15	0.26667	0.826	0.220
3	3/15	0.20000	0.751	0.150
4	2/15	0.13333	0.683	0.091
5	1/15	0.06667	0.621	0.042
	Totals 1.00	$1.00000	Factor =	$0.806

---

1. For a discussion of accelerated depreciation methods, see Appendix B at the end of the book.

dance with the sum-of-years-digits over a five-year period, discounted at 10 percent:

4. We now find the *PV* of the depreciation tax savings (DTS) as follows:

$$PV_{DTS} = T \text{ (Depreciable cost)(Factor)}$$
$$= .4 \ (\$2)(.806) = \$0.6448.$$

Thus, the present value of the depreciation tax savings resulting from an investment of $2 is $0.6448.

5. Table B10−1 gives factors for both the sum-of-years-digits and double-declining depreciation methods, for various asset lives, and for different discount rates. The factor calculated above, .806, can also be found in the upper half of Table B10−1 in the 10 percent column at period 5.

We may utilize these accelerated depreciation factors to recalculate the Culver example given in Chapter 10, using the alternative, and somewhat streamlined, decision format shown in Table B10−2. The top section of the table presents the cash outflows at the time the investment is made. All these flows occur immediately, so no discounting is required, and the present value factor is 1.0. No tax adjustment is necessary on the invoice price of the new machine, but, as we saw above, the $4,000 loss on the old machine gives rise to a $1,600 tax reduction, which is deducted from the price of the new machine. Also, the $1,000 salvage value on the old machine is treated as a reduction in cash outflows necessary to acquire the new machine. Notice that since the $1,000 is a recovery of capital investment, it is not considered to be taxable income; hence, no tax adjustment is made for the salvage value.

In the lower section of the table we see that revenues increase by $3,000 a year—a sales increase of $1,000 plus a cost reduction of $2,000. However, this amount is taxable, so with a 40 percent tax, the after-tax benefits are reduced to $1,800. This $1,800 is received each year for ten years, so it is an annuity. The present value of the annuity, discounted at the 10 percent cost of capital, is $11,061.

Cash inflows also come from the depreciation on the new machine— depreciation on the new machine totals $10,000, and the tax saving totals $4,000. In Table B10−2, we assume that the new investment is depreciated by the double-declining balance *(DDB)* method over a ten-year period; hence a factor taken from Table B10−1, 0.685, is applied to the after-tax depreciation figure of $4,000, to obtain a present value of $2,740 for the depreciation "tax shelter."[2]

---

2. The term "tax shelter" or "tax shield" is frequently used to denote the value of depreciation and other items which "shelter" or "shield" income from taxes. The *DDB* method is discussed in Appendix B at the end of the book.

Table B10–1

Tables for Present Value of Depreciation for Sum-of-Years'-Digits and Double-Declining Balance Methods at Different Costs of Capital

Sum-of-years'-digits (SYD)

Period	6%	8%	10%	12%	14%	15%	16%
1	—	—	—	—	—	—	—
2	—	—	—	—	—	—	—
3	0.908	0.881	0.855	0.831	0.808	0.796	0.786
4	0.891	0.860	0.830	0.802	0.776	0.763	0.751
5	0.875	0.839	0.806	0.775	0.746	0.732	0.719
6	0.859	0.820	0.783	0.749	0.718	0.703	0.689
7	0.844	0.801	0.761	0.725	0.692	0.676	0.661
8	0.829	0.782	0.740	0.702	0.667	0.650	0.635
9	0.814	0.765	0.720	0.680	0.643	0.626	0.610
10	0.800	0.748	0.701	0.659	0.621	0.604	0.587
11	0.786	0.731	0.683	0.639	0.600	0.582	0.565
12	0.773	0.715	0.665	0.620	0.581	0.562	0.545
13	0.760	0.700	0.648	0.602	0.562	0.543	0.526
14	0.747	0.685	0.632	0.585	0.544	0.525	0.508
15	0.734	0.671	0.616	0.569	0.527	0.508	0.491
16	0.722	0.657	0.601	0.553	0.511	0.492	0.475
17	0.711	0.644	0.587	0.538	0.496	0.477	0.460
18	0.699	0.631	0.573	0.524	0.482	0.463	0.445
19	0.688	0.618	0.560	0.510	0.468	0.449	0.432
20	0.677	0.606	0.547	0.497	0.455	0.436	0.419

Double-declining balance (DDB)

Period	6%	8%	10%	12%	14%	15%	16%
1	—	—	—	—	—	—	—
2	—	—	—	—	—	—	—
3	0.920	0.896	0.873	0.851	0.831	0.821	0.811
4	0.898	0.868	0.840	0.814	0.789	0.777	0.766
5	0.878	0.843	0.811	0.781	0.753	0.739	0.727
6	0.858	0.819	0.783	0.749	0.718	0.704	0.689
7	0.840	0.796	0.756	0.720	0.687	0.671	0.656
8	0.821	0.774	0.731	0.692	0.657	0.641	0.625
9	0.804	0.753	0.708	0.667	0.630	0.614	0.597
10	0.787	0.733	0.685	0.643	0.605	0.588	0.571
11	0.771	0.714	0.664	0.620	0.582	0.564	0.547
12	0.755	0.696	0.644	0.599	0.559	0.541	0.524
13	0.740	0.678	0.625	0.579	0.539	0.521	0.504
14	0.725	0.661	0.607	0.560	0.520	0.501	0.484
15	0.711	0.645	0.590	0.542	0.502	0.483	0.466
16	0.697	0.630	0.573	0.526	0.485	0.466	0.450
17	0.684	0.615	0.558	0.510	0.469	0.451	0.434
18	0.671	0.601	0.543	0.495	0.454	0.436	0.419
19	0.659	0.587	0.529	0.480	0.440	0.422	0.405
20	0.647	0.574	0.515	0.467	0.427	0.409	0.392

**Table B10–2
Calculations for
Replacement
Decision:
Accelerated
Depreciation**

	Amount before Tax	Amount after Tax*	Year Event Occurs	Present Value Factor at 10%	Present Value
Outflows at time investment is made					
Investment in new equipment	$12,000	$12,000	—	1.00	$12,000
Salvage value of old†	(1,000)	(1,000)	0	1.00	(1,000)
Tax loss on sale	(4,000)	(1,600)	0	1.00	(1,600)
Total outflows					
(present value of costs)					$ 9,400
Inflows, or annual returns					
Benefits	3,000	1,800	1–10	6.145	$11,061
Depreciation on new (total)	10,000	4,000	1–10	0.685	2,740
Depreciation on old (annual)	(500)	(200)	1–10	6.145	(1,229)
Salvage value on new†	2,000	2,000	10	0.386	772
Total inflows					
(present value of benefits)					$13,344

Present value of inflows less present value of outflows = $3,944

*The "tax loss on sale" and depreciation figures are multiplied by T, the tax rate, to obtain the "after tax" figures, while the benefits are multiplied by $(1 - T)$.
†Salvage value is not an issue in this example. However, the table is structured to show how salvage values would be handled in cases where they are applicable.

The old machine was being depreciated by the straight-line method; hence it provides a cash flow of $500 before taxes and $200 after taxes for ten years. Observe that the depreciation on the old machine is *subtracted* from the inflows section. The logic here is that, had the replacement *not* been made, the company would have had the benefit of the $500 depreciation each year for the next ten years. With the replacement, however, all this depreciation is taken as an operating loss immediately and is shown as the tax loss on sale in the upper section of the table.

When the present values of the inflows and outflows are summed, we obtain the project's *NPV*. In this example, the *NPV* is $3,944 versus $3,662 for the straight-line text example. In general, *NPV*s are higher when accelerated depreciation is used, as the *PV* of the depreciation benefit is higher than it would be under straight line.

11 Investment Decisions under Uncertainty

In order to develop the theory and methodology of capital budgeting in a systematic manner, the "riskiness" of alternative projects was not treated explicitly in the preceding chapter. However, since investors and financial managers are generally risk averters, they should take into account whether one project is more risky than another when choosing between projects. Several approaches to risk analysis are discussed in this chapter.[1]

Risk in Financial Analysis

The riskiness of an asset is defined in terms of the likely variability of future returns from the asset. For example, if one buys a $1 million short-term government bond expected to yield 5 percent, then the return on the investment, 5 percent, can be estimated quite precisely, and the investment is defined as relatively risk free. However, if the $1 million is invested in the stock of a company just being organized to prospect for uranium in Central Africa, then the probable return cannot be estimated precisely. The rate of return on the $1 million investment could range from minus 100 percent to some extremely large figure, and because of this high variability, the project is defined as relatively risky. Similarly, sales forecasts for different products of a single firm might exhibit differing degrees of riskiness. For example, Union Carbide might be quite sure that sales of its Eveready batteries will range between 50 and 60 million for the coming year, but be highly uncertain about how many units of a new laser measuring device will be sold during the year.

Risk, then, is associated with project variability—the more variable the expected future returns, the riskier the investment. However, we can define risk more precisely, and it is useful to do so. This more precise definition requires a step-by-step development, which constitutes the remainder of this section.

---

1. This chapter is long and introduces some important new concepts that will be applied in subsequent chapters as well.

**Probability
Distributions**

Any investment decision—or, for that matter, almost *any* kind of business decision—implies a forecast of future events that is either explicit or implicit. Ordinarily, the forecast of annual cash flow is a single figure, or *point estimate*, frequently called the "most likely" or "best" estimate. For example, one might forecast that the cash flows from a particular project will be $500 a year for three years.

How good is this point estimate; that is, how confident is the forecaster of his predicted return? Is he very certain, very uncertain, or somewhere in between? This degree of uncertainty can be defined and measured in terms of the forecaster's *probability distribution*—the probability estimates associated with each possible outcome. In its simplest form, a probability distribution could consist of just a few potential outcomes. For example, in forcasting cash flows, we could make an optimistic estimate, a pessimistic estimate, and a most likely estimate; or, alternatively, we could make high, low, and "best guess" estimates. We might expect our high, or optimistic, estimate to be realized if the national economy booms, our pessimistic estimate to hold if the economy is depressed, and our best guess to occur if the economy runs at a normal level. These ranges are illustrated in Table 11–1. The figures in the table represent some improvement over our earlier best-guess estimate of $500, as additional information has been provided. However, some critical information is still missing: How likely is it that we will have a boom, a recession, or normal economic conditions? If we have estimates of the probabilities of these events, we can develop a weighted average cash flow estimate and a measure of our degree of confidence in this estimate. This point is explored in the next section.

**Table 11–1
Expected Cash Flows under
Different Economic Conditions**

State of the Economy	Cash Flows
Recession	$400
Normal	500
Boom	600

**Risk
Comparisons**

To illustrate how the probability distribution concept can be used to compare the riskiness of alternative investment projects, suppose we are considering two investment decisions each calling for an outlay of $1,000 and each expected to produce a cash flow of $500 a year for three years. (The best-estimate cash flow is $500 a year for each project.) If the discount rate is 10 percent, we can use the methods developed in the preceding chapter to estimate each project's net present value:

$$NPV = \$500 \times 2.487 - \$1,000$$
$$= \$1,243.50 - \$1,000$$
$$= \$243.50 \text{ for each project.}$$

The projects have the same expected returns; does this mean that they are equally desirable? To answer this question, we need to know whether the projects are also equally risky, since "desirability" depends upon both returns and risk.

Let us suppose that project A calls for the replacement of an old machine used in normal operations by a more efficient one, and the benefits are labor and raw material savings that will result. Project B, on the other hand, calls for the purchase of an entirely new machine to produce a new product, the demand for which is highly uncertain. The replacement machine (project A) will be used more, hence savings will be greater, if demand for the product is high. Expected demand for the new product (project B) is also greatest when the economy is booming.

We stated above that the expected annual returns from each project are $500. Let us assume that these figures were developed in the following manner:

1. First, we estimate project returns under different states of the economy as in Table 11–2. Tables of this kind are typically referred to as *payoff matrices*.

**Table 11–2
Payoff Matrix for Projects A and B**

State of the Economy	Annual Cash Flows	
	Project A	Project B
Recession	$400	$ 0
Normal	500	500
Boom	600	1,000

2. Next, we estimate the likelihood of different states of the economy. Assume our economic forecasts indicate that, given current trends in economic indicators, the chances are two out of ten that recession will occur, six out of ten that the economy will be normal, and two out of ten that there will be a boom.

3. Redefining the word "chance" as *probability*, we find that the probability of a recession is $2/10 = .2$, or 20 percent; the probability of normal times is $6/10 = .6$, or 60 percent; and the probability of a boom is $2/10 = .2$, or 20 percent. Notice that the probabilities add up to 1.0, or 100 percent: $.2 + .6 + .2 = 1.0$, or 100 percent.

4. Finally, in Table 11–3 we calculate weighted averages of the possible returns by multiplying each dollar return by its probability of occur-

rence. When column 4 of the table is summed, we obtain a weighted average of the outcomes for each alternative under various states of the economy; this weighted average is defined as the *expected value* of the cash flows from the project. It need not, of course, be equal to the project's outcome for a normal state of the economy, although this is the case for both projects in this example.

Table 11–3 **Calculation of** **Expected Values**	State of the Economy (1)	Probability of This State Occurring (2)	Outcome If This State Occurs (3)	(2) × (3) (4)
Project A				
	Recession	0.2	$ 400	$ 80
	Normal	0.6	500	300
	Boom	0.2	600	120
		1.0	Expected value =	$500
Project B				
	Recession	0.2	$ 0	$ 0
	Normal	0.6	500	300
	Boom	0.2	1,000	200
		1.0	Expected value =	$500

We can graph the results shown in Table 11–3 to obtain a picture of the variability of actual outcomes; this is shown in the bar charts in Figure 11–1. The height of each bar signifies the probability that a given outcome will occur. The range of probable outcomes for project A is from $400 to $600, with an average or *expected value* of $500. The expected value for project B is also $500, but the range of possible outcomes is from $0 to $1,000.

Continuous Distributions. Thus far we have assumed that only three states of the economy can exist: recession, normal, and boom. Actually, of course, the state of the economy could range from a deep depression, as in the early 1930s, to a fantastic boom; and there are an unlimited number of possibilities in between. Suppose we had the time and patience to assign a probability to each possible state of the economy (with the sum of the probabilities still equaling 1.0) and to assign a monetary outcome to each project for each state of the economy. We would have a table similar to Table 11–3 except that it would have many more entries for "Probability" and "Outcome if this state occurs." These tables could be used to calculate expected values as shown above,

Figure 11–1
Relationship between
the State of the
Economy and Project
Returns

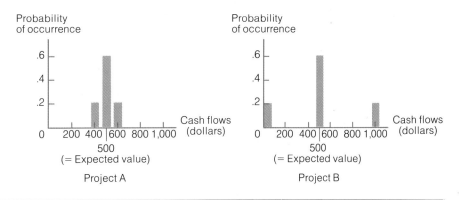

Project A

Project B

and the probabilities and outcomes could be graphed as the continuous
curves presented in Figure 11–2. Here we have changed the assumptions so that there is zero probability that project A will yield less than
$400 or more than $600, and so that there is zero probability that project B will yield less than $0 or more than $1,000.

Figure 11–2 is a graph of the *probability distributions* of returns on
projects A and B. In general, the tighter the probability distribution, or,
alternatively stated, the more peaked the distribution, the more likely it

Figure 11–2
Probability Distribution
Showing Relationship
between State of the
Economy and Project
Returns

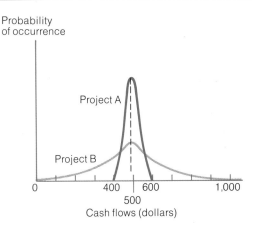

is that the actual outcome will be close to the expected value. Since project A has a relatively tight probability distribution, its *actual* profits are likely to be closer to the *expected* $500 than are those of project B.

Risk versus Uncertainty

Sometimes a distinction is made between *risk* and *uncertainty*. When this distinction is made, risk is associated with those situations in which a probability distribution of the returns on a given project can be estimated; uncertainty is associated with those situations in which insufficient evidence is available even to estimate a probability distribution. We do not make this distinction; risk and uncertainty are used synonymously in this chapter.

We do, however, recognize that probability distributions of expected returns can themselves be estimated with greater or lesser precision. In some instances, the probability distribution can be estimated *objectively* with statistical techniques. For example, a large oil company may be able to estimate from past recovery data the probability distribution of recoverable oil reserves in a given field. When statistical procedures can be used, risk is said to be measured by *objective probability distributions*. There are, however, many situations in which statistical data cannot be used. For example, a company considering the introduction of a totally new product will have some idea about the required investment outlay, the demand for the product, the production costs, and so forth. These estimates will not, however, be determined by statistics; they will be determined subjectively and are defined as *subjective probability distributions*.

Traditional Measures of Risk of Individual Projects

Risk is difficult to measure unambiguously. The traditional measures of risk have been applied to individual projects in isolation. Newer approaches have recognized that individual projects can be combined with other projects into groups of projects or portfolios. Viewing an individual project in its broader portfolio context changes the appropriate measure of risk to be applied. These relationships will be explained in the remainder of this chapter. We start with a discussion of the traditional measures of risk applied to individual projects so that the relationships between the different approaches can be seen.

The traditional measure of risk applied to individual projects is stated in terms of probability distributions such as those presented in Figure 11–2. The tighter the probability distribution of expected future returns, the smaller the risk of a given project. According to this traditional view, Project A is less risky than Project B because each of the possible returns for (A) is closer to the expected return than is true for (B).

**Measuring Risk:
Standard
Deviation**

The traditional approach utilizes a measure of the tightness of the probability distribution of project returns. The measure of tightness it utilizes is the standard deviation, the symbol for which is σ, read "sigma." The tighter the probability distribution, the smaller the standard deviation. We can confirm this statement by the actual calculation of the standard deviation as presented in Table 11–4.

**Table 11–4
Calculation of
Standard
Deviations**

State of the Economy (1)	Probability of State Occurring (2)	Outcome If State Occurs (3)	Expected Value (2) × (3) (4)	Deviation (5)	Squared Deviation (6)	Variance (2) × (6) (7)
Project A						
Boom	.2	600	120	100	10,000	2,000
Normal	.6	500	300	0	0	0
Recession	.2	400	80	(100)	10,000	2,000
		Expected value = $500			Variance = $4,000	
					Standard deviation (σ) = $63.25	
Project B						
Boom	.2	1,000	200	500	250,000	50,000
Normal	.6	500	300	0	0	0
Recession	.2	0	0	(500)	250,000	50,000
		Expected value = $500			Variance = $100,000	
					Standard deviation (σ) = $ 316.23	

Column (1) lists the alternative states of the world as portrayed by alternative states of the economy. Column (2) lists the probability of each of the states. Column (3) lists the outcome if a particular state occurs. These are the possible returns from a given project under alternative states. Column (4) is the expected values obtained by multiplying the probability with the associated outcome. The sum of Column (4) is the expected value for the distribution of probable returns representing a weighted average of the various possible outcomes. We then proceed to calculate the variance and standard deviation of the probability distribution. In Column (5) we subtract the expected value from each possible outcome to obtain a set of deviations about the expected value. In Column (6) we square each deviation. In Column (7) we multiply the squared deviation by the probability of occurrence for its related outcome and sum these products to obtain the variance of the probability distribution. The standard deviation is then obtained by taking the square root of the variance.

Using the procedures described, we observe in Table 11–4 that the standard deviation of Project A is $63.25; that of Project B is $316.23.

By the standard deviation criterion, Project B is "riskier" since its standard deviation is much larger than the standard deviation for Project A. Since the expected values of the net present values for returns from the two projects are equal at $500, Project A would be preferred. It has the same expected value but a smaller variance and smaller standard deviation.

**Measuring Risk:
The Coefficient
of Variation**

Certain problems can arise when the standard deviation is used as a measure of risk. To illustrate, consider Figure 11–3, which shows the probability distributions for investments C and D. Investment C has an expected return of $1,000 and a standard deviation of $300. Investment D also has a standard deviation of $300, but its expected return is $4,000. The likely percentage deviation from the mean of investment C is considerably higher than that from the mean of investment D, or, put another way, C has more risk *per dollar of return* than D. On this basis, it is reasonable to assign a higher degree of risk to investment C than to investment D even though they have identical standard deviations.

Figure 11–3
Probability
Distributions of Two
Investments with
Different Expected
Returns

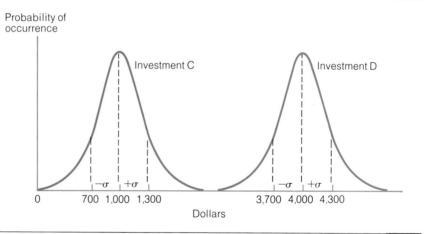

The standard procedure for handling this problem is to divide the standard deviation (σ_j) by the mean, or expected value of net cash flows ($\bar{F}_j$), to obtain the *coefficient of variation (CV):*

$$CV_j = \frac{\sigma_j}{\bar{F}_j}.$$

For investment C we divide the $300 standard deviation by the $1,000 expected value or mean, obtaining .30 as the coefficient of variation.

Similarly, for investment D we divide the standard deviation of $300 by the mean value $4,000 to obtain .075. This is a much lower coefficient of variation than for investment C. Since investment D has a lower coefficient of variation, it has less risk per unit of return than investment C. For the higher expected return and a lower standardized measure of risk, investment D would be unambiguously preferred. Thus, if the standard deviation is to be used as a measure of risk for investments viewed in isolation, the normalization obtained by dividing through by the respective means to obtain the coefficient of variation should be performed.

Riskiness over Time

We can also use Figure 11–2 to consider the riskiness of a stream of receipts over time. Visualize, for example, investment A as being the expected cash flow from a particular project during year 1, and investment B as being the expected cash flow from the *same* project in the tenth year. The expected return is the same for each of the two years, but the subjectively estimated standard deviation (hence the coefficient of variation) is larger for the more distant return. In this case, riskiness is *increasing over time*.

Figure 11–4 may help to clarify the concept of increasing riskiness over time. Figure 11–4(a) simply shows the probability distribution of expected cash flows in two years—years 1 and 10. The distribution is

Figure 11–4
Risk as a Function of Time

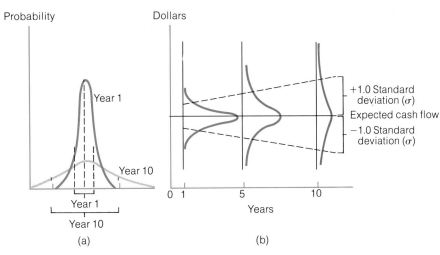

flatter in year 10, indicating that there is more uncertainty about expected cash flows in distant years. Figure 11–4(b) represents a three-dimensional plot of the expected cash flows over time and their probability distributions. The probability distributions should be visualized as extending out from the page. The dashed lines show the standard deviations attached to the cash flows of each year; the fact that these lines diverge from the expected cash flow line indicates that riskiness is increasing over time. If risk was thought of as being constant over time — that is, if the cash flow in a distant year could be estimated equally as well as the cash flow of a close year — then the standard deviation would be constant and the boundary lines would not diverge from the expected cash flow line. The fact that the standard deviation is increasing over time, while the expected return is constant, would, of course, cause the coefficient of variation to increase similarly.

Portfolio Risk

When considering the riskiness of a particular investment, it is frequently useful to consider the relationship between the investment in question and other existing assets or potential investment opportunities. To illustrate, a steel company may decide to diversify into residential construction materials. It knows that when the economy is booming, the demand for steel is high and the returns from the steel mill are large. Residential construction, on the other hand, tends to be countercyclical: when the economy as a whole is in a recession, the demand for construction materials is high.[2] Because of these divergent cyclical patterns, a diversified firm with investments in both steel and construction could expect to have a more stable pattern of revenues than would a firm engaged exclusively in either steel or residential construction. In other words, the deviations of the returns on the *portfolio of assets*, σ, may be less than the sum of the deviations of the returns from the individual assets.[3]

This point is illustrated in Figure 11–5: 11–5(a) shows the rate of return variations for the steel plant, 11–5(b) shows the fluctuations for the residential construction material division, and 11–5(c) shows the rate of

---

2. The reason for the countercyclical behavior of the residential construction industry has to do with the availability of credit. When the economy is booming, interest rates are high. High interest rates seem to discourage potential home buyers more than they do other demanders of credit. As a result, the residential construction industry has historically shown marked countercyclical tendencies.

3. These conclusions obviously hold also for portfolios of financial assets — stocks and bonds. In fact the basic concepts of portfolio theory were developed specifically for common stocks by Harry Markowitz and were first presented in his article, "Portfolio Selection," *Journal of Finance* 7, no. 1 (March 1952), pp. 77–91. The logical extension of portfolio theory to capital budgeting calls for considering firms as having "portfolios of tangible assets."

return for the combined company. When the returns from steel are large, those from residential construction are small, and vice versa. As a consequence, the combined rate of return is relatively stable.

If we calculate the correlation between rates of return on the steel and construction divisions, we find the correlation coefficient to be negative — whenever rates of return on the steel plant are high, those on the construction material plants are low. If any two projects, A and B, have a high degree of *negative correlation*, then taking on the two investments reduces the firm's overall risk. This risk reduction is defined as a *portfolio effect*.

On the other hand, if there had been a high *positive correlation* between projects A and B — that is, if returns on A were high at the same time those on B were high — overall risk could not have been reduced significantly by diversification. If the corrleation between A and B had been +1.0, the risk reduction would have been zero, so no portfolio effects would have been obtained.

Figure 11–5
Relationship of Returns on Two Hypothetical Investments

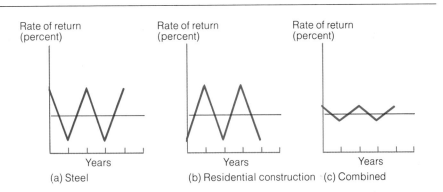

(a) Steel (b) Residential construction (c) Combined

If the returns from the two projects were completely uncorrelated — that is, if the correlation coefficient between them was zero — then diversification would benefit the firm to at least some extent. The larger the number of uncorrelated, or independent, projects the firm takes on, the smaller will be the variation in its overall rate of return.[4] Uncorrelated projects are not as useful for reducing risk as are negatively correlated ones, but they are better than positively correlated projects.

Correlation coefficients range from +1.0, indicating perfect positive

4. The principle involved here is the so-called law of large numbers. As the number of independent projects is increased, the standard deviation of the returns on the portfolio of projects will decrease with the square root of the number of projects taken on.

correlations, to -1.0, indicating perfect negative correlation. If the correlation coefficient is zero, then the projects are independent, or uncorrelated.

We can summarize the arguments on portfolio risk that have been presented thus far:

1. If *perfectly negatively correlated* projects are available in sufficient number, then diversification can completely eliminate risk. Perfect negative correlation is, however, almost never found in the real world.
2. If *uncorrelated* projects are available in sufficient number, then diversification can reduce risk significantly — to zero at the limit.
3. If all alternative projects are *perfectly positively correlated*, then diversification does not reduce risk at all.

In fact, most projects are *positively* correlated but not *perfectly* correlated. The degree of intercorrelation among projects depends upon economic factors, and these factors are usually amenable to analysis. Returns on investments in projects closely related to the firm's basic products and markets will ordinarily be highly correlated with returns on the remainder of the firm's assets, and such investments will not generally reduce the firm's risk. However, investments in other product lines and in other geographic markets may have a low degree of correlation with other components of the firm and may, therefore, reduce overall risk. Accordingly, if an asset's returns are not too closely related to the firm's other major assets (or, better still, are negatively correlated with other investments), this asset is more valuable to a risk-averting firm than is a similar asset whose returns are positively correlated with the bulk of the assets.

**Expected
Return on a
Portfolio**

A portfolio is defined as a combination of assets, and portfolio theory deals with the selection of optimal portfolios; that is, portfolios that provide the highest possible return for any specified degree of risk, or the lowest possible risk for any specified rate of return. Since portfolio theory has been developed most thoroughly for *financial assets* — stocks and bonds — we shall, for the most part, restrict our discussion to these assets.[5] However, extensions of financial asset portfolio theory to physical assets are readily made, and certainly the concepts are relevant in capital budgeting.

---

5. Financial assets are highly divisible and available in large numbers, and a great deal of data is available on such assets. Capital assets such as plant and equipment, on the other hand, are "lumpy," and the data needed to apply portfolio theory to such assets are not readily available.

The rate of return on a portfolio is always a linear function — it is simply a weighted average of the returns of the individual securities in the portfolio. For example, if 50 percent of the portfolio is invested in a security with a 6 percent expected return (security L), and 50 percent in one with a 10 percent expected return (security M), the expected rate of return on the portfolio is

$$E(k_p) = w(6\%) + (1 - w)\ (10\%)$$
$$= .5(6\%) + .5(10\%) = 8\%.$$

Here, $E(k_p)$ is the expected return on the portfolio, w is the percent of the portfolio invested in L, and $(1 - w)$ is the percent invested in M. If all of the portfolio is invested in L, the expected return is 6 percent. If all is invested in M, the expected return is 10 percent. If the portfolio contains some of each, the expected portfolio return is a linear combination of the two securities' expected returns — for example, 8 percent in our present case. Therefore, given the expected returns on the individual securities, the expected return on the portfolio depends upon the amount of funds invested in each security.

Figure 11–6 illustrates the possible returns for our two-asset portfolio. Line LM represents all possible expected returns when securities L

Figure 11–6
Rates of Return on a
Two-Asset Portfolio

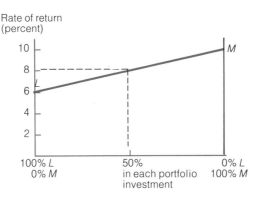

and M are combined in different proportions. Note that when 50 percent of the portfolio is invested in each asset, the expected return on the portfolio is seen to be 8 percent, just as we calculated above.

In general, the expected return on an n-asset portfolio is defined by Equation 11–1a:

$$E(k_p) = \sum_{j=1}^{n} w_j k_j. \tag{11–1a}$$

Here w_j is the percent of the portfolio invested in the jth asset, and k_j is the expected return on the jth asset. To illustrate, if the portfolio consists of five securities, whose individual returns are shown in the parentheses, then the expected return would be computed as follows:

$$E(k_p) = w_1k_1 + w_2k_2 + w_3k_3 + w_4k_4 + w_5k_5$$
$$= .05(20\%) + .10(15\%) + .20(5\%) + .25(10\%) + .40(25\%) = 16\%.$$

Thus, the portfolio's expected return is a weighted average of the returns on each included asset, with the weights being the proportion of funds invested in each security. Of course, the sum of the weights is always equal to 1; for example,

$$\sum_{j=1}^{n} w_j = .05 + .10 + .20 + .25 + .40 = 1.$$

**Riskiness of a
Portfolio**

The riskiness of a portfolio is measured by the standard deviation of expected returns. Equation 11–2 is used to calculate any standard deviation:

$$\sigma_p = \sqrt{\sum_{s=1}^{n} (k_{ps} - \bar{k}_p)^2 P_s}. \tag{11–2}$$

Here σ_p is the standard deviation of the portfolio's expected returns; k_{ps} is the expected portfolio return given the sth state of the economy; $\bar{k}_p$ is the mean value of the n possible returns; and P_s is the probability of

Figure 11–7
Distributions of
Portfolio Returns

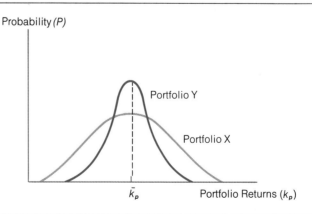

6. Equation 11–2 is derived from the general definition of the standard deviation, and it may be interpreted similarly; that is, the actual returns earned on a portfolio should lie within $\pm 1\sigma_p$ approximately 68 percent of the time.

occurrence of the sth state of the economy.[6] Figure 11–7 illustrates two possible distributions of expected portfolio returns for two portfolios. Portfolio X has more variability than portfolio Y; consequently, investors view portfolio X as being riskier than Y.

A fundamental aspect of portfolio theory is the idea that the riskiness inherent in any single asset held in a portfolio is different from the riskiness of that asset held in isolation. As we shall see, it is possible for a given asset to be quite risky when held in isolation, but not very risky if held in a portfolio. The impact of a single asset on a portfolio's riskiness— which is the riskiness of the asset when it is held in a portfolio—is discussed later in this chapter.

Measuring the Riskiness of a Portfolio: The Two-Asset Case

Equation 11–2 could be used to calculate the riskiness of a portfolio, but, under the assumption that the distributions of returns on the individual securities are normal, a complicated looking but operationally simple equation can be used to determine the risk of a two-asset portfolio:[7]

$$\sigma_p = \sqrt{w^2\sigma_A^2 + (1-w)^2\sigma_B^2 + 2w(1-w)\ Cov_{AB}}. \tag{11-3}$$

The *covariance (Cov)* between two securities depends upon (1) the *correlation* between the two securities, and (2) the *standard deviation* of each security's returns; it is calculated as follows:

$$Cov_{AB} = \rho_{AB}\ \sigma_A\ \sigma_B. \tag{11-4}$$

Here Cov_{AB} is the covariance between securities A and B; ρ_{AB} is the correlation coefficient between A and B; and σ_A and σ_B are the standard deviations of the securities' returns.

Substituting Equation 11–4 for Cov_{AB} in 11–3, we may rewrite Equation 11–3 as 11–5:

$$\sigma_p = \sqrt{w^2\ \sigma_A^2 + (1-w)^2\ \sigma_B^2 + 2w(1-w)\ \rho_{AB}\ \sigma_A\ \sigma_B}. \tag{11-5}$$

Here w is the percentage of the total portfolio value invested in security A; $(1-w)$ is the percent of the portfolio invested in security B; σ_A is the standard deviation of security A; σ_B is the standard deviation of security B; Cov_{AB} is the covariance between securities A and B; and ρ_{AB} is the correlation coefficient between the securities. Stated another way, if

---

7. Equation 11–3 is derived from 11–2 in the standard statistics books. Notice that if $w = 1$, all of the portfolio is invested in project A and Equation 11–2 reduces to

$$\sigma_p = \sqrt{\sigma_A^2} = \sigma_A.$$

The portfolio contains but a single asset, so the risk of the portfolio and that of the asset are identical. It may also be noted that Equations 11–2 and 11–3 can be expanded to include any number of assets by adding additional variance and covariance terms.

σ_A is the standard deviation of security A and σ_B is the standard deviation of security B, then σ_p, the standard deviation of a *portfolio* containing both A and B, is a function of σ_A, σ_B, ρ_{AB}, and w; the specific functional relationship is given as Equation 11–3 or 11–5. Examples of the use of Equation 11–5 are given in a later section.

If $\rho_{AB} = +1.0$, then Equation 11–5 may be simplified to the following linear expression: $\sigma_p = w\sigma_A + (1 - w)\sigma_B$; otherwise, 11–5 is a quadratic equation, and some value of w causes σ_p to be minimized. If we differentiate 11–5 with respect to w, set this derivative equal to zero, and solve for w, we obtain:

$$w_A = \frac{\sigma_B(\sigma_B - \rho_{AB}\,\sigma_A)}{\sigma_A{}^2 + \sigma_B{}^2 - 2\rho_{AB}\,\sigma_A\,\sigma_B}. \qquad (11–6)$$

A usual condition assumed in using the equation is that $0 \le w \le 1.0$; that is, no more than 100 percent of the portfolio can be in any one asset, and negative positions (short positions) cannot be maintained in any asset.

Two special cases of 11–6 are worthy to note. First, notice that when the returns of securities A and B are negatively correlated, that is, $\rho_{AB} = -1.0$, then substituting $\rho_{AB} = -1.0$ in Equation 11–6 yields Equation 11–6a:

$$w_A = \frac{\sigma_B}{\sigma_A + \sigma_B}. \qquad \text{(Use only if } \rho_{AB} = -1.0.) \qquad (11–6a)$$

To illustrate the use of 11–6a, suppose the returns of securities A and B are perfectly negatively correlated, that is, $\rho_{AB} = -1.0$, $\sigma_A = 2.0$, and $\sigma_B = 4.0$. The riskiness of the portfolio (σ_p) consisting of securities A and B will be completely eliminated, or equal to zero, if and only if 67 percent of the portfolio is invested in security A:

$$w_A = \frac{4}{2 + 4} = \frac{4}{6} = .67 = 67\%.$$

The second special case is when the returns of securities A and B are independent ($\rho_{AB} = 0$); now substituting $\rho_{AB} = 0$ in Equation 11–6 yields Equation 11–6b:

$$w_A = \frac{\sigma_B{}^2}{\sigma_A{}^2 + \sigma_B{}^2}. \qquad \text{(Use only if } \rho_{AB} = 0.) \qquad (11–6b)$$

To illustrate the use of 11–6b, suppose $\rho_{AB} = 0$, $\sigma_A = 8$, and $\sigma_B = 6$. The riskiness of the portfolio (σ_p) is minimized if and only if the percentage of the portfolio invested in security A is equal to 36 percent, computed as follows:

$$w_A = \frac{36}{64 + 36} = \frac{36}{100} = .36 = 36\%.$$

Measuring the Riskiness of a Portfolio: The N-Asset Case

An expanded form of Equation 11-3 has been developed to compute the standard deviation of a portfolio consisting of any number of securities:

$$\sigma_p = \sqrt{\sum_{i=1}^{N} w_i^2 \, \sigma_i^2 + 2 \sum_{i=1}^{N-1} \sum_{j=i+1}^{N} w_i w_j \rho_{ij} \, \sigma_i \, \sigma_j}. \tag{11-7}$$

Here w_i is the proportion of the individual's investment allocated to security i, w_j is the proportion of the individual's investment allocated to security j, ρ_{ij} is the correlation coefficient between security i and security j, and N is the number of securities contained in the portfolio.

Since Equation 11-7 has N securities, there are N variance terms (that is, $w_i^2 \, \sigma_i^2$) and $N^2 - N$ covariance terms (that is, $w_i w_j \rho_{ij} \sigma_i \sigma_j$). Since the covariance terms increase quadratically as the number of assets increases, the expanded equation becomes quite complex if N is large. For example, if N is 500, Equation 11-7 will have 250,000 terms under the radical! The index model utilized by Sharpe reduces the computational requirements substantially.[8]

Portfolio Opportunities

Suppose we are considering N assets, with N being any number greater than one. These assets can be combined into an almost limitless number of portfolios, and each possible portfolio will have an expected rate of return, $E(k_p)$, and risk, σ_p. The hypothetical set of all possible portfolios — defined as the *attainable set* — is graphed as the shaded area in Figure 11-8.

Given the full set of potential portfolios that can be constructed from the available assets, which portfolio should *actually* be constructed? This choice involves two separate decisions: (1) determining the *efficient set of portfolios* and (2) choosing from the efficient set the single portfolio that is best for the individual investor. In the remainder of this section we discuss the concept of the efficient set of portfolios; then in the next section we consider choices among efficient portfolios.

8. W. F. Sharpe, *Portfolio Theory and Capital Markets* (New York: McGraw-Hill, 1970), chap. 7, Index Models.

Figure 11–8
The Efficient Set of
Investments

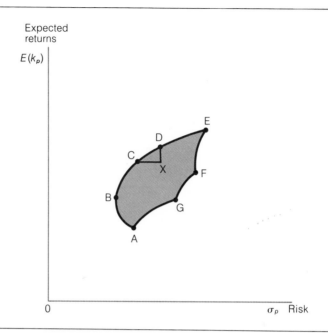

An *efficient portfolio* is defined as a portfolio that provides the highest possible expected return for any degree of risk, or the lowest possible degree of risk for any expected return. In Figure 11–8 the boundary *BCDE* defines the *efficient set of portfolios*.[9] Portfolios to the left of the efficient set are not possible, because they lie outside the attainable set; that is, there is no set of k_i values that will yield a portfolio with an expected rate of return $E(k_p)$ and risk σ_p represented by a point to the left of *BCDE*. Portfolios to the right of the efficient set are inefficient, because some other portfolio could provide either a higher return with the same degree of risk or a lower risk for the same rate of return. To illustrate, consider point *X*. Portfolio *C* provides the same rate of return as does portfolio *X*, but *C* is less risky. At the same time, portfolio *D* is as risky as portfolio *X*, but *D* provides a higher expected rate of return. Points *C* and *D* (and other points on the boundary of the efficient set between *C* and *D*) are said to *dominate* point *X*.

9. A computational procedure for determining the efficient set of portfolios was developed by Harry Markowitz and first reported in his article, "Portfolio Selection," *Journal of Finance* 7, no. 1 (March 1952), pp. 77–91.

Utility Theory and Portfolio Choices

The assumption of risk aversion is basic to many decision models used in finance. Since this assumption is so important, it is appropriate to discuss why risk aversion generally holds.

In theory, we can identify three possible attitudes toward risk: a desire for risk, an aversion to risk, and an indifference to risk. A *risk seeker* is one who prefers risk; given a choice between more and less risky investments with identical expected monetary returns, he would prefer the riskier investment. Faced with the same choice, the *risk averter* would select the less risky investment. The person who is indifferent to risk would not care which investment he received. *There undoubtedly are individuals who prefer risk and others who are indifferent to it, but both logic and observation suggest that business managers and stockholders are predominately risk averters.*

Why do you suppose risk aversion generally holds? Given two investments, each with the same expected dollar returns, why would most investors prefer the less risky one? Several theories have been advanced in answer to this question, but perhaps the most logically satisfying one involves *utility theory*.

At the heart of utility theory is the notion of *diminishing marginal utility for money*. If an individual with no money received $100, he could satisfy his most immediate needs. If he then received a second $100, he could utilize it, but the second $100 would not be quite as necessary to him as the first $100. Thus, the "utility" of the second, or *marginal*, $100 is less than that of the first $100, and so on for additional increments of money. Therefore, we say that the marginal utility of money is diminishing.

Figure 11–9 graphs the relationship between income or wealth and its utility, where utility is measured in units called *utils*. Curve A, the one of primary interest, is for someone with a diminishing marginal utility for money. If this particular individual had $5,000, then he would have 10 utils of "happiness" or satisfaction. If he received an additional $2,500, his utility would rise to 12 utils, *an increase of two units*. However, if he lost $2,500, his utility would fall to six utils, *a loss of four units*.

Most investors (as opposed to people who go to Las Vegas) appear to have a declining marginal utility for money, and this directly affects their attitudes toward risk. Our measures of risk estimate the likelihood that a given return will turn out to be above or below the expected return. Someone who has a constant marginal utility for money will value each dollar of "extra" returns just as highly as each dollar of "lost" returns. On the other hand, someone with a diminishing marginal utility for money will get more "pain" from a dollar lost than "pleasure" from a dollar gained. Because of his utility of money function, the second individual will be very much opposed to risk, and he will require a very

Figure 11–9
Relationship between
Money and Its Utility

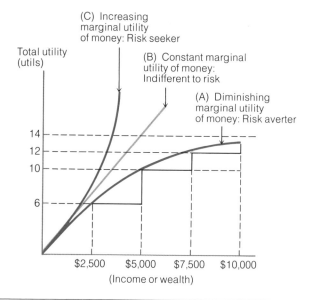

high return on any investment that is subject to much risk. In curve A of Figure 11–5, for example, a gain of $2,500 from a base of $5,000 would bring 2 utils of additional satisfaction, but a $2,500 loss would cause a 4-util satisfaction loss. Therefore, a person with this utility function and $5,000 would be unwilling to make a bet with a 50–50 chance of winning or losing $2,500. However, the risk-indifferent individual with curve B would be indifferent to the bet, and the risk lover would be eager to make it.

Diminishing marginal utility leads directly to risk aversion, and this risk aversion is reflected in the capitalization rate investors apply when determining the value of a firm. To make this clear, let us assume that government bonds are riskless securities and that such bonds currently offer a 5 percent rate of return.[10] Thus, if someone bought a $5,000 United States Treasury bond and held it for one year, he would end up with $5,250, a profit of $250. Suppose he had an alternative investment opportunity that called for the $5,000 to be used to back a wildcat oil-drilling operation. If the drilling operation is successful, the investment will be worth $7,500 at the end of the year. If it is unsuccessful, the investor can liquidate his holdings and recover $2,500. There is a 60 per-

---

10. We shall abstract from any risk of price declines in bond prices caused by increases in the level of interest rates. Thus, the risk with which we are concerned at this point is *default risk*, the risk that principal and interest payments will not be made as scheduled.

cent chance that oil will be discovered, and a 40 percent chance of a "dry hole." If he has only $5,000 to invest, should our investor choose the riskless government bond or the risky drilling operation?

Let us first calculate the expected monetary values of the two investments; this is done in Table 11–5. The calculation for the oil venture shows that the expected value of this venture, $5,500, is higher than that of the bond. (Also, the expected return on the oil venture is 10 percent [calculated as $500 expected profit/$5,000 cost] versus 5 percent for the bond.) Does this mean that our investor should put his money in the wildcat well? Not necessarily—it depends on his utility function. If his

Table 11–5 **Expected Returns from Two Projects**	States of Nature	Drilling Operation			Government Bond		
		Probability (1)	Outcome (2)	(1) × (2) (3)	Probability (1)	Outcome (2)	(1) × (2) (3)
	Oil	.6	$7,500	$4,500	1.0	$5,250	$5,250
	No oil	.4	2,500	1,000			
			Expected value = $5,500				$5,250

marginal utility for money is sharply diminishing, then the potential loss of utility that would result from a dry hole, or no oil, might not be fully offset by the potential gain in utility that would result from the development of a producing well. If the utility function that is shown in curve A of Figure 11–9 is applicable, this is exactly the case. To show this, we modify the expected monetary value calculation to reflect utility considerations. Reading from Figure 11–9, curve A, we see that this particular risk-averse investor would have approximately 12 utils if he invests in the wildcat venture and oil is found, 6 utils if he makes this investment and no oil is found, and 10.5 utils with certainty if he chooses the government bond. This information is used in Table 11–6 to calculate the *expected utility* for the oil investment. No calculation is needed for the government bond; we know its utility is 10.5 regardless of the outcome of the oil venture.

Since the *expected utility* from the wildcat venture is only 9.6 utils versus 10.5 from the government bond, we see that for this investor the government bond is the preferred investment. Thus, even though the *expected monetary value* for the oil venture is higher, *expected utility* is

Table 11–6 **Expected Utility of Oil-drilling Project**	States of Nature	Probability (1)	Monetary Outcome (2)	Associated Utility (3)	(1) × (3) (4)
	Oil	.6	$7,500	12.0	7.2
	No oil	.4	2.500	6.0	2.4
				Expected utility = 9.6 utils	

higher for the bond; risk considerations therefore lead us to choose the safer government bond.

Risk-Return Indifference Curves

Given the efficient set of portfolio combinations, which specific portfolio should an investor choose? To determine the optimal portfolio for a particular investor, we must know his attitude toward risk, or his risk-return tradeoff function.

An investor's risk-return preference function is based on the standard economic concept of indifference curves as illustrated in Figure 11–10. The curves labelled I_A and I_B represent the indifference curves of individuals A and B. Mr. A is equally well satisfied with a riskless 4 percent return, an expected 6 percent return with risk of $\sigma_p = 4$ percent, and so on. Mr. B is indifferent between the riskless 4 percent portfolio, a portfolio with an expected return of 6 percent but with a risk of $\sigma_p = 2$ percent, and so on.

Figure 11–10
Indifference curves
for Risk and
Expected Rate of
Return

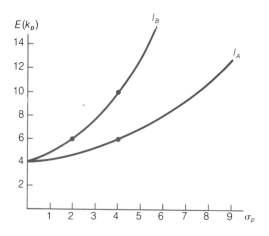

Notice that B requires a higher expected rate of return to compensate him for a given increase in risk than does A; thus, B is more *risk averse* than A. For example, if $\sigma_p = 4$ percent, Mr. B requires a return of 10 percent, while Mr. A has a required return of only 6 percent. In other words, Mr. B requires a *risk premium*—defined as the difference between the riskless return (4 percent) and the required return—of 6 percentage points to compensate for a risk $\sigma_p = 4$ percent, while Mr. A's risk premium for this degree of risk is only 2 percentage points.

An infinite number of utility curves could be drawn for each individual representing the risk-return tradeoff for different levels of satis-

Figure 11–11
Family of Indifference
Curves for Individuals
A and B

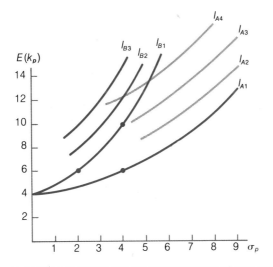

faction. For a given level of σ_p, a greater $E(k_p)$ is received as the curves move farther out to the left. Each point on curve I_{A2} represents a higher level of satisfaction, or greater utility, than any point on I_{A1}, and I_{A3} represents more utility than I_{A2}. Also, different individuals are likely to have different sets of curves or different risk-return tradeoffs. Since the curves of B start from the same point and have a greater slope in the risk-return plane than the curves of A, this indicates that investor B requires a higher return for the same amount of risk. Then similarly for investor B, as the curves move to the left this represents high levels of satisfaction.

**The Optimal
Portfolio for an
Investor**

We can now combine the efficient set of portfolios with indifference curves to determine an individual investor's optimal portfolio. In Figure 11 − 12 we see that the optimal portfolio is found at the tangency point between the efficient set of portfolios and an indifference curve − this tangency point marks the highest level of satisfaction the investor can attain. Mr. A picks a combination of securities (a portfolio) that provides an expected return of about 13 percent and has a risk of about $\sigma_p = 5$ percent. Mr. B, who is more risk averse than Mr. A, picks a portfolio with a lower expected return (about 11 percent) but a riskiness of only $\sigma_p = 3.7$ percent.

To complete the analysis, we note that Mr. A's portfolio contains a larger amount of the more risky securities, while our risk averter, Mr. B, selects a portfolio more heavily weighted with low-risk securities.

Figure 11–12
Optimal Portfolio
Selection

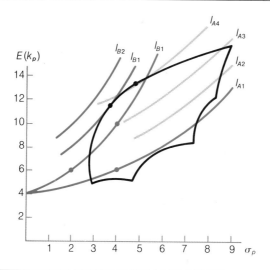

Investment Decisions under Uncertainty in the CAPM Framework

In Figure 11–12 we graphed a set of portfolio opportunities provided by the market and illustrated a method for selecting the optimal portfolio. In Figure 11–13 the relationships are developed still further to convey the underlying logic of the capital asset pricing model (CAPM). Figure 11–13 shows a feasible set of portfolios of risky assets and a set of utility indifference curves (I_1, I_2, I_3), which represent the tradeoff between risk and return for an investor. Point N, where the utility curve is tangent to the portfolio opportunities curve, $ANMB$, represents an equilibrium: it is the point where the investor obtains the highest return for a given amount of risk, σ_N or the smallest risk while obtaining a given expected return, $E(k_N)$.[11]

However, the investor can do better than portfolio N—i.e., he can reach a higher indifference curve. In addition to the risky securities represented in the feasible set of portfolios, there is a risk-free asset that yields R_F; this is also shown in Figure 11–13. With the additional alternative of investing in the risk-free asset, the investor can create a new portfolio that combines the risk-free asset with a portfolio of risky assets. This enables him to achieve any combination of risk and return lying along a straight line connecting R_F and the point of tangency of the straight line at M on the portfolio opportunities curve. All portfolios on the line $R_F MZ$ are preferred to the other risky portfolio opportunities on curve $ANMB$; the points on the line $R_F MZ$ represent the highest attainable combinations of risk and return.

11. To economize on notation we shall usually write σ_p for $\sigma_{(k_p)}$ and σ_m for $\sigma_{(k_M)}$, etc.

Figure 11–13
Investor Equilibrium
Combining the Risk-
free Asset with the
Market Portfolio

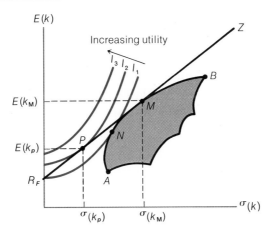

Given the new opportunity set R_FMZ, our investor will move to point P, where he will be on a higher risk-return indifference curve. Note that line R_FMZ dominates the opportunities that could have been achieved from the portfolio opportunities curve $ANMB$ alone. In general, if an investor can include both the risk-free security and a fraction of the risky portfolio, M, in his own portfolio, he will have the opportunity to move to a point such as P. In addition, if he can borrow as well as lend (lending is equivalent to buying risk-free securities) at the riskless rate R_F, he can move out the line segment MZ, and he would do so if his utility indifference curve were tangent to R_FMZ in that section.

Under the conditions set forth in Figure 11–13, all investors would hold portfolios lying on the line R_FMZ; this implies that they would hold only efficient portfolios which are linear combinations of the risk-free security and the risky portfolio M. For the capital market to be in equilibrium, M must be a portfolio that contains every asset in exact proportion to that asset's fraction of the total market value of all assets; that is, if security j is w percent of the total market value of all securities, w percent of the market portfolio M will consist of security j. In effect, M represents "the market." Thus, in equilibrium, all investors will hold efficient portfolios with standard deviation-return combinations along the line R_FMZ. The particular location of a given individual on the line will be determined by the point at which his indifference curve is tangent to the line, and this in turn reflects his attitude toward risk, or his degree of risk aversion.

The line R_FMZ in Figure 11–13 (using the "rise over run" concept) is given by Equation 11–8:

$$E(k_p) = R_F + \frac{E(k_M) - R_F}{\sigma_{(k_M)}} \sigma_{(k_p)}. \tag{11-8}$$

Thus, the expected return on any portfolio is equal to the riskless rate plus a risk premium equal to $[E(k_M) - R_F]/\sigma(k_M)$ times the portfolio's standard deviation. Therefore, the capital market line for efficient portfolios bears a linear relationship between expected return and risk, and it may be rewritten as follows:

$$E(k_p) = R_F + \lambda^* \sigma_p. \tag{11-8a}$$

Here

$E(k_p)$ = expected return on an efficient portfolio

R_F = risk-free interest rate

$$\lambda^* = \text{market price of risk; } \lambda^* = \frac{E(k_M) - R_F}{\sigma_M}$$

σ_p = standard deviation of returns on an efficient portfolio

$E(k_M)$ = expected return on the market portfolio

σ_M = standard deviation of returns on the market portfolio.

All efficient portfolios, including the market portfolio, lie on the CML. Hence:

$$E(k_M) = R_F + \lambda^* \sigma_M. \tag{11-8b}$$

Both Equations 11-8a and 11-8b state that the expected return on an efficient portfolio in equilibrium is equal to a risk-free return plus the market price of risk multiplied by the standard deviation of the portfolio returns. This relationship is graphed in Figure 11-14. The CML is drawn as a straight line with an intercept at R_F, the risk-free return, and a slope equal to the market price of risk (λ^*), which is the market risk

Figure 11-14
Expected Return on an
Efficient Portfolio

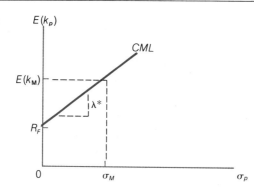

premium $[E(k_M) - R_F]$ divided by σ_M. Thus, the market price of risk, λ^*, is a normalized risk premium. The market price of risk reflects the attitudes of individuals in the aggregate (that is, all individuals) toward risk; thus, it reflects a composite of the utility functions of all individuals.

The Security Market Line (SML)

Thus far we have developed the market model with respect to *portfolios*. Our next step is to relate the model to individual securities. First, note that the expected returns for an individual security or investment can be represented as points on the following *security market line*:[12]

$$E(k_j) = R_F + \lambda \; \text{Cov}(k_j, k_M). \tag{11–9}$$

Here:

$$\lambda = \text{price of risk for securities} = [E(k_M) - R_F]/\sigma_M^2$$

$\text{Cov}(k_j, k_M) =$ covariance of the returns of security j with returns on the market.

$E(k_j) =$ expected return on an individual security j.

Equation 11–9 for the security market line (*SML*) is graphed in Figure 11–15, which relates the covariance of the returns on the individual security to the expected return on the individual security.[13] The *SML*

---

12. For a simple derivation, see Jensen, *Bell Journal* (1972).
13. The relationship between *SML* and *CML* can be shown as follows:

$$(SML): E(k_j) = R_F + \frac{[E(k_M) - R_F]}{\sigma^2_M} \text{Cov}(k_j, k_M)$$

$$\text{Cov}(k_j, k_M) = \rho(k_j, k_M)\sigma_j\sigma_M,$$

where

$\rho(k_j, k_M) =$ correlation coefficient between the return of security j and the market portfolio

$\sigma_j =$ standard deviation of the return of security j

$\sigma_M =$ as defined before.

So,

$$E(k_j) = R_F + \frac{[E(k_M) - R_F]}{\sigma^2_M} \rho(k_j, k_M)\sigma_j\sigma_M$$

$$= R_F + \frac{[E(k_M) - R_F]}{\sigma_M} \rho(k_j, k_M)\sigma_j$$

If j is an efficient portfolio, $\rho(k_j, k_M) = 1$. Then *SML* reduces to *CML*.

$$E(k_j) = R_F + \frac{[E(k_M) - R_F]}{\sigma_M} \sigma_j$$

$$= R_F + \lambda^*\sigma_j.$$

Figure 11–15
The SML for Individual
Securities

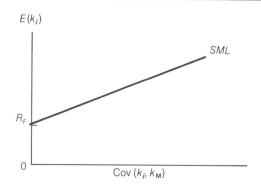

differs from the *CML* in two respects. First, for the individual securities or individual firm, the risk measure is the covariance instead of the standard deviation. This is an important conceptual difference because it conveys the recognition that the risk of an individual security or firm is measured in terms of its contribution to the risk of the portfolio into which it is placed. Second, the price of risk is shown as the excess market return normalized by the *variance* of market returns in the denominator instead of the standard deviation. The effect is to change the dimensionality or scale of the security market line as compared with the capital market line.

Beta Coefficients

The final step in the development of the CAPM framework is to express risk in terms of the beta coefficient. Rearranging Equation 11–9 by dividing the covariance of the individual securities by σ^2_M, we obtain Equation 11–10, which is another version of the security market line with a different scaling:

$$E(k_j) = R_F + [E(k_M) - R_F]\beta_j. \tag{11-10}$$

Here $\beta_j = \text{Cov}(k_j, k_M)/\sigma^2_M$; $E(k_j)$ is the expected return on an asset; and β_j is a measure of the volatility of the individual security's returns relative to market returns. In this form, we see that the individual security's risk premium is the market risk premium weighted by the relative risk or volatility of the individual security.

Required Return on an Investment

Equation 11–10 states that the expected return on an individual security or real investment is represented by a risk-free rate of interest plus a risk premium. Earlier literature did not provide a theory for the determination of the risk premium. Capital market theory shows the risk premium to be equal to the market risk premium weighted by the index of the systematic risk of the individual security or real investment.

The β for an individual security reflects industry characteristics and management policies that determine how returns fluctuate in relation to variations in overall market returns. If the general economic environment is stable, if industry characteristics remain unchanged, and if management policies have continuity, the measure of β will be relatively stable when calculated for different time periods. However, if these conditions of stability do not exist; the value of β would vary.

The great advantage of Equation 11–10 is that all its factors other than β are market-wide constants. If βs are stable, the measurement of expected returns is straightforward. For example, the returns on the market for long periods have been shown by the studies of Fisher and Lorie to be at the 9 to 11 percent level.[14] The level of R_F has been characteristically at the 4 to 6 percent level. Thus the expected return on an individual investment, using the lower of each of the two numbers and a β of 1.2, would be:

$$E(k_j) = 4\% + (9\% - 4\%)1.2 = 10\%. \tag{11–10a}$$

The higher of each of the two figures gives an $E(k_j)$ of 15%:

$$E(k_j) = 6\% + (11\% - 6\%)1.2 = 12\%. \tag{11–10b}$$

Thus we have numerical measures of the amount of the risk premium that is added to the risk-free return to obtain a risk-adjusted discount rate. The risk-free rate and the market risk premium (the excess of the market return over the risk-free rate) are economy-wide measures. They vary for different time periods, but provide a basis for measurements that can be used in making judgmental decisions. In the numerical illustrations above, if a firm has a beta of 1.2, we would expect its required return according to the security market line to be between 10 and 12 percent, depending upon general interest levels. This provides us with a relatively narrow boundary of returns within which managerial judgments may be exercised.

14. L. Fisher and J. Lorie, "Rates of Return on Investments in Common Stocks," *Journal of Business* 37 (January 1964), pp. 1–21. L. Fisher, "Some New Stock-Market Indexes," *Journal of Business* 39 (January 1966), pp. 191–218.

Risk Adjusted Investment Hurdle Rates

The capital asset pricing model permits the criteria for asset expansion decisions under uncertainty to be set out unambiguously and compactly. The basic relation expressed in Equation 11–10 can also be used to formulate a criterion for capital budgeting decisions;[15] that is, the relation in Equation 11–10 can be extended to apply to the expected return $E(k_j^o)$ on an individual project and its volatility measure, β_j^o, as set forth in Equation 11–11.[16]

$$E(k_j^o) > R_F + [E(k_M) - R_F] \, \beta_j^o. \tag{11–11}$$

In inequality 11–11 the market constants remain the same. However, the variables for the individual firm now become variables for the individual project by addition of an appropriate superscript. Inequality 11–11 expresses the condition that must hold if the project is to be acceptable. The expected return on the new project must exceed the pure rate of interest plus the market risk premium weighted by β_j^o, the measure of the individual project's systematic risk.

The general relationships are illustrated in Figure 11–15. The criterion in graphical terms is to accept all projects that plot above the market line and reject all those that plot below the market line. Managers seek to find new projects such as A and B with returns in excess of the levels required by the risk-return market equilibrium relation illustrated in Figure 11–16. When such projects are added to the firm's operations,

Figure 11–16
Illustration of the Use
of Investment Hurdle
Rates

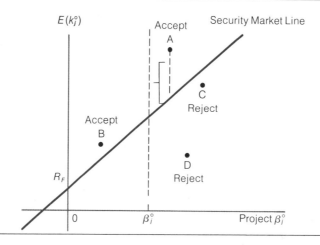

15. M. E. Rubinstein, "A Synthesis of Corporate Financial Theory," *Journal of Finance* (March 1973), p. 167.

16. The superscript^o indicates an individual investment project.

the expected returns on the firm's common stock (at its previous existing price) will be higher than required by the market line. These "excess returns" induce a rise in price until the return on the stock $E(k_j)$ is
at an equilibrium level represented by the security market line in Figure
11–16. These general concepts may now be illustrated more concretely
in a numerical example.

The Morton Company Case. In the case that follows, four states-of-the-
world are considered with respect to future prospects for real growth in
Gross National Product. State 1 represents a relatively serious recession,
State 2 is a mild recession, State 3 is a mild recovery, and State 4 is a
strong recovery. The probabilities of these alternative future states-of-
the world are set forth in Column 2 of Table 11–7. Estimates of market
returns and project rates of return are set forth in the remaining
columns.

Table 11–7 **Summary of Information— Morton Case**	(1) State of World (s)	(2) Subjective Probability (P_s)	(3) Market Return k_{Ms}	(4) Proj. #1	(5) Proj. #2	(6) Proj. #3	(7) Proj. #4
				Project Rates of Return			
	1	.1	−.15	−.30	−.30	−.09	−.05
	2	.3	.05	.10	−.10	.01	.05
	3	.4	.15	.30	.30	.05	.10
	4	.2	.20	.40	.40	.08	.15

The Morton Company is considering four projects in a capital expansion program. The economics staff projected the future course of the
market portfolio over the estimated life span of the projects under each
of the four states-of-the-world (first three columns in Table 11–7); it
recommended the use of a risk-free rate of return of 5 percent. The finance department provided the estimates of project returns conditional
on the state-of-the-world (columns 4 through 7 in Table 11–7). Each
project involves an outlay of approximately $50,000.

Assuming that the projects are independent and that the firm can
raise sufficient funds to finance all four projects, which projects would
be accepted using the market price of risk (MPR) criterion?

Solution Procedure. In Table 11–8 the data provided by market relationships are utilized to calculate the expected return on the market
along with its variance and standard deviation. The probabilities of the
future states-of-the-world are multiplied by the associated market returns and their products are summed to obtain the expected market
return $E(k_M)$ of 10 percent.

Table 11–8
Calculation of
Market Parameters

s	P_s	k_M	$P_s k_M$	$(k_M - \bar{k}_M)$	$(k_M - \bar{k}_M)^2$	$P_s(k_M - \bar{k}_M)^2$
1	.1	−.15	−.015	−.25	.0625	.00625
2	.3	.05	.015	−.05	.0025	.00075
3	.4	.15	.060	.05	.0025	.00100
4	.2	.20	.040	.10	.0100	.00200
			$\bar{k}_M = .10$			$\text{Var}(k_M) = .01$

The expected market return $E(k_M)$ is used in calculating the variance and standard deviation of the market returns. This is shown in columns 4 through 6. The expected return is deducted from the return under each state, and deviations from $E(k_M)$ in column 4 are squared in column 5. In column 6 the squared deviations are multiplied by the probabilities of each expected future state (which appear in column 1). These products are summed to give the variance of the market return. The square root of the variance is its standard deviation.

A similar procedure is followed in Table 11–9 for calculating the expected return and the covariance for each of the four individual projects. The expected return is obtained by multiplying the probability of each state times the associated forecasted return. The deviations of the return under each state from the expected return are next calculated in

Table 11–9
Calculation of
Expected Returns
and Covariances
for the Four
Hypothetical
Projects

s	P_s	k_j	$P_s k_j$	$(k_1 - \bar{k}_1)(k_M - \bar{k}_M)$	$P_s(k_1 - \bar{k}_1)(k_M - \bar{k}_M)$
1	.1	−.30	−.03	$(-.50)(-.25) = .125$	.0125
2	.3	.10	.03	$(-.10)(-.05) = .005$	.0015
3	.4	.30	.12	$(+.10)(+.05) = .005$	.002
4	.2	.40	.08	$(+.20)(+.10) = .020$	.0040
			$\bar{k}_1 = .20$		$\text{Cov}(k_1, k_M) = .0200$
1	.1	−.30	−.03	$(-.44)(-.25) = .110$	.0110
2	.3	−.10	−.03	$(-.24)(-.05) = .012$	.0036
3	.4	.30	.12	$(+.16)(+.05) = .008$	.0032
4	.2	.40	.08	$(+.26)(+.10) = .026$	.0052
			$\bar{k}_2 = .14$		$\text{Cov}(k_2, k_M) = .0230$
1	.1	−.09	−.009	$(-.12)(-.25) = .030$	.0030
2	.3	.01	.003	$(-.02)(-.05) = .001$	.0003
3	.4	.05	.020	$(+.02)(+.05) = .001$	.0004
4	.2	.08	.016	$(+.05)(+.10) = .005$	.0010
			$\bar{k}_3 = .030$		$\text{Cov}(k_3, k_M) = .0047$
1	.1	−.05	−.005	$(-.13)(-.25) = .0325$	.00325
2	.3	.05	.015	$(-.03)(-.05) = .0015$	.00045
3	.4	.10	.04	$(+.02)(+.05) = .0010$	.00040
4	.2	.15	.03	$(+.07)(+.10) = .0070$	.00140
			$\bar{k}_4 = .08$		$\text{Cov}(k_4, k_M) = .00550$

column 5. The deviations of the market returns from their mean are re-peated for convenience. In column 8, the deviations of project returns are multiplied by the deviations of the market returns and by the proba-bility factors to determine the covariance for each of the four projects.

In Table 11–10, the beta for each project is calculated as the ratio of its covariance to the variance of the market return, and they are employed in Table 11–5 to estimate the required return on each project in terms of the market line relationship. The risk-free rate of return is assumed to be 5 percent, with a market risk premium of 5 percent.

**Table 11–10
Calculation of
the Betas**

$$\beta_1^\circ = .0200/.01 = 2.00$$
$$\beta_2^\circ = .0230/.01 = 2.30$$
$$\beta_3^\circ = .0047/.01 = 0.47$$
$$\beta_4^\circ = .0055/.01 = 0.55$$

**Table 11–11
Calculation of
Excess Returns**

(1) Project Number	(2) Measurement of Required Return	(3) Estimated Return	(4) Excess Return %
P1	$E(k_1) = .05 + .05(2.0) = .150$	.200	5.00
P2	$E(k_2) = .05 + .05(2.3) = .165$	.140	−2.50
P3	$E(k_3) = .05 + .05(.47) = .0735$	.030	−4.35
P4	$E(k_4) = .05 + .05(.55) = .0775$	.080	0.25

Required returns as shown in column 2 of Table 11–11 are deducted from the estimated returns for each individual project to derive the "ex-cess returns." These relations are depicted graphically in Figure 11–17. The MPR criterion accepts the projects with positive excess returns, which appear above the MPR line. It rejects those with negative excess returns (plotted below the MPR line).

**Figure 11–17
Application of the
CAPM Investment
Criterion**

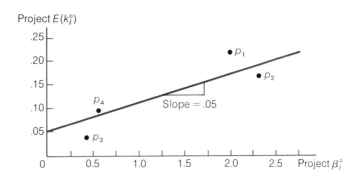

Risk Adjusted Discount Rates versus the Certainty Equivalent Method

The capital asset pricing model as a market price of risk measure provides a risk-adjusted required rate of return for analyzing risky projects. Recall that $E(k_j) = R_F + (k_M - R_F)\beta_j$ with the final term representing the risk adjustment added to the risk-free return, R_F. This is the discount rate that can then be utilized in the basic capital budgeting equation as shown in Equation 11–12.

$$\text{NPV}_j^o = \sum_{t=0}^{n} \frac{F_t}{[1 + E(k_j)]^t} \tag{11–12}$$

where

NPV^o = net present value of a project

F_t = project net cash flows

$E(k_j)$ = risk-adjusted discount factor.

Thus with no capital rationing, if the net present value of a project when discounted at the risk-adjusted required rate of return is greater than zero, then we should accept the project. This technique can be used to compare projects of all different risk classes. It is, therefore, superior to a net present value technique that uses only one discount rate for all projects even though the risk among projects is different. In concept, therefore, the risk-adjusted required rate of return is superior to a method in which only one discount rate is used for projects of different risks.

Project risk can be handled by making adjustments to the numerator of the present value equation (the certainty equivalent method) or to the denominator of the equation (the risk-adjusted discount rate method). The risk-adjusted discount rate method is the one most frequently used, probably because it is easier to estimate suitable discount rates than it is to derive certainty equivalent factors. However, Robichek and Myers[17] in 1966 advocated the certainty equivalent approach as being theoretically superior to the risk-adjusted discount rate method. Still, they, as well as H. Y. Chen, showed that if risk is perceived to be an increasing function of time, then using a risk-adjusted discount rate is a theoretically valid procedure.[18]

Robichek and Myers showed that risk-adjusted rates tend to lump together the pure rate of interest, a risk premium, and time (through the compounding process), while the certainty equivalent approach keeps

---

17. A. A. Robichek and S. C. Myers, "Conceptual Problems in the Use of Risk-Adjusted Discount Rates," *Journal of Finance* 21 (December 1966), pp. 727–30.

18. H. Y. Chen, "Valuation Under Uncertainty," *Journal of Financial and Quantitative Analysis* 2 (September 1967), pp. 313–26.

risk and the pure rate of interest separate. This separation gives an advantage to certainty equivalents. However, financial managers are more familiar with the concept of risk-adjusted discounts, and it is easier to use market data to develop adjusted discount rates. We do feel, however, that the certainty equivalent method deserves further study and that it may eventually turn out to be the generally accepted method of taking risk into account in the capital budgeting process.

The use of the capital asset pricing model is sufficiently flexible so that if it is preferred to use a certainty equivalent formulation, the risk adjustment term can be deducted from the numerator and the risk-free rate employed as the discount factor. Begin with equation (11–9) presented earlier.

$$E(k_j) = R_F + \lambda \text{Cov}(k_j, k_M) \tag{11–9}$$

By definition: $k_j = \dfrac{E(X_j)}{V_j}$. So $\dfrac{E(X_j)}{V_j} = R_F + \lambda \text{Cov}\left(\dfrac{X_j}{V_j}, k_M\right)$ and

$$\frac{1}{V_j}[E(X_j) - \lambda \text{Cov}(X_j, k_M)] = R_F$$

$$V_j = \frac{E(X_j) - \lambda \text{Cov}(X_j, k_M)}{R_F} \tag{11–13}$$

For projects: $V_j^o = \dfrac{E(X_j^o) - \lambda \text{Cov}(X_j^o, k_M)}{R_F}$ (11–14a)

$$NPV_j^o = (V_j^o - \text{Cost}_j^o). \tag{11–14b}$$

Thus the use of the market price of risk criterion provides us with a very flexible tool for making an adjustment for risk in analyzing investment projects of differing risks. To illustrate the application of the last two equations, we will use the data for project 4 in the Morton Company Case discussed above. The required rate of return was:

$$E(k_4^o) = R_F + [E(k_M) - R_F]\,\beta_4^o. \qquad \text{Inserting values:}$$

$$7.75\% = 5\% + [10\% - 5\%].55.$$

The $E(k_4^o)$ value of 7.75 percent represents a risk-adjusted required rate of return on the project based on the beta risk measure equal to .55. We can also express this equation with covariance, using the relationship:

$$\text{Cov}(k_4^o, k_M) = \beta_4^o \, \text{Var}(k_M)$$

$$= .55(.01)$$

$$= .0055.$$

The returns from the project that we actually observe are the dollar returns indicated by the X_4^o values. Suppose that the cost of the project ($Cost_4^o$) or investment outlay is $1,000. We can then calculate $Cov(X_4^o, k_M)$:

$$Cov(k_4^o, k_M) = Cov\left(\frac{X_4^o}{Cost_4^o}, k_M\right) = \frac{1}{Cost_4^o} Cov(X_4^o, k_M). \text{ Hence,}$$

$$Cov(X_4^o, k_M) = Cost_4^o \, Cov(k_4^o, k_M)$$

$$= 1,000(.0055)$$

$$= 5.5.$$

We now have the information to utilize equation (11–14a) for project 4:

$$V_4^o = \frac{E(X_4^o) - \lambda Cov(X_4^o, k_M)}{R_F}$$

$$= \frac{80 - 5(5.5)}{.05} = \frac{80 - 27.5}{.05}$$

$$V_4^o = \$1,050.$$

Since the cost of project 4 is $1,000 and its value is $1,050, the net gain or the net present value for the investment in project 4 (NPV_4^o) is $50. Note that the risk adjustment factor is 27.5 or .344 times the expected dollar returns from the project.[19] This illustrates how the CAPM can provide a measure of the risk adjustment factor.

We recognize that the computations of beta for individual firms are sometimes not statistically significant and often not stable over time. Nevertheless, the methodology described provides a starting point. In addition, a risk adjustment factor taking other dimensions of risk into account as well as judgmental factors may be used in estimating a project's net present value.[20]

Summary

Two facts of life in finance are (1) that investors are averse to risk and (2) that at least some risk is inherent in most business decisions. Given investor aversion to risk and differing degrees of risk in different financial alternatives, it is necessary to consider risk in financial analysis.

Our first task is to define what we mean by risk; our second task is to

---

19. The certainty equivalent adjustment factor (ϕ) would be $(1 - .344)$, which equals .656.
20. See Appendix E to this chapter for further material on making certainty equivalent adjustments.

measure it. The concept of *probability* is a fundamental element in both the definition and the measurement of risk. A *probability distribution* shows the probability of occurrence of each possible outcome, assuming a given investment is undertaken. The mean, or weighted average, of the distribution is defined as the *expected value* of the investment. The *coefficient of variation* of the distribution or, sometimes, the *standard deviation*, both of which measure the extent to which actual outcomes are likely to vary from the expected value, are used as measures of risk.

Under most circumstances, more distant returns are considered to be more risky than near-term returns. Thus, the standard deviation and coefficient of variation for distant cash flows are likely to be higher than those for cash flows expected relatively soon, even when the cash flows are from the same project.

In appraising the riskiness of an individual capital investment, not only the variability of the expected returns of the project itself but also the correlation between expected returns on this project and the remainder of the firm's assets must be taken into account. This relationship is called the *portfolio effect* of the particular project. Favorable portfolio effects are strongest when a project is negatively correlated with the firm's other assets and weakest when positive correlation exists. Portfolio effects lie at the heart of the firm's efforts to diversify into product lines not closely related to the firm's main line of business.

The riskiness of a portfolio is measured by the standard deviation of expected returns. From any group of risky assets it is possible to develop an investment portfolio opportunity set in terms of risk and expected returns. Within the opportunity set there will be a smaller group of alternative portfolios that provide the maximum return for a given level of risk. This is the efficient set of portfolios. Given equal expected returns, a risk averse investor would choose the one that minimizes his risk.

The trade-off between risk and expected return is expressed graphically as indifference curves. For any individual there is a unique set of indifference curves that can be used to determine the individual's optimum portfolio including the fraction that should be invested in risk-free assets. The availability of a risk-free asset enables the investor to combine the risk-free asset with a portfolio of risky assets. A straight line drawn from the return on the risk-free asset to a point through a point of tangency with the portfolio opportunities curve defines the risk-return relations for the market, and the line is the capital market line (CML). The highest utility level is achieved for the investor by the point of tangency of his indifference curve for risk and returns with the capital market line. If this point is to the left of the market portfolio tangency, the investor holds risk-free assets as well as risky assets, so he has both less risk and less return on his total portfolio. If the investor is less risk averse, his point of tangency with the CML is to the right of the market portfolio. He borrows to invest more in risky assets, so has more risk and higher expected returns.

The risk-return relationships for individual securities (imperfect portfolios) use the covariance of individual security returns with the market returns as the measure of risk. The relation between returns and the covariance for individual securities defines the security market line (SML).

Another way to describe the return-risk relationship is in terms of beta coefficients. β is simply the covariance standardized by the market variance. With risk expressed in this way, expected return can be stated as a β multiple of the market risk premium (expected return on the market less the risk-free rate) plus the risk-free rate. All factors except β are market-wide constants.

The capital asset pricing model provides a means for determining a market adjusted discount rate that is project specific and appropriate for determining the NPV of risky capital budgeting projects. The CAPM can be used with either the certainty equivalent or the risk adjusted discount rate formulation of the NPV equation.

Questions

11–1. Define the following terms:

a. risk	h. market price of risk
b. uncertainty	i. covariance
c. probability distribution	j. coefficient of correlation
d. expected value	k. variance
e. standard deviation	l. beta
f. coefficient of variation	m. risk-adjusted discount rate
g. portfolio effects	

11–2. The probability distribution of a less risky expected return is more peaked than that of a risky return. What shape would the probability distribution have (1) for completely cetain returns and (2) for completely uncertain returns?

11–3. Project A has an expected return of $500 and a standard deviation of $100. Project B also has a standard deviation of $100 but an expected return of $300. Which project is the more risky? Why?

11–4. Assume that residential construction and industries related to it are countercyclical to the economy in general and to steel in particular. Does this negative correlation between steel and construction-related industries necessarily mean that a savings and loan association, whose profitability tends to vary with construction levels, would be less risky if it diversified by acquiring a steel distributor?

11–5. "The use of the security market line as a basis for determining risk-adjusted discount rates is all right in theory, but it cannot be applied in practice. Investors' reactions to risk cannot be measured precisely, so it is impossible to construct a set of risk-adjusted discount rates for different classes of investment." Comment on this statement.

11–6. The risk-free rate is 6%, the market price of risk is 4, and the covariance of the project return with the market return is .015. (a) If the variance of the market returns is 1%, what is the beta of the project? (b) What is an estimate of the required risk adjusted return for the project?

11–7. The correlation of the project's return with the market is .6 and the standard deviation of the project's return is .3. The variance of the market returns is 1%, the market price of risk is 5, and the risk-free rate is 6%. What is the covariance of the project returns with the market returns? Its beta? Its required risk-adjusted return?

11–8. For the project in question 11–7, the required investment outlay is $1,800. The expected net cash flows after taxes are estimated at $600 for 5 years. Should the project be accepted?

Problems

11–1. The Jacobs Company is analyzing two mutually exclusive investment projects. Each project costs $4,500, and each has an expected life of three years. Annual net cash flows from each project begin one year after the initial investment is made and have the following probability distributions:

Probability	Cash Flow
Project A: .2	$ 4,000
.6	4,500
.2	5,000
Project B: .2	0
.6	4,500
.2	12,000

Jacobs has decided to evaluate the riskier project at a 12 percent rate and the less risky project at a 10 percent rate.
a. What is the expected value of the annual net cash flows from each project?
b. What is the risk-adjusted *NPV* of each project?
c. If it were known that project B was negatively correlated with other cash flows of the firm, while project A was positively correlated, how would this knowledge affect your decision?

11–2. Danly, Inc.'s, marketing division is reviewing its advertising plans in conjunction with the firm's annual capital budget. Because of management's desire to retain a controlling equity position, each division has been given a budget limitation; $120,000 has been allocated to the marketing division, which is considering two mutually exclusive investments for promotion of new business for the firm's children's furniture.

The first is the continuation of the firm's direct mail advertising program. Costs are 12 cents a mailing, enabling the firm to mail 1,000,000 pieces a year. Over many years, responses have averaged 1 percent of pieces mailed—ranging from 0.8 to 1.2 percent in 95 percent of the years for which experience is available. Probability estimates for these response percentages are: 10 percent chance for 0.8 percent response, 70 percent chance for 1 percent response, and 20 percent chance for 1.2 percent response. One-third of these responses are converted to sales that average $125, with a $50 pretax profit margin after all costs except advertising. There are no substantial lagged effects for direct mail returns. However, there may be additional lagged benefits from the second alternative, a newspaper advertising campaign that the company is seriously considering.

The local sales representative of a five-city national newspaper chain has proposed the following contract to the director of marketing: A four-column, four-inch advertisement (usual cost $210 a day) running 365 days in five major newspapers with an average circulation of 750,000 each (3,000,000 guaranteed minimum average circulation) for a total cost of $120,000. This represents an average daily cost of $329 versus a $1,050 normal daily rate for the five papers. The newspaper chain also agrees to provide one hundred hours of free copywriting consulting time. Depending upon the effectiveness of the advertising copy, responses per day could be expected to range from 200 to only 20. Profits per response should be the same as with direct mail advertising. The marketing director has assigned the following subjective probabilities to the possible responses:

Daily Responses	Probability
200	.25
100	.50
20	.25

The applicable tax rate is 50 percent.

a. Construct a payoff matrix of profits and probabilities for each of the two marketing programs, and determine the expected after-tax net profit under each plan.

b. Construct a simple bar graph of the three possible profit outcomes for each plan. On the basis of the appearance of the two graphs, which plan seems to be the more risky?

c. Calculate the risk (coefficient of variation of the profit distribution) associated with the direct mail campaign ($cv = .75$ for the newspaper advertising program).

d. Which project should the division accept? What other important factors should be considered?

11–3. During union negotiations this year, the Spitzer Company management realized that it must offer its employees greater retirement benefits. The company is considering offering either one of the following: plan A, an increase in the amount of the company's share of the annual contribution to the funded pension plan now in existence, or plan B, elimination of the existing pension plan and its replacement by a new plan calling for variable payback where the amount of the company's payment would depend upon the level of profits for the year.

The actual cost of the pension plan to Spitzer will depend upon many factors, such as age of employees, number of years they have been with the company, and employees' current earnings. However, the prime causes of uncertainty for the new retirement offers are these: since employees are given options as to the extent to which they wish to participate in the pension plan, their individual decisions will determine the amount of the employer's contribution under plan A. This uncertainty will be resolved in the first year of the new plan. For plan B, the level of future profits is the big question; however, the success or failure of a new product line to be introduced the last part of the coming year will greatly reduce this uncertainty.

Management wishes to make a two-year cost comparison for the two plans, and has therefore made the following cost and probability estimates:

Probability	Cost First Year
Plan A: .1	$ 60,000
.3	75,000
.6	90,000
Plan B: .2	50,000
.5	75,000
.3	$100,000

In the second year for plan A, uncertainty is negligible, since all employees will have elected their participation in the program. Management estimates the second-year cost of plan A to be $6,000 greater than its first-year cost. For plan B, uncertainty about second-year profits will still exist, so estimates of costs are also still uncertain.

Given First-year Cost	Probability	Second-year Cost
$ 50,000	.6	$ 50,000
50,000	.4	75,000
75,000	.5	85,000
75,000	.5	100,000
100,000	.4	110,000
100,000	.6	130,000

a. Construct a decision tree for management to use in evaluating the two plans. Assuming that all costs occur at the end of the year for which they apply and that an 8 percent discount rate is appropriate, compute the PV of costs for each plan at each branch terminal of the tree. Next, find the expected PV costs of each project as a weighted average of these terminal *PVs*. (Note: the *PVs* of the two plans could be computed in a simpler manner, but information needed for the risk analysis would not be generated.)

b. Which project is the more risky? (Do not calculate standard deviations.)

c. Which plan should the firm offer to the union? What other factors might be relevant considerations of management?

11-4. Your firm is considering two mutually exclusive investment projects — project A at a cost of $110,000 and project B at a cost of $140,000. The planning division of your firm has estimated the following probability distribution of cash flows to be generated by each project in each of the next five years:

Project A		Project B	
Probability	Cash Flow	Probability	Cash Flow
.2	$15,000	.2	$10,000
.6	30,000	.6	40,000
.2	35,000	.2	60,000

a. Which of those projects is the riskier? Why?

b. Each project's risk is different from that of the firm as a whole. The firm's management adjusts for risk by means of the formula:

$$k_j = R_F + 10cv,$$

where

k_j = the required rate of return on the jth project;

R_F = the risk-free rate, and is equal to 6 percent;

cv = coefficient of variation of the project's cash flows.

What are the required rates of return on projects A and B?

c. Which of those projects, if either, should be accepted by your firm? Explain and support your answer. In calculating the *NPVs*, round the cost of capital figures calculated in part (b) to the nearest whole number.

11-5. The chief financial officer of Worldcorp seeks to determine the value and the required return for the Industrial Products Project (without taxes or leverage). He has gathered the following data.

Year (t)	Return on the Market (k_{Mt})	Earnings before Interest and Taxes (X_{jt})
19X1	.27	$ 25
19X2	.12	5
19X3	(.03)	(5)
19X4	.12	15
19X5	(.03)	(10)
19X6	.27	30

The yield to maturity on Treasury bills is .066 and is expected to remain at this level in the forseeable future. For the unlevered project, compute (a) the value of the project and (b) the required rate of return on the project. (Assume five degrees of freedom for the covariance and variance calculations and six degrees for the means).

11–6. You are given the following information for an investment project: $P = \$3$ per unit; $vc = \$2$ per unit; $FC = \$300$. The risk free rate is 5 percent $= R_F$. (Use Var $k_M = .01$.)

Also:

P_s	k_M	Q	Where:	$P =$ Selling price per unit sold
.2	−.05	0		$vc =$ Variable costs per unit sold
.5	.10	600		$c = (P - vc) =$ Contribution margin per unit
.3	.20	1,000		$Q =$ Units of output sold
				$FC =$ Total fixed costs

(a) What is lambda or the market risk measure?
(b) What is the value of the investment project?
(c) What is the required return on the investment project?

11–7. Given the following facts (the investment cost of each project is equal):

S	P_s	k_{Ms}	Return to Project 1	Return to Project 2
1	.1	−.3	−.4	−.4
2	.2	−.1	−.2	−.2
3	.3	.1	0	.6
4	.4	.3	.7	0

Calculate:

(a) The three means, the variances, the standard deviations, and the covariance of Project 1 with the market, covariance of Project 2 with the market, covariance of Project 1 with Project 2, the correlation coefficients ρ_{1M}, ρ_{2M}, and the correlation coefficient of Project 1 with Project 2.

(b) If 1 and 2 were to be combined into a portfolio, what would be the weights of each project, w_1 and w_2 in the portfolio, to minimize the portfolio standard deviation?

Calculate the expected return on that portfolio and its standard deviation.

(c) $R_F = .04$. Calculate the security market line.

On a graph:

(1) Plot the security market line.

(2) Plot points for Project 1 and for Project 2.

(d) If you had to choose between the two projects, which would be selected?

Selected References

Adler, Michael. "On Risk-Adjusted Capitalization Rates and Valuation By Individuals." *Journal of Finance* 25 (Sept. 1970): 819–36.

Baesel, Jerome B. "On the Assessment of Risk: Some Further Considerations." *Journal of Finance* 29 (Dec. 1974): 1491–94.

Bierman, Harold Jr., and Hass, Jerome E. "Capital Budgeting Under Uncertainty: A Reformulation." *Journal of Finance* 28 (Mar. 1973): 119–30.

Bierman, Harold Jr., and Hausman, Warren H. "The Resolution of Investment Uncertainty Through Time." *Management Science* 18 (Aug. 1972): 654–62.

Blume, Marshall E. "On the Assessment of Risk." *Journal of Finance* 26 (Mar. 1971): 1–10.

Bogue, Marcus C., and Roll, Richard. "Capital Budgeting of Risky Projects with 'Imperfect' Markets for Physical Capital." *Journal of Finance* 29 (May 1974): 601–13.

Bonini, Charles P. "Capital Investment Under Uncertainty with Abandonment Options." *Journal of Financial and Quantitative Analysis* 12 (Mar. 1977): 39–54.

Brumelle, Shelby L., and Schwab, Bernhard. "Capital Budgeting with Uncertain Future Opportunities: A Markovian Approach." *Journal of Financial and Quantitative Analysis* 7 (Jan. 1973): 111–22.

Bussey, Lynn E., and Stevens, G. T., Jr. "Formulating Correlated Cash Flow Streams." *The Engineering Economist* 18 (Fall 1972):1–30.

Byrne, R.; Charnes, A.; Cooper, A.; and Kortanek, K. "Some New Approaches to Risk." *Accounting Review* 63 (Jan. 1968):18–37.

Chen, Houng-Yhi. "Valuation under Uncertainty." *Journal of Financial and Quantitative Analysis* 2 (Sept. 1967): 313–25.

Cooley, Philip L.; Roenfeldt, Rodney L.; and It-Keong Chew. "Capital Budgeting Procedures under Inflation." *Financial Management* 4 (Winter 1975): 18–27.

Edelman, Franz, and Greenberg, Joel S. "Venture Analysis: The Assessment of Uncertainty and Risk." *Financial Executive* 37 (Aug. 1969): 56–62.

Elton, Edwin J., and Gruber, Martin J. "On the Maximization of the Geometric Mean with Lognormal Return Distribution." *Management Science* 21 (Dec. 1974): 483–88.

Fairley, William B., and Jacoby, Henry D. "Investment Analysis Using the Probabiltiy Distribution of the Internal Rate of Return." *Management Science* 21 (Aug. 1975): 1428–37.

Gentry, James, and Pike, John. "An Empirical Study of the Risk-Return Hypothesis Using Common Stock Portfolios of Life Insurance Companies." *Journal of Financial and Quantitative Analysis* 5 (June 1970): 179–86.

Grayson, C. Jackson, Jr. *Decisions Under Uncertainty: Drilling Decisions by Oil and Gas Operators.* Boston: Division of Research, Harvard Business School, 1960.

Greer, Willis R., Jr. "Capital Budgeting Analysis with the Timing of Events Uncertain." *Accounting Review* 45 (Jan. 1970): 103–14.

Hayes, Robert H. "Incorporating Risk Aversion into Risk Analysis." *The Engineering Economist* 20 (Winter 1975): 99–121.

Hertz, David B. "Investment Policies that Pay Off." *Harvard Business Review* 46 (Jan.–Feb. 1968): 96–108.

———. "Risk Analysis in Capital Investment." *Harvard Business Review* 42 (Jan.–Feb. 1964): 95–106.

Hespos, Richard F., and Strassmann, Paul A. "Stochastic Decision Trees for the Analysis of Investment Decisions." *Management Science* 11 (Aug. 1965): 244–59.

Hillier, Frederick S. "The Derivation of Probabilistic Information for the Evaluation of Risky Investments." *Management Science* 9 (Apr. 1963).

Hillier, Frederick S., and Heebink, David V. "Evaluation of Risky Capital Investments." *California Management Review* 8 (Winter 1965): 71–80.

Joy, O. Maurice. "Abandonment Values and Abandonment Decisions: A Clarification." *The Journal of Finance* 31 (Sept. 1976): 1225–28.

Keeley, Robert, and Westerfield, Randolph. "A Problem in Probability Distribution Techniques for Capital Budgeting." *Journal of Finance* 27 (June 1972): 703–9.

Kryzanowski, Lawrence; Lusztig, Peter; and Schwab, Bernhard. "Monte Carlo Simulation and Capital Expenditure Decisions—A Case Study." *The Engineering Economist* 18 (Fall 1972): 31–48.

Latane, H. A., and Tuttle, Donald L. "Decision Theory and Financial Management." *Journal of Finance* 21, no. 2 (May 1966): 228–44.

Lerner, Eugene M., and Rappaport, Alfred. "Limit DCF in Capital Budgeting." *Harvard Business Review* 46 (July–Aug. 1968):133–39.

Lessard, Donald R., and Bower, Richard S. "An Operational Approach to Risk Screening." *Journal of Finance* 28 (May 1973):321–38.

Lewellen, Wilbur G., and Long, Michael S. "Simulation versus Single-Value Estimates in Capital Expenditure Analysis." *Decision Sciences* 3 (1973): 19–33.

Lintner, John. "Security Prices, Risk and Maximal Gains from Diversification." *Journal of Finance* 20 (Dec. 1965): 587–616.

———. "The Evaluation of Risk Assets and the Selection of Risky Investments in Stock Portfolios and Capital Budgets." *Review of Economics and Statistics* 47 (Feb. 1965): 13–37.

Litzenberger, Robert H., and Budd, Alan P. "Corporate Investment Criteria and the Valuation of Risk Assets." *Journal of Financial and Quantitative Analysis* 5 (Dec. 1970): 395–420.

Litzenberger, Robert H., and Joy, O. M. "Target Rates of Return and Corporate

Asset and Liability Structure under Uncertainty." *Journal of Financial and Quantitative Analysis* 6 (Mar. 1971): 675–86.

Litzenberger, Robert H., and Joy, O. M. "Decentralized Capital Budgeting Decisions and Shareholder Wealth Maximization." *Journal of Finance* 30 (June 1975):993–1002.

Lockett, A. Geoffrey, and Gear, Anthony E. "Multistage Capital Budgeting under Uncertainty." *Journal of Financial and Quantitative Analysis* 10 (Mar. 1975): 21–36.

Lockett, A. Geoffrey, and Tomkins, Cyril. "The Discount Rate Problem in Capital Rationing Situations: Comment." *Journal of Financial and Quantitative Analysis* 5 (June 1970): 245–60.

Magee, J. F. "How to Use Decision Trees in Capital Investment." *Harvard Business Review* 42 (Sept.–Oct. 1964): 79–96.

Maier, Steven F., and Vander Weide, James H. "Capital Budgeting in the Decentralized Firm." *Management Science* 23 (Dec. 1976): 433--43.

Mao, James C. T. "Survey of Capital Budgeting: Theory and Practice." *Journal of Finance* 25 (May 1970): 349–60.

Mao, James C. T., and Helliwell, John F. "Investment Decisions under Uncertainty: Theory and Practice." *Journal of Finance* 24 (May 1969): 323–38.

Moag, Joseph S., and Lerner, Eugene M. "Capital Budgeting Decisions under Imperfect Market Conditions—A Systems Framework." *Journal of Finance* 24 (Sept. 1969): 613–21.

Modigliani, Franco, and Pogue, Gerald A. "An Introduction to Risk and Return." *Financial Analysts' Journal* 30 (Mar.–Apr. 1974):68–80, and (May–June 1974):69–88.

Myers, Stewart C. "Procedures for Capital Budgeting under Uncertainty." *Industrial Management Review* 9 (Spring 1968): 1–15.

Page, Alfred N., ed. *Utility Theory.* New York: Wiley, 1968.

Paine, Neil R. "Uncertainty and Capital Budgeting." *Accounting Review* 39 (Apr. 1964): 330–32.

Perrakis, Stylianos. "Certainty Equivalents and Timing Uncertainty." *Journal of Financial and Quantitative Analysis* 10 (Mar. 1975): 109–18.

Peterson, D. E., and Laughhunn, D. J. "Capital Expenditure Programming and Some Alternative Approaches to Risk." *Management Science* 17 (Jan. 1971): 320–36.

Quirin, G. David. *The Capital Expenditure Decision.* Homewood, Ill.: Irwin, 1967.

Robichek, A., and Myers, S. *Optimal Financing Decisions.* Englewood Cliffs, N.J.: Prentice-Hall, 1965, chap. 5.

——— "Risk-Adjusted Discount Rates." *Journal of Finance* 21, no. 4 (Dec. 1966): 727–30.

Robichek, A.; Ogilvie, Donald G.; and Roach, John D. C. "Capital Budgeting: A Pragmatic Approach." *Financial Executive* 37 (Apr. 1969): 26–38.

Robichek, A., and Van Horne, James C. "Abandonment Value and Capital Budgeting." *Journal of Finance* 22 (Dec. 1967), 577–89; Dyl, Edward A. and Long, Hugh W. "Comment." *Journal of Finance* 24 (Mar. 1969): 88–95; and Robichek, A., and Van Horne, James C. "Reply." *ibid.,* 96–97.

Robichek, Alexander A. "Interpreting the Results of Risk Analysis." *Journal of Finance* 30 (Dec. 1975): 1384–86.

Schwab, Bernhard, and Schwab, Helmut. "A Method of Investment Evaluation for Smaller Companies." *Management Services* (July–Aug. 1969): 43–53.

Schwendiman, Carl J., and Pinches, George E. "An Analysis of Alternative Measures of Investment Risk." *Journal of Finance* 30 (Mar. 1975): 193–200.

Stapleton, Richard C. "Portfolio Analysis, Stock Valuation and Capital Budgeting Rules for Risky Projects." *Journal of Finance* 26 (Mar. 1971): 95–118.

Stevens, Bussey. "A Solution Methodology for Probabilistic Capital Budgeting Problems Using Complex Utility Functions." *The Engineering Economist* 21 (Winter 1976): 89–110.

Swalm, Ralph O. "Utility Theory—Insights into Risk Taking." *Harvard Business Review* 44 (Nov.–Dec. 1966):123–36.

Thompson, Howard E. "Mathematical Programming, The Capital Asset Pricing Model and Capital Budgeting of Inter-Related Projects." *Journal of Finance* 31 (Mar. 1976): 125–31.

Tuttle, Donald L., and Litzenberger, Robert H. "Leverage, Diversification and Capital Market Effects on a Risk-Adjusted Capital Budgeting Framework." *Journal of Finance* 23 (June 1968): 427–44.

U.S. Congress, Subcommittee on Economy in Government of the Joint Economic Committee. *Economic Analysis of Public Investment Decisions: Interest Rate Policy and Discounting Analysis.* Washington, D.C.: U.S. Government Printing Office, 1968.

Van Horne, James. "Capital Budgeting Decisions Involving Combinations of Risky Investments." *Management Science* 13 (Oct. 1966): 84–92.

––––––. "The Analysis of Uncertainty Resolution in Capital Budgeting for New Products." *Management Science* 15 (Apr. 1969): 376–86.

––––––. "The Variation of Project Life as a Means for Adjusting for Risk." *The Engineering Economist* 21 (Spring 1976): 151–58.

Wallingford, B. A. "A Survey and Comparison of Portfolio Selection Models." *Journal of Financial and Quantitative Analysis* 3 (June 1967): 85–106.

Waters, Robert C., and Bullock, Richard L. "Inflation and Replacement Decisions." *The Engineering Economist* 21 (Summer 1976): 249–57.

Weston, J. Fred. "Investment Decisions Using the Capital Asset Pricing Model." *Financial Management* 2 (Spring 1973): 25–33.

Woods, Donald H. "Improving Estimates That Involve Uncertainty." *Harvard Business Review* 45 (July–Aug. 1966): 91–98.

Young, Donovan, and Contreras, Luis E. "Expected Present Worths of Cash Flows Under Uncertain Timing." *The Engineering Economist* 20 (Summer 1975): 257–68.

Appendix A to Chapter 11
Formal Analysis of Risk

In Chapter 11, we saw that probability distributions can be viewed in either of two ways: (1) as a series of *discrete values* represented by a bar chart, such as Figure 11-1, or (2) as a *continuous function* represented by a smooth curve, such as that in Figure 11-2. Actually, there is an important difference in the way these two graphs are interpreted: The probabilities associated with the outcomes in Figure 11-1 are given by the *height* of each bar, while in Figure 11-2 the probabilities must be found by calculating the *area* under the curve between points of interest. Suppose, for example, that we have the continuous probability distribution shown in Figure A11-1. This is a normal curve with a mean of 20 and a standard deviation of 5; x could be dollars, percentage rates of return, or any other units. If we want to know the probability that an outcome will fall between 15 and 30, we must calculate the area beneath the curve between these points, or the shaded area in the diagram.

Figure A11-1
Continuous Probability
Distribution

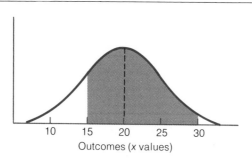

Outcomes (x values)

The area under the curve between 15 and 30 can be determined by integrating the curve over this interval, or, since the distribution is normal, by reference to statistical tables of the area under the normal curve such as Table A11-1 or Appendix C to this book.[1] To use these

---

1. The equation for the normal curve is tedious to integrate, thus making the use of tables much more convenient. The equation for the normal curve is

$$f(x) / \frac{1}{\sqrt{2\pi\sigma^2}} \, e^{-(x-\mu)^2/2\sigma^2},$$

tables, it is necessary only to know the mean and standard deviation of the distribution.[2]

z	Area from the Mean to the Point of Interest	Ordinate
0.0	.0000	.3989
0.5	.1915	.3521
1.0	.3413	.2420
1.5	.4332	.1295
2.0	.4773	.0540
2.5	.4938	.0175
3.0	.4987	.0044

$z =$ number of standard deviations from the mean. Some area tables are set up to indicate the area to the left or right of the point of interest; in this book we indicate the area between the mean and the point of interest.

The distribution to be investigated must first be standardized by using the following formula:

$$z = \frac{x - \mu}{\sigma}, \qquad\qquad (A11–1)$$

where z is the standardized variable, or the number of standard deviations from the mean;[3] x is the outcome of interest; and μ and σ are the mean and standard deviation of the distribution, respectively. For our example, where we are interested in the probability that an outcome will fall between 15 and 30, we first normalize these points of interest using Equation A11–1:

$$z_1 = \frac{15 - 20}{5} = -1.0; \; z_2 = \frac{30 - 20}{5} = 2.0.$$

The areas associated with these z values are found in Table A11–1 to be .3413 and .4773.[4] This means that the probability is .3413 that the actual outcome will fall between 15 and 20, and .4773 that it will fall between 20 and 30. Summing these probabilites shows that the probability of an outcome falling between 15 and 30 is .8186, or 81.86 percent.

where π and e are mathematical constants; μ (read mu) and σ denote the mean and standard deviation of the probability distribution, and x is any possible outcome.

2. The calculating procedure for means and standard deviations is illustrated in Chapter 11, Table 11–4.

3. Note that if the point of interest is 1σ away from the mean, then $x - \mu = \sigma$, so $z = \sigma/\sigma = 1.0$. Thus, when $z = 1.0$, the point of interest is 1σ away from the mean; when $z = 2$ the value is 2σ, and so forth.

4. Note that the negative sign on z_1 is ignored, since the normal curve is symmetrical around the mean; the minus sign merely indicates that the point lies to the left of the mean.

Suppose we had been interested in determining the probability that the actual outcome would be greater than 15. Here we would first note that the probability is .3413 that the outcome will be between 15 and 20, then observe that the probability is .5000 of an outcome greater than the mean, 20. Thus, the probability is .3413 + .5000 = .8413, or 84.13 percent, that the outcome will exceed 15.

Some interesting properties of normal probability distributions can be seen by examining Table A11–1 and Figure A11–2, which is a graph of the normal curve. For any normal distribution, the probability of an outcome falling within plus or minus one standard deviation from the mean is .6826, or 68.26 percent: .3413 percent × 2.0. If we take the range within two standard deviations of the mean, the probability of an occurrence within this range is 95.46 percent, and 99.74 percent of all outcomes will fall within three standard deviations of the mean. Although the distribution theoretically runs from minus infinity to plus infinity, the probability of occurrences beyond about three standard deviations is very near zero.

Figure A11–2
The Normal Curve

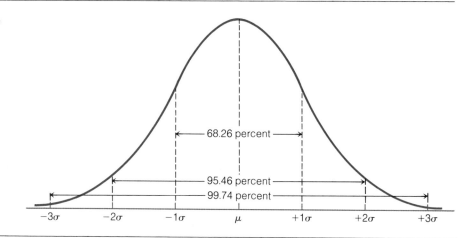

**Illustrating
the Use of
Probability
Concepts**

The concepts discussed both in the chapter and in the preceding section can be clarified by a numerical example. Consider three states of the economy: boom, normal, and recession. Next, assume that we can attach a probability of occurrence to each state of the economy, and, further, that we can estimate the dollar returns that will occur on each of two projects under each possible state. With this information, we construct Table A11–2.

The expected values of projects A and B are calculated by Equation A11–2,

$$\bar{F}_j = \sum_{s=1}^{n} F_{js}P_s \tag{A11–2}$$

and the standard deviations of their respective returns are found by Equation A11–3,

$$\sigma_j = \sqrt{\sum_{s=1}^{n} (F_{js} - \bar{F}_j)^2 P_s}. \tag{A11–3}$$

Table A11–2 **Means and Standard Deviations of Projects A and B**	State of the Economy	Probability of Its Occurring, P_s	Return F_{js}	$F_{js}P_s$
	Project A			
	Recession	.2	$400	$ 80
	Normal	.6	500	300
	Boom	.2	600	120
		1.0	Expected value =	$500
	Standard deviation = σ_A = $63.20.			
	Project B			
	Recession	.2	$300	$ 60
	Normal	.6	500	300
	Boom	.2	700	140
		1.0	Expected value =	$500
	Standard deviation = σ_B = $126.50.			

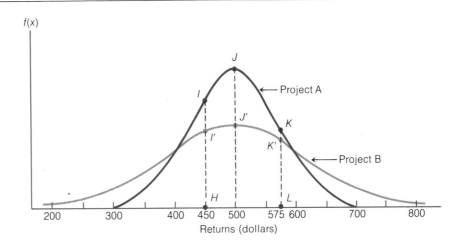

Figure A11–3
Probability
Distributions for
Projects A and B

On the assumption that the returns from projects A and B are normally distributed, knowing the mean and the standard deviation as calculated in Table A11–2 permits us to graph probability distributions for projects A and B; these distributions are shown in Figure A11–3.[5] The expected value of each project's cash flow is seen to be $500; however, the flatter graph of B indicates that this is the riskier project.

Suppose we want to determine the probabilities that the actual returns of projects A and B will be in the interval $450 to $575. Using Equation A11–1 and Figure A11–3, we can calculate the respective probability distributions. The first step is to calculate the z values of the interval limits for the two projects:

Project A

$$\text{lower } z_1 = \frac{\$450 - \$500}{\$63.20} = -.79.$$

$$\text{upper } z_2 = \frac{\$575 - \$500}{\$63.20} = 1.19.$$

Project B

$$\text{lower } z_1 = \frac{\$450 - \$500}{\$126.50} = -.40.$$

$$\text{upper } z_2 = \frac{\$575 - \$500}{\$126.50} = .59.$$

5. Normal probability distributions can be constructed once the mean and standard deviation are known, using a table of *ordinates* of the normal curve. (See column 3 of Table A11–1.) This table is similar to the table of areas used above, except that the ordinate table gives relative *heights* of probability curve $f(x)$ at various z values rather than areas beneath the curve. Figure A11–3 was constructed by plotting points at various z values according to the following formula:

$$f(x) = \frac{1}{\sigma} \times (\text{ordinate for } z \text{ value}),$$

where the ordinate value is read from a table of ordinates.

For example, the points corresponding to the mean and +1 standard deviation for projects A and B were calculated as follows:

(1)	z (2)	Ordinate at z (3)	$1/\sigma$ (4)	$f(x)$ (5) = (3) × (4)
Project A				
mean = 500.00	0	.3989	1/63.2	.0063
+1σ = 563.20	1	.2420	1/63.2	.0038
+2σ = 626.40	2	.0540	1/63.2	.0008
Project B				
Mean = 500.00	0	.3989	1/126.5	.0032
+1σ = 626.50	1	.2420	1/126.5	.0019
+2σ = 753.00	2	.0540	1/126.5	.0004

Column 5 above gives the relative heights of the two distributions: Thus, if we decide (for pictorial convenience) to let the curve for project B be 3.2 inches high at the mean, then the curve should be 1.9 inches high at $\mu \pm 1\sigma$, and the curve for project A should be 6.3 inches at the mean and 3.8 inches at $\pm 1\sigma$. Other points in Figure A11–3 were determined in like manner.

In Appendix C at the end of the book, which is a more complete table of z values, we find the areas under a normal curve for each of these four z values:

Project A	z Value	Area
lower z:	− .79	.2852
upper z:	1.19	.3830
	Total area =	.6682 or 66.82 percent

Project B	z Value	Area
lower z:	−.40	.1554
upper z:	.59	.2224
	Total area =	.3778 or 37.78 percent

Thus, there is about a 67 percent chance that the actual cash flow from project A will lie in the interval $450 to $575, and about a 38 percent probability that B's cash flow will fall in this interval.

Now look back at Figure A11–3 and observe the two areas that were just calculated. For project A, the area bounded by *HIJKL* represents

Figure A11–4
Cumulative Probability
Distributions for
Projects A and B

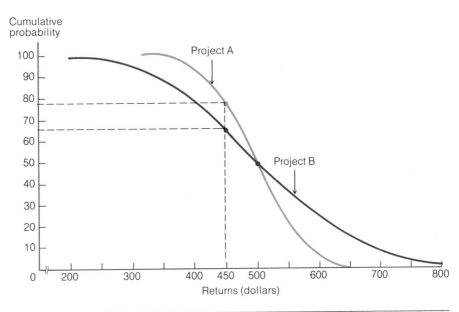

about 67 percent of the area under A's curve. For project B, that area bounded by $HI'J'K'L$ includes about 38 percent of the total area.

Cumulative Probability

Suppose we ask these questions: What is the probability that the cash flows from project A will be at least $100? $150? $200? and so on. Obviously, there is a higher probability of their being at least $100 rather than $150, $150 rather than $200, and so on. In general, the most convenient way of expressing the answer to such "at least" questions is through the use of *cumulative probability distributions*; these distributions for projects A and B are calculated in Table A11–3 and plotted in Figure A11–4.

Suppose projects A and B each cost $450; then, if each project returns at least $450, they will both break even. What is the probability of breaking even on each project? From Figure A11–4 we see that the probability is 78 percent that project A will break even, while the break-

Table A11–3 Cumulative Probability Distributions for Projects A and B	Expected Return	z Value	Cumulative Probability
	Project A		
	300	−3.16	.9990*
	400	−1.58	.9429
	450	− .79	.7855
	500	0.00	.5000†
	575	1.19	.1170‡
	600	1.58	.0571
	700	3.16	.0001
	Project B		
	200	−2.37	.9911*
	300	−1.58	.9429
	400	− .79	.7855
	450	− .39	.6517
	500	0.00	.5000†
	575	.59	.2776‡
	600	.79	.2148
	700	1.58	.0571
	800	2.37	.0089

*.5000 plus areas under left tail of the normal curve; for example, for Project A, .5000 + .4990 = .9990 = 99.9 percent for $z = -3.16$.

†The mean has a cumulative probability of .5000 = 50 percent.

‡.5000 less area under right tail of the normal curve; for example, for Project A, .5000 − .3830 = .1170 = 11.7 percent for $z = 1.19$.

even probability is only 65 percent for the riskier project B. However, there is virtually no chance that A will yield more than $650, while B has a 5 percent chance of returning $700 or more.

**Other
Distributions**

Thus far we have assumed that project returns fit a probability distribution that is approximately normal. Many distributions do fit this pattern, and normal distributions are relatively easy to work with. Therefore, much of the work done on risk measurement assumes a normal distribution. However, other distributions are certainly possible; Figure A11–5 shows distributions skewed to the right and left, respectively. For two possible investments with equal expected returns, F, would an investor prefer a normal, left-skewed, or right-skewed distribution? A distribution skewed to the right, such as the one in Figure A11–5(a), would probably be chosen because the odds on a very low return are small, while there is some chance of very high returns. For the left-skewed distributions, there is little likelihood of large gains but some possibility of losses.

Figure A11–5
Skewed Distributions

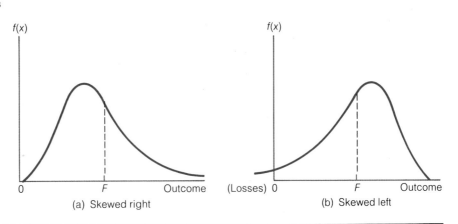

(a) Skewed right　　　　　(b) Skewed left

Summary

In this appendix we have reviewed some of the basics of probability theory and showed how it can be used in evaluating risky investments. More advanced concepts for multiperiod cash flows, and for various return patterns, are presented in Appendices B, C, D, E, and F.

Problems

A11–1. The sales of the Cleveland Company for next year have the following probability distribution:

Probability	Sales (millions)
.1	$10
.2	12
.4	15
.2	18
.1	20

a. On graph paper, plot sales on the horizontal axis and probability of sales on the vertical axis, using the points given above. Draw a smooth curve connecting your plotted points. What can you say about this curve?

b. Compute the mean of the probability distribution.

c. Compute the standard deviation of the probability distribution.

d. Compute the coefficient of variation of the probability distribution.

e. What is the probability that sales will exceed $16 million?

f. What is the probability that sales will fall below $13 million?

g. What is the probability that sales will be between $13 and $16 million?

h. What is the probability that sales will exceed $17 million?

A11–2. Mutual of Poughkeepsie offers to sell your firm a $1 million one-year term insurance policy on your corporate jet for a premium of $7,500. The probability that the plane will be lost or incur damages in that amount in any 12-month period is .001.

a. What is the insurance company's expected gain from sale of the policy?

b. What is the insurance company's expected gain or loss if the probability of a $1 million fire loss is .01? Would the insurance company still offer your firm the same policy for the same premium? Explain.

Appendix B to Chapter 11
Evaluating Uncertain Cash
Flows Over Time

In Appendix A to Chapter 11 we presented some of the statistical theory upon which risk analysis is based. In this appendix, somewhat more advanced theory is used to deal with the problem of uncertain returns over time. Our discussion is divided into two cases: (1) where expected returns are normally distributed and are independent from one period to another, and (2) where normality and intertemporal independence do not hold.

Independent Returns Over Time

In Appendix A to Chapter 11 we calculated an investment's one-year expected return, and the standard deviation of that return, as follows:

Expected return for year t:

$$\overline{F}_t = \sum_{s=1}^{n} (F_{ts}P_{ts}).$$ (B11–1)

Variation of expected return for year t:

$$\sigma_t = \left[\sum_{s=1}^{n} (F_{ts} - \overline{F}_t)^2 P_{ts} \right]^{1/2}.$$ (B11–2)

If the probability distribution P_{ts} is normally distributed, and if the cash flow in year t, $\overline{F}_t$, is independent of the cash flow in year $(t-1)$, then we can find the present value of an uncertain stream of returns by use of Equation B11–3, and the standard deviation of this PV by use of Equation B11–4:

Expected present value of investment:

$$PV = \sum_{t=1}^{n} \left[\frac{\overline{F}_t}{(1+k)^t} \right].$$ (B11–3)

Variation of expected present value of the investment:[1]

$$\sigma_{PV} = \left[\sum_{t=0}^{n} \frac{\sigma_t^2}{(1 + k)^{2t}} \right]^{1/2}$$ (B11–4)

Here

F_{ts} = cash flow return associated with the sth probability in year t

P_{ts} = probability of the sth return in year t

$\overline{F}_t$ = expected cash flow return from the investment in the tth year, an average weighted by probabilities

σ_t = standard deviation of the expected returns in the tth year

PV = present value of all expected returns over the n-year life of the investment

k = appropriate rate of discount for the future returns

σ_{PV} = standard deviation of the present value of expected returns.

Equation B11–1 calculates the expected returns of an investment for a given year, t, as a weighted average, the items to be averaged being the possible outcomes and the weights being the probabilities associated with each possible outcome for the year. Equation B11–2 calculates the standard deviation of the expected return in year t. Equation B11–3 discounts the expected returns over each year of the project's life to find the present value of the project, and Equation B11–4 calculates the standard deviation of the expected PV of the project. The first two equations deal with the returns and risk for individual years, while the last two equations deal with returns and risk of the project as a whole.

Comparison of Two Investments with Uncertain Returns Over Future Time Periods

The application and significance of the basic formulas can best be conveyed by illustrative examples. The relevant data and calculations are set forth in Tables B11–1 for project A and B11–2 for project B. Project A's cash investment is $100. Returns are expected over three periods. There are five possible "states of the world"; that is, $s = 1 \ldots 5$, and the outcomes for each of these states are given in the columns headed F_{1s}, F_{2s}, F_{3s}. Note that the range of possible returns widens in the later periods.

---

1. For a proof of Equation B11–4, see Frederick S. Hillier, "The Derivation of Probabilistic Information for the Evaluation of Risky Investments," *Management Science* 9 (April 1963), pp. 443–57.

**Table B11-1
Probable Returns from Risky Investment A**

Investment A $100 (cash outflow in period 0)
(1) Calculation of Expected Returns

	Period 1			Period 2			Period 3		
State$_{(s)}$	F_{1s}	P_{1s}	$F_{1s}P_{1s}$	F_{2s}	P_{2s}	$F_{2s}P_{2s}$	F_{3s}	P_{3s}	$F_{3s}P_{3s}$
1	50	.10	5	20	.10	2	− 40	.10	− 4
2	60	.20	12	40	.25	10	30	.30	9
3	70	.40	28	60	.30	18	50	.30	15
4	80	.20	16	80	.25	20	80	.20	16
5	90	.10	9	100	.10	10	140	.10	14

$$\sum_{s=1}^{5} (F_{1s}P_{1s}) = \bar{F}_1 = 70 \qquad \bar{F}_2 = 60 \qquad \bar{F}_3 = 50$$

(2) Calculation of Standard Deviation

State$_{(s)}$	$(F_{1s} - \bar{F}_1)^2$	P_{1s}	$(F_{1s} - \bar{F}_1)^2 P_{1s}$	$(F_{2s} - \bar{F}_2)^2$	P_{2s}	$(F_{2s} - \bar{F}_2)^2 P_{2s}$	$(F_{3s} - \bar{F}_3)^2$	P_{3s}	$(F_{3s} - \bar{F}_3)^2 P_{3s}$
1	400	.10	40	1600	.10	160	8100	.10	810
2	100	.20	20	400	.25	100	400	.30	120
3	0	.40	0	0	.30	0	0	.30	0
4	100	.20	20	400	.25	100	900	.20	180
5	400	.10	40	1600	.10	160	8100	.10	810

$$\sum_{s=1}^{5} (F_{1s} - \bar{F}_1)^2 P_{1s} = 120 = \sigma_1^2 \qquad \sigma_2^2 = 520 \qquad \sigma_3^2 = 1920$$

$$\sigma_1 = \sqrt{120} = 10.95 \qquad \sigma_2 = \sqrt{520} = 22.80 \qquad \sigma_3 = \sqrt{1920} = 43.82$$

$$(3)\ PV_A = \frac{70}{1.06} + \frac{60}{(1.06)^2} + \frac{50}{(1.06)^3} = \frac{70}{1.060} + \frac{60}{1.124} + \frac{50}{1.191} = \$161.40$$

$$(4)\ \sigma_{PV} = \left[\frac{120}{(1.06)^2} + \frac{520}{(1.06)^4} + \frac{1920}{(1.06)^6}\right]^{1/2} = \left[\frac{120}{1.124} + \frac{520}{1.262} + \frac{1920}{1.419}\right]^{1/2}$$

$$= [106.76 + 412.04 + 1,353.07]^{1/2} = [1,871.87]^{1/2} = 43.25$$

The associated probabilities are in the columns headed P_{1s}, P_{2s}, and P_{3s}. It should be noted that in period 2 the probability distribution is somewhat flatter than in period 1, and that in period 3 the probability distribution is even more flat and is also skewed somewhat to the left, or toward the possibility of lower returns. Thus, the combination of a wider range of outcomes and flatter probability distribution for periods 2 and 3 indicates that greater uncertainty is associated with returns expected in the more distant future. This type of situation is shown in Figure 11-4, in the body of Chapter 11.

Given these data, the expected returns for project A for each period are calculated and found to be $70, $60, and $50, respectively. The standard deviation of each of these returns is then calculated, using Equation B11-2. Next, Equation B11-3 is used to calculate project A's ex-

Table B11–2			
Probable Returns from Risky Investment B	Investment B = \$100 Cash Inflows		

P_{ts}	F_{1s}	F_{2s}	F_{3s}
.10	40	30	20
.20	50	40	30
.40	60	50	40
.20	70	60	50
.10	80	70	60
$\overline{R}_t$	60	50	40

(2) $\sigma_t = [.10(20)^2 + .20(10)^2 + .20(10)^2 + .10(20)^2]^{1/2} = [120]^{1/2} = \$10.95$

(3) $PV_B = \dfrac{60}{1.060} + \dfrac{50}{1.124} + \dfrac{40}{1.191} = 56.60 + 44.48 + 33.58 = \$134.66$

(4) $\sigma_{PV} = \left[\dfrac{120}{1.124} + \dfrac{120}{1.262} + \dfrac{120}{1.419}\right]^{1/2} = [106.76 + 95.08 + 84.57]^{1/2} = [286.40]^{1/2} = \$16.91$

pected present value, \$161.40. Finally, Equation B11–4 is used to find the standard deviation of that present value, \$43.25.

In Table B11–2, similar calculations are performed for project B, which also involves an outlay of \$100. To simplify the calculations, we assume that the indicated probabilities are the same for each of the three periods, but note that the expected returns drop with each successive year. Thus, the standard deviation of expected returns, $\sigma_t = \$10.95$, is the same for each of the three periods, but the coefficient of variation, which is the standard deviation divided by the mean return, is lower for the earlier returns, because expected returns are declining. Thus, the riskiness of project B is also increasing over time. Equations B11–3 and B11–4 are again used to calculate the present value of the expected returns, \$134.66, and the standard deviation of the expected value, \$16.91.

Knowing the mean (PV) and the standard deviation (σ_{NPV}) as calculated in Tables B11–1 and B11–2, and assuming that the returns from projects A and B are normally distributed, we can construct probability distribution graphs for the two projects; these distributions are shown in Figure B11–1. The expected PV of A is seen to be \$161, while that of B is \$134. However, the larger standard deviation and flatter graph of A indicate that A is the riskier project.

The decision-maker must still choose between the riskier but probably more profitable project A and the less risky but probably less profitable project B. How is this choice made? Conceptually, the information on relative project riskiness could be used to establish risk-adjusted discount rates, which could then be used to calculate risk-adjusted NPVs, using the market price of risk theory described in Chapter 11. This would require the calculation of the systematic risk measures,

Figure B11–1
Probability
Distributions of *PV* for
Projects A and B

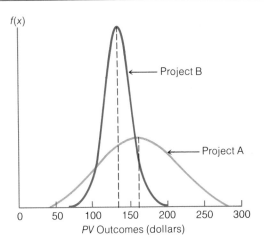

covariance or beta, over multi-time periods.[2] Further discussion of the relationship between risk and the cost of capital will be deferred to Chapter 17.

Cumulative Probability

A useful and practical way of expressing the distributions of projects A and B is in terms of cumulative probabilities (discussed in detail in Appendix A to Chapter 11). We know that projects A and B each have a cost of $100; what is the probability that the present value of the cash flows from each of these projects will be *at least* $100, that is, that the *NPV* will be zero or greater? Cumulative probabilities are used to answer this question.

Cumulative probabilities are developed from the data on the area under the normal curve given in Appendix C. In Table B11–3, the data on projects A and B are combined with the information on the area under the normal curve. The various entries in columns 1 and 2 of this table represent possible outcomes for the *PV* of projects A and B. Since the investment outlay for each project is $100, this sum can be subtracted from the *PV* figures in columns 1 and 2 to obtain the *NPV* values in columns 3 and 4. The z values in column 5 simply denote the number of standard deviations each entry is from the mean, and column 6 gives

2. See Marcus Bogue and Richard Roll, "Capital Budgeting of Risky Projects with 'Imperfect' Markets for Physical Capital," *Journal of Finance* 29 (May 1974), 601–13.

**Table B11–3
Cumulative
Probabilities of
Expected Present
Values of
Investments
A and B**

Expected PV of at Least		Expected NPV of at Least		z Value*	Cumulative Probability
A (1)	B (2)	A (3)	B (4)	(5)	(6)
$ 31.65	$ 83.93	(68.35)	(16.07)	−3z	99.9%†
74.90	100.84	(25.10)	.84	−2z	97.7
118.15	117.75	18.15	17.75	−1z	84.1
161.40	134.66	61.40	34.66	−	50.0
204.65	151.57	104.65	51.57	+1z	15.9‡
247.90	168.48	147.90	68.48	2z	2.3
291.15	185.39	191.15	85.39	3z	.1
$100.0		0.0		1.42	92.2%§
	$100.0		0.0	2.05	98.0‖

*z = number of standard deviations from mean PV.

†.5000 *plus* areas under *left* tail of normal curve; for example, .5000 + .4987 = 99.9 percent for $z = −3$.

‡.5000 *less* areas under *right* tail of normal curve; for example, .500 − .4773 = 2.3 percent for $z = 2$.

§$NPV = PV −$ Cost.

$z = \dfrac{PV}{\sigma_{NPV}}$ where $NPV = 0$.

Since the PV differs from the NPV by a constant, $\sigma_{NPV} = \sigma_{PV}$.

$z = \dfrac{61.40}{43.25} = 1.42$ for project A.

The area under the right tail of the normal curve associated with $z = 1.42$ is .4222, so

Area = .5000 + .4222 = .9222,

and the probability of $NPV \geq 0$ is 92.2 percent.

‖For project B,

$z = \dfrac{34.66}{16.91} = 2.05$ where $NPV = 0$,

and the associated area = .5000 + .4798 = .9798, so the probability of $NPV \geq 0$ is 98 percent for project B.

the probability of realizing *PVs* and *NPVs at least* as large as those shown in columns 1 through 4. From Appendix C, we see that for the first line of Table B11 – 3, the probability of an outcome's lying to the left of −3σ is .0013, or .13 percent, so the probability of the outcome's lying to the right of −3σ; that is, the probability of NPV_A being at least ($68.35) or NPV_B being at least ($16.07) is 100.00 percent: .13 percent = 99.87 percent ≈ 99.9 percent. The other values in Table B11–3 are developed similarly. Note that the last two rows of the table indicate that the probability of at least breaking even is 92.2 percent for project A and 98.0 percent for project B.

Figure B11 – 2 shows these data on cumulative probabilities in graph

Figure B11–2
Cumulative Probability
Analysis of *NPV*
Values for Projects A
and B

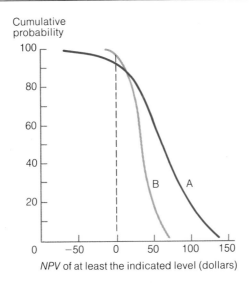

form. Here it is easy to see that project B has only a small chance of not breaking even, but it also has virtually no chance of earning an *NPV* of over about $60. Project A, on the other hand, has a higher probability of losing money, but it also has a fairly high probability of achieving an *NPV* of over $100.

It is clear that investment A has a higher expected return than investment B. However, disregarding portfolio effects, investment B is less risky. Selection between A and B would depend upon the decision-maker's attitude toward risk, as well as upon how the two investments might fit in with the firm's other assets.

Interdependent Returns Over Time: The Hillier and Hertz Approaches

The foregoing presentation represents a general method for dealing with risk when the returns of one period do not depend upon outcomes in other years; that is, when the returns are *independent* and when the expected returns for a given year are normally distributed. When these conditions of independence and normality do not hold, the calculations become more complicated. The models for which expected net cash flows between periods are correlated (the expected returns between time periods are dependent), and for which some of the returns of an investment are correlated and some are independent, have been treated by Frederick Hillier.[3] Mathematical techniques are also available for dealing with nonnormal probability distributions. We shall not go into the technical methodology involved, but Hillier's approach has proved to be a useful way of dealing with uncertainty in at least some practical situations.

Another approach to capital budgeting under uncertainty is presented in an article by David Hertz.[4] He is particularly persuasive in indicating that, taking probabilities into account, the expected rate of return may be quite different from the conventional best-single-estimate approach. Hertz illustrates the use of the probability information in an approach that requires only a range of high and low values around expected values of such key variables as sales, profit margins, and so forth. Under his method, the decision-maker is not required to assign probabilities to the variables; he must choose only (1) the expected value, (2) an upper estimate, and (3) a lower estimate. The Monte Carlo[5] method, which involves using a table of random numbers to generate the possible probabilities, is used to generate the required probability distributions.

The Monte Carlo method also permits assignment of values that reflect differing degrees of dependence between some events and some subsequent events. For example, the expected sales for the firm, as well as its selling prices, might be determined by the intensity of competition in conjunction with the total size of market demand and its growth rate. A further advantage of the Hertz technique is that, by separating the individual factors that determine profitability, the separate effects of each factor can be estimated and the sensitivity of profitability to each factor can be determined. If the effects of a particular factor on the final results are negligible, it is not necessary for management to analyze that particular factor in any great detail.

Sensitivity Analysis

The *NPV* of a project will, in the final analysis, depend upon such factors as quantity of sales, sales prices, input costs, and the like. If these values turn out to be favorable—that is, output and sales prices are high, and costs are low—then profits, the realized rate of return, and the actual *NPV* will be high, and conversely if poor results are experienced.

---

3. See Frederick S. Hillier, "The Derivation of Probabilistic Information for the Evaluation of Risk Investments," *Management Science* 9 (April 1963), pp. 44–57, and Frederick S. Hillier and David V. Heebink, "Evaluating Risky Capital Investments," *California Management Review* 8 (Winter 1965), pp. 71–80.

4. David B. Hertz, "Uncertainty and Investment Selection," in J. F. Weston and M. B. Goudzwaard, eds., *The Treasurer's Handbook* (Homewood, Ill.: Dow Jones-Irwin, 1976), Chapter 18, pp. 376–420.

5. For a discussion of the nature of the Monte Carlo method and some applications, see C. McMillan and R. F. Gonzalez, *Systems Analysis* (Homewood, Ill.: Irwin, 1965), pp. 76–121.

Recognizing these causal relationships, businessmen often calculate projects' *NPV*s under alternative assumptions, then see just how sensitive *NPV* is to changing conditions. One example that recently came to the authors' attention involves a fertilizer company that was comparing two alternative types of phosphate plants. Fuel represents a major cost, and one plant uses coal, which may be obtained under a long-term, fixed-cost contract, while the other uses oil, which must be purchased at current market prices. Considering present and projected future prices, the oil-fired plant looks better—it has a considerably higher *NPV*. However, oil prices are volatile, and if prices rise by more than the expected rate, this plant will be unprofitable. The coal-fired plant, on the other hand, has a lower *NPV* under the expected conditions, but this *NPV* is not sensitive to changing conditions in the energy market. The company finally selected the coal plant because the sensitivity analysis indicated it to be less risky.

Monte Carlo Simulation Analysis

Sensitivity analysis as practiced by the fertilizer company described above is informal in the sense that no probabilities are attached to the likelihood of various outcomes. Monte Carlo *simulation analysis* represents a refinement that does employ probability estimates. In this section we first describe how *decision trees* can be used to attach probabilities to different outcomes, and then we illustrate how full-scale computer simulation can be employed to analyze major projects.

Decision Trees. Most important decisions are not made once-and-for-all at one point in time. Rather, decisions are made in stages. For example, a petroleum firm considering the possibility of expanding into agricultural chemicals might take the following steps: (1) spend $100,000 for a survey of supply-demand conditions in the agricultural chemical industry; (2) if the survey results are favorable, spend $500,000 on a pilot plant to investigate production methods; and (3) depending on the costs estimated from the pilot study and the demand potential from the market study, either abandon the project, build a large plant, or build a small one. Thus, the final decision actually is made in stages, with subsequent decisions depending on the results of previous decisions.

The sequence of events can be mapped out like the branches of a tree, hence the name *decision tree*. As an example, consider Figure B 11–3. There it is assumed that the petroleum company has completed its industry supply-demand analysis and pilot plant study, and has determined that it should proceed to develop a full-scale production facility. The firm must decide whether to build a large plant or a small one. Demand expectations for the plant's products are 50 percent for high demand, 30 percent for medium demand, and 20 percent for low demand. Depending upon demand, net cash flows (sales revenues minus operating costs, all discounted to the present) will range from $8.8 million to $1.4 million if a large plant is built, and from $2.6 million to $1.4 million if a small plant is built.

The initial costs of the large and small plants are shown in column 5; when these investment outlays are subtracted from the *PV* of cash flows, the result is the set of possible *NPV*s shown in column 6. One, but only one, of these *NPV*s will actually occur. Finally, we multiply column 6 by column 3 to obtain column 7, and the sums in column 7 give the expected *NPV*s of the large and small plants.

Because the expected *NPV* of the larger plant ($730,000) is larger than that of the small plant ($300,000), should the decision be to build the large plant? Perhaps, but not necessarily. Notice that the range of outcomes is greater if the large plant is built, with the actual *NPV*s (column 6 in Figure B11–3 minus the investment cost) varying from $3.8 million to *minus* $3.6 million. However, a range of only $600,000 to minus $600,000 exists for the small plant. Since the required investments for

Figure B11–3
Illustrative Decision Tree

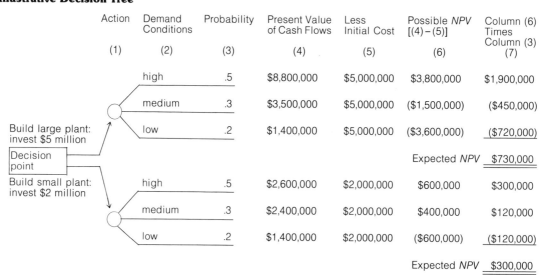

Action (1)	Demand Conditions (2)	Probability (3)	Present Value of Cash Flows (4)	Less Initial Cost (5)	Possible *NPV* [(4)−(5)] (6)	Column (6) Times Column (3) (7)
	high	.5	$8,800,000	$5,000,000	$3,800,000	$1,900,000
	medium	.3	$3,500,000	$5,000,000	($1,500,000)	($450,000)
Build large plant: invest $5 million	low	.2	$1,400,000	$5,000,000	($3,600,000)	($720,000)
Decision point					Expected *NPV*	$730,000
Build small plant: invest $2 million	high	.5	$2,600,000	$2,000,000	$600,000	$300,000
	medium	.3	$2,400,000	$2,000,000	$400,000	$120,000
	low	.2	$1,400,000	$2,000,000	($600,000)	($120,000)
					Expected *NPV*	$300,000

Note: The figures in column 4 are the annual cash flows from operations—sales revenues minus cash operating costs—discounted at an appropriate rate. For reasons explained later in the chapter appendices, the riskless rate of interest is usually the appropriate discount rate. Variations of *NPV*s at the riskless rate are then analyzed to provide insights into the appropriate risk-adjusted discount rate for each alternative, and these rates are used, together with expected cash flows, to determine a true expected *NPV* for the alternatives.

the two plants are not the same, we must examine the coefficients of variation of the net present value possibilities in order to determine which alternative actually entails the greater risk. The coefficient of variation for the large plant's present value is 4.3, while that for the small plant is only 1.5.[6] Thus, risk is greater if the decision is to build the large plant.

The decision-maker could take account of the risk differentials in a variety of ways. He could assign utility values to the cash flows given in column 4 of Figure B11−3, thus stating column 6 in terms of expected utility. He would then choose the plant size that provided the greatest utility. Alternatively, he could use the certainty equivalent or risk-adjusted discount rate methods in calculating the present values given in column 4. The plant that offered the larger risk-adjusted net present value would then be the optimal choice.

The decision tree illustrated in Figure B11−3 is quite simple; in actual use, the trees are frequently far more complex and involve a number of sequential decision points. As an example of a more complex tree, consider Figure B11−4. The boxes numbered 1, 2, and so on, are *decision points*, that is, instances when the firm must choose between alternatives, while the circles represent the possible actual outcomes, one of which will follow these decisions. At decision point 1, the firm has three choices: to invest $3 million in a large plant, to invest $1.3 million in a small plant, or to spend $100,000 on market research. If the large plant is built, the firm follows the upper branch, and its position has been fixed—it can only hope that demand will be high. If it builds the small plant, then it follows the lower branch. If demand is low, no further action is required. If demand is high, decision point 2 is reached, and the firm must either do nothing or else expand the plant at a cost of another $2.2 million. (Thus, if it obtains a large plant through expansion, the cost is $500,000 greater than if it had built the large plant in the first place.)

If the decision at point 1 is to pay $100,000 for more information, the firm moves to the center branch. The research modifies the firm's information about potential demand. Initially, the probabilities were 70 percent for high demand and 30 percent for low demand. The research survey will show either favorable (positive) or unfavorable (negative) demand prospects: If they are positive, we assume that the probability for high final demand will be 87 percent and that for low demand will be 13 percent; if the research yields negative results, the odds on high

---

6. Using Equation 11−3 and the data on possible returns in Figure B11−3 the standard deviation of returns for the larger plant is found to be $3.155 million, and that for the smaller one is $458,260. Dividing each of these standard deviations by the expected returns for their respective plant size gives the coefficients of variation.

final demand are only 35 percent and those for low demand are 65 percent. These results will, of course, influence the firm's decision whether to build a large or a small plant.

If the firm builds a large plant and demand is high, then sales and profits will be large. However, if it builds a large plant and demand is weak, sales will be low and losses, rather than profits, will be incurred. On the other hand, if it builds a small plant and demand is high, sales and profits will be lower than they could have been had a large plant been built, but the chances of losses in the event of low demand will be eliminated. Thus, the decision to build the large plant is riskier than the one to build the small plant. The decision to commission the research is, in effect, an expenditure to reduce the degree of uncertainty in the decision on which plant to build; the research provides additional information on the probability of high versus low demand, thus lowering the level of uncertainty.

The decision tree in Figure B11–4 is incomplete in that no dollar outcomes (or utility values) are assigned to the various situations. If this step were taken, along the lines shown in the last two columns of Figure B11–3, then expected values could be obtained for each of the alternative actions. These expected values could then be used to aid the decision-maker in choosing among the alternatives.

Computer Simulation

The concepts embodied in decision tree analysis can be extended to computer simulation. To illustrate the technique, let us consider a proposal to build a new textile plant. The cost of the plant is not known for certain, although it is expected to run about $150 million. If no problems are encountered, the cost can be as low as $125 million, while an unfortunate series of events—strikes, unprojected increases in materials costs, technical problems, and the like—could result in the investment outlay running as high as $225 million.

Revenues from the new facility, which will operate for many years, will depend on population growth and income in the region, competition, developments in synthetic fabrics research, and textile import quotas. Operating costs will depend on production efficiency, materials and labor cost trends, and the like. Since both sales revenues and operating costs are uncertain, annual profits are also uncertain.

Assuming that probability distributions can be assigned to each of the major cost and revenue determinants, a computer program can be constructed to simulate what is likely to happen. In effect, the computer selects one value at random from each of the relevant distributions, combines it with other values selected from the other distributions, and produces an estimated profit and net present value or rate of return on

Figure B11-4
Decision Tree with
Multiple Decision
Points

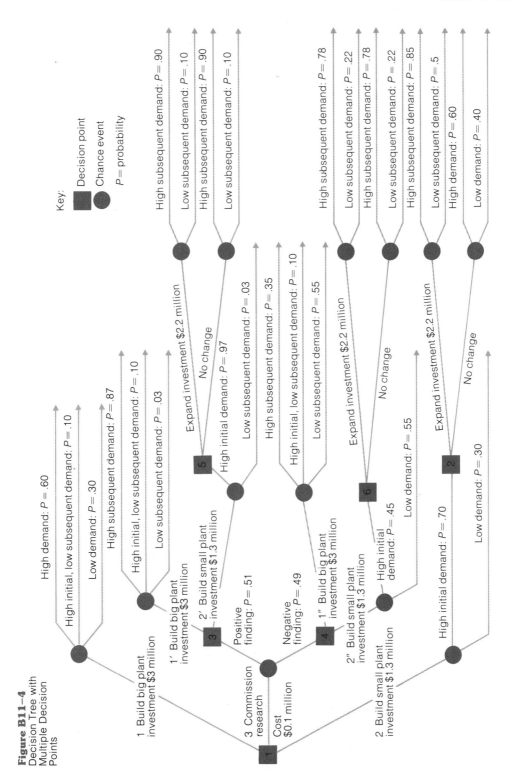

Key:

■ Decision point

● Chance event

P = probability

Figure B11-5
Simulation for
Investment Planning

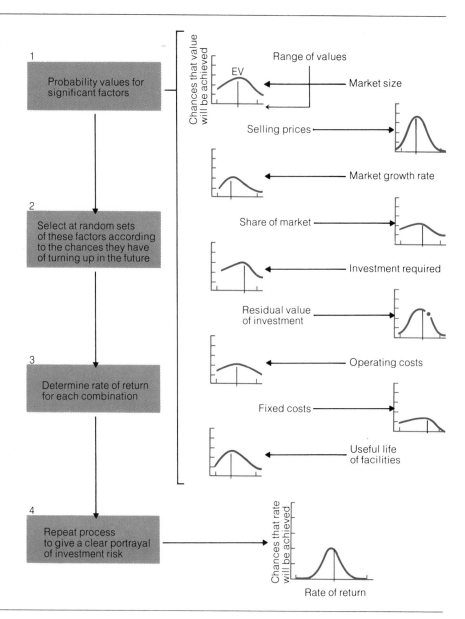

investment.[7] This particular profit and rate of return occur, of course, only for the particular combination of values selected during this trial. The computer goes on to select other sets of values and to compute other profits and rates of return repeatedly, for perhaps several hundred trials. A count is kept of the number of times each rate of return is computed, and when the computer runs are completed, the frequency with which the various rates of return occurred can be plotted as a frequency distribution.

The procedure is illustrated in Figures B11−5 and B11−6.[8] Figure B11−5 is a flowchart outlining the simulation procedure described above, while Figure B11−6 illustrates the frequency distribution of rates of return generated by such a simulation for two alternative projects, X and Y, each with an expected cost of $20 million. The expected rate of return on investment X is 15 percent, and that of investment Y is 20 percent. However, these are only the *average* rates of return generated by the computer; simulated rates range from −10 percent to +45 percent for investment Y and from 5 to 25 percent for investment X. The standard deviation generated for X is only 4 percentage points—68 percent of the computer runs had rates of return between 11 and 19 percent—while that for Y is 12 percentage points. Clearly, then, investment Y is riskier than investment X.

The computer simulation has provided us with both an extimate of

Figure B11-6
Expected Rates of
Return on Investments
X and Y

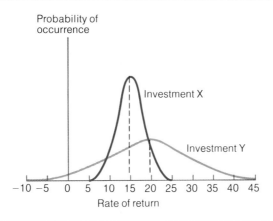

7. If the variables are not independent, then conditional probabilities must be employed. For example, if demand is weak, then both sales in units and sales prices are likely to be low, and these interrelationships must be taken into account in the simulation.

8. Figure B11−5 is adapted from Hertz, *Treasurer's Handbook*, Chapter 18.

the expected returns on the two projects and an estimate of their relative risks. A decision about which alternative should be chosen can now be made, perhaps by using the risk-adjusted discount rate method or perhaps in a judgmental, informal manner by the decision-maker.

However, computer simulation is not always feasible for risk analysis. The technique involves obtaining probability distributions about a number of variables—investment outlays, unit sales, product prices, input prices, asset lives, and so on—and a fair amount of programming and machine-time costs. Therefore, full-scale simulation is not generally worthwhile except for large and expensive projects, such as major plant expansions or new-product decisions. In those cases, however, when a firm is deciding whether to accept a major undertaking involving millions of dollars, computer simulation can provide valuable insights into the relative merits of alternative strategies.

Problems

B11–1. The financial vice-president for the Atkins Manufacturing Company is analyzing the potential of a $1,500 investment in a new machine. His estimate of the cash-flow distribution for the three-year life of the machine is shown below:

Period 1		Period 2		Period 3	
Probability	Cash Flow	Probability	Cash Flow	Probability	Cash Flow
.10	$800	.10	$800	.20	$1,200
.20	600	.30	700	.50	900
.40	400	.40	600	.20	600
.30	200	.20	500	.10	300

Probability distributions are assumed to be independent. Treasury bills are yielding 5 percent. To evaluate the investment, the vice-president has asked you to make the following calculations:
a. The expected net present value of the project.
b. The standard deviation about the expected value.
c. The probability that the net present value will be zero or less (assume the distribution is normal and continuous).
d. The probability that the net present value will be greater than zero.
e. The probability that the net present value will at least equal the mean.
f. The profitability index of the expected value.
g. The probability that the profitability index will be (i) less than 1 or (ii) greater than 2.

B11–2. The Eastern Tool and Die Company is considering an investment in a project that requires an initial outlay of $3,000 with an expected net cash flow generated over three periods as follows:

Period 1		Period 2		Period 3	
Probability	Cash Flow	Probability	Cash Flow	Probability	Cash Flow
.10	800	.10	800	.20	800
.20	1,000	.30	1,000	.50	1,000
.40	1,500	.40	1,500	.20	1,500
.30	2,000	.20	2,000	.10	2,000

a. What is the expected net present value of this project? (Assume that the probability distributions are independent and that Treasury bills are yielding 5 percent.)

b. Calculate the standard deviation about the expected value.

c. Find the probability that the net present value will be zero or less. (Assume that the distribution is normal and continuous.) What is the probability that the NPV will be greater than zero?

d. Calculate the profitability index of the expected value. What is the probability that the index will be (i) less than 1 and (ii) greater than 2?

B11–3. The Parker Company has the following probability distributions for net cash flows during the first year for a potential project:

Probability	Cash Flow
.50	$100
.30	200
.20	300

Performance of similar projects in the past has indicated that the net cash flow distributions are not independent. The level of demand and the related net cash flow returns experienced in period 1 influence the achievements in period 2 in the following way:

If year 1 = $100, the distribution for year 2 is:

.70	$100
.20	200
.10	300

If year 1 = $200, the distribution for year 2 is:

.10	$100
.60	200
.30	300

If year 1 = $300, the distribution for year 2 is:

.10	$100
.20	200
.50	300
.20	400

a. If $200 is earned in year 1, what is the probability that the second year's earnings will be $200 or less?
b. What is the probability that earnings for year 1 will be $100 and for year 2, $200?
c. What is the probability that the Parker Company will earn more than $300 on this project in the second year?
d. If earnings for the first year are $300, what is the probability that $200 or more will be earned the second year?
e. What is the probability that Parker will earn at least $600 over the life of the project?

Appendix C to Chapter 11
Abandonment Value [1]

At some future time, usually because of some unforeseen problems, it may become more profitable to abandon a project, even though its economic life has not yet ended, than to continue its operation. Taking this possibility into consideration in the capital budgeting process may increase the project's expected net present value and reduce its standard deviation of returns. In this discussion we first show how to include *abandonment value* in the analysis when making accept-reject decisions, and then we look at criteria for actually abandoning a project after it has been accepted.

The analysis required for taking abandonment value into account in evaluating an investment project involves no principles beyond those already set forth. However, because it does represent an important aspect of the decision process, it is useful to have a decision model that includes abandonment value in its framework. The principles involved may best be conveyed through a specific example illustrating the role of abandonment value in evaluating projects under uncertainty.

The Palmer Corporation has invested $300 in new machinery with expected cash flows over two years. This is shown in Table C11–1.

Table C11–1 **Expected Cash Flows**	Year 1		Year 2	
	Cash Flow	Initial Probability P (1)	Cash Flow	Conditional Probability P (2|1)
	$200	(.3)	$100	(.3)
			200	(.5)
			300	(.2)
	300	(.4)	200	(.3)
			300	(.5)
			400	(.2)
	400	(.3)	300	(.3)
			400	(.4)
			500	(.3)

1. For an early treatment of abandonment value, see Alexander A. Robichek and James C. Van Horne, "Abandonment Value and Capital Budgeting," *Journal of Finance* 22, no. 4 (December 1967), pp. 577–90.

Table C11–2
Calculation of Expected Net Present Value

Year 1			Year 2			Probability Analysis				
Cash Flow	PV Factor	Present Value	Cash Flow	PV Factor	Present Value	Present Value of Total Cash Flow	Initial Probability	Conditional Probability	Joint Probability	Expected Value
(1)	(2)	(3) = (1 × 2)	(4)	(5)	(6) = (4 × 5)	(7) = (3 + 6)	(8)	(9)	(10) = (8 × 9)	(11) = (7 × 10)
$200	.893	179	$100	.797	80	$259	.3	.3	.09	$ 23
			200	.797	159	338		.5	.15	51
			300	.797	239	418		.2	.06	25
300	.893	268	200	.797	159	427	.4	.3	.12	51
			300	.797	239	507		.5	.20	101
			400	.797	319	587		.2	.08	47
400	.893	357	300	.797	239	596	.3	.3	.09	54
			400	.797	319	676		.4	.12	81
			500	.797	398	755		.3	.09	68
									1.00	$501

Expected present value = $501
Expected net present value = $201

There are two sets of probabilities associated with the project: The initial probabilities should be interpreted as probabilities of particular cash flows from the first year only; the conditional probabilities are the probabilities of particular cash flows in the second year, given that a specific outcome has occurred in the first year. Thus, the results in the second year are *conditional* upon the results of the first year. If high profits occur in the first year, chances are that the second year will also bring high profits. To obtain the probability that a particular first-year outcome and a particular second-year outcome will both occur, we must multiply the initial probability by the conditional probability to obtain what is termed the *joint probability*.

These concepts are applied to the data of Table C11–1 to construct Table C11–2. The project is not expected to have any returns after the second year. The firm's cost of capital is 12 percent. To indicate the role of abandonment value, we first calculate the expected net present value of the investment and its expected standard deviation without considering abandonment value. This calculation is made in Table C11–2, where we find the expected *NPV* to be $201.

Next, in Table C11–3, we calculate the standard deviation of the future cash flows, finding $\sigma = \$145$.

Table C11–3 Calculation of Standard Deviation	Exp. NPV^*	$- NPV$	$=$ Deviations	Squared Deviations*	$\times$ Joint Probability	$=$ Amount
	(41)	201	(242)	58,564	.09	5,271
	38	201	(163)	26,569	.15	3,985
	118	201	(83)	6,889	.06	413
	127	201	(74)	5,476	.12	657
	207	201	6	36	.20	7
	286	201	85	7,225	.08	578
	296	201	95	9,025	.09	812
	375	201	174	30,276	.12	3,633
	455	201	254	64,516	.09	5,806
					1.00	21,162

Expected standard deviation $= \sigma = (21,162)^{1/2} = \$145$

*Value from column 7, Table C11–2, minus $300 cost (some rounding differences).

The decision-maker can expand this analysis to take abandonment value into account. Suppose the abandonment value of the project at the end of the first year is estimated to be $250. This is the amount that can be obtained by liquidating the project after the first year, and the $250 is independent of actual first-year results. If the project is abandoned after one year, then the $250 will replace any second-year returns. In other words, if the project is abandoned at the end of year 1, then year 1 returns will increase by $250 and year 2 returns will be zero. The present value of this estimated $250 abandonment value is, therefore, compared with the expected present values of the cash flows that would occur during the second year if abandonment did not take place. But to make the comparison valid, we must use the second year flows based on the conditional probabilities only, rather than the joint probabilities that were used in the preceding analysis. This calculation is shown in Table C11 – 4.

Table C11–4 Expected Present Values of Cash Flows During the Second Year	Cash Flow	PV Factor	PV	Conditional Probability		Expected Present Value
	$100	.797	80	.3		$ 24
	200	.797	159	.5		80
	300	.797	239	.2		48
					Branch total	$152
	200	.797	159	.3		$ 48
	300	.797	239	.5		120
	400	.797	319	.2		64
					Branch total	$232
	300	.797	239	.3		$ 72
	400	.797	319	.4		128
	500	.797	398	.3		119
					Branch total	$319

We next compare the present value of the $250 abandonment value, $250 × .893 = $223, with the branch expected present values for each of the three possible cash flow patterns (branches) depicted above. If the $223 present value of abandonment exceeds one or more of the expected present values of the possible branches of cash flows, taking abandonment value into account will improve the indicated returns from the project. This alternative calculation is presented in Table C11–5 to show expected present values with abandonment taken into consideration, and the new calculation of the standard deviation is shown in Table C11–6.

We may now compare the results when abandonment value is taken into account with the results when it is not considered. Including abandonment value in the calculations increases the expected net present value from $201 to $223, or by about 10 percent; and it reduces the expected standard deviation of returns from $145 to $118 and the coefficients of variation from .72 to .53. Thus, for this problem, abandonment value improves the attractiveness of the investment.

**Table C11–5
Expected Net
Present Value with
Abandonment
Value Included**

Year 1 Cash Flow	× Factor	= PV	Year 2 Cash Flow	× Factor	= PV	Present Value of Total Cash Flow	× Joint Proba-bility	= Expected Value
$450	.893	$402	0	.797	0	$402	.30	$121
			200	.797	$159	427	.12	51
300	.893	268	300	.797	239	507	.20	101
			400	.797	319	587	.08	47
			300	.797	239	596	.09	54
400	.893	357	400	.797	319	676	.12	81
			500	.797	398	755	.09	68
							1.00	

Expected present value = $523

Expected net present value = 223

**Table C11–6
Calculation of
Standard Deviation
for Net Cash Flow
with Abandonment
Value Included**

NPV_s	− NPV	= Deviation	Deviation^2	× Joint Probability	= Amount
102	223	(121)	14,641	.30	4,392
127	223	(96)	9,216	.12	1,106
207	223	(16)	256	.20	51
287	223	64	4,096	.08	328
296	223	73	5,329	.09	480
376	223	153	23,409	.12	2,809
455	223	232	53,824	.09	4,844
					14,010

Expected standard deviation = $(14,010)^{1/2}$ = $118

Abandonment value is important in another aspect of financial deci-sion-making: the reevaluation of projects in succeeding years after they have been undertaken. The decision whether to continue the project or to abandon it sometime during its life depends upon which branch occurs during each time period. For example, suppose that during year 1 the cash flow actually obtained was $200. Then the three possibilities associated with year 2 are the three that were conditionally dependent upon a $200 outcome in year 1. The other six probabilities for year 2, which were considered in the initial evaluation, were conditional upon other first-year outcomes and, thus, are no longer relevant. A calcula-tion (Table C11–7) is then made of the second-year net cash flows, discounted back one year.

At the end of the first year the abandonment value is $250. This is compared with the expected present value of the second-year net cash flow series, discounted one year. This value is determined to be $171, so the abandonment value of $250 exceeds the net present value of returns for the second year. Therefore, the project should be abandoned at the

Table C11–7					Discounted
Calculation of				Probability	Expected
Expected Net Cash	Cash Flow $\times$ PV Factor $=$		PV	$\times$ Factor	$=$ Cash Flow
Flow for Second					
Period When $200	$100	.893	$ 89	.3	$ 27
Was Earned During	200	.893	179	.5	90
the First Year	300	.893	268	.2	54
			Expected present value $=$ $171		

end of the first year. Note that it is not necessary to compare the standard deviations, because with abandonment the standard deviation of returns is zero, which is certainly lower than the standard deviation of any set of uncertain second-year cash flows.

In summary, it is sometimes advantageous to abandon a project even though the net present value of continued operation is positive. The basic reason is that the present value of abandonment after a shorter time may actually be greater than the present value of continued operation. For example, consider a truck with two years of remaining useful life. The present value of continued use is, say, $900, but the current market value of the truck is $1,000. Clearly, if the proceeds from the sale can be invested to earn at least the applicable cost of capital, the better decision would be to sell the truck.

Further Developments in Abandonment Decision Rules[2]

The traditional abandonment decision rule is that the project should be abandoned in the first year that abandonment value exceeds the present value of remaining expected cash flows from continued operation. More recently it has become evident that this decision rule may not result in the optimal abandonment decision. Abandonment at a later date may result in an even greater net present value. Returning to our example of the truck, there is one option that has not been considered: that is, to operate the truck for another year with a present value of $500, and then abandon it, with the present value of abandonment in a year being $600. Thus, the present value of this alternative is $1,100. The truck should be used for one year and then sold.

The optimal abandonment decision rule is to determine the combination of remaining operating cash flows and future abandonment that has the maximum expected net present value. This decision rule is, un-

---

2. See E. A. Dyl and H. W. Long, "Abandonment Value and Capital Budgeting: Comment," *Journal of Finance* (March 1969), pp. 88–95; "Reply" by A. A. Robichek and J. C. Van Horne, pp. 96–97; O. Maurice Joy, "Abandonment Values and Abandonment Decisions: A Clarification," *Journal of Finance* (September 1976), pp. 1225–28.

fortunately, difficult to implement, especially when the project life is long and there are numerous opportunities for abandonment over time. If a piece of equipment can be used for 20 years or abandoned at the end of any year then 20 different net present value calculations would be required to determine the optimum pattern, resulting in maximum expected net present value.

It is argued that this approach is too cumbersome and that all that is required is to find that there is at least one pattern of cash flows that yields an expected net present value greater than the value of abandonment. Thus the rule becomes an accept-reject decision; continue to operate the project so long as expected present value of continued operation and abandonment at any later period is greater than the value of abandonment now. There is no need ever to determine the maximum expected net present value. Furthermore, since it is impossible to predict accurately future abandonment value, whatever the expected net present value is, it will surely be inaccurate.

The accept-reject decision has one shortcoming, however; it does not provide a means of selecting between mutually exclusive investments or of making capital rationing decisions. To return to our truck example a final time, we have shown that the present value is $1,100, when the truck is operated for another year. Using the accept-reject rule we would continue to operate the truck. But suppose a truck could be leased for $1,000 for one year and would produce cash flows worth $1,200 at net present value. If only one truck is required (mutually exclusive choice decision) or the only source of the $1,000 to lease the truck is the sale of the old truck (capital rationing) then the value to the firm is maximized if the truck is sold, and the new truck leased.

It is evident that both rules (the maximum net present value rule, and the accept-reject rule) have merit. Maximum net present value should be employed whenever capital rationing or mutually exclusive choices are involved. Accept-reject can be used to reduce the cumbersomeness of the problem whenever one decision is independent of all others. (Problem C11–3 provides an opportunity to explore both of these approaches.)

Problems

C11–1. In its first year of operation at Delta Steel Corporation, a new electric furnace employed in the scrap steel division produced a savings of $400 a month over the basic oxygen furnace. The scrap steel division at Delta Steel is quite old and inefficient. Before the new electric furnace was installed, management estimated that the company could save $4,980 a year if the scrap-melting division was eliminated. Management must decide what action to take for the second year. The new

furnace has no scrap value. The required rate of return for the firm is 6
percent.

a. If the savings in the second year are equal to those obtained in the
first year, should the scrap division be abandoned?

b. What decision would be reached if the cost analysis of savings per
month with the electric furnace for the second year is:

Probability	Amount
.05	$200
.15	300
.50	400
.20	500
.10	600

C11–2. A firm has invested $4,000 in automated machinery with the probable
net cash flows over two years as follows:

Year 1		Year 2	
Net Cash Flow	Initial Probability P (1)	Net Cash Flow	Conditional Probability P (2/1)
		$2,500	(.3)
$3,000	(.3)	3,000	(.5)
		3,500	(.2)
		3,000	(.3)
4,000	(.4)	4,000	(.5)
		5,000	(.2)
		4,000	(.3)
5,000	(.3)	5,000	(.4)
		6,000	(.3)

The firm's cost of capital is 12 percent.

a. Calculate the expected net present value of the investment and standard deviation without considering abandonment value.

b. If the abandonment value at the end of year 1 is $2,800, calculate the
new expected net present value and standard deviation of the project.

c. During period 1, the cash flow actually experienced was $3,000.
Should the project now be abandoned or should it be continued
through period 2?

C11–3. The following investment decision is being considered by Citrus
Farms. For $7,000 the company can acquire ownership of ten acres of
15-year-old orange trees and a 15-year lease on the land. The productive life of an orange tree is divided into stages as follows:

Stage	Age of Trees	Expected Annual Profit from 10 Acres
Peak	16–20 years	$1,000
Adult	21–25 years	900
Mature	26–30 years	800

There is a market for decorative orange trees. Suppliers will buy trees and remove them according to a schedule based on age of the tree. Expected prices that could be obtained for the ten-acre total are: $9,000 at end of age 20, $12,000 at age 25, and $8,000 at age 30.

a. Citrus Farms has a 10 percent cost of capital. What is the present value of each alternative? Since the land and anything on it will belong to the lessor in 15 years, assume that once the trees are harvested the land will not be replanted by Citrus.

b. As an alternative to this investment, Citrus can use the $7,000 to buy a new orange sorting machine. The machine would reduce sorting expense by $1,300 a year for 15 years. Which investment would you make? Why? Assume all other investment opportunities for the next 15 years will earn the cost of capital.

c. In the tenth year you discover that everyone else with 25-year-old trees has sold them. As a consequence, the price you can get for your trees is only $8,000. Since so many trees have been sold for decoration, small orange crops are expected for the next five years. As a result, the price will be higher. Your acreage will yield $1,200 a year. The selling price of your trees in another five years is expected to still be depressed to $6,000. What should you do?

d. What was the net present value of your actual investment over the 15-year period given the developments in part C?

e. What would have been the outcome if you had sold the trees in year 10 for $8,000?

Appendix D to Chapter 11
Some Implications of
Portfolio Theory:
The Capital Asset Pricing Model

Effects of Diversification: Some Illustrations with a Two-Asset Portfolio

The concepts of portfolio diversification discussed in Chapter 11 are here further clarified by some additional illustrations. Assume that two investment securities, A and B, are available, and that we have a specific amount of money to invest in these securities. We can allocate our funds between the securities in any proportion. Security A has an expected rate of return $E(k_A) = 5$ percent and a standard deviation of expected returns $\sigma_A = 4$ percent; for security B, the expected return $E(k_B) = 8$ percent and the standard deviation $\sigma_B = 10$ percent.

Our ultimate task is to determine the optimal portfolio, that is, the optimal percentage of our available funds to invest in each security. Intermediate steps include (1) determining the attainable set of portfolios, (2) determining the efficient set from among the attainable set, and (3) selecting the best portfolio from the efficient set.

There is not yet sufficient information to select the best portfolio — we need data on the degree of correlation between the two securities' returns, ρ_{AB}, in order to construct the attainable and efficient portfolios. Let us assume three different degrees of correlation: $\rho_{AB} = +1.0$, $\rho_{AB} = 0$, and $\rho_{AB} = -1.0$, and then develop the portfolios' expected returns $E(k_p)$ and standard deviations of returns σ_p for each case.

To calculate $E(k_p)$ and σ_p, we use Equations D11–1 and D11–2:

$$E(k_p) = w\, E(k_A) + (1 - w)\, E(k_B), \tag{D11-1}$$

and

$$\sigma_p = \sqrt{w^2\, \sigma_A^2 + (1 - w)^2\, \sigma_B^2 + 2w(1 - w)\, \rho_{AB}\, \sigma_A\, \sigma_B}. \tag{D11-2}$$

We may now substitute in the given values for k_A and k_B, then solve Equation D11–1 for $E(k_p)$ at different values of w. For example, when w equals .75, then

$$E(k_p) = .75\ (5\%) + .25\ (8\%) = 5.75\%.$$

Similarly, we can substitute in the given values for σ_A, σ_B, and ρ_{AB}, then solve Equation D11–2 for σ_p at different values of w. For example, when $\rho_{AB} = 0$ and $w = 75$ percent, then

$$\sigma_p = \sqrt{(.5625)(16) + (.0625)(100) + 2(.75)(.25)(0)(4)(10)}$$
$$= \sqrt{9 + 6.25} = \sqrt{15.25} = 3.9\%.$$

The equations can be solved for other values for w and for the three cases, $\rho_{AB} = +1.0$, 0, and -1.0; Table D11–1 gives the solution values for $w = 100$ percent, 75 percent, 50 percent, 25 percent, and 0 percent, and Figure D11–1 gives plots of $E(k_p)$, σ_p, and the attainable set of portfolios for each case. In both the table and the graphs, note the following points:

Figure D11–1
Illustrations of Portfolio
Returns, Risk, and the
Attainable Set of
Portfolios

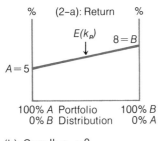
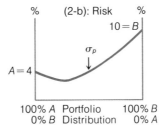
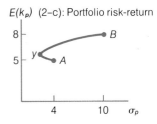

(a) Case I: $\rho_{AB} = +1.0$

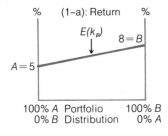
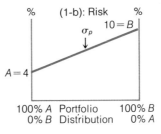
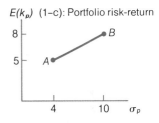

(b) Case II: $\rho_{AB} = 0$

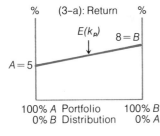
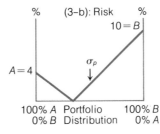
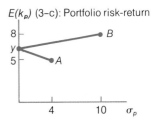

(c) Case III: $\rho_{AB} = -1.0$

1. $E(k_p)$ is a linear function of w, and the graphs of $E(k_p)$ are identical in the three cases because $E(k_p)$ is independent of the correlation between securities A and B.
2. σ_p is linear in Case I, where $\rho_{AB} = +1.0$; it is nonlinear in Case II; and Case III of the figure shows that risk can be completely diversified away when $\rho_{AB} = -1.0$.[1]

Table D11–1
$E(k_p)$ and σ_p Under Various Assumptions

Percent of Portfolio in Security A (value of w)	Percent of Portfolio in Security B (value of $1 - w$)	$\rho_{AB} = +1.0$		$\rho_{AB} = 0$		$\rho_{AB} = -1.0$	
		$E(k_p)$	σ_p	$E(k_p)$	σ_p	$E(k_p)$	σ_p
100	0	5.00	4.0	5.00	4.0	5.00	4.0
75	25	5.75	5.5	5.75	3.9	5.75	0.5
50	50	6.50	7.0	6.50	5.1	6.50	3.0
25	75	7.25	8.5	7.25	7.6	7.25	6.5
0	100	8.00	10.0	8.00	10.0	8.00	10.0

3. Panels (1-c), (2-c), and (3-c) give the attainable set of portfolios consisting of securities A and B. With only two securities, the attainable set is a curve or line rather than an area. If more securities were added, then the shaded area shown in Figure 11–8 would develop.
4. That part of the attainable set from Y to B in cases 2 and 3 is efficient; that part from A to Y is inefficient. In case 1, all parts of the attainable set are efficient.

Figure D11–2
Attainable Sets of
Portfolios for the Three
Cases

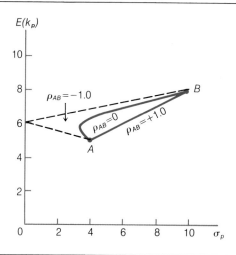

Figure D11–2 consolidates the attainable sets for the three cases to facilitate comparison. The most interesting aspect of the graph is the clear demonstration that the lower the value of ρ_{AB}, the better the portfolios that can be constructed. For any specified rate of return as shown on the horizontal axis, σ_p is lowest for $\rho_{AB} = -1$, and highest for $\rho_{AB} = +1$, while the rate of return that can be achieved at any specified degree of risk is highest for $\rho_{AB} = -1$, and lowest for $\rho_{AB} = +1$ (except for the point B at which all the curves converge, since the total investment is 100 percent in B).

Obviously, only one correlation coefficient can exist between securities A and B; assume that the actual ρ_{AB} is 0. It now remains to select the best portfolio (that is, the percentage of the total funds to be invested in each security). This decision depends upon the individual investor's risk aversion as represented by his risk-return indifference curves. In Figure D11–3 we show the attainable set of portfolios for $\rho_{AB} = 0$ from Figure D11–2 and the indifference curves for Mr. A and Mr. B taken from Figure 11–11 in Chapter 11. Given these possibilities, Mr. B would choose a portfolio providing an expected rate of return of 7.2 percent with $\sigma_p = 7.3$, while Mr. A would choose a portfolio with $E(k_p) =$

Figure D11–3
Selecting the Optimal
Portfolio

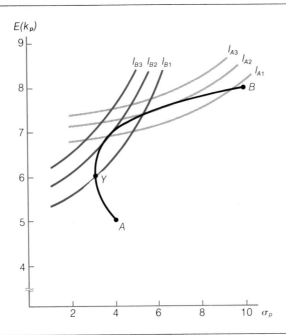

6.2 and $\sigma_p = 4.2$. Mr. A's portfolio would consist of 60 percent security A and 40 percent security B, while Mr. B's portfolio would contain 27 percent security A and 73 percent security B.[2]

Relationship Between Correlation and Expected Rates of Return

If a security or other asset has returns that are less than perfectly correlated with the returns on other assets, then combining this new asset with other assets will produce favorable portfolio effects. Further, the lower the degree of correlation, the larger the portfolio effects. Now suppose you hold a portfolio of securities with an expected return $E(k_p)$ = 8 percent and $\sigma_p = 6$ percent. You hear of a new security Z that has an expected return of 8 percent, $\sigma_z = 6$ percent, and the correlation of Z's returns with those on your present portfolio is -0.5.

If you sell off part of your present portfolio and use the proceeds to purchase security Z, your expected rate of return will remain at 8 percent, but your portfolio's risk will decline, so you would make this shift. If others have favorable portfolio effects from security Z, they too will seek to buy it, and the collective action will tend to drive Z's price up and its expected yield down. We see, then, that a security's degree of correlation with other securities influences the rate of return on the security in the marketplace. This aspect of portfolio theory is vitally important in analyzing the riskiness of a firm's securities, hence its cost of capital. Accordingly, we shall return to portfolio theory in Chapter 19, where it is extended and used to obtain an index of a firm's risk.

Security Risk versus Portfolio Risk

An empirical study by Wagner and Lau can be used to demonstrate the effects of diversification.[3] They divided a sample of 200 NYSE stocks into six subgroups based on the Standard and Poor's quality ratings as of June 1960. Then they constructed portfolios from each of the subgroups, using 1 to 20 randomly selected securities and applying equal weights to each security. For the first subgroup (A + quality stocks), Table D11–2 can be used to summarize some effects of diversification. As the number of securities in the portfolio increases, the standard deviation of portfolio returns decreases, but at a decreasing rate, with further reductions in risk being relatively small after about ten securi-

---

2. These percentages can be determined by Equation D11–1, by simply seeing what percentage of the two securities is consistent with $E(k_p) = 7.2\%$ and 6.2%.

3. W. H. Wagner and S. C. Lau, "The Effect of Diversification on Risk," *Financial Analysts' Journal* (November–December 1971), pp. 48–53.

Table D11–2 **Reduction in Portfolio Risk Through Diversification**	No. of Securities in Portfolio	Standard Deviation of Portfolio Returns (σ_p) (% per month)	Correlation with Return on Market Index[a]
	1	7.0	.54
	2	5.0	.63
	3	4.8	.75
	4	4.6	.77
	5	4.6	.79
	10	4.2	.85
	15	4.0	.88
	20	3.9	.89

[a]The "market" here refers to an unweighted index of all NYSE stocks.

ties are included in the portfolio. More will be said about the third column of the table, correlation with the market, shortly.

These data indicate that even well-diversified portfolios possess some level of risk that cannot be diversified away. Indeed, this is exactly the case, and the general situation is illustrated graphically in Figure D11–4. The risk of the portfolio, σ_p, has been divided into two parts. The part that can be reduced through diversification is defined as *unsystematic* risk, while the part that cannot be eliminated is defined as *systematic*, or market-related, risk.[4]

Now refer back to the third column of Table D11–2. Notice that as the number of securities in each portfolio increases, and as the standard deviation decreases, the correlation between the return on the portfolio and the return on the market index increases. Thus, a broadly diversi-

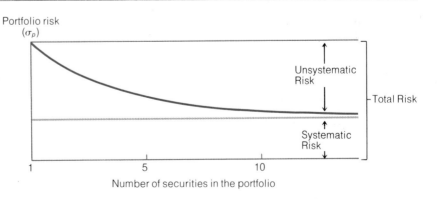

Figure D11–4
Reduction of Risk
through Diversification

4. In the real world, it is extremely difficult to find stocks with zero or negative correlations; hence, some risk is inherent in any stock portfolio.

fied portfolio is highly correlated with the market, and its risk (1) is largely systematic and (2) arises because of general market movements.

We can summarize our analysis of risk to this point as follows:

1. The risk of a portfolio can be measured by the standard deviation of its rate of return, σ_p.
2. The risk of an individual security is its contribution to the portfolio's risk.
3. The standard deviation of a stock's return, σ_j, is the relevant measure of risk for an undiversified investor who holds only stock j.
4. A stock's standard deviation reflects both unsystematic risk that can be eliminated by diversification and systematic or market-related risk; only the systematic component of security risk is relevant for the well-diversified investor, so only this element is reflected in the risk premium.
5. A stock's systematic risk is measured by its volatility in relation to the general market. This factor is analyzed next.

Efficient versus Inefficient Portfolios

Professor Sharpe derived the following relationship between total risk and its components, unsystematic (diversifiable) and systematic risk:[5]

$$(\sigma_j^2) = (\sigma_j^s)^2 + (\sigma_j^u)^2 \qquad \text{(D11-3)}$$

where σ_j = standard deviation of k_j
σ_j^s = security j's systematic risk ($= b_j \sigma_M$)
σ_j^u = security j's unsystematic risk.

These relationships apply to portfolios as well:

$$(\sigma_p)^2 = (\sigma_p^s)^2 + (\sigma_p^u)^2 \qquad \text{(D11-4)}$$

where σ_p = standard deviation of rate of return on portfolio
σ_p^s = portfolio's systematic risk
σ_p^u = portfolio's unsystematic risk.

The relationship between systematic risk and volatility is the same for securities and portfolios. Thus,

$$\sigma_p^s = b_p \sigma_M \qquad \text{(D11-5)}$$

Efficient portfolios have no unsystematic risk. Thus a portfolio with some unsystematic risk that has not been diversified away is inefficient. Individual securities are likely to include some unsystematic risk so they are inefficient portfolios.

Equation D11-3 divides the variance of stock j's return into two

5. William F. Sharpe, *Portfolio Theory and Capital Markets* (New York: McGraw-Hill, 1970), pp. 96-97.

parts, (1) the systematic risk component, $[\sigma^s]^2$, which is $(b_j\sigma_M)^2$ — its beta coefficient and the variability of market returns, and (2) the unsystematic residual risk component, $(\sigma_j^u)^2$. The unsystematic component can be eliminated through diversification, but the systematic component can only be reduced by altering the firm's correlation with the "market," that is, by attempting to change its beta coefficient through a change in investment or financial policy.

The logical conclusion of all this is that if investors think in portfolio terms then they should not worry about the unsystematic risk because it can be diversified away. Thus, investors should consider only systematic risk, in Equation D11−3. Since the variance of the market is a given, the determinant of relative riskiness among stocks is the beta coefficient.

This type of analysis provides the foundations for the development of the capital asset pricing model (CAPM) summarized in the chapter. In this appendix we shall now set forth other aspects of the capital asset pricing model. The riskiness of a portfolio of assets as measured by its standard deviation of returns is generally less than the average of the risks of the individual assets as measured by their standard deviations. Since investors generally hold portfolios of securities, not just one security, it is reasonable to consider the riskiness of a security in terms of its contribution to the riskiness of the portfolio rather than in terms of its riskiness if held in isolation. *The significant contribution of the capital asset pricing model (CAPM) is that it provides a measure of the risk of a security in the portfolio sense.*

Basic Assumptions of the CAPM

Like all financial theories, a number of assumptions were made in the development of the CAPM; these were summarized by Jensen (1972, *Bell Journal*) as follows:

1. All investors are single-period expected utility of terminal wealth maximizers who choose among alternative portfolios on the basis of mean and variance (or standard deviation) of returns.
2. All investors can borrow or lend an unlimited amount at an exogenously given risk-free rate of interest, R_F, and there are no restrictions on short sales of any asset.
3. All investors have identical subjective estimates of the means, variances, and covariances of return among all assets, i.e., investors have homogeneous expectations.
4. All assets are perfectly divisible, perfectly liquid (that is, marketable at the going price), and there are no transactions costs.
5. There are no taxes.

6. All investors are price takers.
7. The quantities of all assets are given.

While these assumptions may appear to be severely limiting, they are similar to those made in the standard economic theory of the firm and in the basic models of Modigliani-Miller, Gordon, and others. Further, theoretical extensions in the literature that seek to relax the basic CAPM assumptions yield results that are generally consistent with the basic theory. Finally, the CAPM has been used in several rate cases and civil court cases, where its advocates have stood up quite well under intense and expert cross-examination.

The Tradeoff between Risk and Return

Since investors as a group are averse to risk, the higher the risk of a stock, the higher its required rate of return. Figure D11−5 illustrates this concept. Here, the required rate of return is plotted on the vertical axis, and risk is shown on the horizontal axis. The line showing the relationship between risk and rate of return is defined as the *security market line* (SML). The intercept of the security market line, R_F, is the riskless rate of return, generally taken as the return on U.S. Treasury securities. Riskless securities have beta coefficients equal to zero; since

Figure D11−5
The Tradeoff between
Risk and Return: The
Security Market Line
(SML)

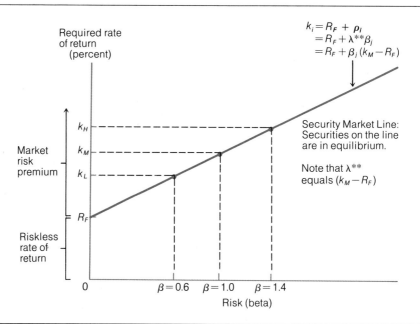

$$k_i = R_F + \rho_i$$
$$= R_F + \lambda^{**}\beta_j$$
$$= R_F + \beta_j (k_M - R_F)$$

Required rate
of return
(percent)

Security Market Line:
Securities on the line
are in equilibrium.

Note that λ^{**}
equals $(k_M - R_F)$

k_H
k_M
Market
risk
premium
k_L

R_F
Riskless
rate of
return

0      $\beta = 0.6$ $\beta = 1.0$ $\beta = 1.4$

Risk (beta)

returns on riskless securities are fixed and constant, they do not move at all with changes in the market. An "average" stock has a beta of 1.0, and such a stock has a required rate of return, k_M, equal to the market average return. A relatively low-risk stock might have a beta of .6 and a required rate of return equal to k_L, while a relatively high-risk stock might have a beta of 1.4 and a required return equal to k_H.

Betas of Portfolios

It should be noted that a portfolio made up of low beta securities will itself have a low beta, as the beta of any set of securities is a weighted average of the individual securities:

$$\beta_p = \sum_{i=1}^{n} w_i \beta_j. \tag{D11-6}$$

Here β_p is the beta of the portfolio, which reflects how volatile the portfolio is in relation to the market index; w_i is the percentage of the portfolio invested in the ith stock; and β_j is the beta coefficient of the jth stock.

The beta coefficients of mutual funds, pension funds, and other large portfolios are presently being calculated and used to judge the riskiness of these portfolios, and funds are actually being constructed to provide investors with specified degrees of riskiness. It is too early to judge how well betas will work as a measure of long-term risk, but the financial community is actually using these concepts in security selection and portfolio construction.

Cost of Capital Dynamics

The expected return on any stock i is equal to the riskless rate of return plus a risk premium: $k_j = R_F + \rho_j$. Since the risk premium for the entire market is equal to $(\bar{k}_M - R_F)$, we can develop the following equation for any individual stock j:[6]

$$\bar{k}_j = R_F + \beta_j(\bar{k}_M - R_F). \tag{D11-7}$$

Stated in words, the expected return on any stock is equal to the sum of the riskless rate of return plus the product of the stock's beta coefficient times the risk premium on the market as a whole. If beta is less than 1.0,

---

6. Equation D11–7 is developed as follows: First, the risk premium is a linear function of the stock's beta coefficient—that is, $\rho_j = \lambda^{**}\beta_j$. Accordingly, $\bar{k}_j = R_F + \lambda^{**}\beta_j$. By definition, the market as a whole has a beta of 1.0—the average stock must move in proportion to the market, and if this is so, then beta is 1.0. Therefore, this average or market risk premium must be equal to λ^{**}—that is, $\lambda^{**} = \rho_M$. Thus, $\bar{k}_j = R_F + \beta_j\rho_M$. But the market risk premium is equal to $(\bar{k}_M - R_F)$, so for any stock i we have the following equation:

$$k_j = R_F + \beta_j(\bar{k}_M - R_F)_j.$$

then the stock has a smaller than average risk premium, while if beta is larger than 1.0, the converse holds.

Interest rates change over time, and when they do, the change in R_F is reflected in the cost of equity both for the "average" stock k_M, and for any individual stock, k_i. Such changes cause the capital market line in Figure D11−5 to shift. The intercept term, R_F, goes up or down, while the slope of the line could increase, decrease, or remain constant.[7]

Risk premiums, which are reflected in the slope of the security market line, may also change over time. When investors are pessimistic and worried, the market line of Figure D11−5 will tend to be steep, implying a high "price of risk," whereas when investors are less risk averse, the price of risk declines and the market line is less steeply inclined.

A number of careful studies confirm that rates of return rise with risk. However, the empirical tests do not show neat, stable relationships; rather, depending on the test period analyzed and the methodology used, many security market lines could be generated. This instability is to be expected for two reasons: First, we would expect the market line to change over time as both interest rates and investors' outlooks change, so a stable market line over time would be strange indeed. Second, we are forced to estimate the market line on the basis of imperfect data, and where errors in the data exist, estimating problems are bound to arise.[8]

Questions

D11−1. The return on project j is 80 percent and on project k is 20 percent. Their standard deviations are 2 percent and 5 percent respectively. The correlation between their returns is 0.1. What is the portfolio return and standard deviation when the proportion of project j in the portfolio is 0 percent?

D11−2. Define "systematic" and "unsystematic" risk.

D11−3. Risk premiums increase with risk. Would risk premiums be more dependent on systematic or unsystematic risk? Explain.

D11−4. The expected return on the existing "portfolio" of projects of a firm is 12 percent with a standard deviation of 8 percent. Another project is added with an expected return of 10 percent and a standard deviation of 2 percent. The new project has zero correlation with the existing projects and will be 10 percent of the enlarged portfolio. What will be the

---

7. R. H. Litzenberger and A. P. Budd, "Secular Trends in Risk Premiums," *Journal of Finance* (September 1972), pp. 857−64.

8. However, these problems are probably less severe in the capital asset pricing model than are the problems encountered using alternative approaches.

expected return and standard deviation of the new portfolio of investment projects of the firm?

D11-5. The market risk premium is 5 percent. The risk-free rate is 6 percent. Projects A, B, and C are added with estimated betas of .8, 1.2, and 2, respectively. What will be the required rates of return on these projects?

D11-6. Suppose that inflation causes the nominal risk-free return and the market return to rise by an equal amount. Will the market risk premium be affected?

Problems

D11-2. You are planning to invest $100,000. Two securities, i and j, are available. The expected return for A is 9 percent and $\sigma_A = 4$ percent; the expected return for B is 10 percent and $\sigma_B = 5$ percent; $\rho_{AB} = 0.5$:

   a. Construct a table similar to Table D11-1 giving $E(k_p)$ and σ_p for 100 percent, 75 percent, 50 percent, 25 percent, and 0 percent investment in stock A.
   b. Use your calculated $E(k_p)$ and σ_p values to graph the attainable set of portfolios, and indicate which part of the attainable set is efficient.
   c. Using hypothetical indifference curves, show how an investor might choose a portfolio consisting of stocks A and B.

D11-2. You are planning to invest $100,000. Two securities, i and j, are available, and you can invest in either of them or in a portfolio with some of each. You estimate that the following probability distributions of returns are applicable:

Security i		Security j	
.1	− 5 %	.1	0 %
.2	0	.2	5
.4	11.25	.4	8.75
.2	15	.2	10
.1	20	.1	15

The expected returns are 9 percent and 8 percent for i and j, respectively; i.e., $E(k_i) = 9$ percent and $E(k_j) = 8$ percent. $\sigma_i = 7.56$ percent and $\sigma_j = 3.75$ percent.
   a. Assume $\rho_{ij} = -.5$. What percentage of your portfolio should be invested in each security in order to minimize your investment risk?
   b. Calculate σ_p and $E(k_p)$ for portfolios consisting of 100 percent i and 0 percent j; 100 percent j and 0 percent i; and the minimum risk portfolio as calculated in (a). (Hint: Notice that some of these data are given above.)
   c. Graph the *feasible* set of portfolios, and identify the *efficient* section of the feasible set.

d. Suppose your risk-return tradeoff function, or indifference curve, is a linear family of lines with a slope of .15. Use this information, plus the graph constructed in (c), to locate (approximately) your optimal portfolio. Give the percentage of your funds invested in each security, and the optimal portfolio's σ_p and $E(k_p)$. [Hint: Estimate σ_p and $E(k_p)$ graphically, then use the equation for $E(k_p)$ to determine w.]

e. What is the probability that your optimal portfolio will, in fact, yield less than 4.15 percent?

f. Demonstrate *why* a graph of the efficient set such as the one you constructed in (c) above is always linear if portfolios are formed between a riskless security (a bond) and a risky asset (a stock or perhaps a portfolio of stocks).

D11–3. You are planning to invest $200,000. Two securities, C and D, are available, and you can invest in either of them or in a portfolio with some of each. You estimate that the following probability distributions of returns are applicable:

Security C		Security D	
.2	− 4	.2	2
.3	0	.3	4
.3	12	.3	8
.2	26	.2	10

The expected returns are 8 percent and 6 percent for up-down and down-up, respectively; i.e., $E(k_C) = 8$ percent and $E(k_D) = 6$ percent. $\sigma_C = 10.84$ percent and $\sigma_D = 2.97$ percent.

a. Assume $\rho_{CD} = -.5$. What percentage of your portfolio should be invested in each security in order to minimize your investment risk?

b. Calculate σ_p and $E(k_p)$ for portfolios consisting of 100 percent C and 0 percent D; 100 percent D and 0 percent C; and the minimum risk portfolio as calculated in (a). (Hint: Notice that some of these data are given above.)

c. Graph the *feasible* set of portfolios, and identify the *efficient* section of the feasible set.

d. Suppose your risk-return tradeoff function, or indifference curve is a linear family of lines with a slope of .25. Use this information, plus the graph constructed in (c), to locate (approximately) your optimal portfolio. Give the percentage of your funds invested in each security, and the optimal portfolio's σ_p and $E(k_p)$. [Hint: Estimate σ_p and $E(k_p)$ graphically, then use the equation for $E(k_p)$ to determine w.]

e. What is the probability that your optimal portfolio will, in fact, yield less than 1.15 percent?

f. Demonstrate *why* a graph of the efficient set such as the one you constructed in (c) above is always linear if portfolios are formed between a riskless security (a bond) and a risky asset (a stock or perhaps a portfolio of stocks).

**Selected
References**

Blume, Marshall E. "Betas and Their Regression Tendencies." *The Journal of Finance* 30 (June 1975): 785–95.

Hagerman, Robert L., and Kim, E. Han. "Capital Asset Pricing with Price Level Changes." *The Journal of Financial and Quantitative Analysis* 11 (Sept. 1976): 381–92.

Hakansson, Nils H., and Miller, Bruce L. "Compound-Return Mean-Variance Efficient Portfolios Never Risk Ruin." *Management Science* 22 (Dec. 1975): 391–400.

Mayers, David. "Nonmarketable Assets, Market Segmentation, and the Level of Asset Prices." *The Journal of Financial and Quantitative Analysis* 11 (Mar. 1976): 1–12.

Modigliani, Franco, and Pogue, Gerald A. "An Introduction to Risk and Return." *Financial Analysts' Journal* 30 (Mar.–Apr. 1974): 68–80; (May–June 1974): 69–86.

Robichek, Alexander A., and Cohn, Richard A. "The Economic Determinants of Systematic Risk." *The Journal of Finance* 29 (May 1974): 439–47.

Thompson, Donald J., II. "Sources of Systematic Risk in Common Stocks." *The Journal of Business* 49 (Apr. 1976): 173–88.

Appendix E to Chapter 11
Certainty Equivalent Adjustments

Subjective Certainty Equivalent Adjustments

In Chapter 11 we used the capital asset pricing model to show the precise relationship between a risk adjusted discount factor and a certainty equivalent discount factor. Because the parameters of the real world may be changing over time, some decision-makers employ subjective risk adjustment factors similar to the procedures described in this section.

The *certainty equivalent* method follows directly from the concepts of utility theory presented in Chapter 11. Under the subjective certainty equivalent approach, the decision-maker must specify how much money is required with certainty to make him or her indifferent between this certain sum and the expected value of a risky sum. To illustrate, suppose a rich eccentric offered you the following two choices.

1. Flip a fair coin. If a head comes up, you receive $1 million, but if a tail comes up you get nothing. The expected value of the gamble is $500,000 (= .5 × $1,000,000 + .5 × 0).
2. You do not flip a coin; you simply pocket $300,000 cash.

If you find yourself indifferent between the two alternatives, then $300,000 is your certainty equivalent for the risky $500,000 expected return. In other words, the certain or riskless amount provides exactly the same utility as the risky alternative. Any certainty equivalent less than $500,000 indicates risk aversion.

The certainty equivalent concept is illustrated in Figure E11–1. The curve shows a series of risk-return combinations to which the decision-maker is indifferent. For example, point A represents an investment with a perceived degree of risk as measured by its beta value, β_A, and with an expected dollar return of $2,000. The individual whose risk-return tradeoff function, or indifference curve, is shown here is indifferent between a sure $1,000, an expected $2,000 with risk β_A, and an expected $3,000 with risk β_B.

Given the risk-return indifference curve of investors in general, the firm could adjust the *NPV* equation as follows:

1. Substitute R_F for k in the denominator of the equation

$$NPV = \sum_{t=1}^{n} \frac{F_t}{(1 + R_F)^t} - I,$$

**Figure E11–1
Certainty
Equivalent
Returns**

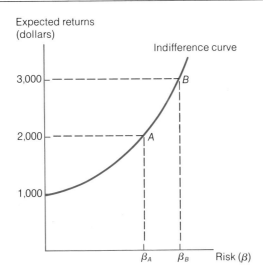

where R_F is the discount rate applicable for riskless investments such as United States government bonds.

2. Divide the certainty equivalent of a risky return by the risky return to obtain a *certainty equivalent adjustment factor,*

$$\phi_A = \frac{\text{certain return}}{\text{risky return}} = \frac{\$1,000}{\$2,000} = .50 \text{ for } \beta_A$$

and

$$\phi_B = \frac{\$1,000}{\$3,000} = .33 \text{ for } \beta_B.$$

3. Conceptually, ϕ values could be developed for all possible values of β. The range of ϕ would be from 1.0 for $\beta = 0$ to a value close to zero for large values of β, assuming risk aversion.[1]

4. The risk-aversion functions of all individuals could, conceptually, be averaged to form a "market risk-aversion function." An example of such a function is shown in Figure E11–2.

5. Given the market risk-aversion function and the degree of risk in-

---

1. Of course, different individuals may have different ϕ functions, depending on their degrees of risk aversion. Further, an individual's own α function might shift over time as personal situations, including wealth and family status, changed.

herent in any risky return, the risky return could be replaced by its certainty equivalent:

Certainty equivalent of $F_t = \phi_t F_t$.

6. The basic *NPV* equation could then be converted to Equation E11−1, a model that explicitly accounts for risk:

$$NPV = \sum_{t=1}^{n} \frac{F_t}{(1+k)^t} - I = \sum_{t=1}^{n} \frac{\phi_t F_t}{(1+R_F)^t} - I \qquad \text{(E11−1)}$$

In this form, the effects of different courses of action with different risk (β) and returns (F_t) can be appraised.

Risk-Adjusted Discount Rates. An alternative procedure for taking risk into account utilizes the security market line discussed in Chapter 11, whose logic was further developed in the preceding Appendix D11. The security market line provides a risk-return tradeoff function. The general form of the security market line is shown in Equation E11−2.

$$E(k_j) = R_F + \lambda\, Cov(k_j,\, k_M) \qquad \text{(E11−2)}$$

Suppose that we are given the economy-wide parameters of a value of R_F equal to 5 percent and a λ of 4. The risk characteristics of the investment, security, firm, or other capital asset are defined by the value of the covariance term. Some illustrative values of the covariance term and the associated expected returns are shown in Table E11−1.

**Table E11−1
Returns Related to
Risk**

	Expressed as Decimals		Expressed as Percents	
	$Cov(k_j,\, k_M)$	$E(k_j)$	$Cov(k_j,\, k_M)$	$E(k_j)$
A	0	.05	0	5
B	.005	.07	.5	7
C	.015	.11	1.5	11
D	.0175	.12	1.75	12
E	.025	.15	2.50	15

The relationships shown in Table E11−1 can also be graphed as in Figure E11−2. The security market line depicted in Figure E11−2 is a risk-return tradeoff function. The average investor is indifferent to a riskless asset with a certain 5 percent return, a moderately risky asset with an 11 percent return, or a very risky asset with a 15 percent expected return. As risk increases, higher and higher returns on investment are required to compensate investors for the additional risk.

The difference between the required rate of return on a particular

**Figure E11-2
Illustrative
Risk-Return
Relationships**

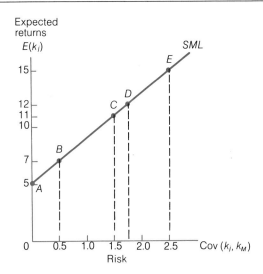

risky asset and the rate of return on a riskless asset is defined as the risk premium on the risky asset. For the security market line depicted in Figure E11–2 the riskless rate is 5 percent; a 2 percent risk premium is required to compensate for a covariance of .5 percent, and a 10 percent risk premium is attached to an investment with a covariance of 2.5 percent. The average investor is indifferent between risky investments B, C, D, and E and the riskless asset A.

If a particular firm's stock is located at point D on the security market line, investors expect the rate of return on the stock to be 12 percent. If the firm changes the nature of its investment projects so that it takes on projects that reduce the covariance of its returns with the market, then a lower required rate of return results; it may move down to point C on the security market line. Conversely, if the firm changes its investment program so that its covariance moves up to 2.5 percent, the return that is required by investors will be 15 percent.

Because compounding over time has a compounding effect on the risk premium, it is sometimes desirable to be able to use a certainty equivalent discount rate. The security market line expression lends itself to this reformulation. To do this, we first make use of the following definition:

$$E(k_j) = \frac{E(X_j)}{V_j}$$

This enables us to rewrite the security market line relationship as shown in Equation E11–2a, which, after we rearrange terms, becomes Equation E11–2b.

$$\frac{E(X_j)}{V_j} = R_F + \lambda\ Cov\left(\frac{X_j}{V_j}, k_M\right) \tag{E11-2a}$$

$$\frac{1}{V_j}\ [E(X_j) - \lambda\ Cov(X_j, k_M)] = R_F$$

$$V_j = \frac{E(X_j) - \lambda\ Cov(X_j, k_M)}{R_F} \tag{E11-2b}$$

Equation E11–2b makes an adjustment to the numerator representing the asset returns. This adjustment converts the returns to a certainty equivalent amount. When this is done, the risk-free rate of return can be used as a discount rate. To illustrate what is involved let us assume some values related to the previous example. Let: $X_j = \$120$; $\lambda = 4$; $Cov(X_j, k_M) = 17.5$; $R_F = .05$.

These values can then be utilized in Equation E11–2b as shown in Equation E11–2b':

$$V_j = \frac{120 - 4(17.5)}{.05} = \frac{120 - 70}{.05} = \frac{50}{.05} = \$1,000 \tag{E11-2b'}$$

Thus we see that the risky returns are $120. The risk adjustment is $70. Hence, the certainty equivalent returns are $50. When we discount the certainty equivalent returns at the risk-free rate of 5 percent, we obtain a value for the asset of $1,000. However, for a one-period model such as the CAPM reflected in the security market line, we will obtain the same results if we use risk-adjusted values both in the numerator and in the denominator. To illustrate, let us first recognize the relationship in Equation E11–3.

$$Cov\left(\frac{X_j}{V_j}, k_M\right) = Cov(k_j, k_M) \tag{E11-3}$$

Rearranging terms and inserting values known to this point we obtain:

$$Cov(X_j, k_M) = V_j\ Cov(k_j, k_M) \tag{E11-3a}$$

$$17.5 = 1,000\ Cov(k_j, k_M) \tag{E11-3b}$$

$$Cov(k_j, k_M) = 17.5/1,000 = .0175 \tag{E11-3c}$$

In developing the expression for the value of the asset in risk-adjusted terms, we express the security market line in the form of Equation E11–4:

$$\frac{E(X_j)}{V_j} = R_F + \lambda\ Cov(k_j,\ k_M) \tag{E11-4}$$

Solving for the value of the asset we obtain Equation (E11-4a):

$$V_j = \frac{E(X_j)}{R_F + \lambda\ Cov(k_j,\ k_M)} \tag{E11-4a}$$

We can now use Equation (E11-4a) to obtain the value of the firm, using a risk-adjusted discount rate.

$$V_j = \frac{120}{.05 + 4(.0175)}$$

$$V_j = \frac{120}{.05 + .07} = \frac{120}{.12} = \$1,000$$

Thus we obtain the same value whether we use the certainty equivalent formulation and the risk-free return or the risk-adjusted values in both the numerator and the denominator.

Traditionally it has been customary to convert the risky return to a certainty equivalent return by applying a certainty equivalent factor, ϕ. In the informal approaches to the treatment of risk the value of ϕ was formulated on a judgmental basis. However, with the use of the security market line we were able to develop a data-based estimate of ϕ. Using the information from the example above we found that the certainty equivalent return was $50, while the risky return was $120. The ratio between the two was .4167. Hence, we can take Equation E11-2a and, instead of subtracting the risk adjustment factor, multiply by the certainty equivalent factor, ϕ, as shown in Equation E11-5:

$$V_j = \frac{\phi E(X_j)}{R_F} \tag{E11-5}$$

When we insert the appropriate values, we again obtain a value of the asset of $1,000.

$$V_j = \frac{.4167(120)}{.05} = \frac{50}{.05} = \$1,000$$

Thus the use of the security market line enables us to express valuation relationships in either the risk-adjusted form or in their certainty equivalent form.

Risk and the Timing of Returns

By its nature, the discount rate serves both to allow for the time value of money *and* to provide an allowance for the relative riskiness of a project's returns. In other words, both *time* and *risk* are accounted for by one adjustment process. Since time and risk are really separate variables, this combination value must be carefully chosen if it is to be appropriate for its intended purpose. It should be noted that the certainty equivalent method *does not* combine risk and time but, rather, keeps them separate, adjusting for risk in the numerator and for time in the denominator. As a result, it can be argued that certainty equivalents are superior to risk-adjusted discount rates. However, as was pointed out in Chapter 11, risk-adjusted discount rates are used by financial managers more frequently because of their greater convenience and familiarity.

If the risk-adjusted discount rate method is to be used, it is important to choose the values of these rates carefully. We will now consider the particular assumptions that are implicit in the choice of a constant risk-adjusted discount rate over time. Here the "risk index" ϕ is calculated as the ratio of the present value interest factor for a risky cash flow divided by the present value interest factor of a riskless asset.[2]

$$\text{Index of risk} = \phi_t = \frac{PVIF_{\text{risky asset}}}{PVIF_{\text{riskless asset}}} = \frac{(1 + \text{risky rate})^{-t}}{(1 + \text{riskless rate})^{-t}}. \qquad \textbf{(E11–6)}$$

To illustrate, suppose we are calculating ϕ, the risk index, for a cash flow expected after 10 years when the riskless rate is 5 percent and the risky rate is 10 percent. The interest factors are found in Appendix Table D–2 to be .614 and .386 for the riskless and risky assets, respectively, so the certainty equivalent risk index is found as follows:

$$\text{Risk index} = \phi_{10} = \frac{.386}{.614} = .629.$$

Equation E11–6 has some interesting implications that can be seen in Table E11–1, which works out the ϕ values for a pair of interest rates over time, and in Figure E11–3, where these values (and others) are plotted. Risk, as measured by ϕ_t, is an increasing function of both *time* and the *differential between the riskless and risky discount rates*. In other words, a given risk premium has a larger and larger impact on the risk index as the time horizon is lengthened. This phenomenon occurs, of course, because of the compounding effect.

This concept can be expressed analytically. Let the risk index for any year t, ϕ_t, be designated as

$$\phi_t = \frac{(1 + R_F + \rho)^{-t}}{(1 + R_F)^{-t}} = \frac{(1 + R_F)^t}{(1 + R_F + \rho)^t}$$

---

2. This discussion parallels that of Robichek and Myers, "Risk Adjusted Discount Rates," *Journal of Finance* 21, no. 4 (December 1966), pp. 727–30.

Figure E11–3
Changes in Perceived
Risk Over Time

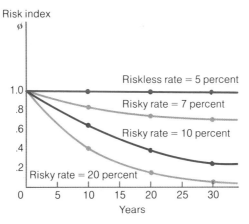

Risk index

Notes: 1. The smaller the value of ϕ, the index of risk, the greater the perceived risk.
2. For a given riskless rate (for example, 5 percent) and risky rate (for example, 10 percent), the value of ϕ_t declines over time; that is, with a constant risk premium (5 percent = 10 percent − 5 percent), the declining curve indicates that perceived risk increases with time. Therefore, a constant risk premium (and risk-adjusted discount rate) implies that risk of an individual cash flow is perceived to be higher and higher the further into the future the cash flow is due.
3. At any given future point in time (other than $t = 0$), ϕ, the index of perceived risk, is lower the higher the risk premium. At the point 10 years, for example, the ϕ for the 7 percent risky rate, with a 2 percent risk premium, is .826; it is .629 for the 10 percent rate; and it is .403 for the 15 percent rate.

where R_F is the riskless rate and ρ is the risk premium. For a longer period of $t + 1$ years, and holding constant ρ and R_F,

$$\phi_{t+1} = \frac{(1 + R_F)^{t+1}}{(1 + R_F + \rho)^{t+1}}$$

$$= \frac{(1 + R_F)^t}{(1 - R_F + \rho)^t} \cdot \frac{(1 + R_F)}{(1 + R_F + \rho)}$$

$$= \phi_t\left(\frac{1 + R_F}{1 + R_F + \rho}\right).$$

Therefore, $\phi_{t+1} < \phi_t$ provided $\rho > 0$. Since smaller values of ϕ are associated with higher risk, risk must be perceived to be *increasing* over time whenever the risk premium, ρ, is a constant. Further, note that the risk-adjusted discount rate, k, is equal to $R_F + \rho$. If R_F and ρ are both constants, then R_F is also a constant and

$$\phi_{t+1} = \phi_c\left(\frac{1 + R_F}{1 + k}\right).$$

Therefore, a constant k implies that ϕ_t is declining and that risk is thought to be increasing over time.

Table E11-2	Discount Rate—Years	Riskless Project 5%	Risky Project 10%	RI
Calculation of Certainty Equivalents	0	1.000	1.000	1.000
	1	.952	.909	.955
	10	.614	.386	.629
	20	.377	.149	.395
	30	.231	.057	.247

Note: The $RI = 1.0$ when $t = 0$ because

$$\frac{PVIF_{risky\ rate}}{PVIF_{riskless\ rate}} = \frac{(1 + k)^0}{(1 + R_F)^0} = \frac{1}{1} = 1.0$$

where R_F = riskless rate and k = risky rate.

The relationship between k, risk, and time is graphed in Figure E11-4. If risk is thought to increase over time (in terms of Figure 11-4, the estimated coefficient of variation of returns is increasing), then the risk index should also increase over time. A constant value of k implies increasing risk; this condition is shown in Figure E11-4(a). However, if the riskiness of returns is not higher for distant than for close-at-hand returns, then distant returns should be discounted at a *lower k* than close returns; this condition is shown in Figure E11-4(b). Note again that the reason behind this result is the fact that the risk premium component of k is being compounded.

Implications

A firm using the risk-adjusted discount rate approach for its capital budgeting decisions will have an overall rate that generally reflects its overall, market-determined riskiness. This rate will be used for "average" projects. Lower rates will be used for less risky projects, and higher rates will be used for riskier projects. To facilitate the decision process, corporate headquarters may prescribe rates for different divisions and for different classes of investments (for example, replacement, expansion of existing lines, expansion into new lines). Then, investments of a given class within a given division are analyzed in terms of the prescribed rate. For example, replacement decisions in the retailing division of an oil company might all be evaluated with an 8 percent cost of capital, while exploration and production investments might require a 20 percent return.

Notice what such a procedure implies about risk: risk increases with time, and it imposes a relatively severe burden on long-term projects. This means that short-payoff alternatives will be selected over those with longer payoffs when, for example, there are alternative ways of

Figure E11-4
Relationship between
Risk and Time

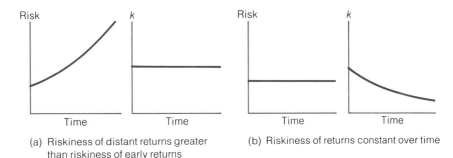

(a) Riskiness of distant returns greater
   than riskiness of early returns

(b) Riskiness of returns constant over time

performing a given task, and that less capital-intensive methods of performing given tasks will be employed.

However, there are a substantial number of projects for which distant returns are *not* more difficult to estimate than near-term returns. For example, the estimated returns on a water pipeline serving a developing community may be quite uncertain in the short run, because the rate of growth of the community is uncertain. However, the water company may be quite sure that in time the community will be fully developed and will utilize the full capacity of the pipeline. Similar situations could exist in many public projects—water projects, highway programs, schools, and so forth; in public utility investment decisions; and when industrial firms are building plants to serve specified geographic markets.

To the extent that this implicit assumption of rising risk over time reflects the facts, then a constant discount rate, k, may be appropriate. In the vast majority of business situations, risk actually is an increasing function of time, so a constant risk-adjusted discount rate is reasonable. There are, however, situations for which this is not true; one should be aware of the relationships described in this appendix and avoid the pitfall of unwittingly penalizing long-term projects when they are not, in fact, more risky than shorter-term projects.

Appendix F to Chapter 11
Capital Budgeting Procedures
Under Inflation[1]

The United States has experienced persistent inflation since 1966 at levels exceeding the moderate price level changes of previous peacetime periods. What effects does this have on the results of capital budgeting analysis? We can analyze the impacts of inflation by using an illustrative example to clarify the new influences introduced.

Let us begin with the standard capital budgeting case in which inflation is absent. The expression for calculating the net present value of the investment is shown in equation F11–1.

$$\overline{NPV} = \sum_{t=1}^{N} \frac{\overline{F}_t}{(1+k)^t} - I \qquad\qquad \textbf{(F11–1)}$$

The symbols used have the following meanings and values:

$\overline{NPV}$ = expected net present value of the project
$\overline{F}_t$ = expected net cash flows per year from the project = \$20,000
k = cost of capital applicable to the risk of the project = 9 percent
N = number of years the net cash flows are received = 5
I = required investment outlay for the project = \$75,000.

With the data provided, we can utilize F11–1 as follows:

$$
\begin{aligned}
\overline{NPV}_0 &= \sum_{t=1}^{N} \frac{\$20,000}{(1.09)^t} - \$75,000 \\
&= 20,000(3.8896) - \$75,000 \\
&= 77,792 - 75,000 \\
&= \$2,792.
\end{aligned}
$$

We find that the project has an expected net present value of \$2,792, and under the simple conditions assumed, we would accept the project. Now let us consider the effects of inflation. Suppose that inflation at an annual rate of 6 percent is expected to take place during the five years of

1. For articles on this subject see J. C. Van Horne, "A Note on Biases in Capital Budgeting Introduced by Inflation," *Journal of Financial and Quantitative Analysis* 6 (Jan. 1971), pp. 653–58; and P. L. Cooley, R. L. Roenfeldt, and It-Keong Chew, "Capital Budgeting Procedures under Inflation," *Financial Management* 4 (Winter 1975), pp. 18–27; also see their exchange with M. C. Findlay and A. W. Frankle in *Financial Management* (August 1976), pp. 83–90.

the project. Since investment and security returns are based on expected future returns, the anticipated inflation rate will be reflected in
the required rate of return on the project or the applicable cost of capital
for the project. This relationship has long been recognized in financial
economics and is known as the Fisher effect. In formal terms we have:

$$(1 + k_j)\,(1 + n) = (1 + K_j) \tag{F11-2}$$

where k_j is the required rate of return in nominal terms and n is the anticipated annual inflation rate over the life of the project. For our example, equation F11-2 would be:

$$(1 + .09)\,(1 + .06) = (1 + .09 + .06 + .0054).$$

If the cross product term .0054 is included in the addition, we would
have .1554 as the required rate of return in nominal terms. However,
since the cross product term is generally small and since both k_j, the
required rate of return in real terms, and the anticipated inflation rate
are estimates, it is customary practice to make a simple addition of the
real rate and the inflation rate. The required nominal rate of return that
would be used in the calculation would therefore be 15 percent.

It is at this point that some biases in capital budgeting under inflationary conditions may be introduced. The market data utilized in the
estimated current capital costs will include the premium for anticipated
inflation. But while the market remembers to include an adjustment for
inflation in the capitalization factor, in the capital budgeting analysis,
the cash-flow estimates may fail to include an element to reflect future
inflation. As a consequence, the analysis would appear as in the calculations below for $\overline{NPV}_1$.

$$\overline{NPV}_1 = \sum_{t=1}^{N} \frac{\$20,000}{(1.09)^t(1.06)^t} - \$75,000 \doteq \sum_{t=1}^{N} \frac{\$20,000}{(1.15)^t} - \$75,000$$
$$\doteq 20,000(3.3522) - 75,000$$
$$\doteq 67,044 - 75,000 \doteq (\$7,956).$$

It now appears that the project will have a negative net present value
of almost $8,000. With a negative net present value of substantial mag-
nitude, the project would be rejected. However, a sound analysis requires that the anticipated inflation rate also be taken into account in
the cash flow estimates as well. Initially, for simplicity, let us assume
that the same inflation rate of 6 percent is applicable to the net cash
flows. We take this step in setting forth the expression for $\overline{NPV}_2$ as follows:

$$\overline{NPV}_2 = \sum_{t=1}^{N} \frac{\$20,000(1.06)^t}{(1.09)^t(1.06)^t} - 75,000 = \sum_{t=1}^{N} \frac{\$20,000}{(1.09)^t} - \$75,000.$$

Since the inflation factors are now in both the numerator and the denominator and are the same, they can be cancelled. The result for the calculation of $\overline{NPV}_2$ will therefore be the same as for $\overline{NPV}_0$, which was a positive $2,792. Thus when anticipated inflation is properly reflected in both the cash flow estimates in the numerator and the required rate of return from market data in the denominator, the resulting $\overline{NPV}$ calculation will be both in real and nominal terms. This was noted by Professor Findlay as follows: "Any properly measured, market-determined wealth concept is, simultaneously, *both nominal and real* . . . Hence, $\overline{NPV}$, or any other wealth measure, gives the amount for which one can 'cash out' now (nominal) and also the amount of today's goods that can be consumed at today's prices (real)."[2] Thus if inflation is reflected in both the cash flow estimates and in the required rate of return, the resulting $\overline{NPV}$ estimate will be free of inflation bias.

To this point we have purposely kept the analysis simple to focus on the basic principles involved since controversy has erupted over the issues involved. In applying these concepts, the anticipated inflation might be expected to affect the required rate of return and the cash flow estimates differently. Indeed, the components of the net cash flows, the cash outflows and the cash inflows, may themselves be influenced by the anticipated inflation by different magnitudes. These complications will not, however, change the basic method of analysis, only the specifics of the calculations. The nature of the more complex case is indicated by equation F11-3.

$$\overline{NPV}_0 = \sum_{t=1}^{N} \frac{[\overline{(\text{Inflows})}_t(1+n_i)^t - \overline{(\text{Outflows})}_t(1+n_0)^t](1-T) + \overline{(\text{Depr})}_t(T)}{(1+K)^t}$$

$$\text{(F11-3)}$$

The cash inflows may be subject to a rate of inflation that is different from the rate of inflation in the cash outflows. Both may differ from the anticipated rate of inflation reflected in the required rate of return in the denominator. Some illustrative data will demonstrate the application of F11-3.

Table F11-1 sets forth data for expected cash flows without inflation effects. The pattern is a constant $20,000 per year for five years as in the original example. In Table F11-2 the estimates of expected net cash flows include inflation effects. The cash inflows are subject to a 7 percent inflation rate, while the cash outflows are subject to an 8 percent inflation rate. The resulting expected net cash flows are shown in the bottom line of the table. The required rate of return of 15 percent is assumed to reflect a 6 percent inflation rate as before.

---

2. *Financial Management*, Autumn 1976, p. 85.

Table F11–1 Expected Net Cash Flows Without Inflation Effects		1	2	3	4	5
	Expected cash inflows	$40,000	$50,000	$60,000	$70,000	$80,000
	Expected cash outflows	15,000	25,000	35,000	45,000	55,000
		25,000	25,000	25,000	25,000	25,000
	Times (1 − tax rate)	.50	.50	.50	.50	.50
		12,500	12,500	12,500	12,500	12,500
	Depreciation (tax rate)	7,500	7,500	7,500	7,500	7,500
	Expected net cash flows ($\bar{F}_t$)	$20,000	$20,000	$20,000	$20,000	$20,000

Table F11–2 Expected Net Cash Flows Including Inflation Effects		1	2	3	4	5
	Expected cash inflows ($\eta = 7\%$)	$42,800	$57,250	$73,500	$91,770	$112,240
	Expected cash outflows ($\eta = 8\%$)	16,200	29,150	44,100	61,200	80,795
		26,600	28,100	29,400	30,570	31,445
	Times (1 − tax rate)	.50	.50	.50	.50	.50
		13,300	14,050	14,700	15,285	15,722
	Depreciation (tax rate)	7,500	7,500	7,500	7,500	7,500
	Expected net cash flows ($\bar{F}_t$)	$20,800	$21,550	$22,200	$22,785	$ 23,222

The calculation of the expected net present value $(\overline{NPV}_3)$ is shown in Table F11–3. Taking all the inflation influences into account, $\overline{NPV}_3$ is a negative $1,430. The project would be rejected. In this example, the inflationary forces on the cash outflows were greater than for the cash inflows. Some have suggested that this influence has been sufficiently widespread and that it accounts for the sluggish rate of capital investment in the United States since the early 1970s.

The situation we illustrated initially was that failure to take inflation into account in the expected cash flows resulted in an erroneous capital budgeting analysis. A project was rejected that, measured correctly, produced a return exceeding the required rate of return. There would be an unsound allocation of capital if the bias in the analysis due to inflation had not been taken into account. In our second and more complex

Table F11–3 Calculation of $\overline{NPV}_3$	Year	Cash Flow (1)	Discount Factor (15%) (2)	Present Value (1) × (2)
	1	20,800	.870	18,096
	2	21,550	.756	16,292
	3	22,200	.658	14,608
	4	22,785	.572	13,033
	5	23,222	.497	11,541

$$\overline{NPV}_3 = \$73,570 - \$75,000$$
$$= (\$1,430)$$

example, inflation caused the cash outflows to grow at a higher rate than the cash inflows. As a consequence, the expected net present value of the project was negative. Making the inflation adjustment does not always necessarily result in a positive net present value for the project — it simply results in a more accurate estimate of the net benefits from the project, positive or negative.

Problems

F11–1. Your firm is considering an investment in a machine that produces bowling balls. The cost of the machine is $100,000 with zero expected salvage value. Annual production in units during the five-year life of the machine is expected to be: 5,000; 8,000; 12,000; 10,000; and 6,000.

 The price of bowling balls is expected to rise from $20 during year 1 at a rate of 2 percent per year for the following four years. Production cash outflows are expected to grow at 10 percent per year from the first-year production costs of $10 per unit.

 Depreciation of the machine will be on a straight line basis. The applicable tax rate is 40 percent, and the applicable cost of capital is 15 percent. Should the investment in the machine be made?

F11–2. You are given the following information about an investment of $40,000: It is expected to yield benefits over a five-year period. It is also expected that there will be annual cash inflows of $90,000 and annual cash outflows of $75,000, excluding taxes and the depreciation tax shelter. The tax rate is 40 percent, and the cost of capital is .08 percent.

 a. Compute the net present value of the investment.

 b. On investigation you discover that no adjustments have been made for inflation or price level changes. Year 1 data are correct, but after that inflows are expected to increase at 4 percent per year and outflows at 6 percent per year. The general rate of inflation is expected to be about 6 percent, causing the cost of capital to rise to 14 percent. Reevaluate the net present value of the project in light of this information.

Part IV

Sources and Forms of Long-term Financing

In the introductory section, we analyzed the firm in an overall, aggregate sense. Next, in Part II, we considered the top half of the balance sheet, analyzing current assets, current liabilities, and the interactions between the two. Then, in Part III, we moved to the lower left side of the balance sheet, examining the process by which firms decide on investments in fixed assets. Now, in Part IV, we move to the lower right side of the balance sheet, to consider the various types of long-term funds available to the firm when it seeks long-term external capital.

Chapter 12 presents an overview of the capital markets, explaining briefly certain institutional material without which no basic finance course is complete. Chapter 13 analyzes the financial characteristics of common stock; Chapter 14 examines bonds and preferred stock; Chapter 15 analyzes term loans and leases; and Chapter 16 discusses the nature and use of warrants and convertibles. This institutional background is essential for an understanding of Part V, Financial Structure and the Cost of Capital, where we take up the question of the optimal mix of financing.

12 The Market for Long-term Securities

One fundamental basis for classifying securities markets is the distinction between *primary markets* in which stocks and bonds are initially sold and *secondary* markets in which they are subsequently traded. Initial sales of securities are made by investment banking firms who purchase them from the issuing firm and sell them through an underwriting syndicate or group. The subsequent transactions in the securities take place in organized securities exchanges or in less formal markets. The operations of securities markets provide a framework within which the nature of investment banking and the new issue market can better be understood. Accordingly, we first develop the background provided by a study of the secondary markets.

Securities Markets

The securities markets are in a state of flux and change. After four years of research and investigation, Congress enacted the Securities Acts Amendments of 1975.[1] This new law departs from the concept of self-regulation that had previously been followed in the relationships between the government and the securities industry. In order to understand the matters dealt with in the amendments of 1975 and the changes that they are likely to bring about, it is necessary to describe the major institutions of the securities markets and how they have operated. We shall describe in turn, the organized security exchanges, the over-the-counter markets, the third market, and the fourth market.

The major exchange is the New York Stock Exchange (NYSE) on which about 1,500 common stocks are listed, accounting for over 80 percent of the almost $200 billion value of annual dollar volume of trading and somewhat less than 80 percent of the over 6 billion annual share volume of trading. The American Stock Exchange is second in volume with 1,300 stocks traded, accounting for under 10 percent of dollar volume and somewhat over 10 percent of share volume. Some 350 stocks are traded solely on one or more of the 11 registered regional exchanges, accounting for about 2 to 5 percent of volume in the three largest and accounting for less than 1 percent of total volume in the remaining.

---

1. The original Securities Acts of 1933 and 1934 are discussed later in this chapter.

The organized security exchanges are tangible, physical entities. Each of the larger ones occupies its own building, has specifically designated members, and has an elected governing body—its board of governors. Members are said to have "seats" on the exchange, although everybody stands up. These seats, which are bought and sold, represent the right to trade on the exchange. In 1968, seats on the New York Stock Exchange (NYSE) sold at a record high of $515,000; in 1974 they sold for about $85,000. During 1975, NYSE seat sales ranged between a high of $138,000 and a low of $55,000.[2]

Most of the larger stock brokerage firms own seats on the exchanges and designate one or more of the officers of the firm as members of the exchange. The exchanges are open daily, and the members meet in a large room equipped with telephones and telegraphs that enable each brokerage house member to communicate with the offices of his firm throughout the country.

Like other markets, a security exchange facilitates communication between buyers and sellers. For example, Merrill Lynch, Pierce, Fenner and Smith, Inc., (the largest brokerage firm) might receive an order in its Atlanta office from a customer who wants to buy 100 shares of General Motors stock. Simultaneously, a brokerage house in Denver might receive an order from a customer wishing to sell 100 shares of GM. Each broker would communicate by wire with his firm's representative on the NYSE. Other brokers throughout the country are also communicating with their own exchange members. The exchange members with *sell orders* offer the shares for sale, and they are bid for by the members with *buy orders*. Thus, the exchanges operate as *auction markets*.[3]

Stock Market Reporting

Securities that are traded on the organized security exchanges are called *listed securities*, and are distinguished from other securities, known as *unlisted securities*. (Unlisted securities are traded in the over-the-counter market, which is discussed below.)

Considerable information is available dealing with transactions among listed securities, and the very existence of this information reduces the uncertainty inherent in security investments. This reduction of uncertainty, of course, makes listed securities relatively attractive to investors, and it lowers the cost of capital to firms.[4] We cannot delve

---

2. New York Stock Exchange, *1976 Fact Book*, p. 58.

3. This discussion is highly simplified. The exchanges have members known as "specialists," who facilitate the trading process by keeping an inventory of shares of the stocks in which they specialize. If a buy order comes in at a time when no sell order arrives, the specialist may sell off some of his inventory. Similarly, if a sell order comes in, the specialist will buy and add to his inventory.

4. If you think the stock markets today are risky, just imagine what it was like in the era *before* the existence of the SEC, routine reporting, and the like!

deeply into the matter of financial reporting—this is more properly the field of investment analysis—but it is useful to explain the most widely used service, the New York Stock Exchange reporting system.

Figure 12–1
Stock Market
Transactions

−1977− High	Low	Stocks	Div.	P-E Ratio	Sales 100s	High	Low	Close	Net Chg.
				−A−A−A−					
37½	32⅜	ACF Ind	1.80	9	41	36¼	36	36¼	....
23¼	19¾	AMF	1.24	10	164	20¾	20½	20⅝	....
15⅜	13½	APL Cp	1	5	1	13¾	13¾	13¾+	⅛
50¾	38⅛	ARASv	1.32	10	53	42¾	41¼	41⅜−	1⅛
23⅝	17¼	ASALtd	.80	..	183	19¾	19½	19½−	⅜
10¾	9⅜	ATOInc	.40	6	101	10	9⅞	9⅞−	¼
49⅛	42¼	AbbtLab	1	13	247	43¾	42½	42⅞−	1
3½	2¾	AdmDg	.04	5	3	2⅞	2⅞	2⅞	....
13¼	11⅝	AdmEx	1.15e	..	55	12⅜	12¼	12⅜	....
5	3⅞	AdmMil	.05e	8	6	4⅛	4	4⅛+	⅛
14⅜	10½	Addrssg	.10e	17	94	11	10⅝	10⅞−	⅛
35¾	28⅜	AetnaLf	1.20	8	547	32⅜	31½	31¾+	½
51	44⅝	AetnaLf	pf 2	..	3	48	47½	48 +	3
14½	10½	Aguirre		..	47	13¾	13½	13⅝−	⅛
20	15⅛	Ahmans	.40	6	104	19⅛	18⅞	19 −	¼
3⅞	3	Aileen		60	55	3⅛	3	3	....
35⅞	25	AirProd	.20b	11	245	26½	26	26¼−	¼
15½	12⅞	AirbnFrt	.60	11	27	14¼	13⅞	13⅞−	½
32⅜	28¼	Airco	1.15	7	40	31⅝	31⅛	31⅝+	⅜
19⅛	16	Akzona	1.20	78	31	18⅜	17⅝	18 −	¼
16⅞	14⅜	AlaGas	1.28	7	2	15⅜	15⅛	15⅛−	¼

Source: *Wall Street Journal*, 20 April 1977
(reporting transactions on 19 April 1977).

Figure 12−1 is a section of "the stock market page" taken from the *Wall Street Journal* reporting of NYSE-Composite Transactions, which include trades on five regional exchanges, trades reported by the National Association of Securities Dealers, and from Instinet (explained below). Stocks are listed alphabetically with the stocks whose names consist of capital letters listed first. The items are explained by reference to the information on Abbott Labs, a drug company. The two columns on the left show the highest and the lowest prices at which the stocks have sold during the year; Abbott has traded in the range from $42 ¼ to $49 ⅛ (or $42.25 to $49.125). The figure just to the right of the company's abbreviated name is the dividend rate based on the most recent regular quarterly payment. Abbott Labs is expected to pay $1.00 a share in 1977. Next comes the P/E ratio, or the current price of the stock divided by its earnings per share during the last year. (Price/earnings ratios are discussed at some length in Chapter 17.)

After the P/E ratio comes the volume of trading for the day; 24,700 shares of Abbott Labs stock were traded on April 19, 1977. Following the volume come the high and the low prices for the day and the closing price. On April 19 Abbott traded as high as $43 ³/₄ (or $43.75) and as low as $42 ¹/₂, while the last trade was at $42 ⁷/₈. The last column gives the change from the closing price on the previous day. Abbott Labs was down $1.00, so the previous close must have been $43 ⁷/₈ (since $43 ⁷/₈ − 1 = $42 ⁷/₈, the indicated closing price on April 18). A set of footnotes always accompanies the stock market quotes, giving additional information about specific issues.

Margin Trading and Short Selling

Two practices—margin trading and short selling—that are said to contribute to the securities markets' efficiency are described next.

Margin trading involves the buying of securities on credit. For example, when margin requirements are 80 percent, 100 shares of a stock selling for $100 a share can be bought by putting up, in cash, only $8,000, or 80 percent of the purchase price, and borrowing the remaining $2,000. The stockbroker lends the margin purchaser the funds, retaining custody of the stock as collateral. Margin requirements are determined by the Federal Reserve Board (the Fed). When the Fed judges that stock market activity and prices are unduly stimulated by easy credit, it raises margin requirements and thus reduces the amount of credit available for the purchase of stocks. On the other hand, if the Fed desires to stimulate the market as part of its overall monetary policy operations, it reduces margin requirements. In January 1974, for example, the margin was lowered from 65 to 50 percent.

Short selling is somewhat more complicated. Suppose you own 100 shares of ZN, which is currently selling for $80 a share. If you become convinced that ZN is overpriced and that it is going to fall to $40 within the next year, you would probably sell your stock. Now suppose you do not own any ZN, but you still think the price will fall from $80 to $40. If you are really convinced that this drop will occur, you can do what is called *go short* in ZN, or *sell ZN short*.

Short selling means selling a security that is not owned by the seller. To effect a short sale, you borrow, say, 100 shares of ZN from your broker, then sell these shares in the normal manner for $80 a share, or $8,000 in total. Suppose you are correct and ZN declines to $40 a share. You could buy 100 shares, and record a $4,000 profit. Of course, if ZN had gone up to $150 instead of declining, you would have had to pay $15,000 to replace the stock you borrowed to sell for $8,000, so you would have lost $7,000. The advantage claimed for short selling is that it increases the number of participants operating in the market, makes a more "continuous" market, and thereby reduces fluctuations in stock prices. This is, however, a controversial subject.

Insofar as margin trading and short selling do make a more continuous market, they encourage stock ownership and have two beneficial effects: (1) They broaden ownership of securities by increasing the ability of people to buy securities. (2) They provide for a more active market, and more active trading makes for narrower price fluctuations. However, when a strong speculative psychology grips the market, margin trading can be a fuel that feeds the speculative fervor, while short selling can aggravate pessimism on the downside. The downside effects of short selling are somewhat restricted, however, in that a short sale may not be made at a lower price than that of the last previously recorded sale. Thus, if a stock is in a continuous decline, short selling cannot occur; hence it cannot be used to push the stock down. In the 1920s, before this rule was put into effect, market manipulators could and did use short sales to drive prices down. Today most short selling occurs when stocks are rising rapidly, and this has a stabilizing influence.

Benefits Provided by Security Exchanges

Organized security exchanges are said to provide important benefits to businesses in at least four ways.

1. Security exchanges facilitate the investment process by providing a marketplace in which to conduct transactions efficiently and relatively inexpensively. Investors are thus assured that they will have a place in which to sell their securities, if they decide to do so. The increased liquidity thus provided by the exchanges makes investors willing to accept a lower rate of return on securities than they would otherwise require. This means that exchanges lower the cost of capital to businesses.

2. By providing a market, exchanges create an institution in which continuous transactions test the values of securities. The purchases and sales of securities record judgments on the values and prospects of companies and their securities. Companies whose prospects are judged favorably by the investment community will have higher values, thus facilitating new financing and growth.

3. Security prices are relatively more stable because of the operation of the security exchanges. Organized markets improve liquidity by providing continuous markets which make for more frequent, but smaller, price changes. In the absence of organized markets, price changes would be less frequent but more violent.

4. The securities markets aid in the digestion of new security issues and facilitate their successful flotation.

These benefits are important, but not all firms are in a position to utilize the exchanges. Such firms can, however, get many of the same benefits by having their securities traded in the over-the-counter market.

In the recent changes affecting the trading in securities, two are particularly worthy of note. The 1975 Securities Acts Amendments state that no national securities exchange may impose a schedule of minimum fixed commission rates after May 1, 1976. It is still too early to judge its impact. One likely effect is the "unbundling" of joint services such as research reports from the activities provided by brokerage firms.

The Securities Acts Amendments of 1975 also provide for the development of a national market system. Two concepts of a central market system have emerged. One, sponsored by the NYSE, envisions a single trading exchange. The other concept sees trading in a number of places with competition among them, but linked by a system of communications between participants, including clearing and settlement facilities. The SEC is empowered to exercise leadership in developing such a system.

Over-the-Counter Security Markets (OTC)

The over-the-counter securities market is the term used for all of the buying and selling activity in securities that does not take place on a stock exchange. The OTC market includes stocks of all types and sizes of U.S. corporations as well as some foreign issues. In the OTC market there are approximately 30,000 common stocks of public corporations, but only about 10,000 are actively traded. This is about three times the number of companies listed on the organized exchanges. In addition, it is in the OTC market that transactions take place in: (1) almost all bonds of U.S. corporations, (2) almost all bonds of federal, state, and local governments, (3) open-end investment company shares or mutual funds, (4) new issues of securities, (5) most secondary distributions of large blocks of stock, whether or not listed on an exchange, and (6) stocks of most of the country's banks and insurance companies.

The exchanges operate as auction markets in which the trading process is achieved through agents making transactions at one geographically centralized exchange location. On an exchange, firms known as specialists are responsible for matching buy and sell orders and for maintaining an orderly market in a particular security. In contrast, the OTC market is a dealer market—meaning that business is conducted across the country by broker/dealers known as market makers. These are dealers who stand ready to buy and sell securities in a manner similar to a wholesale supplier of goods or merchandise. The exchanges are used to match buy and sell orders that come in more or less simultaneously. But if a stock is traded less frequently, perhaps because it is a new or a small firm, matching buy and sell orders might require an extended period of time. To avoid this problem, some broker/dealer firms maintain an inventory of the stocks. They buy when individual investors wish to sell, and sell when investors want to buy. At one time the inventory of securities was kept in a safe, and when bought and sold, they were literally passed "over the counter."

The brokers and dealers operating in the over-the-counter markets communicate through a network of private wires, telephone lines, and since 1971 by an electronic quotation system called NASDAQ, whose letters stand for the National Association of Securities Dealers Automated Quotation system. NASDAQ is a computerized system which provides for current price quotations to be displayed on terminals in subscribers' offices.

The term "third market" refers to over-the-counter trading in listed securities by nonmembers of an exchange. It generally represents trades of large blocks of listed stocks off the floor of the exchange, with a brokerage house acting as an intermediary between two institutional investors.

The "fourth market" refers to direct transfers of blocks of stock among institutional investors without an intermediary broker. A well-known example was the arrangement between the Ford Foundation and the Rockefeller Foundation to exchange the common stocks of the Ford Motor Co. and Standard Oil of New Jersey. Such transactions have led to the development of *Instinet,* a computerized quotation system with display terminals to provide communications between major institutional investors.

The development of the third and fourth markets reflects the increased importance of institutional investors in stock trading. During the decade of the 1960s, for example, the equity holdings of private, noninsured pension funds rose by over 500 percent, of state and local retirement funds by over 2,800 percent, and of investment companies (mutual funds) by over 300 percent. New York Stock Exchange studies indicate that the institutions by the mid-1970s held one-third of NYSE-listed stocks and accounted for over one-half the dollar volume on the NYSE.

In terms of numbers of issues, the majority of stocks are traded over the counter. However, because the stocks of larger companies are listed on the exchanges, it is estimated that two-thirds of the dollar volume of stock trading takes place on the exchanges. The situation is reversed in the bond market. Although the bonds of a number of the larger companies are listed on the NYSE bond list, over 95 percent of bond transactions take place in the over-the-counter market. The reason for this is that bonds typically are traded among the large financial institutions, for example, life insurance companies and pension funds, which deal in very large blocks of securities. It is relatively easy for the over-the-counter bond dealers to arrange the transfer of large blocks of bonds among the relatively few holders of the bonds. It would be impossible to conduct similar operations in the stock market among the literally millions of large and small stockholders.

Decision to List Stock

The exchanges have certain requirements that firms must meet before their stock can be listed—these requirements relate to size of company, number of years in business, earnings record, number of shares outstanding and their market value, and the like. In general, requirements become more stringent as we move from the regional exchanges toward the NYSE.

The firm itself makes the decision to seek to list or not to list its securities on an exchange. Typically, the stocks of new and small companies are traded over-the-counter—there is simply not enough activity to justify the use of an auction market for such stocks. As the company grows, establishes an earnings record, expands the number of shares outstanding, and increases its list of stockholders, it may decide to apply for listing on one of the regional exchanges. For example, a Chicago company might list on the Midwest Stock Exchange, or a West Coast company might list its stock on the Pacific Coast Exchange. As the company grows still more, and as its stock becomes distributed throughout the country, it may seek a listing on the American Stock Exchange, the smaller of the two national exchanges. Finally, if it becomes one of the nation's leading firms, it could switch to the Big Board, the New York Stock Exchange.

Assuming a company qualifies, many people believe that listing is beneficial both to it and to its stockholders. Listed companies receive a certain amount of free advertising and publicity, and their status as a listed company enhances their prestige and reputation. This probably has a beneficial effect on the sales of the products of the firm, and it probably is advantageous in terms of lowering the required rate of return on the common stock. Investors respond favorably to increased information, increased liquidity, and increased prestige; by providing investors with these services in the form of listing their companies' stocks, financial managers lower their firms' costs of capital.[5]

Investment Banking

In the American economy, saving is done by one group of persons, while investing is done by another. ("Investing" is used here in the sense of actually putting money into plant, equipment, and inventory, not in the sense of buying securities.) Thus, savings are placed with financial intermediaries who, in turn, make the funds available to firms wishing to acquire plant and equipment and to hold inventories.

One of the major institutions performing this channeling role is the *investment banking* institution. The term "investment banker" is somewhat misleading in that investment bankers are neither investors nor bankers. That is, they do not invest their own funds permanently; nor are they repositories for individuals' funds, as are commercial banks or savings banks. What, then, is the nature of investment banking?

The many activities of investment bankers may be described first in general terms and then with respect to specific functions. The historical and traditional function of the investment banker has been to act as the middleman in channeling driblets of savings and funds of individuals into the purchase of business securities. The investment banker does this by purchasing and distributing the new securities of individual companies. Specifically, the investment banker performs the functions of underwriting, distribution of securities, and advice and counsel.

Underwriting

Underwriting is the insurance function of bearing the risks of adverse price fluctuations during the period in which a new issue of securities is being distributed. The nature of the underwriting function of the investment banker can best be conveyed by an example. A business firm needs $10 million. It selects an investment banker, conferences are

5. Two industries, banking and insurance, have a tradition against listing their stocks. The historic reason given by banks was that they were afraid that a falling market price of their stocks would lead depositors to think the bank itself was in danger and, thus, would cause a run on the bank. Some basis for such fears may have existed before the creation of the Federal Deposit Insurance Corporation in 1935, but the fear is no longer justified. The other reason for banks' not listing has to do with reporting financial information. The exchanges require that quarterly financial statements be sent to all stockholders; banks have been reluctant to provide financial information. Increasingly, bank regulatory agencies are requiring public disclosure of additional financial information. As this trend continues, it is expected that banks will increasingly seek to list their securities on exchanges. A notable first is the Chase Manhattan Bank, which was listed on the New York Stock Exchange in 1965.

held, and the decision is made to issue $10 million of bonds. An underwriting agreement is drawn up; on a specific day, the investment banker presents the company with a check for $10 million (less commission). In return, the investment banker receives bonds in denominations of $1,000 each, which he sells to the public.

The company receives the $10 million before the investment banker has sold the bonds. Between the time the investment banker pays the firm the $10 million and the time he has sold the bonds, the investment banker bears all the risk of market price fluctuations in the bonds. Conceivably, it can take the investment banker 10, 20, 30 days, 6 months, or longer to sell bonds. If in the interim the bond market collapses, the investment banker will be carrying the risk of loss on the sale of the bonds.

There have been dramatic instances of bond market collapses within one week after an investment banker has bought $50 million or $100 million of bonds. For example, in the spring of 1974 an issue of New Jersey Sporting Arena bonds dropped $140 per $1,000 bond during the underwriting period, costing the underwriters an estimated $8 million loss. However, the issuing firm does not need to be concerned about the risk of market price fluctuations while the investment banker is selling the bonds. The firm has received its money. *One fundamental economic function of the investment banker, then, is to underwrite the risk of a decline in the market price between the time the investment banker transmits the money to the firm and the time the bonds are placed in the hands of their ultimate buyers.* For this reason, the investment banker is often called an underwriter: he is an underwriter of risk during the distribution period.

Distribution

The second function of the investment banker is marketing new issues of securities. The investment banker is a specialist who has a staff and dealer organization to distribute securities. He can, therefore, perform the physical distribution function more efficiently and more economically than could an individual corporation. Sporadically, whenever it wished to sell an issue of securities, each corporation would find it necessary to establish a marketing or selling organization. This would be a very expensive and ineffective method of selling securities. The investment banker has a permanent, trained staff and dealer organization continually available to distribute the securities. In addition, the investment banker's reputation for selecting good companies and pricing securities fairly builds up a broad clientele over a period, further increasing the efficiency with which he can sell securities.

**Advice and
Counsel**

Since the investment banker is engaged in the origination and sale of securities, through experience he becomes an expert in advising about terms and characteristics of securities that will appeal to investors. The advice and guidance of the investment banker in determining the characteristics and provisions of securities so that they will be successfully marketed is valuable. Furthermore, the reputation of the investment banker, as a seller of the securities, depends upon the subsequent performance of the securities. Therefore, he often will sit on the boards of directors of firms whose securities he has sold. In this way he is able to provide continuing financial counsel and to increase the firm's probability of success.

**Investment
Banking
Operation**

Probably the best way to gain a clear understanding of the investment banking function is to trace the history of a new issue of securities.[6] Accordingly, in this section we describe the steps necessary to issue new securities.

**Preunderwriting
Conferences**

First, the members of the issuing firm and the investment banker hold preunderwriting conferences, at which they discuss the amount of capital to be raised, the type of security to be issued, and the terms of the agreement.

Memorandums will be written by the treasurer of the issuing company to the firm's directors and other officers, describing alternative proposals suggested at the conferences. Meetings of the board of directors of the issuing company will be held to discuss the alternatives and to attempt to reach a decision.

At some point, the issuer enters an agreement with the investment banker that a flotation will take place. The investment banker will then begin to conduct an underwriting investigation. If the company is proposing to purchase additional assets, the underwriter's engineering staff may make an analysis of the proposed acquisition. A public accounting firm will be called upon to make an audit of the issuing firm's

---

6. The process described here relates primarily to situations where the firm doing the financing picks an investment banker, then negotiates with him over the terms of the issue. An alternative procedure, used extensively only in the public utility industry, is for the selling firm to specify the terms of the new issue, then to have investment bankers bid for the entire new issue by use of *sealed bids*. The very high fixed costs that an investment banker must incur to investigate thoroughly the company and its new issue rule out sealed bids except for the very largest issues. The operation described in this section is called *negotiated underwriting;* competition is keen among underwriters, of course, to develop and maintain working relations with business firms.

financial situation, and they will also aid in the preparation of the registration statements for the Securities and Exchange Commission (SEC) in connection with these issues.

A firm of lawyers will be called in to interpret and judge the legal aspects of the flotation. In addition, the originating underwriter, who will be the manager of the subsequent underwriting syndicate, will make an exhaustive investigation of the prospects of the company.

When the investigations are completed but before registration with the SEC, an underwriting agreement will be drawn up by the investment banker. Terms of the tentative underwriting agreement may be modified through discussions between the underwriter and the issuing company, but finally an agreement will be reached on all underwriting terms except the actual price of the securities.

Registration Statement

A registration statement will then be filed with the SEC. The statutes set a 20-day waiting period (which in practice may be shortened or lengthened by the SEC) during which time its staff analyzes the registration statement to determine whether there are any omissions or misrepresentations of fact. The SEC may file exceptions to the registration statement or may ask for additional information from the issuing company or the underwriters during the examination period. During this period, the investment bankers are not permitted to offer the securities for sale, although they may print preliminary prospectuses with all the customary information except the offering price.

Pricing the Securities

The actual price the underwriter pays the issuer is not generally determined until the close of the registration period. There is no universally followed practice, but one common arrangement for a new issue of stock calls for the investment banker to buy the securities at a prescribed number of points below the closing price on the last day of registration. For example, in October 1977 the stock of Wilcox Chemical Company had a current price of $38, and had traded between $35 and $40 a share during the previous three months. The firm and the underwriter agreed that the investment banker would buy 200,000 new shares at $2.50 below the closing price on the last day of registration. The stock closed at $36 on the day the SEC released the issue, so the firm received $33.50 a share. Typically, such agreements have an escape clause that provides for the contract to be voided if the price of the securities ends below some predetermined figure. In the illustrative case, this "upset" price was set at $34 a share. Thus, if the closing price of the shares on the last day of registration had been $33.50, Wilcox would have had the option of withdrawing from the agreement.

The preceding arrangement holds, of course, only for additional offerings of the stock of firms whose old stock was previously traded. When a company "goes public" for the first time, the investment banker and the firm will negotiate a price in accordance with the valuation principles described in Chapter 17.

The investment banker will have an easier job if the issue is priced relatively low. The issuer of the securities naturally wants as high a price as possible. Some conflict of interest on price therefore arises between the investment banker and the issuer. If the issuer is financially sophisticated and makes comparisons with similar security issues, the investment banker is forced to price close to the market.

Underwriting Syndicate

The investment banker with whom the issuing firm has conducted its discussions will not typically handle the purchase and distribution of the issue alone, unless the issue is a very small one. If the sums of money involved are large and the risks of price fluctuations are substantial, the investment banker forms a syndicate in an effort to minimize the amount of risk he carries. A syndicate is a temporary association for the purpose of carrying out a specific objective. The nature of the arrangements for a syndicate in the underwriting and sale of a security through an investment banker may best be understood with the aid of Figure 12–2.

The managing underwriter invites other investment bankers to participate in the transaction on the basis of their knowledge of the particular kind of offering to be made and on the basis of their strength and dealer contacts in selling securities of this type. Each investment banker has business relations with other investment bankers and dealers; thus, each investment banker has a selling group consisting of himself and other investment bankers and dealers.

Some firms combine all these characteristics. For example, Merrill Lynch, Pierce, Fenner and Smith underwrites some issues and manages the underwriting of others. On still other flotations, it will be invited by the manager to join in the distribution of the issue. It also purchases securities as a dealer and carries an inventory of those securities. It publishes lists of securities it has for sale. In addition to being a dealer, Merrill Lynch, of course, carries on substantial activity as a broker. An individual investment firm may carry on all these functions, just as a department store sells many varieties of merchandise.

There are also firms with a narrower range of functions—specialty dealers, specialty brokers, and specialty investment counselors. Thus, in the financial field there is specialization of financial functions, as well as department store types of operations. A *dealer* purchases securities outright, holds them in inventory as a grocery store would hold its inventory, and sells them at whatever price he can get. He may benefit from price appreciation or he may suffer a loss on declines, as any merchandiser does. A *broker*, on the other hand, takes orders for purchases and transmits them to the proper exchange; his gain is the commission he charges for the service.

Figure 12–2
Diagram of Sales of
$100 Million of Bonds
through Investment
Bankers

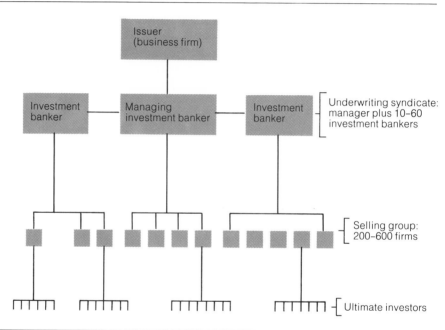

Syndicates are used in the distribution of securities for three reasons: (1) A single investment banker may be financially unable to handle a large issue alone. (2) The originating house may desire to spread the risk even if it is financially able to handle the issue alone. (3) The utilization of several selling organizations, as well as other underwriters, permits an economy of selling effort and expense and encourages broader, nationwide distribution.

Participating underwriters and dealers are provided with full information on all phases of these financing transactions, and they share in the underwriting commission. Suppose that an investment banker buys $10 million worth of bonds to be sold at par, or $1,000 each. If the investment banker receives a two-point spread, he will buy the bonds from the issuer at 98; thus, he must pay the issuer $9.8 million for the issue of

$10 million. Typically, on a two-point spread, the managing underwriter will receive the first one-quarter of 1 percent for originating and managing the syndicate. Next, the entire underwriting group will receive about three-quarters of 1 percent. Members of the selling group receive about 1 percent as a sales commission.

If the manager of the underwriting group makes a sale to an ultimate purchaser of the securities, he will receive the $1/4$ percent as manager, $3/4$ percent as underwriter, and 1 percent as seller—the full 2 percent. If he wholesales some of the securities to members of the selling group who make the ultimate sale, the latter will receive the 1 percent selling commission and the manager will receive the other 1 percent for managing and underwriting the issue. If the issue is managed by one firm, underwritten by a second, and sold by a third, the 2 percent commission is divided, with 1 percent going to the selling firm, $3/4$ percent to the underwriter, and $1/4$ percent to the manager of the underwriting group.

Ordinarily, each underwriter's liability is limited to his agreed-upon commitment. For example, if an investment banker participates in a $20 million offering and agrees to see to it that $5 million of the securities are sold, his responsibility ends when he sells his $5 million.

Selling Group

The selling group is formed primarily for the purpose of distributing securities; it consists of dealers, who take relatively small participations from the members of the underwriting group. The underwriters act as wholesalers; members of the selling group act as retailers. The number of houses in a selling group depends partly upon the size of the issue. A selling group may have as many as 300 to 400 dealers.

The operation of the selling group is controlled by the *selling group agreement*, which usually covers the following major points.

Description of the Issue. The description is set forth in a report on the issue, the prospectus, which fully describes the issue and the issuer.

Concession. Members of the selling group subscribe to the new issue at a public offering price less the *concession* given to them as a commission for their selling service. In the preceding example, this was 1 percent.

Handling Purchased Securities. The selling group agreement provides that no member of the selling group be permitted to sell the securities below the public offering price. The syndicate manager invariably "pegs" the quotation in the market by placing continuous orders to buy at the public offering price. A careful record is kept of bond or stock certificate numbers so that repurchased bonds may be identified with the member of the selling group who sold them. The general practice is to cancel the commission on such securities and add brokerage costs incurred in the repurchase. Repurchased securities are then placed with other dealers for sale.[7]

Duration of Selling Group. The most common provision in selling group agreements is that the group has an existence of 30 days, subject to earlier termination by the manager. The agreement may be extended, however, for an additional 80 days by members representing 75 percent of the selling group.

Offering and Sale

After the selling group has been formed, the actual offering takes place. Publicity for the sale is given in advance of the offering date. Advertising material is prepared for release as soon as permissible. The actual day of the offering is chosen with a view to avoiding temporary congestion in the security market and other unfavorable events or circumstances.

The formal public offering is called "opening the books," an archaic term reflecting ancient customs of the investment banking trade. When the books are opened, the manager accepts subscriptions to the issue from both selling group participants and outsiders who may wish to buy. If the demand is great, the books may be closed immediately and an announcement made that the issue is oversubscribed; the issue is said to "fly out the window." If the reception is weak, the books may remain open for an extended period.

Market Stabilization

During the period of the offering and distribution of securities, the manager of the underwriting group typically stabilizes the price of the issue. The duration of the price-pegging operation is usually 30 days. The price is pegged by placing orders to buy at a specified price in the market. The pegging operation is designed to prevent a cumulative downward movement in the price, which would result in losses for all members of the underwriting group. As the manager of the underwriting group has the major responsibility, he assumes the task of pegging the price.

If the market deteriorates during the offering period, the investment banker carries a rather substantial risk. For this reason, the pegging operation may not be sufficient to protect the underwriters. In one Pure

---

7. Without these repurchase arrangements, a member of the selling group could sell his share of the securities on the open market instead of to new purchasers. Since the pegging operation is going on, there would be a ready market for the securities; consequently, a penalty is necessary to avoid thwarting of the syndicate operation.

Oil Company issue of $44 million convertible preferred stock, only $1 million of shares were sold at the $100 offering price. At the conclusion of the underwriting agreement, initial trading took place at $74, incurring for the investment bankers a loss of over $11 million ($43 million $\times$ 26 percent). In the Textron issue of June 1967, the offering was reduced from $100 million to $50 million because of market congestion, and still 5 percent of the bonds were unsold after the initial offering. Other such cases can be cited.

It has been charged that pegging the price during the offering period constitutes a monopolistic price-fixing arrangement. Investment bankers reply, however, that not to peg the price would increase the risk and therefore the underwriting cost to the issuer. On balance, it appears that the pegging operation has a socially useful function. The danger of monopolistic pricing is avoided, or at least mitigated substantially, by competitive factors. If an underwriter attempts to set a monopolistic price on a particular issue of securities, the investor can turn to thousands of other securities that are not price pegged. The degree of control over the market by the underwriter in a price-pegging operation seems negligible.

Costs of Flotation

The cost of selling new issues of securities is put into perspective in Table 12–1. The table summarizes recent data on costs of flotation compiled from data on the subject by the SEC. Two important generalizations can be drawn from this data:

1. The cost of flotation for common stock is greater than for preferred stock, and the costs of both are greater than the cost of flotation for bonds.
2. The cost of flotation as a percentage of the gross proceeds is greater for small issues than for large ones.

What are the reasons for these relationships? The explanations are found in the amount of risk involved and in the job of physical distribution. Bonds are generally bought in large blocks by a relatively few institutional investors, whereas stocks are bought by millions of individuals. For this reason the distribution job is harder for common stock, and the expenses of marketing it are greater. Similarly, stocks are more volatile than bonds, so underwriting risks are larger for stock than for bond flotations.

The explanation for the variation in cost with the size of issue is also easily found. In the first place, certain fixed expenses are associated with any distribution of securities: the underwriting investigation, the

**Table 12–1
Costs of Flotation as a Percentage of Proceeds for Common Stock Issues, 1971–1975***

Size of Issue ($ millions)	Underwriting				Rights with Standby Underwriting				Rights	
	Number	Compensation as a Percentage of Proceeds	Other Expenses as a Percentage of Proceeds	Total Cost as a Percentage of Proceeds	Number	Compensation as a Percentage of Proceeds	Other Expenses as a Percentage of Proceeds	Total Cost as a Percentage of Proceeds	Number	Total Cost as a Percentage of Proceeds
Under .50	0	—	—	—	0	—	—	—	3	8.99
.50–.99	6	6.96	6.78	13.74	2	3.43	4.80	8.24	2	4.59
1.00–1.99	18	10.40	4.89	15.29	5	6.36	4.15	10.51	5	4.90
2.00–4.99	61	6.59	2.87	9.47	9	5.20	2.85	8.06	7	2.85
5.00–9.99	66	5.50	1.53	7.03	4	3.92	2.18	6.10	6	1.39
10.00–19.99	91	4.84	0.71	5.55	10	4.14	1.21	5.35	3	0.72
20.00–49.99	156	4.30	0.37	4.67	12	3.84	0.90	4.74	1	0.52
50.00–99.99	70	3.97	0.21	4.18	9	3.96	0.74	4.70	2	0.21
100.00–500.00	16	3.81	0.14	3.95	5	3.50	0.50	4.00	9	0.13
Total/AVG	484	8.02	1.15	6.17	56	4.32	1.73	6.05	38	2.45

*Issues are included only if the company's stock was listed on the NYSE, AMEX, or regional exchanges prior to the offering; any associated secondary distribution represents less than 10 percent of the total proceeds of the issue, and the offering contains no other types of securities.

Source: Clifford W. Smith, Jr., "Substitute Methods for Raising Additional Capital: Rights Offerings versus Underwritten Issues," University of Rochester, GSM Working Paper Series No. 7616, August 1976, Table 2.

preparation of the registration statement, legal fees, and so forth. Since these expenses are relatively large and fixed, their percentage of the total cost of flotation runs high on small issues. Second, small issues are typically those of relatively less well-known firms, so underwriting expenses may be larger than usual because the danger of omitting vital information is greater. Furthermore, the selling job is more difficult: salesmen must exert greater effort to sell the securities of a less well-known firm. For these reasons the underwriting commission, as a percentage of the gross proceeds, is relatively high for small issues.

Flotation costs are also influenced by whether or not the issue is a "rights offering," and if it is, by the extent of the underpricing.[8] If rights are used and if the underpricing is substantial, then the investment banker bears little risk of inability to sell the shares. Further, very little selling effort will be required in such a situation. These two factors combine to enable a company to float new securities to its own stockholders at a relatively low cost. However, rights offerings without use of underwriters accounted for only 38 of the 578 issues sold — less than 7 percent, during the 1971–75 period covered in Table 12–1.

Regulation of Security Trading

The operations of investment bankers, exchanges, and over-the-counter markets described in the previous sections of this chapter are significantly influenced by a series of federal statutes enacted during and after 1933. The financial manager is affected by these laws for several reasons: (1) Corporate officers are subjected to personal liabilities. (2) The laws affect the ease and costs of financing, and they also affect the behavior of the money and capital markets in which the corporation's securities are sold and traded. (3) Investors' willingness to buy securities is influenced by the existence of safeguards provided by these laws.

Securities Act of 1933

The first of the securities acts, the Securities Act of 1933, followed congressional investigations of the stock market collapse of 1929–1932. The reasons motivating the act were (1) the large losses to investors, (2) the failures of many corporations on which little information had been provided, and (3) the misrepresentations that had been made to investors.

The basic objective of the Securities Act of 1933 is to provide for both *full disclosure* of relevant information and a *record of representations*. It seeks to achieve these objectives by the following means:

---

8. "Rights offerings" involve the sale of stock to existing stockholders. This topic is discussed extensively in Chapter 13.

1. It applies to all interstate offerings to the public (some exemptions are government bonds and bank stocks) in amounts of $500,000 or more.
2. Securities must be registered at least 20 days before they are publicly offered. The registration statement provides financial, legal, and technical information about the company. A prospectus summarizes this information for use in selling the securities. If information is inadequate or misleading, the SEC will delay or stop the public offering. (Obtaining the information required to review the registration statement may result in a waiting period that exceeds 20 days.)
3. After the registration has become effective, the securities may be offered if accompanied by the prospectus. Preliminary or "red herring" prospectuses may be distributed to potential buyers during the waiting period.
4. If the registration statement or prospectus contains misrepresentations or omissions of material facts, any purchaser who suffers a loss may sue for damages. Liabilities and severe penalties may be imposed on the issuer, its officers, directors, accountants, engineers, appraisers, underwriters, and all others who participated in the preparation of the registration statement.

The Act of 1933 provides for full disclosure. It also has resulted in a procedure for obtaining a record of representations.

Securities Exchange Act of 1934

The Securities Exchange Act of 1934 extends the disclosure principle, as applied to new issues by the Act of 1933, to trading in already issued securities (the "secondhand" securities market). It seeks to accomplish this by the following measures:

1. It establishes a Securities and Exchange Commission (the Federal Trade Commission had been administering the Act of 1933).
2. It provides for registration and regulation of national securities exchanges. Companies whose securities are listed on an exchange must file reports similar to registration statements with both the SEC and the stock exchange and must provide periodic reports as well.
3. It provides control over corporate "insiders." Officers, directors, and major stockholders of a corporation must file monthly reports of changes in holdings of the stock of the corporation. Any short-term profits from such transactions are payable to the corporation.
4. The Act of 1934 gives the SEC the power to prohibit manipulation by such devices as pools (aggregations of funds used to affect prices

artificially), wash sales (sales between members of the same group to record artificial transaction prices), and pegging the market other than during stock flotations.

5. The SEC is given control over the proxy machinery and practices.
6. Control over the flow of credit into security transactions is established by giving the board of governors of the Federal Reserve System the power to control margin requirements.

Appraisal of Regulation of Security Trading

Why should security transactions be regulated? It may be argued that a great body of relevant knowledge is necessary to make an informed judgment of the value of a security. Moreover, security values are subject to great gyrations, which influence stability and business conditions generally. Hence, social well-being requires that orderly markets be promoted.

The objectives of the regulation may be summarized into three points:

1. To protect the amateur investor from fraud and to provide him with a basis for more informed judgments.
2. To control the volume of bank credit to finance security speculation.
3. To provide orderly markets in securities.

Progress has been made on all three counts. There has been some cost in the increased time and expense involved in new flotations by companies, although the benefits seem worth their costs. The regulations are powerless to prevent investors from investing in unsound ventures or to prevent stock prices from skyrocketing during booms and falling greatly during periods of pessimism. Still, requirements for increased information have been of value in preventing fraud and gross misrepresentations.

From the standpoint of the financial manager, regulation has a twofold significance: (1) It affects the costs of issuing securities. (2) It affects the riskiness of securities, hence the rate of return investors require when they purchase stocks and bonds. As we will see in subsequent chapters, these two factors have an important bearing on the firm's cost of capital, and, through the capital budgeting process, on its investment decisions. Further, since business investment is a key determinant of employment and production in the economy, we will see that efficient capital markets have an important impact on all of society.

Summary

Securities are traded both on *exchanges* and in the *over-the-counter market*. The stocks of larger industrial and utility companies are generally listed on an exchange; stocks of financial institutions, small industrial firms, and practically all bonds are traded over the counter. From the standpoint of the financial manager, listing on an exchange seems advantageous for seasoned issues. The over-the-counter market may aid in the seasoning process until the security can meet the requirements for listing.

The investment banker provides middleman services to both the seller and the buyer of new securities. He helps plan the issue, underwrites it, and handles the job of selling the issue to the ultimate investor. The cost of this service to the issuer is related to the magnitude of the total job the banker must perform to place the issue. The investment banker must also look to the interests of his brokerage customers; if these investors are not satisfied with the banker's products, they will deal elsewhere.

Flotation costs are lowest for bonds, higher for preferred stocks, and highest for common stock. Larger companies have lower flotation costs than smaller ones for each type of security, and most companies can cut their stock flotation costs by issuing the new securities to stockholders through rights offerings. (Rights offerings are discussed in Chapter 13.)

The financial manager should be familiar with the federal laws regulating the issuance and trading of securities, because they influence his liabilities and affect financing methods and costs. Regulation of securities trading seeks (1) to provide information that investors can utilize as a basis for judging the merits of securities, (2) to control the volume of credit used in securities trading, and (3) to provide orderly securities markets. The laws do not, however, prevent either purchase of unsound issues or wide price fluctuations. They raise somewhat the costs of flotation but have probably decreased the cost of capital by increasing public confidence in the securities markets.

Questions

12–1. State several advantages to a firm that lists its stock on a major stock exchange.

12–2. Would you expect the cost of capital of a firm to be affected if it changed its status from one traded over the counter to one traded on the New York Stock Exchange? Explain.

12–3. Evaluate the following statement: Buying stocks is in the nature of true investment; stock is purchased in order to receive a dividend return on the invested capital. Short selling, on the other hand, is fundamentally a form of gambling; it is simply betting that a stock's price will decline. Consequently, if we do not wish to see Wall Street turned into an eastern Las Vegas, all short selling should be forbidden.

12–4. Evaluate the following statement: The fundamental purpose of the federal security laws dealing with new issues is to prevent investors, principally small ones, from sustaining losses on the purchase of stocks.

12–5. Suppose two firms were each selling $10 million of common stock. The firms are similar—that is, they are of the same size, are in the same industry, have the same leverage, and have other similarities—except that one is publicly owned and the other is closely held. Would their costs of flotation by the same? If different, state the probable relationships. If the issue were $10 million of bonds, would your answer be the same?

12–6. Define these terms: brokerage firm, underwriting group, selling group, and investment banker.

12–7. Each month the Securities and Exchange Commission publishes a report of the transactions made by the officers and directors of listed firms in their own companies' equity securities. Why do you suppose the SEC makes this report?

12–8. The SEC forbids officers and directors to sell short the shares of their own company. Why do you suppose this rule is on the books?

12–9. Prior to 1933, investment banking and commercial banking were both carried on by the same firm. In that year, however, the Banking Act required that these functions be separated. On the basis of your knowledge of investment banking and commercial banking, discuss the pros and cons of this forced separation.

12–10. Before entering a formal agreement, investment bankers investigate quite carefully the companies whose securities they underwrite; this is especially true of the issues of firms going public for the first time. Since the bankers do not themselves plan to hold the securities but plan to sell them to others as soon as possible, why are they so concerned about making careful investigations? Does your answer to the question have any bearing on the fact that investment banking is a very difficult field to "break into"?

12–11. If competitive bidding was required on all security offerings, would flotation costs be higher or lower? Would the size of the issuing firm be material in determining the effects of required competitive bidding?

12–12. Since investment bankers price new issues in relation to outstanding issues, should a spread exist between the yields on the new and the outstanding issues? Discuss this matter separately for stock issues and bond issues.

12–13. What issues are raised by the increasing purchase of equities by institutional investors?

Problems

12–1.[9] In March 1975, three executives of the Hughes Aircraft Company, one of the largest privately owned corporations in the world, decided to break away from Hughes and to set up a company of their own. The principal reason for this decision was capital gains; Hughes Aircraft stock is all privately owned, and the corporate structure makes it impossible for executives to be granted stock purchase options. Hughes's executives receive substantial salaries and bonuses, but this income is all taxable at normal tax rates, and no capital gains opportunities are available.

The three men, Jim Adcock, Robert Goddard, and Rick Aiken, have located a medium-size electronics manufacturing company available for purchase. All the stock of this firm, Baynard Industries, is owned by the founder, Joseph Baynard. Although the company is in excellent shape, Baynard wants to sell it because of his failing health. A price of $5.7 million has been established, based on a price/earnings ratio of 12 and annual earnings of $475,000. Baynard has given the three prospective purchasers an option to purchase the company for the agreed price; the option is to run for six months, during which time the three men are to arrange financing with which to buy the firm.

Adcock has consulted with Jules Scott, a partner in the New York investment banking firm of Williams Brothers and an acquaintance of some years' standing, to seek his assistance in obtaining the funds necessary to complete the purchase. Adcock, Goddard, and Aiken each have some money available to put into the new enterprise, but they need a substantial amount of outside capital. There is some possibility of borrowing part of the money, but Scott has discouraged this idea. His reasoning is, first, that Baynard Industries is already highly leveraged, and if the purchasers were to borrow additional funds, there would be a very severe risk that they would be unable to service this debt in the event of a recession in the electronics industry. Although the firm is currently earning $475,000 a year, this figure could quickly turn into a loss in the event of a few canceled defense contracts or cost miscalculations.

Scott's second reason for discouraging a loan is that Adcock, Goddard, and Aiken plan not only to operate Baynard Industries and seek internal growth but also to use the corporation as a vehicle for making further acquisitions of electronics companies. This being the case, Scott believes that it would be wise for the company to keep any borrowing potential in reserve for use in later acquisitions.

Scott proposes that the three partners obtain funds to purchase Baynard Industries in accordance with the figures shown in Table P12–1.

Baynard Industries would be reorganized with an authorized 5,000,000 shares, with 1,125,000 to be issued at the time the transfer takes place and the other 3,875,000 to be held in reserve for possible issuance in connection with acquisitions. Adcock, Goddard, and Aiken would each purchase 100,000 shares at a price of $1 a share, the par

9. This case study is taken from E. F. Brigham, Timothy J. Nantell, Robert T. Aubey, and Richard H. Pettway, *Cases in Managerial Finance*, 2d ed. (New York: Holt, Rinehart and Winston, 1974).

Table P12–1 Baynard Industries	Price paid to Joseph Baynard (12 × $475,000 earnings)		$5,700,000
	Authorized shares	5,000,000	
	Initially issued shares	1,125,000	
	Initial distribution of shares:		
	Adcock	100,000 shares at $1.00	$ 100,000
	Goddard	100,000 shares at $1.00	100,000
	Aiken	100,000 shares at $1.00	100,000
	Williams Brothers	125,000 shares at $7.00	875,000
	Public stockholders	700,000 shares at $7.00	4,900,000
		1,125,000	$6,075,000
	Underwriting costs: 5% of $4,900,000	$245,000	
	Legal fees, and so on, associated with issue	45,000	$ 290,000
			$5,785,000
	Payment to Joseph Baynard		5,700,000
	Net funds to Baynard Industries		$ 85,000

value. Williams Brothers would purchase 125,000 shares at a price of $7. The remaining 700,000 shares would be sold to the public at a price of $7 a share.

Williams Brothers' underwriting fee would be 5 percent of the shares sold to the public, or $245,000. Legal fees, accounting fees, and other charges associated with the issue would amount to $45,000, for a total underwriting cost of $290,000. After deducting the underwriting charges and the payment to Baynard from the gross proceeds of the stock sale, the reorganized Baynard Industries would receive funds in the amount of $85,000, which would be used for internal expansion purposes.

As a part of the initial agreement, Adcock, Goddard, and Aiken each would be given options to purchase an additional 80,000 shares at a price of $7 a share for one year. Williams Brothers would be given an option to purchase an additional 100,000 shares at $7 a share in one year.

a. What is the total underwriting charge, expressed as a percentage of the funds raised by the underwriter? Does this charge seem reasonable in the light of published statistics on the cost of floating new issues of common stock?

b. Suppose that the three men estimate the following probabilities for the firm's stock price one year from now:

Price	Probability
$ 1	.05
5	.10
9	.35
13	.35
17	.10
21	.05

Assuming Williams Brothers exercises its options, calculate the following ratio (ignore time-discount effects):

$$\frac{\text{Gross profit to Williams Brothers}}{\text{Funds raised by underwriter}}.$$

Disregard Williams Brothers' profit on the 125,000 shares it bought outright at the initial offering. Comment on the ratio.

c. Are Adcock, Goddard, and Aiken purchasing their stock at a "fair" price? Should the prospectus disclose the fact that they would buy their stock at $1 a share, whereas public stockholders would buy their stock at $7 a share?

d. Would it be reasonable for Williams Brothers to purchase its initial 125,000 shares at a price of $1?

e. Do you foresee any problems of control for Adcock, Goddard, and Aiken?

f. Would the expectation of an exceptionally large need for investment funds next year be a relevant consideration in deciding on the amount of funds to be raised now?

12-2. The Algonquin Table Company is planning to issue $5 million of new common stock. In reaching the decision as to the form of offering, two alternatives were considered:
1. A rights offering. Out-of-pocket cost as a percentage of new capital would be 1.4 percent.
2. An underwriting. Out-of-pocket cost as a percentage of new capital would be 7.0 percent.

Given the difference in cost, Algonquin's choice of the second alternative seems paradoxical.

a. From Table 12-1, what proportion of issues this size are made by rights offerings as compared to the use of underwriters?

b. Discuss the influence of other factors, in addition to direct costs cited, that must be taken into account in choosing between the two alternative methods of offering. In your answer consider the following as well as other factors that may occur to you:
(1) Timing of receipt of flows
(2) Risk
(3) Other internal benefits and costs
(4) Distribution
(5) Effect on stock price.

12-3. Each of three companies is considering a new offering.

The Crown Company in the paint manufacturing industry has total assets of $30 million. It contemplates a new common stock issue of $1.5 million. It has determined that use of an underwriter would be desirable.

The Apache Company in the "small aircraft" industry has assets of $1 billion. It intends a $40 million offering using rights with a standby underwriting.

AT&T plans a $500 million common stock offering using rights, and direct sale without use of an investment banker.

    a. What will the compensation costs as a percent of proceeds be for each of the three companies?

    b. Explain the reasons for the differences in costs.

Selected References

Altman, Edward I. "A Financial Early Warning System for Over-the-Counter Broker-Dealers." *Journal of Finance* 31 (Sept. 1976): 1201–17.

Archer, Stephen H., and Faerber, LeRoy G. "Firm Size and the Cost of Equity Capital." *Journal of Finance* 21 (Mar. 1966): 69–84.

Baumol, William J. *The Stock Market and Economic Efficiency.* New York: Fordham University Press, 1965.

Benston, George J., and Smith, Clifford W., Jr. "A Transactions Cost Approach to the Theory of Financial Intermediation." *Journal of Finance* 31 (May 1976): 215–31.

Brown, J. Michael. "Post-Offering Experience of Companies Going Public." *Journal of Business* (Jan. 1970): 10–18.

Burnham, I. W. "The Securities Industry: Financing Corporate America." *Financial Executive* 44 (Mar. 1976): 26–31.

Cohan, A. B. *Private Placements and Public Offerings: Market Shares since 1935.* Chapel Hill, N.C.: School of Business Administration, University of North Carolina, 1961.

———. "Yields on New Underwritten Corporate Bonds." *Journal of Finance* 17 (Dec. 1962): 585–605.

Copeland, Thomas E. "A Model of Asset Trading Under the Assumption of Sequential Information Arrival." *Journal of Finance* 31 (Sept. 1976): 1149–68.

Dann, Larry Y.; Mayers, David; and Raab, Robert J., Jr. "Trading Rules, Large Blocks and the Speed of Price Adjustment." *Journal of Financial Economics* 4 (Jan. 1977): 3–22.

Dougall, Herbert E. *Capital Markets and Institutions,* 2d ed. Englewood Cliffs, N.J.: Prentice-Hall, 1970.

Eiteman, David K. "The S.E.C. Special Study and the Exchange Markets." *Journal of Finance* 21 (May 1966): 311–23.

Friend, Irwin, and Blume, Marshall. "Competitive Commissions on the New York Stock Exchange." *Journal of Finance* 28 (Sept. 1973): 795–819.

Friend, Irwin; Hoffman, G. W.; and Winn, W. J. *The Over-the-Counter Securities Market.* New York: McGraw-Hill, 1958.

Friend, Irwin; Longstreet, James R.; Mendelson, Morris; Miller, Ervin; and Hess, Arleigh R., Jr. *Investment Banking and the New Issue Market.* Cleveland: World Publishing Co., 1967.

Furst, Richard W. "Does Listing Increase the Market Price of Common Stocks?" *Journal of Business* 43 (Apr. 1970): 174–80.

Goldsmith, Raymond W. *The Flow of Capital Funds in the Postwar Economy.* New York: National Bureau of Economic Research, 1965.

Goulet, Waldemar M. "Price Changes, Managerial Actions and Insider Trading at the Time of Listing." *Financial Management* 3 (Spring 1974): 30–36.

Hayes, Samuel L., III. "Investment Banking: Power Structure in Flux." *Harvard Business Review* 49 (Mar. – Apr. 1971): 136 – 52.

Ibbotson, Roger G., and Jaffe, Jeffrey F. " 'Hot Issue' Markets." *Journal of Finance* 30 (June 1975): 1027 – 42.

Johnson, Keith B.; Morton, T. Gregory; and Findlay, M. Chapman, III. "An Empirical Analysis of the Flotation Cost of Corporate Securities, 1971 – 1972." *Journal of Finance* 30 (June 1975): 1129 – 33.

Karna, Adi S. "The Cost of Private Versus Public Debt Issues." *Financial Management* 1 (Summer 1972): 65 – 67.

Krainer, Robert E. "A Reexamination of the Theory of Monopsonistic Discrimination in the Capital Market." *The Journal of Business* 47 (July 1974): 429 – 39.

Logue, Dennis E., and Lindvall, John R. "The Behavior of Investment Bankers: An Econometric Investigation." *Journal of Finance* 29 (Mar. 1974): 203 – 15.

Nelson, J. Russell. "Price Effects in Rights Offerings." *Journal of Finance* 20 (Dec. 1965): 647 – 50.

Robinson, Roland, and Bartell, H. Robert, Jr. "Uneasy Partnership: SEC/NYSE." *Harvard Business Review* 43 (Jan. – Feb. 1965): 76 – 88.

Sears, Gerald A. "Public Offerings for Smaller Companies." *Harvard Business Review* 46 (Sept. – Oct. 1968): 112 – 20.

Shaw, David C. "The Cost of Going Public in Canada." *Financial Executive* (July 1969): 20 – 28.

Soldofsky, Robert M. "Classified Common Stock." *The Business Lawyer* (Apr. 1968): 899 – 902.

———. "Convertible Preferred Stock: Renewed Life in an Old Form." *The Business Lawyer* (July 1969), 1385 – 92.

Soldofsky, Robert M., and Johnson, Craig R. "Rights Timing." *Financial Analysts' Journal* 23 (July – Aug. 1967): 101 – 4.

Stoll, Hans R., and Curley Anthony J. "Small Business and the New Issues Market for Equities." *Journal of Financial and Quantitative Analysis* 5 (Sept. 1970): 309 – 22.

Sullivan, Brian. "An Introduction to 'Going Public.' " *Journal of Accountancy* (Nov. 1965).

Van Horne, James C. "New Listings and Their Price Behavior." *Journal of Finance* 25 (Sept. 1970): 783 – 94.

———. *Function and Analysis of Capital Market Rates.* Englewood Cliffs, N.J.: Prentice-Hall, 1970.

West, Richard R., and Tinic, Seha M. "Corporate Finance and the Changing Stock Market." *Financial Management* 3 (Autumn 1974): 14 – 23.

13   **Common Stock**

Common equity, or if unincorporated firms are being considered, partnership or proprietorship interests, constitute the first source of funds to a new business and the base of support for borrowing by existing firms. Accordingly, our discussion of specific forms of long-term financing will begin with an analysis of common stock.

Apportionment of Income, Control, and Risk

The nature of equity ownership depends upon the form of the business or organization. The central problem revolves around an apportionment of certain rights and responsibilities among those who have provided the funds necessary for the operation of the business.

The rights and responsibilities attaching to equity consist of positive considerations—income potential and control of the firm—and negative considerations—loss potential, legal responsibility, and personal liability.

General Rights of Holders of Common Stock

The rights of holders of common stock in a business corporation are established by the laws of the state in which the corporation is chartered and by the terms of the charter granted by the state. The characteristics of charters are relatively uniform on many matters, including the following two:

Collective Rights. Certain collective rights are usually given to the holders of common stock. Some of the more important rights allow stockholders (1) to amend the charter with the approval of the appropriate officials in the state of incorporation; (2) to adopt and amend bylaws; (3) to elect the directors of the corporation; (4) to authorize the sale of fixed assets; (5) to enter into mergers; (6) to change the amount of authorized common stock; and (7) to issue preferred stock, debentures, bonds, and other securities.

Specific Rights. Holders of common stock also have specific rights as individual owners. (1) They have the right to vote in the manner prescribed by the corporate charter. (2) They may sell their stock certificates, their evidence of ownership, and in this way transfer their ownership interest to other persons. (3) They have the right to inspect the corporate books.[1] (4) They have the right to share residual assets of the corporation on dissolution; however, the holders of common stock are last among the claimants to the assets of the corporation.

Apportionment of Income

Two important positive considerations are involved in equity ownership: income and control. The right to income carries risks of loss. Control also involves responsibility and liability. In an individual proprietorship, using only funds supplied by the owner, the owner has a 100 percent right to income and control and to loss and responsibility. As soon as the proprietor incurs debt, however, he has entered into contracts that place limitations on his complete freedom to control the firm and to apportion the firm's income.

In a partnership, these rights are apportioned among the partners in an agreed manner. In the absence of a formal agreement, a division is made by state law. In a corporation more significant issues arise concerning the rights of the owners.

Apportionment of Control

Through the right to vote, holders of common stock have legal control of the corporation. As a practical matter, however, in many corporations the principal officers constitute all, or a majority of, the members of the board of directors. In such circumstances the board of directors may be controlled by the management, rather than vice versa. Management control, or control of a business by other than its owners, results. However, numerous examples demonstrate that stockholders can reassert their control if they are dissatisfied with the policies of the corporation. In recent years, proxy battles with the aim of altering corporate policies have occurred fairly often, and firms whose managers are unresponsive to stockholders' desires are subject to takeover bids by other firms.

As receivers of residual income, holders of common stock are frequently referred to as the ultimate entrepreneurs in the firm. They are the ultimate owners, and they have the ultimate control. Presumably the firm is managed on behalf of its owners, the holders of common stock, but there has been much dispute about the actual situation. The point of view has been expressed that the corporation is an institution with an existence separate from the owners', and that the corporation exists to fulfill certain functions for stockholders as only one among

---

1. Obviously, a corporation cannot have its business affairs disturbed by allowing every stockholder to go through any record the stockholder would like to inspect. A corporation could not wisely permit a competitor who happened to buy shares of its common stock to look at all the corporation records. There must be, and there are, practical limitations to this right.

other important groups, such as workers, consumers, and the economy as a whole. This view may have some validity, but it should also be noted that ordinarily the officers of a firm are also large stockholders. In addition, more and more firms are relating officers' compensation to the firm's profit performance, either by granting executives stock purchase options or by giving bonuses. These actions are, of course, designed to make managers' personal goals more consistent with those of the stockholders — to increase the firm's earnings and stock price.

Apportionment of Risk

Another consideration involved in equity ownership is risk. Because, on liquidation, holders of common stock are last in the priority of claims, the portion of capital they contribute provides a cushion for creditors if losses occur on dissolution. The equity-to-total-assets ratio indicates the percentage by which assets may shrink in value on liquidation before creditors will incur losses.

For example, compare two corporations, A and B, whose balance sheets are shown in Table 13–1. The ratio of equity to total assets in corporation A is 80 percent. Total assets would therefore have to shrink by 80 percent before creditors would lose money. By contrast, in corporation B the extent by which assets may shrink in value on liquidation before creditors lose money is only 40 percent.

Table 13–1
Balance Sheets for Corporations A and B

Corporation A			Corporation B		
	Debt	$ 20		Debt	$ 60
	Equity	80		Equity	40
Total assets $100	Total claims $100		Total assets $100	Total claims $100	

Common Stock Financing

Before undertaking an evaluation of common stock financing, it is desirable to describe some of its additional important characteristics. These topics include (1) the nature of voting rights, (2) the nature of the preemptive right, and (3) variations in the forms of common stock.

Nature of Voting Rights

For each share of common stock owned, the holder has the right to cast one vote at the annual meeting of stockholders of the corporation or at such special meetings as may be called.

Proxy. Provision is made for the temporary transfer of the right to vote by an instrument known as a *proxy*. The transfer is limited in its duration, typically for a specific occasion such as the annual meeting of stockholders.

The SEC supervises the use of the proxy machinery and issues frequent rules and regulations seeking to improve its administration. SEC supervision is justified for several reasons. First, if the proxy machinery is left wholly in the hands of management, there is a danger that the incumbent management will be self-perpetuated. Second, if it is made easy for minority groups of stockholders and opposition stockholders to oust management, there is danger that they may gain control of the corporation for temporary advantages or to place their friends in management positions.

Cumulative Voting. A method of voting that has come into increased prominence is cumulative voting. Cumulative voting for directors is required in 22 states, including California, Illinois, Pennsylvania, Ohio, and Michigan. It is permissible in 18, including Delaware, New York, and New Jersey. Ten states make no provision for cumulative voting.

Cumulative voting permits multiple votes for a single director. For example, suppose six directors are to be elected. The owner of 100 shares can cast 100 votes for each of the six openings. Cumulatively, then, he has 600 votes. When cumulative voting is permitted, the stockholder may accumulate his votes and cast 600 votes for *one* director, instead of 100 each for *six* directors. Cumulative voting is designed to enable a minority group of stockholders to obtain some voice in the control of the company by electing at least one director to the board.

The nature of cumulative voting is illustrated by use of the following formula:

$$req. = \frac{des.(n)}{\# + 1} + 1. \tag{13-1}$$

Here,

$req.$ = number of shares required to elect a desired number of directors
$des.$ = number of directors stockholder desires to elect
n = total number of shares of common stock outstanding and entitled to vote[2]
$\#$ = total number of directors to be elected

---

2. An alternative that may be agreed to by the contesting parties is to define *(n)* as the number of shares *voted*, not *authorized to vote*. This procedure, which in effect gives each group seeking to elect directors the same percentage of directors as their percentage of the voted stock, is frequently followed. When it is used a group that seeks to gain control with a minimum investment must estimate the percentage of shares that will be voted and then obtain control of more than 50 percent of that number.

The formula may be made more meaningful by an example. The ABC company will elect six directors. There are fifteen candidates and 100,000 shares entitled to vote. If a group desires to elect two directors, how many shares must it have?

$$req. = \frac{2 \times 100,000}{6 + 1} + 1 = 28,572. \tag{13-2}$$

Observe the significance of the formula. Here, a minority group wishes to elect one-third of the board of directors. They can achieve their goal by owning less than one-third the number of shares of stock.[3]

Alternatively, assuming that a group holds 40,000 shares of stock in this company, how many directors would it be possible for the group to elect, following the rigid assumptions of the formula? The formula can be used in its present form or can be solved for *des.* and expressed as

$$des. = \frac{(req. - 1)(\# + 1)}{n}. \tag{13-3}$$

Inserting the figures, the calculation would be

$$des. = \frac{39,999 \times 7}{100,000} = 2.8 \tag{13-4}$$

The 40,000 shares could elect two and eight-tenths directors. Since directors cannot exist as fractions, the group can elect only two directors.

As a practical matter, suppose that in the above situation the total number of shares is 100,000. Hence 60,000 shares remain in other hands. The voting of all the 60,000 shares may not be concentrated. Suppose the 60,000 shares (cumulatively, 360,000 votes) not held by our group are distributed equally among ten candidates, 36,000 shares held by each candidate. If our group's 240,000 votes are distributed equally for each of six candidates, we could elect all six directors even though we do not have a majority of the stock.

Actually, it is difficult to make assumptions about how the opposition votes will be distributed. What is shown here is a good example of game theory. One rule in the theory of games is to assume that your opponents will do the worst they can do to you and to counter with actions to minimize the maximum loss. This is the kind of assumption followed in the formula. If your opposition concentrates its votes in the optimum manner, what is the best you can do to work in the direction of your goal? Other plausible assumptions can be subsitituted if there

---

3. Note also that at least 14,287 shares must be controlled to elect one director. As far as electing a director goes, any number less than 14,287 constitutes a useless minority.

are sufficient facts to support alternative hypotheses about the behavior of the opponents.

Preemptive Right

The preemptive right gives holders of common stock the first option to purchase additional issues of common stock. In some states the preemptive right is made a part of every corporate charter; in others, it is necessary to insert the preemptive right specifically in the charter.

The purpose of this right is twofold. First, it protects the power of control of present stockholders. If it were not for this safeguard, the management of a corporation under criticism from stockholders could prevent stockholders from removing it from office by issuing a large number of additional shares at a very low price and purchasing these shares itself. Management would thereby secure control of the corporation to frustrate the will of the current stockholders.

The second, and by far the more important, protection that the preemptive right affords stockholders regards dilution of value. For example, assume that 1,000 shares of common stock, each with a price of $100, are outstanding, making the total market value of the firm $100,000. An additional 1,000 shares are sold at $50 a share, or for $50,000, thus raising the total market value of the firm to $150,000. When the total market value is divided by the new total shares outstanding, a value of $75 a share is obtained. Thus, selling common stock at below market value will dilute the price of the stock and will be detrimental to present stockholders and beneficial to those who purchased the new shares. The preemptive right prevents such occurrences. This point is discussed at length later in this chapter.

Forms of Common Stock[4]

Classified. Classified common stock was used extensively in the late 1920s, sometimes in ways that misled investors. During that period, class A common stock was usually nonvoting, and class B was typically voting. Thus promoters could control companies by selling large amounts of class A stock while retaining class B stock.

---

4. Accountants also use the term "par value" to designate an arbitrary value assigned when stock is sold. When a firm sells newly issued stock, it must record the transaction on its balance sheet. For example, suppose a newly created firm commences operations by selling 100,000 shares at $10 a share, raising a total of $1 million. This $1 million must appear on the balance sheet, but what will it be called? One choice would be to assign the stock a "par value" of $10 and label the $1 million "common stock." Another choice would be to assign a $1 par value and show $100,000 ($1 par value times 100,00 shares) as "common stock" and $900,000 as "paid-in surplus." Still another choice would be to disregard the term "par value" entirely—that is, use no-par stock—and record the $1 million as "common stock." Since the choice is quite arbitrary for all practical purposes, more and more firms are adopting the last procedure and abolishing the term "par value." Because there are quite enough useful concepts and terms in accounting and finance, we heartily applaud the demise of useless ones such as this.

In more recent years there has been a revival of class B common for sound purposes. It is used by small, new companies seeking to acquire funds from outside sources. Common stock A is sold to the public and typically pays dividends; it has full voting rights. Common stock B, however, is retained by the organizers of the company, but dividends are not paid on it until the company has established its earning power. By the use of the classified stock, the public can take a position in a conservatively financed growth company without sacrificing income.

Founders' Shares. Founders' shares are somewhat like class B stock except that they carry *sole* voting rights and typically do not have the right to dividends for a number of years. Thus the organizers of the firm are able to maintain complete control of the operations in the crucial initial development of the firm. At the same time, other investors are protected against excessive withdrawals of funds by owners.

Evaluation of Common Stock as a Source of Funds

Thus far, the chapter has covered the main characteristics of common stock, frequently referred to as equity shares. By way of a summary of the important aspects of common stock, we now appraise this type of financing from the standpoint of the issuer.

From Viewpoint of Issuer

Advantages. First, common stock does not entail fixed charges. If the company generates the earnings, it can pay common stock dividends. In contrast to bond interest, however, there is no legal obligation to pay dividends. Second, common stock carries no fixed maturity date. Third, since common stock provides a cushion against losses for creditors, the sale of common stock increases the credit-worthiness of the firm.

Fourth, common stock may at times be sold more easily than debt. Common stock appeals to certain investor groups for two reasons: (1) it typically carries a higher expected return than does preferred stock or debt, and (2) it provides the investor with a better hedge against inflation than does straight preferred stock or bonds because it represents the ownership of the firm. Ordinarily, common stock increases in value when the value of real assets arises during an inflationary period.[5]

Fifth, returns from common stock in the form of capital gains are subject to the lower personal income tax rates on capital gains. Hence

---

5. During the inflation of the last decade, the lags of product price increases behind the rise of input costs have depressed corporate earnings and increased the uncertainty of earnings growth, causing price/earnings multiples to fall.

the effective personal income tax rates on returns from common stock may be lower than the effective tax rates on the interest on debt.

Disadvantages. First, the sale of common stock extends voting rights or control to the additional stockowners who are brought into the company. For this reason, among others, additional equity financing is often avoided by small and new firms. The owner-managers may be unwilling to share control of their companies with outsiders.

Second, common stock gives more owners the right to share in income. The use of debt may enable the firm to utilize funds at a fixed low cost, whereas common stock gives equal rights to new stockholders to share in the net profits of the firm.

Third, as we saw in Chapter 12, the costs of underwriting and distributing common stock are usually higher than those for underwriting and distributing preferred stock or debt. Flotation costs for selling common stock are characteristically higher because (1) costs of investigating an equity security investment are higher than investigating the feasibility of a comparable debt security, and (2) stocks are more risky, which means equity holdings must be diversified, which in turn means that a given dollar amount of new stock must be sold to a greater number of purchasers than the same amount of debt.

Fourth, as we shall see in Chapter 19, if the firm has more equity or less debt than is called for in the optimum capital structure, the average cost of capital will be higher than necessary.

Fifth, common stock dividends are not deductible as an expense for calculating the corporation's income subject to the federal income tax, but bond interest is deductible. The impact of this factor is reflected in the relative cost of equity capital vis-à-vis debt capital.

From a Social Viewpoint

Common stock should also be considered from a social standpoint. Common stock is a desirable form of financing because it renders business firms, hence a major segment of the economy, less vulnerable to the consequences of declines in sales and earnings. If sales and earnings decline, common stock financing involves no fixed charges, the payment of which might force the firm into reorganization or bankruptcy.

However, another aspect of common stock financing may have less desirable social consequences. Common stock prices fall in recessions, representing a rise in the cost of equity capital. The rising cost of equity raises the overall cost of capital, which in turn reduces investment. This reduction further aggravates the recession. However, an expanding economy is accompanied by rising stock prices, and with rising stock prices comes a drop in the cost of capital. This, in turn, stimulates investment, which may add to a developing inflationary boom. In summary, a consideration of its effect on the cost of capital suggests that stock financing may tend to amplify cyclical fluctuations.

Just how these opposing forces combine to produce a net effect is unknown, but the authors believe that the first is the stronger; that is, stock financing tends to stabilize the economy.

Use of Rights in Financing

If the preemptive right is contained in a particular firm's charter, then it must offer any new common stock to existing stockholders. If the charter does not prescribe a preemptive right, the firm has a choice of making the sale to its existing stockholders or to an entirely new set of investors. If the sale is to the existing stockholders, the stock flotation is called a *rights offering*. Each stockholder is issued an option to buy a certain number of the new shares, and the terms of the option are contained on a piece of paper called a *right*. Each stockholder receives one right for each share of stock he owns. The advantages and disadvantages of rights offerings are described in this section.

Theoretical Relationships

Several issues confront the financial manager who is deciding on the details of a rights offering. The various considerations can be made clear by the use of illustrative data on the Southeast Company, whose balance sheet and income statement are given in Table 13–2.

Southeast earns $4 million after taxes and has one million shares outstanding, so earnings per share are $4. The stock sells at 25 times earnings, or for $100 a share. The company plans to raise $10 million of new

Table 13–2
Southeast Company Financial Statements Before Rights Offering

Partial balance sheet

Total debt, 5%		$ 40,000,000
Common stock		10,000,000
Retained earnings		50,000,000
Total assets	$100,000,000	Total liabilities and capital	$100,000,000

Partial income statement

Total earnings	$10,000,000
Interest on debt	2,000,000
Income before taxes	8,000,000
Taxes (50% assumed)	4,000,000
Earnings after taxes	4,000,000
Earnings per share (1,000,000 shares)	$4
Market price of stock (price/earnings ratio of 25 assumed)	$100

equity funds through a rights offering and decides to sell the new stock to shareholders for $80 a share. The questions now facing the financial manager are:

1. How many rights will be required to purchase a share of the newly issued stock?
2. What is the value of each right?
3. What effect will the rights offering have on the price of the existing stock?

We will now analyze each of these questions.

Number of Rights Needed to Purchase a New Share

Southeast plans to raise $10 million in new equity funds and to sell the new stock at a price of $80 a share. Dividing the subscription price into the total funds to be raised gives the number of shares to be issued:

$$\text{Number of new shares} = \frac{\text{funds to be raised}}{\text{subscription price}} = \frac{\$10,000,000}{\$80}$$
$$= 125,000 \text{ shares.}$$

The next step is to divide the number of new shares into the number of previously outstanding shares to get the number of rights required to subscribe to one share of the new stock. Note that stockholders always receive one right for each share of stock they own:

$$\frac{\text{Number of rights needed to}}{\text{buy a share of the stock}} = \frac{\text{old shares}}{\text{new shares}} = \frac{1,000,000}{125,000} = 8 \text{ rights.}$$

Therefore, a stockholder will have to surrender eight rights plus $80 to receive one of the newly issued shares. Had the subscription price been set at $95 a share, 9.5 rights would have been required to subscribe to each new share; if the price had been set at $10 a share, only one right would have been needed.

Value of a Right

It is clearly worth something to be able to buy for less than $100 a share of stock selling for $100. The right provides this privilege, so the right must have a value. To see how the theoretical value of a right is established, we continue with the example of the Southeast Company, assuming that it will raise $10 million by selling 125,000 new shares at $80 a share.

First, notice that the *market value* of the old stock was $100 million: $100 a share times one million shares. (The book value is irrelevant.) When the firm sells the new stock, it brings in an additional $10 million.

As a first approximation, we assume that the market value of the common stock increases by exactly this $10 million. Actually, the market value of all the common stock will go up by more than $10 million if investors think the company will be able to invest these funds at a yield substantially in excess of the cost of equity capital, but it will go up by less than $10 million if investors are doubtful of the company's ability to put the new funds to work profitably in the near future.

Under the assumption that market value exactly reflects the new funds brought in, the total market value of the common stock after the new issue will be $110 million. Dividing this new value by the new total number of shares outstanding, 1.125 million, we obtain a new market value of $97.78 a share. Therefore, we see that after the financing has been completed, the price of the common stock will have fallen from $100 to $97.78.

Since the rights give the stockholders the privilege of buying for only $80 a share of stock that will end up being worth $97.78, thus saving $17.78, is $17.78 the value of each right? The answer is "no," because eight rights are required to buy one new share; we must divide $17.78 by 8 to get the value of each right. In the example each one is worth $2.22.

Ex Rights

The Southeast Company's rights have a very definite value, and this value accrues to the holders of the common stock. But what happens if stock is traded during the offering period? Who will receive the rights, the old owners or the new? The standard procedure calls for the company to set a "holder of record date," then for stock to go *ex rights* after the holder-of-record date. If the stock is sold prior to the ex rights date, the new owner will receive the rights; if it is sold on or after the ex rights date, the old owner will receive them. For example, on October 15, Southeast Company might announce the terms of the new financing, stating that rights will be mailed out on December 1 to stockholders of record as of the close of business on November 15. Anyone buying the old stock on or before November 15 will receive the rights; anyone buying the stock on or after November 16 will *not* receive the rights. Thus, November 16 is the *ex rights date;* before November 16 the stock sells *rights on.* In the case of Southeast Company, the *rights-on price* is $100, the *ex rights price* is $97.78.

Formula Value of a Right

Rights On. Equations have been developed for determining the value of rights without going through all the procedures described above. While the stock is still selling rights on, the value at which the rights will sell when they are issued can be found by use of the following formula:

$$\text{Value of} \atop \text{one right} = \frac{\text{market value of stock, rights on} - \text{subscription price}}{\text{number of rights required to purchase one share plus 1}}$$

$$v_r = \frac{p_o - p^s}{\# + 1} \tag{13-5}$$

Here

p_o = the rights-on price of the stock
p^s = the subscription price
$\#$ = the number of rights required to purchase a new share of stock
v_r = the value of one right.

Substituting the appropriate values for the Southeast Company, we obtain

$$v_r = \frac{\$100 - \$80}{8 + 1} = \frac{\$20}{9} = \$2.22.$$

This agrees with the value of the rights we found by the step-by-step analysis.

Ex Rights. Suppose you are a stockholder in the Southeast Company. When you return to the United States from a trip to Europe, you read about the rights offering in the newspaper. The stock is now selling ex rights for $97.78 a share. How can you calculate the theoretical value of a right? Simply using the following formula, which follows the logic described in preceding sections, you can determine the value of each right to be $2.22:

$$\text{Value of} \atop \text{one right} = \frac{\text{market value of stock, ex rights} - \text{subscription price}}{\text{number of rights required to purchase one share}}$$

$$v_r = \frac{p_e - p^s}{\#}$$

$$v_r = \frac{\$97.78 - \$80}{8} = \frac{\$17.78}{8} = \$2.22.$$

Here p_e is the ex rights price of the stock.[6] $\tag{13-6}$

---

6. We developed Equation 13-6 directly from the verbal explanation given in the above section, "Value of a Right." Equation 13-5 can then be derived from Equation 13-6 as follows:
1. Note that

$$p_e = p_o - v_r \tag{13-7}$$

2. Substitute Equation 13-7 into Equation 13-6, obtaining

$$v_r = \frac{p_o - v_r - p^s}{\#} \tag{13-8}$$

Effects on Position of Stockholders

A stockholder has the choice of exercising his rights or selling them. If he has sufficient funds and if he wants to buy more shares of the company's stock, the stockholder will exercise the rights. If he does not have the money or does not want to buy more stock, he will sell his rights. In either case, provided the formula value of the rights holds true, the stockholder will neither benefit nor lose by the rights offering. This statement can be made clear by considering the position of an individual stockholder in the Southeast Company.

The stockholder had eight shares of stock before the rights offering. The eight shares each had a market value of $100 a share, so the stockholder had a total market value of $800 in the company's stock. If he exercises his rights, he will be able to purchase one additional share at $80 a share, a new investment of $80; his total investment is now $880. He now owns nine shares of his company's stock, which, after the rights offering, has a value of $97.78 a share. The value of his stock is $880, exactly what he has invested in it.

Alternatively, if he sold his eight rights, which have a value of $2.22 a right, he would receive $17.78. He would now have his original eight shares of stock plus $17.78 in cash. But his original eight shares of stock now have a market price of $97.78 a share. The $782.22 market value of his stock plus the $17.78 in cash is the same as the original $800 market value of stock with which he began. From a purely mechanical or arithmetical standpoint, the stockholder neither benefits nor gains from the sale of additional shares of stock through rights. Of course, if he forgets to exercise or sell his rights, or if brokerage costs of selling the rights are excessive, then a stockholder can suffer a loss. But, in general, the issuing firm makes special efforts to minimize brokerage costs, and adequate time is given to enable the stockholder to take some action, so losses are minimal.

---

3. Simplify Equation 13–8 as follows, ending with Equation 13–5. This completes the derivation.

$$v_r = \frac{p_o - p^s}{\#} - \frac{v_r}{\#}$$

$$v_r + \frac{v_r}{\#} = \frac{p_o - p^s}{\#}$$

$$v_r \left(\frac{\# + 1}{\#} \right) = \frac{p_o - p^s}{\#}$$

$$v_r = \frac{p_o - p^s}{\#} \cdot \frac{\#}{\# + 1}$$

$$v_r = \frac{p_o - p^s}{\# + 1}$$

Even though the rights are very valuable and *should* be exercised, some stockholders will doubtless neglect to do so. Still, all the stock *will* be sold because of the *oversubscription privilege* contained in most rights offerings. The oversubscription privilege gives subscribing stockholders the right to buy, on a pro rata basis, all shares not taken in the initial offering. To illustrate, if John Doe owns 10 percent of the stock in Southeast Company and if 20 percent of the rights offered by the company are not exercised (or sold) by the stockholders to whom they were originally given, then John Doe could buy an additional 2.5 percent of the new stock.[7] Since this stock is a bargain—$80 for stock worth $97.78—John Doe and other stockholders would use the oversubscription privilege, thus assuring the full sale of the new stock issue.

Relation between Market Price and Subscription Price

We can now investigate the factors influencing the use of rights and, if the rights are used, the level at which the subscription price will be set. The articles of incorporation of the Southeast Company permit it to use rights or not, depending on whether it judges their use to be advantageous to the company and its stockholders. The financial vice-president of the company is considering three alternative methods of raising the additional sum of $10 million.

Alternative 1. Southeast Company could sell to the public through investment bankers additional shares at approximately $100 a share, the company netting approximately $96 a share; thus, it would need to sell 105,000 shares in order to cover the underwriting commission.

Alternative 2. The company could sell additional shares through rights, using investment bankers and paying a commission of 1 percent on the total dollar amount of the stock sold plus an additional ¾ percent on all shares unsubscribed and taken over by the investment bankers. Allowing for the usual market pressure when common stock is sold, the new shares would be sold at a 20 percent discount, or at $80. Thus, 125,000 additional shares would be offered through rights. With eight rights, an additional share could be purchased at $80.

We noted above that stockholders are given the right to subscribe to any unexercised rights on a pro rata basis. Only shares not subscribed

---

7. Eighty percent of the stock was subscribed. Doe subscribed to 10/80, or 12.5 percent of the stock that was taken; he can obtain 12.5 percent of the unsubscribed stock. Therefore, his oversubscription allocation is 12.5 percent × 20 = 2.5 percent of the new stock.

to on an original or secondary basis are sold to the underwriters and subjected to the ¾ percent additional commission.

Alternative 3. The company could sell additional shares through rights at $10 a share. Investment bankers would not be employed at all. The number of additional shares of common stock to be sold would be one million. For each right held, existing stockholders would be permitted to buy one share of the new common stock.

Under alternative 1, investment bankers are used and rights would not be utilized at all. In this circumstance the underwriting commission, or flotation cost, is approximately 4 percent. In alternative 2, where rights are used with a small discount, the underwriting commission is reduced, because the discount removes much of the risk of not being able to sell the issue. The underwriting commission consists of two parts—1 percent on the original issue and an additional three-quarters of 1 percent commission on all unsubscribed shares the investment bankers are required to take over and sell. Thus, the actual commission will range somewhere between 1 percent and 1¾ percent. Under alternative 3, the subscription price is $10 a share. With such a large concession, the company does not need to use investment bankers at all, because the rights are certain to have value and to be either exercised or sold. Which of the three alternatives is superior?

Alternative 1 will provide a wider distribution of the securities sold, thus lessening any possible control problems. Also, it provides assurance from the investment bankers that the company will receive the $10 million involved in the new issue. In addition, the firm receives continuing financial counsel from the investment bankers. The company pays for these services in the form of underwriting charges. The stock price, after the issue, should be approximately $100.

Under alternative 2, by utilizing rights, the company reduces its underwriting expenses. There is also a small reduction in the unit price per share, from $100 to $97.78 a share. Moreover, some stockholders may neither exercise nor sell their rights, thus suffering a loss. Existing stockholders will buy some of the new shares, so the distribution is likely to be less wide. Because of the underwriting contract, the firm, under alternative 2, is also assured of receiving the funds sought. Finally, it is often argued that investors like the opportunity of purchasing additional shares through rights offerings and that the use of rights offerings increases "stockholder loyalty."

Alternative 3 involves no underwriting expense, and it results in a substantial decrease in the unit price of shares. Initially, however, the shares will be less widely distributed. Note that alternative 3 has a large stock-split effect, which results in a much lower final stock price per share.[8] Many people feel that there is an optimal stock price—one that will produce a maximum total market value of the shares—and that this price is generally in the range of $30 to $60 a share. If this is the feeling of Southeast's directors, they may believe that alternative 3 permits them to reach this more desirable price range, while at the same time reducing flotation costs on the new issue. However, since the rights have a substantial value, any stockholder who fails either to exercise or to sell them would suffer a serious loss.

The three alternatives are summarized in Table 13–3.

Table 13–3 **Summary of Three Methods of Raising Additional Money**		Advantages	Disadvantages
	Alternative 1	1. Wider distribution 2. Certainty of receiving funds	1. High underwriting costs
	Alternative 2	1. Smaller underwriting costs 2. Lower unit price of shares 3. Certainty of receiving funds 4. Increase stockholder loyalty	1. More narrow distribution 2. Losses to forgetful stockholders
	Alternative 3	1. No underwriting costs 2. Substantial decrease in unit price of shares 3. Increase stockholder loyalty	1. More narrow distribution 2. Severe losses to forgetful stockholders

The alternative that is most advantageous depends upon the company's needs. If the company is strongly interested in a wider distribution of its securities, alternative 1 is preferable. If it is most interested in reducing the unit price of its shares and is confident that the lower unit price will induce wider distribution of its shares, alternative 3 will be chosen. If the company's needs are moderate in both directions, alternative 2 may offer a satisfactory compromise. Whether rights will be used and the level of the subscription price both depend upon the needs of the company at a particular time.

Exercise of Rights

Interestingly enough, it is expected that in most cases a small percentage of stockholders may neglect to exercise their rights or to sell them. In a recent offering, the holders of 1½ percent of the shares of General Motors common stock did not exercise their rights. The loss involved to

8. Stock splits are discussed in Chapter 20. Basically, a stock split is simply the issuance of additional shares to existing stockholders for *no* additional funds. Stock splits "divide the pie into more pieces."

these stockholders was $1.5 million. In a recent AT&T issue, the loss to shareholders who neglected to exercise their rights was $960,000.

Market Price and Subscription Price

Measured from the registration date for the new issue of the security, the average percentage by which the subscription prices of new issues were below their market prices has been about 15 percent in recent years. Examples of price concessions of 40 percent or more are observed in a small percentage of issues, but the most frequently encountered discounts are from 10 to 20 percent.

Effect on Subsequent Behavior of Market Price of Stock

It is often stated that new issues of stock through rights will depress the price of the existing common stock of the company. To the extent that a subscription price in connection with the rights offering is lower than the market price, there will be a "stock-split effect" on the market price of the common stock. With the prevailing market price of Southeast Company's stock at $100 and a $10 subscription price, the new market price will probably drop to about $55.

But the second question is whether, because of the rights offering, the actual new market price will be $55 or lower or higher. Again, empirical analysis of the movement in stock prices during rights offerings indicates that generalization is not practical. What happens to the market prices of the stock ex rights and after the rights trading period depends upon the future earnings prospects of the issuing company.

Advantages of Use of Rights in New Financing

We have seen that the preemptive right gives the shareholders the protection of preserving their pro rata share in the earnings and control of the company. The firm also benefits. By offering new issues of securities to the existing stockholders, it increases the likelihood of a favorable reception for the stock. By their ownership of common stock in the company, these investors have already indicated a favorable evaluation of the company. They may be receptive to the purchase of additional shares, particularly when the additional reasons indicated below are taken into account.

The shares purchased with rights are also subject to lower margin requirements. For example, margin requirements since January 1974 have been 50 percent; in other words, a person buying listed stocks must have at least $50 of his own funds for every $100 of securities purchased. However, if shares of new issues of stocks are purchased with rights, only $25 per $100 of common stock purchased must be furnished by the investor himself; he is permitted by law to borrow up to 75 percent of the purchase price. Furthermore, the absence of a clear pattern in the price behavior of the adjusted market price of the stocks and rights before, during, and after the trading period may enhance interest in the investment possibilities of the instruments.

These factors may offset the tendency toward a downward pressure on the price of the common stock occurring at the time of a new issue.[9] With the increased interest in, and advantages afforded by, the rights offering, the "true" or "adjusted" downward price pressure may actually be avoided.

A related advantage is that the flotation costs to an issuer associated with a rights offering will be lower than the cost of a public flotation. Costs referred to here are cash costs. For example, the flotation costs of issues of common stock during 1971–75 were 6.17 percent on public issues compared with 2.45 percent of the proceeds to the company on rights offerings.[10]

The financial manager may obtain positive benefits from underpricing. Since a rights offering is a stock split to a certain degree, it will cause the market price of the stock to fall to a level lower than it otherwise would have been. But stock splits may increase the number of shareholders in a company by bringing the price of a stock into a more attractive trading level. Furthermore, a rights offering may be associated with increased dividends for the stock owners.[11]

Finally, the total effect of the rights offering may be to stimulate an enthusiastic response from stockholders and the investment market as a whole, with the result that opportunities for financing become more attractive to the firm. Thus, the financial manager may be able to engage in common stock financing at lower costs and under more favorable terms.

Summary

In this chapter, the characteristics of common stock financing have been presented. The advantages and disadvantages of external equity financing, compared with the use of preferred stock and debt, have been described. The purpose of the descriptive background mate-

9. The downward pressure develops because of an increase in the supply of securities without a necessarily equivalent increase in the demand. Generally it is a temporary phenomenon, and the stock tends to return to the theoretical price after a few months. Obviously, if the acquired funds are invested at a very high rate of return, the stock price benefits; if the investment does not turn out well, the stock price suffers.

10. C. W. Smith, Jr., "Substitute Methods for Raising Additional Capital: Rights Offerings versus Underwritten Issues," August 1976, MS.

11. The increased dividends may convey information that the prospective earnings of the firm have improved and may result in a higher market price for the firm's stock.

rial has been to provide a basis for making sound decisions when financing by common stock is being considered as a possible alternative.

The chapter also discussed the key decisions confronting the financial manager when he considers a rights offering, and indicated the major features bearing on such decisions. Rights offerings may be used effectively by financial managers to increase the goodwill of shareholders. If the new financing associated with the rights represents a sound decision—one likely to result in improved earnings for the firm—a rise in stock values will probably result. The use of rights will permit shareholders to preserve their positions or to improve them. However, if investors feel that the new financing is not well advised, the rights offering may cause the price of the stock to decline by more than the value of the rights. Because the rights offering is directed to existing shareholders, it may be possible to reduce the costs of floating the new issue.

A major decision for financial managers in a rights offering is to set the subscription price, or the amount of the concession, from the existing market price of the stock. Formulas reflecting the static effects of a rights offering indicate that neither the stockholders nor the company benefits or loses from the price changes. The rights offering has the effect of a stock split. The level set for the subscription price will, to a great degree, reflect the objectives and effects of a stock split.

The subsequent price behavior of the rights and the common stock in the associated new offering will reflect the earnings and dividends prospects of the company, as well as the underlying developments in the securities markets. The new financing associated with the rights offering may be an indicator of prospective growth in the sales and earnings of the company. The stock-split effects of the rights offering may be used to alter the company's dividend payments. The effects of these developments on the market behavior of the rights and the securities before, during, and after the rights trading period will reflect the expectations of investors toward the outlook for the earnings and dividends of the firm.

Questions

13–1. By what percentage could total assets shrink in value on liquidation before creditors incur losses in each of the following cases:
  a. Equity to total asset ratio, 50 percent?
  b. Debt to equity ratio, 50 percent ?
  c. Debt to total asset ratio, 40 percent?

13–2. How many shares must a minority group own in order to assure election of two directors if nine new directors will be elected and 200,000 shares are outstanding? Assume cumulative voting exists.

13–3. Should the preemptive right entitle stockholders to purchase convertible bonds before they are offered to outsiders?

13–4. What are the reasons for not letting officers and directors of a corporation make short sales in their company's stock?

13–5. It is frequently stated that the primary purpose of the preemptive right is to allow individuals to maintain their proportionate share of the ownership and control of a corporation. Just how important do you suppose this consideration is for the average stockholder of a firm whose shares are traded on the New York or the American stock exchanges? Is the preemptive right likely to be of more importance to stockholders of closely held firms?

13–6. How would the success of a rights offering be affected by a declining stock market?

13–7. What are some of the advantages and disadvantages of setting the subscription price on a rights offering substantially below the current market price of the stock?

13–8. Is a firm likely to get wider distribution of shares if it sells new stock through a rights offering or directly to underwriters? Why would a company be interested in getting a wider distribution of shares?

Problems

13–1. The common stock of Arlington Development Company is selling for $32 on the market. Stockholders are offered one new share at a subscription price of $20 for every three shares held. What is the value of each right?

13–2. United Appliance Company common stock is priced at $40 a share on the market. Notice is given that stockholders may purchase one new share at a price of $27.50 for every four shares held. You hold 250 shares at the time of the notice.
   a. At approximately what market price will each right sell?
   b. Why will this be the approximate price?
   c. What effect will the issuance of rights have on the original market price?

13–3. Eileen has 600 shares of Fisher Industries. The market price per share is $81. The company now offers stockholders one new share to be purchased for $45 for every five shares held.
   a. Determine the value of each right.
   b. Assume that Eileen (i) uses 160 rights and sells the other 440, or (ii) sells 600 rights at the market price you have calculated. Prepare a statement showing the changes in her position, under the above assumptions.

13–4. As a shareholder of Younger Corporation, you are notified that for each seven shares you own you have the right to purchase one additional share at a price of $15. The current market price of Younger stock is $63 per share.

a. Determine the value of each right.
b. At the time of the offering your total assets consist of 490 shares of Younger stock and $1,500 in cash. Prepare a statement to show total assets before the offering, and total assets after the offering if you exercise all of the rights.
c. Prepare a statement to show total assets after the offering if you sell all of the rights.

13–5. The Northridge Company has the following balance sheet and income statement:

The Northridge Company
Balance sheet before rights offering

		Total debt (6%)	$ 7,000,000
		Common stock (100,000 shares)	3,000,000
		Retained earnings	4,000,000
Total assets	$14,000,000	Total liabilities and capital	$14,000,000

Income Statement

Earning rate: 12% on total assets

Total earnings	$ 1,680,000
Interest on debts	420,000
Income before taxes	$ 1,260,000
Taxes (50% rate assumed)	630,000
Earnings after taxes	$ 630,000
Earnings per share	$ 6.30
Dividends per share (56% of earnings)	$ 3.53
Price/earnings ratio	15 times
Market price per share	$94.50

The Northridge Company plans to raise an additional $5 million through a rights offering. The additional funds will continue to earn 12 percent. The price/earnings ratio is assumed to remain at 15 times, the dividend payout will continue to be 56 percent, and the 50 percent tax rate will remain in effect. (Do not attempt to use the formulas given in the chapter for this problem. Additional information is given here which violates the "other things constant" assumption inherent in the formula.)
a. Assuming subscription prices of $25, $50, and $80 a share:
  (i) How many additional shares of stock will have to be sold?
  (ii) How many rights will be required to purchase one new share?
  (iii) What will be the new earnings per share?
  (vi) What will be the new market price per share?
  (v) What will be the new dividend per share if the dividend payout ratio is maintained?
b. What is the significance of your results?

13–6. As one of the minority shareholders of the Belmont Corporation you are dissatisfied with the current operations of the company. You feel that if you could gain membership to the company's board of directors you could persuade them to make some improvements. The problem is that current management controls 75 percent of the stock. You personally control 7 percent. The balance is held by other minority shareholders. There is a total of 500,000 voting shares. Ten directors will be elected at the next annual stockholders meeting.

a. If voting is noncumulative, can you alone elect yourself director?

b. Suppose you are able to persuade all the minority shareholders that you should be elected. If voting is noncumulative, can they elect you?

c. If voting is cumulative, can you, acting alone, elect yourself director?

d. What percent of the minority shares other than your own would you need to have voted for you to be certain of election?

e. What is the number of directors the minority shareholders could elect with certainty?

13–7. The Frost Crop Food Company is engaged principally in the business of growing, processing, and marketing a variety of frozen vegetables and is a major company in this field. High-quality products are produced and marketed at premium prices.

During each of the past several years the company's sales have increased and the needed inventories have been financed from short-term sources. The officers have discussed the idea of refinancing their bank loans with long-term debt or common stock. A common stock issue of 310,000 shares sold at this time (present market price $72 a share) would yield $21 million after expenses. This same sum could be raised by selling 12-year bonds with an interest rate of 8 percent and a sinking fund to retire the bonds over their 12-year life. (See financial statements below.)

a. Should Frost Crop Food refinance the short-term loans? Why?

b. If the bank loans should be refinanced, what factors should be considered in determining which form of financing to use? (This question should not be answered in terms of precise cost of capital calcula-

Food Processing Industry Financial Ratios

Current ratio	2.2 times
Sales to total assets	2.0 times
Sales to inventory	5.6 times
Average collection period	22.0 days
Current debt/total assets	25–30%
Long-term debt/total assets	10–15%
Preferred/total assets	0.5%
Net worth/total assets	60–65%
Profits to sales	2.3%
Net profits to total assets	4.0%
Profits to net worth	8.4%
Expected growth rate of earnings and dividends	6.5%

Frost Crop Food Company
Consolidated balance sheet
March 31, 1978*
(in millions of dollars)

Current assets	$141	Accounts payable	$12	
Fixed plant and equipment	57	Notes payable	36	
Other assets	12	Accruals	15	
		Total current liabilities		$ 63
		Long-term debt, 5%		63
		Preferred stock		9
		Common stock (par $6)	$12	
		Retained earnings	63	
		Net worth		75
Total assets	$210	Total claims on assets		$210

*The majority of harvesting activities do not begin until late April or May.

Frost Crop Food Company
Consolidated statement of income
Year ended March 31
(in millions of dollars)

	1975	1976	1977	1978
Net sales	225.0	234.6	292.8	347.1
Cost of goods sold	146.1	156.6	195.3	230.4
Gross profit	78.9	78.0	97.5	116.7
Other expenses	61.8	66.0	81.0	88.5
Operating income	17.1	12.0	16.5	28.2
Other income (net)	(3.3)	(4.2)	(5.7)	(9.3)
Earnings before tax	13.8	7.8	10.8	18.9
Taxes	7.2	3.3	5.4	9.6
Net profit	6.6	4.5	5.4	9.3
Preferred dividend	0.3	0.3	0.3	0.3
Earnings available to common stock	$ 6.3	$ 4.2	$ 5.1	$ 9.0
Earnings per share	$ 3.15	$ 2.10	$ 2.55	$ 4.50
Cash dividends per share	1.29	1.44	1.59	1.80
Price range for common stock				
High	$ 66.00	$ 69.00	$ 66.00	$ 81.00
Low	30.00	42.00	51.00	63.00

tions. Rather, a more qualitative and subjective analysis is appropriate. The only calculations necessary are some simple ratios. Careful interpretation of these ratios is necessary, however, to understand and discuss the often complex, subjective judgment issues involved.)

Selected References

Bacon, Peter W. "The Subscription Price in Rights Offerings." *Financial Management* 1 (Summer 1972): 59–64.

Bear, Robert M., and Curley, Anthony J. "Unseasoned Equity Financing." *Journal of Financial and Quantitative Analysis* 10 (June 1975): 311–25.

Donaldson, Gordon. "Financial Goals: Management vs. Stockholders." *Harvard Business Review* 41 (May–June 1963): 116–29.

Duvall, Richard M., and Austin, Douglas V. "Predicting the Results of Proxy Contests." *Journal of Finance* 20 (Sept. 1965): 467–71.

Furst, Richard W. "Does Listing Increase the Market Price of Common Stocks?" *Journal of Business* 43 (Apr. 1970): 174–80.

Ibbotson, R. R. "Price Performance of Common Stock New Issues." *The Journal of Financial Economics* 2 (Sept. 1975): 235–72.

Keane, Simon M. "The Significance of the Issue Price in Rights Issues." *Journal of Business Finance* 4, no. 3 (1972): 40–45.

Lee, Steven James. "Going Private." *Financial Executive* 42 (Dec. 1974): 10–15.

Logue, Dennis E. "On the Pricing of Unseasoned Equity Issues: 1965–1969." *Journal of Financial and Quantitative Analysis* 8 (Jan. 1973): 91–104.

Lowe, H. D. "The Classification of Corporate Stock Equities." *Accounting Review* 36 (July 1961): 425–33.

McDonald, J. G., and Fisher, A. K. "New Issue Stock Price Behavior." *Journal of Finance* 27 (Mar. 1972): 97–102.

Nelson, J. Russell. "Price Effects in Rights Offerings." *Journal of Finance* 20 (Dec. 1965): 647–50.

Stevenson, Harold W. *Common Stock Financing.* Ann Arbor, Mich.: University of Michigan, 1957.

Stoll, Hans R., and Curley, Anthony J. "Small Business and the New Issues Market for Equities." *Journal of Financial and Quantitative Analysis* 5 (Sept. 1970): 309–22.

Thompson, Howard E. "A Note on the Value of Rights in Estimating the Investor Capitalization Rate." *Journal of Finance* 28 (Mar. 1973): 157–60.

Van Horne, James C. "New Listings and their Price Behavior." *Journal of Finance* 25 (Sept. 1970): 783–94.

Young, Alan, and Marshall, Wayne. "Controlling Shareholder Servicing Costs." *Harvard Business Review* 49 (Jan.–Feb. 1971): 71–78.

14 Fixed Income Securities: Debt and Preferred Stock

There are many classes of fixed income securities: long term and short term, secured and unsecured, marketable and nonmarketable, participating and nonparticipating, senior and junior, and so on.

Different classes of investors favor different classes of securities, and tastes change over time. An astute financial manager knows how to "package" his securities at a given point in time to make them most attractive to the most potential investors, thereby keeping his cost of capital to a minimum. This chapter deals with the two most important types of long-term, fixed income securities—bonds and preferred stocks.

Instruments of Long-term Debt Financing

For an understanding of long-term forms of financing, we need some familiarity with technical terminology. The discussion of long-term debt therefore begins with an explanation of several important instruments and terms.

Bond

Most people have had some experience with short-term promissory notes. A *bond* is simply a long-term promissory note.

Mortgage

A *mortgage* represents a pledge of designated property for a loan. Under a *mortgage bond*, the corporation pledges certain real assets as security for the bond. A mortgage bond is therefore secured by real property.[1] The pledge is a condition of the loan.

Debenture

A *debenture* is a long-term bond that is *not* secured by a pledge of any specific property. However, like other general creditor claims, it is secured by any property not otherwise pledged.

---

1. There is also the *chattel mortgage*, which is secured by personal property, but this is generally an intermediate-term instrument. *Real property* is defined as real estate—land and buildings. *Personal property* is defined as anything else, including equipment, inventories, furniture, and so on.

Indenture

Since a bond is a long-term promissory note, a long-term relation between borrower and lender is established in a document called an *indenture*. When it is a matter of an ordinary 60- or 90-day promissory note, few new developments are likely to occur in the life or affairs of the borrower to endanger repayment. The lender looks closely at the borrower's current position, because current assets are the main source of repayment. A bond, however, is a long-term contractual relationship between the issuer of the bond and the bondholders; over such an extended period the bondholder has cause to worry that the firm's position might change materially.

In the ordinary common stock or preferred stock certificate or agreement, the details of the contractual relation can be summarized in a few paragraphs. The bond indenture, however, may be a document of several hundred pages covering a large number of factors that will be important to the contractual parties. It discusses the form of the bond and the instrument. It provides a complete description of property pledged. It specifies the authorized amount of the bond issue. It contains protective clauses, or *covenants*, which are detailed and which usually include limits on indebtedness, restrictions on dividends, and a sinking fund provision. Generally a minimum current ratio requirement, as well as provisions for redemption or call privileges, are also added.

Trustee

Not only is a bond of long duration, but the issue is also likely to be of substantial size. Before the rise of the large aggregations of savings through insurance companies or pension funds, no single buyer was able to buy an issue of such size. Bonds were therefore issued in denominations of $1,000 each and were sold to a large number of purchasers. To facilitate communication between the issuer and the numerous bondholders, another device was instituted, the trustee, who is the representative of the bondholders. The trustee is presumed to act at all times for the protection of the bondholders and on their behalf.

Any legal person, including a corporation, is considered competent to act as a trustee. Typically, however, the duties of the trustee are handled by a department of a commercial bank.

The trustee has three main responsibilities. (1) The trustee certifies the issue of bonds. This duty involves making certain that all the legal requirements for drawing up the bond contract and the indenture have been carried out. (2) The trustee polices the behavior of the corporation in its performance of the responsibilities set forth in the indenture provisions. (3) The trustee is responsible for taking appropriate action on behalf of the bondholders if the corporation defaults on payment of interest or principal.

It is said that in many corporate bond defaults in the early 1930s, trustees did not act in the best interests of the bondholders. The trustees did not conserve the assets of the corporation effectively. Often they did not take early action, so that corporation executives continued their salaries and disposed of assets under conditions favorable to themselves but detrimental to the bondholders. Assets pledged as security for the bonds were sold; specific security was, thus, no longer available. The result in many instances was that holders of mortgage bonds found themselves more in the position of general creditors than in that of secured bondholders.

As a consequence of such practices, the Trust Indenture Act of 1939 was passed in order to give more protection to bondholders. It provides that trustees must be given sufficient power to act on behalf of bondholders. The indenture must fully disclose rights and responsibilities and must not be deceptive. There is provision for changes in the indenture at the option of the bondholders. It is specifically required that prompt, protective action be taken by the trustees for bondholders if default occurs. Provision is made for making certain that an arm's-length relation exists between the issuing corporation and the trustee, and the corporation must make periodic reports to its trustee to enable him to carry out his protective responsibilities.

Call Provision

A *call provision* gives the issuing corporation the right to call in the bond for redemption. If it is used, the call provision generally states that the company must pay an amount greater than the par value of the bond, with this additional sum being defined as the *call premium.* The call premium is typically set equal to one year's interest if the bond is called during the first year, with the premium declining at a constant rate each year thereafter. For example, the call premium on a $1,000 par value, 20-year, 6 percent bond would generally be $60 if called during the first year, $57 if called during the second year (calculated by reducing the $60, or 6 percent, premium by one-twentieth), and so on.

As pointed out later in this chapter, the call privilege is valuable to the firm but potentially detrimental to the investor, especially if the bond is issued in a period when interest rates are thought to be cyclically high. Accordingly, the interest rate on a new issue of callable bonds will exceed that on a new issue of noncallable bonds. For example, on May 24, 1974, Great Falls Power Company sold an issue of AA-rated bonds to yield 9.375 percent. These bonds were callable immediately. On the same day, Midwest Electric sold an issue of AA-rated bonds to yield 9.20 percent. Midwest's bonds were noncallable for ten years. Investors were apparently willing to accept a 0.175 percent lower interest rate on Midwest's bonds for the assurance that the relatively high (by historic standards) rate of interest would be earned for at least ten years. Great Falls, on the other hand, had to incur a 0.175 percent higher annual interest rate for the privilege of calling the bonds in the event of a subsequent decline in interest rates. We will discuss the analysis for determining when to call an issue later in this chapter.

Sinking Fund

A *sinking fund* is a provision that facilitates the orderly retirement of a bond issue (or, in some cases, an issue of preferred stock). Typically, the sinking fund provision requires the firm to buy and retire a portion of the bond issue each year. Sometimes the stipulated sinking fund payment is tied to sales or earnings of the current year, but usually it is a mandatory fixed amount. If it is mandatory, a failure to meet the sinking fund payment causes the bond issue to be thrown into default and could lead the company into bankruptcy. Obviously, then, a sinking fund can constitute a dangerous cash drain on the firm.

In most cases the firm is given the right to handle the sinking fund in either of two ways. (1) It may call a certain percentage of the bonds at a stipulated price each year—for example, 2 percent of the original amount at a price of $1,050; the actual bonds to be called, which are numbered serially, are determined by a lottery. (2) It may spend the funds provided by the sinking fund payment to buy the bonds on the open market. The firm will do whichever results in the greatest reduction of outstanding bonds for a given expenditure. Therefore, if interest rates have risen (and the price of the bonds has fallen), the firm will choose the open market alternative. If interest rates have fallen and bond prices have risen, the company will elect to use the option of calling bonds.

It must be recognized that the call provision of the sinking fund may at times work to the detriment of bondholders. If, for example, the bond carries a 7 percent interest rate, and if yields on similar securities are 4 percent, the bond will sell for well above par. A sinking fund call at par would thus greatly disadvantage some bondholders. On balance, securities that provide for a sinking fund and continuing redemption are likely to be offered initially on a lower yield basis than are securities without such a fund. Since sinking funds provide additional protection to investors, sinking fund bonds are likely to sell initially at higher prices; hence, they have a lower cost of capital to the issuer.

Funded Debt

Funded debt is simply long-term debt. When a firm is said to be planning to "fund" its floating debt, it will replace short-term securities by long-term securities. Funding does not imply placing money with a trustee or other repository; it is simply part of the jargon of finance and means "long term."[2]

Secured Bonds

Secured long-term debt may be classified according to (1) the priority of claims, (2) the right to issue additional securities, and (3) the scope of the lien.

Priority of Claims

A senior mortgage has prior claims on assets and earnings. Senior railroad mortgages, for example, have been called the "mortgages next to the rail," implying that they have the first claim on the land and assets of the railroad corporations.

A junior mortgage is a subordinate lien, such as a second or a third mortgage. It is a lien or claim junior to others.

Right to Issue Additional Securities

Mortgage bonds may also be classified with respect to the right to issue additional obligations pledging already encumbered property.

In the case of a *closed-end mortgage*, a company may not sell additional bonds, beyond those already issued, secured by the property specified in the mortgage. For example, assume that a corporation with plant and land worth $5 million has a $2 million mortgage on these properties. If the mortgage is closed end, no more bonds having first liens on this property may be issued. Thus a closed-end mortgage provides greater security to the bond buyer. The ratio of the amount of the senior bonds to the value of the property will not be increased by subsequent issues.

If the bond indenture is silent on this point, it is called an *open-end mortgage*. Its nature may be illustrated by referring to the example cited above. Against property worth $5 million, bonds of $2 million are sold. If an additional first mortgage bond of $1 million is subsequently sold, the property has been pledged for a total of $3 million of bonds. If, on liquidation, the property sold for $2 million, the original bondholders would receive 67 cents on the dollar. If the mortgage had been closed end, they would have been fully paid.

Most characteristic is the *limited open-end mortgage*. Its nature may be

---

2. Tampa Electric Company provides a good example of funding. This company has a continuous construction program. Typically, it uses short-term debt to finance construction expenditures. However, once short-term debt has built up to about $75 million, the company sells a stock or bond issue, uses the proceeds to pay off its bank loans, and starts the cycle again. The high flotation costs of small security issues make this process desirable.

indicated by continuing the example. A first mortgage bond issue of $2 million, secured by the property worth $5 million, is sold. The indenture provides that an additional $1 million worth of bonds—or an additional amount of bonds up to 60 percent of the original cost of the property—may be sold. Thus, the mortgage is open only up to a certain point.

Scope of the Lien

Bonds may also be classified with respect to the scope of their lien. When a *specific lien* exists, the security for a first mortgage or a second mortgage is a specifically designated property. A lien is granted on certain specified property. On the other hand, a *blanket mortgage* pledges all real property currently owned by the company. Real property includes only land and those things affixed thereto, so a blanket mortgage would not be a mortgage on cash, accounts receivables, or inventories because these items are personal property. A blanket mortgage gives more protection to the bondholder than does a specific mortgage because it provides a claim on all real property owned by the company.

Unsecured Bonds
Debentures

A *debenture* is an unsecured bond and, as such, provides no lien on specific property as security for the obligation. Debenture holders are therefore general creditors whose claim is protected by property not otherwise pledged. The advantage of debentures from the standpoint of the issuer is that he leaves his property unencumbered for subsequent financing. However, in practice the use of debentures depends on the nature of the firm's assets and its general credit strength.

If the credit position of a firm is exceptionally strong, it can issue debentures—it simply does not need specific security. However, the credit position of a company may be so weak that it has no alternative to the use of debentures—all its property may already be encumbered. American Telephone & Telegraph's vast financing program since the end of World War II has been mainly through debentures, both convertible and straight debentures. AT&T is such a strong institution that it does not have to provide security for its debt issues.

Debentures are also issued by companies in industries where it would not be practical to provide a lien through a mortgage on fixed assets. Examples of such an industry would be the large mail order houses and the finance companies, which characteristically do not have large fixed assets in relation to their total assets. The bulk of their assets is in the form of inventory or receivables, neither of which is satisfactory security for a mortgage lien.

Subordinated Debentures

The term "subordinate" means below or inferior. Thus, *subordinated debt* has claims on assets after unsubordinated debt in the event of liquidation. Debentures may be subordinated to designated notes payable — usually bank loans — or to any or all other debt. In the event of liquidation or reorganization, the debentures cannot be paid until senior debt *as named in the indenture* has been paid. Senior debt typically does not include trade accounts payable. How the subordination provision strengthens the position of senior-debt holders is shown in Table 14-1.

Where $200 is available for distribution, the subordinated debt has a claim on 25 percent of $200, or $50. However, this claim is subordinated only to the bank debt (the only senior debt) and is added to the $100 claim of the bank. As a consequence, 75 percent of the bank's original claim is satisfied.

Where $300 is available for distribution, the $75 allocated to the subordinated debt is divided into two parts: $50 goes to the bank and the other $25 remains for the subordinated debt holders. In this situation, the senior bank debt holders are fully paid off, 75 percent of other debt is paid, and the subordinated debt receives only 25 percent of its claim.

Subordination is frequently required. Alert credit managers of firms supplying trade credit, or commercial bank loan officers, typically will insist upon subordination, particularly where debt is owed to the principal stockholders or officers of a company. Subordinated debentures are also often convertible into the common stock of the issuing company.

Preferred stock, in comparison to subordinated debt, suffers from the disadvantage that preferred stock dividends are not deductible as an expense for tax purposes. The interest on subordinated debentures is an expense for tax purposes. Some people have referred to subordinated debentures as being much like a special kind of preferred stock, the dividends of which are deductible as an expense for tax purposes. Subordinated debt has therefore become an increasingly important source of corporate capital.

The reasons for the use of subordinated debentures are clear. They offer a great tax advantage over preferred stock, yet they do not restrict the ability of the borrower to obtain senior debt, as would be the case if all debt sources were on an equal basis.

Subordinated debentures are further stimulated by periods of tight money when commercial banks may require a greater equity base for short-term financing. Subordinated debentures provide a greater equity cushion for loans from commercial banks or other forms of senior debt. The use of subordinated debentures also illustrates the development of hybrid securities that emerge to meet changing situations that develop in the capital market.

Table 14–1 **Illustration of Bankruptcy Payments to Senior Debt, Other Debt, and Subordinated Debt**	Financial Structure	Book Value (1)	Percent of Total Debt (2)	Initial Allocation (3)	Actual Payment (4)	Percent of Original Claim Satisfied (5)
	I. $200 available for claims on liquidation					
	Bank debt	$200	50%	$100	$150	75%
	Other debt	100	25	50	50	50
	Subordinated debt	100	25	50	0	0
	Total debt	$400	100%	$200	$200	50%
	Net worth	300				0
	Total	$700				29%
	II. $300 available for claims on liquidation					
	Bank debt	$200	50%	$150	$200	100%
	Other debt	100	25	75	75	75
	Subordinated debt	100	25	75	25	25
	Total debt	$400	100%	$300	$300	75%
	Net worth	300				0
	Total	$700				43%

Steps: 1. Express each type of debt as a percentage of total debt (column 2).
2. Multiply the debt percentages (column 2) by the amount available, obtaining the initial allocations shown in column 3.
3. The subordinated debt is subordinate to bank debt. Therefore, the initial allocation to subordinate debt is added to the bank debt allocation until it has been exhausted or until the bank debt is finally paid off. This is given in column 4.

Income Bonds

Income bonds typically arise from corporate reorganizations, and these bonds pay interest only if income is actually earned by the company. Because the company, having gone through reorganization, has been in difficult financial circumstances, interest is not a fixed charge; the principal, however, must be paid when due.

Income bonds are like preferred stock in that management is not required to pay interest if it is not earned. However, they differ from preferred stock in that if interest has been earned, management is required to pay it, and also in that interest paid on income bonds is deductible for income tax purposes while preferred dividends are not.

The main characteristic and distinct advantage of the income bond is that interest is payable only if the company achieves some earnings. Since earnings calculations are subject to differing interpretations, the indenture of the income bond carefully defines income and expenses. If it did not, long, drawn-out litigation might result.

Some income bonds are cumulative indefinitely (if interest is not paid, it "accumulates" and must be paid at some future date); others are cumulative for the first three to five years, after which time they become noncumulative.

Income bonds usually contain sinking fund provisions to provide for their retirement. The annual payments to the sinking funds range between $1/2$ and 1 percent of the face amount of the original issue. Because the sinking fund payment requirements are typically contingent on earnings, a fixed-cash drain on the company is avoided.

Sometimes income bonds are convertible. There are sound reasons for their being convertible if they arise out of a reorganization. Creditors who receive income bonds in exchange for defaulted obligations have a less desirable position than they had previously. Since they have received something based on an adverse and problematical forecast of the future of the company, it is appropriate that if the company should prosper, income bondholders should be entitled to participate. When income bonds are issued in situations other than reorganization, the convertibility feature is a "sweetener" likely to make the issue more attractive to prospective bond buyers.

Typically, income bonds do not have voting rights when they are issued. Sometimes bondholders are given the right to elect one, two, or some specified number of directors if interest is not paid for a certain number of years.

Characteristics of Long-term Debt

Risk. Debt is favorable to the holder because it gives him priority both in earnings and in liquidation. Debt also has a definite maturity and is protected by the covenants of the indenture.

From Viewpoint of Holder

Income. The bondholder has a fixed return; except in the case of income bonds, interest payments are not contingent on the level of earnings of the company. However, debt does not participate in any superior earnings of the company, and gains are limited in magnitude. Note particularly that bondholders suffer during inflationary periods. A 20-year, 6 percent bond pays $60 of interest each year. Under inflation, the purchasing power of this $60 is eroded, causing a loss in real value to the bondholder.[3] Frequently, long-term debt is callable. If bonds are

---

3. Recognizing this fact, investors demand higher interest rates during inflationary periods. This point is discussed at length in Chapters 17 and 21.

called, the investor receives funds that must be reinvested to be kept active.

Control. The bondholder usually does not have the right to vote. However, if the bonds go into default, then bondholders will, in effect, take control of the company.

An overall appraisal of the characteristics of long-term debt indicates that for the investor it is good from the standpoint of risk, has limited advantages with regard to income, and is weak with respect to control.

From Viewpoint of Issuer

Advantages. The issuer of a bond has the following advantages.

1. The cost of debt is definitely limited. Bondholders do not participate in superior profits if earned.
2. Not only is the cost limited, but typically the expected yield is lower than the cost of common stock.
3. The owners of the corporation do not share their control when debt financing is used.
4. The interest payment on debt is deductible as a tax expense.
5. Flexibility in the financial structure of the corporation may be achieved by inserting a call provision in the bond indenture.

Disadvantages. Following are the disadvantages to the bond issuer.

1. Debt is a fixed charge; there is greater risk if the earnings of the company fluctuate because the corporation may be unable to meet these fixed charges.
2. As we will see in Chapter 17, higher risk brings higher capitalization rates on equity earnings. Thus, even though leverage is favorable and raises earnings per share, the higher capitalization rates attributable to leverage may drive the common stock value down.
3. Debt usually has a definite maturity date. Because of the fixed maturity date, the financial officer must make provision for repayment of the debt.
4. Since long-term debt is a commitment for a long period, it involves risk; the expectations and plans on which the debt was issued may change. The debt may prove to be a burden, or it may prove to have been advantageous. For example, if income, employment, the price level, and interest rates all fall greatly, the assumption of a large amount of long-term debt may prove to have been an unwise financial policy. The railroads are always given as an example in this regard. They were able to meet their ordinary operating expenses dur-

ing the 1930s but were unable to meet the heavy financial charges they had undertaken earlier, when the prospects for the railroads looked more favorable than they turned out to be.

5. In a long-term contractual relationship, the indenture provisions are likely to be much more stringent than they are in a short-term credit agreement. Hence the firm may be subject to much more disturbing and crippling restrictions in the indenture of a long-term debt arrangement than would be the case if it had borrowed on a short-term basis or had issued common stock.

6. There is a limit on the extent to which funds can be raised through long-term debt. Generally accepted standards of financial policy dictate that the debt ratio shall not exceed certain limits. These standards of financial prudence set limits or controls on the extent to which funds may be raised through long-term debt. When debt gets beyond these limits, its cost rises rapidly.

Decisions on Use of Long-term Debt

When a number of alternative methods of long-term financing are under consideration, the following conditions favor the use of long-term debt:

1. Sales and earnings are relatively stable, or a substantial increase in future sales and earnings is expected to provide a substantial benefit from the use of leverage.

2. A substantial rise in the price level is expected in the future, making it advantageous for the firm to incur debt that will be repaid with cheaper dollars.

3. The existing debt ratio is relatively low for the line of business.

4. Management thinks the price of the common stock in relation to that of bonds is temporarily depressed.

5. Sale of common stock would involve problems of maintaining the existing control pattern in the company.

Decisions about the use of debt may also be considered in terms of the average cost of capital curve as developed in Chapter 19. There we will see that firms have optimal capital structures, or perhaps optimal ranges, and that the average cost of capital is higher than it need be if the firm uses a nonoptimal amount of debt. The factors listed above all relate to the optimal debt ratio: Some cause the optimal ratio to increase; others cause it to decrease.

Whenever the firm is contemplating raising new outside capital and is choosing between debt and equity, it is implicitly making a judgment about its actual debt ratio in relation to the optimal ratio. For example, consider Figure 14–1, which shows the assumed shape of the Long-street Company's average cost of capital schedule. If Longstreet is planning to raise outside capital, it must make a judgment about whether it is presently at point A or point B. If it decides that it is at A, it should issue debt; if it believes that it is at B, the decision should be to sell new common stock. This, of course, is a judgment decision, but all the factors discussed in this chapter must be considered when the decision is being made. This subject is discussed further in Chapter 19.

Figure 14–1
The Longstreet
Company's Average
Cost of Capital
Schedule

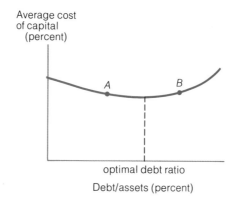

Nature of Preferred Stock

Preferred stock has claims and rights ahead of common stock, but behind all bonds. The preference may be a prior claim on earnings, a prior claim on assets in the event of liquidation, or a preferential position with regard to both earnings and assets.

Hybrid Form

The hybrid nature of preferred stock becomes apparent when we try to classify it in relation to bonds and common stock. The priority feature and the (generally) fixed dividend indicate that preferred stock is similar to bonds. Payments to the preferred stockholders are limited in amount so that the common stockholders receive the advantages (or disadvantages) of leverage. However, if the preferred dividends are not earned, the company can forego paying them without danger of bankruptcy. In this characteristic, preferred stock is similar to common stock. Moreover, failure to pay the stipulated dividend does not cause default of the obligation, as does failure to pay bond interest.

Debt and Equity. In some types of analysis, preferred stock is treated similarly to debt. For example, if the analysis is being made by a *potential stockholder* considering the earnings fluctuations induced by fixed-charge securities, preferred stock would be treated like debt. Suppose, however, that the analysis is by a *bondholder* studying the firm's vulnerability to *failure* brought on by declines in sales or in income. Since the dividends on preferred stock are not a fixed charge in the sense that failure to pay them would represent a default of an obligation, preferred stock represents a cushion; it provides an additional equity base. From the point of view of *stockholders*, it is a leverage-inducing instrument much like debt. From the point of view of *creditors*, it constitutes additional net worth. Preferred stock may therefore be treated either as debt or as equity, depending on the nature of the problem under consideration.[4]

Major Provisions of Preferred Stock Issues

Because the possible characteristics, rights, and obligations of any specific security vary so widely, a point of diminishing returns is quickly reached in a descriptive discussion of different kinds of securities. As economic circumstances change, new kinds of securities are manufactured. The possibilities are numerous. The kinds and varieties of securities are limited chiefly by the imagination and ingenuity of the managers formulating the terms of the security issues. It is not surprising, then, that preferred stock can be found in a variety of forms. We will now look at the main terms and characteristics in each case and examine the possible variations in relation to the kinds of situations or circumstances in which they could occur.[5]

Priority in Assets and Earnings

Many provisions in a preferred stock certificate are designed to reduce risk to the purchaser in relation to the risk carried by the holder of common stock. Preferred stock usually has priority with regard to earnings and assets. Two provisions designed to prevent undermining these preferred stock priorities are often found. The first states that, without the consent of the holders of the preferred stock, there can be no subsequent sale of securities having a prior or equal claim on earnings. The second provision seeks to hold earnings in the firm. It re-

---

4. Accountants generally include preferred stock in the equity portion of the capital structure. But preferred is *very different* from common equity.

5. Much of the data in this section is taken from a study by Donald E. Fischer and Glenn A. Wilt, Jr., "Non-Convertible Preferred Stocks as a Financing Instrument," *Journal of Finance* 23 (September 1968), pp. 611–24.

quires a minimum level of retained earnings before common stock dividends are permitted. In order to assure the availability of liquid assets that may be converted into cash for the payment of dividends, the maintenance of a minimum current ratio may also be required.

Par Value

Unlike common stock, preferred stock usually has a par value; this value is a meaningful quantity. First, it establishes the amount due to the preferred stockholders in the event of liquidation. Second, the preferred dividend is frequently stated as a percentage of the par value. For example, J. I. Case has preferred stock outstanding that has a par value of $100, and the dividend is stated to be 7 percent of par. It would, of course, be just as appropriate for the Case preferred stock to state simply that the annual dividend is $7; on many preferred stocks the dividends are stated in this manner rather than as a percentage of par value.

Cumulative Dividends

A high percentage of dividends on preferred stocks is cumulative—all past preferred dividends must be paid before common dividends may be paid. The cumulative feature is therefore a protective device. If the preferred stock was not cumulative, preferred and common stock dividends could be passed by for a number of years. The company could then vote a large common stock dividend, but only the stipulated payment to preferred stock. Suppose the preferred stock with a par value of $100 carried a 7 percent dividend. Suppose the company did not pay dividends for several years so that it accumulated funds that would enable it to pay in total about $50 in dividends. It could pay one $7 dividend to the preferred stock and a $43 dividend to the common stock. Obviously, this device could be used to evade the preferred position that the holders of preferred stock have tried to obtain. The cumulative feature prevents such evasion.[6]

Large arrearages on preferred stock would make it difficult to resume dividend payments on common stock. To avoid delays in beginning common stock dividend payments again, a compromise arrangement with the holders of common stock is likely to be worked out. A package offer is one possibility; for example, a recapitalization plan may provide for an exchange of shares. The arrearage will be wiped out by the donation of common stock with a value equal to the amount of the preferred dividend arrearage, and the holders of preferred stock are thus given an

---

6. Note, however, that compounding is absent in most cumulative plans. In other words, the arrearages themselves earn no return.

ownership share in the corporation. In addition, resumption of current dividends on the preferred may be promised. Whether these provisions are worth anything depends on the future earnings prospects of the company.

The advantage to the company of substituting common stock for dividends in arrears is that it can start again with a clean balance sheet. If earnings recover, dividends can be paid to the holders of common stock without making up arrearages to the holders of preferred stock. The original common stockholders, of course, will have given up a portion of their ownership of the corporation.

Convertibility

Approximately 40 percent of the preferred stock that has been issued in recent years is convertible into common stock. For example, one share of a particular preferred stock could be convertible into 2.5 shares of the firm's common stock at the option of the preferred shareholder. The nature of convertibility is discussed in Chapter 16.

Some Infrequent Provisions

Some of the other provisions occasionally encountered in preferred stocks include the following.

Voting Rights. Sometimes a preferred stock is given the right to vote for directors. When this feature is present, it generally permits the preferred stock to elect a *minority* of the board, say three out of nine directors. The voting privilege becomes operative only if the company has not paid the preferred dividend for a specified period, for example, six, eight, or ten quarters.

Participating. A rare type of preferred stock is one that participates with the common stock in sharing the firm's earnings. The following factors generally relate to participating preferred stocks: (1) the stated preferred dividend is paid first—for example, $5 a share; (2) next, income is allocated to common stock dividends *up* to an amount equal to the preferred dividend—in this case, $5; (3) any remaining income is shared equally between the common and the preferred stockholders.

Sinking Fund. Some preferred issues have a sinking fund requirement. When they do, the sinking fund ordinarily calls for the purchase and retirement of a given percentage of the preferred stock each year.

Maturity. Preferred stocks almost never have maturity dates on which they must be retired. However, if the issue has a sinking fund, this effectively creates a maturity date.

Call Provision. A call provision gives the issuing corporation the right to call in the preferred stock for redemption, the same as for bonds. If it is used, the call provision generally states that the company must pay an amount greater than the par value of the preferred stock, with this additional sum being defined as the *call premium*. For example, a $100 par value preferred stock might be callable at the option of the corporation at $108 a share.

Evaluation of Preferred Stock From Viewpoint of Issuer

An important advantage of preferred stock from the viewpoint of the issuer is that, in contrast to bonds, the obligation to make fixed interest payments is avoided. Also, a firm wishing to expand because its earning power is high may obtain higher earnings for the original owners by selling preferred stock with a limited return rather than by selling common stock.

Advantages. By selling preferred stock the financial manager avoids the provision of equal participation in earnings that the sale of additional common stock would require. Preferred stock also permits a company to avoid sharing control through participation in voting. In contrast to bonds, it enables the firm to conserve mortgagable assets. Since preferred stock typically has no maturity and no sinking fund, it is more flexible than bonds.

Disadvantages. Characteristically, preferred stock must be sold on a higher yield basis than that for bonds. Preferred stock dividends are not deductible as a tax expense, a characteristic that makes their cost differential very great in comparison with that of bonds.[7] As we shall see in Chapter 19, the after-tax cost of debt is approximately half the

---

7. Historically, a given firm's preferred stock generally carried higher rates than its bonds because of the greater risk inherent in preferred stocks from the holder's viewpoint. However, as is noted below, the fact that preferred dividends are largely exempt from the corporate income tax has made preferred stock attractive to corporate investors. In recent years, high-grade preferreds, on average, have sold on a lower yield basis than high-grade bonds. Fischer and Wilt ("Non-Convertible Preferred Stocks as a Financing Instrument") found that bonds in 1965 had a yield 0.39 percentage points *above* preferred stocks. Thus, a very strong firm could sell preferreds to yield about 0.3 percent less than bonds. As an example, on March 27, 1973, AT&T sold a preferred issue that yielded 7.28 percent to an investor. On that same date, AT&T bonds yielded 7.55 percent, or 0.27 percent more than the preferred. The tax treatment accounted for this differential; the *after-tax* yield was greater on the preferred stock than on the bonds.

stated coupon rate for profitable firms. The cost of preferred, however, is the full percentage amount of the preferred dividend.[8]

From Viewpoint of Investor

In fashioning securities, the financial manager needs to consider the investor's point of view. Frequently it is asserted that preferred stocks have so many disadvantages both to the issuer and to the investor that they should never be issued. Nevertheless, preferred stock is issued in substantial amounts.

Advantages. Preferred stock provides the following advantages to the investor. (1) Preferred stocks provide reasonably steady income. (2) Preferred stockholders have a preference over common stockholders in liquidation; numerous examples can be cited where the prior-preference position of holders of preferred stock saved them from losses incurred by holders of common stock. (3) Many corporations (for example, insurance companies) like to hold preferred stocks as investments because 85 percent of the dividends received on these shares is not taxable.

Disadvantages. Preferred stock also has some disadvantages to investors. (1) Although the holders of preferred stock bear a substantial portion of ownership risk, their returns are limited. (2) Price fluctuations in preferred stock are far greater than those in bonds, yet yields on bonds are frequently higher than those on preferred stock. (3) The stock has no legally enforceable right to dividends. (4) Accrued dividend arrearages are seldom settled in cash comparable to the amount of the obligation that has been incurred.

Recent Trends

Because of the nondeductibility of preferred stock dividends as a tax expense, many companies have retired their preferred stock. Often debentures or subordinated debentures will be offered to preferred stockholders in exchange. The interest on the debentures is deductible as a tax expense, whereas preferred stock dividends are not deductible.

When the preferred stock is not callable, the company must offer terms of exchange that are sufficiently attractive to induce the preferred stockholders to agree to the exchange. Characteristically, bonds or other

---

8. By far the most important issuers of nonconvertible preferred stocks are the utility companies. For these firms, taxes are an expense for rate-making purposes—that is, higher taxes are passed on to the customers in the form of higher prices—so tax deductibility is not an important issue. This explains why utilities issue about 85 percent of all nonconvertible preferreds.

securities in an amount somewhat above the recent value of the preferred stock will be issued in exchange. Sometimes bonds equal in market value to the preferred stock will be issued, along with additional cash or common stock, to provide an extra inducement to the preferred stockholders. Sometimes the offer will be bonds equal to only a portion of the current market value of the preferred with an additional amount, represented by cash or common stock, that will bring the total amount offered to the preferred stockholders to something over its market value as of a recent date.

U.S. Steel's replacement of its 7 percent preferred stock in 1965 illustrates one of these exchange patterns. U.S. Steel proposed that its 7 percent preferred stock be changed into $4\frac{5}{8}$ percent 30-year bonds at a rate of $175 principal amount of bonds for each preferred share. On August 17, 1965, when the plan was announced, the preferred stock was selling at $150. U.S. Steel also announced that the conversion would increase earnings available to common stock by $10 million yearly, or 18 cents a share at 1965 federal income tax rates; this was sufficient inducement to persuade the company to give the preferred stockholders the added $25 a share.

Decision Making on Use of Preferred Stock

We can now distill the circumstances favoring the use of preferred stock from the foregoing analysis. As a hybrid security, the use of preferred stock is favored by conditions that fall between those favoring the use of common stock and those favoring the use of debt.

When a firm's profit margin is high enough to more than cover preferred stock dividends, it will be advantageous to employ leverage. However, if the firm's sales and profits are subject to considerable fluctuations, the use of debt with fixed interest charges may be unduly risky. Preferred stock may offer a happy compromise. The use of preferred stock will be strongly favored if the firm already has a debt ratio that is high in relation to the reference level maximum for the line of business.

Relative costs of alternative sources of financing are always important considerations. When the market prices of common stocks are relatively low, the costs of common stock financing are relatively high; this is shown in Chapter 17. The costs of preferred stock financing follow interest rate levels more than common stock prices; in other words, when interest rates are low, the cost of preferred stock is also likely to be low. When the costs of fixed-income instruments, such as preferred stock, are low and the costs of variable value securities, such as common stock, are high, the use of preferred stock is favored.

Preferred stock may also be the desired form of financing whenever the use of debt would involve excessive risk, but the issuance of common stock would result in problems of control for the dominant ownership group in the company.

Rationale for Different Classes of Securities

At this point, the following questions are likely to come to mind: Why are there so many different forms of long-term securities? Why would anybody ever be willing to purchase subordinated bonds or income bonds? The answers to both questions may be made clear by reference to Figure 14–2. The now familiar tradeoff function is drawn to show the risk and the expected returns for the various securities of the Longstreet Company. Longstreet's first mortgage bonds are slightly more risky than U.S. Treasury bonds and sell at a slightly higher expected return. The second mortgage bonds are yet more risky and have a still higher expected return. Subordinated debentures, income bonds, and preferred stocks all are increasingly risky and have increasingly higher expected returns. Longstreet's common stock, the riskiest security the firm issues, has the highest expected return of any of its offerings.

Why does Longstreet issue so many different classes of securities? Why not just offer one type of bond plus common stock? The answer lies in the fact that different investors have different risk-return tradeoff

Figure 14–2
Risk and Expected
Returns on Different
Classes of Securities,
the Longstreet
Company

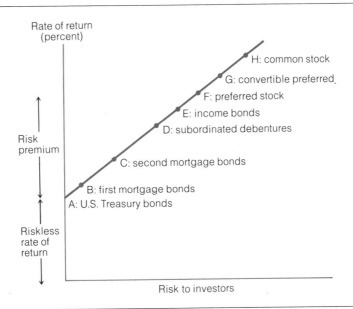

preferences, so if its securities are to appeal to the broadest possible market, Longstreet must offer securities that appeal to as many investors as possible. Used wisely, a policy of selling differentiated securities can lower a firm's overall cost of capital below what it would be if it issued only one class of debt and common stock.

Refunding a Bond or a Preferred Stock Issue

Suppose a company sells bonds or preferred stock at a time when interest rates are relatively high. Provided the issue is callable, as many are, the company can sell a new issue of low-yielding securities if and when interest rates drop and use the proceeds to retire the high-rate issue. This is called a *refunding operation*.[9]

The decision to refund a security issue is analyzed in much the same manner as a capital budgeting expenditure. The costs of refunding — the "investment outlay" — are (1) the call premium paid for the privilege of calling the old issue and (2) the flotation costs incurred in selling the new issue. The annual receipts, in the capital budgeting sense, are the interest payments that are saved each year; for example, if interest expense on the old issue is $1 million while that on the new issue is $700,000, the $300,000 saving constitutes the annual benefits.

In analyzing the advantages of refunding, the net present value method is the recommended procedure — discount the future interest savings back to the present and compare the discounted value with the cash outlays associated with the refunding. *In the discounting process, the after-tax cost of the new debt, not the average cost of capital, should be used as the discount factor.* The reason for this is that there is relatively little risk to the savings — their value is known with relative certainty, which is quite unlike most capital budgeting decisions. The following case illustrates the calculations needed in a refunding decision.

As discussed in Chapters 6 and 21, interest rate levels peaked cyclically in the autumn of 1974 when the rates on new issues of triple A corporate bonds exceeded 10 percent. By December 1976, these yields had declined to almost 8 percent, representing a swing of approximately 200 basis points. The last half of 1976 was characterized by a substantial activity in refunding of bond and preferred stock issues at lower interest rates. A moderate increase in interest rates occurred during the early part of January 1977, but refundings continued to be attractive. Also, interest rates were considered to be near their cyclical lows. Illustrative of the bond refunding activity that occurred in 1976–77 is the South

---

9. For an excellent discussion of refunding, see O. D. Bowlin, "The Refunding Decision," *Journal of Finance* 21 (March 1966), pp. 55–68.

Carolina Electric & Gas Company's $30 million First and Refunding Mortgage Bond issue dated February 17, 1977, at 8⅜ percent interest rate, maturing March 1, 2007.[10] The net proceeds from the sale of these bonds were applied to the redemption of Carolina's First and Refunding Mortgage bonds, 9⅞ percent series due in the year 2000 at a redemption price of 107.04 percent of the principal amount plus accrued interest to the date of redemption at April 1, 1977.

The relevant data on the old issue and on the new refunding issues are summarized below:

	Old Issue	New Issue
Face amount	$30,000,000	$30,000,000
Interest rate	9⅞%	8⅜%
Life of bond	30 years	30 years
Maturity date	June 1, 2000	March 1, 1977
Total issue proceeds	$29,700,000	29,918,100
Flotation costs	600,000	262,500
Net proceeds of sale	$29,100,000	$29,655,600

Step 1. What is the investment outlay required to refund the issue? There are four components to the required investment outlay; the call premium on the old issue, flotation costs on the new issue, flotation costs on the old issue, and additional interest expense.

a. Call premium:
The call premium is 7.04 percent of face value as given by the bond indenture on the old issue. Since this is a tax deductible expense, the actual cost is reduced by the company's tax rate of 40 percent.

$$\text{Before-tax call premium} = \text{Call rate} \times \text{face amount}$$

$$\$2,112,000 = .0704 \times \$30,000.00$$

$$\text{After-tax call premium} = \text{Before-tax call premium} \times (1 - \text{tax rate})$$

$$\$1,267,200 = \$2,112,000 \times (1 - .40).$$

Although South Carolina Electric & Gas must expend $2.112 million on the call premium, this is a deductible expense. Since the company is in a 40 percent tax bracket, it saves $844,800 in taxes. The after-tax cost of the call is, therefore, only $1,267,200.

b. Flotation costs on new issue:
Total flotation costs are $262,500. For tax purposes costs are amortized

---

10. This is an actual refunding operation based on the company prospectus dated February 17, 1977, and information obtained on the old issue from *Moody's Public Utilities* volume.

over the life of the new bond, or 30 years. Assuming straight-line amortization, the annual tax deduction is given by:

$$\text{Annual tax deduction} = \frac{\text{Flotation costs}}{\text{Life of bond (new issue)}}$$

$$\$8,750 = \frac{\$262,500}{30}.$$

Since South Carolina E & G is in the 40 percent tax bracket, it has a tax saving of $3,500 a year ($8,750 × .40) for 30 years. This is an annuity of $3,500 for 30 years. The present value of the annuity is found by discounting at the after-tax cost of the new debt issue. The after-tax cost of debt is the before-tax interest rate times one minus the tax rate (8.375 × .60) or 5 percent.

$$
\begin{aligned}
PV \text{ of tax saving} &= PVIF_a \times \text{Annual after-tax saving} \\
&= 15.373 \times \$3,500 \\
&= \$53,805.
\end{aligned}
$$

Net after tax effect of new flotation cost is:

New flotation costs	$262,500
PV of tax savings	53,805
Net cost	$208,695

c. Flotation costs on old issue:

The old issue has an unamortized flotation cost of $460,000 (23/30 × $600,000). This may be recognized immediately as an expense, thus creating an after-tax savings of $184,000. The firm will, however, lose a deduction of $20,000 a year for 23 years, or an after-tax benefit of $8,000 a year. The present value of this lost benefit, discounted at 5 percent is:

$$
\begin{aligned}
PV \text{ of lost benefit} &= PVIF_a \times \$8,000 \\
&= 13.488 \times \$8,000 \\
&= \$107,906.
\end{aligned}
$$

The net after-tax effect of old flotation costs is:

Tax savings on old flotation costs	($184,000)
	−107,906
Net after-tax effect of old flotation costs	($76,084)

d. Additional interest:

The old bond will not be retired until one month after the new bond is issued. Thus, there will be a period of one month when interest is accruing on both bonds. During this period the proceeds of the new issue are invested in short term treasury bills to earn 4.5 percent.

One month "extra" interest on new issue
Face Amount $\times$ $\frac{1}{12}$ $\times$ 8.375% = before-tax interest costs
$30,000,000 $\times$ $\frac{1}{12}$ $\times$ .08375 = $209,375
One month income from treasury bill investment
Net proceeds $\frac{1}{12}$ $\times$ .045 = $111,209
Net after-tax interest cost:
(Interest cost − interest revenue) $\times$ (1 − tax rate) = cost
(209,375 − 111,209) (1 − .4) = $58,900

e. Total after-tax investment:
The total investment outlay required to refund the bond issue is thus:

Call premium	$1,267,200
Flotation cost, new	208,695
Flotation cost, old	(76,096)
Additional interest	58,900
Total investment	$1,458,699

Step 2. What are the annual savings?
a. Old bond interest after tax:

Face amount $\times$ interest rate $\times$ (1 − tax rate) = interest
$30,000,000 $\times$ .09875 $\times$ (1 − .4) = $1,777,500

b. New bond interest after tax:

$30,000,000 $\times$ .08375 $\times$ (1 − .4) = $1,507,500

c. Annual savings: $ 270,000

Step 3. What is the present value of the savings?
a. Twenty-three years *PV* of annuity factor at 5 percent = 13.488
b. *PV* of $270,000 a year for 23 years:

$$13.488 \times \$270,000 = \$3,641,760.$$

Step 4. Conclusion: Since the present value of the receipts ($3,641,760) exceeds the required investment ($1,458,699), the issue should be refunded.

Two other points should be mentioned. First, since the $270,000 savings is an essentially riskless investment, its present value is found by discounting at the firm's least risky rate—its after-tax cost of debt. Second, since the refunding operation is advantageous to the firm, it must be disadvantageous to bondholders—they must give up their $9\frac{7}{8}$ per-

cent bond and reinvest in one yielding 8⅜ percent. This points out the
danger of the call provision to bondholders and explains why, at any
given time, bonds without a call provision command higher prices than
callable bonds.[11]

Summary

Bonds. A *bond* is a long-term promissory note. A *mortgage bond* is secured by real property. An *indenture* is an agreement between the firm
issuing a bond and the numerous bondholders, represented by a
trustee.

Secured long-term debt differs with respect to (1) the priority of claims,
(2) the right to issue additional securities, and (3) the scope of the lien
provided. These characteristics determine the amount of protection
provided to the bondholder by the terms of the security. Giving the
investor more security will induce him to accept a lower yield but will
restrict the future freedom of action of the issuing firm.

The main classes of unsecured bonds are (1) *debentures*, (2) *subordinated debentures*, and (3) *income bonds*. Holders of debentures are unsecured
general creditors. Subordinated debentures are junior in claim to bank
loans. Income bonds are similar to preferred stock in that interest is
paid only when earned.

The characteristics of long-term debt determine the circumstances
under which it will be used when alternative forms of financing are
under analysis. The cost of debt is limited, but it is a fixed obligation.
Bond interest is an expense deductible for tax purposes. Debt carries a
maturity date and may require sinking fund payments to prepare for
extinguishing the obligation. Indenture provisions are likely to include
restrictions on the freedom of action of the management of the firm.

The nature of long-term debt encourages its use under the following
circumstances:

1. Sales and earnings are relatively stable.
2. Profit margins are adequate to make leverage advantageous.
3. A rise in profits or the general price level is expected.
4. The existing debt ratio is relatively low.
5. Common stock price/earnings ratios are low in relation to the levels
   of interest rates.
6. Control considerations are important.

11. See F. C. Jen and J. E. Wert, "The Effects of Call Risk on Corporate Bond Yields," *Journal of Finance* 22 (December 1967), pp. 637–52; and G. Pye, "The Value of Call Deferment on a Bond: Some
Empirical Results," *Journal of Finance* 22 (December 1967), pp. 623–36.

7. Cash flow requirements under the bond agreement are not burdensome.
8. Restrictions of the bond indenture are not onerous.

Although seven of the eight factors may favor debt, the eighth can swing the decision to the use of equity capital. The list of factors is, thus, simply a checklist of things to be considered when deciding on bonds versus stock; the actual decision is based on a judgment about the relative importance of the several factors.

Preferred Stocks. The *characteristics of preferred stock* vary with the requirements of the situation under which it is issued. However, certain patterns tend to remain. Preferred stocks usually have priority over common stocks with respect to earnings and claims on assets in liquidation. Preferred stocks are usually cumulative; they have no maturity but are sometimes callable. They are typically nonparticipating and have only contingent voting rights.

The advantages to the issuer are limited dividends and no maturity. These advantages may outweigh the disadvantages of higher cost and the nondeductibility of the dividends as an expense for tax purposes. But their acceptance by investors is the final test of whether they can be sold on favorable terms.

Companies sell preferred stock when they seek the advantages of financial leverage but fear the dangers of the fixed charges on debt in the face of potential fluctuations in income. If debt ratios are already high or if the costs of common stock financing are relatively high, the advantages of preferred stock will be reinforced.

The use of preferred stock has declined significantly since the advent of the corporate income tax, because preferred dividends are not deductible for income tax purposes, while bond interest payments are deductible. In recent years, however, there has been a strong shift back to a new kind of preferred stock—convertible preferred, used primarily in connection with mergers. If the stockholders of the acquired company receive cash or bonds, they are required to pay capital gains taxes on any gains that might have been realized. If convertible preferred stock is given to the selling stockholders, this constitutes a tax-free exchange of securities. The selling stockholders can obtain a fixed income security and at the same time postpone the payment of capital gains taxes.

Refunding. If a bond or a preferred stock issue was sold when interest rates were higher than they are at present, and if the issue is callable, it may be profitable to call the old issue and refund it with a new, lower-cost issue. An analysis similar to capital budgeting is required to determine whether a refunding operation should be undertaken.

Questions

14–1. A sinking fund is set up in one of two ways:
   a. The corporation makes annual payments to the trustee, who invests the proceeds in securities (frequently government bonds) and uses the accumulated total to retire the bond issue on maturity.
   b. The trustee uses the annual payments to retire a portion of the issue each year, either calling a given percentage of the issue by a lottery and paying a specified price per bond or buying bonds on the open market, whichever is cheaper.

   Discuss the advantages and disadvantages of each procedure from the viewpoint of both the firm and the bondholders.

14–2. Since a corporation often has the right to call bonds at will, do you believe individuals should be able to demand repayment at any time they so desire?

14–3. What are the relative advantages and disadvantages of issuing a long-term bond during a recession versus during a period of prosperity?

14–4. Missouri Pacific's 4¾ percent income bonds due in 2020 are selling for $770, while the company's 4¼ percent first mortgage bonds due in 2005 are selling for $945. Why would the bonds with the lower coupon sell at a higher price? (Each has a $1,000 par value.)

14–5. When a firm sells bonds, it must offer a package acceptable to potential buyers. Included in this package of terms are such features as the issue price, the coupon interest rate, the term to maturity, sinking fund provisions, and other features. The package itself is determined through a bargaining process between the firm and the investment bankers who will handle the issue. What particular features would you, as a corporate treasurer, be especially interested in having, and which would you be most willing to give ground on, under each of the following conditions:
   a. You believe that the economy is near the peak of a business cycle.
   b. Long-run forecasts indicate that your firm may have heavy cash inflows in relation to cash needs during the next five to ten years.
   c. Your current liabilities are presently low, but you anticipate raising a considerable amount of funds through short-term borrowing in the near future.

14–6. Bonds are less attractive to investors during periods of inflation because a rise in the price level will reduce the purchasing power of the fixed-interest payments and also of the principal. Discuss the advantages and disadvantages to a corporation of using a bond whose interest payments and principal would increase in direct proportion to increases in the price level (an inflation-proof bond).

14–7. If preferred stock dividends are passed for several years, the preferred stockholders are frequently given the right to elect several members of the board of directors. In the case of bonds that are in default on interest payments, this procedure is not followed. Why does this difference exist?

14–8. Preferred stocks are found in almost all industries, but one industry is the really dominant issuer of preferred shares. What is this industry, and why are firms in it so disposed to using preferred stock?

14–9. If the corporate income tax were abolished, would this raise or lower the amount of new preferred stock issued?

14–10. Investors buying securities have some expected or required rate of return in mind. Which would you expect to be higher, the required rate of return (before taxes) on preferred stocks or that on common stocks (a) for individual investors and (b) for corporate investors (for example, insurance companies)?

14–11. Do you think the before-tax required rate of return is higher or lower on very high grade preferred stocks or on bonds (a) for individual investors and (b) for corporate investors?

14–12. For purposes of measuring a firm's leverage, should preferred stock be classified as debt or as equity? Does it matter if the classification is being made (a) by the firm itself, (b) by creditors, or (c) by equity investors?

Problems

14–1. The Longmont Corporation has a $600,000 long-term bond issue outstanding. This debt has an additional ten years to maturity and bears a coupon interest rate of 9 percent. The firm now has the opportunity of refinancing the debt with ten-year bonds at a rate of 7 percent. Further declines in the interest rate are unanticipated. The bond redemption premium (call premium) on the old bond would be $30,000; issue cost on the new would be $20,000. If tax effects are ignored, should the firm refund the bonds?

14–2. In late 1978 the Coaltown Cas & Electric Company sought to raise $6 million to refinance present preferred stock issues at a lower rate. The company could sell additional debt at 9 percent, preferred stock at 8.84 percent, or common stock at $50 a share. How should the company raise the money? Relevant financial information is provided below.

(This question should not be answered in terms of precise cost of capital calculations. Rather, a more qualitative and subjective analysis is appropriate. The only calculations necessary are some simple ratios. Careful interpretation of these ratios is necessary, however, to understand and discuss the often complex, subjective judgment issues involved.)

Public Utilities Financial Ratios

Current ratio (times)	1.0
Interest earned (before taxes) (times)	4.0
Sales to total assets (times)	0.3
Average collection period (days)	28.0
Current debt/total assets (percent)	5–10

Long-term debt/total assets (percent)	45–50
Preferred/total assets (percent)	10–15
Common equity/total assets (percent)	30–35
Earnings before interest and taxes to total assets (percent)	8.9
Profits to common equity (percent)	12.1
Expected growth in earnings and dividends (percent)	4.5

**Coaltown Gas &
Electric Company**
Balance sheet,
July 31, 1978
(in millions of dollars)

Cash	$ 0.75	Current liabilities		$ 3.00
Receivables	1.50	Long-term debt, 3.5%		27.00
Material and supplies	1.20	Preferred stock, 5.60%		6.00
Total current assets	$ 3.45	Common stock, $25 par value		11.25
		Capital surplus		6.60
Net property	56.55	Retained earnings		6.15
Total assets	$60.00	Total claims		$60.00

**Coaltown Gas &
Electric Company**
Income statement
for year ended
July 31, 1978
(in millions of dollars)

Operating revenues	$18.9000
Operating expenses	12.5000
Earnings before interest and taxes	$ 6.4000
Interest deduction	.9450
Earnings before taxes	$ 5.4550
Income taxes at 50%	2.7275
Earnings after taxes	$ 2.7275
Preferred dividends	.3360
Net income available to common	$ 2.3915
Earnings per share	$ 5.31
Dividends per share	$ 4.25

14–3. Cathode Electronics is planning a capital improvement program to provide greater efficiency and versatility in its operations. It is estimated that by mid-1979 the company will need to raise $200 million. Cathode is a leading electronics producer with an excellent credit rating.

You are asked to set up a program for obtaining the necessary funds. Using the following information, indicate the best form of financing. Some items you should include in your analysis are profit margins, relative costs, control of the voting stock, cash flows, ratio analysis, pro forma analysis, and implicit cost of capital. Cathode's common stock is selling at $64 a share. The company could sell debt (25 years) at 8.0 percent or preferred stock at 8.5 percent.

Electronics Industry Financial Ratios

Current ratio (times)	2.1
Sales to total assets (times)	1.8

Coverage of fixed charges (times)	7.0
Average collection period (days)	42.0
Current debt/total assets (percent)	20–25
Long-term debt/total assets (percent)	10.0
Preferred/total assets (percent)	0–5
Net worth/total assets (percent)	65–70
Profits to sales (percent)	3.3
Profits to total assets (percent)	6.0
Profits to net worth (percent)	9.5
Expected growth rate in earnings and dividends	5.3

Cathode Electronics Company
Consolidated balance sheet, December 31, 1978 (in millions of dollars)

Assets

Current	$ 760	
Other investments	140	
Properties (net)	1,140	
Prepaid expenses	40	
Total assets		$2,080

Liabilities

Current	$ 320	
Long-term debt, 5.5%	180	
Total liabilities		$ 500
Common stock, $10 par	$ 320	
Capital surplus	300	
Retained earnings	880	
Reserves	80	
Total net worth		1,580
Total liabilities and net worth		$2,080

Cathode Electronics Company
Consolidated income statement for years ended December 31, 1976, 1977, and 1978 (in millions of dollars)

	1976	1977	1978
Sales	$2,440	$1,820	$2,160
Other income	20	20	20
Total	$2,460	$1,840	$2,180
Cost and expenses	2,113	1,591	1,910
Income before interest and taxes	$ 347	$ 249	$ 270
Interest on long-term debt	$ 7	$ 9	$ 10
Federal income tax	172	120	128
Net income	$ 168	$ 120	$ 132
Cash dividends	92	92	92
Shares outstanding (widely held)	40,000,000 for all three years		

Selected References

Ang, James S. "The Two Faces of Bond Refunding." *Journal of Finance* 30 (June 1975): 869–74.

———. "The Intertemporal Behavior of Corporate Debt Policy." *Journal of Financial and Quantitative Analysis* 11 (Nov. 1976): 555–66.

Ang, James S., and Patel, Kiritkumar A. "Empirical Research on Capital Markets Bond Rating Methods: Comparison and Validation." *Journal of Finance* 30 (May 1975): 631–40.

Bierman, Harold. *Financial Policy Decisions.* New York: Macmillan, 1970. Chaps. 2 and 12.

———. "The Bond Refunding Decision." *Financial Management* 1 (Summer 1972): 22–29.

———. "The Bond Refunding Decision as a Markov Process." *Management Science* 12 (Aug. 1966): 545–51.

Bierman, Harold, and Barnea, Amir. "Expected Short-Term Interest Rates in Bond Refunding." *Financial Management* 3 (Spring 1974): 75–79.

Bildersee, John S. "Some New Bond Indexes." *Journal of Business* 48 (Oct. 1975): 506–25.

———. "Some Aspects of Performance of Non-Convertible Preferred Stocks." *Journal of Finance,* forthcoming.

Black, Fischer, and Cox, John C. "Valuing Corporate Securities: Some Effects of Bond Indenture Provisions." *Journal of Finance* 31 (May 1976): 351–67.

Bloch, Ernest. "Pricing a Corporate Bond Issue: A Look Behind the Scenes." *Essays in Money and Credit.* New York: Federal Reserve Bank of New York, 1964, pp. 72–76.

Boquist, John A.; Racette, George A.; and Schlarbaum, Gary G. "Duration and Risk Assessment for Bonds and Common Stocks." *Journal of Finance* 30 (Dec. 1975): 1360–65.

Bowlin, Oswald D. "The Refunding Decision: Another Special Case in Capital Budgeting." *Journal of Finance* 21 (Mar. 1966): 55–68.

Brown, Bowman. "Why Corporations Should Consider Income Bonds." *Financial Executive* 35 (Oct. 1967): 74–78.

Bullington, Robert A. "How Corporate Debt Issues are Rated." *Financial Executive* 42 (Sept. 1974): 28–37.

Caks, John. "The Coupon Effect on Yield to Maturity." *Journal of Finance* 32 (Mar. 1977): 103–15.

Cohan, Avery B. *Private Placements and Public Offerings: Market Shares Since 1935.* Chapel Hill, N.C.: School of Business Administration, University of North Carolina, 1961.

Donaldson, Gordon. "In Defense of Preferred Stock." *Harvard Business Review* 40 (July–Aug. 1962): 123–36.

———. "New Framework for Corporate Debt Policy." *Harvard Business Review* 40 (Mar.–Apr. 1962): 117–31.

Dyl, E. A., and Joehnk, M. D. "Competitive Versus Negotiated Underwriting of Public Utility Debt." *Bell Journal of Economics* 7 (Autumn 1976): 680–89.

Ederington, Louis H. "The Yield Spread on New Issues of Corporate Bonds." *Journal of Finance* 29 (Dec. 1974): 1531–43.

————. "Uncertainty, Competition, and Costs in Corporate Bond Underwriting." *Journal of Financial Economics* 2 (Mar. 1975): 71–94.

————. "Negotiated Versus Competitive Underwritings of Corporate Bonds." *Journal of Finance* 31 (Mar. 1976): 17–26.

Elsaid, Hussein H. "The Function of Preferred Stock in the Corporate Financial Plan." *Financial Analysts' Journal* (July–Aug. 1969): 112–17.

Elton, Edwin J., and Gruber, Martin J. "The Economic Value of the Call Option." *Journal of Finance* 27 (Sept. 1972): 891–902.

Everett, Edward. "Subordinated Debt—Nature and Enforcement." *Business Lawyer* 20 (July 1965): 953–87.

Fischer, Donald E., and Wilt, Glenn A., Jr. "Non-Convertible Preferred Stock as a Financing Instrument, 1950–1965." *Journal of Finance* 23 (Sept. 1968): 611–24.

Fisher, Lawrence. "Determinants of Risk Premiums on Corporate Bonds." *Journal of Political Economy* 67 (June 1959): 217–37.

Gritta, Richard D. "The Impact of Lease Capitalization." *Financial Analysts' Journal* 30 (Mar.–Apr. 1974): 47–52.

Grove, M. A. "On 'Duration' and the Optimal Maturity Structure of the Balance Sheet." *Bell Journal of Economics and Management Science* 5 (Autumn 1974): 696–709.

Hickman, W. B. *Corporate Bonds: Quality and Investment Performance*, Occasional Paper 59. New York: National Bureau of Economic Research, 1957.

Jen, Frank C., and Wert, James E. "The Value of the Deferred Call Privilege." *National Banking Review* 3 (Mar. 1966): 369–78.

————. "The Effects of Call Risk on Corporate Bond Yields." *Journal of Finance* 22 (Dec. 1967): 637–52.

————. "The Deferred Call Provision and Corporate Bond Yields." *Journal of Financial and Quantitative Analysis* 3 (June 1968): 157–69.

Johnson, Ramon E. "Term Structures of Corporate Bond Yields as a Function of Risk of Default." *Journal of Finance* 22 (May 1967): 313–45.

Johnson, Robert W. "Subordinated Debentures: Debt That Serves as Equity." *Journal of Finance* 10 (Mar. 1955): 1–16.

Johnson, Rodney, and Klein, Richard. "Corporate Motives in Repurchases of Discounted Bonds." *Financial Management* 3 (Autumn 1974): 44–49.

Kelly, Paul E. "New Financing Techniques on Wall Street." *Financial Executive* 44 (Nov. 1974): 30–43.

Kolodny, Richard. "The Refunding Decision in Near Perfect Markets." *Journal of Finance* 29 (Dec. 1974): 1467–77.

Litzenberger, Robert H., and Rutenberg, David P. "Size and Timing of Corporate Bond Flotations." *Journal of Financial and Quantitative Analysis* 8 (Jan. 1972): 1343–59.

Mayor, Thomas H., and McCoin, Kenneth G. "The Rate of Discount in Bond Refunding." *Financial Management* 3 (Autumn 1974): 54–58.

Morris, James R. "On Corporate Debt Maturity Strategies." *Journal of Finance* 31 (Mar. 1976): 29–37.

————. "A Model for Corporate Debt Maturity Decisions." *Journal of Financial and Quantitative Analysis* 11 (Sept. 1976): 339–58.

Ofer, Aharon R., and Taggart, Robert A., Jr. "Bond Refunding: A Clarifying Analysis." *Journal of Finance* 32 (Mar. 1977): 21–30.

Pinches, George E. "Financing With Convertible Preferred Stock, 1960–1967." *Journal of Finance* 25 (Mar. 1970): 53–63.

Pinches, George E., and Mingo, Kent A. "A Multivariate Analysis of Industrial Bond Ratings." *Journal of Finance* 28 (Mar. 1973): 1–18.

———. "The Role of Subordination and Industrial Bond Ratings." *Journal of Finance* 30 (Mar. 1975): 201–06.

Pogue, Thomas F., and Soldofsky, Robert M. "What's in a Bond Rating." *Journal of Financial and Quantitative Analysis* 4 (June 1969): 201–28.

Pye, Gordon. "The Value of Call Deferment on a Bond: Some Empirical Results." *Journal of Finance* 22 (Dec. 1967): 623–36.

———. "The Value of the Call Option on a Bond." *Journal of Political Economy* 74 (Apr. 1966): 200–05.

Racette, George A., and Lewellen, Wilbur G. "Corporate Debt Coupon Rate Strategies." *National Tax Journal* 29 (June 1976): 165–78.

Reilly, Frank K., and Joehnk, Michael D. "The Association Between Market-Determined Risk Measures for Bonds and Bond Ratings." *Journal of Finance* 31 (Dec. 1976): 1387–1403.

Shapiro, Eli, and Wolf, Charles R. *The Role of Private Placements in Corporate Finance.* Boston: Division of Research, Graduate School of Business Administration, Harvard University, 1972.

Sibley, A. M. "Some Evidence on the Cash Flow Effects of Bond Refunding." *Financial Management* 3 (Autumn 1974): 50–53.

Sprecher, C. Ronald. "A Note on Financing Mergers with Convertible Preferred Stock." *Journal of Finance* 26 (June 1971): 683–86.

Stevenson, Richard A. "Retirement of Non-Callable Preferred Stock." *Journal of Finance* 25 (Dec. 1970): 1143–52.

Tallman, Gary D.; Rush, David F.; and Melicher, Ronald W. "Competitive Versus Negotiated Underwriting Costs for Regulated Industries." *Financial Management* 3 (Summer 1974): 49–55.

Tinic, Seha M., and West, Richard R. "Marketability of Common Stocks in Canada and the U.S.A.: A Comparison of Agent Versus Dealer Dominated Markets." *Journal of Finance* 29 (June 1974): 729–46.

Van Horne, James C. "Implied Fixed Costs in Long-Term Debt Issues." *Journal of Financial and Quantitative Analysis* 8 (Dec. 1973).

Weingartner, H. Martin. "Optimal Timing of Bond Refunding." *Management Science* 13 (Mar. 1967): 511–24.

White, William L. "Debt Management and the Form of Business Financing." *Journal of Finance* 29 (May 1974): 565–77.

Winn, Willis J., and Hess, Arleigh, Jr. "The Value of the Call Privilege." *Journal of Finance* 14 (May 1959): 182–95.

Wishner, Maynard I. "Coming: Significantly Larger Roles for Secured Corporate Financing." *Financial Executive* 45 (May 1977): 18–23.

15　Term Loans and Leases

Intermediate-term financing is defined as *debt originally scheduled for repayment in more than one year but in less than ten years.* Anything shorter is a current liability and falls in the class of short-term credit, while obligations due in ten or more years are thought of as long-term debt. This distinction is arbitrary, of course — we might just as well define intermediate-term credit as loans with maturities of one to five years. However, the one-to-ten year distinction is commonly used, so we shall follow it here.

The major forms of intermediate-term financing include (1) *term loans* and (2) *lease financing.*

Term Loans

A term loan is a business loan with a maturity of more than one year. Ordinarily, term loans are retired by systematic repayments (often called *amortization payments*) over the life of the loan, although there are exceptions to the rule. Security, generally in the form of a chattel mortgage on equipment, is often employed, but the larger, stronger companies are able to borrow on an unsecured basis.

The primary lenders of term credit are commercial banks, life insurance companies, and, to a lesser extent, pension funds. Bank loans are generally restricted to maturities of between one and five years, while insurance companies and pension funds make the bulk of their term loans for between five and fifteen years. Therefore, many insurance company term loans are long-term, not intermediate-term, financing. Sometimes, when relatively large loans ($10 million and up) are involved, banks and insurance companies combine to make a loan, with the bank taking the short maturities and the insurance company the long maturities. Some specific features of term loans are discussed in the following sections.

Repayment Schedule

Because the repayment, or amortization, schedule is a particularly important feature of almost all term loans, it is useful to describe how it is determined. The purpose of amortization, of course, is to have the loan repaid gradually over its life rather than fall due all at once. Amortization forces the borrower to retire the loan slowly, thus protecting both the lender and the borrower against the possibility that the borrower will not make adequate provisions for retirement during the life of the loan. This is especially important where the loan is for the purpose of purchasing a specific item of equipment; here the amortization schedule will be geared to the productive life of the equipment, and payments will be made from cash flows resulting from use of the equipment.

To illustrate how the amortization schedule is determined, let us assume that a firm borrows $1,000 on a ten-year loan, that interest is computed at 8 percent on the declining balance, and that the principal and interest are to be paid in ten equal installments. What is the amount of each of the ten annual payments? To find this value we must use the present value concepts developed in Chapter 9.

First, notice that the lender advances $1,000 and receives in turn a 10-year annuity of a dollars each year. In the section headed Annual Receipts from an Annuity in Chapter 9, we saw that these receipts could be calculated as

$$a = \frac{PV_{at}}{PVIF_a},$$

where a is the annual receipt, PV_{at} is the present value of the annuity, and $PVIF_a$ is the appropriate interest factor found either in Table 9−5 or in Appendix Table D−4. Substituting the $1,000 for PV_{at} and the interest factor for a 10-year, 8 percent annuity, or 6.710, for $PVIF_a$, we find

$$a = \frac{\$1,000}{6.710} = \$149.$$

Therefore, if our firm makes ten annual installments of $149 each, it will have retired the $1,000 loan and provided the lender an 8 percent return on his investment.

	Year	Total Payment	Interest*	Amortization Repayment	Remaining Balance
Table 15−1 **Term-Loan** **Schedule**	1	$149	$80	$ 69	$931
	2	149	74	75	856
	3	149	68	81	775
	4	149	62	87	688
	5	149	55	94	594
	6	149	48	101	493
	7	149	39	110	383
	8	149	31	118	265
	9	149	21	128	137
	10	149	11	138	—

*Interest for the first year is .08 × $1,000 = $80; for the second year, .08 × $931 = $74; and so on.

Table 15–1 breaks down the annual payments into interest and repayment components and, in the process, proves that level payments of $149 will, in fact, retire the $1,000 loan and give the lender his 8 percent return. This breakdown is important for tax purposes, because the interest payments are deductible expenses to the borrower and taxable income to the lender.

Characteristics of Term Loans

Maturity. For commercial banks, the term loan runs 5 years or less, typically 3 years. For insurance companies, the most typical maturities have been 5 to 15 years. This difference reflects the fact that liabilities of commercial banks are shorter term than are those of insurance companies. As we pointed out above, banks and insurance companies occasionally cooperate in their term lending. For example, if a firm (usually a large one) seeks a 15-year term loan, a bank may take the loan for the first 5 years and an insurance company for the last 10 years.

Collateral. Commercial banks require security on about 60 percent of the volume and 90 percent of the number of term loans made. They take as security mainly stocks, bonds, machinery, and equipment. Insurance companies also require security on nearly one-third of their loans, frequently using real estate as collateral on the longer ones.

Options. In recent years institutional investors have increasingly taken compensation in addition to fixed interest payments on directly negotiated loans. The most popular form of additional compensation is an option to buy common stock, the option being in the form of detachable warrants permitting the purchase of the shares at stated prices over a designated period.[1]

Repayment Provisions. Most term loans are repayable in equal installments. Only a small percentage of the loans have any balloon segment, or unamortized balance, at the end. It is possible to prepay term loans ahead of schedule, but a prepayment penalty equal to 8 to 10 percent of the outstanding balance is usually assessed in such cases.

Terms of Loan Agreements

A major advantage of a term loan is that it assures the borrower of the use of the funds for an extended period. On a 90-day loan, since the

---

1. See Chapter 16 for more details on warrants.

commercial bank has the option to renew or not renew, the bank has frequent opportunities to reexamine the situation of the borrower. If it has deteriorated unduly, the loan officer simply does not renew the loan. On a term loan, however, the bank or the insurance company has committed itself for a period of years. Because of this long-term commitment, restrictive provisions are incorporated into the loan agreement to protect the lender for the duration of the loan. The most important of the typical restrictive provisions are listed below.

Current Ratio. The current ratio must be maintained at some specified level—$2\frac{1}{2}$ to 1; 3 to 1; $3\frac{1}{2}$ to 1, depending upon the borrower's line of business. Net working capital must also be maintained at some minimum level.

Additional Long-term Debt. Typically, there are prohibitions against incurring additional long-term indebtedness except with the permission of the lender. Furthermore, the lender does not ordinarily permit the pledging of assets. The loan agreement may also prohibit the borrower from assuming any contingent liabilities, such as guaranteeing the indebtedness of a subsidiary. Finally, the loan agreement probably restricts the borrower from circumventing these provisions by signing long-term leases beyond specified amounts.

Management. The loan agreement may require that any major changes in management personnel, or in its composition, must be approved by the lender. The loan agreement may require life insurance on the principals or key people in the business. In addition, the loan agreement may provide for the creation of a voting trust or a granting of proxies for a specified period to ensure that the management of the company will be under the control of the group on which the lender has relied in making the loan.

Financial Statements. The lender will require the borrower to submit periodic financial statements for his review.

This list does not exhaust all terms found in loan agreements, but it is illustrative. It serves to indicate the kind of protective provisions the bank or the insurance company seeks to embody in the loan agreement.

Cost of Term Loans

Another major aspect of term lending is its cost. As with other forms of lending, the interest rate on term loans varies with the size of the loan and the quality of the borrower. Surveys show that on smaller term loans the interest rate may run up to 15 percent. On loans of $1 million and above, term loan rates have been close to the prime rate. The size of the loan reflects the quality of the borrower as well as the fixed cost involved in making small loans.

The interest rate could be fixed for the life of the loan, or it could vary. Often the loan agreement specifies that the interest rate will be based on the average of the rediscount rate[2] in the borrower's federal reserve district during the previous three months, generally 1 or 2 percent above the rediscount rate. In other words, the loan rate can fluctuate during the life of the loan and is often tied to the rediscount rate. It may also be geared to the published prime rate charged by New York City banks.

Lease Financing

Firms are generally interested in *using* buildings and equipment, not in owning them per se. One way of obtaining the use of facilities and equipment is to buy them, but an alternative is to lease them. Prior to the 1950s, leasing was generally associated with real estate — land and buildings — but today it is possible to lease virtually any kind of fixed asset. The following quotation from a recent issue of *Fortune* will give an idea of the importance of equipment leasing; leases for real estate increase the significance of this financing technique:

Capital equipment with an original cost of somewhat more than $60 billion is now on lease in the U.S. to corporations, institutions, and governments. New equipment worth over $11 billion was leased last year, and it accounted for about 14 percent of all business investment in capital equipment. Overall, the volume of leasing is expanding by around 20 percent a year. If leasing continues to grow at its recent rate, by 1977 about one-fifth of all new capital equipment put in use by business will be leased.[3]

In a number of respects, leasing is quite similar to borrowing. However, unlike debt or equity financing, which, as a part of a general pool of financing sources cannot be associated with specific assets, leasing is typically identified with particular assets. Leasing provides for the acquisition of assets and their "complete financing" simultaneously.

A lease has an advantage compared to debt in that the lessor has a better position than a creditor if the user firm experiences financial difficulties. If the lessee does not meet his lease obligations, the lessor has a stronger legal right to take back the asset because the lessor still legally

---

2. The rediscount rate is the rate of interest at which a bank may borrow from a Federal Reserve bank.
3. Peter Vanderwicken, "The Powerful Logic of the Leasing Boom," *Fortune* (November 1973), p. 136.

owns the asset. A creditor, even a secured creditor, encounters costs and delays in recovering assets that he has directly or indirectly financed. So the lessor has less risk than other financing sources used in acquiring assets. Hence the riskier the firm that is seeking financing, the greater the reason for the supplier of financing to formulate a leasing arrangement rather than a loan. While banks, which provide term loans as well as leases, may prefer a lease or shift to a lease for risky applicants, the extent to which this differential risk position accounts for the growth of leasing activity is not known.

Types of Leases

Conceptually, as we show below, leasing is quite similar to borrowing, so leasing provides financial leverage. Leasing takes several different forms, the most important of which are sale and leaseback service leases, and straight financial leases. These three major types of leases are described below.

Sale and Leaseback

Under a sale and leaseback arrangement, a firm owning land, buildings, or equipment sells the property to a financial institution and simultaneously executes an agreement to lease the property back for a specified period under specific terms. If real estate is involved, the financial institution is generally a life insurance company; if the property consists of equipment and machinery, the financial institution could be an insurance company, a commercial bank, or a specialized leasing company.

Note that the seller, or *lessee*, immediately receives the purchase price put up by the buyer, or *lessor*. At the same time, the seller-lessee retains the use of the property. This parallel is carried over to the lease payment schedule. Under a mortgage loan arrangement, the financial institution would receive a series of equal payments just sufficient to amortize the loan and to provide the lender with a specified rate of return on his investment. The nature of the calculations was described above in the section on term loans. Under a sale and leaseback arrangement, the lease payments are set up in exactly the same manner—the payments are sufficient to return the full purchase price to the financial institution, in addition to providing it with a stated return on its investment.

Service Leases

Service, or operating, leases include both financing and maintenance services. IBM is one of the pioneers of the service lease contract; computers and office copying machines, together with automobiles and trucks, are the primary types of equipment involved in service leases. These leases ordinarily call for the lessor to maintain and service the leased equipment, and the costs of this maintenance are built into the lease payments or contracted for separately.

Another important characteristic of the service lease is the fact that it is frequently not fully amortized. In other words, the payments required under the lease contract are *not* sufficient to recover the full cost of the equipment. Obviously, however, the lease contract is written for considerably less than the expected life of the leased equipment, and the lessor expects to recover his cost either in subsequent renewal payments or on disposal of the leased equipment.

A final feature of the service lease is that it frequently contains a cancellation clause giving the lessee the right to cancel the lease and return the equipment before the expiration of the basic lease agreement. This is an important consideration for the lessee, for it means that he can return the equipment if technological developments render it obsolete, or if he simply no longer needs it.

**Financial
Leases**

A strict financial lease is one that does *not* provide for maintenance services, is *not* cancellable, and *is* fully amortized (that is, the lessor receives rental payments equal to the full price of the leased equipment). The typical arrangement involves the following steps:

1. The firm that will use the equipment selects the specific items it requires and negotiates the price and delivery terms with the manufacturer or the distributor.
2. Next, the user firm arranges with a bank or a leasing company to buy the equipment from the manufacturer or the distributor, and the user firm simultaneously executes an agreement to lease the equipment from the financial institution. The terms call for full amortization of the financial institution's cost, plus a return of from 6 to 12 percent a year on the unamortized balance. The lessee is generally given an option to renew the lease at a reduced rental on expiration of the basic lease, but he does not have the right to cancel the basic lease without completely paying off the financial institution.

Financial leases are almost the same as sale and leaseback arrangements, the main difference being that the leased equipment is new and the lessor buys it from a manufacturer or a distributor instead of from the user-lessee. A sale and leaseback may, then, be thought of as a special type of financial lease.

Internal Revenue Service Requirements for a Lease

The full amount of the annual lease payments is deductible for income tax purposes *provided the Internal Revenue Service agrees that a particular contract is a genuine lease and not simply an installment loan called a lease.* This makes it important that a lease contract be written in a form acceptable to the Internal Revenue Service. The following are the major requirements for bona fide lease transactions from the standpoint of the IRS:

1. The term must be less than thirty years; otherwise the lease is regarded as a form of sale.
2. The rent must represent a reasonable return to the lessor, "reasonable" being in the range of 7 to 12 percent on the investment.
3. The renewal option must be bona fide, and this requirement can best be met by giving the lessee the first option to meet an equal bona fide outside offer.
4. There shall be no repurchase option; if there is, the lessee should merely be given parity with an equal outside offer.

Accounting for Leases

In November 1976, the Financial Accounting Standards Board issued Statement of Financial Accounting Standards No. 13, *Accounting for Leases.* Like other FASB statements, the standards set forth must be followed by business firms if their financial statements are to receive certification by auditors. FASB No. 13 has implications both for the utilization of leases and for their accounting-financial treatment. Those elements of FASB No. 13 most relevant for financial analysis of leases will therefore be summarized.

For some types of leases, FASB No. 13 requires that the obligation be capitalized on the asset side with a related lease obligation on the liability side of the balance sheet. Since the treatment depends on the types of leases, the criteria for classification are first set forth. A lease is classified as a capital lease if it meets any one or more of four paragraph 7 criteria:

a. The lease transfers ownership of the property to the lessee by the end of the lease term.
b. The lease gives the lessee the option to purchase the property at a price sufficiently below the expected fair value of the property that the exercise of the option is highly probable.
c. The lease term is equal to 75 percent or more of the estimated economic life of the property.
d. The present value of the minimum lease payments exceeds 90 percent of the fair value of the property at the inception of the lease.

The discount factor to be used in calculating the present value is the implicit rate used by the lessor or the lessee's incremental borrowing rate, whichever is lower. (Note that the use of the lower discount factor represents a higher present value factor and therefore a higher calculated present value for a given pattern of lease payments. It therefore increases the likelihood that the 90 percent test will be met and that the lease will be classified as a capital lease.)

From the standpoint of the lessee, if a lease is not a capital lease, it is classified as an operating lease. From the standpoint of the lessor, four types of leases are defined: (1) sales-type leases, (2) direct financing leases, (3) leveraged leases, and (4) operating leases representing all leases other than the first three types. A sales-type lease or a direct financing lease meets one or more of the four paragraph 7 criteria *and* both of two paragraph 8 criteria, which are: (1) Collectibility of the minimum lease payments is reasonably predictable. (2) No important uncertainties surround the amount of unreimbursable costs yet to be incurred by the lessor under the lease. Sales-type leases give rise to profit (or loss) to the lessor — the fair value of the leased property at the inception of the lease is greater (or less) than its cost of carrying amount. Sales-type leases normally arise when manufacturers or dealers use leasing in marketing their products. Direct financing leases are leases other than leveraged leases for which the cost of carrying amount is equal to the fair value of the leased property at the inception of the lease. Leveraged leases are direct financing leases in which substantial financing is provided by a long-term creditor on a nonrecourse basis with respect to the general credit of the lessor.

Accounting by Lessees

For operating leases, rentals shall be charged to expense over the lease term with disclosures of future rental obligations in total as well as by each of the following five years. For lessees, capital leases are to be capitalized and shown on the balance sheet both as a fixed asset and as a noncurrent obligation. Capitalization will represent the present value of the minimum lease payments less that portion of lease payments representing executory costs such as insurance, maintenance, and taxes to be paid by the lessor (including any profit return he includes in such charges). The discount factor would be as described in paragraph 7 (d), the lower of the implicit rate used by the lessor and the incremental borrowing rate of the lessee. The asset is to be amortized in a manner consistent with the lessee's normal depreciation policy for owned assets. During the lease term, each lease payment is to be allocated between a reduction of the obligation and the interest expense to produce a constant rate of interest on the remaining balance of the obligation.

Thus for capital leases, the balance sheet would include items as follows:

**Company X
Balance Sheet**

Assets	December 31,		Liabilities	December 31,	
	1977	1976		1977	1976
Leased property under capital leases, less accumulated amortization	XXX	XXX	Current: Obligations under capital leases	XXX	XXX
			Noncurrent: Obligations under capital leases	XXX	XXX

In addition to the balance sheet capitalization of capital leases, substantial additional footnote disclosures would be required for both capital and operating leases. These would include a description of leasing arrangements, an analysis of leased property under capital leases by major classes of property, a schedule by years of future minimum lease payments with executory and interest costs broken out for capital leases, and contingent rentals for operating leases.

FASB No. 13 sets forth requirements for capitalizing capital leases and for standardized disclosures for both capital leases and operating leases by lessees. Lease commitments will therefore not represent "off-balance sheet" financing for capital assets, and standard disclosure requirements will make general the footnote reporting of information on operating leases. Hence, the argument that leasing represents a form of financing that lenders may not take into account in their analysis of the financial position of firms seeking financing will be even less valid in the future. We do not regard it plausible that sophisticated lenders were fooled by off-balance sheet leasing obligations. However, the capitalization of capital leases and standard disclosure requirements for operating leases will make it easier for general users of financial reports to obtain additional information on the leasing obligations of firms. Hence, the requirements of FASB No. 13 are useful. We doubt whether the extent of use of leasing will be substantially altered since the particular circumstances that have provided a basis for the use of leasing in the past are not likely to be greatly affected by the increased disclosure requirements.

Cost Comparison between Lease and Purchase[4]

For an understanding of the possible advantages and disadvantages of lease financing, the cost of leasing must be compared with the cost of owning the equipment. To make the leasing versus owning cost comparison clear, we will first take the point of view of the lessor to understand the basic financial factors that are involved. Assume the following:

I = cost of an asset = \$20,000

Dep = the annual economic and tax depreciation charge

k = the cost of capital appropriate or the competitive risk-adjusted return of the project associated with the asset
= 10%

T = the lessor's corporate tax rate = 40%

N = the economic life and tax depreciation life of the asset = 5 years

NPV_{LOR} = the net present value of the lease-rental income from the assets to the lessor.

With the above facts we can calculate the equilibrium lease rental rate in a competitive market of lessors. What we have posed is a standard capital budgeting problem question. What cash flow return from the use of an asset will earn the applicable cost of capital? The investment or cost of the capital budgeting project is $-I$. The return is composed of two elements. One is the cash inflow from the lease rental; the other is the tax shelter from depreciation. The discount factor is the weighted cost of capital reflecting the appropriate debt leverage applicable to the kinds of equipment that are being leased. These factors represent the basic capital budgeting analysis discussed in Chapter 10. Consistent with the foregoing analysis, the equation to solve for the (uniform annual) lease rental rate, L_t, is equation (15–1).

$$NPV_{LOR} = -I + \sum_{t=1}^{N} \frac{L_t(1-T) + TDep_t}{(1+k)^t} \tag{15–1}$$

$$= -I + (PVIF_a)[L_t(1-T) + TDep_t]$$

Given the above facts and assuming straight-line depreciation, the solution to equation (15–1) is shown in equation (15–1a). The competi-

---

4. These materials on the financial analysis of leasing reflect collaborative research by Fred Weston and Professor Larry Y. Dann, who provided valuable insights.

tive market assumption constrains the net present value of the lessor in equation (15–1a) to be zero. Hence the NPV of the lessor in equation (15–1) is set equal to zero. We then solve equation (15–1a) for the competitive equilibrium rental rate.

$$0 = -20{,}000 + \sum_{t=1}^{5} \frac{L_t(1 - .4) + .4(4{,}000)}{(1.1)^t} \qquad \textbf{(15–1a)}$$

$$3.791(.6L_t) = 20{,}000 - 3.791(1{,}600)$$

$$.6L_t = 13{,}934.4/3.791$$

$$L_t = \$6{,}126.$$

At an equilibrium rental (under the facts assumed) of $6,126 the lessor companies earn their cost of capital of 10 percent. Next we take the position of the user of the asset. The user faces the decision of whether to lease the asset or to own it. The new symbols and facts are:

NPV_0 = the net present value to the user if the firm owns the assets.

NPV_L = the net present value to the user if the firm leases the assets.

F_t' = the marginal product of the asset to a specific user firm or the cash flow benefits from the use of the capital assets (excluding depreciation effects) = $6,126.

k = the cost of capital to the user firm reflecting the risk in use when the marginal value product of the machine varies systematically with the return on total wealth = 10%.

Let us first consider the results if the user is the owner of the equipment. The user's position is exactly the same as the lessor. The leverage position of the user and therefore the user's weighted average cost of capital would be the same as for the leasing company. The formula would be exactly the same as equation (15–1) except that the cash flows represent the marginal value of product of the equipment used, so that these benefits are indicated as F_t rather than L_t. The expression for determining the net present value of owning is set forth in equation (15–2):

$$NPV_0 = \sum_{t=1}^{N} \frac{F_t'(1 - T)}{(1 + k)^t} - I + \sum_{t=1}^{N} \frac{TDep_t}{(1 + k)^t} \qquad \textbf{(15–2)}$$

$$= -I + (PVIF_a)\,[F_t(1 - T) + TDep_t].$$

The first term represents the net cash flows from the use of the asset. These would be the same whether the asset is leased or owned. If the asset is owned, it would be purchased at the cost of the asset, which is I. The third term in equation (15–2) represents the benefits that the owner of the asset will have by virtue of tax shelter of the depreciation outlays. We can then use equation (15–2) to calculate the net present value of owning the asset. The calculation is shown in equation (15–2a):

$$NPV_0 = -20,000 + 3.791[6,126(.6) + 4,000(.4)] \qquad (15\text{–}2a)$$

$$= -20,000 + 3.791 (5,275.6)$$

$$NPV_0 = 0.$$

We next consider the user's alternative of leasing the equipment. The net present value of leasing is determined by taking the net present value of the net benefits from the use of the assets and calculating their present value over the life of the lease. From this is deducted the annual lease rental payments made by the lessee.[5] In formal terms this is expressed in equation (15–3).

$$NPV_L = \sum_{t=1}^{N} \frac{F'_t(1-T)}{(1+k)^t} - \sum_{t=1}^{N} \frac{L_t(1-T)}{(1+k)^t} \qquad (15\text{–}3)$$

$$= (PVIF_a) [F_t(1-T) - L_t(1-T)].$$

Using the facts of the case as set forth above and assuming that F_t, the cash benefits from the use of the capital assets, is equal to $6,126, equation (15–3) can be solved as shown in equation (15–3a):

$$NPV_L = 3.791[6,126(1-T) - 6,126(1-T)] \qquad (15\text{–}3a)$$

$$= 0$$

This result is the same as for the position of the user as owner. It is also the same as the result for the lessor. These indifference results illustrate the principles set forth in recent articles by Miller and Upton and by Lewellen, Long, and McConnell.[6] The zero net present values reflect equilibrium in the equipment leasing market as well as in the equipment user's market.

However, it would not be unreasonable to have the particular uses to which users put the equipment represent some disequilibrium gains. For example, if the benefits from the use of the equipment by particular users with some special advantages were $6,500 per year, the net present value of owning would be shown by equation (15–2b):

5. The actual pattern of payment on leases is different from the equal annual payment schedule assumed in the above analysis. Typically, monthly payments are required at the start to initiate the leasing contract. In fact, the payment patterns vary greatly depending on the requirements of the lessee and the circumstances of the lessor. The solution framework set forth in the text is sufficiently flexible to be used for whatever pattern of payments may be agreed upon in the leasing contract.

6. *Journal of Finance*, June 1976.

$$NPV_0 = -20,000 + 3.791[6,500(.6) + 4,000(.4)] \qquad (15-2b)$$

$$= -20,000 + 3.791(5,500)$$

$$= -20,000 + 20,850.5$$

$$NPV_0 = \$850.5.$$

The net present value if the user leases the equipment is shown by equation (15–3b):

$$NPV_0 = 3.791[6,500(.6) - 6,126(.6)]$$

$$= 3.791(3,900 - 3,675.6)$$

$$= 3.791(224.4) \qquad (15-3b)$$

$$= \$850.7.$$

Again, the indifference result between owning and leasing by the user is found. In the absence of some specified market imperfections, this indifference result between owning and leasing will result. A sound method of analyzing leasing versus owning must obtain this indifference result, unless some specific market imperfections can be identified to account for differences. For example, it will require some differences in the applicable tax rates for the lessor versus user firm, or differences in the amount of tax subsidies available, or differences in transactions costs to cause differences in the costs of leasing versus owning for the user firm.

Next, let us consider the use of accelerated depreciation. In Appendix B to chapter 10, Table B10–1 provides in convenient form the present value of depreciation for the sum-of-year's digits and for the double declining balance methods of depreciation over a range of values of the cost of capital. In the present example, we will illustrate the use of the sum-of-year's digits method of depreciation with the cost of capital of 10 percent for five years. We can read the depreciation factor of .806 directly from Table B10–1. To utilize the depreciation factor we separate the cash inflow factors in the last term of equation (15–1) into two parts as shown in equation (15–1b).

$$NPV_{LOR} = -I + \sum_{t=1}^{N} \frac{L_t(1-T)}{(1+k)^t} + \sum_{t=1}^{N} \frac{T\,Dep_t}{(1+k)^t} \qquad (15-1b)$$

We can then proceed to make the calculations. In equation (15–1c), we utilize the data from the illustrative example we have been using throughout this discussion. However, instead of straight-line depreciation, we utilize the present value factor for the sum-of-years'-digits method of depreciation. This is .806 for the 10 percent cost of capital for the five-year life of the asset. We then solve for the uniform annual lease-rental rate that would be required by the lessor in order to earn his cost of capital of 10 percent.

$$NPV_{LOR} = -20,000 + \sum_{t=1}^{N} \frac{L_t(.6)}{(1.1)^t} + \sum_{t=1}^{N} \frac{TDep_t}{(1+k)^t} \qquad (15\text{--}1c)$$

$$= -20,000 + 3.791(.6L) + .4(20,000)(.806)$$

$$3.791(.6L) = 20,000 - 6,448$$

$$.6L = 13,552/3.791$$

$$.6L = 3,575$$

$$L = \$5,958.$$

The resulting uniform annual lease-rental charge that would be required by the lessor in order to earn his cost of capital of 10 percent would be $5,958. Note that this is lower than the required lease rental for the lessor to earn his cost of capital when straight-line depreciation was used. The reason for this is that with accelerated depreciation the tax shelter provided comes in larger amounts in the earlier years when the present value factors are higher. Thus, since the amount of tax shelter is increased and since under competitive conditions the lease rental moves to the level at which lessors earn their cost of capital, the lease-rental would be reduced.

If the benefits of accelerated depreciation were not available to the user firm, the net present value from owning would remain at $850.[7] But we shall show below that the net present value from leasing would be $1,233 if the leasing firms can utilize accelerated depreciation and competition results in passing these tax advantages on in the form of lower lease rental charges. This illustrates the kind of market frictions that can result in an advantage to leasing as compared with owning an asset. But it is specific frictions of this kind that must be brought in to a previous equilibrium result to establish why leasing or owning may be advantageous to the user firm.

In the present illustration, if the user firm can also utilize the benefits of accelerated depreciation, the indifference result will again obtain. We can therefore examine the effects of accelerated depreciation on the user firm that leases or buys the asset. When the user firm leases the asset, equation (15–3) is unchanged—we simply insert the lower rental rate for the L_t in equation (15–3). We then obtain equation (15–3c).

---

7. This could occur if the user firm has tax loss carryovers that render the accelerated depreciation benefits of no benefit to the user firm.

$$NPV_L = 3.791 \ (6,500).6 - 5,958 \ (.6) \ (3.791) \qquad \qquad \textbf{(15-3c)}$$

$$= 14,785 - 13,552$$

$$= \$1,233.$$

The net present value to the lessee now is $1,233, which is higher than the net present value when straight-line depreciation was being used. We next consider the position of the user firm that owns the asset. In this case we again use the same equation (15–2). However, we now utilize the sum-of-the-years'-digits depreciation factor as shown in the last term in equation (15–2c).

$$NPV_o = 3.791 \ (6,500).6 - 20,000 + .4 \ (20,000) \ (.806) \qquad \qquad \textbf{(15-2c)}$$

$$= 14,785 - 20,000 + 6,448$$

$$= \$1,233.$$

We see that the net present value of owning is $1,233, which was exactly the net present value of leasing. Thus the effect of accelerated depreciation is to provide larger tax shelters. Given competitive conditions among lessors, this results in a lower rental rate and a higher net present value of using the asset whether the use of the asset is achieved through leasing (renting) or through buying and owning the asset. But again, assuming competitive financial markets, the terms on which leasing versus owning will be available to the user firm will result in no advantage to one form of acquiring the use of the assets as compared with another. It is only when there are some forms of frictions in the markets that result in more favorable terms to lessees versus user-owners that some advantage to leasing versus owning results.

Additional Factors That May Affect the Leasing versus Owning Decision

A number of other factors could influence the costs of leasing versus owning capital assets by the user firm. These include:

1. Different costs of capital for the lessor versus the user firm.
2. Financing costs higher in leasing.
3. Differences in maintenance costs.
4. The benefits of residual values to the owner of the assets.
5. The possibility of reducing obsolescence costs by the leasing firms.
6. The possibility of increased credit availability under leasing.
7. More favorable tax treatment such as more rapid write-off.
8. Possible differences in the ability to utilize tax reduction opportunities.

In connection with each of these factors various arguments are encountered with respect to the advantages and disadvantages of leasing. Many of the arguments carry with them a number of implicit assumptions, so that their applicability to real world conditions is subject to considerable qualifications. Each of the factors will be considered in turn.

Different Costs of Capital for the Lessor versus the User Firm. It can be argued that if the leasing company has a lower cost of capital than the user firm, the lower cost of capital will, in competitive markets, result in a lease-rental whose costs will be lower than the costs of owning by the user firm. This follows in a quite straightforward way from the type of financial analysis made in equations (15–1) through (15–3). But under what circumstances will the cost of capital be different for the leasing firm as compared with the user firm? We have to consider the basic risks involved in using capital assets. Miller and Upton have demonstrated that two broad types of risks are present.[8] One risk is that an asset's economic depreciation will vary in some systematic way with the level of the economy from the rate of depreciation expected when the lease rental rate is determined, that is, the risk that the agreed lease payments, which are based on expected depreciation, will be insufficient to cover the subsequent realized depreciation. This risk is borne by the owner, whether a leasing firm or a user-buyer.

Another risk is the risk associated with F_t, the (uncertain) future net cash flows to be derived from employing the capital services of the asset. This risk is borne by the leasing company if the lease contract is cancellable at any time with no penalty, by the user firm if the lease contract is noncancellable over the life of the asset, and shared by them under any contractual arrangement between these two extremes. But competitive capital markets will insure that the implicit discount rate in the leasing arrangement, as negotiated, will reflect the allocation of the risks under the particular sharing arrangement specified. Under the standard price equals marginal cost condition of competitive markets, it is the cost of capital of the project that is the relevant discount rate. Hence it is difficult to visualize why the risk in use of a capital asset will be different whether the asset is owned by a leasing company or by the user firm.

Another possibility is that the user firm may have a lower cost of cap-

---

8. M. H. Miller and C. W. Upton, "Leasing, Buying, and the Cost of Capital Services," *Journal of Finance* 31 (June 1976), pp. 761–86.

ital than the leasing company. Miller and Upton evaluate this possibility as follows: "It is true that such a company, looking only at the conventional formulas, might find it profitable to buy rather than rent. But it would find it even more profitable, under those circumstances, to enter the leasing business."[9] This would eliminate any divergence.

Under competitive market conditions, it is not likely that the disequilibrium conditions implied by the different costs of capital will long persist. The supply of financial intermediaries of the leasing kind will either increase or decrease to restore equilibrium in the benefits from leasing versus owning an asset by a user firm.

Financing Costs Higher in Leasing. A similar view is that leasing always involves higher implicit financing costs. This argument is also of doubtful validity. First, when the nature of the lessee as a credit risk is considered, there may be no difference. Second, it is difficult to separate the money costs of leasing from the other services that may be embodied in a leasing contract. If, because of its specialized operations, the leasing company can perform nonfinancial services such as maintenance of the equipment at a lower cost than the lessee or some other institution can perform them, then the effective cost of leasing may be lower than for funds obtained from borrowing or other sources. The efficiencies of performing specialized services may thus enable the leasing company to operate by charging a lower total cost than the lessee would have to pay for the package of money plus services on any other basis.

Differences in Maintenance Costs. Another argument frequently encountered is that leasing may be less expensive because no explicit maintenance costs are involved. But this is because the maintenance costs are included in the lease-rental rate. The key question is whether the maintenance can be performed at a lower cost when performed by the lessor as compared with having a separate maintenance contract with an independent firm which specializes in performing maintenance on capital assets of the type involved. Whether maintenance costs would be different if supplied by one type of specialist firm as compared with another type of specialist firm is a factual matter depending upon the industries and particular firms involved.

Residual Values. One important point that must be mentioned in connection with leasing is that the lessor owns the property at the expiration of the lease. The value of the property at the end of the lease is

9. Miller and Upton, "Cost of Capital Services," p. 767.

called the *residual value.* Superficially, it would appear that where residual values are large, owning will be less expensive than leasing. However, even this apparently obvious advantage of owning is subject to substantial qualification. On leased equipment, the obsolescence factor may be so large that it is doubtful whether residual values will be of a great order of magnitude. If residual values appear favorable, competition between leasing companies and other financial sources, as well as competition among leasing companies themselves, will force leasing rates down to the point where the potentials of residual values are fully recognized in the leasing contract rates. Thus, the existence of residual values of equipment is not likely to result in materially lower costs of owning. However, in connection with decisions whether to lease or to own land, the obsolescence factor is not involved except to the extent of deterioration in areas with changing population or use patterns. In a period of optimistic expectations about land values, there may be a tendency to overestimate rates of increase in land values. As a consequence, the current purchase of land may involve a price so high that the probable rate of return on owned land may be relatively small. Under this condition, leasing may well represent a more economical way of obtaining the use of land than does owning. Conversely, if the probable increase in land values is not fully reflected in current prices, it will be advantageous to own the land.

Thus it is difficult to generalize about whether residual value considerations are likely to make the effective cost of leasing higher or lower than the cost of owning. The results depend on whether the individual firm has opportunities to take advantage of overoptimistic or overpessimistic evaluations of future value changes by the market as a whole and whether the firm or market is correct on average.

Obsolescence Costs. Another popular notion is that leasing costs will be lower because of the rapid obsolescence of some kinds of equipment. If the obsolescence rate on equipment is high, leasing costs must reflect such a rate. Thus, in general terms, it might be argued that neither residual values nor obsolescence rates can basically affect the cost of owning versus leasing.

In connection with leasing, however, it is possible that certain leasing companies may be well equipped to handle the obsolescence problem. For example, the Clark Equipment Company is a manufacturer, reconditioner, and specialist in materials handling equipment, with its own sales organization and system of distributors. This may enable Clark to write favorable leases for equipment. If the equipment becomes obsolete to one user, it may still be satisfactory for other users with different materials handling requirements, and Clark is well situated to locate these other users. The position is similar in computer leasing.

This illustration indicates how a leasing company, by combining lending with other specialized services, may reduce the social costs of obsolescence and increase effective residual values. By such operations the total cost of obtaining the use of such equipment is reduced. Possibly other institutions that do not combine financing and other specialist functions, such as manufacturing, reconditioning, servicing, and sales, may, in conjunction with financing institutions, perform the overall functions as efficiently and at as low cost as do integrated leasing companies. However, this is a factual matter depending upon the relative efficiency of the competing firms in different lines of business and different kinds of equipment.

Increased Credit Availability. Two possible situations may exist to give leasing an advantage to firms seeking the maximum degree of financial leverage. First, it is frequently stated that firms can obtain more money for longer terms under a lease arrangement than under a secured loan agreement for the purchase of a specific piece of equipment. Second, leasing may not have as much of an impact on future borrowing capacity as does borrowing to buy the equipment. This point is illustrated by the balance sheets of two hypothetical firms, A and B, in Table 15–2.

Table 15–2
Balance Sheet Effects of Leasing

Before Asset Increase				After Asset Increase							
Firms A and B				Firm A				Firm B			
		Debt	$ 50			Debt	$150			Debt	$ 50
Total	____	Equity	50	Total	____	Equity	50	Total	____	Equity	50
assets	$100		$100	assets	$200		$200	assets	$100		$100

Initially, the balance sheets of both firms are identical, and they both have debt ratios of 50 percent. Next, they each decide to acquire assets costing $100. Firm A borrows $100 to make the purchase, so an asset and a liability go on its balance sheet, and its debt ratio is increased to 75 percent. Firm B leases the equipment. The lease may call for fixed charges as high as or even higher than the loan, and the obligations assumed under the lease can be equally or more dangerous to other creditors, but the fact that its reported debt ratio is lower may enable firm B to obtain additional credit from other lenders. The amount of the annual rentals is shown as a note to B's financial statements, so credit analysts are aware of it, but evidence suggests that many of them still give less weight to firm B's lease than to firm A's loan.

This illustration indicates quite clearly a weakness of the debt ratio — if two companies are being compared and if one leases a substantial amount of equipment, then the debt ratio as we calculate it does not accurately show their relative leverage positions.[10]

Rapid Write-off. If the lease is written for a period that is much shorter than the depreciable life of the asset, with renewals at low rentals after the lessor has recovered his costs during the basic lease period, then deductible depreciation is small in relation to the deductible lease payment in the early years. In a sense, this amounts to a very rapid write-off, which is advantageous to the lessee. However, the Internal Revenue Service correctly disallows as deductions lease payments under leases (1) that call for a rapid amortization of the lessor's costs and (2) that have a relatively low renewal or purchase option.

Differences in Tax Rates or Tax Subsidies. There will frequently be an advantage to leasing versus buying when the tax rates of the lessor firm are lower as compared with the user firm. If the tax rates of the lessor firms are lower than the tax rates of the user firms, then competition among leasing firms would result in reduced lease-rental rates to the user firms. Then there would be an advantage to leasing as compared with owning if the user firm has higher applicable tax rates than the leasing firms. Similarly, if the user firm is unable to use tax subsidies (e.g., investment tax credits), it may be advantageous for a leasing firm to be organized that can utilize the tax shelters from tax subsidies. (Consider, for example, the airline industry when substantial amounts of new equipment are being required.)

For example, the investment tax credit, discussed in Appendix A to this book, can be taken only if the firm's profits and taxes exceed a certain level. If a firm is unprofitable, or if it is expanding so rapidly and generating such large tax credits that it cannot use them all, then it may be profitable for it to enter a lease arrangement. Here the lessor (a bank or leasing company) will take the credit and give the lessee a corresponding reduction in lease charges. Railroads and airlines have been large users of leasing for this reason in recent years, as have industrial companies faced with particular situations. Anaconda, for example, fi-

---

10. Three comments are appropriate here. First, financial analysts sometimes attempt to reconstruct the balance sheets of firms such as B by "capitalizing the lease payments," that is, estimating the value of both the lease obligation and the leased assets and transforming B's balance sheet into one comparable to A's. Second, as we indicated in Chapter 2, lease charges are included in the fixed charge coverage ratio, and this ratio will be approximately equal for firms A and B, thus revealing the true state of affairs. Thus it is unlikely that lenders will be fooled into granting greater credit with a lease than with a conventional loan having terms similar to those of the lease. Third, FASB No. 13 provides for including capital leases in the firm's balance sheet.

nanced most of the cost of a $138 million aluminum plant built in 1973 through a lease arrangement.[11] Anaconda had suffered a $356 million tax loss when Chile expropriated its copper mining properties, and the carry-forward of this loss would hold taxes down for years. Thus, Anaconda could not use the tax credit associated with the new plant. By entering a lease arrangement, Anaconda was able to pass the tax credit on to the lessees, who in turn gave Anaconda lower lease payments than would have existed under a loan arrangement. Anaconda's financial staff estimated that financial charges over the life of the plant would be $74 million less under the lease arrangement than under a borrow-and-buy plan.

Incidentally, the Anaconda lease was set up as a "leveraged lease."[12] A group of banks and Chrysler Corporation provided about $38 million of equity and were the owner-lessors. These owner-lessors borrowed the balance of the required funds from Prudential, Metropolitan, and Aetna — large life insurance companies. The banks and Chrysler received not only the investment tax credit but also the tax shelter associated with accelerated depreciation on the plant. Such leveraged leases, often with wealthy individuals seeking tax shelters acting as owner-lessors, are an important part of the financial scene today and help explain why leasing has reached a total volume of over $60 billion.

Summary

Intermediate-term financing is defined as any liability originally scheduled for repayment in more than one year but in less than ten years. Anything shorter is a current liability, while obligations due in ten or more years are thought of as long-term debt. The major forms of intermediate-term financing include (1) *term loans* and (2) *lease financing*.

Term Loans. A term loan is a business credit with a maturity of more than one year but of less than 15 years. There are exceptions to the rule, but ordinarily term loans are retired by systematic repayments (amortization payments) over the life of the loan. Security, generally in the form of a chattel mortgage on equipment, is often employed; the larger, stronger companies are able to borrow on an unsecured basis. Commercial banks and life insurance companies are the principal suppliers of term loan credit. Commercial banks typically make smaller, shorter-term loans; life insurance companies grant larger, longer-term credits.

11. Vanderwicken, "Powerful Logic of the Leasing Boom," pp. 132–94.
12. Technically, a "leveraged lease" is one in which the financial intermediary, a bank or other lessor, uses borrowed funds to acquire the assets it leases, as illustrated by the Anaconda example.

The interest cost of term loans, like rates on other credits, varies with the size of the loan and the strength of the borrower. For small loans to small companies, rates may go up as high as 15 percent; for large loans to large firms, the rate will be close to prime. Since term loans run for long periods, during which interest rates can change radically, many loans have variable interest rates, with the rate set at a certain level above the prime rate or above the Federal Reserve rediscount rate.

Another aspect of term loans is the series of *protective covenants* contained in most loan agreements. The lender's funds are tied up for a long period, and during this time the borrower's situation can change markedly. To protect himself, the lender will include in the loan agreement stipulations that the borrower will maintain his current ratio at a specified level, limit acquisitions of additional fixed assets, keep his debt ratio below a stated amount, and so on. These provisions are necessary from the lender's point of view, but they necessarily restrict the borrower's actions.

Lease Financing. Leasing has long been used in connection with the acquisition of equipment by railroad companies. In recent years, it has been extended to a wide variety of equipment.

Three different forms of lease financing were considered: (1) sale and leaseback, in which a firm owning land, buildings, or equipment sells the property and simultaneously executes an agreement to lease the property for a specified period under specific terms; (2) service leases or operating leases, which include both financing and maintenance services, are often cancellable, and call for payments under the lease contract which may not fully recover the cost of the equipment; and (3) financial leases, which do not provide for maintenance services, are not cancellable, and do fully amortize the cost of the leased asset during the basic lease contract period.

To understand the possible advantages and disadvantages of lease financing, the cost of leasing an asset must be compared with the cost of owning the same asset. In the absence of major tax advantages, whether or not leasing is advantageous turns primarily on the firm's ability to acquire funds by other methods. A financial lease contract is very similar to a straight-debt arrangement and uses some of the firm's debt-carrying ability.

Questions   15–1. "The type of equipment best suited for leasing has a long life in relation to the length of the lease, is a removable, standard product that could be used by many different firms, and is easily identifiable. In short, it is the kind of equipment that could be repossessed and sold readily. However, we would be quite happy to write a ten-year lease on paper towels for a firm such as General Motors." Discuss the statement.

15–2. Leasing is often called a hedge against obsolescence. Under what conditions is this actually true?

15–3. Is leasing in any sense a hedge against inflation for the lessee? For the lessor?

15–4. One alleged advantage of leasing is that it keeps liabilities off the balance sheet, thus making it possible for a firm to obtain more leverage than it otherwise could. This raises the question of whether or not both the lease obligation and the asset involved should be capitalized and shown on the balance sheet. Discuss the pros and cons of capitalizing leases and the related assets.

15–5. A firm is seeking a term loan from a bank. Under what conditions would it want a fixed interest rate, and under what condition would it want the rate to fluctuate with the prime rate?

15–6. Under what conditions would a "balloon note," or loan that is not fully amortized, be advantageous to a borrower?

Problems

15–1. a. The Clarkton Company produces industrial machines. The machines have five year lives. Clarkton sells the machines for $30,000. Alternatively, Clarkton offers a lease arrangement at a rental that, because of competitive factors, yields a return to Clarkton of 12 percent, its cost of capital. What will their competitive lease rental rate be? (Assume straight-line depreciation, zero salvage value, and $T = 40\%$.)

b. The Stockton Machine Shop, Inc., is contemplating the purchase of a machine exactly like those rented by Clarkton. The machines produce net benefits of $10,000 per year. They can also buy the machine for $30,000, or the machines can be rented from Clarkton at the competitive lease rental rate. Stockton's cost of capital is 12 percent, and $T = 40\%$. Which alternative is preferred?

c. If Clarkton's cost of capital is 9 percent and competition exists among lessors, solve for the new equilibrium rental rate. Would Stockton's decision be altered?

15–2. The Scott Brothers Department Store is considering a sale and leaseback of its major property, consisting of land and a building, because it is 30 days late on 80 percent of its accounts payable. The recent balance sheet of Scott Brothers is shown below. Profit before taxes in 1975 is $36,000; after taxes, $20,000.

Annual depreciation charges are $57,600 on the building and $72,000 on the fixtures and equipment. The land and building could be sold for a total of $2.8 million. The annual net rental will be $240,000.

a. How much capital gains tax will Scott Brothers pay if the land and building are sold? (Assume all capital gains are taxed at the capital

Scott Brothers **Department Store** Balance sheet December 31, 1975 (thousands of dollars)	Cash		$ 288	Accounts payable	$1,440
	Receivables		1,440	Bank loans, 8%	1,440
	Inventories		1,872	Other current liabilities	720
	Total current assets		$3,600	Total current debt	$3,600
	Land	$1,152		Common stock	1,440
	Building	720		Retained earnings	720
	Fixtures and equipment	288			
	Net fixed assets		2,160		
	Total assets		$5,760	Total claims	$5,760

gains tax rate; that is, disregard such items as recapture of depreciation, tax preference treatment, and so on.)

b. Compare the current ratio before and after the sale and leaseback if the after-tax net proceeds are used to "clean up" the bank loans and to reduce accounts payable and other current liabilities.

c. If the lease had been in effect during 1975, what would Scott Brothers' profit for 1975 have been?

d. What are the basic financial problems facing Scott Brothers? Will the sale and leaseback operation solve them?

Selected References

Axelson, Kenneth S. "Needed: A Generally Accepted Method for Measuring Lease Commitments." *Financial Executive* 39 (July 1971): 40–52.

Beechy, Thomas H. "Quasi-Debt Analysis of Financial Leases." *Accounting Review* 44 (Apr. 1969): 375–81.

Bower, Richard S. "Issues in Lease Financing." *Financial Management* 2 (Winter 1973), 25–34.

Bower, Richard S.; Herringer, Frank C.; and Williamson, J. Peter. "Lease Evaluation." *Accounting Review* 41, no. 2 (Apr. 1966): 257–65.

Brigham, Eugene F. "The Impact of Bank Entry on Market Conditions in the Equipment Leasing Industry." *National Banking Review* 2 (Sept. 1964): 11–26.

Doenges, R. Conrad. "The Cost of Leasing." *Engineering Economist* 17 (Fall 1971): 31–44.

Fawthrop, R. A., and Terry, Brian. "Debt Management and the Use of Leasing Finance in UK Corporate Financing Strategies." *Journal of Business Finance & Accounting* 2 (Autumn 1975): 295–314.

————. "The Evaluation of an Integrated Investment and Lease-financing." *Journal of Business Finance & Accounting* 3 (Autumn 1976): 79–112.

Ferrara, William L. "Should Investment and Financing Decisions Be Separated?" *Accounting Review* 41 (Jan. 1966): 106–14.

Ferrara, William L., and Wojdak, Joseph F. "Valuation of Long-Term Leases." *Financial Analysts' Journal* 25 (Nov.–Dec. 1969): 29–32.

Findlay, M. Chapman, III, "Financial Lease Evaluation: Survey and Synthesis."

Paper presented at the Eastern Finance Association Meetings, Storrs, Conn., Apr. 12, 1973.

———. "A Sensitivity Analysis of IRR Leasing Models." *Engineering Economist* 20 (Summer 1975): 231–41.

Gant, Donald R. "Illusion in Lease Financing." *Harvard Business Review* 37 (Mar.–Apr. 1959): 121–42.

———. "A Critical Look at Lease Financing." *Controller* 29 (June 1961).

Gordon, Myron J. "A General Solution to the Buy or Lease Decision: A Pedagogical Note." *Journal of Finance* 29 (Mar. 1974): 245–50.

Hamel, H. G. "Leasing in Industry." *Studies in Business Policy* no. 127 (New York: National Industrial Conference Board, 1968).

Hawkins, David F. "Objectives, not Rules for Lease Accounting." *Financial Executive* 38 (Nov. 1970): 30–38.

Hayes, Douglas A. *Bank Lending Policies: Issues and Practices.* Ann Arbor, Mich.: Bureau of Business Research, University of Michigan, 1964. Chap. 6.

Honig, Lawrence E., and Coley, Stephen C. "An After-Tax Equivalent Payment Approach to Conventional Lease Analysis." *Financial Management* 4 (Winter 1975): 18–27.

Johnson, Robert W., and Lewellen, Wilbur G. "Analysis of the Lease-or-Buy Decision." *Journal of Finance* 27 (Sept. 1972): 815–23.

Keller, Thomas F., and Peterson, Russell J. "Optimal Financial Structure, Cost of Capital, and the Lease-or-Buy Decision." *Journal of Business Finance & Accounting* 1 (Autumn 1974): 405–14.

Knutson, Peter H. "Leased Equipment and Divisional Return on Capital." *N.A.A. Bulletin* 44 (Nov. 1962): 15–20.

Law, Warren A., and Crum, M. Colyer. *Equipment Leasing and Commercial Banks.* Chicago, Ill.: Association of Reserve City Bankers, 1963.

Lewellen, Wilbur G.; Long, Michael S.; and McConnell, John J. "Asset Leasing in Competitive Capital Markets." *Journal of Finance* 31 (June 1976): 787–98.

Miller, Merton H., and Upton, Charles W. "Leasing, Buying, and the Cost of Capital Services." *Journal of Finance* 31 (June 1976): 761–86.

Mitchell, G. B. "After-Tax Cost of Leasing." *Accounting Review* 45 (Apr. 1970): 308–14.

Moyer, Charles R. "Lease Evaluation and the Investment Tax Credit: A Framework for Analysis." *Financial Management* 4 (Summer 1975): 39–44.

Myers, John H. *Reporting of Leases in Financial Statements.* New York: American Institute of Certified Public Accountants, 1962.

Myers, Stewart C.; Dill, David A.; and Bautista, Alberto J. "Valuation of Financial Lease Contracts." *Journal of Finance* 31 (June 1976): 799–819.

Nantell, Timothy J. "Equivalence of Lease versus Buy Analyses." *Financial Management* 2 (Autumn 1973): 61–65.

Nelson, A. Thomas. "Capitalized Leases—The Effect on Financial Ratios." *Journal of Accountancy* 116 (July 1963): 49–58.

Ofer, Aharon R. "The Evaluation of the Lease Versus Purchase Alternatives." *Financial Management* 5 (Summer 1976): 67–72.

Roenfeldt, Rodney L., and Osteryoung, Jerome S. "Analysis of Financial Leases." *Financial Management* 2 (Spring 1973): 74–87.

Sartoris, William L., and Paul, Ronda S. "Lease Evaluation—Another Capital Budgeting Decision." *Financial Management* 2 (Summer 1973): 46–52.

Schall, Lawrence D. "The Lease-or-Buy and Asset Acquisition Decisions." *Journal of Finance* 29, no. 4 (Sept. 1974): 1203–14.

Vancil, Richard F. "Lease or Borrow: New Method of Analysis." *Harvard Business Review* 39 (Sept.–Oct. 1961).

————. "Lease or Borrow: Steps in Negotiation." *Harvard Business Review* 39 (Nov.–Dec. 1961): 238–59.

Vancil, Richard F., and Anthony, Robert N. "The Financial Community Looks at Leasing." *Harvard Business Review* 37 (Nov.–Dec. 1959), 113–30.

Zinbarg, Edward D. "The Private Placement Loan Agreement." *Financial Analysts Journal* 31 (July-Aug. 1975): 33–35.

Appendix A to Chapter 15
Alternative Approches to
Leasing Decisions

Other points of view have been presented as applicable to formulating the appropriate framework for leasing decisions. Particularly, there has been considerable disagreement on the appropriate discount rate to be used in the analysis. In the presentation in the body of the chapter we have utilized the cost of capital applicable to the risk of the project.

Cost of Debt as the Discount Factor

An alternative view is to use the after-tax cost of debt as the discount factor. The reasons given for using the cost of debt as the discount factor emphasize that leasing is a substitute for borrowing. If one form of borrowing is being compared with another form of borrowing, it is argued that the cost of debt can be used in comparing the costs. If this were true, the only elements that would be compared would be the interest costs and interest tax shields. But since other elements such as the costs of ownership to both the lessor and user-owner and other types of tax shields such as depreciation enter into the analysis, the comparison involves more than one form of borrowing with another form of borrowing. Myers, Dill and Bautista describe the alternatives as follows:[1]

A firm that signs a lease contract really undertakes two simultaneous transactions:

Transaction 1A Purchase the asset for cash.

Transaction 1B: Purchase the necessary cash by giving up the asset's depreciation tax shields, salvage value and investment tax credit, and by agreeing to make a stream of cash payments to the lessor.

The alternative is a second set of two transactions:

Transaction 2A: Purchase the asset for cash.

Transaction 2B: Purchase the necessary cash by selling whatever package of financing instruments is optimal when leasing is excluded.

We are concerned with how the market value of the firm changes if the lease is used as a substitute for "normal" financing. . . . To repeat, we define the value of the lease contract as the advantage of leasing vs. normal financing. (p. 801).

---

1. Stewart C. Myers, David A. Dill, and Alberto J. Bautista, "Valuation of Financial Lease Contracts," *Journal of Finance* 31 (June 1976), pp. 799–820.

We agree that the comparison is between leasing and the normal mix of debt and equity financing since the lease provides for the acquisition of the asset as well as its financing. Although leasing is an alternative to debt financing, debt financing itself requires an equity base. Hence a weighted marginal cost of capital should be used to discount the differential cash flows involved in leasing versus owning an asset. Nevertheless, a widely respected body of opinion would argue for using the after-tax cost of debt as the discount factor. This approach will be illustrated so that the reader will see the nature of its application.

We shall return to our previous illustration contained in the body of Chapter 15 to continue it with the use of the cost of debt as the discount factor. We had determined that the lease rental rate under competitive conditions in the leasing market would be $6,126 per year. The cost of leasing can be determined by discounting the lease payments at the after-tax cost of debt. Let us assume that the cost of debt is 10 percent. Assuming a uniform stream of payments as before, the present value of the cost of leasing can be expressed compactly.[2] We have:

$$\text{Present value of the cost of leasing} = \sum_{t=1}^{N} \frac{L_t\,(1-T)}{[1+k_b\,(1-T)]^t} \qquad \textbf{(A15–1)}$$

Equation A15–1 consists of the lease payments less the tax shield on the lease payments. If the cost of debt, k_b, is 10 percent, its after-tax cost is 6 percent since the tax rate is 40 percent. We can now insert the numerical values as shown in equation A15–1a.

$$\text{Present value of the cost of leasing} = \sum_{t=1}^{5} \frac{6{,}126(.6)}{(1.06)^t} = 3{,}675.6(4.212) = \$15{,}482 \qquad \textbf{(A15–1a)}$$

The conventional analysis of the cost of owning formulates it in a "borrow-own" framework. It is assumed that the alternative to leasing is to borrow the full amount of the value of the asset, which is $20,000 in our example. Then a schedule of debt payments is made in order to determine the amount of the annual interest charges. The procedure is illustrated in Table A15–1.

It is assumed that the loan of $20,000 is paid off in a level annual amount to cover annual interest charges plus amortization of the princi-

---

2. We emphasize again that a wide variety of payment patterns may be encountered in leasing. One is to require the first payment or the first and last payments in advance. Or the pattern could start with high payments, scaling them down to lower ones. Or the payment schedule could start with low payments and increase them toward the end of the lease payment. Or a balloon payment might be required at some point. But since these are mechanical matters in the calculation, we shall assume the simplest pattern to focus on the central conceptual matters involved.

Table A15–1	End of Year	Balance of Principal Owed End of Year	Principal plus Interest Payments	Annual Interest 10% times (2)	Reduction of Principal
Schedule of Debt Payments	(1)	(2)	(3)	(4)	(5)
	1	$20,000	$ 5,276	$2,000	$ 3,276
	2	16,724	5,276	1,672	3,604
	3	13,120	5,276	1,312	3,964
	4	9,156	5,276	916	4,360
	5	4,796	5,276	480	4,796
	Totals		$26,380	$6,380	$20,000

pal. The amount is an annuity that can be determined by use of the present value of an annuity formula as shown in equation A15–2.

$$20,000 = \sum_{t=1}^{N} \frac{a_t}{(1 + k_b)^t} \tag{A15-2}$$

$$a_t = \frac{\$20,000}{(PVIF_a)}$$

$$a_t = \frac{\$20,000}{3.791} = \$5,276$$

Solving equation A15–2 for the level annual annuity we obtain $5,276. This represents the principal plus interest payments set forth in column (3) of Table A15–1. The sum of these five annual payments is shown to be $26,380. This represents repayment of the principal of $20,000 plus the sum of the annual interest payments. The interest payments for each year are determined by multiplying column (2), the balance of principal owed at the end of the year, by 10 percent, the assumed cost of borrowing. The sum of the annual interest payments does, in fact, equal the total interest of $6,380 obtained by deducting the principal of $20,000 from the total of the five annual payments shown in column (3).

A schedule of cash outflows for the borrow and own alternative is then developed to determine the present value of the after-tax cash flows. This is illustrated in Table A15–2.

The analysis of cash outflows begins with a listing of the loan payments as shown in column (2). Next the annual interest payments from Table A15–1 are listed in column (3). Since straight-line depreciation is assumed, the annual depreciation charges are $4,000 per year as shown in column (4). The tax shelter to the owner of the equipment is the sum of the annual interest plus depreciation multiplied by the tax rate. The amounts of the annual tax shield are shown in column (5). Column (6) is

Table A15–2
Schedule of Cash Outflows:
Borrow and Own

End of Year	Loan Payment	Annual Interest	Depreciation	Tax Shield [(3) + (4)].4	Cash Flows After Taxes (2)−(5)	Present Value Factor @ 6%	Present Value of Cash Flows
(1)	(2)	(3)	(4)	(5)	(6)	(7)	(8)
1	$ 5,276	$2,000	$ 4,000	$ 2,400	$ 2,876	.943	$ 2,712
2	5,276	1,672	4,000	2,269	3,007	.890	2,676
3	5,276	1,312	4,000	2,125	3,151	.840	2,647
4	5,276	916	4,000	1,966	3,310	.792	2,622
5	5,276	480	4,000	1,792	3,484	.747	2,603
Totals	$26,380	$6,380	$20,000	$10,552	$15,828		$13,260

cash flow after taxes obtained by deducting column (5) from column (2).

Since the cost of borrowing is 10 percent, its after-tax cost with a 40 percent tax rate is 6 percent. The present value factors at 6 percent are listed in column (7). They are multiplied by the after-tax cash flows to obtain column (8), the present value of after-tax cash flows.

The total of column (8) represents the present value of the after-tax cost of the borrow and own alternative. This amount is then compared with the $15,482 obtained as the present value of the cost of leasing in equation A15–1a. The borrow and own alternative is shown to involve a cost that is lower than the cost of leasing by $2,222.

The usual explanation for this difference is that under the borrow and own alternative the annual interest expenses are higher in the early years when the present value factors are higher. This provides a larger tax shield in the earlier years and is said to result in a lower cost under the borrow and own alternative.

However, this method of analysis is suspect because we have utilized the data from our example in the body of Chapter 15 in which the indifference result was found to obtain. There was no advantage to leasing versus owning consistent with competitive market equilibrium conditions. Since the use of the after-tax cost of debt as the discount factor produces something other than an indifference result, its underlying theoretical validity is suspect. In addition, as a practical matter the terms of the lease payments would not necessarily be an equal annual amount. The annual lease payments could readily be increased in the earlier years and decreased in the later years to result in the same present value of after-tax cost of leasing as for the borrow and own alternative.

Our framework is sufficiently broad and flexible to accommodate alternative choices of the discount rate to be employed in the valuation relationships. If one prefers to substitute the cost of debt for the weighted marginal cost of capital, this can be done. However, the symmetry between the position of the lessor and lessee which is generally agreed to be necessary for a correct analysis will not be possible to achieve if the cost of debt is used as the discount factor. Clearly, a 100 percent debt ratio for the lessor firm would not be realistic, so a weighted cost to reflect some use of equity would be required. By symmetry, the use of the cost of debt alone is inappropriate for analyzing the position of the lessee.

Use of an Internal-Rate-Return Analysis

A related second approach to analyzing the cost of leasing versus alternative sources of financing utilizes the internal rate of return. In this approach the cost of leasing is the internal rate of return or discount rate that equates the present value of leasing payments, net of their tax shields plus the tax shields for depreciation and the investment tax credit that would be obtained if the asset were purchased, with the cost of the asset. In this method the cost of leasing includes not only the after-tax lease payments but the investment tax credit foregone and the depreciation tax deductions that otherwise would have been obtained if the asset had been purchased.

The cost of the asset that is avoided by leasing is treated as a cash inflow, while the costs of leasing just described are treated as cash outflows. A column of cash flows after taxes is calculated. It begins with a positive figure, which is the cost of the asset avoided, and then moves to negative figures representing the costs of leasing. A rate of discount is then determined that equates the negative cash flows with the positive cash flows in the column. (This would be 10 percent in our example.)

This discount rate is taken as a measure of the after-tax cost of lease financing. In the procedure, this after-tax cost of lease financing is then compared with the after-tax cost of debt financing. The after-tax cost of debt financing is 6 percent in our example, so the 10 percent after-tax cost of leasing would be considered more costly.

One of the advantages claimed for this approach is that it avoids the problem of having to determine a rate of discount. However, this claim is illusory. The internal rate of return approach to the leasing comparison is fundamentally no different from the use of the after-tax cost of debt method described in the previous section. The reason this is so is that when the discount rate, which is treated as the after-tax cost of lease financing, is compared with the after-tax cost of debt financing, this implies that the relevant measure for comparison is the after-tax cost of debt financing rather than the firm's cost of capital. Since leasing involves the acquisition of an asset as well as its financing and generally provides "complete financing," which substitutes for a "normal mix of financing," many authors agree that the appropriate discount factor to apply to lease payments is the firm's cost of capital. Hence the calculation of the discount factor called the after-tax cost of lease financing based on leasing payments could well be argued to be appropriately compared with the firm's cost of capital rather than with the firm's cost of debt. Hence, the internal rate of return analysis does not avoid the problem of selecting the appropriate rate of discount.

Use of Multiple Discount Rates

Still a third view is to vary the discount rate with the risk of the component cash flows. The counterargument here is that the flows are part of one transaction whose risks are determined by the underlying risks of the cash flows which should not be broken into segments. Since this third view is also widely held, it is useful to summarize this approach.

The most complete statement of this alternative approach was provided by Professor Schall.[3] Schall emphasizes that the cost of capital applicable is the risk of the project rather than the cost of capital of the firm as a whole. Schall also argues that in analyzing the leasing versus buy-own decision it is inappropriate to always require a one-to-one debt displacement between leasing and borrowing. He holds that the alternative to leasing should not be constrained to debt but may include a number of alternative combinations of financing.

Schall summarizes the comparison between leasing and purchasing in his formulations reproduced here as equations A15−3 and A15−4.

$$NPV_L = \sum_{t=1}^{N} \frac{(1-T)\bar{F}_t}{(1+k_X)^t} - \sum_{t=1}^{N} \frac{(1-T)\bar{L}_t}{(1+k_L)^t} \tag{A15−3}$$

$$NPV_0 = \sum_{t=1}^{N} \frac{\overline{G}_t}{(1+k_G)^t} + \sum_{t=1}^{N} \frac{Tk_b\overline{B}_t}{(1+k_R)^t} - I. \tag{A15−4}$$

$$= \sum_{t=1}^{N} \frac{(1-T)(\bar{F}_t - z_{mt}) + T\overline{Dep}_t}{(1+k_G)^t} + \sum_{t=1}^{N} \frac{Tk_bB_t}{(1+k_R)^t} - I + \frac{\overline{Z}_N}{(1+k_s)^{N'}},$$

where:

F_t = Cash revenues less cash expenses associated with the asset at time t if it is leased

L_t = Lease payment at time t

---

3. Lawrence B. Schall, "The Lease-or-Buy and Asset Acquisition Decisions," *Journal of Finance* 29 (September 1974), pp. 1203–14.

$k =$ Discount rate used by investors in valuing a stream

$k_b B_t =$ Interest paid on any new debt at time t issued to finance a purchase

$T =$ Tax rate on ordinary firm income

$z_{mt} =$ Cash costs at time t that are incurred under ownership of the asset but not if it is leased; for example, state and local taxes, certain upkeep expenses, etc.

$I =$ Cash purchase cost of the asset

$Z_N =$ After tax salvage value of the asset at the end of the lease period

$Dep_t =$ Depreciation deduction for period t allowed for tax purposes

$N =$ Economic life of the asset

$G_t =$ Operating cash flow with purchase $= (1 - T)(X_t - z_{mt}) + TDep_t.$

Equation A15–3, used by Schall to calculate the net present value of leasing, is exactly the same as our equation 15–4 in the text of Chapter 15 except that he applies different discount rates to the cash inflows as compared with the lease payments. In addition, he correctly indicates an uncertainty model since he places a bar above the F and L to convey that it is the expected cash flows and the expected lease payments that are discounted.

Schall's formulation reproduced here as equation A15–4 is related to our equation 15–2. He introduces an additional term, z_{mt}, representing some costs incurred under ownership of the asset such as state and local taxes and certain maintenance expenses. In our formulation we assume that a separate contract could be written for maintenance whether the asset is owned or leased. In addition, state and local taxes can be assumed to be included in the lease payment and carried separately in the analysis of purchasing or netted out of both as we have done in equation 15–2. In addition, the term containing the Z covers an expected salvage value of the asset at the end of the lease period. This is presented on an after-tax basis. Finally, there is an expression for the present value of the tax shelter associated from interest payments on the debt utilized as a part of the financing of the asset purchased.[4]

Professor Schall explains how he would determine the different dis-

---

4. As will be shown in Appendix B to Chapter 19, when the discount factor used is the weighted cost of capital, the interest tax shelter is embodied in the discount factor. However, when the cost of *equity* capital is used to discount the net operating cash inflows, the interest tax shelter is shown as a separate term. The relationships appear as follows:

$$V = \frac{X(1 - T)}{k} \text{ where } k \text{ is the weighted average cost of capital}$$

$$V = \frac{X(1 - T)}{k_e} + \frac{Tk_b B}{k_b} \text{ where } k_e \text{ is the cost of equity capital}$$

Or $V = V_u + TB$. This is one of the relationships set forth by Modigliani and Miller in their "tax correction" article in the *American Economic Review* of June 1963.

count rates to be employed in the analysis. To estimate k_x in equation A15–3 the firm would observe the returns and values of all equity firms that own similar assets. The k_G is somewhat different because maintenance costs and depreciation flows are combined into the cash flow expression he refers to as G.[5] The k_R is a borrowing cost, and k_L is a cost related to "leasing cash flows," indicated in his numerical example to be somewhat higher than k_R. The k_s is a higher discount factor than the others since the salvage value of the asset at the end of the life of the lease is judged to be more risky than the other cash flows.

The meaning of the Schall formulation can be conveyed by utilizing the specific example he provides to illustrate the application of his methodology.[6] The value of the items used in his example are summarized and their relationships indicated in Table A15–3.

**Table A15–3
Illustrative Data
Utilized in Schall's
Example of the
Lease versus
Purchase Analysis**

		Lease Analysis	Purchase Analysis
F_t	Earnings before interest, taxes and lease payments	$700	$700
L_t	Lease payment or depreciation, if purchase	600	300
z_{mt}	Taxes, maintenance, etc., if purchase		100
$EBIT$	Earnings before interest and taxes	100	300
$k_b B$	Interest paid on debt		72
	Profit before taxes	100	228
T	Tax rate on ordinary income = .5; Taxes	50	114
	Net income	50	114
Z_N	After tax salvage value of the asset at the end of the lease period = $50		
G_t	Operating cash flows with purchase = $(1 - T)(F_t - z_{mt}) + T\,Dep = 300 + 150 = 450$		

Schall further assumes that the cost of the asset of $1,500 is covered by borrowing $1,200 and by utilizing equity funds of $300. He postulates in addition that only interest is payable annually on the debt so that, with a 6 percent debt interest cost, the annual interest expense is $72. He makes no provision in his analysis for repayment of the debt, on the assumption that if repaid, it could immediately be borrowed elsewhere. Nor does he explicitly take account of the cash outflows associated with the use of equity funds of $300. Their cost would appear to be encompassed in the discount factors he utilizes.

The data are then used to evaluate the net present value from leasing as set forth in equation A15–5. The k_x utilized by Schall appears to be the applicable cost of equity for firms that own assets similar to the as-

---

5. Note that Schall's approach implies that he could have treated each of the components of G as separate cash flows so that different discount rates could have been applied to each.
6. We have modified Schall's example slightly to simplify this presentation.

set under consideration here. The discount factor for G is somewhat lower because the G expression includes maintenance expenses and depreciation representing cash flows that are somewhat less risky than the net operating income of the firm. The k_R is the cost of borrowing, assumed to be given at 6 percent. Schall assumes that the cost of leasing, K_L, is somewhat higher and utilizes an 8 percent cost of leasing. The cost of capital applied to the expected salvage value k_s is 10 percent, which coincides with the 10 percent he utilizes for k_G.[7]

The applicable values and discount factors are inserted in his formulation as shown in (A15–5). The result is that the net present value of leasing is $64.

$$NPV_L = \sum_{t=1}^{5} \frac{.5(700)}{(1.12)^t} - \sum_{t=1}^{5} \frac{.5(600)}{(1.08)^t} \qquad \text{(A15–5)}$$

$$= \sum_{t=1}^{5} \frac{350}{(1.12)^t} - \sum_{t=1}^{5} \frac{300}{(1.08)^t}$$

$$= 350(3.605) - 300(3.993)$$

$$= 1,262 - 1,198$$

$$= \$64.$$

Similarly, the analysis of the purchase decision is made in equation (A15–6). When evaluated, the net present value of purchasing is $389.[8]

$$NPV_0 = \sum_{t=1}^{5} \frac{.5(700 - 100) + .5(300)}{(1.10)^t} + \sum_{t=1}^{5} \frac{.5(72)}{(1.06)^t} - \$1,500 + \frac{50}{(1.10)^5}$$

$$= \sum_{t=1}^{5} \frac{450}{(1.10)^t} + \frac{36}{(1.06)^t} - 1,500 + 50(.621) \qquad \text{(A15-6)}$$

$$= 450(3.791) + 36(4.212) - 1,500 + 31$$

$$= 1,706 + 152 - 1,500 + 31$$

$$= \$389.$$

The conclusion reached is that purchase is preferred to leasing since the increase in the value of the firm resulting from the purchase is greater than the increase in the value of the firm resulting from leasing. In

7. We are conveying the methodology applied by Professor Schall. As indicated, we do not necessarily agree with the assumptions employed in his approach to the lease versus purchase decision.

8. The $64 we obtain for the net present value of leasing is the same as the amount obtained by Professor Schall. However, Professor Schall obtained $425 for the net present value of the purchase alternative. This is because he used accelerated depreciation. In contrast, we used straight-line depreciation so that the calculations could be made compactly using the conventional present value of annuity expressions.

addition, purchasing meets the capital budgeting hurdle rate since the change in the value of the firm when the use of the asset is obtained by purchase (using the applicable project discount rate or rates) is a positive value.

The Value Additivity Principle in Leasing Analysis

The underlying model which Schall employs is the value additivity principle which holds that neither fragmenting cash flows nor recombining them will affect the resulting total values. This is the underlying model that he applies to his leasing analysis. From this stems his procedures under which each cash flow involved under either leasing or buying-owning must be discounted at its appropriate capitalization rate subject to the constraint that the value additivity principle holds. Otherwise, in his model of no transactions costs there would be profitable arbitrage opportunities. The discount rate employed is the discount rate for a stream that already exists in the market and is perfectly correlated with the cash flow stream under analysis. Or if the stream does not already exist, it can be created without cost.

Under the value additivity principle, in his numerical example one would have expected Schall to show that there was no net advantage to either leasing or purchasing. Yet in his original example there was an advantage to purchasing of the order of magnitude described here. Professor Schall's presentation would, therefore, seem to involve an internal inconsistency. If value additivity holds, there should be no advantage to either purchasing or leasing. Since his example portrayed an advantage to purchasing, he would be required to describe the imperfections such as monopolistic elements, transactions costs, or segmented markets to account for differences in the cost of leasing versus owning; then, the underlying model of his paper, the value additivity principle, no longer holds.

However, Schall's model can be modified to be consistent with his underlying value additivity principle model. Equation A15−5' reflects the requisite modification. The lease rental rate is changed so that there is now no advantage to leasing versus owning the asset.

$$NPV_L = \sum_{t=1}^{5} \frac{.5(700)}{(1.12)^t} - \sum_{t=1}^{5} \frac{.5(437.20)}{(1.08)^t} \tag{A15−5'}$$

$$= \sum_{t=1}^{5} \frac{350}{(1.12)^t} - \sum_{t=1}^{5} \frac{218.60}{(1.08)^t}$$

$$= 350(3.605) - 218.60(3.993)$$

$$= 1,262 - 873$$

$$= \$389.$$

The advantage of leasing is now as high as the advantage of owning. This is a result guaranteed by competitive market conditions and the value additivity principle upon which the Schall analysis is based.

Finally, Schall suggests that his method is applicable regardless of whether the lease provides for complete financing of the asset required or whether some combination of financing is utilized to acquire the use of the asset. If one believes that the cash flows associated with the financing of an asset that utilizes leasing as one of the sources of financing involves cash flows with segments of varying risk, the method set forth by Schall can be utilized. The methodology employed in our presentation of the approach to leasing is sufficiently general so that the particular discount rate the analyst prefers to use can be employed.

Multiple Discounts with a Break-even Approach

Closely related to the Schall approach is the formulation set forth by Professor Bower.[9] Bower sets forth a general formulation he suggests can be used to express any of the approaches to the leasing question in equation A15–7.

$$NAL = I - \sum_{t=1}^{N} \frac{L_t}{(1 + X_2)^t} + \sum_{t=1}^{N} \frac{T L_t}{(1 + X_3)^t} - \sum_{t=1}^{N} \frac{T Dep_t}{(1 + X_4)^t} \qquad \textbf{(A15–7)}$$

$$- \sum_{t=1}^{N} \frac{T I_t}{(1 + X_5)^t} + \sum_{t=1}^{N} \frac{O_j(1 - T)}{(1 + X_6)^t} - \frac{V_N}{(1 + X_7)^N}$$

We have translated his symbols into those used in Chapter 15. Three additional symbols we have not used to this point: O_j represents maintenance costs of the equipment, I_t represents the interest component of the loan payment, and V_n is the after-tax realized salvage value of the asset at the expiration of the lease period.

Professor Bower observes that there is general agreement on the handling of the first term and the last two terms in the expression. The first term is the purchase price of the asset to be leased, representing the outlay that will be avoided if the asset is acquired through the lease. No discounting is involved. As Bower states, "The last two terms include conventional project flows with risk characteristics and financing mix implications that fail to distinguish them from the flows usually considered in capital budgeting." He observes that these two are typically discounted at the company's cost of capital. An alternative approach he

9. Richard S. Bower, "Issues in Lease Financing," *Financial Management* 2 (Winter 1973), pp. 25–34.

describes is to adjust the flows to their certainty equivalence and then use a risk-free discount factor.[10]

In his key analysis framework Bower focuses on his decision format number 2. After some analysis he concludes that the cost of capital as the appropriate discount factor is applicable not only to the after-tax salvage and the after-tax operating savings but to the lease payments as well. The remaining areas of disagreement involve three factors each of which represents a tax shelter. He then applies a range of discount factors to determine the tax shelter discount factor, which makes the cost of leasing equal to the cost of purchasing. This is an after-tax interest rate, which can be converted into a before-tax borrowing rate based on the income tax rate of the firm. He then suggests that the executives of the firm can form their own judgment as to the appropriate pre-tax borrowing rate to apply and take into account as well "the wide variety of other considerations that influence executives' actions."

But this leaves unsettled analytically the question of whether the applicable break-even discount factor is a cost of debt or whether it is the applicable cost of capital. Bower's approach can be used to demonstrate the generality of the indifference result employed in our general approach set forth in the body of Chapter 15. Bower's general equation is set forth in modified form in (A15−8). This differs from Bower's formulation in A15−7 in using the cost of capital as the discount factor throughout and not listing the interest tax shelter separately since it is embedded in the weighted cost of capital employed.[11]

$$NAL = I - \sum_{t=1}^{N} \frac{L_t}{(1 + k)^t} + \sum_{t=1}^{N} \frac{T L_t}{(1 + k)^t} - \sum_{t=1}^{N} \frac{T Dep}{(1 + k)^t} + \sum_{t=1}^{N} \frac{O_j(1 - T)}{(1 + k)^t}$$

$$- \frac{V_N}{(1 + k)^N} \qquad\qquad \text{(A15−8)}$$

To illustrate the application of equation A15−8 assume the following additional information.

$I = 25,000$
$Z_N = 5,000$
$O_j = 2,000$

---

10. Professor Schall correctly suggests that the appropriate cost of capital is that applicable to the project risk under analysis. This is also the weighted cost of capital that we have been employing.

11. As we have observed, for an infinite time horizon the same result is produced whether the weighted cost of capital is used as the discount factor or alternatively all flows except the interest tax shelter are discounted at the firm's cost of equity and the interest tax shelter is discounted at the cost of debt. In the leasing analysis finite time periods are involved. However, it is customary to consider repetitions of the contracts to be equivalent to an infinite time horizon problem.

The additional factors that need to be taken into account can now be included in the solution process. Based on equation (A15−8) the net present value from the standpoint of the lessor is shown in (A15−9).

$$NPV_{LOR} = -I + \sum_{t=1}^{N} \frac{L_t(1 - T) + T\,Dep + O_j(1 - T)}{(1 + k)^t} - \frac{Z_N}{(1 + k)^N}. \qquad \text{(A15−9)}$$

Utilizing equation (A15−9) and the facts provided for this example, we obtain the formulation shown in equation (A15−9a).

$$NPV_{LOR} = -20{,}000 + 3.791\,[.6L_t + 1{,}600 + 1{,}200] - .784(5{,}000)$$
$$3.791(.6L_t) = 20{,}000 - 3.791[2{,}800] + 3{,}920$$
$$2.2746L_t = 23{,}920 - 10{,}614.8 \qquad \text{(A15−9A)}$$
$$2.2746L_t = 13{,}305.2$$
$$L_t = \$5{,}850.$$

For competitive conditions in the leasing industry in which the net present value is zero the equilibrium lease rental rate is $5,850.

We can now turn to the analysis of the owning versus leasing decision. Again, we will assume that there is equilibrium in the market for the use of the equipment. The net present value of owning is shown by equation A15−10.

$$NPV_0 = -I + \sum_{t=1}^{N} \frac{F_t(1 - T) + T\,Dep + O_j(1 - T)}{(1 + k)^t} - \frac{Z_N}{(1 + k)^N} \qquad \text{(A15−10)}$$

Again, the facts can be utilized to solve for the net present value of owning as shown in equation A15−10a.

$$NPV_0 = -20{,}000 + 3.791[.6(5{,}850) + 1{,}600 + 1{,}200] - .784(5{,}000)$$
$$= -20{,}000 + 3.791(6{,}310) - 3{,}920 \qquad \text{(A15−10a)}$$
$$= -23{,}920 + 23{,}921$$
$$\cong 0.$$

The solution is zero, indicating no net present value from owning. The firm simply earns its cost of capital. The analysis for leasing requires the use of equation A15−11, which is the same as the original equation 15−3 utilized in the body of the chapter in analyzing leasing. There are no new additional factors to be taken into consideration. All of the new elements affect the owning alternative only. Equation A15−11 is utilized in equation A15−11a.

$$NPL_L = \sum_{t=1}^{N} \frac{F_t(1 - T) - L_t(1 - T)}{(1 + k)^t} \qquad \text{(A15−11)}$$

$$NPV_L = 3.791[.6(5{,}850) - .6(5{,}850)] \qquad \text{(A15−11a)}$$
$$= 0.$$

The net present value of leasing is shown to be zero. Thus the indifference result again obtains. We have illustrated equilibrium in both the market for leasing companies as well as the market for the use of the equipment. As indicated in the body of the chapter, we could have illustrated net benefits over and above the firm's cost of capital in a market for the use of equipment. However, the indifference result would still have obtained whatever the size of the benefits. The size of the net present value would have been the same for owning as for leasing.

Summary

We have illustrated that alternative approaches to leasing can be reformulated to obtain the necessary indifference result as the foundation for further analysis. Departures from the indifference result would require that the market frictions or market imperfections that produce an advantage to owning versus leasing be specified. If these frictions are appropriately specified, they can then be logically related to the quantitative differences in the analysis that may be found. Unless the analysis starts with the indifference result and is able to track clearly how a result other than the indifference result is produced, the comparison between the costs of leasing and the costs of owning may be unreliable. No matter how complicated or sophisticated the procedure is, it will yield a false security unless a clear relation to the indifference result can be tracked and set out clearly. A major source of advantages or disadvantages of leasing is the unequal tax positions of lessors and users of the assets.

Problems

A15–1. The Bradley Steel Company seeks to acquire the services of a rolling machine at the lowest possible cost. The choice is to either lease one at $17,142 annually or purchase one for $54,000. Their cost of capital is 14 percent, and their tax rate is 40 percent. The machine has an economic life of six years and no salvage value. The company uses straight-line depreciation. Which is the less costly method of financing?

A15–2. The Nelson Company is faced with the decision of whether it should purchase or lease a new fork-lift truck. The truck can be leased on an eight-year contract for $6,280.50 a year, or it can be purchased for $24,000. The lease includes maintenance and service. The salvage value of the truck eight years hence is $2,000. The company uses straight-line depreciation. If the truck is owned, service and maintenance charges (deductible costs) will be $500 per year. The company can borrow at 10 percent and has a 40 percent marginal tax rate and 12 percent cost of capital.

a. Analyze the lease versus purchase decision using the firm's cost of capital of 12 percent as the discount factor.
b. Make the analysis using the after-tax cost of debt as the discount factor.
c. Compare your results.

16   **Warrants and Convertibles**

Thus far in the discussion of long-term financing, we have examined the nature of common stock, preferred stock, various types of debt, and leasing. We have also seen how offering common stock through the use of rights can facilitate low-cost stock flotations. In this chapter, we see how the financial manager, through the use of warrants and convertibles, can make his company's securities attractive to an even broader range of investors, thereby lowering his cost of capital. As we show in Chapter 21, "The Timing of Financial Policy," the use of warrants and convertibles has greatly increased in recent years.

Therefore, it is important to understand the characteristics of these two types of securities.

Warrants

A *warrant* is an option to buy a stated number of shares of stock at a specified price. For example, Trans Pacific Airlines has warrants outstanding that give the warrant holders the right to buy one share of TPA stock at a price of $22 for each warrant held. The warrants generally expire on a certain date—TPA's warrants expire on December 1, 1981—although some have perpetual lives.

Formula Value of a Warrant

Warrants have a calculated, or formula, value and an actual value, or price, that is determined in the marketplace. The formula value is found by use of the following equation:

$$\text{Formula value} = \left(\begin{array}{c}\text{market price of}\\\text{common stock}\end{array} - \begin{array}{c}\text{option}\\\text{price}\end{array}\right) \times \left(\begin{array}{c}\text{number of shares each}\\\text{warrant entitles owner}\\\text{to purchase.}\end{array}\right)$$

For instance, a TPA warrant entitles the holder to purchase one share of common stock at $22 a share. If the market price of the common stock is $64.50, the formula price of the warrant may be obtained as follows:

$(\$64.50 - \$22) \times 1.0 = \$42.50.$

The formula gives a negative value when the stock is selling for less than the option price. For example, if TPA stock is selling for $20, the formula value of the warrants is minus $2. This makes no sense, so we define the formula value to be zero when the stock is selling for less than the option price.

Actual Price of a Warrant

Generally, warrants sell above their formula values. When TPA stock was selling for $64.50, the warrants had a formula value of $42.50 but were selling at a price of $46.87. This represented a premium of $4.37 above the formula value.

A set of TPA stock prices, together with actual and formula warrant values, is given in Table 16–1 and plotted in Figure 16–1. At any stock price below $22, the formula value of the warrant is zero; beyond $22, each $1 increase in the price of the stock brings with it a $1 increase in the formula value of the warrant. The actual market price of the warrants lies above the formula value at each price of the common stock. Notice, however, that the premium of market price over formula value declines as the price of the common stock increases. For example, when the common sold for $22 and the warrants had a zero formula value, their actual price, and the premium, was $9. As the price of the stock rises, the formula value of the warrants matches the increase dollar for dollar, but for a while the *market price* of the warrant climbs less rapidly and the premium declines. The premium is $9 when the stock sells for $22 a share, but it declines to $1 by the time the stock price has risen to $75 a share. Beyond this point the premium seems to be constant.

Why do you suppose this pattern exists? Why should the warrant

Figure 16–1
Formula and Actual
Values of TPA
Warrants at Different
Common Stock Prices

Table 16–1
Formula and Actual
Values of TPA
Warrants at
Different Market
Prices

	Value of Warrant		
Price of Stock	Formula Price	Actual Price	Premium
$ 0.00	$ 0.00	Not available	—
22.00	0.00	$ 9.00	$9.00
23.00	1.00	9.75	8.75
24.00	2.00	10.50	8.50
33.67	11.67	17.37	5.70
52.00	30.00	32.00	2.00
75.00	53.00	54.00	1.00
100.00	78.00	79.00	1.00
150.00	128.00	Not available	—

ever sell for more than its formula value, and why does the premium decline as the price of the stock increases? The answer lies in the speculative appeal of warrants—they enable a person to gain a high degree of personal leverage when buying securities. To illustrate, suppose TPA warrants always sold for exactly their formula value. Now suppose you are thinking of investing in the company's common stock at a time when it is selling for $25 a share. If you buy a share and the price rises to $50 in a year, you have made a 100 percent capital gain. However, had you bought the warrants at their formula value ($3 when the stock sells for $25), your capital gain would have been $25 on a $3 investment, or 833 percent. At the same time, your total loss potential with the warrant is only $3, while the potential loss from the purchase of the stock is $25. The huge capital gains potential, combined with the loss limitation, is clearly worth something—the exact amount it is worth to investors is the amount of the premium.[1]

But why does the premium decline as the price of the stock rises? The answer is that both the leverage effect and the loss protection feature decline at high stock prices. For example, if you are thinking of buying the stock at $75 a share, the formula value of the warrants is $53. If the stock price doubles to $150, the formula value of TPA warrants goes from $53 to $128. The percentage capital gain on the stock is still 100 percent, but the percentage gain on the warrant declines from 833 percent to 142 percent. Moreover, notice that the loss potential on the warrant is much greater when the warrant is selling at high prices. These two factors, the declining leverage impact and the increasing danger of losses, explain why the premium diminishes as the price of the common stock rises.

1. However, a $3 decline in the stock price produces only a 12 percent loss if the stock is purchased, and a 100 percent loss if you buy the warrant and it declines to its formula value.

Warrant Valuation[2]

The formula defines the value of a warrant to be zero whenever the price of the stock is below the option, or *exercise*, price. We know, however, that warrants frequently sell for a nonzero price even though the formula value is zero—for example, see Table 16–1. Why would someone pay a positive price for a warrant that permits him to buy stock for *more than* the current market price of the stock?

The answer to this question can be seen in Figure 16–2. The curve is the probability distribution of the "average" investor regarding the future price of a share of stock. The current market price, $p_m = \$50$, is at the mean of the distribution. Now suppose the exercise price is *less than* the current market price, say at $p_A = \$40$. In this case, assuming the warrant entitles the holder to buy one share, the warrant has a formula value of $10. But suppose the exercise price had been $p_B = \$50$ or any higher price; now the formula value is zero.

Figure 16–2
Probability Distribution
of Future Stock Prices

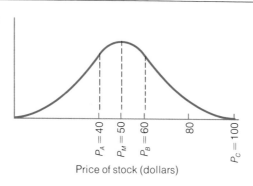

Price of stock (dollars)

Suppose you owned 100 of these warrants, saw that the exercise price was $60, and calculated the formula value to be zero. Suppose you gave the warrants to your instructor, thinking they were worthless. A year later the price of the stock rises to $80—after all, there was a reasonably good chance that it would reach this level. You now see that you gave away for nothing something that later turned out to be worth ($80 − $60) (100 warrants) = $2,000. This example shows why the price of a warrant may be greater than zero even though its formula value is zero.

Further inspection of Figure 16–2 suggests three generalizations:

2. This section is rather technical and may be omitted without loss of continuity.

(1) Only if the exercise price is beyond the outer bound of the distribution (that is, there is a zero probability of the market price getting as high as the exercise price) will the warrant ever fall to a zero price. Further, *all* stockholders must share this view. (2) The flatter the distribution (that is, the higher the standard deviation), the higher the probability of an extremely high stock price. It is these high stock prices that give warrants value, so the larger the standard deviation, the higher the value of the warrant. (3) The life of the warrant is a consideration; if the warrant is due to expire in a few months, the stock price will not be likely to reach an extreme value (that is, the shorter the time interval, the narrower the distribution of stock prices), so the warrant will be less valuable than one that has a longer life.

Statistical models, including as independent variables the market price of the stock, the exercise price, the expected growth rate of the stock price, the variance of the stock price, and the life of the warrant, have been developed to determine empirically the value of warrants. These models are discussed in the appendix to this chapter.

Use of Warrants in Financing

In the past, warrants have generally been used by small, rapidly growing firms as "sweeteners" when selling either debt or preferred stocks. Such firms are frequently regarded by investors as being highly risky. Their bonds could be sold only if the firms were willing to accept extremely high rates of interest and very restrictive indenture provisions, to offer warrants, or to make the bonds convertible. In April 1970, however, AT&T raised $1.57 billion by selling bonds with warrants. This was the largest financing of any type ever undertaken by a business firm, and it marked the first use ever of warrants by a large, strong corporation.[3] It may safely be anticipated that other large firms will follow AT&T's lead, so we can expect to see a more widespread use of warrants in the future than has been true in the past.[4]

Giving warrants along with bonds enables investors to share in the company's growth, if it does, in fact, grow and prosper; therefore, investors are willing to accept a lower bond interest rate and less restrictive indenture provisions. A bond with warrants has some characteristics of debt and some characteristics of equity. It is a hybrid security that provides the financial manager with an opportunity to expand his

---

3. It is also interesting to note that before the AT&T issue, the New York Stock Exchange had a policy against listing warrants. The NYSE's stated policy was that warrants could not be listed because they were "speculative" instruments rather than "investment" securities. When AT&T issued warrants, however, the Exchange changed its policy and agreed to list warrants that met certain specifications.

4. In fact, the number of warrants listed on the New York Stock Exchange increased to 38 by the end of 1975. *Fact Book, 1976*, New York Stock Exchange, p. 34.

mix of securities, appealing to a broader group of investors, and, thus, possibly lowering his firm's cost of capital.

Warrants can also bring in additional funds. The option price is generally set 15 to 20 percent above the market price of the stock at the time of the bond issue. If the firm does grow and prosper, and if its stock price rises above the option price at which shares may be purchased, warrant holders will surrender their warrants and buy stock at the stated price. There are several reasons for this. First, warrant holders will *surely* surrender warrants and buy stock if the warrants are about to expire with the market price of the stock above the option price. Second, warrant holders will *voluntarily* surrender and buy as just mentioned if the company raises the dividend on the common stock. No dividend is earned on the warrant, so it provides no current income. However, if the common stock pays a high dividend, it provides an attractive dividend yield. This induces warrant holders to exercise their option to buy the stock. Third, warrants sometimes have *stepped-up option prices.* For example, the Williamson Scientific Company has warrants outstanding with an option price of $25 until December 31, 1979, at which time the option price rises to $30. If the price of the common stock is over $25 just before December 1979, many warrant holders will exercise their option before the stepped-up price takes effect.

One desirable feature of warrants is that they generally bring in additional funds only if such funds are needed. If the company grows and prospers, causing the price of the stock to rise, the warrants are exercised and bring in needed funds. If the company is not successful and cannot profitably employ additional money, the price of its stock will probably not rise sufficiently to induce exercise of the options.

Convertibles

Convertible securities are bonds or preferred stocks that are exchangeable into common stock at the option of the holder and under specified terms and conditions. The most important of the special features relates to how many shares of stock a convertible holder receives if he converts. This feature is defined as the *conversion ratio*, which gives the number of shares of common stock the holder of the convertible receives when he surrenders his security on conversion. Related to the conversion ratio is the *conversion price*, or the effective price paid for the common stock when conversion occurs. In effect, a convertible is similar to a bond with an attached warrant.

The relationship between the conversion ratio and the conversion price is illustrated by Adams Electric Company convertible debentures, issued at their $1,000 par value in 1975. At any time prior to maturity on July 1, 1995, a debenture holder can turn in his bond and receive in its place 20 shares of common stock; therefore, the conversion ratio is 20 shares for one bond. The bond has a par value of $1,000, so the holder is giving up this amount when he converts. Dividing the $1,000 by the 20 shares received gives a conversion price of $50 a share:

$$\text{Conversion price} = \frac{\text{par value of bond}}{\text{shares received}} = \frac{\$1,000}{20} = \$50.$$

The conversion price and the conversion ratio are established at the time the convertible bond is sold. Generally, these values are fixed for the life of the bond, although sometimes a stepped-up conversion price is used. Litton Industries' convertible debentures, for example, were convertible into 12.5 shares until 1972, and they may be exchanged into 11.76 shares from 1972 until 1982 and into 11.11 shares from 1982 until they mature in 1987. The conversion price thus started at $80, rose to $85, then to $90. Litton's convertibles, like most, are callable at the option of the company.

Another factor that may cause a change in the conversion price and ratio is a standard feature of almost all convertibles—the clause protecting the convertible against dilution from stock splits, stock dividends, and the sale of common stock at low prices (as in a rights offering). The typical provision states that no common stock can be sold at a price below the conversion price and that the conversion price must be lowered (and the conversion ratio raised) by the percentage amount of any stock dividend or split. For example, if Adams Electric had a two-for-one split, the conversion ratio would automatically be adjusted to 40 and the conversion price lowered to $25. If this protection was not contained in the contract, a company could completely thwart conversion by the use of stock splits and dividends. Warrants are similarly protected against dilution.

Like warrant option prices, the conversion price is characteristically set from 15 to 20 percent above the prevailing market price of the common stock at the time the convertible issue is sold. Exactly how the conversion price is established can best be understood after examining some of the reasons why firms use convertibles.

Advantages of Convertibles

Convertibles offer advantages to corporations as well as to individual investors. The most important of these advantages are discussed below.

As a "sweetener" when selling debt. A company can sell debt with lower interest rates and less restrictive covenants by giving investors a chance to share in potential capital gains. Convertibles, like bonds with warrants, offer this possibility.

To sell common stock at prices higher than those currently prevailing. Many companies actually want to sell common stock, not debt, but feel that the price of the stock is temporarily depressed. Management may know, for example, that earnings are depressed because of a strike but that they will snap back during the next year and pull the price of the stock up with them. To sell stock now would require giving up more shares to raise a given amount of money than management thinks is necessary. However, setting the conversion price 15 to 20 percent above the present market price of the stock will require giving up 15 to 20 percent fewer shares when the bonds are converted than would be required if stock was sold directly.

Notice, however, that management is counting on the stock's price rising above the conversion price to make the bonds actually attractive in conversion. If the stock price does not rise and conversion does not occur, then the company is saddled with debt.

How can the company be sure that conversion will occur when the price of the stock rises above the conversion price? Characteristically, convertibles have a provision that gives the issuing firm the opportunity of calling the convertible at a specified price. Suppose the conversion price is $50, the conversion ratio is 20, the market price of the common stock has risen to $60, and the call price on the convertible bond is $1,050. If the company calls the bond (by giving the usual notification of 20 days), bondholders can either convert into common stock with a market value of $1,200 or allow the company to redeem the bond for $1,050. Naturally, bondholders prefer $1,200 to $1,050, so conversion occurs. The call provision therefore gives the company a means of forcing conversion, provided that the market price of the stock is greater than the conversion price.

To have low-cost capital during a construction period. Another advantage from the standpoint of the issuer is that a convertible issue may be used as a temporary financing device. During the years 1946 through 1957, AT&T sold $10 billion of convertible debentures. By 1959 about 80 percent of these convertible debentures had been converted into common stock. AT&T did not want to sell straight debt in that amount because its financial structure would have been unbalanced. On the other hand, if AT&T had simply issued large amounts of common stock periodically, there would have been price pressure on its stock because the market is slow to digest large blocks of stock.

By using convertible debentures, which provided for a lag of some six to nine months before they were convertible into common stock, AT&T received relatively cheap money to finance growth. Transmission lines and telephone exchange buildings must first be built to provide the basis for ultimately installing phones. While AT&T is making such installations, these investments are not earning any money. Therefore, it was important to AT&T to minimize the cost of money during the construction period. After six to nine months had elapsed and the installations were translated into telephones that were bringing in revenues, AT&T was better able to pay the regular common stock dividend.

Disadvantages of Convertibles

From the standpoint of the issuer, convertibles have a possible disadvantage. Although the convertible bond does give the issuer the opportunity to sell common stock at a price 15 to 20 percent higher than it could otherwise be sold, if the common stock greatly increases in price the issuer may find that he would have been better off if he had waited and simply sold the common stock. Further, if the company truly wants to raise equity capital and if the price of the stock declines after the bond is issued, then it is stuck with debt.

Analysis of Convertible Debentures[5]

A convertible security is a hybrid, having some of the characteristics of common stocks and some characteristics of bonds or preferred stocks. Investors expect to earn an interest yield as well as a capital gains yield. Moreover, the corporation recognizes that it incurs an interest cost and a potential dilution of equity when it sells convertibles. In this section, we first develop a theoretical model to combine these two cost components and then discuss the conditions under which convertibles should be used.

Model of Convertible Bonds

Since an investor who purchases a convertible bond expects to receive interest plus capital gains, his total expected return is the sum of these two parts. His expected interest return is dependent primarily upon the bond's coupon interest rate and upon the price paid for the bond, while the expected capital gains yield is dependent basically upon the relationship between the stock price at the time of issue and the conversion price, and upon the expected growth rate in the price of the stock. We will now examine these two yield components.

Consider the graph in Figure 16–3, which we will examine in detail. In this analysis, think of the graph as showing the *ex ante*, or expected, relationships. We are now at year $t = 0$ and are projecting events into

5. This section is relatively technical, and it may be omitted on a first reading without loss of continuity.

the future. The symbols used in Figure 16–3 and the remainder of this chapter are listed in Table 16–2.

Call Price and Maturity Value. Our hypothetical bond is a new issue that can be purchased for $M = \$1,000$, and this initial price is also the par (and maturity) value. The bond is callable at the option of the corporation, with the call price originating at $V_0 = \$1,040$, somewhat above par, and declining linearly over the 20-year term to maturity to equal $M'' = \$1,000$ at maturity.

Value in Conversion. At any point in time, the bond could be converted to stock, and the value of the stock received on conversion is defined as the *conversion value* of the bond. The original conversion value (C_0) is established by multiplying the market price of the stock at the time of issue by the number of shares into which the bond may be converted (the conversion ratio). The stock price is expected to grow at a rate (g), causing the conversion value curve (C_t) to rise at this same rate. This establishes the curve C_t, which shows the expected conversion value at each point in time. All of this is expressed by Equation 16–1:

$$C_t = p_0(1 + g)^t \#, \tag{16–1}$$

where

C_t = conversion value at time t

Table 16–2
Summary of Symbols Used in Chapter 16

B_t = straight debt value of a bond at time t
c = dollars of interest paid each year; $\$40 = 4$ percent of M
C_N = conversion value = $p_0(1 + g)^N \#$
C_t = conversion value at time t
g = expected rate of growth of the stock's price
k_b = market rate of interest on equivalent risk, nonconvertible debt issues
k_c = internal rate of return, or expected yield, on the convertible
M = price paid for the bond
M' = market value of the convertible bond when its conversion value becomes equal to its market value
M'' = maturity value
N = number of years bond is expected to be held
$\#$ = conversion ratio, or number of shares received on conversion
p_c = conversion price = $M/\#$
p_0 = current market price of the stock
t = number of years since date of issue
t^* = number of years remaining until maturity = original term to maturity
T = marginal corporate income tax rate
V_0 = original call price of an option

p_0 = initial price of the common stock = \$45 per share

g = expected rate of growth of the stock's price = 4 percent

\# = conversion ratio, or number of shares received on conversion = 20.

Figure 16–3
Model of a Convertible
Bond

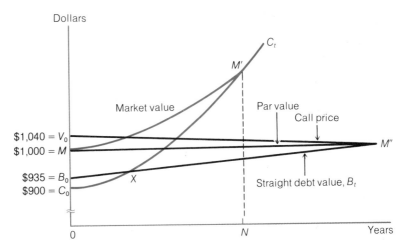

The initial conversion value of the bond, when $t = 0$, is simply \$45 ×
20, or \$900. One year later it is expected to be \$45 (1.04)(20) = \$936; after
two years it is expected to rise to \$973.44; and so on. We see, then, that
the expected conversion value curve C_t is a function of the expected
growth in the price of the stock.

Bond Value. In addition to its value in conversion, the bond also has a
straight-debt value, B_t, defined as the price at which the bond would
sell in any year t if it did not have the conversion option. At each point
in time, B_t is determined by the following equation:

$$B_t = \sum_{j=1}^{t^*} \frac{c}{(1 + k_b)^j} + \frac{M''}{(1 + k_b)^{t^*}}. \tag{16–2}$$

Here,

t = number of years since date of issue

t^* = number of years remaining until maturity = original term to
maturity (20 years) minus t

j = time subscript from 1 to t^*

k_b = market rate of interest on equivalent risk, nonconvertible debt issues = $4\frac{1}{2}$ percent (Note that k_b > coupon interest on the convertible.)

c = dollars of interest paid each year; $40 = 4$ percent of M

M'' = maturity value.

Equation 16–2 is used to calculate the bond value B_t from each point t to the maturity date. To illustrate the use of the equation, we will calculate B_t at $t=0$ and $t=8$. First, note that $t=0$ is the point in time when the bond is issued, while $t=8$ means the bond is eight years old and has 12 years remaining to maturity. So, for B_0, the summation term refers to an annuity of $40 per year for $t^*=20-0=20$ years, while for B_8, the summation represents a 12-year annuity; $t^*=20-8=12$ years:

$$B_0 = \sum_{j=1}^{20} \frac{\$40}{(1.045)^j} + \frac{\$1,000}{(1.045)^{20}}$$

$$= \$40\,(13.026) + \$1,000\,(0.416)$$

$$= \$521.04 + \$416 = \$937.04.$$

$$B_8 = \sum_{j=1}^{12} \frac{\$40}{(1.045)^j} + \frac{\$1,000}{(1.045)^{12}}$$

$$= \$40\,(9.124) + \$1,000\,(0.591)$$

$$= \$364.96 + \$591 = \$955.96.$$

We see, then, that B_t rises over time and that $B_{20} = \$1,000$.[6]

Market Value Floor. The convertible will never sell below its value as a straight bond—if it did, investors interested in buying debt instruments would see it as a bargain, start buying the bonds, and drive their value up to B_t. Similarly, the convertible could never sell below its conversion value—if it did, investors interested in the stock would buy the bonds, convert, and obtain shares at a bargain price, but drive the price of the convertible up to C_t in the process. Thus, the lines C_0C_t and B_0M'' in Figure 16–3 serve as floors below which the market price of the bond cannot fall. The higher of these two floors dominates, with the dark, discontinuous curve B_0XC_t forming the *effective market value floor.*

---

6. In Equation 16–2, bond values are calculated at the beginning of each period, just after the last interest payment has been made. Most bonds (convertible and nonconvertible alike) are actually traded on the basis of a basic price, determined as in Equation 16–2, plus interest accrued since the last payment date. Thus, if one were to buy this bond a few days before the end of year 20, he would pay approximately $1,000 plus $40 accrued interest, and the invoice from the broker would indicate these two components.

Expected Market Value. Ordinarily, convertibles sell at premiums over their bond and conversion value floors. For our illustrative bond, the expected market value is represented in Figure 16–3 by the curve MM', which lies above the effective floor (B_0XC_t) over most of the range but converges with B_0XC_t in year N. The rationale behind this price action is developed in the following two subsections.

Why the Market Value Exceeds the B_0XC_t Floor. The spread between MM' and B_0XC_t, which represents the premium marginal investors[7] are willing to pay for the conversion option, may be explained by several factors. First, since the convertible bond may be converted into common stock if the company prospers and the stock price rises, it usually commands a premium over its value as straight debt (that is, the right of conversion has a positive value). Second, the convertible bond usually commands a premium over its conversion value because, by holding convertibles, an investor is able to reduce his risk exposure. To illustrate, suppose someone buys the hypothetical bond for $1,000. At the time, it is convertible into 20 shares of stock with a market price of $45, giving a conversion value of $900. If the stock market turns sharply down and the stock price falls to $22.50 per share, a stock investor would suffer a 50 percent loss in value. Had he held a convertible bond, its price would have fallen from $1,000 to the bond value floor, B_0M'' in Figure 16–3, which is at least $937. Hence, holding the convertible entails less risk than holding common stock; this also causes convertibles to sell at a premium above their conversion value.[8]

Why the Market Value Approaches the Conversion Value. The MM' curve in Figure 16–3 rises less rapidly than the C_0C_t curve, indicating that the market value approaches the conversion value as the conversion value increases. This is caused by three separate factors. First, and probably most important, the bondholders realize that the issue is callable; if it is in fact called, they have the option of either surrendering for redemption or converting. In the former case, they receive the call price; in the latter, they receive stock with a value designated by C_t. If the market price of the bond is above both of these values, the holder

---

7. Marginal investors, often called "the market," are defined as those just willing to hold the bond at its going price. These investors are, in fact, the ones who actually determine the level of the bond's price.
   8. Two institutional factors may also contribute to convertibles' premiums. First, margin requirements are typically lower for convertibles than for stock; thus, speculators can speculate with less money in the convertible than the stock market. Second, certain institutional investors, such as life insurance companies, have more freedom to invest in convertibles than in stocks, so if these institutions want to invest in stocks to a greater extent than their regulators permit, they may expand stock holdings "through the back door" with convertibles.

is in danger of a potential loss in wealth in the event of a call; this fact prevents wide spreads between MM' and B_0XC_t whenever the market value exceeds the call price.

The second factor driving MM' toward C_0C_t is related to the loss protection characteristic of convertibles. Barring changes in the interest rate on the firm's straight-debt securities, the potential loss on a convertible is equal to the spread between MM' and B_0M''. Since this spread increases at high conversion values, the loss potential also increases, causing the premium attributable to the loss protection to diminish.

The third factor causing the gap between MM' and C_0C_t to close has to do with the relationship between the yield on a convertible and that on the common stock for which it may be exchanged. The yield on most common stocks consists of two components: a dividend yield and an expected capital gain yield. In the next section we will see that convertibles also have two yield components, one from interest payments and one from capital gains. After some point, the expected capital gain is the same for both instruments, but the current yield on the bond declines vis-à-vis that on the common stock because dividends on stocks whose prices are rising are typically also rising, while interest payments are fixed. This causes the gap between MM' and C_0C_t to close and would eventually lead to a negative premium except for the fact that voluntary conversion occurs first.

Expected Rate of Return on a Convertible

The purchaser of a convertible generally expects the price of the stock to rise, the conversion value to rise with the stock, and the conversion to take place after some period of time, say N years. Thus, the purchaser expects first to receive a series of interest payments of $\$c$ per year for N years and then to have stock with a value equal to $C_N = p_0(1+g)^N \#$. The expected rate of return on the convertible, k_c, is found by solving for k_c in the following equation:

$$M = \sum_{t=1}^{N} \frac{c}{(1+k_c)^t} + \frac{p_0(1+g)^N \#}{(1+k_c)^N}. \tag{16–3}$$

Here

$M =$ maturity value, also equal to par value. Note also that M is the price paid for the bond

$c =$ dollars of interest received per year

$C_N =$ conversion value $= p_0(1+g)^N \#$

N = number of years bond is expected to be held

k_c = internal rate of return, or expected yield, on the convertible.

The equation is purely definitional; it simply states that if an investor pays M dollars for a convertible bond, holds it for N years, and receives a series of interest payments plus a terminal value, then he will receive a return on his investment equal to k_c.[9]

The *ex ante* yield on a convertible (k_c) is probabilistic—it is dependent upon a set of variables subject to probability distributions and hence must itself be a random variable. It is possible, however, to define each of the determinants of k_c in terms of its mean expected value; $E(g)$, for example, is the expected value of the growth rate in the stock's price over N years. For simplicity, $E(g)$ and other random variables are shortened to g, C_N, and so on. With the variables defined in this manner, it is possible to work sequentially through two equations to find the expected rate of return on a convertible bond.

Remembering that bondholders are assumed to cash out in year N, presumably reinvesting the terminal value received in some other security, we may establish the determinants of C_N; they are (1) the corporation's policy in regard to calling the bond to force conversion; or (2) the investor's decision to hold the bond until it is called, to sell it, or to convert voluntarily.

Corporation's Call Policy. Corporations issuing convertible bonds generally have policies regarding just how far up the C_0C_t curve they will allow a bond to go before calling to force conversion. These policies range from calling as soon as they are "sure" conversion will take place (this generally means a premium of about 20 percent over the par value) to never calling at all. If the policy is never to issue a call, however, the firm generally relies on the dividend-interest differential to cause voluntary conversion.

It is apparent that call policy has a very direct influence on the expected number of years a convertible will remain outstanding, hence on the value of C_N found by Equation 16–3. Naturally, expectations about call policy influence the expected rate of return on a convertible bond. Because of this, the issuing firm must take investor expectations into account. A policy that may be in the apparent short-run interest of the corporation may penalize the investor with such a low effective actual

---

9. Three simplifications are made in this analysis. First, taxes are ignored. Second, the problem of reinvestment rates is handled by assuming that all reinvestment is made at the internal rate of return. Third, it is assumed that the bondholder does not hold stock after conversion; he cashes out, as would be true of an institutional investor precluded from holding common stock.

yield that the firm may have difficulties when it subsequently attempts to market additional securities. This point is illustrated in one of the problems at the end of the chapter.[10]

Investors' Cash-Out Policy. Investors' cash-out policy is similar to the corporate call policy in that it sets a limit on how far up the C_0C_t curve an investor is willing to ride. The decision is influenced by the interest-dividend relationship, by the investor's aversion to risk (recall that risk due to a stock price decline increases as one moves up the C_0C_t curve), and by his willingness to hold securities providing low current yields. In general, it appears that investors are willing to ride higher up $C_0C_{t'}$ given the dividend-interest relationship, than the firm is willing to let them ride; hence, corporate call policy generally supersedes investor cash-out policy.

Years the Bond is Held

As we have seen, the path of the conversion value curve is traced out by Equation 16–1:

$$C_t = p_0(1 + g)^t \; \#. \tag{16–1}$$

Recognizing that $\# = M/p_c$, where p_c is defined as the initial conversion price of the shares, Equation 16–1 may be rewritten:

$$C_t = \frac{p_0}{p_c} (1 + g)^t M. \tag{16–4}$$

Setting Equation 16–4 equal to the C_t defined by corporate policy (for example, $1,200 if a 20 percent premium is used), we find

$$C_N = \frac{p_0}{p_c} (1 + g)^N M = \$1,200 \tag{16–5}$$

$$\$1,200 = \frac{\$45}{\$50} (1.04)^N \; \$1,000 = \$900 \; (1.04)^N$$

$$\frac{\$1,200}{\$900} = 1.333 = (1.04)^N.$$

The 1.333 is the *CVIF* for the compound sum of $1 growing at 4 percent

---

10. We might also mention that some firms seek to encourage *voluntary conversion* rather than call to force conversion. One way of getting voluntary conversion is to include a provision for periodic stepped-up conversion prices; for example, Litton Industries' conversion price goes up every three years (so the number of shares received upon conversion goes down), and this stimulates voluntary conversion at the step-up date provided the conversion value of the bond is above the straight-debt value. In addition, voluntary conversion occurs when the dividend yield on stock received on conversion exceeds the interest yield on the convertibles.

for N years. Looking up this factor in the 4 percent column of Table D–1, we find that the factor 1.333 lies between the seventh and eighth years, so $N \approx 7\frac{1}{2}$ years.

We may now substitute this value of N (rounded to eight years for simplicity), together with the other known data, into Equation 16–3:

$$M = \sum_{t=1}^{N} \frac{c}{(1 + k_c)^t} + \frac{p_0(1 + g)^N \#}{(1 + k_c)^N} \qquad (16\text{--}3)$$

$$\$1{,}000 = \sum_{t=1}^{8} \frac{c}{(1 + k_c)^t} + \frac{\$45\,(1.04)^8 20}{(1 + k_c)^8}$$

$$= \$40(PVIF_a) + \$1{,}232(PVIF).$$

Using the interest factors for 6 percent, we find

$$PV = \$40(6.210) + \$1{,}232(.627)$$

$$= \$248 + \$772 = \$1{,}020 > \$1{,}000.$$

Therefore, k_c is a little larger than 6 percent. Using interest factors for 7 percent, we find

$$PV = \$239 + \$717 = \$956 < \$1{,}000.$$

Thus, k_c is between 6 and 7 percent; interpolating, we find $k_c = 6.3$ percent, so someone purchasing this convertible for \$1,000 could expect to obtain a return of 6.3 percent on his investment.[11]

Setting the Terms of a Convertible Issue

As we know, investors have a risk-determined required rate of return for any security. They will not purchase a given security unless its terms are such that they can reasonably expect to earn at least their required rate of return. For our convertible issue, the expected rate of return is 6.3 percent. If 6.3 percent is also the required rate of return on securities with this degree of risk, then the bonds can be issued at a price of \$1,000. If they are offered at that price, all the bonds will be sold. However, the price of the bonds after the flotation will remain in the vicinity of \$1,000.

A corporation raising funds through convertibles will seek to set terms that will cause its bonds to just clear the market. What terms can the firm adjust, and what will happen if it sets these terms incorrectly? Actually, we can separate the key variables into two classes, those over

---

11. We have not done so, but, conceptually, k_c could be split into two separate rates of return, one applicable to the expected interest payments and the other applicable to the conversion value in Equation 16–3. If this was done, the rate used to discount interest payments would probably be the lower one, as interest payments are more certain than capital gains.

which the firm has no direct control at the time the convertible is issued, and those over which the firm does have control.

Variables outside the firm's direct control:

1. p_0 = current market price of the stock
2. g = expected growth rate
3. the value of C_t at which investors expect the firm to call and force conversion. (However, if the bond is made noncallable for a period of years, this does have a bearing on C_t.)
4. the riskiness of the firm and its securities as seen by investors
5. k_b = interest rate on nonconvertible debt.

Controllable variables:

1. M = par value = maturity value = issue price
2. p_c = conversion price = $M/\#$
3. c = coupon interest (Note that c/M = initial interest yield on the bonds; c/M is generally $< k_b$, that is, the interest yield on convertibles is generally less than that on straight debt of the same risk.).

Typically, M is set at $1,000. The value of M is really not very important, as a low value of M simply means the firm will have to issue more bonds, while a high M means that fewer, more valuable bonds will be issued.

Naturally, the firm would like to set c as low as possible, in order to hold down interest expense, and also to set p_c as high as possible (and $\#$ as low as possible) to minimize the number of shares it will have to issue upon conversion. Investors, on the other hand, want a high value for c and a low p_c. The corporation and its investment bankers will seek to find a set of c and p_c values that will cause the issue to just clear the market; more generous terms would lead to a price run-up and unnecessarily penalize the firm, while insufficient terms would keep investors from buying the issue and prevent the firm from attracting the capital it needs.

The issuing firm can make tradeoffs between p_c and c. Assume that the required rate of return on our illustrative bond is 6.3 percent and that all terms and conditions are as specified above. The bond will just clear the market at a price of $1,000. However, suppose the issuing firm wants conversion to occur earlier than eight years—perhaps it plans a major expansion program and wants to issue straight bonds and, therefore, needs to have conversion occur to lower the debt ratio prior to the new issue. In that case, the firm would lower p_c by raising $\#$ above 20. That action, taken alone, would raise the value of the convertible above $1,000, but it could be offset by lowering c below $40. Thus, investors would be getting a lower interest yield but higher expected capital gains. If the changes were made precisely so as to keep Equation 16–3 in balance, the package of expected interest plus expected capital gains could continue to equal 6.3 percent. Exactly that kind of logic is used when firms set the terms on convertibles.

| **Decisions on Use of Warrants and Convertibles** | The Winchester Company, an electronic circuit and component manufacturer with assets of $12 million, illustrates a typical case where convertibles are useful. |

Winchester's profits have been depressed as a result of its heavy expenditures on research and development for a new product. This situation has held down the growth rate of earnings and dividends; the price/earnings ratio is only 18 times, as compared with an industry average of 22. At the current $2 earnings per share and P/E of 18, the stock is selling for $36 a share. The Winchester family owns 70 percent of the 300,000 shares outstanding, or 210,000 shares. It would like to retain majority control but cannot buy more stock.

The heavy R & D expenditures have resulted in the development of a new type of printed circuit that management believes will be highly profitable. Five million dollars is needed to build and equip new production facilities, and profits will not start to flow into the company for some eighteen months after construction on the new plant is started. Winchester's debt amounts to $5.4 million, or 45 percent of assets, well above the 25 percent industry average. Present debt indenture provisions restrict the company from selling additional debt unless the new debt is subordinate to that now outstanding.

Investment bankers inform J. H. Winchester, Jr., the financial vice-president, that subordinated debentures cannot be sold unless they are convertible or have warrants attached. Convertibles or bonds with warrants can be sold with a 5 percent coupon interest rate if the conversion price or warrant option price is set at 15 percent above the present market price of $36, or at $41 a share. Alternatively, the investment bankers are willing to buy convertibles or bonds with warrants at a 5½ percent interest rate and a 20 percent conversion premium, or a conversion (or exercise) price of $43.50. If the company wants to sell common stock directly, it can net $33 a share.

Which of the alternatives should Winchester choose? First, note that if common stock is used, the company must sell 151,000 shares ($5 million divided by $33). Combined with the 90,000 shares held outside the family, this amounts to 241,000 shares versus the Winchester holdings of 210,000, so the family will lose majority control if common stock is sold.

If the 5 percent convertibles or bonds with warrants are used and the bonds are converted or the warrants are exercised, 122,000 new shares will be added. Combined with the old 90,000, the outside interest will then be 212,000, so again the Winchester family will lose majority control. However, if the 5½ percent convertibles or bonds with warrants are used, then after conversion or exercise only 115,000 new shares will be created. In this case the family will have 210,000 shares versus 205,000 for outsiders; absolute control will be maintained.

In addition to assuring control, using the convertibles or warrants also benefits earnings per share in the long run—the total number of shares is less because fewer new shares must be issued to get the $5 million, so earnings per share will be higher. Before conversion or exercise, however, the firm has a considerable amount of debt outstanding. Adding $5 million raises the total debt to $10.4 million against new total assets of $17 million, so the debt ratio will be over 61 percent versus the 25 percent industry average. This could be dangerous. If delays are encountered in bringing the new plant into production, if demand does not meet expectations, if the company should experience a strike, if the economy should go into a recession—if any of these things occur—the company will be extremely vulnerable because of the high debt ratio.

In the present case, the decision was made to sell the 5½ percent convertible debentures. Two years later, earnings climbed to $3 a share, the *P/E* ratio to 20, and the price of the stock to $60. The bonds were called, but, of course, conversion occurred. After conversion, debt amounted to approximately $5.5 million against total assets of $17.5 million (some earnings had been retained), so the debt ratio was down to a more reasonable 31 percent.

Convertibles were chosen rather than bonds with warrants for the following reason. If a firm has a high debt ratio and its near-term prospects are favorable, it can anticipate a rise in the price of its stock and thus be able to call the bonds and force conversion. Warrants, on the other hand, have a stated life, and even though the price of the firm's stock rises, the warrants may not be exercised until near their expiration date.[12] If, subsequent to the favorable period (during which convertibles could have been called), the firm encounters less favorable developments and the price of its stock falls, the warrants may lose their value and may never be exercised. The heavy debt burden will then become aggravated. Therefore, the use of convertibles gives the firm greater control over the timing of future capital structure changes. This

---

12. To our knowledge, no company has ever issued a "callable" warrant; that is, one that the issuer would call for exercise under specific conditions. We recently recommended to a company that it consider issuing perpetual, but callable, warrants. These could be called to force exercise if the price of the stock exceeded the exercise price by, say, 30 percent; they would otherwise have no expiration date. Such warrants would probably be viewed with favor by investors afraid of warrants that might expire valueless, and they would still give the company control over the warrants similar to that over convertibles.

factor is of particular importance to the firm if its debt ratio is already high in relation to the risks of its line of business.

Reporting Earnings if Convertibles or Warrants Are Outstanding

Before closing the chapter, we should note that firms with convertibles or warrants outstanding are required to report earnings per share in two ways: (1) *primary EPS*, which in essence is earnings available to common stock divided by the number of shares actually outstanding, and (2) *fully diluted EPS*, which shows what EPS would be if all warrants had been exercised or convertibles converted prior to the reporting date. For firms with large amounts of option securities outstanding, there can be a substantial difference between the two EPS figures. The purpose of the provision is, of course, to give investors a more accurate picture of the firm's true profit position.[13]

Summary

Both warrants and convertibles are forms of options used in financing business firms. The use of such long-term options is encouraged by an economic environment combining prospects of both boom or inflation and depression or deflation. The senior position of the securities protects against recessions. The option feature offers the opportunity for participation in rising stock prices.

Both the convertibility privilege and warrants are used as "sweeteners." The option privileges they grant may make it possible for small companies to sell debt or preferred stock that otherwise could not be sold. For large companies, the "sweeteners" result in lower costs of the securities sold. In addition, the options provide for the future sale of the common stock at prices higher than could be obtained at present. The options thereby permit the delayed sale of common stock at more favorable prices.

The conversion of bonds by their holders does not ordinarily bring additional funds to the company. The exercise of warrants will provide such funds. The conversion of securities will result in reduced debt ratios. The exercise of warrants will strengthen the equity position but will still leave the debt or preferred stock on the balance sheet. In comparing the use of convertibles to senior securities carrying warrants, a firm with a high debt ratio should choose convertibles. A firm with a moderate or low debt ratio may employ warrants.

13. For further analysis of the issues treated in this chapter, see E. F. Brigham, "An Analysis of Convertible Debentures: Theory and Some Empirical Evidence," *Journal of Finance* (March 1966).

In the past, larger and stronger firms tended to favor convertibles over bonds with warrants, so most warrants have been issued by smaller, weaker concerns. AT&T's use of warrants in its $1.57 billion 1970 financing has caused other large firms to reexamine their positions on warrants, and we anticipate that warrants will come into increasing use in the years ahead.

Questions

16–1. Why do warrants typically sell at prices greater than their formula values?

16–2. Why do convertibles typically sell at prices greater than their formula values (the higher of the conversion value or straight-debt value)? Would you expect the percentage premium on a convertible bond to be more or less than that on a warrant? (The percentage premium is defined as the market price minus the formula value, divided by the market price.)

16–3. What effect does the trend in stock prices (subsequent to issue) have on a firm's ability to raise funds (a) through convertibles and (b) through warrants?

16–4. If a firm expects to have additional financial requirements in the future, would you recommend that it use convertibles or bonds with warrants? Why?

16–5. How does a firm's dividend policy affect each of the following?
a. the value of long-term warrants
b. the likelihood that convertible bonds will be converted
c. the likelihood that warrants will be exercised

16–6. Evaluate the following statement: "Issuing convertible securities represents a means by which a firm can sell common stock at a price above the existing market."

16–7. Why do corporations often sell convertibles on a rights basis?

Problems

16–1. The Garnet Lumber Company's capital consists of 24,000 shares of common stock and 8,000 warrants, each good for buying three shares of common at $30 a share. The warrants are protected against dilution (that is, the subscription price is adjusted downward in the event of a stock dividend or if the firm sells common stock at less than the $30 exercise price). The company issues rights to buy one new share of common for $25 for every four shares. With the stock selling rights on at $35, compute:
a. The theoretical value of the rights before the stock sells ex-rights.
b. The new subscription price of the warrants after the rights issue.

16–2. The Ironhill Manufacturing Company was planning to finance an expansion in the summer of 1978. The principle executives of the company were agreed that an industrial company such as theirs should finance growth by means of common stock rather than debt. However, they felt the price of the company's common stock did not reflect its true worth, so they were desirous of selling a convertible security. They considered a convertible debenture but feared the burden of fixed interest charges if the common stock did not rise in price to make conversion attractive. They decided on an issue of convertible preferred stock.

The common stock was currently selling at $48 a share. Management projected earnings for 1979 at $3.60 a share and expected a future growth rate of 12 percent a year. It was agreed by the investment bankers and the management that the common stock would sell at 13.3 times earnings, the current price/earnings ratio.

a. What conversion price should be set by the issuer?

b. Should the preferred stock include a call price provision? Why?

16-3. Quality Photocopy, Inc., has the following balance sheet:

Balance Sheet 1

Current assets	$125,000	Current debt (free)	$ 50,000
Net fixed assets	125,000	Common stock, par value $2	50,000
		Retained earnings	150,000
Total assets	$250,000	Total claims	$250,000

a. The firm earns 18 percent on total assets before taxes (assume a 50 percent tax rate). What are earnings per share? Twenty-five thousand shares are outstanding.

b. If the price/earnings ratio for the company's stock is 16 times, what is the market price of the company's stock?

c. What is the book value of the company's stock?

In the following few years, sales are expected to double and the financing needs of the firm will double. The firm decides to sell debentures to meet these needs. It is undecided, however, whether to sell convertible debentures or debentures with warrants. The new balance sheet would appear as follows:

Balance Sheet 2

Current assets	$250,000	Current debt	$100,000
Net fixed assets	250,000	Debentures	150,000
		Common stock, par value $2	50,000
		Retained earnings	200,000
Total assets	$500,000	Total claims	$500,000

The convertible debentures would pay 7 percent interest and would be convertible into 40 shares of common stock for each $1,000 debenture. The debentures with warrants would carry an 8 percent coupon and entitle each holder of a $1,000 debenture to buy 25 shares of common stock at $50.

d. Assume that convertible debentures are sold and all are later converted. Show the new balance sheet, disregarding any changes in retained earnings.

Balance Sheet 3

	Current debt	_____
	Debentures	_____
	Common stock, par value $2	_____
	Paid-in capital	_____
	Retained earnings	_____
Total assets _____	Total claims	_____

e. Complete the firm's income statement after the debentures have all been converted:

Income Statement 1

Net income after all charges except debenture interest and before taxes (18% of total assets)	_____
Debenture interest	_____
Federal income tax, 50%	_____
Net income after taxes	_____
Earnings per share after taxes	_____

f. Now, instead of convertibles, assume that debentures with warrants were issued. Assume further that the warrants were all exercised. Show the new balance sheet figures.

Balance Sheet 4

	Current debt	_____
	Debentures	_____
	Common stock, par value $2	_____
	Paid-in capital	_____
	Retained earnings	_____
Total assets _____	Total claims	_____

g. Complete the firm's income statement after the debenture warrants have all been exercised.

Income Statement 2

Net income after all charges except debenture interest and before taxes	_____
Debenture interest	_____
Taxable income	_____
Federal income tax	_____
Net income after taxes	_____
Earnings per share after taxes	_____

16-4. The Printomat Company has grown rapidly during the past five years. Recently its commercial bank has urged the company to consider increasing permanent financing. Its bank loan under a line of credit has risen to $175,000, carrying 7 percent interest. Printomat has been 30 to 60 days late in paying trade creditors.

Discussions with an investment banker have resulted in the suggestion to raise $350,000 at this time. Investment bankers have assured the company that the following alternatives will be feasible (flotation costs will be ignored):

Alternative 1: Sell common stock at $7.

Alternative 2: Sell convertible bonds at a 7 percent coupon, convertible into common stock at $8.

Alternative 3: Sell debentures at a 7 percent coupon, each $1,000 bond carrying 125 warrants to buy common stock at $8.

Additional information is given below.

Printomat Company Balance Sheet

		Current liabilities	$315,000
		Common stock, par $1.00	90,000
		Retained earnings	45,000
Total assets	$450,000	Total liabilities and capital	$450,000

Printomat Company Income Statement

Sales	$900,000
All costs except interest	810,000
Gross profit	$ 90,000
Interest	10,000
Profit before taxes	$ 80,000
Taxes at 50%	40,000
Profits after taxes	$ 40,000
Shares	90,000
Earnings per share	$0.44
Price/earnings ratio	17 ×
Market price of stock	$7.48

Larry Anderson, the president, owns 70 percent of the common stock of Printomat Company and wishes to maintain control of the company. Ninety thousand shares are outstanding.

a. Show the new balance sheet under each alternative. For alternatives 2 and 3, show the balance sheet after conversion of the debentures or exercise of warrants. Assume that one-half the funds raised will be used to pay off the bank loan and one-half to increase total assets.

b. Show Anderson's control position under each alternative, assuming that he does not purchase additional shares.

c. What is the effect on earnings per share of each alternative, if it is assumed that profits before interest and taxes will be 20 percent of total assets?

d. What will be the debt ratio under each alternative?

e. Which of the three alternatives would you recommend to Anderson and why?

16–5. Continental Chemical Company is planning to raise $25 million by selling convertible debentures. Its stock is currently selling for $50 per share ($P_0 = \$50$). The stock price has grown in the past, and is expected to grow in the future, at the rate of 5 percent per year. Continental's current dividend is $3 per share, so investors appear to have an expected (and required) rate of return of 11 percent ($k = D/P_0 + g = \$3/\$50 + 5\%$) on investments as risky as the company's common stock.

Continental recently sold nonconvertible debentures that yield 7 percent. Investment bankers have informed the treasurer that he can sell convertibles at a lower interest yield, offering him these two choices:

A. $P_c = \$55.55$ (# = 18)
   $C = \$60$ (6% coupon yield)
   $M = \$1,000$
   25-year maturity

B. $P_c = \$62.50$ (# = 16)
   $C = \$65$ (6½% coupon yield)
   $M = \$1,000$
   25-year maturity

In either case, the bonds are not callable for two years; they are callable thereafter at $1,000; investors do not expect the bonds to be called unless $C_t = \$1,266$; but investors do expect the bonds to be called if $C_t = \$1,266$.

a. Determine the expected yield on bond A; that on bond B is 8.5%.

b. Do the terms offered by the investment bankers seem consistent? Which bond would an investor prefer? Which would Continental's treasurer prefer?

c. Suppose the company decided on bond A, but wanted to step up the conversion price from $55.55 to $58.82 after 10 years. Should this stepped-up conversion price affect the expected yield on the bonds and the other terms on the bonds?

d. Suppose, contrary to investors' expectations, Continental called the bonds after two years. What would the *ex post* effective yield be on bond A? Would this early call affect the company's credibility in the financial markets?

e. Sketch out a rough graph similar to Figure 16–3 for Continental. Use the graph to illustrate what would happen to the wealth position of an investor who bought Continental bonds the day before the announcement of the unexpected two-year call.

f. Suppose the expected yield on the convertible had been less than that on straight debt (actually, it was higher). Would this appear logical? Explain.

16–6. The Seaboard Development Company plans to sell a 5 percent coupon, 25-year convertible bond on January 1, 1978, for $1,000. The bond is callable at $1,050 in the first year, and the call price declines by $2 each year thereafter. The bond may be converted into 14 shares of stock that now (January 1, 1977) sells for $60 per share. The stock price is expected to increase at a rate of 4 percent each year. Nonconvertible bonds with the same degree of risk would yield 7 percent. Investors expect Seaboard to call the convertibles if and when the conversion value exceeds the call price by 20 percent.

a. Graph a model that represents investors' expectations for the bond. Include as points on the graph B_0 and B_5; C_0, C_5, and C_{10}; and the call price at $t = 0$ and $t = 5$. Approximate the other points, and also the market price line.

b. What rate of return do investors appear to be expecting on the bond? Is this expected rate reasonable in view of the rate on Seaboard's straight (nonconvertible) bonds? If not, what does this suggest about (i) probable success of the issue, (ii) the wisdom of the company's use of convertibles with the terms given above, and (iii) possible changes in the terms if your answer to (i) is that the bonds would probably not sell?

16–7. Inspiration Enterprises plans to issue convertible debt. The terms of the 10-year bonds have been tentatively set at 6 percent interest with a 15 percent conversion premium. However, if management will accept a 10 percent premium, interest can be reduced to 4.5 percent. Alternatively for only three-fourths of one percent more interest the conversion premium can be raised to 20 percent.

a. What would be the net present value of the decrease or increase in interest expense for one $1,000 bond? Inspiration is in a 50 percent tax bracket and the cost of capital is 12 percent.

b. The current stock price is $25 per share. Determine the value of the differences from the 15 percent conversion premium.

c. Discuss the implications of parts (a) and (b).

16–8. The Piper Company plans to issue convertible debt with a 5 percent coupon and $1,000 par value. The convertible will have a five-year life, but management hopes that future developments will make it advantageous to call the issue at an earlier date.

a. Straight debt with equal risk, coupon, and maturity is selling with a market rate of interest of 8 percent. Determine the straight debt value at time equal zero, and at the end of years one and two. Use these three points plus the maturity value to graph the straight debt value of the convertible.

b. At time zero the conversion value of the bond is $790 since initial price of the common stock is $79 and the conversion ratio is 10. The stock is expected to appreciate at a rate of 15.0% per year. Graph the conversion value of the bond (C_t) on the same graph.

c. What is the minimum price the convertible can sell for at year zero, one, two, and three, assuming the stock value increases as predicted?

d. Assume that the bond is expected to be called when the conversion value of the bond reaches 120 percent of par value, and that the bonds sell originally at par value. On the graph, locate the maturity conversion value (M') on C_t and draw a curve between the issue price (M) and M' with curvature similar to C_t.

e. In what year is the debt expected to be called?

f. Assume the call price at year zero is $1,050, decreasing by $10 per year. Show the call price of debt on the same graph. What would the debt holders do if the bond was called at year one, two, or three?

g. What return on their investment is earned by purchasers of the convertible bonds at their issuance if the bonds are called in three years?

Selected References

Bacon, Peter W., and Winn, Edward L., Jr. "The Impact of Forced Conversion on Stock Prices." *Journal of Finance* 24 (Dec. 1969):871–74.

Baumol, William J.; Malkiel, Burton G.; and Quandt, Richard E. "The Valuation of Convertible Securities." *Quarterly Journal of Economics* 80 (Feb. 1966): 48–59.

Black, Fischer. "Fact and Fantasy in the Use of Options." *Financial Analysts Journal* 31 (July–Aug. 1975):36–41.

Black, Fischer, and Scholes, Myron. "The Valuation of Option Contracts and a Test of Market Efficiency." *Journal of Finance* 27 (May 1972):399–417.

Bond, F. M. "Yields on Convertible Securities: 1969–1974." *The Journal of Business Finance & Accounting* 3 (Summer 1976): 93–114.

Brigham, Eugene F. "An Analysis of Convertible Debentures: Theory and Some Empirical Evidence." *Journal of Finance* 21 (Mar. 1966):35–54.

Chen, Andrew H. Y. "A Model of Warrant Pricing in a Dynamic Market." *Journal of Finance* 25 (Dec. 1970):1041–59.

Cretien, Paul D., Jr. "Premiums on Convertible Bonds: Comment." *Journal of Finance* 25 (Sept. 1970):917–22.

Dawson, Steven M. "Timing Interest Payments for Convertible Bonds." *Financial Management* 3 (Summer 1974): 14–16.

Duvel, David Tell. "Premiums on Convertible Bonds: Comment." *Journal of Finance* 25 (Sept. 1970):923–27.

Frank, Werner G., and Kroncke, Charles. "Classifying Conversions of Convertible Debentures Over Four Years." *Financial Management* 3 (Summer 1974): 33–42.

Frank, Werner G., and Weygandt, Jerry J. "Convertible Debt and Earnings Per Share: Pragmatism vs. Good Theory." *Accounting Review* 45 (Apr. 1970): 280–89.

Frankle, A. W., and Hawkins, C. A. "Beta Coefficients for Convertible Bonds." *Journal of Finance* 30 (Mar. 1975), 207–10.

Hayes, Samuel L., III. "New Interest in Incentive Financing." *Harvard Business Review* 44 (July–Aug. 1966):99–112.

Hettenhouse, G. W., and Puglisi, D. J. "Investor Experience with Options." *Financial Analysts' Journal* 31 (July–Aug. 1975):53–58.

Horrigan, James O. "Some Hypotheses on the Valuation of Stock Warrants." *Journal of Business Finance & Accounting* 1 (Summer 1974):239–47.

Pilcher, C. James. *Raising Capital with Convertible Securities.* Ann Arbor, Mich.: Bureau of Business Research, University of Michigan, 1955.

Pinches, George E. "Financing with Convertible Preferred Stocks, 1960–1967." *Journal of Finance* 25 (Mar. 1970):53–64.

Poensgen, Otto H. "The Valuation of Convertible Bonds." Parts I and II. *Industrial Management Review* 6 and 7 (Fall 1965 and Spring 1966):77–92 and 83–98.

Reback, Robert. "Risk and Return in Option Trading" *Financial Analysts' Journal* 31 (July–Aug. 1975):42–52.

Rush, David F., and Melicher, Ronald W. "An Empirical Examination of Factors Which Influence Warrant Prices." *Journal of Finance* 29 (Dec. 1974):1449–66.

Samuelson, Paul A., and Merton, Robert C. "A Complete Model of Warrant Pricing That Maximizes Utility." *Industrial Management Review* 10 (Winter 1969):17–46.

Schwartz, Eduardo S. "The Valuation of Warrants: Implementing a New Approach." *Journal of Financial Economics* 4 (Jan. 1977):79–94.

Shelton, John P. "The Relation of the Price of a Warrant to the Price of its Associated Stock." *Financial Analysts' Journal* 23 (May–June and July–Aug. 1967): 143–51 and 88–99.

Smith, C. W. "Option Pricing; A Review." *Journal of Financial Economics* 3 (Jan.–Mar. 1976):3–52.

Soldofsky, Robert M. "Yield-Rate Performance of Convertible Securities." *Financial Analysts' Journal* 27 (Mar.–Apr. 1971):61–65.

Sprecher, C. Ronald. "A Note on Financing Mergers with Convertible Preferred Stock." *Journal of Finance* 26 (June 1971):683–86.

Stone, Bernell K. "Warrant Financing." *Journal of Financial and Quantitative Analysis* 11 (Mar. 1976):143–54.

Walter, James E., and Que, Agustin V. "The Valuation of Convertible Bonds." *Journal of Finance* 28 (June 1973):713–32.

Weil, Roman L., Jr.; Segall, Joel E.; and Green, David, Jr. "Premiums on Convertible Bonds." *Journal of Finance* 23 (June 1968):445–64.

———. "A Reply to Premiums on Convertible Bonds: Comment." *Journal of Finance* 25 (Sept. 1970):931–33.

Appendix A to Chapter 16
The Option Pricing Model (OPM)

Introduction to Options

Options are contracts that give their holder the right to buy (or sell) an asset at a predetermined price, called the striking or exercise price, for a given period of time. For example, on December 6, 1976, a call option on Dow Chemical common stock gave its holder the right to buy one share of common at an exercise price of $45 until July 1977. The price of a share of Dow was $39½ and the call option sold for $1.75. This would be referred to as an out-of-the-money option because the exercise price was more than the current price of the common stock. An in-the-money option has an exercise price that is less than the current price of the common stock. An option to buy the Dow common stock at $35 when the common was selling at $39½ would be an in-the-money option; it would sell for (39½ − 35) = $4½ plus the premium of about $1.75, or at about $6.25.

In recent years models for pricing options (OPM) have been derived, which enable us to treat the variables discussed in Chapter 16 and in Appendix A16 with numerical solutions.[1] These models are applicable to a wide range of option-type contracts, including warrants and convertibles discussed in Chapter 16.

The considerable increase in interest in options and option pricing has been associated with the development of new options markets and important new theoretical developments. In April 1973, organized trading in call options began on the Chicago Board Options Exchange (CBOE), followed by call option trading on the American Stock Exchange (AMEX options). The path-breaking paper by Fischer Black and Myron Scholes appeared at about the same time. In addition to deriving the general equilibrium option pricing equation as well as conducting empirical tests, Black and Scholes suggested other implications of option pricing that have significance for many other important aspects of business finance.

Black and Scholes observed that option pricing principles can be used to value other complex contingent claim assets such as the equity of a

---

1. F. Black and M. Scholes, "The Pricing of Options and Corporate Liabilities," *Journal of Political Economy* 81 (May/June 1973), pp. 637–54; Black and Scholes, "The Valuation of Option Contracts and a Test of Market Efficiency," *Journal of Finance* 27 (May 1972), pp. 399–417; R. C. Merton, "Theory of Rational Option Pricing," *Bell Journal* 4 (Spring 1973), pp. 141–83.

levered firm. From this viewpoint, the shareholders of a firm have a call that gives them the right to buy back the firm from the bondholders by paying the face value of the bonds at maturity or exercising other alternatives for buying the bonds. A number of important applications of the option pricing model were then made. As observed by Clifford Smith in his comprehensive review article,[2] "the model is also applied by Merton (1974) to analyze the effects of risk on the value of corporate debt; by Galai and Masulis (1976) to examine the effect of mergers, acquisitions, scale expansions, and spin-offs on the relative values of the debt and equity claims of the firm; by Ingersoll (1976) to value the shares of dual purpose funds; and by Black (1976) to value commodity options, forward contracts, and future contracts" (p. 5).

Because of the large number of additional areas on which the option pricing models provide new insights, it is useful to develop an understanding of the basic ideas involved. First, some of the fundamental characteristics of the use of options will be developed. Second, some of the basic relationships will be developed in an intuitive way as a background for the presentation and application of the Black and Scholes option pricing model.

The Use of Call Options

The underlying nature of options can be explained most concretely by comparing four alternative strategies with regard to gains or losses from fluctuations in the price of the stock. Consider 100 shares of stock whose current price is $50 per share. The results of four alternative investment positions is depicted in Figure A16–1. If an investor buys the stock and holds it (has a long position in the stock), he gains or loses if the stock increases or decreases in price. For a $10 rise or fall in the stock price, the investor gains or loses $10 per share or plus or minus 20%. (Brokerage costs, taxes, and other factors not central to the main issues under analysis here are not taken into consideration.) This is a simple relationship that is used as the benchmark for comparison with the other possible strategies.

Next we consider the alternative of buying a call that gives an option to buy the stock at $50 for six months. A rough indication of the price (a pricing formula is presented later) would be $300 for the call or $3 per share of the 100 shares of stock under consideration. Assume that the stock rises to $60 near the end of the six-month period. The value of the call would be $10 since it enables a purchase of a share of stock worth

---

2. Clifford W. Smith, Jr., "Option Pricing; A Review," *Journal of Financial Economics* 3 (Jan/March 1976), pp. 3–51.

Figure A16–1
Results for Alternative
Investment Positions

(1) Long in stock

(2) Buy a call

(3) Sell a naked call

(4) Sell a covered call

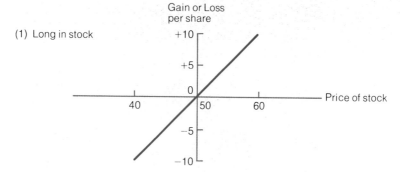
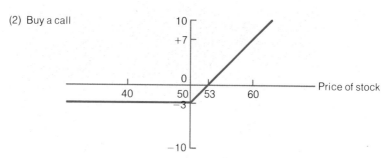
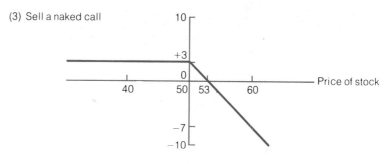
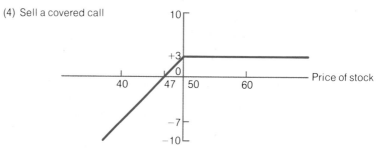

$60 for $50. (As will be shown in the option pricing formula, since we have assumed that this opportunity becomes available only just before the end of the sixth-month option period, very little premium will be added to the difference between the stock value (S) and the exercise price of the call (X_0). The net gain will be the $10 less the price paid for the call of $3, which equals $7. If the stock declines by $10, the holder of the option would simply not exercise it. He would lose the $3 per share he had paid for the call. Treating the $3 as the investment, the buyer of the call either gains 233% or loses 100%.

A third position is that a call is sold without owning the stock (a naked call). The seller would receive the $3 (the brokerage house will hold the $300 and will require additional deposits if the stock declines in value). If the stock increases in price to $60 just before the end of the expiration of the call option, the option will be worth $10. To supply the stock or to balance off his option position will cost the seller of the naked option $10, so he has lost $7 net. If the stock declines in value to $40, the option will have no value and the seller has netted $3.

The percentage gain or loss cannot be meaningfully calculated since it will depend upon how the investment position of the seller of the naked option is defined. Should it be an estimate of some contingent liability which he has? Or shall we infer some estimate of his investment worth, which enables him to trade in naked options? Since there is no clear number for his investment position, we shall not attempt to measure his percentage gain or loss. We can observe that his upside gain is limited to the selling price of the option. However, there is no downside limit on his loss since the rising price of the stock will increase the price of the option he would have to buy to balance the options he has sold or increase without limit the price of the stock he would have to buy to satisfy the call he has sold. Obviously, one would not sell a naked call unless he judged that the probability of a decline in the price of the stock was very high.

The fourth and final position we consider is the sale of a covered call by an investor who already owns the 100 shares of the stock (the sale of a covered call). Since he already owns the stock, we may view the sale of the call as a sale of the stock at $53 if the price of the stock rises to $60 or a shift in his investment basis for the stock to $47 if the price of the stock declines to $40. Thus a rise in the price of the stock to $60 represents a 6 percent gain and a decline to $40 represents a 14 percent loss.

Each of the four alternative strategies is depicted graphically in Figure A16-1. The results of the four strategies are summarized in Table A16-1. Buying a call greatly magnifies the possible percentage gains and losses. Selling a naked call results in a pattern that is a mirror image of buying a call. Selling a covered call limits the upside percentage gain and reduces somewhat the downside percentage loss. Note that since the seller of a naked call is hurt most by a substantial rise in the price of the stock and the seller of a covered call is hurt most by a substantial decline in the price of the stock, divergent views of the price prospects of the stock may still result in the sale of calls on the stock. Thus transactions in calls may magnify gains or losses or dampen gains or losses, depending upon the position of the investor and the strategy that he elects to follow.

Table A16–1
Results of Four
Alternative
Investment
Strategies Involving
Options

	Gain or (loss) Per Share with Change in Stock Price			
	Stock Price Increases by $10		Stock Price Decreases by $10	
	Amount	Percent	Amount	Percent
1. Long in stock	$10	20%	($10)	(20%)
2. Buy a call	$ 7	233%	($ 3)	(100%)
3. Sell a naked call	($ 7)	*	$ 3	*
4. Sell a covered call	$ 3	6%	($ 7)	(14%)

*Depends upon the definition of the "investment" made.

Basic Price Relations

With this background on the mechanics of option trading and its implications, we can begin the analysis of the determinants of option prices. An intuitive approach to option pricing is to consider the terminal call price under certainty.[3] Let C^* be the terminal call price, S^* be the terminal stock price, and X_0 the exercise price of the option. The following relationship will obtain:

$$C^* = S^* - X_0$$

This is similar to the simple warrant formula. The call price will be equal to the difference between the stock price and the exercise price, or zero if the exercise price is greater than the stock price. Thus if the terminal stock price just before the expiration of a call is $60 and the exercise price of the option is $50, the terminal call price, C^*, will be $10. In an equilibrium world of certainty, the return to all assets is equal to the rate, r. Hence the terminal values of the stock price and option price may be written:

$$S_0^* = S_0 e^{rt} \quad \text{and} \quad C_0^* = C_0 e^{rt}$$

Substituting, we have

---

3. Based on the presentation in Clifford W. Smith, Jr., "Option Pricing."

$$C_0 e^{rt^*} = e^{rt^*} S_0 - X_0$$
$$C_0 = e^{-rt^*} [e^{rt^*} S_0 - X_0]$$
$$C_0 = e^{-rt^*} e^{rt^*} S_0 - e^{-rt^*} X_0$$
$$C_0 = S_0 - e^{-rt^*} X_0$$

Thus the value of a call is equal to the price of the stock less the exercise price discounted at r over the time of its remaining maturity period. This expression differs from the Black-Scholes pricing equation only in the multiplication of each of the terms on the right-hand side of the equation, S_0 and X_0, by probability factors. These probability terms reflect the uncertainty about the terminal prices of the stock. With this background, we can now turn to the Black-Scholes option pricing model.

Calculations of Options Values

In the Black-Scholes model, the derivation is based on the creation of a perfect hedge by simultaneously being long (short) in the underlying security and holding an opposite, short (long) position on a number of options. The return on a completely hedged position will then be equal to the risk-free return on the investment in order to eliminate arbitrage opportunities. A call option that can be exercised only at some future maturity date[4] can then be evaluated by the following expressions:

$$C_0 = S_0 N(\text{dist. } 1) - X_0 e^{-R_F t^*} N (\text{dist. } 2) \qquad \text{(A16–1)}$$

$$\text{dist. } 1 = \frac{ln(S_0/X_0) + [R_F + (\sigma^2/2)] t^*}{\sigma\sqrt{t^*}} \qquad \text{(A16–2)}$$

$$\text{dist. } 2 = \text{dist. } 1 - \sigma\sqrt{t^*} \qquad \text{(A16–3)}$$

where:

C_0 = the option price or value of the option
S_0 = current value of the underlying asset
X_0 = the exercise or striking price of the option
$N(\cdot)$ = the standardized normal cumulative probability density function
R_F = the riskless interest rate
σ^2 = the instantaneous rate of variance of percentage returns
t^* = time to maturity or duration of the option.

---

4. This is called a "European Option." It is not unnatural to use a formula for the value of a European call option that can be exercised only at the maturity data of the option. Merton, in a purely probabilistic formulation for nondividend paying stocks, demonstrated that it is always advantageous to delay exercising a call option until the latest possible date, its maturity.

The application of these expressions follows readily from the material we have previously set forth in Appendix A to Chapter 11.[5] For example, the $N(\cdot)$ expressions were treated in Table A11–3 and the corresponding Figure A11–4, both dealing with cumulative probability distributions. Some specific numerical examples will illustrate the application of equations A16–1 through A16–3.

Suppose we are valuing a warrant to purchase a share of common stock. The following facts could be directly observed or estimated from market data:

$S_0 = \$10$
$X_0 = \$10$
$t^* = 4$ years
$R_F = 6\%$
$\sigma^2 = 9\%$

The value of S could be read from the financial quotation page of a current newspaper. X_0 and t^*, the exercise price of a warrant and its maturity, respectively, are shown on the face of the warrant certificate. The risk-free rate can be estimated from the rates on short term U.S. treasury bills. The rate of variance can be estimated by taking the daily prices of the stock for one year, from which a variance of prices could be calculated.[6] We can now proceed to make the calculations as shown in equations A16–1a, A16–2a, and A16–3a.

$$C_0 = 10\ N(\text{dist. 1}) - 10e^{-.06(4)}\ N(\text{dist. 2}) \tag{A16–1a}$$

$$\text{dist. }1 = \frac{ln(10/10) + [.06 + (.09/2)]4}{.3(2)} \tag{A16–2a}$$

$$= \frac{(.105)4}{.6} = .7$$

$$\text{dist. }2 = .7 - .3(2) = .1 \tag{A16–3a}$$
$$C_0 = 10(.758) - 10(.787)(.5398)$$
$$= 7.58 - 4.25$$
$$C_0 = \$3.33$$

5. Equations A16–1 through A16–3 can also be combined into one equation:

$$C_0 = S_0 \cdot N\left[\frac{ln(S_0/X_0) + (r + \sigma^2/2)t^*}{\sigma\sqrt{t^*}}\right] - e^{-rt^*}X_0 N\left[\frac{ln(S_0/X_0) + (r - \sigma^2/2)t^*}{\sigma\sqrt{t^*}}\right]$$

6. The model presented here assumes no dividend payments, so that dividends would be ignored in calculating the variance of the percentage value changes. This is precisely correct for non-cash-dividend paying stocks but only approximately correct for others.

First, we calculate the value of the cumulative distribution function as shown in A16–2a. It should be noted that the logarithm is the natural logarithm. The *ln* of 10/10 or 1, the first term in the numerator, is zero. The value of dist. 1 is found to be .7. We use Table C on page 995 and find the value of .7 in the z column. We find a value of .2580. This represents the shaded area in Figure A16–2.

Figure A16–2
Graph of an Appendix
Table C Value

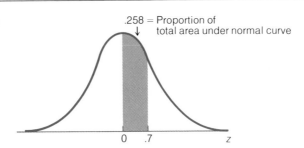

.258 = Proportion of
total area under normal curve

0 .7   z

Since the formula calls for the cumulative distribution, we add the total area under the left-hand tail of the distribution, which has a value of .5000 exactly. Thus the value of dist. 1 equals .758, which is used in A16–1a. Because dist. 2 is related to dist. 1 by a simple relationship, we place .7 in A16–2a to obtain a dist. 2 value of .1. In Table C on p. 995, we find a value of .0398 to which we add .5 to obtain .5398 to use in A16–1a.

The evaluation of the $e^{-.06(4)}$ term involves continuous compounding. In Appendix A to Chapter 9 we described how the Table A9–1 of natural logarithms could be used to perform continuous compounding. Looking in Table A9–1 for .24 and interpolating, we obtain 1.27125 for the future sum. We take the reciprocal to obtain the present value factor of .786628 or .787 used in A16–1a.[7] Performing the remaining calculations, we obtain $3.33 for the option price.

Next let us assume that the current price of the stock is $20 rather than $10. We now utilize equations A16–1b, A16–2b, and A16–3b.

$$\text{dist. } 1 = \frac{ln(20/10) + .42}{.6} = \frac{.693 + .42}{.6} = 1.85 \qquad \textbf{(A16–2b)}$$

7. We could obtain an approximate result by using Table C–2 for the present value factors with annual compounding.

$$\text{dist. } 2 = 1.85 - .6 = 1.25 \tag{A16-3b}$$

$$C_0 = 20 \, N(\text{dist. 1}) - 10e^{-.06\,(4)} \, N(\text{dist. 2}) \tag{A16-1b}$$
$$C_0 = 20(.968) - 10(.787)(.8940)$$
$$C_0 = \$12.32$$

Proceeding as described before, we now obtain \$12.32 as the value of the option. Thus we are enabled to derive the relationship for the predicted market value of the option as depicted in Figure 16–1. We will utilize another set of data to derive the values shown in Table A16–2 to develop the lines shown in Figure A16–3 for the indicated market price of a warrant as a function of the following key variables:

S_0—the price of the stock varies from \$10 to \$40
t^*—duration of the warrant of 4 to 9 years
X_0—exercise price of \$20.

Table A16–2 Relations Between the Values of an Option for a Range of Values of Stock Price and Option Maturity*	−1− t^*	−2− $V	−3− % Change	−4− N(dist. 1)	−5− N(dist. 2)	−6− C_0	−7− % Change	−8− Ratio, Percent Change in Option Price to Percent Change in Stock Price
	4	2		.0000†	.0000†	\$ 0.00†		
	4	10		.3246	.1457	0.93		
	4	20	100	.7580	.5398	6.67	617	6.2
	4	30	50	.9155	.8085	14.74	121	2.4
	4	40	33	.9677	.8940	24.64	67	2.0
	4	60	50	.9943	.9732	44.35	80	1.6
	9	10		.6103	.2676	\$ 2.98		
	9	20	100	.8531	.5590	10.54	354	3.5
	9	30	50	.9332	.7257	19.54	85	1.7
	9	40	33	.9656	.8212	29.05	49	1.5
	9	60	50	.9884	.9147	48.64	67	1.3

*For $C_0 = \$20$, $R_F = .06$ and $\sigma^2 = .09$.
†These values approach zero.

Factors Influencing Options Values

A number of relationships can be observed from the patterns in Table A16–2 and Figure A16–3. The higher the price of the stock, the greater the value of the option for fixed values of the other variables. The longer the maturity of the option, the higher its value. Line A represents the maximum value of the option, since it cannot be worth more than the stock. Line B represents the minimum value of the option, corresponding to the formula value of the warrant given in Figure 16–1 of Chapter

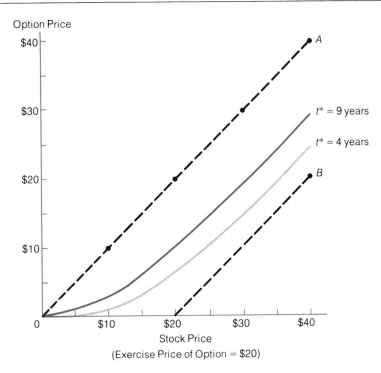

Figure A16–3
The Relation between Option Value and Stock Price for a Given Exercise Price of the Option

(Exercise Price of Option = $20)

16. Its value cannot be negative and will be no less than the formula value of an option given on page 581 of Chapter 16.

The longer the maturity of the option, the closer it moves toward Line A, its maximum value. Conversely, the shorter the maturity of a warrant the closer it moves toward its minimum value, Line B. In Chapter 16 in Figure 16–1, the market price of the TPA warrants is shown to be close to the formula value of a warrant that corresponds to Line B of Figure A16–3. Hence it is likely that the remaining maturity of the TPA warrants must be relatively short.

When the stock price is substantially higher than the exercise price, the option will have a high value and is almost certain to be exercised. The value of the option we have been computing can also be approximated by calculating the current price of a pure discount bond with a face value equal to the exercise price of the option and a maturity equal to the maturity of the option.[8] This current price is deducted from the

8. For an explanation see Black and Scholes, "The Pricing of Options," p. 638.

current stock value to give the value of the option. For example, for a current stock value of $60 and an option maturity of four years,

$$C_0 = 60 - 20e^{-.24} = 60 - 20(.7866) = 60 - 15.73 = 44.27.$$

This result for the value of the option differs only slightly from the result of $44.35 we obtained using the option pricing model (OPM). The option has a high value and is likely to be exercised. On the other hand, if the price of the stock is considerably less than the exercise price of the option, such as the $2 value in Table A16–2, the option will have no value and will be likely to expire without being exercised.

We observe also that the curves depicting the value of an option as the stock price varies are concave from above and lie below the 45° line drawn from the origin (line A). For an option of given maturity, any percentage change in the stock price will result in a larger percentage change in the option value. This is demonstrated by the percentage change columns in Table A16–2 and by the final column of Table A16–2, which presents the ratio of the percent change in the option price to the percent change in the stock price. For the longer maturity, the volatility of the option price is reduced somewhat. Also, at higher stock prices for a given maturity, the volatility of the option prices relative to the stock price changes is reduced.

Thus the use of the option pricing models enables us to observe some fundamental patterns in the relationships between stock prices and the related option values. These relationships depend upon the level of stock prices, the duration and exercise price of the option, the risk-free interest rate, and the variance of the percentage returns on the stock values.

The Pricing of Corporate Securities

The option pricing model also provides us with additional insights on the nature of debt and equity in a firm.[9] Since the debt has a maturity, the equity of a firm can be regarded as a European call option on the total value of the firm. The shareholders of the firm have an option to buy back the firm from the bondholders at an exercise price equal to the face value of the bonds at time N, the maturity date of the bonds. If the value of the firm, V_N, is above the face value of the bonds, the equity will have a positive value. If the value of the firm is below the face value of

9. R. C. Merton, "On the Pricing of Corporate Debt: The Risk Structure of Interest Rates," *Journal of Finance* 29 (May 1974), pp. 449–70; D. D. Galai and R. W. Masulis, "The Option Pricing Model and the Risk Factor of Stock," *Journal of Financial Economics* 3 (1976), pp. 53–81.

the bonds, the value of the equity is zero, but it cannot become negative because of the limited liability nature of the equity. The limited liability feature of corporate equity helps explain why the corporate form has facilitated raising large amounts of equity funds. The shareholders have protection against a decline in the firm's value below C_0 (the face value of the bonds, the option exercise price) and have a right to the differential in the firm's value above C_0.

The OPM enables us to price out the value of the equity, given the value of the debt, or C_0, the option exercise price. It also enables us to analyze the effect of the riskiness of the firm's investment or production programs (the firm's degree of operating leverage) on the interests and positions of the shareholders in relationship to the creditors. A numerical example will illustrate the ideas involved.

Let us begin by pricing the value of the equity. Assume the following: The current value of the firm, V_0 is $3,000,000; the face value of the debt, C_0, is $1,000,000, and has a remaining maturity of four years. The variance of the percentage returns on the value of the firm (σ^2) is .01 and R_F is equal to 5 percent. By using the OPM we can calculate the indicated market value of the firm's equity, S_0. First we calculate the two distribution functions:

$$\text{dist. } 1 = \frac{ln3 + (.05 + .005)4}{.1(2)} = \frac{1.0986 + .22}{.2} = \frac{1.3186}{.2} = 6.593$$

$N(\text{dist. } 1) \cong 1$
dist. $2 = 6.593 - .2 = 6.393$
$N(\text{dist. } 2) \cong 1$

Second, we calculate the value of the common stock:

$$S_0 = \$3,000,000(1) - 1,000,000(1)e^{-.2} = 3,000,000 - 818,731$$
$$S_0 = \$2,181,000$$

Given that the value of the firm is $3,000,000 and the calculated value of the equity shares is $2,181,000, the indicated market value of the debt is $818,731. We can now investigate the effects of the firm's changing the riskiness of its investment program. Assume that the firm takes on more risky investments so that the variance rises to a .16 level. We can now recalculate the values of the equity and debt under the assumption that the value of the firm remains at $3,000,000. We begin with the distribution functions:

$$\text{dist. } 1 = \frac{(1.0986) + (.05 + .08)4}{.4(2)} = \frac{1.0986 + .52}{.8} = \frac{1.6186}{.8} = 2.0233$$

$N(\text{dist. } 1) = .9785$
dist. $2 = 2.0233 - .8 = 1.2233$
$N(\text{dist. } 2) = .8894$

We can next calculate the value of the equity in the firm by the OPM.

$$S_0 = \$3,000,000(.9785) - \$1,000,000(.8894)(.81873)$$
$$= 2,936,500 - 728,200$$
$$S_0 = 2,208,300$$

The market value of the debt therefore drops to $791,700. Hence, increasing the riskiness of the firm's production operations increases the value of the equity and reduces the value of the debt. Thus the OPM indicates some inherent divergence of interests between the shareholders and the creditors of the firm. Since the shareholders possess voting control of the firm, they may take actions that may be adverse to the interests of the creditors. It is for such reasons that various "me first" rules are written into the bond indentures representing restrictions on what the firm (through actions of the controlling group, the shareholders and its designated managerial group) may or may not do.[10] This is for the purpose of protecting the position of the creditors of the firm.

The OPM thus enables us to quantify a number of relations for which we formerly were unable to obtain solutions without making *ad hoc* assumptions about critical variables. In contrast the OPM model provides a logical and internally consistent framework for valuing options and pricing out corporate securities. In addition, all of the elements of the OPM model are measurable by marketplace data. Thus the OPM provides us with new insights on how to value options and new insights on the relative positions of the equity holders and the creditors of the firm. The OPM has been put to considerable practical applications by financial houses during recent years. In addition, it opens up new interesting theoretical paths, many of which remain to be explored fully, especially in the areas of further large-scale empirical testing of a number of aspects of the options pricing model.

Problems

A16-1. The common stock of Atom Sporting Goods, Inc., sells for $30 per share. Warrants to purchase the stock at a price of $20 are also available. The warrants have four years to maturity. The instantaneous variance of returns on the common stock is 4 percent. The risk-free rate is 5 percent.
  a. Using the option pricing model, determine the value of a warrant.
  b. What would be the value of the warrant if the maturity were nine years? Why does the value of the warrant change with the change in maturity?

10. Cf. E. F. Fama and M. H. Miller, *The Theory of Finance* (New York: Holt, Rinehart and Winston, 1972), pp. 150–70.

A16–2. Cold Water Land Development Company is currently valued at $10,000,000. Seventy-five percent of current value is the face value of debt, all of which will mature in four years. Because land sales is a volatile business, the variance of percentage returns is 64 percent. The risk-free rate is 6 percent.

    a. Determine the market value of the equity.

    b. Determine the market value of the debt.

    c. Should the equity holders exercise their option to acquire the firm from its creditors? Explain.

A16–3. Great Plains Distributing Company is currently valued at $10,000,000. Ten percent of current value is the face value of debt, all of which matures in four years. The variance of percentage returns is 64 percent. The risk-free rate is 6 percent.

    a. Determine the value of the equity.

    b. Determine the value of the debt.

    c. Should the equity holders exercise their option to acquire the firm from its creditors? Explain.

Selected References

Black, F. "The Pricing of Commodity Contracts." *Journal of Financial Economics* 3 (Jan.–Mar. 1976); 167–79.

Cox, J. C., and Ross, S. A. "The Valuation of Options for Alternative Stochastic Processes." *Journal of Financial Economics* 3 (Jan.–Mar. 1976):145–66.

———. "A Survey of Some New Results in Financial Option Pricing Policy." *Journal of Finance* 31 (May 1976); 383–402.

Galai, D., and Masulis, R. W. "The Option Pricing Model and the Risk Factor of Stock." *Journal of Financial Economics* 3 (Jan.–Mar. 1976):53–82.

Ingersoll, J. E. "A Theoretical and Empirical Investigation of the Dual Purpose Funds: An Application of Contingent-Claims Analysis." *Journal of Financial Economics* 3 (Jan.–Mar. 1976):83–124.

Latane, Henry A., and Rendleman, Richard J., Jr. "Standard Deviations of Stock Price Ratios Implied in Option Prices." *Journal of Finance* 31 (May 1976): 369–81.

Leabo, Dick A., and Rogalski, Richard J. "Warrant Price Movements and the Efficient Market Model." *Journal of Finance* 30 (Mar. 1975):163–77.

Merton, Robert C. "On the Pricing of Corporate Debt: The Risk Structure of Interest Rates." *Journal of Finance* 29 (May 1974):449–70.

———"Option Pricing When Underlying Stock Returns Are Discontinuous." *Journal of Financial Economics* 3 (Jan.–Mar. 1976):125–44.

Rubinstein, M. E. "The Valuation of Uncertain Income Streams and the Pricing of Options." *Bell Journal of Economics* 7 (Autumn 1976):407–25.

Scholes, Myron. "Taxes and the Pricing of Options." *Journal of Finance* 31 (May 1976):319–32.

Part V

Financial Structure and the Cost of Capital

In Part IV we examined the major sources and forms of long-term external capital, considering the market for long-term securities and the principal types of securities—common and preferred stocks, bonds, term loans, leases, convertibles, and warrants. We compared the advantages and disadvantages of these different instruments and considered some of the factors that financial managers keep in mind as they decide which form of financing to use at a specific time. Now, in Part V, we examine the long-term financing decision in a somewhat different manner, searching for the *optimal* financial structure, or the financial structure that simultaneously minimizes the firm's cost of capital and maximizes the market value of its common stock. As we shall see, financing decisions and investment decisions are interdependent—the optimal financing plan and the optimal level of investment must be determined simultaneously—so Part V also serves the important function of integrating the theory of capital budgeting and the theory of capital structure.

Part V contains four chapters: First, Chapter 17, Valuation and Rates of Return, examines the way risk and return interact to determine value. Next, Chapter 18, Financial Structure and the Use of Leverage, highlights the manner in which debt not only generally increases expected earnings, but also increases the firm's risk position. Chapter 19, The Cost of Capital, draws on the two preceding chapters to establish the firm's optimal capital structure as well as its cost of capital. Finally, in Chapter 20, Dividend Policy and Internal Financing, we analyze the decision of whether to pay out earnings in the form of dividends or to retain earnings for reinvestment in the business, and we show the interrelationship between capital budgeting and the cost of capital.

17 Valuation and Rates of Return[1]

One of the financial manager's principal goals is to maximize the value of his firm's stock; accordingly, an understanding of the way the market values securities is essential to sound financial management. Also, the rate of return concepts developed in this chapter are used extensively in Chapters 18 and 19, where we analyze the optimal capital structure and show how to calculate a marginal cost of capital for use in capital budgeting.

Definitions of Value

While it may be difficult to ascribe monetary returns to certain kinds of assets—works of art, for instance—the fundamental characteristic of business assets is that they give rise to income flows. Sometimes these flows are easy to determine and measure—the interest return on a bond is an example. At other times, the cash flows attributable to the asset must be estimated, as was done in Chapters 10 and 11 in the evaluation of projects. Regardless of the difficulties of measuring income flows, it is the prospective income from business assets that gives them value.

Liquidating Value versus Going-concern Value

Several different definitions of "value" exist in the literature and are used in practice, with different ones being appropriate at different times. The first distinction that must be made is that between liquidating value and going-concern value. *Liquidating value* is defined as the amount that could be realized if an asset or a group of assets (the entire assets of a firm, for example) are sold separately from the organization that has been using them. If the owner of a machine shop decides to retire, he might auction off his inventory and equipment, collect his accounts receivable, then sell his land and buildings to a grocery wholesaler for use as a warehouse. The sum of the proceeds from each category of assets would be the liquidating value of the assets. If his debts are subtracted from this amount, the difference would represent the liquidating value of his ownership in the business.

1. This chapter is relatively long and difficult, but quite important. Students should allow for this in their preparation schedules.

On the other hand, if the firm is sold as an operating business to a corporation or to another individual, the purchaser would pay an amount equal to the *going-concern value* of the company. If the going-concern value exceeds the liquidating value, the difference represents the value of the organization as distinct from the value of the assets.[2]

**Book Value
versus Market
Value**

We must also distinguish between *book value*, or the accounting value at which an asset is carried, and *market value*, the price at which the asset can be sold. If the asset in question is a firm, it actually has two market values — a liquidating value and a going-concern value. Only the higher of the two is generally referred to as *the* market value.

For stocks, an item of primary concern in this chapter, book value per share is the firm's total common equity — common stock, capital or paid-in surplus, and accumulated retained earnings — divided by shares outstanding. For a given firm, book value per share might be $50. The market value, which is what people will actually pay for a share of the stock, could be above or below the book value. Nuclear Research, for example, has a book value per share of $8.27 and a market value of $25.50; West Virginia Railroad, on the other hand, has a book value of $112.80 versus a market value of only $6.75. Nuclear Research's assets produce a high and rapidly growing earnings stream; West Virginia Railroad's assets are far less productive. Since market value is dependent upon earnings, while book value reflects historical cost, it is not surprising to find deviations between book and market values in a dynamic, uncertain world.

**Market Value
versus "Fair" or
"Reasonable"
Value**

The concept of a fair or reasonable value (sometimes called the "intrinsic" value) is widespread in the literature on stock market investments. Although the market value of a security is known at any given time, the security's fair value as viewed by different investors could differ. Graham, Dodd, and Cottle, in a leading investments text, define fair value as "that value which is justified by the facts; e.g., assets, earnings, dividends . . . The computed [fair] value is likely to change at least from year to year, as the factors governing that value are modified."[3]

Although Graham, Dodd, and Cottle develop this concept for security (that is, stock and bond) valuation, the idea is applicable to all business assets. What it involves, basically, is estimating the future net cash

---

2. Accountants have termed this difference "goodwill," but "organization value" would be a more appropriate description.

3. B. Graham; D. L. Dodd; and S. Cottle, *Security Analysis* (New York: McGraw-Hill, 1961), p. 28.

flows attributable to an asset; determining an appropriate capitalization, or discount, rate; and then finding the present value of the cash flows. This, of course, is exactly what was done in Chapters 9, 10 and 11, where the concept of reasonable value was developed for application in finding the present value of investment opportunities.

The procedure for determining an asset's value is known as the *capitalization-of-income method of valuation*. This is simply a fancy name for the present value of a stream of earnings, discussed at length in Chapter 9. *In going through the present chapter, keep in mind that value, or the price of securities, is exactly analogous to the present value of assets as determined in Chapters 10 and 11.* From this point on, whenever the word "value" is used, we mean the *present value* found by capitalizing expected future cash flows.

The Required Rate of Return

The first step in using the capitalization of income procedure is to establish the proper capitalization rate, or discount rate, for the security. *This rate is defined as the required rate of return, and it is the minimum rate of return necessary to induce investors to buy or hold the security.* For any given risky security, j, the expected rate of return, k_j, is equal to the riskless rate of interest, R_F, plus a risk premium, ρ_j (read "rho" of security):[4]

$$\bar{k}_j = R_F + \rho_j = R_F + (\bar{k}_M - R_F)\beta_j \tag{17-1}$$

Equation 17-1 is the security market line (SML), which specifies the relationship between risk and the expected rate of return.[5] One advantage of the use of the SML is that the components of risk can be identified and estimated from readily available published data. The risk premium is composed of two parts: the risk premium on the market as a whole and a risk measure for the individual security. The risk premium for the market as a whole is the amount by which the return on a broad market index such as the Standard and Poor's 500 stock index exceeds a risk-free return measured by the current yield on U.S. government se-

---

4. In Appendix E-11 the application of the capital asset pricing model to analyzing investment decisions under uncertainty was set forth. Here the application of the CAPM to the determination of the required rate of return on different types of securities and therefore to valuation questions is set forth.

5. Although not necessary to our use and application of the SML concepts, the interested reader can find a formal development of the SML relationships in Appendix E to Chapter 11 and a more intuitive development of its applications in Appendix A to the present chapter. These SML relationships are now standard in finance literature and in general use among financial firms such as Merrill, Lynch, the Wells Fargo Bank, and Value Line. The terms are now used in advertisements and discussions in the financial press such as the *Wall Street Journal*.

curities, which are free of default risk. The return on the market may be referred to as $\bar{k}_M$ so that the risk premium on the market is: $(\bar{k}_M - R_F)$.

$$\text{Market risk premium} = (\bar{k}_M - R_F) \tag{17–1a}$$

It can be demonstrated that the securities market pays a premium only for that part of the risk of a security that cannot be eliminated by diversification. Risk that cannot be diversified away is called systematic risk and is measured by the covariance of the returns on the individual security with the returns on the market portfolio. The systematic risk of a security, when normalized by the variance of the market returns, is referred to as the "beta" of the security. We have:

$$\beta_j = \frac{\text{Cov}(k_j, k_M)}{\text{Var}(k_M)}$$

where:

$$\beta_j = \text{the risk of an individual security } j$$
$$\text{Cov}(k_j, k_M) = \text{the covariance of the returns on the individual security}$$
$$\text{with the returns on the market}$$
$$\text{Var}(k_M) = \text{the variance of the returns on the market}$$

To illustrate the application of these concepts, we shall use some realistic magnitudes for each of the terms involved. The return on the market $(\bar{k}_M)$ has ranged from 9 percent to 13 percent; the variance of the returns on the market $[\text{Var}(k_M)]$ is about 1 percent; the risk-free rate (R_F) has ranged from about 5 percent to 7 percent. Using the mid-point of the ranges of values for the market returns for the risk-free rate we have:

$$(\bar{k}_M - R_F) = (.11 - .06) = .05 = 5\% \tag{17–1b}$$

The risk premium, ρ_j, is the product of the market risk premium times the risk of the individual security, β_j, which varies somewhat above and below 1.[6] Hence for a β_j of 1.2 the value of the risk premium, ρ_j, on the individual security j is:

$$\rho_j = (\bar{k}_M - R_F)\beta_j = (.11 - .06)1.2 = .06 = 6\%.$$

This indicates that 6 percent would be added to the risk-free return, R_F, to obtain an expected return of 12 percent on an individual security j. Note that the two measures, the risk-free return, R_F, and the market risk premium, $(\bar{k}_M - R_F)$, are economy-wide parameters. Thus we can

---

6. The covariance of the market returns with the market returns is its variance, so the beta of the market is $\text{Var}(k_M)/(\text{Var}(k_M))$, which equals 1. Normal values of the betas of individual securities would be from about .5 to 1.5.

use them with the beta of any security to obtain its expected return. This can be demonstrated by the use of the graph of the SML.

Figure 17–1 presents a graph of the SML. The expected rate of return is shown on the vertical axis, while risk, measured here as the beta of the security is shown on the horizontal axis.

Figure 17–1
The Relationship between Risk and the Expected Rate of Return: The Security Market Line (SML)

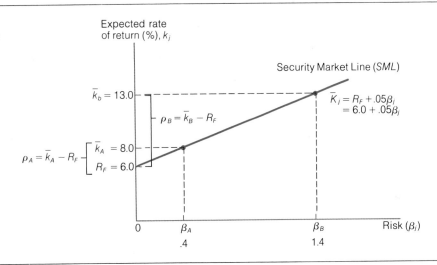

Since a riskless asset, by definition, has no risk, R_F lies on the vertical axis. As risk increases, the expected rate of return also increases. A relatively low-risk security, such as that of firm A, might have a risk index of $\beta_A = .4$ and an expected rate of return of $\bar{k}_A = 8$ percent. A more risky security, such as that of firm B, might have a risk index of $\beta_B = 1.4$ and an expected rate of return of $k_B = 13$ percent.

In the illustrative case, the slope of the SML is .05, indicating that the expected rate of return rises by one percent for each .2 increase in the security's beta. The beta is .4 for firm A, so the risk premium on that security is 2 percent $(.05 \times .4 = 2$ percent), while the beta on security B is 1.4, making its risk premium 7 percent $(.05 \times 1.4 = 7$ percent). When these two risk premiums are added to the riskless rate, R_F, we obtain the expected rates of return:

$$\bar{k}_A = 6\% + 2\% = 8\%.$$

$$\bar{k}_B = 6\% + 7\% = 13\%.$$

Notice that the graph can also be used to analyze the securities of a single firm. Since a company's bonds have a smaller standard deviation of expected returns than its common stock, $\bar{k}_A$ might be the expected rate of return on the firm's bonds, while $\bar{k}_B$ might refer to its common stock. The company's preferred stock and convertibles would lie on the SML between $\bar{k}_A$ and $\bar{k}_B$.

Shifts in the SML: Changing Interest Rates

We noted in Chapter 6 that interest rates shift markedly over time, and when such shifts occur, the SML can also be expected to shift. Figure 17–2 illustrates the effects of an increase in the riskless rate from 6 percent to 8 percent, with the increase perhaps resulting from an increase in the rate of inflation. If it is assumed that $\bar{k}_M$ also increases by 2 percentage points as R_F increases by 2 percentage points, the slope of the SML remains constant, but the intercept shifts upward:

Original SML equation: $\bar{k}_j = 6.0\% + .05\beta_j$

Revised SML equation: $\bar{k}_j = 8.0\% + .05\beta_j$

This results in increases in the expected rates of return for firms A and B, with $\bar{k}_A$ rising from 8 to 10 percent and $\bar{k}_B$ from 13 to 15 percent.

Figure 17–2
The Effect of Rising Interest Rates on the Expected Rate of Return

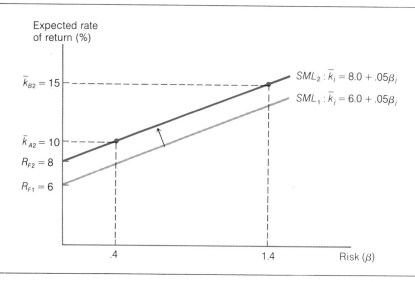

Shifts in the SML: Investor Psychology

The slope of the SML depends upon investors' attitudes toward risk. When investors are gloomy and pessimistic, they are highly averse to risk, and at such times the SML has a relatively steep slope. Conversely, when investors on the whole are optimistic and have a bright outlook, the slope of the SML is not so steep. When investors' attitudes change, the SML shifts. Figure 17–3 illustrates a change in attitudes toward increased pessimism, or an increase in risk aversion. The slope of the SML increases from .05 to .07 as shown:[7]

Original SML equation: $\bar{k}_j = 6\% + .05\beta_j$

Revised SML equation: $\bar{k}_j = 6\% + .07\beta_j$

This results in increases in the expected rates of return for firms A and B, with $\bar{k}_A$ rising from 8 to 8.8 percent and $\bar{k}_B$ from 13 to 15.8 percent.

Figure 17–3
The Effect of Changing Investor Attitudes on the Expected Rate of Return

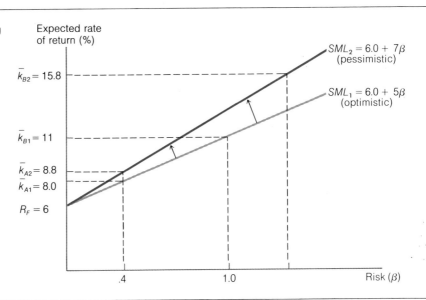

Since the SML is a market-wide relationship, the "expected" return on a security is "required" for market equilibrium relationships. In the subsequent section on common stock valuation, the return on stock equity *required* by equilibrium relationships will be designated as k_s^* in contrast to $\bar{k}_s$, a return *expected* from individual security earnings and price relationships.

---

7. R_F may also change when the slope of the SML curve shifts owing to the changed relationship between returns on risky and riskless assets.

Bond Valuation

The rate of return concepts developed above may now be used to explain the process of security valuation. In this section we examine bond values; in the two following sections, we go on to study preferred and common stocks. Bond values are relatively easy to determine. As long as the bond is not expected to go into default, the expected cash flows are the annual interest payments plus the principal amount due when the bond matures. Depending upon differences in the risk of default on interest or principal, the appropriate capitalization (or discount) rate applied to different bonds will vary. A U.S. Treasury security, for example, would have less risk than one issued by the Westbrig Corporation; consequently, a lower discount (or capitalization) rate would be applied to its interest payments. The actual calculating procedures employed in bond valuation are illustrated by the following examples.

Perpetual Bond

After the Napoleonic Wars (1814), England sold a huge bond issue, which was used to pay off many smaller issues that had been floated in prior years to pay for the war. Since the purpose of the new issue was to consolidate past debts, the individual bonds were called Consols. Suppose the bonds paid $50 interest annually into perpetuity. (Actually, interest was stated in pounds.) What would the bonds be worth under current market conditions?

First, note that the value v_b of any perpetuity is computed as follows:[8]

---

8. A perpetuity is a bond that never matures; it pays interest indefinitely. Equation 17–2 is simply the present value of an infinite series; its proof is demonstrated below: Rewrite Equation 17–2 as follows:

$$v_b = c\left[\frac{1}{(1+k_b)^1} + \frac{1}{(1+k_b)^2} + \cdots + \frac{1}{(1+k_b)^N}\right]. \tag{1}$$

Multiply both sides of Equation (1) by $(1 + k_b)$:

$$v_b(1 + k_b) = c\left[1 + \frac{1}{(1+k_b)^1} + \frac{1}{(1+k_b)^2} + \cdots + \frac{1}{(1+k_b)^{N-1}}\right] \tag{2}$$

Subtract Equation (1) from Equation (2), obtaining:

$$v_b(1 + k_b - 1) = c\left[1 - \frac{1}{(1+k_b)^N}\right]. \tag{3}$$

As $N \to \infty$, $\frac{1}{(1+k_b)^N} \to 0$, so Equation (3) approaches

$$v_b k_b = c,$$

and

$$v_b = \frac{c}{k_b}. \tag{17-2}$$

$$v_b = \frac{c}{(1 + k_b)^1} + \frac{c}{(1 + k_b)^2} + \cdots$$

$$= \frac{c}{k_b}. \tag{17–2}$$

Here c is the constant annual interest in dollars and k_b is the appropriate interest rate, or required rate of return, for the bond issue. (In this chapter, we use k_b, k_{ps}, and k_s to designate the required rates of return on debt, preferred stock, and common stock, respectively.) Equation 17–2 is an infinite series of $1 a year, and the value of the bond is the discounted sum of the infinite series.

We know that the Consol's annual interest payment is $50; therefore, the only other thing we need in order to find its value is the appropriate interest rate. This is commonly taken as the going interest rate, or yield, on bonds of similar risk. Suppose we find such bonds to be paying 4 percent under current market conditions. Then the Consol's value is determined as follows:

$$v_b = \frac{c}{k_b} = \frac{\$50}{0.04} = \$1,250.$$

If the going rate of interest rises to 5 percent, the value of the bond falls to $1,000 ($50/0.05 = $1,000). If interest rates continue rising, when the rate goes as high as 6 percent the value of the Consol will be only $833.33. Values of this perpetual bond for a range of interest rates are given in the following tabulation:

Current Market Interest Rate	Current Market Value
0.02	$2,500.00
0.03	1,666.67
0.04	1,250.00
0.05	1,000.00
0.06	833.33
0.07	714.29
0.08	625.00

Short-term Bond

Now suppose the British government issues bonds with the same risk of default as the Consols, but with a three-year maturity. The new bonds also pay $50 interest and have a $1,000 maturity value. What will the value of these new bonds be at the time of issue if the going rate of interest is 4 percent? To find this value, we must solve Equation 17–3:

$$v_b = \frac{c_1}{(1 + k_b)^1} + \frac{c_2}{(1 + k_b)^2} + \frac{c_3 + M}{(1 + k_b)^3}. \tag{17–3}$$

Here M is the maturity value of the bond. The solution is given in the following tabulation.[9]

Year	Receipt	4 Percent Discount Factors	Present Value
1	$50	.962	$ 48.10
2	$50	.925	46.25
3	$50 + $1,000	.889	933.45
		Bond value =	$1,027.80

At the various rates of interest used in the perpetuity example, this three-year bond would have the following values:

Current Market Interest Rate	Current Market Value
.02%	$1,086.15
.03	1,056.45
.04	1.027.80
.05	1,000.00
.06	973.65
.07	947.20
.08	922.85

**Interest-rate
Risk**

Figure 17–4 shows how the values of the long-term bond (the Consol) and the short-term bond change in response to changes in the going market rate of interest. Note how much less sensitive the short-term bond is to changes in interest rates. At a 5 percent interest rate, both the perpetuity and the short-term bonds are valued at $1,000. When rates rise to 8 percent, the long-term bond falls to $625, while the short-term security falls only to $923. A similar situation occurs when rates fall below 5 percent. This differential responsiveness to changes in interest rates depends on interest rate levels. When the securities bear low or moderate interest rate levels, for a given change in required yields, the greater will be the resulting change in the prices of the securities. However, at yields of 10 percent or more such as would be found on deep discount bonds, for a further change in required yields, the resulting change in price is smaller for the longer term bonds than for the shorter maturity deep discount bonds. This helps explain why corporate treasurers are reluctant to hold their low interest rate near-cash reserves in

---

9. If the bond has a longer maturity, 20 years for example, we would certainly want to calculate its present value by finding the present value of a 20-year annuity and then adding to that the present value of the $1,000 principal amount received at maturity. Special bond tables have been devised to simplify the calculation procedure. Note also that k_b will frequently differ for the long- and short-term bonds; as we saw in Chapter 6, unless the yield to maturity curve is flat, long- and short-term rates differ.

reserves in the form of long-term debt instruments—these near-cash reserves are held for precautionary purposes, and a treasurer would be unwilling to sacrifice safety for a little higher yield on a long-term bond.

Figure 17–4
Values of Long-term
and Short-term Bonds,
5 Percent Coupon
Rate, at Different
Market Interest Rates

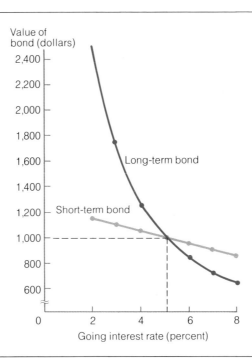

Yield to Maturity

The rate of return that is expected if a bond is held to its maturity date is defined as the *yield to maturity*. Suppose a perpetuity has a stated par value of $1,000, has a 5 percent coupon rate (that is, pays 5 percent, or $50 annually, on this stated value), and is currently selling for $625. We can solve Equation 17–2 for k_b to find the yield on the bond:

$$k_b = \frac{c}{v_b} = \frac{\$50}{\$625} = 8\% = \text{yield on a perpetuity.}$$

If the bond sells for $1,250, the formula will show that the yield is 4 percent.

For the three-year bond paying $50 interest a year, if the price of the bond is $922.85, the yield to maturity is found by solving Equation 17–3; the solution *PVIF* is the one for 8 percent:

$$\$922.85 = \$50(PVIF) + \$50(PVIF) + \$1,050(PVIF)$$

$$= \$50(.926) + \$50(.857) + \$1,050(.794)$$

$$= \$46.30 + \$42.85 + \$833.70 = \$922.85 \text{ when } PVIF = 8\%.$$

The interest factors are taken from the 8 percent column of Table D-2. The solution procedure is exactly like that for finding the internal rate of return in capital budgeting, and the trial-and-error method is required unless special tables are available.[10]

Preferred Stock Valuation

Most preferred stocks entitle their owners to regular, fixed dividend payments similar to bond interest. Although some preferred issues are eventually retired, most are perpetuities whose value is found as follows:

$$v_{ps} = \frac{d_{ps}}{k_{ps}} \qquad (17\text{-}4)$$

In this case, d_{ps} is the dividend on the preferred stock, and k_{ps} is the appropriate capitalization rate for investments of this degree of risk. For example, General Motors has a preferred stock outstanding that pays a $3.75 annual dividend. The average annual yield on preferred stocks in late 1946 when the stock was issued was 3.79 percent. The GM preferred stock was a no par stock that sold at 100 to yield 3.75 percent at the issue date. Preferred stock yields during March 1977 averaged 7.14 percent. On April 21, 1977, the $3.75 preferred stock of General Motors closed at $52. The yield on a preferred stock is similar to that on a perpetual bond and is found by solving Equation 17-4 for k_{ps}. For the GM issue, we can observe the current price of the stock from newspaper market quotations to be $52; its annual dividend is $3.75, so the yield is 7.21 percent, calculated as follows:

$$k_{ps} = \frac{d_{ps}}{v_{ps}} = \frac{\$3.75}{\$52} = 7.21\%$$

The valuation relationship expressed by Equation 17-4 is also implied. If we know the promised dividend payment on the preferred stock and its current yield, we can determine its value:

$$v_{ps} = \frac{\$3.75}{.0721} = \$52$$

10. We first tried the *PVIFs* for 6 percent, found that the equation did not "work," then raised the *PVIF* to 8 percent, where the equation did "work." This indicated that 8 percent was the yield to maturity on the bond. In practice, specialized interest tables called *bond tables*, generated by a computer, are available to facilitate determining the yield to maturity on bonds with different maturities, with different stated interest rates, and selling for various discounts below or premiums above their maturity values.

Common Stock Valuation and Rates of Return

While the same principles apply to the valuation of common stocks as to bonds or preferred stocks, two features make their analysis much more difficult. First is the degree of certainty with which receipts can be forecast. For bonds and preferred stocks, this forecast presents little difficulty, as the interest payments or preferred dividends are known with relative certainty. However, in the case of common stocks, forecasting future earnings, dividends, and stock prices is exceedingly difficult, to say the least. The second complicating feature is that, unlike interest and preferred dividends, common stock earnings and dividends are generally expected to grow, not remain constant. Hence, while standard annuity formulas can be applied, more difficult conceptual schemes must also be used.

Estimating the Value of a Stock: The Single Period Case

The price today of a share of common stock, p_0, depends upon (1) the cash flows investors expect to receive if they buy the stock and (2) the riskiness of these expected cash flows. The expected cash flows consist of two elements: (1) the dividend expected in each year t, defined as d_t, and (2) the price investors expect to receive when they sell the stock at the end of year n, defined as p_n, which includes the return of the original investment plus a capital gain (or minus a capital loss): If investors expect to hold the stock for one year, and if the stock price is expected to grow at the rate g, the valuation equation is

$$p_0 = \frac{\text{expected dividend} + \text{expected price (both at end of year 1)}}{1.0 + \text{required rate of return}}$$

$$= \frac{d_1 + p_1}{(1 + k_s)} = \frac{d_1 + p_0(1 + g)}{(1 + k_s)}, \tag{17-5}$$

which can be simplified to yield Equation 17-6.[11]

$$p_0 = \frac{d_1}{k_s - g} \tag{17-6}$$

11. $p_0 = \dfrac{d_1 + p_0(1 + g)}{(1 + k_s)}$ (17-5)

$p_0(1 + k_s) = d_1 + p_0(1 + g)$

$p_0(1 + k_s - 1 - g) = d_1$

$p_0(k_s - g) = d_1$

$p_0 = \dfrac{d_1}{k_s - g}.$ (17-6)

Notice that this equation is developed for a one-year holding period. In a later section, we will show that it is also valid for longer periods, provided the expected growth rate is constant.

Equations 17–5 and 17–6 represent the present value of the expected dividends and the year-end stock price, discounted at the required rate of return. Solving Equation 17–6 gives the "expected" or "intrinsic" price for the stock. To illustrate, suppose you are thinking of buying a share of Universal Rubber common stock. If you buy the stock, you will hold it for one year. You note that Universal Rubber earned $3.43 per share last year, and paid a dividend of $1.90. Earnings and dividends have been rising at about 5 percent a year, on the average, over the last 10 to 15 years, and you expect this growth to continue. Further, if earnings and dividends grow at the expected rate, you think the stock price will likewise grow by 5 percent.

The next step is to determine the required rate of return on Universal Rubber stock. The current rate of interest on U.S. Treasury securities, R_F, is 6 percent, but Universal Rubber is clearly more risky than government securities: competitors could erode the company's market; labor problems could disrupt operations; an economic recession could cause sales to fall below the breakeven point; auto sales could decline, pulling down Universal Rubber's own sales and profits; and so on. Further, even if sales, earnings, and dividends meet projections, the stock price could still fall as a result of a generally weak market.

Given all these risk factors, you conclude that a 6 percent risk premium is justified, so your required rate of return on Universal Rubber's stock, k_s is calculated as follows:

$$k_s^* = R_F + \rho = 6\% + 6\% = 12\%.$$

Next, you estimate the dividend for the coming year, d_1, as follows:

$$d_1 = d_0(1 + g) = \$1.90\ (1.05) = \$2.$$

Now we have the necessary information to estimate the fair value of the stock by the use of Equation 17–6:

$$p_0 = \frac{d_1}{k_s^* - g} \tag{17–6}$$

$$= \frac{\$2}{.12 - .05} = \$28.57.$$

To you, $28.57 represents a reasonable price for Universal Rubber's stock. If the actual market price is less, you will buy it; if the actual price is higher, you will not buy it, or you will sell if you own it.[12]

---

12. Notice the similarity between this process and the *NPV* method of capital budgeting described in Chapter 10. In the earlier chapter, we (1) estimated a cost of capital for the firm, which compares with estimating k_s, our required rate of return, (2) discounted expected future cash flows, which are analogous to dividends plus the future stock price, (3) found the present value of future cash flows, which corre-

**Estimating the
Rate of Return
on a Stock**

In the preceding section we calculated the "expected price" of Universal Rubber's stock to a given investor. Let us now change the procedure somewhat, and calculate the rate of return the investor can expect if he purchases the stock at the current market price per share. The expected rate of return, which we define as $\bar{k}_s$, is analogous to the internal rate of return on a capital project: $\bar{k}_s$ is the discount rate that equates the present value of the expected dividends (d_1) and final stock price (p_1) to the present stock price (p_0):

$$p_0 = \frac{d_1 + p_1}{(1 + \bar{k}_s)} = \frac{d_1 + p_0(1 + g)}{(1 + \bar{k}_s)}.$$

Suppose Universal Rubber is selling for $40 per share. We can calculate $\bar{k}_s$ as follows:

$$\$40 = \frac{\$2 + \$40(1.05)}{(1 + \bar{k}_s)} = \frac{\$2 + \$42}{(1 + \bar{k}_s)}$$

$$\$40(1 + \bar{k}_s) = \$44$$

$$1 + \bar{k}_s = 1.10$$

$$\bar{k}_s = .10 \text{ or } 10\%.$$

Thus, if you expect to receive a $2 dividend and a year-end price of $42, then your expected rate of return on the investment is 10 percent.

Notice that the expected rate of return, $\bar{k}_s$, consists of two components, an expected dividend yield and an expected capital gains yield:

$$\bar{k}_s = \frac{\text{expected dividend}}{\text{present price}} + \frac{\text{expected increase in price}}{\text{present price}}$$

$$= \frac{d_1}{p_0} + g. \tag{17-6}$$

For Universal Rubber bought at a price of $40,

$$\bar{k}_s = \frac{\$2}{\$40} + \frac{\$2}{\$40} = 5\% + 5\% = 10\%.$$

Given an expected rate of return of 10 percent, should you make the purchase? This depends upon how the expected return compares with the required return. If $\bar{k}_s$ exceeds k_s^*, buy; if $\bar{k}_s$ is less than k_s^*, sell; and if

---

sponds to the "fair value" of the stock, (4) determined the initial outlay for the project, which compares with finding the actual price of the stock, and (5) accepted the project if the *PV* of future cash flows exceeded the initial cost of the project, which is similar to comparing the "fair value" of the stock to its market price.

$\bar{k}_s$ equals k_s^*, the stock price is in equilibrium and you should be indifferent. In this case, your 12 percent required rate of return for Universal Rubber exceeds the 10 percent expected return, so you should not buy the stock.[13]

Market Equilibrium: Required versus Expected Returns

In the two preceding sections we calculated (1) expected and required rates of return and (2) "expected" stock prices. Further, we saw that buy/no-buy decisions can be based upon a comparison of either k_s^* versus $\bar{k}_s$ or "expected" stock value versus actual market price. In this section, we first show that the two decision rules are entirely consistent, then illustrate the process by which stock market equilibrium is maintained.

Consider again the Universal Rubber example, when the following data are applicable:

Expected dividend at year end $= \bar{d}_1 = \$2.$
Expected growth rate in stock price $= \bar{g} = 5\%.$
Required rate of return $= k_s^* = 12\%.$

We calculated an "expected" price of $28.57. We next found that the actual market price, as read from a newspaper or obtained from a stockbroker, is $40, and on the basis of that price we calculated a 10 percent expected rate of return.

By either the rate of return or calculated price criteria, Universal Rubber's stock is overvalued:

Actual price $= \$40 >$ "expected" price $= \$28.57,$

and

Required rate of return $(k_s^*) = 12\% >$ expected rate of return $(\bar{k}_s) = 10\%.$

You should not buy this stock at the $40 price, and if you own it, you should sell.

Now let us assume that you are a "typical" or "representative" investor, so that your expectations and actions actually determine stock market prices. You and others will start selling Universal Rubber stock, and this selling pressure will cause the price to decline. The decline will continue until the price reaches $28.57, which you, the typical investor, feel is its intrinsic value. At this price, the expected rate of return will also equal the required rate of return:

---

13. Notice the similarity between this process and the *IRR* method of capital budgeting. The expected rate of return, $\bar{k}_s$, corresponds to the *IRR* on a project, and the required rate of return, k_s^*, corresponds to cost-of-capital cutoff rate used in capital budgeting.

$$\bar{k}_s = \frac{d_1}{p_0} + g = \frac{\$2}{\$28.57} + 5\% = 7\% + 5\% = 12\%,$$

and

$$k_s^* = R_F + \rho = 6\% + 6\% = 12\%.$$

This situation will always hold—whenever the actual market price is equal to the "fair" price as calculated by a "typical" investor, required and expected returns will also be equal, and the market will be in equilibrium; that is, there will be no tendency for the stock price to go up or down.

Factors Leading to Changes in Market Prices	Let us assume that Universal Rubber's stock is in equilibrium, selling at a price of $28.57 per share. If all expectations are exactly met, over the next year the price will gradually rise to $30, or by 5 percent. However, many different events could occur to cause a change in the equilibrium price of the stock. To illustrate the forces at work, consider again the stock price model, the set of inputs used to develop the price of $28.57, and a new set of assumed input variables:

	Variable Value	
	Original	New
Riskless rate (R_F)	6%	5%
Risk aversion coefficient (λ^{**})	.04	.05
Index of stock's risk (β)	1.5	1.2
Expected growth rate (g)	5%	6%

The first three variables influence k_s^*, which declines as a result of the new set of variables from 12 percent to 11 percent:

Original: $k_s^* = 6\% + (.04)(1.5) = 12\%.$

New: $k_s^* = 5\% + (.05)(1.2) = 11\%.$

Using these values, together with the new d and g values, we find that p_0 rises from $28.57 to $40.20:

Original: $p_0 = \dfrac{\$1.90(1.05)}{.12 - .05} = \dfrac{\$2}{.07} = \$28.57.$

New: $p_0 = \dfrac{\$1.90(1.06)}{.11 - .06} = \dfrac{\$2.01}{.05} = \$40.20.$

At the new price, the expected and required rate of return will be equal:

$$\bar{k}_s = \frac{\$2.01}{\$40.20} + 6\% = 11\% = k_s^*,$$

as found above.

Evidence suggests that securities adjust quite rapidly to disequilibrium situations. Consequently, equilibrium ordinarily exists for any given stock, and in general the required and expected returns are equal. Stock prices certainly change, sometimes violently and rapidly, but this simply reflects changing conditions and expectations. There are, of course, times when a stock continues to react for several months to a favorable or unfavorable development, but this does not signify a long adjustment period; rather, it merely shows that as more information about the situation becomes available, the market adjusts to these new bits of information. Throughout the remainder of this book, we will assume that security markets are in equilibrium, with $k^* = \bar{k}$. Hence, we shall generally use k (with the appropriate subscript) for the required return or applicable discount rate unless we are directly contrasting the required return, k^*, with the expected return, $\bar{k}$.

Multiperiod Stock Valuation Models

Thus far, our discussion of stock values and rates of return has focused on a single-period model, where we expect to hold the stock for one year, receive one dividend, and then sell the stock at the end of the year. In this section, we expand the analysis to deal with more realistic, but more complicated, multiperiod models.

Expected Dividends as the Basis for Stock Values

According to generally accepted theory, stock prices are determined as the present value of a stream of cash flows. In other words, the capitalization of income procedure applies to stocks as well as to bonds and other assets. What are the cash flows that corporations provide to their stockholders? What flows do the markets in fact capitalize? A number of different models have been formulated. At least four different categories of flows have been capitalized in alternative formulations: (1) the stream of dividends, (2) the stream of earnings, (3) the current earnings plus flows resulting from future investment opportunities, and (4) the discounting of cash flows as in capital budgeting models. Miller and Modigliani have demonstrated that these different approaches are equivalent and yield the same valuations.[14] Since multiperiod valuation

14. See their "Dividend Policy, Growth, and the Valuation of Shares," *Journal of Business* 34 (October 1961), pp. 411–33.

models are inherently complicated, we shall illustrate the methodology involved by use of the least complicated form—the stream of dividends approach. In this formulation, a share of common stock may be regarded as being similar to a perpetual bond or share of perpetual preferred stock, and its value may be established as the present value of its stream of dividends:

Value of stock $= p_0 = PV$ of expected future dividends

$$= \frac{d_1}{(1 + k_s)^1} + \frac{d_2}{(1 + k_s)^2} + \cdots$$

$$= \sum_{t=1}^{\infty} \frac{d_t}{(1 + k_s)^t}. \tag{17-7}$$

Unlike bond interest and preferred dividends, common stock dividends are not generally expected to remain constant in the future; hence we cannot work with the convenient annuity formulas. This fact, combined with the much greater uncertainty about common stock dividends than about bond interest or preferred dividends, makes common stock valuation a more complex task than bond or preferred stock valuation.

Equation 17–7 is a quite general stock valuation model in the sense that the time pattern of d_t can be anything; d_t can be rising, falling, constant, or it can even fluctuate randomly, and Equation 17–7 will still hold. For many purposes, however, it is useful to estimate a particular time pattern for d_t and then develop a simplified (that is, easier to evaluate) version of the stock valuation model expressed in Equation 17–7. In the following sections, we consider the special cases of zero growth, constant growth, and "supernormal" growth.

Stock Values with Zero Growth

Suppose the rate of growth is measured by the rate at which dividends are expected to increase. If future growth is expected to be zero, the value of the stock reduces to the same formula as was developed for a perpetual bond:

$$\text{price} = \frac{\text{dividend}}{\text{capitalization rate}}$$

$$p_0 = \frac{d_1}{k_s}. \tag{17-8}$$

Solving for k_s, we obtain

$$k_s = \frac{d_1}{p_0}, \tag{17-8a}$$

which states that the required rate of return on a share of stock that has no growth prospects is simply the dividend yield.

"Normal," or Constant, Growth

Year after year, the earnings and dividends of most companies have been increasing. In general, this growth is expected to continue in the foreseeable future at about the same rate as GNP. On this basis, it is expected that an average, or "normal," company will grow at a rate of from 3 to 5 percent a year. Thus, if such a company's previous dividend, which has already been paid, was d_0, its dividend in any future year t may be forecast as $d_t = d_0(1 + g)^t$, where g = the expected rate of growth. For example, if Universal Rubber just paid a dividend of $1.90 (that is, $d_0 = \$1.90$), and investors expect a 5 percent growth rate, the estimated dividend one year hence will be $d_1 = (\$1.90)(1.05) = \$2$; d_2 will be $2.10; and the estimated dividend five years hence will be

$$d_t = d_0(1 + g)^t$$

$$= \$1.90(1.05)^5$$

$$= \$2.42.$$

Using this method of estimating future dividends, the current price, P_0, is determined as follows:

$$p_0 = \frac{d_1}{(1 + k_s)^1} + \frac{d_2}{(1 + k_s)^2} + \frac{d_3}{(1 + k_s)^3} + \cdots$$

$$= \frac{d_0(1 + g)^1}{(1 + k_s)^1} + \frac{d_0(1 + g)^2}{(1 + k_s)^2} + \frac{d_0(1 + g)^3}{(1 + k_s)^3} + \cdots$$

$$= \sum_{t=1}^{\infty} \frac{d_0(1 + g)^t}{(1 + k_s)^t}. \tag{17-9}$$

If g is constant, Equation 17-9 may be simplified as follows:[15]

$$p_0 = \frac{d_1}{k_s - g}. \tag{17-10}$$

15. The proof of Equation 17-10 is as follows. Rewrite Equation 17-9 as

$$p_0 = d_0\left[\frac{(1 + g)}{(1 + k_s)} + \frac{(1 + g)^2}{(1 + k_s)^2} + \frac{(1 + g)^3}{(1 + k_s)^3} + \cdots + \frac{(1 + g)^N}{(1 + k_s)^N}\right]. \tag{1}$$

Multiply both sides of Equation (1) by $(1 + k_s)/(1 + g)$:

$$\left[\frac{(1 + k_s)}{(1 + g)}\right]p_0 = d_0\left[1 + \frac{(1 + g)}{(1 + k_s)} + \frac{(1 + g)^2}{(1 + k_s)^2} + \cdots + \frac{(1 + g)^{N-1}}{(1 + k_s)^{N-1}}\right]. \tag{2}$$

Notice that the constant growth model expressed in Equation 17–10 is identical to the single-period model, Equation 17–5, developed in an earlier section.

A necessary condition for the constant growth model is that k_s be greater than g; otherwise, Equation 17–10 gives nonsense answers. If k_s equals g, the equation blows up, yielding an infinite price; if k_s is less than g, a *negative* price results. Since neither infinite nor negative stock prices make sense, it is clear that in equilibrium k_s must be greater than g.

Note that Equation 17–10 is sufficiently general to encompass the no-growth case described above. If growth is zero, this is simply a special case, and Equation 17–10 is equal to Equation 17–8.[16]

"Supernormal" Growth

Firms typically go through "life cycles" during part of which their growth is much faster than that of the economy as a whole. Automobile manufacturers in the 1920s and computer and office equipment manufacturers in the 1960s are examples. Figure 17–5 illustrates such supernormal growth and compares it with normal growth, zero growth, and negative growth.[17]

The illustrative supernormal growth firm is expected to grow at a 20 percent rate for ten years, then to have its growth rate fall to 4 percent,

---

Subtract Equation (1) from Equation (2) to obtain

$$\left[\frac{(1 + k_s)}{(1 + g)} - 1\right]p_0 = d_0\left[1 - \frac{(1 - g)^N}{(1 - k_s)^N}\right].$$

$$\left[\frac{(1 - k_s) - (1 + g)}{(1 + g)}\right]p_0 = d_0\left[1 - \frac{(1 + g)^N}{(1 + k_s)^N}\right].$$

Assuming $k_s > g$, as $N \to \infty$ the term in brackets on the right side of the equation $\to 1.0$, leaving

$$\left[\frac{(1 + k_s) - (1 + g)}{(1 + g)}\right]p_0 = d_0,$$

which simplifies to

$$(k_s - g)p_0 = d_0(1 + g) = d_1$$

$$p_0 = \frac{d_1}{k_s - g}. \tag{17–10}$$

16. One technical point should at least be mentioned here. The logic underlying the analysis implicitly assumes that investors are indifferent to dividend yield or capital gains. Empirical work has not conclusively established whether this is true or not, but the question is discussed in Chapter 20.

17. A *negative* growth rate represents a declining company. A mining company whose profits are falling because of a declining ore body is an example.

Figure 17–5
Illustrative Dividend
Growth Rates

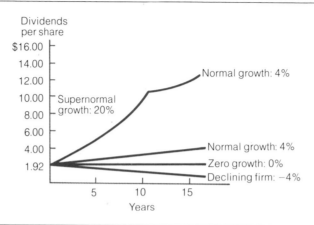

the norm for the economy. The value of a firm with such a growth pattern is determined by the following equation:

Present price = PV of dividends during supernormal growth period +
Value of stock price at end of supernormal growth
period discounted back to present

$$P_0 = \sum_{t=1}^{N} \frac{d_0(1 + g_s)^t}{(1 + k_s)^t} + \left(\frac{d_{N+1}}{k_s - g_n}\right)\left(\frac{1}{(1 + k_s)^N}\right). \qquad (17\text{–}11)$$

Here g_s is the supernormal growth rate, g_n is the normal growth rate, and N is the period of supernormal growth.

Working through an example will help make this clear. Consider a supernormal growth firm whose previous dividend was $1.92 (that is, $d_0 = \$1.92$), with the dividend expected to increase by 20 percent a year for ten years and thereafter at 4 percent a year indefinitely. If stockholders' required rate of return is 9 percent on an investment with this degree of risk, what is the value of the stock? On the basis of the calculations in Table 17–1, the value is found to be $138.19, the present value of the dividends during the first ten years plus the present value of the stock at the end of the tenth year.

**Comparing
Companies with
Different
Expected
Growth Rates**

It is useful to summarize this section by comparing the four illustrative firms whose dividend trends were graphed in Figure 17–5. Using the valuation equations developed above, the conditions assumed in the preceding examples, and the additional assumptions that each firm had earnings per share during the preceding reporting period of $3.60 (that is, $EPS_0 = \$3.60$) and paid out 53.3 percent of its reported earnings

**Table 17–1
Method of
Calculating the
Value of a Stock
with Supernormal
Growth**

Assumptions:

a. Stockholders' capitalization rate is 9 percent; i.e., $k_s = 9\%$.
b. Growth rate is 20 percent for ten years, 4 percent thereafter; i.e., $g_s = 20\%$, $g_n = 4\%$, and $N = 10$.
c. Last year's dividend was $1.92; i.e., $d_0 = \$1.92$.

Step 1. Find present value of dividends during rapid growth period:

End of Year	Dividend $1.92(1.20)^t	$PVIF = 1/(1.09)^t$	Present Value
1	$ 2.30	.917	$ 2.11
2	2.76	.842	2.32
3	3.32	.772	2.56
4	3.98	.708	2.82
5	4.78	.650	3.11
6	5.73	.596	3.42
7	6.88	.547	3.76
8	8.26	.502	4.15
9	9.91	.460	4.56
10	11.89	.422	5.02

$$\text{PV of first ten years' dividends} = \sum_{t=1}^{10} \frac{d_0(1 + g_s)^t}{(1 + k_s)^t} = \underline{\underline{\$33.83}}$$

Step 2. Find present value of year 10 stock price:
a. Find value of stock at end of year 10:

$$P_{10} = \frac{d_{11}}{k_s - g_n} = \frac{\$11.89(1.04)}{.05} = \$247.31.$$

b. Discount p_{10} back to present:

$$PV = P_{10}\left(\frac{1}{1 + k_s}\right)^{10} = \$247.31(.422) = \$104.36.$$

Step 3. Sum to find total value of stock today:

$$p_0 = \$33.83 + \$104.36 = \$138.19.$$

(therefore dividends per share last year, d_0, were $1.92 for each company), we show prices, dividend yields, and price/earnings ratios (hereafter written P/E) in Table 17–2.

Investors require and expect a return of 9 percent on each of the stocks. For the declining firm, this return consists of a relatively high current dividend yield combined with a capital *loss* amounting to 4 percent a year. For the no-growth firm, there is neither a capital gain nor a capital loss expectation, so the 9 percent return must be obtained entirely from the dividend yield. The normal growth firm provides a relatively low current dividend yield, but a 4 percent a year capital gain expectation. Finally, the supernormal growth firm has the lowest current dividend yield but the highest capital gain expectation.

What is expected to happen to the prices of the four illustrative firms' stocks over time? Three of the four cases are straightforward: The zero growth firm's price is expected to be constant (that is, $p_t = p_{t+1}$); the declining firm is expected to have a falling stock price; and the constant growth firm's stock is expected to grow at a constant rate, 4 percent. The supernormal growth case is more complex, but what is expected can be seen from the data in Table 17–1.

It can readily be shown that[18]

$$\sum_{t=1}^{N} \frac{(1+g_s)^t}{(1+k_s)^t} = \frac{(1+g_s)[(1+h)^{10}-1]}{g_s-k_s} = \frac{(1+g_s)h}{(g_s-k_s)}\left[\frac{(1+h)^{10}-1}{h}\right]$$

where $\dfrac{(1+g_s)}{(1+k_s)} = (1+h)$ for ease of expression.

The third term is expressed in the sum of an annuity form by multiplying the second term by h/h as shown above.

For the example in Table 17–1, we have:

$$1+h = \frac{(1+g_s)}{(1+k_s)} = \frac{1.20}{1.09} = 1.100917431 \qquad \frac{(1+g_s)}{(g_s-k_s)} = \frac{1.2}{.11} = 10.909$$

$$(1+h)^{10} = (1.100917431)^{10} = 2.615456$$

$$(1+h)^{10} - 1 = 1.615456$$

---

18. Numerical calculation procedure for a summation expression.

$$\sum_{t=1}^{10} \frac{D_o(1+g_s)^t}{(1+k_s)^t} = D_o \sum_{t=1}^{10} \frac{(1+g_s)^t}{(1+k_s)^t} \quad \text{Write out the summation expression:}$$

$$\sum_{t=1}^{10} \left(\frac{1+g_s}{1+k_s}\right)^t = \left(\frac{1+g_s}{1+k_s}\right) + \left(\frac{1+g_s}{1+k_s}\right)^2 + \cdots + \left(\frac{1+g_s}{1+k_s}\right)^{10} \quad \text{Factor} \left(\frac{1+g_s}{1+k_s}\right) \text{ from all terms.}$$

$$= \left(\frac{1+g_s}{1+k_s}\right)\left[1 + \left(\frac{1+g_s}{1+k_s}\right) + \cdots + \left(\frac{1+g_s}{1+k_s}\right)^9\right] \quad \text{Use the formula for the summation of a}$$

geometric progression over N periods and simplify.

$$S_N = \frac{r^N-1}{r-1} = \frac{1+g_s}{1+k_s}\frac{\left[\left(\frac{1+g_s}{1+k_s}\right)^{10}-1\right]}{\left(\frac{1+g_s}{1+k_s}\right)-1} = \frac{(1+g_s)\left[\left(\frac{1+g_s}{1+k_s}\right)^{10}-1\right]}{(1+k_s)\frac{1+g_s-1-k_s}{(1+k_s)}} = \frac{(1+g_s)}{(g_s-k_s)}\left[\left(\frac{1+g_s}{1+k_s}\right)^{10}-1\right]$$

Let $\left(\dfrac{1+g_s}{1+k_s}\right) = (1+h)$. Then $S_N = \dfrac{(1+g_s)}{(g_s-k_s)}[(1+h)^{10}-1]$ Multiply by $\dfrac{h}{h}$

$$S_N = \left[\frac{(1+g_s)(h)}{(g_s-k_s)}\right]\left[\frac{[(1+h)^{10}-1]}{h}\right] \quad \text{The second term is the sum of an annuity.}$$

Thus $\displaystyle\sum_{t=1}^{N} \frac{D_o(1+g_s)^t}{(1+k_s)^t} = D_o\left(\frac{1+g_s}{g_s-k_s}\right)[(1+h)^N-1] = D_o\frac{(1+g_s)(h)}{(g_s-k_s)}\left[\frac{(1+h)^{10}-1}{h}\right]$

$$\frac{(1 + g_s)[(1 + h)^{10} - 1]}{(g_s - k_s)} = 10.909 \times 1.615456 = 17.623$$

$$D_0(17.623) = 1.92(17.623) = 33.836$$

The *PV* of the first ten years' dividends shown in Table 17–1 is $33.83, approximately the same. Note that the present price, P_0, is $138.19 and that the expected price in year 10, P_{10}, is $247.31. This represents an average growth rate of 6 percent.[19] We do not show, but we could, that the expected growth rate of the stock's price is higher than 6 percent in the early part of the ten-year supernormal growth period and less than 6 percent toward the end of the period, as investors perceive the approaching end of the supernormal period. From year 11 on, the company's stock price and dividend are expected to grow at the "normal" rate, 4 percent.

The relationships among the P/E ratios, shown in the last column of Table 17–2, are similar to what one would intuitively expect—the higher the expected growth (all other things the same), the higher the P/E ratio.[20]

Table 17–2 Prices, Dividend Yields, and Price/ Earnings Ratios for 9 Percent Returns under Different Growth Assumptions		Price	Current Dividend Yield	P/E Ratio*
Declining firm:	$P_0 = \dfrac{d_1}{k_s - g} = \dfrac{\$1.84}{0.09 - (-0.04)}$	$ 14.15	13%	3.9
No-growth firm:	$P_0 = \dfrac{d_1}{k_s} = \dfrac{\$1.92}{0.09}$	$ 21.33	9%	5.9
Normal growth firm:	$P_0 = \dfrac{d_1}{k_s - g} = \dfrac{\$2.00}{0.09 - 0.04}$	$ 40.00	5%	11.1
Supernormal growth firm:	$P_0 = $ (See Table 17–1)	$138.19	1.7%	38.4

*It was assumed at the beginning of this example that each company is earning $3.60 initially. This $3.60, divided into the various prices, gives the indicated P/E ratios.

We might also note that as the supernormal growth rate declines toward the normal rate (or as the time when this decline will occur becomes more imminent), the high P/E ratio must approach the normal P/E ratio; that is, the P/E of 38.4 will decline year by year and equal 11.1, that of the normal growth company, in the tenth year. See A. A. Robichek and M. C. Bogue, "A Note on the Behavior of Expected Price/Earnings Ratios over Time," *Journal of Finance* (June 1971).

Note also that d_1 differs for each firm, being calculated as follows:

$d_1 = EPS_0(1 + g)(\text{payout}) = \$3.60(1 + g)(0.533)$.

19. Found from Table 17–1; $247.31/$138.19 = 1.79, and this is approximately the CVIF for a 6 percent growth rate.

20. Differences in P/E ratios among firms can also arise from differences in the rates of return, k_s, which investors use in capitalizing the future dividend streams. If one company has a higher P/E than another, this could be caused by a higher g, a lower k, or a combination of these two factors.

A General Valuation Formulation

The most general valuation formula is the Modigliani-Miller temporary growth formula:

$$V(0) = \frac{X(0)(1 + g)(1 - T)}{k}\left\{1 + \frac{b(r - k)}{br - k}\left[\left(\frac{1 + br}{1 + k}\right)^N - 1\right]\right\}$$

Where: $V(0)$ = value of the firm in period 0

$X(0)$ = net operating income of the firm in period 0

T = effective corporate income tax rate

g = growth rate in $X(t) = br$

b = ratio of $I(t)$ to $X(t)$

$I(t)$ = investment of the firm per year

r = internal profitability rate of the firm

k = applicable capitalization rate; k_u for an unlevered firm; k, the weighted cost of capital for a levered firm

For example, an investment has earned $5 million after corporate income taxes during the most recent year. Its internal profitability rate is expected to be 24 percent per annum for the next five years, after which it will drop to 12 percent, which is the applicable cost of capital for an investment of its risk characteristics. The ratio of new investment to annual earnings is expected to be .8 for a long period of time. What is the appropriate value to be placed on this investment?

$$V(0) = \frac{5(1.192)}{.12}\left\{1 + \frac{.8(.24 - .12)}{.192 - .12}\left[\left(\frac{1.192}{1.12}\right)^5 - 1\right]\right\}$$

$$= \frac{5.96}{.12}\left\{1 + \left[\frac{.096}{.072} \quad (1.3655 - 1)\right]\right\}$$

$$= 49.67\left\{1 + .4873\right\}$$

$V(0)$ = $73.87 million

Note that of the total value of $73.87 million, $49.67 million comes from capitalization of $X(1)(1 - T)$ of $5.96 million at 12 percent. The remaining $24.20 million reflects the addition to total value due to the supernormal $(r > k)$ earning power for five years.

Marketability and Rates of Return

Throughout the chapter, whenever we discussed the required rate of return on securities, we concentrated on two factors, the riskless rate of interest and the risk inherent in the security in question. Before closing, however, we should also note that investors also value flexibility, or maneuverability. If one becomes disenchanted with a particular investment, or if he needs funds for consumption or other investments, it is highly desirable for him to be able to liquidate his holdings. Other things the same, the higher the liquidity, or marketability, the lower an investment's required rate of return. Accordingly, one would expect to find listed stocks selling on a lower yield basis than over-the-counter stocks, and widely traded stocks selling at lower yields than stocks with no established market. Since investments in small firms are generally less liquid than those in large companies, we have another reason for expecting to find higher required returns among smaller companies.

Summary

In the discussion of the capital budgeting process in Chapter 10, the discount rate used in the calculations was seen to be of vital importance. At that time, we simply assumed that the cost of capital—the discount rate used in the present value process—was known, and we used this assumed rate in the calculations. In this chapter, however, we began to lay the foundations for actually calculating the cost of capital.

Since the cost of capital is integrally related to investors' returns on capital, the basic principles underlying valuation theory were discussed, and a number of definitions of value were presented: (1) liquidating value versus going-concern value, (2) book value versus market value, and (3) "fair" value versus current market price. Market value is fundamentally dependent upon discounted cash flow concepts and procedures; it involves estimating future cash flows and discounting them back to the present at an appropriate rate of interest.

Rates of return on bonds and preferred stocks are simple to understand and to calculate, but common stock returns are more difficult. First, common stock returns consist (1) of dividends and (2) of capital gains, not a single type of payment, as in the case of bonds and preferred stocks. This fact necessitates the development of a rate of return formula that considers both dividends and capital gains; the rate of return formula for common stock is, therefore, a two-part equation:

Rate of return = dividend yield + capital gains yield.

The second complicating feature of common stock is the degree of uncertainty involved. Bond and preferred stock payments are relatively predictable, but forecasting common stock dividends and, even more, capital gains, is a highly uncertain business.

The expected rate of return for common stocks can be expressed as $\bar{k}_s = d_1/p_0 + g$ if the growth rate is a constant. p_0 is the price, d_1 is the dividend expected this year, and g refers to expected *future* growth.

Stock values are determined as the present value of a stream of cash flows. Therefore, the time pattern of these expected cash flows is very important in valuation of stock. The earnings and dividends of most companies have been increasing at a rate of 3 to 5 percent a year—this is considered a normal growth rate. Some companies may have prospects for no growth at all; others may anticipate a period of "supernormal" growth before settling down to a normal growth rate; still others may grow in a random fashion.

The required rate of return on any security, k_j^*, is the minimum rate of return necessary to induce investors to buy or to hold the security. This rate of return is a function of the riskless rate of interest and the investment's risk characteristics:

$$\bar{k}_j = R_F + \rho_j = R_F + (\bar{k}_M - R_F)\beta_j$$

This equation, when graphed, is called the *security market line* (SML), from which the required return, k_j^*, is specified. Because investors generally dislike risk, the required rate of return is higher on riskier securities. Bonds, as a class, are less risky then preferred stocks, and preferred stocks, in turn, are less risky than common stocks. As a result, the required rate of return is lowest for bonds, next for preferred stocks, and highest for common stocks. Within each of these security classes, there are variations among the issuing firms' risks; hence, required rates of return vary among firms.

In equilibrium, the expected rate of return $(\bar{k})$ and the required rate of return (k^*) for a firm j will be equal. If, however, some disturbance causes them to be different, the market price of the stock (and thus its dividend yield) will quickly change to establish a new equilibrium where k_j^* and $\bar{k}_j$ are again equal.

The required rate of return also depends upon the marketability of a given security issue—the stocks and bonds of larger, better known firms are more marketable, hence the required rates of return on such securities are lower than those on smaller, less well-known firms. As we shall see in Chapter 19, the required rate of return is, in essence, a firm's cost of capital, so if small firms have relatively high required rates of return, they also have relatively high costs of capital.

Questions

17–1. Explain what is meant by the term "yield to maturity" (a) for bonds and (b) for preferred stocks. (c) Is it appropriate to talk of a yield to maturity on a preferred stock that has no specific maturity date?

17–2. Explain why bonds with longer maturities experience wider price movements from a given change in interest rates than do shorter maturity bonds. Preferably give your answer (a) in words (intuitively) and (b) mathematically.

17-3. Explain why a share of no-growth common stock is similar to a share of preferred stock. Use one of the equations developed in the chapter in your explanation.

17-4. Explain the importance in common stock valuation (a) of current dividends, (b) of current market price, (c) of the expected future growth rate, and (d) of the market capitalization rate.

17-5. Suppose a firm's charter explicitly precludes it from ever paying a dividend. Investors *know* that this restriction will never be removed. Earnings for 1974 were $1 a share, and they are expected to grow at a rate of 4 percent forever. If the required rate of return is 10 percent, what is the firm's theoretical P/E ratio?

17-6. Describe the factors that determine the market rate of return on a particular stock at a given point in time.

17-7. Explain how (a) interest rates and (b) investors' aversion to risk influence stock and bond prices.

17-8. Most inheritance tax laws state that for estate tax purposes, property shall be valued on the basis of "fair market value." Describe how an inheritance tax appraiser might use the valuation principles discussed in this chapter to establish the value (a) of shares of a stock listed on the New York Stock Exchange and (b) of shares representing 20 percent of a stock that is not publicly traded.

Problems

17-1a. The Valuation Corporation has outstanding a series of *perpetual* bonds that pay $100 interest annually. Bonds of this type currently yield 8 percent. At what price should Valuation's bonds sell?

b. Assume that the required yield for bonds of this type rises to 12 percent. What will be the new price of Valuation's bonds?

c. Assume that the required yield drops to 10 percent. What will be the new price of Valuation's bonds?

d. Now suppose that Valuation has another series of bonds that pay $100 annual interest, mature in five years, and pay $1,000 on maturity. What will be the value of these bonds when the going rate of interest is (i) 8 percent, (ii) 12 percent, and (iii) 10 percent? (Hint: Use both the PV of an annuity and the PV of $1 tables.)

e. Why do the longer term bonds (the perpetuities) fluctuate more when interest rates change than do the shorter term (the five-year bonds)?

17-2. What will be the "yield to maturity" of a perpetual bond with a $1,000 par value, an 8 percent coupon rate, and a current market price of (a) $800, (b) $1,000, and (c) $1,200? Assume interest is paid annually.

17–3a. Assuming that a bond has four years remaining to maturity and that interest is paid annually, what will be the yield to maturity on the bond with a $1,000 maturity value, an 8 percent coupon interest rate, and a current market price (i) of $825 or (ii) of $1,107? (Hint: Try 14 percent and 5 percent for the two bonds, but *show your work.*)

b. Would you pay $825 for the bond described in part a if your required rate of return for securities in the same risk class is 10 percent; that is, k_b = 10 percent? Explain your answer.

17–4a. The bonds of the Stanroy Corporation are perpetuities bearing a 9 percent coupon. Bonds of this type yield 8 percent. What is the price of Stanroy bonds? Their par value is $1,000.

b. Interest rate levels rise to the point where such bonds now yield 12 percent. What will be the price of the Stanroy bonds now?

c. Interest rate levels drop to 9 percent. At what price will the Stanroy bonds sell?

d. How would your answers to parts a, b, and c change if the bonds had a definite maturity date of 19 years?

17–5a. Trans-Atlantic Aviation is currently earning $8 million a year after taxes. A total of 4,500,000 shares are authorized, and 4,000,000 shares are outstanding. What are the company's earnings per share?

b. Investors require a 16 percent rate of return on stocks in the same risk class as Trans-Atlantic (k_e = 16%). At what price will the stock sell if the pervious dividend was $1 ($d_0$ = $1), and investors expect dividends to grow at a constant compound annual rate of (i) *minus* 6 percent, (ii) 0 percent, (iii) 6 percent, and (iv) 12 percent? (Hint: Use $d_1 = d_0(1 + g)$, not d_0, in the formula.)

c. In part b, what is the "formula price" if the required rate of return is 16 percent and the expected growth rate is (i) 16 percent or (ii) 21 percent? Are these reasonable results? Explain.

d. At what price/earnings (P/E) ratio will the stock sell, assuming each of the growth expectations given in part b?

17–6. Kathy Kobb plans to invest in common stocks for a period of 12 years, after which she will sell out, buy a lifetime room-and-board membership in a retirement home, and retire. She feels that Ogden Mines is currently, but temporarily, undervalued by the market. Kobb expects Ogden Mines' current earnings and dividend to double in the next 12 years. Ogden Mines' last dividend was $2, and its stock currently sells for $45 a share.

a. If Kobb requires a 10 percent return on her investment, will Ogden Mines be a good buy for her?

b. What is the maximum that Kobb could pay for Ogden Mines and still earn her required 10 percent?

c. What might be the cause of such a market undervaluation?

d. Given Kobb's assumptions, what market capitalization rate for Ogden Mines does the current price imply?

17-7. In 1936 the Canadian government raised $55 million by issuing perpetual bonds at a 3 percent annual rate of interest.* Unlike most bonds issued today, which have a specific maturity date, these perpetual bonds can remain outstanding forever; they are, in fact, perpetuities.

At the time of issue, the Canadian government stated that cash redemption was *possible* at face value ($100) on or after September 1966; in other words, the bonds were callable at par after September 1966. Believing that the bonds would in fact be called, many investors in the early 1960s purchased these bonds with expectations of receiving $100 in 1966 for each perpetual they held. In 1963 the bonds sold for $55, but a rush of buyers drove the price to just below the $100 par value by 1966. Prices fell dramatically, however, when the Canadian government announced that these perpetual bonds were indeed perpetual and would *not* be paid off. A new 30-year supply of coupons was sent to each bondholder, and the bond's market price declined to $42 in December 1972.

Because of their severe losses, hundreds of Canadian bondholders have formed the Perpetual Bond Association to lobby for face value redemption of the bonds. Government officials in Ottawa insist that claims for face value payment are nonsense, that the bonds were clearly identified as perpetuals, and that they did not mature in 1966 or at any other time. One Ottawa official states, "Our job is to protect the taxpayer. Why should we pay $55 million for less than $25 million worth of bonds?"

a. Would it make sense for a business firm to issue bonds such as the Canadian bonds described above? Would it matter if the firm was a proprietorship or a corporation?

b. If the United States government today offered a five-year bond, a 50-year bond, a "regular perpetuity," and a Canadian-type perpetuity, what do you think the relative order of interest rates would be; that is, rank the bonds from the one with the lowest to the one with the highest rate of interest. Explain your answer.

c. (i) Suppose that because of pressure by the Perpetual Bond Association, you believe that the Canadian government will redeem this particular perpetual bond issue in five years. Which course of action is more advantageous to you: (1) to sell your bonds today at $42 or (2) to wait five years and have them redeemed? Similar risk bonds earn 8 percent today, and are expected to remain at this level for the next five years.

(ii) If you have the opportunity to invest your money in bonds of similar risk, at what rate of return are you indifferent between selling your perpetuals today or having them redeemed in five

---

*This case is based on an article that appeared in the *Wall Street Journal* on December 26, 1972.

years; that is, what is the expected yield to maturity on the Ca-
nadians?

d. Show, mathematically, the perpetuities' value if they yield 7.15 percent, pay $3 interest annually, and are considered as regular perpetu-
ities. Show what would occur to the price of the bonds if the interest
rate fell to 2 percent.

e. Are the Canadian bonds more likely to be valued as "regular perpetuities" if the going rate of interest is above or below 3 percent?
Why?

f. Do you think the Canadian government would have taken the same
action with regard to retiring the bonds if the interest rate had fallen
rather than risen between 1936 and 1966?

g. Do you think the Canadian government was "fair" or "unfair" in its
actions? Give pros and cons, and justify your reason for thinking
that one outweighs the other.

17–8. In a 1972 study prepared for the Federal Recreation Commission, it was
determined that the following equation can be used to estimate the
required rates of return on various types of long-term capital market
securities (stocks and bonds of various companies): $k_j^* = R_F + .04\beta_j$.
Here k_j^* is the required rate of return on the jth security; R_F is the riskless rate of interest as measured by the yield on long-term United States
government bonds; and β_j is the beta of the jth security's rate of return
during the past five years.

a. What is the required rate of return, k_j^* if the riskless rate of return is 6
percent and the security in question has a beta of (i) .2, (ii) .5, (iii)
1.0, and (iv) 1.5? Graph your results.

b. What is the required rate of return, k_j^*, using the betas given in part a
but assuming the riskless rate (i) rises to 8 percent or (ii) falls to 4
percent? Graph these results.

c. Suppose the required rate of return equation changes from $k_j^* = 6\% +
.04\beta_j$ to $k_j^* = 6\% + .05\beta_j$. What does this imply about investor's risk
aversion? Illustrate with a graph.

d. Suppose the equation $k_j^* = 6\% + .04\beta_j$ is the appropriate one; that is,
this is the equation for the security market line (SML). Further, suppose a particular stock sells for $20 a share, is expected to pay $1 dividend at the end of the current year, and has a beta of expected returns of .8; that is, $\beta_j = .8$. Information reaches investors that causes
them to expect a future growth rate of 3 percent, which is different
from the former expected growth rate. β_j does not change. (i) What
was the former growth rate, assuming the stock was in equilibrium
before the changed expectations as to growth? (ii) What will happen
to the price of the stock? That is, calculate the new equilibrium price,
and explain the process by which this new equilibrium will be
reached. The expected dividend for the current year is still $1.

17–9. Because of ill health and old age, John Ashby contemplates the sale of
his shoe store. His corporation has the following balance sheet:

Assets		Liabilities and Net Worth	
Cash	$ 6,000	Notes payable — bank	$ 2,000
Receivables, net	2,000	Accounts payable	4,000
Inventories	13,000	Accruals	1,000
Fixtures and equipment less $10,000 reserve for depreciation	14,000	Common stock plus surplus	28,000
Total assets	$35,000	Total liabilities and net worth	$35,000

Annual before-tax earnings (after rent, interest, and salaries) for the preceding three years have averaged $8,000.

Ashby has set a price of $40,000, which includes all the assets of the business except cash; the buyer assumes all debts. The assets include a five-year lease on the building in which the store is located and the goodwill associated with the name of Ashby Shoes. Assume that both Ashby and the potential purchaser are in the 50 percent tax bracket.

a. Is the price of $40,000 a reasonable one? Explain.

b. What other factors should be taken into account in arriving at a selling price?

c. What is the significance, if any, of the five-year lease?

17–10. The Ellis Company is a small jewelry manufacturer. The company has been successful and has grown. Now, Ellis is planning to sell an issue of common stock to the public for the first time, and it faces the problem of setting an appropriate price on its common stock. The company feels that the proper procedure is to select firms similar to it with publicly traded common stock and to make relevant comparisons.

The company finds several jewelry manufacturers similar to it with respect to product mix, size, asset composition, and debt/equity proportions. Of these, Bonden and Seeger are most similar.

Relation	Bonden	Seeger	(Ellis Totals)
Earnings per share, 1978	$ 5.00	$ 8.00	$ 1,500,000
Average, 1972–78	4.00	5.00	1,000,000
Price per share, 1978	48.00	65.00	—
Dividends per share, 1978	3.00	4.00	700,000
Average, 1972–78	2.50	3.25	500,000
Book value per share	45.00	70.00	12,000,000
Market-book ratio	107%	93%	—

a. How would these relations be used in guiding Ellis in arriving at a market value for its stock?

b. What price would you recommend if Ellis sells 500,000 shares?

17–11. The Mid-America Consulting Corporation is expected to grow at a rate of about 18 percent for the next four years, then at 12 percent for another three years, and finally settle down to a growth rate of 6 percent for the indefinite future. The company's common stock currently pays a $0.60 dividend, but dividends are expected to increase in proportion to the growth of the firm.

a. What values would you place on the common stock if you require a 12 percent return on your investment?

b. How would your valuation be affected if you intend to hold the stock for only three years?

c. What would you expect the trend (i) of market price, (ii) of price/earnings ratio, and (iii) of dividend yield to be over the next ten years (up, down, or constant)?

17–12. An investor requires a 20 percent return on the common stock of the M Company. During its most recent complete year, the M Company stock earned $4 and paid $2 per share. Its earnings and dividends are expected to grow at a 32 percent rate for five years, after which they are expected to grow at 8 percent per year. At what value of the M Company stock would the investor earn his required 20 percent return?

17–13. The Mason Company is contemplating the purchase of the Norton Company. During the most recent year, Norton had earnings of $2 million and paid dividends of $1 million. The earnings and dividends of Norton were expected to grow at an annual rate of 30 percent for five years, after which they will grow at an 8 percent rate per year. The required return on an investment with the risk characteristics of the Norton Company is 16 percent.

What is the maximum that the Mason Company could pay for the Norton Company to earn at least a 16 percent return on its investment?

Selected References

Arditti, Fred D. "Risk and the Required Return on Equity." *Journal of Finance* (Mar. 1967):19–36.

———. "A Note on Discounting the Components of an Income Stream." *Journal of Finance* 29 (June 1974):995–99.

Barnea, Amir, and Logue, Dennis E. "Evaluating the Forecasts of a Security Analyst." *Financial Management* 2 (Summer 1973):38–45.

Bauman, W. Scott. "Investment Returns and Present Values." *Financial Analysts' Journal* 25 (Nov.–Dec. 1969):107–18.

Ben-Shahar, Haim, and Sarnat, Marshall. "Reinvestment and the Rate of Return on Common Stocks." *Journal of Finance* 21 (Dec. 1966):737–42.

Bower, Richard S., and Bower, Dorothy H. "Risk and the Valuation of Common Stock." *Journal of Political Economy* 77 (May–June 1969):349–62.

Brigham, Eugene F., and Pappas, James L. "Duration of Growth, Changes in Growth Rates, and Corporate Share Prices." *Financial Analysts' Journal* 24 (May–June 1966):157–62.

Carr, J. L.; Halpern, P. J.; and McCallum, J. S. "Correcting the Yield Curve: A Re-Interpretation of the Duration Problem." *Journal of Finance* 29 (Sept. 1974):1287–94.

Draper, P. R. "Industry Influences on Share Price Variability." *Journal of Business Finance & Accounting* 2 (Summer 1975):169–86.

Edwards, Charles E., and Hilton, James G. "High-Low Averages as an Estimator of Annual Average Stock Prices." *Journal of Finance* 21 (Mar. 1966): 112–15.

Elton, Edwin J., and Gruber, Martin J. "Earnings Estimates and the Accuracy of Expectational Data." *Management Science* 18 (Apr. 1972):409–24.

———. "Valuation and Asset Selection Under Alternative Investment Opportunities." *Journal of Finance* 31 (May 1976):525–39.

Elton, Edwin J.; Gruber, Martin J.; and Lieber, Zvi. "Financial Models of Regulated Firms Valuation, Optimum Investment and Financing for the Firm Subject to Regulation." *Journal of Finance* 30 (May 1975):401–25.

Fewings, David R. "The Impact of Growth on the Risk of Common Stocks." *Journal of Finance* 30 (May 1975):525–31.

Fisher, Lawrence. "Determinants of Risk Premiums on Corporate Bonds." *Journal of Political Economy* 67 (June 1959):217–37.

Foster, Earl M. "Price-Earnings Ratio and Corporate Growth." *Financial Analysts' Journal* (Jan.–Feb. 1970):96–99.

Gentry, James A., and Pyhrr, Stephen A. "Simulating an EPS Growth Model." *Financial Management* 2 (Summer 1973):68–75.

Granger, Clive W. J. "Some Consequences of the Valuation Model When Expectations are Taken to be Optimum Forecasts." *Journal of Finance* 30 Mar. 1975):135–45.

Haugen, Robert A. "Expected Growth, Required Return, and the Variability of Stock Prices." *Journal of Financial and Quantitative Analysis* 5 (Sept. 1970): 297–308.

Haugen, Robert A., and Heins, A. James. "Risk and the Rate of Return on Financial Assets." *Journal of Financial and Quantitative Analysis* 10 (Dec. 1975): 775–84.

Haugen, Robert A., and Wichern, Dean W. "The Elasticity of Financial Assets." *Journal of Finance* 29 (Sept. 1974):1229–40.

Herzog, John P. "Investor Experience in Corporate Securities: A New Technique for Measurement." *Journal of Finance* 19 (Mar. 1964):46–62.

Holt, Charles C. "The Influence of Growth Duration on Share Prices." *Journal of Finance* 17 (Sept. 1962):465–75.

Ibbotson, Roger G., and Sinquefield, Rex A. "Stocks, Bonds, Bills, and Inflation: Simulations of the Future (1976–2000)." *Journal of Business* 49 (July 1976): 313–38.

Jaffe, Jeffrey F., and Mandelker, Gershon. "The Value of the Firm Under Regulation." *Journal of Finance* 31 (May 1976):701–13.

Lintner, John. "Inflation and Security Returns." *Journal of Finance* 30 (May 1975):259–80.

Logue, Dennis E., and Merville, Larry J. "Financial Policy and Market Expectations." *Financial Management* 1 (Summer 1972):37–44.

Malkiel, Burton G. "Equity Yields, Growth, and the Structure of Share Prices." *American Economic Review* 53 (Dec. 1963):467–94.

Malkiel, Burton G., and Gragg, John G. "Expectations and the Structure of Share Prices." *American Economic Review* 40 (Sept. 1970):601–17.

Mao, James C. T. "The Valuation of Growth Stocks: The Investment Opportunities Approach." *Journal of Finance* 21 (Mar. 1966):95–102.

McDonald, John G., and Osborne Alfred E., Jr. "Forecasting the Market Return on Common Stocks." *Journal of Business Finance & Accounting* 1 (Summer 1974):217–37.

McEnally, Richard W. "A Note on the Return Behavior of High Risk Common Stocks." *Journal of Finance* 29 (Mar. 1974):199–202.

Melicher, Ronald W., and Rush, David F. "Systematic Risk, Financial Data, and Bond Rating Relationships in a Regulated Industry Environment." *Journal of Finance* 29 (May 1974):537–44.

Norgaard, Richard L. "An Examination of the Yields of Corporate Bonds and Stocks." *Journal of Finance* 29 (Sept. 1974):1275–86.

Ofer, Aharon R. "Investors Expectations of Earnings Growth, Their Accuracy and Effects on the Structure of Realized Rates of Return." *Journal of Finance* 30 (May 1975):509–23.

Pinches, George E., and Mingo, Kent A. "A Multivariate Analysis of Industrial Bond Ratings." *Journal of Finance* 28 (Mar. 1973):1–18.

Pringle, John J. "Price/Earnings Ratios, Earnings Per Share, and Financial Management." *Financial Management* 2 (Spring 1973):34–40.

Ricketts, Donald E., and Barrett, Michael J. "Corporate Operating Income Forecasting Ability." *Financial Management* 2 (Summer 1973):53–62.

Robichek, Alexander A., and Bogue, Marcus C. "A Note on the Behavior of Expected Price/Earnings Ratios Over Time." *Journal of Finance* 26 (June 1971):731–36.

Silvers, J. B. "An Alternative to the Yield Spread as a Measure of Risk." *Journal of Finance* 28 (Sept. 1973):933–55.

Soldofsky, Robert M. "The History of Bond Tables and Stock Valuation Models." *Journal of Finance* 21 (Mar. 1966):103–11.

Soldofsky, Robert M., and Murphy, James T. *Growth Yields on Common Stock—Theory and Tables.* Iowa City, Iowa: State University of Iowa, 1963.

Stone, B. K. "The Conformity of Stock Values Based on Discounted Dividends to a Fair-return Process." *Bell Journal of Economics* 6 (Autumn 75):698–702.

Thompson, Howard E. "A Note on the Value of Rights in Estimating the Investor Capitalization Rate." *Journal of Finance* 28 (Mar. 1973):157–60.

Van Horne, James C., and Glassmire, William F., Jr. "The Impact of Unanticipated Changes in Inflation on the Value of Common Stocks." *Journal of Finance* 7 (Dec. 1972):1081–92.

Walter, James E. "Investment Planning Under Variable Price Change." *Financial Management* 1 (Winter 1972):36–50.

Warren, James M. "An Operational Model for Security Analysis and Valuation." *Journal of Financial and Quantitative Analysis* 9 (June 1974):395–422.

Wendt, Paul F. "Current Growth Stock Valuation Methods." *Financial Analysts' Journal* 33 (Mar.–Apr. 1965):3–15.

18 Financial Structure and the Use of Leverage

In the last chapter, we saw that each security has a required rate of return, k^*, and an expected rate of return, $\bar{k}$. The required rate of return is determined in part by the level of interest rates (the risk-free rate) in the economy, and in part by the riskiness of the individual security. The expected rate of return on a bond or a share of preferred stock is determined primarily by the interest or preferred dividends, while the expected rate of return on common stock depends upon earnings available for distribution as cash dividends and growth. Both risk and expected returns may be affected by financial leverage, as we see in this chapter.

Basic Definitions

To avoid ambiguity in the use of key concepts, the meanings of frequently used expressions are given here. *Financial structure* refers to the way the firm's assets are financed: it is the entire right-hand side of the balance sheet. *Capital structure* is the permanent financing of the firm, represented primarily by long-term debt, preferred stock, and common equity, but excluding all short-term credit. Thus, a firm's capital structure is only a part of its financial structure. *Common equity* includes common stock, capital surplus, and accumulated retained earnings.

Our key concept for this chapter is *financial leverage*, or the *leverage factor*, defined as the ratio of total debt to total assets or the total value of the firm. For example, a firm having a total value of $100 million and a total debt of $50 million would have a leverage factor of 50 percent.[1] Thus B/V = 50 percent. The B/V ratio implies a debt to common stock (B/S) ratio. B/S is equal to B/V ÷ (1 − B/V). Thus if B/V = .5, then B/S = 1.

Finally, we should distinguish at the outset between business risk and financial risk. By *business risk* we mean the inherent uncertainty or variability of expected pretax returns on the firm's "portfolio" of assets. This kind of risk was examined in Chapter 11, where it was defined in terms of the probability distribution of returns on the firm's assets. By *financial risk* we mean the additional risk that is induced by the use of financial leverage.

---

1. The present discussion will consider variations in financial leverage in the context of a debt-equity tradeoff. No distinction will be made between long- and short-term debt.

Theory of Financial Leverage

Perhaps the best way to understand the proper use of financial leverage is to analyze its impact on profitability and fluctuations in profitability under various leverage conditions.[2] As an example, consider four alternative financial structures for the Universal Machine Company, a manufacturer of equipment used by industrial firms. The alternative balance sheets are displayed in Table 18–1.

Table 18–1
Four Alternative Financial Structures, Universal Machine Company (Based on Book Values) ($000)

Structure 1: $B/S = 0\%$; $B/TA = 0\%$

		Total debt	$ 0
		Common stock ($10 par)	10,000
Total assets	$10,000	Total claims	$10,000

Structure 2: $B/S = 25\%$; $B/TA = 20\%$

		Total debt (10%)	$ 2,000
		Common stock ($10 par)	8,000
Total assets	$10,000	Total claims	$10,000

Structure 3: $B/S = 100\%$; $B/TA = 50\%$

		Total debt (10%)	$ 5,000
		Common stock ($10 par)	5,000
Total assets	$10,000	Total claims	$10,000

Structure 4: $B/S = 400\%$; $B/TA = 80\%$

		Total debt (10%)	$ 8,000
		Common stock ($10 par)	2,000
Total assets	$10,000	Total claims	$10,000

Structure 1 uses no debt and consequently has a leverage factor of zero. Structure 2 has a leverage factor of 20 percent. Structure 3 has a leverage factor of 50 percent, and structure 4 has a leverage factor of 80 percent.

How do these different financial patterns affect stockholder returns? As can be seen from Table 18–2, the answer depends partly upon the

---

2. We shall initially hold the level of investment constant, considering only different financial structures for a firm of the same size. Since firms also face decisions that require a choice between debt versus equity for financing an increase in investment, this second type of decision will next be analyzed with the benefit of the perspective provided by the more general analysis of the financial structure decision in its pure form.

Table 18–2
**Stockholders'
Returns and
Earnings per Share
under Various
Leverage and
Economic
Conditions,
Universal Machine
Company ($000)**

	.1	.3	.4	.2
Probability of indicated sales				
Sales in Dollars	$ 0	$6,000	$10,000	$20,000
Fixed costs	2,000	2,000	2,000	2,000
Variable costs (40% of sales)	−	2,400	4,000	8,000
Total costs (except interest)	$2,000	$4,400	$ 6,000	$10,000
Earnings before interest and taxes (EBIT)	$(2,000)	$1,600	$ 4,000	$10,000
Capital Structure 1				
EBIT				
Less: Interest				
Less: Income taxes (50%)*	(1,000)	800	2,000	5,000
Net profit after taxes	$(1,000)	$ 800	$ 2,000	$ 5,000
Earnings per share on 1,000 shares	−$1.00	$ .80	$2.00	$5.00
Return on stockholders' equity	−10%	8%	20%	50%
Capital Structure 2				
EBIT				
Less: Interest (10% × 2,000)	200	200	200	200
Earnings before taxes	(2,200)	$1,400	$ 3,800	$ 9,800
Less: Income taxes (50%)*	(1,100)	700	1,900	4,900
Net profit after taxes	$(1,100)	$ 700	$ 1,900	$ 4,900
Earnings per share on 800 shares	−$1.38	$ .88	$2.38	$6.13
Return on stockholders' equity	−13.8%	8.8%	23.8%	61.3%
Capital Structure 3				
EBIT				
Less: Interest (10% × 5,000)	500	500	500	500
Earnings before taxes	(2,500)	1,100	3,500	9,500
Less: Income taxes (50%)*	(1,250)	550	1,750	4,750
Net profit after taxes	$(1,250)	$ 550	$ 1,750	$ 4,750
Earnings per share on 500 shares	−$2.50	$ 1.10	$3.50	$9.50
Return on stockholders' equity	−25%	11%	35%	95%
Capital Structure 4				
EBIT				
Less: Interest (10% × 8,000)	800	800	800	800
Earnings before taxes (50%)*	(2,800)	800	3,200	9,200
Less: Income taxes	(1,400)	400	1,600	4,600
Net profit after taxes	$(1,400)	$ 400	$ 1,600	$ 4,600
Earnings per share on 200 shares	−$7.00	$ 2.00	$8.00	$23.00
Return on stockholders' equity	−70%	20%	80%	230%

*The tax calculation assumes that losses are carried back and result in tax credits.

level of sales of the firm and partly upon the probability assessments associated with the alternative potential sales levels of Universal. The probability distribution for future sales was constructed by Universal's marketing department in cooperation with representatives from the general staff group of top management based on their knowledge of present supply and demand conditions along with estimates for future economic conditions and sales. The alternative probable conditions range from very poor (zero sales due to the possibility of a labor strike resulting from some very difficult labor negotiations currently underway) to very good under an optimistic assessment of the future outlook. It is assumed that the firm has total assets of $10,000,000.[3] The rate of interest on debt is 10 percent and the assumed tax rate is 50 percent. Variable costs are estimated to be 40 percent of sales and fixed costs equal $2,000,000.

Table 18–2 lays out the pattern of the analysis. It begins by listing the probability of sales at levels indicated by the next line. The fixed costs as shown remain the same for each level of sales. The total amount of variable costs increases with the level of sales since variable costs are 40 percent of sales. The fixed costs and variable costs are added to obtain total costs. Sales less total costs equals earnings before interest and taxes *(EBIT)*. Based on the indicated level of earnings before interest and taxes for the four sales levels associated with probabilities ranging from .1 to .4, the effects of the four alternative capital structures are analyzed.

Capital structure 1 is first considered. Since structure 1 employs no leverage, the interest expense is zero. *EBIT* divided by the 1,000,000 shares of common stock gives earnings per share associated with each of the probability factors and with each of the alternative levels of sales. The rate of return on common stock is *EBIT* minus taxes divided by stockholder's equity.

When debt is introduced into the capital structure, interest on the debt is deducted from the earnings before interest and taxes *(EBIT)* before the tax rate is applied and the net profit after tax is calculated. Then earnings per share on the indicated number of shares and the return on stockholders' equity is calculated as before. The capital structure with no debt is now compared with capital structure 3 with the 50 percent leverage factor since this leverage factor approximates that for all manufacturing industries in the United States for 1976. For the capital structure with no debt, earnings per share range from a loss of $1 per share to profit of $5 a share, a range of $6. Under the capital structure with a leverage factor of 50 percent, the range in earnings per share is from a

---

3. The numbers are rounded for convenience and in most tables and calculations the analysis will be made in thousands of dollars, so that the last three zeros will be omitted explicitly.

negative $2.50 to a positive $9.50. This is a range of $12, which is double the range in earnings per share with zero leverage. Similarly the return on shareholders' equity for the unlevered firm has a range of 60 percentage points, while the return on stockholders' equity for the 50 percent levered firm has a range of 120 percentage points.

Table 18–2 shows the two return relationships, earnings per share and return on stockholders' equity, associated with leverage. Under any given financial structure earnings per share and the return on stockholders' equity increase with improved sales levels. Also, these earnings are magnified as leverage is increased. Thus increased leverage increases the degree of fluctuations in earnings per share and in returns on equity for any given degree of fluctuation in sales and its related return on total assets. Leverage increases the returns to the owners of the firm if used successfully. But if leverage is unsuccessful, it may result in inability to pay fixed charge obligations and ultimately result in financial difficulties leading to financial reorganization or bankruptcy.[4]

In Table 18–3 a return-risk analysis of the four financial structure alternatives is performed. Applying the probability factors to each of the associated earnings per share results, the expected earnings per share is calculated for each financial structure and the associated variance and standard deviation for each financial structure is calculated as well. Then the standard deviation is divided by the expected earnings per share to obtain the coefficient of variation. These are all presented in

Figure 18–1
Relationship Between
Return and Leverage

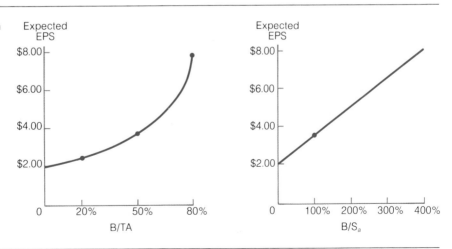

4. See Chapter 23 for an explanation of the nature of financial reorganization and bankruptcy.

Table 18–3 for each of the four alternative financial structures considered. Figure 18–1 provides a graph of the expected earnings per share
as calculated in Table 18–3 in relation to the four alternative debt to
equity and debt to total asset ratios. It will be seen that the expected
earnings per share increase linearly with the debt to equity ratio and
increase at an increasing rate when the leverage factor is measured by
the debt to total asset ratio.

Table 18–3 **Return-risk Analysis** **of the Four** **Financial Structure** **Alternatives**		s	p_s	EPS	$p_s EPS$	$EPS - E(EPS)$	$[EPS - E(EPS)]^2$	$p_s[EPS - E(EPS)]^2$
	Structure 1	1	.1	−$1.00	−.1	−2.94	8.6436	.8644
		2	.3	$ .80	.24	−1.14	1.2996	.3899
		3	.4	$2.00	.8	.06	.0036	.0014
		4	.2	$5.00	1.0	3.06	9.3636	1.8727
				$E(EPS) = \$1.94$				$\sigma^2 = 3.1284$
								$\sigma = 1.7687$
					$CV = \sigma/E(EPS) = .912$			
	Structure 2	1	.1	−$1.38	−.138	−3.68	13.5424	1.3542
		2	.3	$ .88	.264	−1.42	2.0164	.6049
		3	.4	$2.38	.952	.08	.0064	.0026
		4	.2	$6.13	1.226	3.83	14.6689	2.9338
				$E(EPS) = \$2.30$				$\sigma^2 = 4.8955$
								$\sigma = 2.2126$
					$CV = .962$			
	Structure 3	1	.1	−$2.50	−.25	−5.88	34.5744	3.4574
		2	.3	$1.10	.33	−2.28	5.1984	1.7155
		3	.4	$3.50	1.40	.12	.0144	.0058
		4	.2	$9.50	1.90	6.12	37.4544	7.4909
				$E(EPS) = \$3.38$				$\sigma^2 = 12.6696$
								$\sigma = 3.5594$
					$CV = 1.05$			
	Structure 4	1	.1	−$7.00	−.7	−14.70	216.09	21.609
		2	.3	$2.00	.6	−5.70	32.49	9.747
		3	.4	$8.00	3.20	.30	.09	.036
		4	.2	$23.00	4.60	15.30	234.09	46.818
				$E(EPS) = \$7.70$				$\sigma^2 = 78.21$
								$\sigma = 8.8436$
					$CV = 1.15$			

We now turn to a consideration of some alternative measures of the
riskiness of the expected returns in relation to the alternative levels of
sales and the alternative financial structures employed. We have noted

how leverage increases the variability of earnings per share and the variability of returns to stockholders. For example, using no leverage, earnings per share range from a loss of $1 to a gain of $5. With a leverage of 80 percent the range is from a loss of $7 to a gain of $23 per share.

There are three alternative measures of this variability in earnings induced by leverage, each of which in some sense is a measure of risk. These three alternative measures of risk are the standard deviation, the coefficient of variation and the beta coefficient. The standard deviation and coefficient of variation of expected earnings per share are calculated in Table 18−3. In each case the coefficient of variation is calculated by dividing the standard deviation by the average earnings per share. The coefficient of variation rises from .912 in structure 1 to 1.15 in structure 4. Clearly, both of these measures of risk rise with increased leverage.

The third measure of risk is the beta coefficient (β) for the various leverage factors illustrated. First, the market return parameters must be estimated. The basic estimates of the market return are shown for the four probability factors in Table 18−4. Applying the probability factors to the four alternative estimates of the return on the market, the expected or average return on the market is shown to be 10 percent. When the expected return on the market is deducted from each of the four estimates of market returns, the deviations of the market returns from their mean are calculated as in Column 5. In Column 6 these deviations are squared. In Column 7 the probability factors are applied, then the items are summed to obtain the variance of the market, which is approximately 1 percent. The standard deviation of the market returns would, therefore, be .1.

Table 18−4
Estimation of Market Parameters

(1)	(2)	(3)	(4)	(5)	(6)	(7)
s	p_s	k_M	$p_s k_M$	$[k_M - E(k_M)]$	$[k_M - E(k_M)]^2$	$p_s[k_M - E(k_M)]^2$
1	.1	(.15)	(.015)	(.25)	.0625	.00625
2	.3	.05	.015	(.05)	.0025	.00075
3	.4	.15	.60	.05	.0025	.00100
4	.2	.20	.040	.10	.01	.00200
			$E(k_M) = .10$			Var $k_M = .01000$
						$\sigma k_M \cong .10$

With the use of the market parameters calculated in Table 18−4, we can utilize the procedures illustrated near the end of Chapter 11 to calculate the βs for each level of leverage of the Universal Machine Company, as shown in Table 18−5.

**Table 18–5
Calculation of the
Beta Coefficients*
for Four Alternative
Leverage Ratios
Universal Machine
Company (Based
on Market Values)†**

Financial Structure	B_j/V_j	B_j/S_j	B_j
1	0%	0%	.65
2	8.16%	8.89%	.68
3	19.2%	23.8%	.73
4	29.1%	41.0%	.79

*Recall that $\beta_j^* = \text{Cov}(k_j, k_M)/\text{Var}(k_M)$ where β_j^* is the beta for an unlevered firm, and as will be developed in Chapter 19, $\beta_j = \beta_j^* + \beta_j^*(B_j/S_j)(1 - T)$.

†First, V_u is obtained by the method discussed in Chapter 11, which establishes that $V_u = \dfrac{E(X) - \lambda\,\text{Cov}(X, k_M)}{R_F}$. For this example, we have $V_u = \dfrac{1940 - 5(153)}{.05} = \$23,500$. Second, we use the relation developed in Appendix B to Chapter 19, $V_L = V_u + TB$ where V_L is the value of the levered firm and V_u is the value of the unlevered firm. By definition, $S_j = V_j - B$.

The results in Table 18–5 are calculated as follows:

1. First obtain $E(X)$ and $\text{Cov}(X, k_u)$. Note that X is after taxes.

s	P_s	X	P_sX	$(X - \overline{X})(k_M - \bar{k}_M)P_s$
1	.1	−1,000	− 100	$(-2,940)(-.25).1 = 73.5$
2	.3	800	240	$(-1,140)(-.05).3 = 17.1$
3	.4	2,000	800	$(\quad 60)(\ .05).4 = 1.2$
4	.2	5,000	1,000	$(\ 3,060)(\ .10).2 = 61.2$
			$\overline{X} = 1,940$	$\text{Cov}(X, k_M) = 153.0$

Recall that $(k_M - \bar{k}_M)$ is in column (5) of Table 18–4.
$\text{Cov}(k_j, k_M) = \text{Cov}(X_j, k_M)/V_u = 153/23,500 = .0065$
$\beta_j^* = \text{Cov}(k_j, k_M)/\text{Var}(k_M) = .0065/.01 = .65$

2. Calculate beta for the leveraged financial structures.

Financial Structure (1)	TB (2)	V_L (3)	B (4)	B/V_L (4) − (3) (5)	S (3) − (4) (6)	B/S (4) − (6) (7)	$B/S(1 - T)$ .5(7) (8)	$B/S(1 - T)\beta^*$ .65(8) (9)	B_j .65 + (9) (10)
1	0	—	0	—	—	—	—	—	.65
2	$1,000	$24,500	$2,000	8.16%	$22,500	8.89%	.0444	.0289	.68
3	2.500	26,000	5,000	19.2	21,000	23.8	.1190	.0774	.73
4	4,000	27,500	8,000	29.1	19,500	41.0	.2051	.1333	.78

In Table 18–5 one risk measure, the beta coefficient, is exhibited in relationship to the leverage ratios of debt to the total market value of the firm and debt to the total market value of the equity. Since the leverage ratios are measured in market values in Table 18–5, as is required by the theoretical relationship between β and leverage, the leverage ratios at market values for the four financial structures are different from the leverage ratios measured at book in Table 18–6.

In Table 18–6 other risk-return tradeoffs for various leverage ratios for Universal Machine Company are set forth. The table shows how the leverage ratio measured by both debt/assets and debt/equity influences expected earnings per share. In addition, two of the associated risk measures are exhibited. The risk measures are the standard deviation and the coefficient of variation. The leverage ratios are measured at book values.

Table 18–6 **Risk-return Tradeoff** **for Various** **Leverage Ratios,** **Universal Machine** **Company (Based** **on Book Values)**	Debt/Assets	Debt/Equity	Expected *EPS*	Standard Deviation	Coefficient of Variation
	0%	0%	$1.94	1.77	.912
	20%	25%	$2.30	2.21	.962
	50%	100%	$3.38	3.56	1.050
	80%	400%	$7.70	8.84	1.150

These numerical relationships between leverage and the three risk measures are summarized in Figure 18–2. The relationship between risk as measured by the standard deviation and the leverage ratio of debt/equity measured at book, as well as risk as measured by the β coefficient and the debt/equity ratio measured at market are both linear. Also, the relationship between the coefficient of variation and the debt/equity ratio measured at book is curvilinear but curved down from above. The relationship when leverage is measured by debt/total assets is curvilinear upward for the standard deviation and for the β coefficient. However, when risk is measured by the coefficient of variation in relation to the debt/total asset leverage ratio, a linear relationship obtains. The different shapes of the relationship stem from the basic underlying theory of the computations involved. But what is common to all of the six portrayals of the relationship between risk and leverage is that to obtain the higher expected earnings, whether measured by earnings per share or return on stockholders' equity that go with increased leverage, the firm must incur more risk. As previously indicated, there is a positive relationship between return and risk and there is also a positive relationship between risk and the degree of leverage employed.

Another dimension of the return-leverage-risk relationship is exhibited by Figure 18–3. Figure 18–3 sets forth a relationship between rates of return on assets and rates of return on net worth under different leverage conditions. For zero leverage, the line of relationship begins at the origin and has a slope that is less steep than the slope of the relationship when leverage is employed. With leverage, the intercept of the

Figure 18–2
Relationships Between
Risk and Leverage

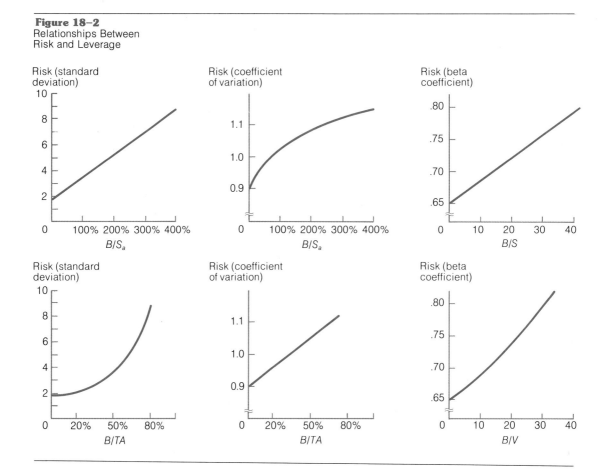

line is negative, indicating that at low rates of return on total assets, the return on net worth is negative, representing a loss. The intersection of the three lines is at the 10 percent rate of return on total assets, which is equal to the before-tax interest cost of debt. At this intersection point the return on net worth is 5 percent. The 50 percent tax rate reduces the 10 percent return on total assets to a return of 5 percent on net worth regardless of the degree of leverage. When returns on assets are higher than 10 percent, debt-financed assets can cover interest cost and still leave something over for the stockholders. But the reverse holds if assets earn less than 10 percent. Figure 18–3 illustrates a general proposition: Whenever the return on assets exceeds the cost of debt, leverage is favorable, and the higher the leverage factor the higher the rate of return on common equity.

Figure 18–3
Relationship Between
Rates of Return on
Assets and Rates of
Return on Net Worth
under Different
Leverage Conditions

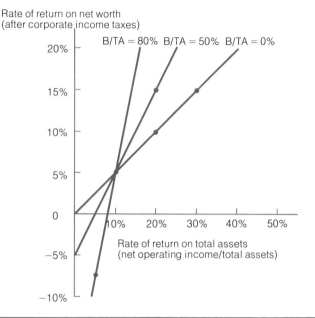

Analysis of Alternative Methods of Financing

Thus far in the analysis we have simply varied leverage, holding the total amount of investment by the firm constant. In real world decision making it is often necessary to perform an analysis in which alternative leverage structures are being considered along with financing which increases the amount of the investment of the firm and the size of total assets. This further aspect of combining the financing and leverage decisions will be developed by a continuation of the Universal Machine Company example. The latest balance sheet of the Universal Machine Company is set forth in Table 18–7. Universal Machine Company manufactures equipment used in industrial manufacturing. The major product is a lathe used to trim the rough edges off sheets of fabricated steel. The lathes sell for $100,000 each. As is typically the case for producers of

Table 18–7
Universal Machine Company
Balance Sheet,
December 31,
1977 ($000)

Cash	$ 300	Total liabilities having	
Receivables (net)	1,200	an average cost of 10%	$ 5,000
Inventories	1,400		
Plant (net)	3,000	Common stock ($10 par)	5,000
Equipment (net)	4,100		
Total assets	$10,000	Total claims on assets	$10,000

durable capital assets, the company's sales fluctuate widely, far more than does the overall economy. For example, during nine of the preceding 25 years, sales of the Universal Machine Company have been below the breakeven point, so losses have been relatively frequent.

Although future sales are uncertain, current demand is high and appears to be headed higher. Thus, if Universal is to continue its sales growth, it will have to increase capacity. A capacity increase involving $2,000,000 of new capital is under consideration. James Watson, the financial vice-president, learns that he can raise $2,000,000 by selling bonds with a 10 percent coupon. Alternatively, he can raise the additional funds by selling 100,000 shares of common stock at a market price of $20 per share. Fixed costs after the planned expansion will be $2,000,000 a year. Variable costs excluding interest on the debt will be 40 percent of sales.[5] The probability distribution for future sales possibilities is the same as was set forth in the previous section analyzing the pure leverage decision for Universal.

Although Watson's recommendation will be given much weight, the final decision for the method of financing rests with the company's board of directors. Procedurally, the financial vice president will analyze the situation, evaluate all reasonable alternatives, come to a conclusion, and then present the alternatives with his recommendations to the board. For his own analysis, as well as for presentation to the board, Watson prepares the materials shown in Table 18–8.

In the top third of the table, earnings before interest and taxes *(EBIT)* are calculated for different levels of sales ranging from $0 to $2 million. The firm suffers an operating loss until sales are $3.3 million, but beyond that point it enjoys a rapid rise in gross profit.

The middle third of the table shows the financial results that will occur at the various sales levels if bonds are used. First, the $700,000 annual interest charges ($500,000 on existing debt plus $200,000 on the new bonds) are deducted from the earnings before interest and taxes. Next, taxes are taken out; notice that if the sales level is so low that losses are incurred, the firm receives a tax credit. Then, net profits after taxes are divided by the 500,000 shares outstanding to obtain earnings per share *(EPS)* of common stock.[6] The various *EPS* figures are multiplied by the corresponding probability estimates to obtain an expected *EPS* of $3.18. Finally, the coefficient of variation is calculated and used as a measure of the riskiness of the financing plan.

In the bottom third of the table, the financial results that will occur

---

5. The assumption that variable costs will be a constant percentage of sales over the entire range of output is not valid, but variable costs are relatively constant over the output range likely to occur.

6. The number of shares initially outstanding can be calculated by dividing the $5 million common stock figure given on the balance sheet by the $10 par value.

Table 18–8 Universal Machine Company, Profit Calculations at Various Sales Levels	Probability of indicated sales	.1	.3	.4	.2
	Sales in units	0	60	100	200
	Sales in dollars	$ 0	$6,000	$10,000	$20,000
	Fixed costs	2,000	2,000	2,000	2,000
	Variable costs (40% of sales)	0	2,400	4,000	8,000
	Total costs (except interest)	$ 2,000	$4,400	$ 6,000	$10,000
	Earnings before interest and taxes (EBIT)	$(2,000)	$1,600	$ 4,000	$10,000

Financing with bonds ($B/A = 58.3\%$; $B/S = 140\%$)

Less: Interest (10% × 7,000)	700	700	700	700
Earnings before taxes	(2,700)	900	3,300	9,300
Less: Income taxes (50%)	(1,350)	450	1,650	4,650
Net profit after taxes	(1,350)	450	1,650	4,650
EPS on 500 shares*	−$2.70	$ .90	$ 3.30	$ 9.30
Expected EPS $3.18				

Financing with stock ($B/A = 41.7\%$; $B/S_j = 71.4\%$)

Less: Interest (10% × 5,000)	500	500	500	500
Earnings before taxes	(2,500)	1,100	3,500	9,500
Less: Income taxes (50%)	(1,250)	550	1,750	4,750
Net profit after taxes	(1,250)	550	1,750	4,750
EPS on 600 shares*	$ (2.08)	$ .92	$ 2.92	$ 7.91
Expected EPS $2.82				

*The EPS figures can also be obtained using the following formula:

$$EPS = \frac{(\text{sales} - \text{fixed costs} - \text{variable costs} - \text{interest})(1 - \text{tax rate})}{\text{shares outstanding}}$$

For example, at sales = $10 million,

$$EPS_{stock} = \frac{(10 - 2 - 4 - .5)(.5)}{.6} = \$2.92$$

$$EPS_{bonds} = \frac{(10 - 2 - 4 - .7)(.5)}{.5} = \$3.30$$

with stock financing are calculated. Net profit after interest and taxes is divided by 600,000—the original 500,000 plus the new 100,000 ($20 × 100,000 = $2 million)—to find earnings per share. Expected *EPS* is computed in the same way as for the bond financing.

Figure 18–4 shows the probability distribution of earnings per share. Stock financing has the tighter, more peaked distribution. We know from Table 18–3 that it will also have a smaller coefficient of variation than bond financing. Hence, stock financing is less risky than bond financing. However, the expected earnings per share is lower for stock than for bonds, so we are again faced with the kind of risk-return trade-off that characterizes most financial decisions.

The nature of the tradeoff can be made more specific. In Table 18–9

Figure 18–4
Probability Curves for
Stock and Bond
Financing

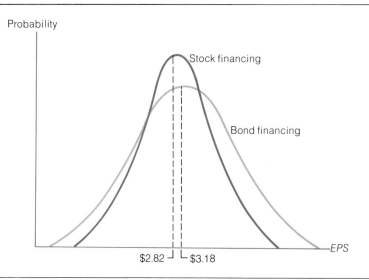

we present two measures of the leverage return and risk relationships. In Part A of the table the leverage ratio as measured by debt to total assets at book values are related to expected earnings per share and the coefficient of variation. In Part B the leverage as measured by debt to equity at market values is related to the expected return on equity and the beta measure of risk.

The nature of these relationships is depicted graphically in Figure 18–5. There is an upward curvilinear relationship between the coefficient of variation and earnings per share when the leverage ratio is measured by debt to total assets at book value. There is a linear relationship between beta and the return on equity when leverage is measured

Table 18–9

Leverage, Return, and Risk Relationships

		Leverage Ratio B/TA%	Expected EPS	Coefficient of Variation
Part A		0	1.94	.912
		20	2.30	.962
		50	3.38	1.05
		80	7.70	1.15
Part B		Leverage B/V%	Required Return on Equity	Beta Coefficient
		0	8.25	.65
		8.16%	8.40	.68
		19.2%	8.65	.73
		29.1%	8.95	.79

by the debt to equity ratio at market values.[7] But regardless of whether the relationship is linear or nonlinear there is agreement that in order to obtain the higher expected earnings that go with increased leverage, the firm must accept more risk.

Figure 18–5
Part A—EPS and
Coefficient of Variation;
Part B—Return on
Equity and Beta

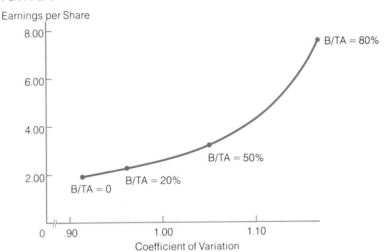

Part A: EPS and Coefficient of Variation

Earnings per Share

Part B: Return on Equity and Beta

Return on Equity

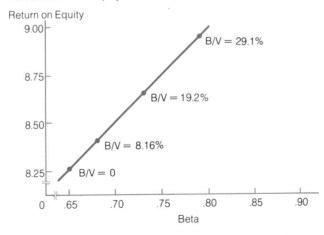

7. These linearities result because we are implicitly employing the Modigliani-Miller model in a world with taxes but with no bankruptcy cost penalties. In Chapter 19 when we bring in bankruptcy cost penalties we indicate that there will be nonlinearities in these relationships. Equation 17–1 is used to calculate the required return on equity.

What choice should Watson recommend to the board? How much leverage should Universal Machine use? These questions cannot be answered at this point—we must defer answers until we have covered some additional concepts and examined the effects of leverage on the cost of both debt and equity capital.

Breakeven Analysis

Another way of presenting the data on Universal's two financing methods is shown in Figure 18–6, a breakeven chart similar to the charts used in Chapter 3. If sales are depressed to zero, the debt financing line would cut the Y axis at −$2.70, below the −$2.08 intercept of the common stock financing line. The debt line has a steeper slope and rises faster, however, showing that earnings per share will go up faster with increases in sales if debt is used. The two lines cross at sales of $6.2 million. Below that sales volume the firm would be better off issuing common stock; above that level, debt financing would produce higher earnings per share.[8]

Figure 18–6
Earnings per Share for Stock and Debt Financing

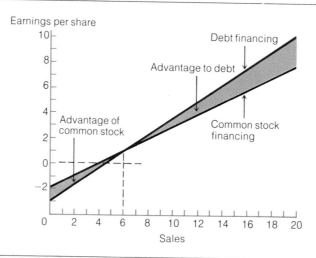

8. Since in this case the equation is linear, the breakeven or indifference level of Sales ($P \cdot Q$) can be found as follows:

$$EPS_S = \frac{(P \cdot Q - 2 - .4P \cdot Q - .5)(.5)}{.6} = \frac{(P \cdot Q - 2 - .4P \cdot Q - .7)(.5)}{.5} = EPS_B$$

$$P \cdot Q = \$6.2 \text{ million}$$

If Watson and his board of directors *know with certainty* that sales will never again fall below $6.2 million, bonds would be the preferred method of financing the asset increase. But they cannot know this for certain. They know that in previous years sales, in fact, have fallen below this critical level. Further, if any detrimental long-run events occur, future sales may again fall well below $6.2 million. If sales continue to expand, however, there would be higher earnings per share from using bonds; no officer or director would want to forego these substantial advantages.

Watson's recommendation, and the decision of each director, will depend (1) upon each person's appraisal of the future and (2) upon his psychological attitude toward risk.[9] The pessimists, or risk averters, will prefer to employ common stock, while the optimists, or those less sensitive to risk, will favor bonds. This example, which is typical of many real-world situations, suggests that the major disagreements over the choice of forms of financing are likely to reflect uncertainty about the future levels of the firm's sales. Such uncertainty, in turn, reflects the characteristics of the firm's environment—general business conditions, industry trends, and quality and aggressiveness of management.

Relationship of Financial Leverage to Operating Leverage[10]

In Chapter 3 it was shown that a firm has some degree of control over its production processes; it can, within limits, use either a highly automated production process with high fixed costs but low variable costs or a less automated process with lower fixed costs but higher variable costs. If a firm uses a high degree of operating leverage, it was seen that its breakeven point is at a relatively high sales level and that changes in the level of sales have a magnified (or "leveraged") impact on profits. Notice that financial leverage has exactly the same kind of effect on profits: the higher the leverage factor, the higher the breakeven sales volume and the greater the impact on profits from a given change in sales volume.

9. Theory suggests that the decision should be based upon stockholders' utility preferences, or the market risk-return tradeoff function discussed in Chapter 11. In practice, it is difficult to obtain such information as *data*, so decisions such as this one are generally based upon the subjective judgment of the decision-maker. A knowledge of the theory, even if it cannot be applied directly, is extremely useful in making good judgmental decisions. Further, knowing the theory permits us to structure research programs and data-collecting systems that will make direct application of the theory increasingly feasible in future years.

10. This section may be omitted without loss of continuity.

The *degree of operating leverage* was defined as the percentage change in operating profits associated with a given percentage change in sales volume, and Equation 3–2 was developed for calculating operating leverage:

$$\text{Degree of operating leverage at point } Q = \frac{Q(P - vc)}{Q(P - vc) - FC} \qquad (3\text{–}2)$$

$$= \frac{P \cdot Q - VC}{P \cdot Q - VC - FC}. \qquad (3\text{–}2a)$$

Here Q is units of output, P is the average sales price per unit of output, vc is the variable cost per unit, and FC is total fixed costs, while PQ is sales in dollars and VC is total variable costs. Applying the formula to Universal Machine at a sales level of $10,000 (see Table 18–2 above) and assuming one machine sells for $100, we find its operating leverage to be 1.50, so a 100 percent increase in volume produces a 150 percent increase in profit:

$$\text{Degree of operating leverage} = \frac{100(\$100 - \$40)}{100(\$100 - 40) - 2{,}000}$$

$$= \frac{10{,}000 - 4{,}000}{10{,}000 - 4{,}000 - 2{,}000}$$

$$= \frac{\$6{,}000}{\$4{,}000} = 1.50 \text{ or } 150\%$$

Operating leverage affects *earnings before interest and taxes (EBIT)*, while financial leverage affects *earnings after interest and taxes*, the earnings available to common stockholders. In terms of Table 18–4, operating leverage affects the top section of the table, financial leverage the lower sections. Thus, if Universal Machine had more operating leverage, its fixed costs would be higher than $2,000, its variable cost ratio would be lower than 40 percent of sales, and earnings before interest and taxes would vary with sales to a greater extent. Financial leverage takes over where operating leverage leaves off, further magnifying the effect on earnings per share of a change in the level of sales. For this reason, operating leverage is sometimes referred to as *first-stage leverage* and financial leverage as *second-stage leverage*.

Degree of Financial Leverage

The *degree of financial leverage* is defined as the percentage change in earnings available to common stockholders that is associated with a given percentage change in earnings before interest and taxes *(EBIT)*.

An equation has been developed as an aid in calculating the degree of financial leverage for any given level of *EBIT* and interest charges *(iB)*.[11]

$$\text{Degree of financial leverage} = \frac{EBIT}{EBIT - iB} \qquad (18\text{--}1)$$

For Universal Machine at 100 units of output and an *EBIT* of $4,000, the degree of financial leverage with bond financing is

$$\text{Financial leverage: bonds} = \frac{\$4,000}{\$4,000 - \$700} = 1.21$$

Therefore, a 100 percent increase in *EBIT* would result in a 121 percent increase in earnings per share. If stock financing is used, the degree of financial leverage may be calculated and found to be 1.14, so a 100 percent increase in *EBIT* would produce a 114 percent increase in *EPS*.

**Combining
Operating and
Financial
Leverage**

Operating leverage causes a change in sales volume to have a magnified effect on *EBIT*, and if financial leverage is superimposed on operating leverage, changes in *EBIT* will have a magnified effect on earnings per share. Therefore, if a firm uses a considerable amount of both operating leverage and financial leverage, even small changes in the level of sales will produce wide fluctuations in *EPS*.

Equation 3–2 for the degree of operating leverage can be combined

11. The equation is developed as follows:
1. Notice that $EBIT = Q(P - vc) - FC$.
2. Earnings per share $(EPS) = \dfrac{(EBIT - iB)(1 - T)}{N}$, where *EBIT* is earnings before interest and taxes, *iB* is interest paid, *T* is the corporate tax rate, and *N* is the number of shares outstanding.
3. *iB* is a constant, so ΔEPS, the change in *EPS*, is

$$\Delta EPS = \frac{\Delta EBIT(1 - T)}{N}$$

4. The percentage increase in *EPS* is the change in *EPS* over the original *EPS*, or

$$\frac{\dfrac{\Delta EBIT(1 - T)}{N}}{\dfrac{(EBIT - iB)(1 - T)}{N}} = \frac{\Delta EBIT}{EBIT - iB}.$$

5. The degree of financial leverage is the percentage change in *EPS* over the percentage change in *EBIT*, so

$$\text{Financial leverage} = \frac{\dfrac{\Delta EBIT}{EBIT - iB}}{\dfrac{\Delta EBIT}{EBIT}} = \frac{EBIT}{EBIT - iB}$$

with Equation 18–1 for financial leverage to show the total leveraging effect of a given change in sales on earnings per share.[12]

$$\text{Combined leverage effect} = \frac{Q(P - vc)}{Q(P - vc) - FC - iB} \tag{18-2}$$

For Universal Machine at an output of 200 units (or $2 million of sales), the combined leverage effect, using debt financing, is

$$\text{Combined leverage effect} = \frac{100(\$100 - \$40)}{100(\$100 - \$40) - \$2,000 - \$700}$$

$$= \frac{\$6,000}{\$6,000 - \$2,000 - \$700}$$

$$= 181.8 \text{ percent}$$

Therefore, a 100 percent increase in sales from 100 units to 200 units would cause *EPS* to increase by 181.8 percent, so the new *EPS* figure would be 1.818 times the original *EPS*:

$$EPS_{(200 \text{ units})} = EPS_{(100 \text{ units})} + (EPS_{(100 \text{ units})}) \times 1.81$$
$$= EPS_{(100 \text{ units})} \times (1 + 1.81)$$
$$= \$3.30 \times 2.818 = \$9.30.$$

These figures agree, of course, with those worked out in Table 18–8.

Financial and operating leverage can be employed in various combinations. In the Universal Machine example, the combined leverage factor of 1.818 was obtained by using operating leverage of degree 1.50 and financial leverage of 1.21, but many other combinations of financial and operating leverage would have produced the same combined leverage factor. Within limits, firms can and do make tradeoffs between financial and operating leverage.

The usefulness of the degree of leverage concept lies in the facts

---

12. Equation 18–2 is developed as follows:
1. Recognize that $EBIT = Q(P - vc) - FC$, then rewrite Equation 18–1 as

$$\frac{EBIT}{EBIT - iB} = \frac{Q(P - vc) - FC}{Q(P - vc) - FC - iB}. \tag{18-1a}$$

2. The total leverage effect is equal to the degree of operating leverage times the degree of financial leverage, or Equation 3–2 times Equation 18–1a:

Combined leverage effect = Equation 3–2 × Equation 18–1a

$$= \frac{Q(P - vc)}{Q(P - vc) - FC} \cdot \frac{Q(P - vc) - FC}{Q(P - vc) - FC - iB} \tag{18-2}$$

$$= \frac{Q(P - vc)}{Q(P - vc) - FC - iB}.$$

(1) that it enables us to specify the precise effect of a change in sales volume on earnings available to common stock and (2) that it permits us to show the interrelationship between operating and financial leverage. The concept can be used to show a businessman, for example, that a decision to automate and to finance new equipment with bonds will result in a situation wherein a 10 percent decline in sales will produce a 50 percent decline in earnings, whereas a different operating and financial leverage package will be such that a 10 percent sales decline will cause earnings to decline by only 20 percent. In our experience, having the alternatives stated in this manner gives the decision-maker a better idea of the ramifications of his actions.[13]

Variations in Financial Structure

As might be expected, wide variations in the use of financial leverage may be observed among industries and among the individual firms in each industry. Illustrative of these differences is the range of ratios of debt to total assets shown in Table 18–10. Service industries use the most leverage, reflecting (1) that services include financial institutions, which as a group have high liabilities, and (2) that there are many smaller firms in the service industries, and small firms as a group are heavy users of debt. Public utility use of debt stems from a heavy fixed asset investment, coupled with extremely stable sales. Mining and manufacturing firms use less debt, because of their exposure to fluctuating sales.

Within the broad category "manufacturing," wide variations are observed for individual industries. Table 18–11 presents an array of total-debt-to-total-assets ratios for selected manufacturing industries. The lowest ratios are found among soft drink companies and sawmills, in which cost pressures have been severe. Low debt ratios are also found among the durable goods industries. The highest debt ratios are found in consumer nondurable goods, where demand is relatively insensitive to fluctuations and general business activity.

Even within a given industry, there are wide variations in the use of financial leverage, as illustrated for the electric utility industry in Table 18–12. These variations reflect a number of different considerations, including the volatility of business in the companies' operating areas, the extent to which they use preferred stock, and their managements' willingness to assume risk.

---

13. The concept is also useful for investors. If firms in an industry are classified as to their degrees of total leverage, an investor who is optimistic about prospects for the industry might favor those firms with high leverage, and vice versa if he expects industry sales to decline.

Table 18–10
Variations in
Financial Leverage
in Selected
Industries and
Industry Groups

Category	Total Liabilities to Total Assets
Miscellaneous	
Farms	64
Metal mining, iron ores	44
Coal mining	50
Crude petroleum and natural gas	44
Contract construction	31
Manufacturing	
Grain mill products	47
Tobacco manufacturers	47
Textile mill products	41
Paper and allied products	50
Chemicals and allied products	41
Petroleum refining	38
Farm machinery	57
Electronic components	58
Utilities	
Railroad transportation	52
Air transportation	72
Telephone and telegraph	50
Electric utilities	60
Wholesale trade	
Motor vehicles	63
Petroleum	57
Retail trade	
Retail food stores	52
Retail drugstores	55
Retail furniture	58
Services, hotels	72

Source: Leo Troy, *Almanac of Business and Industrial Financial Ratios* (Englewood Cliffs, N.J.: Prentice-Hall, 1974).

(Based on *Statistics of Income* data of the Internal Revenue Service).

Factors Influencing Financial Structure

Thus far the discussion has touched on the factors that are generally considered when a firm formulates basic policies relating to its financial structure. The more important of these financial structure determinants are now listed and briefly discussed.

1. Growth rate of future sales.
2. Stability of future sales.
3. Competitive structure of the industry.
4. Asset structure of the firm.

Table 18–11 **Financial Leverage** **in Selected** **Manufacturing** **Industries, 1975**	Category	Total Debt to Total Assets
	Soft Drinks	32%
	Sawmills and planing mills	36
	Industrial chemicals	41
	Blast furnaces and steel works	44
	Motor vehicles	46
	Farm machinery and equipment	49
	Electrical industrial apparatus	50
	Toys and sporting goods	51
	Textiles	55

Source: Dun & Bradstreet, "The Ratios of Manufacturing, 1975," *Dun's Review*, December 1976.

Table 18–12 **Debt-to-Total-** **Capitalization** **Ratios (Selected** **Electric Utility** **Companies, 1975)**		
	Central Illinois Public Service	47%
	Detroit Edison	49
	Consolidated Edison of New York	50
	Montana Power	51
	Dayton Power & Light	51
	Middle South Utilities	54
	American Electric Power	56

Source: *Moody's Handbook of Common Stocks*,
Spring 1977

5. Control position and attitudes toward risk of owners and management.
6. Lenders' attitudes toward the firm and the industry.

Growth Rate of Sales

The future growth rate of sales is a measure of the extent to which the earnings per share of a firm are likely to be magnified by leverage. If sales and earnings grow at a rate of 8 to 10 percent a year, for example, financing by debt with limited fixed charges should magnify the returns to owners of the stock.[14] This can be seen from Figure 18–6 above.

However, the common stock of a firm whose sales and earnings are growing at a favorable rate commands a high price; thus, it sometimes appears that equity financing is desirable. The firm must weigh the benefits of using leverage against the opportunity of broadening its equity base when it chooses between future financing alternatives. Such firms may be expected to have a moderate-to-high level of debt financing.

14. Such a growth rate is also often associated with a high profit rate.

Sales Stability

Sales stability and debt ratios are directly related. With greater stability in sales and earnings, a firm can incur the fixed charges of debt with less risk than it can when its sales and earnings are subject to periodic declines; in the latter instance it will have difficulty in meeting its obligations. The stability of the utility industry, combined with relatively favorable growth prospects, has resulted in high leverage ratios in that industry.

Competitive Structure

Debt-servicing ability is dependent upon the profitability, as well as the volume, of sales. Hence, the stability of profit margins is as important as the stability of sales. The ease with which new firms may enter the industry and the ability of competing firms to expand capacity will influence profit margins. A growth industry promises higher profit margins, but such margins are likely to narrow if the industry is one in which the number of firms can be easily increased through additional entry. For example, the franchised fast-service food companies were a very profitable industry in the early 1960s, but it was relatively easy for new firms to enter this business and go into competition with the older firms. As the industry matured during the late 1960s and early 1970s, the capacity of the old and the new firms grew at an increased rate. As a consequence, profit margins declined.

Asset Structure

Asset structure influences the sources of financing in several ways. Firms with long-lived fixed assets, especially when demand for their output is relatively assured (for example, utilities), use long-term mortgage debt extensively. Firms whose assets are mostly receivables and inventory whose value is dependent on the continued profitability of the individual firm — for example, those in wholesale and retail trade — rely less on long-term debt financing and more on short term.

Management Attitudes

The management attitudes that most directly influence the choice of financing are those concerning (1) control of the enterprise and (2) risk. Large corporations whose stock is widely owned may choose additional sales of common stock because they will have little influence on the control of the company. Also, because management represents a stewardship for the owners, it is often less willing to take the risk of heavy fixed charges.[15]

---

15. It would be inappropriate to delve too far into motivational theory in a finance book, but it is interesting to note that the managers of many larger, publicly owned corporations have a relatively small ownership position and derive most of their income from salaries. Some writers assert that in such cases

In contrast, the owners of small firms may prefer to avoid issuing common stock in order to be assured of continued control. Because they generally have confidence in the prospects of their companies and because they can see the large potential gains to themselves resulting from leverage, managers of such firms are often willing to incur high debt ratios.

The converse can, of course, also hold—the owner-manager of a small firm may be *more* conservative than the manager of a large company. If the net worth of the small firm is, say, $1 million, and if it all belongs to the owner-manager, he may well decide that he is already prosperous enough, and may elect not to risk using leverage in an effort to become still more wealthy.

Lender Attitudes

Regardless of managements' analyses of the proper leverage factors for their firms, there is no question but that lenders' attitudes are frequently important—sometimes the most important—determinants of financial structures. In the majority of cases, the corporation discusses its financial structure with lenders and gives much weight to their advice. But when management is so confident of the future that it seeks to use leverage beyond norms for the industry, lenders may be unwilling to accept such debt increases. They will emphasize that excessive debt reduces the credit standing of the borrower and the credit rating of the securities previously issued. The lenders' point of view has been expressed by a borrower, a financial vice-president, who stated, "Our policy is to determine how much debt we can carry and still maintain an AA bond rating, then use that amount less a small margin for safety."

Summary

Financial leverage, which means using debt to boost rates of return on net worth over the returns available on assets, is the primary topic covered in this chapter. Whenever the return on assets exceeds the cost

---

managements do not strive for profits, especially if this effort involves using leverage with its inherent risk. Presumably, these managers feel that the risks of leverage for them, the ones who actually decide to use debt or equity, outweigh the potential gains from successful leverage. If sales are low, there is a chance of failure and the loss of their jobs, whereas if sales and profits are high, it is the stockholders, not management, who receive the benefits. Another way of looking at the situation is to say that most stockholders are more diversified than most managers—if the firm fails, a stockholder loses only that percentage of his net worth invested in the firm, but the manager loses 100 percent of his job. While there is undoubtedly some merit to this argument, it should be pointed out that companies are increasingly using profit-based compensation schemes—bonus systems and stock-option plans—to motivate management to seek profitability, and low leverage companies are subject to take-over bids (see Chapter 22).

of debt, leverage is favorable and the return on equity is raised by using it. However, leverage is a two-edged sword, and if the returns on assets are less than the cost of debt, then leverage reduces the returns on equity. This reduction is greater the more leverage a firm employs. As a net result, leverage may be used to boost stockholder returns, but it is used at the risk of increasing losses if the firm's economic fortunes decline.

Probability data, whenever it is available, can be used to make the risk-return tradeoff involved in the use of financial leverage more precise. The expected earnings per share *(EPS)* and coefficient of variation *(CV)* of these earnings may be calculated under alternative financial plans, and these *EPS* versus *CV* comparisons aid in making choices among plans.

Financial leverage is similar to operating leverage, a concept discussed in Chapter 3. As is true for operating leverage, financial leverage can be defined rigorously and measured in terms of the *degree of financial leverage.* In addition, the effects of financial and operating leverage may be combined, with the *combined leverage factor* showing the percentage changes in earnings per share that will result from a given percentage change in sales.

In the following chapter the concepts developed to this point in the book will be extended to the formal theory of the cost of capital. The way investors appraise the relative desirability of increased returns versus higher risks is seen to be a most important consideration — one that, in general, invalidates the theory that firms should strive for maximum earnings per share regardless of the risks involved.

Questions

18–1. How will each of the occurrences listed below affect a firm's financial structure, capital structure, and net worth?
   a. The firm retains earnings of $100 during the year.
   b. A preferred stock issue is refinanced with bonds.
   c. Bonds are sold for cash.
   d. The firm repurchases 10 percent of its outstanding common stock with excess cash.
   e. An issue of convertible bonds is converted.

18–2. From an economic and social standpoint, is the use of financial leverage justifiable? Explain by listing some advantages and disadvantages.

18–3. Financial leverage and operating leverage are similar in one very important respect. What is this similarity and why is it important?

18–4. How does the use of financial leverage affect the breakeven point?

18–5. Would you expect risk to increase (a) proportionately, (b) more than proportionately, or (c) less than proportionately, with added financial leverage? Give reasons for your answer.

18–6. What are some reasons for variations of debt ratios among the firms in a given industry?

18–7. Why is the following statement true? "Other things being the same, firms with relatively stable sales are able to incur relatively high debt ratios."

18–8. Why do public utility companies usually pursue a different financial policy from that of trade firms?

18–9. The use of financial ratios and industry averages in the financial planning and analysis of a firm should be approached with caution. Why?

18–10. Some economists believe that swings in business cycles will not be as wide in the future as they have been in the past. Assuming that they are correct in their analysis, what effect might this added stability have on the types of financing used by firms in the United States? Would your answer be true for all firms?

Problems

18–1. The Peterson Company plans to raise a net amount of $240 million for new equipment financing and working capital. Two alternatives are being considered. Common stock may be sold at a market price of $42 a share to net $40, or debentures yielding 9 percent may be issued with a 2 percent flotation cost.

The balance sheet and income statement of the Peterson Company prior to financing are given below:

The Peterson Company
Balance sheet
December 31, 1978
(in millions of dollars)

Current assets	$800	Accounts payable	$150
Net fixed assets	400	Notes payable to bank	250
		Other current liabilities	200
		Total current liabilities	600
		Long-term debt	250
		Common stock $2 par	50
		Retained earnings	300
Total assets	$1,200	Total claims	$1,200

The Peterson Company
Income statement
for year ended December 31, 1978
(in millions of dollars)

Sales	$2,200
Net income before taxes (10%)	220
Interest on debt	40
Net income subject to tax	180
Tax (50%)	90
Net income after tax	$ 90

Annual sales are expected to be distributed according to the following probabilities.

Annual Sales	Probability
$1400	.20
2000	.30
2500	.40
3200	.10

a. Assuming that net income before interest and taxes remains at 10 percent of sales, calculate earnings per share under both the stock financing and the debt financing alternatives at each possible level of sales.
b. Calculate expected earnings per share under both debt and stock financing.

18–2. American Battery Corporation produces one product, a long-life rechargeable battery for use in small calculators. Last year 50,000 batteries were sold at $20 each. American Battery's income statement is shown below.

American Battery Corporation
Income statement
for year ended December 31, 1978

Sales		$1,000,000
Less: Variable cost	$400,000	
Fixed cost	200,000	600,000
EBIT		$ 400,000
Less: Interest		125,000
Net income before tax		$ 275,000
Less: Income tax ($T = 0.40$)		110,000
Net income		$ 165,000
EPS (100,000 shares)		$1.65

a. Calculate (i) the degree of operating leverage, (ii) the degree of financial leverage, and (iii) the combined leverage effect for American Battery for the 1978 level of sales.
b. American Battery is considering changing to a new production process for manufacturing the batteries. Highly automated and capital intensive, the new process will double fixed costs to $400,000 but will decrease variable costs to $4 a unit. If the new equipment is financed with bonds, interest will increase by $70,000; if the equipment is financed by common stock, total stock outstanding will increase by 20,000 shares. Assuming that sales remain constant, calculate for each financing method (i) earnings per share and (ii) the combined leverage if the new process is employed.
c. Under what conditions would you expect American Battery to want to change its operations to the more automated plant?

d. If sales are expected to increase, which alternative will have the greatest impact on *EPS?* Illustrate with an example.

18-3. The Hunter Corporation plans to expand assets by 50 percent; to finance the expansion, it is choosing between a straight 7 percent debt issue and common stock. Its current balance sheet and income statement are shown below.

Hunter Corporation
Balance sheet
December 31, 1980

		Debt, 6%	$140,000
		Common stock, $10 par	350,000
		Retained earnings	210,000
Total assets	$700,000	Total claims	$700,000

Hunter Corporation
Income statement
for year ended December 31, 1980

Sales	$2,100,000
Total costs (excluding interest)	1,881,600
Net income before taxes	$ 218,400
Debt interest	8,400
Income before taxes	$ 210,000
Taxes at 50%	105,000
Net income	$ 105,000

Earnings per share: $\dfrac{\$105,000}{35,000} = \$3$

Price/earnings ratio = 10×*

Market price: 10 × 3 = $30

*The price/earnings ratio is the market price per share divided by earnings per share. It represents the amount of money an investor is willing to pay for $1 of current earnings. The higher the riskiness of a stock, the lower its *P/E* ratio, other things held constant. The concept of price/earnings ratio is discussed at some length in Chapter 17.

If Hunter Corporation finances the $350,000 expansion with debt, the rate on the incremental debt will be 7 percent and the price/earnings ratio of the common stock will be 8 times. If the expansion is financed by equity, the new stock can be sold at $25, the rate on debt will be 6 percent, and the price/earnings ratio of all the outstanding common stock will remain at 10 times earnings.

a. Assuming that net income before interest and taxes *(EBIT)* is 10 percent of sales, calculate earnings per share at sales levels of $0, $700,000, $1,400,000, $2,100,000, $2,800,000, $3,500,000, and $4,200,000, when financing is with (i) common stock and (ii) debt. Assume no fixed costs of production.

b. Make a breakeven chart for *EPS* and indicate the breakeven point in sales (that is, where *EPS* using bonds = *EPS* using stock).

c. Using the price/earnings ratio, calculate the market value per share of common stock for each sales level for both the debt and the equity financing.

d. Make a breakeven chart of market value per share for the company using data from part c, and indicate the breakeven point.

e. If the firm follows the policy of seeking to maximize (i) *EPS* or (ii) market price per share, which form of financing should be used?

f. Now assume that the following probability estimates of future sales have been made: 5 percent chance of $0; 7.5 percent chance of $700,000; 20 percent chance of $1,400,000; 35 percent chance of $2,100,000; 20 percent chance of $2,800,000; 7.5 percent chance of $3,500,000; and 5 percent chance of $4,200,000. Calculate expected values for *EPS* and market price per share under each financing alternative.

g. What other factors should be taken into account in choosing between the two forms of financing?

h. Would it matter if the presently outstanding stock were all owned by the final decision-maker, the president, and that this represented his entire net worth? Would it matter if he was compensated entirely by a fixed salary? that he had a substantial number of stock options?

Selected References

Altman, Edward I. "Corporate Bankruptcy Potential, Stockholder Returns, and Share Valuation." *Journal of Finance* 24 (Dec. 1969):887–900.

Arditti, Fred D. "Risk and the Required Return on Equity." *Journal of Finance* 22 (Mar. 1967):19–36.

Donaldson, Gordon. *Corporate Debt Capacity.* Boston: Division of Research, Harvard Business School, 1961.

———. "New Framework for Corporate Debt Capacity." *Harvard Business Review* 40 (Mar.–Apr. 1962):117–31.

———. "Strategy for Financial Emergencies." *Harvard Business Review* 47 (Nov.–Dec. 1969):67–79.

Ghandhi, J. K. S. "On the Measurement of Leverage." *Journal of Finance* 21 (Dec. 1966):715–26.

Haslem, John A. "Leverage Effects on Corporate Earnings." *Arizona Review* 19 (Mar. 1970):7–11.

Hunt, Pearson. "A Proposal for Precise Definitions of 'Trading on the Equity' and 'Leverage.'" *Journal of Finance* 16 (Sept. 1961):377–86.

Krainer, Robert E. "Interest Rates, Leverage, and Investor Rationality." *Journal of Financial and Quantitative Analysis* 12 (Mar. 1977):1–16.

Kraus, Alan, and Litzenberger, Robert. "A State-Preference Model of Optimal Financial Leverage." *Journal of Finance* 28 (Sept. 1973):911–22.

Lev, Baruch, and Pekelman, Dov. "A Multiperiod Adjustment Model for the Firm's Capital Structure." *The Journal of Finance* 30 (Mar. 1975):75–91.

Lloyd-Davies, Peter R. "Optimal Financial Policy in Imperfect Markets." *Journal of Financial and Quantitative Analysis* 10 (Sept. 1975): 457–81.

Scott, David F., and Martin, John D. "Industry Influence on Financial Structure." *Financial Management* 4 (Spring 1975):67–73.

Tepper, Irwin, and Affleck, A. R. P. "Pension Plan Liabilities and Corporate Financial Strategies." *Journal of Finance* 29 (Dec. 1974):1549–64.

Toy, Norman; Stonehill, Arthur; Remmers, Lee; Wright, Richard; and Beekhuisen, Theo. "A Comparative International Study of Growth, Profitability, and Risk as Determinants of Corporate Debt Ratios in the Manufacturing Sector." *Journal of Financial and Quantitative Analysis* 9 (Nov. 1974):875–86.

Vickers, Douglas. "Disequilibrium Structures and Financing Decisions in the Firm." *Journal of Business Finance & Accounting* 1 (Autumn 1974):375–88.

Williams, Edward E. "Cost of Capital Functions and the Firm's Optimal Level of Gearing." *Journal of Business Finance* 4, no. 2, 78–83.

Wippern, Ronald F. "Financial Structure and the Value of the Firm." *Journal of Finance* 21 (Dec. 1966):615–34.

19   The Cost of Capital[1]

The cost of capital is a critically important topic. First, as we saw in Chapter 10, capital budgeting decisions have a major impact on the firm, and proper capital budgeting requires an estimate of the cost of capital. Second, in Chapter 18 we saw that financial structure can affect both the size and riskiness of the firm's earnings stream, hence the value of the firm. A knowledge of the cost of capital, and how it is influenced by financial leverage, is useful in making capital structure decisions. Finally, a number of other decisions, including those related to leasing, to bond refunding, and to working capital policy, require estimates of the cost of capital.[2]

In this chapter, we first point out the necessity of using a weighted average cost of capital. Second, the cost of the individual components of the capital structure—debt, preferred stock, and equity—are considered: because investors perceive different classes of securities to have different degrees of risk, there are variations in the costs of different types of securities. Third, the individual component costs are brought together to form a weighted cost of capital. Fourth, the concepts developed in the earlier sections are illustrated with an example of the cost of capital calculation for an actual company. Finally, the interrelationship between the cost of capital and the investment opportunity schedule is developed, and the simultaneous determination of the marginal cost of capital and the marginal return on investment is discussed.

Composite, or Overall, Cost of Capital

Suppose a particular firm's cost of debt is estimated to be 8 percent, its cost of equity is estimated to be 12 percent, and the decision has been made to finance next year's projects by selling debt. The argument is sometimes advanced that the cost of these projects is 8 percent, because

---

1. This chapter is relatively long and difficult; students should allow for this in their preparation schedules.

2. The cost of capital is also vitally important in regulated industries, including electric, gas, telephone, and transportation. In essence, regulatory commissions seek to measure a utility's cost of capital, then set prices so that the company will just earn this rate of return. If the estimate is too low, then the company will not be able to attract sufficient capital to meet long-run demands for service, and the public will suffer. If the estimate of capital costs is too high, customers will pay too much for service.

debt will be used to finance them. However, this position contains a basic fallacy. To finance a particular set of projects with debt implies that the firm is also using up some of its potential for obtaining new low-cost debt. As expansion occurs in subsequent years, at some point the firm will find it necessary to use additional equity financing or else the debt ratio will become too large.

To illustrate, suppose the firm has an 8 percent cost of debt and a 12 percent cost of equity. In the first year it borrows heavily, using up its debt capacity in the process, to finance projects yielding 9 percent. In the second year it has projects available that yield 11 percent, well above the return on first-year projects, but it cannot accept them because they would have to be financed with 12 percent equity money. To avoid this problem, the firm should be viewed as an on-going concern, and its cost of capital should be calculated as a weighted average, or composite, of the various types of funds it uses: debt, preferred, and equity.

Basic Definitions

Both students and practitioners are often confused about how to calculate and use the cost of capital. To a large extent, this confusion results from imprecise, ambiguous definitions, but a careful study of the following definitions will eliminate such unnecessary difficulties.

Capital, or Financial, Components

Capital (or financial) components are the items on the right-hand side of the balance sheet: various types of debt, preferred stock, and common equity. Any net increase in assets must be financed by an increase in one or more capital components.

Component Costs

Capital is a necessary factor of production, and like any other factor, it has a cost. The cost of each component is defined as the *component cost* of that particular component. For example, if the firm can borrow money at 8 percent, the component cost of debt is defined as 8 percent.[3] Throughout most of this chapter, we concentrate on debt, preferred stock, retained earnings, and new issues of common stock. These are the capital structure components, and their component costs are identified by the following symbols:

---

3. We will see that there is a before-tax cost of debt; 8 percent is the before-tax component cost of debt. Also, the effects of debt on the cost of equity will be considered later.

k_b = interest rate on firm's new debt = component cost of debt, before tax.

$k_b(1 - T)$ = component cost of debt, after tax, where T = marginal tax rate; $k_b(1 - T)$ is the debt cost used to calculate the marginal cost of capital.

k_{ps} = component cost of preferred stock.

k_r = component cost of retained earnings (or internal equity).

k_e = component cost of new issues of common stock (or external equity). k_s was defined as the required rate of return on common equity in Chapter 17. Here we distinguish between equity obtained from retained earnings and selling new stock, hence the distinction between k_e and k_r.

k = an average, or "composite," cost of capital. If a firm raises $1 of new capital to finance asset expansion, and if it is to keep its capital structure in balance (that is, if it is to keep the same percentage of debt, preferred, and equity), then it will raise part of the dollar as debt, part as preferred, and part as common equity (with equity coming either as retained earnings or from the sale of new common stock).[4] k is also a *marginal cost:* there is a value of k for each dollar the firm raises during the year. k is, in effect, the marginal cost of capital used in Chapter 10, and the relationship between k and the amount of funds raised during the year is expressed as the *MCC* schedule in Figure 10–1.[5]

These definitions and concepts are explained in detail in the remainder of this chapter, where we seek to accomplish two goals: (1) to develop a marginal cost of capital schedule $(k = MCC)$ that can be used in capital budgeting, and (2) to determine the mix of types of capital that will minimize the *MCC* schedule. If the firm finances so as to minimize its *MCC*, uses this *MCC* to calculate *NPVs*, and makes capital budgeting decisions on the basis of the *NPV* method, this will lead to a maximization of stock prices.

---

4. Firms do try to keep their debt, preferred stock, and common equity in balance, but they *do not* try to maintain any proportional relationship between the common stock and retained earnings accounts as shown on the balance sheet.

5. k also reflects the riskiness of the firm's various assets as discussed in Chapter 11, Investment Decisions Under Uncertainty. If a firm uses risk-adjusted discount rates for different capital projects, the average of these rates, weighted by the sizes of the various investments, should equal k.

Before-Tax Component Cost of Debt (k_b)

If a firm borrows $100,000 for one year at 6 percent interest, the investors who purchase the debt receive, and the firm must pay them, a total of $6,000 annual interest on their investment:

$$k_b = \text{before-tax cost of debt} = \frac{\text{interest}}{\text{principal}} = \frac{\$6,000}{\$100,000} = 6\%. \qquad (19\text{–}1)$$

For now, assume that there is no corporate income tax on the firm; the effect of income taxes on the analysis of cost of capital is treated in a later section of the chapter. Under this assumption, the firm's dollar interest cost is $6,000, and its percentage cost of debt is 6 percent. As a first approximation, *the component cost of debt is equal to the rate of return earned by investors, or the interest rate on debt.*[6] If the firm borrows and invests the borrowed funds to earn a return just equal to the interest rate, then the earnings available to common stock remain unchanged.[7] This is demonstrated below.

The ABC Company has sales of $1 million, operating costs of $900,000, and no debt. Its income statement is shown in the Before column of Table 19–1. Then it borrows $100,000 at 6 percent and invests the funds

---

6. The cost of convertible debt is slightly more complicated, but it can be calculated using the following formula:

$$M = \sum_{t=1}^{N} \frac{c}{(1 + k_c)^t} + \frac{tv}{(1 + k_c)^N}.$$

Here M is the price of the convertible bond; c is the annual interest rate in dollars; tv is the expected terminal value of the bond in year N; N is the expected number of years that the bond will be outstanding; and k_c is the required rate of return on the convertible. The risk to an investor holding a convertible is somewhat higher than that on a straight bond, but somewhat less than that on common stock. Accordingly, the cost of convertibles is generally between that on bonds and that on stock. This concept is discussed in detail in Chapter 16. We should also note that the after-tax cost of a convertible is found as k_c in the equation, but here c is multiplied by $(1 - T)$, where T is the marginal corporate tax rate.

7. Note that this definition is a *first approximation;* it is modified later to take account of the deductibility of interest payments for income tax purposes. Note also that here the cost of debt is considered in isolation. The impact of debt on the cost of equity, as well as on future increments of debt, is treated when the weighted cost of a combination of debt and equity is derived. Finally, flotation costs, or the costs of selling the debt, are ignored. Flotation costs for debt issues are generally quite low; in fact, most debt is placed directly with banks, insurance companies, pension funds, and the like, and involves no flotation costs. If flotation costs are involved, the cost of debt can be approximated by the following equation:

$$k_b = \frac{c_t + \dfrac{M - p_b}{N}}{\dfrac{M + p_b}{2}}.$$

Here c_t is the periodic interest payment in dollars, M is the par or maturity value of the bond, p_b is the bond's issue price (hence $M - p_b$ is the premium or discount), and N is the life of the bond. The equation is an approximation, as it does not consider compounding effects. However, the approximation is quite close; for example, with a 5 percent, 25-year, $1,000 par value bond sold at $980, the formula gives $k_b =$ 5.13 versus 5.15 as found from a bond table.

in assets whose use causes sales to rise by $7,000 and operating costs to rise by $1,000. Hence, profits before interest rise by $6,000. The new situation is shown in the After column. Earnings are unchanged, as the investment just earns its component cost of capital.

Table 19–1 **Income Statement** **for the ABC** **Company**	Before	After
Sales	$1,000,000	$1,007,000
Operating costs	900,000	901,000
Earnings before interest	$ 100,000	$ 106,000
Interest	–	6,000
Earnings	$ 100,000	$ 100,000

Note that the cost of debt is applicable to *new* debt, not to the interest on any old, previously outstanding debt. In other words, we are interested in the cost of new debt, or the *marginal* cost of debt. The primary concern with the cost of capital is to use it in a decision-making process — the decision whether to obtain capital to make new investments; whether the firm borrowed at high or low rates in the past is irrelevant.[8]

Preferred Stock

Preferred stock, described in detail in Chapter 14, is a hybrid between debt and common stock. Like debt, preferred stock carries a fixed commitment on the part of the corporation to make periodic payments, and, in liquidation, the claims of the preferred stockholders take precedence over those of the common stockholders. Failure to make the preferred dividend payments does not result in bankruptcy, as does nonpayment of interest on bonds. Preferred stock is thus somewhat more risky *to the firm* than common stock, but it is less risky than bonds. Just the reverse holds for investors. To the investor, preferred is less risky than common but more risky than debt. Thus, if an investor is willing to buy the firm's bonds on the basis of a 6 percent interest return, he might, because of risk aversion, be unwilling to purchase the firm's preferred stock at a yield of less than 8 percent. Assuming the preferred issue is a perpetuity that sells for $100 a share and pays an $8 annual dividend, its yield is calculated as follows:

---

8. The fact that the firm borrowed at high or low rates in the past is, of course, important in terms of the effect of the interest charges on current profits, but this past decision is not relevant for *current* decisions. For current financial decisions, only current interest rates are relevant.

$$\text{Preferred yield} = \frac{\text{preferred dividend}}{\text{price of preferred stock}} = \frac{d_{ps}}{p_{ps}} = \frac{\$8}{\$100} = 8\%. \qquad (19-2)$$

Assuming the firm can sell additional preferred stock at $100 a share, its cost of preferred is also 8 percent. In other words, *as a first approximation, the component cost of preferred stock (k_{ps}) is equal to the return investors receive on the shares as calculated in Equation 19-2.*

If the firm receives less than the market price of preferred stock when it sells new preferred, p_{ps} in the denominator of Equation 19-2 should be the net price received by the firm. Suppose, for example, the firm must incur a selling or *flotation* cost of $4 a share. In other words, buyers of the preferred issue pay $100 a share, but brokers charge a selling commission of $4 a share, so the firm nets $96 a share. The cost of new preferred to the firm is calculated as shown in Equation 19-2a:

$$k_{ps} = \text{cost of preferred} = \frac{d_{ps}}{p_{ps}} = \frac{\$8}{\$96} = 8.33\%. \qquad (19-2a)$$

Tax Adjustment

As they stand, the definitions of the component costs of debt and preferred stock are incompatible when we introduce taxes into the analysis, because interest payments are deductible expense whereas preferred dividends are not. The following example illustrates the point.

The ABC Company can borrow $100,000 at 6 percent, or it can sell 1,000 shares of $6 preferred stock to net $100 a share. Assuming a 48 percent tax rate, its before-investment situation is given in the Before column of Table 19-2. At what rate of return must the company invest the proceeds from the new financing to keep the earnings available to common shareholders from changing?

As can be seen from the tabulations in Table 19-2, if the funds are invested to yield 6 percent before taxes, earnings available to common stockholders are constant if debt is used, but they decline if the financing is with preferred stock. To maintain the $52,000 net earnings requires that funds generated from the sale of preferred stock be invested to yield 11.538 percent before taxes or 6 percent after taxes.[9]

Since stockholders are concerned with after-tax rather than before-tax earnings, only the cost of capital *after* corporate taxes should be used.

---

9. The 11.538 percent is found as follows: 6%/(1 − tax rate) = 6%/0.52.

Table 19-2
Tax Adjustment
for Cost of Debt

		Before	Invest in Assets Yielding		
			6%		11.538%
		Before	Debt	Preferred	Preferred
Earnings before interest and taxes *(EBIT)*		$100,000	$106,000	$106,000	$111,538
Interest		–	6,000	–	–
Earnings before taxes *(EBT)*		$100,000	$100,000	$106,000	$111,538
Taxes 48% *(T)*		(48,000)	(48,000)	(50,880)	(53,538)
Preferred dividends		–	–	(6,000)	(6,000)
Available for common dividends		$ 52,000	$ 52,000	$ 49,120	$ 52,000

The cost of preferred stock is already on an after-tax basis as defined, but a simple adjustment is needed to arrive at the after-tax cost of debt. It is recognized that interest payments are tax deductible—the higher the firm's interest payments, the lower its tax bill. In effect, the federal government pays part of a firm's interest charges. Therefore, the cost of debt capital is calculated as follows:

$$k_b(1 - T) = \text{after-tax cost of debt}$$

$$= (\text{before-tax cost}) \times (1.0 - \text{tax rate}). \qquad (19\text{--}3)$$

Whenever the weighted cost of capital (k) is calculated, k_b $(1 - T)$ and not k_b is used.

Example

Before-tax cost of debt = 6 percent; tax rate = 48 percent.
$k_b(1 - T) = \text{after-tax cost} = (0.06)(1 - 0.48) = (0.06)(0.52) = 3.12$ percent.

Cost of Retained Earnings (k_r)[10]

The cost of preferred stock is based on the return investors require if they are to purchase the preferred stock; the cost of debt is based on the interest rate investors require on debt issues, adjusted for taxes. The cost of equity obtained by retaining earnings can be defined similarly:

10. The term "retained earnings" can be interpreted to mean the balance sheet item "retained earnings," consisting of all the earnings retained in the business throughout its history, or it can mean the income statement item "additions to retained earnings." This latter definition is used in the present chapter: *"Retained earnings" for our purpose here refers to that part of current earnings that is not paid out in dividends but, rather, is retained and reinvested in the business.*

"Equity" is defined in this chapter to *exclude* preferred stock. Equity is the sum of capital stock, capital surplus, and accumulated retained earnings. Note that our treatment of the cost of retained earnings abstracts from certain complications caused by personal income taxes on dividend income and by brokerage costs incurred in reinvesting dividend income. Similarly, we do not explicitly treat the cost of depreciation-generated funds in the chapter. These topics are, however, discussed at length in Appendix A to this chapter.

it is k_r, *the rate of return stockholders require on the firm's common stock.* (k_r is identical to k_s as developed in Chapter 17.)

As we saw in Chapter 17, the value of a share of common stock depends, ultimately, on the dividends paid on the stock:

$$p_0 = \frac{d_1}{(1 + k_r)} + \frac{d_2}{(1 + k_r)^2} + \cdots \qquad \text{(19-4)}$$

Here p_0 is the current price of the stock; d_t is the dividend expected to be paid at the end of year t; and k_r is the required rate of return. If dividends are expected to grow at a constant rate, we saw in Chapter 17 that Equation 19-4 reduces to

$$p_0 = \frac{d_1}{k_r - g}. \qquad \text{(19-5)}$$

In equilibrium, the expected and required rates of return must be equal, so we can solve for k_r to obtain the required rate of return on common equity:

$$k_r = \frac{d_1}{p_0} + \text{expected } g. \qquad \text{(19-6)}$$

Example

To illustrate this calculation, consider Aubey Rents, a firm expected to earn $2 a share and to pay a $1 dividend during the coming year. The company's earnings, dividends, and stock price have all been growing at about 5 percent a year, and this growth rate is expected to continue indefinitely. The stock is in equilibrium and currently sells for $20 a share. Using this information, we compute the required rate of return on the stock in equilibrium, using Equation 19-6 as follows:

$$k_r = \frac{\$1}{\$20} + 5\% = 10\%.$$

The expected growth rate for the price of the shares in 5 percent, which, on the $20 initial price, should lead to a $1 increase in the value of the stock, to $21. This price increase will be attained (barring changes in the general level of stock prices) if Aubey invests the $1 of retained earnings to yield 10 percent. However, if the $1 is invested to yield only 5 percent, then earnings will grow by only 5 cents during the year, not by the expected 10 cents a share. The new earnings will be $2.05, a growth of only 2½ percent, rather than the expected $2.10, or 5 percent increase. If investors believe that the firm will earn only 5 percent on retained earnings in the future and attain only a 2½ percent growth rate, they will reappraise the value of the stock downward according to Equation 19-5 as follows:

$$p_0 = \frac{d_1}{k_r - g} = \frac{\$1}{.10 - .025} = \frac{\$1}{.075} = \$13.33.$$

Note, however, that Aubey Rents will suffer this price decline *only if it invests equity funds—retained earnings—at less than its component cost of capital.*

If Aubey refrains from making new investments and pays all its earnings in dividends, it will cut its growth rate to zero. However, the price of the stock will not fall, because investors will still get the required 10 percent rate of return on their shares:

$$k_r = \frac{d_1}{p_0} + g = \frac{\$2}{\$20} + 0 = 10\%, \text{ or}$$

$$p_0 = \frac{\$2}{.10 - 0} = \$20.$$

All the return would come in the form of dividends, but the actual rate of return would match the required 10 percent.

The preceding example demonstrates a fundamentally important fact: *If a firm earns its required rate of return, k_r, then when it retains earnings and invests them in its operations, its current stock price will not change as a result of this financing and investment. However, if it earns less than k_r the stock price will fall; if it earns more, the stock price will rise.*

Cost of Newly Issued Common Stock, or External Equity (k_e)

The cost of new common stock, or *external* equity capital, k_e is higher than the cost of retained earnings, k_r because of flotation costs involved in selling new common stock. What rate of return must be earned on funds raised by selling stock to make the action worthwhile? To put it another way, what is the cost of new common stock? The answer is found by applying the following formula:[11]

$$k_e = \frac{d_1}{p_0(1-f)} + g = \frac{d_1}{p_n} + g = \frac{\text{dividend yield}}{(1 - \text{flotation percentage})} + \text{growth.} \tag{19-7}$$

---

11. The equation is derived as follows:

Step 1. The old stockholders expect the firm to pay a stream of dividends, d_t; this income stream will be derived from existing assets. New investors will likewise expect to receive the same stream of dividends, d_t. For new investors to obtain this stream *without impairing the d_t stream of the old investors,* the new funds obtained from the sale of stock must be invested at a return high enough to provide a dividend stream whose present value is equal to the price the firm receives:

$$p_n = \sum_{t=1}^{\infty} \frac{d_t}{(1 + k_e)^t}. \tag{19-8}$$

Here f is the percentage cost of selling the issue, so $p_0(1-f)=p_n$ is the net price received by the firm. For example, if $p_0=\$10$ and $f=10$ percent, then the firm receives $9 for each new share sold; hence $p_n=\$9$. Notice that Equation 19–7 is strictly applicable only if future growth is expected to be constant.

For Aubey Rents, the cost of new outside equity is computed as follows:

$$k_e = \frac{\$1}{\$20(1-.10)} + 5\% = 10.55\%.$$

Investors require a return of $k_r=10$ percent on Aubey's stock. However, because of flotation costs, Aubey must earn *more* than 10 percent on stock-financed investments to provide this 10 percent. Specifically, if Aubey Rents earns 10.55 percent on investments financed by new common stock issues, then earnings per share will not fall below previously expected earnings; its expected dividend can be maintained; the growth rate for earnings and dividends will be maintained; and as a result of all this, the price per share will not decline. If Aubey earns less than 10.55 percent, then earnings, dividends, and growth will fall below expectations, causing the price of the stock to decline. Since the cost of capital is *defined* as the rate of return that must be earned to prevent the price of the stock from falling, we see that the company's cost of external equity, k_e, is 10.55 percent.[12]

Here p_n is the net price to the firm; d_t is the dividend stream to new stockholders; and k_e is the cost of new outside equity.

Step 2. If flotation costs are expressed as a percentage, f, of the gross price of the stock, p_0, we may express p_n as follows:

$$p_n = p_0(1-f).$$

Step 3. When growth is a constant, Equation 19–8 reduces to

$$p_n = p_0(1-f) = \frac{d_1}{k_e - g}. \tag{19–8a}$$

Step 4. Equation 19–8a may be solved for k_e.

$$k_e = \frac{d_1}{p_0(1-f)} + g. \tag{19–7}$$

12. The cost of external equity is sometimes defined as follows:

$$k_e = \frac{k_r}{1-f}$$

This equation is correct if the firm's expected growth rate is zero; see Equation 19–7. In other cases it tends to overstate k_e.

Finding the Basic Required Rate of Return on Common Equity

It is obvious by now that the basic rate of return investors require on a firm's common equity, k_s as developed in Chapter 17, is a most important quantity. This required rate of return is the cost of retained earnings, and it forms the basis for the cost of capital obtained from new stock issues. How is this all-important quantity estimated?

Although one *can* use very involved, highly complicated procedures for making this estimation, satisfactory estimates may be obtained in one of three ways:

1. Estimate the security market line (SML) as described in Chapter 17; estimate the relative riskiness of the firm in question; and then use these estimates to obtain the required rate of return on the firm's stock:[13]

$$k_s = R_F + \rho.$$

Under this procedure, the estimated cost of equity (k_s) will move up or down with changes in interest rates and with changes in "investor psychology."

2. An alternative procedure, the use of which is recommended in conjunction with the one described above, is to estimate the basic required rate of return as follows:

a. Assume that investors expect the past-realized rate of return on the stock, to be earned in the future, so the expected return is equal to $\bar{k}_s$.

b. Assume that the stock is in equilibrium, with $k_s^* = \bar{k}_s$.

c. Under these assumptions, the required rate of return may be estimated as equal to the past realized rate of return:

$$k_s^* = \bar{k}_s = \frac{d_1}{p_0} + \text{past growth rate.}$$

Stockholder returns are derived from dividends and capital gains, and the total of the dividend yield plus the average growth rate over the past five to ten years may give an estimate of the total returns that stockholders expect in the future from a particular share of stock.

3. For "normal" companies in "normal" times, past growth rates may be projected into the future, and the second method will give satisfactory results. *However, if the company's growth has been abnormally high or low, either because of its own unique situation or because of general economic conditions, then investors will not project the past growth rate into the future, so method 2 will not yield a good estimate of k_s^*.* In this case, g must be estimated in some other manner. Security analysts regularly make earnings growth forecasts, looking at such factors as projected sales, profit margins, competitive factors, and the like. Someone making a

---

13. See Appendix C to this chapter for illustrations of the use of the capital asset pricing model in calculating the cost of equity capital and the cost of capital for firms.

cost of capital estimate can obtain such analysts' forecasts and use them as a proxy for the growth expectations of investors in general, combine g with the current dividend yield, and estimate $\bar{k}_s$ as

$$k_s^* = \frac{d_1}{p_0} + \text{growth rate as projected by security analysts.}$$

Again, note that this estimate of k_s^* is based upon the assumption that g is expected to remain constant in the future.

Based on our own experience in estimating equity capital costs, we recognize that both careful analysis and some very fine judgments are required in this process. It would be nice to pretend that these judgments are unnecessary and to specify an easy, precise way of determining the exact cost of equity capital. Unfortunately, this is not possible. Finance is, in large part, a matter of judgment, and we simply must face this fact.

Effect of Leverage on the Cost of Equity

We have seen in earlier chapters that investors in general are averse to risk, and that risk aversion leads investors to require higher yields on riskier investments. In Chapter 18, we used the Universal Company case to demonstrate that for any given degree of business risk, the higher the debt ratio, the larger will be the measures of variability in earnings per share and return on equity.[14] Combining these results leads us to conclude that the more debt a given company employs, other things held constant, the higher its required rate of return on equity capital will be.

To illustrate this relationship consider Figure 19–1, which presents a

Figure 19–1
Distribution of EBIT for Universal Machine Company

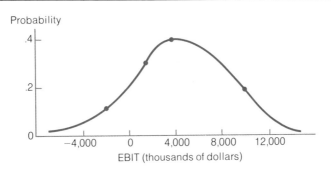

EBIT (thousands of dollars)

---

14. These relationships were worked out for Universal in Table 18–5.

probability distribution of *EBIT* for the Universal Machine Company.[15] The area under the curve in Figure 19-1 to the left of any level of fixed charges represents the probability of not covering these charges. The higher the level of debt, the larger the fixed charges and the higher the probability of not being able to cover fixed charges. The inability to meet fixed charges may trigger a number of penalty clauses in the debt indentures (agreements) and lead to reorganization or bankruptcy (see Chapter 23) with attendant costs of attorneys and court proceedings. Even before such legal difficulties, the increasing risk of financial difficulties may result in the loss of key employees who find positions with firms whose financial outlook is safer, in the reduced availability of goods from key suppliers as well as in the reduced availability of financing.[16]

The existence of substantial bankruptcy penalties would cause the linear relationship between leverage and the related risks of equity and debt to become curvilinear upward as well as to increase the required

Table 19-3

Universal Machine Company: Leverage, Risk Indexes, and the Required Rates of Return on Equity

Leverage (debt/equity) (B/S)	No bankruptcy penalties*		With bankruptcy penalties†		Required Return on Equity	
					No bankruptcy penalties‡	With bankruptcy penalties§
	ρ_1^*	ρ_2^*	ρ_1	ρ_2		
0	6%	0%	6%	0%	12.00	12.00
.25	6%	.75%	6%	.75%	12.75	12.75
.43	6%	1.29%	6%	1.29%	13.29	13.29
.67	6%	2.01%	6%	3.51%	14.00	15.51
1.00	6%	3.00%	6%	6.00%	15.00	18.00
1.50	6%	4.50%	6%	11.86%	16.50	23.86
4.00	6%	12.00%	6%	33.54%	24.00	45.54

*The columns are calculated as follows:
$\rho_1^* = \beta_u (k_M - R_F)$ $\rho_2^* = (B/S)(1 - T) \rho_1^*$

†Calculations
$\rho_1 = \beta_u (k_M - R_F)$
For ρ_2 we have:

B/S ≤ .43	$\rho_2 = (B/S)(1 - T) \rho_1$
B/S = .67	$\rho_2 = (.5 + B/S)(1 - T) \rho_1$
B/S = 1.00	$\rho_2 = (1 + B/S)(1 - T) \rho_1$
B/S = 1.50	$\rho_2 = (1 + B/S)^{1.5}(1 - T) \rho_1$
B/S = 4.00	$\rho_2 = (1 + B/S)^{1.5}(1 - T) \rho_1$

‡Calculations
$6\% + \rho_1^* + \rho_2^*$
§Calculations
$6\% + \rho_1 + \rho_2$

15. This is based on the data in Table 18-2 from the previous chapter.
16. The possibilities that bankruptcy penalties may be substantial are developed in Appendix D to this chapter.

returns on equity and debt. In the present section we will analyze the effect on required returns on equity. The greater probability of not covering fixed charges, which also increases the probabilities of bankruptcy, will cause the relationship between leverage and the risk measures for Universal Machine to curve up more rapidly than discussed in Chapter 18 under the assumptions of no bankruptcy penalties. Accordingly, the relationship between leverage, the indexes of risk, and the required rates of return may be as set forth in Table 19–3.

In Chapter 17 we indicated that the required rate of return consisted of the riskless rate plus a risk premium: $k_s = R_F + \rho$. Here we divide ρ into two components, ρ_1 (read "rho one"), a premium for business risk; and ρ_2, a premium required to compensate equity investors for the additional risk brought on by financial leverage. Expressed as an equation,

$$k_s = R_F + \rho_1 + \rho_2. \tag{19–9}$$

The riskless rate of return, R_F, is a function of general economic conditions, Federal Reserve policy, and the like. The premium for business risk, ρ_1, is a function of the nature of the firm's industry, its degree of operating leverage, its diversification, and so on. Financial risk, ρ_2, depends upon the degree of financial leverage employed.[17]

In Table 19–3 we illustrate how the magnitudes of business and financial risk might be measured in relation to leverage and then indicate their plausible impact on the required rates of return on equity.[18] The calculations of ρ_1^* and ρ_2^* are based on the assumptions of no substantial bankruptcy costs. ρ_1^* is simply the beta for an unlevered firm times the market risk premium and ρ_2^* is ρ_1^* times $[B/S] [1-T]$.

With bankruptcy costs, however, the indexes of financial risk are likely to increase at an increasing rate when leverage passes some critical point and become curvilinear upward as measured in Table 19–3, which is also graphed in Figure 19–2. The required rate of return on equity is 12 percent if the company uses no debt, but k_s^* increases after

---

17. ρ_2 increases at an increasing rate with leverage because bankruptcy, as opposed to simply lower earnings, becomes an increasing threat as the debt ratio rises, and bankruptcy may have high costs of its own (see Chapter 23). As we saw in Chapter 14, the specific terms of the firm's debt also affect its financial risk. Especially important here is the maturity structure of the debt. We might also note that some financial theorists argue that the relationship between ρ_2 and leverage is linear; see Appendix B to this chapter. Further, ρ_1 is always smaller for any firm whose asset returns are not perfectly correlated, or are negatively correlated, with most other firms, if negative correlation exists, ρ_1 could even be negative, as this firm's stock would be sought to reduce the overall risk in investors' portfolios. This covariance effect is discussed in Appendix C to this chapter.

18. Keep in mind that throughout this analysis we are holding constant the firm's assets and the *EBIT* on these assets. We wish to consider the effect of leverage on the cost of capital *holding other things constant.*

Figure 19–2
Illustrative
Relationship Between
the Cost of Equity and
Financial Leverage

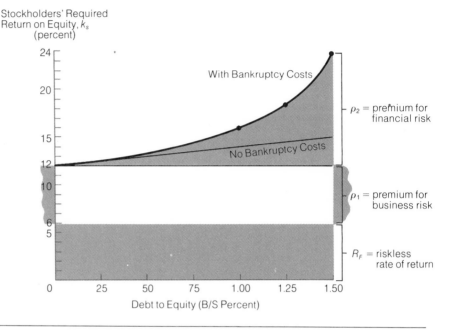

debt passes some critical level and is 23.86 percent if the debt to value ratio is as high as 60 percent.[19] With leverage beyond 60 percent, it is likely that the required cost of equity is so high that the funds for all practical purposes are not available.

Effect of Leverage on the Component Cost of Debt

The component cost of debt is also affected by leverage: the higher the leverage ratio, the higher the cost of debt. Further, the cost of debt can be expected to rise at an increasing rate with leverage. To see why this is so, we can again consider the Universal Machine Company example. The probability distribution of earnings before interest and taxes(*EBIT*) is represented by Figure 19–1.

19. This corresponds to a debt-to-equity ratio of 150 percent. In this example we assume that the risk-return tradeoff function has been estimated, perhaps in a subjective manner, by the financial manager. The precise specification of such risk-return functions is one of the more controversial areas of finance, and having attempted to measure them empirically ourselves, we can attest to the difficulties involved. However, even though the precise shape of the function is open to question, it is generally agreed (1) that the curve is upward sloping and (2) that some estimate, be it better or worse, is necessary if we are to obtain a cost of capital for use in capital budgeting. In this chapter our main concern is that the broad concepts be grasped.

Table 19–4 Universal Machine Company: Effect of Leverage on the Cost of Debt	Leverage (Debt/Equity)	Interest Rate (k_b)	After-tax Cost of Debt $k_b(1 - T)$
	0%	10%	5.0%
	20	10	5.0
	30	11	5.5
	40	13	6.5
	50	16	8.0
	60	27	13.5

The more debt the firm has, the higher the interest requirements; and the higher the interest charges, the greater the probability that earnings *(EBIT)* will not be sufficient to meet these charges.[20] Creditors will perceive this increasing risk as the debt ratio rises, and they will begin charging a risk premium above the riskless rate, causing the firm's interest rate to rise: Since creditors are risk averters and are assumed to have a diminishing marginal utility for money, they will demand that interest rates be increased to compensate for the increased risk.

One other effect that may operate to raise interest rates at an increasing rate is the fact that a firm may need to use a variety of sources in order to borrow large amounts of funds in relation to its equity base. For example, a firm may be able to borrow from banks only up to some limit set by bank policy or bank examiner regulations. In order to increase its borrowings, the firm would have to seek other institutions, such as insurance companies, finance companies, and so on, that may

Figure 19–3
Universal Machine, Weighted Average Cost of Capital

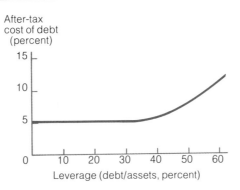

After-tax cost of debt (percent)

Leverage (debt/assets, percent)

20. Recall that the area under the curve in Figure 19–1 to the left of any level of fixed charges represents the probability of not covering these charges.

demand higher interest rates than those charged by banks. Such an effect might tend to cause interest rates to jump whenever the firm was forced to find new lenders.

Table 19–4 shows the estimated relationships between leverage, the interest rate, and the after-tax cost of debt for Universal Machine. Assuming a 50 percent tax rate, the after-tax cost of debt is one-half the interest rate; these figures are also shown in Figure 19–3, where they are plotted against the debt ratio. In the example, Universal's cost of debt is constant until the debt ratio passes 20 percent or $2 million; then it begins to climb.

Combining Debt and Equity: Weighted Average, or Composite, Cost of Capital

Debt and equity may now be combined to determine Universal Machine's average, or composite, cost of capital, and Table 19–5 shows the calculations used to determine the weighted average cost.[21] The average cost, together with the component cost of debt and equity, is plotted against the debt ratio in Figure 19–4. Here we see that the composite cost of capital is minimized when its debt ratio is approximately 35 percent, so Universal's optimal capital structure calls for about 35 percent debt, 65 percent equity.

It is important to note that the average cost of capital curve is relatively flat over a fairly broad range: if Universal Machine's debt ratio is in the range of 20 to 40 percent, the average cost of capital cannot be lowered very much by moving to the optimal point. This appears to be a fairly typical situation, as almost any "reasonable" schedule for the component costs of debt and equity will produce a saucer-shaped average cost of capital schedule similar to that shown in Figure 19–4. This gives financial managers quite a degree of flexibility in planning their financing programs, permitting them to sell debt one year, equity the next, in order to take advantage of capital market conditions and to avoid high flotation costs associated with small security issues.

Table 19–5 and Figure 19–4 are based on the assumption that the

---

21. A generalized equation can be used to calculate the weighted cost of capital:

$$k = \sum_{i=1}^{n} w_i k_i$$

where w_i is the weight of the ith type of capital and k_i is the cost of the ith component. If the firm had one class of debt, preferred stock, and equity, k would be found as

$$k = w_b k_b + w_{ps} k_{ps} + w_s k_s.$$

It would, of course, be possible to expand this equation to encompass long- and short-term debt, convertibles, "free" capital, and the like.

Table 19–5
Calculation of Points on Average Cost of Capital Curve (percent), or the Composite Cost of Capital for Different Capital Structures

	Percent of Total (1)	Component Costs (2)	Weighted, or Composite, Cost: $k = (1) \times (2) \div 100$ (3)*
Debt	0	5.0	0
Equity	100	12.0	12.0
	100		12.0
Debt	20	5.0	1.0
Equity	80	12.6	10.1
	100		11.1
Debt	30	5.5	1.7
Equity	70	12.9	9.0
	100		10.7
Debt	40	6.5	2.6
Equity	60	14.4	8.6
	100		11.2
Debt	50	8.0	4.0
Equity	50	17.0	8.5
	100		12.5
Debt	60	13.5	8.1
Equity	40	21.4	8.6
	100		16.7

*We divide by 100 to obtain percentages; figures rounded to nearest hundredth.

Figure 19–4
Universal Machine Company: Cost of Capital Curves

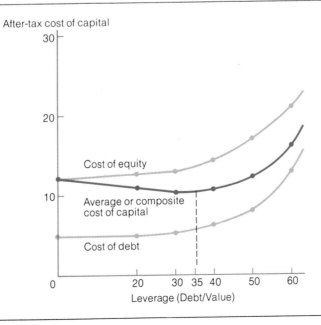

firm is planning to raise a given amount of new capital during the year. For a larger or smaller amount of new capital, some other cost figures might be applicable; the optimal capital structure might call for a different debt ratio, and the minimum average cost of capital *(k)* might be higher or lower. This point is discussed in detail later in the chapter.

Figure 19–5
Hypothetical Cost of
Capital Schedules for
High-risk (R) and Low-
risk (S) Firms

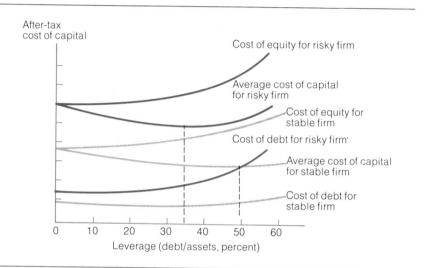

High-risk and Low-risk Firms

Shown in Figure 19–5 are the cost of capital schedules for a firm in a risky industry (R) and for one in a stable industry (S). Firm R, the one on which Figure 19–4 was based, is Universal Machine; firm S is a relatively stable, safe company. We have already examined the interrelationships of the curves of Universal Machine—after declining for a while as additional low-cost debt is averaged in with equity, the average cost of capital for firm R begins to rise after debt has reached 35 percent of total capital. Beyond this point, the fact that both debt and equity are becoming more expensive offsets the fact that the component cost of debt is less than that of common equity.

While the same principles apply to the less risky firm, its cost functions are quite different from those of Universal Machine. In the first place, S's overall business risk is lower, giving rise to lower debt and equity costs at all debt levels. Further, its relative stability means that less risk is attached to any given percentage of debt; therefore, its costs of both debt and equity—and, consequently, its average cost of capital—turn up further to the right than do the corresponding curves for Universal Machine. The optimum debt ratio for the firm in the stable industry is 50 percent as compared to only 30–35 percent for Universal.

Determining the actual optimal capital structure for a specific firm requires both analysis and judgment, and it is up to a firm's financial manager to decide on the best capital structure for his company. Once this decision has been reached, the weighting system for the average cost of capital calculation is also determined. Unless otherwise noted, we will assume that management deems its present book value capital structure to be optimal, and we shall use this set of weights in our calculations.[22]

Calculating the Marginal Cost of Capital for an Actual Company

The procedures discussed above are now applied to an actual company, the Continental Container Company, to illustrate the cost of capital calculation. Continental Container is a large firm, with assets of over $950 million and sales of over $1 billion. Sales and earnings are relatively stable, as food and beverage companies make up the bulk of the firm's customers. Dividends have been paid since 1923, even during the depression of the 1930s. On the basis of an indicated dividend rate of $2 and a current price of $33.50 a share, the dividend yield is 6 percent. Over the past ten years, earnings, dividends, and the price of the stock have grown at a rate of about 5 percent; all indications suggest that this same rate of growth will be maintained in the foreseeable future.[23] Since internally generated funds provide sufficient equity, only the costs of internal equity, found in this case to be the 6 percent dividend yield plus the 5 percent growth rate, or a total of 11 percent, need be considered.

The average interest rate on Continental Container's outstanding debt is 4.5 percent, but much of this debt was issued in earlier years when interest rates were much lower than they are now. Current market yields on both long-term and short-term debt are about 8 percent, and approximately this cost will be associated with new debt issues. After a

22. The weights used to calculate the marginal cost of capital, k, should theoretically be based on market values.

23. Earnings per share for 1964 were $2.26, while *EPS* for 1974 were $3.65. Dividing $3.65 by $2.25 gives 1.62, which is the *CVIF* for 10 years at 5 percent from Table D–1. Thus, *EPS* grew at a 5 percent rate over the ten-year period from 1964 through 1974. Dividends grew similarly, and security analysts are projecting a continuation of these rates.

48 percent income tax, the cost of debt is estimated to be 4.2 percent. The preferred stock is stated to be 3.75 percent preferred, but it was also issued when rates were low. On the basis of current market yields, the estimated cost of new preferred stock is 7.5 percent.

The right-hand side of Continental Container's balance sheet is given in Table 19–6. A large portion (24 percent) of the firm's funds are "free" in the sense that no interest is charged for them — accounts payable and accruals are in this class. Some would argue that in the calculation of the overall cost of capital, this "free" capital should be included. Under certain circumstances this procedure is valid; usually, however, only "non-free" capital need be considered.[24] Of the target, or chosen long-term capital structure, 22 percent is debt, 1 percent is preferred stock, and 77 percent is common equity. This means, in effect, that each $1.00 of new capital is raised as $0.22 of debt, $0.01 of preferred stock, and $0.77 as common equity (retained earnings or new stock).

If management believes that some other capital structure is optimal, then other weights would be used; for purposes of illustration it is assumed that the existing structure has been determined to be the optimum. Further, let us assume that Continental Container plans to raise $20 million during the current year. To maintain the target capital struc-

Table 19–6 Continental Container Company: Right-hand Side of Balance Sheet (Millions of Dollars)			Non-free funds only	
Payables and accruals	$186	19.4%		
Tax accruals	44	4.6		
Total "free" current funds	$230	24.0%		
Interest-bearing debt	$160	16.7%	$160	22%
Preferred stock	7	0.8	7	1
Common equity	560	58.5	560	77
Non-free funds	727	76.0%	$727	100%
Total financing	$957	100.0%		

24. The primary justification for ignoring "free" capital is that, in the capital budgeting process, these spontaneously generated funds are netted out against the required investment outlay, then ignored in the cost of capital calculation. To illustrate, consider a retail firm thinking of opening a new store. According to customary practices, the firm should (1) estimate the required outlay, (2) estimate the net receipts (additions to profits) from the new store, (3) discount the estimated receipts at the cost of capital, and (4) accept the decision to open the new store only if the net present value of the expected revenue stream exceeds the investment outlay. The estimated accruals, trade payables, and other costless forms of credit are deducted from the investment to determine the "required outlay" before making the calculation. Alternatively, "free" capital could be costed in, and working capital associated with specific projects added in when determining the investment outlay. In most instances, the two procedures will result in similar decisions.

ture, this $20 million must be raised as follows: $4.4 million as debt, $0.2 million as preferred stock, and $15.4 million as equity. Also, note that all equity is obtained in the form of retained earnings. On the basis of these weights and the previously determined costs of debt, equity, and preferred stock, the calculations shown in Table 19–7 indicate that Continental Container's composite cost of new capital is 9.5 percent. As long as Continental Container finances in the indicated manner and uses only retained earnings of equity, each dollar of new funds should cost this amount.

Table 19–7 **Continental** **Container** **Illustrative** **Calculation of** **Average Cost of** **Capital: $20** **Million New** **Capital**		Amount of Capital (1)	Proportions (2)	Component Costs (3)	Product $(2) \times (3) = (4)$
	Debt	$ 4.4	22.0%	4.2%	.0092
	Preferred stock	.2	1.0	7.5	.0008
	Common equity	15.4	77.0	11.0	.0847
		$20.0	100.0%		$k = .0947 = 9.5\%$

Marginal Cost of Capital When New Common Stock Is Used

In the preceding example of Continental Container, we assumed that the company would finance only with debt, preferred stock, and *internally generated equity*. On this basis we found the weighted average cost of new capital, or the marginal cost of capital, to be 9.5 percent. What would have occurred, however, if the firm's need for funds had been so great that it was forced to sell new common stock? The answer is that its marginal cost of new capital would have increased. To show why this is so, we shall extend the Continental Container example.

First, suppose that during 1975 Continental Container had total earnings of $59 million available for common stockholders, paid $27 million in dividends, and retained $32 million. We know that to keep the capital structure in balance, the retained earnings should equal 77 percent of the net addition to capital, the other 23 percent being debt and preferred stock. Therefore, the total amount of new capital that can be obtained on the basis of the retained earnings is

Retained earnings = (percent equity)(new capital)

$$\text{New capital} = \frac{\text{retained earnings}}{\text{percent equity}}$$

$$= \frac{\$32 \text{ million}}{0.77} = \$41.6 \text{ million.}$$

Next, we note that 1 percent of the new capital, or about $400,000, should be preferred stock and that 22 percent, or $9.2 million, should be debt. In other words, Continental Container can raise a total of $41.6 million — $32 million from retained earnings, $9.2 million in the form of debt, and $400,000 in the form of preferred stock — and still maintain its target capital structure in exact balance.

If all financing up to $41.6 million is in the prescribed proportions, the composite cost of each dollar of new capital *up to $41.6 million* is still 9.5 percent, the previously computed weighted average cost of capital. In Table 19−7, we showed the calculation of the weighted average cost of raising $20 million; had we made the calculation for any other amount *up to $41.6 million*, the weighted average cost would have also been 9.5 percent. Thus, each dollar of new capital costs 9.5 percent, so this is the marginal cost of capital.

As soon as the total of the required funds exceeds $41.6 million, however, Continental must begin relying on more expensive new common stock. Therefore, beyond $41.6 million we must compute a new marginal cost of capital. Assuming Continental Container would incur a flotation cost on new equity issues equal to 10 percent, we could compute the cost of capital for funds over $41.6 million as shown in Table 19−8.

Table 19−8 **Calculation of** **Continental** **Container's** **Marginal Cost of** **Capital Using** **New Common Stock**	1. Find the cost of new equity: $$\text{Cost of new common stock} = \frac{\text{dividend yield}}{(1 - \text{flotation percentage})} + \text{growth}$$ $$k_e = \frac{.06}{.90} + 5\% = 11.7\%.$$

2. Find a new weighted or composite cost of each dollar of new capital in excess of $41.6 million, using only new common stock for the equity component:

	Proportion ×	component cost =	product
Debt	22%	4.2	.0092
Preferred stock	1	7.5	.0008
Equity (new)	77	11.7	.0901
	100%		$k = .1001 \approx 10\%$

According to Table 19−7, as long as Continental Container raises no more than $41.6 million, its weighted average and marginal cost of new or incremental capital is 9.5 percent, but as we have shown in Table 19−8, every dollar over $41.6 million has a cost of 10 percent, so the marginal cost beyond $41.6 million is 10 percent.

Other Breaks in the MCC Schedule

The *marginal cost of capital schedule* shows the relationship between the weighted average cost of each dollar raised (k) and the total amount of capital raised during the year, other things, such as the riskiness of the assets acquired, held constant. In the preceding section, we saw that Continental Container's *MCC* schedule increases at the point where its retained earnings are exhausted and it begins to use more expensive new common stock.

Actually, any time any component cost rises, a similar break will occur. For example, if Continental could obtain only $10 million of debt at 8 percent, with additional debt costing 9 percent, then this rise in k_b would produce a higher $k_b(1 - T)$, which in turn would lead to a higher k. Where would this break occur? Under the assumptions made thus far for Continental Container, it would occur at $45.5 million, found as:

$$\begin{array}{l} \text{Break in } MCC \\ \text{schedule caused by} \\ \text{rising debt cost} \end{array} = \frac{\begin{array}{c}\text{amount of lower-cost}\\\text{debt}\end{array}}{\begin{array}{c}\text{debt as percentage}\\\text{of capital raised}\end{array}}$$

$$= \frac{\$10}{0.22} = \$45.5 \text{ million.}$$

Now suppose only an additional $5 million, over and above the first $10 million, can be borrowed at 9 percent, after which the component cost of new debt rises to 10 percent. A new break will occur, this one at $68.2 million:

$$\frac{\begin{array}{c}\text{amount of lower-cost}\\\text{debt}\end{array}}{\text{debt/total capital}} = \frac{\$10 + \$5}{0.22} = \$68.2 \text{ million.}$$

Similar breaks could be caused by increases in the cost of preferred stock, higher common stock flotation costs as more stock is sold, and perhaps even a change in k_s, the basic required rate of return on the firm's common equity as discussed in Chapter 17.[25]

In general, breaks in the *MCC* schedule will occur whenever any component cost increases as a result of the volume of capital raised, and the breaking points can be calculated by use of Equation 19–10:

---

25. It has been argued that, as a company sells more and more stock or other types of securities, it must attract investors who are less and less familiar with and impressed by the company, hence that the securities must be sold at lower prices and higher yields. This pressure could affect all securities, new and old. If the sale of additional stock (permanently) lowers the price of old stock, then this reduction in value must be assessed as a marginal cost of the new stock. This situation is said to exist for the utilities, whose huge, recurrent issues of securities in recent years have been depressing the prices of their outstanding securities.

$$\text{Break in } MCC = \frac{\begin{array}{c}\text{total amount of lower-cost capital}\\ \text{for a given component}\end{array}}{\begin{array}{c}\text{percentage of total capital}\\ \text{represented by the component}\end{array}} \qquad \textbf{(19–10)}$$

If we determined that Continental Container would experience higher component costs for debt at $10 million and at $15 million, for preferred at $5 million, and for common equity at $32 million (when retained earnings are exhausted) and at $50 million, then Equation 19–10 could be used to compute breaks in the company's MCC schedule:

Point Where Break Occurs	Cause of Break	k in Interval before Break
$ 41.5 million	(shift from k_r to k_e)	9.5%
45.5	(rising k_b)	10.0
64.9	(rising k_e)	10.6
68.2	(rising k_b)	11.2
500.0	(rising k_{ps})	11.6

It is necessary to calculate a different $MCC = k$ for the interval between each of the breaks in the MCC schedule. For example, we have already calculated the MCC from zero to $41.5 million as 9.5 percent, and that from $41.5 to $45.5 million as 10 percent. The values of k for each interval are shown above, and they are plotted as the step-function MCC schedule shown in Figure 19–6, panel a.

Figure 19–6
Relationship between Marginal Cost and Amount of Funds Raised

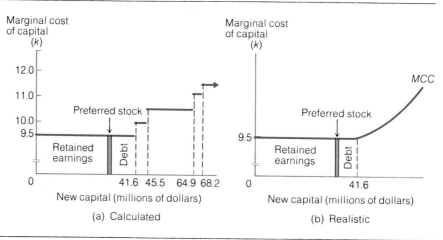

(a) Calculated

(b) Realistic

This graph is highly idealized; in fact, the actual MCC curve looks much more like that shown in Figure 19–6(b). Here we see that the curve is flat until it reaches the vicinity of $41.6 million; it then turns up gradually and continues rising. It will go up gradually rather than suddenly because the firm will probably make small adjustments to its target debt ratio, its dividend payout ratio, the actual types of securities it uses, and so on. And the curve will continue to rise, because, as more and more of its securities are put on the market during a fairly short period, it will experience more and more difficulty in getting the market to absorb the new securities.

Ordinarily, a firm will calculate its MCC schedule as a step-function similar to the one shown in Figure 19–6(a), then "smooth it out" by connecting the values of k shown in the middle of each interval. When one recognizes the types of estimates and approximations that go into the step-function curve, the smoothing process is less arbitrary than it might first appear to be.

In the earlier analysis associated with Figure 19–5, we were investigating the influence of the financing mix or financial structure on the firm's cost of capital. The financing mix was being varied, but not the total amount of capital raised. Since a marginal cost is the increment in cost as the total amount of financing is increased, when we vary the financing mix holding the total amount of financing constant, the relevant cost of capital is the weighted average cost of capital (WACC). We can say either that no marginal cost of capital is involved or that the marginal cost of capital is equal to the WACC. We use the symbol, k, as the WACC.

In the present analysis, Figure 19–6 portrays the effects of increasing the total amount of new financing, holding the financing mix fixed at the optimal proportions. We then calculate the weighted marginal cost of capital. In Figure 19–6 over the flat segment of the MCC curve, the average cost of capital is equal to the marginal cost of capital. When the marginal cost of capital begins to rise, the curve that is an average cost in relation to the MCC lies below the MCC. (If nine people all 6 feet tall come into a room in sequence, the average and marginal height will be 6 feet. If the tenth person entering is 7 feet tall, the marginal height will be 7 feet, but the average height will be 6.1 feet.) We exhibit only the MCC in Figure 19–6 because we are analyzing the determination of the size of the total capital budget for a firm, and hence the MCC is relevant as the investment hurdle rate. But recall that we are holding the financing mix at its optimal proportions, so that the MCC for each amount of new financing is also the WACC for the optimal mix of financing that minimizes the level of the MCC curve. For these reasons, we again use k as the symbol for the cost of capital along the MCC curve.

Combining the MCC and the Investment Opportunity Schedules

Having developed the firm's *MCC* schedule, and planned its financing mix so as to minimize the schedule, the financial manager's next task is to utilize the *MCC* in the capital budgeting process. How is this done? First, suppose that the *k* value in the flat part of the *MCC* schedule is used as the discount rate for calculating the *NPV* and that the total cost of all projects with *NPV* > 0 is less than the dollar amount at which the *MCC* schedule turns up. In this case, the value of *k* that was used is the correct one. For example, if Continental Container used 9.5 percent as its cost of capital and found that the acceptable projects totalled $41.6 million or less, then 9.5 percent is the appropriate cost of capital for capital budgeting.[26]

But suppose the acceptable projects totalled *more than* $41.6 million with a 9.5 percent discount rate. What do we do now? The most efficient procedure is given below:

Step 1. Calculate and plot the *MCC* schedule as shown in Figure 19–6.

Step 2. Ask the operating personnel to estimate the dollar volume of acceptable projects at a range of discount rates, say 14 percent, 13 percent, 12 percent, 11 percent, 10 percent, and 9 percent. There will, thus, be an estimate of the capital budget at a series of *k* values. For Continental Container, these values were estimated as follows:

k	Capital Budget
14%	$20 million
13	30
12	40
11	50
10	60
9	70

Step 3. Plot the *k*, capital budget points, as determined in Step 2 on the same graph as the *MCC*; this plot is labeled *IRR* in Figure 19–7.[27]

---

26. We are, of course, abstracting from project risk; here we assume that the average riskiness of all projects undertaken is equal to the average riskiness of the firm's existing plant. Some projects may be more risky than average, hence call for a risk-adjusted cost of capital > 9.5 percent, while others are less risky than average and call for a cost of capital < 9.5 percent.

27. To see why the *k*, capital budget line, is a type of *IRR* curve, consider the following:
   1. The *NPV* of a project is zero if the project's *IRR* is equal to *k*.
   2. Now suppose we determine that no projects have *NPV* ≥ 0 at *k* = 15%. This means that no projects have *IRR* ≥ 15%.
   3. Next, suppose we determine that $20 million of projects have *NPV* ≥ 0 at *k* = 14%. This means that these projects all have 14% ≤ *IRR* ≤ 15%.
   4. If the projects were completely divisible, and if we examined very small changes in *k*, then we would have a continuous *IRR* curve. As it is, the curve labeled *IRR* in Figure 19–7 is an approximation. In any event, the example does illustrate how an *IRR* curve can be developed even though a company uses the *NPV* capital budgeting method.

Figure 19–7
Interfacing the *MCC* and *IRR* Curves to Determine the Total Capital Budget for a Given Time Period

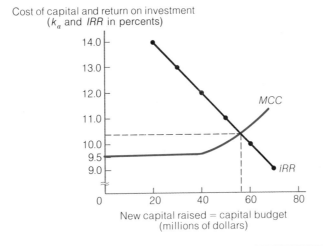

Cost of capital and return on investment
(k_a and *IRR* in percents)

Step 4. The correct *MCC* for use in capital budgeting—assuming both the *MCC* and *IRR* curves are developed correctly—is the value at the intersection of the two curves, 10.4 percent. If this value of k is used to calculate *NPV*s, then projects totalling $56 million will have *NPV*s greater than zero. This is the capital budget that will maximize the value of the firm.

Dynamic Considerations

Conditions change over time; when they do, the firm must make adjustments. First, the firm's own individual situation may change. For example, as it grows and matures, its business risk may decline; this may, in turn, lead to an optimal capital structure that includes more debt. Second, capital market conditions could undergo a pronounced, long-run change, making either debt or equity relatively favorable. This too could lead to a new optimal capital structure. Third, even though the long-run optimal structure remains unchanged, temporary shifts in the capital markets could suggest that the firm use either debt or equity, departing somewhat from the optimal capital structure, then adjust back to the long-run optimum in subsequent years. Fourth, the supply and demand for funds varies from time to time, causing shifts in the cost of both debt and equity, and, of course, in the marginal cost of capital. Finally, the firm may experience an almost unconscious change in capital structure because of retained earnings unless its growth rate is sufficient to call for the employment of more debt on a continual basis.

For all these reasons, it is important that the firm reexamine its cost of capital periodically, especially before determining the annual capital budget or engaging in new long-term financing.[28]

Large Firms versus Small Firms[29]

Before closing this chapter, we should note that significant differences in capital costs exist between large and small firms; these differences are especially pronounced in the case of privately owned small firms. The same concepts are involved, and the methods of calculating the average and marginal costs of capital are similar, but several points of difference arise:

1. It is especially difficult to obtain reasonable estimates of equity capital costs for small, privately owned firms.
2. Tax considerations are generally quite important for privately owned companies, as owner-managers may be in the top personal tax brackets. This factor can cause the effective after-tax cost of retained earnings to be considerably lower than the after-tax cost of new outside equity.
3. Flotation costs for new security issues, especially new stock issues, are much higher for small than for large firms (see Chapter 12).

Points 2 and 3 both cause the marginal cost curves for small firms to rise rapidly once retained earnings are exhausted. These relationships have implications for the growth and development of large versus small firms; recognizing the plight of smaller companies, the federal government has set up programs to aid small businesses to obtain capital.

Summary

In Chapter 17, the nature of the valuation process and the concept of expected rates of return were considered in some detail. The present chapter used these valuation concepts to develop an average cost of capital for the firm. First, the cost of the individual components of the capital structure—debt, preferred stock, and equity—were analyzed. Next, these individual component costs were brought together to form an

---

28. Note that an exact calculation of a firm's need for funds cannot be made until the marginal cost of capital to be used in the capital budgeting process has been calculated. Thus, the marginal cost of capital and the amount of financing required for new projects should be simultaneously determined. This simultaneous determination is considered in Chapter 20, where dividend policy and internal financing decisions are discussed.
29. For an extended discussion of this subject, see Eugene F. Brigham and Keith V. Smith, "The Cost of Capital to Small Firms," in *Readings in Managerial Finance* (New York: Holt, Rinehart and Winston, 1971).

average, or composite, cost of capital. Finally, the conceptual ideas developed in the first two sections were illustrated with an example of the cost of capital for an actual company—Continental Container Company.

Cost of Individual Capital Components. The *cost of debt*, $k_b (1 - T)$, is defined as the interest rate that must be paid on new increments of debt capital multiplied by (1 − tax rate). The *preferred stock cost* to the company is the effective yield and is found as the annual preferred dividend divided by the net price the company receives when it sells new preferred stock. In equation form, the cost of preferred stock is

$$\text{cost of preferred stock} = k_{ps} = \frac{\text{preferred dividend}}{\text{net price of preferred}}.$$

The *cost of common equity* is defined as the minimum rate of return that must be earned on equity-financed investments to keep the value of the existing common equity unchanged. This required rate of return is the rate of return that investors expect to receive on the company's common stock—the dividend yield plus the capital gains yield. Sometimes, we assume that the investors expect to receive about the same rates of return in the future that they have received in the past; in this case, we can estimate the required rate of return on the basis of actual historical returns.

Equity capital comes from two sources, retained earnings and sale of new issues of common stock. The basic required rate of return (k_r) is used for the cost of retained earnings. However, new stock has a higher cost because of the presence of flotation costs associated with the sale of stock. The cost of new common stock issues is computed as follows:

$$\text{Cost of new stock} = k_e = \frac{\text{dividend yield}}{(1 - \text{flotation percentage})} + \text{growth}.$$

New common stock is therefore more expensive than retained earnings.

Weighted Average, or Composite, Cost of Capital. The first step in calculating the weighted average cost of capital, k, is to determine the cost of the individual capital components as described above. The next step is to establish the proper set of weights to be used in the averaging process. Unless we have reason to think otherwise, we generally assume that the present capital structure of the firm is at an optimum, where optimum is defined as the capital structure that will produce the minimum average cost of capital for raising a given amount of funds, or a minimum cost of incremental capital. The optimal capital structure varies from industry to industry, with more stable industries having optimal capital structures that call for the use of more debt than in the case of unstable industries.

Marginal cost. The marginal cost of capital schedule, defined as the cost of each additional dollar raised during the current year, is of interest for two reasons. First, the firm should finance in a manner that minimizes the MCC schedule, and therefore it must measure the MCC. Second, the MCC is the rate that should be used in the capital budgeting process—the firm should take on new capital projects only if their net present values are positive when evaluated at the marginal cost of capital.

The marginal cost of capital is constant over a range, then begins to rise. The rise is probably gradual, not abrupt, because firms make small adjustments in their target debt ratios, begin to use an assortment of securities, retain more of their earnings, and so on, as they reach the limit of internally generated equity funds.

Questions

19–1. Suppose that basic business risks to all firms in any given industry are similar.
   a. Would you expect all firms in each industry to have approximately the same cost of capital?
   b. How would the averages differ among industries?

19–2. Why are internally generated retained earnings less expensive than equity raised by selling stock?

19–3. Prior to the 1930s the corporate income tax was not very important, as rates were fairly low. Also prior to the 1930s preferred stock was much more important than it has been since that period. Is there a relation between the rise of corporate income taxes and the decline in importance of preferred stock?

19–4. Describe how each of the following situations would affect the cost of capital to corporations in general.
   a. The federal government solves the problem of business cycles (that is, cyclical stability is increased).
   b. The Federal Reserve Board takes action to lower interest rates.
   c. The cost of floating new stock issues rises.

19–5. The firm's covariance is .014, the risk free rate is 7 percent, the market risk premium $(\bar{k}_M - R_F)$ is 5 percent and the variance of the market returns is 1 percent. With no bankruptcy costs, what is the cost of capital, k, for an unlevered firm? What is the beta of the firm?

19–6. Now assume that the information in 19–5 is all on an after-tax basis, the corporate tax rate is 50 percent, and the firm has a debt to equity ratio of 100 percent, with a debt cost of 7 percent. What is the new beta of the firm? What is its required return on equity? What is the cost of capital for the levered firm?

19-7. An unlevered firm has a beta of .8. How much leverage can it employ if its corporate tax rate is 50 percent and it aims to have a beta of 1.2?

19-8. The formula $k_r = (d_1/p_0) + g$, where d_1 = expected current dividend, p_0 = the current price of a stock, and g = the past rate of growth in dividends, is sometimes used to estimate k_r, the cost of equity capital. Explain the implications of the formula.

19-9. What factors operate to cause the cost of debt to increase with financial leverage?

19-10. Explain the relationship between the required rate of return on common equity (k_s^*) and the debt ratio.

19-11. How would the various component costs of capital, and the average cost of capital, be likely to change if a firm expands its operations into a new, more risky industry?

19-12. The stock of XYZ Company is currently selling at its low for the year, but management feels that the stock price is only temporarily depressed because of investor pessimism. The firm's capital budget this year is so large that the use of new outside equity is contemplated. However, management does not want to sell new stock at the current low price and is therefore considering a departure from its "optimal" capital structure by borrowing the funds it would otherwise have raised in the equity markets. Does this seem to be a wise move?

19-13. Explain the following statement: "The marginal cost of capital is an average in some sense."

Problems

19-1. On January 1, 1977, the total assets of the Rossiter Company were $60 million. By the end of the year total assets are expected to be $90 million. The firm's capital structure, shown below, is considered to be optimal. Assume there is no short-term debt.

Debt (6% coupon bonds)	$24,000,000
Preferred stock (7%)	6,000,000
Common equity	30,000,000
	$60,000,000

New bonds will have an 8 percent coupon rate and will be sold at par. Preferred will have a 9 percent rate and will also be sold at par. Common stock, currently selling at $30 a share, can be sold to net the company $27 a share. Stockholders' required rate of return is estimated to be 12 percent, consisting of a dividend yield of 4 percent and an expected growth of 8 percent. Retained earnings are estimated to be $3 million (ignore depreciation). The marginal corporate tax rate is 50 percent.

a. Assuming all asset expansion (gross expenditures for fixed assets plus related working capital) is included in the capital budget, what is the dollar amount of the capital budget? (Ignore depreciation.)

b. To maintain the present capital structure, how much of the capital budget must be financed by equity?

c. How much of the new equity funds needed must be generated internally? externally?

d. Calculate the cost of each of the equity components.

e. At what level of capital expenditures will there be a break in the MCC schedule?

f. Calculate the MCC (i) below and (ii) above the break in the schedule.

g. Plot the MCC schedule. Also, draw in an IRR schedule that is consistent with the MCC schedule and the projected capital budget.

19–2. The Austen Company has the following capital structure as of December 31, 1977:

Debt (8%)		$12,000,000
Preferred (8½%)		4,000,000
Common stock	$ 4,000,000	
Retained earnings	12,000,000	
Common equity		16,000,000
Total capitalization		$32,000,000

Earnings per share have grown steadily from $0.93 in 1967 to $2 estimated for 1977. The investment community, expecting this growth to continue, applies a price/earnings ratio of 18 to yield a current market price of $36. Austen's last annual dividend was $1.25, and it expects the dividend to grow at the same rate as earnings. The addition to retained earnings for 1977 is projected at $4 million; these funds will be available during the next budget year. The corporate tax rate is 50 percent.

Assuming that the capital structure relations set out above are maintained, new securities can be sold at the following costs:

Bonds: Up to and including $3 million of new bonds, 8 percent yield to investor on all new bonds.

From $3.01 to $6 million of new bonds, 8½ percent yield to investor on this increment of bonds.

Over $6 million of new bonds, 10 percent yield to investor on this increment of bonds.

Preferred: Up to and including $1 million of preferred stock, 8½ percent yield to investor on all new preferred stock.

From $1.01 to $2 million of preferred stock, 9 percent yield to investor on this increment of preferred stock.

Over $2 million of preferred stock, 10 percent yield to investor on this increment of preferred stock.

Common: Up to $4 million of new outside common stock, $36 a share less $2.50 a share flotation cost.

Over $4 million of new outside common stock, $36 a share less $5 a share flotation cost on this increment of new common.

a. At what dollar amounts of new capital will breaks occur in the *MCC*?
b. Calculate the *MCC* in the interval between each of these breaks, then plot the *MCC* schedule.
c. Discuss the breaking points in the marginal cost curve. What factors in the real world would tend to make the marginal cost curve smooth?
d. Assume now that Austen has the following investment opportunities:
   (i) It can invest any amount up to $4 million at an 11 percent rate of return.
   (ii) It can invest an additional $8 million at a 10.2 percent rate of return.
   (iii) It can invest still another $12 million at a 9.3 percent rate of return.

Thus, Austen's total potential capital budget is $24 million. Determine the size of the company's optimal capital budget for the year.

19-3. The following tabulation gives earnings-per-share figures for the Burnham Corporation during the preceding ten years. The firm's common stock, 140,000 shares outstanding, is now selling for $50 a share, and the expected dividend for the current year is 50 percent of the 1977 *EPS*. Investors expect past trends to continue.

Year	EPS
1968	$2.00
1969	2.16
1970	2.33
1971	2.52
1972	2.72
1973	2.94
1974	3.18
1975	3.43
1976	3.70
1977	4.00

New preferred stock paying a $5 dividend could be sold to the public at a price of $52.50, which includes a $2.50 flotation cost (that is, the net price to Burnham is $50). The current interest rate on new debt is 8 percent. The firm's marginal tax rate is 40 percent. The firm's capital structure, considered to be optimal, is as follows:

Debt (6%)	$ 2,500,000
Preferred stock (7%)	500,000
Common equity	7,000,000
	$10,000,000

a. Calculate the after-tax cost (i) of new debt, (ii) of new preferred stock, and (iii) of common equity, assuming new equity comes only from retained earnings. Calculate the cost of equity as $k_r = d_1/p_0 + g$.

b. Find the marginal cost of capital, again assuming no new common stock is sold.

c. How much can be spent for capital investments before external equity must be sold? (Assume that retained earnings available for 1978 investment is 50 percent of 1977 earnings.)

d. What is the marginal cost of capital (cost of funds raised in excess of the amount calculated in part c) if the firm can sell new common stock at $50 a share to net $45 a share? The cost of debt and of preferred stock is constant.

e. In the problem, we assume that the capital structure is optimal. What would happen if the firm deviated from this capital structure? Use a graph to illustrate your answer.

19-4. The New River Manufacturing Company has the following capital structure as of December 31, 1978:

Debt (9%)		$ 8,000,000
Common stock	3,000,000	
Retained earnings	9,000,000	
Common equity		12,000,000
Total capitalization		$20,000,000

The company is planning its investment program for the next year. It expects the following funds to be available as needed for capital investment.

Additional retained earnings of 10 percent $1 million at a cost
Outside equity 0 to 2 million at 11.1 percent
   2.1 to 5 million at 12 percent
   5.1 to 8 million at 15 percent
Debt financing 0 to 2 million at 9 percent
   2.1 to 4 million at 10 percent
   4.1 to 6 million at 11.5 percent

The company is in a 50 percent tax bracket and intends to maintain debt at 40 percent of total assets.

a. Assume the company has investment possibilities of $15 million and that the average return after tax is expected to be 11 percent. Compute the weighted average cost of the $15 million of new capital required. Should the investments be made?

b. Assume the investment can be broken up into three $5 million blocks, each yielding 11 percent. Compute the marginal cost of capital for each increase of $5 million. What should be the total investment?

c. Would your answer be any different if the expected return on the three blocks of investment were different—say 10 percent on one, 11 percent on another, and 12 percent on a third? (Assume the investments are independent of one another.)

Selected References

Adler, Michael. "On the Risk-Return Trade-Off in the Valuation of Assets." *Journal of Financial and Quantitative Analysis* (Dec. 1969):493–512.

———. "The Cost of Capital and Valuation of a Two Country Firm." *Journal of Finance* 29 (Mar. 1974):119–32.

Alberts, W. W., and Archer, S. H. "Some Evidence on the Effect of Company Size on the Cost of Equity Capital." *Journal of Financial and Quantitative Analysis* 8 (Mar. 1973):229–45.

Ang, James S. "Weighted Average versus True Cost of Capital." *Financial Management* 2 (Autumn 1973):56–60.

Archer, Stephen H., and Faerber, LeRoy G. "Firm Size and the Cost of Equity Capital." *Journal of Finance* 21 (Mar. 1966):69–84.

Arditti, Fred D. "Risk and the Required Return on Equity." *Journal of Finance* 22 (Mar. 1967):19–36.

———. "The Weighted Average Cost of Capital: Some Questions on Its Definition, Interpretation and Use." *Journal of Finance* 28 (Sept. 1973):1001–07.

Arditti, Fred D., and Tysseland, Milford S. "Three Ways to Present the Marginal Cost of Capital." *Financial Management* 2 (Summer 1973):63–67.

Barges, Alexander. *The Effect of Capital Structure on the Cost of Capital.* Englewood Cliffs, N.J.: Prentice-Hall, 1963.

Baron, David P. "Firm Valuation, Corporate Taxes, and Default Risk." *Journal of Finance* 30 (Dec. 1975):1251–64.

Baxter, Nevins D. "Leverage, Risk of Ruin, and the Cost of Capital." *Journal of Finance* 22 (Sept. 1967):395–404.

Ben-Shahar, Haim. "The Capital Structure and the Cost of Capital: A Suggested Exposition." *Journal of Finance* 23 (Sept. 1968):639–53.

Ben-Shahar, Haim, and Ascher, Abraham. "Capital Budgeting and Stock Valuation: Comment." *American Economic Review* 57 (Mar. 1967):209–14.

Beranek, William. *The Effects of Leverage on the Market Value of Common Stocks.* Madison, Wisc.: Bureau of Business Research and Service, University of Wisconsin, 1964.

———. "The Cost of Capital, Capital Budgeting, and the Maximization of Shareholder Wealth." *Journal of Financial and Quantitative Analysis* 10 (Mar. 1975):1–20.

———. "A Little More on the Weighted Average Cost of Capital." *Journal of Financial and Quantitative Analysis* 10 (Dec. 1975):892.

———. "The Weighted Average Cost of Capital and Shareholder Wealth Maximization." *Journal of Financial and Quantitative Analysis* 12 (Mar. 1977):17–32.

Bierman, Harold, Jr. "Risk and the Addition of Debt to the Capital Structure." *Journal of Financial and Quantitative Analysis* 3 (Dec. 1968):415–23.

Blume, Marshall E. "On the Assessment of Risk." *Journal of Finance* 26 (Mar. 1971):1–10.

Blume, Marshall E., and Friend, Irwin. "A New Look at the Capital-Asset Pricing Model." *Journal of Finance* 28 (Mar. 1973):19–34.

Bodenhorn, Diran. "A Cash Flow Concept of Profit." *Journal of Finance* 19 (Mar. 1964):16–31.

Boness, A. James. "A Pedagogic Note on the Cost of Capital." *Journal of Finance* 19 (Mar. 1964):99–106.

Boot, John C. G., and Frankfurter, George M. "The Dynamics of Corporate Debt Management, Decision Rules, and Some Empirical Estimates." *Journal of Financial and Quantitative Analysis* 7 (Sept. 1972):1956–66.

Bower, Richard S., and Bower, Dorothy H. "Risk and Valuation of Common Stock." *Journal of Political Economy* 77 (May–June 1969):349–62.

Brennan, Michael J. "A New Look at the Weighted Average Cost of Capital." *Journal of Business Finance* 5, no. 1 (1973):24–30.

Brewer, D. E., and Michaelson, J. "The Cost of Capital, Corporation Finance, and the Theory of Investment: Comment." *American Economic Review* 55 (June 1965):516–24.

Brigham, Eugene F., and Smith, Keith V. "The Cost of Capital to the Small Firm." *The Engineering Economist* 13 (Fall 1967):1–26.

Crockett, Jean, and Friend, Irwin. "Capital Budgeting and Stock Valuation: Comment." *American Economic Review* 57 (Mar. 1967):214–20.

Davis, E. W., and Yeomans, K. A. "Market Discount on New Issues of Equity: The Influence of Firm Size, Method of Issue and Market Volatility." *Journal of Business Finance & Accounting* 3 (Winter 1976):27–42.

Donaldson, Gordon. *Corporate Debt Capacity.* Boston: Division of Research, Harvard Business School, 1961.

——. "New Framework for Corporate Debt Capacity." *Harvard Business Review* 40 (Mar.–Apr. 1962):117–31.

——. "Strategy for Financial Emergencies." *Harvard Business Review* 47 (Nov.–Dec. 1969):67–79.

Durand, David. "Cost of Debt and Equity Funds for Business: Trends and Problems of Measurement." Reprinted in Ezra Solomon, ed., *The Management of Corporate Capital.* New York: Free Press, 1959, 91–116.

Elton, Edwin J., and Gruber, Martin J. "The Cost of Retained Earnings—Implications of Share Repurchase." *Industrial Management Review* 9 (Spring 1968): 87–104.

——. "Valuation and the Cost of Capital for Regulated Industries." *Journal of Finance* 26 (June 1971):661–70.

Ezzell, John R., and Porter, R. Burr. "Flotation Costs and the Weighted Average Cost of Capital." *Journal of Financial and Quantitative Analysis* 11 (Sept. 1976): 403–14.

Fama, Eugene F. "Risk, Return, and Equilibrium: Some Clarifying Comments." *Journal of Finance* 23 (Mar. 1968):29–40.

Fama, Eugene F., and Miller, Merton H. *The Theory of Finance.* New York: Holt, Rinehart and Winston, Inc., 1972.

Glenn, David W. "Super Premium Security Prices and Optimal Corporate Financing Decisions." *Journal of Finance* 31 (May 1976):507–24.

Gordon, Myron. *The Investment, Financing, and Valuation of the Corporation.* Homewood, Ill.: Irwin, 1962.

Gordon, Myron and Halpern, Paul J. "Cost of Capital for a Division of a Firm." *Journal of Finance* 29 (Sept. 1974):1153–63.

Grinyer, John R. "The Cost of Equity, The C.A.P.M. and Management Objectives Under Uncertainty." *Journal of Business Finance & Accounting* 3 (Winter 1976):101–21.

Hakansson, Nils H. "On the Dividend Capitalization Model under Uncertainty." *Journal of Financial and Quantitative Analysis* 4 (Mar. 1969):65–87.

Haley, Charles W. "A Note on the Cost of Debt." *Journal of Financial and Quantitative Analysis* 1 (Dec. 1966):72–93.

———. "Taxes, The Cost of Capital, and the Firm's Investment Decisions." *Journal of Finance* 26 (Sept. 1971):901–17.

Hamada, Robert S. "Portfolio Analysis, Market Equilibrium and Corporation Finance." *Journal of Finance* 24 (Mar. 1969):13–32.

Haugen, Robert A., and Kumar, Prem. "The Traditional Approach to Valuing Levered-Growth Stocks: A Clarification." *Journal of Financial and Quantitative Analysis* 9 (Dec. 1974):1031–44.

Haugen, Robert A., and Pappas, James L. "Equilibrium in the Pricing of Capital Assets, Risk-Bearing Debt Instruments, and the Question of Optimal Capital Structure." *Journal of Financial and Quantitative Analysis* 6 (June 1971):943–54.

Haugen, Robert A., and Wichern, Dean W. "The Intricate Relationship Between Financial Leverage and the Stability of Stock Prices." *Journal of Finance* 30 (Dec. 1975):1283–92.

Heins, A. James, and Sprenkle, Case M. "A Comment on the Modigliani-Miller Cost of Capital Thesis." *American Economic Review* 59 (Sept. 1969):590–92.

Henderson, Glenn V., Jr. "On Capitalization Rates for Riskless Streams." *Journal of Finance* 31 (Dec. 1976):1491–93.

Higgins, Robert C. "Growth, Dividend Policy and Capital Costs in the Electric Utility Industry." *Journal of Finance* 29, no. 4 (Sept. 1974):1189–1201.

Hirshleifer, Jack. "Investment Decisions under Uncertainty: Applications of the State-Preference Approach." *Quarterly Journal of Economics* (May 1966):252–77.

Hite, Gailen L. "Leverage, Output Effects, and the M-M Theorems." *Journal of Financial Economics* 4 (Mar. 1977):177–202.

Jensen, Michael C. "Risk, the Pricing of Capital Assets, and the Evaluation of Investment Portfolios." *Journal of Business* 42 (Apr. 1969):167–247.

Jensen, Michael C., and Meckling, William H. "Theory of the Firm: Managerial Behavior, Agency Costs and Ownership Structure." *Journal of Financial Economics* 3 (Oct. 1976):305–60.

Keenan, Michael. "Models of Equity Valuation: The Great Serm Bubble." *Journal of Finance* 25 (May 1970):243–73.

Keenan, Michael, and Maldonado, Rita M. "The Redundancy of Earnings Leverage in a Cost of Capital Decision Framework." *Journal of Business Finance & Accounting* 3 (Summer 1976):43–56.

Krouse, Clement G. "Optimal Financing and Capital Structure Programs for the Firm." *Journal of Finance* 27 (Dec. 1972):1057–72.

Kumar, Prem. "Growth Stocks and Corporate Capital Structure Theory." *Journal of Finance* 30 (May 1975):532–47.

Lee, Wayne Y., and Barker, Henry H. "Bankruptcy Costs and the Firm's Optimal Debt Capacity: A Positive Theory of Capital Structure." *Southern Economic Journal* 43 (Apr. 1977):1453–65.

Lerner, Eugene M., and Carleton, Willard T. "Financing Decisions of the Firm." *Journal of Finance* 21 (May 1966):202–14.

———. "The Integration of Capital Budgeting and Stock Valuation." *American Economic Review* 54 (Sept. 1964):683–702. "Reply." *American Economic Review* 57 (Mar. 1967), 220–22.

———. *A Theory of Financial Analysis.* New York: Harcourt, 1966.

Lewellen, Wilbur G. *The Cost of Capital.* Belmont, Calif.: Wadsworth, 1969, chaps. 3–4.

———. "A Conceptual Reappraisal of Cost of Capital." *Financial Management* 3 (Winter 1974):63–70.

Lintner, John. "The Cost of Capital and Optimal Financing of Corporate Growth." *Journal of Finance* 18 (May 1963):292–310.

———. "Dividends, Earnings, Leverage, Stock Prices and the Supply of Capital to Corporations." *Review of Economics and Statistics* 44 (Aug. 1962):243–69.

———. "Security Prices, Risk, and Maximal Gains from Diversification." *Journal of Finance* 20 (Dec. 1965):587–616.

———. "The Aggregation of Investors' Judgments and Preferences in Purely Competitive Security Markets." *Journal of Financial and Quantitative Analysis* 4 (Dec. 1969):347–400.

Long, Michael S., and Racette, George A. "Stochastic Demand, Output and the Cost of Capital." *Journal of Finance* 29 (May 1974):499–506.

Machol, Robert E., and Lerner, Eugene M. "Risk, Ruin, and Investment Analysis." *Journal of Financial and Quantitative Analysis* 4 (Dec. 1969):473–92.

Malkiel, Burton G. "Equity Yields, Growth, and the Structure of Share Prices." *American Economic Review* 53 (Dec. 1963):467–94.

Mao, James C. T. "The Valuation of Growth Stocks: The Investment Opportunities Approach." *Journal of Finance* 21 (Mar. 1966):95–102.

McDonald, John G. "Market Measures of Capital Cost." *Journal of Business Finance* (Autumn 1970):27–36.

Melnyk, Lew Z. "Cost of Capital as a Function of Financial Leverage." *Decision Sciences* (July–Oct. 1970):327–56.

Miller, M. H., and Modigliani, Franco. "Cost of Capital to Electric Utility Industry." *American Economic Review* (June 1966):333–91.

Modigliani, Franco, and Miller, M. H. "The Cost of Capital, Corporation Finance and the Theory of Investment." *American Economic Review* 48 (June 1958):261–97.

———. "The Cost of Capital, Corporation Finance and the Theory of Investment: Reply." *American Economic Review* 49 (Sept. 1958):655–69. "Taxes and the Cost of Capital: A Correction." *American Economic Review* 53 (June 1963):433–43. "Reply." *American Economic Review* 55 (June 1965):524–27.

Mossin, Jan. "Security Pricing and Investment Criteria in Competitive Markets." *American Economic Review* 59 (Dec. 1969):749–56.

Mumey, Glen A. *Theory of Financial Structure.* New York: Holt, Rinehart and Winston, 1969.

Myers, Stewart C. "A Time-State Preference Model of Security Valuation." *Journal of Financial and Quantitative Analysis* 3 (Mar. 1968):1–34.

———. "Interactions of Corporate Financing and Investment Decisions—Implications for Capital Budgeting." *Journal of Finance* 29 (Mar. 1974):1–25.

———. "The Application of Finance Theory to Public Utility Rate Cases." *Bell Journal of Economics and Management Science* 3 (Spring 1972):58–97.

Nantell, Timothy J., and Carlson, C. Robert. "The Cost of Capital as a Weighted Average." *Journal of Finance* 30 (Dec. 1975):1343–55.

Petry, Glenn H. "Empirical Evidence on Cost of Capital Weights." *Financial Management* 4 (Winter 1975):58–65.

Pettit, R. Richardson, and Westerfield, Randolph. "Using the Capital Asset Pricing Model and the Market Model to Predict Security Returns." *Journal of Financial and Quantitative Analysis* 9 (Sept. 1974):579–605.

Pfahl, John K.; Crary, David T.; and Howard, R. Hayden. "The Limits of Leverage." *Financial Executive* (May 1970):48–55.

Pfahl, John K., and Crary, David T. "Leverage and the Rate of Return Required by Equity." *The Investment Process*. Scranton, Pa.: The International Textbook Company, 1970, 175–91.

Pogue, G. A. "An Extension of the Markowitz Portfolio Selection Model to Include Variable Transactions Costs, Short Sales, Leverage Policies and Taxes." *Journal of Finance* 25 (Dec. 1970):1005–27.

Porterfield, James T. S. *Investment Decisions and Capital Costs*. Englewood Cliffs, N.J.: Prentice-Hall, 1965.

Quirin, G. David. *The Capital Expenditure Decision*. Homewood, Ill.: Irwin, 1967, chaps. 5–6.

Reilly, Raymond R., and Wecker, William E. "On the Weighted Average Cost of Capital." *Journal of Financial and Quantitative Analysis* 8 (Jan. 1973): 123–26.

Resek, Robert W. "Multidimensional Risk and the Modigliani-Miller Hypothesis." *Journal of Finance* 25 (Mar. 1970):47–52.

Robichek, Alexander A. "Risk and the Value of Securities." *Journal of Financial and Quantitative Analysis* 4 (Dec. 1969):513–38.

Robichek, Alexander A.; McDonald, J. G.; and Higgins, R. C. "Some Estimates of the Cost of Capital to Electric Utilities, 1954–1957: Comment." *American Economic Review* 57 (Dec. 1967):1278–88.

Robichek, Alexander A., and McDonald, John G. "The Cost of Capital Concept: Potential Use and Misuse." *Financial Executive* 33 (June 1965):2–8.

Robichek, Alexander A., and Myers, Stewart C. *Optimal Financial Decisions*. Englewood Cliffs, N.J.: Prentice-Hall, 1965.

Rosenberg, Barr, and Guy, James. "Beta and Investment Fundamentals." *Financial Analysts' Journal* 32 (May–June 1976):60–72.

Schwartz, Eli. "Theory of the Capital Structure of the Firm." *Journal of Finance* 14 (Mar. 1959):18–39.

Schwartz, Eli, and Aronson, J. Richard. "Some Surrogate Evidence in Support of the Concept of Optimal Capital Structure." *Journal of Finance* 22 (Mar. 1967): 10–18.

Scott, David F., Jr. "Evidence on the Importance of Financial Structure." *Financial Management* 1 (Summer 1972):45–50.

Scott, J. H. "A Theory of Optimal Capital Structure." *Bell Journal of Economics* 7 (Spring 1976):33–54.

———. "Bankruptcy, Secured Debt, and Optimal Capital Structure." *Journal of Finance* 32 (Mar. 1977):1–19.

Sharpe, William F. "A Simplified Model for Portfolio Analysis." *Management Science* 10 (Jan. 1963):277–93.

———. "Capital Asset Prices: A Theory of Market Equilibrium." *Journal of Finance* 19 (Sept. 1964):425–42.

———. *Portfolio Analysis and Capital Markets.* New York: McGraw-Hill, 1970.

———. "Security Prices, Risk, and Maximal Gains from Diversification." *Journal of Finance* 21, no. 4 (Dec. 1966):743–44.

Sloane, William R., and Reisman, Arnold. "Stock Evaluation Theory: Classification, Reconciliation, and General Model." *Journal of Financial and Quantitative Analysis* 3 (June 1968):171–204.

Soldofsky, Robert M., and Miller, Roger L. "Risk-Premium Curves for Different Classes of Long-Term Securities, 1950–1966." *Journal of Finance* (June 1969): 429–45.

Solomon, Ezra. "Leverage and the Cost of Capital." *Journal of Finance* 18 (May 1963).

———. "Measuring a Company's Cost of Capital." *Journal of Business* 28 (Oct. 1955):240–52.

———. *The Theory of Financial Management.* New York: Columbia University Press, 1963.

———. *The Management of Corporate Capital.* New York: Free Press, 1959.

Stapleton, R. C. "A Note On Default Risk, Leverage and the MM Theorem." *Journal of Financial Economics* 2 (Dec. 1975):377–382.

Stiglitz, Joseph E. "A Re-Examination of the Modigliani-Miller Theorem." *American Economic Review* 59 (Dec. 1969):784–93.

Tinsley, P. A. "Capital Structure, Precautionary Balances, and Valuation of the Firm: The Problem of Financial Risk." *Journal of Financial and Quantitative Analysis* 5 (Mar. 1970):33–62.

Tobin, James. "Liquidity Preference as Behavior Towards Risk." *Review of Economic Studies* 25 (Feb. 1958):65–86.

Vandell, Robert F., and Pennell, Robert M. "Tight-Money Financing." *Harvard Business Review* 49 (Sept.–Oct. 1971):82–97.

Vickers, Douglas. "Profitability and Reinvestment Rates: A Note on the Gordon Paradox." *Journal of Business* 39 (July 1966):366–70.

———. "The Cost of Capital and the Structure of the Firm." *Journal of Finance* 25 (Mar. 1970):35–46.

Weston, J. Fred. "A Test of Cost of Capital Propositions." *Southern Economic Journal* 30 (Oct. 1963):105–212.

———. "Investment Decisions Using the Capital Asset Pricing Model." *Financial Management* 1 (Spring 1973):25–33.

Whitmore, G. A. "Market Demand Curve for Common Stock and the Maximization of Market Value." *Journal of Financial and Quantitative Analysis* 5 (Mar. 1970):105–14.

Wippern, Ronald F. "Financial Structure and the Value of the Firm." *Journal of Finance* 21 (Dec. 1966):615–34.

Appendix A to Chapter 19
Some Unresolved Issues on
the Cost of Capital

In this appendix we will show how some of the issues glossed over earlier can affect the cost of capital calculation. The purpose here is as much to raise questions as to answer them, yet the material has important practical implications. Moreover, anyone engaged in financial management must understand all the implications underlying the practical judgments that the financial manager will necessarily be forced to make.

Cost of Retained Earnings

Whenever a firm retains a portion of its net income rather then paying it out in dividends, there is an "opportunity cost" to stockholders. If the firm in question has a required rate of return of 12 percent on its stock (i.e., $k_s = 12\%$), then presumably its shareholders could have invested the retained earnings, had they been paid out in dividends, in other firms of similar risk and received a 12 percent return. This 12 percent is, under certain assumptions, the opportunity cost of retained earnings. The two assumptions are (1) that the stockholder pays no income tax on dividends and (2) that he incurs no brokerage costs when reinvesting dividend receipts.[1] *To the extent that these assumptions are not met, the opportunity cost of retained earnings, hence the cost of capital from retained earnings, is lower than the cost of new common stock.* The following example is an illustration.

The ABC Company has net earnings of $1 million, and all of its stockholders are in the 30 percent marginal tax bracket. Management estimates that under present conditions stockholders' required rate of return is 12 percent. If the earnings are paid out as dividends, the recipients will pay income taxes, then reinvest the proceeds in the stock of similar firms and obtain a 12 percent return. The brokerage costs to the stockholders will average 3 percent of the new investments. What rate of return must be earned internally to provide the stockholders with incremental earnings equal to what they would receive externally?

---

1. There is also a question of whether investors prefer to receive their rewards from stock investments in the form of dividends or as capital gains. The question is considered in some detail in Chapter 20, but here it is assumed that investors are indifferent between dividends and capital gains.

1. After-tax proceeds
   of dividend payment $= \$1,000,000 -$ personal taxes
   $= \$1,000,000 - \$300,000$
   $= \$700,000.$
2. Net investment after brokerage costs $= \$700,000 -$ brokerage
   $= \$700,000 - \$21,000$
   $= \$679,000.$
3. Earnings on new investment $= (679,000)(0.12) = \$81,480$
4. Internal rate of return (k_r) necessary to provide stockholders with incremental income of $81,480:

$$\$81,480 = (\$1,000,000)(k_r)$$
$$k_r = 8.148\%.$$

5. If the firm is able to earn 8.148 percent on retained earnings, the stockholders will be as well off as they would be if all earnings were paid out and then reinvested to yield 12 percent.
6. Therefore, the internal opportunity cost, or the required rate of return on retention-financed investments, is less than the stockholders' required rate of return and may be calculated as follows:

$$k_r = k_s(1 - T)(1 - f),$$

where k_r = the required return on retention-financed investments, k_s is stockholders' required rate of return, T = the stockholders' marginal tax rate, and f = the percentage brokerage cost. In the example being considered,

$$k_r = 0.12(0.7)(0.97) = 0.081, \text{ or } 8.1\%.$$

This procedure actually involves an overstatement. The retained earnings will give rise to an increase in the price of the stock; if the investor sells it, he will be subject to a capital gains tax. The capital gains tax rate is lower than the rate applicable to dividends (generally); also, as this tax is deferred, it has a lower present value.

Two limiting cases can be applied. First, it can be assumed that the stockholder never sells the stock, passing it on to his heirs, who do the same, *ad infinitum.* In this case, the procedures in the example are correct. At the other limit, it can be assumed that the investor holds the stock for the minimum hold-period (one year) to receive capital gains tax treatment, then sells the stock and pays a tax at one half his normal tax rate (or 25 percent, if this is lower). In this case, the value of T for the example should be 15 percent, and the resultant cost of retained earnings is computed to be:

$$k_r = 0.12(0.85)(0.97) = 0.099, \text{ or } 9.9\%.$$

The correct figure probably lies somewhere between these two extremes, but there is no way of knowing exactly where.

The example shows that, in general, the required rate of return on retention-financed investment (k_r) is less than investors' required rate of return (k_s) by the amount of brokerage costs on reinvested dividends receipts and by stockholders' marginal tax rates. But suppose there are many stockholders, and their marginal tax rates range from zero to 70 percent. Now what should be done? There simply is no one correct answer. One could use one half the average marginal tax rate of individual stockholders in general (one estimate places this average at about 40 percent),[2] the 25 percent maximum capital gains tax, the tax rate of the controlling stockholder, or one could try to estimate the average tax rate of all the firm's stockholders and use one half that number.[3]

Stock Purchases

Under certain circumstances, the procedure discussed in the preceding section is invalid or, at least, unnecessary. If k_s, the market-determined rate of return on the stock of the firm in question or of firms in the same risk class, is 12 percent, and if the firm can buy its own or similar stocks to yield 12 percent, then this sets a lower limit on project returns. The firm would never invest in assets yielding less than 12 percent, the value of k_s, because it can obtain this yield on market securities.

Several points make this line of reasoning questionable. First, a company whose stock is not publicly traded cannot buy its own stock on the open market. Second, privately held firms could not buy large amounts of the stock of publicly owned firms for investment purposes only without the Internal Revenue Service stepping in and imposing penalties under the improper accumulation of retained earnings tax (see Appen-

---

2. Vincent Jolivet, "The Weighted Average Marginal Tax Rate on Dividends Received by Individuals in the U.S.," *American Economic Review* (June 1966).

3. Another equation for determining a tax-and-brokerage adjusted cost of retained earnings is the following:

$$k_r = k_s \left[\frac{(1-f)(1-T_p)}{(1-T_g)} \right].$$

Here T_p is the personal tax on dividend income and T_g is the tax on capital gains. Using our illustrative values, we find k_r as follows:

$$k_r = 12 \left[\frac{(.97)(.7)}{.85} \right] = 12(.7988) = 9.59\%. \tag{A19-1}$$

Thus, this estimate of k_r lies between our extreme cases, 8.1 percent and 9.9 percent. See W. G. Lewellen, *The Cost of Capital* (Belmont, Ca.: Wadsworth, 1969), chapter 5, for a discussion of the logic behind this formula.

dix A to this book). Third, publicly owned companies that can legally buy their own stock on the open market under certain conditions may be averse to doing so, thereby admitting that they are unable to generate acceptable projects in a growing economic setting.[4] Also, if a firm engages in large-scale purchases of its own stock, it will probably run the price up and the yield down during the period in which it is making the acquisition.

The question of open-market purchases has not been fully resolved.[5] We are convinced that many firms, especially privately owned companies, cannot use open-market purchases (or mergers either) to avoid the effects of personal taxes on dividends; at least, for these companies, the cost of retained earnings is somewhat lower than the basic required rate of return. In our own experience, we have seen situations in which the stockholders of closely held firms were in high tax brackets and, therefore, directed the firms to make internal investments at rates of return less than the expected market returns on common stock for precisely the reasons outlined here. Further, we find it difficult to question their logic and their judgment that their cost of retained earnings is less than their external required rate of return. Certainly, the cost of external equity is higher than the cost of retained earnings, because of flotation and other transactions costs. In addition, the differential tax rate on dividends and capital gains must be taken into account.[6] In our own work with public companies, we reflect the higher cost of external equity by assigning a cost equal to 15 to 20 percent above the basic required return, that is, $k_e \approx 1.15\, k_s$. The adjustment factor used depends upon the stockholder characteristics, as indicated by management, of the firm in question. We must, however, admit to a feeling of uneasiness when we make this adjustment.

Cost of Depreciation-generated Funds

The very first increment of cash flow used to finance any year's capital budget is depreciation-generated funds. In their statements of sources and uses of funds, corporations generally show depreciation charges to be one of the most important sources of funds, if not the most important. For capital budgeting purposes, should depreciation

---

4. A special factor has been developed during the 1970's. The prices of products sold by firms do not cover the replacement cost of the assets used to produce them. Real rates of return (adjusted for inflation) have been depressed and stock prices in general are below book values. Firms purchase their own shares, stating that it is the highest yielding investment we can make."

5. See Chapter 20 for an extended discussion of stock repurchases.

6. See the 1976 presidential address to the American Finance Association by Merton H. Miller, "Debt and Taxes," *Journal of Finance* 32 (May 1977), pp. 261–76.

be considered "free" capital; should it be ignored completely; or should a charge be assessed against it? The answer is that a charge should indeed be assessed against these funds, and that this cost is approximately equal to the average cost of capital before outside equity is used.

The reasoning here is that the firm could, if it so desired, distribute the depreciation-generated funds to its stockholders and creditors, the parties who financed the assets in the first place. For example, if $10 million of depreciation-generated funds were available, the firm could either reinvest them or distribute them. If they are to be distributed, the distribution must be to both bondholders and stockholders in proportion to their shares of the capital structure; otherwise the capital structure will change. Obviously, this distribution should take place if the funds cannot be invested to yield the cost of captial, but retention should occur if the internal rate of return exceeds the cost of capital. Since the cost of depreciation-generated funds is equal to the average cost of capital, depreciation does not enter the calculation of the average cost of capital.

Depreciation does, however, affect the cost of capital *schedule* in a very significant way. Consider Figure 19–6: here we see that the cost of capital schedule begins to rise once the total funds raised goes beyond $41.6 million. However, if depreciation were considered to be a source of funds available for capital budgeting purposes, then the flat part of the curve would be extended out by the amount of the depreciation. In the Continental Container example, if depreciation amounted to $20 million, then the cost of capital schedule would begin to rise at $61.6 million rather than at $41.6 million.

What difference does all this make, and should we be concerned with a cost of capital schedule that includes or excludes depreciation? If we are concerned with the effects of *net increases* in assets, then the schedule without depreciation is appropriate. However, if we are concerned with gross capital expenditures—including replacement as well as expansion investments—then the schedule that includes depreciation is the relevant one.

Appendix B to Chapter 19
The Effect of Capital Structure on Valuation and the Cost of Capital

A firm's value is dependent upon its expected earnings stream and the rate used to discount this stream, or the cost of capital; therefore, if capital structure is to affect value, it must do so by operating either on expected earnings or on the cost of capital, or on both. Because interest is tax-deductible, leverage generally increases expected earnings, at least so long as the firm does not use so much leverage that bankruptcy seriously threatens its continued existence. The effect of leverage on the cost of capital is much less clear; indeed, this issue has been one of the major controversies in finance for the past 20 or so years, and perhaps more theoretical and empirical work has been done on this subject than on any other in the field. In this appendix we set forth the major theories on the relationship between leverage and the cost of capital.

The Net Income (NI) and Net Operating Income (NOI) Approaches

Economists have identified two basic market structures—pure competition and pure monopoly—and they can determine the optimal price-quantity solution for firms in either of these two positions. Most firms in the real world are in the gray area of oligopoly, which lies somewhere between the pure cases, but an understanding of the pure cases is helpful in understanding oligopoly and real-firm behavior.

The situation is similar with respect to leverage—there are two extreme positions corresponding to pure competition and pure monopoly, and a middle ground actually occupied by most if not all firms. David Durand, in a key article,[1] identified the two extreme cases:

Net Income Approach (NI). Under the NI approach to valuation, the interest rate and the cost of equity are independent of the capital structure, but the weighted average or overall cost of capital declines, and the total value (value of stock plus value of debt) rises, with increased use of leverage.

Net Operating Income Approach (NOI). Under the NOI approach, the cost of equity increases, the weighted average cost of capital

---

1. See David Durand, "Costs of Debt and Equity Funds for Business: Trends and Problems of Measurement," reprinted in Ezra Solomon, ed., *The Management of Corporate Capital* (New York: Free Press, 1959), pp. 91–116.

remains constant, and the total value of the firm also remains constant as leverage is changed.

Thus, if the NI approach is the correct one, leverage is an important variable, and debt policy decisions have a significant influence on the value of the firm. However, if the NOI approach is the correct one, then the firm's management need not be too concerned with financial structure, because it simply does not greatly matter.

Basic Assumptions and Definitions

In order to focus on the key elements of the controversy, we begin by making several simplifying assumptions:

1. Only two types of capital are employed, long-term debt and common stock.
2. There is no tax on corporate income. This assumption is later relaxed.
3. The firm's total assets are given, but its capital structure can be changed by selling debt to repurchase stock, or stock to retire debt.
4. All earnings are paid out as dividends.
5. All investors have the same subjective probability distributions of expected future operating earnings *(EBIT)* for a given firm; that is, investors have homogeneous expectations.
6. The operating earnings of the firm are not expected to grow; that is, the firm's expected *EBIT* is the same in all future periods.
7. The firm's business risk is constant over time and is independent of its capital structure and financial risk.
8. The firm is expected to continue indefinitely.

In addition to these assumptions, we shall use the following basic definitions and symbols:

S = total market value of the stock (equity).
B = total market value of the bonds (debt).
V = total market value of the firm = $S + B$.
$EBIT$ = earnings before interest and taxes = net operating income (NOI).
IC = interest payments in dollars.

Our next task is to specify and define the key cost of capital and valuation relationships:

1. *Debt*

$$\text{Cost of debt capital} = k_b = \frac{IC}{B}.$$

$$\text{Value of debt} = B = \frac{IC}{k_b}.$$

2. *Equity, or Common Stock*

$$\text{Cost of equity capital} = k_s = \frac{d_1}{p_0} + g.$$

Here d_1 is the next dividend, p_0 is the current price per share, and g is the expected growth rate. According to assumption 4 above, the percentage of earnings retained, or the retention rate (b), is zero; since $g = br$, where r is the rate of return on equity, $g = br = 0 \times r = 0$; in other words, the growth rate is zero. This is consistent with assumption 6 above. Note also that $d_1 = (1 - b)(e_1)$, and with $b = 0$, $d_1 = (1)(e_1) = e_1$. Thus,

$$k_s = \frac{d_1}{p_0} + g = \frac{e_1}{p_0} + 0 = \frac{e_1}{p_0}.$$

This equation is on a per share basis; multiplying both the numerator and denominator by the number of shares outstanding (n), we obtain

$$k_s = \frac{e_1(n)}{p_0(n)} = \frac{EBIT - IC}{S} = \frac{\text{Net income available to stockholders}}{\text{Total market value of stock}}.$$

Thus, k_s may be defined on either a per share or a total basis.

The value of the stock, or common equity, is equal to earnings divided by the cost of equity. On a per share basis:

$$p_0 = \frac{e_1}{k_s},$$

or on a total firm basis:

$$S = \left(\frac{EBIT - IC}{k_s}\right) = p_0 n.$$

3. *Overall, or Weighted Average, Cost of Capital*

The overall, or weighted average, cost of capital is

$$k = w_b k_b + w_s k_s$$

$$= \left(\frac{B}{V}\right)k_b + \left(\frac{S}{V}\right)k_s$$

$$= \left(\frac{B}{B+S}\right)k_b + \left(\frac{S}{B+S}\right)k_s.$$

4. The total value of the firm is thus

$$V = B + S$$

$$= \frac{IC}{k_b} + \frac{(EBIT - IC)}{k_s}.$$

These equations are not controversial—they are simply definitions that apply under either the NI or NOI approaches. However, there are major differences between the NI and NOI theories, as we shall see in the next sections.

The Net Income (NI) Approach

The basic difference between NI and NOI relates to what happens to k_s as the firm's use of debt changes. Under NI, k_s is assumed to be fixed and constant regardless of the firm's degree of financial leverage, while under NOI, k_s is assumed to change. (Both theories assume that k_b, the interest rate on debt, is constant.) To illustrate the NI approach, assume that a firm has $4 million of debt at 7.5 percent, an expected annual net operating earnings *(EBIT)* of $900,000, and an equity capitalization rate (k_s) of 10 percent. With no corporate income taxes, the NI approach gives the value of the firm as follows:

Net operating earnings *(EBIT)*	$ 900,000
Interest on debt ($4 million × 7.5%)	− 300,000
Available to common	$ 600,000
Market value of equity = S = $600,000/.10	$ 6,000,000
Market value of bonds = B = $300,000/.075	4,000,000
Total market value of firm = $V = S + B$	$10,000,000

Notice that the component costs of capital under the NI approach are

$k_b = 7.5$ percent, given as constant, and

$k_s = 10$ percent, given as constant,

so

$$k = 7.5\left(\frac{4,000,000}{10,000,000}\right) + 10\left(\frac{6,000,000}{10,000,000}\right)$$

$$= 7.5(.4) + 10(.6)$$

$$= 3\% + 6\% = 9\%.$$

Now we can examine the effect of a change in financing mix on the firm's cost of capital and market value. Suppose the firm increases its leverage by selling $1 million of debt and using the proceeds to retire stock: What effect will this change have on the value of the firm and its cost of capital? Under the NI approach, it is assumed that the component costs of debt and equity are held constant at 7.5 percent and 10 percent, respectively, so the new situation will be as follows:

Net operating earnings *(EBIT)*	$ 900,000
Less: Interest on debt ($5 million × 7.5 percent)	− 375,000
Available to common	$ 525,000
$S = \$525{,}000/.10 =$	$ 5,250,000
$B = \$375{,}000/.075 =$	5,000,000
$V = B + S =$	$10,250,000

The overall, or average, cost of capital is calculated as follows:

$$k = 7.5\left(\frac{5{,}000{,}000}{10{,}250{,}000}\right) + 10\left(\frac{5{,}250{,}000}{10{,}250{,}000}\right)$$

$$= 7.5\left(\frac{5}{10.25}\right) + 10\left(\frac{5.25}{10.25}\right) = 8.78\%.$$

Thus, using additional leverage has caused the total value of the firm to rise and the average cost of capital to fall.

Table B19–1 shows the firm's overall cost of capital and total market value at different degrees of financial leverage, while the cost of capital figures are plotted in Figure B19–1. Notice, in the table, that the firm's value rises steadily as the debt ratio increases, and, in both the table and the figure, that the overall, or average, cost of capital declines continuously.

Figure B19–1
Cost of Capital under
the NI Approach

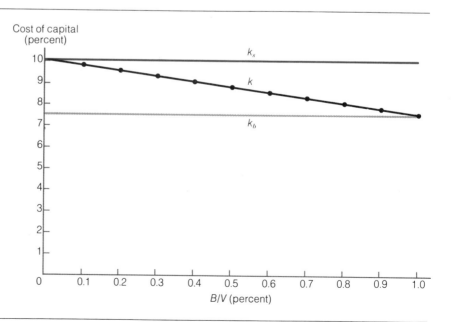

Table B19–1 **Effect of Capital Structure on Value and Cost of Capital: NI (EBIT = \$900,000; Other Dollars in Millions)**	Leverage Ratio $\dfrac{B}{V}$	0%	30.77%	65.12%	80.00%	93.62%	100.00%
	Value of debt (B)	0	\$3.000	\$ 7.000	\$ 9.000	\$11.000	\$12.000
	Value of equity (S)	\$9.000	\$6.750	\$ 3.750	\$ 2.250	\$ .750	\$ 0
	Total value (V)	\$9.000	\$9.750	\$10.750	\$11.250	\$11.750	\$12.000
	k_b	7.5%	7.5%	7.5%	7.5%	7.5%	7.5%
	k_s	10.0%	10.0%	10.0%	10.0%	10.0%	10.0%
	k	10.0%	9.2308%	8.3720%	8.000%	7.6595%	7.5000%

The Net Operating Income (NOI) Approach

The second major approach, NOI, is closely identified with the works of Franco Modigliani and Merton Miller (MM), who strongly support NOI on the basis of their theoretical and empirical research.[2] In this section, we set forth the key features of the NOI approach, illustrate the cost of capital and valuation that result under NOI, and summarize Modigliani and Miller's theoretical arguments in support of NOI.

The major assumptions of the NOI approach (in addition to the set of assumptions common to both NI and NOI shown in the first section) are as follows:

1. In a world of no taxes, the total market value of the firm (V) is found by capitalizing net operating income (EBIT = NOI) at the overall cost of capital, k, which is a constant. Thus,

$$V = \frac{EBIT}{k}.$$

Since k is independent of financial mix, as is EBIT, V is also a constant and is independent of capital structure.

2. The value of the equity, or the total value of the stock (S), is found by subtracting the value of the debt (B) from V. Thus, $S = V - B$, which implies that S is a *residual* obtained by deducting the stated value of the bonds from the total value of the firm, *which was found by capitalizing* EBIT *or* NOI *at the constant overall cost of capital.*

3. The cost of equity was defined earlier as follows:

$$k_s = \frac{EBIT - IC}{S}.$$

2. See F. Modigliani and M. H. Miller, "The Cost of Capital, Corporation Finance and the Theory of Investment," *American Economic Review* 48 (June 1958), pp. 261–97, and "The Cost of Capital, Corporation Finance and the Theory of Investment: Reply," *American Economic Review* 49 (September 1958), pp. 655–69; "Taxes and the Cost of Capital: A Correction," *American Economic Review* 53 (June 1963), pp. 433–43; and "Reply," *American Economic Review* 55 (June 1965), pp. 524–27.

As we shall see below, *this implies that* k_s *increases as leverage increases.*

4. The overall cost of capital is an average of the costs of debt and equity:

$$k = w_b k_b + w_s k_s = k_b\left(\frac{B}{V}\right) + k_s\left(\frac{S}{V}\right).$$

If the values of k and S are determined as shown above, then this value of k will equal the given and constant k for the firm. This point is also demonstrated in the examples given below.

We can use the data employed in the NI section to illustrate the NOI approach. Thus, the firm is assumed to have $EBIT = \$900,000$; a cost of debt $(k_b) = 7.5\%$; an initial debt of \$4 million; and an average cost of capital $(k) = 10\%$. Under the NOI approach, the total value of the firm is calculated as follows:

Net operating income *(EBIT)*	$\underline{\$\ \ 900,000}$
$V = B + S = EBIT/k = \$900,000/.10$	$\$9,000,000$
$B = \$4,000,000$	$-\ 4,000,000$
$S = $ a residual $=$	$\underline{\$5,000,000}$

Given the value of the stock, we can now calculate the cost of equity capital as follows:

$$k_s = \frac{EBIT - IC}{S} = \frac{\$900,000 - .075(\$4,000,000)}{\$5,000,000}$$

$$= \frac{\$600,000}{\$5,000,000} = .12 \text{ or } 12\%.$$

The weighted average cost of capital can now be calculated:

$$k = k_b\left(\frac{B}{V}\right) + k_s\left(\frac{S}{V}\right) = 7.5\%\left(\frac{4}{9}\right) + 12\%\left(\frac{5}{9}\right) = 3.33 + 6.67 = 10\%.$$

**Table B19–2
Effect of Capital
Structure on Value
and Cost of
Capital: NOI
(EBIT = $900,000;
Other Dollars
in Millions)**

$\frac{B}{V}$	0%	22.22%	44.44%	88.89%	100.00%
Debt *(B)*	$ 0	$2.000	$4.000	$8.000	$9.000
Equity *(S)*	$9.000	$7.000	$5.000	$1.000	$ 0
Total value *(V)*	$9.000	$9.000	$9.000	$9.000	$9.000
k_b	7.5%	7.5%	7.5%	7.5%	7.5%
k_s	10.0%	10.71%	12.0%	30.0%	—
k	10.0%	10.0%	10.0%	10.0%	10.0%
$\frac{B}{S}$	0%	28.57%	80.00%	800.00%	—

Thus, the average cost of capital is 10 percent, just as the NOI theory says it should be.

If debt were increased to $5 million, the value of the firm would remain constant at $9 million, the value of the stock would drop to $4 million, and the cost of equity would rise to 13.12 percent:

$$k_s = \frac{\$900,000 - .075(\$5,000,000)}{\$4,000,000} = \frac{\$525,000}{\$4,000,000} = 13.12\%,$$

and

$$k = 7.5\%\left(\frac{5}{9}\right) + 13.12\left(\frac{4}{9}\right) = 4.17 + 5.83 = 10\%.$$

Figure B19–2
Cost of Capital under the NOI Approach, No Taxes

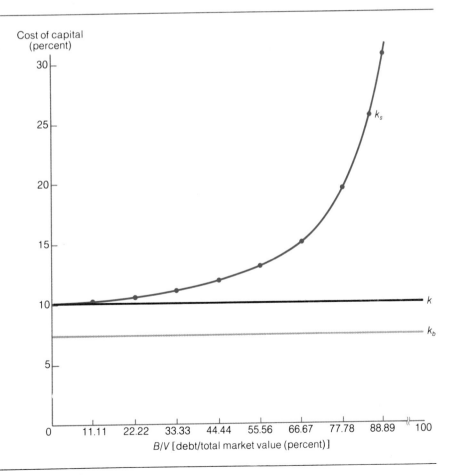

Again, we see that the calculated average cost of capital is a constant.

Values for V, B, S, k and k_s at different debt ratios are shown in Table B19–2, and a plot of the NOI cost of capital is shown in Figure B19–2. The key features of these two exhibits are as follows:

1. Both the cost of debt (k_b) and the overall, or average, cost of capital (k) are constant.
2. The cost of equity (k_s) increases exponentially with leverage as measured by the ratio (B/V).[3]

Modigliani and Miller's Support for NOI: The Arbitrage Argument

Modigliani and Miller base their support of the NOI hypothesis on arbitrage, arguing that if two companies differ only in the way they are financed and in their total market value, investors will sell shares of the overvalued firm, buy those of the undervalued firm, and continue this process until the companies have the same market value. To illustrate the arbitrage argument, assume that two firms L (for levered) and U (for unlevered) are identical in all respects except financial structure. Firm L

---

3. A firm's leverage can be measured (at market values) by either the debt-to-total-value ratio (B/V), or the debt/equity (B/S) ratio. Under the NOI-MM theory, the cost of equity is an exponential function of the B/V ratio (see Figure B19–2) but a linear function of the B/S ratio. For a demonstration of this linear relationship, consider the following:

$$k = k_b(B/V) + k_s(S/V) \qquad \text{(B19–1)}$$

or

$$k_s = \frac{k - k_b\left(\frac{B}{V}\right)}{\frac{S}{V}}. \qquad \text{(B19–2)}$$

Now note that $V = B + S$, and that the equity ratio S/V may be rewritten as

$$\frac{S}{V} = 1 - \frac{B}{B + S}. \qquad \text{(B19–3)}$$

We may substitute (B19–2) and (B19–3) into (B19–1), then simplify as follows:

$$k_s = \frac{k - k_b\dfrac{B}{B + S}}{1 - \dfrac{B}{B + S}} = \frac{\dfrac{k(B + S) - k_bB}{B + S}}{\dfrac{B + S - B}{B + S}}$$

$$= \frac{kB + kS - k_bB}{S} = k + (k - k_b)\frac{B}{S}. \qquad \text{(B19–4)}$$

k and k_b are constants, so Equation (B19–4) is of the form $y = a + bx$, which is linear. Equation (B19–4) states that the required rate of return on common stock (k_s) is equal to the appropriate capitalization rate for a pure equity stream for that class (k) plus a premium for financial risk equal to the spread between that capitalization rate (k) and the yield on debt (k_b) times the debt-equity ratio (B/S). This expression for the cost of equity capital is referred to as MM's Proposition II.

has $4 million of 7.5 percent debt; firm U is all equity financed. Both firms have $EBIT = \$900,000$. In the initial situation, before arbitrage, both firms have an equity capitalization rate $k_s = 10$ percent. Under these conditions, and assuming the NI approach is correct, the following situation will exist:

	Firm U	Firm L
Net operating income *(EBIT)*	$ 900,000	$ 900,000
Less interest on debt	0	− 300,000
Available to common	$ 900,000	$ 600,000
Value of stock *(S)*	$9,000,000	$ 6,000,000
Value of debt *(B)*	0	4,000,000
Total market value *(V = B + S)*	$9,000,000	$10,000,000

This is the NI solution, and MM argue that it cannot persist.

An investor in firm L can, according to MM, increase his total returns without increasing his financial risk. For example, suppose the investor owns 10 percent of L's stock, so that his investment is $600,000. He can sell his stock in L, borrow an amount equal to 10 percent of L's debt ($400,000), and then buy 10 percent of U's stock for $900,000. Notice that the investor received $1 million from sale of stock plus borrowing, and spent $900,000 on U's stock, so he has $100,000 in uncommitted funds.

Now consider the investor's income position:

Old income:	10% of L's $600,000 =		$60,000
New income:	10% of U's $900,000	$90,000	
	Less 7.5% on $400,000 loan	− 30,000	$60,000

Thus, his stock investment income is exactly the same as before, but he has $100,000 left over for investment elsewhere, so his total return will rise. Further, his risk, according to MM, is the same as before—he has simply substituted "homemade" leverage for corporate leverage.

MM argue that this arbitrage process will occur, with sales of L's stock driving its price down and purchases of U's stock driving its price up, until the market values of the two firms are equal. When this equality is reached, the NOI conditions are fulfilled, and the value of the firms and their overall costs of capital are equal; that is, value and k are independent of capital structure. However, in reaching this conclusion, MM must make some important assumptions:

1. Their analysis implies that personal and corporate leverage are perfect substitutes. In the case of corporate borrowings, the individual investing in the levered firm has only limited liability. If, however,

he engages in arbitrage transactions, there is the possibility that he may lose not only his holdings in the unlevered firm but also his other assets.

2. In the analysis, transaction costs were assumed away, yet such costs may retard the arbitrage process.

3. Corporations and individuals are assumed to borrow at the same rate. The cost of borrowing could be higher for the individual than for the firm.

4. At times, institutional restrictions may retard the arbitrage process. Institutional investors dominate stock markets today, yet most institutional investors are prohibited from engaging in "homemade" leverage.

MM's critics argue that the assumptions of the MM model are invalid, and that, in the real world, firms' values and costs of capital are functions of financial leverage. We shall return to this debate later, after examining the situation when the assumption of no corporate taxes is relaxed.

The Modigliani-Miller View with Taxes

When taxes are introduced, MM's position changes: with corporate taxes, they recognize that the levered firm commands a higher value because interest on debt is a deductible expense. Specifically, MM state that L's value exceeds that of U by an amount equal to L's debt multiplied by the tax rate:

$$V = V_U + BT$$

Here V = value of firm L, V_U = value of Firm U, B = amount of debt in L, and T = tax rate. Their proof goes as follows. Consider two firms that are identical in all respects except capital structure. Assume that firm U has no debt in its capital structure, while L employs debt, and that expected operating earnings, $EBIT = X$, is identical for each firm. Under these assumptions, the operating earnings after tax available to investors, X_U and X_L, for firms U and L respectively, are computed as follows:

$$X_U = X(1 - T) \tag{B19-5}$$

and

$$X_L = (X - k_bB)(1 - T) + k_bB \tag{B19-6}$$

where T = tax rate, k_b = interest rate on debt, and B = amount of debt. The first term to the right of the equal sign in Equation B19-6 is the income available to stockholders; the second term is that available to bondholders.

Since firm U does not employ debt, its value (V_U) may be determined by discounting its annual net income after corporate taxes, $X(1-T)$, by its capitalization rate, k_U:

$$V_U = \frac{X(1-T)}{k_U}. \tag{B19-7}$$

The levered firm's after-tax income, X_L, as set forth in Equation B19−6, can be restated as follows:

$$X_L = (X - k_b B)(1-T) + k_b B$$
$$= X - k_b B - XT + kB_b T + k_b B$$
$$= X - XT + k_b BT$$
$$= X(1-T) + k_b BT$$

The first term in the final equation, $X(1-T)$, is equivalent to U's income, while the second part, $k_b BT$, represents the tax savings that occur because interest is deductible.

The value of the levered firm is found by capitalizing both parts of its after-tax earnings. MM argue that because L's "regular" earnings stream is precisely as risky as is the income of firm U, it should be capitalized at the same rate (k_U). However, since the debt is assumed to be riskless, interest on the debt must be paid, and the tax saving represents a certain, riskless stream that should be discounted at the riskless rate (k_b). Thus, we obtain Equation B19−8:

$$V = \frac{X(1-T)}{k_U} + \frac{k_b BT}{k_b} = \frac{X(1-T)}{k_U} + BT. \tag{B19-8}$$

However, since

$$V_U = \frac{X(1-T)}{k_U},$$

we may also express V as

$$V = V_U + BT,$$

which is what we set out to prove.

We may now illustrate the MM valuation and cost of capital hypotheses in a world with corporate taxes.[4] Assume (1) that a firm starts in

---

4. First, it must be recognized that with the introduction of corporate income taxes, either (1) the values of business firms will be lower because of the decline in earnings, or (2) rates of return before taxes (*EBIT*/Assets) will rise to offset the tax revenue; which condition holds depends upon the incidence of corporate income taxes, a long-standing question among economists. We simply note that something must change when taxes are imposed, although in our example we let the rate of return change.

business with total capital of \$5.4 million; (2) that this capital is used to purchase assets costing \$5.4 million; (3) that the before-tax rate of return on these assets is 16.67 percent, producing $EBIT = \$900,000$; (4) that the leverage-free equity capitalization rate is $k_s = 10$ percent; and (5) that the corporate income tax rate is 40 percent. We may compute the value of the unlevered firm as follows:

$$V_U = \frac{X(1-T)}{k_U} = \frac{\$900,000(1-.4)}{.10} = \$5,400,000.$$

As debt is added, the total market value of the firm rises by BT per unit of debt; for example, if \$1 million of debt is used, then

$$V = V_U + BT = \$5,400,000 + \$400,000 = \$5,800,000.$$

Note also that if we divide $EBIT$ by V, the quotient is the before-tax rate of return on total market value, and this rate of return declines as debt is increased. Values of V and $EBIT/V$, together with several rates of return calculations which are explained below, are shown in Table B19-3.

**Table B19-3
Effect of Leverage
on Valuation and
the Cost of
Capital: MM
Assumptions in a
World with Taxes
(Dollars in Millions)**

Debt (B)	Equity (S)	Total Value (V)	B/S	EBIT/V	After-tax Rate of Return on Equity		Average Cost of Capital (k)
					Book	Market (k_s)	
\$0	\$5.4	\$5.4	0%	16.67%	10.00%	10.00%	10.00%
\$2	\$4.2	\$6.2	47.6%	14.52%	13.23%	10.71%	8.72%
\$4	\$3.0	\$7.0	133.0%	12.86%	17.14%	12.00%	7.77%
\$6	\$1.8	\$7.8	333.3%	11.54%	n.a.	15.00%	6.92%
\$8	\$0.6	\$8.6	1333.3%	10.47%	n.a.	30.00%	6.28%

n.a. = not applicable; implies debt greater than assets (\$5,400,000), which would imply a negative accounting net worth, so the rate of return on book equity is not meaningful.

The book value and market value of common equity, and the rates of return on these two values, will vary with leverage under the MM tax model. Total corporate assets are \$5,400,000 by assumption, and we can establish other items as follows:

1. Net profit after interest and taxes $= (X - IC)(1 - T)$.
2. Book value of equity $= \$5,400,000 - B$.
3. Market value of equity $= V - B$.
4. Rate of return on book equity $= [(X - IC)(1 - T)]/(\$5,400,000 - B)$.
5. Rate of return on market value of equity $= k_s = [(X - IC)(1 - T)]/$

$(V - B)$ = the required rate of return on equity, or the cost of equity capital.

6. Overall cost of capital $= k = (B/V)(1 - T)(k_b) + (S/V)(k_s)$.

Using these relationships, and values of V and B as shown in Table B19–3, we can find the rates of return on book and market equity at different degrees of leverage:

Debt = $0:

$$\text{Rate of return on book equity} = \frac{(\$900,000 - \$0)(.6)}{\$5,400,000 - \$0} = 10.0\%.$$

$$\text{Rate of return on market equity} = k_s = \frac{\$540,000}{\$5,400,000} = 10.0\%.$$

Average cost of capital $= k = (0)(.6)(7.5) + (1.00)(10.0) = 10.0\%$.

Debt = $2 million:

$$\text{Rate of return on book equity} = \frac{(\$900,000 - \$150,000)(.6)}{\$5,400,000 - \$2,000,000}$$

$$= \frac{\$450,000}{\$3,400,000} = 13.23\%.$$

$$\text{Rate of return on market equity} = \frac{\$450,000}{\$4,200,000} = 10.71\%.$$

Average cost of capital $= k = (.32)(.6)(7.5) + (.68)(10.71) = 8.72$.

The cost-of-capital situation under the MM assumptions in a world with taxes is graphed in Figure B19–3. The materials in Figure B19–3 and Table B19–3 illustrate the following points:

1. The total value of the firm rises with leverage (Table B19–3).
2. The rate of return on the book value of equity rises rapidly with leverage, but is meaningless for debt > $5.4 million (Table B19–3).
3. The rate of return on the market value of equity, which is also the cost of equity capital, rises with leverage, but less rapidly than the rate of return on book values (Table B19–3 and Figure B19–3).
4. The after-tax cost of debt is constant (4.5 percent in our example as shown in Figure B19–3).
5. The overall, or average, cost of capital declines linearly as the debt ratio is increased. However, it would be difficult, if not impossible, for the firm to increase its market value debt ratio to or beyond the point where the book value debt ratio is 100 percent, that is, beyond the point where $B = $5.4 million (Table B19–3 and Figure B19–3).

Figure B19–3
The Cost of Capital
under the MM
Assumptions, with
Taxes

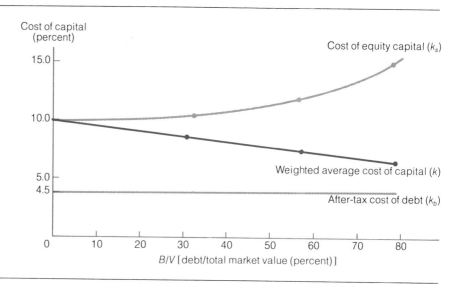

Thus, the MM model in a world of corporate taxes leads to the conclusion that the value of a firm will be maximized, and its cost of capital minimized, if it uses only debt in its capital structure. Of course, firms do not engage in 100 percent debt financing.

The Modigliani-Miller Arbitrage Process in a World with Taxes

With corporate taxes, both the NI and NOI approaches produce higher values for the levered than for the unlevered firms. However, the two theories differ with respect both to the size of this difference and to the manner in which it is generated. To illustrate, we shall use the same data as given previously. The tax rate is 40 percent. Firm L has $4 million of 7.5 percent debt; firm U is all equity financed; and both firms have $EBIT = \$900,000$. To begin, assume that both firms have an equity capitalization rate $k_s = 10$ percent. Under these conditions, the NI approach establishes the value of firms U and L as follows:

	Firm U	Firm L
Net operating income *(EBIT)*	$ 900,000	$ 900,000
Less: interest on debt	— 0	— 300,000
Taxable income	$ 900,000	$ 600,000
Less: Taxes at 40 percent	— 360,000	— 240,000
Available to common	$ 540,000	$ 360,000

Value of stock	$5,400,000	$3,600,000
Value of debt *(B)*	0	4,000,000
Total market value (*V* = *B* + *S*)	$5,400,000	$7,600,000

MM would argue that this NI solution represents a fundamental disequilibrium and therefore cannot persist. Using the MM equations developed above, we see that the equilibrium value of the levered firm is $V = V_u + BT = 5,400,000 + (4,000,000)(.40) = \$7,000,000$, or $0.6 million less than the value calculated above. Firm L is thus overvalued, and, in a reasonably perfect market, a situation like this cannot exist — arbitrage will force the value of the firm back to equilibrium in accordance with the equation $V = V_u + BT$.

The arbitrage process with taxes works as follows. Assume an investor owns 5 percent of L's stock (that is, $.05 \times \$3,600,000 = \$180,000$). His income from this investment is $.10 \times \$180,000 = \$18,000$. Now this investor can obtain a higher income, without increasing his risk, by moving from L to U. He would reduce his percentage holdings in L's debt (5 percent) times $(1 - T)$ — that is, $.05(1 - .4)(\$4 \text{ million}) = \$120,000$. Finally, he would purchase 5 percent of U's stock ($.05 \times 5,400,000 = \$270,000$). The switch from L to U provides the investor with the following income and uncommitted funds:

Income = .10 × $270,000	$ 27,000
Less: Cost of personal debt	
= 7.5 percent × 120,000 borrowed capital	9,000
Net income from new investment	$ 18,000
Total funds: Original capital	$180,000
Borrowed funds	120,000
	$300,000
Total outlay	$270,000
Uncommitted funds	$ 30,000

Through arbitrage and the substitution of personal for corporate leverage, the investor can switch from the levered company into the unlevered one, earn the same total return ($18,000) on his net worth, be exposed to the same leverage as formerly (but on personal rather than corporate account), and have funds left over to invest elsewhere. According to MM, many investors would recognize this arbitrage opportunity, attempt to make the switch, and in the process drive the price of L's stock down to establish an equilibrium where the total market values of the two firms are consistent with the MM equation, that is, $V_U = \$5.4$ million, and $V = V_U + BT = \$5.4$ million $+ \$1.6$ million $= \$7$ million.

The Weighted Cost of Capital Again

A simple expression for the weighted cost of capital can also be developed from the above relationships. Recall that k_u is the after-tax cost of capital for an unlevered firm. With taxes, MM's proposition II is expressed by Equation B19–9:[5]

$$k_s = k_u + (k_u - k_b) \frac{B(1-T)}{S} \tag{B19-9}$$

But the weighted cost of capital is:

$$k = k_b(1-T)\frac{B}{V_L} + k_s \frac{S}{V_L}$$

Substitute from Equation B19–9 for k_s.

$$k = k_b(1-T)\frac{B}{V_L} + \left[k_u + (k_u - k_b)\frac{B(1-T)}{S} \right] \frac{S}{V_L} \tag{B19-10}$$

We multiply through in Equation B19–10.

$$k = \frac{k_b B}{V_L} - \frac{k_b TB}{V_L} + \frac{k_u S}{V_L} + \frac{k_u B}{V_L} - \frac{k_u TB}{V_L} - \frac{k_b B}{V_L} + \frac{k_b + B}{V_L}$$

The terms with opposite signs can be cancelled to obtain:

$$k = \frac{k_u B}{V_L} + \frac{k_u S}{V_L} - \frac{k_u TB}{V_L} \tag{B19-11}$$

Since $B + S = V_L$, the first two terms on the right-hand side of Equation B19–11 equal k_u. We can factor k_u to obtain:

$$k = k_u \left(1 - \frac{TB}{V_L} \right) \tag{B19-12}$$

Equation B19–12 states that the weighted cost of capital for a levered firm (in a world with corporate income taxes) is equal to the (after-tax) cost of capital for an unlevered firm times (one minus the firm's tax rate multiplied by its leverage ratio). Thus if:

$$k_u = .15$$
$$T = .5$$
$$B/V_L = .4$$

5. See footnote 3 for MM's proportion II without taxes.

We can obtain k from Equation B19–12:

$$k = .15[1 - .5(.4)]$$

$$k = .12$$

The Effect of Leverage on the Cost of Capital: A Summary of Alternative Positions

A review of the literature on the leverage question suggests that three alternative positions have, in the past, been advocated: the "traditional" view, the MM view, and what can best be described as a compromise view. Figure B19–4 gives graphic representations of these three views. (No one has ever argued seriously that the NI approach holds.)

The Traditional View

Prior to the appearance of the 1958 MM article, most writers dealing with the cost of capital seemed to advocate a position roughly consistent with that shown in panel (a) of Figure B19–4. We say "roughly" because, prior to MM's work, academic writers on the subject were not sufficiently rigorous to enable us to pin down their views. At any rate, most academicians who did express views on this subject seemed to go along with the net income approach up to a point—they seemed to feel that the cost of both debt and equity was independent of the debt ratio until some unspecified amount of debt was employed, after which the cost of equity and debt begin to rise rather sharply. As a result, the average or overall cost of capital in the traditional view declined rather sharply, then rose sharply beyond the optimum debt ratio.

Figure B19–4
Alternative Views of the Relationship between the Use of Debt and the Cost of Capital

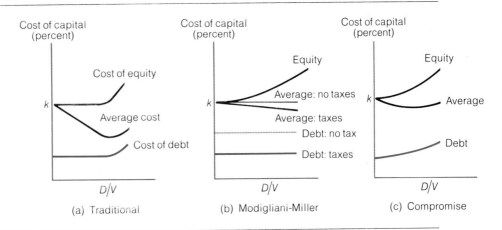

Modigliani-Miller View

Panel (b) of Figure B19–4 shows the MM view with and without corporate taxes. This figure combines Figures B19–2 and B19–3 from Appendix B to Chapter 19 and reflects that related discussion.

Compromise View

Panel (c) of Figure B19–4 shows what might be described as a compromise view of the relationship between debt and the cost of capital. Unlike the traditional view, which has the cost of debt and equity constant when relatively little debt is used, and the MM view, which is that the cost of equity rises at a rate that causes the average cost of capital to be constant (no taxes) or to decline linearly (with taxes), the compromise view holds that the cost of both debt and equity rises with the degree of financial leverage, with the result being a relatively shallow average cost of capital curve.

To summarize, the traditional view suggests that the average cost of capital declines rapidly with debt over a certain range and then begins to rise rapidly. The result is something approximating a V-shaped average cost of capital curve. The average cost of capital, according to MM, is constant in a world with no taxes, but declines continuously with increases in debt when corporate income taxes are considered. Thus, the MM model suggests that a firm that pays no corporate taxes need not worry about its capital structure, while a firm that does pay taxes should take on as much debt as it can get. Under the compromise view—which reflects our own feelings—the average cost of capital curve is saucer-shaped rather than V-shaped. There is an optimum capital structure, so it pays the financial manager to give careful consideration to his firm's capital structure. But the curve does not have a sharply defined minimum, so the firm is not penalized greatly by departing somewhat from the optimal debt structure. This permits flexibility in financial planning.

Neither theory nor empirical analysis has been able to specify precisely the optimal capital structure for an actual firm, or the precise cost of capital at any given capital structure—capital structure decisions are largely matters of informed judgment. However, *informed* judgment requires that some analysis of the type described in this book be undertaken, and an awareness of the theoretical considerations described here is very useful in such analyses.

Problems

B19–1. Companies U and L are identical in every respect except that U is unlevered while L has $10 million of 5 percent bonds outstanding. Assume (1) that all of the MM assumptions are met, (2) that the tax rate is 40 percent, (3) that *EBIT* is $2 million, and (4) that the equity capitalization rate for company U is 10 percent.

a. What value would MM estimate for each firm?

b. Suppose $V_U = \$8$ million and $V_L = \$18$ million. According to MM, do these represent equilibrium values? If not, explain the process by which equilibrium will be restored. No calculations are necessary.

B19-2. You are provided the following information: The firm's expected net operating income (X) is $400. Its value as an unlevered firm (V_U) is $2,000. The tax rate is 40 percent. The cost of debt is 8.7 percent. The ratio of debt to equity for the levered firm, when it is levered, is 1. Using the NOI approach.

a. Calculate the after-tax cost of equity capital for both the levered and unlevered firm.

b. Calculate the after-tax weighted average cost of capital for each.

c. Why is the cost of equity capital higher for the levered firm, but the weighted average cost of capital lower?

B19-3. Company A and Company B are in the same risk class, and are identical in every respect except that Company A is levered, while Company B is not. Company A has $3 million in 5 percent bonds outstanding. Both firms earn 10 percent *before interest and taxes* on their $5 million of total assets. Assume perfect capital markets, rational investors, and so on, a tax rate of 60 percent, and a capitalization rate of 10 percent for an all equity company.

a. Compute the value of firms A and B using the net income (NI) approach.

b. Compute the value of each firm using the net operating income (NOI) approach.

c. Using the NOI approach, calculate the after-tax weighted average cost of capital, k, for firms A and B. Which of these two firms has an optimal capital structure according to the NOI approach? Why?

d. According to the NOI approach, the values for firms A and B computed in part a above are not in equilibrium. If a situation like this exists, an investor in the overvalued firm can, through the arbitrage process, secure the same income at lower cost. Assuming that you own 1 percent of A's stock, show the process which will give you the same amount of income but at less cost. At what point would this process stop?

e. Company B (the wholly equity financed firm) wants to change its capital structure by introducing debt. Management believes that the cost of equity to the firm will take the form

$$k_s = R_F + \rho_1 + \rho_2$$

where

k_s = the cost of equity,

R_F = the after-tax riskless interest rate, currently at about 6 percent,

p_1 = a premium demanded by the firm as a result of its particular business activity, currently estimated to be 4 percent, and

p_2 = a premium demanded as a result of the firm's financial leverage.

Management believes that the premium, p_2, can be approximated by taking the firm's *debt-assets* ratio, squaring it, and multiplying by .10 to give the additional percentage points of premium required by the market. Management also feels that the firm's cost of debt is a function of the debt ratio, and estimates that this function is approximately equal to the following schedule:

Ratio Debt/Assets	After-tax Cost of Debt
0%	.05
20%	.05
30%	.06
40%	.07
60%	.12

Under these assumptions, is there an optimal capital structure for firm B? If so, what is this optimal debt-equity ratio?

B19–4. The cost of debt before taxes is 10 percent. The cost of equity for a leveraged firm is 14 percent. The debt to total value of the levered firm is 50 percent. The corporate tax rate is 40 percent.
a. What is the cost of capital of the levered firm?
b. What is the cost of capital of the firm if it were unlevered?

Appendix C to Chapter 19
Using the CAPM to Estimate a
Firm's Cost of Capital

Three steps are required in using the capital asset pricing model (CAPM) to estimate a firm's cost of equity capital:

1. estimate the market parameters in order to estimate the security market line;
2. estimate the firm's beta coefficient; and,
3. utilize the estimates to formulate a judgment of the firm's cost of equity capital.

Each of these steps will be covered, first explaining the formal methodology involved and then indicating the kinds of judgments required to arrive at a number or range of numbers for the firm's cost of equity capital.

Estimating the Market Parameters

The key market parameters to estimate are the risk-free rate of return, the expected return on the market and the variance of the market return. With these we have estimates of the key market-determined variables of the security market line. For example, suppose that we estimated the risk-free return to be 5 percent, the return on the market to be 10 percent, and the variance of the market to be 1 percent. The security market line could then be expressed as shown in Equations C19–1 and C19–2:

$$\bar{k}_j = R_F + \lambda \operatorname{Cov}(k_j, k_M) \text{ where } \lambda = \frac{k_M - R_F}{\operatorname{Var}(k_M)} \tag{C19–1}$$

$$\bar{k}_j = R_F + (k_M - R_F)\beta_j \tag{C19–2}$$

When we fill in the illustrative market parameters we would obtain Equations C19–1a and C19–2a:

$$\bar{k}_j = .05 + \frac{(.10 - .05)}{.01} \operatorname{Cov}(k_j, k_M) \tag{C19–1a}$$
$$= .05 + 5 \operatorname{Cov}(k_j, k_M)$$

$$\bar{k}_j = .05 + .05(\beta_j) \text{ where } \beta_j = \frac{\operatorname{Cov}(k_j, k_M)}{\operatorname{Var}(k_M)} \tag{C19–2a}$$

Thus if we knew that the beta for the firm under analysis was 1.5, using Equation C19–2a we would have:

$$\bar{k}_j = .05 + .05(1.5) \qquad \bar{k}_j = .05 + 5(.015) \text{ since } \text{Cov}(k_j, k_M) = \beta_j \text{ Var}(k_M)$$

$$\bar{k}_j = .125 \qquad\qquad\qquad\qquad \text{Cov}(k_j, k_M) = 1.5(.01) = .015$$

Thus the cost of equity capital for the firm would be 12.5 percent. This brief overview indicates the power of the CAPM approach. Once we have good estimates of the market parameters all we need to know is the systematic risk measure for the firm or project to obtain an estimate of the required return on that investment. Much empirical work has been performed on the estimates of the market parameters. Some of these represent formal scholarly studies analyzing the empirical validity of the capital asset pricing model.[1] Other estimates of market parameters are available from various financial firms and services such as Merrill Lynch, Pierce, Fenner and Smith, Wells Fargo Bank, and the Value Line. The sophisticated methodologies utilized include analysis over a number of periods typically using intervals of one month, but some services use intervals as short as one week or one day. The nature of the sophisticated procedures for estimating the market parameters can be conveyed by the data in Table C19–1, which provides an approximation to the market parameters for the period 1960 through 1976. The percent returns listed in Column (5) are obtained by adding the dividend yield in Column (4) plus the capital gain calculated in Column (3) from the information on the Standard & Poor 500 stock price index data listed in Column (2). Taking the mean value of the data in Column (5) we can obtain the mean market return over the period of approximately 8 percent.

In Column (6) the deviations from the market return are listed. In Column (7) the deviations are squared, then summed and divided by 15 to obtain the .0143 estimate of market variance.[2]

The risk-free return is estimated by use of the six-month treasury bill rate. The average for the years indicated are listed in Column (8). These average annual values are summed and divided by 16 to obtain

1. F. Black; M. C. Jensen; and M. Scholes, "The Capital Asset Pricing Model: Some Empirical Tests," in *Studies in the Theory of Capital Markets,* ed. M. C. Jensen (New York: Praeger, 1972); E. F. Fama, and J. MacBeth, "Risk, Return and Equilibrium: Empirical Tests," *Journal of Political Economy* 81 (May–June 1973), pp. 607–36; I. Friend, and M. Blume, "Measurement of Portfolio Performance under Uncertainty," *American Economic Review* 60 (September 1970), pp. 561–75; N. Jacob, "The Measurement of Systematic Risk for Securities and Portfolios: Some Empirical Results," *Journal of Financial and Quantitative Analysis* 6 (March 1971), pp. 815–34; M. C. Jensen, ed., in *Studies in the Theory of Capital Markets;* M. H. Miller, and M. Scholes, "Rates of Return in Relation to Risk: A Re-examination of Some Recent Findings," in *Studies in the Theory of Capital Markets,* pp. 47–78.

2. We divide by 15 rather than 16 since one degree of freedom has been lost in that the calculation of the variance involves the use of the mean return on the market which has already been calculated.

	Year	S&P 500 Price Index	% Change in Price	Dividend Yield	Percent Return	Return Deviation	Market Variance	Risk Free Return
	(t)	p_t	$\dfrac{p_t}{p_{t-1}} - 1$	$\dfrac{d_t}{p_t}$	k_{Mt} $(3+4)$	$(k_{Mt} - \bar{k}_M)$ $(5 - \bar{k}_M)$	$(k_{Mt} - \bar{k}_M)^2$ (6^2)	R_F
	(1)	(2)	(3)	(4)	(5)	(6)	(7)	(8)
	1960	55.85						
	1961	66.27	.1866	.0298	.2164	.1371	.018796	.03
	1962	62.38	(.0587)	.0337	(.0250)	(.1043)	.010878	.03
	1963	69.87	.1201	.0317	.1518	.0725	.005256	.03
	1964	81.37	.1646	.0301	.1947	.1154	.013317	.04
	1965	88.17	.0836	.0300	.1136	.0343	.001176	.04
	1966	85.26	(.0330)	.0340	.0010	(.0783)	.006131	.04
	1967	91.93	.0782	.0320	.1102	.0309	.000955	.05
	1968	98.70	.0736	.0307	.1043	.0250	.000625	.05
	1969	97.84	(.0087)	.0324	.0237	(.0556)	.003091	.07
	1970	83.22	(.1494)	.0383	(.1111)	(.1904)	.036252	.06
	1971	98.29	.1811	.0314	.2125	.1332	.017742	.05
	1972	109.20	.1110	.0284	.1394	.0601	.003612	.05
	1973	107.43	(.0162)	.0306	.0144	(.0649)	.004212	.07
	1974	82.85	(.2288)	.0447	(.1824)	(.2617)	.068487	.08
	1975	85.17	.0280	.0431	.0711	(.0082)	.000067	.06
	1976	102.01	.1977	.0376	.2353	.1560	.024336	.06
					1.2699		.214933	.81

Table C19–1 Estimates of Market Parameters

$R_F = .81/16 = .051$

$\bar{k}_M = 1.2699/16 = .079 \approx .080$ $\text{Var}(k_M) = .2149/15 = .0143$

Sources: *Economic Report of the President*, 1975, and individual issues of the *Federal Reserve Bulletin*.

an estimate of the risk-free return for the time period covered of 5.1 percent.

The estimates we have obtained reflect the characteristics of the market with the turbulence introduced by unsettled economic conditions following 1966. Other studies of market behavior over more extended time periods and utilizing monthly intervals rather than annual time periods suggest a range of about 9 to 11 percent for market returns. Thus our 8 percent estimate dominated by the weak market in recent years, is slightly low. Most previous studies of market parameters utilize at least 60 months of returns so have at least 60 observations as compared with the 16 observations in Table C19–1. Of course, a larger number of observations will reduce the variance measured so that the longer term studies suggest that 1 percent is a good estimate of market variance on the average. Inspection of Column (8) containing the risk-free return measures indicates a range of from 3 percent to 8 percent. Thus the higher values of R_F have predominated in the later years.

Hence to make current estimates of the cost of equity or to make estimates for use in future periods, a range of 4 to 6 percent as estimates of the risk-free return would be plausible. The somewhat unusual nature of the general economic conditions in recent years is suggested by a paradox observed in the results from Table C19−1. The higher rate of inflation after 1966 is reflected in the rising levels of the risk-free return. The sharper market declines and relatively weaker recoveries in market returns indicate that stock market returns have not been able to fully capture the inflation premium.

Because of these shifts in the estimates of market parameters (their apparent underlying nonstationarities) our use of the CAPM is more as a normative model (normative indicates the way people ought to behave or a way of thinking rather than precise numbers). Thus in applying the market parameters we have an estimate of 4 to 6 percent for the risk-free return, 8 to 11 percent for the return on the market, and 1 percent for the variance of the market. We can use these ranges in two ways: (1) we could apply the ranges to provide a sensitivity analysis of the range of possible estimates of the cost of equity capital for a firm or project; or (2) we could select from the range the single figures that would appear to be most appropriate for the time period for which the analysis is being made. To illustrate the methodology for calculating a cost of equity capital for individual firms, we shall use the estimates closer to C19−1a and C19−2a. These are: $k_M = 9\%$; $\text{Var}(k_M) = 1\%$; and $R_F = 5\%$. With these estimates of market parameters, we turn to their application to individual firms.

Estimating the Beta Coefficient for Individual Firms

In Tables C19−2 and C19−3 we set forth the calculations of beta for General Motors Corporation and Chrysler Corporation. The first seven columns of these two tables exactly parallel the first seven columns of Table C19−1 used to estimate the market parameters. Thus no furthur explanation is required. In Column (8) we calculate the covariance of the returns for the individual companies with the market returns. Thus we use Column (6) in Tables C19−2 and C19−3 along with Column (6) representing the market deviations shown in Table C19−1. The data in Column (8) for General Motors and Chrysler are used to calculate the covariance of the two firms. The covariance for General Motors is approximately 2 percent while the covariance for Chrysler is approximately 3.5 percent. When we use our previous measure of the variance of the market obtained from the data in Table C19−1 we obtain an estimate of beta of 1.35 for General Motors and an estimate of beta of 2.47 for Chrysler. We are now ready to apply these results in estimating the cost of equity for General Motors and Chrysler.

Table C19-2 Calculation of Beta for General Motors	Year	GM Price	% Change in Price	Dividend Yield	Percent Return	Deviation of Returns	Variance of Returns	Covariance with Market
	(t)	p_t	$\dfrac{p_t}{p_t - 1} - 1$	$\dfrac{d_t}{p_t}$	k_{jt}	$(k_{jt} - \bar{k}_j)$	$(k_{jt} - \bar{k}_j)^2$	$(k_{jt} - \bar{k}_j)(k_{Mt} - \bar{k}_M)$
					$(3 + 4)$	$(5 - \bar{k}_M)$	(6^2)	$(6 \times 6 \text{ market})$
	(1)	(2)	(3)	(4)	(5)	(6)	(7)	(8)
	1960	48						
	1961	49	.02	.05	.07	(.029)	.000841	(.003976)
	1962	52	.06	.06	.12	.021	.000441	(.002190)
	1963	74	.42	.05	.47	.371	.137641	.026898
	1964	90	.22	.05	.27	.171	.029241	.019733
	1965	102	.13	.05	.18	.081	.006561	.002778
	1966	87	(.15)	.05	(.10)	(.199)	.039601	.015582
	1967	78	(.10)	.05	(.05)	(.149)	.022201	(.004604)
	1968	81	.04	.05	.09	(.009)	.000081	(.000225)
	1969	74	(.09)	.06	(.03)	(.069)	.004761	.003836
	1970	70	(.05)	.05	.00	(.099)	.009801	.018850
	1971	82	.17	.04	.21	.111	.012321	.014785
	1972	78	(.05)	.06	.01	(.089)	.007921	(.005349)
	1973	65	(.17)	.08	(.09)	(.189)	.035721	.012266
	1974	42	(.35)	.08	(.27)	(.369)	.136161	.096567
	1975	45	.07	.05	.12	.021	.000961	(.000172)
	1976	68	.51	.07	.58	.481	.231361	.075036
					1.58		.675616	.269815

$\bar{k}_j = 1.58/16 = .099 \approx .100$

$\text{Var}(k_j) = .6756/15 = .0450$

$\text{Cov}(k_j, k_M) = .2698/14 = .0193$

$\beta_j = \dfrac{.0193}{.0143} = 1.35$

$\beta_j' = \dfrac{.02}{.01} = 2$

Use of the Security Market Line to Estimate the Cost of Equity Capital

The security market line we are using has been set forth in equations C19-1a and C19-2a. With the two estimates of beta for General Motors and for Chrysler, we obtain estimates of the cost of equity of 12 percent for General Motors and 17.35 percent for Chrysler. The actual historical average returns of the two companies were on the low side of the range of their indicated costs of equity capital.

Our own judgment is that the relevant cost of equity capital for the two companies would be somewhat higher than the estimates we have produced. Our reasons are related to the underlying economic characteristics of the automobile industry currently and prospectively along with the respective position of each of the firms in the automobile industry. It is generally acknowledged that the automobile industry has become substantially more risky in recent years. The addition of safety

Table C19-3 Calculation of Beta for Chrysler	Year	Chrysler Price	% Change in Price	Dividend Yield	Percent Return	Deviation of Return	Variance of Return	Covariance with Market
	(t)	p_t	$\dfrac{p_t}{p_t-1}-1$	$\dfrac{d_t}{p_t}$	k_{jt}	$(k_{jt}-\bar{k}_j)$	$(k_{jt}-\bar{k}_j)^2$	$(k_{jt}-\bar{k}_j)(k_{Mt}-\bar{k}_M)$
					$(3+4)$	$(5-k_M)$	(6^2)	$(6\times 6 \text{ market})$
	(1)	(2)	(3)	(4)	(5)	(6)	(7)	(8)
	1960	13						
	1961	12	(.08)	.02	(.06)	(.184)	.0339	(.025226)
	1962	14	.17	.02	.19	.066	.0044	(.006884)
	1963	33	1.36	.01	1.37	1.246	1.5525	.090335
	1964	51	.55	.02	.57	.446	.1989	.051468
	1965	54	.06	.02	.08	(.044)	.0019	(.001509)
	1966	45	(.17)	.04	(.13)	(.254)	.0645	.019888
	1967	44	(.02)	.05	.03	(.094)	.0088	(.002905)
	1968	60	.36	.03	.39	.266	.0708	.006650
	1969	44	(.27)	.05	(.22)	(.344)	.1185	.019126
	1970	25	(.43)	.02	(.41)	(.534)	.2852	.101674
	1971	30	.20	.02	.22	.096	.0092	.012787
	1972	35	.17	.03	.20	.076	.0058	.004568
	1973	33	(.06)	.04	(.02)	(.144)	.0207	.009346
	1974	14	(.58)	.10	(.48)	(.604)	.3648	.158067
	1975	11	(.21)	0	(.21)	(.334)	.1116	.002739
	1976	16	.45	.02	.47	.346	.1197	.053976
					1.99		2.9712	.494100

$\bar{k}_j = 1.99/16 = .124$

$\text{Var}(k_j) = 2.9712/15 = .1981$

$\text{Cov}(k_j, k_M) = .4941/14 = .0353$

$\beta_j = \dfrac{.0353}{.0143} = 2.47$

$\beta' = \dfrac{.035}{.01} = 3.5$

devices and pollution controls has added substantially to the cost of automobiles. There are also increased risks whether the automobile manufacturers can meet the pollution control standards and gasoline mileage standards that have been set by Congress for future years. The energy shortage may result in new and substantial excise taxes on larger automobiles which are said to be the more profitable line for companies such as General Motors and Chrysler. Thus we would add 1.25 percent to make the estimate of the cost of equity 13 percent for General Motors and add 1.65 percent to make the estimate of the cost of equity 19 percent for Chrysler. The estimate of the betas would rise to 1.6 for General Motors and 2.8 for Chrysler.

However, we are here only illustrating the methodology. Without substantial additional analysis we would not seek to defend any particular estimate of the costs of equity for General Motors and Chrysler. We believe, however, that the indicated ranges of 12 to 13 percent for General Motors and 17 to 19 percent for Chrysler are "in the ball park." Other financial data would support our result that the cost of equity is greater for Chrysler, reflecting its much more volatile performance than General Motors. This suggests further analysis of the components of the beta measures for the two companies.

Measuring Business and Financial Risks

The capital asset pricing model enables us to separate the components of business and financial risks. Proposition II of MM in their original (partial equilibrium) formulation can be expressed both without and with taxes:

$$\text{No taxes} \quad k_s = k_u + (k_u - k_b)\frac{B}{S}$$

$$\text{With taxes} \quad k_s = k_u + (k_u - k_b)\frac{B(1-T)}{S}$$

From a paper by Hamada,[3] the corresponding formulations in the CAPM framework are:

$$\text{No taxes} \quad \bar{k}_s = R_F + \lambda \text{Cov}(k_u, k_M)\left[1 + \frac{B}{S}\right]$$

$$\text{With taxes} \quad \bar{k}_s = R_F + \lambda \text{Cov}(k_u, k_M)\left[1 + \frac{B(1-T)}{S}\right]$$

Under both:

$$k_u = \frac{E(X)(1-T)}{V_u} \qquad k = \frac{E(X)(1-T)}{V_L}$$

Recall that: k_u = the cost of capital of an unlevered firm

k_s = the cost of equity capital of a levered firm

k = the weighted average cost of capital of a levered firm

The CAPM formulations can also be expressed in the form that utilizes beta as the measure of risk as follows:

$$\bar{k} = R_F + [\bar{k}_M - R_F]\beta_u\left[1 + \frac{B(1-T)}{S}\right] \tag{C19-3}$$

---

3. Robert S. Hamada, "Portfolio Analysis, Market Equilibrium and Corporation Finance," *Journal of Finance* 24 (March 1969), pp. 13–31.

where β_u is for an unlevered firm. When we multiply the terms we have the expression as shown in C19–3a:

$$\bar{k}_s = R_F + [\bar{k}_M - R_F]\beta_u + [\bar{k}_M - R_F]\beta_u \frac{B(1-T)}{S} \tag{C19–3a}$$

The beta that we observe is thus composed of the elements as shown in equation C19–4:

$$\beta_j = \beta_u\left[1 + \frac{B(1-T)}{S}\right] \tag{C19–4}$$

We can thus separate the elements of business risk and financial risk as shown in Equation C19–4a.

$$\beta_j = \beta_u + \beta_u\left[\frac{B(1-T)}{S}\right] \tag{C19–4a}$$

Then solving C19–4 for the business risk term from the observed data we have the relationship shown in Equation C19–4b:

$$\beta_u = \frac{\beta_j}{\left[1 + \frac{B(1-T)}{S}\right]} \tag{C19–4b}$$

We may now apply these relationships using the data for General Motors and for Chrysler.

Based on an analysis of the capital structures of General Motors and Chrysler over a period of years, we have estimated the debt equity ratio of General Motors to be .25 and the debt equity ratio of Chrysler to be 1.0. We have utilized a tax rate of .5 for both companies. We can, therefore, proceed to calculate the beta measuring business risk for each company, utilizing the high values of beta, as shown in Equation C19–4c:

$$\text{General Motors: } \beta_u = \frac{1.6}{1 + (.25)(.5)} = \frac{1.6}{1.125} = 1.4$$

$$\text{Chrysler: } \qquad \beta_u = \frac{3.5}{1 + (1)(.5)} = \frac{3.5}{1.5} = 2.3 \tag{C19–4c}$$

As shown, we obtain a β_u for General Motors of 1.4. The β_u for Chrysler is 1.9. This enables us to now set forth the relationships that show the components that make up the cost of equity capital for each company. This is shown in Table C19–4.

In Table C19–4 we see that the risk-free element in the cost of equity capital for both General Motors and Chrysler is 5 percent. This is a mar-

Table C19-4
Components of the
Firm's Cost of
Equity Capital

	After-tax Cost of Equity Capital		Risk Free Element		Premium for Business Risk		Premium for Financial Risk
	$\bar{k}_s$	$=$	R_F	$+$	$(\bar{k}_M - R_F)\beta_j^*$	$+$	$(\bar{k}_M - R_F)\beta_j^* \left[\dfrac{B(1-T)}{S}\right]$
GM			5%	$+$	4%(1.8)	$+$	4%(1.8)(.25)(.5)
	13%	$\cong$	5%	$+$	7.2%	$+$	0.9%
Chrysler			5%	$+$	4%(2.3)	$+$	4%(2.3)(1)(.5)
	19%	$\cong$	5%	$+$	9.2%	$+$	4.6%

Differences due to rounding in calculation of β_j^*.

ket parameter. The premium for business risk is the market risk premium multiplied times each firm's beta as an unlevered firm. This component is 7.2 percent for General Motors, 2.0 percentage points lower than the 9.2 percent for Chrysler. The third element in the cost of equity capital requirement for each firm is the premium for business risk multiplied by the leverage element. This adds slightly less than 1 percent to the cost of equity for General Motors because of its low leverage ratio. Chrysler, which has a debt to equity ratio of 1, adds a premium for financial risk of 4.6 percent. Thus the differential in the cost of equity capital for General Motors reflects its lower premium for business risk, and more significantly its lower premium for financial risk.

In this appendix we have illustrated the application of some of the central concepts of the capital asset pricing model. In actual use, much more sophisticated computations of each of the elements that we have used would be employed. However, one way of checking the results from the use of more complex methods is to make rough estimates utilizing the procedures here described.

Estimate of the Firm's Cost of Capital

We can now calculate the cost of capital for each of the two companies. We have estimated the market cost of debt as 8.2 percent for General Motors and 9.4 percent for Chrysler on the basis of the current yields to maturity of their outstanding debt, as well as their movements in recent years. Recall that we had already analyzed their leverage ratios in separating the components of business and financial risk.

We utilize the standard expression for the cost of capital:

$$k = k_b(1-T)\frac{B}{V} + k_s\frac{S}{V}$$

We can then calculate the cost of capital for each company:

General Motors

$$k = .082(.5)(.2) + .13(.8)$$

$$= .0082 + .104$$

$$= .1182 \cong 12\%$$

Chrysler

$$k = .094(.5)(.5) + .19(.5)$$

$$= .0235 + .095$$

$$= .1185 \cong 12\%$$

Although Chrysler has a higher cost of debt as well as a higher cost of equity, the weighted cost of capital for Chrysler is about equal to the 12 percent cost of capital of General Motors. Since Chrysler uses a higher proportion of debt, it benefits to a higher degree from the tax advantages of debt.

Problems

C19–1. The following data have been developed for the Donovan Company, the manufacturer of an advanced line of adhesives.

State	Probability	Market Return k_M	Return for the Firm k_j
1	.1	−.15	−.30
2	.3	.05	.00
3	.4	.15	.20
4	.2	.20	.50

The risk-free rate is 6 percent. Make calculations of the following:
a. The market return.
b. The variance of the market.
c. The expected return for the Donovan Company.
d. The covariance of the returns of the Donovan Company with the returns on the market.
e. Write the equation of the security market line.
f. What is the expected return for the Donovan Company?
g. What is the required return for the Donovan Company?

C19 – 2. The following data have been developed for the Milliken Company.

Year	Return on the Market	Company Returns
1978	.27	.25
1977	.12	.05
1976	(.03)	(.05)
1975	.12	.15
1974	(.03)	(.10)
1973	.27	.30

The yield to maturity on Treasury bills is .066 and is expected to remain at this point for the forseeable future. (Assume 5 degrees of freedom for the covariance and variance calculations and 6 degrees for the means.) Make calculations of the following:

a. The market return.
b. The variance of the market.
c. The expected return for the Milliken Company.
d. The covariance of the returns of the Milliken Company with the returns on the market.
e. Write the equation of the security market line.
f. What is the expected return for the Milliken Company?
g. What is the required return for the Milliken Company?

C19 – 3. The chief financial officer of Worldcorp seeks to determine the value of the division and of the cost of capital for the Industrial Products Division (without any leverage). He has gathered the following data. (Ignore taxes).

Year	Return on the Market	Earnings before Interest and Taxes
19X1	.27	$ 25
19X2	.12	5
19X3	(.03)	(5)
19X4	.12	15
19X5	(.03)	(10)
19X6	.27	30

The yield to maturity on Treasury bills is .066 and is expected to remain at this level in the foreseeable future. For the unlevered division, compute (a) the value of the division and (b) the cost of capital. Assume 5 degrees of freedom for the covariance and variance calculations and 6 degrees for the means.

C19 – 4. The Myers Corporation has a total investment of $200 million in five divisions.

Division	Divisional Investment	Divisional Beta Coefficient (estimated)
A	$60	0.5
B	50	2.0
C	30	4.0
D	40	1.0
E	20	3.0

Management believes that there is a systematic relationship between each division's return and market returns as described by the beta coefficients and these relationships are assumed to be stable over time.

The current risk-free rate is 5 percent, while expected market returns have the following probability distribution for the next period:

Probability	Market Return
.1	6%
.2	8
.4	10
.2	12
.1	14

a. What is the estimated equation for the security market line (SML)?
b. Compute the expected return on the Myers Corporation for the next period.
c. Suppose management receives a proposal for a new division. The investment needed to create the new division is $50 million; it will have an expected return of 15 percent, and its estimated beta coefficient is 2.5. Should the new division be created? At what expected rate of return would management be indifferent to starting the new division?

C19–5. You are given the following data on market returns (k_M) and the returns on stocks A and B.
a. The risk-free rate of return is 6 percent. Determine the market return and variance.
b. For stocks A and B determine the following:
   expected return $(\bar{k}_i)$
   covariance with the market $[Cov(k_i,k_M)]$
   beta (β_i)
   required return (k_i^*)

Returns by Year						
Return	1973	1974	1975	1976	1977	1978
k_M	.20	.10	−.05	.15	.30	−.10
k_A	.25	.05	−.15	.15	.55	−.25
k_B	−.20	.30	.70	−.10	.50	−.60

variance of historic returns (σ_i^2)

c. What percent of the risk of stocks A and B is systematic? Explain.

d. Graph the security market line and the returns of the two stocks.

e. Assuming no changes in variance or covariance of returns what would you expect to happen to the prices of the two stocks? Why?

f. If both stocks were priced on the SML which would have the higher yield? Which has the higher variance? Explain this apparent paradox.

Selected References

Black, F. "Capital Market Equilibrium with Restricted Borrowing." *Journal of Business* 45 (July 1972):444–54.

Black, F.; Jensen, M. C.; and Scholes, M. "The Capital Asset Pricing Model: Some Empirical Tests." In *Studies in the Theory of Capital Markets*. Edited by M. C. Jensen. New York:Praeger, 1972.

Black, F., and Scholes, M. "The Pricing of Options and Corporate Liabilities." *Journal of Political Economy* 81 (May–June 1973):637–54.

Brennan, M. J. "Capital Market Equilibrium with Divergent Borrowing and Lending Rates." *Journal of Financial and Quantitative Analysis* 6 (Dec. 1971): 1197–1205.

———. "Investor Taxes, Market Equilibrium and Corporate Finance." Ph.D. dissertation, M.I.T., June 1970.

Brigham, E. F., and Pappas, J. "Rates of Return on Common Stock." *Journal of Business* 42 (July 1969).

Douglas, George W. "Risk in the Equity Markets: An Empirical Appraisal of Market Efficiency." *Yale Economic Essays* 9 (Spring 1969):3–45.

Evans, J. L., and Archer, S. H. "Diversification and the Reduction of Dispersion: An Empirical Analysis." *Journal of Finance* 23 (Dec. 1968):761–67.

Fama, E. F. "Efficient Capital Markets: A Review of Theory and Empirical Work." *Journal of Finance* 25 (May 1970):383–417.

———. "Risk, Return, and Equilibrium." *Journal of Political Economy* 79 (Jan.–Feb. 1971):30–55.

———. "Risk, Return, and Equilibrium: Some Clarifying Comments." *Journal of Finance* 23 (Mar. 1968):29–40.

Fama, E. F., and MacBeth, J. "Risk, Return and Equilibrium: Empirical Tests." *Journal of Political Economy* 81 (May–June 1973):607–36.

Fama, E. F., and Miller, M. H. *The Theory of Finance.* New York: Holt, Rinehart and Winston, 1972.

Friend, I., and Blume, M. "Measurement of Portfolio Performance under Uncertainty." *American Economic Review* 60 (Sept 1970):561–75.

Friend, I., Landskroner, Yoram; and Losq, Etienne. "The Demand for Risky Assets Under Uncertain Inflation." *Journal of Finance* 31 (Dec. 1976): 1287–97.

Gordon, Myron J., and Halpern, Paul J. "Cost of Capital for a Division of a Firm." *Journal of Finance* 29, no. 4 (Sept. 1974):1153–63.

Hakansson, N. "Capital Growth and the Mean-Variance Approach to Portfolio Selection." *Journal of Financial and Quantitative Analysis* 6 (Jan. 1971): 517–58.

Hamada, R. S. "Portfolio Analysis, Market Equilibrium and Corporation Finance." *Journal of Finance* 24 (Mar. 1969):13–32.

———. "The Effect of the Firm's Capital Structure on the Systematic Risk of Common Stocks." *Journal of Finance* 27 (May 1972):435–52.

Haugen, Robert A., and Pappas, James L. "Equilibrium in the Pricing of Capital Assets, Risk-Bearing Debt Instruments, and the Question of Optimal Capital Structure." *Journal of Financial and Quantitative Analysis* 6 (June 1971):943–53. See also Imai, Yutaka, and Rubinstein, Mark. "Comment." *Journal of Financial and Quantitative Analysis* 7 (Sept. 1972):2001–3; and Haugen and Pappas. "Reply." Ibid., 2005–8.

Hirshleifer, J. "Efficient Allocation of Capital in an Uncertain World." *American Economic Review* 54 (May 1964):77–85.

———. *Investment, Interest and Capital.* Englewood Cliffs, N.J.: Prentice-Hall, 1970.

Hsia, C. C. "Inflation Risk and Capital Asset Pricing." Typescript. Los Angeles: University of California, 1973.

Jacob, N. "The Measurement of Systematic Risk for Securities and Portfolios: Some Empirical Results." *Journal of Financial and Quantitative Analysis* 6 (Mar. 1971):815–34.

Jensen, M. C. "The Foundations and Current State of Capital Market Theory." In *Studies in the Theory of Capital Markets.* Edited by M. C. Jensen. New York: Praeger, 1972.

———. "The Performance of Mutual Funds in the Period 1945–1964." *Journal of Finance* 23 (May 1968):389–416.

———. "Risk, the Pricing of Capital Assets, and the Evaluation of Investment Portfolios." *Journal of Business* 42 (Apr. 1969):167–247.

———, ed. *Studies in the Theory of Capital Markets.* New York: Praeger, 1972.

———. "Capital Markets: Theory and Evidence." *Bell Journal of Economics and Management Science* 3 (Autumn 1972).

Kraus, A., and Litzenberger, R. H. "Skewness, Preference and the Valuation of Risk Assets." Stanford, Calif.: Stanford University, 1972.

Kumar, Prem. "Market Equilibrium and Corporation Finance: Some Issues." *Journal of Finance* 29, no. 4 (September 1974):1175–88.

Latane, H. "Criteria for Choice among Risky Ventures." *Journal of Political Economy* 67 (April 1959):144–55.

Lintner, J. "The Aggregation of Investors' Diverse Judgment and Preferences in Purely Competitive Securities Markets." *Journal of Financial and Quantitative Analysis* 4 (Dec. 1969):347–400.

———. "Security Prices, Risk, and Maximal Gains from Diversification." *Journal of Finance* 20 (Dec. 1965):587–616.

———. "The Valuation of Risk Assets and the Selection of Risky Investments in Stock Portfolios and Capital Budgets." *Review of Economics and Statistics* 47 (Feb. 1965):13–37.

Litzenberger, R. H., and Budd, A. P. "Secular Trends in Risk Premiums." *Journal of Finance* 27 (Sept. 1972):857–64.

Litzenberger, Robert H., and Rao, C. U. "Portfolio Theory and Industry Cost-of-Capital Estimates." *Journal of Financial and Quantitative Analysis* 7 (Mar. 1972): 1443–62.

Long, J. B., Jr. "Consumption-Investment Decisions and Equilibrium in the Securities Market." In *Studies in the Theory of Capital Markets.* Edited by M. C. Jensen. New York: Praeger, 1972.

———. "Stock Prices, Inflation, and the Term Structure of Interest Rates." Working Paper Series No. 7310 (April 1973), University of Rochester.

Markowitz, H. M. "Portfolio Selection." *Journal of Finance* 7 (Mar. 1952):77–91.

———. *Portfolio Selection: Efficient Diversification of Investments.* New York: Wiley, 1959.

Mayers, D. "Non-Marketable Assets and Capital Market Equilibrium under Uncertainty." In *Studies in the Theory of Capital Markets.* Edited by M. C. Jensen. New York: Praeger, 1972.

———. "Non-Marketable Assets and the Determination of Capital Asset Prices in the Absence of a Riskless Asset." *Journal of Business* 46 (April 1973):258–67.

Mossin, J. "Equilibrium in a Capital Asset Market." *Econometrica* 34 (Oct. 1966): 768–83.

———. "Security Pricing and Investment Criteria in Competitive Markets." *American Economic Review* 59 (Dec 1969):749–56.

Myers, S. C. "Procedures for Capital Budgeting Under Uncertainty." *Industrial Management Review* (Spring 1968).

Myers, S. C., and Pogue, G. A. *An Evaluation of the Risk of Comsat's Common Stock* (August 1973), submitted to the FCC in connection with Comsat's rate case (FCC Docket 16070).

Radner, R. "Problems in the Theory of Markets under Uncertainty." *American Economic Review* 60 (May 1970):454–60.

Roll, R. "Bias in Fitting the Sharpe Model to Time Series Data." *Journal of Financial and Quantitative Analysis* 4 (Sept. 1969):271–89.

———. "Investment Diversification and Bond Maturity." *Journal of Finance* 26 (Mar. 1971):51–66.

———. "Assets, Money, and Commodity Price Inflation under Uncertainty: Demand Theory." Working Paper 48–71–2 (August 1972), Carnegie-Mellon University.

Rubinstein, M. E. "A Mean-Variance Synthesis of Corporate Financial Theory." *Journal of Finance* 28 (Mar. 1973):167–81.

Schall, Lawrence D. "Asset Valuation, Firm Investment, and Firm Diversification." *Journal of Business* 45 (Jan. 1972):11–28.

Sharpe, W. F. "A Simplified Model for Portfolio Analysis." *Management Science* 9 (Jan. 1963):277–93.

———. "Capital Asset Prices: A Theory of Market Equilibrium under Conditions of Risk." *Journal of Finance* 19 (Sept. 1964):425–42.

———. *Portfolio Theory and Capital Markets.* New York: McGraw-Hill, 1970.

Tobin, J. "Liquidity Preference as Behavior toward Risk." *Review of Economic Studies* 25 (Feb. 1958):65–85.

Treynor, J. L. "How to Rate Management of Investment Funds." *Harvard Business Review* 43 (Jan.–Feb. 1965):63–75.

Wagner, W. H., and Lau, S. C. "The Effect of Diversification on Risk." *Financial Analysts' Journal* (Nov. Dec. 1971):48–53.

Weston, J. F. "Investment Decisions Using the Capital Asset Pricing Model." *Financial Management* (Spring 1973):25–33.

Appendix D to Chapter 19
The State-Preference Model and
Optimal Financial Leverage[1]

Three important recent developments in finance are the capital asset pricing model (CAPM), the options pricing model (OPM) and the state-preference model (SPM). The Capital Asset Pricing Model has been discussed in Appendix E to Chapter 10 and in Appendix A to Chapter 17. The Option Pricing Model has been set forth in Appendix C to Chapter 16. We now utilize the State-Preference Model to provide a wrap-up of the discussion of financial leverage.

Alternative Future States-of-the-World

The state-preference model provides a useful way of looking at the world and the nature of securities. One way of describing uncertainty about the future is to say that one of a set of alternative possible states-of-the-world will occur. Definition of a set of states provides a means of describing characteristics of securities, since any security can be regarded as a contract to pay an amount that depends on the state that actually occurs.

For example, the decision to invest in the securities of a machinery manufacturer or of a machinery manufacturer to issue securities under a favorable set of conditions will depend upon the potential future states of the economy. Will the economy be sufficiently strong so that the demand for capital goods will provide favorable demand factors for a machinery manufacturer? Similarly, in the production plans of an automobile manufacturer or in contemplating investment in securities of an automobile company, will the future state of the economy be sufficiently strong to stimulate consumer optimism, resulting in a high volume of automobile purchases? Some of the main factors influencing the future states-of-the-world that will influence the sales of a firm or the prospects for investments in a firm are set forth in Table D19-1.

As a practical matter a person will explicitly consider only a small number of factors in making a decision. Hence, individual decision makers are likely to select those variables judged to be most critical for influencing the payoff possibilities of securities in which a position or investment is contemplated. For practical reasons, therefore, alternative

1. This section was written with the valuable counsel of Professor Harry DeAngelo.

Table D19–1
Central Factors
Influencing
Estimates of Future
States of the World
for Use in
Forecasting the
Sales of the Firm
	A. Economy
	  1. Growth rate of GNP—real terms
	  2. Growth rate of GNP—inflation
	  3. Growth rate of monetary base (availability)
	  4. Long-term interest rates
	  5. Short-term interest rates
	
	B. Competition
	  1. Prices of rivals products
	  2. New products by rivals
	  3. Changes in products by rivals
	  4. New advertising campaigns by rivals
	  5. Salesman and other selling efforts by rivals
	  6. Prices of products in industry-substitute products
	  7. Quality of industry-substitute products
	
	C. Cultural and political factors
	  1. Externalities and their influences on sales of our products
	  2. Product liabilities

future states-of-the-world might be summarized into forecasts of alternative levels or rates of growth in the gross national product. Ultimately a wide variety of the factors listed in Table D19–1 are likely to be reflected in levels of gross national product. Furthermore, the rate of growth and the performance of most individual industries in the economy are greatly influenced with movements in gross national product. Thus alternative future states-of-the-world may be characterized in terms of four possibilities with respect to gross national product. These might be a strong rate of growth, a moderate rate of growth, a moderate decline, or a substantial decline.

While for practical problems we might limit the number of alternative future states-of-the-world, from another standpoint—that of personal portfolio construction—we would like to provide for all possible future states-of-the-world. If we could always find a security that provided some payoff under one of the many possible future states-of-the-world, we could hedge by combining a large number of securities so that regardless of the future state of the world that occurs, we would receive some payoff. The actual securities we encounter in the real world are complex securities in the sense that their payoffs are positive, but generally different, amounts under alternative states-of-the-world. If actual securities could provide some payoff for every possible future state-of-the-world by appropriately combining long and short positions in securities, we could create a pure or primitive security.

The Concept of a Pure Security

A pure or primitive security is one that pays off $1 if one particular future state-of-the-world occurs and pays off nothing if any other state-of-the-world occurs. This seems like an abstract concept so let us develop the idea further by means of an example. We shall take the case of the Mistinback Company, which sells baskets of fruit. This particular company limits its sales to only two types of baskets. Basket 1 is composed of 10 bananas and 20 apples and sells for $8. Basket 2 is composed of 30 bananas and 10 apples and sells for $9. The question is posed what is the price of one banana or one apple only?

The situation may be summarized by the following pay-offs set forth in Table D19−2.

Table D19−2
Payoffs in Relation to Prices of Baskets of Fruit

	Bananas	Apples	Prices
Basket #1	10	20	$8
Basket #2	30	10	$9

To calculate the value of a banana or an apple, we set up two equations:

$$10 \, V_B + 20 \, V_A = \$8$$
$$30 \, V_B + 10 \, V_A = \$9$$

Solving simultaneously, we obtain

$$V_A = \$.30$$
$$V_B = \$.20$$

We may now apply this same analysis to securities. Any individual security is similar to a mixed basket of goods with regard to alternative future states-of-the-world. Recall that a pure security is a security that pays $1 if a specified state occurs and nothing if any other state occurs.[2]

We may proceed to determine the price of a pure security in a manner analogous to that employed for the fruit baskets. Consider security j, which pays $10 if state 1 occurs and $20 if state 2 occurs. The current price of security j is $8. Security k pays $30 if state 1 occurs and $10 if state 2 occurs. Its current price is $9. Note that state 1 might be a GNP growth during the year of 8 percent in real terms, while state 2 might represent a growth in real national product of only 1 percent. In Table D19−3 the pay-off for the two securities is set forth. Here, F_{j_1} is the pay-off in state 1 to security j, F_{k_1} is the payoff in state 1 to security k, etc. The

---

2. Observe that this is a clear form of nondiversification. It represents putting all of one's financial resources into one state-basket.

equations for determining the prices for the two pure securities related to the situation described are:

$$p_1 F_{j1} + p_2 F_{j2} = p_j$$
$$p_1 F_{k1} + p_2 F_{k2} = p_k$$

Table D19–3 **Payoff Table for** **Securities 1 and 2**	State 1	State 2	
Security j	$p_{j1} = \$10$	$p_{j2} = \$20$	$p_j = \$8$
Security k	$p_{k1} = \$30$	$p_{k2} = \$10$	$p_k = \$9$

Proceeding analogously to the situation for the fruit baskets, we insert the value of security payoffs into the two equations to obtain the price of pure security 1 as $.20 and the price of pure security 2 as $.30.

$$10p_1 + 20p_2 = \$8$$
$$30p_1 + 10p_2 = \$9$$
$$p_1 = \$.20$$
$$p_2 = \$.30$$

It should be emphasized that the p_1 of $.20 and the p_2 of $.30 are not assigned to securities j and k.

In sum, securities j and k represent bundles of returns under alternative future states. Any actual security provides different payoffs for different future states. But under appropriately defined conditions, from the prices of actual securities the prices of pure securities can be determined. The concept of a pure security is useful for analytical purposes as well as for providing a useful point of view in financial analysis as illustrated in the following section, which provides an application of the state-preference model to leverage decisions.

Use of the SPM to Determine the Optimal Financial Leverage

The state-preference model has been used to analyze the question of optimal financial leverage.[3] The ideas will be conveyed by a specific example. It is assumed that there are four possible states-of-the-world and that the capital markets are complete in that there exists at least one security for every possible state-of-the-world such that there is a full set of primitive securities.

The symbols that will be utilized are listed in Table D19–4.

3. Alan Kraus and Robert Litzenburger, "A State-Preference Model of Optimal Financial Leverage," *Journal of Finance* 28 (September 1973), pp. 911–22.

Table D19–4 Symbols Used in the SPM Analysis of Optimal Financial Leverage	
	p_s = the market price of the primitive security that represents a claim on one dollar in state s and zero dollars in all other states. X_s = the earnings before interest and taxes that the firm will achieve in state s (EBIT). B = the nominal payment to debt, representing a promise to pay fixed amount B, irrespective of the state that occurs. $S(B)$ = the market value of the firm's equity as a function of the amount of debt issued by the firm. $V(B)$ = the market value of the firm as a function of the amount of debt issued. f_s = the costs of failure in state s; $0 < f_s \leq X_s$. T = the corporate tax rate.

The data that will be analyzed in this example are summarized in Table D19–5.

Table D19–5
Data for SPM Analysis of Optimal Financial Leverage

(1)	(2)	(3)	(4)
s	X_s	p_s	f_s
1	100	0.30	100
2	500	0.50	400
3	1,000	0.20	500
4	2,000	0.10	1,200

In Table D19–5 we have ordered the states by the size of the *EBIT* that the firm will achieve under alternative states. Column (3) of the table lists the prices of primitive securities for each of the four states. In Column (4) we list the failure or bankruptcy costs associated with the inability to meet debt obligations.

In this state-preference framework let us analyze the position of debt holders and equity holders. Table D19–6 analyzes the amounts received under alternative condtions. Under condition 1 the *EBIT* is equal to or exceeds the debt obligation. Under that condition debt holders will receive B and equity holders will receive the income remaining after deduction of B and of taxes. Under condition 2 the *EBIT* is positive, but less than the amount of the debt obligation, B. The debt holders will receive whatever *EBIT* remains after payment less the failure or

Table D19–6
Amounts Received under Alternative Conditions

Condition	(1) Amount of X_s in Relation to B	(2) Debt Holders Receive	(3) Equity Holders Receive
1.	$X_s \geq B$	B	$(X_s - B)(1 - T)$
2.	$0 \leq X_s < B$	$(X_s - f_s)$	0
3.	$X_s < 0$	0	0

bankruptcy costs. Equity holders will receive nothing. If the *EBIT* is negative, neither the debt holders nor equity holders receive anything. These relationships are quite logical and straightforward.

The amounts received under alternative conditions as outlined in Table D19–7 are multiplied by the prices of the primitive securities to obtain the value of debt holders' receipts and of equity holders' receipts as well as the value of the firm under alternative conditions. The value of debt holders' receipts is obtained by simply multiplying what the debt holders receive by p_s and similarly for the value of equity holders' receipts. The value of the firm is obtained by adding the value of the debt holders' receipts to the value of the equity holders' receipts.

Table D19–7
Formulas for the Value of the Firm under Alternative Conditions

Condition	(1) Amount of X_s in Relation to B	(2) Debt Holders Receive	(3) Value of Debt Holders' Receipts in State s	(4) Equity Holders Receive	(5) Value of Equity Holders' Receipts in State s	(6) Value of the Firm in State s
1.	$X_s \geq B$	B	Bp_s	$(X_s - B)(1 - T)$	$(X_s - B)(1 - T)p_s$	$Bp_s + (X_s - B)(1 - T)p_s$
2.	$0 < X_s < B$	$(X_s - f_s)$	$(X_s - f_s)p_s$	0	0	$(X_s - f_s)p_s$
3.	$X_s < 0$	0	0	0	0	0

In Table D19–8 we utilize the preceding information to calculate the value of the firm under alternative debt levels. On the left-hand side of the table we begin by specifying the amount of debt and the resulting relationships between X_s, the *EBIT* under alternative states, in relationship to the promised payment to debt. The subsequent lines on the left then set forth the applicable formulas for calculating the state contingent value of the firm depending upon the level of debt utilized. For example, when the firm is unlevered its value is equal to the sum of (*EBIT*) times (1 minus the tax rate) times (the price of the primitive security for each state). Using the illustrative data from Table D19–5, we obtain the amounts on the right-hand column of Table D19–8.

When debt is 100, EBIT is equal to or greater than debt for all states-of-the-world. The formula employed, therefore, is set forth in Table D19–7 under condition 1 and shown in Column (6). Again, the numbers from Table D19–5 are inserted to obtain a current market value of the firm, $V(100)$, of \$385 for debt level 2 in Table D19–8.

We shall discuss the pattern for debt of \$1,000 as illustrative of the remaining sections of Table D19–8. When B is equal to \$1,000 the *EBIT* is less than the promised payment to debt for states 1 and 2 and equal to

Table D19–8
Calculations of the Value of the Firm under Alternative Debt Levels

Condition	State	Value of Firm's State s Payoff	
1. $B = 0$, $X_s \geq B$ for all s $$V_s(0) = \sum_{s=1}^{4} X_s(1 - T)p_s$$	1 2 3 4	$100(.5).3 =$ $500(.5).5 =$ $1,000(.5).2 =$ $2,000(.5).1 =$	15 125 100 100
		$V(0) = \$340$	
2. $B = 100$, $X_s \geq B$ for all s $$V_s(100) = \sum_{s=1}^{4} Bp_s + \sum_{s=1}^{4} (X_s - B)(1 - T)p_s$$	1 2 3 4	$100(.3) + (100 - 100)(.5).3 =$ $100(.5) + (500 - 100)(.5).5 =$ $100(.2) + (1,000 - 100)(.5).2 =$ $100(.1) + (2,000 - 100)(.5).1 =$	30 150 110 95
		$V(100) = \$385$	
3. $B = 500$, $X_s < B$ for $s = 1$ $X_s > B$ for $s = 2, 3, 4$ $$V_s(500) = (X_s - f_s)p_s \text{ for } s = 1$$ $$V_s(500) = \sum_{s=2}^{4} Bp_s + \sum_{s=2}^{4} (X_s - B)(1 - T)p_s$$	1 2 3 4	$(100 - 100).3 =$ $500(.5) + (500 - 500)(.5).5 =$ $500(.2) + (1,000 - 500)(.5).2 =$ $500(.1) + (2,000 - 500)(.5).1 =$	0 250 200 75
		$V(500) = \$525$	
4. $B = 1,000$, $X_s < B$ for $s = 1, 2$ $X_s \geq B$ for $s = 3, 4$ $$V_s(1,000) = \sum_{s=1}^{2} (X_s - f_s)p_s$$ $$V_s(1,000) = \sum_{s=3}^{4} Bp_s + \sum_{s=3}^{4} (X_s - B)(1 - T)p_s$$	1 2 3 4	$(100 - 100)(.3) =$ $(500 - 400)(.5).5 =$ $1,000(.2) + (1,000 - 1,000)(.5).2 =$ $1,000(.1) + (2,000 - 1,000)(.5).1 =$	0 25 200 150
		$V(1,000) = \$375$	
5. $B = 2,000$, $X_s < B$ for $s = 1, 2, 3$ $X_s \geq B$ for $s = 4$ $$V_s(2,000) = \sum_{s=1}^{3} (X_s - f_s)p_s$$ $$V_s(2,000) = Bp_s + (X_s - B)(1 - T)p_s \text{ for } s = 4$$	1 2 3 4	$(100 - 100)(.3) =$ $(500 - 400)(.5).5 =$ $(1,000 - 500)(.5).2 =$ $2,000(.1) + (2,000 - 2,000)(.5).1 =$	0 25 50 200
		$V(2,000) = \$275$	

or greater than debt for states 3 and 4. As Table D19–7 indicates, condition 2, therefore, obtains for states 1 and 2 while condition 1 obtains for states 3 and 4. The applicable formulas are, therefore, utilized to obtain a $V(1,000)$ of \$375, as shown in Table D19–8.

An analysis of Table D19–8 shows that the highest value of the firm is obtained when debt leverage of \$500 is employed by the firm. For any other level of debt obligations the value of the firm is lower. This example illustrates that with taxes and bankruptcy costs there exists an optimal amount of leverage.[4]

Implications for Leverage Decisions

Our use of the state-preference model has thereby enabled us to analyze some conditions under which an optimal capital leverage exists.[5] This result is, of course, not perfectly general since it was based on a specific illustration. Some more general relationships will now be set forth. First we need to introduce the concept of complete capital markets. Complete capital markets are those in which a security exists for every possible state-of-the-world so that it is possible to create a full set of primitive securities. In complete capital markets, in the absence of imperfections such as taxes, agency costs, and bankruptcy costs, capital structure would not matter (the Modigliani-Miller propositions would obtain).

The leverage policy of a firm consists of repackaging the claims on its *EBIT*. The only reason why repackaging of claims on the firm's *EBIT* would have an effect on the value of the firm would be because the firm had thereby provided investors with a new set of market opportunities for forming portfolios or taking a position with regard to future states-of-the-world. But if the capital markets are already complete, the firm has added nothing by a repackaging of claims on *EBIT* since no new independent investment opportunities can be provided. All possible future states-of-the-world have already been covered by existing securities.

The proof of the Modigliani-Miller independence thesis does not depend on the assumption that the firm will always meet its debt obligations. For some debt levels the firm may not meet its debt obligations in some states-of-the-world and would be bankrupt. If there are no bankruptcy penalties or bankruptcy costs (the situation in a perfect market), the *nature* of the claims on the firm's *EBIT* have been fundamentally unaltered. Thus the value of the firm remains unchanged.

Thus complete and perfect capital markets constitute sufficient conditions for the Modigliani-Miller propositions to hold. But as the foregoing example illustrated, the taxation of corporate profits and the exis-

---

4. Kraus and Litzenburger conclude with regard to their analysis as follows: "Contrary to the traditional net income approach to valuation, if the firm's debt obligation exceeds its earnings in some states the firm's market value is *not* necessarily a concave (from below) function of its debt obligation" (p. 918). However, this result follows only from their formulation of the problem in discontinuous terms. The problem could equally well be formulated with continuous functions in such a way that the resulting value of the firm would be continuous and concave (from below) in B.

5. Problem D19–4 illustrates that the production decisions and capital structure decisions of the firm can be interdependent given the presence of imperfections.

tence of bankruptcy-agency penalties represent market imperfections under which the capital structure choice will affect the value of the firm. We conclude that Modigliani and Miller are correct under properly specified conditions.

Furthermore, it is the absence of complete and perfect capital markets that makes capital structure matter. It is not clear whether the actual number of securities approximates the condition of completeness of the capital markets. However, without question there are corporate income taxes as well as agency and bankruptcy costs. The extent to which agency and bankruptcy costs affect capital structure significantly is an empirical matter.

The existence of market imperfections will cause the value of the firm to behave as generally depicted in Figure D19–1. As the amount of debt in the financial structure increases, the present value of tax savings will initially cause the market value of the firm to rise as a linear function. The slope of the line will be equal to the corporate tax rate. However, at some point agency and bankruptcy costs will cause the market value of the firm to bend down from what it would be if the only imperfection were corporate income taxes.

Figure D19–1
Influence of Debt on Market Value of the Firm

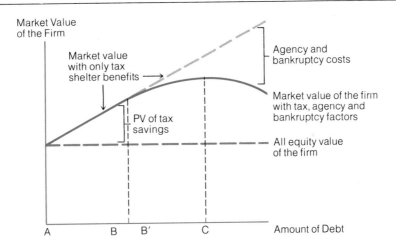

The Nature of Agency Costs

The nature of agency costs has been indicated in Appendix A to Chapter 16 dealing with the options pricing model. It was shown that if the shareholders move the firm into a more risky production plan, the value of the equity will rise in relation to the value of the debt. Thus there is a divergence of interest between shareholders and debtholders. In addition, if the managers of firms are paid on the basis of the size of the firm rather than its profitability rate, managers may seek to increase the size of the firm subject to achieving some profit ratio which will avoid confrontation with the shareholders. Bondholders will be concerned if the inefficiencies and low profitability that may result from seeking size for its own sake potentially impair the coverage of fixed charges.

Because of the possible divergences of interests, the bond indenture will contain restrictions on the freedom of action of both the shareholders and the managers of the firm. These restrictions limit the freedom of action of the managers and shareholders and, therefore, represent some "costs." In addition, it is not possible to cover every possible contingency by indenture restrictions. As a consequence, another agency cost will be "residual losses."[6] Residual loss represents a divergence between agents' decisions and decisions that would maximize the welfare of the principal. Thus the greater the amount of debt the greater the protection that is likely to be sought by the bondholders and hence the more restrictive will be indenture provisions.

In addition, "costs of bankruptcy" arise before actual formal legal procedures of bankruptcy take place. As the operating performance of the firm deteriorates in relation to its fixed contractual obligations, or as the amount of debt increases in relation to the firm's equity for a given level of operating performance, the financial markets may become increasingly reluctant to provide additional financing. Thus as conditions of this kind deteriorate, a number of costs will arise resulting from different degrees of financial inadequacy or failure on the part of the firm. These "costs of bankruptcy" that may be incurred successively include the following:

1. Financing under increasingly onerous terms, conditions, and rates. These represent increased costs.
2. Loss of key employees. The prospects of the firm are unfavorable so that able employees and executives seek alternative employment.
3. The loss of suppliers of the most saleable types of goods. The suppliers may fear that they will not be paid or that this customer does not represent one who will achieve growth in sales in the future.
4. The loss of sales due to lack of confidence on the part of customers that the firm will be around to stand behind the product.
5. Lack of financing under any terms, conditions, and rates to carry out

---

6. For a more complete explanation of agency costs and related terms see M. C. Jensen and W. H. Meckling, "Theory of the Firm: Managerial Behavior, Agency Costs and Ownership Structure," *Journal of Financial Economics* 3 (1976), pp. 305–60.

favorable but risky investments. This is because the overall prospects of the firm are not favorable in relation to its existing obligations.

6. The need to liquidate fixed assets to meet working capital requirements. A forced reduction in the scale of operations.
7. Formal bankruptcy proceedings. Legal and administrative costs will be incurred. In addition, a receiver will be appointed to conduct the operation of the firm, which may involve a disruption of operations.

As a consequence of agency and bankruptcy costs, the market value of the firm may begin to diverge from the straight line representing market value with only tax shelter benefits shown in Figure D19–1. At some point, agency and bankruptcy costs may become so large that the indicated market value of the firm actually begins to turn down, point C in Figure D19–1. This point would represent the target leverage ratio at which the market value of the firm is maximized—the optimal financial structure.

Problems

D19–1. Security A pays $30 if state 1 occurs and $10 if state 2 occurs. Security B pays $20 if state 1 occurs $40 if state 2 occurs The price of security A is $5 and the price of security B is $10.
   a. Set up the payoff table for securities A and B.
   b. Determine the prices of the two pure securities.

D19–2. The Sand Corporation is evaluating alternatives for financing its production. There are essentially three possible levels of production depending on which state-of-the-world occurs. Cost of failure and earnings before interest and taxes are different for each state. The company is considering use of debt in the amount of $0, $1,000, $3,000 or $6,000, and would like to know which alternative will maximize the expected value of the firm, given the probabilities (or primitive security prices) associated with each state. The tax rate is 50 percent.

State (s)	Planned Production EBIT (X_s)	Price of Primitive Security (p_s)	Cost of Failure (f_s)
1	2,000	.30	500
2	4,000	.50	1,500
3	8,000	.20	4,000

D19–3. The Kendrick Company is evaluating three alternative production plans $(X_s, Y_s$ and $Z_s)$ as shown below. Cost of failure is the same for each plan. Prices of primitive securities for the four possible states are as indicated.

Financial Structure and
the Cost of Capital

State	Price of Primitive Security	Cost of Failure	Planned Production EBIT		
(s)	(p_s)	(f_s)	(X_s)	(Y_s)	(Z_s)
1	.10	100	200	600	100
2	.40	600	1,200	1,500	800
3	.30	1,500	3,000	2,800	3,200
4	.20	2,000	3,500	3,000	3,800

Assuming the production will be financed with funds including $3,000 of debt, which of the three production plans would maximize the value of the firm? The tax rate is 50 percent.

D19–4. Under production plan A the *EBIT* of the firm for alternative states-of-the-world is indicated by the X_s column. The price of the primitive pure securities in state s is p_s. The failure or bankruptcy costs are f_s. Under production plan B, the *EBIT* of the firm is indicated by X'_s. Production plan B involves giving up 300 in state 3 to add 300 in state 2. Since the prices of pure securities and bankruptcy costs are given by the market, they remain unchanged under production plan B. The tax rate is 50 percent.

s	X_s	p_s	f_s	X'_s
1	500	.20	100	500
2	600	.40	300	900
3	1,400	.30	500	1,100
4	2,000	.10	800	2,000

a. What is the optimal financial leverage for production plan A by the criterion of maximizing the value of the firm?
b. Is the optimal financial leverage changed by new production plan B?
c. What implications do the results under A and B have for the interdependence between production plans and financial structure?

Selected References

Arrow, K. J. "The Role of Securities in the Optimal Allocation of Risk-Bearing." *Review of Economic Studies* 31 (Apr. 1964): 91–96.

Hirshleifer, J. "Investment Decisions Under Uncertainty: Application of the State-Preference Approach." *Quarterly Journal of Economics* 80 (May 1966): 262–77.

Kraus, Alan, and Litzenberger, Robert. "A State-Preference Model of Optimal Financial Leverage." *Journal of Finance* 28 (Sept. 1973): 911–22.

Myers, S. C. "A Time-State Preference Model of Security Valuation." *Journal of Financial and Quantitative Analysis* 3 (Mar. 1968):1–33.

Sharpe, W. F. *Portfolio Theory and Capital Markets.* New York: McGraw-Hill, 1970. Chap. 10, "State-Preference Theory."

20 Dividend Policy and Internal Financing

Dividend policy determines the division of earnings between payments to stockholders and reinvestment in the firm. Retained earnings are one of the most significant sources of funds for financing corporate growth, but dividends constitute the cash flows that accrue to stockholders. The factors that influence the allocation of earnings to dividends or retained earnings are the subject of this chapter.

Factors Influencing Dividend Policy

What factors determine the extent to which a firm will pay out dividends instead of retain earnings? As a first step toward answering this question, we shall consider some of the factors that influence dividend policy.

Legal Rules

Although state statutes and court decisions governing dividend policy are complicated, their essential nature may be stated briefly. The legal rules provide that dividends must be paid from earnings, either from the current year's earnings or from past years' earnings as reflected in the balance sheet account "retained earnings."

State laws emphasize three rules: (1) the net profits rule, (2) the capital impairment rule, and (3) the insolvency rule. The *net profits* rule provides that dividends may be paid from past and present earnings. The *capital impairment* rule protects creditors by forbidding the payment of dividends from capital. Paying dividends from capital would be distributing the investment in a company rather than its earnings.[1] The *insolvency* rule provides that corporations may not pay dividends while insolvent. Insolvency is here defined in the bankruptcy sense that liabilities exceed assets, and to pay dividends under such conditions would mean giving stockholders funds that rightfully belong to the creditors.

Legal aspects are significant. They provide the framework within

---

1. It is possible, of course, to return stockholders' capital; when this is done, however, it must be clearly stated as such. A dividend paid out of capital is called a *liquidating* dividend.

which dividend policies can be formulated. Within these boundaries, however, financial and economic factors have a major influence on policy.

Liquidity Position

Profits held as retained earnings (which show up in the right-hand side of the balance sheet in the account labeled "retained earnings") are generally invested in assets required for the conduct of the business. Retained earnings from preceding years are already invested in plant and equipment, inventories, and other assets; they are not held as cash. Thus, although a firm has had a record of earnings, it may not be able to pay cash dividends because of its liquidity position. Indeed, a growing firm, even a very profitable one, typically has a pressing need for funds. In such a situation the firm may elect not to pay cash dividends.

If this point is not clear, refer back to Table 2–1, the Walker-Wilson Company's balance sheet. The retained earnings account shows $400,000, but the cash account shows only $50,000. Since some cash must be retained to pay bills, it is clear that Walker-Wilson's cash position precludes a dividend of even $50,000.

Need to Repay Debt

When a firm has sold debt to finance expansion or to substitute for other forms of financing, it is faced with two alternatives: it can refund the debt at maturity by replacing it with another form of security, or it can make provision for paying off the debt. If the decision is to retire the debt, this will generally require the retention of earnings.

Restrictions in Debt Contracts

Debt contracts, particularly when long-term debt is involved, frequently restrict a firm's ability to pay cash dividends. Such restrictions, which are designed to protect the position of the lender, usually state (1) that future dividends can be paid only out of earnings generated *after* the signing of the loan agreement (that is, future dividends cannot be paid out of past retained earnings), and (2) that dividends cannot be paid when net working capital (current assets minus current liabilities) is below a specified amount. Similarly, preferred stock agreements generally state that no cash dividends can be paid on the common stock until all accrued preferred dividends have been paid.

Rate of Asset Expansion

The more rapid the rate at which the firm is growing, the greater will be its needs for financing asset expansion. The greater the future need for funds, the more likely the firm is to retain earnings rather than pay them out. If a firm seeks to raise funds externally, natural sources are the present shareholders who already know the company. But if earnings are paid out as dividends and are subjected to high personal income tax rates, only a portion of the earnings would be available for reinvestment.

Profit Rate

The rate of return on assets determines the relative attractiveness of paying out earnings in the form of dividends to stockholders who will use them elsewhere, compared with the productivity of their use in the present enterprise.

Stability of Earnings

If earnings are relatively stable, a firm is better able to predict what its future earnings will be. A stable firm is therefore more likely to pay out a higher percentage of its earnings than is a firm with fluctuating earnings. The unstable firm is not certain that in subsequent years the hoped-for earnings will be realized, so it is more likely to retain a high proportion of earnings. A lower dividend will be easier to maintain if earnings should fall off in the future.

Access to the Capital Markets

A large, well-established firm with a record of profitability and some stability of earnings will have easy access to capital markets and other forms of external financing. The small, new, or venturesome firm, however, is riskier for potential investors. Its ability to raise equity or debt funds from capital markets is restricted, and it must retain more earnings to finance its operations. A well-established firm is thus likely to have a higher dividend payout rate than is a new or small firm.

Control

Another important variable is the effect of alternative sources of financing on the control situation in the firm. Some corporations, as a matter of policy, will expand only to the extent of their internal earnings. This policy is defended on the grounds that raising funds by selling additional common stock dilutes the control of the dominant group in the company. At the same time, selling debt increases the risks of fluctuating earnings to the present owners of the company. Reliance on internal financing in order to maintain control reduces the dividend payout.

Tax Position of Stockholders

The tax position of the owners of the corporation greatly influences the desire for dividends. For example, a corporation closely held by a few taxpayers in high income tax brackets is likely to pay a relatively low dividend. The owners of the corporation are interested in taking their income in the form of capital gains rather than as dividends, which are subject to higher personal income tax rates. However, the stockholders of a large, widely held corporation may be interested in a high dividend payout.

At times there is a conflict of interest in large corporations between stockholders in high income tax brackets and those in low tax brackets. The former may prefer to see a low dividend payout and a high rate of earnings retention in the hope of an appreciation in the capital stock of the company. The lower income stockholders may prefer a relatively high dividend payout rate. The dividend policy of such a firm may be a compromise between a low and a high payout — an intermediate payout ratio. If, however, one group dominates and sets, let us say, a low payout policy, those stockholders who seek income are likely to sell their shares over time and shift into higher yielding stocks. *Thus, to at least some extent, a firm's payout policy determines its stockholder types, as well as vice versa.* This has been called the "clientele influence" on dividend policy.

Tax on Improperly Accumulated Earnings

In order to prevent wealthy stockholders from using the corporation as an "incorporated pocketbook" by which they can avoid the high rates of personal income tax, tax regulations applicable to corporations provide for a special surtax on improperly accumulated income. However, Section 531 of the Revenue Act of 1954 places the burden of proof on the Internal Revenue Service to justify penalty rates for accumulation of earnings. That is, earnings retention is justified unless the Internal Revenue Service can prove otherwise.

Dividend Policy Decisions

A fundamental relation observed in dividend policy is the widespread tendency of corporations to pursue a relatively stable dividend policy. Profits of firms fluctuate considerably with changes in the level of business activity, but Figure 20–1 shows that dividends are more stable than earnings.

Most corporations seek to maintain a target dividend per share. However, dividends increase with a lag after earnings rise. Dividends are increased only after an increase in earnings appears clearly sustainable and relatively permanent. When dividends have been increased, strenuous efforts are made to maintain them at the new level. If earnings decline, the existing dividend will generally be maintained until it is clear that an earnings recovery will not take place.

Figure 20–1
Figure 20–1
Corporate Earnings
after Taxes and
Dividends

Figure 20–2 illustrates these ideas by showing the earnings and dividends patterns for the Walter Watch Company over a 30-year period. Initially earnings are $2 and dividends $1 a share, providing a 50 percent payout ratio. Earnings rise for four years, while dividends remain constant; thus, the payout ratio falls during this period. During 1955 and 1956, earnings fall substantially; however, the dividend is maintained and the payout rises above the 50 percent target. During the period

Figure 20–2
Dividends and
Earnings Patterns,
Walter Watch
Company

between 1956 and 1960, earnings experience a sustained rise. Dividends are held constant for a time, while management seeks to determine whether the earnings increase is permanent. By 1961, the earnings gains seem permanent, and dividends are raised in three steps to reestablish the 50 percent target payout. During 1965 a strike causes earnings to fall below the regular dividend; expecting the earnings decline to be temporary, management maintains the dividend. Earnings fluctuate on a fairly high plateau from 1966 through 1972, during which time dividends remain constant. A new increase in earnings induces management to raise the dividend in 1973 to reestablish the 50 percent payout ratio.

Rationale for Stable Dividends

Walter Watch, like the great majority of firms, kept its dividend at a relatively steady dollar amount but allowed its payout ratio to fluctuate. Why would it follow such a policy?

Consider the stable dividend policy from the standpoint of the stockholders as owners of a company. Their acquiescence with the general practice must imply that stable dividend policies lead to higher stock prices on the average than do alternative dividend policies. Is this a fact? Does a stable dividend policy maximize equity values for a corporation? There has been no truly conclusive empirical study of dividend policy, so any answer to the question must be regarded as tentative. On logical grounds, however, there is reason to believe that a stable dividend policy will lead to higher stock prices. First, investors might be expected to value more highly dividends they are more sure of receiving, since fluctuating dividends are riskier than stable dividends. Accordingly, the same average amount of dividends received under a fluctuating dividend policy is likely to have a higher discount factor applied to it than is applied to dividends under a stable dividend policy. In the terms used in Chapter 19, this means that a firm with a stable dividend would have a lower required rate of return—or cost of equity capital—than one whose dividends fluctuate.

Second, many stockholders live on income received in the form of dividends. Such stockholders would be greatly inconvenienced by fluctuating dividends, and they would likely pay a premium for a stock with a relatively assured minimum dollar dividend.

A third advantage of a stable dividend from the standpoint of a corporation and its stockowners is the requirement of *legal listing*. Legal lists are lists of securities in which mutual savings banks, pension funds, insurance companies, and other fiduciary institutions are permitted to invest. One of the criteria for placing a stock on the legal list is that dividend payments be maintained. Thus, legal listing encourages pursuance of a stable dividend policy.

On the other hand, if a firm's investment opportunities fluctuate from year to year, should it not retain more earnings during some years in order to take advantage of these opportunities when they appear, then increase dividends when good internal investment opportunities are scarce? This line of reasoning would lead to the recommendation of a fluctuating payout for companies whose investment opportunities are unstable. However, the logic of the argument is diminished by recognizing that it is possible to maintain a reasonably stable dividend by using outside financing, including debt, to smooth out the differences between the funds needed for investment and the amount of money provided by retained earnings.

Alternative Dividend Policies

Before going on to consider dividend policy at a theoretical level, it is useful to summarize the three major types of dividend policies.

Stable Dollar Amount per Share. The policy of a stable dollar amount per share, followed by most firms, is the policy that is implied when we say "stable dividend policy."

Constant Payout Ratio. A very few firms follow a policy of paying out a constant percentage of earnings. Earnings will surely fluctuate, so following this policy necessarily means that the dollar amount of dividends will fluctuate. For reasons discussed in the preceding section, this policy is not likely to maximize the value of a firm's stock. Before its bankruptcy, Penn-Central Railroad followed the policy of paying out one-half its earnings: "A dollar for the stockholders and a dollar for the company," as one director put it.

Low Regular Dividend plus Extras. The low-regular-dividend-plus-extras policy is a compromise between the first two. It gives the firm flexibility, but it leaves investors somewhat uncertain about what their dividend income will be. But if a firm's earnings are quite volatile, this policy may well be its best choice.

The relative merits of these three policies can be evaluated better after a discussion of the residual theory of dividends, the topic covered in the next section.

Residual Theory of Dividends[2]

In the preceding chapters on capital budgeting and the cost of capital, we indicated that, generally, the cost of capital schedule and the investment opportunity schedule must be combined before the cost of capital can be established. In other words, the optimum capital budget, the marginal cost of capital, and the marginal rate of return on investment are determined *simultaneously*. In this section we examine this simultaneous solution in the framework of what is called *the residual theory of dividends.* The theory draws on materials developed earlier in the book — capital budgeting and the cost of capital — and serves to provide a bridge between these key concepts.

The starting point in the theory is that investors prefer to have the firm retain and reinvest earnings rather than pay them out in dividends *if the return on reinvested earnings exceeds the rate of return the investor could, himself, obtain on other investments of comparable risk.* If the corporation can reinvest retained earnings at a 20 percent rate of return, while the best rate the stockholder can obtain if the earnings are passed on to him in the form of dividends is 10 percent, then the stockholder would prefer to have the firm retain the profits.

We saw in Chapter 19 that the cost of equity capital obtained from retained earnings is an *opportunity cost* that reflects rates of return open to equity investors. If a firm's stockholders could buy other stocks of equal risk and obtain a 10 percent dividend-plus-capital-gains yield, then 10 percent is the firm's cost of retained earnings. The cost of new outside equity raised by selling common stock is higher because of the costs of floating the issue.

Most firms have an optimum debt ratio that calls for at least some debt, so new financing is done partly with debt and partly with equity. Debt has a different, and generally lower, cost than equity, so the two forms of capital must be combined to find the *weighted average cost of capital.* As long as the firm finances at the optimum point, using an optimum amount of debt and equity, and provided it uses only internally generated equity (retained earnings), its marginal cost of each new dollar of capital will be minimized.

Internally generated equity is available for financing a certain amount of new investment; beyond this amount, the firm must turn to more expensive new common stock. At the point where new stock must be sold, the cost of equity and, consequently, the marginal cost of capital, rises.

These concepts, which were developed in Chapter 19, are illustrated in Figure 20–3. The firm has a marginal cost of capital of 10 percent so

2. "Residual" implies *left over.* The residual theory of dividend policy implies that dividends are paid after internal investment opportunities have been exhausted.

Figure 20–3
The Marginal Cost of
Capital

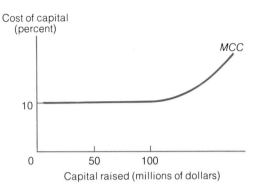

Cost of capital
(percent)

MCC

10

0   50   100

Capital raised (millions of dollars)

long as retained earnings are available; the marginal cost of capital begins to rise when new stock must be sold.

Our hypothetical firm has $50 million of earnings and a 50 percent optimum debt ratio. It can make net investments (investments in addition to asset replacements financed from depreciation) up to $100 million: $50 million from retained earnings plus $50 million new debt supported by the retained earnings if it does not pay dividends. Therefore, its marginal cost of capital is constant at 10 percent for up to $100 million of capital. Beyond $100 million, the marginal cost of capital begins rising as the firm begins to use more expensive new common stock.

Next, suppose the firm's capital budgeting department draws up a list of investment opportunities, ranked in the order of each project's *IRR*, and plots them on a graph. The investment opportunity curves of

Figure 20–4
Investment
Opportunities

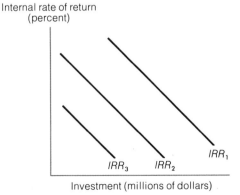

Internal rate of return
(percent)

*IRR*₃   *IRR*₂   *IRR*₁

Investment (millions of dollars)

three different years — one for a good year (IRR_1), one for a normal year (IRR_2), and one for a bad year (IRR_3) — are shown in Figure 20–4. IRR_1 shows that the firm can invest more money, and at higher rates of return, than it can when the investment opportunities are those given by IRR_2 and IRR_3.

Now we combine the investment opportunity schedule with the cost of capital schedule; this is done in Figure 20–5. The point where the investment opportunity curve cuts the cost of capital curve defines the proper level of new investment. When investment opportunities are relatively poor, the optimum level of investment is $25 million; when opportunities are about normal, $75 million should be invested; and when opportunities are relatively good, the firm should make new investments in the amount of $125 million.

Figure 20–5
Interrelationship
among Cost of Capital,
Investment
Opportunities, and
New Investment

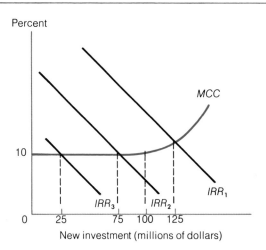

Consider the situation where IRR_1 is the appropriate schedule. Suppose the firm has $50 million in earnings and a 50 percent target debt ratio, so it can finance $100 million, $50 million earnings plus $50 million debt, from retained earnings plus new debt *if it retains all its earnings*. If it pays part of the earnings in dividends, then it will have to begin using expensive new common stock sooner, so the cost of capital curve will rise sooner. This suggests that under the conditions of IRR, the firm should retain all its earnings and actually sell some new common stock in order to take advantage of its investment opportunities. Its payout ratio would thus be zero percent.

Under the conditions of IRR_2, however, the firm should invest only $75 million. How should this investment be financed? First, notice that if it retains the full amount of its earnings, $50 million, it will need to sell only $25 million of new debt. However, by retaining $50 million and selling only $25 million of new debt, the firm will move away from its target capital structure. To stay on target, the firm must finance the required $75 million half by equity—retained earnings—and half by debt, or $37.5 million by retained earnings and $37.5 million by debt. Now if the firm has $50 million in total earnings and decides to retain and reinvest $37.5 million, it must distribute the $12.5 million residual to its stockholders. In this case, the payout ratio is 25 percent ($12.5 million divided by $50 million).

Finally, under the bad conditions of IRR_3, the firm should invest only $25 million. Because it has $50 million in earnings, it could finance the entire $25 million out of retained earnings and still have $25 million available for dividends. Should this be done? Under the assumptions, this would not be a good decision, because it would move the firm away from its target debt ratio. To stay in the 50-50 debt/equity position, the firm must retain $12.5 million and sell $12.5 million of debt. When the $12.5 million of retained earnings is subtracted from the $50 million of earnings, the firm is left with a residual of $37.5, the amount that should be paid out in dividends. In this case the payout ratio is 75 percent.

Long-run Viewpoint

There seems to be a conflict between the residual theory and the statement made in an earlier section that firms should and do maintain reasonably stable cash dividends. How can this conflict be reconciled?

A firm may have a target capital structure without being at that target at all times. In other words, we would not recommend that a firm adjust its dividend each and every year—indeed, this is not necessary. Firms do have target debt ratios, but they also have a certain amount of flexibility—they can be moderately above or below the target debt position in any one year with no serious adverse consequences. This means that if an unusually large number of good investments are available in a particular year, the firm does not necessarily have to cut its dividend to take advantage of them—it can borrow somewhat more heavily than usual in that particular year without getting its debt ratio too far out of line. Obviously, however, this excessive reliance on debt could not continue for too many years without seriously affecting the debt ratio, necessitating either a sale of new stock or a cut in dividends and an attendant increase in the level of retained earnings.

High and Low Dividend Payout Industries

Some industries are experiencing rapid growth in the demand for their products, affording firms in these industries many good investment opportunities. Electronics, office equipment, and entertainment are examples of such industries in recent years. Other industries have experienced much slower growth, or perhaps even declines. Examples of such slow-growth industries are cigarette manufacturing and textiles. Still other industries are growing at about the same rate as the general economy—oil, autos, and banking are representative.

The theory suggests that firms in rapidly growing industries should generally have IRR curves that are relatively far out to the right on graphs such as Figure 20–5; for example, Xerox, Polaroid, and IBM might have investment opportunities similar to IRR_1. The tobacco companies, on the other hand, could be expected to have investment schedules similar to IRR_3, while IRR_2 might be appropriate for Union Carbide.

Each of these firms would, of course, experience shifts in investment opportunities from year to year, but the curves would *tend* to be in about the same part of the graph. In other words, firms such as Xerox would *tend* to have more investment opportunities than money, so they would *tend* to have zero (or very low) payout ratios. Reynolds Tobacco, on the other hand, would *tend* to have more money than good investments, so we would expect to find Reynolds paying out a relatively high percentage of earnings in dividends. These companies do, in fact, conform with our expectations.

Conflicting Theories on Dividends[3]

Two basic schools of thought on dividend policy have been expressed in the theoretical literature of finance. One school, associated with Myron Gordon and John Lintner, among others, holds that the capital gains expected to result from earnings retention are more risky than are dividend expectations. Accordingly, this school suggests that the earnings of a firm with a low-payout ratio will typically be capitalized at higher rates than the earnings of a high-payout firm, other things held constant.

The other school, associated with Merton Miller and Franco Modigliani, holds that investors are basically indifferent to returns in the form of dividends or capital gains. If, when firms raise or lower their divi-

---

3. See the references at the end of this chapter for an extended discussion of the theory of dividend policy.

dends, their stock prices tend to rise or fall in like manner, does this prove that investors prefer dividends? Miller and Modigliani argue that it does not, that any effect a change in dividends has on the price of a firm's stock is related primarily to *information about expected future earnings conveyed by a change in dividends.* Recalling that corporate managements dislike cutting dividends, Miller and Modigliani argue that increases in cash dividends raise expectations about the level of future earnings—dividend increases have favorable *information content.* In terms of Figure 20–2, Miller and Modigliani would say that Walter Watch's dividend increases in 1961, 1962, 1963, and 1973 had information content about future earnings—these dividend increases signaled to stockholders that management expected the recent earnings increases to be permanent.

Dividends are probably subject to less uncertainty than capital gains, but dividends are taxed at a higher rate than capital gains. How do these two forces balance out? Some argue that the uncertainty factor dominates; others feel that the differential tax rate is the stronger force and causes investors to favor corporate retention of earnings; still others—and we put ourselves in this group—argue that it is difficult to generalize. Depending on the tax status and the current income needs of its set of stockholders (both brokerage costs and capital gains taxes make it difficult for individual stockholders to shift companies), as well as the firm's internal investment opportunities, the optimum dividend policy will vary from firm to firm. We thus place heavy emphasis on the "clientele effect."

Dividend Payments

Dividends are normally paid quarterly. For example, Liggett Group has paid annual dividends of $2.50. In common financial language, we say that Liggett Group's *regular quarterly dividend is 62.5 cents,* or that its *regular annual dividend* is $2.50. The management of a company such as Liggett Group, sometimes by an explicit statement in the annual report and sometimes by implication, conveys to stockholders an expectation that the regular dividend will be maintained if at all possible. Further, management conveys its belief that earnings will be sufficient to maintain the dividend.

Under other conditions, a firm's cash flows and investment needs may be too volatile for it to set a very high regular dividend; on the average, however, it needs a high dividend payout to dispose of funds not necessary for reinvestment. In such a case, the directors can set a relatively low regular dividend—low enough that it can be maintained even in low profit years or in years when a considerable amount of reinvestment is needed — and supplement it with an extra dividend in years when excess funds are available. General Motors, whose earnings fluctuate widely from year to year, has long followed the practice of supplementing its regular dividend with an *extra dividend* paid in addition to the regular fourth quarter dividend.

Payment Procedure

The actual payment procedure is of some importance, and the following is an outline of the payment sequence.

1. *Declaration Date* The directors meet, say on November 15, and declare the regular dividend. On this date, the directors issue a statement similar to the following: "On November 15, 1977, the directors of the XYZ Company met and declared the regular quarterly dividend of 50 cents a share, plus an extra dividend of 75 cents a share, to holders of record on December 15, payment to be made on January 2, 1978."

2. *Holder-of-Record Date* On December 15, the *holder-of-record date*, the company closes its stock transfer books and makes up a list of the shareholders as of that date. If XYZ Company is notified of the sale and transfer of some stock before December 16, the new owner receives the dividend. If notification is received on or after December 16, the old stockholder gets the dividend.

3. *Ex Dividend Date* Suppose Edward Johns buys 100 shares of stock from Robert Noble on December 13; will the company be notified of the transfer in time to list Johns as the new owner and, thus, pay the dividend to him? To avoid conflict, the stock brokerage business has set up a convention of declaring that the right to the dividend remains with the stock until four days prior to the holder-of-record date; on the fourth day before the record date, the right to the dividend no longer goes with the shares. The date when the right to the dividend leaves the stock is called the *ex dividend date.*

In this case, the ex dividend date is four days prior to December 15, or December 11. Therefore, if Johns is to receive the dividend, he must buy the stock by December 10. If he buys it on December 11 or later, Noble will receive the dividend.

The total dividend, regular plus extra, amounts to $1.25, so the ex dividend date is important. Barring fluctuations in the stock market, we would normally expect the price of a stock to drop by approximately the amount of the dividend on the ex dividend date.

4. *Payment Date* The company actually mails the checks to the holders of record on January 2, the payment date.

Stock Dividends and Stock Splits

One of the significant aspects of dividend policy is that of *stock dividends* and *stock splits*. A *stock dividend* is paid in additional shares of stock instead of in cash, and simply involves a bookkeeping transfer from retained earnings to the capital stock account.[4] In a *stock split* there is no change in the capital accounts. A larger number of shares of common stock is issued. In a two-for-one split, each stockholder would receive two shares for each one previously held. Book value per share would be cut in half. The par, or stated, value per share of common stock is similarly changed.

From a practical standpoint there is little difference between a stock dividend and a stock split. The New York Stock Exchange considers any distribution of stock totaling less than 25 percent of outstanding stock to be a stock dividend. Any distribution of stock of 25 percent or more is regarded as a stock split. Since the two are similar, the issues outlined below are discussed in connection with both stock dividends and stock splits.

Price Effects

The results of a careful empirical study of the effects of stock dividends are available and can be used as a basis for observations on the price effects of stock dividends.[5] The findings of the study are presented in Table 20–1. When stock dividends were associated with a cash dividend increase, the value of the company's stock six months after the ex dividend date had risen by 8 percent. On the other hand, where stock dividends were not accompanied by cash dividend increases, stock values fell by 12 percent during the subsequent six-month period.

These data seem to suggest that stock dividends are seen for what they are—simply additional pieces of paper—and that they do not represent true income. When they are accompanied by higher earnings and cash dividends, investors bid up the value of the stock. However, when stock dividends are not accompanied by increases in earnings and cash dividends, the dilution of earnings and dividends per share

---

4. One point that should be made in connection with stock dividends is that the transfer from retained earnings to the capital stock account must be based on market value. In other words, if a firm's shares are selling for $100 and it has 1,000,000 shares outstanding, a 10 percent stock dividend requires the transfer of $10 million (100,000 × $100) from retained earnings to capital stock. Quite obviously, stock dividends are thus limited by the size of retained earnings. The rule was put into effect to prevent the declaration of stock dividends unless the firm has had earnings. This is another in a long series of rulings designed to prevent investors from being fooled by the practices of unscrupulous firms.

5. C. A. Barker, "Evaluation of Stock Dividends," *Harvard Business Review* 36 (July–August 1958), pp. 99–114. Barker's study has been replicated several times in recent years, but his results are still valid—they have withstood the test of time.

Table 20–1		Price at Selected Dates (in Percentages)		
Price Effects of		Six Months	At	Six Months
Stock Dividends		Prior to	ex Dividend	after
		ex Dividend	Date	ex Dividend
		Date		Date
	Cash dividend increase	100	109	108
	No cash dividend increase	100	99	88

causes the price of the stock to drop. The fundamental determinant is underlying earnings and dividend trends.

Effects on Extent of Ownership

Table 20-2 shows the effect of stock dividends on common stock ownership. Large stock dividends resulted in the largest percentage increases in stock ownership. The use of stock dividends increased shareholders by 25 percent on the average. For companies and industries that did not offer stock splits or stock dividends, the increase in ownership was only 5 percent. Furthermore, the degree of increase in ownership increased with the size of the stock dividend.

Table 20–2		Percentage Increase in Stockholders, 1950–1953
Effect of Stock		
Dividends on		
Stock Ownership		
	Stock dividend, 25% and over	30
	Stock dividend, 5–25%	17
	All stock dividends	25
	No stock dividends or splits	5

Source: C. Austin Barker, "Evaluation of Stock Dividends," *Harvard Business Review* 36 (July–August 1958), pp. 99–114.

This evidence suggests that stock dividends increase share ownership. Regardless of the effect on the total market value of the firm, the use of stock dividends and stock splits effectively increases stock ownership by lowering the price at which shares are traded to a more popular range.

Stock Repurchases as an Alternative to Dividends

Treasury stock is the name given to common stock that has been repurchased by the issuing firm, and the acquisition of treasury stock represents an alternative to the payment of dividends. If some of the outstanding stock is repurchased, fewer shares will remain outstanding; and assuming the repurchase does not adversely affect the firm's earnings, the earnings per share of the remaining shares will increase. This increase in earnings per share may result in a higher market price per share, so capital gains will have been substituted for dividends. These effects can be seen from the following example.

Example

American Development Corporation (ADC) earned $4.4 million in 1978; of this amount, 50 percent, or $2.2 million, has been allocated for distribution to common shareholders. There are currently 1,100,000 shares outstanding, and the market value is $20 a share. ADC can use the $2.2 million to repurchase 100,000 of its shares through a tender offer for $22 a share, or it can pay a cash dividend of $2 a share.[6]

The effect of the repurchase on the *EPS* and market price per share of the remaining stock can be determined in the following way:

1. Current *EPS* $= \dfrac{\text{total earnings}}{\text{number of shares}} = \dfrac{\$4.4 \text{ million}}{1.1 \text{ million}}$

$$= \$4 \text{ per share.}$$

2. Current *P/E* ratio $= \dfrac{\$20}{\$4} = 5\text{X.}$

3. *EPS* after repurchase of 100,000 shares $= \dfrac{\$4.4 \text{ million}}{1 \text{ million}} = \$4.40 \text{ per share.}$

4. Expected market price after repurchase $= (P/E)(EPS) = (5)(\$4.40) = \$22 \text{ per share.}$

It should be noticed from this example that investors would receive benefits of $2 a share in any case, either in the form of a $2 cash dividend or a $2 increase in stock price. The result occurs because we assumed (1) that shares could be repurchased at $22 a share, (2) that *EPS* would remain unchanged, and (3) that the *P/E* ratio would remain constant. If shares could be bought for less than $22, the operation would be even better for *remaining* stockholders, but the reverse would hold if ADC paid more than $22 a share. Furthermore, the *P/E* ratio might change as a result of the repurchase operation, rising if

6. Stock repurchases are commonly made in three ways. First, a publicly owned firm can simply buy its own stock through a broker on the open market. Second, it can issue a *tender* under which it permits stockholders to send in (that is, "tender") their shares to the firm in exchange for a specified price per share. When tender offers are made, the firm generally indicates that it will buy up to a specified number of shares within a specified time period (usually about two weeks); if more shares are tendered than the company wishes to purchase, then purchases are made on a pro rata basis. Finally, the firm can purchase a block of shares from one large holder on a negotiated basis. If the latter procedure is employed, care must be taken to insure that this one stockholder does not receive preferential treatment not available to other stockholders.

investors view it favorably, falling if they view it unfavorably. Some factors that might affect *P/E* ratios are considered next.

Advantages of Repurchases from the Stockholder's Viewpoint

1. Profits earned on repurchases are taxed at the capital gains rate, whereas a dividend distribution would be taxed at the stockholder's marginal tax rate. This is significant. For example, it has been estimated that, on the average, stockholders pay a tax of about 45 percent on marginal income. Since the capital gains tax rate is generally only one-half the ordinary tax rate, the typical shareholder would clearly benefit, other things the same, if the distribution is in the form of a stock repurchase rather than a dividend.
2. The stockholder has a choice: He can either sell or not sell. On the other hand, with a dividend, he has to accept the payment and pay the tax.
3. A qualitative advantage advanced by market practitioners is that repurchase can often remove a large block of stock overhanging the market.

Advantages of Repurchases from Management's Viewpoint

1. Studies have shown that dividends are *sticky* in the short run because managements are reluctant to raise dividends if the new dividend cannot be maintained in the future. Managements dislike cutting cash dividends, so they are reluctant to raise dividends if they are not confident that the dividend can be maintained in the future. Hence, if the excess cash flow is thought to be only *temporary*, management may prefer to "conceal" the distribution in the form of share repurchases rather than to declare a cash dividend they believe cannot be maintained.
2. Repurchased stock can be used for acquisitions or released when stock options are exercised. Discussions with financial managers indicate that it is frequently more convenient and less expensive to use repurchased stock rather than newly issued stock for these purposes, and also when convertibles are converted or warrants exercised.
3. If directors have large holdings themselves, they may have especially strong preferences for repurchases rather than dividend payments because of the tax factor.
4. One interesting use of stock repurchases was Standard Products' strategy of repurchasing its own stock to thwart an attempted takeover. Defiance Industries, Inc., attempted to acquire a controlling interest in Standard Products through a tender offer of $15 a share. Standard's management countered with a tender offer of its own at $17.25 a share, financed by $1.725 million in internal funds and by

$3.525 million in long-term debt. This kept stockholders from accepting the outside tender offer and enabled Standard Products' management to retain control.

5. Repurchases can be used to effect large-scale changes in capital structure. For example, at one time American Standard had virtually no long-term debt outstanding. The company decided that its optimal capital structure called for the use of considerably more debt, but even if it financed *only* with debt it would have taken years to get the debt ratio up to the newly defined optimal level. What could the company do? It sold $22 million of long-term debt and used the proceeds to repurchase its common stock, thus producing an instantaneous change in its capital structure.

6. Treasury stock can be resold in the open market if the firm needs additional funds.

Disadvantages of Repurchases from the Stockholder's Viewpoint

1. Stockholders may not be indifferent between dividends and capital gains, and the price of the stock might benefit more from cash dividends than from repurchases. Cash dividends are generally thought of as being relatively dependable, but repurchases are not. Further, if a firm announces a regular, dependable repurchase program, the improper accumulation tax discussed below would probably become more of a threat.

2. The *selling* stockholders may not be fully aware of all the implications of a repurchase or may not have all pertinent information about the corporation's present and future activities. For this reason, firms generally announce a repurchase program before embarking on it.

3. The corporation may pay too high a price for the repurchased stock, to the disadvantage of remaining stockholders. If the shares are inactive and if the firm seeks to acquire a relatively large amount of its stock, the price may be bid above a maintainable price and then fall after the firm ceases its repurchase operations.

4. By reducing the proportion of cash or marketable securities in the asset structure, the risk composition of the firm's assets and earnings may be increased. The *P/E* ratio may therefore drop.

Disadvantages of Repurchases from Management's Viewpoint

1. Studies have shown that firms which repurchase substantial amounts of stock have poorer growth rates and investment opportunities than ones that do not. Thus, some people feel that announcing a repurchase program is like announcing that management cannot locate good investment projects. One could argue that instituting a repurchase program should be regarded in the same manner as announcing a higher dividend payout, but if repurchases are regard-

ed as indicating especially unfavorable growth opportunities, then repurchases can have an adverse impact on the firm's image, and also on the price of its stock.

2. Repurchases might involve some risk from a legal standpoint. If the Internal Revenue Service can establish that the repurchases are primarily for the avoidance of taxes on dividends, then penalties may be imposed on the firm under the improper accumulation of earnings provision of the tax code. Actions have been brought against closely held companies under Section 531, but we know of no case where such an action has been brought against a publicly owned firm, even though some firms have retired over one-half their outstanding stock. Also, the SEC may raise serious questions if it appears that the firm may be manipulating the price of its shares.

Conclusion on Stock Repurchases

When all the pros and the cons on stock repurchases are totaled, where do we stand? Our own conclusions may be summarized as follows:

1. Repurchases on a regular, systematic, dependable basis, like quarterly dividends, are not feasible because of uncertainties about the tax treatment of such a program and uncertainties about such things as the market price of the shares, how many shares would be tendered, and so forth.
2. However, repurchases do offer some significant advantages over dividends, so this procedure should be given careful consideration on the basis of the firm's own unique situation.
3. Repurchases can be especially valuable to effect a significant shift in capital structure within a short period.
4. Repurchases may increase the riskiness of the firm's assets and earnings.

Summary

Dividend policy determines the extent of internal financing by a firm. The financial manager decides whether to release corporate earnings from the control of the enterprise. Because dividend policy may affect the financial structure, the flow of funds, corporate liquidity, stock prices, and investor satisfaction — to list a few ramifications — it is clearly an important aspect of financial management.

In theory, once the firm's debt policy and cost of capital have been determined, dividend policy should automatically follow. Under our theoretical model, dividends are simply a residual after investment needs have been met; if this policy is followed and if investors are indifferent to receiving their investment returns in the form of dividends or of capital gains, stockholders are better off than they are under any other possible dividend policy. However, the financial manager simply does not have all the information assumed in the theory, and judgment must be exercised.

As a guide to financial managers responsible for dividend policy, the following check list summarizes the major economic and financial factors influencing dividend policy:

1. Rate of growth and profit level.
2. Stability of earnings.
3. Age and size of firm.
4. Cash position.
5. Need to repay debt.
6. Control.
7. Maintenance of a target dividend.
8. Tax position of stockholders.
9. Tax position of the corporation; improper accumulation considerations.

Of the factors listed, some lead to higher dividend payouts, some to lower payouts. It is not possible to provide a formula that can be used to establish the proper dividend payout for a given situation; this is a task requiring the exercise of judgment. The considerations summarized above provide a check list for guiding dividend decisions.

Empirical studies indicate a wide diversity of dividend payout ratios not only among industries but also among firms in the same industry. Studies also show that dividends are more stable than earnings. Firms are reluctant to raise dividends in years of good earnings, and they resist dividend cuts as earnings decline. In view of investors' observed preference for stable dividends and of the probability that a cut in dividends is likely to be interpreted as forecasting a decline in earnings, stable dividends make good sense.

Stock Dividends and Splits. Neither stock dividends nor stock splits alone exert a fundamental influence on prices. The fundamental determinant of the price of the company's stock is the company's earning power compared with the earning power of other companies. However, both stock splits and stock dividends can be used as an effective instrument of financial policy. They are useful devices for reducing the price at which stocks are traded, and studies indicate that stock dividends and stock splits tend to broaden the ownership of a firm's shares.

Stock Repurchases. Stock repurchases have been used as an alternative to cash dividends. Although repurchases have significant advantages over dividends, they also have disadvantages, in particular the fact that stock repurchases necessarily involve greater uncertainty than cash dividends. As with so much in finance, generalizations about stock repurchases are difficult—each firm has its own unique problems and conditions, and repurchase policy must be formulated within the context of the firm's characteristics and circumstances as a whole.

Questions

20–1. As an investor, would you rather invest in a firm with a policy of maintaining (a) a constant payout ratio, (b) a constant dollar dividend per share, or (c) a constant regular quarterly dividend plus a year-end extra when earnings are sufficiently high or corporate investment needs are sufficiently low? Explain your answer.

20–2. How would each of the following changes probably affect aggregate payout ratios? Explain your answer.
a. An increase in the personal income tax rate.
b. A liberalization in depreciation policies for federal income tax purposes.
c. A rise in interest rates.
d. An increase in corporate profits.
e. A decline in investment opportunities.

20–3. Discuss the pros and cons of having the directors formally announce what a firm's dividend policy will be in the future.

20–4. Most firms would like to have their stock selling at a high P/E ratio and also have an extensive public ownership (many different shareholders). Explain how stock dividends or stock splits may be compatible with these aims.

20–5. What is the difference between a stock dividend and a stock split? As a stockholder, would you prefer to see your company declare a 100 percent stock dividend or a two-for-one split?

20–6. In theory, if we had perfect capital markets, we would expect investors to be indifferent between cash dividends and an equivalent repurchase of stock outstanding. What factors might in practice cause investors to value one over the other?

20–7. "The cost of retained earnings is less than the cost of new outside equity capital. Consequently, it is totally irrational for a firm to sell a new issue of stock and to pay dividends during the same year." Discuss this statement.

20–8. Would it ever be rational for a firm to borrow money in order to pay dividends? Explain.

20–9. Union spokesmen have presented arguments similar to the following: "Corporations such as General Foods retain about one-half their profits for financing needs. If they financed by selling stock instead of by retained earnings, they could cut prices substantially and still earn enough to pay the same dividend to their shareholders. Therefore, their profits are too high." Evaluate this statement.

20–10. "Executive salaries have been shown to be more closely correlated to size of firm than to profitability. If a firm's board of directors is controlled by management instead of by outside directors, this might result in the firm's retaining more earnings than can be justified from the stockholders' point of view." Discuss the statement, being sure (a) to use Figure 20–5 in your answer and (b) to explain the implied relationship between dividend policy and stock prices.

Problems

20–1. The directors of Northwest Lumber Supply have been comparing the growth of their market price with the growth of one of their competitors, Parker Panels, Inc. Their findings are summarized below.

Northwest Lumber Supply

Year	Earnings	Dividend	Payout	Price	P/E
1978	$4.30	$2.58	60%	$68	15.8
1977	3.85	2.31	60	60	15.6
1976	3.29	1.97	60	50	15.2
1975	3.09	1.85	60	42	13.6
1974	3.05	1.83	60	38	12.5
1973	2.64	1.58	60	31	11.7
1972	1.98	1.19	60	26	13.1
1971	2.93	1.76	60	31	10.6
1970	3.48	2.09	60	35	10.1
1969	2.95	1.77	60	30	10.2

Parker Panels, Inc.

Year	Earnings	Dividend	Payout	Price	P/E
1978	$3.24	$1.94	60%	$70	21.6
1977	2.75	1.79	65	56	20.4
1976	2.94	1.79	61	53	18.0
1975	2.93	1.73	59	48	16.4
1974	2.90	1.65	57	44	15.2
1973	2.86	1.57	55	41	14.3
1972	2.61	1.49	57	35	13.4
1971	1.55	1.50	97	20	12.9
1970	2.24	1.50	67	34	15.2
1969	2.19	1.49	68	30	13.7

Both companies are in the same markets, and both are similarly organized (approximately the same degrees of operating and financial leverage). Northwest has been consistently earning more per share yet, for some reason, has not been valued at as high a P/E ratio as Parker. What factors would you point out as possible causes for this lower market valuation of Northwest's stock?

20-2. New Life Tobacco Company has for many years enjoyed a moderate but stable growth in sales and earnings. However, cigarette consumption and, consequently, New Life sales have been falling off recently, partly because of a national awareness of the dangers of smoking to health. Anticipating futher declines in tobacco sales for the future, New Life management hopes eventually to move almost entirely out of the tobacco business and, instead, develop a new diversified product line in growth-oriented industries.

New Life has been especially interested in the prospects for pollution-control devices—its research department having already done much work on problems of filtering smoke. Right now, the company estimates that an investment of $24 million is necessary to purchase new facilities and begin operations on these products, but the investment could return about 18 percent within a short time. Other investment opportunities total $9.6 million and are expected to return about 12 percent.

The company has been paying a $2.40 dividend on its 6,000,000 shares outstanding. The announced dividend policy has been to maintain a stable dollar dividend, raising it only when it appears that earnings have reached a new, permanently higher level. The directors might, however, change this policy if reasons for doing so are compelling. Total earnings for the year are $22.8 million, common stock is currently selling for $45, and the firm's current leverage ratio (B/A) is 45 percent. Current costs of various forms of financing are:

New bonds	7%
New common stock sold at $45 to yield the firm	$41
Investors required rate of return on equity	9%
Tax rate	50%

a. Calculate the marginal cost of capital above and below the point of exhaustion of retained earnings for New Life.
b. How large should New Life's capital budget be for the year?
c. What is an appropriate dividend policy for New Life? How should the capital budget be financed?
d. How might risk factors influence New Life's cost of capital, capital structure, and dividend policy?
e. What assumptions, if any, do your answers to the above make about investors' preference for dividends versus capital gain—that is, investors preference regarding different d/p and g components of k?

20-3. General Industries, Inc., has earnings this year of $16.5 million, 50 percent of which is required to take advantage of excellent investment opportunities of the firm. The firm has 206,250 shares outstanding, selling currently at $320 a share. Bruce Newton, a major stockholder (18,750 shares), has expressed displeasure with a great deal of managerial policy.

Management has approached him with the prospect of selling his holdings back to the firm, and he has expressed a willingness to do this at a price of $320 a share. Assuming that the market uses a constant P/E ratio of 4 in valuing the stock, answer the following questions:

a. Should the firm buy Newton's shares? Assume that dividends will not be paid on Newton's shares if repurchased.

b. How large a cash dividend should be declared?

c. What is the final value of General Industries' stock after all cash payments to shareholders?

20–4. Listed below are pertinent financial data for the common stocks of International Metals Corporation, Precision Systems, and Amalgamated Fuel & Gas. International Metals is a leading producer of copper, zinc, and lead, whose product demand is quite cyclical. Precision Systems is a computer manufacturer. Amalgamated Fuel & Gas is an integrated gas system serving the northeastern United States.

What differences are revealed by the data on the dividend policies of the three firms? What explanations can be given for these differences? What is the relationship of dividend policy to the market price of the stock?

International Metals Corporation

Year	Earnings	Dividends	Price Range	Payout	P/E Ratio
1978	$4.59	$1.15	46–19	25%	10–4
1977	2.25	0.72	21–12	32	9–5
1976	0.99	0.69	21–11	70	18–10
1975	0.87	0.66	27–18	76	25–17
1974	2.01	0.58	24–15	29	11–7
1973	1.73	0.54	27–19	31	14–9
1972	0.95	0.46	25–13	48	20–10
1971	1.11	0.79	29–12	71	22–9
1970	2.19	0.74	37–26	34	12–8
1969	2.78	0.64	28–16	23	7–4

Precision Systems

Year	Earnings	Dividends	Price Range	Payout	P/E Ratio
1978	$1.16	$0.06	46–32	5%	40–28
1977	0.71	0.05	53–30	7	88–32
1976	0.63	0.05	55–20	8	115–85
1975	0.52	0.05	60–44	10	116–72
1974	0.56	0.05	65–41	9	68–35
1973	0.69	0.05	47–24	7	59–23
1972	0.47	0.05	27–11	11	37–18
1971	0.36	0.04	13–6	11	30–13
1970	0.22	0.03	7–3	14	21–11
1969	0.13	0.02	3–2	15	23–15

**Amalgamated
Fuel & Gas**

Year	Earnings	Dividends	Price Range	Payout	P/E Ratio*
1978	$2.17	$1.37	34–31	63%	16–14
1977	2.29	1.31	37–29	57	16–13
1976	2.15	1.23	31–23	57	14–11
1975	1.84	1.20	33–24	65	18–13
1974	1.86	1.19	24–22	64	13–12
1973	1.74	1.15	25–21	66	14–12
1972	1.78	1.10	24–17	62	13–10
1971	1.30	1.10	20–16	85	15–13
1970	1.58	1.03	22–19	65	14–12
1969	1.57	1.00	23–20	64	15–12

*Price/earnings ratios are the high and the low for the year according to Standard & Poor's Reports.

20–5. Listed below are pertinent financial data for the common stocks of United States Steel Corporation and Kellogg Company. U.S. Steel is the largest domestic steelmaker, accounting for 23.4 percent of the industry's steel products. Kellogg is the worlds' largest manufacturer of ready-to-eat breakfast cereals and accounts for about 42 percent of the total domestic output.

What differences are revealed by the data on the dividend policies of the two firms? What explanations can be given for these differences? What is the relationship of dividend policy to the market price of the stock? What information content and legal listing differences are present?

**United States Steel
Corporation**

Year	Earnings	Dividends	Price Range	Payout	P/E Ratio
1975	$10.33	$2.80	71–38	27%	5.1
1974	11.72	2.20	48–35	19	5.3
1973	6.01	1.60	38–27	27	4.9
1972	2.90	1.60	35–27	55	5.2
1971	2.85	2.00	36–25	70	6.6
1970	2.72	2.40	39–28	88	7.1
1969	4.01	2.40	49–33	60	5.9
1968	4.69	2.40	45–38	51	5.7
1967	3.19	2.40	50–38	75	5.4
1966	4.60	2.00	56–35	43	4.4

Kellogg Company

Year	Earnings	Dividends	Price Range	Payout	P/E Ratio
1975	$1.40	$0.73	11–8	52	13.3
1974	0.98	0.59	11–9	60	14.5
1973	0.89	0.55	12–9	62	17.2
1972	0.83	0.52	11–9	63	16.9
1971	0.76	0.50	12–9	66	16.7
1970	0.68	0.45	14–11	66	15.8
1969	0.62	0.40	17–11	65	16.8
1968	0.59	0.38	18–13	64	18.0
1967	0.57	0.33	18–10	58	17.7
1966	0.53	0.30	23–14	57	17.6

Source: *Moody's Handbook of Common Stocks*, Spring 1976.

Selected References

Austin, Douglas V. "Treasury Stock Reacquisition by American Corporations: 1961–67." *Financial Executive* 37 (May 1969): 41–49.

Barker, C. A. "Effective Stock Splits." *Harvard Business Review* 34 (Jan.–Feb. 1956):101–6.

———. "Stock Splits in a Bull Market." *Harvard Business Review* 35 (May–June 1957): 72–79.

———. "Evaluation of Stock Dividends." *Harvard Business Review* 36 (July–Aug. 1958):99–114.

———. "Price Effects of Stock Dividend Shares, at Ex-Dividend Dates." *Journal of Finance* 14(Sept. 1959):373–78.

Baumol, William J. "On Dividend Policy and Market Imperfection." *Journal of Business* 36 (Jan. 1963):112–15.

Ben-Zion, Uri, and Shalit, Sol S. "Size, Leverage, and Dividend Record as Determinants of Equity Risk." *Journal of Finance* 30 (June 1975):1015–26.

Bierman, Harold, Jr., and West, Richard. "The Acquisition of Common Stock by the Corporate Issuer." *Journal of Finance* 21 (Dec. 1966):687–96.

Black, F., and Scholes, M. "The Effects of Dividend Yield and Dividend Policy on Common Stock Prices and Returns." *Journal of Financial Economics* 1 (May 1974):1–22.

Brennan, Michael. "A Note on Dividend Irrelevance and the Gordon Valuation Model." *Journal of Finance* 26 (Dec. 1971):1115–23.

Brigham, Eugene. "The Profitability of a Firm's Repurchase of Its Own Common Stock." *California Management Review* 7 (Winter 1964):69–75.

Brigham, Eugene, and Gordon, Myron J. "Leverage, Dividend Policy, and the Cost of Capital." *Journal of Finance* 23 (Mar. 1968):85–104.

———. "A Reply to Leverage, Dividend Policy and the Cost of Capital: A Comment." *Journal of Finance* 25 (Sept. 1970):904–8.

Brittain, John A. *Corporate Dividend Policy*. Washington, D.C.: The Brookings Institution, 1966.

Davenport, Michael. "Leverage, Dividend Policy and the Cost of Capital: A Comment." *Journal of Finance* 25 (Sept. 1970):893–97.

Dobrovolsky, S. P. "Economics of Corporate Internal and External Financing." *Journal of Finance* 13 (Mar. 1958):35–47.

Ellert, James C. "Mergers, Antitrust Law Enforcement and Stockholder Returns." *Journal of Finance* 31 (May 1976):715–32.

Ellis, Charles D. "New Framework for Analyzing Capital Structure." *Financial Executive* 37 (Apr. 1969):75–86.

––––––. "Repurchase Stock to Revitalize Equity." *Harvard Business Review* 43 (July–Aug. 1965):119–28.

Elton, Edwin J., and Gruber, Martin J. "Marginal Stockholder Tax Rates and the Clientele Effect." *Review of Economics and Statistics* 52 (Feb. 1970):68–74.

––––––. "The Cost of Retained Earnings–Implications of Share Repurchase." *Industrial Management Review* 9 (Spring 1968):87–104.

––––––. "The Effect of Share Repurchases on the Value of the Firm." *Journal of Finance* 23 (Mar. 1968):135–50.

Fama, E. F. "The Empirical Relationships Between the Dividend and Investment Decisions of Firms." *American Economic Review* 64 (June 1974):304–18.

Fama, E. F., and Babiak, Harvey. "Dividend Policy: An Empirical Analysis." *Journal of the American Statistical Association* 63 (Dec. 1968):1132–61.

Fama, E. F.; Fisher, Lawrence; Jensen, Michael; and Roll, Richard. "The Adjustment of Stock Prices to New Information." *International Economic Review* 10 (Feb. 1969): 1–21.

Friend, Irwin, and Puckett, Marshall. "Dividends and Stock Prices." *American Economic Review* 54 (Sept. 1964):656–82.

Gordon, Myron J. "Dividends, Earnings and Stock Prices." *Review of Economics and Statistics* 41 (May 1959):99–105.

––––––. *The Investment, Financing and Valuation of the Corporation.* Homewood, Ill.: Irwin, 1962.

––––––. "Optimal Investment and Financing Policy." *Journal of Finance* 18 (May 1963).

Guthart, Leo A. "Why Companies Are Buying Back Their Own Stock." *Financial Analysts' Journal* 23 (Apr.–May 1967):105–10.

––––––. "More Companies Are Buying Back Their Stock." *Harvard Business Review* 43 (Mar.–Apr. 1965):40–45.

Hausman, W. H.; West, R. R.; and Largay, J. A. "Stock Splits, Price Changes, and Trading Profits: A Synthesis." *Journal of Business* 44 (Jan. 1971):69–77.

Higgins, Robert C. "The Corporate Dividend-Saving Decision." *Journal of Financial and Quantitative Analysis* 7 (Mar. 1972):1527–41.

––––––. "Dividend Policy and Increasing Discount Rate: A Clarification." *Journal of Financial and Quantitative Analysis* 7(June 1972):1757–62.

––––––. "Growth, Dividend Policy and Capital Costs in the Electric Utility Industry." *Journal of Finance* 29 (Sept. 1974): 1189–1201.

Johnson, Keith B. "Stock Splits and Price Changes." *Journal of Finance* 21 (Dec. 1966):675–86.

Lee, Cheng F. "Functional Form and the Dividend Effect in the Electric Utility Industry," *Journal of Finance* 31 (Dec. 1976):1481–86.

Lerner, Eugene M., and Carleton, Williard T. *A Theory of Financial Analysis.* New York: Harcourt Brace Jovanovich, 1966.

Lintner, John. "Distribution of Incomes of Corporations Among Dividends,

Retained Earnings, and Taxes." *American Economic Review* 46 (May 1956): 97–113.

——. "Dividends, Earnings, Leverage, Stock Prices and the Supply of Capital to Corporations." *Review of Economics and Statistics* 44 (Aug. 1962):243–69.

——. "Dividend Policy and Market Valuations: A Reply." *Journal of Business* 36 (Jan. 1963):116–19.

——. "Optimal Dividends and Corporate Growth Under Uncertainty." *Quarterly Journal of Economics* 88 (Feb. 1964):49–95.

Mehta, Dileep R. "The Impact of Outstanding Convertible Bonds on Corporate Dividend Policy." *Journal of Finance* 31 (May 1976):489–506.

Mendelson, Morris. "Leverage, Dividend Policy and the Cost of Capital: A Comment." *Journal of Finance* 25 (Sept. 1970):898–903.

Millar, James A., and Fielitz, Bruce D. "Stock-Split and Stock-Dividend Decisions." *Financial Management* 2 (Winter 1973):35–45.

Miller, Merton H., and Modigliani, Franco. "Dividend Policy, Growth, and the Valuation of Shares." *Journal of Business* 34 (Oct. 1961):411–33.

——. "Dividend Policy and Market Valuation: A Reply." *Journal of Business* 36 (Jan. 1963):116–19.

——. "Some Estimates of the Cost of Capital to the Electric Utility Industry." *American Economic Review* 56 (June 1966):333–91.

Norgaard, Richard, and Norgaard, Corine. "A Critical Examination of Share Repurchase." *Financial Management* 3, no. 1 (Spring 1974):44–50.

Pettit, R. Richardson. "Dividend Announcements, Security Performance, and Capital Market Efficiency." *Journal of Finance* 27 (Dec. 1972):993–1007.

——. "The Impact of Dividend and Earnings Announcements: A Reconciliation." *Journal of Business* 49 (Jan. 1976):86–96.

Pettway, Richard H., and Malone, R. Phil. "Automatic Dividend Reinvestment Plans of Nonfinancial Corporations." *Financial Management* 2 (Winter 1973): 11–18.

Porterfield, James T. S. "Dividends, Dilution, and Delusion." *Harvard Business Review* 37 (Nov.–Dec. 1959):156–61.

Robichek, Alexander A., and Myers, Stewart C. *Optimal Financing Decisions.* Englewood Cliffs, N.J.: Prentice-Hall, 1965. Chap. 4.

Stapleton, Richard C. "Portfolio Analysis, Stock Valuation, and Capital Budgeting Decision Rules for Risky Projects." *Journal of Finance* 26 (Mar. 1971): 95–118.

Stevenson, Richard. "Corporate Stock Reacquisitions." *Accounting Review* 41 (Apr. 1966):312–17.

Stewart, Samuel S., Jr. "Should a Corporation Repurchase its Own Stock?" *Journal of Finance* 31 (June 1976):911–21.

Sussman, M. R. *The Stock Dividend.* Ann Arbor, Mich.: Bureau of Business Research, University of Michigan, 1962.

Walter, James E. "Dividend Policies and Common Stock Prices." *Journal of Finance* 11 (Mar. 1956):29–41.

——. *Dividend Policy and Enterprise Valuation.* Belmont, Calif.: Wadsworth Publishing Company, 1967.

——. "Dividend Policy: Its Influence on the Value of the Enterprise." *Journal of Finance* 18 (May 1963):280–91.

Watts, Ross. "The Information Content of Dividends." *Journal of Business* 46 (Apr. 1973):191–211.

West, Richard R., and Bierman, Harold, Jr. "Corporate Dividend Policy and Preemptive Security Issues." *Journal of Business* 42 (Jan. 1968):71–75.

West, Richard R. and Brouilette, Alan B. "Reverse Stock Splits." *Financial Executive* 38 (Jan. 1970):12–17.

Weston, C. R. "Adjustment to Future Dividend Rates in the Prediction of Ex-rights Prices." *Journal of Business Finance & Accounting* 1 (Autumn 1974): 335–42.

Whittington, G. "The Profitability of Retained Earnings." *Review of Economics and Statistics* 54 (May 1972):152–60.

Woods, Donald H., and Brigham, Eugene F. "Stockholder Distribution Decisions: Share Repurchase or Dividends." *Journal of Financial and Quantitative Analysis* 1 (Mar. 1966):15–28.

Wrightsman, Dwayne, and Horrigan, James O. "Retention, Risk of Success, and the Price of Stock." *Journal of Finance* 30 (Dec. 1975):1357–59.

Young, Allan. "Financial, Operating, and Security Market Parameters of Repurchasing." *Financial Analysts' Journal* 25 (July–Aug. 1969):123–28.

————. "The Effects of Share Distribution on Price Action." *Financial Review* Eastern Finance Association (1975).

Part VI

Integrated Topics in Financial Management

In the final five chapters we take up important but somewhat specialized topics, which draw on the concepts developed in earlier sections.

Chapter 21, "Timing of Financial Policy," introduces dynamics into the decision process, showing how financial managers react to changing conditions in the capital markets. Chapter 22 deals with the growth of firms through mergers and holding companies, and the reasoning behind this development. Throughout the text, we have dealt with growing and successful firms; however, many firms face financial difficulties, and the causes and possible remedies to these difficulties are discussed in Chapter 23. Next, in Chapter 24, we discuss some of the financial aspects of multinational corporations, a topic of increasing importance in today's economy. Finally, in Chapter 25, we apply many of the topics covered throughout the book to the specific situation faced by a small firm; small business finance is an important and practical subject, but we also use the chapter to summarize and integrate many of the principles set forth throughout the book.

Timing of Financial Policy

This chapter deals with the timing of financial policy. Although the topic has always been important, the new inflationary environment has caused timing to take on greater significance than ever before. Since the mid-1960s, the U.S. economy has experienced a series of "credit crunches," during which the costs of financing have risen substantially. Minimizing the need to raise capital during these crunches is important. Also, a key question facing financial managers is whether financing costs will return to lower levels in the reasonably near future, or whether the continued upward trends in recent years will continue. How this question is resolved will greatly influence the costs, amounts, and types of capital raised by business firms.

In an inflationary environment, changes in asset requirements are magnified by rising price levels; financial managers must consider this when planning their requirements. Also, when analyzing prospective returns from capital assets, the financial manager must realize that the prices of similar capital assets will increase substantially in future years because of inflation. Finally, it is exceedingly difficult to raise the requisite amount of funds in an inflationary environment, and, as a consequence, the problem of planning to meet future maturing obligations is crucial.

Significance to Financial Management

The significance of financial timing is suggested by the following quotation from *Business Week*:

Even a modest increase in monetary restraint will be hard for most companies to handle. Ever since the end of last year's credit drought, companies have worked hard to rebuild liquidity.

However, there's a "difference between actual and desired liquidity," says an economist for a major New York City Bank, "and companies haven't succeeded in loosening up balance sheets."

In contrasting money market conditions that lie ahead with 1966, economists stress the expected impact of inflation itself. During late 1966, the wholesale price index remained relatively stable. But if price increases get larger in coming months, interest rates are almost sure to climb.

"People who borrow under conditions of sharp inflation are willing to pay

*any amount for money," says Milton Friedman of the University of Chicago,
"and people who lend ask high rates to protect themselves from loss of purchasing power." If the Fed doesn't tighten, Friedman expects prices to rise by
at least 5 percent and possibly 7 percent during 1968 and predicts that interest rates will be in the 9 percent to 10 percent range.*[1]

Milton Friedman's forecast was subsequently borne out. But financial
managers have also had to face another problem—fluctuating rates.
This increased volatility is highlighted by a study of interest rate patterns in recent years. Interest rates have fluctuated very sharply over the
past decade, although the trend in yields has generally been upward. In
1969 and early 1970, when inflationary expectations were strong and
bank credit expansion was curtailed, market rates reached the highest
levels in U.S. history. Then during 1970 and early 1971, as economic activity slowed and monetary policy eased, interest rates dropped more
sharply than in most earlier periods of decline. In 1974, under the stimulus of "double-digit inflation," new records were set; major corporations and the U.S. government paid record amounts for long-term debt,
and the prime rate hit a new high of 12 percent late in that year. Interest
rates then turned down in the effort to reverse the economic decline
which began in the fourth quarter of 1974. On December 22, 1976, the
prime rate was reduced to 6 percent by the Chase Manhattan bank, but
most banks held their prime rate at 6 ¼ percent.

Financial managers are divided on the question of whether major
fluctuations in money costs will continue to occur in the future, and also
about whether interest rates will continue their upward trend. Experience suggests that both possibilities should be taken into account in financial planning. Accordingly, in this chapter we first analyze cyclical
patterns in the costs of financing and then review the nature of monetary and fiscal policies, focusing particular attention on the implications
of these policies for future patterns in the cost of external financing.

Historical Patterns in the Costs of Financing

Table 21–1 highlights changes in recent years, while Figure 21–1 presents the broad pattern of long- and short-term interest rates since the
turn of the century. One outstanding characteristic of interest rate behavior is the wide magnitude of the changes in the price of money over
the years. For example, the borrowing rate on four-to-six months' commercial paper, which is the best indication of the cost of short-term

1. "Is a Money Crunch on Its Way?" *Business Week* (29 September 1967), p. 36.

money to large corporations, reached a low of 0.53 percent in 1941. By 1953, this rate stood at 2.52 percent, but it declined to 1.58 percent during the business recession of the following year. In the early 1960s prime commercial paper rates rose to over 3 percent; during the credit stringency of the late 1960s, they rose to almost 9 percent. Between December 1969 and February 1972, commercial paper rates declined from 8.84 percent to a low of 3.93 percent. Rates fluctuated slightly between 4.5 percent and 5.2 percent for the remainder of 1972, but during 1973 and 1974, under inflationary pressures after price controls were lifted, rates rose again and hit new highs in the autumn of 1974. Efforts to stimulate the economy were associated with declining interest rates that appeared to bottom out in December 1976. Short-term rates fell to one-half or less of their 1974 highs.

Table 21–1

Selected Interest Rates* (Percent)

Category	Earlier Highs	1971 Lows	1974 Highs	1976 Lows
Short-term				
Treasury bills, 3 months	7.87 (January 1970)	3.38 (March)	9.4 (August)	4.3 (December)
Commercial paper, 4–6 months	8.84 (December 1969)	4.19 (March)	11.80 (August)	4.7 (December)
Long-term				
10-year U.S. government	6.91 (May 1970)	5.70 (March)	8.10 (October)	7.0 (December)
Corporate AAA new issues	9.12	7.00	10.10 (October)	8.0 (December)

*Monthly averages
Source: Federal Reserve bulletins and Federal Reserve chart books.

Yields on high-grade, long-term corporate bonds have fluctuated similarly, but not to the same degree. For example, the corporate AAA bond rate reached a low of 2.53 percent in 1946. It rose to over 3 percent in 1953 and, after declining to 2.90 percent during the business downturn of 1954, it climbed to 4.41 percent by 1960. During August 1966, yields on AAA corporates rose above 5½ percent, and the rise continued to over 9 percent in 1970. A cyclical low of 7 percent was reached in February 1971, but subsequently the long-term rates rose and eclipsed the earlier high. The subsequent decline in long-term rates was about 1.5 to 2.0 percentage points.

The cost of equity capital is more difficult to measure than debt, and time series data on equity costs are not available. However, as the cost

Figure 21–1
Long- and Short-term
Interest Rates

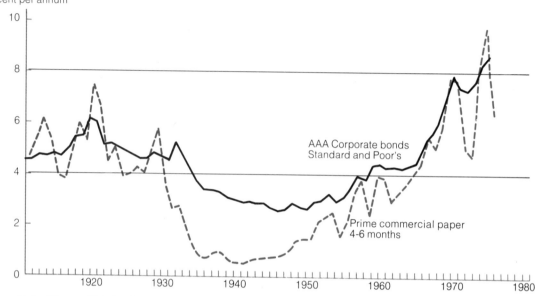

Percent per annum

AAA Corporate bonds
Standard and Poor's

Prime commercial paper
4-6 months

Sources: Federal Reserve Historical Chart Book, Financial and Business Statistics, 1976

of equity is dependent upon the cost of debt ($k_s = k_f +$ risk premium), fluctuations in the cost of debt are indicators of corresponding fluctuations in the cost of equity.

This brief review of fluctuations in short- and long-term interest rates is sufficient to demonstrate that the cost of capital is one of the most volatile inputs purchased by firms. Within relatively short time periods, money costs have fluctuated by over 100 percent.

Interest Rates as an Index of Availability of Funds

While the cost variations associated with interest rate fluctuations are substantial, the greatest significance of interest rates is their role as an index of the availability of funds. A period of high interest rates reflects tight money, which is in turn associated with tight reserve positions at commercial banks. At such times interest rates rise, but there are conventional limits on interest rates. Consequently, a larger quantity of funds is demanded by borrowers than banks are able to make available. Banks therefore begin to ration funds among prospective borrowers by continuing lines of credit to traditional customers but restricting loans to new borrowers.

Small firms characteristically have greater difficulty obtaining financing during periods of tight money, and even among large borrowers, the bargaining position of financial institutions is stronger. It is a lender's rather than a borrower's market. Consequently, the conditions in all loan agreements are more restrictive when the demand for funds is high.

Interest rates are therefore of very great significance to financial managers as an index of the availability of funds. For small- and medium-sized firms, a period of rising interest rates may indicate increasing difficulty in obtaining any financing at all. Or, if financing is obtained, it will be at a higher cost and under less favorable conditions.

A period of tight money will have a particularly strong impact on the utilities and other heavy industries, state and local governments, and the housing and construction sectors. The heavy, long-term investments in these areas cause the impact of interest rates on profitability to be especially significant. Thus, during the credit crunch of 1974, the sectors listed above saw funds become virtually unavailable. Utility companies were forced to reduce planned expansions, state and local financing has become onerous, and the housing and construction sectors declined substantially. The tightness of monetary conditions in the late autumn of 1977 again affected these same sectors.

Costs of Different Kinds of Financing Over Time

The preceding section showed that interest rates vary widely over time. In addition, the relative costs of debt, preferred stock, and equity fluctuate. Data on these relative costs are presented in Figure 21–2, which shows that earnings/price ratios have fluctuated from 16 percent to 1 percent.[2] During the 1960s, E/P ratios averaged about 6 percent, ranging from 4.7 to 6.7 percent. However, the rising costs of capital associated with inflation in the 1970s drove stock prices down and E/P ratios up to over 14 percent by 1974. Yields on bonds have fluctuated to a much lesser extent. Furthermore, since bonds and preferred stocks both

---

2. An earnings/price ratio, the reciprocal of a *P/E* ratio, does not measure exactly the cost of equity capital, but it does indicate *trends* in this cost. In other words, when earnings/price ratios are high, the cost of equity capital tends to be high, and vice versa.

Figure 21–2
Long-term Security
Yields

Percent per annum

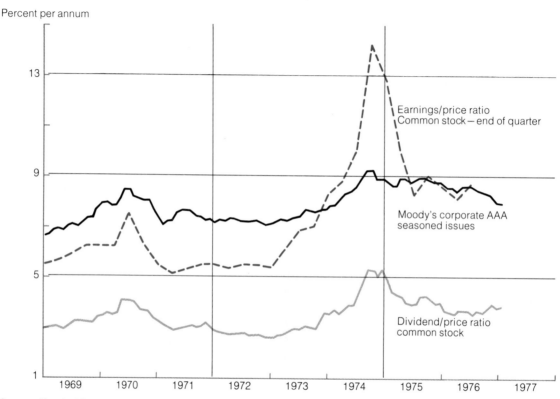

Sources: Historical Supplement to Federal Reserve Chart Book on Financial and Business Statistics, 1976; Board of Governors of the Federal Reserve System.

provide a stable, fixed income to investors, they are close substitutes for each other, and their yields parallel each other closely.[3]

The pronounced decline in earnings/price ratios that began in the early 1950s resulted largely from investors' increasing awareness of the growth potential in common stock earnings, dividends, and stock prices. The economy was strong during this period, and security ana-

3. We have not shown preferred stock yields in Figure 21–2 since they have been so close to the AAA corporate bond yields, lower by five to 50 basis points during the period covered by the figure. Historically, bond yields have tended to lie below those on preferred stocks. This relationship resulted from the fact that bonds have priority over preferred stocks and, hence, are less risky. However, preferred

lysts and investors became aware of the importance of the g component in the expected rate of return equation $k_s = d/p + g$. A recognition of the dangers of inflation and of its effect on fixed income securities was driving bond and preferred stock yields up, further closing the gap between interest rates and earnings/price ratios.

Relation Between Long-term and Short-term Interest Rates

One of the important elements in the financial manager's timing decisions is an understanding of the relationship between long-term and short-term interest rates.[4] Long-term interest rates are rates on securities with maturities in excess of ten years. Short-term interest rates are those on securities with maturities of under one year.

Figure 21–3 is an enlarged version of Figure 21–1; it shows the relationship between long- and short-term interest rates from 1962 to 1974. In some periods, short-term interest rates were higher than long-term interest rates; this was true in 1966 and again in 1969, 1973, and 1974, when the money market was extremely tight. Under certain conditions there is greater risk to holding long-term securities than short-term securities. The longer the maturity of the security, the greater the danger that the issuer may not make an effective adaptation to its environment and therefore may not be able to meet its obligations in 10, 15, or 20 years. Furthermore, the *prices* of long-term bonds are much more volatile than those of short-term bonds when interest rates change; the reason for this is largely arithmetic and was described in Chapter 17.

The *expectations theory* states that long-term interest rates may in general be regarded as an average of expected future short-term interest rates. Thus the relation between long and short rates will depend on what is expected to happen in the future to short-term interest rates, as illustrated in Table 21–2.

In section A it is assumed that short-term interest rates will rise 1 percent each year, beginning at 2 percent in year one. The corresponding long-term interest rate in year one for a five-year period is approximate-

---

stock dividends are largely tax exempt to corporate owners, so after-tax yields (to corporations) are considerably higher than those on bonds. Recall that 85 percent of the dividends received by a corporate stockholder are tax exempt to the receiver, whereas interest income is fully taxable to the recipient. During the 1960s, certain corporations (insurance companies, savings and loans, mutual savings banks) which had previously paid very low taxes became subject to higher taxes; these firms bought preferred stocks, pushing preferred stock before-tax yields below those of bonds in the late 1960s and early 1970s.

4. The relationship between long-term and short-term interest rates—generally referred to as the "term structure of interest rates"—is developed in detail in the Appendix to Chapter 6.

Figure 21–3
Long-term and Short-
term Interest Rates

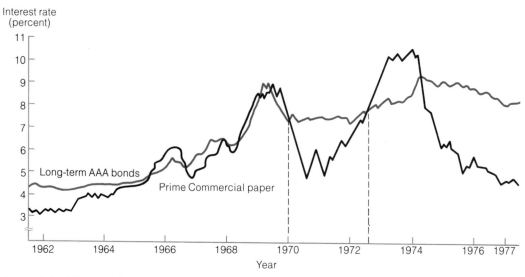

Source: *Federal Reserve Bulletin*, various issues.

ly 4 percent; that is, the average of the five short-term rates. Thus, in year one, the long-term rate is double the short-term rate.

Consider, however, the situation under section B—in a tight-money situation in year one, short-term rates are 6 percent, but they are expected to decline by 1 percent each year. The average of these rates is the same as in section A, because the numbers are identical—their order is simply reversed. Now, however, the long-term rate of 4 percent lies below the initial short-term rate of 6 percent.

These examples do not prove the relation between short- and long-term rates. They do, however, illustrate the pattern that would exist if

Table 21–2
**Relation between
Short-Term and
Long-Term Interest
Rates**

Year	A 5-Year Note	A Short-Term Rates	B 5-Year Note	B Short-Term Rates
1	4	2	4	6
2		3		5
3		4		4
4		5		3
5		6		2

the only factor operating was expected changes in interest rate movements, which themselves reflect a broad group of supply and demand factors. However, many other factors operate in the market. Some of these include differences in the risks of loss and failure among individual business firms, in the economic outlook for different industries, in the degree to which price-level changes affect different products and industries, and in the impact that changes in government legislation will have on different firms in an industry.

Characteristic Patterns in Cost of Money

In Figure 21–4, we depict in a general way the pattern between GNP and interest rates. Short-term interest rates show the widest amplitude of swings. Since the long-term interest rates are *averages* of short-term rates, they are not as volatile as short-term rates — short-term rates move more quickly and fluctuate more than long-term rates. The cost of debt money tends to coincide with movements in general business conditions, both at the peak and at the trough. Thus, as we see in Table 21–3, the economy slowed significantly in 1967 and 1971, and interest rates declined during those periods, while the booming economy in 1965–66 precipitated an increase in rates; in all three periods short rates changed more than long rates.

The cost of equity funds may best be approximated by expected equity yields — dividends plus capital gains. To understand the behavior of equity yields, one must analyze the behavior of earnings, dividends,

Figure 21–4
Relation Between
Movements of Gross
National Product and
Interest Rates

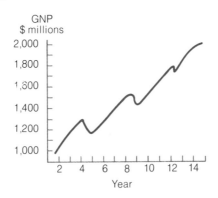

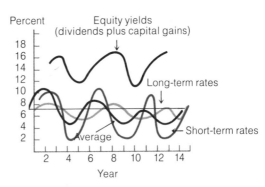

Table 21–3
Brief Summary of Supply and Demand
in U.S. Credit Markets
(Annual net increases in amounts outstanding, $ billions)

	1971	1972	1973	1974	1975	1976e	1977p
Realized net demands:							
Privately held mortgages	44.3	68.8	68.7	42.8	38.5	61.3	69.5
Corporate and foreign bonds	25.6	19.9	14.5	29.7	39.0	36.9	34.5
Business loans and open market paper	7.6	26.4	46.7	50.9	−15.8	4.5	21.0
Consumer and other loans	17.0	26.6	27.1	12.2	9.7	26.0	33.0
Privately held treasury and agency debt	21.7	24.2	19.2	28.1	83.5	74.9	68.0
State and local debt	21.7	12.8	14.1	14.5	15.7	13.7	17.0
Total demand for credit	137.9	178.7	190.3	178.2	170.6	217.3	243.0
Invested net supply:							
Thrift institutions	41.2	48.8	36.3	28.1	57.5	69.8	72.9
Insurance and pension funds	12.8	15.0	18.9	28.7	35.5	38.3	39.7
Investment companies	0.5	1.6	1.6	1.9	3.4	3.5	4.6
Other investing institutions	12.1	14.2	19.1	5.5	0.6	8.7	14.1
Commercial banks	50.9	73.3	77.6	59.8	31.0	44.5	58.0
Various other (primarily money market) investors*	25.3	15.5	8.8	20.1	17.6	28.0	31.5
Residual: Households direct	−4.9	10.3	28.0	34.1	25.0	24.5	22.2
Total supply of credit	137.9	178.7	190.3	178.2	170.6	217.3	243.0

e = estimated
p = preliminary
*Consists of business corporations, state and local governments, and foreign investors.
Source: Henry Kaufman, James McKeon, and Jeffrey Cohn *Prospects for the Credit Markets in 1977*
(New York: Salomon Brothers, 1977), p. 5.

and stock prices. Corporate earnings are highly volatile – they lead the business cycle both on the upturn and on the downturn, and dividends follow earnings. Prices of common stocks anticipate changes in corporate earnings. Prices of equities are also influenced by money market conditions. Owing to the gradual tightening in money market conditions as expansion continues, bond yields rise and attract money out of stocks and into bonds, causing the prices of equities to turn down before corporate profits reach their peak. Hence, the cost of equity financing turns up because firms receive lower prices for the stocks they sell.[5]

5. Recall that in Chapter 17 we showed that, at least conceptually, stock prices may be determined by the equation

$$p = \frac{d}{k_s - g}$$

where p = the price of a share of stock, d = the dividend on the stock, k_s = the required rate of return on the stock (or the cost of equity capital), and g = the expected growth rate. Since stocks and bonds compete with each other for investors' funds, if monetary policy drives interest rates up, k_s will likewise rise and p must decline.

In other words, the cost of equity capital begins to rise in the later stages of the business cycle.

The relationships between the costs of financing over time illustrated in Figure 21–4 represent generalizations that provide a frame of reference for the financial manager; the patterns are not intended as precise guidelines. A basic requirement for sound financial management is the ability to make judgments about future economic and financial conditions that will affect financial timing and the forms and sources of financing that are used. The next section seeks to provide a foundation for evaluating trends in financial markets.

Money and Capital Market Behavior
Federal Reserve Policy

Fundamental to an understanding of the behavior of the money and capital markets is an analysis of the role of the central bank, which in the United States is the Federal Reserve System. The Fed, as it is called, has a set of instruments with which to influence the operations of commercial banks, whose loan and investment activities in turn have an important influence on the cost and availability of money. The most powerful of the Fed's instruments, hence the one used most sparingly, is changing *reserve requirements* (the percentage of deposits that must be kept on reserve with the Fed). The one most often used is changing the pattern of *open-market operations* (the Fed's buying and selling of securities, which expands and contracts the amount of funds in the public's hands).

Changes in the *discount rate* (the interest rate charged to commercial banks when they borrow from Federal Reserve Banks) are likely to have more of a psychological influence than direct quantitative effects. These changes represent an implicit announcement by Federal Reserve authorities that a change in economic conditions has occurred and that these new conditions call for a tightening or easing of monetary conditions. The data demonstrate that increases in the Federal Reserve bank discount rate have been followed by rising interest rate levels, and conversely.

When the Federal Reserve System purchases or sells securities in the open market, makes changes in the discount rate, or varies reserve requirements, such actions change interest rates on most securities.

Fiscal Policy

The fiscal policy of the federal government has a great impact on movements in interest rates. A cash budget deficit represents a stimulating influence by the federal government, and a cash surplus exerts a restraining influence from the government-spending sector of the economy. However, this generalization must be modified to reflect the way a deficit is financed and the way a surplus is used. To have the most stimulating effect, the deficit should be financed by sale of securities through the banking system, particularly the central bank—this provides a maximum amount of bank reserves and permits a multiple expansion in the money supply. To have the most restrictive effect, the surplus should be used to retire bonds held by the banking system, particularly the central bank, thus reducing bank reserves and causing a multiple contraction in the supply of money.

The impact of Treasury financing programs varies. Ordinarily, when the Treasury needs to draw funds from the money market, it competes with other potential users of funds; the result may be a rise in interest rate levels. However, the desire to hold down interest rates also influences Treasury and Federal Reserve policy. To ensure the success of a large new offering, Federal Reserve authorities may temporarily ease money conditions, an action that will tend to soften interest rates. If the Treasury encounters resistance in selling securities in the nonbanking sector, they may be sold in large volume to the commercial banking system, which expands its reserves and thereby increases the monetary base. This change in turn tends to lower the level of interest rates.

Interest Rate Forecasts

Within this framework of general economic and financial patterns, short-term interest rate patterns and forecasts may be analyzed through the use of flow of funds accounts. The flow of funds accounts are summarized in Table 21–4 to depict the behavior of the major categories of suppliers and demanders of funds. By projecting the sources and uses of funds in different categories, we can estimate the direction of the pressure on interest rates.[6]

The table can be used in the following way: Historical patterns can be established to show uses and sources of funds in relation to the growth of the economy as a whole as measured by GNP. When in any particular year the demand for funds grows faster than the supply in relation to historical patterns, interest rates are likely to rise. These extra funds are supplied by drawing on the commercial banking system, which is the pivot in the financial mechanism. Whenever the demand for funds must be met by drawing on the commercial banking system to a greater-than-normal degree, interest rates rise.

Another significant statistic in the table is the rise in the supply of

---

6. Compilations of studies of this kind are facilitated by the flow of funds data developed by the Federal Reserve System and published monthly in the *Federal Reserve Bulletin*.

Table 21–4
Selected Components of Sources and Uses of Corporate Funds, 1963–77

	1963	1968	1971	1972	1973	1974	1975	1976e	1977p
	Percentages of Annual Net Increases in Sources or Uses								
Uses									
Total physical investment	81	97	83	79	87	93	81	88	88
Net trade and consumer credit	6	4	2	6	4	4	2	4	5
Other	13	(1)	15	15	9	3	17	8	7
Total uses	100%	100%	100%	100%	100%	100%	100%	100%	100%
Sources									
Retained earnings	22	8	11	12	10	1	12	21	20
Depreciation	53	52	49	46	44	47	60	52	51
Internal cash generation	75	60	60	58	54	48	72	73	71
Bank loans	6	12	3	9	18	19	(12)	(2)	5
Mortgage debt	*	5	10	13	12	9	7	5	4
Other	*	8	1	3	4	7	4	3	3
Net new bond issues	7	12	17	9	7	14	22	14	10
Net new stock issues	†	3	10	8	5	3	7	7	7
Total external sources	21	40	40	42	46	52	28	27	29
Total sources	100%	100%	100%	100%	100%	100%	100%	100%	100%

e = estimated
p = preliminary
*not available
†less than 1 percent
Source: Based on materials in Henry Kaufman, James McKeon, and Jeffrey Cohn, *Supply and Demand
for Credit in 1977* (New York: Salomon Brothers, 1977), p. 5.

funds from "Residual: households direct"; funds from this source increased greatly between 1973 and 1974. Because of restrictive Federal Reserve policies, the ability of the commercial banks and other financial institutions to supply funds was held back in relation to demand. This produced high interest rates (see Figure 21–1), and these high rates induced individuals, businesses, and others to make their surplus funds available to borrowers. Thus, the supply of funds was augmented from nonbanking sources, but only at substantially higher interest rates.

Most longer term predictions for the financial market call for continued high interest rates with only moderate declines of short duration from time to time. The causes are diverse, but a major factor reflects efforts of governments throughout the world to achieve full employment and high growth rates. A worldwide capital shortage has resulted.

The outlook for continued price level increases and high interest rates has had a number of effects on corporate financial policy. Table 21–4 presents the sources and uses of corporate funds for the period 1963–1977, expressed as a percentage of the annual net increases. Dramatic fluctuations have taken place in the role of internal financing. Total internal cash generation declined from 79 percent of total sources in 1963 to 48 percent in 1974. By 1977 internal cash generation again accounted for 71 percent of total sources.

Another significant change has been an increase in the use of external long-term financing from stocks and bonds. New common stock financing rose from negligible amounts in 1963 to 10 percent in 1971 and has been stable at about 7 percent during 1975, 1976, and 1977. The use of common stock financing to strengthen the equity position of firms was even greater in certain industries and for some individual firms. Long-term bond financing likewise grew from 7 percent in 1963 to 22 percent by 1975. It has remained relatively high—at something over 10 percent—for both 1976 and 1977.

These relations are further emphasized in Table 21–5. Part I of the table presents data on gross proceeds (total funds raised before using part of the cash proceeds to retire obligations previously outstanding). Part II presents data on net proceeds after refundings and other adjustments. Part III analyzes some patterns in convertible debt financing. These data indicate, as one would expect, a changing pattern of financing as interest rates rose during the 1960s and 1970s.

1. Stock financing as a percentage of long-term external financing almost quadrupled on a gross basis and rose from a negative 4 percent to a plus 40 percent on a net basis.
2. Bond financing on a gross basis dropped from over 90 percent to under 70 percent of the total.
3. Between 1963 and 1968 private placement of debt dropped from over one-half of total long-term debt financing to as low as 24 percent on a gross basis and to as low as 15 percent on a net basis. The declines in the private placement of debt reflect the periodic impact of tight money on the financing demands placed on insurance companies, a major source of direct placement of financing. As the table shows, the private placement of debt has increased somewhat after the mid-1970s.
4. With the onset of inflation in 1966 the role of convertible debt increased substantially, representing 17 percent of gross financing in 1968. In subsequent years, however, the use of convertibles moderated. The reduced attractiveness of convertibles may reflect the relatively weak stock market after 1967.
5. Convertible debt issued in mergers rose from less than 2 percent before 1967 to over 10 percent in 1968, but in the 1970s declined to 1 percent or less.
6. The percentage of convertible debt reduced by conversion into stock

Table 21-5
Long-Term Corporate Capital by Type, 1963-77

I. Gross Proceeds of Bond and Stock Financing (percentages)

	1963	1968	1972	1973	1974	1975	1976	1977
Straight debt, public	42	42	57	54	73	73	63	60
Straight debt, private	53	29	35	42	23	24	34	35
Convertible debt for cash	3	17	8	3	2	3	3	4
Convertible debt in mergers	2	12	*	1	2	*	*	1
Total bonds	100%	100%	100%	100%	100%	100%	100%	100%
Total bonds	91	79	68	67	84	80	73	69
Total stocks	9	21	32	33	16	20	27	31
Total bonds and stocks	100%	100%	100%	100%	100%	100%	100%	100%

II. Net Proceeds of Bond and Stock Financing (percentages)

	1963	1968	1972	1973	1974	1975	1976	1977
Straight debt, public	41	48	70	79	84	83	74	71
Straight debt, private	55	19	28	27	15	16	26	27
Convertible debt	4	33	2	(6)	1	1	*	2
Total bonds	100%	100%	100%	100%	100%	100%	100%	100%
Total bonds	104	107	60	60	86	76	68	60
Total stocks	(4)	(7)	40	40	14	24	32	40
Total bonds and stocks	100%	100%	100%	100%	100%	100%	100%	100%

III. Analysis of Convertible Bond Offerings
(Annual Net Increases in Amounts Outstanding in Billions of Dollars)

	1963	1968	1972	1973	1974	1975	1976	1977
Total convertibles	0.5	5.6	2.3	0.9	1.1	1.5	1.2	1.8
Less convertibles called, retired or converted	2.0	1.7	.7	1.2	1.2	1.4	.3	1.0
Called, retired, or converted as a percentage of total	60	18	87	188	64	80	100	78
Yearly net convertible debt	0.2	4.6	0.3	(.8)	0.4	0.3	*	0.4
Cumulative outstanding†	0.2	11.5	20.1	19.3	19.7	20.0	20.0	20.4

*Less than 1 percent
†Cumulative 1963 through 1977.
Source: Based on material in Henry Kaufman, James McKeon, and Jeffrey Cohn, *Supply and Demand for Credit in 1977* (New York: Salomon Brothers, 1977), tables 3A and 3C.

was relatively high in 1963, but it declined substantially in 1968 and thereafter again increased significantly.

7. The cumulative total of net convertible debt outstanding rose from $11.5 billion in 1968 to $20.4 billion by 1977. It is clear that the increased uncertainties about the rate of inflation and the increased difficulties of forecasting interest rate patterns during this period

have led to the greater use of hybrid forms of financing—debt with equity participation such as convertibles or warrants. The percentage of direct loans with such equity sweeteners, or interest adjustment provisions, is reported to be even higher than was true in the public flotations on which data are available.

8. The credit stringency that reached a climax in May 1970 with the Penn Central bankruptcy led to a massive effort to restructure corporate balance sheets. Long-term financing accounted for about 84 percent of total external financing in 1970, versus an average of 62 percent for the five years prior to 1969.[7] The use of net short-term external financing sources, including bank loans and commercial paper,

Figure 21–5
Business Loans in the First 24 Months of Recoveries (All Commercial Banks, Seasonally Adjusted, Trough Equals 100)

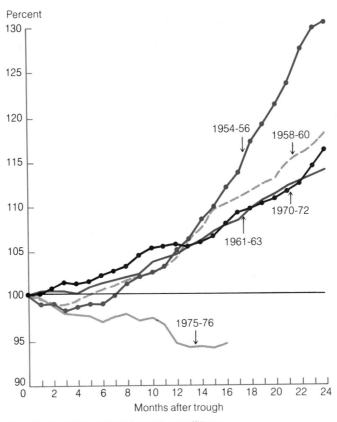

Note: Business loans include loan sales to affiliates.
Source: Board of Governors of the Federal Reserve System.

actually declined by $500 million during the first quarter of 1971. Thus short-term debt was repaid as longer term debt and equity were used to improve corporate liquidity.

Of particular interest is the unusual behavior of business loans made by commercial banks during the recovery of 1975–76. The historical pattern is presented in Figure 21–5.[8]

During the first 16 months of the previous four business recoveries, commercial bank business loans had expanded to approximately 110 percent of their level at the low turning point of business activity. In 1975–76, however, commercial bank business loans had actually declined to some 95 percent of the earlier level.

The explanation for this atypical behavior is found in a number of basic economic and financial factors. One set of factors is shown in Table 21–6:

In contrast with the previous four recoveries, investment by firms in inventories and fixed assets has lagged. In the 1975–76 recovery there was virtually no change in the book value of business inventories. The percentage increase in business fixed investment represented about one-half the rate of growth for corresponding periods of earlier recovery.

The behavior of financial variables was also different during the 1975–76 recovery as shown by Table 21–7.

Table 21–6
Business Spending in Early Stages of Economic Recoveries
Percentage changes from trough quarter

Period	Change in book value of business inventories	Current-dollar change in business fixed investment
1954-III – 1955-III	3.4	18.2
1958-III – 1959-III	5.1	12.6
1961-II – 1962-II	4.5	12.5
1971-I – 1972-I	6.1	13.4
1975-II – 1976-II	0.6	7.1

Source: United States Department of Commerce.

7. Richard L. Gady, "Recent Patterns in Corporate Financing," *Economic Commentary* (Federal Reserve Bank of Cleveland, June 14, 1971).

8. In the following two tables and two figures the original sources of the data are indicated. The tables and figures were taken from Maury N. Harris, "The Weakness of Business Loans in the Current Recovery," Federal Reserve Bank of New York *Monthly Review*, vol. 58 (Aug. 1976), pp. 208–14.

**Table 21-7
Financial Variables in the Early Stages of Economic Recoveries**

	Commercial bank average prime rate less average rate on 4- to 6-month commercial paper*	Net funds raised through		Nonfinancial corporations Growth of internal funds	
		Stock sales	Bond sales	Aftertax profits	Corporate cash flow less inventory profits†
	Percent	(Billions of dollars)		(Percentage changes from trough quarter)	
Period					
(1)	(2)	(3)	(4)	(5)	(6)
1954-III – 1955-II	1.32	1.02	2.95	36.9	27.0
1958-III – 1959-II	0.82	2.14	4.10	61.3	34.5
1961-II – 1962-I	1.45	1.51	5.16	31.6	25.5
1971-I – 1971-IV	0.65	11.44	18.81	40.0	23.8
1975-II – 1976-I	1.33	9.78	21.79	53.5	46.2

*Average of first five quarters of recoveries.
†Corporate cash flow is the sum of undistributed aftertax profits plus tax depreciation.
Sources: United States Department of Commerce and Board of Governors of the Federal Reserve System.

Corporate cash flow less inventory profits represented a much higher percentage change from the trough quarter during the 1975–76 recovery than for the previous four recoveries. The spread between the commercial bank prime rate and the average rate on short-term commercial paper was 133 basis points during the 1975–76 recovery. This is about equal to the spread during two of the previous four recoveries, but substantially higher than the spread during the other two recoveries. This spread was almost double the difference between commercial bank rates and commercial paper rates in the previous recovery. The 1971 recovery was similar to the 1975–76 recovery in that both were characterized by a substantial volume of funds raised through the sales of stocks and bonds. In each of the two recoveries about $10 billion was raised through stock sales sharply above the $1–2 billion raise during the previous recoveries.

Approximately $20 billion dollars was raised by bond sales during the 1971 and 1975–76 recoveries as compared with an average of $4–5 billion during the preceding three recoveries. The data on stock and bond sales demonstrate that during the 1971 and 1975–76 recoveries corporations made strong efforts to improve their liquidity position. The pattern is exhibited by Figure 21–6.

After trending downward from 1952 into the recession of 1970, the

Figure 21–6
Selected Balance-
sheet Measures for
Nonfinancial
Corporations

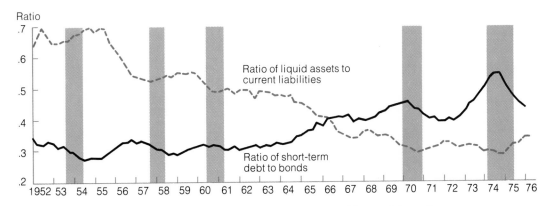

Note: Shaded areas represent periods of recession as defined by the National Bureau of Economic Research, except for the latest recession, which is tentatively judged to have ended in March 1975.
Source: Board of Governors of the Federal Reserve System.

ratio of liquid assets/current liabilities stabilized somewhat. But after the recession of 1974 the ratio of liquid assets/current liabilities has been improved. Corporations have also sought to reverse the rising ratio of short-term debt to bonds. This ratio is about .30 over the period 1952–64. With the onset of inflation in the later part of the 1960s, the ratio of short-term debt to bonds reached a peak of approximately .55 during the recession of 1974. Subsequently, this ratio has been brought down to about .43.

Thus, a number of factors were going on to explain the unusual behavior of the volume of business loans during the first 18 months of the 1975–76 recovery. Commercial banks themselves were seeking to strengthen the quality of their own business loan portfolios. They were more selective and permitted a wider spread between the average commercial bank prime rate and the average rate on short-term commercial paper to encourage some borrowers to utilize the commercial paper market for their short-term borrowing. In addition, the rate of increase in investment by business firms during the early stages of the 1975–76 recovery was far below the rate of four previous recoveries. Corporate cash flows in nominal dollar terms were much larger than in previous recoveries. In addition, business firms were seeking to strengthen their working capital position by utilizing long-term financing in the form of bonds and permanent financing in the form of stocks. This was an effort that began during the 1971 recovery and was resumed during the recovery of 1971–76.

Data on recent trends in preferred stock offerings are presented in Table 21–8. By far the largest sources of offerings are the utilities: electric power, water and gas companies, telephone. The new issue preferred stock volume was reduced in 1976 because the Bell System was out of the market that year. Other utilities also issued common stock

Table 21–8
Recent Trends in the Volume of New Preferred Stock Offerings, by Type of Issue and Issuer in Historical Perspective ($ Billions)

	1971	1972	1973	1974	1975	12 Months Ending Nov. 1976
Utility	1.9	2.4	1.9	2.0	2.5	2.1
Telephone	1.4	0.7	1.2	0.1	0.1	0.1
Manufacturing and Mining	0.3	0.2	0.1	0.1	0.6	0.5
Financial and real estate	*	*	0.1	*	0.1	0.2
Other	*	*	*	*	0.1	*
Total	3.7	3.4	3.3	2.3	3.5	2.9
Memo: Public offerings	3.6	2.4	2.4	1.7	3.1	2.5
Private placements	0.1	1.0	0.9	0.5	0.4	0.4

*Less than $50 million.
Note: Columns may not add to totals due to rounding.
Source: *Comments on Credit*, Salomon Brothers, April 1, 1977, p. 4.

rather than preferred stock during 1976. However, the volume of industrial and financial preferreds remained high, as did the volume of private placements.

Thus the interactions of the higher rates of inflation since 1966 and fluctuating interest rate levels have produced changing patterns of financial policies in business firms. It is useful to analyze the relations between price level changes and interest rate levels to understand better the implications for financing developments that are likely to continue to evolve.

Effects of Price Level Changes on Interest Rates

Price level trends affect interest rates in two important ways. First, the "nominal" interest rate—the contract, or stated, interest rate—reflects expectations about future price level behavior. If prices are rising, and are expected to rise further, the expected rate of inflation is added to the interest rate that would have prevailed in the absence of inflation to adjust for the decline in purchasing power represented by price increases.

This concept is illustrated in Table 21–9 and in Figure 21–7. In Table 21–9, column (1) gives the nominal interest rate on prime commercial

**Table 21–9
Calculation of Real
Interest Rates**

Year	(Nominal Rate) on Prime Commercial Paper	One Plus Commercial Paper Rate	$\dfrac{CPI^*_{t-1}}{CPI_t}$	Col. (2) times Col. (3)	Real Rate of Interest Col. (4) Minus 1.0 Times 100(%)
	(1)	(2)	(3)	(4)	(5)
1962	3.26	1.0326	.989	1.021	2.1%
3	3.55	1.0355	.988	1.023	2.3
4	3.97	1.0397	.987	1.026	2.6
5	4.38	1.0438	.983	1.026	2.6
6	5.55	1.0555	.972	1.026	2.6
7	5.10	1.0510	.972	1.022	2.2
8	5.90	1.0590	.962	1.019	1.9
9	7.83	1.0783	.947	1.021	2.1
1970	7.72	1.0772	.944	1.017	1.7
1	5.11	1.0511	.959	1.008	0.8
2	4.69	1.0469	.968	1.013	1.3
3	8.15	1.0815	.941	1.018	1.8
4	9.87	1.0987	.914	1.004	0.4
1975	6.33	1.0633	.916	0.974	(2.6)
6	5.35	1.0535	.945	0.996	(0.4)
7	5.70	1.0570	.930	0.983	(1.7)

*CPI refers to the Consumer Price Index.
Source: *Economic Report of the President, 1976* and *Economic Indicators, 1977.*

paper. This is expressed as one plus a decimal in column (2). Column (3) represents the year-to-year decline in purchasing power as measured by the consumer price index (CPI). Column (4) gives the interest minus inflation value of the original principal amount plus the interest rate presented in column (2). Column (5) presents the real or inflation-adjusted rate of interest. The real and nominal rates obtained from Table 21–8 are graphed in Figure 21–7. The real rates of interest have

Figure 21–7
Nominal and Real
Interest Rates on
Prime Commercial
Paper, 1963–1977

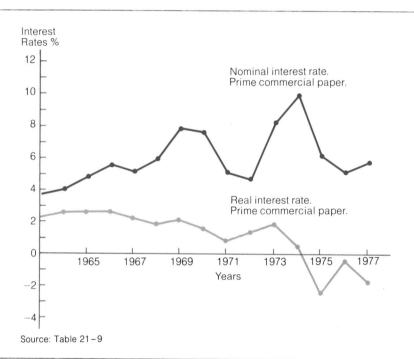

Source: Table 21–9

generally been in the 1–3 percent range. However, during the period 1975–77 nominal rates of interest on prime commercial paper have not been sufficient to offset the decline in purchasing power as measured by the consumer price index. The real rate of return during these years has, in fact, been negative.

CPI refers to the Consumer Price Index. We also used other measures of price level changes such as the Gross National Product price deflator, but the results were not changed significantly.

Implications of Interest Rate Patterns for Financial Timing

Variations in the cost of money and its availability are likely to be of great significance to financial managers. The importance of sound financial timing is further underscored by the mistakes observed in the past and the uncertainties of the future.

A question that is continuously challenging financial managers is whether interest rates, which appeared to have bottomed in late 1976 at levels above their previous 1971 lows, will continue to trend upward. In terms of cyclical movements, long-term financing appeared attractive in 1976. However, if interest rates again move to the lower levels experienced in previous decades, the financing of 1976 would represent locking the company into high-cost, long-term capital.

Easy answers to these questions are not available, and the uncertainties have given rise to new forms and patterns of financing as documented throughout this book. No one can give definitive answers to the questions raised above, but financial executives must make decisions, and they must, therefore, make judgments about these issues.

Summary

Financial managers have at least some flexibility in their operations. Even though a firm may have a target debt/assets ratio, it can deviate from this target to some extent in a given year to take advantage of favorable conditions in either the bond market or the stock market. Similarly, although it may have a target relationship between its long-term and short-term debt, it can vary from this target if market conditions suggest that such action is appropriate.

As a basis for making sound decisions with respect to financial timing, we have analyzed data covering both cyclical and long-term trends. Uncertainties about the future have increased in recent years, with a resultant increase in the importance of sound financial timing. Moreover, attempts to deal with an increasing level of uncertainty in the economy have given rise to new innovations in financing techniques and patterns. Some important changes in financing that have developed in response to changes in the economy, especially in the money and capital markets, are listed below.

1. Long-term financing has increased in comparison with the use of short-term commercial bank financing. Bond flotations in the capital markets have risen to record levels.

2. Public flotations of equity issues have increased substantially.

3. A large increase in debt ratios has occurred in response to the inflationary environment. From 1966 to 1976 the ratio of debt to assets for all manufacturing companies rose from 33 to 46 percent.

4. An increase has occurred in the use of equity participations in the form of convertibles or warrants.

5. Insurance companies and other institutional lenders have virtually ceased to provide credit to small- and medium-sized borrowers on a straight debt basis. For business loans, warrants are usually required, while on mortgages, supplementary payments based on a percentage of gross or net income are stipulated in loan contracts.

6. Since larger firms have greater access to the financial markets, an increase in the volume of trade credit has occurred, with larger firms increasing their extension of credit to smaller ones.

7. New equity issues have taken place with each cyclical recovery in stock prices. In the middle and late stages of business recoveries short-term financing has increased. After economic downturns when interest rates have been reduced, corporations have increasingly utilized long-term financing to decrease the ratio of short-term financing to long-term financing. As equity prices recovered during the early stages of business upswings, business firms have sought to strengthen their leverage positions by selling new equity issues.

These developments indicate that trends in the money and capital markets are increasing in importance to financial managers. The changes have been so massive that not only has financial timing been involved but also innovations in forms of financing used have been stimulated. Thus, financial policies have been broadened and have taken on greater importance in the overall management of business firms.

Questions

21-1. "It makes good sense for a firm to fund its floating debt, because this relieves the possibility that it will be called upon to pay off debt at an awkward time. From the standpoint of cost, however, it is always cheaper to use short-term debt than long-term debt." Discuss the statement.

21-2. Historical data indicate that more than twice as much capital is raised yearly by selling bonds than by selling common stocks. Does this indicate that corporate capital structures are becoming overburdened with debt?

21-3. Is the Federal Reserve's tight money policy restraining the country's economic growth? Discuss the pros and cons from the corporation's viewpoint.

21-4. Why do interest rates on different types of securities vary widely?

21–5. What does GNP represent? Why are its levels and growth significant to the financial manager?

21–6. When are short-term interest rates higher than long-term rates? What is indicated if short-term rates are high in relation to long-term rates for a prolonged period of time such as 20 years in a given country?

21–7. During a period of 10 years, the price level in a particular country has doubled. But during the following ten years, the price level is relatively stable. Discuss the effects on interest rates during the two ten-year periods.

Problems

21–1. In mid-1958 the Towers Company made a reappraisal of its sales forecasts for the next one, two, and five years. It was clear that the product development program that had been underway for the previous five years was then coming to fruition. The officers of Towers were confident that a sales growth of 12 to 15 percent a year (on a compound basis) for the next five years was strongly indicated unless general business declined.

The Towers Company had total assets of $10 million. It had a debt-to-total assets ratio of 29 percent. Since it had been spending heavily on research and development during the past five years, its profits had been depressed and the stock had not been favorably regarded by investors.

The Towers Company learned that it could borrow on a short-term basis at 2.5 percent (the rate for prime commercial paper at mid-1958 was 1.6 percent) and sell some common stock or float some nonconvertible long-term bonds at 4 percent. Towers financed by selling $2 million of common stock (the maximum to avoid control problems) and by short-term loans at the lower rates until early 1960, when it found that its growing financial requirements could not be met by short-term borrowing. Its need for financing was so great that Towers sold $10 million of convertible debentures at 5.5 percent (the rate on prime commercial paper at this time was almost 5 percent) and with terms requiring a strong current ratio and limitations on fixed-asset purchases. The price of its common stock had quadrupled by mid-1959 but had dropped by 10 percent in early 1960.

Evaluate the timing and the selection of forms of financing by the Towers Company.

21–2. In July 1975, as the economy in general was emerging from the 1973–74 downturn and the Video Industries Corporation's business was resuming its strong growth in sales, Sam Lincoln, the treasurer, concluded that the firm would require more working capital financing during the year ending June 30, 1976. Below are the historical and the *pro forma* income statements and balance sheets of the Video Industries Corporation.

**Video Industries Corporation
Income Statements
for Years Ended June 30, 1975 and 1976
(in Thousands of Dollars)**

	1975	Pro Forma 1976
Sales, net	$20,000	$28,000
Cost of sales	16,000	20,000
Gross profit	4,000	8,000
Operating expenses	2,000	3,000
Operating profit	2,000	5,000
Other income, net	400	200
Profits before taxes	2,400	5,200
Taxes	1,200	2,600
Net profit after taxes	1,200	2,600
Dividends	200	400
To retained earnings	$ 1,000	$ 2,200

**Video Industries Corporation
Balance Sheets, June 30, 1975 and 1976
(in Thousands of Dollars)**

Assets	1975	Pro Forma 1976
Cash	$ 400	$ 1,200
Receivables	1,600	2,400
Inventories	2,000	3,200
Total current assets	$4,000	$ 6,800
Fixed assets, net	2,000	4,000
Total assets	$6,000	$10,800

Liabilities and Capital		
Accounts payable	600	$ 1,000
Accruals	200	400
Reserves for taxes	1,200	1,600
Total current liabilities	$2,000	$ 3,000
Additional financing needed	0	1,600
Common stock, $10 par	2,000	2,000
Retained earnings	2,000	4,200
Total liabilities and capital	$6,000	$10,800

How should the financing needs be met? Why? (Although the $1,600,000 *pro forma* financial requirements are shown in the long-term section of the balance sheet, they can be met with either long- or short-term funds.)

21-3. On January 21, 1970, the American Telephone & Telegraph Company announced plans for new corporate financing. The financing offered to shareholders of record on April 10, 1970, consisted of rights to bonds with detachable warrants. The debentures had a par value of $100, and each bond carried two warrants entitling the holder to purchase a share of AT&T stock for $52. Thirty-five shares of common stock (that is, 35 rights) would be required to purchase one debenture. It was provided that the rights would expire on May 18, 1970. The financing was a success, as all the debentures were sold.

About 549,500,000 shares were outstanding. The bonds had a 30-year maturity and carried an interest rate of 8.75 percent. The two warrants each allowed the holder to purchase a share of stock for $52 at any time from November 15, 1970, through May 15, 1975.

Data on the number of telephones in service, average conversations per day, net income to AT&T common stock, construction expenditures, total capital, debt to total capital, earnings per share, dividends per share, price range, return on total capital, and return on equity are shown in Table P21–3.

a. The financing provided for the sale of how many debentures?
b. At a price of $100 each, how much financing would be obtained initially by the sale of the debentures?
c. What was the total number of warrants issued?
d. If all the warrants were exercised at the exercise price of $52, how much additional financing would be raised by AT&T by May 15, 1975?
e. What total amount of funds is AT&T raising for the five-year period from this financing?
f. What was the total of construction expenditures less the total of depreciation charges ($9.8 billion) during the years 1965–1969?
g. On the basis of the answer to part f, we may take as an approximate measure of AT&T's future financing needs the sum of construction expenditures less the total of depreciation charges for the same period. On this basis, estimate AT&T's total financing needs for the period 1970–1975, if construction expenditures grow at a 10 percent rate and depreciation expenses, which were $2.316 million in 1969, grow at an 8 percent rate.
h. What would retained earnings be for the period 1970–1975, if net income grows at a 7 percent rate and a 60 percent dividend payout policy is followed?
i. What portion of total financing requirements estimated under part g would not be covered by retained earnings plus the financing under consideration?
j. In 1969 AT&T had a debt ratio of 39 percent, or $15.7 billion in debt and $24.5 billion in equity. If the company decides to move to a 45 percent debt ratio, how much additional debt and outside equity financing would be required for the 1970–1975 period?
k. In the years immediately after World War II, AT&T utilized convertible debentures in connection with its financing. In this present in-

Table P21–3
Some Basic Data on the American Telephone & Telegraph Company, 1959–1969

Year	Number of Telephones in Service, Year End (in Millions)	Average Number of Conversations per Day (in Millions)	Operating Revenues (in Billions)	Net Income to AT&T Shares (in Billions)	Total Number of Shares (in Millions)	Construction Expenditures (in Billions)
1959	57.9	208	$ 7.4	$1.113	427	$2.249
1960	60.7	219	7.9	1.213	438	2.658
1961	63.2	226	8.4	1.285	465	2.696
1962	66.0	242	9.0	1.388	479	2.976
1963	68.6	251	9.6	1.480	488	3.136
1964	72.0	262	10.3	1.659	512	3.519
1965	75.9	280	11.1	1.796	527	3.918
1966	70.0	295	12.1	1.979	536	4.193
1967	83.8	307	13.0	2.049	540	4.310
1968	88.0	323	14.1	2.052	547	4.742
1969	92.7	350	15.7	2.199	549	5.731
5-year growth rate:						
1959–1964	4.5	4.7	6.8	8.3	3.7	9.4
1964–1969	5.2	6.0	8.8	5.8	1.4	10.2

Year	Total Capital (in Billions)	Debt to Total Capital (Percent)	Earnings per Share (in Dollars)	Dividends per Share (in Dollars)	Price Range (Rounded)	Return on Total Capital (in Percents)	Return on Equity (in Percents)
1959	$18.9	36	2.61	1.58	44–37	7.55	9.77
1960	20.5	36	2.79	1.65	54–40	7.69	10.00
1961	22.3	35	2.76	1.72	70–52	7.41	9.46
1962	24.3	35	2.90	1.80	68–49	7.45	9.47
1963	25.6	35	3.03	1.80	71–57	7.45	9.49
1964	28.0	33	3.24	1.95	75–65	7.56	9.51
1965	29.8	33	3.41	2.00	70–60	7.65	9.53
1966	32.0	33	3.69	2.20	64–50	7.91	9.86
1967	34.5	35	3.79	2.20	63–50	7.77	9.73
1968	36.9	36	3.75	2.40	58–48	7.50	9.26
1969	40.2	39	4.00	2.45	58–48	7.73	9.04
5-year growth rate:							
1959–1964	8.2	—	4.4	4.3	11.5*	7.52†	9.62†
1964–1969	7.5	—	4.3	4.7	−5.5*	7.69‡	9.49‡

*Based on average of high and low values.
†Average for years 1959–1964.
‡Average for years 1964–1969.
Source: American Telephone & Telegraph Annual Reports and Prospectus, April 13, 1970.

stance, it utilized warrants rather than convertibles. Can you suggest some reasons for the shift from convertibles to debentures with warrants?

l. Discuss how the amount, timing, and form of financing employed by AT&T in the 1970 financing episode was influenced by the economic and financial developments of the late 1960s.

21–4. Drake Manufacturing Company has decided to undertake a two-part capital expansion program, from which no benefits will accrue until both phases are completed. As treasurer of Drake it is your responsibility to examine the various sources of funds available to the company to finance each phase. The first phase will cost $5 million and will be undertaken immediately. It is anticipated that the company will begin the second phase, which also has an estimated cost of $5 million, approximately one year from now. The estimate for the second phase includes an adjustment for the rate of inflation, which is expected to increase from the current rate of 6 percent to approximately 9 percent at the end of the coming year. Drake's common stock is widely held and is traded on the over-the-counter market. Drake's balance sheet, income statement and market information for the last fiscal year are given here:

Drake Manufacturing Company
Balance Sheet
December 31, 1976
(Dollars in Millions)

Current Assets:		Current liabilities:	
Cash	$ 2.0	Accounts payable	$ 5.0
Accounts receivable (net)	10.0	Accruals	2.4
Inventory	20.0	Current portion of LTD	2.0
Total current assets	$32.0	Total current liabilities	$ 9.4
		Long-term debt (7%) (LTD)	16.0
Net property plant and equipment	50.0	Common stock ($10 par)	21.5
Total assets	$82.0	Paid in capital	13.0
		Retained earnings	22.1
		Total	$82.0

Drake Manufacturing Company
Income Statement
for Year Ending December 31, 1976
(Dollars in Millions)

Sales	$150.00	
Gross margin	60.00	
Operating expenses	39.00	
Operating income	21.00	
Interest	1.26	EPS = $4.59
Pretax earnings	$ 19.74	DPS = 1.60
Taxes (50 percent)	9.87	P/E = 10×
Net income	$ 9.87	Market price = $45.90

After a thorough review of the situation, and discussions with several
banks and underwriters, you conclude that the following options are
open to Drake. (Note: in any given year, assume that only one source of
funds may be used.)

1. Use short-term debt to cover phases 1 and 2 of the construction program, then refund this debt with any of the long-term methods noted in 2 below at the end of the construction period.
2. Obtain long-term financing now for phase 1 of the construction
   program, then obtain additional financing next year for phase 2.
   The long-term financing methods available are bank term loans,
   debentures, and common stock.
3. Obtain long-term financing now to cover both phases of the expansion program, using one of the methods outlined in 2 above, to
   raise $10 million.

A review of the latest issue of the *Wall Street Journal* indicated that the
following interest rates are now prevailing:

Bank Loans

Prime bank rate	6.75%
Revolving loan	8.75
Long-term	9.25

Commercial Paper

90–119 days	5.93%
4–6 months	6.27

U. S. Treasury Securities

3 months	4.93%
6 months	5.33
1 year	5.78

Corporate Bonds (20 years)

Aa	8.8%

Your analysis of the economy shows that economic activity began showing strong signs of improvement about two months ago, following a long
period of sluggishness. You also notice that, according to today's *Wall
Street Journal*, the average *P/E* ratio for Dow Jones Industrials is 13.1
compared to 8.6 less than one year ago.

You are concerned about the effect the additional financing will have
on Drake's EPS and market price, as the benefits from the expansion will
not begin to be realized for about three years. You also wish to maintain
a strong, liquid balance sheet. The maximum acceptable ratio of long-
term debt to total long-term capital is 33 percent. Discussions with underwriters have indicated that a stock issue could be sold at the current
market price. However, the discussion of a public or private debt issue,

or the rating for a public issue of bonds, was not conclusive. Management believed that a public bond issue would probably be rated A.

As treasurer, you are requested to analyze the situation completely, and to support what you feel is the optimum financing plan and timing.

21–5. The objective of this assignment is to evaluate the timing decision associated with a recent issue of corporate bonds.

a. From an issue of the *Wall Street Journal* published within the most recent 30-day period, in the pages that describe new issues of stock and bonds sold to the public, identify a public issue of corporate bonds that came to market (were issued) the preceding day. Record information identifying the issuer, the date of issue, the amount of the issue, its maturity, coupon rate, issue price, yield to maturity, rating, any other stated terms of the issue, and the degree of success of the first day sales. Much of this information can be found in the "tombstone" advertisement for the issue. Somewhere on the immediate surrounding pages will be a paragraph or a very short statement about the issue, its rating, and the way the issue was received by the market.

b. In the most recent monthly issue of the *Federal Reserve Bulletin (FRB)*, locate in the index the item "Interest Rates: Bond and Stock Yields," and in that table under "Corporate Bonds" locate the column headed "Total." Record the yields under "Total" for each of the last 15 months reported, and also the yield reported for each of the five years preceding the monthly data. Plot these data. Also, indicate the yield for your new issue as determined in part a above on this graph.

c. Briefly explain what has happened to long-term corporate interest rates in general in the interim between the most recent *FRB* data and the date of your new issue in part a. Given the current state of the economy, what is the outlook for interest rates over the next six months to one year?

d. Discuss the percentage interest cost incurred by the issuer of your bonds, and the timing of the new issue.

Selected References

Andersen, Leonal C. "Is There a Capital Shortage: Theory and Recent Evidence." *Journal of Finance* 31 (May 1976):257–68.

Freund, William C. "The Dynamic Financial Markets." *Financial Executive* 33 (May 1965):11–26, 57–58.

Friedman, Milton. "Factors Affecting the Level of Interest Rates." In *Savings and Residential Financing.* Chicago: U.S. Savings and Loan League, 1968, pp. 10–27.

Gibson, William E. "Price Expectations Effects on Interest Rates." *Journal of Finance* 25 (Mar. 1970):19–34.

Grossman, Herschel I. "The Term Structure of Interest Rates." *Journal of Finance* 22 (Dec. 1967):611–22.

Johnson, Ramon E. "Term Structures of Corporate Bond Yields as a Function of Risk of Default." *Journal of Finance* 22 (May 1967):313–45.

Kessel, Reuben A. *Cyclical Behavior of the Term Structure of Interest Rates.* New York: National Bureau of Economic Research, 1965.

Malkiel, Burton G. *The Term Structure of Interest Rates.* Princeton, N.J.: Princeton University Press, 1966.

Moor, Roy E. "The Timing of Financial Policy." In *The Treasurer's Handbook*, J. Fred Weston and Maurice B. Goudzwaard, eds. Homewood, Illinois: Dow Jones-Irwin, 1976, pp. 43–67.

Ritter, L. S. *Money and Economic Analysis.* 3rd ed. New York: Houghton Mifflin, 1967.

Robinson, Roland I. *Money and Capital Markets.* New York: McGraw-Hill, 1964.

Tussing, A. Dale. "Can Monetary Policy Influence the Availability of Credit?" *Journal of Finance* 21 (Mar. 1966):1–14.

Van Horne, James. "Interest-Rate Expectations, the Shape of the Yield Curve and Monetary Policy." *Review of Economics and Statistics* 48 (May 1966): 211–15.

Wachtel, Paul; Sametz, Arnold; and Shuford, Harry. "Capital Shortages: Myth or Reality." *Journal of Finance* 31 (May 1976):269–86.

22 External Growth: Mergers and Holding Companies

Growth is vital to the well-being of a firm; without it, a business cannot attract able management because it cannot give recognition in promotions or offer challenging creative activity. Without able executives, the firm is likely to decline and die. Much of the material in the previous chapters dealing with analysis, planning, and financing has a direct bearing on the financial manager's potential contribution to the growth of a firm. Because of the central importance of the growth requirement, the present chapter focuses on strategies for promoting growth.

Merger activity has played an important part in the growth of firms in the United States, and financial managers are required both to appraise the desirability of a prospective purchase and to participate directly in evaluating the respective companies involved in a merger.[1] Consequently, it is essential that the study of financial management provide the background necessary for effective participation in merger negotiations and decisions.

Financial managers—and intelligent laymen—also need to be aware of the broader significance of mergers. Despite the heightened merger activities in the 1920s, again after World War II, and during the 1960s, recent merger movements have neither approached the magnitude nor had the social consequences of those that took place from 1890 to 1905. During this period, more than two hundred major combinations were effected, resulting in the concentration that has characterized the steel, tobacco, and other important industries. Regardless of the business objectives and motives of merger activity, its social and economic consequences must also be taken into account.

While the frenzied merger movement of the 1960s peaked in the last two years of that decade, mergers of major magnitude have continued to take place. It was reported that merger activity in 1976 was up 30 percent over the previous year.[2] In addition, between 1971 and 1975 approximately 40 companies with assets exceeding $100 million were

---

1. As we use the term, "merger" means any combination that forms one economic unit from two or more previous ones. For legal purposes there are distinctions between the various ways these combinations can occur, but our emphasis is on fundamental business and financial aspects of mergers or acquisitions.

2. *Business Week*, 19 July 1976.

merged into acquiring companies. Table 22-1 provides information on these major mergers during the first half of the 1970s.

Table 22-1
Acquired Companies with Assets of $100 million or More during 1971-75

Year	Acquiring company	Acquired company	Assets ($Millions)
1971	Imperial Chemical Ind. Ltd.	Atlas Chemical Ind. Ltd.	139.6
1971	U.S. Smelting, Refining & Mining Co.	Federal Pacific Electric Co.	135.0
1971	National Steel Corp.	Granite City Steel Co.	312.7
1971	Omega-Alpha, Inc.	Okonite Co. (from Ling-Temco-Vought)	174.9
1971	Charter Company	Signal Complex (oil refining and marketing properties of Signal Cos.)	114.2
1972	Williams Companies	Continental Oil Co. (Plant Foods Division)	125.5
1972	Colgate-Palmolive Co.	Kendall Co.	194.4
1972	Jim Walter Corp.	Panacon Corp. (from Rapid American Corp.)	106.0
1972	Pepsico Inc.	Rheingold Corp.	101.4
1972	Federal Paper Board Co.	Riegel Paper Corp. (paper, forest products, and real estate divisions)	102.9
1972	U.S. Filter Corp.	Slick Corp.	120.7
1973	Red River Valley Sugarbeet Grower Association, Inc.	American Crystal Sugar Co.	114.8
1973	Rockwell International Corp.	Collins Radio Co.	278.9
1973	Coastal State Gas Producing Co.	Colorado Interstate Corp.	376.2
1973	Fruehauf Corp.	Kelsey Hayes Co.	273.8
1973	Norton Simon, Inc.	Max Factor & Co.	175.7
1973	North American Rockwell Corp.	Rockwell Manufacturing Co.	224.6
1973	Time, Inc.	Temple Industries, Inc.	118.8
1974	Rockwell International Corp.	Admiral Corp.	275.9
1974	International Nickel Co. of Canada, Ltd.	E.S.B., Inc.	315.1
1974	United Aircraft Corp.	Essex International, Inc.	464.8
1974	Hoechst, Farbwerke A.G.	Foster Grant Co., Inc. (subsidiary of United Brands Co.)	118.5
1974	Thyssen-Bornemisza Group N.V.	Indian Head, Inc.	328.9
1974	Dresser Industries, Inc.	Jeffrey Galion, Inc.	206.4
1974	Philips Incandescent Lamp Works (Philips N.V.)	Magnavox Co.	330.7
1974	Matsushita Electric Industrial Co.	Motorola, Inc. (Color TV Division)	150.6
1974	Knight Newspapers, Inc.	Ridder Publications, Inc.	163.8
1974	Burmah Oil, Ltd.	Signal Oil & Gas. Co. (subsidiary, of the Signal Companies, Inc.)	340.1

Table 22–1 Continued

1974	Murphy Oil Corp.	Storm Drilling & Marine, Inc.	101.4
1975	Babcock & Wilcox Ltd.	American Chain & Cable Co.	235.1
1975	International Minerals & Chemical Corp.	Commerical Solvents Corp.	153.8
1975	Imetal Societe	Copperweld Corp.	158.3
1975	Colt Industries, Inc.	Garlock, Inc.	113.0
1975	International Paper Co.	General Crude Oil Co.	108.4
1975	Gulf & Western Ind.	Kayser-Roth Corp.	402.0
1975	United Technologies Corp.	Otis Elevator Co.	764.2
1975	Baker Oil Tools, Inc.	Reed Tool Co.	125.8
1975	Signal Companies, Inc.	Universal Oil Products Co.	443.1
1975	Emhart Corp.	USM Corp.	604.3

Source: *FTC Statistical Report on Mergers and Acquisitions*, November 1976, pp. 109–10.

The years 1976 and 1977 have been characterized as a "merger binge" in which companies of substantial size were involved. For example, twelve major mergers took place during 1976 and 1977 or were pending as of November 1977. The total value of the transactions involved cumulates to $6.3 billions. The participants were:

Acquiring Company	Acquired Company	Value of transaction (in millions)
General Electric	Utah International	$2,170
Atlantic Richfield	Anaconda	536
R. J. Reynolds	Burmah Oil & Gas	520
J. Ray McDermott	Babcock & Wilcox	510
Gulf Oil	Kewanee Industries	440
Getty Oil	Mission; Skelly Oil	356
Champion International	Hoerner Waldorf	351
Pepsico	Pizza Hut	313
Continental Group	Richmond	293
Nestlé	Alcon Laboratories	268
Marathon Oil	Pan Ocean Oil	265
ITT	Carbon Industries	264

Source: *Business Week*, November 14, 1977, p. 177.

Mergers versus Internal Growth

Many of the objectives of size and diversification may be achieved either through internal growth or by external growth through acquisitions and mergers. In the post-World War II period, considerable diversification was achieved by many firms through external acquisition.

Some financial reasons for utilizing external acquisition instead of internal growth to achieve diversification are discussed below.

Financing

Sometimes it is possible to finance an acquisition when it is not possible to finance internal growth. A large steel plant, for example, involves a large investment. Steel capacity may be acquired in a merger through an exchange of stock more cheaply than it can be obtained by buying the facilities themselves. Sellers may be more willing to accept the stock of the purchaser in payment for the facilities sold than would investors in a public offering. The use of stock reduces cash requirements for the acquisition of assets.

Market Capitalization Rates

While it is not strictly an operating factor, the fact that the earnings of larger economic units are frequently capitalized at lower rates and hence produce higher market values has stimulated many mergers. The securities of larger firms have better marketability; these firms are more able to diversify and thus reduce risks, and they are generally better known. All these factors lead to lower required rates of return and higher price/earnings ratios. As a result, it may be possible to consolidate firms and have the resulting market value greater than the sum of their individual values, even if there is no increase in aggregate earnings. To illustrate, three companies may each be earning $1 million and selling at 10 times earnings, for a total market value of ($1 million)(10)(3) equals $30 million. When these companies combine, the new company may obtain a stock exchange listing or may take other actions to improve the price of its stock. If so, the price/earnings ratio may rise to 15, in which case the market value of the consolidated firm would be $45 million.[3]

The major reason for the increase in takeovers in 1976–77 is that the replacement values of corporate assets have been rising with inflation while inflation has depressed real earnings, resulting in lower stock prices. It has been estimated that by the end of 1977, the replacement costs of corporate net assets (for nonfarm, nonfinancial corporations) were about 25 percent higher than the market values of the corporate securities representing ownership of the corporate assets (*Business*

---

3. The market capitalization rate is related to the cost of equity, as we discussed in Chapter 19. A lower capitalization rate results in a lower cost of capital. Therefore, the same actions that raise the market value of the equity also lower the firm's cost of new capital.

Week, November 14, 1977, p. 179). Because selling prices of products have been based on the historical costs of assets, the prospective returns on new investments at current, higher replacement costs have been unattractively low. With the market values of other companies substantially below their replacement costs, acquisitions provide the opportunity of higher returns than would be earned by investments in physical assets either in the firm's own line of business or in new areas.

Taxes

Without question, the high level of taxation was a factor stimulating merger activity in the postwar period. Studies have indicated that taxes appear to have been a major reason for the sale of about one-third of the firms acquired by merger. Inheritance taxes precipitated these sales in some cases; in others, the advantage of buying a company with a tax loss provided the motivation.

Terms of Mergers

For every merger actually consummated, a number of other potentially attractive combinations fail during the negotiating stage. In some of these cases, negotiations are broken off when it is revealed that the companies' operations are not compatible. In others, tangible benefits would result, but the parties are unable to agree on the merger terms. Of these terms, the most important is the price to be paid by the acquiring firm for the firm acquired. Factors that influence this important aspect of a merger are now considered.

Effects on Price and Earnings

A merger carries potentialities for either favorable or adverse effects on earnings, on market prices of shares, or on both. Previous chapters have shown that investment decisions should be guided by the effects on market values, and these effects should in turn be determined by the effects on future earnings and dividends. These future events are difficult to forecast, however, so stockholders, as well as managers, attribute great importance to the immediate effects of a contemplated merger on earnings per share. Directors of companies will often state, "I do not know how the merger will affect the market price of the shares of my company because so many forces influencing market prices are at work. But the effect on earnings per share can be seen directly."

An example will illustrate the effects of a proposed merger on earnings per share and thus suggest the kinds of problems that are likely to arise. Assume the following facts for two companies:

	Company A	Company B
Total earnings	$20,000	$50,000
Number of shares of common stock	5,000	10,000
Earnings per share of stock	$ 4.00	$ 5.00
Price/earnings ratio per share	15×	12×
Market price per share	$ 60.00	$ 60.00

Suppose the firms agree to merge, with B, the surviving firm, acquiring the shares of A by a one-for-one exchange of stock. The exchange ratio is determined by the respective market prices of the two companies. Assuming no increase in earnings, the effects on earnings per share are shown in the following tabulation:

	Shares of Company B Owned after Merger	Earnings per Share	
		Before merger	After merger
A's stockholders	5,000	$4	$4.67
B's stockholders	10,000	5	4.67
Total	15,000		

Since total earnings are $70,000 and a total of 15,000 shares will be outstanding after the merger has been completed, the new earnings per share will be $4.67. Earnings will increase by 67 cents for A's stockholders, but they will decline by 33 cents for B's.

The effects on market values are less certain. If the combined company sells at company A's price/earnings ratio of 15, the new market value per share of the new company will be $70. In this case, shareholders of both companies will have benefited. This result comes about because the combined earnings are now valued at a multiplier of 15, whereas prior to the merger one portion of the earnings was valued at a multiplier of 15 and another portion was valued at a multiplier of 12.

If, on the other hand, the earnings of the new company are valued at B's multiplier of 12, the indicated market value of the shares will be $56. The shareholders of each company will have suffered a $4 dilution in market value.

Because the effects on market value per share are less certain than those on earnings per share, the impact of earnings per share tends to be given great weight in merger negotiations. Because of this, the following analysis also emphasizes effects on earnings per share, while recognizing that maximizing market value is the valid rule of investment decisions.

If the merger takes place on the basis of earnings, neither earnings dilution nor earnings appreciation will take place, as shown below.

	Shares of Company B Owned after Merger	Earnings per Old Share	
		Before merger	After merger
A's stockholders*	4,000	$4	$4
B's stockholders	10,000	5	5
Total	14,000		

*On the basis of earnings, the exchange ratio is 4:5; that is, company A's shareholders receive four shares of B stock for each five shares of A stock they own. Earnings per share of the merged company is $5. But, since A's shareholders now own only 80 percent of the number of their old shares, their equivalent earnings per *old* share is the same $4. For example, suppose one of A's stockholders formerly held 100 shares. He will own only 80 shares of B after the merger, and his total earnings will be 80 × $5 = $400. Dividing his $400 total earnings by the number of shares he formerly owned, 100, gives the $4 per *old* share.

It is clear that the equivalent earnings per share after the merger are the same as before the merger. The effects on market values will depend upon whether the 15-times multiplier of A or the 12-times multiplier of B prevails.

Of the numerous factors affecting the valuation of the constituent companies in a merger, all must ultimately be reflected in the earnings per share, or market price, of the companies. Hence, all the effects on the earnings position or wealth position of stockholders are encompassed by the foregoing example. We will now consider both quantitative and qualitative factors that will influence the terms on which a merger is likely to take place.

Quantitative Factors Affecting Terms of Mergers

Five factors have received the greatest emphasis in arriving at merger terms:

1. Earnings and the growth rate of earnings.
2. Dividends.
3. Market values.
4. Book values.
5. Net current assets.

Analysis is typically based on the per share values of the foregoing factors. The relative importance of each factor and the circumstances under which each is likely to be the most influential determinant in arriving at terms will vary. The nature of these influences is described below.

Earnings and Growth Rates. Both expected earnings and capitalization rates as reflected in P/E ratios are important in determining the values that will be established in a merger. The analysis necessarily begins with historical data on the firms' earnings, whose past growth rates, future trends, and variability are important determinants of the earnings multiplier, or P/E ratio, that will prevail after the merger.

How future earnings growth rates affect the multiplier can be illustrated by extending the preceding example. First, we know that high P/E ratios are commonly associated with rapidly growing companies. Since company A has the higher P/E ratio, it is reasonable to assume that its earnings are expected to grow more rapidly than those of company B. Suppose A's expected growth rate is 10 percent and B's is 5 percent. Looking at the proposed merger from the point of view of company B and its stockholders, and assuming that the exchange ratio is based on present market prices, it can be seen that B will suffer a dilution in earnings when the merger occurs. However, B will be acquiring a firm with more favorable growth prospects; hence, its earnings after the merger should increase more rapidly than before. In this case, the new growth rate is assumed to be a weighted average of the growth rates of the individual firms, weighted by their respective total earnings before the merger. In the example, the new expected growth rate is 6.43 percent.

With the new growth rate it is possible to determine just how long it will take company B's stockholders to regain the earnings dilution — that is, how long it will take earnings per share to revert back to their previous position before the merger. This can be determined graphically from Figure 22–1.[4] Without the merger, B would have initial earnings of $5 a share, and these earnings would have grown at a rate of 5 percent a year. With the merger, earnings drop to $4.67 a share, but the rate of growth increases to 6.43 percent. Under these conditions, the earnings dilution is overcome after five years; from the fifth year on, B's earnings will be higher, assuming the merger is consummated.

This same relationship could be developed from the point of view of the faster growing firm. Here there would be an immediate earnings increase but a reduced rate of growth. Working through the analysis would show the number of years before the earnings accretion would be eroded.

It is apparent that the critical variables are (1) the respective rates of

---

4. The calculation could also be made algebraically by solving for N in the following equation: $E_1(1 + g_1)^N = E_2(1 + g_2)^N$, where E_1 = earnings before the merger, E_2 = earnings after the merger, g_1 and g_2 are the growth rates before and after the merger, and N is the break-even number of years.

growth of the two firms; (2) their relative sizes, which determine the actual amount of the initial earnings per share dilution or accretion, as well as the new weighted average growth rate; (3) the firms' *P/E* ratios; and (4) the exchange ratio. These factors interact to produce the resulting pattern of earnings per share for the surviving company. It is possible to generalize the relationships somewhat; for our purposes, it is necessary simply to note that in the bargaining process the exchange ratio is the variable that must be manipulated in an effort to reach a mutually satisfactory earnings pattern.[5]

Figure 22–1
Effect of Merger
on Future Earnings

5. We should also mention at this point that certain companies, especially the "conglomerates," are reported to have used mergers to produce a "growth illusion" designed to increase the prices of their stocks. When a high *P/E* ratio company buys a low *P/E* ratio company, the earnings per share of the acquiring firm rise *because* of the merger. Thus, mergers can produce growth in reported earnings for the acquiring firm. This growth by merger, in turn, can cause the acquiring firm to keep its high *P/E* ratio. With this ratio, the conglomerates can seek new low *P/E* merger candidates and thus continue to obtain growth through mergers. The chain is broken (1) if the rate of merger activity slows, or (2) if the *P/E* ratio of the acquiring firm falls. In 1968 and 1969 several large conglomerates reported profit declines caused by losses in certain of their divisions. This reduced the growth rate in *EPS*, which in turn led to a decline in the *P/E* ratio. A change in tax laws and antitrust suits against some conglomerate mergers also made it more difficult to consummate favorable mergers. All these factors, along with tight money and depressed conditions in some industries, caused a further reduction in the *P/E* ratio and compounded these firms' problems. The net result was a drastic revaluation of conglomerate share prices, with such former favorites as LTV falling from a high of $169 to $7½ and Litton Industries, from $115 to $6¾.

Dividends. Because they represent the actual income received by stock-holders, dividends may influence the terms of merger. As the material in Chapter 20 suggests, however, dividends are likely to have little influence on the market price of companies with a record of high growth and high profitability. Some companies have not yet paid cash dividends but command market prices representing a high multiple of current earnings. For example, some nondividend paying companies with high price/earnings ratios reported in the April 19, 1977, *Wall Street Journal* were Continental Materials with a price/earnings ratio of 113, Ranger Oil with 58 and Viatech, Inc., with 100. However, for utility companies and for companies in industries where growth rates and profitability have declined, the dollar amount of dividends paid may have a relatively important influence on the market price of the stock. Dividends may therefore influence the terms on which these companies would be likely to trade in a merger.[6]

Market Values. The price of a firm's stock reflects expectations about its future earnings and dividends, so current market values are expected to have a strong influence on the terms of a merger. However, the value placed on a firm in an acquisition is likely to exceed its current market price for a number of reasons. (1) If the company is in a depressed industry, its stockholders are likely to overdiscount the dismal outlook for the company; this will result in a very low current market price. (2) The prospective purchaser may be interested in acquiring the company for the contribution that it may make to the acquiring company. Thus, the acquired company is worth more to an informed purchaser than it is in the general market. (3) Stockholders are offered more than current market prices for their stock as an inducement to sell. For these reasons, the offering price is usually in the range of 10 to 20 percent above the market price before the merger announcement.

Book Value per Share. Book values are generally considered to be relatively unimportant in determining the value of a company, as they merely represent the historical investments that have been made in the company. These investments may have little relation to current values or prices. At times, however, especially when book values substantially exceed market values, they may well have an impact on merger terms. The book value is an index of the amount of physical facilities made available in the merger. Despite a past record of low earning power, it

---

6. If a company that does not pay dividends on its stock is seeking to acquire a firm whose stockholders are accustomed to receiving dividends, the exchange can be on a convertibles-for-common-stock basis. This will enable the acquired firm's stockholders to continue receiving income.

is always possible that, under effective management, a firm's assets may once again achieve normal earning power, in which case the market value of the company will rise. Because of the potential contribution of physical properties to improved future earnings, book values may have an influence on actual merger terms.

Net Current Assets per Share. Net current assets (current assets minus current liabilities) per share are likely to have an influence on merger terms because they represent the amount of liquidity that may be obtained from a company in a merger. In the postwar textile mergers, net current assets were very high, and this was one of the characteristics making textile companies attractive to the acquiring firms. By buying a textile company, often with securities, an acquiring company was in a position to look for still other merger candidates, paying for the new acquisition with the just-acquired liquidity. Similarly, if an acquired company is debt-free, the acquiring firm may be able to borrow funds required for the purchase, using the acquired firm's assets and earning power to pay off the loan after the merger or to provide security for renewing or even increasing the borrowing.[7]

Relative Importance of Quantitative Factors

Attempts have been made to determine statistically the relative weights assigned to each of the above factors in actual merger cases. These attempts have been singularly unsuccessful. In one case, one factor seems to dominate; in another, some other determinant appears to be most important. This absence of consistent patterns among the quantitative factors suggests that qualitative forces are also at work, and we now turn our attention to these management factors.

Qualitative Influences: Synergy

Sometimes the most important influence on the terms of a merger is a business consideration not reflected at all in historical quantitative data. A soundly conceived merger is one in which the combination produces what may be called a *synergistic*, or "two-plus-two-equals-five," effect. By the combination, more profits are generated than could be achieved by the sum of the individual firms operating separately.

To illustrate, in the merger between Merck and Company and Sharp and Dohme, it was said that each company complemented the other in an important way. Merck had a strong reputation for its research organization. Sharp and Dohme had a most effective sales force. The combi-

---

7. By the same token, a firm seeking to *avoid* being acquired will reduce its liquid position and use up its borrowing potential.

nation of these two pharmaceutical companies added strength to both. Another example is the merger between Carrier Corporation and Affiliated Gas Equipment, Inc. The merger enabled the combined company to provide a complete line of air-conditioning and heating equipment. The merger between Hilton Hotels and Statler Hotels led to economies in the purchase of supplies and materials. One Hilton executive estimated that the savings accruing simply from the combined management of the Statler Hotel in New York and Hilton's New York Hotel amounted to $700,000 a year. The bulk of the savings were in laundry, food, advertising, and administrative costs.

The qualitative factors may also reflect other influences. The merger or acquisition may enable one company that lacks general management ability to obtain it from the other company. Another factor may be the acquisition of a technically competent scientific or engineering staff if one of the companies has fallen behind in the technological race. In such a situation, the company needing the technical competence possessed by the other firm may be willing to pay a substantial premium over previous levels of earnings, dividends, market values, or book values of the acquired firm.

The purpose of the merger may be to develop a production capability a firm does not possess. Some firms are strong in producing custom-made items with high performance characteristics, yet these firms, on entering new markets, must make use of mass-production techniques. If the firm has had no such experience, this skill may have to be obtained by means of a merger. The firm may perhaps need to develop an effective sales organization. For example, some of the companies previously oriented to the defense market, such as those in aerospace, found that they had only a limited industrial sales organization; merger was the solution to the problem.

The foregoing are the kinds of qualitative considerations that may have an overriding influence on the actual terms of merger, and the values of these contributions are never easy to quantify. The all-encompassing question, of course, is how these factors will affect the contribution of each company to future earnings per share in the combined operation. The historical data and the qualitative considerations described, in addition to judgment and bargaining, combine to determine merger terms.

Accounting Policies in Mergers

After merger terms have been agreed upon, the financial manager must be familiar with the accounting principles for recording the financial results of the merger and for reflecting the initial effect on the earnings of the surviving firm. This section deals with these matters.

The financial statements of the survivor in a merger must follow the regulations and supervision of the Securities and Exchange Commission. The SEC's requirements follow the recommendations of professional accounting societies on combinations, but interpretations of actual situations require much financial and economic analysis.

On August 2, 1970, the 18-member Accounting Principles Board (APB) of The American Institute of Certified Public Accountants issued Opinion 16, dealing with guidelines for corporate mergers, and Opinion 17, dealing with goodwill arising from mergers. The recommendations, which became effective October 31, 1970, modify and elaborate previous pronouncements on the "pooling of interests" and "purchase" methods of accounting for business combinations. For reasons that will become clear later in this section, corporate managements generally prefer pooling. Six broad tests are used to determine whether the conditions for the pooling of interest treatment are met. If all of these are met, then the combination is, in a sense, a "merger among equals," and the *pooling of interests* method may be employed.

1. The acquired firm's stockholders maintain an ownership position in the surviving firm.
2. The basis for accounting for the assets of the acquired entity is unchanged.
3. Independent interests are combined; each entity had autonomy for two years prior to the initiation of the plan to combine; no more than 10 percent ownership of voting common stock is held as intercorporate investments.
4. The combination is effected in a single transaction; contingent payouts are not permitted in poolings but may be used in purchases.
5. The acquiring corporation issues only common stock with rights identical to its outstanding voting common stock in exchange for substantially all the voting common stock of the other company; "substantially" is defined as 90 percent.
6. The combined entity does not intend to dispose of a significant portion of the assets of the combining companies within two years after the merger.

In contrast, a *purchase* involves (1) new owners, (2) an appraisal of the acquired firm's physical assets and a restatement of the balance sheet to reflect these new values, and (3) the possibility of an excess or deficiency of consideration given up vis-à-vis the book value of equity. Point (3) refers to the creation of goodwill. In a purchase, the excess of the purchase price paid over the book value (restated to reflect the appraisal value of physical assets) is set up as goodwill, and capital surplus is increased (or decreased) accordingly. In a pooling of interests, the combined total assets after the merger represent a simple sum of the asset contributions of the constituent companies.

In a *purchase*, if the acquiring firm pays more than the acquired net worth, the excess is associated either with tangible depreciable assets or with goodwill. Asset write-offs are deductible, but goodwill written off is not deductible for tax purposes, even though the new recommendations require that goodwill be written off over some reasonable period but no longer than 40 years. This requires a write-off of at least 2.5 percent a year of the amount of goodwill arising from a purchase. Therefore, if a merger is treated as a purchase, reported profits will be lower than if it is handled as a pooling of interests. This is one of the reasons that pooling is popular among acquiring firms.

Previous to issuance of APB Opinion 16, another stimulus to pooling was the opportunity to dispose of assets acquired at depreciated book values, selling them at their current values, and recording subsequent profits on sales of assets. Opinion 16 attempted to deal with this practice by the requirement that sales of major portions of assets are not to be contemplated for at least two years after the merger has taken place. For example, suppose firm A buys firm B, exchanging stock worth $100 million for assets worth $100 million but carried at $25 million. After the merger, A could, before the change in rules, sell the acquired assets and report the difference between book value and the purchase price, or $75 million, as earned income. Thus, mergers could be used in still another way to create an illusion of profits and growth.

These general statements may be made more meaningful by concrete illustrations of first a purchase and then a pooling of interests.[8]

Financial Treatment of a Purchase

The financial treatment of a purchase may best be explained by use of a hypothetical example. The Mammoth Company has just purchased the Petty Company under an arrangement known as a *purchase*. The facts are as given in Table 22–2, which also shows the financial treatment. The illustration conforms to the general nature of a purchase. Measured by total assets, the Mammoth Company is 20 times as large as Petty, while its total earnings are 15 times as large. Assume that the terms of the purchase will be one share of Mammoth for two shares of Petty, based on the prevailing market value of their shares of common stock. Thus, in terms of Mammoth's stock, Mammoth is giving to Petty's stockholders $30 of market value and $7 of book value for each share of Petty stock. Petty's market value is $30 a share, its book value is $3 a

---

8. The material in this section is technical and is generally covered in accounting courses. The reader may skip to the section on holding companies without loss of continuity.

share, and the fair value of the equity is $6,000.[9] The total market value of Mammoth paid for Petty is $60,000. The goodwill involved may be calculated as follows:

Value given by Mammoth	$60,000
Fair value of net worth of Petty purchased	6,000
Goodwill	$54,000

Table 22-2
Financial Treatment of a Purchase

	Mammoth Company	Petty Company	Adjustments		Pro Forma Balance Sheet
			Debit	Credit	
Assets					
Current	$ 80,000	$ 4,000			$ 84,000
Other assets	20,000	2,000			22,000
Net fixed assets	100,000	4,000			104,000
Goodwill			$54,000		54,000
Total assets	$200,000	$10,000			$264,000
Liabilities and net worth					
Current liabilities	$ 40,000	$ 4,000			$ 44,000
Long-term debt	20,000				20,000
Common stock	40,000	1,000	1,000	4,000	44,000
Capital surplus	20,000			56,000	76,000
Retained earnings	80,000	5,000	5,000		80,000
Total liab. and net worth	$200,000	$10,000	$60,000	$60,000	$264,000
Explanation					
Par value per share, common stock	$4	$0.50			
Number of shares outstanding	10,000	2,000			
Book value per share	$14	$3			
Total earnings	$30,000	$2,000			
Earnings per share	$3	$1			
Price/earnings ratio	20×	30×			
Market value per share	$60	$30			

9. Under purchase accounting, the acquiring company "should allocate the cost of an acquired company to the assets acquired and liabilities assumed." (*APB Opinion No. 16*, p. 318, par. 87.) A specific procedure is set forth. First, all identifiable assets acquired should be assigned a portion of the cost of the acquired company, normally equal to their fair (market or appraised) values at date of acquisition. Second, the excess of the cost of the acquired company over the sum of the amounts assigned to net assets should be recorded as goodwill. The sum of fair market values assigned may exceed the cost of the acquired company. If so, values otherwise assignable to noncurrent assets should be reduced by a proportionate part of the excess. If noncurrent assets are reduced to zero and some excess still remains, it should be set up as a deferred credit.

The $54,000 goodwill represents a debit in the "Adjustments" column and is carried to the pro forma balance sheet. The pro forma balance sheet is obtained by simply adding the balance sheets of the constituent companies, together with adjustments.

A total value of $60,000 has been given by Mammoth for a book value of $6,000. This amount represents, in addition to the debt, a payment of $1,000 for the common stock of Petty, $5,000 for the retained earnings, and $54,000 goodwill. The corresponding credit is the 1,000 shares of Mammoth given in the transaction at their par value of $4 a share, resulting in a credit of $4,000, and the capital surplus of Mammoth is increased by $56,000 (equals $60,000 paid minus $4,000 increase in common stock). The net credit to the net worth account is $54,000, which balances the net debit to the asset accounts. When these adjustments are carried through to the *pro forma* balance sheet, total assets are increased from the uncombined total of $210,000 to a new total of $264,000. Total tangible assets, however, still remain $210,000.

The effects on earnings per share for stockholders in each company are shown below:

Total earnings (before write-off of goodwill)	$32,000
Amortization of goodwill	1,350
Total net earnings	$30,650
Total shares	11,000
Earnings per share	$2.79
For Petty shareholders	
New earnings per share*	$1.40
Before-purchase earnings per share	$1.00
Accretion per share	$0.40
For Mammoth shareholders	
Before-purchase earnings per share	$3.00
New earnings per share	$2.79
Dilution per share	$0.21

*Petty shareholders, after the one-for-two exchange, have only one-half as many shares as before the merger.

Total earnings represent the combined earnings of Mammoth and Petty. Mammoth believes that the value reflected in goodwill will be permanent, but under *APB Opinion 17*, it is required to write off the goodwill account over a minimum of 40 years. The annual charge of $1,350 is the goodwill of $54,000 divided by 40. The total amount of net earnings is, therefore, $30,650.

The total shares are 11,000, because Mammoth has given one share of stock for every two shares of Petty previously outstanding. The new earnings per share are therefore $2.79. The calculation of earnings accretion or dilution proceeds on the same principles as the calculations set forth earlier in the chapter. The results require two important comments, however.

It will be noted that although the earnings accretion per share for Petty is 40 cents, the earnings dilution per share for Mammoth is relatively small, only 21 cents a share. The explanation is that the size of Mammoth is large in relation to that of Petty. This example also illustrates a general principle—when a large company acquires a small one, it can afford to pay a high multiple of earnings per share of the smaller company. In the present example, the price/earnings ratio of Petty is 30, whereas that of Mammoth is 20. If the acquiring company is large in relation to the acquired firm, it can pay a substantial premium and yet suffer only small dilution in its earnings per share.

It is, however, unrealistic to assume that the same earnings on total assets will result after the merger. After all, the purpose of the merger is to achieve something that the two companies could not have achieved alone. When Philip Morris & Company purchased Benson & Hedges, maker of Parliament, a leading filter-tip brand, it was buying the ability and experience of Benson & Hedges. By means of this merger, Philip Morris & Company was able to make an entry into the rapidly growing filter-cigarette business more quickly than it could otherwise have done. The combined earnings per share were expected to rise.

In the Mammoth-Petty illustration, the earnings rate on the tangible assets of Mammoth is 15 percent and on the total assets of Petty is 20 percent. Let us now assume that the return on total tangible assets of the combined companies rises to 20 percent. The 20 percent of tangible assets of $210,000 equals $42,000; less the amortization of goodwill over 40 years of $1,350 per year, equals $40,650 net earnings. With the same total shares of 11,000 outstanding, the new earnings per share will be $3.70. Thus there will be accretion of $2.70 for the Petty shareholders and an accretion of 70 cents for the Mammoth shareholders as well.

This illustrates another general principle—if the purchase of a small company adds to the earnings of the consolidated enterprise, earnings per share may increase for both participants in the merger. Even if the merger results in an initial dilution in earnings per share of the larger company, it may still be advantageous. The initial dilution in the earnings per share may be regarded as an investment that will have a payoff at some future date in terms of increased growth in earnings per share of the consolidated company.

Treatment of Goodwill

In a purchase, goodwill is likely to arise; since goodwill represents an intangible asset, its treatment is subject to the exercise of judgment. It will therefore be useful to set out a few generalizations on good practice in the treatment of goodwill.

1. When goodwill is purchased, it should not be charged to surplus immediately on acquisition. Preferably, goodwill should be written off against income and should go through the income statement. Since goodwill is to be written off against income, it is not appropriate to write it off entirely on acquisition, because this would be of such magnitude that distortion of earnings for that year would result.

2. The general view is not to write off purchased goodwill by charges to capital surplus. Purchased goodwill is supposed to represent, and to be reflected in, a future rise of income. It should be written off against income rather than against capital surplus.

3. When goodwill is purchased, an estimate should be made of its life. Annual charges, based on the estimated life of the goodwill, should then be made against income to amortize the goodwill over the estimated period of the usefulness of the goodwill purchased.

4. Intangibles must be written off over a maximum of 40 years by *APB Opinion 17.*

When goodwill is purchased, it should be treated like any other asset. It should be written off to the extent that the value represented by any part of goodwill has a limited life, as is likely to be the situation. In a free enterprise economy, the existence of high profits represented by superior earning power attracts additional resources into that line of business. The growth of capacity and the increase in competition are likely to erode the superior earning power over time.

Financial Treatment of Pooling of Interests

When a business combination is a *pooling of interests* rather than a purchase, the accounting treatment is simply to combine the balance sheets of the two companies. Goodwill will not ordinarily arise in the consolidation.

The financial treatment may be indicated by another example, which reflects the facts as they are set forth in Table 22–3. In order to focus on the critical issues, the balance sheets are identical in every respect. However, a difference in the amount and rate of profit (after interest) of the two companies is indicated.

Book value per share is $10. The amount of profit after interest and taxes is $42,000 for company A and $21,000 for company B. Earnings per share are therefore $3.50 and $1.75, respectively. The price/earnings ra-

Table 22–3
Financial Treatment of Pooling of Interests

	A	B	Net Adjustments on A's Books — Debit	Net Adjustments on A's Books — Credit	Acquiring Firm A's New Balance Sheets and Earnings if the Exchange Basis is 2/1	Acquiring Firm A's New Balance Sheets and Earnings if the Exchange Basis is 3/1
Current assets	$100,000	$100,000			$200,000	$200,000
Fixed assets	100,000	100,000			200,000	200,000
Total assets	$200,000	$200,000			$400,000	$400,000
Current liabilities	$ 50,000	$ 50,000			$100,000	$100,000
Long-term debt	30,000	30,000			60,000	60,000
Total debt	80,000	80,000			160,000	160,000
Common stock, par value $5	60,000	60,000	$30,000* $40,000†		90,000	80,000
Capital surplus	50,000	50,000		$30,000* $40,000†	130,000	140,000
Retained earnings	10,000	10,000			20,000	20,000
Total claims on assets	$200,000	$200,000			$400,000	$400,000
			Ratios A/B			
Number of shares of stock	12,000	12,000			18,000	16,000
Book value	$ 10	$ 10	1.0			
Amount of profit after interest and taxes	$ 42,000	$ 21,000			$ 63,000	$ 63,000
Earnings per share	$ 3.50	$ 1.75	2.0		$ 3.50	$ 3.94
Price/earnings ratio	18	12				
Market price of stock	$ 63.00	$ 21.00	3.0			
Net working capital per share	$ 4.17	$ 4.17	1.0			
Dividends per share	$ 1.75	$ 0.875	2.0		Shareholders' New *EPS*	

					A	B
Exchange ratio No. 1: earnings basis	2/1					
Equivalent earnings per share (new basis)					$3.50	$1.75
Exchange ratio No. 2: price basis	3/1					
Equivalent earnings per share (new basis)					$3.94	$1.31

*2/1 ratio basis.
†3/1 ratio basis.

tio is 18 for A and 12 for B, so the market price of stock for A is $63 and for B $27. The net working capital per share is $4.17 in each instance. The dividends per share are $1.75 for A and $0.875 for B.

Now assume that the terms of the merger would reflect either

(1) earnings or (2) market price per share. In both cases it is assumed that A is the acquiring and surviving firm. If A buys B on the basis of earnings, it exchanges 0.5 shares of A's common stock for 1 share of B's common stock. The total number of shares of A's common stock that will be outstanding after the acquisition is 18,000, of which 6,000 shares will be held by the old stockholders of B. The new earnings per share in the now larger A company will be the total earnings of $63,000 divided by 18,000, which equals $3.50 per share. Thus, the earnings per share for A remain unchanged. The old shareholders of B now hold 0.5 shares of A for each share of B held before the acquisition. Hence, their equivalent earnings per share from their present holdings of A shares are $1.75, the same as before the acquisition. We see that the stockholders of neither A nor B have experienced earnings dilution or earnings accretion.

When the terms of exchange are based on market price per share, the terms of acquisition would be the exchange of $1/3$ share of A stock for 1 share of B stock. The number of A shares is increased by the 4,000 exchanged for the 12,000 shares of B. The combined earnings of $63,000 are divided by 16,000 shares to obtain an increase in A's earnings per share to $3.94, which represents earnings accretion of $0.44 per share for the A shareholders. The old B shareholders now hold $1/3$ share of A for each 1 share of B held before the acquisition. Their equivalent earnings are now $3.94 divided by 3, or $1.31, representing earnings dilution of $0.44 per share.

The adjustment to the common stock account in surviving company A's balance sheet reflects the fact that only 6,000 shares of A were used to buy 12,000 shares of B when the acquisition is made on the basis of earnings. The decrease of 6,000 shares times the par value of $5 requires a net debit of $30,000 to the common stock account of A ($60,000 + $60,000 − $30,000 = $90,000) with an offsetting increase of $30,000 in the capital surplus account of company A ($50,000 + $50,000 + $30,000 = $130,000). When the exchange is made on the basis of market values, only 4,000 shares of A are needed to acquire the 12,000 shares of B. Hence, the net decrease in the common stock account of A is $40,000, with an offsetting increase in the same amount in A's capital surplus.

The general principle is that when terms of merger are based on the market price per share and the price/earnings ratios of the two companies are different, earnings accretion and dilution will occur. The company with a higher price/earnings ratio will attain earnings accretion; the company with the lower price/earnings ratio will suffer earnings dilution. If the sizes of the companies are greatly different, the effect on the larger company will be relatively small, whether in earnings dilution or in earnings accretion. The effect on the smaller company will be large.

Holding Companies

In 1889, New Jersey became the first state to pass a general incorporation law permitting corporations to be formed for the sole purpose of owning the stocks of other companies. This law was the origin of the holding company. The Sherman Act of 1890, which prohibits combinations or collusion in restraint of trade, gave an impetus to holding company operations as well as to outright mergers, because companies could do as one company what they were forbidden to do, by the terms of the act, as separate companies.

Many of the advantages and disadvantages of holding companies are no more than the advantages and disadvantages of large-scale operations already discussed in connection with mergers and consolidations. Whether a company is organized on a divisional basis or with the divisions kept as separate companies does not affect the basic reasons for conducting a large-scale, multiproduct, multiplant operation. However, the holding company form of large-scale operations has different advantages and disadvantages from those of completely integrated divisionalized operations.

Advantages of Holding Companies

Control with Fractional Ownership. Through a holding company operation, a firm may buy 5, 10, or 50 percent of the stock of another corporation. Such fractional ownership may be sufficient to give the acquiring company effective working control or substantial influence over the operations of the company in which it has acquired stock ownership. An article in the *New York Times* states this point clearly.

Working control is often considered to entail more than 25 percent of the common stock, but it can be as low as 10 percent if the stock is widely distributed. One financier says that the attitude of management is more important than the number of shares owned, adding that "if they think you can control the company, then you do." In addition, control on a very slim margin can be held through friendship with large stockholders outside the holding company group.

Sometimes holding company operations represent the initial stages of the transformation of an operating company into an investment company, particularly when the operating company is in a declining industry. When the sales of an industry begin to decline permanently and the firm begins to liquidate its operating assets, it may use these liquid funds to invest in industries having a more favorable growth potential. An illustration of this is provided by the same *New York Times* article.

Former investment banker Gordon W. Wattles, who holds many corporate directorships, is the architect of the pyramid built on Century Investors and Webster Investors. The former was once an aviation investment concern, while the latter began as a cigar maker.

Isolation of Risks. Because the various operating companies in a holding company system are separate legal entities, the obligations of any one unit are separate from those of the other units. Catastrophic losses incurred by one unit of the holding company system are therefore not transmitted as claims on the assets of the other units.

Although this is the customary generalization of the nature of a holding company system, it is not completely valid. In extending credit to one of the units of a holding company system, an astute financial manager or loan officer will require a guarantee or a claim on the assets of all the elements in a complete holding company system. To some degree, therefore, the assets in the various elements of a holding company are joined. The advantage remains to the extent that unanticipated catastrophes that may occur to one unit in a holding company system will not be transmitted to the other units.

Approval Not Required. If a holding company group is seeking to obtain effective working control of a number of companies, it may quietly purchase a portion of their stock. This is a completely informal operation, and the permission or approval of the stockholders of the acquired company or companies is not required. Thus the guiding personalities in a holding company operation are not dependent upon negotiations and approval of the other interest groups in order to obtain their objectives. This feature of holding company operations has, however, been limited somewhat by the recent SEC actions described later in the chapter.

**Disadvantages
of Holding
Companies**

Partial Multiple Taxation. Provided the holding company owns at least 80 percent of a subsidiary's voting stock, the Internal Revenue regulations permit the filing of consolidated returns, in which case dividends received by the parent are not taxed. However, if less than 80 percent of the stock is owned, returns may not be consolidated, but 85 percent of the dividends received by the holding company may be deducted. With a tax rate of 48 percent, this means that the effective tax on intercorporate dividends is 7.2 percent. This partial double taxation somewhat offsets the benefits of holding company control with limited ownership, but whether the penalty of 7.2 percent of dividends received is sufficient to offset other possible advantages is a matter that must be decided in individual situations.[10]

Ease of Enforced Dissolution. In the case of a holding company operation that falls into disfavor with the U.S. Department of Justice, it is relatively easy to require dissolution of the relationship by disposal of stock ownership; for instance, in the late 1950s du Pont was required to dispose of its 23 percent stock interest in General Motors Corporation, acquired in the early 1920s. Because there was no fusion between the corporations, there were no difficulties, from an operating standpoint, in requiring the separation of the two companies. However, if complete amalgamation had taken place, it would have been much more difficult to break up the company after so many years, and the likelihood of forced divestiture would have been reduced.

Risks of Excessive Pyramiding. While pyramiding magnifies profits if operations are successful, as was seen in the financial leverage analysis, it also magnifies losses. The greater the degree of pyramiding, the greater the degree of risk involved for any fluctuations in sales or earnings of the company. This potential disadvantage of pyramiding operations through holding companies is discussed in the next section.

Leverage in Holding Companies

The problem of excessive leverage is worthy of further note, for the degree of leverage in certain past instances has been truly staggering. For example, in the 1920s, Samuel Insull and his group controlled electric utility operating companies at the bottom of a holding company pyramid by a one-twentieth of 1 percent investment. As a ratio, this represents 1/2,000. In other words, $1 of capital at the top holding company level controlled $2,000 of assets at the operating level. A similar situation existed in the railroad field. It has been stated that Robert R. Young, with an investment of $254,000, obtained control of the Allegheny system, consisting of total operating assets of $3 billion.

The nature of leverage in a holding company system and its advantages and disadvantages are illustrated by the hypothetical example developed in Table 22-4.[11] Although, as in the previous example, this is

---

10. The 1969 Tax Reform Law also empowers the Internal Revenue Service to prohibit the deductibility of debt issued to acquire another firm where the following conditions hold: (1) the debt is subordinated to a "significant portion" of the firm's other creditors; (2) the debt is convertible or has warrants attached; (3) the debt/assets ratio exceeds 67 percent; and (4) on a *pro forma* basis, the times-interest-earned ratio is less than 3. The IRS can use discretion in invoking this power.

11. Corrections in computations were supplied by Dr. Narendra C. Bhandari, University of Baltimore.

a hypothetical case, it illustrates actual situations. One-half of the operating company's class B common stock is owned by holding company 1; in fact, it is the only asset of holding company 1. Holding company 2 holds as its total assets one-half of the class B common stock of holding company 1. Consequently, $1,000 of class B common stock of holding company 2 controls $2 million of assets at the operating company level. Further leverage could, of course, have been postulated in this situation by setting up a third company to own common stock B of holding company 2.

Table 22–4
Leverage in a
Holding Company
System

Holding Company 2

Common stock B of holding		Debt	$2,000
company 1	$5,000	Preferred stock	1,000
		Common stock: class A*	1,000
		Common stock: class B	1,000
	$5,000		$5,000

Holding Company 1

Common stock B of		Debt	$ 50,000
operating company	$100,000	Preferred stock	10,000
		Common stock: class A*	30,000
		Common stock: class B	10,000
	$100,000		$100,000

Operating Company

Total assets	$2,000,000	Debt	$1,000,000
		Preferred stock	150,000
		Common stock: class A*	650,000
		Common stock: class B	200,000
	$2,000,000		$2,000,000

*Common stock A is nonvoting.

Table 22–5 shows the results of holding company leverage on gains and losses at the top level. In the first column, it is assumed that the operating company earns 12 percent before taxes on its $2 million of assets; in the second column it is assumed that the return on assets is 8 percent. The operating and holding companies are the same ones described in Table 22–4.

A return of 12 percent on the operating assets of $2 million represents a total profit of $240,000. The debt interest of $40,000 is deducted from this amount, and the 50 percent tax rate applies to the remainder. The amount available to common stock after payment of debt interest, pre-

Table 22–5
Results of Holding
Company Leverage
on Gains and
Losses

Assume that each company pays: 4% on debt
5% on preferred stock
8% on common stock A

	Earnings before Taxes	
Operating Company	12%	8%
Amount earned	$240,000	$160,000
Less tax*	100,000	60,000
Available to meet fixed charges	$140,000	$100,000
Debt interest	$ 40,000	$ 40,000
Preferred stock	7,500	7,500
Common stock A	52,000	52,000
Total charges	$ 99,500	$ 99,500
Available to common B	40,500	500
Dividends to common B	40,000	500
Holding Company 1		
Amount earned	$ 20,000	$ 250
Less tax (0.5 × 0.5 × $1,000)*	500	0
Available to meet fixed charges	$ 19,500	$ 250
Debt interest	$ 2,000	$ 2,000
Preferred stock	500	500
Common stock A	2,400	2,400
Total charges	$ 4,900	$ 4,900
Available to common B	$ 14,600	loss
Dividends to common B	10 000	
Holding Company 2		
Amount earned	$ 5,000	
Less taxes (0.5 × 0.5 × $670)*	335	
Available to meet fixed charges	$ 4,665	
Debt interest	$ 80	
Preferred stock	50	
Common stock A	80	
Total charges	$ 210	
Available to common B	$ 4,455	
Percent return on common B	445.5%	

*Tax computed on earnings less interest charges at a 50 percent tax rate. Since earnings are entirely in the form of intercorporate dividends, only 15 percent of the holding company's earnings are taxable.

ferred stock dividends, and an 8 percent return to the nonvoting common stock A is $40,500. Assuming a $40,000 dividend payout, holding company 1, on the basis of its 50 percent ownership of the operating company, earns $20,000. If the same kind of analysis is followed through, the amount available to common stock B in holding company 2 would be $4,455. This return is on an investment of $1,000, representing a return on the investment in common stock B of holding company 2 of about 445 percent. The power of leverage in a holding company system can indeed be great.

On the other hand, if a decline in revenues caused the pretax earnings to drop to 8 percent of the total assets of the operating company, the results would be disastrous. The amount earned under these circumstances is $160,000. After deducting the bond interest, the amount subject to tax is $120,000, resulting in a tax of $60,000. The after-tax-but-before-interest earnings are $100,000. The total prior charges are $99,500, leaving $500 available to common stock B. If all earnings are paid out in dividends to common stock B, the earnings of holding company 1 are $250. This is not enough to meet the debt interest. The holding company system would be forced to default on the debt interest of holding company 1 and, of course, holding company 2.

This example illustrates the potential for tremendous gains in a holding company system. It also illustrates that a small decline in earnings on the assets of the operating companies would be disastrous.

Tender Offers

In a tender offer, one party, generally a corporation seeking a controlling interest in another corporation, asks the stockholders of the firm it is seeking to control to submit, or "tender," their shares in exchange for a specified price. The price is generally stated as so many dollars per share of acquired stock, although it can be stated in terms of shares of stock in the acquiring firm. Tender offers have been used for a number of years, but the pace greatly accelerated after 1965 and was at a crescendo in 1976 and 1977.

If one firm wishes to gain control over another, it typically approaches the other firm's management and board of directors seeking its approval of the merger. An alternative approach is termed the "bear hug" in which a company mails a letter to the directors of the takeover target announcing the acquisition proposal, requiring the directors to make a quick decision on the bid. If approval cannot be obtained, the acquiring company can appeal directly to stockholders by means of the tender offer, unless the management and directors of the target firm hold enough stock to retain control. When the acquiring company goes directly to the shareholders, this technique had been called a "Saturday night special," implying that a gun has been aimed at the directors since if the shareholders respond favorably to the tender offer, the acquiring company will gain control and have the power to replace the directors who have not cooperated in their takeover efforts.

During 1967, congressional investigations were conducted to obtain information that could be used to legislate controls over tender offers. The reasons for the investigations were (1) the frequency of tender offers, (2) the thought that the recent merger trend was leading to "too much concentration" in the economy, and (3) the feeling that tender offers were somehow "unfair" to the managements of the firms acquired through this vehicle. A new law became effective on July 29, 1968, placing tender offers under full SEC jurisdiction. Disclosure requirements written into the statute include the following: (1) The acquiring firm must give both to the management of the target firm and to the SEC 30 days' notice of its intentions to make the acquisition. (2) When substantial blocks are purchased through tender offers (or through open market purchases—that is, on the stock exchange), the beneficial owner of the stock must be disclosed, together with the name of the party putting up the money for the transaction.

In addition to the new powers granted to the SEC to require disclosure of takeover intentions, other tactics may be used by the intended target. More than 30 states have adopted antitakeover laws that can delay tender offers so that an alternative may be pursued. The takeover target may also utilize other legal tactics such as court suits alleging that antitrust laws and other regulatory guidelines are violated. Such tactics may forestall a takeover. For example, when Anderson, Clayton, & Co. made a bid for Gerber Products Co., the latter instituted a number of legal suits. After five months of legal maneuvers on both sides, Anderson, Clayton dropped its bid in September 1977. The Hart-Scott-Rodino Act of 1976 amending the antitrust laws contained a provision that requires premerger notification to the FTC of large mergers. This provision is to become effective in 1978.

As a consequence of the disclosure requirements in connection with intended tender offers, competition between bidders in takeover efforts may cause the acquisition price to rise well above the market price of the stock before the initial tender offer. This is illustrated by some examples.

The first example is Tenneco's acquisition of Kern County Land Company. Kern was a relatively old, conservatively managed company whose assets consisted largely of oil properties and agricultural land, together with some manufacturing subsidiaries. Many informed investors believed that Kern's assets had a potential long-run value in excess of its current market price. Occidental Petroleum, a relatively aggressive company, made an investigation of Kern's assets and decided to make a tender offer for the company. At that time, Kern's market price on the New York Stock Exchange was about $60 a share, while the price Occidental decided to offer Kern's stockholders was $83.50 a share. According to Kern's management, Occidental's management got in touch with the former over a weekend and informed Kern that the tender offer would be made the following Monday.

Kern's management resisted the offer. Because the published statements of Occidental indicated that it felt Kern's undervalued position was partly the result of an unimaginative management, Kern's management could anticipate being replaced in the event that Occidental effected the takeover. Naturally, Kern's management resisted the takeover. Kern's president wrote a letter to stockholders condemning the merger and published the letter as an advertisement in the *Wall Street Journal*. His position was that Kern's stock was certainly valuable and that it was worth more than had been offered by Occidental Petroleum.

How would Kern County's stockholders react to this exchange? In the first place, the stock had been selling at about $60 a share, and now they were offered $83.50 a share. With this differential, stockholders would certainly accept the tender unless Kern's management could do something to keep the price above $83.50. What Kern did was to obtain "marriage proposals" from a number of other companies. Kern's management reported to the newspapers—while Occidental's tender offer was still outstanding—that it had received a substantial number of proposals calling for the purchase of Kern's stock at a price substantially in excess of $83.50.

The offer Kern's management finally accepted—and presumably the one giving Kern's stockholders the highest price—was from Tenneco Corporation. Tenneco offered one share of a new $5.50 convertible preferred stock for each share of Kern's stock. At the time of Tenneco's offer, the market value of this convertible preferred was estimated to be worth about $105 a share. Further, Kern's stockholders would not have to pay capital gains tax on this stock at the time of the exchange. (Had they accepted Occidental's offer, the difference between $83.50 and the cost of their stock would be taxable income to Kern's stockholders.) According to newspaper reports, Tenneco planned to keep Kern's existing management after the merger was completed.

When the Kern–Tenneco merger was completed, Tenneco owned the Kern stock and thus became a holding company, with Kern being one of its operating subsidiaries.

If the takeover company bids too low initially, it may stimulate a bidding contest. But if it makes the initial bid at a substantial premium over the prevailing market price of the takeover target, it may be criticized by its stockholders for having paid an excessive amount. Both situations have occurred, so a difficult challenge is posed in formulating the right takeover bid. Examples are provided by dramatic episodes that occurred during 1977,

United Technologies (UT) bid $42 per share in March 1977 for Babcock & Wilcox (BW), whose common stock was then selling for less than $35 per share. United Technologies is a producer of aircraft engines, rocket motors and engines, automotive and space equipment, helicopters, elevators, escalators, and other industrial equipment. Babcock & Wilcox was mainly in steam-generating equipment such as the massive boilers used in both fossil-fuel and nuclear-powered turbine generator systems. In addition, it produced pollution control equipment and other equipment for the handling and transfer of heat. The 1976 sales of UT were $5.2 billion, while the 1976 sales of BW were $1.7 billion. Shortly after UT's tender offer, J. Ray McDermott & Co. (JRM) entered the contest. JRM was smaller than either of the other two companies with sales of $1.2 billion in 1976. JRM was mainly in the engineering, fabrication, and installation of facilities for the production of oil and gas. By May 1977, JRM announced that it had bought nearly 9 percent of BW's stock on the open market. BW proceeded to take legal actions against both takeover rivals. In August 1977, UT upped its bid for BW to $48. Shortly thereafter, JRM bid $55, which the BW directors urged its shareholders to accept. A complicated series of counterbids ensued, with McDermott winning the competition for a final price of $65 a share, nearly double the pretender market price.

In an example of a bid that might have been too high, Kennecott Copper was motivated by the fear of becoming a takeover target itself. In accordance with a requirement by the Federal Trade Commission of divestiture of Peabody Coal, Kennecott had agreed to a sale to a group of companies for $1.2 billion to be paid in installments. Since Kennecott was in process of becoming cash rich as it received installment payments for the purchase price, it wanted to utilize the cash. It sought to avoid being acquired by a company that might use debt to buy Kennecott and then use the cash flowing into Kennecott to pay off the debt. Kennecott, with 1976 sales of slightly under $1 billion, is an integrated producer of metals (mainly copper) and mineral products.

Eaton Corporation (formerly Eaton Yale & Towne) with 1976 revenues of $1.8 billion, in early November 1977, had made an offer of $47 per share for the stock of the Carborundum Company then selling at $33.25 per share. Eaton produces locks and other security systems as well as automotive parts and components. Carborundum, a leading producer of carbon products, other abrasives, refractory and electric products, had 1976 revenues of $614 million. In mid-November 1977, Kennecott made an offer to Carborundum of $66 per share. On November 17, 1977, it was announced that the directors of both companies had unanimously approved the offer. Some stockholders stated that they were stunned by this "squandering of Kennecott's cash." Others praised Kennecott for avoiding the "ridiculous newspaper auction that marked the Babcock & Wilcox battle." The reader is invited to make his own judgment of the appropriateness of the $66 price paid by Kennecott.

Summary

Growth is vital to the well-being of a firm, for without it a business cannot attract able management because it cannot give recognition in promotions and challenging creative activity. Mergers have played an important part in the growth of firms, and since financial managers are required both to appraise the desirability of a prospective merger and to participate in evaluating the respective companies involved in the merger, the present chapter has been devoted to background materials on merger decisions.

Terms of Mergers. The most important term that must be negotiated in a merger arrangement is the price the acquiring firm will pay for the acquired business. The most important *quantitative* factors influencing the terms of a merger are (1) current earnings, (2) current market prices, (3) book values, and (4) net working capital. *Qualitative* considerations may suggest that *synergistic*, or "two-plus-two-equals-five," effects may be present to a sufficient extent to warrant paying more for the acquired firm than the quantitative factors would suggest. Recently, the current values of corporate stock have exceeded the market values of the related corporate securities.

Accounting Policies and Mergers. A merger may be treated as either a *purchase* or a *pooling of interests*. In a *purchase*, a larger firm generally takes over a smaller one and assumes all management control. The amount actually paid for the smaller firm is reflected in the acquiring firm's balance sheet; if more was paid for the acquired firm than the book value of its assets, goodwill is reflected on the acquiring firm's financial statements. In a *pooling of interests*, the merged firms should be about the same size, both managements should carry on important functions after the merger, and common stock rather than cash or bonds should be used in payment. The total assets of the surviving firm in a pooling are equal to the sum of the assets of the two independent companies, so no goodwill is required to be written off as a charge against earnings.

Holding Companies. In mergers, one firm disappears. However, an alternative is for one firm to buy all or a majority of the common stock of another and to run the acquired firm as an operating subsidiary. When this occurs, the acquiring firm is said to be a *holding company*. A number of advantages arise when a holding company is formed.

1. It may be possible to control the acquired firm with a smaller investment than would be necessary in a merger.
2. Each firm in a holding company is a separate legal entity, and the

obligations of any one unit are separate from the obligations of the other units.
3. Stockholder approval is required before a merger can take place. This is not necessary in a holding company situation.

There are also some disadvantages to holding companies, some of which are listed below.

1. If the holding company does not own 80 percent of the subsidiary's stock and does not file consolidated tax returns, it is subject to taxes on 15 percent of the dividends received from the subsidiary.
2. The leverage effects possible in holding companies can subject the holding company to magnification of earnings fluctuations and related risks.
3. The Antitrust Division of the U.S. Department of Justice can much more easily force the breakup of a holding company situation than it can bring about the dissolution of two completely merged firms.

Questions

22-1. The number of mergers tends to fluctuate with business activity, rising when GNP rises and falling when GNP falls. Why does this relationship exist?

22-2. A large firm has certain advantages over a smaller one. What are some of the *financial* advantages of large size?

22-3. What are some of the potential benefits that can be expected by a firm that merges with a company in a different industry?

22-4. Distinguish between a holding company and an operating company. Give an example of each.

22-5. Which appears to be more risky, the use of debt in the holding company's capital structure or the use of debt in the operating company's? Why?

22-6. Is the public interest served by an increase in merger activity? Give arguments both pro and con.

22-7. Would the book value of a company's assets be considered the absolute minimum price to be paid for a firm? Why? Is there any value that would qualify as an absolute minimum?

22-8. Discuss the situation where one firm, Mic vest Motors, for example, calls off merger negotiations with anothe American Data Labs, because the latter's stock price is overvalued. hat assumption concerning dilution is implicit in the above situatio.?

22-9. There are many methods by which a company can raise additional capital. Can a merger be considered a means of raising additional equity capital? Explain.

22-10. A particularly difficult problem regarding business combinations has been whether to treat the new company as a *purchase* or as a *pooling of interests.*
   a. What criteria can be set down to differentiate between these two forms of business combinations?
   b. Would you as a stockholder in one of the firms prefer a purchase or a pooling arrangement? Why?
   c. Which combination would you prefer if you were a high-ranking manager in one of the firms?

22-11. Question 22-10 discusses purchase and pooling arrangements. Why is it important to make a distinction between these two combination forms?

22-12. Are the negotiations for merger agreements more difficult if the firms are in different industries or in the same industry? If they are about the same size or quite different in size? If the ages of the firms are about the same or if they are very different? Why?

22-13. How would the existence of long-term debt in a company's financial structure affect its valuation for merger purposes? Could the same be said for any debt account regardless of its maturity?

22-14. During 1964-65, the Pure Oil Company was involved in merger negotiations with at least three other firms. The terms of these arrangements varied from a transfer of stock to a direct cash purchase of Pure Oil. Discuss the relative advantages to a corporation of paying for an acquisition in cash or in stock.

22-15. In late 1968 the SEC and the New York Stock Exchange each issued sets of rulings on disclosure of information that, in effect, required that firms disclose that they have entered into merger discussions as soon as they start such discussions. Since the previous procedure had been to delay disclosure until it was evident that there was a reasonably good expectation the merger under discussion would actually go through (and not to bring the matter up at all if the merger died in the early stages), it can safely be predicted that, in a statistical sense, a larger percentage of prospective mergers will be "abandoned" in the future than in the past.
   a. Why do you suppose the new rulings were put into effect?
   b. Will the new rulings have any adverse effects? Why?

Problems

22-1. You are given the following balance sheets:

**Rocky Mountain Services Company
Consolidated Balance Sheet**

Cash	$1,500	Borrowings	$1,125
Other current assets	1,125	Common stock	1,875
Net property	1,875	Retained earnings	1,500
Total assets	$4,500	Total claims on assets	$4,500

White Lighting Company
Balance Sheet

Cash	$375	Net worth	$750
Net property	375		
Total assets	$750	Total net worth	$750

a. The holding company, Rocky Mountain, buys the operating company, White, with "free" cash of $750. Show the new consolidated balance sheet for Rocky Mountain after the acquisition.

b. Instead of buying White, Rocky Mountain buys Conner Company with free cash of $1,125. The balance sheet of Conner follows:

Conner Company
Balance Sheet

Cash	$ 750	Borrowings	$ 750
Net property	1,125	Net worth	1,125
Total assets	$1,875	Total claims on assets	$1,875

Show the new consolidated balance sheet for Rocky Mountain after acquisition of Conner.

c. What are the implications of your consolidated balance sheets for measuring the growth of firms resulting from acquisitions?

22–2. Southern Realty Company is a holding company owning the entire common stock of Bryant Company and Sunther Company. The balance sheet as of December 31, 1975, for each subsidiary is identical with the following one.

Balance Sheet
December 31, 1975

Current assets	$ 7,500,000	Current liabilities	$ 1,250,000
Fixed assets, net	5,000,000	First mortgage bonds (9%)	2,500,000
		Preferred stock (7%)	2,500,000
		Common stock	5,000,000
		Retained earnings	1,250,000
Total assets	$12,500,000	Total claims on assets	$12,500,000

Each operating company earns $1,375,000 annually before taxes and before interest and preferred dividends. A 50 percent tax rate is assumed.

a. What is the annual rate of return on each company's net worth (common stock plus retained earnings)?

b. Construct a balance sheet for Southern Realty Company based on the following assumptions: (i) The only asset of the holding company is the common stock of the two subsidiaries; this stock is carried at par (not book) value. (ii) The holding company has $1.2 million of 8 percent coupon debt and $2.8 million of 6 percent preferred stock.

c. What is the rate of return on the book value of the holding company's common stock if (i) Southern Realty files a consolidated income tax return, and (ii) subsidiary earnings available to common are taken as dividends by the holding company?

d. With regard to part c, which method of income taxation should Southern Realty employ?

e. How can the rate of return in part c be increased?

f. What determines the percentage ownership required to control the holding company?

g. If ownership of 25 percent of the holding company's common stock ($6 million of common) could control all three firms, what percentage would this be of the total operating assets?

22–3. You are given the following data on two companies:

	Company I	Company II	Adjustments	Consolidated Statement
Current assets	$56,000	$56,000		_____
Fixed assets	34,000	34,000		_____
Total assets	$90,000	$90,000		_____
Current liabilities	$31,000	$31,000		_____
Long-term debt	19,000	19,000		_____
Total debt, 5%*	$50,000	$50,000		_____
Common stock, par value $4	24,000	24,000	_____	_____
Capital surplus	11,000	11,000	_____	_____
Retained earnings	5,000	5,000	_____	_____
Total claims on assets	$90,000	$90,000		_____

			Ratios	
1. Number of shares of stock	6,000	6,000		1. _____
2. Book value per share	_____	_____	1. _____	2. _____
3. Amount of profit before interest and taxes†	$29,000	$15,000		3. _____
4. Earnings per share	_____	_____	2. _____	4. _____
5. Price/earnings ratio	22.6	12		
6. Market price of stock	_____	_____	3. _____	
7. Working capital per share	_____	_____	4. _____	
8. Dividends per share, 50% payout	_____	_____	5. _____	
9. Exchange ratio	_____	_____	6. _____	(I/II)
10. Equivalent earnings per old share	_____	_____		

*Average rate on interest-bearing and noninterest-bearing debt combined.
†Assume a 50 percent tax rate.

a. In your judgment, what would be a reasonable basis for determining the terms at which shares in company I and in company II would be exchanged for shares in a new company III? What exchange ratio would you recommend and why?

b. Use the market price of stock relation as the basis for the terms of ex-change of stock in the old company for stock in the new company (two shares of III for one share of I, and one-half share of III for one share of II). Then complete the calculations for filling in all the blank spaces, including the adjustments for making the consolidated state-ment. Treat this problem as a situation that the SEC and accountants would refer to as a pooling of interests.

22–4. The Vertical Company has just purchased the Horizontal Company under an arrangement known as a purchase. The purchase was made by stock in a settlement based exactly on the indicated market prices of the two firms. The data on the two companies are given below.

    a. Fill in the blank spaces and complete the adjustments and pro forma balance sheet columns and show the journal entries for the stock pur-chase. Give an explanation for your entries.

    b. Calculate earnings dilution or accretion for both companies on the assumption that total earnings are unchanged.

    c. Calculate the earnings dilution or accretion on the assumption that the return on combined tangible assets rises to 20 percent after inter-est and taxes.

    d. Comment on your findings.

	Vertical	Horizontal	Adjustments Debits	Credits	Pro Forma Balance Sheet
Current assets	$ 450,000	$ 7,000			
Other assets	150,000	5,000			
Fixed assets	400,000	8,000			
Intangibles (goodwill)					
Total assets	$1,000,000	$20,000			
Current liabilities	$ 200,000	$ 8,000			
Long-term debt	150,000				
Common stock	200,000	2,000			
Capital surplus	150,000				
Retained earnings	300,000	10,000			
Total claims	$1,000,000	$20,000			
Par value	$4.00	$0.50			
Number of shares					
Total earnings available to common	$ 125,000	$ 8,000			
Book value					
Earnings per share					
Price/earnings ratio	10 times	25 times			
Market value per share					

22–5. Every merger agreement is subject to negotiation between the compa-nies involved. One significant indicator of the compensation received by the acquired company is the respective market price of the companies' stocks in relation to the merger terms. Some actual merger data are given below.

Calculate the percent premium, or discount, received by the acquired company, using market prices as the criteria. Compare the results of your calculations on the basis of the stock prices of the two previous quarters with that of your results on the basis of the prices immediately preceding the merger. Which is the proper measure of the actual discount or premium received: the one indicated by the earlier stock prices or the one indicated by the stock prices immediately preceding the merger? Explain.

Company	Terms	Market Price Two Quarters before Merger		Market Price Immediately Preceding Merger	
		A	B	A	B
1 {A Celanese Corporation / B Champlain Oil	2 shares of Celanese for every 3 shares of Champlain	62	34	67	42
2 {A Cities Service Company / B Tennessee Corporation	0.9 shares (2.25 pref.) for each Tenn. Corp. share (common)	65	48	61	55
3 {A Ford Motor Company / B Philco Corporation	1 share of Ford for every 4½ shares of Philco	81	22	113	25
4 {A General Telephone / B Sylvania Electric	Share-for-share basis	52	46	69	69

Selected References

Ackerman, Robert W., and Fray, Lionel L. "Financial Evaluation of a Potential Acquisition." *Financial Executive* (October 1967):34–54.

Adler, Michael, and Dumas, Bernard. "Optimal International Acquisitions." *Journal of Finance* 30 (Mar. 1975):1–19.

Alberts, William W., and Segall, Joel E., eds. *The Corporate Merger.* Chicago: University of Chicago Press, 1966.

Austin, Douglas V. "The Financial Management of Tender Offer Takeovers." *Financial Management* 3, no. 1 (Spring 1974):37–43.

Boczar, Gregory E. "Market Characteristics and Multibank Holding Company Acquisitions." *Journal of Finance* 32 (Mar. 1977):131–46.

Buckley, Adrian. "A Review of Acquisition Valuation Models—A Comment." *Journal of Business Finance & Accounting* 2 (Spring 1975):147–52.

Cheney, Richard E. "What's New on the Corporate Takeover Scene." *Financial Executive* 40 (Apr. 1972):18–21.

———. "Remedies for Tender-Offer Anxiety." *Financial Executive* 43 (Aug. 1975):16–19.

Cohen, Manuel F. "Takeover Bids." *Financial Analysts' Journal* 26 (Jan.–Feb. 1970):26–31.

Crowther, John F. "Peril Point Acquisition Prices." *Harvard Business Review* 47 (Sept.–Oct. 1969):58–62.

Cunitz, Jonathan A. "Valuing Potential Acquisitions." *Financial Executive* 39 (Apr. 1971):16–28.

Folz, David F., and Weston, J. Fred. "Looking Ahead in Evaluating Proposed Mergers." *NAA Bulletin*, 43 (Apr. 1962):17–27.

Gaskill, William J. "Are You Ready for the New Merger Boom?" *Financial Executive* 42 (Sept. 1974):38–41.

Gort, Michael. *Diversification and Integration in American Industry.* Princeton, N.J.: Princeton University Press, 1962.

Gort, Michael, and Hogarty, Thomas E. "New Evidence on Mergers." *Journal of Law and Economics* 13 (Apr. 1970):167–84.

Goudzwaard, Maurice B. "Conglomerate Mergers, Convertibles, and Cash Dividends." *Quarterly Review of Business and Economics* (Spring 1969):53–62.

Haugen, Robert A., and Langetieg, Terence C. "An Empirical Test for Synergism in Merger." *Journal of Finance* 30 (June 1975):1003–14.

Hayes, Samuel L., III, and Taussig, Russell A. "Tactics in Cash Takeover Bids." *Harvard Business Review* 45 (Mar.–Apr. 1967):135–48.

Heath, John, Jr. "Valuation Factors and Techniques in Mergers and Acquisitions." *Financial Executive* 40 (Apr. 1972):34–44.

Hexter, Richard M. "How to Sell Your Company." *Harvard Business Review* 46 (May–June 1968):71–77.

Higgins, Robert C., and Schall, Lawrence D. "Corporate Bankruptcy and Conglomerate Merger." *Journal of Finance* 30 (Mar. 1975):93–113.

Hogarty, Thomas F. "The Profitability of Corporate Mergers." *Journal of Business* 44 (July 1970):317–27.

Howell, Robert A. "Plan to Integrate Your Acquisitions." *Harvard Business Review* 48 (Nov.–Dec. 1970):66–76.

Kelly, Eamon M. *The Profitability of Growth Through Mergers.* Pa.: Pennsylvania State University, 1967.

Kitching, John. "Winning and Losing with European Acquisitions." *Harvard Business Review* 52 (Mar.–Apr. 1974):124–36.

Kraber, Richard W. "Acquisition Analysis: New Help from Your Computer." *Financial Executive* (March 1970):10–15.

Larson, Kermit D., and Gonedes, Nicholas J. "Business Combinations: An Exchange-Ratio Determination Model." *Accounting Review* 44 (Oct. 1969): 720–28.

Lev, Baruch, and Mandelker, Gershon. "The Microeconomic Consequences of Corporate Mergers." *Journal of Business* 45 (Jan. 1972):85–104.

Lewellen, Wilbur G. "A Pure Financial Rationale for the Conglomerate Merger." *Journal of Finance* 26 (May 1971):521–37.

Lorie, J. H., and Halpern, P. "Conglomerates: The Rhetoric and the Evidence." *Journal of Law and Economics* 13 (Apr. 1970):149–66.

MacDougal, Gary E., and Malek, Fred V. "Master Plan for Merger Negotiations." *Harvard Business Review* 48 (Jan.–Feb. 1970):71–82.

Mandelker, G. "Risk and Return: The Case of Merging Firms." *Journal of Financial Economics* 1 (Dec. 1974):303–36.

Mason, R. Hal, and Goudzwaard, Maurice B. "Performance of Conglomerate Firms: A Portfolio Approach." *Journal of Finance* 31 (Mar. 1976):39–48.

Mead, Walter J. "Instantaneous Merger Profit as a Conglomerate Merger Motive." *Western Economic Review* 7 (Dec. 1969):295–306.

Melicher, Ronald W. "Financing with Convertible Preferred Stock: Comment." *Journal of Finance* 25 (Mar. 1971):144–47.

Melicher, Ronald W., and Rush, David F. "Evidence on the Acquisition-Related Performance of Conglomerate Firms." *Journal of Finance* 29 (Mar. 1974): 141–49.

Melicher, Ronald W., and Harter, Thomas R. "Stock Price Movements of Firms Engaging in Large Acquisitions." *Journal of Financial and Quantitative Analysis* 7 (Mar. 1972):1469–75.

Mueller, Dennis C. "A Theory of Conglomerate Mergers." *Quarterly Journal of Economics* 83 (Nov. 1969):643–59.

Reid, Samuel Richardson. *Mergers, Managers, and the Economy.* New York: McGraw-Hill, 1968.

Reilly, Frank K. "What Determines the Ratio of Exchange in Corporate Mergers?" *Financial Analysts' Journal* 18 (Nov.–Dec. 1962):47–50.

Reinhardt, Uwe E. *Mergers and Consolidations: A Corporate-Finance Approach.* Morristown: General Learning Press, 1972.

Reum, W. Robert, and Steele, Thomas A., III. "Contingent Payouts Cut Acquisition Risks." *Harvard Business Review* 48 (Mar.–Apr. 1970):83–91.

Rockwell, Willard F., Jr. "How to Acquire a Company." *Harvard Business Review* 46 (May–June 1968):121–32.

Shad, John S. R. "The Financial Realities of Mergers." *Harvard Business Review* 47 (Nov.–Dec. 1969):133–46.

Shick, Richard A. "The Analysis of Mergers and Acquisitions." *Journal of Finance* 27 (May 1972):495–502.

Shick, Richard A., and Jan, Frank C. "Merger Benefits to Shareholders of Acquiring Firms." *Financial Management* 3 (Winter 1974):45–53.

Silberman, Irwin H. "A Note on Merger Valuation." *Journal of Finance* 23 (June 1968):528–34.

Smalter, Donald J., and Lancey, Roderic C. "P/E Analysis in Acquisition Strategy." *Harvard Business Review* 44 (Nov.–Dec. 1966), 85–95.

Smith, Keith V., and Weston, J. Fred. "Further Evaluation of Conglomerate Performance," *Journal of Business Research* 5 (1977):5–14.

Sprecher, C. Ronald. "A Note on Financing Mergers with Convertible Preferred Stock." *Journal of Finance* 26 (June 1971):683–86.

Stapleton, R. C. "The Acquisition Decision as a Capital Budgeting Problem." *Journal of Business Finance & Accounting* 2 (Summer 1975):187–202.

Troubh, Raymond S. "Purchased Affection: A Primer on Cash Tender Offers." *Harvard Business Review* 54 (July–Aug. 1976):79–91.

Vancil, Richard F., and Lorange, Peter. "Strategic Planning in Diversified Companies." *Harvard Business Review* 53 (Jan.–Feb. 1975):81–90.

Weston, J. Fred. *The Role of Mergers in the Growth of Large Firms.* Berkeley: University of California Press, 1953.

Weston, J. Fred; Smith, Keith V.; and Shrieves, Ronald E. "Conglomerate Performance Using the Capital Asset Pricing Model." *Review of Economics and Statistics* (November 1972):357–63.

Weston, J. Fred, and Peltzman, Sam, eds. *Public Policy Toward Mergers.* Pacific Palisades, Calif.: Goodyear, 1969.

Weston, J. Fred and Mansinghka, Surendra K. "Tests of the Efficiency of Conglomerate Firms." *Journal of Finance* 26 (Sept. 1971):919–36.

Woods, Donald H., and Caverly, Thomas A. "Development of a Linear Programming Model for the Analysis of Merger/Acquisition Situations." *Journal of Financial and Quantitative Analysis* 4 (Jan. 1970):627–42.

Wyatt, Arthur R., and Kieso, Donald E. *Business Combinations: Planning and Action.* Scranton: International Textbook Company, 1969.

23 Failure, Reorganization and Liquidation

Thus far the text has dealt with issues associated mainly with the growing, successful enterprise. Not all businesses are so fortunate, however, so we must examine financial difficulties, their causes, and their possible remedies. This material is significant for the financial manager of successful, as well as potentially unsuccessful, firms. The successful firm's financial manager must know his firm's rights and remedies as a creditor and must participate effectively in efforts to collect from financially distressed debtors. Conversely, the financial manager of a less successful firm must know how to handle his own firm's affairs if financial difficulties arise. Such understanding may often mean the difference between loss of ownership of the firm and rehabilitation of the operation as a going enterprise.

Some dramatic major bankruptcies have occurred in recent years. Most notable was the huge Penn Central Company, which involved total assets at the end of 1969 amounting to almost $7 billion with total debts outstanding of over $4 billion. The W. T. Grant bankruptcy was also of substantial magnitude, involving $1.2 billion of assets. A number of bankruptcies raised questions of improprieties in the management of the companies. Illustrative is the Equity Funding Company bankruptcy which involved writing up fictitious life insurance.

The instabilities of the early 1970s involved large commercial banks as well as nonfinancial enterprises. The Franklin National Bank, which failed in 1974, had reached an asset size of $5 billion and was the twentieth largest of the nation's more than 14,000 FDIC-insured banks. In 1974, also, the Beverly Hills Bancorp went into bankruptcy. Earlier the U.S. National Bank of San Diego had to be taken over by the Federal Deposit Insurance Corporation with questions of fraud raised in connection with its prior management. Even large foreign banks ran into difficulties in 1974. The failure in 1974 of Bankhaus I. D. Herstatt, one of Germany's largest private banks, sent shock waves through the international money markets.

The Firm's Life Cycle

The life cycle of an industry or firm is often depicted as an S-shaped curve, as shown in Figure 23–1. The figure represents a hypothetical life cycle of a firm, and although it is an oversimplification, it does provide a useful framework for analysis. The hypothesis represented by the four-stage life-cycle concept is based on a number of assumptions — competent management in the growth periods and insufficient management foresight prior to the decline phase. Obviously, one of management's primary goals is to prolong phase B and to completely forestall phase D; many firms are apparently successful in these endeavors.

Figure 23–1
Hypothetical Life Cycle
of a Firm

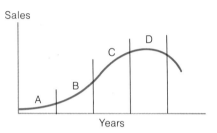

If an industry experiences the period of decline, financial readjustment problems will arise, affecting most firms in the industry. Furthermore, specific events may result in business failure — for example, a prolonged strike, a fire not adequately covered by insurance, or a bad decision on a new product.

Failure

Although failure can be defined in several ways according to various applications of the term, it does not necessarily result in the collapse and dissolution of a firm.

Economic Failure

Failure in an economic sense usually signifies that a firm's revenues do not cover costs. Another definition of economic failure states that a firm has failed if the rate of earnings on the historical cost of investment is less than the firm's cost of capital. According to still another definition, a firm can be considered a failure if its actual returns have fallen below expected returns. There is no consensus on the definition of failure in an economic sense.[1]

---

1. In still another economic sense, a firm that goes bankrupt may not be a failure at all. To illustrate, suppose someone starts a business to *attempt* to develop a product that, if successful, will produce very large returns and, if unsuccessful, will result in a total loss of invested funds. The entrepreneur *knows* that he is taking a risk but thinks the potential gains are worth the chance of loss. If a loss in fact results, then the outcome simply occurred in the left tail of the distribution of returns.

**Financial
Failure**

Although financial failure is a less ambiguous term than the concept of economic failure, even here, two aspects are generally recognized:

Technical Insolvency. A firm can be considered a failure if it is insolvent in the sense that it cannot meet its current obligations as they fall due, even though its total assets may exceed its total liabilities. This is defined as *technical insolvency*.

Bankruptcy. A firm is a failure, or is *bankrupt*, if its total liabilities exceed a fair valuation of its total assets. The "real" net worth of the firm is negative.

When we use the word "failure" hereafter, we include both technical insolvency and bankruptcy.

**Causes of
Failures**

Different studies assign the causes of failure to different factors. The Dun & Bradstreet compilations assign these causes as follows:[2]

Cause of Failure	Percentage of Total
Neglect	2.0
Fraud	1.5
Disaster	.9
Management incompetence	93.1
Unknown	2.5

A number of other studies of failures may be generalized into the following groups:[3]

Cause of Failure	Percentage of Total
Unfavorable industry trends (secular)	20
Management incompetence	60
Catastrophes	10
Miscellaneous	10

Both classifications include the effects of recessions and place the resulting failures in the category of managerial incompetence. This method is logical—managements should be prepared to operate in en-

---

2. *The Failure Record, 1972* (New York: Dun & Bradstreet, Inc., 1973).

3. See studies referred to in A. S. Dewing, *The Financial Policy of Corporations* (New York: Ronald, 1953), vol. 2, chap. 28.

vironments in which recessions occur and should frame their policies to cope with downturns as well as to benefit from business upswings. Also, managements must anticipate unfavorable industry trends.

A number of financial remedies are available to management when it becomes aware of the imminence or occurrence of insolvency. These remedies are described in the remainder of this chapter.

The Failure Record[4]

How widespread is business failure? Is it a rare phenomenon, or do failures occur fairly often? In Table 23–1, we see that a fairly large number of businesses do fail, although the failures in any one year are not a large percentage of the business population. In 1974, for example, there were 10,158 failures, but these represented only 0.39 percent of all business firms. The average failed firm owed $306,600 when it "went under." It is interesting to note that the failure rate rose significantly in

**Table 23–1
Historical Failure Rate Experience of United States Businesses**

Years	Number of Failures	Average Failure Rate*	Average Liability per Failure†
1857–1968	1,258,141	87	$ 28,292
(average per year)	(11,233)		
1900–1968	942,447	70	32,889
(average per year)	(13,659)		
1946–1968	255,041	42	61,101
(average per year)	(11,089)		
1959–1968	138,805	54	84,724
(average per year)	(13,881)		
1961	17,075	64	63,843
1965	13,514	53	97,800
1966	13,061	52	106,091
1967	12,364	49	102,332
1968	9,636	39	97,654
1969	9,154	37	124,767
1970	10,748	44	175,638
1971	10,326	42	185,641
1972	9,566	38	209,099
1973	9,345	36	245,912
1974	9,915	38	307,931
1975	11,432	43	383,150

*Per 10,000 concerns.
†"Average" here means the median; that is, one-half the failed firms had more liabilities while one-half had less. The arithmetic average is much larger.
Source: Edward I. Altman, *Corporate Bankruptcy in America* (Lexington, Mass.: Heath Lexington Books, 1972); Dun & Bradstreet, *The Failure Record.*

4. This section draws heavily from Edward I. Altman, *Corporate Bankruptcy in America* (Lexington, Mass.: Heath Lexington Books, 1972).

1970–71, and again in 1974; in both periods, high interest rates, a shortage of credit, and a weakened economy combined to cause weaker firms to declare bankruptcy.

Large firms are not immune to bankruptcy; this is clear from Table 23–2, which lists the major corporate bankruptcies during 1970 and 1971. In a sense, Table 23–2 understates financial problems among larger firms, because, as Altman notes, except in cases of fraud or where the failing company is too large to be absorbed by another firm, mergers or governmental intervention are generally arranged as an alternative to outright bankruptcy. Thus, in recent years the Federal Home Loan Bank System arranged the mergers of several very large "problem" savings and loan associations into sound institutions, and the Federal Reserve System has done the same thing for banks. Several United States government agencies, principally the Defense Department, arranged to "bail out" Lockheed when it would have otherwise failed in 1970; the

Table 23–2	1970 Bankruptcies	1969 Assets*
Large Corporate Bankruptcies in America, by Asset Size, 1970 and 1971	Penn Central Transportation Company	4,700.0
	Boston & Maine Railroad	224.1
	Lehigh Valley Railroad	173.8
	Beck Industries	156.9
	Dolly Madison Industries	92.4
	Four Seasons Nursing Centers	37.7
	Roberts Company	36.8
	Visual Electronics	24.3
	Bishop Industries	16.3
	Milo Electronics	13.0
	National Radio Company	10.2
	RIC International Industries, Inc.	10.2
	GF Industries, Inc.	9.6
	Century Geophysical Corp.	8.9
	1971 Bankruptcies†	1970 Assets*
	King Resources Company	176.7
	Bermac Corporation	102.3
	Farrington Manufacturing Company	37.6
	Computer Applications	28.9
	Remco Industries	25.1
	Transogram, Inc.	21.5
	Cle-ware Industries	20.0
	Executive House, Inc.	13.6

*In millions of dollars
†Through July, 1971
Source: Edward I. Altman, *Corporate Bankruptcy in America* (Lexington Mass.: Heath Lexington Books, 1972); Dun & Bradstreet, *The Failure Record, 1975.*

"shotgun marriage" of Douglas Aircraft and McDonnell was designed to prevent Douglas' failure in the late 1960s. Similar instances could be cited in the securities brokerage industry in the late 1960s and early 1970s.

Why do government and industry seek to avoid bankruptcy among larger firms? There are many reasons—to prevent an erosion of confidence in the case of financial institutions, to maintain a viable supplier in the cases of Lockheed and Douglas, and to avoid disrupting a local community. Also, bankruptcy is a very expensive process, so even when "the public interest" is not at stake, private industry has strong incentives to avoid out-and-out bankruptcy. The costs of bankruptcy, as well as some further alternatives to it, are discussed in subsequent sections.

Extension and Composition

Extension and *composition* are discussed together because they both represent voluntary concessions by creditors. Extension postpones the date of required payment of past-due obligations. Composition voluntarily *reduces* the creditors' claims on the debtor. Both have the purpose of keeping the debtor in business and avoiding court costs. Although creditors absorb a temporary loss, the recovery is often greater than if one of the formal procedures had been followed, and the hope is that a stable customer will emerge.

Procedure

A meeting of the debtor and his creditors is held. The creditors appoint a committee consisting of four or five of the largest creditors and one or two of the smaller ones. These meetings are typically arranged and conducted by *adjustment bureaus* associated with local credit managers' associations or by trade associations.

After a meeting is held at the adjustment bureau and it is judged that the case can be worked out, the bureau assigns investigators to make an exhaustive report. The bureau and the creditors' committee use the facts of the report to formulate a plan for adjustment of claims. Another meeting between the debtor and his creditors is then held in an attempt to work out an extension or a composition, or a combination of the two. Subsequent meetings may be required to reach final agreements.

Necessary Conditions

At least three conditions are usually necessary to make an extension or a composition feasible:

1. The debtor is a good moral risk.
2. The debtor shows ability to make a recovery.
3. General business conditions are favorable to recovery.

Extension

An extension is preferred by creditors because it provides for payment in full. The debtor buys current purchases on a cash basis and pays off his past balance over an extended time. In some cases, creditors may agree not only to extend time of payment but also to subordinate existing claims to new debts incurred in favor of vendors extending credit during the period of the extension. The creditors must have faith that the debtor will solve his problems. Because of the uncertainties involved, however, creditors will want to exercise controls over the debtor while waiting for their claims to be paid.

As examples of controls, the committee may insist that an assignment (turnover of assets to the creditors' committee) be executed, to be held in escrow in case of default. Or, if the debtor is a corporation, the committee may require that stockholders transfer their stock certificates into an escrow until repayment as called for under the extension has been completed. The committee may also designate a representative to countersign all checks. Furthermore, the committee may obtain security in the form of notes, mortgages, or assignment of accounts receivable.

Composition

In a composition, a pro rata cash settlement is made. Creditors receive in cash from the debtor a uniform percentage of the obligations. The cash received is taken as full settlement of the debt. The ratio may be as low as 10 percent. Bargaining will take place between the debtor and the creditors over the savings that result from avoiding certain costs associated with the bankruptcy: costs of administration, legal fees, investigators, and so on. In addition to avoiding such costs, the debtor gains in that he avoids the stigma of bankruptcy, and thus he may be induced to part with most of the savings that result from avoiding bankruptcy.

Combination Settlement

Often the bargaining process will result in a compromise involving both an extension and a composition. For example, the settlement may provide for a cash payment of 25 percent of the debt and six future installments of 10 percent each. Total payment would thereby aggregate 85 percent. Installment payments are usually evidenced by notes. Creditors will also seek protective controls.

Appraisal of Voluntary Settlements

The advantages of voluntary settlements are informality and simplicity. Investigative, legal, and administrative expenses are held to a minimum. The procedure is the most economical and results in the largest return to creditors.

One possible disadvantage is that the debtor is left in control of his business. This situation may involve legal complications or erosion of assets still operated by the debtor. However, numerous controls are available to give the creditors protection.

A second disadvantage is that small creditors may take a nuisance role in that they may insist on payment in full. As a consequence, settlements typically provide for payment in full for claims under $50 or $100. If a composition is involved and all claims under $50 are paid, all creditors will receive a base of $50 plus the agreed-on percentage of the balance of their claims.

Reorganization

Reorganization is a form of extension or composition of the firm's obligations. However, the legal formalities are much more involved than the procedures thus far described. Regardless of the legal procedure followed, the reorganization processes have several features in common.

1. The firm is insolvent either because it is unable to meet cash obligations as they come due or because claims on the firm exceed its assets. Hence, some modifications in the nature or amount of the firm's obligations must be made. A scaling down of terms or amounts must be formulated. This procedure may represent scaling down fixed charges or converting short-term debt into long-term debt.
2. New funds must be raised for working capital and for property rehabilitation.
3. The operating and managerial causes of difficulty must be discovered and eliminated.

The procedures involved in effecting a reorganization are highly legalistic and are, in fact, thoroughly understood only by attorneys who specialize in bankruptcy and reorganization. We shall therefore confine our remarks to the general principles involved.

A reorganization is, in essence, a composition, a scaling down of claims. In any composition, two conditions must be met: (1) the scaling down must be fair to all parties, and (2) in return for the sacrifices, the likelihood of successful rehabilitation and profitable future operation of the firm must be feasible. These are the standards of *fairness* and *feasibility*, which are analyzed further in the next section.

Financial Decisions in Reorganization

When a business becomes insolvent, a decision must be made whether to dissolve the firm through liquidation or to keep it alive through reorganization. Fundamentally, this decision depends upon a determination of the value of the firm if it is rehabilitated versus the value of the sum of the parts if it is dismembered.

Liquidation values depend upon the degree of specialization of the capital assets used in the firm and hence their resale value. In addition, liquidation itself involves costs of dismantling, including legal costs. Successful reorganization also involves costs. Typically, better equipment must be installed, obsolete inventories must be disposed of, and improvements in management must be made.

Net liquidation values are compared with the value of the firm after reorganization, net of the costs of rehabilitation. The procedure that promises the higher returns to the creditors and owners will be the course of action favored. Often the greater indicated value of the firm in reorganization, compared with its value in liquidation, is used to force a compromise agreement among the claimants in a reorganization, even when they feel that their relative position has not been treated fairly in the reorganization plan.

In reorganizations, both the SEC and the courts are called upon to determine the *fairness* and the *feasibility* of proposed plans of reorganization.[5] In developing standards of fairness in connection with such reorganizations, both the courts and the SEC have adhered to two court decisions that established precedent on these matters.[6]

Standards of Fairness

The basic doctrine of fairness states that claims must be recognized in the order of their legal and contractual priority. Junior claimants may participate only to the extent that they have made an additional cash contribution to the reorganization of the firm.

Carrying out this concept of fairness involves the following steps:

1. An estimate of future sales must be made.
2. An analysis of operating conditions must be made so that the future earnings on sales can be estimated.
3. A determination of the capitalization rate to be applied to these future earnings must be made.

---

5. The federal bankruptcy laws specify that reorganization plans be worked out by court-appointed officials and be reviewed by the SEC.

6. *Case V. Los Angeles Lumber Products Co.*, 308 U.S. 106 (1939) and *Consolidated Rock Products Co. v. duBoise*, 213 U.S. 510 (1940). Securities and Exchange Commission, Seventeenth Annual Report, 1951 (Washington, D. C.: U. S. Government Printing Office), p. 130.

4. The capitalization rate must be applied to the estimated future earnings to obtain an indicated value of the properties of the company.
5. Provision for distribution to the claimants must then be made.

Example of Reorganization and Standards of Fairness

The meaning and content of these procedures may best be set out by the use of an actual example of reorganization involving the Northeastern Steel Corporation. Table 23–3 gives the balance sheet of the Northeastern Steel Corporation as of March 31, 1957. The company had been suffering losses running to $2.5 million a year, and, as will be made clear below, the asset values in the March 31, 1957, balance sheet are overstated. Accordingly, the company filed a petition for reorganization with a federal court. The court, in accordance with the law, appointed a disinterested trustee. On June 13, 1957, the trustee filed with the court a plan of reorganization, which was subsequently analyzed by the SEC.

Table 23–3
Northeastern Steel Corporation Balance Sheet, March 31, 1957 (Millions of Dollars)

Assets

Current assets	$ 3.50
Net property	12.50
Miscellaneous assets	0.70
Total assets	$16.70

Liabilities and capital

Accounts payable	$ 1.00
Taxes	0.25
Notes payable	0.25
Other current liabilities	1.75
4½% First-mortgage bonds, due 1970	6.00
6% Subordinated debentures, due 1975	7.00
Common stock ($1)	1.00
Paid-in capital	3.45
Retained earnings	(4.00)
Total liabilities and capital	$16.70

The trustee found that the company could not be internally reorganized, and he concluded that the only feasible program would be to combine Northeastern with an established producer of stainless and alloyed steel. Accordingly, the trustee solicited the interest of a number of steel companies. Late in March 1957, Carpenter Steel Company showed an interest in Northeastern. On June 3, 1957, Carpenter made a formal proposal to take over the $6 million of 4½ percent first-mortgage bonds of Northeastern, to pay $250,000 in taxes owed by Northeastern, and to pay 40,000 shares of Carpenter Steel common stock to the company.

Since the stock had a market price of $75 a share, the value of the stock was equivalent to $3 million. Thus, Carpenter was offering $3 million, plus the $6 million loan takeover and the $250,000 taxes, a total of $9.2 million on assets that had a net book value of $16.7 million.

Trustee's Plan. The trustee's plan, based on 40,000 shares at $75 equaling $3 million, is shown in Table 23–4. The total claims of the unsecured creditors equals $10 million. However, the amounts available total only $3 million. Thus, each claimant would be entitled to receive 30 percent before the adjustment for subordination. Before this adjustment, holders of notes payable would receive 30 percent of their $250,000 claim, or $75,000. However, the debentures are subordinated to the *notes payable*, so an additional $175,000 would be transferred to notes payable from the subordinated debentures. In the last column of Table 23–4, the dollar claims of each class of debt are restated in terms of the number of shares of Carpenter common stock received by each class of unsecured creditors.

**Table 23–4
Northeastern Steel
Corporation
Trustee's plan**

Prior claims	Amount	Receives
Taxes	$ 250,000	Cash paid by Carpenter
Mortgage bonds, 4½%, 1970	6,000,000	Same assumed by Carpenter

Trustee's plans for remainder of claims

Valuation based on 40,000 shares at $75 equals $3 million, or 30% of $10 million liabilities

Claims	Amount	30 Percent × Amount of Claim	Claim after Subordination	Number of Shares of Common Stock
Notes payable	$ 250,000	$ 75,000	$ 250,000	3,333
General unsecured creditors	2,750,000	825,000	825,000	11,000
Subordinated debentures	7,000,000	2,100,000	1,925,000	25,667
	$10,000,000	$3,000,000	$3,000,000	40,000

SEC Evaluation. The Securities and Exchange Commission, in evaluating the proposal from the standpoint of fairness, made the following analysis. The SEC began with an evaluation of the prospective value of Northeastern Steel (Table 23–5). After a survey and discussion with various experts, it arrived at estimated sales of Northeastern Steel Corporation of $25 million a year. It was further estimated that the profit margin on sales would equal 6 percent, thus giving an indicated future earnings of $1.5 million a year.

The SEC analyzed price/earnings ratios for comparable steel companies and arrived at 8 times future earnings for a capitalization factor. Multiplying 8 by $1.5 million gave an indicated total value of the company of $12 million. Since the mortgage bonds assumed by Carpenter totaled $6 million, a net value of $6 million was left for the other claims. This value is double that of the 40,000 shares of Carpenter Steel stock offered for the remainder of the company. Because the SEC felt that the value of these claims was $6 million rather than $3 million, it concluded that the trustee's plan for reorganization did not meet the test of fairness. Note that under both the trustee's plan and the SEC plan, the holders of common stock were to receive nothing, while the holders of the first-mortgage bonds were to be paid in full.

Because no better alternative offer could be obtained, the proposal of Carpenter Steel was accepted despite the SEC disagreement with the valuation.

**Table 23–5
Northeastern Steel
Corporation: SEC
Evaluation of
Fairness**

Valuation

Estimated sales of Northeastern Steel Corp.	$25,000,000 per year
Earnings at 6% of sales	1,500,000
Price/earnings ratio of 8 times earnings	12,000,000
Mortgage bonds assumed, $6,000,000	6,000,000
Net value	$ 6,000,000

Claims	Amount	Claim	Claim after Subordination
Notes payable	$ 250,000	$ 150,000	$ 250,000*
General unsecured creditors	2,750,000	1,650,000	1,650,000
Subordinated debentures (subordinate to notes payable)	7,000,000	4,200,000	4,100,000*
Totals	$10,000,000	$6,000,000	$6,000,000
Total available	6,000,000		
Percentage of claims	60%		

*Notes payable must be satisfied before subordinated debenture holders receive anything.

**Standard of
Feasibility**

The primary test of feasibility is that the fixed charges on the income of the corporation after reorganization are amply covered by earnings or, if a value for a firm that is to be sold is established, that a buyer can be found at that price. Adequate coverage of fixed charges for a company that is to continue in operation generally requires an improvement in earnings or a reduction of fixed charges, or both.

Policies Required. Among the actions that will have to be taken to improve the earning power of the company are the following:

1. Where the quality of management has been inefficient and inadequate for the task, new talents and abilities must be brought into the company if it is to operate sucessfully subsequent to the reorganization.
2. If inventories have become obsolete, they should be disposed of and the operations of the company streamlined.
3. Sometimes the plant and the equipment of the firm need to be modernized before it can operate and compete successfully on a cost basis.
4. Reorganization may also require an improvement in production, marketing, advertising, and other functions, to enable the firm to compete successfully and earn satisfactory profits.
5. It is sometimes necessary to develop new products so that the firm can move from areas where economic trends have become undesirable into areas where the growth and stability potential is greater.

Application of Feasibility Tests. Let us refer again to the Northeastern Steel Corporation example. The SEC observed that the reorganization involved taking over the properties of the Northeastern Steel Corporation by the Carpenter Steel Company. It judged that the direction and aid of the Carpenter Steel Company would remedy the production deficiencies that had troubled Northeastern Steel. Whereas the debt-to-assets ratio of Northeastern Steel had become unbalanced, the Carpenter Steel Company went into the purchase with only a moderate amount of debt. After consolidation, the total debt of Carpenter Steel was approximately $17.5 million compared with total assets of more than $63 million. Therefore the debt ratio of 27 percent after the reorganization was not unreasonable.

The net income after taxes of Carpenter Steel had been running at a level of approximately $6 million. The interest on the long-term debt of Carpenter Steel would be $270,000 and, taking short-term borrowings into account, would total a maximum of $600,000 a year. The $6 million profit after taxes would therefore provide a ten-times coverage of fixed charges; this exceeds the standard of eight times for the industry.

Notice that the question of feasibility would have been irrelevant (from the standpoint of the SEC) if Carpenter Steel had offered $3 million in cash rather than in stock. It is the SEC's function to protect the interests of Northeastern Steel's creditors. Since they are being forced to take common stock in another firm, the SEC must look into the feasibility of the transaction. If Carpenter had made a cash offer, however, the feasibility of Carpenter's own operation after the transaction was completed would have been none of the SEC's concern. Notice that the SEC feasibility study is much more important if a small, weak firm buys the assets of a reorganized firm for stock than if the purchase is made by a stronger firm. Thus, the SEC would be more concerned with the feasibility of a takeover of Northeastern by Wesbrig Corporation than it would be if General Motors made the takeover.

Liquidation Procedures

Liquidation of a business occurs when the estimated value of the firm is greater "dead than alive."

Assignment is a liquidation procedure that does not go through the courts, although it can be used to achieve full settlement of claims on the debtor. *Bankruptcy* is a legal procedure carried out under the jurisdiction of special courts in which a business firm is formally liquidated and claims of creditors are completely discharged.

Assignment

Assignment (as well as bankruptcy) takes place when the debtor is insolvent and the possibilities of restoring profitability are so remote that the enterprise should be dissolved—that is, when the firm is "worth more dead than alive." Assignment is a technique for liquidating a debt and yielding a larger amount to the creditors than is likely to be achieved in formal bankruptcy.

Technically, there are three classes of assignments: (1) common-law assignment, (2) statutory assignment, and (3) assignment plus settlement.

Common-Law Assignment. The common law provides for an assignment whereby a debtor transfers his title to assets to a third person, known as an assignee or a trustee. The trustee is instructed to liquidate the assets and to distribute the proceeds among the creditors on a pro rata basis.

Typically, an assignment is conducted through the adjustment bureau of the local credit managers' association. The assignee may liquidate the assets through what is known as a bulk sale, which is a public sale through an auctioneer. The auction is preceded by sufficient advertising so that there will be a number of bids. Liquidation may also be by a piecemeal auction sale conducted on the premises of the assignor by a competent licensed auctioneer, rather than by a bulk sale. On-premises sales are particularly advantageous in the liquidation of large machine shops of manufacturing plants.

The common-law assignment, as such, does not discharge the debtor from his obligations. If a corporation goes out of business and does not satisfy all its claims, there will still be claims against it, but in effect the corporation has ceased to exist. The people who have been associated with the company can then proceed to organize another corporation free of the debts and obligations of the previous corporation. There is always the danger, however, that the court may hold the individuals responsible: therefore, it is usually important to obtain a statement from creditors that claims have been completely settled. Such a statement is, of course, even more important for an unincorporated business.

Although a common-law assignment has taken place, the assignee, in drawing up checks paying the creditors, may write on the check the requisite legal language to make the payment a complete discharge of the obligation. There are technical legal requirements for this process, which are best carried out with the aid of a lawyer, but essential is a statement that endorsement of this check represents acknowledgment of full payment for the obligation.

Statutory Assignment. Statutory assignment is similar in concept to common-law assignment. Legally, it is carried out under state statutes regulating assignment; technically, it requires more formality. The debtor executes an instrument of assignment, which is recorded. This recordation provides notice to all third parties. The proceedings are handled under court order: the court appoints an assignee and supervises the proceedings, including the sale of the assets and distribution of the proceeds. As in the common-law assignment, the debtor is not automatically discharged from the balance of his obligations. He can discharge himself, however, by printing the requisite statement on the settlement checks.

Assignment Plus Settlement. Both the common-law assignment and the statutory assignment may take place with recognition and agreement beforehand by the creditors that the assignment will represent a complete discharge of obligation. Normally, the debtor communicates with the local credit managers' association. The adjustment bureau of the association arranges a meeting of all the creditors, and a trust instrument of assignment is drawn up. The adjustment bureau is designated to dispose of the assets, which are sold through regular trade channels, by bulk sales, by auction, or by private sales. The creditors will, typically, leave all responsibility for the liquidation procedure with the assignee, the adjustment bureau of the local credit managers' association.

Having disposed of the assets and obtained funds, the adjustment bureau will then distribute the proceeds pro rata among the creditors, with the designation on the check that this is in full settlement of the claims on the debtor. Ordinarily, a release is not agreed upon before the execution of the assignment. After full examination of the facts, the creditors' committee will usually make a recommendation for the granting of a release following the execution of the assignment. If releases are not forthcoming, the assignor may, within four months of the date of the assignment, file a voluntary petition in bankruptcy. In this event the assignment is terminated and the assignee must account and report to the trustee and the referee in bankruptcy, and deliver to the trustee all assets in the estate (usually by that time assets have been reduced to cash).

Assignment has substantial advantages over bankruptcy. Bankruptcy through the courts involves much time, legal formalities, and accounting and legal expenses. An assignment saves the costs of bankruptcy proceedings, and it may save time as well.

Furthermore, an assignee usually has much more flexibility in disposing of property than does a bankruptcy trustee. He may be more familiar with the normal channels of trade. Since he takes action much sooner, before the inventories become more obsolete, he may achieve better results.

Bankruptcy

Although the bankruptcy procedures leave room for improvement, the Federal Bankruptcy Acts themselves represent two main achievements: (1) They provide safeguards against fraud by the debtor during liquidation, and, simultaneously, they provide for an equitable distribution of the debtor's assets among his creditors. (2) Insolvent debtors may discharge all their obligations and start new businesses unhampered by a burden of prior debt.

Prerequisites for Bankruptcy

A *voluntary petition of bankruptcy* may be filed by the debtor, but if an *involuntary petition* is to be filed, three conditions must be met.

1. The total debts of the insolvent must be $1,000 or more.
2. If the debtor has fewer than 12 creditors, any one of the creditors may file the petition if the amount owed him is $500 or more. If there are 12 or more creditors, the petition must be signed by three or more creditors, each having provable total claims of $500 or more.
3. Within the four preceding months, the debtor must have committed one or more of the following six acts of bankruptcy.

Acts of Bankruptcy

The six acts of bankruptcy can be summarized briefly.

1. Concealment or Fraudulent Conveyance. Concealment constitutes hiding of assets with intent to defraud creditors. Fraudulent conveyance is transfer of property to a third party without adequate consideration and with intent to defraud creditors.

2. Preferential Transfer. A preferential transfer is the transfer of money or assets by an insolvent debtor to a creditor, giving the creditor a greater portion of his claim than other creditors would receive on liquidation.

3. Legal Lien or Distraint. If an insolvent debtor permits any creditor to obtain a lien on his property and fails to discharge the lien within 30 days, or if the debtor permits a landlord to distrain (to seize property that has been pledged as security for a loan) for nonpayment of rent, he has committed an act of bankruptcy. In this way, creditors, by obtaining a lien, may force an insolvent but obdurate debtor into bankruptcy.

4. Assignment. If a debtor makes a general assignment for the benefit of his creditors, an act of bankruptcy likewise exists. Again, this enables creditors who have become distrustful of the debtor in the process of assignment to transfer the proceedings to a bankruptcy court. As a matter of practice, typically in common-law assignments, creditors will require that a debtor execute a formal assignment document to be held in escrow, to become effective if informal and voluntary settlement negotiations fail. If they do fail, the assignment becomes effective and the creditors have the right to throw the case into the bankruptcy court.

5. Appointment of Receiver or Trustee. If an insolvent debtor permits the appointment of a receiver or a trustee to take charge of his property, he has committed an act of bankruptcy. In this event, the creditors may remove a receivership or an adjustment proceeding to a bankruptcy court.

6. Admission in Writing. If the debtor admits in writing his inability to pay his debts and his willingness to be judged bankrupt, he has committed an act of bankruptcy. The reason for this sixth act of bankruptcy is that debtors are often unwilling to engage in voluntary bankruptcy because it carries some stigma of avoidance of obligations. Sometimes, therefore, negotiations with a debtor reach an impasse. Admission in writing is one of the methods of forcing the debtor to commit an act of bankruptcy and of moving the proceedings into a bankruptcy court, where the debtor will no longer be able to reject all plans for settlement.

Adjudication and the Referee

On the filing of the petition of involuntary bankruptcy, a subpoena is served on the debtor. There is usually no contest by the debtor, and the court adjudges him bankrupt. On adjudication, the case is transferred by the court to a referee in bankruptcy. A referee in bankruptcy is generally a lawyer appointed for a specified term by the judge of the bankruptcy court to act in his place after adjudication.

In addition, on petition of the creditors, the referee in voluntary proceedings or the judge in involuntary proceedings may appoint a receiver, who serves as the custodian of the property of the debtor until the appointment of a trustee. This arrangement was developed because a long period elapses between the date of the filing of a petition in bankruptcy and the election of a trustee at the first creditors' meeting. To safeguard the creditors' interest during this period, the court, through either the referee or the judge, may appoint a receiver in bankruptcy. The receiver in bankruptcy has full control until the trustee is appointed.

First Creditors' Meeting: Election of Trustee

At the first meeting of the creditors, a trustee is elected. If different blocks of creditors have a different candidate for trustee, the election may become drawn out. Frequently, the trustee will be the adjustment bureau of the local credit managers' association. At this first meeting the debtor may also be examined for the purpose of obtaining necessary information.

Subsequent Procedure

The trustee and the creditors' committee act to convert all assets into cash. The trustee sends a letter to people owing the debtor money, warning that all past-due accounts will result in instant suit if immediate payment is not made, and that, if necessary, he will institute such suit. Appraisers are appointed by the courts to set a value on the property. With the advice of the creditors' committee and by authorization of the referee, the merchandise is sold by approved methods. As in an assignment, auctions may be held.

Property may not be sold without consent of the court at less than 75 percent of the appraised value that has been set by the appraisers appointed by the court. Cash received from the disposition of the property is used first to pay all expenses associated with the proceedings of the bankruptcy and then to pay any remaining funds to the claimants.

Final Meeting and Discharge

When the trustee has completed his liquidation and has sent out all the claimants' checks, he makes an accounting, which is reviewed by the creditors and the referee. The bankruptcy is then discharged and the debtor is released from all debts.

If the hearings before the referee indicate the probability of fraud, the FBI is required to undertake an investigation. If the fraud was not committed and the bankruptcy is discharged, the debtor is again free to engage in business. Since business is highly competitive in many fields, the debtor will probably not have great difficulty in obtaining credit again. Under the National Bankruptcy Act, however, a debtor may not be granted a discharge more often than at six-year intervals.

Priority of Claims on Distribution of Proceeds of a Bankruptcy

The order of priority of claims in bankruptcy is as follows:

1. Costs of administering and operating the bankrupt estate.
2. Wages due workers if earned within three months prior to the filing of the petition in bankruptcy. The amount of wages is not to exceed $600 per person.
3. Taxes due the United States, state, county, or any other government agency.
4. Secured creditors, with the proceeds of the sale of specific property pledged for a mortgage.
5. General or unsecured creditors. This claim consists of the remaining

**Table 23–6
Bankrupt Firm
Balance Sheet**

Current assets	$80,000,000	Accounts payable	$20,000,000
Net property	$10,000,000	Notes payable (due bank)	10.000,000
		Accrued wages, 1,400 @ $500	700,000
		U.S. taxes	1,000,000
		State and local taxes	300,000
		Current debt	$32,000,000
		First mortgage	$ 6,000,000
		Second mortgage	1,000,000
		Subordinated debentures*	8,000,000
		Long-term debt	$15,000,000
		Preferred stock	2,000,000
		Common stock	26,000,000
		Capital surplus	4,000,000
		Retained earnings	11,000,000
		Net worth	$43,000,000
Total assets	$90,000,000	Total claims	$90,000,000

*Subordinated to $10 million notes payable to the First National Bank.

balances after payment to secured creditors from the sale of specific property, and includes trade credit, bank loans, and debenture bonds. Holders of subordinated debt fall into this category, but they must turn over required amounts to the holders of senior debt.

6. Preferred stock.
7. Common stock.

To illustrate how this priority of claims works out, let us take a specific example. The balance sheet of a bankrupt firm is shown in Table 23–6. Assets total $90 million. The claims are those indicated on the right-hand side of the balance sheet. It will be noted that the subordinated debentures are subordinated to the notes payable to commercial banks.

Now assume that the assets of the firm are sold. These assets, shown in the balance sheet in Table 23–6, are greatly overstated—they are, in fact, worth much less than the $90 million at which they are carried. The following amounts are realized on liquidation:

Current assets	$28,000,000
Net property	5,000,000
Total assets	$33,000,000

The order of priority of payment of claims is shown by Table 23–7. Fees and expenses of administration are typically about 20 percent of gross proceeds, and in this example they are assumed to be $6 million. Next in priority are wages due workers, which total $700,000. The total amount of taxes to be paid is $1.3 million. Thus far, the total of claims paid for the $33 million is $8 million. The first mortgage is then paid from the net proceeds of $5 million from the sale of fixed property, leaving $20 million available to the general creditors.

The claims of the general creditors total $40 million. Since $20 million is available, each claimant would receive 50 percent of his claim before the subordination adjustment. This adjustment requires that the subordinated debentures turn over to the notes to which they are subordinated all amounts received until the notes are satisfied. In this situation, the claim of the notes payable is $10 million, but only $5 million is available; the deficiency is therefore $5 million. After transfer by the subordinated debentures of $4 million, there remains a deficiency of $1 million, which will be unsatisfied. It will be noted that 90 percent of the bank claim is satisfied, whereas only 50 percent of other unsecured claims will be satisfied. These figures illustrate the usefulness of the subordination provision to the security to which the subordination is

**Table 23–7
Bankrupt Firm
Order of Priority
of Claims**

Distribution of Proceeds on Liquidation

1. Proceeds of sale of assets	$33,000,000
2. Fees and expenses of administration of bankruptcy	$ 6,000,000
3. Wages due workers earned three months prior to filing of bankruptcy petition	700,000
4. Taxes	1,300,000
	$25,000,000
5. First mortgage, paid from sale of net property	5,000,000
6. Available to general creditors	$20,000,000

Claims of General Creditors	Claim (1)	Application of 50 Percent (2)	After Subordination Adjustment (3)	Percentage of Original Claims Received (4)
Unsatisfied portion of first mortgage	$ 1,000,000	$ 500,000	$ 500,000	92
Unsatisfied portion of second mortgage	1,000,000	500,000	500,000	50
Notes payable	10,000,000	5,000,000	9,000,000	90
Accounts payable	20,000,000	10,000,000	10,000,000	50
Subordinated debentures	8,000,000	4,000,000	0	0
	$40,000,000	$20,000,000	$20,000,000	56

Notes: 1. Column 1 is the claim of each class of creditor. Total claims equal $40 million.
2. From line 6 in the upper section of the table we see that $20 million is available. This sum, divided by the $40 million of claims, indicates that general creditors will receive 50 percent of their claims. This is shown in column 2.
3. The debentures are subordinated to the notes payable. Four million dollars is transferred from debentures to notes payable in column 3.
4. Column 4 shows the results of dividing the column 3 figure by the original amount given in Table 23–6, except for first mortgage, where $5 million paid on sale of property is included. The 56 percent total figure includes the first mortgage transactions, that is, ($20,000,000 + $5,000,000) ÷ ($40,000,000 + $5,000,000) = 56%.

made. Since no other funds remain, the claims of the holders of preferred and common stocks are completely wiped out.

The order of priority may be altered by special subordination agreements. For example, in the W. T. Grant bankruptcy during the mid-1970s, the commercial banks had agreed to subordinate their loans to the payables to trade creditors in order to induce suppliers of W. T. Grant to continue the flow of merchandise to the company. As a consequence of the $400 million that appeared to be realizable from W. T. Grant, the order of priority seemed to be the following: First in line was the $24 million worth of senior debentures. Second, because of an unusual lien arrangement, came trade creditors with $110 million owed.

Third were the banks, which subordinated to the trade creditors $300 million of their $640 million loan to Grant with an additional $90 million loaned after the filing for reorganization. Next came junior debenture holders with claims of $94 million. Last in line was unsecured debt including $300 million in landlord claims and utility bills. In addition, it was estimated that administrative costs of the reorganization would total $30 million. There was also an unresolved Internal Revenue Service claim of $60 million plus interest. Further, there would be legal fees that were estimated to run into the millions and would assume a priority status.[7]

Studies of the proceeds in bankruptcy liquidations reveal that unsecured creditors receive, on the average, about 15 cents on the dollar. Consequently, where assignment to creditors is likely to yield more, assignment is to be preferred to bankruptcy.

Summary

Problems associated with the decline and failure of a firm, and methods of rehabilitating or liquidating one that has failed, were the subjects treated in this chapter. The major cause of failure is incompetent management. Bad managers should, of course, be removed as promptly as possible; if failure has occurred, a number of remedies are open to the interested parties.

The first question to be answered is whether the firm is better off "dead or alive"—whether it should be liquidated and sold off piecemeal or be rehabilitated. Assuming the decision is made that the firm should survive, it must be put through what is called a *reorganization*. Legal procedures are always costly, especially in the case of a business failure. Therefore, if it is at all possible, both the debtor and the creditors are better off if matters can be handled on an informal basis rather than through the courts. The informal procedures used in reorganization are (1) *extension*, which postpones the date of settlement, and (2) *composition*, which reduces the amount owed.

If voluntary settlement through extension or composition is not possible, the matter is thrown into the courts. If the court decides on reorganization rather than liquidation, it will appoint a trustee (1) to control the firm going through reorganization and (2) to prepare a formal plan of reorganization. The plan, which must be reviewed by the SEC, must meet the standards of *fairness* to all parties and *feasibility* in the sense that the reorganized enterprise will stand a good chance of surviving instead of being thrown back into the bankruptcy courts.

7. *Business Week*, 1 March, 1976, p. 21.

The application of standards of fairness and feasibility developed in this chapter can help to determine the probable success of a particular plan for reorganization. The concept of *fairness* involves the estimation of sales and earnings and the application of a capitalization rate to the latter to determine the appropriate distribution to each claimant.

The *feasibility* test examines the ability of the new enterprise to carry the fixed charges resulting from the reorganization plan. The quality of management and the company's assets must be assured. Production and marketing may also require improvement.

Finally, where liquidation is treated as the only solution to the debtor's insolvency, the creditors should attempt procedures that will net them the largest recovery. *Assignment* of the debtor's property is the cheaper and the faster procedure. Furthermore, there is more flexibility in disposing of the debtor's property and thus providing larger returns. *Bankruptcy* provides formal procedures in liquidation to safeguard the debtor's property from fraud and provides equitable distribution to the creditors. The procedure is long and cumbersome. Moreover, the debtor's property is generally poorly managed during bankruptcy proceedings unless the trustee is closely supervised by the creditors.

Questions

23-1. "A certain number of business failures is a healthy sign. If there are no failures, this is an indication (a) that entrepreneurs are overly cautious, hence not as inventive and as willing to take risks as a healthy, growing economy requires, (b) that competition is not functioning to weed out inefficient producers, or (c) that both situations exist." Discuss, giving pros and cons.

23-2. How can financial analysis be used to forecast the probability of a given firm's failure? Assuming that such analysis is properly applied, can it always predict failure?

23-3. Why do creditors usually accept a plan for financial rehabilitation rather than demand liquidation of the business?

23-4. Would it be possible to form a profitable company by merging two companies, both of which are business failures? Explain.

23-5. Distinguish between a reorganization and a bankruptcy.

23-6. Would it be a sound rule to liquidate whenever the liquidation value is above the value of the corporation as a going concern? Discuss.

23-7. Why do all liquidations usually result in losses for the creditors or the owners, or both? Would partial liquidation or liquidation over a period limit their losses? Explain.

23-8. Are liquidations likely to be more common for public utility, railroad, or industrial corporations? Why?

Problems

23-1. The financial statements of the Hamilton Publishing Company for 1978 are shown below:

Hamilton Publishing Company Balance Sheet, December 31, 1978 (in Thousands of Dollars)

Current assets	$130,000	Current liabilities	$ 53,000
Investments	40,000	Advance payments for subscriptions	78,000
Net fixed assets	200,000	Reserves	8,000
Goodwill	14,000	$8 preferred stock, $100 par	
		(1,500,000 shares)	150,000
		$9 preferred stock, no par	
		(100,000 shares, callable at $110)	11,000
		Common stock, $1.50 par	
		(8,000,000 shares)	12,000
		Retained earnings	72,000
Total assets	$384,000	Total claims	$384,000

Hamilton Publishing Company Income Statement, December 31, 1978 (in Thousands of Dollars)

Operating income		$ 194,400
Operating expenses		172,800
Earnings before income tax		21,600
Income tax at 50 percent		10,800
Income after taxes		10,800
Dividends on $8 preferred stock	12,000	
Dividends on $9 preferred stock	900	12,900
Income available for common stock		$(2,100)

A recapitalization plan is proposed in which each share of $8 preferred will be exchanged for one share of $2 preferred (stated value $20), plus $80 of stated principal in 8 percent subordinated income debentures with par value $1,000. The $9 preferred would be retired from cash.

a. Show the pro forma balance sheet (in thousands of dollars) giving effect to the recapitalization and showing the new preferred at its stated value and the common stock at par value.

b. Present the pro forma income statement (in thousands of dollars).

c. How much does the firm increase income available to common stock by the recapitalization?

d. How much less is the required pretax earnings after the recapitalization compared to before the change? (Required earning is the amount necessary to meet fixed charges, debenture interest, and preferred dividends.)

e. How is the debt to net worth position of the company affected by the recapitalization?

f. Would you vote for the recapitalization if you were a holder of the $8 preferred stock?

23-2. The Accurate Instrument Company produces precision instruments. The company's products are designed and manufactured according to specifications set out by its customers and are highly specialized.

Declines in sales and increases in development expenses in recent years resulted in a large deficit at the end of 1975.

Accurate Instrument Company Balance Sheet December 31, 1975 (in Thousands of Dollars)

Current assets	$375	Current liabilities		$450
Fixed assets	375	Long-term debt (unsecured)		225
		Capital stock		150
		Retained earnings (deficit)		(75)
Total assets	$750	Total claims		$750

Accurate Instrument Company Sales and Profits, 1972–1975 (in Thousands of Dollars)

Year	Sales	Net Profit after Tax before Fixed Charges
1972	$2,625	$262.5
1973	$2,400	$ 225.0
1974	$1,425	$(75.0)
1975	$1,350	$(112.5)

Independent assessment led to the conclusion that the company would have a liquidation value of about $600,000. As an alternative to liquidation, the management concluded that a reorganization was possible with additional investment of $300,000. The management was confident of eventual success of the company and stated that the additional investment would restore earnings to $125,000 a year after taxes and before fixed charges. The appropriate multiplier to apply is eight times. The management is negotiating with a local investment group to obtain the additional investment of $300,000. If the funds are obtained, the holders of the long-term debt would be given one-half the common stock in the reorganized firm in place of their present claims.

Should the creditors agree to the reorganization or should they force liquidation of the firm?

Selected References

Altman, Edward I. *Corporate Bankruptcy in America*. Lexington, Mass.: Heath Lexington Books, 1971.

———. "Corporate Bankruptcy Potential, Stockholder Returns and Share Valuation." *Journal of Finance* 24 (Dec. 1969):887–900.

———. "Equity Securities of Bankrupt Firms." *Financial Analysts' Journal* 25 (July–Aug. 1969), 129–33.

———. "Financial Ratios, Discriminant Analysis and the Prediction of Corporate Bankruptcy." *Journal of Finance* 23 (Sept. 1968):589–609.

———. "Railroad Bankruptcy Propensity." *Journal of Finance* 26 (May 1971): 333–46.

Appleyard, A. R., and Yarrow, G. K. "The Relationship Between Take-Over Activity and Share Valuation." *Journal of Finance* 30 (Dec. 1975):1239–49.

Beaver, William H. "Financial Ratios as Predictors of Failure." *Empirical Re-*

search in Accounting: Selected Studies. Supplement to *Journal of Accounting Research* (1966):71–111.

———. "Market Prices, Financial Ratios, and the Prediction of Failure." *Journal of Accounting Research* 6 (Autumn 1968):179–92.

Calkins, Francis J. "Corporate Reorganization under Chapter X: A Post-Mortem." *Journal of Finance* 3 (June 1948):19–28.

———. "Feasibility in Plans of Corporate Reorganizations under Chapter X." *Harvard Law Review* 61 (May 1948), 763–81.

Edmister, Robert O. "An Empirical Test of Financial Ratio Analysis for Small Business Failure Prediction." *Journal of Financial and Quantitative Analysis* 7 (Mar. 1972):1477–93.

Ferguson, D. A. "Preferred Stock Valuation in Recapitalizations." *Journal of Finance* 13 (Mar. 1958):48–69.

Gordon, Myron J. "Towards a Theory of Financial Distress." *Journal of Finance* 26 (May 1971):347–56.

Green, Steven J. "Bankruptcy: Help or Hindrance?" *Financial Executive* 43 (Dec. 1975):30–35.

Johnson, Craig G. "Ratio Analysis and the Prediction of Firm Failure." *Journal of Finance* 25 (Dec. 1970):1166–68. See also Edward A. Altman, "Reply." *Ibid.*, pp. 1169–72.

Murray, Roger F. "The Penn Central Debacle: Lessons for Financial Analysis." *Journal of Finance* 26 (May 1971):327–32.

Pye, Gordon. "Gauging the Default Premium." *Financial Analysts' Journal* 30 (Jan.–Feb. 1974):49–52.

Stapleton, R. C. "Some Aspects of the Pure Theory of Corporate Finance: Bankruptcies and Take-overs: Comment." *Bell Journal of Economics* 6 (Autumn 1975):708–10.

Stiglitz, J. E. "Some Aspects of the Pure Theory of Corporate Finance; Bankruptcies and Take-overs: Reply." *Bell Journal of Economics* 6 (Autumn 1975):711–14.

Van Arsdell, Paul M. *Corporation Finance.* New York: Ronald, 1968, chaps. 48–53.

Van Horne, James C. "Optimal Initiation of Bankruptcy Proceedings." *Journal of Finance* 31 (June 1976):897–910.

Walter, James E. "Determination of Technical Insolvency." *Journal of Business* 30 (Jan. 1957):30–43.

Weston, J. Fred. "The Industrial Economics Background of the Penn Central Bankruptcy." *Journal of Finance* 26 (May 1971):311–26.

Multinational Business Finance[1]

Although the basic concepts underlying financial management in a multinational firm are essentially the same as those for a domestic company, a multinational financial manager must make decisions within the framework of at least three separate economic and political environments: his own country's, the international economy, and that of at least one foreign country. This chapter shows how these different environmental influences affect the financial manager as he attempts to apply the concepts developed in previous chapters.

Trend Toward International Operations

Table 24–1 is a list of the 50 largest industrial firms in the world ranked by sales. Although it is apparent the U.S. firms, which account for eight of the first 12, dominate that list, it is equally important to note that of the total 50, there are only 23 U.S. firms. In terms of total sales and total net income, U.S. firms accounted for 45 percent and 38 percent respectively.

Table 24–1
The Fifty Largest Industrial Companies in the World

Rank	Company	Headquarters	Sales ($000)	Net Income ($000)
1	Exxon	New York	44,864,824	2,503,013
2	General Motors	Detroit	35,724,911	1,253,092
3	Royal Dutch/Shell Group	London/The Hague	32,105,096	2,110,927
4	Texaco	New York	24,507,454	830,583
5	Ford Motor	Dearborn, Mich.	24,009,100	322,700
6	Mobil Oil	New York	20,620,392	809,877
7	National Iranian Oil	Teheran	18,854,547	16,947,071
8	British Petroleum	London	17,285,854	369,202
9	Standard Oil of California	San Francisco	16,822,077	772,509
10	Unilever	London	15,015,994	322,108

1. This chapter was written by Robert T. Aubey, Professor of Finance, The University of Wisconsin.

Table 24–1 Continued

Rank	Company	Headquarters	Sales ($000)	Net Income ($000)
11	International Business Machines	Armonk, N.Y.	14,436,541	1,989,877
12	Gulf Oil	Pittsburgh	14,268,000	700,000
13	General Electric	Fairfield, Conn.	13,399,100	580,800
14	Chrysler	Highland Park, Mich.	11,699,305	(259,535)
15	International Tel. & Tel.	New York	11,367,647	398,171
16	Philips' Gloeilampenfabrieken	Eindhoven (Netherlands)	10,746,485	152,190
17	Standard Oil (Ind.)	Chicago	9,955,248	786,987
18	Cie Française des Pétroles	Paris	9,145,778	168,472
19	Nippon Steel	Tokyo	8,796,902	111,935
20	August Thyssen-Hütte	Duisburg (Germany)	8,764,899	99,926
21	Hoechst	Frankfurt on Main	8,462,322	100,972
22	ENI	Rome	8,334,432	(134,869)
23	Daimler-Benz	Stuttgart	8,194,271	125,768
24	U.S. Steel	Pittsburgh	8,167,269	559,614
25	BASF	Ludwigshafen on Rhine	8,152,318	152,831
26	Shell Oil	Houston	8,143,445	514,827
27	Renault	Boulogne-Billancourt (France)	7,831,330	(128,702)
28	Siemens	Munich	7,759,909	201,275
29	Volkswagenwerk	Wolfsburg (Germany)	7,680,786	(63,971)
30	Atlantic Richfield	Los Angeles	7,307,854	350,395
31	Continental Oil	Stamford, Conn.	7,253,801	330,854
32	Bayer	Leverkusen (Germany)	7,223,302	128,229
33	E.I. du Pont de Nemours	Wilmington, Del.	7,221,500	271,800
34	Toyota Motor	Toyoda-City (Japan)	7,194,139	250,848
35	ELF-Aquitaine	Paris	7,165,390	199,875
36	Nestlé	Vevey (Switzerland)	7,080,160	309,365
37	ICI (Imperial Chemical Industries)	London	6,884,219	424,294
38	Petrobrás (Petróleo Brasileiro)	Rio de Janeiro	6,625,516	703,586
39	Western Electric	New York	6,590,116	107,308
40	British-American Tobacco	London	6,145,979	314,041
41	Procter & Gamble	Cincinnati	6,081,675	333,862
42	Hitachi	Tokyo	5,916,135	94,084
43	Westinghouse Electric	Pittsburgh	5,862,747	165,224
44	Mitsubishi Heavy Industries	Tokyo	5,693,994	40,699
45	Union Carbide	New York	5,665,000	381,700
46	Tenneco	Houston	5,599,709	342,936
47	Nissan Motor	Tokyo	5,479,562	115,532
48	Goodyear Tire & Rubber	Akron, Ohio	5,452,473	161,613
49	Montedison	Milan	5,417,741	(183,912)
50	British Steel	London	5,340,183	171,867
	Totals		568,317,431	37,311,850

Source: *Fortune,* August 1976, p. 243.

Many countries, particularly in Europe, have had foreign economic interests for centuries, but only recently has foreign commerce begun to represent a significant percentage of total United States economic activity. Before World War II, just a handful of American companies had important overseas investments. There were two or three international oil companies, a few mining groups, several banks, and some manufacturers of automobiles, machinery, and electrical equipment. Since 1945, however, American business has become much more world-oriented, and today over 10,000 U.S. firms have significant foreign-based operations. The nature of international business has also changed: traditional "foreign trade," with its emphasis on exporting goods manufactured in the United States, has declined dramatically in importance, being replaced by full-fledged overseas divisions with their own manufacturing plants.

When the emphasis was on export sales, foreign investments were minimal. Today, however, a great deal of investment is required to establish and support this country's overseas operations. In fact, direct foreign investment of U.S. firms climbed sharply from $11.8 billion in 1950 to $133 billion by year-end 1975.[2] Table 24–2, which gives another indication of the growth of U.S. private foreign investment, shows that during the period 1961–73 American firms established over 8,404 new facilities overseas.

This rapid increase in foreign investments has had a tremendous impact on the operations of many American firms. Such companies are highly dependent upon their overseas operations because significant amounts of their total assets, sales, and profits are accounted for by their foreign operating units. Table 24–3 gives the percentage of total earnings represented by foreign earnings for selected industries in 1972. Some of the firms whose data is included in the table—for example, IBM, Pfizer, Mobil, Foster Wheeler, International Systems & Controls, LRC International, Hoover, and F. W. Woolworth—obtained nearly half of their total earnings from their foreign operations.

Overseas expansion has not been limited to American firms; in fact, there is an increasing flow of foreign business investment into the United States.

According to an extensive survey undertaken by the U. S. Department of Commerce, foreign direct investment in the United States

---

2. "Direct foreign investment" involves the ownership of 10 percent or more of the stock of a foreign firm. Other investment is defined as "portfolio investment," where neither control nor influence over the foreign firm is presumed to exist.

reached $26.5 billion by year-end 1974.[3] This compared to $13.7 billion in 1971, $7.6 billion in 1962, and about $3 billion in 1950. The continuation of the growth of foreign investment in the United States is virtually assured with such recent ventures as Volkswagen's $400 million plant in Pennsylvania, Sweden's $100 million investment in Virginia to assemble Volvos, and Michelin's (France) $300 million tire plant in South Carolina.

Although U.S. direct private investment abroad is larger than that of all other countries combined, U.S. firms face strong and increasing competition from foreign-based multinational firms. A good example of this competition is the Dutch firm of Phillips, which has plants in more than 40 countries and sales subsidiaries in 60 more, employs more than 360,000 people worldwide, and manufactures nearly one million different products.

Changing Organization and Structure of Multinational Business

Multinational corporations seldom use the word "foreign": their involvement in overseas business is such that they now regard the world, rather than a single nation, as their area of operations.[4] The sheer size of many corporations' foreign direct investments has caused profound changes in their organizations and operating strategies. The way a firm can be affected by growing international interests is illustrated by the experience of Mid-State Manufacturing Company, Inc. Originally a manufacturer of food processing machinery, Mid-State, through domestic mergers and overseas investments, is now active in several separate lines of business.

In 1955 Mid-State, then a well-known company and highly respected for the quality of its food processing machinery, had its major plants and markets in the midwestern states. During that year, the firm received its first tentative orders from foreign countries. Although it could supply the products ordered, the firm had had no experience with the various regulations, means of transportation, or special skills necessary to complete these transactions. Accordingly, it turned to special-

3. *International Letter*, Federal Reserve Bank of Chicago, No. 280, June 25, 1976. It is also reported that foreign portfolio investment in U.S. stocks and bonds reached $67 billion by year-end 1974. Of that amount, $25 billion was in stock, and $16 billion in government bonds and notes. Government bonds and notes are held primarily by foreign official institutions as part of their international reserves. The total figure for 1975 is estimated at $86 billion.

4. There is no generally accepted definition of the term "multinational corporation." In the purest sense, the term probably should be applied to only a few large firms that have undisputed international ownership, operation, and management. However, the term is commonly applied to any business that has significant operations in several different countries.

**Integrated Topics in
Financial Management**

**Table 24–2
U.S. Firms Overseas: Patterns of Expansion (1961–1972) (in Number of Activities)**

Type of Activity	1961	1962	1963	1964	1965	1966	1967	1968	1969	1970	1971	1972	1973	Total
New Establishments														
Manufacturing	382	445	516	507	426	398	363	371	524	469	311	368	391	5,476
Nonmanufacturing	178	139	202	254	259	190	182	202	348	275	193	242	264	2,928
Subtotal	560	584	718	761	685	588	545	573	872	744	504	510	660	8,404
Expansions														
Manufacturing	185	176	159	155	171	96	54	63	119	90	53	59	65	1,445
Nonmanufacturing	70	100	43	13	17	17	6	8	18	12	5	5	6	320
Subtotal	255	276	202	168	188	113	60	71	137	102	58	64	71	10,169
Licensing Agreements	340	247	304	282	259	174	139	133	177	129	113	128	117	2,542
Total	1,155	1,107	1,224	1,211	1,132	875	744	777	1,186	975	675	802	848	12,711

Source: John B. Rhodes, "U.S. New Business Activities Abroad," *Columbia Journal of World Business*, vol. 9, no. 2, Summer 1974, p. 100.

Table 24–3	Industry	Number of Companies	Total Earnings	Foreign Earnings to Total Earnings (Percent)	Foreign Net Assets to Total Net Assets (Percent)
Industry Comparison of Foreign Operations, Selected Industries, 1972	Chemicals	9	$ 926,109	36.8	30.3
	Construction	11	467,653	19.8	25.5
	Consumer goods	36	2,860,856	51.3	*
	Electricals	16	870,113	32.1	35.8
	Foodstuffs	15	708,504	21.6	22.4
	Machinery	26	420,368	34.9	28.9
	Metals	11	604,972	17.7	21.7
	Office Equipment	9	1,694,171	49.5	28.3
	Petroleum	8	2,962,404	46.9	45.7
	Pharmaceuticals	15	894,355	38.6	31.5

*Not available.
Source: *Business International*, July 20, 1973, p. 230.

ized export brokers and international bankers for the required expertise.

As the volume of overseas orders increased, Mid-State created an export section within its sales department. Because most of the complexities of these export sales were handled by international intermediaries, the export section was basically an extension of the domestic sales department, and the scope of its activities was quite limited. This type of organization was adequate so long as Mid-State was satisfied simply to accept and fill orders as they were received.

In 1957, to acquaint himself with this overseas business and to investigate ways of expanding it, Edward Bronson, Mid-State's president, visited several Latin American countries to which substantial amounts of machinery had been shipped. He became convinced that because of growing industrialization in the region, Mid-State Manufacturing could easily increase its overseas business if it had a sales force in the field. Accordingly, Bronson authorized the recruitment and training of a foreign sales force. The venture proved to be highly productive: foreign sales increased at about twice the rate of domestic sales in 1958, 1959, and 1960.

During 1960, the firm's managers began to realize that, along with the advantages of the international market, there were complications. At first the problems were rather simple, consisting mainly of requests for small modifications in the machinery to meet local conditions. Such minor modifications were easily accomplished, but as the salesmen gained experience and expanded the territories they covered, the requested modifications became more complex. This forced the export section to expand its activities and to work more and more with Mid-State's engineering and production departments. At the same time, increasing foreign requests for credit required contacts between the export and finance departments. By 1961, even though foreign sales had increased to about 10 percent of the company's total sales, it had become apparent that Mid-State's growth in foreign markets was not up to potential. Modifications of domestic machinery could not satisfy all the requests received, and the firm faced some problems servicing the modified machinery it sold.

Bronson decided to explore the feasibility of establishing a foreign production unit, so he again traveled to Latin America. The urgency of his investigation was emphasized by two events. First, a reliable source had reported that one of Mid-State's competitors was studying the possibility of building a plant in Venezuela. Second, in an effort to stimulate its own local industry, Peru, one of Mid-State's largest South American markets, was planning to impose a 50 percent tariff on all imports of food processing machinery. These two events not only underscored the necessity of going ahead with plans for an overseas unit, but also gave a focus to these plans, for it was clear that those two market locations should be examined first.

Immediately upon his return to the United States, Bronson created a study group to inquire into the whole question of the international market and to recommend what actions the firm should take. The report of the international market study group, which was submitted in December 1961, recommended that a subsidiary for international operations be formed to meet the problems and challenges of the international market. Accordingly, in 1962, Mid-State International Corporation was established as a separate company, with its president reporting directly to Bronson.[5]

The proposed organization was put into effect in 1963, and it proved to be a reasonably satisfactory arrangement. By 1970, both the parent company and Mid-State International had grown substantially and had diversified into a number of related lines. Mid-State International, particularly, had found it advantageous to go into the food processing field. It then had units operating in 23 countries, and overseas sales accounted for about 35 percent of total corporate sales.

During its overseas buildup, Mid-State International used several methods to establish itself in the various markets. In countries such as Honduras, where much of the processed food was imported, the company started from scratch and built its own plants. In countries where there were already previously established operations, or where the po-

---

5. For a more complete discussion of why companies go international and the various methods used to become established overseas, see Myles L. Mace, "The President and International Operations," *Harvard Business Review*, November–December 1966, p. 72.

litical conditions were highly uncertain, the company used a licensing arrangement through which Mid-State would supply a local manufacturing firm with financial and technical assistance, trademarks, and general know-how. In countries such as Mexico and Japan, where host government regulations require at least some local ownership, the company went into joint ventures with local investors. Finally, in several European countries, Mid-State acquired local firms. Each time the firm went into a new market, it gained experience that made the next penetration easier.

Edward Bronson, who became chairman of the board in 1971, anticipated that overseas sales would eventually represent 50 percent or more of Mid-State's total sales. Although Bronson realized that it had not yet happened, he looked forward to the time when the foreign and domestic operations would be completely integrated and the Mid-State Manufacturing Company would be a truly multinational firm. This line of thought evolved because of various difficulties encountered in the coordination of the activities of domestic and international operations. It was Mr. Bronson's belief that if the company was to realize its full potential and to take advantage of world developments, reorganization toward the complete integration of domestic and foreign operations would be necessary. This idea was reinforced in June 1971, when he read in *Business Week* that Eaton Corporation was already in the process of developing this type of structure.[6] Bronson understood that because of the nationalistic government policies and legal requirements of many of the host countries, it would be several years before any company could make all its decisions concerning such things as transfer of funds, pricing policies, and shifting of assets as a true multinational firm. However, to the extent possible, Bronson believed that Mid-State should view all operating units as interrelated parts of a single system.

Evaluation of Foreign Investment Opportunities

Since 1972, when Mid-State achieved full integration of its domestic and international capital budgeting procedures, all investment proposals, domestic and foreign, have been required to go through an established screening process: each proposal is subjected to a cash flow analysis, which results in a net present value calculation, and all proposals compete for funds on their individual merits.

Although Mid-State uses the *NPV* method to evaluate projects, the firm's management realizes that there are some significant differences between domestic and international investments. These differences re-

6. *Business Week* 12 June 1971, p. 87.

late primarily to two factors: (1) the political and financial environments of the host countries, and (2) the fact that two cash flow analyses must be performed for each of the foreign investment proposals—one for the project itself, and one for cash flows from the foreign project to the parent. The effects of these two factors on the application of capital budgeting theory are discussed in this section.

The Screening Process

Analysis of the Host Country

In November 1975 Mr. Bronson was approached by the government of Andovia, a West African republic, with a request that his company establish a cocoa processing plant there. Although this request was received as a direct result of one of Bronson's visits to Africa, it was immediately referred to Mid-State International for screening and analysis, as all foreign proposals are, regardless of their origin.

For administrative purposes, Mid-State International has separated the countries of the world into four areas: Europe, Africa and the Middle East, Latin America, and the Far East. The manager of each area group is responsible for the initial screening of all investment proposals for any country within his area. The primary function of this initial screening is to analyze the political environment of the proposed host country and to determine whether or not the economic environment would be receptive to the proposed project.

The initial screening of the cocoa processing plant proposal showed that Andovia was generally receptive to foreign direct investments. Further, according to the latest industrial policy statement of the Andovian government, food processing plants were to be given highest priority because they would reduce the nation's need for imports and thus save foreign exchange. The country had no plans to nationalize any business, and its constitution states that if nationalization becomes desirable in the public interest, adequate, prompt, and effective compensation is guaranteed. At the time of the analysis, no foreign firm had ever been nationalized, although the electric utilities and railroads were nationalized shortly after the country gained its independence in 1948.

Andovia is one of the world's largest producers of cocoa, but virtually the entire crop of 2.5 million tons a year is exported unprocessed. For such products as chocolate, chocolate milk, Ovaltine, and other beverages made of cocoa, the 62 million Andovians depended almost entirely on imports. Thus, the country found itself in the position of first exporting the raw material and then importing the finished product. The government viewed the correction of this situation as an important economic task, making it likely that Mid-State International would experience very favorable tax treatment.

**Analysis of the
International
Environment**

The favorable preliminary report on the project was sent to the office of Robert Harris, the president of Mid-State International, for the second screening stage. Here, the analysis shifts from sole concern with the host country environment to what may be called the "international environment." At this stage, the emphasis centers on such factors as whether the company has the experience to handle the project; whether the project conflicts with other proposals; whether the market could be better served in some other way; and how the project could be intergrated into Mid-State's continuing efforts to manage and allocate working capital on a worldwide basis.

Since Mid-State International already had overseas units in the food processing industry, the Andovian proposal would benefit from the company's prior experience. Also, since the host government had indicated that it was willing to place an import tax on cocoa products once production was started, the market would enjoy a protected status. Finally, it was determined that although minor adjustments in some working capital allocations would be required, the anticipated export sales of the project was expected to provide an inflow of hard currency that would reduce the need for some hedging operations and thus reduce costs.

**Financial
Analysis**

The third stage of the screening process involves a standard financial analysis. Although foreign investment proposals are subject to a number of political and international constraints not associated with domestic investments, once these constraints have been considered, Mid-State's policy is that each project should undergo a financial cash flow evaluation to determine whether the project has a positive risk-adjusted *NPV*. There is, however, an important difference in the application of cash flow analysis to a foreign investment: for foreign investments, there must be two sets of cash flow analyses—one for the project itself and one for the parent company.

**Factors
Affecting the
Cash Flows**

Demand Forecast. As with any investment proposal, the first step in the analysis of the Andovian project was a forecast of demand. For Andovia, as is often the case for developing countries, there simply were no reliable figures on past cocoa consumption. There were, however, fairly good data on imports of cocoa products, and since almost no cocoa was then processed locally, these figures could be used to estimate past consumption. These past usage estimates were correlated with population, income, and other factors, and, on the basis of population and income projections, were used to develop the estimated demand figures given in Table 24–4.

Table 24–4	Year	Tons
Estimated Demand for Cocoa Products	1975	285,000
	1976	291,000
	1977	297,000
	1978	304,000
	1979	310,000
	1980	316,000
	1981	322,000
	1982	328,000
	1983	335,000
	1984	342,000

Duties and Taxes. In arriving at the cash flow figures for a foreign investment, particular attention must be given to the fact that since the transactions to be analyzed flow across national boundaries, a unique set of tax laws and customs duties may be applicable. In the case of Andovia, the government agreed that Mid-State could, under the Andovian Industrial Development Act of 1969, enjoy an income tax holiday for five years, and could also import, duty-free, any new production equipment and materials that could not be obtained from local sources. Used equipment could be imported under a relatively low duty of 10 percent. After five years of production, Mid-State International would be subject to a 40 percent income tax, plus a "super-tax" of 25 percent of all income over 15 percent of equity capital. The super-tax, introduced in 1967 as part of Andovia's Social Reform Act, was originally scheduled to expire in 1977, but it appears that the tax will be extended. If this tax is ever eliminated or reduced, Mid-State's profit potential will, of course, increase.

Applicable Exchange Rates. Another unique feature of foreign investment analysis is that the transactions being examined frequently involve currency transfers, so foreign exchange rates and restrictions must be taken into account. When there is an official rate of exchange and that rate is stable, no problems are presented. However, if changes in the exchange rate are expected (through devaluation or revaluation), or if the exchange rate is allowed to "float," the evaluation process is more complicated; it becomes necessary to forecast the rate of exchange that may be applicable to future transactions.[7] Although the Andovian gov-

---

7. Prior to August 15, 1971, the United States operated under an international monetary system established toward the end of World War II at Bretton Woods, New Hampshire. At the Bretton Woods Conference, the participating nations agreed to adhere to an international monetary policy calling for fixed exchange rates between currencies. The dollar was based on gold, at $35 per ounce of gold, and

ernment allowed the pound to float for a few months after the dollar devaluation of February 1973, it soon became apparent that an equilibrium rate of exchange had been reached at about \$2.80 to one Andovian pound. The Andovian government announced in June 1973 that this new rate would be established as the official rate. Mid-State International's screening report indicated that it was safe to assume that the current rate of exchange of \$2.80 to one Andovian pound (\$2.80:1) would be maintained for the foreseeable future.

Recognizing that many countries closely regulate who may purchase foreign exchange, the screening report also discussed exchange availability. In Andovia, the Central Bank is responsible for the administration of the exchange control regulations. Under those regulations, permission is required to purchase U.S. dollars with Andovian pounds for payment of loan interest, management fees, royalties, home office administration expenses, and most other billings for services rendered by an overseas supplier. Moreover, even if permission to purchase foreign exchange is given, Andovia is frequently so short of foreign exchange that it is simply not available. The screening report indicated that, because of the heavy burden that the armament program has imposed on the country's exchange reserves, applications for permission are subject to considerable delay. Furthermore, the granting of permission does not ensure that the related exchange will be available. In general, the allocation of foreign exchange is administered by the country's commercial banks, and each bank can allocate to its customers only such amounts as are made available to it by the Central Bank.

---

all other currencies were stated in terms of their relationship to the dollar. For example, the British pound was stated to be worth \$2.80. The U.S. Treasury agreed to buy or sell gold to foreigners freely at the rate of \$35 per ounce. President Nixon's action of August 1971, when he announced that the United States would no longer convert dollars to gold, ended the international monetary system formulated at Bretton Woods. The responsibility for deciding whether to let exchange rates "float"—that is, find their own level in relation to other currencies in accordance with supply and demand forces—or to continue maintaining a stable relationship with other currencies was placed on the individual nations. For a time it appeared that fixed exchange rates would be permanently abolished, but they were reinstated in early 1972 when the United States devalued the dollar by raising the price of gold to \$38 per ounce. It was hoped that this action would correct the overvaluation of the dollar and lead to a more stable balance of payment situation. This, however, did not happen; in February 1973, the dollar was again devalued by about 10 percent when the official price of gold was raised to \$42.20 per ounce.

As a result of the second dollar devaluation and the international monetary crisis that followed, all major European exchange markets were officially closed on March 1, 1973. On March 11, eight members of the European Economic Community agreed to maintain fixed exchange rates among themselves within 2¼ percent margins—the so-called floating snake. These eight currencies would then be allowed to float as a bloc against the dollar. The Japanese yen, Swiss franc, British sterling, and Italian lira each continued to float independently. Most of the smaller nations have continued to maintain fixed rates of exchange.

Reinvestment and Restrictions on Repatriation of Profit. Andovian law restricts repatriation of profits to 70 percent of the net income, as defined by law, during a given accounting period. Thus, regardless of the actual cash flows that might be generated during any period, there is a limit on the amount that can be transferred to the parent company. Since there was nothing to indicate that there would be any change in this law, it would have the effect of forcing Mid-State International to reinvest 30 percent of net income each year in its Andovian operation.

To satisfy this required reinvestment, Mid-State International's analysis suggested that the initial plant should be smaller than actual demand requirements. Then it could use the required retained earnings to expand in later years. Between the expansion required to meet current demand and the normal demand growth, it was anticipated that there would be no difficulty in profitably employing the required investment.

Analysis of Cash Flows

One of the major modifications that must be made when the capital budgeting process is applied to a foreign investment is that two sets of interrelated cash flows must be analyzed. Mid-State invests funds to generate cash flows that can, ultimately, be paid out as dividends to its stockholders. For domestic investments, because no restrictions are placed on the use of funds, simple *NPV* analysis of cash flows is sufficient to evaluate the project. In the case of overseas projects, attention must be given to how and when cash flows can be made available to the parent company. As we have already seen, transfers of funds may be constrained either by direct restrictions or because the host country does not have foreign exchange available.

If the earnings in country A are restricted, while the earnings in country B's currency are freely convertible to dollars and are transferable either to the parent company or to other operating units, a rate of return of 25 percent in country A may be less desirable than a 20 percent return in country B. Although a multinational firm is certainly concerned with the profitability of each investment, it is equally concerned with the amount of earnings that are freely convertible and transferable. Thus, the multinational firm is ultimately concerned with the present value of the *net available inflows to the parent company.*

The general procedures for cash flow analysis are the same for a foreign investment as for a domestic investment. For the foreign investment, however, there are several inflow and outflow items that are not usually associated with domestic investment. The flow involved in Mid-State's proposed cocoa processing plant investment serves both to illustrate these items and to show the interrelations between cash flows from the project and cash flows to the parent company.

Project Cash Inflows. The major cash inflows shown in the top section of Table 24–5 are from sales in Andovia. These sales show a rapid increase during the first three years as the operation moves toward full production; after that, projected increases in sales are closely related to the growth in population.[8] It is also anticipated that once full production is reached, any surplus over local demand will be exported. Because all foreign exchange earnings must be turned over to the Central Bank, the export sales, like all the amounts in Table 24–5, are in Andovian pounds.

Project Cash Outflows. The lower portion of Table 24–5 shows the expected project outflows. The projected outflows for the first year—the construction period—consist primarily of expenditures for new and used assets and costs of preparing for operations. After the first year, the major expenditures are for raw materials, labor, and other normal operating expenses as outlined in the table. Since Mid-State would be expanding the capacity of the processing plant, expenditures for fixed assets would continue, but at a much lower rate.

There are two expenses that are somewhat unusual. The first is a supervisory fee—Mid-State Manufacturing Company would supply the Andovian unit with certain supervisory personnel, for a fee. The second is local taxes—in accordance with Mid-State's agreement with the Andovian government, there would be no tax liability for the first five years of operations. After that, income taxes would be paid at the normal Andovian corporate tax rate.

The final row in Table 24–5 shows the net cash receipts for each year. Cash flows are negative for the first three years, but they rise rapidly thereafter.

Parent Company Cash Flows. If this analysis were for a domestic investment, the yearly cash flow figures obtained in Table 24–5 would be discounted at the cost of capital to arrive at a net present value figure. For a foreign proposal, however, this is only the first stage; the multinational firm must be concerned with net inflows that will be available for dividends or employment elsewhere. Since net cash flows calculated in Table 24–5 might be restricted because of various laws and regula-

---

8. The sales figures given in Table 24–5 are expected values derived from a probability distribution that incorporates the various elements of risk associated with the project.

Table 24–5
Andovian Cocoa Processing Plant Proposal, 10-Year Cash Flow (Thousands of Andovian Pounds)*

Year	1	2	3	4	5	6	7	8	9	10
Cash inflows										
Andovian sales		22,500	47,200	72,100	76,400	78,600	81,400	83,600	86,000	88,900
Export sales				500	500	500	500	500	500	500
Terminal value										200
Total Inflows		22,500	47,200	72,600	76,900	79,100	81,900	84,100	86,500	89,600
Cash outflows										
New fixed assets	2,500	178	178	178	178	178	178	178	178	178
Used equipment	1,000									
Plant expansion		200	200							
Out-of-pocket set-up costs	400	200								
Raw material		20,700	41,400	62,000	62,400	62,800	63,000	63,200	63,400	63,600
Labor costs		379	782	1,258	1,332	1,408	1,479	1,553	1,724	1,775
Sales and administrative expense		2,500	5,000	7,500	7,700	7,800	8,200	8,400	8,600	8,800
Supervisory fee		43	57	89	89	89	89	89	89	89
Local taxes							2,890	3,605	4,220	5,075
Total Outflows	3,900	24,200	47,617	71,025	71,699	72,275	75,836	77,025	78,211	79,517
Net Cash Receipts	−3,900	−1,700	−417	1,575	5,201	6,825	6,064	7,075	8,289	10,083

*A token terminal value of 200 Andovian pounds is used for the project.

Table 24–6
Cash Flows Associated with Andovian Proposal (Thousands of U.S. Dollars)

Year	1	2	3	4	5	6	7	8	9	10
Cash inflows										
Yearly inflows from project	−10,924	−4,641	−1,008	4,661	14,817	19,366	17,235	20,067	23,467	28,492
Terminal value										500
Total inflows	−10,924	−4,641	−1,008	4,661	14,817	19,377	17,235	20,067	23,467	28,992
Cash outflows										
U.S. income tax*	−200	−100	−25	2,237	7,112	9,295	117			
U.S. tax on supervisory fee		57	76	119	119	119	119	119	119	119
Div. Withholding tax†		42	132	225	331	438	627	735	832	1,053
Export sales loss (after tax)				800	800	800	800	800	800	800
Total outflows	−200	−1	183	3,381	8,362	10,652	1,723	1,654	1,751	1,972
Net available inflows	−10,724	−4,640	−1,191	1,280	6,455	8,714	15,512	18,413	21,716	27,020
Discount factor (10%)	.91	.83	.75	.68	.62	.56	.51	.47	.42	.39
Present value	−9,759	−3,851	−893	870	4,002	4,880	7,911	8,654	9,121	10,538
Cumulative net present value‡	−9,759	−13,610	−14,503	−13,633	−9,631	−4,751	3,160	11,814	20,935	31,473

*U.S. income taxes decline in the seventh year and disappear thereafter because the firm is given a credit on U.S. taxes for payments of Andovian taxes.

†Tax paid to Andovian government on dividends.

‡If the project terminates after any given year, its NPV will be the figure in this last row under the year in question. For example, if the project operates as projected for ten years, its NPV will be $31,473,000.

tions, it is necessary to develop a second cash flow analysis to show the unencumbered net present values that would be available to the parent company.

Inflows to the parent company would come primarily from the project's net cash flows, the figures on the bottom line of Table 24–5. The parent company would also receive supervisory fees, so total potential repatriated cash flows, shown in dollars on the top line of Table 24–6, are the sum of these two items. Note that Table 24–6 is stated in United States dollars, whereas Table 24–5 was stated in Andovian pounds.[9] A terminal value for the project is expected in year 10; this figure, added to those in row one, constitutes the tenth year cash inflow.

Offsetting these inflows, however, are the several outflows shown in the lower section of Table 24–6, the first of which is for U.S. income tax. There is a tax liability offset for the first three years, resulting from a U.S. tax regulation that permits Mid-State to offset the losses of the foreign subsidiary against income from its other operations. After the initial loss period, parent company income results in a U.S. tax liability. However, this liability may be reduced by the amount of taxes paid by the subsidiary in the host country. Since, under Andovian law, Mid-State would not be required to pay any taxes for the first five years of operation, this provision would not be effective until the sixth year of the project. Other U.S. tax liabilities that would be incurred by the parent company are also shown in Table 24–6.

Recall that after the cocoa processing reaches full production, any surplus will be sold in the export market. Since any export sales made by the Andovian operations would be, to some extent, at the expense of Mid-State's other units serving those markets, the after-tax sales losses suffered by those units should be taken into account. This factor is shown as export sales losses (after tax) in Table 24–6.

Assuming that the project works out as planned, the *NPV* for the parent company is obtained by subtracting the present value of the required outflows from the present value of the anticipated inflows. As shown in Table 24–6, cash flows are discounted at the project's estimated cost of capital to arrive at a present value figure for each year;[10] the final amounts given in the table are cumulative net present values. We see that the project, from the parent company's standpoint, is in the black in the fourth year and has broken even on a discounted cash flow basis — that is, the *NPV* is zero — during the seventh year.

9. The official rate of exchange established by the Andovian government was $2.8011:£1, and this is the rate used to calculate the cash inflow amounts used in Table 24–6.

10. A cost of capital of 10 percent was used on the assumption that 10 percent is the overall company cost of capital and that this project carries about the same risk as the average investment of the company. If the investment were considered to be more risky, then a higher discount rate should be used.

Problems Faced by Multinational Firms

Mid-State's board of directors must give final approval for all capital expenditures in excess of $1 million; since the Andovian project fell into this category, the board had to approve it before the project could be undertaken. Robert Harris, who is president of Mid-State International, and several members of his staff were requested to attend the board's budget meeting in order to answer any questions that might be raised.

During the discussion on the project, Everett Anderson, one of the board members, mentioned that he had just finished reading a survey of 166 international executives who had been asked to list the problems that concerned them most. The consequences of both foreign and domestic government actions, which most of those surveyed saw as beyond their control, were uppermost in their minds. Anderson, to demonstrate that this fear of foreign government action was certainly a legitimate concern, cited the nationalizations that had taken place in Peru and Chile, and the restrictions on foreign businesses being formulated by other South American countries. Specifically, Anderson wondered whether the Andovian government, although it presently had no intention of nationalizing any foreign firms, might not do so in the future if this was deemed to be in the Andovian public interest. He went on to say that if nationalization should occur, all of Mid-State's carefully developed cash flow analyses would be useless.

President Harris agreed that since nationalization appeared to be on the rise throughout the world, there was always some risk that a country might decide to nationalize foreign firms. He pointed out, however, that Andovia had recently emphasized its intention of adhering to international law and had promised to pay prompt and adequate compensation if it should ever nationalize a foreign firm. He added that, as long as Mid-State made a net contribution to the Andovian economy, the likelihood of nationalization was relatively small.

Harris explained his position, noting that in some cases host countries do have reasons for being unhappy with foreign businesses: When an industry is controlled from outside, the host country may pay quite a price. For one thing, if exhaustible natural resources such as minerals or oil are involved, the primary wealth of the host nation may be drained off without regard for the local economy. Further, the host country may lose tax revenue because the foreign corporation can report lower profits by manipulating transfer prices between subsidiaries. Also, when the parent company uses its financial network to pull money out of a country with balance of payment problems, or to move money into one struggling to reduce inflation, then the host government rightfully feels that it is losing control over its domestic economy. In addition, if a company uses its international flexibility to reroute a subsidiary's purchases through some other country, then it may cause a sudden drop in the host country's exports. Harris stated that, finally, a country's economy can be upset if a foreign company suddenly decides to pull out, as several had done in Europe because they had overinvested and wanted to consolidate their operations.

Here Bronson, the chairman of the board, entered the discussion to add that it was company policy to maintain good relations with its host governments, and the cocoa processing plant would make several major contributions toward that end. In the first place, according to Bronson, building a large plant and starting a new industry would benefit Andovia's economy in output, employment, and expanded tax revenues. Second, since Mid-State would introduce more advanced equipment than was presently being used, local labor skills would be upgraded. Since Mid-State planned to train local administrators for almost all positions, management talent would be increased. Bronson held that of great importance was the fact that Mid-State would provide Andovian consumers with a better and cheaper product.

To summarize the discussion, Harris pointed out that the presence of foreign businesses could have both advantages and disadvantages for a host country. He felt that the issue was not which side was right or wrong but, rather, whether the two parties could work together to arrive at a mutually beneficial arrangement. He felt that the best way to counter nationalism was to demonstrate that the investment would make a net contribution to the host country's economy. Harris reminded the group that the Andovian government had been first to suggest the project. Since then, there had been several meetings with various Andovian government agencies, and Mid-State had agreed to consult with them on any decision that could adversely affect their country. Harris concluded that, although there was certainly no way to be sure that the situation would remain stable, at the present time nationalization did not appear to be a problem. Still, he did concede that in the analysis of the Andovian project, Mid-State had not given much weight to the possibility of nationalization when developing the estimated cash flows.[11]

Another board member, Jan Merriam, vice-president of Mid-State's New York bank, spoke up. He pointed out that many countries had recently experienced devaluation. Although the report on the Andovian project mentioned that the official position of the government was to maintain the present exchange, it also stated that foreign exchange had been in short supply recently. He said that it had been Merriam's experience that a short supply of foreign exchange often preceded de-

---

11. The values given in Tables 24–5 and 24–6 are expected values determined from probability distributions of cash flows. The probability of nationalization, and of the losses in this event, was given a low weight in the analysis.

valuation, and he wanted to know if a full investigation of the Andovian situation had been made.

In reply, Harris explained that as a result of some unanticipated devaluations in the first year of foreign operations, Mid-State International had developed a devaluation monitoring procedure that, under normal circumstances, is applied on a monthly basis to each country in which the firm has operations. For potentially troublesome areas, the procedure is repeated more frequently either until the trouble has passed or until action has been taken to minimize the loss. The devaluation monitoring procedure consists, basically, of a constant examination of several items that often are indicators of currency weakness: inflation, balance of trade, balance of payments, deficits in the national budget, trends in interest rates, the international reserve position, and foreign exchange quotations.

Harris assured the board members that Andovia had been subjected to the same examination as other countries. It had been determined that, while there was a shortage of foreign exchange and a trade deficit until recently, most of the problems could be attributed to the civil war of three years ago. Improvement had been made in the balance of trade, and for each of the last two years there had been a small net increase in Andovia's international reserve position. In addition, the rate of inflation had been rather low, at about 2 to 3 percent, and the government had been successful in its efforts to hold down budget deficits. With the new petroleum tax decreed in 1970, and with the foreign exchange savings anticipated from import substitutions, it was most probable that the situation would continue to improve. Nevertheless, a close watch over the condition would be maintained.

Harris was also questioned about the steps that were taken when the devaluation monitoring procedure indicated that a given currency was vulnerable to devaluation. Before he could answer, Don March, manager of the research division and a new member of the board, asked a more fundamental question: How would an Andovian devaluation hurt Mid-State Manufacturing? Harris replied that there would be two effects. First, the cash flows (shown in Table 24–5) were stated in Andovian pounds. These pounds were converted to dollars at the current rate of 2.80 dollars to 1 pound. If the Andovian pound was devalued, fewer dollars could be obtained for each pound, so the dollar value of the Andovian project would be reduced. The second effect of devaluation follows directly from the first: recognizing that a foreign subsidiary is only a collection of "projects," and that the value to the parent of all projects declines when a devaluation occurs, the accounting profession requires an immediate write-down to reflect the effect of the devaluation.

To illustrate the second effect, suppose that devaluation reduced the value of the Andovian pound in relation to the dollar by 50 percent, causing the exchange rate to drop from $2.80:£1 to $1.40:£1. Further, assume that the Andovian company was financed entirely by Mid-State—that is, the Andovian subsidiary has no debt, only equity, and the equity is all owned by the parent company. Although the devaluation would have no effect on the balance sheet of the Andovian subsidiary, the parent company's consolidated balance sheet is stated in dollars, so that portion of consolidated assets represented by the subsidiary, as well as the consolidated net worth, would have to be reduced. The reduction in net worth is a loss and must be reported as a reduction of earnings by the parent. For example, if the subsidiary had assets with a value of 1 million pounds, or 2.8 million dollars, and a 50 percent devaluation occurred, the parent would have to report a loss of $1.4 million from devaluation during the year in which devaluation occurred. This could, of course, have a drastic effect on earnings per share if foreign operations were important and if the devaluation was a large one.

Harris hastened to explain that most subsidiaries are not 100 percent equity financed—most buy supplies and materials locally and, hence, have accounts payable, and many also have long-term debt outstanding. In these cases, creditors bear part of the decline in asset value in the sense that although the liability in pounds is not reduced, the dollar value of the liability is reduced; this partly offsets the decline in asset dollar value. As a result, the parent company's write-down and loss are limited to its equity position. He went on to point out that, while this is *roughly* what happens, the accounting is actually considerably more complex.[12] He was about to explain these details when March stopped him, saying that he felt he now understood the general nature of the problem and doubted if he would be able to grasp the details. He did, however, wonder what could be done if devaluation appeared imminent.

Harris stated that in such cases the company attempted to accelerate funds flows to the parent, and to take on liabilities payable in local currencies, in order to minimize the danger of losses. In the Andovian case, not very much could be done along those lines, but since Harris felt there was little danger of devaluation, he thought the possibility of devaluation losses should not stand in the way of accepting the project.

At this point, Bronson noted that Mid-State had a $15 million reserve set up for devaluation losses. Thus, if such a loss occurred, it would be charged against the reserve, and current reported earnings would be penalized only if the write-off exceeded $15 million.

---

12. A method for determining "exposure" to devaluation is contained in *Hedging Foreign Exchange Risks*, Management Monograph No. 49, published by *Business International*.

Jan Merriam, the banker on the board who had first brought up the topic of devaluation, reentered the conversation, noting that it was the United States that had twice devalued the dollar with the result that the major trading nations were allowing their currencies to float. Merriam then quizzed Harris as to what action, if any, Mid-State was taking to prevent losses that could arise from changes in the floating rates. Harris readily admitted that the company had little experience in this field but that since March of 1973, when the float was put into effect, the "forward market" had been used several times to hedge certain international transactions. As an example, Harris described a recent contract to purchase machinery made in Germany for delivery six months hence for the equivalent of $200,000 in marks. To lock the dollar price of this machinery, the company had simply purchased a six-month forward contract for marks at a dollar price only slightly higher than the current dollar-to-mark exchange rate. Harris explained that although there was a slight cost involved, the use of the forward market effectively reduced the risk involved with floating exchange rates.

Following this explanation, Merriam and several other directors began to discuss the current international monetary situation and how the trends might affect Mid-State's overseas operations. During this discussion one of the directors pointed out that the International Monetary Fund meeting in September 1973 had as its main topic international monetary reforms. Merriam noted that as a result of this meeting, it was clear that the direction of future reforms would be toward reestablishment of a modified fixed-rate system, one with a semiautomatic exchange procedure determined by some indicator such as a country's foreign exchange reserves or balance of payments surplus or deficit. Merriam cautioned, however, that it would take some time for the details to be worked out and that implementation of any such reforms would take even longer to analyze.

After these comments, Chairman Bronson moved that the board vote to approve the Andovian project. The motion was seconded, and the project received the board's unanimous approval.

Financing the Project

Once the project was approved, Bronson asked Harris to outline his financing plans. Since the board had to approve any external financing that involved issues in excess of $1 million, Bronson felt that time would be saved by clearing that point up immediately.

Harris outlined the following: Plant construction and equipment costs for the project are estimated at $10 million, with another $7 million required for working capital, or $17 million in total. The Andovian Industrial Development Bank will make a loan of $1.5 million, and two local commercial banks will jointly lend another $1.5 million. Mid-State will supply $5 million of new equipment for which it will accept an 8 percent note; the Andovian government agrees that the interest payment on the note will in no way affect the allowable remittance of earnings.[13] Mid-State will also be permitted to supply, as part of its investment, $3 million worth of used equipment. Since there is no effective capital market in Andovia, the remaining $6 million will have to come from other sources. In accordance with Mid-State's policy of further development of international sources of funds, Harris proposed that the final $6 million be raised in the Euro-currency market.

Although Euro-dollar[14] loans were currently available at about 9 percent, well below their 1969–1970 high of 11 percent, Euro-bond rates were also very advantageous. Harris noted that one U.S. company had just sold a German mark denominated Euro-bond issue with a yield of 7.26 percent. He felt that the Andovian subsidiary could float an issue at about the same rate if it were denominated in German marks and guaranteed by the parent company. A Mid-State issue in the U.S. would probably carry an 8½ percent rate. Thus, it was clear that Euro-bonds were less costly at the present time. Following a lengthy discussion of the capital restrictions prevailing in European countries and how they would effect a bond issue, the board approved a $3 million Euro-dollar loan to finance working capital and a Euro-bond issue of 7.3 million German marks (equivalent to $3 million) to finance the remaining requirements. Then, with the project approved and the financing settled, the board adjourned.

Questions

24–1. If it were known that Andovia's head of state was leaning toward a Cuban alliance, what effect might this have on the expected profitability of Mid-State's Andovian project?

---

13. An intercompany loan has an advantage over an equity investment in that it is unaffected by remittance restrictions and will return the full principal at maturity. Therefore, this aspect of Harris' plan got around the 30 percent freeze on earnings imposed by the Andovian government. Of course, Andovia realized this too, and consequently restricted the extent of intercompany loan financing.

14. A "Euro-dollar" is a U.S. dollar deposited in a European bank, frequently a European branch of a U.S. bank. If a U.S. firm buys goods from a European firm, it pays in dollars, and these dollars can be placed in an interest-bearing account in a European bank. The bank can lend these dollars in the Euro-dollar market. Many U.S. firms, attracted by the high interest rates paid on Euro-dollar deposits, shifted funds to Europe in the late 1960s. (U.S. banks were restricted in the amount of interest they could pay on corporate time deposits or on certificates of deposit; this stimulated the flow of funds to Europe.) U.S. firms (as well as many U.S. banks) in need of funds, on the other hand, borrowed heavily in the Euro-dollar market when their traditional sources of funds in the U.S. dried up in the monetary squeeze of the late 1960s. The Euro-dollar market is, currently, an alternative for both U.S. firms with surplus cash seeking investments and U.S. firms needing loans. The Euro-dollar market is a prime example of the internationalization of business and finance in recent years.

24-2. Do you think that a discount rate of 10 percent is appropriate for each year of the Andovian project's life? Why?

24-3. How does Mid-State take account of uncertainty in the Andovian project example? What alternatives might it consider?

24-4. What factors are responsible for the difference between the cash flow of Mid-State's Andovian subsidiary and the cash flow to the parent firm?

24-5. In what ways might it benefit the parent company *not* to own 100 percent of the foreign subsidiary's common stock?

24-6. How useful is the Andovian "tax holiday" to Mid-State?

24-7. If all markets were "free," that is, if there were no trade restrictions such as import and export quotas and tariffs, would this tend to stimulate or retard the development of overseas subsidiaries vis-à-vis branches of a domestic firm?

24-8. In 1971, West Germany allowed its currency to "float" upward in value in relation to the United States dollar. By December 1971, its relative value had increased about 12 percent. What effect would you expect this to have on U.S. firms with large foreign investments in Germany?

Problems

24-1. The Overseas Manufacturing Company, a wholly owned subsidiary of an American firm, operates in the country of Panagua. Panagua's balance of payments situation has deteriorated, and there has been talk of a possible devaluation. The latest balance sheet for the subsidiary is given below:

Overseas Manufacturing Company
Balance Sheet
(in U.S. Dollars)

Cash	$ 80,000	Accounts payable	$100,000
Accounts receivable	150,000	Notes payable	50,000
Inventory	200,000	Other liabilities	50,000
Investment in marketable securities	100,000	Long-term dollar liabilities	200,000
Fixed assets	300,000	Equity	430,000
Total	$830,000	Total	$830,000

a. Before devaluation, the assets and liabilities of Overseas are simply added to those of the parent and its other subsidiaries to develop the consolidated balance sheet. Now assume that Panagua devalues its currency by 20 percent. What adjustments would have to be made to the dollar value of the accounts when the consolidated statement is made? (Note: The value of the long-term liability would not be reduced, since this is a dollar liability.) What effect would this have on the parent company's reported profits?

b. Assume (i) that fixed assets are imported capital goods whose prices rise to offset the devaluation, and (ii) that 50 percent of the inventory items are imported components whose prices similarly rise to offset the devaluation. Under these conditions, would the adjustments made in part a be "realistic"? If not, what do you feel would be a realistic value for the net write-down?

c. If Panagua had revalued its currency upward, or if the United States had devalued the dollar by 20 percent, what would have happened (i) immediately to the parent company's books, and (ii) to cash flows from the subsidiary to the parent over the next few years?

Selected References

Albach, Horst. "The Development of the Capital Structure of German Companies." *Journal of Business Finance & Accounting* 2 (Autumn 1975):281–94.

Al-Dukheil, Abdulaziz, and Wassink, Darwin. "Oil and the International Finance System." *Business Horizons* 20 (Apr. 1977):69–73.

Anderson, Gerald L. "International Project Financing." *Financial Executive* 45 (May 1977):40–45.

Baker, James C., and Bates, Thomas H. *Financing International Business Operations.* Scranton, Pa.: Intext Educational Publishers, 1971.

Bowditch, Richard L., and Burtle, James L. "The Corporate Treasurer in a World of Floating Exchange Rates," In *The Treasurer's Handbook,* J. Fred Weston and Maurice B. Goudzwaard, eds. Homewood, Illinois: Dow Jones-Irwin, 1976, pp. 84–112.

Davis, Steven I. "How Risky is International Lending?" *Harvard Business Review* 55 (Jan.–Feb. 1977):135–43.

Denis, Jack, Jr. "How to Hedge Foreign Currency Risk," *Financial Analysts' Journal* 32 (Jan–Feb. 1976):50–54.

Dufey, Gunter. "Corporate Finance and Exchange Rate Variations." *Financial Management* 1 (Summer 1972):51–57.

Eiteman, David K., and Stonehill, Arthur I. *Multinational Business Finance.* Menlo Park, Calif.: Addison-Wesley Publishing Company, 1973.

Folks, William R., Jr., "Decision Analysis for Exchange Risk Management." *Financial Management* 1 (Winter 1972):101–12.

Folks, William R., J., and Stansell, Stanley R. "The Use of Discriminant Analysis in Forecasting Exchange Rate Movements." *Journal of International Business Studies* 6 (Spring 1975):33–50.

Fouraker, L., and Stopford, J. "Organization Structure and the Multinational Strategy." *Administrative Science Quarterly* (June 1968).

Franck, Peter, and Young, Allan. "Stock Price Reaction of Multinational Firms to Exchange Realignments." *Financial Management* 1 (Winter 1972):66–73.

Giddy, Ian H. "An Integrated Theory of Exchange Rate Equilibrium." *Journal of Financial and Quantitative Analysis* 11 (Dec. 1976):883–92.

Hackett, John T. "New Financial Strategies for the MNC." *Business Horizons* 15 (Apr. 1975):13–20.

Hagemann, Helmut. "Anticipate Your Long-Term Foreign Exchange Risks." *Harvard Business Review* 55 (Mar.–Apr. 1977):81–88.

Hodgson, Ralphael W., and Uyterhoeven, Hugo. "Analyzing Foreign Investment Opportunities." *Harvard Business Review* (Mar.–Apr. 1962).

Imai, Yutaka. "Exchange Rate Risk Protection in International Business." *Journal of Financial and Quantitative Analysis* 10 (Sept. 1975):447–56.

Jucker, James V., and de Faro, Clovis. "The Selection of International Borrowing Sources." *Journal of Financial and Quantitative Analysis* 10 (Sept. 1975): 381–407.

Lessard, Donald R. "World, National, and Industry Factors in Equity Returns." *Journal of Finance* 29 (May 1974):379–91.

Lillich, Richard B. *The Protection of Foreign Investment*. Syracuse, N.Y.: Syracuse University Press, 1965.

Mueller, Gerhard G. *International Accounting*. New York: Macmillan, 1967.

Nehrt, Lee Charles. *The Political Climate for Private Foreign Investment*. New York: Praeger, 1970.

Ness, Walter L., Jr. "A Linear Programming Approach to Financing the Multinational Corporation." *Financial Management* 1 (Winter 1972):88–100.

Obersteiner, Erich. "Should the Foreign Affiliate Remit Dividends or Reinvest?" *Financial Management* 2 (Spring 1973):88–93.

Petty, J. William, II, and Walker, Ernest W. "Optimal Transfer Pricing for the Multinational Firm." *Financial Management* 1 (Winter 1972):74–87.

Remmers, Lee; Stonehill, Arthur; Wright, Richard; and Beekhuisen, Theo. "Industry and Size as Debt Ratio Determinants in Manufacturing Internationally." *Financial Management* 3 (Summer 1974):24–32.

Robbins, Sidney M., and Stobaugh, Robert B. "Financing Foreign Affiliates." *Financial Management* 1 (Winter 1972):56–65.

Rodriguez, Rita M. "FASB No. 8: What Has It Done To Us?" *Financial Analysts' Journal* 33 (Mar.–Apr. 1977):40–47.

————. "Management of Foreign Exchange Risk in the U.S. Multinationals." *Journal of Financial and Quantitative Analysis* 9 (Nov. 1974):849–57.

Rodriguez, Rita M., and Carter, E. Eugene. *International Financial Management*. Englewood Cliffs, New Jersey: Prentice-Hall, Inc., 1976.

Rolfe, Sidney E., and Damm, Walter, eds. *The Multinational Corporation in the World Economy*. New York: Praeger, 1970.

Shapiro, Alan C. "Evaluating Financing Costs for Multinational Subsidiaries." *Journal of International Business Studies* 6 (Fall 1975):25–32.

————. "Exchange Rate Changes, Inflation, and the Value of the Multinational Corporation." *Journal of Finance* 30 (May 1975):485–502.

————. "International Cash Management—The Determination of Multicurrency Cash Balances." *Journal of Financial and Quantitative Analysis* 11 (Dec. 1976): 893–900.

Shapiro, Alan C., and Rutenbert, David P. "Managing Exchange Risks in a Floating World." *Financial Management* 5 (Summer 1976):48–58.

Smith, Don T. "Financial Variables in International Business." *Harvard Business Review* (Jan.–Feb. 1966).

Solnik, B. H. "The International Pricing of Risk: An Empirical Investigation of the World Capital Market Structure." *Journal of Finance* 29 (May 1974): 365–78.

Stonehill, Arthur; Beekhuisen, Theo; Wright, Richard; Remmers, Lee; Toy, Norman; Pares, Antonio; Shapiro, Alan; Egan, Douglas; and Bates, Thomas. "Financial Goals and Debt Ratio Determinants: A Survey of Practice in Five Countries." *Financial Management* 4 (Autumn 1975):27–41.

Teck, Alan. "Control Your Exposure to Foreign Exchange." *Harvard Business Review* 52 (Jan.–Feb. 1974):66–75.

Verroen, John. "How ITT Manages Its Foreign Exchange." *Management Services* (Jan.–Feb. 1965).

Voupel, James W., and Curhan, Joan P. *The Making of Multinational Enterprise.* Boston: Harvard Business School, Division of Research, 1969.

Weston, J. Fred, and Sorge, Bart W. *International Managerial Finance.* Homewood, Ill.: Irwin, 1972, pp. xv and 388.

———. *Guide to International Financial Management.* New York: McGraw-Hill Book Company, 1977.

Zenoff, David B., and Zwick, Jack. *International Finance Management.* Englewood Cliffs, N.J.: Prentice-Hall, 1969.

25 Financial Management in the Small Firm[1]

Small business is a key element of the U.S. economy. First, of the approximately 8.5 million firms in the U.S., about 8.0 million are defined by the U.S. government as "small." Thus, small businesses are quantitatively important. Second, and of perhaps even greater significance, small businesses often serve as the vehicle through which ideas for new products and services make their way to the consuming public. Many of the large electronics firms of the 1970s were new, small businesses in the 1950s. Third, the very existence of small businesses, and the fact that new ones are continually being started, serves to increase competition and to retard monopoly.

In some respects, there is no need to study small business finance as a separate topic—the same general principles apply to large and small firms alike. However, small firms face a somewhat different set of problems than larger businesses, and the goals of a small firm are likely to be oriented toward the aspirations of an individual entrepreneur rather than toward investors in general. Also, the characteristics of the money and capital markets create both problems and opportunities for small firms, and a special governmental agency, the Small Business Administration, exists to help small firms with their financing problems. For all these reasons, a chapter focusing directly on the small firm is useful in a book on financial management.

Alternative Forms of Business Organization

From a technical and legal standpoint, there are three major forms of business organization: the single proprietorship, the partnership, and the corporation.[2] In terms of numbers, about 80 percent of business firms are operated as sole proprietorships, while the remainder are equally divided between partnerships and corporations. By dollar value of sales, however, about 80 percent of business is conducted by corporations, about 13 percent by sole proprietorships, and about 7 percent by

---

1. We wish to acknowledge the assistance of D. A. Woolard and E. W. Jenks of the Small Business Administration in the preparation of this chapter.
2. Other less common forms of organization include business trusts, joint stock companies, and cooperatives.

partnerships. In the remainder of this section we describe and compare the characteristics of these alternative forms of business organization.

Sole Proprietorship

A proprietorship is a business owned by one individual. To go into business as a single proprietor is very simple—a person merely begins business operations. However, most cities require even the smallest establishments to be licensed; occasionally state licenses are required as well.

The proprietorship has key advantages for small operations. It is easily and inexpensively formed. No formal charter for operations is required, and a proprietorship is subject to few government regulations. Further, it pays no corporate income taxes, although all earnings of the firm are subject to federal personal income taxes, whether they are reinvested in the business or are withdrawn.

The proprietorship also has important limitations. Most significant is its inability to obtain large sums of capital. Further, the proprietor has unlimited personal liability for his business debts: the creditors may look to both his business assets and the proprietor's personal assets to satisfy their claims. Finally, the proprietorship is limited to the life of the individual who created it. For all of these reasons, the individual proprietorship is limited primarily to small business operations. However, businesses frequently are started as proprietorships and then converted to corporations whenever their growth causes the disadvantages of the proprietorship form to outweigh its advantages.

Partnership

When two or more persons associate to conduct a business enterprise, a partnership is said to exist. A partnership may operate under different degrees of formality, ranging from an informal oral understanding, to a written partnership agreement, up to a formal article agreement filed with the secretary of the state. Like the proprietorship, the partnership has the advantages of ease and economy of formation, as well as freedom from special governmental regulations, and partnership profits are taxed as personal income in proportion to the partners' claims whether they are distributed to them or not.

One of the advantages of the partnership over the proprietorship is that it makes possible a pooling of various types of resources. Some partners may contribute particular skills or contacts, while others may contribute funds. However, there are practical limits to the number of co-owners who can join in an enterprise without destructive conflict, so most partnership agreements provide that a partner cannot sell his share in the business unless all the partners agree to accept the new partner or partners.

If a new partner comes into the business, the old partnership ceases to exist and a new one is created. The withdrawal or death of any one of the partners also dissolves the partnership. To prevent disputes under such circumstances, the articles of the partnership agreement should include terms and conditions under which assets are to be distributed upon dissolution. Of course, dissolution of the partnership does not necessarily mean the end of the business—the remaining partners may simply buy out the one who died or otherwise left the firm. To avoid financial pressures caused by the death of one of the partners, it is a common practice for each partner to carry life insurance naming the remaining partners as his beneficiaries. The proceeds of such a policy may then be used to buy out the investment of the deceased partner.

A number of drawbacks stemming from the characteristics of the partnership limit its use. They include impermanence, difficulties of transferring ownership, and unlimited liability. Partners risk their personal assets as well as their investments in the business. Further, under partnership law, the partners are jointly and separately liable for business debts. This means that if any partner is unable to meet the claims on him resulting from the liquidation of the partnership, the remaining partners must take over the unsatisfied claims, drawing on their personal assets if necesary.[3]

Corporation

A corporation is a legal entity created by a state.[4] This type of business is a separate entity, distinct from its owners and managers. This separateness gives the corporation three major advantages: (1) it has an *unlimited life*—it can continue after its original owners and managers are dead; (2) it permits *limited liability*; that is, stockholders are not personally liable for the debts of the firm;[5] and (3) it permits *easy transferability of ownership interest* in the firm, as ownership interests can be divided into shares of stock, which can be transferred far more easily than partnership interests.

While a proprietorship or a partnership can commence operations without much paper work, the chartering of a corporation involves a complicated, but routinized, process. First, a *certificate of incorporation* is drawn up; in most states it includes the following information: (1) name of proposed corporation, (2) purposes, (3) amount of capital

---

3. However, it is possible to limit the liabilities of certain partners by establishing a *limited partnership*, wherein certain partners are designated *general partners* and others *limited partners*. Limited partnerships are quite common in the area of real estate investment.

4. Certain types of firms—for example, banks—are also chartered by the federal government.

5. In the case of small corporations, the limited liability feature is often a fiction, as bankers and credit managers frequently require personal guarantees from the stockholders of small , weak businesses.

stock, (4) number of directors, (5) names and addresses of directors, and (6) duration (if limited). The certificate is notarized and sent to the secretary of the state in which the business seeks incorporation. The secretary examines the certificate, and if it is satisfactory, he files the certificate, notifies the applicant, and sends a copy to the clerk of the county in which the corporation will have its principal office. The corporation is then officially in existence.

The actual operations of the firm are governed by two documents, the *charter* and the *bylaws*. The corporate charter technically consists of (1) a certificate of incorporation and, by reference, (2) the general corporation laws of the state. Thus, the corporation is bound by the general corporation laws of the state as well as by unique provisions contained in its certificate of incorporation. The bylaws are a set of rules drawn up by the founders of the corporation to aid in governing the internal management of the company. Included are such points as (1) how directors are to be elected (all elected each year or, say, one-third each year, and whether cumulative voting will be used); (2) whether the preemptive right is granted to existing stockholders in the event new securities are sold; and (3) provisions for management committees, such as an executive committee or a finance committee, and their duties. Also included is the procedure for changing the bylaws themselves, should conditions require it.

Economic Aspects of Firm Size

Average firm size varies from industry to industry—steel, auto, and chemical firms tend to be large, while laundries, auto repair shops, and many types of retail firms tend to be relatively small. As a result, the steel, auto, and chemical industries are relatively concentrated (oligopolistic), while even the largest laundry, auto repair shop, or retail operation has no more than a small percentage of its industry's sales.

Why do these differences exist? Perhaps the most obvious reason relates to the extent of economies of scale in the industry: if the cost per unit produced and sold declines up to a high level of output, then firms will tend to be large. However, if costs in an industry only decline over a small range of outputs, then turn up, firms in the industry will tend to be small. Autos, steel, and chemicals are produced more efficiently in large, integrated plants, and distribution costs are lowest if the firms can employ broad-based distribution systems and engage in nationwide advertising campaigns using national media. Certain types of retail stores, on the other hand, are most efficiently operated as smaller, locally owned concerns.

Figure 25–1 graphs the long-run average cost curves in two industries, A and B. For various reasons, costs in industry A turn up at a rela-

Figure 25–1
Long-run Average
Total Cost per Unit of
Output

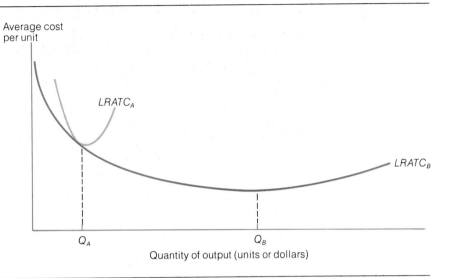

tively small output, so if firms are to be efficient they must produce in
the vicinity of Q_A units of output.[6] Industry B, in contrast, is subject to
economies of scale and declining costs over a much larger range of outputs, so the optimal size of firms in this industry is relatively large.

Firms in an industry may, however, be small simply because the industry is new and the firms have not yet had time to grow and reach
their optimal size. In terms of Figure 25–1, $LRATC_A$ would represent a
short-run cost curve on the long-run curve, not the long-run curve itself.
Virtually all electronics firms were small businesses in the early post-
World War II years, when they were just getting started, even though
economies of scale were inherent in the industry. Today, there are many

6. It should be recognized that the optimal output for many businesses depends on the size of the
market and the locations of potential customers. A retailer has a certain local market whose business is
relatively easy to capture, but to gain additional customers means advertising over a wider area and offering both lower prices and extra services to offset the costs, including inconvenience, to customers
coming to the store. The same thing applies to manufacturers, although here the major cost factor is for
the transportation to ship goods to distant markets. Economies of scale in production or distribution will
lower unit costs, but transportation expenses rise, offsetting these factors to some degree.

In some instances multiplant and multistore operations can be used to reduce the impact of transportation costs in time and money. However, in many businesses the need for close supervision precludes
the possibility of branching, while in others branching is limited because of difficulty of transmitting data
to top management, and top management decisions to field operations. These constraints are being lifted somewhat by computers, data transmission processes, better transportation systems, and new management control processes, all of which are tending to make widely decentralized operations more feasible.

very large electronic firms, such as Hewlett-Packard, LTV, and Teledyne, which were all small when they were organized in the 1950s. The auto industry went through a similar transition in the period 1910–1920.

It is important to recognize that production methods can and do change, and as an industry's technology changes, so may average firm size. Franchised fast-food service operators, such as McDonalds, have revolutionized the hamburger business, just as the chain food operators did the grocery business some years earlier. As mentioned above, better transportation, communications, and data processing systems are increasing the feasibility of some large-scale, geographically diversified operations—these factors have facilitated the development not only of various types of retail chains and franchise operators, but also of branch systems of financial institutions, such as banks, savings and loans, and brokerage firms.

The economies of their industries need to be understood by the managers of small firms. If the most efficient firm of its type is small, then it would be foolish to attempt a major expansion, as smaller, lower-cost operators would have drastic effects on the larger, inefficient firm. On the other hand, if economies of scale are important, then a small firm in the industry is inherently inefficient, and growth is vitally important for survival. It should also be noted that the best way of doing business in a given industry can change over time. Such a change presents not only a real opportunity for perceptive entrepreneurs, but also a serious threat to those who are less alert; the changes that have occurred in other industries in the past should make it clear that today's small business industries may not remain so in the future.[7]

Life Cycle of the Firm

The life cycle of an industry or firm is often depicted as an S-shaped curve, as shown in Figure 25–2. The four stages in the life cycle are described as follows:

---

7. Some interesting philosophical issues are raised whenever conditions change so that a small business industry is consolidated, because an increase in concentration results. However, competition may actually increase, for small businesses tend to have local monopolies, and a local monopoly is just as much a monopoly as any other monopoly. Studies of the banking industry, for example, suggest that competition is higher in areas where large branch banks exist than where smaller unit banks predominate. In other words, it appears that fewer, large, efficient, and aggressive banks with plenty of branches provide better service at lower cost than do more numerous independent unit banks with their local monopolies. The same thing may also hold for various types of retailing.

We should also make a distinction between concentration resulting from changes that take advantage of new managerial developments to rationalize a small-business industry—for example, the development of supermarket chains in the grocery business—and concentration due to mergers among large firms. While we are not arguing for or against any particular change in industrial organization, we do want to point out some of the issues involved.

1. *Experimentation period:* Sales and profits grow slowly following the introduction of a new product or firm.
2. *Exploitation period:* The firm enjoys rapid growth of sales, high profitability, and acceptance of the product.
3. *Maturity:* The rate of growth of sales begins to slow down; growth is dependent in large part upon replacement demand.
4. *Decline:* The firm faces the appearance of substitute products, technological and managerial obsolescence, and saturation of demand for its goods.

Figure 25–2
Hypothetical Life
Cycle of a Typical
Firm

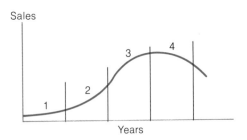

Although it is an oversimplification, Figure 25–2 provides a useful framework for analysis. The hypothesis represented by the four-stage life-cycle concept is based on a number of assumptions. It assumes competent management in the growth periods and insufficient management foresight prior to the decline phase. Obviously, one of management's primary goals is to prolong phase 2, completely forestalling phase 4; a great many firms are apparently successful in this endeavor.

The life cycle is substantially influenced by the form of organization a firm chooses—corporations have potentially long lives, while proprietorships obviously have finite lives: We shall discuss other aspects of the firm's life later, giving special attention to the financing forms employed at each stage.

**Small Firms
in Traditional
Small
Business
Industries**

As noted above, some firms are small because the nature of the industry dictates that small enterprises are more efficient than large ones, while other firms are small primarily because they are new companies—either new entrants to established industries or entrepreneurial enterprises in developing industries. Since these two types of small firms face fundamentally different situations, they have vastly different problems and opportunities. Accordingly, it is useful to treat the two classes separately. We first discuss the small firm in the traditional small business industry, then consider the small firm with growth potential.

Characteristics of Traditional Small Firms

The industries or segments of industries in which small businesses predominate exhibit three common characteristics: (1) a localized market, (2) low capital requirements, and (3) relatively simple technology. Because these characteristics lead to heavy dependence on one man, problems often arise:

1. The key man may not possess the full range of managerial skills required: he may be a good salesman but be unable to handle his employees well; he may fail to keep adequate accounting records, financial control systems, and the like.
2. In a small business with one-man leadership, instead of formal, standardized controls, the control system tends to be informal, direct, and personal. If the business grows, the span of responsibilities may become excessive for the entrepreneur.
3. Because of the businessman's preoccupation with the pressing problems of day-to-day operations, his planning for the future is often inadequate, so changes in the economic environment or competitive shifts can have severe impacts on his firm.
4. A relatively high degree of managerial training, experience, and breadth are necessary, yet often lacking; in his preoccupation with the present, the characteristic small-firm entrepreneur simply does not plan for management succession. Dun & Bradstreet data on business failures indicate that a larger proportion of failures is caused by the lack of experienced management than by any other factor.

Profitability of Small Firms

The problems of a small business may be illustrated by some representative numbers. Most small independent "Mom and Pop" grocery stores have sales of less than $500 per day, but let us assume that a particular store is doing relatively well and has sales of $500 per day. Assume also that the store is open 365 days a year, so its sales for the year total $182,500. According to the *Statement Studies* of the Robert Morris Associates, grocery retailers have a profit margin on sales of about 1 percent after taxes: if our small firm makes 2 percent on sales — to include salaries — that would represent a total profit of only $3,650 for the year. The proprietors of small grocery stores typically work 10 to 12 hours per day, six to seven days a week. Making calculations on the conservative side at 10 hours a day for six days a week implies 60 hours work a week. Assuming a two-week vacation, this would be 50 weeks in the year times 60 hours for a total of 3,000 hours. Three thousand hours divided into $3,650 yields about $1.22 per hour. This is well below the now-prevailing minimum wage for unskilled workers and does not include a return on invested capital.

The owners may suffer even more problems. The average net worth turnover ratio for retail grocery stores is 15 times per year, so on sales of $73,000 the owner would probably need about $5,000 of his or her own capital. Usually he does not have this much initial capital. As a consequence, the typical small firm incurs an inordinate amount of trade credit. It has a weak current ratio, it is slow in paying its bills, and if it is inefficient, what little capital it has is quickly eroded. For reasons such as these, one-third to one-half of all retail firms are discontinued within their first two years of life: the infant mortality rate is high indeed among small businesses!

In the face of these discouraging statistics, why do people open their own businesses? The reasons vary. One is the hope that they will beat the statistics and will be successful — any community, large or small, has a group of very successful small businessmen who, while perhaps not millionaires, can afford $100,000 homes, country clubs, and trips to Europe, not to mention sending their children to college in style. A second reason is the freedom of making one's own decisions, even if the price of this freedom is high. Third, a person may not regard the time he spends working in his own firm as drudgery; there is a wide variety of tasks to be performed in running a small enterprise, and the work can be both interesting and challenging.

Financing the Traditional Small Firm

The typical small business, even the successful one, cannot look to the general capital markets for funds. If the firm owns any real property, it may be able to obtain a mortgage from a bank or a savings and loan. Equipment may perhaps be purchased under a conditional sales contract or be leased. After the business has survived a few years, bank financing may be available on a seasonal basis, but not for permanent growth. Trade credit will, typically, represent the bulk of outside financing (that is, funds not supplied by the owner) available to the firm.

Financial ratio analysis must be of major and overriding importance to the small firm. Such analysis, on a regular basis, is essential to ascertain whether the firm is operating with the requisite managerial efficiency. Whereas a larger, stronger firm may have the financial strength to fall below its industry standards and still recover, the small firm has a smaller margin for error. Thus, anyone interested in a small firm is well advised to look at trends in its financial ratios, and to compare them with industry standards.

Working capital management is of overwhelming importance for most small firms. Because the amount of funds available is limited, liquidity is crucial. Trade credit appears to be an easy way of obtaining funds, yet even trade credit is obtained on terms that generally call for payment within 30 days. Since inventories typically represent a large percentage of total assets, a small firm's inventory policy must also be stressed. Large firms usually offer credit, so to meet competition, small firms may also have to extend credit. The large firm is likely to have an established credit department, but how does the small firm evaluate credit risks? What volume of accounts receivable can be built up without endangering both the solvency and the liquidity of the business? All of these are critical questions for the manager of a small business.

Current liability management is also important for the small firm. Although trade credit is relatively easy to obtain, it is often very costly. If discounts are available but not taken, the effective interest expense of such credit can be extremely high—as we know, not taking discounts on terms of 2/10, net 30 implies a 36 percent interest rate. Also, there is a temptation to be a perpetually slow payer, but this involves dangers: suppliers may refuse any credit whatever, or they may quote higher prices.

As the volume of operations becomes larger, the increased flow of funds through the firm may give the proprietor a false sense of affluence. He moves to a larger home with a spacious yard and pool, and he buys the latest model car. Since his business is growing, he feels the firm can afford to take on more debt. What he may be doing is bleeding the business or, at least, removing retained earnings that are really needed to finance growth.

Many traditional small-business industries are today being conducted under franchise arrangement. Franchising represents a device whereby the training and experience required for a particular line of business is sold to the proprietor on a rental contract basis. Sometimes the franchise also includes a valuable trademark or calls for the supply of some key item. The franchiser may, through bulk buying, be able to sell supplies to the franchisee at lower costs than otherwise would be available. But, as many erstwhile franchise operators know, obtaining a franchise is not necessarily the road to riches—in many such arrangements, the owner of the franchised operation may be required to pay an excessive price for the trademark, specialty inputs and supplies, or managerial advice.

In summary, three areas of finance are of the utmost importance to firms in traditional small business industries. First, the proprietor of the traditional small business must rely on internal financing (retained earnings) to a greater extent than would the management of a larger firm. Second, to survive in the long run, he must be a somewhat better player of a relatively standardized game, in which financial ratio analysis can help him to excel. Third, working capital management is critical to the small entrepreneur; if he fails here, he will not remain solvent, and his firm will go out of business.

The Small Firm with Growth Potential

The second broad category of small business is the small firm with potential for substantial growth. Typically, such a firm has developed a new product or an innovative way of providing an old service: the electronics industry is a good example of the former, while franchised hamburgers and other food operations illustrate the latter. In this section, we discuss the financial aspects of such firms from inception until the business has matured enough to go public. The significant financial aspects of each stage of the firm's life cycle will be set out as a guide to the establishment and development of the new small business enterprise.

Stage 1: Experimentation Period

As indicated above and shown in Figure 25–2, the first stage of a firm's life cycle involves experimentation and simply getting itself firmly entrenched. During this period, management must lay the foundation for future growth, realizing that growth occurs either because the firm can increase its share of the market or because of industry expansion. Market share expansion is difficult due to the reaction of existing firms, and even if the industry is growing, management must recognize that every product and industry has a life cycle. Hence, supernormal growth, for whatever its cause, will continue for only a finite period.

Even though the prospects of growth in an industry are favorable, there will be fluctuations. In addition, managers must be aware of the sales-to-capacity situation in the industry. For example, one of the most favorable growth industries in recent decades has been that of pleasure boats, which has generally grown at about the same rate as the growth in the population with incomes of over $12,000 per annum—10 to 12 percent per year. However, for a number of years capacity grew at a 20 percent rate, so after a point individual firms experienced the problem of excess capacity in spite of the favorable growth.

Particularly in new industries, it is important that the firm identify the techniques needed to succeed in the line of business. When the auto industry was maturing, dealership organizations and the availability of repair parts and service were the critical factors to the success of individual firms. In the computer industry, a backup of software, of marketing, and of maintenance service personnel was vital. In the aerospace industry, the essentials were technological capability and cost control.

Like the owner of a firm in a traditional small business industry, a growth industry entrepreneur must have a knowledge not only of his product and industry, but also of the standard administrative tools essential for effective management in any line of business. Financial planning and control processes are especially important. Financial ratio analysis should be used to develop standards for determining the broad outlines of the balance sheet and the income statement, as well as for guidelines to help isolate developing problem areas.

It is especially important for a small firm that expects growth to plan for it. Initially, such planning will emphasize the expansion of existing operations; later in the firm's life cycle, it must consider possible movements into new product lines. A basic decision that must be made, whatever type of expansion occurs, is to choose between using more or less highly automated productive processes. Standard financial operating leverage, or breakeven analysis, can be employed to measure how changing sales levels will affect the firm's risk and return characteristics. If its forecasts of future sales are optimistic, the firm may make larger investments in fixed assets and choose more highly automated productive processes. As a consequence, its fixed costs will be higher, but its variable costs will be lower. At high operating levels, its total costs per unit will be lower than those of a firm with a smaller ratio of fixed costs to total costs, putting the firm into a strong position in relation to its rivals. However, if volume should fall to low levels, a firm with high operating leverage will face greater risks of bankruptcy.

Stage 2: Exploitation and Rapid Growth Period

After the firm's inception, a successful firm with growth potential will enter stage 2 of its financial cycle. Here, the firm has achieved initial success—it is growing rapidly and it is reasonably profitable. Cash flows and working capital management have become increasingly important. Also, at this stage the firm will have an extraordinary need for additional outside financing; this is shown in Table 25–1, which compares rapid and moderate growth firms. The growth company (Firm 1) expands from $800,000 in sales to $1.2 million in one year; Firm 2 grows by the same amount, but over a four-year period. The percentages in parentheses following the asset-liability accounts indicate the assumed relationships between asset items and the spontaneous sources of funds, which we discussed in Chapter 4 in the section on the percent of sales forecasting method. Note also that profits are assumed to be 6 percent of sales during the year, and that all earnings are retained. Let us further assume that notes payable are increased to cover the financing required—notes payable function as the balancing item. If the firm grows by 50 percent in one year, notes payable almost double. However, if the firm grows from $800,000 to $1.2 million over a four-year period, then notes payable not only do not increase at all, but they can actually be paid off. Hence, current liabilities decline from $200,000 to $148,000, while net worth increases from $200,000 to $452,000.

There is considerable doubt whether the growth firm could actually obtain short-term bank loans of the amount required. Such a large amount of short-term bank financing would cause its current ratio to drop to 1.1, and its debt ratio to rise to 54 percent. This situation develops even with the very favorable 24 percent rate of return on net worth. If the profit rate were lower, the firm's financing problem would be even more serious. When the firm uses four periods to achieve the same amount of growth, the financial ratios indicate a less risky situation. The current ratio never declines—it actually improves over the period. The debt ratio drops from 50 to 25 percent, which is very low compared with the average for all manufacturing firms.

If the rapid growth firm continues to grow at the 50 percent rate, the situation will further deteriorate, and it will become increasingly clear that the firm requires additional equity financing. The debt ratio will become much too high, yet the firm may well be reluctant to bring in

Table 25–1
Financial Effects of Different Rates of Growth (Thousands of Dollars)

	Firm 1		Firm 2				
	Year 1	Year 2	Year 1	Year 2	Year 3	Year 4	Year 5
Sales	$800	$1,200	$800	$900	$1,000	$1,100	$1,200
Current assets (30%)	240	360	240	270	300	330	360
Fixed assets (20%)	160	240	160	180	200	220	240
Total assets	$400	$ 600	$400	$450	$ 500	$ 550	$ 600
Accounts payable (10%)	80	120	80	90	100	110	120
Notes payable	96	172	96	79	56	27	(8)
Other accruals (3%)	24	36	24	27	30	33	36
Current liabilities	$200	$ 328	$200	$196	$ 186	$ 170	$ 148
Common stock	100	100	100	100	100	100	100
Retained earnings*	100	172	100	154	214	280	352
Net worth	$200	$ 272	$200	$254	$ 314	$ 380	$ 452
Total claims	$400	$ 600	$400	$450	$ 500	$ 550	$ 600
Key Ratios							
Current ratio (times)	1.2	1.1	1.2	1.4	1.6	1.9	2.4
Debt ratio (percentage)	50	54	50	44	37	31	25
Sales to total assets (times)	2	2	2	2	2	2	2
Profit to net worth (percentage)	24.0	26.5	24.0	21.3	19.1	17.3	15.9

*Profit is 6 percent of sales; retained earnings are equal to profit plus retained earnings from the previous year.

additional outside equity money because the original owners are unwilling to share control. At this juncture, some financial pitfalls should be recognized and avoided. These are illustrated by the actual experiences of two individual small business owners who explained to the authors the difficulties they encountered. In one instance, the former owner of a firm described the problems that occurred after he obtained additional funds to support growth. He originally owned 100 percent of his company, but the firm needed capital. When two potential suppliers of the necessary funds each requested 30 percent ownership, the founder of the enterprise agreed, figuring that he would still have control with 40 percent, the largest block of the common stock. However, the two new equity owners joined forces, interfered with the creative management of the company, and caused it to fail.

It is also an error to incur debt with an unrealistically short maturity. The former owner of another small firm borrowed on one- and two-year terms, but he failed to realize that if his firm continued to grow at a rapid rate, its needs for financing would increase, not decrease. Subsequently, he simply could not meet his debt maturities. It was convenient to borrow funds that were critically needed for growth on a relatively short-term basis, but when he was unable to make payments as the loans matured, he was forced to give up the controlling share of the equity. Thus, failure to plan properly again caused the founder to lose control of his company.

Risks in the Small Business. Risk is encountered at every stage in a small firm's development. In previous chapters, we have seen that risk results from the impacts of economic conditions, labor problems, competitive pressures, and so on. All firms face such risks, but they are magnified in small businesses. In traditional small-firm industries, entry is easy, competitive pressures drive profit margins to low levels, and there is little margin for error in allowing for adverse developments or managerial mistakes.

For small growth firms, the problem is compounded still further. These firms are typically entering new areas about which little information is available. There may be great potential, but large risks are also involved, and for every glowing success story there are many instances of failure. Further, even after an innovative growth firm has been established, there are continued pressures because of the financial problems noted above. Also, its demonstrated success will stimulate imitators, so its projections must take into account the influx of new firms and the likelihood of a declining market share and increased competitive pressures. Furthermore, high profits may lead to excess capacity, causing problems for every firm in the industry. For all these reasons, the small, rapidly growing firm faces a precarious existence, even when the product-market opportunities upon which it was conceived are sound.

Venture Capital Financing. Small firms that have growth potential face greater risks than almost any other type of business, and their higher risks require special types of financing. This has led to the development of specialized venture capital financing sources. Some venture capital companies are organized as partnerships; others are more formal corporations termed *investment development companies.*[8] The American Research and Development Corporation, one of the first investment development companies, is widely traded in the financial markets; it and other publicly owned investment companies permit individuals and institutions, such as insurance companies, to participate in the venture capital market. Other venture capital companies represent the activities of individuals or partnerships. From time to time the operations of these individual companies are described in the financial press. Notable examples are Arthur Rock[9] and Charles Allen.[10]

When a new business makes an application for financial assistance from a venture capital firm, it receives a rigorous examination. Some development companies use their own staffs for this investigation, while others depend on a board of advisers acting in a consultative capacity. A high percentage of applications is rejected, but if the application is approved, funds are provided. Venture capital companies generally take an equity position in the firms they finance, but they may also extend debt capital. However, when loans are made, they generally involve convertibles or warrants, or are tied in with the purchase of stock by the investment company.

Venture capital companies perform a continuing and active role in the enterprise. Typically, they do not insist on voting control, but they usually have at least one member on the board of directors of the new enterprise. The matter of control has *not* been one of the crucial considerations in investment companies' decisions to invest—indeed, if the management of a small business is not sufficiently strong to make sound decisions, the venture capital firm is not likely to be interested in the first place. However, the investment company does want to maintain continuous contact, provide management counsel, and monitor the progress of its investment.

Another distinctive contribution of the venture capital firm stems

---

8. Under the Investment Company Act of 1940, investment development companies are defined as closed-end, nondiversified investment companies. Closed-end investment companies are like mutual funds, but they differ in that they are under no obligation to buy back the shares they have issued.

9. *Business Week*, 30 May 1970, p. 102.

10. *Wall Street Journal*, August 1970.

from its ownership by wealthy individuals. (Lawrence Rockefeller, for example, is a leading venture capitalist.) For tax reasons, such people are interested in receiving their income in the form of capital gains rather than current income. They are, therefore, in a position to take larger risks. If they lose on the venture, the net after-tax loss is only a portion of the investment since they are in a high personal income tax bracket. For example, a $100,000 loss "costs" only $25,000 for an investor who is in the 75 percent state-plus-federal tax bracket.[11] Their gains, if any, are in the form of capital gains, and therefore are taxed at a rate lower than the rate on ordinary personal income. Thus, for the wealthy individual, the odds are in favor of making higher risk investments.

Another source of venture capital has been developed in recent years—large, well established business firms.[12] A number of large corporations have invested both money and various types of know-how to start or to help develop small business firms. The owner of the small firm is usually a specialist, frequently a technical man who needs both money and help in administrative services such as accounting, finance, production, and marketing. The small firm's owner contributes entrepreneurship, special talents, a taste for risk taking, and "the willingness to work 18 hours a day for peanuts." A number of major corporations have found that there is a mutual advantage for this form of venture capital investment.

Another important source of venture capital financing for small business is the Small Business Investment Company (SBIC). The Small Business Investment Company Act of 1958 empowered the Small Business Administration (SBA) to license and regulate SBICs and to provide them with financial assistance. A minimum of $150,000 in private capital is required for the licensing of an SBIC, and this amount can be doubled by selling subordinated debentures to the SBA (at interest rates generally below prevailing market rates).

In their operations, SBICs have followed two policies similar to investment development or venture capital companies. First, their investments are generally made by the purchase of convertible securities or bonds with warrants, thus giving the SBICs a residual equity position in the companies to which funds are provided. Second, SBICs emphasize management counsel, for which a fee is charged.[13]

At the end of 1972, there were 276 operating SBICs with total equity capital of $350 million. In addition, during the year 1971, Public Law 92-

---

11. Special tax provisions make it possible to offset more than the regular $1,000 of ordinary income by capital losses if the losses are on small businesses as defined by the tax code.

12. "Venture Capital, Corporation Style," *Forbes*, 1 August 1970, pp. 41–42.

13. The larger SBICs have staffs similar to those of holding companies or conglomerates; these staffs provide assistance, for a fee, to the firms in which the SBICs have invested.

213 amended the Small Business Investment Company Act and clarified the SBA's authority to guarantee debentures issued by the SBICs, thus providing the SBIC industry with an expanded source of funding at interest rates somewhat below prevailing market levels.

The SBICs benefited from the aura of government sponsorship and the availability of long-term subordinated debt on attractive terms. Also, the spectacular success of one investment can assure the prosperity of an SBIC or other venture capital company.[14] When SBICs first appeared in the 1950s, these advantages gave rise to very optimistic expectations about SBIC's stock market values. Beginning in 1961, however, investors' appraisals of SBIC common stocks plunged, as it became clear that SBICs were not a guaranteed road to riches. To find and finance successful small businesses requires much work and considerable risks. There was indeed a weeding out of the weaker firms, but since the mid-1960s SBICs have achieved steady progress.

Stage 3: Growth to Maturity

Going Public. With good management, the right economic conditions, and sufficient financing either from a venture capital company or from a government agency, the firm will move into Stage 2, the period of rapid growth. Here the increasing financing requirements will put pressure on the firm to raise capital from the public equity markets. At this point, a full assessment of the critical step in a firm's life, that of "going public," must be made.

Going public represents a fundamental change in life style in at least four respects: (1) The firm moves from informal, personal control to a system of formal controls, and the need for financial techniques such as ratio analysis and the du Pont system of financial planning and control greatly increases. (2) Information must be reported on a timely basis to the outside investors, even though the founders may continue to have majority control. (3) The firm must have a breadth of management in all of the business functions if it is to operate its expanded business effectively. (4) The publicly owned firm typically draws on a board of directors to help formulate sound plans and policies; the board should include representatives of the public owners and other external interest groups to aid the management group in carrying out its broader responsibilities.

The valuation process is particularly important at the time the firm goes public: at what price will stock be sold to new outside investors? In analyzing the investment value of the small and growing firm, some

---

14. American Research and Development Company, for example, made over $100 million on the investment of a few thousand dollars in Digital Equipment.

significant differences in capital costs between large and small firms should be noted:[15]

1. It is especially difficult to obtain reasonable estimates of the cost of equity capital for small, privately owned firms.
2. Because of the risks involved, the required rate of return tends to be high for small firms. However, portfolio effects from a pooling of risks can reduce this factor somewhat.
3. Tax considerations are generally quite important for privately owned companies that are large enough to consider going public, as the owner-managers are probably in the top personal tax brackets. This factor can cause the effective after-tax cost of retained earnings to be considerably lower than the after-tax cost of new outside equity.[16]
4. Flotation costs for new security issues, especially new stock issues, are much higher for small than for large firms. This factor, as well as (3) above, causes the marginal cost of capital curve for small firms to rise rapidly once retained earnings have been exhausted.

The timing of the decision to go public is also especially important, because small firms are more affected by variations in money market conditions than larger companies. During periods of tight money and high interest rates, financial institutions, especially commercial banks, find that the quantity of funds demanded exceeds the supply available at legally permissible and conventionally acceptable rates. One important method employed to ration credit is to raise credit standards. During tight money periods, both a stronger balance sheet record and a longer and more stable record of profitability are required in order to qualify for bank credit. Since financial ratios for small and growing firms tend to be less strong, such firms bear the brunt of credit restraint. Obviously, the small firm that goes public and raises equity capital before a money squeeze is in a better position to ride it out. This firm has already raised some of its needed capital, and its equity cushion enables it to present a stronger picture to the banks, thus helping it to obtain additional capital in the form of debt.

Small Business Administration

It is clear that small firms face difficulties in obtaining capital, and in recognition of this fact, the federal government set up the Small Business Administration (SBA).[17] The SBA operates a number of different

---

15. See Brigham and Smith, "The Cost of Capital to the Small Firm," end-of-chapter references.
16. See Appendix A to Chapter 19.
17. The SBA also helps small companies obtain a fair share of government contracts, and it administers training programs of various types designed to help small entrepreneurs.

programs. One was discussed above in connection with the formation and growth of SBICs. Another, the "Business Loan Program," provides funds for construction, machinery, equipment, and working capital.[18] Loans under this program, which are available only when small businesses are unable to obtain funds on reasonable terms from private sources, are of two types: direct loans and participation loans. In a direct loan, the SBA simply makes a loan to a small business borrower. In a participation loan, the SBA lends part of the funds, while a bank or other private lending institution advances the balance. Under a participation loan, a portion of the funds advanced by the private party may be guaranteed by the SBA. The maximum amount the SBA may lend to any borrower is $350,000; this maximum applies to either a direct loan or to the SBA's portion of a participation loan.

Since SBA loans or guarantees are advantageous to the business recipient, the definition of what constitutes a small business is important. Actually, the definition varies somewhat depending upon the industry. Any manufacturing concern is defined as small if it employs up to 250 people, while it is defined as large if it employs more than 1,000 people. Within this range, the SBA has different standards for different industries. A wholesale firm is classified as small if its annual sales are $5 million or less. Most retail businesses and service firms are defined as small if their total annual receipts are less than $1 million.[19]

Table 25–2 **Financing Patterns at Four Stages of a Firm's Development**	Stage	Financing Pattern
	1. Formation	personal savings, trade credit, government agencies
	2. Rapid growth	internal financing, trade credit, bank credit, venture capital
	3. Growth to maturity	going public, money and capital markets
	4. Maturity and industry decline	internal financing, share repurchase, diversification, mergers

18. In addition to the Business Loan Program, the SBA administers a number of other programs, including the following: (1) Equal Opportunity Loan Program, designed specifically for disadvantaged persons who wish to start or expand an existing business, (2) Development Company Loan Program, which is used to help attract businesses to geographic areas in need of economic stimulation, (3) Displaced Business Loan Program, designed to help small businesses which are forced to relocate because of urban renewal or similar events, (4) Disaster Loan Program, designed to aid both businesses and homeowners who suffer losses as a consequence of some natural disaster, (5) Lease Guarantee Program, designed to help small businesses to obtain rental space in the commercial real estate market, (6) Revolving Line-of-Credit Program, designed to aid small building contractors, (7) Surety Bonding Program, designed to aid small businessmen who must post performance bonds when seeking contracts, and (8) Minority Enterprise SBIC Program, which is designed to stimulate SBICs whose clients are minority-owned firms.

19. A great deal of additional information on the SBA and its various programs may be obtained directly from the Small Business Administration, Washington, D.C., or from regional SBA offices.

Summary

The key factors relating to small business financing are summarized briefly in Table 25–2, which sets forth the financing patterns at the firm's four stages of development. In its formative stage, the new, small firm must rely most heavily on personal savings, trade credit, and government agencies. During its period of rapid growth, internal financing will become an important source of meeting its financing requirements, although continued reliance will be placed on trade credit. At this stage, its record of accomplishment also makes it possible to obtain bank credit to finance seasonal needs, and if the loan can be paid off on an amortized basis over two or three years, the firm may qualify for a term loan as well. If it has the potential for really strong growth, the firm may also be able to attract equity from a venture capital company.

A particularly successful firm may reach the stage where going public becomes feasible—this leads to access to the broader money and capital markets, and it represents a true coming-of-age for the small firm. Even at this point, however, the firm must look ahead, analyzing its products and their prospects. Because every product has a life cycle, the firm must be aware that without the development of new products, growth will cease, and eventually the firm will decline. Accordingly, as product maturity approaches, the firm must plan for the possibility of share repurchases, mergers, or other longer-term strategies. The best time to look ahead and plan for this is while the firm has energy, momentum, and a high price-earnings ratio.

In our coverage of small business financing, the major emphasis has been on providing a framework for analyzing financial needs and opportunities as the characteristics of the firm and its industry evolve. While this type of analysis cannot replace mature judgment, it can certainly aid such judgment and help the financial manager maximize his contribution to the successful development of a small business enterprise.

Questions

25–1. What are the advantages and disadvantages of the use of a sole proprietorship versus a partnership for conducting the operations of a small business firm?

25–2. Under what circumstances does it become advantageous for the small business to incorporate?

25–3. In what sense is the corporation a person?

25–4. Would it be practical for General Motors to be organized as a partnership?

25–5. What influence does each of the following have on possible divergences between the goals and objectives of the managers who control a corporation and those of its stockholders?

a. Profit sharing plans

b. Executive compensation schemes

c. Employee stock option plans

25–6. What is a voting trust? Why is it used?

25–7. What are some sources of information on the past performance of a firm you are thinking of buying?

25–8. A friend of yours has just developed a new product and plans to start a business to produce it. One of his goals is to maintain absolute control, but his own capital is limited. What are some of the ways he can reduce the amount of his initial outlay while still obtaining the use of an efficiently large plant?

25–9. Assume that you are starting a business of your own of the traditional small business type. Develop an outline of the kinds of decisions you will have to make in establishing and financing the small enterprise.

Problems

25–1. Susan Smith, turned off by irrelevant liberal arts courses, decided to leave school at the end of her second year. She plans to open the simplest of retail trade establishments, a grocery store with an emphasis on health foods.

Susan had received an allowance from her parents for some years and was able to save a little over $1,000. She could have saved more, but somehow she "loaned some to friends," and from time to time she was tempted by some interesting new types of apparel. She also drove her car quite a bit, so gas and repairs ate into what otherwise would have been even more savings.

After making some inquiries of her bus. ad. friends, Susan recognized that she must consider such things as location, potential flow of customer traffic, and present and potential competition. Also, she realized that she must analyze the alternatives of buying a building or renting a store and buying or renting the equipment and fixtures she will need— counters, shelving, cash register, and the like. The store space she had in mind had not been occupied by a grocery before, so it lacked shelves and counters.

a. Should Susan buy or rent the store facilities?

b. How should Susan acquire the equipment and fixtures?

c. What kinds of questions is she likely to face with regard to choice of product line?

d. For planning purposes, assume sales per day of $100, $300, and $500, and a profit ratio of net income before taxes to sales of 4 percent. What are her earnings per hour before taxes, assuming that she works 10 hours per day, seven days a week, for 50 weeks per year?

e. With a sales to net worth ratio of 15 times, what investment on her part is indicated at each level of sales? Comment on how she may raise the funds if several years are required to reach each alternative level of sales, and also comment upon the implications of her taking withdrawals from the business.

f. What additional questions must our heroine face if she sells on credit?

g. What are the critical problems likely to be if sales start at $500 per day?

25–2. Fred Thatcher has been employed by the Universal Plastics Company, a Chicago firm, for several years. Because of his industrial engineering background, he has been used in the production department to help develop new plastic products to utilize more extensively the firm's available dies and presses. The product line of Universal Plastics is relatively limited.

While visiting friends in Los Angeles, Thatcher concluded that considerable opportunities for new plastics companies existed in the Southern California area, and he decided on the spot to start his own firm. Initially, he would service the aerospace industry, but he thought the potential existed for later expansion into the airlines generally as well as into a wide variety of products for the food and grocery industries, the school market, hospitals, and department stores. Furthermore, he saw a great opportunity for the substitution of plastics products for wood containers.

Thatcher obtained the services of one of Universal Plastics' ablest salesmen, John Watson, by offering him the opportunity to become the sales manager and marketing vice-president. Accordingly, in 1962 the Hollywood Plastics Company was born. Thatcher received 90 percent of the stock while Watson received 10 percent.

By 1972, 10 years later, Thatcher, the president of Hollywood Plastics, decided he had to give serious consideration to going public. To realize the firm's full growth potential seemed to require financing beyond what Hollywood Plastics could achieve under its present form and method of operations. Through its commercial bank, Security First National, Thatcher was brought into contact with a number of venture capital sources, as well as several investment bankers. They all asked for a report that would cover Hollywood Plastics' background and present a five-year forecast of sales and earnings.

Thatcher had attended an Executive Program at Cal State, where he had worked closely with Kent Smith of the finance faculty. Thatcher had a great deal of respect for Smith, so he asked him to help in the development of the report. Professor Smith utilized a wide range of tools encompassing most of the topics covered in a comprehensive book dealing with mangerial finance; in fact, Smith was especially eager to work on the report so that he could later use it to indicate to his students how the tools and concepts of finance are utilized by a small firm in its growth and development process.

The first segment of the report contained a statement of Hollywood Plastics' product concept. An excerpt from this statement is given below:

The products of Hollywood Plastics consist primarily of the following items: modubox systems for industrial users, trays and cases for the school market, duro nesting boxes for the produce and food markets, duro tote boxes for hospitals, airline service trays, display fixtures, instrument cases, instrument housings and other custom parts, and rocket engine closures.

Most of the products and customers served by Hollywood Plastics are growing rapidly. In addition, Hollywood Plastics has a number of advantages that will enable the company to continue to increase its penetration of these markets. It has the rights and patents to various box design features and has product names which have been copyrighted. Even more important, Hollywood Plastics continues to be the leader in the development of new ideas for materials handling systems. In the food and hospital industries, sanitation requirements are increasingly requiring the substitution of the plastic products for wood containers.

The school market has been only scratched, and Hollywood Plastics is beginning to supply the manufacturers of school equipment with its boxes and trays.

The advantages of Hollywood Plastics' product line are continuing to lead to the substitution of its products for older materials. As a consequence, the replacement of older materials in industries whose total growth is low should result in tremendous further growth for Hollywood Plastics.

Hollywood Plastics has developed customer recognition and loyalty both by the quality of its products and by a 10-year program of national advertising, including full-page advertisements in *Modern Materials Handling Magazine, Western Materials Handling*, etc. This advertising program has strengthened the position of the company, as has its strong national distribution system, which utilizes 200 distributors.

Figure 1 shows actual and projected sales for Hollywood Plastics. Sales have grown from about $300,000 during the first year of operations to $1.4 million in 1971, and to a forecasted level of over $5 million by 1977 [see the middle line of the range of future growth patterns shown in Figure P25–1].

Figure P25–1 is based on Smith's analysis of Hollywood Plastics' product lines and the prospective growth in each of its product areas. Because of Hollywood Plastics' rapid growth rate, Smith used a semilogarithmic chart.

Smith also developed some basic financial relations that he used as the foundation for pro forma balance sheets, income statements, and profitability relations as determined by the sales forecast. Table P25–1 presents abbreviated income statements for each of the past five years, with each element of the income statement stated both in absolute terms and as a percentage of net sales. Table P25–2 gives historical balance sheets for Hollywood Plastics between 1967 and 1971. A related breakeven chart is set forth in Figure P25–2. The historical balance sheet and income statement (and breakeven analysis) are used to construct the projected financial statements to make possible the analysis and valuation involved in

Figure P25–1
Sales Growth of
Hollywood Plastics—
Actual 1965–1971,
Forecast 1972–1977

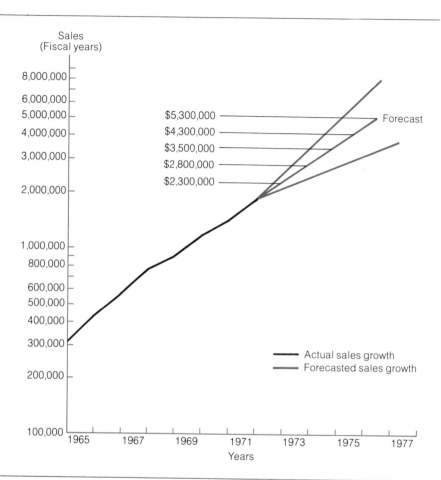

the firm's going public. The following questions indicate the kind of analysis that is required for "taking the firm public."

a. From the data in Table P25–1, plot a scatter diagram of the relation between each of the following items to sales: (1) cost of goods sold, (2) selling expenses, and (3) general and administrative expenses. Plot these in a chart, which we will label Figure P25–3.

b. Using the following equations: cost of goods sold = $24,000 + .69 (sales); selling expense = $90,000 + .08 (sales); general and administrative expenses = $20,000 + .0635 (sales); and federal income tax = .5 (net income before tax), set forth a pro forma income statement forecast for Hollywood Plastics to be Table P25–4 for the years 1972 through 1977 with a percentage analysis as performed in Table P25–1, on the relations that you observe.

Table P25-1
Income Statement Fiscal Years 1967–1971 (in Thousands of Dollars)

	1967 Amount	1967 Percent	1968 Amount	1968 Percent	1969 Amount	1969 Percent	1970 Amount	1970 Percent	1971 Amount	1971 Percent
1. Sales (net)	$403	100.0	$560	100.0	$853	100.0	$1,169	100.0	$1,407	100.0
2. Less: Cost of goods sold	310	76.9	397	70.9	598	70.1	821	70.2	1,000	71.1
3. Gross profit	93	23.1	163	29.1	255	29.9	348	29.8	407	28.9
4. Selling expenses	54	13.4	92	16.4	120	14.1	187	16.0	205	14.6
5. Administrative and general expenses	38	9.4	51	9.1	105	12.3	113	9.7	118	8.4
6. Subtotal	92	22.8	143	25.5	225	26.4	300	25.7	323	23.0
7. Profit from operations	1	.2	20	3.6	30	3.5	48	4.1	85	6.0
8. Other income	9	2.2	4	.7	6	.7	3	.3	—	—
9. Net income before federal income tax	10	2.4	24	4.3	36	4.2	51	4.4	85	6.0
10. Federal income tax	1	.2	8	1.4	13	1.5	21	1.8	39	2.8
11. Net income	$ 9	2.2	$ 16	2.9	$ 23	2.7	$ 30	2.6	$ 46	3.3

Table P25–2	**Assets**	1967	1968	1969	1970	1971
Hollywood Plastics, Inc., Balance Sheet, 1967–1971 (in Thousands of Dollars)	Cash	8	1	8	15	35
	Accounts receivable	44	69	86	102	165
	Inventories	41	59	72	109	86
	Total current assets	93	129	166	226	286
	Gross fixed assets	46	53	72	105	130
	Less: depreciation	27	36	42	55	74
	Net fixed assets	19	17	30	50	56
	Total assets	112	146	196	276	342
	Liabilities	1967	1968	1969	1970	1971
	Notes payable	19	16	12	24	13
	Accounts payable	43	61	81	100	122
	Accruals	13	24	30	45	68
	Total current liabilities	75	101	123	169	193
	Long-term debt	12	4	11	15	11
	Capital stock (par value $.50)	22	22	30	30	30
	Retained earnings	3	19	32	62	108
	Total net worth	25	41	62	92	138
	Total liabilities and net worth	112	146	196	276	342

c. From the balance sheet data in Table P25–2, plot scatter diagrams in six parts of a chart which will be labeled Figure P25–4, the relationship to sales of the following items: accounts receivable, inventory, total fixed assets before depreciation, total assets, accounts payable, and total long-term liabilities. Fit regression lines where possible.

d. Using the following equations: accounts receivable = .12 (sales); total fixed assets before depreciation = 15 + .1 (sales); inventories = 2.8 + .086 (sales); accounts payable = 9.4 + .078 (sales); cash = .04 (sales); accruals = .08 (sales); and annual depreciation = .1 (gross fixed assets), make a forecast of the balance sheets for 1972 through 1977 to be labeled Table P25–5. If more financing is needed, increase notes payable as an adjusting item. If excess cash is available from operations, first pay off notes payable and then create an additional asset account entitled "cash available from operations" (marketable securities).

e. Using the data from Table P25–5, calculate financial ratios. Perform the financial ratio analysis for the years 1967 through 1971 and on a projected basis for 1972 and 1977 for the following ratios: (1) current ratio, (2) average collection period, (3) current liability/total assets, (4) long-term debt/total assets, (5) total debt/total assets, (6) net profits/sales, (7) net profits/total assets, and (8) net profits/net worth. Label this analysis Table P25–6. From the ratios in your Table P25–6, comment on the past financial position of Hollywood Plastics and on the prospects for the forecasted years, 1972 and 1977.

f. Comment on the pattern indicated by the break-even analysis set forth in Figure P25−2.

Figure P25−2
Hollywood Plastics,
Inc.−Breakeven
Analysis

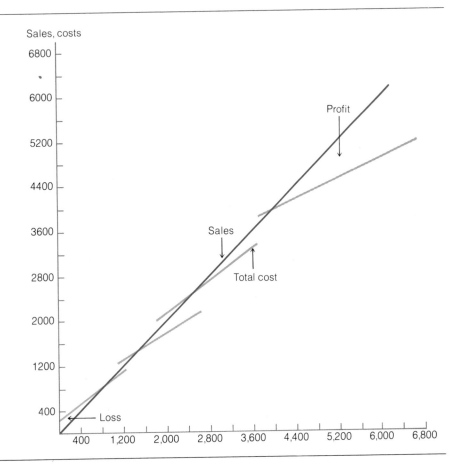

g. From the data in Table P25−2, develop a sources and uses of funds statement for Hollywood Plastics for the five-year period 1967 through 1971. Present your results in a table to be labeled Table P25−7.

h. The valuation is based on the projected net income figures in your Table P25−4, assuming a dividend payout of 50% and assuming that from 1978 on, dividends will grow at a "normal" rate of 10% per annum. Using the method for calculating the value of a company with a supernormal growth period discussed in Chapter 17, set forth a total value for Hollywood Plastics when a cost of capital of 20 percent is used. Some justification for the 20 percent cost of capital is set forth in Table P25−3.

**Table P25–3
Factors Affecting
Valuation of
Hollywood Plastics**

A. *Product-Market Characteristics*
1. Hollywood Plastics is the originator of many materials handling systems and continues to be the leader in the development of new products and uses.
2. Companies in the food and hospital fields are more and more substituting the products of Hollywood Plastics for older and less sanitary materials they have been using in the past.
3. Five of the six markets in which products are sold are strong growth areas.

B. *General Valuation Factors*
1. Strong national distribution with 200 distributors.
2. Can support sales growth to $5 million without expansion of plant.

C. *Additional Valuation Items*
1. Current earnings underestimated by approximately $30,000 per year based on immediate writeoff of tooling expense.
2. Current value of net worth estimated by Kent Smith to be approximately $1,000,000 based on appraisal of individual asset items and cash balances.
3. Selling power built up by ten-year advertising program has capital value.

    i. The investment bankers actually sold 40,000 shares at net proceeds of $600,000. Compare and discuss this implied valuation of the company with your calculation under part h above.

    j. Based on data on costs of flotation by size of issue, indicate what you think might be appropriate compensation to the investment bankers for "taking this company public."

Selected References

Archer, S. H., and Faerber, L. G. "Firm Size and the Cost of Externally Secured Equity Capital." *Journal of Finance* 21 (Mar. 1966):69–83.

Brigham, E. F., and Smith, K. V. "The Cost of Capital to the Small Firm." *Engineering Economist* (Fall 1967):1–26.

Chase, A. G., and Proctor, J. M. "Financial Aid and Venture Capital Programs at SBA." *Bankers Magazine* 153 (Autumn 1970):11–19.

Davis, R. D. "Small Business in the Next Decade." *Advanced Management Journal* 31 (Jan. 1966):5–8.

Edmister, R. O. "Financial Ratios as Discriminant Predictors of Small Business Failure" [abstract]. *Journal of Finance* 27 (Mar. 1972):139–40.

Garvin, W. J. "Small Business Capital Gap: The Special Case of Minority Enterprise." *Journal of Finance* 26 (May 1971):445–57, 466–71.

Gilmore, F. F. "Formulating Strategy in Smaller Companies." *Harvard Business Review* 49 (May 1971):71–81.

Guttentag, J. M., and Herman, E. S. "Do Large Banks Neglect Small Business?" *Journal of Finance* 21 (Sept. 1966):535–38.

Korbel, J. "Micro-Analytic Model of the Generation and Application of Savings in Small Business." *Review of Economics and Statistics* 47 (Aug. 1965):279–86.

Lamont, L. M., and Meticher, R. W. "The Life Cycle and Financial Requirements of Small Technology Based Firms." *Southern Journal of Business* (May 1974): 17–23.

Martin, D. "Can Edge Act Companies Have a Venture Capital Strategy?" *Columbia Journal of World Business* 4 (Nov. 1969):73–80.

McConkey, D. D. "Will Ecology Kill Small Business?" *Business Horizons* 15 (Apr. 1972):61–69.

Pfeffer, Irving. *The Financing of Small Business* New York: Macmillan, 1967.

Rossiter, Bruce G., and Miller, Gene I. "Financing the New Enterprise." In *The Treasurer's Handbook*, J. Fred Weston and Maruice B. Goudzwaard, eds., Homewood, Illinois: Dow Jones-Irwin, 1976, pp. 861–900.

Rubel, S. M. "Important Changes Occur in Venture Capital Industry." *Bankers Monthly* 87 (May 1970):24–25.

Steiner, George. "Approaches to Long-Range Planning for Small Business." *California Management Review* 10 (Fall 1967):3–16.

Wheelright, S. C. "Strategic Planning in the Small Business." *Business Horizons* 14 (Aug. 1971):51–58.

White, L. T. "Management Assistance for Small Business." *Harvard Business Review* 43 (July 1965):67–74.

A   The Tax Environment[1]

The federal government is often called the most important stockholder in the American economy. This is not literally true, as the government does not "own" corporate shares in the strict sense of the word; it is, however, by far the largest recipient of business profits. Income of unincorporated businesses is subject to tax rates ranging up to 70 percent, while income of corporations is taxed at a 48 percent rate. State, and sometimes city or county taxes, must be added to these federal taxes, and dividends received by stockholders are subject to personal income taxes at the stockholders' individual tax rates.

With such a large percentage of business income going to the government, it is not surprising that taxes play an important role in financial decisions. To lease or to buy, to use common stock or debt, to make or not to make a particular investment, to merge or not to merge—all these decisions are influenced by tax factors. This appendix summarizes some basic elements of the tax structure relating to financial decisions.

Fiscal Policy

The federal government uses both monetary policy and fiscal policy to influence the level of economic activity. *Monetary policy*, which is considered in Chapter 21, deals with actions to influence the availability and cost of credit. *Fiscal policy* deals with altering the level and composition of government receipts and expenditures to influence the level of economic activity. Since taxes constitute the primary receipt, they are an important element of fiscal policy.

Three principal methods have been employed to change tax receipts: (1) changing tax rates, (2) changing methods permitted for calculating tax-deductible depreciation (accelerating depreciation), and (3) providing for an investment tax credit for expenditures on new industrial equipment. Each of these points is discussed briefly in this section.

---

1. This appendix has benefited from the assistance of Mr. R. Wendell Buttrey, tax attorney and lecturer on taxation at the University of California, Los Angeles.

Changing Tax Rates

During periods of rapid and unsustainable economic expansion, especially when such expansion has inflationary consequences, the federal government may attempt to dampen the level of economic activity by increasing income tax rates. When tax rates are raised, both personal disposable incomes and corporate profits after taxes are reduced. The reduction in personal disposable incomes reduces individuals' purchasing power and thereby decreases their demand for goods and services. The reduction in corporate after-tax profits reduces the profitability of new investments and, at the same time, reduces corporate funds available for investment. On the other hand, if the economy is depressed and requires some form of stimulation, tax rates can be reduced, providing both consumers and businesses with greater purchasing power and increasing the incentive of business to make investments in plant and equipment.

During the period 1966–69 the economy was operating at a very high level, and prices were increasing at a rate of 3 to 6 percent a year. Military expenditures associated with the Vietnam war were stimulating the economy, while a government deficit was adding to the inflationary pressure. In January 1967, the president asked Congress to increase taxes by 10 percent. After an 18-month delay, Congress did, in June 1968, pass a 10 percent tax surcharge effective for the period January 1, 1968, through December 31, 1969, for corporations, and April 1, 1968, through December 31, 1969, for individuals.[2] Another comprehensive set of tax changes, including some adjustments in basic tax rates, was passed in 1969. Further changes were made throughout the early '70s, their principal effects being a speed-up of tax reductions included in the 1969 act. The Tax Reform Act of 1976 also included comprehensive changes in the federal tax provisions, including adjustment of the corporate tax rate schedule. Some of the provisions of the 1969 and 1976 acts are discussed later in this appendix.

Accelerated Depreciation

Depreciation charges are deductible in computing federal income taxes; the larger the depreciation charge, the lower the actual tax liability. The tax laws specify the allowed methods for calculating depreciation for purposes of computing federal income taxes. If the tax laws are changed

---

2. The tax increase took the form of a surcharge; that is, taxes were computed under the rates given in the following pages of this book; then a surcharge equal to 10 percent of this amount was added to the calculated tax. This surtax was reduced to 5 percent and extended from January 1, 1970, to June 30, 1970, after which date it expired.

to permit more rapid, or *accelerated*, depreciation, this will reduce tax payments and have a stimulating effect on business investments.[3]

A number of different depreciation methods are authorized for tax purposes: (1) straight line, (2) units of production, (3) sum-of-years'-digits, and (4) double declining balance. These methods are explained in Appendix B. The last two methods listed are generally referred to as *accelerated depreciation methods;* ordinarily, they are more favorable from a tax standpoint than is straight line depreciation.

The fiscal policy implications of depreciation methods stem from two factors: (1) using accelerated depreciation reduces taxes in the early years of an asset's life, thus increasing corporate cash flows and making more funds available for investment; and (2) faster cash flows increase the profitability, or rate of return, on an investment. This second point is made clear in Chapter 10, where capital budgeting is discussed.

Depreciation methods, like tax rates, are determined by the Congress and are occasionally altered to influence the level of investment and thereby to stimulate or retard the economy. The most sweeping changes were made in 1954, when the accelerated depreciation methods listed above were first permitted, and in 1962 and 1970, when the depreciable lives of assets for tax purposes were reduced.

Investment Tax Credit

The concept of an investment tax credit was first incorporated into the federal income tax laws in 1962. Under the investment tax credit program, business firms could deduct, as a *credit* against their income tax, a specified percentage of the dollar amount of new investment in each of certain categories of assets. Under the 1962 rules, the tax credit amounted to 7 percent of the amount of new investment in assets having useful lives of eight years or more; two-thirds of 7 percent for assets having lives of six or seven years; one-third of 7 percent for assets having lives of four or five years; and no tax credit for assets having useful lives of less than four years. Thus, if a firm that otherwise would have had a $200,000 tax bill purchased an asset costing $500,000 and having a 20-year life, it would receive a tax credit of $35,000 (equal to 7 percent of $500,000), and its adjusted tax bill would be $165,000.

The investment tax credit, like tax rates and depreciation methods, is subject to congressional changes. During the boom in the early part of 1966, the investment tax credit was suspended in an effort to reduce

---

3. Federal tax statutes also consider the time over which assets must be depreciated. A reduction in the period over which an asset must be depreciated will have the same stimulating effect on the economy as would a change in permitted depreciation *methods* that increased depreciation expenses for tax purposes.

investment, but it was reinstated later in that year; then it was removed again in 1969 and reinstated in 1971.

Corporate Income Tax

Rate Structure

For 1977, the first $25,000 of corporate taxable income is taxed at a 20 percent rate, with 22 percent on the next $25,000 and 48 percent on all corporate income over $50,000. If a firm's taxable income were $100,000, for example, the tax would be computed as follows:

$$20\% \times \$25,000 = \$\ 5,000$$
$$22\% \times\ \ 25,000 = \ \ \ 5,500$$
$$48\% \times\ \ 50,000 = \underline{\ \ 24,000}$$
$$\$34,500$$

Table A-1 shows that the average corporate income tax is moderately progressive up to $1 million, after which it becomes virtually 48 percent.

Table A-1
Marginal and Average Corporate Tax Rates, 1976 (in Percentages)

Corporate Income (in Dollars)	Marginal Tax Rate*	Incremental Taxes Paid	Taxes Paid	Average Tax Rate†
0–25,000	20	5,000	5,000	20
25,001–50,000	22	5,500	10,500	21
50,001–60,000	48	4,800	15,300	25.5
60,001–70,000	48	4,800	20,100	28.7
70,001–80,000	48	4,800	24,900	31.1
80,001–90,000	48	4,800	29,700	33
90,001–100,000	48	4,800	34,500	34.5
100,001–150,000	48	24,000	58,500	39
150,001–200,000	48	24,000	82,500	41.3
200,001–500,000	48	144,000	226,500	45.3
500,001–1,000,000	48	240,000	466,500	46.7
1,000,001–5,000,000	48	1,920,000	2,386,500	47.7
5,000,001–10,000,000	48	2,400,000	4,786,500	47.9
10,000,001–100,000,000	48	43,200,000	47,986,500	48.0
100,000,001–500,000,000	48	192,000,000	239,986,500	48.0

*The *marginal tax rate* is the tax on each additional dollar of taxable income received. The tax on each of the first $25,000 is $.20; on each dollar between $25,001 and $50,000 is $.22; on each dollar over $50,000, the marginal tax rate jumps to $.48.
†The percentage given applies to the upper limit of each class interval. The total taxes paid, when divided by the taxable income, gives the average tax rate.

This relatively simple tax structure has wide implications for business planning. Because the tax rate more than doubles when corporate income rises above $50,000, it clearly would pay to break moderate-sized companies into two or more separate corporations in order to hold the income of each unit under $50,000 and thus keep the tax rate at 22 percent. This was, in fact, done for many years by a number of firms, with some groups (retail chains, small loan companies) having literally thousands of separate corporations. However, the Tax Reform Act of 1969 eliminated the advantages of multiple corporations. If a group of firms having common ownership file separate returns for each company, then only one firm will be taxed at the lower initial rates.

Corporate Capital Gains and Losses[4]

Corporate taxable income consists of two components: (1) profits from the sale of capital assets and (2) all other income, defined as *ordinary income.*

Capital assets—for example, security investments—are defined as assets not bought and sold in the ordinary course of a firm's business. Gains and losses on the sale of capital assets are defined as capital gains and losses, and under certain circumstances they receive special tax treatment. Real and depreciable property used in the business is not defined as a capital asset (Section 1221 of the Internal Revenue Code). However, Section 1231 of the code specifies that such property will be treated as a capital asset in the event of a net gain. In the event of a net loss, the full amount may be deducted from ordinary income without any of the limitations described for capital loss treatments.[5]

Prior to 1977 the sale of a capital asset held for six months or less gave rise to a short-run capital gain or loss; if held for more than six months, the sale produced a long-term gain or loss. For 1977 the definition of long-term for determination of tax liability was changed to assets held over nine months. In 1978 an asset must be held over one year to be classified as long-term.

To determine the amount of capital gains tax, net short-term gains are added to the firm's ordinary income and taxed at regular corporate tax rates. For net long-term capital gains (long-term gains less long-term losses), the tax is limited to 30 percent. For example, if in 1977 a corporation held the common stock of another corporation as an investment for more than nine months, and then sold it at a profit, the gain would have been subject to a maximum tax of 30 percent. Of course, if corpo-

---

4. Corporate capital gains and losses (as well as most other tax matters) are subject to many technical provisions. This section and the others dealing with tax matters include only the most general provisions. For special cases the student is referred to *Federal Tax Course* (Englewood Cliffs, N.J.: Prentice-Hall, 1974).

5. This special treatment of depreciable properties should be kept in mind in connection with the material in Chapter 10 on capital budgeting. The difference between the book value of an asset and its salvage value or abandonment value, if lower than book value, can be deducted from ordinary income, and thus the full amount of this difference represents a deductible expense.

rate income were below $50,000, the regular tax rates of 20 percent or 22 percent would apply.

Depreciable Assets

If an asset — for example, a machine tool — is subject to depreciation, its tax cost is defined as the original purchase price less accumulated depreciation. To illustrate, suppose a machine cost $10,000, and $5,000 of depreciation has been taken on it. Its book value, by definition, is $10,000 − $5,000 = $5,000.

If the company sells the machine for more than its book value, it may incur *either* a capital gain *or* ordinary income for tax purposes. If the gain is a recapture of depreciation, indicating that the firm had been depreciating the asset too rapidly (and charging off this depreciation as an expense to reduce ordinary income), the gain is ordinary income and is taxed accordingly. For example, if the firm sells the machine for $7,000 it incurs a $2,000 gain ($7,000 − $5,000). *However, this gain is not classified as a capital gain but, rather, as the recapture of depreciation. Therefore, it is taxed as ordinary income.*

The sale of a depreciable asset is subject to the capital gains tax when the gain exceeds the amount of depreciation taken. To continue with the preceding example, if our machine had been sold for $12,000, then a total profit of $7,000 ($12,000 − $5,000) would have been realized. Of this amount, $5,000 would represent the recapture of depreciation (since this amount of depreciation had been charged off) and would be taxed as ordinary income; the remaining $2,000 would be classified as a capital gain for tax purposes and would be taxed at a rate of 30 percent.

Finally, if the firm sells the machine for $3,000, it incurs a $2,000 loss ($5,000 book value minus $3,000 received). This net loss can be deducted in full from ordinary income without any limitations.

Deductibility of Capital Losses

A net capital loss is not deductible from ordinary income by a corporation. For example, if in 1976 a corporation had ordinary income of $100,000 and a net capital loss of $25,000 (that is, capital losses for the year exceeded capital gains for the year by $25,000), it still paid a tax on the ordinary income at the normal rate of 20 percent on the first $25,000, 22 percent on the next $25,000 and 48 percent on the remaining $50,000, a total tax of $34,500. The net capital loss may, however, be carried back for three years and then forward five years and may be used to offset capital gains during that period. For example, if this corporation has a net capital gain of $75,000 in 1977, its *taxable net capital gain* in that year is $75,000 less the carry-over of $25,000 or $50,000. The tax on the net gain is 30 percent, or $15,000, which is added to the tax on its ordinary income.

Dividend Income

Another important rule is that 85 percent of dividends received by one corporation from another is exempt from taxation.[6] For example, if corporation H owns stock in corporation S and receives $100,000 in dividends from corporation S, it must pay taxes on only $15,000 of the $100,000. Assuming H is in the 48 percent tax bracket, the tax is $7,200, or 7.2 percent of the dividends received. The reason for this reduced tax is that to subject intercorporate dividends to the full corporate tax rate would eventually lead to triple taxation. First, firm S would pay its regular taxes. Then firm H would pay a second tax. Finally, H's own stockholders would be subject to taxes on their dividends. The 85 percent dividend exclusion thus reduces the multiple taxation of corporate income.

Deductibility of Interest and Dividends

Interest payments made by a corporation are a deductible expense to the firm, but dividends paid on its own stock are not deductible. Thus, if a firm raises $100,000 and contracts to pay the suppliers of this money 7 percent, or $7,000 a year, the $7,000 is deductible if the $100,000 is debt. It is not deductible if the $100,000 is raised as stock and the $7,000 is paid as dividends.[7] This differential treatment of dividends and interest payments has an important effect on the manner in which firms raise capital, as we show in Chapter 19.

Payment of Tax in Installments

Firms must estimate their taxable income for the current year and pay one-fourth of the estimated tax on April 15, June 15, September 15, and December 15 of the current year. The *estimated* taxes paid must be at least 80 percent of actual taxes or the firm will be subjected to penalties. Any differences between estimated and actual taxes are payable by March 15 of the following year. For example, if a firm expects to earn $100,000 in 1977 and to owe a tax of $34,500 on this income, then it must file an *estimated income statement* and pay $8,625 on the 15th of April, June, September, and December of 1976. By March 15, 1977, it must file a final income statement and pay any shortfall (or receive a refund for overages) between estimated and actual taxes.

---

6. If the corporation receiving the dividends owns 80 percent or more of the stock of a dividend-paying firm, it may file a consolidated tax return. In this case, there have been no dividends as far as the Internal Revenue Service is concerned, so there is obviously no tax on dividends received. On the internal books of the related corporations there may be an accounting entry entitled "dividends" used to transfer funds from the subsidiary to the parent, but this is of no concern to the IRS.

7. There are limits on the deductibility of interest payments on some forms of securities issued in connection with mergers. See Chapter 22.

Net Operating Carry-Back and Carry-Forward

Any ordinary corporate operating loss can be carried back three years and forward five years. The law states that the loss must first be carried back to the earliest year, the remainder applied to the second earliest year, and so on. For example, an operating loss in 1974 may be used to reduce taxable income in 1971, 1972, 1973, 1975, 1976, 1977, 1978, and 1979; this sequence *must* be followed.

The purpose of permitting this loss averaging is to avoid penalizing corporations whose incomes fluctuate widely. To illustrate, suppose the Ritz Hotel made $100,000 before taxes in all years except 1974, when it suffered a $600,000 operating loss. The Ritz would use the *carry-back* feature to recompute its taxes for 1971, using $100,000 of the operating losses to reduce the 1971 profit to zero, and would recover the amount of taxes paid in that year; that is, in 1975 Ritz would receive a refund of its 1971 taxes because of the loss experienced in 1974. Since $500,000 of unrecovered losses would still be available, Ritz would do the same thing for 1972 and 1973. Then, in 1975, 1976, and 1977, it would apply the *carry-forward* loss to reduce its profits to zero in each of these years.

The right to carry losses forward and backward has made some corporations attractive buys. For example, Atlas Corporation and Howard Hughes bought RKO Pictures because of a $30 million tax-loss credit. A corporation may acquire another firm that has had a tax loss, operate it as a subsidiary, and then present consolidated returns for tax purposes. In the RKO Pictures case, the $30 million loss would be worth $15 million to Atlas, assuming Atlas pays state and federal income taxes at a 50 percent rate. A loss corporation may be a doubly attractive buy if the purchaser is able to operate the business effectively and turn it into a profitable corporation at the same time that he benefits from the tax-loss carry-forward.

The tax law places severe restrictions on this privilege. First, if the stock ownership of the buying group increases by more than 60 percent within three years after the purchase, then the tax loss carry-forward available may be significantly reduced. The same is true if any aspect of the old business is essentially abandoned. The objective of these limitations is to prevent a firm from merging for the sole purpose of taking advantage of the tax law. If it merges primarily to avoid taxes, the loss privilege may be disallowed.

Improper Accumulation

A special surtax on improperly accumulated income is provided for by Section 531 of the Internal Revenue Code, which states that earnings accumulated by a corporation are subject to penalty rates *if the purpose of the accumulation is to enable the stockholders to avoid the personal income tax.* The penalty rate is 27.5 percent on the first $150,000 of improperly accumulated taxable income for the current year and 38.5 percent on all amounts over $150,000. Of income not paid out in dividends, a cumulative total of $150,000 (the balance sheet item Retained Earnings) is prima facie retainable for the reasonable needs of the business. This is a benefit for small corporations. Although there is a penalty rate on all amounts over $150,000 shown to be unnecessary to meet the reasonable needs of the business, many companies do indeed have legitimate reasons for retaining earnings over $150,000 and are not subject to the penalty rate.

Retained earnings are used to pay off debt, to finance growth, and to provide the corporation with a cushion against possible cash drains caused by losses. How much a firm should properly accumulate for uncertain contingencies is a matter of judgment. Fear of the penalty taxes that may be imposed under Section 531 may cause a firm to pay out a higher rate of dividends than it otherwise would.[8]

Sometimes Section 531 may stimulate mergers. A clear illustration is provided by the purchase of the Toni Company (home permanents) by the Gillette Safety Razor Company.[9] The sale was made at a time when Toni's sales volume had begun to level off. Since earnings retention might have been difficult to justify, the owners of Toni, the Harris brothers, were faced with the alternatives of paying penalty rates for improper accumulation of earnings or of paying out the income as dividends. Toni's income after corporate taxes was $4 million a year; with the Harris brothers' average personal income tax of 75 percent, only $1 million a year would have been left after they paid personal taxes on dividends. By selling Toni for $13 million, they realized a $12 million capital gain (their book value was $1 million). After paying the 25 percent capital gains tax on the $12 million, or $3 million, the Harrises realized $10 million after taxes ($13 million sale price less $3 million tax). Thus, Gillette paid the equivalent of three and one-quarter years' after-corporate-tax earnings for Toni, while the Harris brothers received ten years' after-personal-income-tax net income for it. The tax factor made the transaction advantageous to both parties.

Election of Legal Form for Tax Purposes

The broad aspects of the federal corporate income tax have now been covered. Because the federal income tax on individuals is equally important for many business decisions, the main outlines of this part of the tax system must be discussed. In the next section, the individual tax

8. See materials in James K. Hall, *The Taxation of Corporate Surplus Accumulations* (Washington, D.C.: U.S. Government Printing Office, 1952), especially appendix 3.

9. See J. K. Butters, J. Lintner, and W. L. Cary, *Effects of Taxation, Corporate Mergers* (Boston: Harvard Business School, 1951), pp. 96–111. The lucid presentation by these authors has been drawn on for the general background, but the data have been approximated to simplify the illustration. The principle involved is not affected by the modifications of the facts.

structure is examined and compared with the corporate tax structure, thus providing a basis for making an intelligent choice as to which form of organization a firm should elect for tax purposes.

Personal Income Tax

Of some five million firms in the United States, over four million are organized as individual proprietorships or as partnerships. The income of firms organized as individual proprietorships or as partnerships is taxed as personal income to the owners or the partners. The net income of a proprietorship or a partnership is reported to provide a basis for determining the individual's income tax liability. Thus, as a business tax, the individual income tax may be as important as the corporate income tax.

Individual Income Tax Structure[10]

The tax rates applicable to the single individual are outlined in Table A–2; rates applicable to married couples filing joint returns are shown in Table A–3. Because joint returns are permitted whether or not one spouse earns the entire income, this privilege has the effect of lowering applicable tax rates. Other rate schedules (not shown here) apply to married couples filing separate returns and to unmarried individuals who qualify for head-of-household status.

For some decisions, the taxpayer will compare the marginal tax rates. If a taxpayer has income from other sources and is deciding whether to set up a new venture as a proprietorship or a corporation, he will be concerned with the tax rate applicable to the additional income. In comparing the relative advantages of the corporate versus the noncorporate form of business organization, he is likely to compare the personal individual income tax rates to which his income will be subject with the marginal corporate income tax rates.

When the taxpayer's income will be derived mainly from the enterprise he contemplates forming, he is more likely to compare the average rates of taxation. The relation between the average tax rates of the corporate income tax and the personal income tax is shown in Figure A–1. For single returns, the personal rate rises above the corporate rate at about $8,000, while for joint returns the point at which the personal tax rate begins to exceed the corporate rate is $15,000.[11] Thus, for a firm

10. See instructions to IRS Form 1040 for details on personal income tax matters.

11. The 1969 Tax Reform Act limits the personal income tax rate for both single and joint returns to 50 percent if the income is in the form of salary or income from personal services. The income from a business organized as a partnership or a proprietorship is taxed at rates up to 70 percent, unless the income of the business is primarily attributed to the personal services of the owner (as in the case of a partnership of doctors).

Table A–2 Tax Rates for Single Individuals (1976 Rates)*	Taxable Income Over:	but Not Over:	Tax Equals	of Excess Over:	Average Tax Rate at Upper Limit of Each Class Interval	
					Personal	Corporate
	$ 0	$ 500	$ 0 + 14%	$ 0	14.0%	20.0%
	500	1,000	70 + 15	500	14.5	20.0
	1,000	1,500	145 + 16	1,000	15.0	20.0
	1,500	2,000	225 + 17	1,500	15.5	20.0
	2,000	4,000	310 + 19	2,000	17.3	20.0
	4,000	6,000	690 + 21	4,000	18.5	20.0
	6,000	8,000	1,110 + 24	6,000	19.9	20.0
	8,000	10,000	1,590 + 25	8,000	20.9	20.0
	10,000	12,000	2,090 + 27	10,000	21.9	20.0
	12,000	14,000	2,630 + 29	12,000	22.9	20.0
	14,000	16,000	3,210 + 31	14,000	23.9	20.0
	16,000	18,000	3,830 + 34	16,000	25.1	20.0
	18,000	20,000	4,510 + 36	18,000	26.1	20.0
	20,000	22,000	5,230 + 38	20,000	27.2	20.0
	22,000	26,000	5,990 + 40	22,000	29.2	20.1
	26,000	32,000	7,590 + 45	26,000	32.1	20.4
	32,000	38,000	10,290 + 50	32,000	34.9	20.7
	38,000	44,000	13,290 + 55	38,000	37.7	20.9
	44,000	50,000	16,590 + 60	44,000	40.3	21.0
	50,000	60,000	20,190 + 62	50,000	43.9	25.5
	60,000	70,000	26,390 + 64	60,000	46.8	28.7
	70,000	80,000	32,790 + 66	70,000	49.2	31.1
	80,000	90,000	39,390 + 68	80,000	51.3	33.0
	90,000	100,000	46,190 + 69	90,000	53.1	34.5
	100,000	....	53,090 + 70	100,000	–	–

Example: Taxable income is $7,000; tax is $1,110 + $240 = $1,350. *Note:* The maximum rate on earned income is 50 percent. See footnote 13.

*In 1976, for taxable incomes under $20,000, the IRS provided tables of calculations for the amount of the tax obligation based on the midpoint of $25 intervals up to $3,000 and $50 intervals thereafter up to $20,000.

with a net income of $1 million, there is no question but that the corporate form of business should be used. The tax advantage helps to explain why our largest businesses utilize the corporate form of organization. At incomes in the region of the $15,000 dividing line, whether the corporate or the noncorporate form will be most advantageous depends upon the facts of the case. If a firm finds it necessary to pay out a substantial part of its earnings in dividends, the noncorporate form is likely to be advantageous, because the "double taxation" is avoided. However, the corporate form is satisfactory if most of the earnings are to be retained.

Individual Capital Gains and Losses

As with corporations, the distinction between short-term and long-term gains and losses is the six-month holding period. Net short-term gains are taxed at regular rates; the tax on long-term gains may be

Table A–3 Tax Rates for Married Individuals Filing Joint Returns (1976 Rates)*	Taxable Income Over:	but Not Over:	Tax Equals	of Excess Over:	Average Tax Rate at Upper Limit of Each Class Interval	
					Personal	Corporate
	$ 0	$ 1,000	$ 0 + 14%	$ 0	14.0	20.0
	1,000	2,000	140 + 15	1,000	14.5	20.0
	2,000	3,000	290 + 16	2,000	15.0	20.0
	3,000	4,000	450 + 17	3,000	15.5	20.0
	4,000	8,000	620 + 19	4,000	17.4	20.0
	8,000	12,000	1,380 + 22	8,000	18.8	20.0
	12,000	16,000	2,260 + 25	12,000	20.4	20.0
	16,000	20,000	3,260 + 28	16,000	21.9	20.0
	20,000	24,000	4,380 + 32	20,000	23.6	20.0
	24,000	28,000	5,660 + 36	24,000	25.4	20.2
	28,000	32,000	7,100 + 39	28,000	27.1	20.4
	32,000	36,000	8,660 + 42	32,000	28.7	20.6
	36,000	40,000	10,340 + 45	36,000	30.4	20.8
	40,000	44,000	12,140 + 48	40,000	32.0	20.9
	44,000	52,000	14,060 + 50	44.000	34.7	22.0
	52,000	64,000	18,060 + 53	52,000	38.2	26.9
	64,000	76,000	24,420 + 55	64,000	40.8	30.2
	76,000	88,000	31,020 + 58	76,000	43.2	32.7
	88,000	100,000	37,980 + 60	88,000	45.2	34.5
	100,000	120,000	45,180 + 62	100,000	48.0	36.8
	120,000	140,000	57,580 + 64	120,000	50.3	38.4
	140,000	160,000	70,380 + 66	140,000	52.2	39.6
	160,000	180,000	83,580 + 68	160,000	54.0	40.5
	180,000	200,000	97,180 + 69	180,000	55.5	41.3
	200,000	....	110,980 + 70	200,000	—	—

Note: The maximum rate on earned income is 50 percent. See footnote 13.
*In 1976, for taxable incomes under $20,000, the IRS provided tables of calculations for the amount of the tax obligation based on the midpoint of $25 intervals up to $3,000 and $50 intervals thereafter up to $20,000.

Figure A–1
Comparison between Average Rates of Personal Income Tax and Corporation Income Tax (1974 Tax Rates)

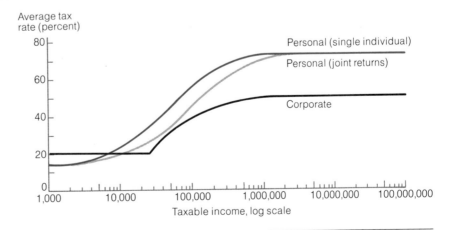

computed in either of two ways. First, the taxpayer may pay a flat rate of 25 percent on net long-term gains up to $50,000 of long-term gains. Alternatively, he may pay the ordinary tax rate on *one-half* the amount of the net long-term gains[12] up to $25,000. The taxpayer should compute his tax under each of these methods and then select the one that results in the lower tax bill.

For example, a married couple with an income of $32,000 from non-capital sources and a $10,000 long-term capital gain would compute their tax in two ways: (1) apply the normal tax rates on $32,000 plus one-half of $10,000 = $37,000, or (2) apply the normal tax on $32,000, plus 25 percent of $10,000. The first method would produce a tax of $10,790; the second, a tax of $11,160. The taxpayer would naturally elect the first method in this case.

In general, for joint returns the 25 percent option is beneficial only if the taxable income exceeds $52,000, the point at which the marginal tax rate exceeds 50 percent. Note that individual and corporate treatments differ in two ways: (1) corporations do not have the option of having only one-half their capital gains taxed at normal rates, and (2) the corporate capital gains tax rate is 30 percent versus 25 percent for individuals.

Personal capital losses, short term or long term, can be carried forward without a time limit and deducted against either short-term or long-term capital gains. In addition, if the capital losses carried forward are not exhausted in the current year, they may be partially charged off against ordinary income. Prior to 1976, 50 percent of long-term capital losses, up to a limit of $1,000 a year, could be deducted. Beginning in 1977 the limit was raised to $2,000 per year. In other words, if an individual has $4,000 of long-term capital losses, he may deduct 50 percent of this amount, or $2,000, from his ordinary income. If the net long-term capital loss is in excess of $4,000, then any amount above $4,000 may be carried forward until it is exhausted. Short-term capital losses are not cut in half; that is, short-term losses can be deducted from ordinary income up to the $2,000 limit. Capital losses may not be carried back by individuals.

Moreover, Section 1244 of the Revenue Act of 1958 provides that individuals who invest in the stock of small corporations and suffer a loss on that stock may, for tax purposes, treat such a loss up to $25,000 a year ($50,000 on a joint return) as an ordinary loss rather than as a capital loss. A corporation is defined for this purpose as a small corporation,

---

12. The 25 percent option is not available on capital gains in excess of $50,000; thus on a $100,000 capital gain, $50,000 would be taxed at 25 percent, while one-half of the remainder would be taxed as ordinary income.

and the loss on its stock can be treated as an ordinary loss, if its common stock does not exceed $500,000 and if its total net worth—common stock plus retained earnings—does not exceed $1 million. This provision also encourages the formation of, and investment in, small corporations.

Dividend Income

The first $100 of dividend income received by an individual stockholder is excluded from taxable income. If stock is owned jointly by a husband and a wife, the exclusion is $200. If only one spouse owns stock, however, the total exclusion is generally only $100.

To illustrate, if a family's gross income consists of $12,000 of salary plus $500 of dividends on stock owned by the husband, the gross taxable income (before deductions) is $12,400. However, if the stock is jointly owned, the taxable gross income would be $12,300, because $200 of the dividend income would be excluded.

Personal Deductions

A $750 deduction is allowed for the taxpayer and each of his dependents. The deduction is doubled on any taxpayer who is over sixty-five years old or is blind. A family of four—husband, wife, and two dependent children, none blind or over sixty-five—would thus have personal deductions of four times $750, or $3,000.[13]

Other Deductions

Certain other items are also deductible from income before computing taxes—medical expenses (subject to limitations), interest payments, state and local taxes, and contributions, among others. A taxpayer has the choice of either itemizing these deductions or taking the standard deduction. In 1976, for those filing a joint return, this was computed as the greater of $2,100 or 16 percent of adjusted gross income up to a maximum of $2,800. For 1977 returns, the standard deduction has been replaced by a flat amount called "zero bracket amount." It is no longer a separate deduction; instead the equivalent amount is built into the new simplified tax tables and tax rate schedules. Taxpayers who itemize deductions will need to make an adjustment as described in the Internal Revenue Service instructions. The "standard deduction" for a joint return is $3,200, or $1,600 each for a married couple filing separate returns. For a single person or unmarried head of household it is $2,200.

13. The personal and standard deductions have been changed frequently in recent years, so check current regulations rather than rely on the data given here.

Partnership, or Proprietorship, or Corporation?

Subchapter S of the Internal Revenue Code provides that some incorporated businesses may elect to be taxed as proprietorships or as partnerships. The main regulations governing permission to make this election include:

1. The firm must be a domestic corporation and must not be affiliated with a group eligible to file consolidated tax returns. (Ordinarily, 80 percent ownership of a subsidiary is required for filing consolidated returns.)
2. The firm may not have more than ten stockholders, all of whom must be individuals.
3. The firm may not derive over 20 percent of its gross receipts from royalties, rents, dividends, interest, annuities, and gains on sales of securities.

Although the foregoing tax factors make it difficult to generalize on whether the corporate or the noncorporate form is more advantageous from a tax standpoint, the essential variables for making an analysis are provided. In general, the advantage now seems to be on the side of the corporation, particularly since a firm may obtain the many benefits of its corporate status and yet elect to be taxed as a proprietorship or a partnership.

Summary

This appendix provides some basic background on the tax environment within which business firms operate.

Corporate Taxes

The *corporate tax rate* structure is simple. The tax rate is 20 percent on income up to $25,000, 22 percent on the next $25,000 and 48 percent on all income over $50,000. Estimated taxes are paid in quarterly installments during the year in which the income is earned; when the returns are filed, the actual tax liability will result either in additional payments or in a refund due. *Operating losses* may be carried back for three years and forward for five years. *Capital losses* may not be treated as a deduction from operating income, but they may be used to offset capital gains. Corporate capital losses may be carried back for three years and forward for five years. Net long-term capital gains are taxed at a 30 percent rate (as compared with 25 percent for individuals).

Eighty-five percent of the *dividends received* by a corporation owning stock in another firm is excluded from the receiving firm's taxable income, and the receiving firm must pay full taxes on the remaining 15 percent of the dividends. *Dividends paid* are not treated as a tax-deductible expense. Regardless of the size of its earnings, a corporation does not have to pay dividends if it needs funds for expansion. If, however, the funds are not used for a legitimate purpose and if earnings are retained merely to enable stockholders to avoid paying personal income taxes on dividends received, the firm will be subject to an *improper accumulations tax. Interest received* is taxable as ordinary income; *interest paid* is a deductible expense.

Personal Income Tax

Unincorporated business income is taxed at the personal tax rates of the owners. Personal income tax rates for both individuals and married persons filing jointly are *progressive* — the higher one's income, the higher his tax rate. Personal income tax rates start at 14 percent of taxable income and rise to either 50 percent or 70 percent of taxable income, depending upon the source of that income. Corporate income tax rates range from 20 to 48 percent. Thus, at lower incomes the personal income tax rate is lower if a business is organized as a proprietorship or a partnership; at higher incomes the corporate tax rate is lower. This fact has a significant bearing on whether a business chooses to be taxed as a corporation or as a proprietorship or a partnership.

Short-term *capital gains* are taxed at ordinary rates; long-term gains, at 25 percent or one-half the normal tax rate, whichever is lower, for individuals (but at 30 percent for corporations). Capital losses can be used to offset capital gains. One-half of an individual's net capital losses in any year can be deducted from ordinary income up to a limit of $1,000 a year. Capital losses in excess of $2,000 can be carried forward indefinitely until used up.

The foregoing material on the United States tax system is not designed to make a tax expert of the reader. It merely provides a few essentials for recognizing the tax aspects of business financial problems and for developing an awareness of the kinds of situations that should be taken to tax specialists for further guidance. These basics are, however, referred to frequently throughout the text, because income taxes are often an important factor in business financial decisions.

Questions

A–1. Compare the marginal and the average tax rates of corporations with taxable incomes of $5,000, $50,000, $500,000, $5,000,000, and $50,000,000. Can you make such a comparison for sole proprietorships or for partnerships?

A–2. Which is the more relevant tax rate, the marginal or the average, in determining the form of organization for a new firm? Have recent changes in the tax laws made the form of organization more or less important than formerly?

A–3. For tax purposes, how does the treatment of interest expense compare with the treatment of common stock dividends from each of the following standpoints: a firm paying the interest or the dividends, an individual recipient, and a corporate recipient?

A–4. Compare the treatment of capital gains and losses with ordinary gains and losses in corporate income tax returns.

A–5. What is the present corporate carry-back and carry-forward tax provision for ordinary income? What is the purpose of this provision?

A–6. What is the purpose of the Internal Revenue Code provision dealing with improper accumulation of corporate surplus revenue?

A–7. Why is personal income tax information important for a study of business finance?

A–8. How do the tax rates for capital gains and losses affect an individual's investment policies and opportunities for financing a small business?

Problems

A–1. A corporation has a net income of $59,800 before interest charges. Assuming interest charges amount to $4,500:
a. How much income tax must the corporation pay?
b. What is the marginal tax rate?

A–2. John Sayles is a married man with two children. His gross income for 1976 is $20,000, which includes $1,600 of corporate dividends received by his wife. He files a joint return and takes the standard deduction. What is his personal income tax liability for 1976?

A–3. The taxable income (losses are shown in parentheses) of the Johnson Corporation formed in 1973, is shown below:

1973	$(250,000)
1974	125,000
1975	175,000
1976	325,000
1977	(125,000)

Based on the 1977 rules and rates, what is the corporate tax liability for each year?

A–4. The Davison Corporation's taxable income statement for 1977 was $150,000. Bond Manufacturing Corporation had a $50,000 loss in 1977. Davison feels that managerial talent can turn Bond into a profitable operation. If the two companies merged prior to January 1, 1978, what would be the merged corporation's income for 1977 after any refund of prepaid taxes? What is the difference in tax liability for Davison before and after the merger?

A–5. In 1977 Grey Manufacturing earned $400,000 before taxes on sales of $8 million. In 1975 it acquired working control of Reaction Products, Inc., for $250,000, and it disposed of the stock in 1977 for $500,000. (Grey controlled less than 80 percent of Reaction.) Dividends paid by Reaction to Grey during 1977 amounted to $25,000.

a. What is Grey's tax for 1977?

b. What would Grey's tax have been if Reaction had declared a further dividend of $50,000 in 1977 and if Grey had sold the stock, purchased in 1975, for $400,000?

A–6. John Mason and Mark Bronson are planning to start a new business, M & B Manufacturing, and they are trying to decide whether to incorporate for tax purposes or to run the business as a partnership. They will each own 50 percent of the business and, if incorporated, all profits will begin to be paid out as dividends in the fourth year. Mason is married and has two children; Bronson is married with no children. Mason has an income (dividends on stocks owned in his own name) of $15,000 per year exclusive of his interest in M & B Manufacturing. Bronson has no outside income, but he has enough savings to support himself until the business starts providing him with an income. Both men take the standard deduction.

a. Assuming the company has the following expected incomes, what will their total personal and corporate taxes be under (i) a partnership and (ii) a corporation?

Year	Income before Tax (Thousands)
1975	$ (30)*
1976	25
1977	95
1978	180
1979	280

*Personal business losses can be carried forward for five years.

b. Should Mason and Bronson form the new business as a partnership or as a corporation? Why?

B   **Depreciation Methods**

The four principal methods of depreciation—straight line, sum-of-years'-digits, double declining balance, and units of production—and their effects on a firm's taxes are illustrated in this appendix. We will begin by assuming that a machine is purchased for $1,100 and has an estimated useful life of ten years or ten thousand hours. It will have a scrap value of $100 after ten years of use or after ten thousand hours, whichever comes first. Table B−1 illustrates each of the four depreciation methods and compares the depreciation charges of each method over the ten-year period.

Table B−1
Comparison of Depreciation Methods for a 10-year, $1,100 Asset with a $100 Salvage Value

Depreciation Methods

Year	Straight Line	Double Declining Balance	Sum-of-Years-Digits	Units of Production*
1	$ 100	$220	$ 182	$ 200
2	100	176	164	180
3	100	141	145	150
4	100	113	127	130
5	100	90	109	100
6	100	72	91	80
7	100	58	73	60
8	100	46	55	50
9	100	37	36	30
10	100	29	18	20
Total	$1,000	$982	$1,000	$1,000

*The assumption is made that the machine is used the following number of hours: first year, 2,000; second year, 1,800; third year, 1,500; fourth year, 1,300; fifth year, 1,000; sixth year, 800; seventh year, 600; eighth year, 500; ninth year, 300; tenth year, 200.

Straight Line   With the straight line method, a uniform annual depreciation charge of $100 a year is provided. This figure is arrived at by simply dividing the economic life into the total cost of the machine minus the estimated salvage value:

$$\frac{(\$1,100 \text{ cost} - \$100 \text{ salvage value})}{10 \text{ years}} = \$100 \text{ a year depreciation charge.}$$

If the estimated salvage value is not in excess of 10 percent of the original cost, it can be ignored, but we are leaving it in for illustrative purposes.

Double Declining Balance

The double declining balance (DDB) method of accelerated depreciation requires the application of a cost rate of depreciation each year to the undepreciated value of the asset at the close of the previous year. In this case, since the annual straight line rate is 10 percent a year ($100 ÷ $1,000), the double declining rate would be 20 percent (2 × 10 percent). This rate is applied to the full purchase price of the machine, not to the cost less salvage value. Therefore, depreciation under the DDB method is $220 during the first year (20 percent × $1,100). Depreciation amounts to $176 in the second year and is calculated by applying the 20 percent rate to the undepreciated value of the asset,

$$20\% \times (1{,}100 - \$220) = \$176,$$

and so on, as the undepreciated balance declines. Notice that under DDB the asset is not fully depreciated at the end of the tenth year. In our example the remaining depreciation would be taken in the tenth year.[1]

Sum-of-years'-digits

Under the sum-of-years'-digits method, the yearly depreciation allowance is determined as follows:

1. Calculate the sum of the years' digits; in our example, there is a total of 55 digits: $1 + 2 + 3 + 4 + 5 + 6 + 7 + 8 + 9 + 10 = 55$. This figure can also be arrived at by means of the sum of an algebraic progression equation where N is the life of the asset:

$$\text{Sum} = N\left(\frac{N+1}{2}\right)$$

$$= 10\left(\frac{10+1}{2}\right) = 55.$$

2. Divide the number of remaining years by the sum-of-years'-digits

---

1. Actually, the company would switch from DDB to straight line whenever straight line depreciation on the remaining book value of the asset exceeds the DDB amount. Thus, in the ninth year the book value is $84, so straight line depreciation would be $42 versus $37 if the change were not made.

and multiply this fraction by the depreciable cost (total cost minus salvage value) of the asset:

Year 1: $\dfrac{10}{55}$ ($1,000) = $182 depreciation.

Year 2: $\dfrac{9}{55}$ ($1,000) = $164 depreciation.

Year 10: $\dfrac{1}{55}$ ($1,000) = $18 depreciation.

Units of Production

Under the units of production method, the expected useful life of 10,000 hours is divided into the depreciable cost (purchase price minus salvage value) to arrive at an hourly depreciation rate of ten cents. Since, in our example, the machine is run for 2,000 hours in the first year, the depreciation in that year is $200; in the second year, $180; and so on. With this method, depreciation charges cannot be estimated precisely ahead of time; the firm must wait until the end of the year to determine what usage has been made of the machine and hence its depreciation.

Effect of Depreciation on Taxes Paid

The effect of the accelerated methods on a firm's income tax payment is easily demonstrated. In the first year, should the firm choose to use the straight line method, only $100 may be deducted from its earnings to arrive at earnings before taxes (the amount of earnings to which the tax rate applies). However, using any one of the other three methods, the firm would have a much greater deduction and, therefore, a lower tax liability.

Changing the Depreciable Life of an Asset

Depreciation charges may actually be accelerated without resorting to changing the depreciation method simply by shortening the estimated life of an asset. The federal government establishes certain guidelines that set legal limits on the minimum life of classes of assets; by lowering these limits, the government can accomplish ends similar to permitting accelerated methods. Halving the minimum depreciable life of an asset, for example, would effectively double the annual rate of depreciation.

C The Normal Curve

Table C
Values of the
Standard Normal
Distribution Function

z	.00	.01	.02	.03	.04	.05	.06	.07	.08	.09
0.0	.0000	.0040	.0080	.0120	.0160	.0199	.0239	.0279	.0319	.0359
0.1	.0398	.0438	.0478	.0517	.0557	.0596	.0636	.0675	.0714	.0753
0.2	.0793	.0832	.0871	.0910	.0948	.0987	.1026	.1064	.1103	.1141
0.3	.1179	.1217	.1255	.1293	.1331	.1368	.1406	.1443	.1480	.1517
0.4	.1554	.1591	.1628	.1664	.1700	.1736	.1772	.1808	.1844	.1879
0.5	.1915	.1950	.1985	.2019	.2054	.2088	.2123	.2157	.2190	.2224
0.6	.2257	.2291	.2324	.2357	.2389	.2422	.2454	.2486	.2517	.2549
0.7	.2580	.2611	.2642	.2673	.2704	.2734	.2764	.2794	.2823	.2852
0.8	.2881	.2910	.2939	.2967	.2995	.3023	.3051	.3078	.3106	.3133
0.9	.3159	.3186	.3212	.3238	.3264	.3289	.3315	.3340	.3365	.3389
1.0	.3413	.3438	.3461	.3485	.3508	.3531	.3554	.3577	.3599	.3621
1.1	.3643	.3665	.3686	.3708	.3729	.3749	.3770	.3790	.3810	.3830
1.2	.3849	.3869	.3888	.3907	.3925	.3944	.3962	.3980	.3997	.4015
1.3	.4032	.4049	.4066	.4082	.4099	.4115	.4131	.4147	.4162	.4177
1.4	.4192	.4207	.4222	.4236	.4251	.4265	.4279	.4292	.4306	.4319
1.5	.4332	.4345	.4357	.4370	.4382	.4394	.4406	.4418	.4429	.4441
1.6	.4452	.4463	.4474	.4484	.4495	.4505	.4515	.4525	.4535	.4545
1.7	.4554	.4564	.4573	.4582	.4591	.4599	.4608	.4616	.4625	.4633
1.8	.4641	.4649	.4656	.4664	.4671	.4678	.4686	.4693	.4699	.4706
1.9	.4713	.4719	.4726	.4732	.4738	.4744	.4750	.4756	.4761	.4767
2.0	.4772	.4778	.4783	.4788	.4793	.4798	.4803	.4808	.4812	.4817
2.1	.4821	.4826	.4830	.4834	.4838	.4842	.4846	.4850	.4854	.4857
2.2	.4861	.4864	.4868	.4871	.4875	.4878	.4881	.4884	.4887	.4890
2.3	.4893	.4896	.4898	.4901	.4904	.4906	.4909	.4911	.4913	.4916
2.4	.4918	.4920	.4922	.4925	.4927	.4929	.4931	.4932	.4934	.4936
2.5	.4938	.4940	.4941	.4943	.4945	.4946	.4948	.4949	.4951	.4952
2.6	.4953	.4955	.4956	.4957	.4959	.4960	.4961	.4962	.4963	.4964
2.7	.4965	.4966	.4967	.4968	.4969	.4970	.4971	.4972	.4973	.4974
2.8	.4974	.4975	.4976	.4977	.4977	.4978	.4979	.4979	.4980	.4981
2.9	.4981	.4982	.4982	.4982	.4984	.4984	.4985	.4985	.4986	.4986
3.0	.4987	.4987	.4987	.4988	.4988	.4989	.4989	.4989	.4990	.4990

D   Interest Tables

Table D–1
Compound
Sum of $1
(CVIF) $S = P(1+r)^N$

Period	1%	2%	3%	4%	5%	6%	7%
1	1.010	1.020	1.030	1.040	1.050	1.060	1.070
2	1.020	1.040	1.061	1.082	1.102	1.124	1.145
3	1.030	1.061	1.093	1.125	1.158	1.191	1.225
4	1.041	1.082	1.126	1.170	1.216	1.262	1.311
5	1.051	1.104	1.159	1.217	1.276	1.338	1.403
6	1.062	1.126	1.194	1.265	1.340	1.419	1.501
7	1.072	1.149	1.230	1.316	1.407	1.504	1.606
8	1.083	1.172	1.267	1.369	1.477	1.594	1.718
9	1.094	1.195	1.305	1.423	1.551	1.689	1.838
10	1.105	1.219	1.344	1.480	1.629	1.791	1.967
11	1.116	1.243	1.384	1.539	1.710	1.898	2.105
12	1.127	1.268	1.426	1.601	1.796	2.012	2.252
13	1.138	1.294	1.469	1.665	1.886	2.133	2.410
14	1.149	1.319	1.513	1.732	1.980	2.261	2.579
15	1.161	1.346	1.558	1.801	2.079	2.397	2.759
16	1.173	1.373	1.605	1.873	2.183	2.540	2.952
17	1.184	1.400	1.653	1.948	2.292	2.693	3.159
18	1.196	1.428	1.702	2.026	2.407	2.854	3.380
19	1.208	1.457	1.754	2.107	2.527	3.026	3.617
20	1.220	1.486	1.806	2.191	2.653	3.207	3.870
25	1.282	1.641	2.094	2.666	3.386	4.292	5.427
30	1.348	1.811	2.427	3.243	4.322	5.743	7.612

Period	8%	9%	10%	12%	14%	15%	16%
1	1.080	1.090	1.100	1.120	1.140	1.150	1.160
2	1.166	1.186	1.210	1.254	1.300	1.322	1.346
3	1.260	1.295	1.331	1.405	1.482	1.521	1.561
4	1.360	1.412	1.464	1.574	1.689	1.749	1.811
5	1.469	1.539	1.611	1.762	1.925	2.011	2.100
6	1.587	1.677	1.772	1.974	2.195	2.313	2.436
7	1.714	1.828	1.949	2.211	2.502	2.660	2.826
8	1.851	1.993	2.144	2.476	2.853	3.059	3.278
9	1.999	2.172	2.358	2.773	3.252	3.518	3.803
10	2.159	2.367	2.594	3.106	3.707	4.046	4.411
11	2.332	2.580	2.853	3.479	4.226	4.652	5.117
12	2.518	2.813	3.138	3.896	4.818	5.350	5.926

Table D-1 Continued

Period	8%	9%	10%	12%	14%	15%	16%
13	2.720	3.066	3.452	4.363	5.492	6.153	6.886
14	2.937	3.342	3.797	4.887	6.261	7.076	7.988
15	3.172	3.642	4.177	5.474	7.138	8.137	9.266
16	3.426	3.970	4.595	6.130	8.137	9.358	10.748
17	3.700	4.328	5.054	6.866	9.276	10.761	12.468
18	3.996	4.717	5.560	7.690	10.575	12.375	14.463
19	4.316	5.142	6.116	8.613	12.056	14.232	16.777
20	4.661	5.604	6.728	9.646	13.743	16.367	19.461
25	6.848	8.623	10.835	17.000	26.462	32.919	40.874
30	10.063	13.268	17.449	29.960	50.950	66.212	85.850

Period	18%	20%	24%	28%	32%	36%
1	1.180	1.200	1.240	1.280	1.320	1.360
2	1.392	1.440	1.538	1.638	1.742	1.850
3	1.643	1.728	1.907	2.067	2.300	2.515
4	1.939	2.074	2.364	2.684	3.036	3.421
5	2.288	2.488	2.932	3.436	4.007	4.653
6	2.700	2.986	3.635	4.398	5.290	6.328
7	3.185	3.583	4.508	5.629	6.983	8.605
8	3.759	4.300	5.590	7.206	9.217	11.703
9	4.435	5.160	6.931	9.223	12.166	15.917
10	5.234	6.192	8.594	11.806	16.060	21.647
11	6.176	7.430	10.657	15.112	21.199	29.439
12	7.288	8.916	13.215	19.343	27.983	40.037
13	8.599	10.699	16.386	24.759	36.937	54.451
14	10.147	12.839	20.319	31.961	48.757	74.053
15	11.974	15.407	25.196	40.565	64.359	100.712
16	14.129	18.488	31.243	51.923	84.954	136.970
17	16.672	22.186	38.741	66.461	112.140	186.280
18	19.673	26.623	48.039	85.071	148.020	253.340
19	23.214	31.948	59.568	108.890	195.390	344.540
20	27.393	38.338	73.864	139.380	257.920	468.570
25	62.669	95.396	216.542	478.900	1033.600	2180.100
30	143.371	237.376	634.820	1645.500	4142.100	10143.000

Period	40%	50%	60%	70%	80%	90%
1	1.400	1.500	1.600	1.700	1.800	1.900
2	1.960	2.250	2.560	2.890	3.240	3.610
3	2.744	3.375	4.096	4.913	5.832	6.859
4	3.842	5.062	6.544	8.352	10.498	13.032
5	5.378	7.594	10.486	14.199	18.896	24.761
6	7.530	11.391	16.777	24.138	34.012	47.046
7	10.541	17.086	26.844	41.034	61.222	89.387
8	14.758	25.629	42.950	69.758	110.200	169.836
9	20.661	38.443	68.720	118.588	198.359	322.688
10	28.925	57.665	109.951	201.599	357.047	613.107

Table D-1 Continued

Period	40%	50%	60%	70%	80%	90%
11	40.496	86.498	175.922	342.719	642.684	1164.902
12	56.694	129.746	281.475	582.622	1156.831	2213.314
13	79.372	194.619	450.360	990.457	2082.295	4205.297
14	111.120	291.929	720.576	1683.777	3748.131	7990.065
15	155.568	437.894	1152.921	2862.421	6746.636	15181.122
16	217.795	656.840	1844.700	4866.100	12144.000	28844.000
17	304.914	985.260	2951.500	8272.400	21859.000	54804.000
18	426.879	1477.900	4722.400	14063.000	39346.000	104130.000
19	597.630	2216.800	7555.800	23907.000	70824.000	197840.000
20	836.683	3325.300	12089.000	40642.000	127480.000	375900.000
25	4499.880	25251.000	126760.000	577060.000	2408900.000	9307600.000
30	24201.432	191750.000	1329200.000	8193500.000	45517000.000	230470000.000

Table D–2
Present Value of $1 (PVIF)
$$P = S(1 + r)^{-N}$$

Period	1%	2%	3%	4%	5%	6%	7%	8%	9%	10%	12%	14%	15%
1	.990	.980	.971	.962	.952	.943	.935•	.926	.917	.909	.893	.877	.870
2	.980	.961	.943	.925	.907	.890	.873	.857	.842	.826	.797	.769	.756
3	.971	.942	.915	.889	.864	.840	.816	.794	.772	.751	.712	.675	.658
4	.961	.924	.889	.855	.823	.792	.763	.735	.708	.683	.636	.592	.572
5	.951	.906	.863	.822	.784	.747	.713	.681	.650	.621	.567	.519	.497
6	.942	.888	.838	.790	.746	.705	.666	.630	.596	.564	.507	.456	.432
7	.933	.871	.813	.760	.711	.665	.623	.583	.547	.513	.452	.400	.376
8	.923	.853	.789	.731	.677	.627	.582	.540	.502	.467	.404	.351	.327
9	.914	.837	.766	.703	.645	.592	.544	.500	.460	.424	.361	.308	.284
10	.905	.820	.744	.676	.614	.558	.508	.463	.422	.386	.322	.270	.247
11	.896	.804	.722	.650	.585	.527	.475	.429	.388	.350	.287	.237	.215
12	.887	.788	.701	.625	.557	.497	.444	.397	.356	.319	.257	.208	.187
13	.879	.773	.681	.601	.530	.469	.415	.368	.326	.290	.229	.182	.163
14	.870	.758	.661	.577	.505	.442	.388	.340	.299	.263	.205	.160	.141
15	.861	.743	.642	.555	.481	.417	.362	.315	.275	.239	.183	.140	.123
16	.853	.728	.623	.534	.458	.394	.339	.292	.252	.218	.163	.123	.107
17	.844	.714	.605	.513	.436	.371	.317	.270	.231	.198	.146	.108	.093
18	.836	.700	.587	.494	.416	.350	.296	.250	.212	.180	.130	.095	.081
19	.828	.686	.570	.475	.396	.331	.276	.232	.194	.164	.116	.083	.070
20	.820	.673	.554	.456	.377	.312	.258	.215	.178	.149	.104	.073	.061
25	.780	.610	.478	.375	.295	.233	.184	.146	.116	.092	.059	.038	.030
30	.742	.552	.412	.308	.231	.174	.131	.099	.075	.057	.033	.020	.015

Period	16%	18%	20%	24%	28%	32%	36%	40%	50%	60%	70%	80%	90%
1	.862	.847	.833	.806	.781	.758	.735	.714	.667	.625	.588	.556	.526
2	.743	.718	.694	.650	.610	.574	.541	.510	.444	.391	.346	.309	.277

Table D-2 Continued

Period	16%	18%	20%	24%	28%	32%	36%	40%	50%	60%	70%	80%	90%
3	.641	.609	.579	.524	.477	.435	.398	.364	.296	.244	.204	.171	.146
4	.552	.516	.482	.423	.373	.329	.292	.260	.198	.153	.120	.095	.077
5	.476	.437	.402	.341	.291	.250	.215	.186	.132	.095	.070	.053	.040
6	.410	.370	.335	.275	.227	.189	.158	.133	.088	.060	.041	.029	.021
7	.354	.314	.279	.222	.178	.143	.116	.095	.059	.037	.024	.016	.011
8	.305	.266	.233	.179	.139	.108	.085	.068	.039	.023	.014	.009	.006
9	.263	.226	.194	.144	.108	.082	.063	.048	.026	.015	.008	.005	.003
10	.227	.191	.162	.116	.085	.062	.046	.035	.017	.009	.005	.003	.002
11	.195	.162	.135	.094	.066	.047	.034	.025	.012	.006	.003	.002	.001
12	.168	.137	.112	.076	.052	.036	.025	.018	.008	.004	.002	.001	.001
13	.145	.116	.093	.061	.040	.027	.018	.013	.005	.002	.001	.001	.000
14	.125	.099	.078	.049	.032	.021	.014	.009	.003	.001	.001	.000	.000
15	.108	.084	.065	.040	.025	.016	.010	.006	.002	.001	.000	.000	.000
16	.093	.071	.054	.032	.019	.012	.007	.005	.002	.001	.000	.000	
17	.080	.060	.045	.026	.015	.009	.005	.003	.001	.000	.000		
18	.089	.051	.038	.021	.012	.007	.004	.002	.001	.000	.000		
19	.060	.043	.031	.017	.009	.005	.003	.002	.000	.000			
20	.051	.037	.026	.014	.007	.004	.002	.001	.000	.000			
25	.024	.016	.010	.005	.002	.001	.000	.000					
30	.012	.007	.004	.002	.001	.000	.000						

Table D–3
Sum of an Annuity of $1 for N Periods (CVIF$_a$)

$$S_{m/r} = \$1\left[\frac{(1+r)^N - 1}{r}\right]$$

Period	1%	2%	3%	4%	5%	6%
1	1.000	1.000	1.000	1.000	1.000	1.000
2	2.010	2.020	2.030	2.040	2.050	2.060
3	3.030	3.060	3.091	3.122	3.152	3.184
4	4.060	4.122	4.184	4.246	4.310	4.375
5	5.101	5.204	5.309	5.416	5.526	5.637
6	6.152	6.308	6.468	6.633	6.802	6.975
7	7.214	7.434	7.662	7.898	8.142	8.394
8	8.286	8.583	8.892	9.214	9.549	9.897
9	9.369	9.755	10.159	10.583	11.027	11.491
10	10.462	10.950	11.464	12.006	12.578	13.181
11	11.567	12.169	12.808	13.486	14.207	14.972
12	12.683	13.412	14.192	15.026	15.917	16.870
13	13.809	14.680	15.618	16.627	17.713	18.882
14	14.947	15.974	17.086	18.292	19.599	21.051
15	16.097	17.293	18.599	20.024	21.579	23.276

Table D-3 Continued

Period	1%	2%	3%	4%	5%	6%
16	17.258	18.639	20.157	21.825	23.657	25.673
17	18.430	20.012	21.762	23.698	25.840	28.213
18	19.615	21.412	23.414	25.645	28.132	30.906
19	20.811	22.841	25.117	27.671	30.539	33.760
20	22.019	24.297	26.870	29.778	33.066	36.786
25	28.243	32.030	36.459	41.646	47.727	54.865
30	34.785	40.568	47.575	56.805	66.439	79.058

Period	7%	8%	9%	10%	12%	14%
1	1.000	1.000	1.000	1.000	1.000	1.000
2	2.070	2.080	2.090	2.100	2.120	2.140
3	3.215	3.246	3.278	3.310	3.374	3.440
4	4.440	4.506	4.573	4.641	4.770	4.921
5	5.751	5.867	5.985	6.105	6.353	6.610
6	7.153	7.336	7.523	7.716	8.115	8.536
7	8.654	8.923	9.200	9.487	10.089	10.730
8	10.260	10.637	11.028	11.436	12.300	13.233
9	11.978	12.488	13.021	13.579	14.776	16.085
10	13.816	14.487	15.193	15.937	17.549	19.337
11	15.784	16.645	17.560	18.531	20.655	23.044
12	17.888	18.977	20.141	21.384	24.133	27.271
13	20.141	21.495	22.953	24.523	28.029	32.089
14	22.550	24.215	26.019	27.975	32.393	37.581
15	25.129	27.152	29.361	31.772	37.280	43.842
16	27.888	30.324	33.003	35.950	42.753	50.980
17	30.840	33.750	36.974	40.545	48.884	59.118
18	33.999	37.450	41.301	45.599	55.750	68.394
19	37.379	41.446	46.018	51.159	63.440	78.969
20	40.995	45.762	51.160	57.275	72.052	91.025
25	63.249	73.106	84.701	98.347	133.334	181.871
30	94.461	113.283	136.308	164.494	241.333	356.787

Period	16%	18%	20%	24%	28%	32%
1	1.000	1.000	1.000	1.000	1.000	1.000
2	2.160	2.180	2.200	2.240	2.280	2.320
3	3.506	3.572	3.640	3.778	3.918	4.062
4	5.066	5.215	5.368	5.684	6.016	6.362
5	6.877	7.154	7.442	8.048	8.700	9.398
6	8.977	9.442	9.930	10.980	12.136	13.406
7	11.414	12.142	12.916	14.615	16.534	18.696
8	14.240	15.327	16.499	19.123	22.163	25.678
9	17.518	19.086	20.799	24.712	29.369	34.895
10	21.321	23.521	25.959	31.643	38.592	47.062
11	25.733	28.755	32.150	40.238	50.399	63.122
12	30.850	34.931	39.580	50.985	65.510	84.320
13	36.786	42.219	48.497	64.110	84.853	112.303

Table D-3 Continued

Period	16%	18%	20%	24%	28%	32%
14	43.672	50.818	59.196	80.496	109.612	149.240
15	51.660	60.965	72.035	100.815	141.303	197.997
16	60.925	72.939	87.442	126.011	181.870	262.36
17	71.673	87.068	105.931	157.253	233.790	347.31
18	84.141	103.740	128.117	195.994	300.250	459.45
19	98.603	123.414	154.740	244.033	385.320	607.47
20	115.380	146.628	186.688	303.601	494.210	802.86
25	249.214	342.603	471.981	898.092	1706.800	3226.80
30	530.312	790.948	1181.882	2640.916	5873.200	12941.00

Period	36%	40%	50%	60%	70%	80%
1	1.000	1.000	1.000	1.000	1.000	1.000
2	2.360	2.400	2.500	2.600	2.700	2.800
3	4.210	4.360	4.750	5.160	5.590	6.040
4	6.725	7.104	8.125	9.256	10.503	11.872
5	10.146	10.846	13.188	15.810	18.855	22.370
6	14.799	16.324	20.781	26.295	33.054	41.265
7	21.126	23.853	32.172	43.073	57.191	75.278
8	29.732	34.395	49.258	69.916	98.225	136.500
9	41.435	49.153	74.887	112.866	167.983	246.699
10	57.352	69.814	113.330	181.585	286.570	445.058
11	78.998	98.739	170.995	291.536	488.170	802.105
12	108.437	139.235	257.493	467.458	830.888	1444.788
13	148.475	195.929	387.239	748.933	1413.510	2601.619
14	202.926	275.300	581.859	1199.293	2403.968	4683.914
15	276.979	386.420	873.788	1919.869	4087.745	8432.045
16	377.690	541.990	1311.700	3072.800	6950.200	15179.000
17	514.660	759.780	1968.500	4917.500	11816.000	27323.000
18	700.940	1064.700	2953.800	7868.900	20089.000	49182.000
19	954.280	1491.600	4431.700	12591.000	34152.000	88528.000
20	1298.800	2089.200	6648.500	20147.000	58059.000	159350.000
25	6053.000	11247.000	50500.000	211270.000	824370.000	3011100.000
30	28172.000	60501.000	383500.000	2215400.000	11705000.000	56896000.000

Table D–4
Present Value of
an Annuity of $1
(PVIF$_a$)

$$A_{n/r} = \$1 \left[\frac{1 - (1 + r)^{-N}}{r} \right]$$

Period	1%	2%	3%	4%	5%	6%	7%	8%	9%	10%
1	0.990	0.980	0.971	0.962	0.952	0.943	0.935	0.926	0.917	0.909
2	1.970	1.942	1.913	1.886	1.859	1.833	1.808	1.783	1.759	1.736
3	2.941	2.884	2.829	2.775	2.723	2.673	2.624	2.577	2.531	2.487
4	3.902	3.808	3.717	3.630	3.546	3.465	3.387	3.312	3.240	3.170
5	4.853	4.713	4.580	4.452	4.329	4.212	4.100	3.993	3.890	3.791
6	5.795	5.601	5.417	5.242	5.076	4.917	4.766	4.623	4.486	4.355
7	6.728	6.472	6.230	6.002	5.786	5.582	5.389	5.206	5.033	4.868
8	7.652	7.325	7.020	6.733	6.463	6.210	5.971	5.747	5.535	5.335
9	8.566	8.162	7.786	7.435	7.108	6.802	6.515	6.247	5.995	5.759
10	9.471	8.983	8.530	8.111	7.722	7.360	7.024	6.710	6.418	6.145
11	10.368	9.787	9.253	8.760	8.306	7.887	7.499	7.139	6.805	6.495
12	11.255	10.575	9.954	9.385	8.863	8.384	7.943	7.536	7.161	6.814
13	12.134	11.348	10.635	9.986	9.394	8.853	8.358	7.904	7.487	7.103
14	13.004	12.106	11.296	10.563	9.899	9.295	8.745	8.244	7.786	7.367
15	13.865	12.849	11.938	11.118	10.380	9.712	9.108	8.559	8.060	7.606
16	14.718	13.578	12.561	11.652	10.838	10.106	9.447	8.851	8.312	7.824
17	15.562	14.292	13.166	12.166	11.274	10.477	9.763	9.122	8.544	8.022
18	16.398	14.992	13.754	12.659	11.690	10.828	10.059	9.372	8.756	8.201
19	17.226	15.678	14.324	13.134	12.085	11.158	10.336	9.604	8.950	8.365
20	18.046	16.351	14.877	13.590	12.462	11.470	10.594	9.818	9.128	8.514
25	22.023	19.523	17.413	15.622	14.094	12.783	11.654	10.675	9.823	9.077
30	25.808	22.397	19.600	17.292	15.373	13.765	12.409	11.258	10.274	9.427

Table D-4 Continued

Period	12%	14%	16%	18%	20%	24%	28%	32%	36%
1	0.893	0.877	0.862	0.847	0.833	0.806	0.781	0.758	0.735
2	1.690	1.647	1.605	1.566	1.528	1.457	1.392	1.332	1.276
3	2.402	2.322	2.246	2.174	2.106	1.981	1.868	1.766	1.674
4	3.037	2.914	2.798	2.690	2.589	2.404	2.241	2.096	1.966
5	3.605	3.433	3.274	3.127	2.991	2.745	2.532	2.345	2.181
6	4.111	3.889	3.685	3.498	3.326	3.020	2.759	2.534	2.339
7	4.564	4.288	4.039	3.812	3.605	3.242	2.937	2.678	2.455
8	4.968	4.639	4.344	4.078	3.837	3.421	3.076	2.786	2.540
9	5.328	4.946	4.607	4.303	4.031	3.566	3.184	2.868	2.603
10	5.650	5.216	4.833	4.494	4.193	3.682	3.269	2.930	2.650
11	5.938	5.453	5.029	4.656	4.327	3.776	3.335	2.978	2.683
12	6.194	5.660	5.197	4.793	4.439	3.851	3.387	3.013	2.708
13	6.424	5.842	5.342	4.910	4.533	3.912	3.427	3.040	2.727
14	6.628	6.002	5.468	5.008	4.611	3.962	3.459	3.061	2.740
15	6.811	6.142	5.575	5.092	4.675	4.001	3.483	3.076	2.750
16	6.974	6.265	5.669	5.162	4.730	4.033	3.503	3.088	2.758
17	7.120	5.373	5.749	4.222	4.775	4.059	3.518	3.097	2.763
18	7.250	6.467	5.818	5.273	4.812	4.080	3.529	3.104	2.767
19	7.366	6.550	5.877	5.316	4.844	4.097	3.539	3.109	2.770
20	7.469	6.623	5.929	5.353	4.870	4.110	3.546	3.113	2.772
25	7.843	6.873	6.097	5.467	4.948	4.147	3.564	3.122	2.776
30	8.005	7.003	6.177	5.517	4.979	4.160	3.569	3.124	2.778

E

Answers to Selected End-of-Chapter Problems

We present here some partial answers to selected end-of-chapter problems. For the most part, the answers given are only the final answers (or answers at intermediate steps) to the more complex problems. Within limits, these answers will be useful to see if the student is "on the right track" toward solving the problem. The primary limitation, which must be kept in mind, is that some questions may have more than one solution, depending upon which of several equally plausible assumptions are made in working the problem. Also, many of the problems involve some verbal discussion as well as numerical calculations. We have not presented any of this verbal material here.

2–4   a. Debt/Assets = 50%, inventory turnover = 5.2, fixed asset turnover = 5.49, return on net worth = 9.30%.

3–1   a. (1) ($14,000); b. 13,750 units; c. (1) −6.86; d. 18,333 units; e. 13,750 units.

3–3   a. (iii) 68,625 units; b. (iii) 9.71; c. (iii) $252,000; f. (iii) 570.4.

3–4   a. Total uses $351.

3–5   b. $130; c. $25,000; d. P = $100, profits $16,000.

4–1   a. Total assets $4,500,000, 5-year addition to retained earnings $630,000.

4–2   a. Total assets $2,434,000.

4–3   a. Total assets $8,280,000; b. $414,000; c. Total assets $9,108,000; d. (3) External funds needed increase by $330,000.

4–5   a. 12%; b. 27%; c. 5.4%.

5–1   a. Surplus cash: $85,250, $233,000, ($151,750), ($26,500), $91,250, $160,250.

6–1   a. 11.3%, 10.4%, 8.8%.

6–2   a. Plan (1) $66,800, (2) $68,000, (3) $67,400; b. Worst: ($25,600), ($4,000), ($14,800), Best: $144,000, $138,000, $141,000.

7–1   a. Net profit from extension (3) $25,610, (4) ($1,600), (5) ($69,600); b. (3) $45,733, (4) $8,600, (5) ($28,400).

7–2   a. $100,000; b. 4 days; c. $75,000, ($325,000); e. $125,000, ($275,000).

7–3   a. $160,000, $200,000, $40,000; b. ($12,500); c. $26,066; d. $26,434.

7–4   a. 4,500 units; b. 89 orders; c. 26,000 units; d. 6,300, 40% increase; e. 40%, .40; f. −.8; g. −.8.

8–1   b. 14.69%; d. 24.49%.

8–2　a. (1) 57%, (2) 34%, (3) 29%.

8–3　a. $300,000.

8–4　a. $134,400; d. Effective annual interest charge, 19.5%.

8–5　b. $160,800, 15.12%.

9–2　Ten years.

9–3　a. $875.48; b. $999.60.

9–4　$7,477.51.

9–5　$59,237.81.

9–6　b. $748.52; c. $906.55.

9–7　b. $56,369.98.

9–8　8%.

9–9　8%.

9–10　7%.

9–11　15%.

9–12　$1,180,000, $1,392,000, $1,643,000, $1,939,000, $2,288,000, $2,700,000.

9–13　a. $5,062, $5,216.

9–14　a. $1.18, $1.39, $1.64, $1.94, $2.29, $2.70; b. $6.00; c. $10; d. $16.

9–15　a. $100,020.

9–16　8.32%.

9–17　a. 8%.

9–18　$73,998.

9–19　a. 16%.

10–1　a. $720,000; b. $160,000; c. $100,000, $NPV = $($51,340).

10–2　a. $\Delta F = \$10,250$, $NPV = \$36,407.50$; b. $NPV = \$44,815$.

10–3　a. ($3,226.45); b. $NPV = $($1,588.65); c. $NPV = \$411.35$; d. $NPV = \$3,519.60$.

10–5　b. A = 17.5%, B = 15.5%; e. 26%.

10–6　Electric powered machine.

10–7　Machine H.

A10–1　a. $NPV^*_A = \$5,834.40$, $NPV^*_B = \$6,285.00$, $IRR_A = 19.9\%$, $IRR_B = 20.6\%$; c. 15.8%.

11–1　a. A $4,500, B $5,100; b. A $6,691.50, B $7,750.20.

11–2　a. Expected profit on mailings = $24,150, expected profit on advertising = $256,182; c. .37.

11–4　a. $E(F_A) = \$28,000$, $\sigma_A = \$6,780$, $CV_A = .242$; b. $k_A = 8.42\%$; c. $NPV_A = \$1,804$.

11–5　a. 56; b. 18%.

11–7　a. $E(k_M) = .10$, $\sigma_M = .2$, $E(k_1) = .20$, $\sigma_1 = .424$, $E(k_2) = .10$, $\sigma_2 = .349$, $Cov(k_1 k_M) = .080$, $Cov(k_2, k_M) = .024$, $Cov(k_1, k_2) = .004$; b. $w_1 = 40\%$, $w_2 = 60\%$, $\sigma_p = .274$, $E(k_p) = .140$; d. Project 1 is preferred.

A11–1　b. $15 million; c. $2.933 million; d. .1955; e. 36.7%; f. 24.8%; g. 38.5%; h. 24.8%.

A11–2　a. $6,500; b. ($2,500).

B11−1 a. NPV = \$197; b. σ = 300; c. 25%; d. 75%; e. 50%; f. 1.13; g. (i) 25%, (ii) .00071%.

B11−2 a. NPV = \$664; b. σ = 623; c. $P(NPV > 0)$ = 86%; d. (i) 14%, (ii) .01%.

B11−3 a. 70%; b. 10%; c. 4%; d. 90%; e. 14%.

C11−1 a. NPV of abandonment value = \$4,696 exceeds NPV of expected savings of continued operation \$4,648.

C11−2 a. NPV = \$6,716, σ = 1,420; b. NPV = \$6,762, σ = 1,359; c. Abandon.

C11−3 a. NPV (sale after 5 years) = \$2,380, NPV (sale after 10 years) = \$3,542, NPV (sale after 15 years) \$1,991; d. \$2,097; e. \$1,998.

D11−1 a.

$E(k_p)$	σ_p
.0900	.0400
.0925	.0378
.0950	.0390
.0975	.0434
.1000	.0500

D11−2 a. 28.12% invested in i, 71.88% in j; d. Invest 55% in i and 45% in j; e. 11.51%.

D11−3 a. 84.28% invested in D, 15.72% in C; d. Invest 35% in C and 65% in D; e. 7.78%.

F11−1 NPV = \$67,939 and project should be undertaken.

12−1 1. 4.24%, 2. 11.2% or 10.0%.

12−2 a. By pure rights 8%, by stand-by underwriting 5%, by underwriting 87%.

13−1 \$3.

13−2 a. \$2.50.

13−3 a. \$6.

13−4 a. \$6.

13−5 For \$25 a share: a. (i) 200,000 shares; (ii) .5 right; (iii) \$3.10; (iv) \$46.50; (v) \$1.74.

13−6 a. No; b. No; c. No; number required = 45,456; d. 11.6%; e. 2.75 directors or 2 for sure.

15−1 a. L_t = \$9,870; b. Indifferent between owning and leasing.

15−2 a. \$278,400; c. (\$31,200).

16−1 a. \$2; b. \$28.

16−2 a. A 5% premium results in \$50.40 conversion price.

16−3 a. \$.90; c. \$8; d. Total claims \$500,000; f. Total claims \$687,500.

16−5 a. 8.9%.

16−6 b. 6.8%.

16−7 a. \$42.38 interest decrease; \$21.19 interest increase.

16−8 e. Year 3; g. Approximately 11 percent.

A16−1 a. \$13.87; b. \$17.63

A16-2 a. $S = \$6,824,500$; b. $B = \$3,175,500$; c. No.

A16-3 a. $S = \$9,298,300$; b. $B = \$701,700$; c. No.

17-1   a. $1,250; c. $1,000; d. (i) $1,080.

17-2   a. 10%.

17-3   a. (i) $825.

17-4   a. $1,125.

17-5   a. $2.00; d. (i) 2.135.

17-6   b. $53; d. 10.7%.

17-7   c. (ii) 24%; d. $41.96, $150.

17-8   a. (i) 6.8%, (ii) 8%; b. (i)(1) 8.8%, (2) 10%, (ii)(1) 4.8%, (2) 6%;
       d. (i) 4.2%, (ii) $16.13.

17-11 a. $18.05.

17-12 $42.42.

17-13 31 million dollars.

18-1   b. Expected $EPS = \$3.16$ (debt alternative), $2.90 (equity alter-
       native).

18-2   a. (i) 1.5, (iii) 2.18; b. bond: (i) $1.23, (ii) 3.90, stock: (i) $1.38,
       (ii) 2.91.

		Sales (in thousands)	
18-3	a.	$0	$2,100	$4,200
	EPS, Debt:	$ −.47	$2.53	$5.53
	EPS, Stock:	$ −.09	$2.06	$4.20

       b. $941,500; d. $2,370,670; f. Debt: $20.24, Stock: $20.60.

19-1   a. $30 million; b. $15 million; c. $12 million externally;
       d. $k_e = 12.4\%$, $k_r = 12\%$; e. $6 million;
       f. (i) 8.5%, (ii) 8.7%.

19-2   a. $8 million, $16 million; b. 9.47%, 9.76%, 10.33%.

19-3   a. (i) 4.8%, (ii) 10%, (iii) 12%; b. 10.10%; c. $400,000; d. 12.44%.

19-4   a. 9.58%; b. 8.24%, 9.20%, 11.30%.

B19-1 a. $12 million, $16 million.

B19-2 a. Unlevered 12%, levered 14.4%; b. Unlevered 12%, levered
       9.6%.

B19-3 a. $V_A = \$4.4$ million, $V_B = \$2$ million; b. $V_A = \$3.8$ million, $V_B =$
       $2 million; c. $k = 5.26\%$ for firm A, $k = 10\%$ for firm B; e. about
       20% debt.

B19-4 a. 10%; b. 12.5%.

C19-1 a. 10%; b. 1%; c. 15%; d. 2.15%; e. 14.6%; f. 15%; g. 14.6%.

C19-2 a. 12%; b. 1.8%; c. 10%; d. 2.1%; e. 12.9%; f. 10%; g. 12.9%.

C19-3 a. $V_j = 56$; b. 17.85%.

C19-4 a. 10%; b. 13.75%; c. No. The expected return of 15 percent is
       below 17.5 percent, the required rate of return.

C19-5 a. $\bar{k}_M = 10\%$; $\sigma_M^2 = .023$; b. $\beta_A = 1.87$, $k_A^* = 13.5\%$; $\beta_B = .78$, $k_B^* =$
       9.1%; c. Percentage for Systematic A = 52%, percentage for Sys-
       tematic B = 8%; e. Price A declines, Price B rises.

D19–1 b. $p_1 = \$.10$, $p_2 = \$.20$.

D19–2 Value is maximized at $B = \$3,000$.

D19–3 Production plan X.

D19–4 a. $B = \$1,400$.

20–2 a. 6.53% (below), 6.82% (above); b. \$33.6 million.

20–3 a. New $EPS = \$88$; b. \$12; c. \$352.

21–3 a. 15,700,000 debentures; c. 31,400,000; d. \$1,632,800,000; e. \$3,202,800,000; f. \$13.1 billion; g. \$30.292 billion; h. \$6.733 billion; i. \$20.356 billion; j. ΔDebt \$14.6 billion, Δequity \$5.8 billion.

22–2 a. 6.4%; c. (i) 9.73%, (ii) 8.73%; g. 6%.

22–4 b. Horizontal \$2.58, Vertical (\$.21); c. Horizontal \$5.04, Vertical \$1.02.

22–5 (1) +20%, (2) +22%, (3) −18%, (4) +13%; vs. (1) +5%, (2) −.2%, (3) 0, (4) 0.

23–1 c. \$5.1 million.

25–1 e. \$2,333, \$7,000, \$11,667.

25–2 b. Net after tax, 1972 = \$81,000 or 4.5%, 1975 = \$222,000 or 6.4%; d. 1977 total assets = \$2,245,000, cash available = \$692,000; e. 1977 current ratio = 1.54, $B/A = 38\%$, profit/net worth = 27%; g. Total sources, 1967–71 = \$294,000; h. \$979,000; i. \$1.5 million with difference about \$100,000.

A–1 a. \$13,044; b. 48%.

A–2 \$2,785

A–3 1973, 1974: \$0; 1975: \$10,500; 1976: \$142,500; 1977: (\$46,500).

A–4 Tax saving after merger \$24,000.

A–5 a. \$255,300; b. \$228,900.

A–6 a. (i) Total tax bill (Bronson & Mason) \$0, \$4,892, \$32,974, \$81,286, \$144,014; (ii) Total tax bill (Bronson & Mason Corporation) \$1,622, \$1,622, \$31,322, \$113,239, \$189,822.

Glossary

Abandonment Value The amount that can be realized by liquidating a project before its economic life has ended.

Accelerated Depreciation Depreciation methods that write off the cost of an asset at a faster rate than the write-off under the straight line method. The three principal methods of accelerated depreciation are: (1) sum-of-years'-digits, (2) double declining balance, and (3) units of production.

Accruals Continually recurring short-term liabilities. Examples are accrued wages, accrued taxes, and accrued interest.

Aging Schedule A report showing how long accounts receivable have been outstanding. It gives the percent of receivables not past due and the percent past due by, for example, one month, two months, or other periods.

Amortize To liquidate on an installment basis; an amortized loan is one in which the principal amount of the loan is repaid in installments during the life of the loan.

Annuity A series of payments of a fixed amount for a specified number of years.

Arbitrage The process of selling overvalued and buying undervalued assets so as to bring about an equilibrium where all assets are properly valued. One who engages in arbitrage is called an arbitrager.

Arrearage Overdue payment; frequently, omitted dividends on preferred stocks.

Assignment A relatively inexpensive way of liquidating a failing firm that does not involve going through the courts.

Balloon Payment When a debt is not fully amortized, the final payment is larger than the preceding payments and is called a "balloon" payment.

Bankruptcy A legal procedure for formally liquidating a business, carried out under the jurisdiction of courts of law.

Beta Coefficient Measures the extent to which the returns on a given stock move with "the stock market."

Bond A long-term debt instrument.

Book Value The accounting value of an asset. The book value of a share of common stock is equal to the net worth (common stock plus retained earnings) of the corporation divided by the number of shares of stock outstanding.

Break-even Analysis An analytical technique for studying the relation between fixed cost, variable cost, and profits. A break-even *chart* graphically depicts the nature of break-even analysis. The break-even *point* represents the volume of sales at which total costs equal total revenues (that is, profits equal zero).

Business Risk The basic risk inherent in a firm's operations. Business risk plus financial risk resulting from the use of debt equals total corporate risk.

Call (1) An option to buy (or "call") a share of stock at a specified price within a specified period. (2) The process of redeeming a bond or preferred stock issue before its normal maturity.

Call Premium The amount in excess of par value that a company must pay when it calls a security.

Call Price The price that must be paid when a security is called. The call price is equal to the par value plus the call premium.

Call Privilege A provision incorporated into a bond or a share of preferred stock that gives the issuer the right to redeem (call) the security at a specified price.

Capital Asset An asset with a life of more than one year that is not bought and sold in the ordinary course of business.

Capital Budgeting The process of planning expenditures on assets whose returns are expected to extend beyond one year.

Capital Gains Profits on the sale of capital assets held for six months or more.

Capital Losses Losses on the sale of capital assets.

Capital Market Line A graphical representation of the relationship between risk and the required rate of return on an efficient portfolio.

Capital Markets Financial transactions involving instruments with maturities greater than one year.

Capital Rationing A situation where a constraint is placed on the total size of the capital investment during a particular period.

Capital Structure The permanent long-term financing of the firm represented by long-term debt, preferred stock, and net worth (net worth consists of capital, capital surplus, and retained earnings). Capital structure is distinguished from *financial structure*, which includes short-term debt plus all reserve accounts.

Capitalization Rate A discount rate used to find the present value of a series of future cash receipts; sometimes called *discount rate*.

Carry-back; Carry-forward For income tax purposes, losses that can be carried backward or forward to reduce federal income taxes.

Cash Budget A schedule showing cash flows (receipts, disbursements, and net cash) for a firm over a specified period.

Cash Cycle The length of time between the purchase of raw materials and the collection of accounts receivable generated in the sale of the final product.

Certainty Equivalents The amount of cash (or rate of return) that someone would require *with certainty* to make him indifferent between this certain sum (or *rate of return*) and a particular uncertain, risky sum (or rate of return).

Characteristic Line A linear least-squares regression line that shows the relationship between an individual security's return and returns on "the market." The slope of the characteristic line is the beta coefficient.

Chattel Mortgage A mortgage on personal property (not real estate). A mortgage on equipment would be a chattel mortgage.

Coefficient of Variation Standard deviation divided by the mean: CV.

Collateral Assets that are used to secure a loan.

Commercial Paper Unsecured, short-term promissory notes of large firms, usually issued in denominations of $1 million or more. The rate of interest on commercial paper is typically somewhat below the prime rate of interest.

Commitment Fee The fee paid to a lender for a formal line of credit.

Compensating Balance A required minimum checking account balance that a firm must maintain with a commercial bank. The required balance is generally equal to 15 to 20 percent of the amount of loans outstanding. Compensating balances can raise the effective rate of interest on bank loans.

Composite Cost of Capital A weighted average of the component costs of debt, preferred stock, and common equity. Also called the "weighted average cost of capital," but it reflects the cost of each additional dollar raised, not the average cost of all capital the firm has raised throughout its history (k).

Composition An informal method of reorganization that voluntarily reduces creditors' claims on the debtor firm.

Compound Interest An interest rate that is applicable when interest in succeeding periods is earned not only on the initial principal but also on the accumulated interest of prior periods. Compound interest is contrasted to *simple interest*, in which returns are not earned on interest received.

Compounding The arithmetic process of determining the final value of a payment or series of payments when compound interest is applied.

Conditional Sales Contract A method of financing new equipment by paying it off in installments over a one-to-five-year period. The seller retains title to the equipment until payment has been completed.

Consolidated Tax Return An income tax return that combines the income statement of several affiliated firms.

Continuous Compounding (Discounting) As opposed to discrete compounding, interest is added continuously rather than at discrete points in time.

Conversion Price The effective price paid for common stock when the stock is obtained by converting either convertible preferred stocks or convertible bonds. For example, if a $1,000 bond is convertible into 20 shares of stock, the conversion price is $50 ($1,000/20).

Conversion Ratio or Conversion Rate The number of shares of common stock that may be obtained by converting a convertible bond or share of convertible preferred stock.

Convertibles Securities (generally bonds or preferred stocks) that are exchangeable at the option of the holder for common stock of the issuing firm.

Correlation Coefficient Measures the degree of relationship between two variables.

Cost of Capital The discount rate that should be used in the capital budgeting process.

Coupon Rate The stated rate of interest on a bond.

Covariance The correlation between two variables multiplied by the standard deviation of each variable:

$$\text{Cov} = r_{xy}\sigma_x\sigma_y.$$

Covenant Detailed clauses contained in loan agreements. Covenants are designed to protect the lender and include such items as limits on total indebtedness, restrictions on dividends, minimum current ratio, and similar provisions.

Cumulative Dividends A protective feature on preferred stock that requires all past preferred dividends to be paid before any common dividends are paid.

Cut-off Point In the capital budgeting process, the minimum rate of return on acceptable investment opportunities.

Debenture A long-term debt instrument that is not secured by a mortgage on specific property.

Debt Ratio Total debt divided by total assets.

Decision Tree A device for setting forth graphically the pattern of relationship between decisions and chance events.

Default The failure to fulfill a contract. Generally, default refers to the failure to pay interest or principal on debt obligations.

Degree of Leverage The percentage increase in profits resulting from a given percentage increase in sales. The degree of leverage may be calculated for financial leverage, operating leverage, or both combined.

Devaluation The process of reducing the value of a country's currency stated in terms of other currencies; e.g., the British pound might be devalued from $2.30 for one pound to $2.00 for one pound.

Discount Rate The interest rate used in the discounting process; sometimes called *capitalization rate.*

Discounted Cash Flow Techniques Methods of ranking investment proposals. Included are (1) internal rate of return method, (2) net present value method, and (3) profitability index or benefit/cost ratio.

Discounting The process of finding the present value of a series of future cash flows. Discounting is the reverse of compounding.

Discounting of Accounts Receivable Short-term financing where accounts receivable are used to secure the loan. The lender does not *buy* the accounts receivable but simply uses them as collateral for the loan. Also called *assigning accounts receivable.*

Dividend Yield The ratio of the current dividend to the current price of a share of stock.

Du Pont System A system of analysis designed to show the relationship between return on investment, asset turnover, and the profit margin.

EBIT Acronym for "earnings before interest and taxes."

Economical Ordering Quantity (EOQ) The optimum (least cost) quantity of merchandise which should be ordered.

EPS Acronym for "earnings per share."

Equity The net worth of a business, consisting of capital stock, capital (or paid-in) surplus, earned surplus (or retained earnings), and occasionally, certain net worth reserves. *Common equity* is that part of the total net worth belonging to the common stockholders. *Total equity* would include preferred stockholders. The terms "common stock," "net worth," and "common equity" are frequently used interchangeably (S).

Exchange Rate The rate at which one currency can be exchanged for another; e.g., $2.30 can be exchanged for one British pound.

Excise Tax A tax on the manufacture, sale, or consumption of specified commodities.

Ex Dividend Date The date on which the right to the current dividend no longer accompanies a stock. (For listed stock, the ex dividend date is four working days prior to the date of record.)

Exercise Price The price that must be paid for a share of common stock when it is bought by exercising a warrant.

Expected Return The rate of return a firm expects to realize from an investment. The expected return is the mean value of the probability distribution of possible returns.

Ex Rights The date on which stock purchase rights are no longer transferred to the purchaser of the stock.

Extension An informal method of reorganization in which the creditors voluntarily postpone the date of required payment on past-due obligations.

External Funds Funds acquired through borrowing or by selling new common or preferred stock.

Factoring A method of financing accounts receivable under which a firm sells its accounts receivable (generally without recourse) to a financial institution (the "factor").

Field Warehousing A method of financing inventories in which a "warehouse" is established at the place of business of the borrowing firm.

Financial Accounting Standards Board (FASB) A private (nongovernment) agency which functions as an accounting standards-setting body.

Financial Intermediation Financial transactions which bring savings surplus units together with savings deficit units so that savings can be redistributed into their most productive uses.

Financial Lease A lease that does not provide for maintenance services, is not cancellable, and is fully amortized over the life of the lease.

Financial Leverage The ratio of total debt to total assets. There are other measures of financial leverage, especially ones that relate cash inflows to required cash outflows. In this book, the debt/total asset ratio is generally used to measure leverage.

Financial Markets Transactions in which the creation and transfer of financial assets and financial liabilities take place.

Financial Risk That portion of total corporate risk, over and above basic business risk, that results from using debt.

Financial Structure The entire right-hand side of the balance sheet—the way in which a firm is financed.

Fisher Effect The increase in the nominal interest rates over real (purchasing power adjusted) interest rates reflecting anticipated inflation.

Fixed Charges Costs that do not vary with the level of output, especially fixed financial costs such as interest, lease payments, and sinking fund payments.

Float The amount of funds tied up in checks that have been written but are still in process and have not yet been collected.

Floating Exchange Rates Exchange rates may be fixed by government policy ("pegged") or allowed to "float" up or down in accordance with supply and demand. When market forces are allowed to function, exchange rates are said to be floating.

Flotation Cost The cost of issuing new stocks or bonds.

Funded Debt Long-term debt.

Funding The process of replacing short-term debt with long-term securities (stocks or bonds).

General Purchasing Power Reporting A proposal by the FASB that the current values of nonmonetary items in financial statements be adjusted by a general price index.

Goodwill Intangible assets of a firm established by the excess of the price paid for the going concern over its book value.

Holding Company A corporation operated for the purpose of owning the common stocks of other corporations.

Hurdle Rate In capital budgeting, the minimum acceptable rate of return on a project; if the expected rate of return is below the hurdle rate, the project is not accepted. The hurdle rate should be the marginal cost of capital.

Improper Accumulation Earnings retained by a business for the purpose of enabling stockholders to avoid personal income taxes.

Income Bond A bond that pays interest only if the current interest is earned.

Incremental Cash Flow Net cash flow attributable to an investment project.

Incremental Cost of Capital The average cost of the increment of capital raised during a given year.

Indenture A formal agreement between the issuer of a bond and the bondholders.

Insolvency The inability to meet maturing debt obligations.

Interest Factor (IF) Numbers found in compound interest and annuity tables.

Internal Financing Funds made available for capital budgeting and working capital expansion through the normal operations of the firm; internal financing is approximately equal to retained earnings plus depreciation.

Internal Rate of Return (IRR) The rate of return on an asset investment. The internal rate of return is calculated by finding the discount rate that equates the present value of future cash flows to the cost of the investment.

Intrinsic Value That value which, in the mind of the analyst, is justified by the facts. It is often used to distinguish between the "true value" of an asset (the intrinsic value) and the asset's current market price.

Investment Banker One who underwrites and distributes new investment securities; more broadly, one who helps business firms to obtain financing.

Investment Tax Credit Business firms can deduct as a credit against their income taxes a specified percentage of the dollar amount of new investments in each of certain categories of assets.

Legal List A list of securities in which mutual savings banks, pensions funds, insurance companies, and other fiduciary institutions are permitted to invest.

Leverage Factor The ratio of debt to total assets.

Lien A lender's claim on assets that are pledged for a loan.

Line of Credit An arrangement whereby a financial institution (bank or insurance company) commits itself to lend up to a specified maximum amount of funds during a specified period. Sometimes the interest rate on the loan is specified; at other times, it is not. Sometimes a commitment fee is imposed for obtaining the line of credit.

Liquidity Refers to a firm's cash position and its ability to meet maturing obligations.

Listed Securities Securities traded on an organized security exchange.

Lock-box Plan A procedure used to speed up collections and to reduce float.

Margin — Profit on Sales The *profit margin* is the percentage of profit after tax to sales.

Margin — Securities Business The buying of stocks or bonds on credit, known as *buying on margin.*

Marginal Cost The cost of an additional unit. The marginal cost of capital is the cost of an additional dollar of new funds.

Marginal Efficiency of Capital A schedule showing the internal rate of return on investment opportunities.

Marginal Revenue The additional gross revenue produced by selling one additional unit of output.

Merger Any combination that forms one company from two or more previously existing companies.

Money Market Financial markets in which funds are borrowed or lent for short periods (i.e., less than one year). (The money market is distinguished from the capital market, which is the market for long-term funds.)

Mortgage A pledge of designated property as security for a loan.

Net Present Value (NPV) Method A method of ranking investment proposals. The NPV is equal to the present value of future returns, discounted at the marginal cost of capital, minus the present value of the cost of the investment.

Net Worth The capital and surplus of a firm — capital stock, capital surplus (paid-in capital), earned surplus (retained earnings), and, occasionally, certain reserves. For some purposes, preferred stock is included; generally, net worth refers only to the common stockholders' position.

Nominal Interest Rate The contracted or stated interest rate, undeflated for price level changes.

Normal Probability Distribution A symmetrical, bell-shaped probability function.

Objective Probability Distributions Probability distributions determined by statistical procedures.

Operating Leverage The extent to which fixed costs are used in a firm's operation. Break-even analysis is used to measure the extent to which operating leverage is employed.

Opportunity Cost The rate of return on the best *alternative* investment that is available. It is the highest return that will *not* be earned if the funds are invested in a particular project. For example, the opportunity cost of *not* investing in bond A yielding 8 percent might be 7.99 percent, which could be earned on bond B.

Options Contracts that give their holder the right to buy (or sell) an asset at a predetermined time for a given period of time.

Ordinary Income Income from the normal operations of a firm. Operating income specifically excludes income from the sale of capital assets.

Organized Security Exchanges Formal organizations having tangible, physical locations. Organized exchanges conduct an auction market in designated ("listed") investment securities. For example, the New York Stock Exchange is an organized exchange.

Overdraft System A system where a depositor may write checks in excess of his balance, with his bank automatically extending a loan to cover the shortage.

Over-the-counter Market All facilities that provide for trading in unlisted securities; that is, those not listed on organized exchanges. The over-the-counter market is typically a "telephone market," as most business is conducted over the telephone.

Par Value The nominal or face value of a stock or bond.

Payback Period The length of time required for the net revenues of an investment to return the cost of the investment.

Payout Ratio The percentage of earnings paid out in the form of dividends.

Pegging A market stabilization action taken by the manager of an underwriting group during the offering of new securities. He does this by continually placing orders to buy at a specified price in the market.

Perpetuity A stream of equal future payments expected to continue forever.

Pledging of Accounts Receivable Short-term borrowing from financial institutions where the loan is secured by accounts receivable. The lender may physically take the accounts receivable but typically has recourse to the borrower; also called *discounting of accounts receivable.*

Pooling of Interest An accounting method for combining the financial statements of firms that merge. Under the pooling-of-interest procedure, the assets of the merged firms are simply added to form the balance sheet of the surviving corporation. This method is different from the "purchase" method, where goodwill is put on the balance sheet to reflect a premium (or discount) paid in excess of book value.

Portfolio Effect The extent to which the variation in returns on a combination of assets (a "portfolio") is less than the sum of the variations of the individual assets.

Portfolio Theory Deals with the selection of optimal portfolios; i.e., portfolios that provide the highest possible return for any specified degree of risk.

Preemptive Right A provision contained in the corporate charter and bylaws that gives holders of common stock the right to purchase on a pro rata basis new issues of common stock (or securities convertible into common stock).

Present Value (PV) The value today of a future payment, or stream of payments, discounted at the appropriate discount rate.

Price/Earnings Ratio (P/E) The ratio of price to earnings. Faster growing or less risky firms typically have higher P/E ratios than either slower growing or riskier firms.

Prime Rate The lowest rate of interest commercial banks charge very large, strong corporations.

Pro Forma A projection. A *pro forma* financial statement is one that shows how the actual statement will look if certain specified assumptions are realized. *Pro forma* statements may be either future or past projections. An example of a backward *pro forma* statement occurs when two firms are planning to merge and shows what their consolidated financial statements would have looked like if they had been merged in preceding years.

Profit Center A unit of a large, decentralized firm that has its own investments and for which a rate of return on investment can be calculated.

Profit Margin The ratio of profits after taxes to sales.

Profitability Index (PI) The present value of future returns divided by the present value of the investment outlay.

Progressive Tax A tax that requires a higher percentage payment on higher incomes. The personal income tax in the United States, which is at a rate of 14 percent on the lowest increments of income to 70 percent on the highest increments, is progressive.

Prospectus A document issued for the purpose of describing a new security issue. The Securities and Exchange Commission (SEC) examines prospectuses to insure that statements contained therein are not "false and misleading."

Proxy A document giving one person the authority or power to act for another. Typically, the authority in question is the power to vote shares of common stock.

Pure (or Primitive) Security A security that pays off $1 if one particular state of the world occurs and pays off nothing if any other state of the world occurs.

Put An option to sell a specific security at a specified price within a designated period.

Rate of Return The internal rate of return on an investment.

Recourse Arrangement A term used in connection with accounts receivable financing. If a firm sells its accounts receivable to a financial institution under a recourse agreement, then, if the accounts receivable cannot be collected, the selling firm must repurchase the account from the financial institution.

Rediscount Rate The rate of interest at which a bank may borrow from a Federal Reserve Bank.

Refunding Sale of new debt securities to replace an old debt issue.

Regression Analysis A statistical procedure for predicting the value of one variable (dependent variable) on the basis of knowledge about one or more other variables (independent variables).

Reinvestment Rate The rate of return at which cash flows from an investment are reinvested. The reinvestment rate may or may not be constant from year to year.

Reorganization When a financially troubled firm goes through reorganization, its assets are restated to reflect their current market value, and its financial structure is restated to reflect any changes on the asset side of the statement. Under a reorganization the firm continues in existence; this is contrasted to bankruptcy, where the firm is liquidated and ceases to exist.

Replacement Cost Accounting A requirement under SEC release no. 190 (1976) that large companies disclose the replacement costs of inventory items and depreciable plant.

Required Rate of Return The rate of return that stockholders expect to receive on common stock investments.

Residual Value The value of leased property at the end of the lease term.

Retained Earnings That portion of earnings not paid out in dividends. The figure that appears on the balance sheet is the sum of the retained earnings for each year throughout the company's history.

Right A short-term option to buy a specified number of shares of a new issue of securities at a designated "subscription" price.

Rights Offering A securities flotation offered to existing stockholders.

Risk The probability that actual future returns will be below expected returns. Measured by standard deviation or coefficient of variation of expected returns.

Risk-adjusted Discount Rates The discount rate applicable for a particular risky (uncertain) stream of income: the riskless rate of interest plus a risk premium appropriate to the level of risk attached to the particular income stream.

Risk Premium The difference between the required rate of return on a particular risky asset and the rate of return on a riskless asset with the same expected life.

Risk-Return Tradeoff Function (See *Security Market Line.*)

Sale and Leaseback An operation whereby a firm sells land, buildings, or equipment to a financial institution and simultaneously executes an agreement to lease the property back for a specified period under specific terms.

Salvage Value The value of a capital asset at the end of a specified period. It is the current market price of an asset being considered for replacement in a capital budgeting problem.

Securities and Exchange Commission (SEC) A federal government agency with which a registration statement must be filed on new issues of securities and which supervises the operation of securities exchanges and related aspects of the securities business.

Securities, Junior Securities that have lower priority in claims on assets and income than other securities *(senior securities).* For example, preferred stock is junior to debentures, but debentures are junior to mortgage bonds. Common stock is the most junior of all corporate securities.

Securities, Senior Securities having claims on income and assets that rank higher than certain other securities *(junior securities).* For example, mortgage bonds are senior to debentures, but debentures are senior to common stock.

Security Market Line A graphic representation of the relation between the required return on a security and the product of its risk times a normalized market measure of risk. Risk-return relationships for individual securities or investments.

Selling Group A group of stock brokerage firms formed for the purpose of distributing a new issue of securities; part of the investment banking process.

Sensitivity Analysis Simulation analysis in which key variables are changed and the resulting change in the rate of return is observed. Typically, the rate of return will be more sensitive to changes in some variables than it will in others.

Service Lease A lease under which the lessor maintains and services the asset.

Short Selling Selling a security that is not owned by the seller at the time of the sale. The seller borrows the security from a brokerage firm and must at some point repay the brokerage firm by buying the security on the open market.

Simulation A technique whereby probable future events are simulated on a computer. Estimated rates of return and risk indexes can be generated.

Sinking Fund A required annual payment designed to amortize a bond or a preferred stock issue. The sinking fund may be held in the form of cash or marketable securities, but more generally the money put into the sinking fund is used to retire each year some of the securities in question.

Small Business Administration (SBA) A government agency organized to aid small firms with their financing and other problems.

Standard Deviation A statistical term that measures the variability of a set of observations from the mean of the distribution (σ).

State Preference Model A framework in which decisions are based on probabilities of payoffs under alternative states of the world.

Stock Dividend A dividend paid in additional shares of stock rather than in cash. It involves a transfer from retained earnings to the capital stock account; therefore, stock dividends are limited by the amount of retained earnings.

Stock Split An accounting action to increase the number of shares outstanding; for example, in a 3-for-1 split, shares outstanding would be tripled and each stockholder would receive three new shares for each one formerly held. Stock splits involve no transfer from surplus to the capital account.

Subjective Probability Distributions Probability distributions determined through subjective procedures without the use of statistics.

Subordinated Debenture A bond having a claim on assets only after the senior debt has been paid off in the event of liquidation.

Subscription Price The price at which a security may be purchased in a rights offering.

Surtax A tax levied in addition to the normal tax. For example, the normal corporate tax rate is 22 percent, but a surtax of 26 percent is added to the normal tax on all corporate income exceeding $25,000.

Synergy A situation where "the whole is greater than the sum of its parts"; in a synergistic merger, the postmerger earnings exceed the sum of the separate companies' premerger earnings.

Systematic Risk That part of a security's risk that cannot be eliminated by diversification.

Tangible Assets Physical assets as opposed to intangible assets such as goodwill and the stated value of patents.

Tender Offers A situation wherein one firm offers to buy the stock of another, going directly to the stockholders, frequently over the opposition of the management of the firm whose stock is being sought.

Term Loan A loan generally obtained from a bank or an insurance company with a maturity greater than one year. Term loans are generally amortized.

Trade Credit Interfirm debt arising through credit sales and recorded as an account receivable by the seller and as an account payable by the buyer.

Treasury Stock Common stock that has been repurchased by the issuing firm.

Trust Receipt An instrument acknowledging that the borrower holds certain goods in trust for the lender. Trust receipt financing is used in connection with the financing of inventories for automobile dealers, construction equipment dealers, appliance dealers, and other dealers in expensive durable goods.

Trustee The representative of bondholders who acts in their interest and facilitates communication between them and the issuer. Typically these duties are handled by a department of a commercial bank.

Underwriting (1) The entire process of issuing new corporate securities. (2) The insurance function of bearing the risk of adverse price fluctuations during the period in which a new issue of stock or bonds is being distributed.

Underwriting Syndicate A syndicate of investment firms formed to spread the risk associated with the purchase and distribution of a new issue of securities. The larger the issue, the more firms typically are involved in the syndicate.

Unlisted Securities Securities that are traded in the over-the-counter market.

Unsystematic Risk That part of a security's risk associated with random events; unsystematic risk can be eliminated by proper diversification.

Utility Theory A body of theory dealing with the relationships among money income, utility (or "happiness"), and the willingness to accept risks.

Value Additivity Principle Neither fragmenting cash flows or recombining them will affect the resulting values of the cash flows.

Warrant A long-term option to buy a stated number of shares of common stock at a specified price. The specified price is generally called the "exercise price."

Weighted Cost of Capital A weighted average of the component costs of debt, preferred stock, and common equity. Also called the "composite cost of capital."

Working Capital Refers to a firm's investment in short-term assets—cash, short-term securities, accounts receivable, and inventories. *Gross working capital* is defined as a firm's total current assets. *Net working capital* is defined as current assets minus current liabilities. If the term "working capital" is used without further qualification, it generally refers to gross working capital.

Yield The rate of return on an investment; the internal rate of return.

Index

Frequently Used Symbols in Managerial Finance

a periodic level payment or annuity

b proportion of net income (NI) retained by the firm

B the market value of the firm's debt

β (beta)   beta of a security, a measure of its riskiness

c coupon payment for a bond

Cov_{jM} covariance of security j returns with market returns

CV coefficient of variation

$CVIF$ compound value interest factor

$CVIF_a$ compound value interest factor for an annuity

d dividend payment per share of common equity

D total dividend payments of the firm for common equity

Dep depreciation

EPS earnings per share; also e

F net after-tax cash flows for capital budgeting analysis of projects

g growth rate or growth factor

i interest rate

I amount of investment

k in general, the discount factor; more specifically, the weighted average cost of capital

     k_b cost of debt

     k_c cost of a convertible issue

     k_j returns to firm j or on security j

     k_s cost of common equity for the levered firm

     k_{ps} cost of senior equity, e.g., preferred stock

     k_u cost of capital for the unlevered firm

     k_M return on the market portfolio

λ (lambda)   slope of the security market line $= (\bar{k}_M - R_F)/\sigma_M^2$

n number of shares outstanding

N life of a project; also terminal year of decision or planning horizon

p price of a security

P sales price per unit of product sold

P_s probability for state of the world s

$PVIF$ present value interest factor

$PVIF_a$ present value interest factor for an annuity

Q quantity produced or sold

r rate of return on new investments; also internal rate of return (IRR)

R_F risk-free rate of interest

ρ_{jk} (rho)   correlation coefficient

s subscript referring to alternative states of the world

S market value of a firm's common equity

σ (sigma)   standard deviation

σ^2 variance

t time period

T the marginal corporate income tax rate

TR total revenues $\equiv$ sales $\equiv$ PQ

V market value of a firm

w weights in capital structure or portfolio proportions

X net operating income of the firm; also equals EBIT $\equiv$ NOI